CRIMINAL LAW & PROCEDURE
Cases, Context, Critique

Third Edition

JENNIE ABELL

ELIZABETH SHEEHY

*Faculty of Common Law
University of Ottawa*

CAPTUS PRESS

Criminal Law & Procedure: Cases, Context, Critique, 3rd Edition

Copyright © 1993–2002 by Jennie Abell, Elizabeth Sheehy and Captus Press Inc.

All rights reserved. No part of this book may be reproduced, stored in a retrieval system, or transmitted, in any form or by any means, electronic, mechanical, photocopying, recording, or otherwise, without prior written permission of the copyright holders.

Care has been taken to trace ownership of copyright materials contained in this book. The publisher will gladly take any information that will enable the rectification of any reference or credit in subsequent editions.

Captus Press Inc.
Units 14 & 15, 1600 Steeles Avenue West
Concord, ON L4K 4M2   Canada
Tel.: (416) 736-5537
Fax: (416) 736-5793
Email: info@captus.com
Internet: http://www.captus.com

National Library of Canada Cataloguing in Publication

Abell, J. (Jennie), 1951 –
   Criminal law & procedure : cases, context, critique / Jennie Abell, Elizabeth Sheehy. — 3rd ed.

Includes bibliographical references and index.
ISBN 1-55322-041-2

   1. Criminal law – Canada.   2. Criminal procedure – Canada.
I. Sheehy, Elizabeth A.   II. Title: Criminal law and procedure.

KE8809.A37 2002   345.71   C2002-904002-7

Canada *We acknowledge the financial support of the Government of Canada through the Book Publishing Industry Development Program (BPIDP) for our publishing activities.*

0 9 8 7 6 5 4 3 2
Printed in Canada

Table of Contents

Introduction 1

1   Definition of Crime 11
    A.   PROBLEMATIZING THE DEFINITION OF "CRIME" 11
        • R. v. Banks 13
    B.   THE CONTINGENCY OF THE DEFINITION OF "CRIME" 22
        • The Dalkon Shield Litigation: Revised Annotated Reprimand 23
    C.   CHALLENGES TO THE DEFINITION OF "CRIME" 29
        • A Feminist Review of Criminal Law 30
        • R. v. Clay 36

2   Colonization and the Imposition of Criminal Law 41
    A.   OUTLAWING THE POTLATCH AND THE SUN DANCE 42
        • The Struggle for Survival: Indian Cultures and the Protestant Ethic
in British Columbia 42
        • Senseless Drumming and Dancing 47
    B.   EARLY "MURDER" TRIALS 50
        • Killing the Shamen 53
    C.   POISONING THE LAND 66
        • No Safe Place 66
        • Killing the Shamen (Continued) 69
    D.   THE APPROPRIATION OF LAND AND THE ROLE OF THE MILITARY 71
    E.   TREATY RIGHTS AND SOVEREIGNTY 73
    F.   FURTHER EXAMPLES OF COLONIALISM 75

3   Aboriginal Peoples and Criminal Law 76
    • A Presentation to the Western Workshop of the Western
Judicial Education Centre 78
    • Royal Commission on the Donald Marshall, Jr. Prosecution:
Digest of Findings and Recommendations 88
    • Submission to the Aboriginal Justice Inquiry 94
    • The Argument for Aboriginal Justice Systems 98

4 Enforcement of the Law 103

A. CLASS 104
- Crime and Class: Unequal Before the Law 104
- R. v. *White* 111

B. SEXUAL ORIENTATION 113
- *Little Sisters Book and Art Emporium* v. *Canada* 113

C. RACISM 121
- Leo LaChance 121
- Wilson Nepoose 123

D. MISCARRIAGES OF JUSTICE 124
- David Milgaard 124
- Guy Paul Morin 125
- Birmingham Six; Guildford Four; Maguire Seven 126
- Lindy Chamberlain 127

E. REMEDIES 127
- Appeals 127
- Extra-Judicial Review 129
- Pardons 130
- Civil Remedies 130

5 Sentencing 132

A. ISSUES IN SENTENCING 132
- Maximum and Minimum Sentences 133
- The Criminal Code Unfair to Women, Manitoba, 1913 . 133
- Sentencing Options 134
- Purpose of Sentence; Aggravating and Mitigating Factors . 137
- Process of Sentencing 138

B. THE POLITICS OF SENTENCING 139

C. CORPORATE CRIMINALITY 140
- R. v. *Manchester Plastics* 140

D. RACE AND RACISM 144
- R. v. *Miloszewski* 145

E. CULTURAL CONFLICTS? THE RELEVANCE OF CULTURE TO SENTENCING 152
- R. v. *Naqitarvik* 153
- Locking Up Natives in Canada 160
- R. v. *Gladue* 164

F. CIRCLE SENTENCING AND FIRST NATION INITIATIVES ... 176
- Circle Sentencing Criteria 177
- Role of Appellate Courts 178
- Critique of Sentencing Circles 180
- The Role of the Victim in the Criminal Justice System: Circle Sentencing in Inuit Communities 182
- Hollow Water First Nation's Community Holistic Circle Healing Project .. 185

Table of Contents

    G. A STUDY IN SENTENCING: VIOLENCE AGAINST WOMEN 188
- *R.* v. *Inwood* (Appellant's Factum) 188
- *R.* v. *Inwood* (Respondent's Factum) 198
- *R.* v. *Inwood* 204

    H. CHARTER IMPLICATIONS 207
- *R.* v. *Hebb* 207

6   Prisons and Parole 216

    A. PUNISHMENT 216
- Discipline 217
  - *Armstrong* v. *Warkworth* 217
- Transfer 221
- Segregation 221
- Criminal Prosecution 222

    B. PRISON CONDITIONS 222
- Overcrowding 222
- Riots 223
- Search and Seizure 224
- Physical Security 224
- Medical Treatment and Rehabilitation 225
- Democratic Rights 226
- Conjugal Visits 226

    C. RACISM IN PRISON 227

    D. WOMEN IN PRISON 230
- Commission of Inquiry into Certain Events at the Prison for Women in Kingston 232

    E. ABORIGINAL PEOPLES 240
- *R.* v. *Daniels* 241

    F. PAROLE 245

7   Law and Order 247

LAW AND ORDER AND THE CANADIAN STATE 247
- Democracy and Terror: October 1970 253

LAW AND ORDER AND THE CANADIAN STATE (Continued) 257
- Blind Justice 258
- The Rambo Spirit 260
- The Men's Club: Rambo Ain't Heavy, He's My Brother 262
- The Media's Hypocrisy and Oka 265

8   Introduction to Criminal Procedure 268
- Classification of Offences 268
- Summary Conviction Offences 269
- Section 553 Offences 269
- Section 469 Offences 269
- Other Indictable Offences 269
- Charter Rights 270

9 Policing ... 271

A. THE ROLE OF THE POLICE ... 271
- The Police: Solutions to or Sources of Crime? ... 271

B. POLICE METHODS ... 277

C. SYSTEMIC BIAS IN POLICING ... 279
- Racism ... 279
  - Spirit-Murdering the Messenger: The Discourse of Fingerpointing as the Law's Response to Racism ... 280
  - Alberta ... 291
  - Manitoba ... 292
  - Québec ... 293
  - Nova Scotia ... 295
    - R. v. Thompson ... 296
    - R. v. R.S.D. ... 300
  - Ontario ... 312
    - **SYNOPSIS**: Law Union of Ontario Presentation to Task Force on Race Relations and Policing ... 312
    - A Report on Attorney-General's Files, Prosecutions and Coroners' Inquests Arising Out of Police Shootings in Ontario to the Commission on Systemic Racism in Ontario Criminal Justice System, 1993 ... 318
      - R. v. Deane ... 325
      - R. v. Brown ... 338
  - Saskatchewan ... 343
  - United States ... 343
- SEXISM ... 344
- *Doe* v. *Metropolitan Toronto Commissioners of Police* ... 345
- HOMOPHOBIA ... 363
  - A Queer Response to Bashing: Legislating Against Hate ... 363

D. POLICING THE POLICE: LEGAL RESPONSES ... 364

E. POLICE RESISTANCE ... 366

10 Search and Seizure ... 368

A. AUTHORIZED BY LAW ... 368

B. LAW MUST BE REASONABLE ... 369
- *Hunter* v. *Southam* ... 369
- The Politics of the Charter ... 379
- *Thomson Newspapers* v. *Canada* ... 382
- *R.* v. *M.R.M.* ... 383
- *R.* v. *Golden* ... 392

C. SEARCH MUST BE REASONABLE ... 404
- *R.* v. *Gogol* ... 404

D. SECTION 24(2): WHEN IS EVIDENCE EXCLUDED? ... 414
- *R.* v. *Collins* ... 414

11 Compelling the Accused's Appearance in Court 420
A. ARREST 420
- Introduction to Powers of Arrest............................420
- Resisting Arrest and Obstruction 421
- *R. v. Biron*..421
- The *Charter* and Arrest: ss. 9 and 10.....................427

B. DETENTION 427
- *R. v. Therens*..428
- *R. v. Grafe*..429
- The *Charter* and Investigative Detention: ss. 9 and 10 ...431
- The *Charter*, Arrest and Detention: s. 15?................432
- *Thurman v. City of Torrington*............................432
- *R. v. Peck*...438

12 Right to Counsel 442
A. RIGHT TO COUNSEL UPON ARREST OR DETENTION 443
- *R. v. Leclair*..443
- *R. v. Brydges*..447

B. RIGHT TO COUNSEL AT TRIAL 453
- Certificates...454
  - *R. v. Rain*...454
- Young persons 465
- Prisoners..465
- Duty Counsel Services 466
- Clinic Services..466
- The Standard of Social Justice Applied to an Evaluation of Criminal Cases Appearing Before the Halifax Courts......466

C. SYSTEMIC BARRIERS TO ACCESS TO COUNSEL: SECTION 15?..... 470

13 Judicial Interim Release 473
- Report of the Aboriginal Justice Inquiry of Manitoba 474
- *R. v. Hall*...476
- *R. v. Li*...484

14 Powers of Prosecution 487
A. POLICE POWERS 488
B. CROWN ATTORNEYS... 489
C. PRIVATE PROSECUTIONS.................................... 491
D. CONTEMPT AND JUDICIAL POWERS 492
- *R. v. Kopyto*...495
- Trials and Tribulations....................................500
- When the Victim Goes to Jail: The Law on Contempt of Court 501
- *R. v. O'Leary*..504

E. SCRUTINY OF JUDGES 507
  - Justice Thomas Berger 509
  - Justice Bertha Wilson 510
  - Judge Andrée Ruffo 510
  - Justice Charles Huband 511
  - Justice Jean-Claude Angers 511
  - Justice John W. McClung 511

Index of Cases 513

Introduction

In some ... areas of the law ... a distinctly male perspective is clearly discernible and has resulted in legal principles that are not fundamentally sound and should be revisited as and when the opportunity presents itself. Canadian feminist scholarship has, in my view, done an excellent job of identifying those areas and making suggestions for reform. Some aspects of the criminal law in particular cry out for change since they are based on presuppositions about the nature of women and women's sexuality that in this day and age are little short of ludicrous.

> Madame Justice Bertha Wilson,
> "Will Women Judges Really Make a Difference?"
> (1989) 28 Osgoode Hall L.J. 507 at 515.

There is no question but that there exists within all of us biases and influences of which we are all unaware, and which cause us to behave and think in certain ways, sometimes to the detriment of others in society. Your education in the public school system, universities, and law schools of this country was permeated with the ethnocidal beliefs about aboriginal people I have spoken about.... [O]ne of the most significant causes of adverse impact upon aboriginal people by the justice system lies in the fact that to this point the culture of the justice system has been white middle class male culture that has not yet learned how to recognize and overcome its own momentum and inertia.

> Murray Sinclair, Associate Chief Judge, Provincial Court of Manitoba,
> "A Presentation to the Western Workshop of
> the Western Judicial Education Centre"
> (14 May 1990) [unpublished].

This book is intended for legal educators and students who are committed to critical and feminist pedagogy and to preparation for issues of systemic bias, such as racism, which will inevitably be confronted in criminal practice. We also intend this book to be of interest to those who work in other disciplines that critically examine law and legal practice. These materials have been years in the making, having their impetus in our political commitments and experience as activists and lawyers, our research and scholarship, and from many years of interactive teaching with these materials at the University of Ottawa, Faculty of Law.

This book reflects critical, feminist, and interdisciplinary frameworks that challenge the objectivity and neutrality of legal doctrine (the definition of law, the evolution of legal doctrine, the specific assumptions of criminal law) and law-in-practice (the enforcement of law at each level: policing, prosecution, and judging). The book is both a law casebook, in that it draws on traditional legal materials, cases, and legislation to illustrate the theoretical points, and a critique of law, in that it examines the impact of traditional legal doctrine and law-in-practice. In particular, the casebook draws out the links between the responses of the criminal justice system to specific groups (for example, Aboriginal peoples,[1] African-Canadians, women, lesbians, gays, and corporations) with reference to contemporary analysis of those issues.

Our materials raise questions about the links between criminal law and the maintenance of relations of dominance and inequality between men and women, and between different manifestations of oppression, such as racism, sexism, lesbophobia, class domination, ableism, and homophobia. These materials are designed to offer sufficient historical and contextual information that the reader can rethink, unexamined and often inarticulate "opinions" about Aboriginal peoples, about the so-called dichotomy between law and politics, about rules that covertly "blame the victim," and so on. The reader is invited to address these materials on an intellectual level, and we enhance this engagement in our classrooms by designing assignments, such as a court report exercise, that require observation and reflection on criminal law-in-practice.

Critical teaching and, more specifically, feminist teaching in this particular subject area has posed many challenges for us. Criminal doctrine and practice have not had to answer to criticisms of their biases from the "inside": that is, from persons trained in law. Most of the critique has been developed and documented by people working "outside" of law, such as criminologists and sociologists, which means that their work has been discounted as "not law." It has also meant that reported cases and legal commentary have been silent on the subject of systemic bias and violence as reinforced through the criminal law.

Only very recently, and under great pressure, has a legal record of these realities begun to be created. For example, the report produced by the Royal Commission on the Prosecution of Donald Marshall, Jr. and Harry Glasbeek's analysis of the legal treatment of eight police shootings of African-Canadian men in Ontario explicitly make points that previously had to be extracted from less "scholarly" sources. While we remain sceptical about whether it is possible to shift relations of power by invoking criminal prosecution or liberal notions of "rights" through litigation, *The Canadian Charter of Rights and Freedoms*, Part I of the *Constitution Act, 1982*, being Schedule B to the *Canada Act 1982* (U.K.), 1982, c. 11 [hereinafter, *Charter*], has at least contributed to the growing body of legal literature exposing inequalities perpetuated through law.

Equality-seeking groups and some lawyers have managed to create the space to use alternative forms of expertise and knowledge to shape legal argumentation. Decisions emerging from the Supreme Court of Canada rely upon interdisciplinary materials and analysis of the impact and implications of particular legal rules. While it remains to be seen how far judges, lawyers, and legal educators will pursue this approach, this book affirms social activism as an important impetus for developments in law and for legal practice.

THEMES

We use the themes of **feminist analysis,** inquiry into **colonization, colonialism, and racism,** and a **class-based critique** of law to explore the impact of criminal law upon women, lesbians, gays, Aboriginal peoples, African-Canadians and other racialized people, and the poor.

Feminism

The profound impact of feminism upon the analysis of criminal law makes it a powerful unifying theme for this book. We define feminism to mean an understanding that women as a group are unequal with men as a group economically, politically, and socially in terms of such indicia as political power, representation among those who create "knowledge," credibility, and physical safety, for example, combined with a commitment to changing women's inequality. While feminists might disagree with one another about the historical and contemporary sources of inequality, the forms and degree of inequality, the ways in which women of diverse physical and mental abilities, racial and ethnic identities, class, and sexual orientation experience gender oppression, and the most effective strategies for change, feminist analyses share certain assumptions. For example, a feminist standpoint assumes that women "matter," that women's accounts of their experiences are valid, and that struggle, in one form or another, is imperative.

The kinds of questions that feminists ask of law are: whether a given legal rule is dependent upon particular assumptions about the nature of men or women, or indeed, "humankind," which need to be interrogated; whether a given issue in law requires additional context prior to resolution, such as further fact-finding or interdisciplinary research and methodology; whether a "neutral" principle or application has a harsh or disparate impact upon women; how a given legal issue of concern to women is linked to other systems of domination, such as racism; and what kind of strategy, legal or otherwise, can effectively challenge the structures that support our current gender relations.

Feminist analysis of law emerged in the 1970s, when issues such as wife battering, abortion, and rape were placed on the public agenda through the work of the women's movement on consciousness-raising and naming of women's experiences, and research about the role and response of law to women's efforts to invoke its protection. Feminists from different political frameworks — liberal, socialist, and radical — participated in the debates and the struggle around criminal law reform of abortion, rape, and wife assault. Specific reforms were, in fact, achieved through this engagement with law. Feminist analysis has also addressed the practices of law enforcement by police, the allegedly "objective" assumptions about criminal responsibility that underpin the legal formulation of defences such as self-defence, the criminal justice structures such as the adversary system, the jury, and prison itself, as well as the ideologies conveyed by the criminal justice system that reproduce coercive gender relations.

Since the coming into force of ss. 15 and 28 of the *Charter*, feminist lawyers have had an impact upon the shape of the law of equality as applied to criminal law, as evidenced by the fact that, in case after case, the Supreme Court has granted standing to feminist groups as intervenors, acknowledging their expertise on equality issues. As a result, the major Supreme Court decisions on equality have been influenced by feminist analysis. For instance, in *R.* v. *Turpin*, [1989] 1 S.C.R. 1296 at 1332 the Supreme Court of Canada held that "A finding that there is discrimination will ... in most but not all cases, necessarily entail a search for disadvantage that exists apart from and independent of the particular legal distinction being challenged." Thus, even the Supreme Court has accepted that meaningful equality is not served by formal notions of "equal treatment," but rather requires attention to questions of systemic oppression. It must be cautioned, however, that the bulk of *Charter* litigation is initiated and, thus, shaped by individuals and groups such as corporations, who can only be viewed as members of the dominant sector. As well, the Court has yet to accept some of the more radical challenges of feminism, as illustrated by recent cases such as *R.* v. *Seaboyer*, [1991] 2 S.C.R. 577 and *R.* v. *O'Connor*, [1995] 4 S.C.R. 411.

Feminist analysis and activism have also been persuasive in numerous other important areas of criminal law and policy outside of litigation strategies: the planned closure of the federal women's prison in Kingston, Ontario; the adoption of new charging policies by police in many provinces for men who batter women; the extension of legal aid, at least in some cases, to women who are complainants in the criminal process; the drafting and passage of legislation designed to limit the use of women's sexual history evidence in rape trials; and the struggle to secure the release from prison of women incarcerated for killing violent partners both before and after the Supreme Court of Canada's decision in *R.* v. *Lavallee*, [1990] 1 S.C.R. 852.

An example of the influence of feminism on criminal law can be found in the legal treatment of wife assault, which winds its way throughout this book. It is first raised in the **Definition of Crime**, where Christine Boyle suggests that women might have specific interests and different priorities as to which values ought to be served by the criminal law, such as physical safety and protection of the integrity of their relationships. Wife assault is next raised by the **Sentencing** materials, both in terms of specific examples of victim-blaming rationales for lenient sentences for wife assault, particularly where the offender is a prominent citizen, such as a judge or a police officer, and in terms of a lengthy case study of the Kirby Inwood case, including the facta and Ontario Court of Appeal decision.

Wife assault is indirectly addressed under **Law and Order** by John Scott's article, which links daily violence against women and a culture of machismo with the Montreal Massacre. Under **Compelling the Accused's Appearance in Court**, we look at the police response to wife assault, and at a United States lawsuit against police for their failure to protect a woman endangered by her former partner. Wife assault is again raised in the **Powers of Prosecution**, where examples of judicial resort to contempt citations against women who have been assaulted but who refuse to fulfil the role of "complainant" are examined.

Colonization, Colonialism, and Racism

A second major theme pursued in this book is the impact of colonization, colonialism, and racism upon Aboriginal peoples in Canada, and upon other racialized groups, such as African-Canadians. We have chosen to focus on these two "groups" because the criminal law system has had a particularly significant impact upon them, both historically and currently. However, it must be recognized that while the criminal law has treated them as "groups" for its purposes, in fact Aboriginal peoples have distinct Nations, laws, and practices, and African-Canadians in Canada are likewise rich in diversity historically, linguistically, and culturally. The forms and implications of racism are thus not only different as between these two groups, but also within each group.

Analysis of systems and forms of white domination informs an understanding of current issues in criminal law. Colonization and slavery enforced specific relations and roles for Aboriginal peoples and African-Canadians in Canada in the social and economic ordering historically. In a Gramscian sense, the ideology of racism has both ideational dimensions and a material base. For example, the Protestant ethic and Christianity were imposed on Aboriginal peoples through specific forms of quasi-criminal law, and racism provided justification, first, for slavery, and then for segregation. Racism also has economic implications through the maintenance of divisions based on constructions of "race" and "ethnicity" and the creation of classes of workers without benefit of "law."

The criminal law has been implicated in the perpetuation of racism through particular policies, laws, and practices. Some of these are motivated by fear and hatred, but others have the effect of furthering white domination by, for instance, invoking stereotypes about Aboriginal peoples, disproportionately affecting African-Canadians, or refusing to acknowledge racism as a component of a particular legal problem. Historically, law was used to strip Aboriginal peoples of their land and identity by the criminalization of their practices of governance, tradition, and spirituality. It was also used to formalize and enforce segregation and the impoverishment of African-Canadians. The roles and relations created historically for Aboriginal and African-Canadians, among others, in the social and economic hierarchy have had very clear implications for current criminal law issues: the "criminalization" and overpolicing of particular groups; the failure of criminal law to investigate and punish violence against members of these communities, including violence perpetrated by police themselves; sentences that have a particularly severe impact on members of these groups; and judicial expansions of the law that criminalize the conduct of targeted groups.

This analysis of the role of racism in shaping the content and application of criminal law, and the role of criminal law in reinforcing dominance through racism, can also be traced for other groups in Canada. For example, in terms of Asian peoples in Canada, the history of the exploitation of Chinese immigrant labourers to build the railways, the use of discriminatory legislation to control immigration through the "head tax," the invocation of criminal law and quasi-criminal law to control employment opportunities and to segregate Chinese people, and the internment and divestment of persons of Japanese descent of their property during the Second World War all provide relevant context for analysis of current policing practices with respect to Asian communities. Links to the criminal law's stance of non-intervention with respect to anti-Semitism in its historical and current forms may also be made. These examples are touched upon in our materials, although they are not fully developed.

Canadian courts have recognized some forms of racism in their interpretations of human rights legislation and in one or two constitutional law cases, such as *R.* v. *Drybones*, [1970] S.C.R. 282. The recent case of *R.* v. *Bob* (1991), 3 C.R. (4th) 348 (Sask. C.A.) found a s. 15 *Charter* violation on the basis of unequal impact of an administrative criminal law decision upon Aboriginal peoples. However, apart from a few cases like *Bob*, the courts have yet to implement these understandings in the criminal law context beyond legislation that is overtly discriminatory. Our materials therefore present the challenge of creating legal responses and rethinking criminal law and practice in opposition to systemic racism.

Issues involving Aboriginal peoples are threaded throughout the book, commencing with **Colonization and the Imposition of Criminal Law**, where the historical materials on the extension of Canadian criminal law to Aboriginal peoples are reproduced. More current examples of the implications of colonization are set out in the section on **Aboriginal Peoples and Criminal Law**, where the results of recent inquiries into criminal "justice" for Aboriginal peoples, the link between criminal law and land claims disputes, and alternative systems of justice are canvassed. The part on **Sentencing** explores the ways in which "culture" and "race" of both victim and accused affect the sentence for a given offence. The section also examines the use of "cultural" defences to mitigate sentences for sexual assault in Northern communities by situating several recent cases within the context of judicial attitudes towards Aboriginal women, academic commentary, and the response of the Inuit women's group, Pauktuutit, to the issue. Finally, the section explores Aboriginal justice initiatives, such as elders panels and circle sentencing.

Under **Prisons and Parole**, we look at the statistics that signal the over-incarceration of Aboriginal women and men. We also note the specific issues that imprisonment presents in terms of spiritual practices, discrimination within prison, and loss of access to community, among others. The link between land claims and criminal law is deepened in the section on **Law and Order** through analysis of the media interest in reporting on the use of violence at Kanehsatake (Oka) and the construction of the Mohawks as "vigilantes" and "criminals." **Policing** presents a province-by-province sketch of racism in terms of both police killings of Aboriginal people and failure to investigate the deaths of Aboriginal people by reference to specific examples and to provincial investigations and reports. In **Compelling the Accused's Appearance in Court**, the materials turn to some of the statistics on the use of arrest powers against Aboriginal people in city streets. Under **Judicial Interim Release**, the effect of the rules and structures governing bail on Aboriginal accused is raised by recommendations for law reform made by the Manitoba Aboriginal Justice Inquiry. In the section dealing with **Powers of Prosecution**, the use of contempt powers against Aboriginal protesters is examined.

The impact of the criminal law upon African-Canadians is also explored in different sections of this book. Racism as an aggravating feature of sentence is examined under **Sentencing**, and **Right to Counsel** reproduces the study by K. Edward Renner and Alan Warner on the impact of an accused's race upon sentencing dispositions in Halifax courts. Reference is made under **Prisons and Parole** to the over-incarceration of African-Canadians in Canadian prisons, to the use of racist language by guards, to the racial segregation of prisoners, and to the differential use of prison discipline. Under **Law and Order**, questions are raised about which racial groups are made the implicit focus of fear campaigns and vigilante actions, such as that perpetrated by Bernhard Goetz in New York.

Policing explores some of these issues in more depth. We use the work of Patricia Williams to examine both the injury and violence of racism and the role of criminal law in its perpetuation. The historical roots of racism in Canada provide context for consideration of current legal claims, such as the *Charter* challenge by African-Canadian students charged in the Cole Harbour, Nova Scotia prosecutions to the bias in the RCMP's investigation and subsequent prosecution. This section utilizes the series of police killings of African-Canadian men in Ontario and Québec and the response of the criminal justice system to highlight the role of unconscious racism and the current "limits" of criminal law, including Glasbeek's analysis of the Attorney-General's files for eight of the Ontario shootings. This issue is returned to under **Search and Seizure** and **Compelling the Accused's Appearance in Court**, where we reproduce some of the challenges to racial profiling.

Class-Based Critique

The third theme explored through these materials is an analysis of economic relations, including the legal treatment of corporate criminality, and the role of the criminal law in reproducing and structuring class relations and in maintaining a capitalist state. The three main contemporary critiques of criminal law have been the work on corporate crime (definition and enforcement), the work on the class and race bias of the administration and enforcement of criminal law (policing, sentencing, and parole), and the feminist work (critiquing both the bias against women and the invisibility of women).

Marxist criminologists have characterized criminal law as the coercive arm of the state and an uncontradictory instrument of class oppression, and have challenged the bias in its doctrine and practice. Marxist analysis has, however, skirted the issue of injury to victims. Calls for increased state intervention have come from both feminists and the New Right. More recently, responding to general attitudes about the rise in crime and the fear of crime, the Left has begun to focus on a more complicated understanding of criminal law. It has taken a bit longer for Left masculinist criminologists to discover the dilemma feminist critical criminologists have been forced to grapple with. Having recognized that "street crime" and appeals to "law and order" were working class issues, and that the victims were primarily poor and working class, progressive criminologists began to rethink their approach to criminal law. This response to the fear of violence was differentiated as Left realism, which took the form of challenges to the basis for the fear of crime, including challenges to the prevalence of particular crimes and an analysis of the ways in which fear and moral panics are constructed. However, this work failed to take seriously the feminist assertion of women's experience of the underreporting of crimes against women.

The corporate crime literature has compared the regulation and enforcement of "street crime" and "suite crime" to point out the class bias in the criminal justice system. It has established that corporate "crime" is treated as a matter of regulation at best, that many "harms," such as corporate homicide, are either not regulated or are essentially treated as private, and that the definition of corporate actors is unnecessarily abstracted. In Canada, that critique has been enlarged with reference to the protection of corporate interests by the *Charter*. Although this work has been important to demonstrate the interests reflected in the definition of criminal law, it would be enhanced by a critical examination of other areas of crime.

While significantly unmasking the bias in law, the corporate crime agenda has also ignored the dilemma of women as victims of violence. The critique of corporate crime is often constructed both too narrowly (restricted to activities such as combines investigation and occupational health) and too instrumentally. A feminist perspective has the potential to enhance that examination. For example, a consideration of injuries to women would refocus the inquiry from such acts of corporate negligence as the design of automobiles like the Ford Pinto to acts with much broader impact, such as the design of contraceptive technology like the Dalkon Shield, a device referred to as an "instrument[s] of death, mutilation and disease" and a "deadly depth charge in [women's] wombs" by Judge Miles Lord.

Similarly, a critical examination that was attentive to racism would refocus the analysis of corporate crime. An examination of environmental crime would pay attention to the ways in which criminal law has been used to enforce the dumping of toxic wastes on lands inhabited by Aboriginal communities, the failure to police such environmental pollution, the resistance to ordering compensation or cleanup, and would consider whether the term "environmental racism" aptly describes these practices. For example, the materials consider the mercury pollution of the Wabigoon river systems by Reed Paper Company, and the effects upon two Ojibway communities in terms of destruction of local economies and the incidence of Minamata disease.

The theme of the class bias of the criminal law is pursued in this book, commencing with the **Definition of Crime**, where the "reprimand" delivered by a U.S. judge to the lawyers and corporate officers implicated in the Dalkon Shield disaster is reproduced to highlight the social, legal, and ethical issues raised by corporate criminality. Recent provincial efforts to criminalize begging are discussed in the context of *Charter* challenges to the definition of crime. Under **Colonization and the Imposition of Criminal Law**, the economic interests pursued through colonization are exposed by examples of corporate destruction of Aboriginal lands and resources. **Enforcement of Law** looks at unequal patterns of criminal law enforcement based on class position, by reference to the work of William Greenaway, and considers the interaction between class and gender in the context of law enforcement against welfare fraud and solicitation for prostitution. **Sentencing** raises questions about the sentencing options available for corporate offenders. The disparate impact of the sentencing process upon poor people, given the individualized basis for consideration of aggravating and mitigating factors at sentencing, and given the severe impact that fines and imprisonment in default of payment of fines have on the poor, is another issue developed under this section.

Search and Seizure takes up the theme of the class-bias of the criminal law in terms of the relative insulation afforded corporations from even regulatory prosecution and by the extension of *Charter* rights to grant immunity from "unreasonable" searches and seizures to these entities. The **Right to Counsel** materials also raise issues of class. Here we canvass the issues around the substance of the formal right to counsel, including challenges to the limited services provided through legal aid schemes, and the implications of access to justice for accused who either appear unrepresented in criminal court or whose lawyers are legal aid lawyers. Access to justice for poor people is raised in a different form under **Judicial Interim Release**, where the criteria for bail and the implications of its denial are considered.

STRUCTURE

We begin in Chapter 1 with the **Definition of Crime** in order to problematize the notion of "crime" as a fixed and "neutral" phenomenon. Instead, we highlight its contingency and its partiality, and investigate the underlying values and assumptions. This section raises questions about the interests and groups served and supported by the current scope of criminal prohibitions, and also puts at issue rigid legal boundaries, such as the one between criminal law and tort law. Two of the major themes of the book, feminism and class-based analysis of criminal law, are introduced in this part. Their relationship can be illuminated by reference to the social construction of crime.

The social construction of particular behaviours as "crime," and the consequent labelling of specific individual actors, both human and corporate, as "criminal" is another sub-theme of this book. The social construction of "criminality" both influences and is shaped by the legal agenda of legislators (e.g. the failure to criminalize racial and sexual harassment), of police (e.g. the relegation of men's violence towards women partners to the "private" sphere or the non-law field of "social work"; the perception that the use of firearms against unarmed, often fleeing African-Canadian men is justified), and of judges (e.g. the use of judicial powers to cite for contempt of court women who refuse the role of "complainant" in the criminal process).

The result is a construction of crime that, in many ways, replicates and reproduces relations of dominance. The construction resonates with ideologies such as those of gender and sexuality, including what Adrienne Rich has described as "compulsory heterosexuality,"[2] the patterns of white domination created by colonization and structured and enforced through "racial" and "ethnic" differentiation, and ideologies of "choice" and "individualism." Similarly, criminal law is shaped by the market "imperatives" of a capitalist economic system.

The sources of the discourse about "crime" and "criminality" are complex. They derive in part from "facts," "accounts," and "statistics" produced by those who have the power to create this "knowledge" about "crime." For example, as the sole agents charged with the responsibility to detect and investigate "crime," the police constitute an important site for the creation of information and statistics about "crime." As well, prison officials and certain media corporations have a virtual monopoly over the creation of information about particular behaviours in specific contexts. Judges, too, interpret and validate the "meaning" and "truth" of this "knowledge" in adjudicating "guilt" and "innocence."

The "knowledge" produced by these sources constructs as crimes the behaviours of a fairly limited group of individuals, and excludes from these understandings other injurious activities of the sources themselves, such as police officers. As Catharine MacKinnon has written:

> Having power means, among other things, that when someone says, "This is how it is," it is taken as being that way. When this happens in law, such a person is accorded credibility. When that person is believed over another speaker, what was said becomes proof. Speaking socially, the beliefs of the powerful become proof, in part because the world actually arranges itself to affirm what the powerful want to see. If you perceive this as a process, you might call it force, or at least pressure or what money can buy. If it is imperceptible as a process, you may consider it voluntary or consensual or free will or human nature, or just the way things are. Beneath this, though, the world is not entirely the way the powerful say it is or want to believe it is. If it appears to be, it is because power constructs the appearance of reality by silencing the voices of the powerless, by excluding them from access to authoritative discourse. Powerlessness means that when you say "This is how it is," it is not taken as being that way. This makes articulating silence, perceiving the presence of absence, believing those who have been socially stripped of credibility, critically contextualizing what passes for

simple fact, necessary to the epistemology of a politics of powerlessness.[3]

Chapter 2 of the book, **Colonization and the Imposition of Criminal Law**, highlights a number of issues about colonization, sovereignty, and the way law has been used historically in colonization. The purpose of this part of the book is to interrogate the role and impact of state use of the criminal law power, and also to provide background to current issues in criminal law. We begin with the historical examples of the use of criminal law and quasi-criminal law to outlaw practices of tradition and governance of Aboriginal peoples, such as the Potlatch and the Sundance. We then turn to early criminal trials of Aboriginal people accused of murder under Canadian law: that is, the imposition of Canadian criminal law on peoples who had a different system of law and justice. The trials raise questions at the level of the individual accused about notions of "culpability" and "blameworthiness," and starkly underline their relationship to colonization and resistance to the appropriation of Aboriginal lands. This part also touches on the imposition of British criminal law upon the Canadien(ne)s of Québec.

Having examined the ways in which criminal law was used in the colonization of Aboriginal peoples historically, we follow with the present day elaboration of the consequences in Chapter 3, **Aboriginal Peoples and Criminal Law**. This part examines the response of criminal law to "crimes" against Aboriginal peoples, including corporate and environmental crimes, as well as the response of criminal law to "crimes" by Aboriginal people, including acts protesting the crimes against them. The exercise of discretion has resulted, historically and contemporarily, in the overpolicing of crimes by Aboriginal people and the underpolicing of crimes against Aboriginal people.

In this part we raise directly some of the most pressing issues in criminal and constitutional justice in contemporary Canada by reference to the Donald Marshall, Jr. Inquiry and its aftermath, the Manitoba Aboriginal Justice Inquiry and the claims of the Manitoba Metis Federation, and the Royal Commission on Aboriginal Peoples. This section links with the earlier sections on colonization and the assumptions embedded in the criminal justice system by exposing the repercussions of "criminalization" and the possibility of alternative systems of Aboriginal justice.

This examination of the historical background, the political context, and the results framed more broadly than simply legal victories or losses demonstrates both how narrowly legal decisions construct the issues and how inadequately the court record describes what has happened. It becomes apparent that the traditional study of legal cases and legal doctrine leaves many questions unanswered or unasked about the criminal process and its results.

Chapter 4 of the book looks at **Enforcement of the Law**, and thus begins to move from the definitions of crime to the criminal process itself. The sources of law are often understood as limited to statutory law, primarily the *Criminal Code*, and judge-made law. Until recently, there has also been a fairly rigid delineation drawn between "substance" and "procedure" in both courses and teaching materials.

Our approach invites a broader examination of the sources of criminal law, including the policies that guide police and prosecutors and the effect of their practices. In order to revitalize criminal procedure by demonstrating its outcomes and effects, we draw on extra-legal materials that provoke reflection about the ways in which law is implicated in the structuring of inequality on the basis of race, class, gender, and sexuality. Many of these issues, for example, racism, have been the subject of public inquiry and criticism by commissions across the country in the past few years, and systemic biases in practice have been identified.

This part, therefore, expands upon the differential patterns of law enforcement by police and Crown attorneys suggested by the materials on Aboriginal peoples, and also looks specifically at the enforcement of the criminal law against poor people, against women who are poor, against gay men by reference to the "bath house" raids in Toronto in 1981, and against gays and lesbians by Canada customs. The theme of homophobia and the use of criminal law to police the boundaries of sex role behaviour is raised by this material. As well, this section invites reflection on the relationship between shifts in social, economic, and political power within communities, and the use of criminal law powers of "enforcement" to attempt to re-establish the structures and relations of dominance. This chapter documents a number of miscarriages of justice, both in Canada and abroad, and canvasses the legal avenues open to wrongfully convicted persons.

Sentencing is the subject of Chapter 5, which traces some of the same patterns in sentencing practices. The **Sentencing** section is extensive, to reflect both its centrality to criminal practice (approximately 85 per cent of criminal charges result in a guilty plea rather than a trial) and its profound significance for accused persons. The major themes of this book are touched upon in this section, including the relevance of race and racism, so-called "cultural" considerations, corporate criminality, violence against women, and the economic impact of sentencing for poor people, particularly the imprisonment of fine defaulters. This chapter also highlights new developments in sentencing, such as the introduction of sentencing circles.

In Chapter 6, **Prisons and Parole**, the book turns to the most restrictive of sentencing options, that of imprisonment. In this context, we look at the role assumed by the courts in implementing a lower level of *Charter* scrutiny for rights violations that occur in prison, the Archambault riots and the report of Amnesty International on the retaliatory violence exerted by the guards against the prisoners, as well as the specific issues confronting gay men, women, and Aboriginal peoples who serve time in prison. This chapter includes extracts from both the *Report of the Commission on Systemic Racism in the Ontario Criminal Justice System* and the Honourable Louise Arbour's report, *Commission of Inquiry into Certain Events at the Prison For Women in Kingston*.

Many of the underlying beliefs and values used to justify imprisonment, the use of discipline in prison, and limitations on rights of prisoners are exposed and challenged in Chapter 7, **Law and Order**. This section raises questions about who is targeted by "law and order" initiatives, and who is empowered by the fear and the budgets that flow from such appeals. In particular, readings on the invocation of the *War Measures Act* in 1970, on vigilantism, on the Montreal Massacre of 1989, and on the Kanehsatake (Oka) conflict permit links to be made between inequalities, the ways in which violence is used to maintain those relations, and the response of the state to that violence. New federal legislation, dubbed the "anti-terrorism" laws, is referenced here in order to make the historical links to current developments more transparent.

In Chapter 8, **Introduction to Criminal Procedure**, we begin the sections that look at criminal procedure in a more detailed fashion. This part is concerned with the classification of offences and the implications of such classification for other process issues, including specific police powers like arrest and the accused's entitlement to select mode of trial, such as trial by jury. It also touches on the many *Charter* claims that can be made by accused persons.

Chapter 9 is the section on **Policing**. It starts with an article that gives an institutional analysis of the role and functioning of police, including their participation in criminal activity. This section then turns to current legal issues in policing, such as sexism and homophobia, and examines racism in more detail by looking at police killings and public inquiries in many provinces. This section provides historical context for racism in Canada by examining the African-Canadian experience. It provides comparative context by looking at United States commentary on the assault on Rodney King, and by reference to the police investigation of the Jeffrey Dahmer case, which implicated both racism and homophobia. Specific strategies in response to policing are posited in this section, and students are invited to assess such strategies critically, including the documentation of police violence and neglect through royal commissions and public inquiries, tort actions against the police, *Charter* challenges to racial profiling, and the possibility of the creation of new categories of "hate crimes."

Police powers of **Search and Seizure** are the subject of Chapter 10. Common law and statutory powers of search are set out, as are the important *Charter* cases and the critique of those cases for class bias and the reification of judicial "neutrality" and "individual rights." This part returns to the issue of the role of the state vis à vis the concentration and exercise of corporate power, specifically in the context of ownership of the media. It also touches on the theme of racism by reference to *Charter* challenges to searches accompanied by racist abuse, and recent cases delineating the power of high school staff to search students and police to engage in strip searches.

Chapter 11 treats the subject of **Compelling the Accused's Appearance in Court**. This section on arrest looks at the common law powers held by police, the *Criminal Code* sections on compelling attendance in court, the impact of police discretion in terms of race, class, and gender, and the way in which the *Charter* is shaping the law of arrest. Chapter 12 focuses on the **Right to Counsel**, both as it emerges in terms of police obligations to advise detained persons of their right to obtain legal advice and judicial obligations to ensure a fair trial. The materials also canvass the limited right to state-funded counsel through legal aid plans, for example. **Judicial Interim Release** is covered in Chapter 13. Here we look at the impact of detention pending trial upon the accused and the outcome of both trial and sentence, the current legal structure for bail determinations, and the reform proposals generated by the Aboriginal Justice Inquiry of Manitoba and the *Report of the Commission on Systemic Racism in the Ontario Criminal Justice System*.

Finally, in Chapter 14 the subject of **Powers of Prosecution** is addressed. Police and Crown attorney powers of prosecution are discussed, with specific reference to the rate at which certain offences, such as sexual assault, are dropped out of the criminal process. This part interrogates the significance of private prosecutions, linking the efforts by private citizens to prosecute the RCMP for *Criminal Code* violations to the earlier materials on **Policing**. We also look at judicial powers of prosecution in the form of contempt citations, illuminating the relationship of these powers to attempts by private actors to invoke the authority of the state, for example, to police private injunctions. This section examines the political meaning and use of contempt powers, and compares this judicial authority with the restrictions on judicial commentary on issues of public concern outside of the courtroom, using the specific examples of Thomas Berger, Bertha Wilson, and Jocelyne Moreau-Bérubé, among others.

In our view, students working with these materials will develop a broad understanding of the context, nature, and impact of the criminal law process in Canada. They will have been exposed to critical methods of analyzing many of the most significant legal issues on the current public policy agenda, and will also have a grounding for working with interdisciplinary materials. Finally, we believe that this book prepares students for further in depth study of criminal law issues and, specifically, for the study of issues of "substantive" criminal law, such as *actus reus* and *mens rea* and the shape and application of defences. These subjects are pursued in Jennie Abell and Elizabeth Sheehy, *Criminal Law and Procedure: Proof, Defences, and Beyond*, 2d ed. (North York: Captus Press, 1999) [hereinafter, Abell and Sheehy, *Proof, Defences, and Beyond*]. The students' ability to appreciate the operative complexity and implications of these other issues is greatly enhanced by materials and links forged in this set of materials.

Notes

1. While we recognize that there are different views on this point, we use the term "Aboriginal peoples" to include First Nations peoples, Metis peoples, and the Inuit. We use this particular term primarily because it has been adopted by a number of Aboriginal organizations (e.g. Aboriginal Women of Saskatchewan) for its importance constitutionally, and for its inclusiveness (e.g. "First Nations" excludes Metis peoples). The Ontario Native Women's Association also chooses the term "Aboriginal" for some of the same reasons in *Breaking Free: A Proposal to Change Aboriginal Family Violence* (Thunder Bay, 1989). We understand that it is important to recognize the many and diverse nations encompassed by the term "Aboriginal peoples," and where possible, we refer specifically to individual nations by their own names.
2. Adrienne Rich, *Compulsory Heterosexuality and Lesbian Existence* (Denver: Antelope Publications, 1980).
3. Catharine MacKinnon, *Feminism Unmodified. Discourses on Life and Law* (Cambridge: Harvard University Press, 1987) at 164.
4. *Royal Commission Report on Newspapers* (Hull: Minister of Supply and Services, 1981) at 9.

1

Definition of Crime

The readings in this chapter are intended to problematize the definition of "crime," to demonstrate its contingency, and to consider challenges to the definition of crime.

A. PROBLEMATIZING THE DEFINITION OF "CRIME"

In the chapter entitled "Street and Suite Crime" of the book, *Corporate Crime in Canada* (Scarborough: Prentice-Hall, 1978), Colin Goff and Charles Reasons raise questions about how we determine which behaviours are "criminal." The formalistic approach, which states that "crime is what the law says it is," is circular, may undermine efforts to confront illegitimate regimes, and seems unhelpful when one considers the sheer volume of *Criminal Code* offences, federal and provincial offences, and municipal laws. As Stephen Hester and Peter Eglin point out in *A Sociology of Crime* (London: Routledge, 1992) at 27 (notes omitted):

> Without criminal law there would be no "crime." Virtually every form of human action — from taking others' property to taking others' lives — has in some time or place been deemed warranted, if not desirable. For example, until recently, slavery, non-consensual intercourse within marriage, and all forms of execution have been widely practised and have received official approval. This is not to say that people have not objected to these forms of behaviour, but until proscribed by criminal law they cannot be considered "crimes." Crime, then, is a relative or legalistic, rather than an absolute, concept. Criminal law is constructed within society. Hence, crime, too, is a social construction.†

To further complicate the definition of "crime," relevant issues must be taken into account, such as who has the legislative authority to define and punish crime, jurisdictional questions of enforcement and prosecution of certain types of offences and offenders, the impact of the *Charter*, the social construction of "crime," the ways in which the law is enforced, and the punishment and censure associated with different offences.

First, the federal government's constitutional authority to legislate with respect to criminal law

---

† Excerpts from Stephen Hester and Peter Eglin, *A Sociology of Crime* (London: Routledge, 1992) at 27. Reproduced with permission of Routledge.

pursuant to s. 91(27) of the *Constitution Act, 1867* (U.K.), 30 & 31 Vict., c. 3 (formerly *British North America Act, 1867*) [hereinafter *Constitution Act, 1867*], has been used to enact not only the *Criminal Code*, but also other statutes that can be described as "criminal law." For example, the *Narcotic Control Act*, R.S.C. 1985, c. N-1, now the *Controlled Drugs and Substances Act*, S.C. 1996, c. 19, the *Food and Drugs Act*, R.S.C. 1985, c. F-27, the *Hazardous Products Act*, R.S.C. 1985, c. H-3, and the *Competition Act*, R.S.C. 1985, c. C-34, are all federal acts that create offences carrying penalties that include fines and imprisonment.

The provinces also have the constitutional authority to legislate offences that carry the possibility of fines and/or imprisonment, thus effectively legislating "crimes." Pursuant to ss. 92(14) and (15) of the *Constitution Act, 1867*, the provinces have the authority to enact laws relating to the administration of justice and that attach penalties to violations of laws that are within their legislative authority, such as property and civil rights in the province.

Thus, for example, the provinces and territories have enacted highway traffic legislation and trespass to property legislation; they have also delegated to the municipalities the power to create "crimes" through by-laws. However, when provincial legislatures enter areas traditionally considered "criminal," they risk declarations by courts that the legislation is invalid as *ultra vires*. Thus, *R. v. Morgentaler*, [1993] 3 S.C.R. 519, held that a Nova Scotia act and regulations that prohibited abortions outside the hospital committee system was beyond the constitutional authority of the province because the true purpose of the law was to restrict abortion as a socially undesirable practice; in *Westendorp v. R.*, [1983] 1 S.C.R. 43, a Calgary municipal by-law prohibiting presence on a city street for the purpose of prostitution was also declared unconstitutional because it was patently an attempt to invade the sphere of legislative authority reserved for the federal government.

Second, although the federal and provincial governments have enacted legislation that creates criminal law outside of the *Criminal Code*, some of these offences are neither detected nor prosecuted by the ordinary police and prosecutorial branches, and some are thus seen as "regulatory" offences rather than "crimes." These offences may be part of regulatory schemes enforced by agencies set up specifically to administer and enforce these laws. For example, provincial laws regulating workplace safety and federal laws limiting corporate behaviour that interferes with marketplace competition are each monitored by separate agencies whose job it is to secure compliance with the legislation, to gather evidence in certain cases, to make decisions as to the pursuit of prosecutions, and even to act as prosecutor.

In addition to separate investigative and prosecutorial agencies that are suggestive of a lesser degree of "criminality," many of these regulatory crimes also use legislative frameworks that reinforce this hierarchy. As Laureen Snider suggests, in her book *Bad Business: Corporate Crime in Canada* (Scarborough: Nelson Canada, 1993) [hereinafter *Bad Business*] at 146 (notes omitted):

> There is no regulatory agency that could be characterized as punitive in its practices by the standards of law enforcement used against traditional criminals. Indeed, by these standards agencies and laws are absurdly permissive. Compared to the Canadian Criminal Code, regulatory acts are full of loopholes.
>
> Canada's Hazardous Products Act, for example, allows action to be taken only after the product is on the market, and therefore after damage has been done. The Food and Drugs Act allows manufacturers to do their own tests of the safety of their products, and accepts these tests as proof. Occupational Health and Safety Acts, both federal and provincial, in Canada and elsewhere, are worded in such a way that safe working conditions must be provided only if doing so will not seriously affect the profitability of the company. The Canadian Environmental Protection Act imposes emission standards only after a "significant danger" to human health has been demonstrated....[†]

Third, while the courts do not have the power to create new "crimes" in a formal sense (with the exception of the common law offence of contempt) because of the prohibition in s. 9(a) of the *Code* ("no person shall be convicted ... of an offence at common law"), judges do have a role in the definition of crime. They interpret: the proof requirements of offences in legislation through statutory interpretation; the defences available both in the *Code* and at common law

---

[†] Excerpts from *Bad Business: Corporate Crime in Canada*, 1st ed., by Laureen Snider. Reproduced with permission of Nelson Thomson Learning, a division of Thomson Learning. Fax: (800) 730-2215.

(s. 8(3) of the *Code*); and the implications of the *Charter* for the obligations of proof imposed on the prosecution. They may also sentence an offender so as to register a judgment that the act was not truly "criminal" (see **Sentencing**, *infra*).

By way of example, the Supreme Court is essentially engaged in defining the scope of "criminal law" when it uses concepts delineating some offences as "true crimes" and carrying "criminal" "stigma" in its rulings interpreting the implications of s. 7 of the *Charter*. According to the Court, any offence that carries the possibility of imprisonment, which would include the vast majority of federal and provincial offences, must require proof of some form of "fault" element: *Reference Re B.C. Motor Vehicle Act*, [1985] 2 S.C.R. 486. However, only for those offences that carry serious social "stigma" will the Court require that fault be assessed subjectively, from the point of view of the accused person: *R. v. Vaillancourt*, [1988] 2 S.C.R. 636. Furthermore, the Court has ruled that the legislature can use an objective measure of "fault" and a reverse onus of proof with respect to those offences such as false advertising that are not "truly criminal," but rather are "instrumental" to achieving some goal of social policy: *R. v. Wholesale Travel Group*, [1991] 3 S.C.R. 154. For further discussion of these cases and concepts, see Abell and Sheehy, *Proof, Defences, and Beyond*, **Mens Rea**.

Fourth, to return to the theme that introduced this chapter, our ideas about what is "true" crime are socially reproduced and reinforced by police, corporate culture, the media and as is implicit in the preceding paragraph, by judges as well. These institutions may also produce contradictory understandings of what is criminal: while sexual assault is widely said to constitute serious criminal behaviour, frequently it is not treated as such by police, media, or judges. Other offences may be regarded and dealt with as serious crimes by police and prosecutors, but find no such support in the notions of criminal justice as expressed by juries. For instance, Constance Backhouse in "Desperate Women and Compassionate Courts" (1984) 34 U.T.L.J. 447 and "Involuntary Motherhood: Abortion, Birth Control and the Law in Nineteenth-Century Canada" (1983) 3 Windsor Y.B. Access Just. 6, documents the surprising leniency in the nineteenth century exhibited by juries and some judges towards women who procured abortions or killed their newborns, but demonstrates that that leniency was reserved, for the most part, for working class women. Similarly, although abortions procured outside the hospital committee process were criminalized under the *Criminal Code* until the offence was declared unconstitutional by the Supreme Court of Canada in 1988 (*R. v. Morgentaler*, [1988] 1 S.C.R. 30), juries consistently acquitted Dr. Henry Morgentaler, doctor and activist, of such charges: see Abell and Sheehy, *Proof, Defences, and Beyond*, **Necessity**.

Thus, patterns of law enforcement by police, prosecutors, and other agencies charged with the administration of regulatory schemes suggest that when certain behaviours are statutorily defined as criminal, they may not be enforced as crimes for certain types of offences, certain classes of offenders, or certain types of victims such as members of a low status group. Further, even if prosecutions are pursued and convictions are obtained, the punishments available and those actually exacted for certain kinds of offences, offenders and victim groups may undermine or reinforce particular understandings of what is "crime."

R. v. Banks†

[BABE J.:]

Introduction

The 13 defendants have all been individually charged with offences under the recently enacted *Safe Streets Act, 1999*, S.O. 1999, c. 8. They have been brought together on consent for a joint trial so that the constitutional validity of the new statutory provisions may be conveniently determined in one proceeding after full argument.

. . . .

---

† (2001), 55 O.R. (3d) 374 (Ct. Just.).

The Challenged Statutory Provisions

The *Safe Streets Act, 1999*, received Royal Assent on December 14, 1999, to come into force upon Proclamation by the Lieutenant Governor. It came into force on January 31, 2000. Its full title is "An Act to promote safety in Ontario by prohibiting aggressive solicitation, solicitation of persons in certain places and disposal of dangerous things in certain places, and to amend the *Highway Traffic Act* to regulate certain activities on roadways."

. . . .

1. In sections 2 and 3,

"solicit" means to request, in person, the immediate provision of money or another thing of value, regardless of whether consideration is offered or provided in return, using the spoken, written or printed word, a gesture or other means.

2.(1) In this section,

"aggressive manner" means a manner that is likely to cause a reasonable person to be concerned for his or her safety or security.

(2) No person shall solicit in an aggressive manner.

(3) Without limiting subsection (1) or (2), a person who engages in one or more of the following activities shall be deemed to be soliciting in an aggressive manner for the purposes of this section:

1. Threatening the person solicited with physical harm, by word or gesture or other means, during the solicitation or after the person solicited responds or fails to respond to the solicitation.
2. Obstructing the path of the person solicited during the solicitation after the person solicited responds or fails to respond to the solicitation.
3. Using abusive language during the solicitation or after the person solicited responds or fails to respond to the solicitation.
4. Proceeding behind, alongside or ahead of the person solicited during the solicitation or after the person solicited responds or fails to respond to the solicitation.
5. Soliciting while intoxicated by alcohol or drugs.
6. Continuing to solicit a person in a persistent manner after the person has responded negatively to the solicitation.

3.(1) In this section,

"public transit vehicle" means a vehicle operated by, for or on behalf of the Government of Ontario, a municipality in Ontario, including a regional and district municipality and the County of Oxford, or a transit commission or authority in Ontario, as part of a regular passenger transportation service;

"roadway" has the same meaning as in the *Highway Traffic Act*;

"vehicle" includes automobile, motorcycle, van, truck, trailer, bus, mobile home, traction engine, farm tractor, road-building machine, bicycle, motor-assisted bicycle, motorized snow vehicle, streetcar and any other vehicle drawn, propelled or driven by any kind of power, including muscular power.

(2) No person shall,

(a) solicit a person who is using, waiting to use, or departing from an automated teller machine;
(b) solicit a person who is using or waiting to use a pay telephone or a public toilet facility;
(c) solicit a person who is waiting at a taxi stop or a public transit stop;
(d) solicit a person who is in or on a public transit vehicle;
(e) solicit a person who is in the process of getting in, out of or off a vehicle or who is in a parking lot; or
(f) while on a roadway, solicit a person who is in or on a stopped, standing or parked vehicle.

...

7.(1) Section 177 of the *Highway Traffic Act* is repealed and the following is substituted:

177.(1) No person, while on the roadway, shall solicit a ride from the driver of a motor vehicle other than a public passenger conveyance.

(2) No person, while on the roadway, shall stop, attempt to stop or approach a motor vehicle for the purpose of offering, selling or providing any commodity or service to the driver or any other person in the motor vehicle;

(3) Subsection (2) does not apply to the offer, sale or provision of towing or repair services or any other commodity or service in an emergency.

...

Prior to its re-enactment in the *Safe Streets Act*, s. 177 of the *Highway Traffic Act*, R.S.O. 1990, c. H.8 already prohibited soliciting rides and stopping motor vehicles to offer commodities or services. The amended section merely adds the words "or approach" to the section, thus covering offers of goods or services to vehicles stopped, for example, at traffic lights.

The Adjudicative Facts

. . . .

Briefly, the defendants Banks, Barrington, Naugle, Beach, Collins, Moran, Stevenson and Coupal were all found engaging in what has come to be popularly called "squeegying" at various locations in the City of Toronto, that is to say, they were approaching vehicles stopped in traffic, mostly at red lights, and offering to clean or cleaning the windshields with the hope or expectation of receiving money from the drivers. Banks, Barrington, Collins and Coupal were charged with committing offences contrary to s. 177(2) of the *Highway Traffic Act*, as amended by the *Safe Streets Act*. Naugle, Moran, Beach and Stevenson were charged with offences contrary to s. 3(2)(f) of the *Safe Streets Act*.

Brydges, Batuskin, Evans and Leonard were all found approaching stopped vehicles in a similar manner, but they simply asked for money without offering to perform a service. All were charged under s. 3(2)(f) of the *Safe Streets Act*.

The defendant Hughes was found panhandling for money on Bloor Street in Toronto. He was approaching pedestrians and would continue to follow them for a short distance continuing to ask for money after a refusal. He would approach everyone whom he observed coming out of restaurants. He was charged with soliciting aggressively contrary to s. 2(2) of the *Safe Streets Act*. This conduct would seem to engage para. 4 and, arguably, para. 6 of the extended definitions of "soliciting in an aggressive manner" contained in s. 2(3).

All of the defendants except Stevenson are described in the agreed statements as being "homeless" or as having "no fixed address". They vary in age from 16 to 50.

. . . .

The Federalism Question

The distribution of powers under Canada's federal constitution has now had more than 130 years of judicial consideration, and the general principles are well established. Criminal law and procedure is one of the heads of "exclusive legislative authority" of Parliament under s. 91(27) of the *Constitution Act, 1867*. A province is, therefore, not competent to create a crime, and any provincial legislation that purports to do so is *ultra vires*. It is, however, within provincial legislative competence to create offences in order to enforce standards imposed by provincial laws that are enacted "in relation to matters coming within the classes of subjects ... enumerated" in s. 92 of the Act. As generations of Canadian law students have learned, in dealing with distribution-of-powers questions under ss. 91 and 92, one must first identify "the matter" to determine which level of government has the competence to legislate in relation to it by looking for the "pith and substance" or "dominant aspect" of the statute in question, while recognizing that a subject may have different aspects that bring it within the legislative competence of both levels of government (the "double aspect doctrine"). Where both levels of government have legislated in relation to a matter, otherwise valid provincial legislation may be rendered "inoperative" by valid federal legislation if there is direct conflict between them. In many cases, however, both provincial and federal legislation may operate side by side "even where the legal effect ... is virtually identical": *R.* v. *Morgentaler*, [1993] 3 S.C.R. 463 at pp. 497–98. See also *Prince Edward Island (Provincial Secretary)* v. *Egan*, [1941] S.C.R. 396 (upholding the right of a province to suspend a driving licence upon conviction for a *Criminal Code* driving offence); *Smith* v. *R.*, [1960] S.C.R. 776 (upholding a prosecution for making a false statement in a prospectus under the *Securities Act* of Ontario notwithstanding the existence of a *Criminal Code* offence for making a false prospectus); *Multiple Access Ltd.* v. *McCutcheon*, [1982] 2 S.C.R. 161 (recognizing that insider trading has both securities law and companies law aspects so that both levels of government could validly enact civil remedies). In *Smith*, *supra*, Martland J. said at p. 800 S.C.R.:

> The fact that both provisions prohibit certain acts with penal consequences does not constitute a conflict. It may happen that some acts might be punishable under both provisions and in this sense that these provisions overlap. However, even in such cases, there is no conflict in the sense that compliance with one law involves a breach of the other. It would appear, therefore, that they can operate concurrently.

Even identical provisions have been held not to conflict. In *Multiple Access* v. *McCutcheon*, *supra*, at p. 189 S.C.R., Dickson J. said:

> The provincial legislation merely duplicates the federal, it does not contradict it. The fact that a plaintiff may have a choice of remedies does not mean that the provisions of both levels of government cannot "live together" and operate concurrently.

These cases lead Professor Hogg, [*Constitutional Law of Canada*, looseleaf], to conclude at p. 16-13 that Canadian constitutional law differs from the American and Australian because:

> The inexorable conclusion is that there is no room for imputed inconsistency based on covering the field or negative implication. The sole

test of inconsistency in Canadian constitutional law is express contradiction. This is the course of judicial restraint, allowing the fullest possible play to provincial legislation.

Applying these well known constitutional principles, it has long been established that the regulation of roads and traffic and conduct on roads is a provincial matter: *Ontario (Attorney General)* v. *Winner*, [1954] A.C. 541; *Prince Edward Island* v. *Egan, supra*, at p. 415 S.C.R.; *O'Grady* v. *Sparling*, [1960] S.C.R. 804. In a succession of cases, the Supreme Court of Canada has upheld the constitutionality of the "careless driving" and "failing to remain at the scene of an accident" sections of the *Highway Traffic Act* notwithstanding the very similar *Criminal Code* offences of "dangerous driving" and "failing to stop": *O'Grady* v. *Sparling, supra*; *Stephens* v. *R.*, [1960] S.C.R. 823; *Mann* v. *R.*, [1966] S.C.R. 238. Subsequent efforts to delineate a clear boundary between the operation of the provincial and federal legislation have not been notably successful: *R.* v. *Binus*, [1967] S.C.R. 594; *R.* v. *Peda*, [1969] S.C.R. 905.

In *P.E.I.* v. *Egan, supra*, a law automatically suspending the licence of anyone convicted of the *Criminal Code* offence of driving while intoxicated was held to be valid provincial legislation, notwithstanding the subsequent enactment of a *Criminal Code* provision whereby a person convicted of such offence may be prohibited from driving anywhere in Canada. In *Reference re s. 92(4) of the Vehicles Act, 1957 (Saskatchewan)*, [1958] S.C.R. 608, the majority extended *P.E.I.* v. *Egan, supra*, and upheld a provincial law that suspended the licence of any driver refusing to comply with a police request for a breath sample, even though at the time federal law expressly provided that "no person is required to give a sample of ... breath ... as evidence" of impaired driving (the *Criminal Code*, S.C. 1953-54, 2-3 Eliz. II, c. 51, s. 224(4)).

Professor Hogg, *supra*, concludes at p. 15-12 that: "It is clear from these cases that laws prescribing rules of conduct on the roads have a "double aspect", and are therefor competent to both the Parliament and a Legislature."

I do not consider that the power to regulate the use of roads can be narrowly confined to the promotion of "traffic safety", although that is no doubt an important factor, as the defendants seem to contend. Further, it is clear that the power to regulate conduct extends to parks, sidewalks and other public places, and includes pedestrian as well as vehicular traffic. Thus in *R.* v. *Jarvis, Warrington and Verge* (1980), 57 C.C.C. (2d) 65, the Court of Appeal of Nova Scotia upheld a provision of the *Towns Act*, R.S.N.S. 1967, c. 309 making it an offence to "incommode peaceful passersby or loiter on the streets or highways or in the doorways or windows of shops or dwellings on the streets or thoroughfares of the town" as "ancillary to" the provincial power to "regulate the use of, and traffic on town streets"; in *R.* v. *Young* (1973), 1 O.R. (2d) 564, the Court of Appeal upheld a by-law that prohibited shouting and making noise likely to disturb as "designed to provide for the quiet enjoyment of residential property"; in *R.* v. *Beattie* (1969), 7 C.R.N.S. 116, the Ontario Court of Appeal upheld a by-law prohibiting "boisterous, unseemly or unlawful conduct" or the use of "profane, indecent or abusive language" in parks as having the object "the regulation of conduct in parks so as to preserve their enjoyment as places of serenity and so as to abate breaches of the peace" and therefore valid municipal legislation; in *R.* v. *Nakashima* (1974), 19 C.C.C. (2d) 279 (B.C.S.C.), a by-law prohibiting making noise on a highway or elsewhere that disturbed the peace was upheld; in *Presseau* v. *Paquette* (1952), 101 C.C.C. 256, Demers J., of the Superior Court of Quebec, upheld a municipal by-law making it an offence "to obstruct pedestrians or traffic by standing or loitering upon the streets, highways, lanes, sidewalks, pavements or public places of the City of Montreal, and by refusing without sufficient excuse to move on when ordered to do so by a constable or peace officer" as concerning "the circulation of pedestrian traffic". It should be noted that in each of these cases the court found no conflict with federal legislation covering similar conduct: in *Jarvis et al., supra*, with the *Criminal Code* offences of causing a disturbance in a public place, now found in s. 175(1)(a) and of loitering in a public place and obstructing persons, now s. 175(1)(c); in *Beattie, supra*; *Young, supra*; and *Nakashima, supra*, with the *Criminal Code* offence of causing a disturbance; and in *Presseau* v. *Paquette, supra*, with the former vagrancy section of the *Code*. Note also the decision of the Supreme Court of Canada in *Canada (Attorney General)* v. *Dupond*, [1978] 2 S.C.R. 770, which upheld a Montreal by-law authorizing the banning of gatherings that endangered the public peace as legislation as a "matter of a merely local or private nature" under s. 92(16) of the *British North America Act* and held that the suppression of conditions "likely to favour the commission of crimes" was within provincial jurisdiction.

Westendorp v. *R.*, [1983] 1 S.C.R. 43 is a case relied upon by the defence. In this case, the defendant was charged under a City of Calgary by-law that made it an offence "to be or remain on the street for the purpose of prostitution". The impugned by-law had been enacted as an amendment to a by-law entitled the *Streets By-Law*, which is described at p. 47 S.C.R. as "an extensive regulatory and prohibitory enactment relating to the use of city streets", controlling street activities such as soliciting or carrying on business, trades or occupations on any street. At pp. 51–52 S.C.R., Laskin C.J.C., for the Court, said:

> It is patent ... that s. 6.1 is of a completely different order from its preceding sections and, certainly, from all those succeeding it. It is specious to regard s. 6.1 as relating to control of the streets. If that were its purpose, it would have dealt with congregation of persons on the streets or with obstruction, unrelated to what the congregating or obstructing persons say or otherwise do. As the by-law stands and reads, it is activated only by what is said by a person, referable to the offer of sexual services.... It is triggered only by an offer of sexual services or a solicitation to that end.... It is clearly distinguishable from *Bédard* v. *Dawson*, [1923] S.C.R. 681, where the provincial legislation under attack there was justified as concerned with the control and enjoyment of property.

I do not read this case as questioning the wide provincial power to legislate in relation to streets. The Court found, however, that the pith and substance of the by-law in question was criminal, and in its terms it is clearly distinguishable from the legislation before us.

Similarly, the regulation of business within the province and the licensing of trades and professions are matters of provincial jurisdiction, exercised either directly or by delegation to municipalities, or to provincially constituted boards, commissions and professional governing bodies. The broad scope of provincial power in this area was laid out in a well-known series of decisions affirming provincial authority over the field of insurance and rebuffing federal attempts to regulate that industry [references excluded]. Professor Hogg, *supra*, summarizes the effect of these cases as follows at p. 21-8: "The insurance cases ... established the proposition that the regulation of business was ordinarily a matter of property and civil rights in the province." Thus trading in securities is in Canada subject to provincial regulation through provincial securities commissions, notwithstanding the obvious national scope of that industry, giving rise to the "double aspect" referred to above. Professor Hogg goes on to state at p. 21-10: "Regulation of professions and trades is no different for constitutional purposes than that for other industries and comes under property and civil rights in the province."

In a footnote, Professor Hogg lists the following examples affirming the provincial jurisdiction over various trades and professions [references excluded, but the cases involved accountants, realtors, pharmacists, engineers and lawyers]. Accordingly, in so far as begging may be considered a trade or occupation, it is subject to provincial regulation under the distribution of powers.

Accordingly, I think that the *Safe Streets Act* on its face is valid provincial legislation under the distribution of powers. Furthermore, I do not think that the fact that the federal government has, in the past, legislated against begging in the vagrancy provisions of the *Criminal Code*, or that much of the conduct covered by the *Safe Streets Act* may arguably be caught by various sections of the *Criminal Code*, to be of any significance to its validity as a provincial law in the light of the foregoing authorities. The provisions preventing solicitation of and offering goods or services to stopped vehicles are consistent with the existing scheme of the *Highway Traffic Act* separating pedestrian and vehicular traffic. ... Insofar as a demonstration that "safety" may be furthered by this measure is necessary to a finding of validity, such need not be proved strictly; it is enough that there be a rational basis for so finding: Hogg, *supra*, pp. 15–20.1 and 15–21, and it seems to me that the rationality of separating pedestrian and vehicular traffic so far as possible is self-evident, both for safety and to enhance the circulation of traffic. As pointed out by the Crown in its factum, several of the affiants concede this. The provisions restricting the place and manner of solicitation are within the provincial jurisdiction to regulate activities on streets and sidewalks and other public places recognized in the cases cited above.

The defence, however, characterizes the *Safe Streets Act* as a "colourable" attempt to legislate in relation to criminal law by re-criminalizing begging under the guise of legislating in relation to streets and traffic. Professor Hogg, *supra*, at pp. 15–17ff, discusses the "colourability" doctrine, which means that not only the form of the legislation must be examined but also its substance and the intent underlying its enactment, which can be gleaned from its legislative history and, in some cases, from how it is in fact administered. In *R.* v. *Morgentaler* [1993], *supra*, Sopinka J. describes it as follows:

> The "colourability doctrine" in the distribution of powers is invoked when a law looks as though it deals with a matter within jurisdiction, but in essence is addressed to a matter outside the jurisdiction.

Thus in the line of cases concerning the regulation of the insurance industry referred to above, various attempts by Parliament to legislate concerning insurance under various heads of federal power including criminal law (*Reciprocal Insurers*, *supra*), taxation (*Re Insurance Act (Canada)*, *supra*), and immigration and aliens (*Re Insurance Act (Canada)*, *supra*) were struck down as colourable attempts to interfere with the exercise of civil rights in the province or intermeddle with the insurance business. In *Re Upper Churchill Water Rights Reversion Act*, [1984] 1 S.C.R. 297, a Newfoundland statute that expropriated the assets of a hydro-electric generating company was struck down. Although the province had the right to expropriated property within its borders, the effect would be to frustrate a long-term contract that obliged the company to supply electric power to Hydro-Quebec at below market rates, and although the contract was not referred to in the legislation, interference with it was held to be the pith and substance or true object of the legislation, which was struck down even though "cloaked in the proper constitutional form".

In *R.* v. *Morgentaler* [1993], *supra*, the Supreme Court struck down a Nova Scotia statute and regulations that required designated medical procedures including abortion, be performed in a hospital. The case is described by Professor Hogg, *supra*, at p. 15-18, as a remarkable application of the "colourability doctrine" even though Sopinka J. said at p. 496 S.C.R. that he did not find it necessary to invoke it, because even on its face the Act invaded the criminal law power by expressly prohibiting the performance of abortions in some circumstances (p. 495 S.C.R.). Based on uncontradicted testimony, supported by the legislative debates surrounding its passage, the Court found that its true purpose was to prevent the establishment by Dr. Morgentaler of free standing abortion clinics in the province. Since they were aimed at "suppressing the perceived harm or evil of abortion clinics" the Act and Regulations were properly characterized as invalid criminal legislation, and not as in relation to health, hospitals and the medical profession, areas of provincial concern, as they purported to be. Rather than regulating "the place for delivery of a medical service with a view to controlling the quality and nature of its health delivery care system", which would be within provincial competence, it had "attempted to prohibit the performance of abortions outside hospitals with a view to suppressing or punishing what it perceives to be the socially undesirable conduct of abortion" which made it criminal law (p. 488 S.C.R.).

In *Morgentaler* [1993], *supra*, the Court admitted and relied on legislative history in coming to its conclusion. *Saumur* v. *Quebec (City)*, [1953] 2 S.C.R. 299 is a case where the Court looked at the actual administration of an Act as an aid to classifying it. A by-law of the City of Quebec made it an offence to distribute literature in the streets without the prior written permission of the Chief of Police. At p. 15-16 to p. 15-17, Professor Hogg, *supra*, says:

> Such a by-law could have been passed for the purpose of protecting pedestrian traffic or controlling litter on the City streets, and indeed four judges of the Supreme Court of Canada did uphold the law as being in relation to streets, a perfectly legitimate topic of provincial regulation. But the other five judges — a majority — took note of the way the by-law was actually administered.

This examination of how the by-law was actually being enforced showed that the chief of police was using it as a vehicle of censorship to prohibit the distribution of literature by the Jehovah's Witnesses. The majority thus classified it as being in relation to speech or religion, and thus *ultra vires* the province.

The defence say that the legislative debates surrounding the enactment of the *Safe Streets Act* demonstrate that the purpose of the *Safe Streets Act* is to re-criminalize begging, which, until 1972, was prohibited by the *Criminal Code* vagrancy section, and submit that legislating for "the security and protection of the public with respect to the perceived threats of panhandlers", the purpose stated by the government, is *ultra vires* the legislature. The defence further assert that the debates show that it was never intended to enforce the provisions against approaching stopped cars or soliciting captive audiences against anyone other than squeegiers and beggars, and point to the introduction of a Private Member's Bill on April 17, 2000, that passed second reading on December 14, 2000, exempting "registered charities" from s. 3(2) (the captive audience section) and s. 7 (amending the *Highway Traffic Act*) of the *Safe Streets Act*. This Bill was introduced by an Opposition Member and narrowly passed second reading with all members of the Cabinet who were present voting against it. Insofar as it is relevant, it is clear from the debates that the members supporting the amending Bill were of the view that the provisions they proposed to amend were not being selectively enforced against squeegiers and beggars, thus contradicting the defence position that the *Safe Streets Act* was solely targeted at them and not at all concerned with traffic safety. I do not consider the evidence of one of the affiants to the effect that he has observed police ignoring conduct that the affiant believes contraravened the Act to be evidence of systematic selective enforcement; indeed, it is as consistent with non-enforcement as selective enforcement; most people could attest to having seen police officers ignore driving infractions of one sort or another. I am dealing with the *Safe Streets Act* as it now stands; it is entirely speculative to forecast whether the pending amendment will ultimately become law, and what the position would be if it does must be for another court to determine.

Furthermore, I am not of the view that legislating to promote a sense of security by users of the streets and other public places is *ultra vires* the Province. The authorities already cited show that traditionally the provinces and their municipalities have had wide scope to control the use of public places. This is not, like abortion, a subject historically regarded as exclusively criminal. In *Morgentaler* [1993], *supra*, as it had in *R.* v. *Morgentaler*, [1988] 1 S.C.R. 30 and *R.* v. *Morgentaler* (1975), [1976] 1 S.C.R. 616 the Supreme Court held that legislation in respect to abortion historically had been considered a matter for the criminal law since Confederation and before, and noted at p. 504 S.C.R. that "public morals" was a strong concern of the Members of the House of Assembly who spoke to the legislation. While conceding that there was "some recognition of a provincial 'morality' power", the valid exercise of it had to "be firmly rooted in an independent provincial head of power". Sopinka J. continued [at pp. 504–505 S.C.R.]:

> While legislation which authorizes the establishment and enforcement of a local standard of morality does not *ipso facto* "invade the field of criminal law" (see *Nova Scotia Board of Censors v. McNeil*, [[1978] 2 S.C.R. 662] at pp. 691–92), it cannot be denied that interdiction of conduct in the interest of public morals was and remains one of the classic ends of the criminal law, as established in the *Margarine Reference* [[1949] S.C.R. 1] at p. 50....

I do not consider the activities legislated against here to be so obviously "interdicted in the interest of public morals" as was the case in *Morgentaler* [1993]. As we have seen, regulation of conduct on streets has a long established "double aspect" that is wholly lacking for regulation of abortion. Accordingly, I am still of the view, having examined material beyond the four corners of the statute that it is properly characterized under the distribution of powers as legislation in relation to traffic and conduct in the streets and to the regulation of occupations.

[The analysis rejecting the s. 7 and 11(d) *Charter* challenges has been omitted.]

. . . .

Section 15(1) — Equality

Section 15(1) of the *Charter* provides:

> **15**(1) Every individual is equal before and under the law and has the right to the equal protection and equal benefit of the law without discrimination and, in particular, without discrimination based on race, national or ethnic origin, colour, religion, sex, age or mental or physical disability.

The purpose of the section was stated in *Law* v. *Canada (Minister of Employment and Immigration)*, [1999] 1 S.C.R. 497 at p. 549 by Iacobucci J. to be:

> ... to prevent the violation of essential human dignity and freedom through the imposition of disadvantage, stereotyping or political or social prejudice, and to promote a society in which all persons enjoy equal recognition at law as human beings or as members of Canadian society, equally deserving of concern, respect and consideration.

. . . .

A majority of the Supreme Court of Canada has consistently held that the general right of an individual to be free from legal discrimination is conditioned by the listed grounds following "in particular", so that the ambit of s. 15(1) extends beyond the enumerated grounds only to "analogous grounds": *Andrews* v. *Law Society of British Columbia*, [1989] 1 S.C.R. 143, holding that preventing non-citizens from being called to the bar was discrimination based on an "analogous ground" (citizenship) that could not be justified under s. 1....

The criteria for characterizing grounds of discrimination as analogous were described by McLachlin and Bastarache JJ. in *Corbiere* v. *Canada (Minister of Indian and Northern Affairs)*, [1999] 2 S.C.R. 203 at pp. 219–20, 173 D.L.R. (4th) 1 as:

> ... grounds based on characteristics that we cannot change or that the government has no legitimate interest in expecting us to change to receive equal treatment under the law. To put it another way, s. 15 targets the denial of equal treatment on grounds that are actually immutable, like race, or constructively immutable, like religion. Other factors identified in the cases as associated with the enumerated and analogous grounds, like the fact that the decision adversely impacts on a discrete and insular minority or a

group that has been historically discriminated against, may be seen to flow from the central concept of immutable or constructively immutable personal characteristics, which too often have served as illegitimate and demeaning proxies for merit-based decision making.

The defence says that the defendants share the personal characteristic of "extreme poverty", that this qualifies as an "analogous ground", and that the *Safe Streets Act* discriminates against them as such. The Crown submits that "extreme poverty" is not an "analogous ground" because it is neither immutable or constructively immutable, and notes the reluctance of the courts to recognize economic factors as creating such grounds....

Thus in *Masse* v. *Ontario (Ministry of Community and Social Services)* (1996), 134 D.L.R. (4th) 20 (Ont. Div. Ct.); leave to appeal to C.A. denied [1996] O.J. No. 1526; leave to appeal to S.C.C. denied [1996] S.C.C.A. No. 373, the Divisional Court refused to recognize welfare recipients as a "discrete and insular minority" in a case in which reductions in the level of welfare were challenged; in *Dunmore* v. *Ontario (Attorney General)* (1997), 37 O.R. (3d) 287 (Gen. Div.); aff'd (1999), 182 D.L.R. (4th) 471 (C.A.); leave to appeal to S.C.C. granted [1999] S.C.C.A. No. 196, Sharpe J. refused to recognize agricultural workers as such a group in a case challenging their exclusion from the right to bargain collectively in the *Labour Relations Act, 1995*, S.O. 1995, c. 1; in *Polewsky* v. *Home Hardware Stores Ltd.* (1999), 68 C.R.R. (2d) 330 (Ont. S.C.J.), Gillese J. rejected a challenge under s. 15 by a would-be Small Claims Court plaintiff to the absence of a provision in the *Courts of Justice Act*, R.S.O. 1990, c. C.43 giving a judge discretion to wave filing fees for impecunious litigants, because:

> The poor in Canadian Society are not a group in which the members are linked by shared personal or group characteristics. The absence of common or shared characteristics means, in my view, that poverty is not an analogous ground to those enumerated. [At p. 346 C.R.R.]

In *Falkiner* v. *Ontario (Director, Income Maintenance Branch, Ministry of Community and Social Services)* (2000), 188 D.L.R. (4th) 52 (Ont. Div. Ct.), however, the court did accept that membership in the group of "sole support mothers on welfare" could be considered to provide grounds for a claim of discrimination because of the definition of "spouse" in a Regulation under the *Family Benefits Act*; such claim could be in part founded on the enumerated ground of "sex" and partly on an analogous ground.

Accordingly, while the weight of authority is against recognizing poverty in itself as an analogous ground, the issue cannot be said to be finally settled. The other difficulty, however, is with the defendants' claim of discrimination. They do not seriously contend that the Act is not neutral on its face; that is, it applies to everyone and makes no distinctions between persons, and only addresses conduct. Rather, it is argued, as I apprehend it, that the *Safe Streets Act* is part of a concerted government campaign against the poor that has exacerbated their historically disadvantaged position in society, so that they are reduced to having to beg for subsistence, and as it is only the "extremely poor" who must do so, the law discriminates by restricting them and only them in how they may do so. I have already rejected the submission that the Act restricts them and only them in the discussion about the "doctrine of colourability" in the section on the "federalism question" above. Much of the affidavit material filed by the defendants consists of complaints about the general thrust of current provincial social policy in Ontario; the affiants all have an obvious socio-economic and political perspective that is diametrically opposed to that of the government of the day. It is, however, frankly difficult to discern how the legislation in question in itself can be said to have a prejudicial effect on their "essential human dignity" by placing restrictions on the place and manner of solicitation. As Sharpe J. said in *Dunmore* v. *Ontario*, *supra*, at p. 311 O.R.:

> There are many forms of injustice in our society, particularly those resulting from uneven distribution of wealth, that cannot be remedied by the courts through interpretation of the *Charter* and that must be remedied through the legislative process.

In conclusion, I do not find that the defendants have been denied legal equality by the *Safe Streets Act* so as to offend s. 15 of the *Charter*.

Section 2(b) — Freedom of Expression

[The court found that s. 2(b) of the *Charter* is violated by the legislation.]

Accordingly, I am of the view that the restrictions on soliciting must be justified under s. 1 of the *Charter*. I note the following passages from the article "Down and Out in Winnipeg and Toronto: The Ethics of Legislating Against Panhandling" (Ottawa: Caledon Institute of Social Policy, 1998) by Arthur Schafer, Director, Centre for Professional and Applied Ethics of the University of Manitoba, filed by the defence:

> Beginning in the 1980's, and continuing into the 1990's, the centre of many Canadian cities experienced a dramatic increase in the number of down-and-out individuals living on the streets ... "squeegee kids" wiping auto windshields without invitation, in the expectation of payment from embarrassed motorists, beggars outside hotels and shopping malls.
>
> ...
>
> Typically, an encounter between a pedestrian and a panhandler is a mundane, non-threatening affair. The beggar will hold out a hand, request spare change or sit quietly on the pavement, eyes down to signal passivity.... The great majority of encounters between passers-by and beggars is of this non-aggressive variety. They may be experienced as a nuisance by many of the targeted population, but they are non threatening.
>
> Occasionally, however, a panhandler or, worse, a group of panhandlers, will aggressively confront a passer-by, possibly obstructing passage or following the targeted pedestrian down the street, reach out to touch him or her, or utter words of threat.
>
> There is a world of difference between these two types of begging behaviour.... Aggressive panhandling ... may be experienced as menacing and frightening no matter what the target otherwise might think about people who panhandle. Yet such crucial distinctions are not being made by Canadian municipalities which are today, seemingly, in a race to legislate against both types of panhandling....
>
> The urbanologist Jane Jacobs, in her enormously influential book *The Death and Life of Great American Cities*, makes the point that the health and viability of a neighbourhood depend critically on the attractiveness of its sidewalks, streets and public spaces:
>
>> The bedrock attributes of a successful city district [are] that a person must feel personally safe and secure on the streets among all these strangers. He must not feel automatically menaced by them. A city district that fails in this respect also does badly in other ways and lays up for itself and for its city at large, mountain on mountain of trouble.

It seems to me that these passages well reflect the objects of the *Safe Streets Act*. They identify the problem that aggressive begging can pose to both the short- and long-term health of urban areas and justify legislating against it. The legislation before me does not reach passive panhandlers (noting that most of the "captive audience" sections are not raised on the facts before me). As noted by Professor Hogg, *supra*, at p. 40-17:

> The least severe form of restriction on expression is the regulation of the time, manner or place of expression. For example, a law might prohibit the use of cartoons in advertising directed at children, or a law might authorize a public official to stipulate the time and place of a parade. These laws restrict expression, and are therefore in violation of s. 2(b), but because they do not regulate the content of expression a court would be likely to uphold the law under s. 1.

It is my view that these comments apply to the restrictions here on place and manner of soliciting. I was referred to a number of United States authorities, which seem to have uniformly found such limited restrictions on begging constitutional under the First Amendment guarantee of freedom of speech, while finding blanket prohibitions unconstitutional. ...

Finally, I would characterize the expression we are concerned with as peripheral to the core values protected by s. 2(b); it is more akin to commercial than to political expression. I find assertions by affiants and authors relied upon by the defence to the contrary unconvincing; it may be that they consider the presence of aggressive beggars in the streets conducive to the advancement of their own socio-political points of view, but there is no evidence at all that the defendants themselves or others like them are intending to make a political point by soliciting for funds.

For these reasons, I find that the test in *Oakes*, [[1986] 1 S.C.R. 103], has been met and that the infringement of freedom of expression is justified under s. 1.

Verdict
I find all defendants guilty as charged.

Defendants convicted.

■

For a collection of essays devoted to the exploration of issues arising under Ontario's *Safe Street Act* see Joe Hermer and Janet Mosher, eds., *Disorderly People: The Politics of Exclusion in Ontario* (Halifax: Fernwood, 2002).

B. THE CONTINGENCY OF THE DEFINITION OF "CRIME"

The form and content of criminal law's prohibitions are contingent on many factors, including the culture and values of the dominant society, the historical moment considered, the economic system and the nature of the state, and the relations of power between various groups. The definitions and underlying ideologies are also a subject of ongoing struggle. For example, the works of Douglas Hay, *et al.*, eds., *Albion's Fatal Tree* (New York: Pantheon, 1975), E.P. Thompson, *Whigs and Hunters: The Origins of the Black Act* (London: Penguin Books, 1975), and Alun Howkins, "Economic Crime and Class Law: Poaching and the Game Laws, 1840–1880" in Sandra B. Burman and Barbara E. Harrell-Bond, eds., *The Imposition of Law* (New York: Academic Press, 1979) 273 explore the legal and political developments in class and property relations in England that corresponded with the creation of criminal law offences to enforce emerging rights of private ownership.

In Canada, definitions of crime were imported from England in the first *Criminal Code* of 1892 (which was essentially an adoption of the English Draft Code of 1879: see *Report of the Royal Commission to consider the Law Relating to Indictable Offences* (London: House of Commons, 1978–1879)), but other "criminal" laws specific to the process of colonization and to the unique conditions in Canada supplemented the *Criminal Code*. A very important example is the body of provisions contained in the Indian Acts and their amendments. These laws criminalized Aboriginal practices to facilitate colonization and the separation of Aboriginal peoples from their lands. They are discussed in more detail in the chapter that follows, **Colonization and the Imposition of Criminal Law**.

Another example in the Canadian context is provided by the series of anti-Chinese laws of the early 1900s, whereby persons of "Chinese" descent were prohibited from employing "white" women in several provinces: *An Act to Prevent the Employment of Female Labour in Certain Capacities*, S.S. 1912, c. 17, s. 1; *An Act to amend An Act to Prevent the Employment of Female Labour in Certain Capacities*, S.S. 1912–13, c. 18, s. 1; *An Act to amend the Factory, Shop and Office Building Act*, S.O. 1914, c. 40, s. 2; *An Act to amend the Manitoba Factories Act*, S.M. 1916, c. 41, s. 1; and *An Act to amend the 'Municipal Act'*, S.B.C. 1919, c. 63, s. 13. Like the laws criminalizing Aboriginal practices as part of colonization, these provincial offences signalled to Chinese Canadians the rigidity of racial boundaries in Canada by rendering all those of "Chinese" descent, regardless of citizenship, as "other," and by rendering all women with "white" skin as "white," regardless of their status as European immigrants: Constance Backhouse, "White Female Help and Chinese-Canadian Labourers: Race, Class, Gender and Law in the Case of Yee Clun, 1924" (1994) 26 Can. Ethnic Stud. 34. Backhouse argues further that these laws reinforced ideas about "race" as immutable "fact," fostered negative images of Asian men as predators, and prevented competitive entrepreneurial enterprise by Chinese Canadians by prohibiting employment from the only available female labour pool. Victor Lee, in "The Law of Gold Mountain" (1992) 21 Man. L.J. 301, notes that these offences directed at employers of "Chinese" descent were linked to a larger state endeavour to discourage settlement by immigrants from China.

Other laws outside of the *Criminal Code* were also used historically in Canada to criminalize conduct and advance colonization and racial segregation. Thus, in Nova Scotia in 1946, Viola Desmond was convicted and fined under *The Theatres, Cinematographs and Amusement Act*, R.S.N.S. 1923, c. 162, for allegedly failing to pay the appropriate tax on her theatre ticket, in violation of s. 8 of that Act. She had purchased a ticket and paid the tax for what was in fact an "upstairs" seat, informally reserved for "Black" customers; instead, she seated herself in the "downstairs" seats, among the "white" customers, and attempted to pay the one-cent difference in the ticket amount. Constance Backhouse points out in her article, "Racial Segregation in Canadian Legal History: Viola Desmond's Challenge, Nova Scotia, 1946" (1994) 17 Dalhousie L.J. 299 at 304–5 that: "Even more problematic was the prosecution's attempt to utilize provincial legislation to buttress community practices of racial discrimination.... As the press would later attest, Viola Desmond 'was being tried for being a negress [*sic*] and not for any felony'." Backhouse's article not only describes Desmond's case in detail, but also gives an overview of the use of law to enforce segregation in Canada (at 321–34) and documents some of the other challenges launched by African-Canadians (at 312, note 42).

As the preceding examples make clear, the definition of crime is shaped by and premised on power and powerlessness: those excluded from political, economic, and social power are more likely to have their activities criminalized and to be unsuccessful in resisting criminalization campaigns. For example, the criminalization of certain drugs, notably not those that injure and kill the most people (e.g. alcohol and tobacco together account, directly and indirectly, for 53,000 deaths per year in Canada, compared to fewer than 1,000 caused by illegal drugs: Doug Fischer, "Truly dangerous drugs are legal ones, researcher says" *The Ottawa Citizen* (4 February 1994) A3 and CP, "Addiction's toll in '92 $18-billion, Study says" *The [Toronto] Globe and Mail* (19 June 1996) A21 (describing alcohol and tobacco as taking the bigger economic toll)) can only be explained by reference to their association with those who are relatively powerless. Thus, for example, when, in the period between 1908 and 1923, narcotics use was first criminalized with the exception of medical use (although physicians created addiction among middle-class and women patients), "there was virtually no opposition to the criminalization of 'non-therapeutic' opiate use associated in the public mind with the low-status immigrant Chinese population. Similarly, producers of the drugs, alcohol and tobacco, were often British, of high status and contributed useful taxes; their activities were not proscribed": Hester and Eglin, *A Sociology of Crime*, supra at 33.

Similarly, marijuana offences were first enacted in the United States when its use was associated with Mexican labourers and African-American musicians: Tony Poveda, *Re-Thinking White-Collar Crime* (Westport, Ct.: Praeger Publishers, 1994) at 53. For further readings on the issues raised by the criminalization of drugs, see R. Solomon and T. Madison, "The Evolution of Non-Medical Opiate Use in Canada 1870–1908" in Robert A. Silverman and James J. Teevan, Jr., eds., *Crime in Canadian Society* (Toronto: Butterworths, 1986) 52 and Charles E. Reasons, "The Addict as a Criminal: Perpetuation of a Legend" (1975) 21 Crime and Delinq. 19.

The forces that produced particular definitions of crime historically also affect our current statutory and social understandings of the appropriate content of criminal law. The narcotics offences referred to in the preceding paragraphs can be understood in light of current ideas about "escalating crime" and by reference to the interests served by a focus on the "war on drugs": Chester Mitchell, "Narcotics: A Case Study in Criminal Law Creation" in Jane Gladstone, Richard Ericson, and Clifford Shearing, eds., *Criminology: A Reader's Guide* (Toronto: Centre of Criminology, 1991) 177; Poveda, *Re-Thinking White-Collar Crime*, supra at 52–57; and Dianne Martin, "Casualties of the Criminal Justice System: Women and Justice Under the War on Drugs" (1993) 6 C.J.W.L. 305. Some of these offences are currently under challenge through *Charter* litigation: see *R.* v. *Clay*, infra.

While quasi-criminal offences have been enacted in certain regulatory schemes that affect health and safety in Canada, they are frequently inadequate to address the criminal conduct of corporations and their managers and directors. Often, the only legal condemnation of such behaviour will come from the tort system. The reprimand by Judge Miles Lord in the context of civil litigation by survivors of the Dalkon Shield, reproduced below, prompts questions as to why the criminal law was not invoked and its role in responding to large-scale injury and death.

The Dalkon Shield Litigation: Revised Annotated Reprimand[†]

[L]et me preface [these remarks] with this — this of course should be part of what one would represent to the Court of Appeals, as you appeal to them — that Judge Lord has concluded that these cases in effect are all one. I have that in the document that I gave to your defense lawyers and to Mr. Robins, Mr. Forrest, Dr. Lunsford, and certain of the comments that are made might well be taken out of context this morning.

I agreed that I would hand this document to them and I thought [that I] could visit with them about it in a rather superficial way just to be sure

---

† By Chief Judge Miles W. Lord, (1986) 9 Hamline L. Rev. 7 at 7–11, 28–29. Notes omitted. Reproduced by permission of the author.

they had read it. One of the reasons I wanted them to read it was so that they would never again testify in any Court that they knew nothing about the dangers inherent in the Dalkon Shield. However, when you get a bifurcated presentation like this, it may lend itself to distortion — and I have seen plenty of that — so, as a consequence, I am going to read the whole speech, my appeal to these gentlemen:

Mr. Robins, Mr. Forrest, and Dr. Lunsford, after months of reflecting, study and cogitation and no small amount of prayer I have concluded it perfectly appropriate to make to you this statement, which will constitute my plea to you to seek new horizons in corporate consciousness and a new sense of personal responsibility for the activities of those who work under you in the name of A.H. Robins Company. It is not enough to say, "I did not know," "It was not me," "Look elsewhere." Time and time again each of you [has] used this kind of argument in refusing to acknowledge your responsibility and pretending to the world that the chief officers and directors of your gigantic multi-national corporation have no responsibility for the company's acts and omissions.

In a speech I made several years ago — the document which I have just asked you to read — I suggested to hundreds of ministers of the Gospel, who constitute the Minnesota Council of Churches, that the accumulation of corporate wrongs is in my mind a manifestation of individual sin.

You, Mr. Robins, Jr., have been heard to boast many times that the growth and prosperity of this company is a direct result of its having been in the Robins family for three generations, the stamp of the Robins family is upon it, the corporation is built in the image of the Robins mentality.

You, Dr. Lunsford, as director of the company's most sensitive and important subdivision, the medical division, have violated every ethical precept to which every doctor under your supervision must pledge as he gives the oath of Hippocrates and assumes the mantle of one who would cure and nurture unto the physical needs of the populace.

You, Mr. Forrest, are a lawyer who, upon finding his client in trouble, should counsel and guide him along a course which will comport with the legal and moral and ethical principles which must bind us all. You have not brought honor to your profession, Mr. Forrest.

Gentlemen, the result of these activities and attitudes on your part [has] been catastrophic. Today, as you sit here, attempting once more to extricate yourselves from the legal consequences of your acts, none of you [has] faced up to the fact that more that 9,000 women have made claims that they gave a part of their womanhood so that your company might prosper. It is alleged that others gave their lives so you might prosper. And there stand behind legions more who have been injured but who have not sought relief in the courts of this land. I dread to think what would have been the consequences if your victims had been men rather than women, women who seem through some strange quirk of our society's mores to be expected to suffer pain, suffering and humiliation.

If one poor young man were by some act of his, without authority or consent, to inflict such damage upon one woman, he would be jailed for a good portion for the rest of his life. And yet your company, without warning to women, invaded their bodies by the millions and caused them injuries by the thousands. And when the time came for these women to make their claims against your company, you attacked their characters, you inquired into their sexual practices and into the identity of their sex partners. You exposed these women and ruined families and reputations and careers in order to intimidate those who would raise their voices against you. You introduced issues that had no relationship whatsoever to the fact that you planted in the bodies of these women instruments of death, mutilation, and of disease.

I wish to make it absolutely clear that I am specifically directing and limiting my remarks to that which I have learned and observed in these consolidated cases before me. If an incident arises involving another product made by A.H. Robins Company, an independent judgment would have to be made as to the conduct of your company concerning that product. Likewise, a product made by any other company must of course be adjudged upon the individual facts of that case.

Gentlemen, you state that your company has suffered enough, that the infliction of further punishment in a form of punitive damages will cause harm to your ongoing business, will punish innocent shareholders and, conceivably, depress your profits to the point where you would not survive as a competitor in this industry. Well, when the poor and downtrodden in this country commit crimes, they too plead that these are crimes of survival and that they should be excused for illegal acts which helped them escape desperate economic straits. On a few occasions when these excuses are made and a contrite and remorseful defendant promises to mend his ways, courts will give heed to such a plea. But no court would heed this plea when the individual denies the wrongful nature of his deed and gives no indication that he will mend his ways. Your company in the face of overwhelming evidence denies its guilt and continues its monstrous mischief.

Mr. Forrest, you have told me that you are working with members of the Congress of the United States to ask them to find a way of forgiving you for punitive damages which might otherwise be imposed. Yet the profits of your company continue to mount. Your last financial report boasts of new records for sales and earnings with a profit of more than fifty-eight million in 1983. And all the while, insofar as this Court is able to determine, you three men and your company still engage in the same course of wrongdoing on which you originally commenced.

Until such time as your company indicates that it is willing to cease and desist this deception and seek out and advise victims, your remonstrances to Congress and to the courts of this country are indeed hollow and cynical.

The company has not suffered, nor have you men personally. You are collectively being enriched by millions of dollars each year. There is as yet no evidence that your company has suffered any penalty whatsoever for these litigations. In fact the evidence is to the contrary.

The case law indicates that the purpose of punitive damages is to make an award which will punish a defendant for his wrongdoing. Punishment traditionally involves the principles of revenge, rehabilitation and deterrence. There is no evidence I have been able to find, in my review of these cases, to indicate that any one of these factors has been accomplished.

Mr. Robins, Mr. Forrest, Dr. Lunsford, you have not been rehabilitated by the punitive damage awards that have been made so far. In fact, I don't think one of them has ever been paid yet, up until this settlement. Under your direction your company has in fact continued to allow women, tens of thousands of them, to wear this device, a deadly depth charge in their wombs, ready to explode at any time. Your attorney, Mr. Alexander Slaughter, denies that tens of thousands of these devices are still in the bodies of women. But I submit to you that Mr. Slaughter has no more basis for his denial than the plaintiffs for stating it as a truth — because we simply do not know how many women are still wearing these devices; and your company, run by you three men, is not willing to find out.

The only conceivable reasons you have not recalled this product are that it would hurt your balance sheet and alert women, who already have been harmed, that you may be liable for their injuries. As I said before, and out of context, you have taken the bottom line as your guiding beacon and the low road as your route. This is corporate irresponsibility at its meanest.

Rehabilitation involves an admission of guilt, a certain contrition, an acknowledgement of wrongdoing, and a resolution to take a new course towards a better life. I find none of this in the instance of you and your corporation.

Confession is good for the soul, Gentlemen. Face up to your misdeeds. Acknowledge the responsibility that you have for the activities of those who work under you. Rectify this evil situation. Warn the potential future victim and recompense those who have already been harmed.

Mr. Robins, Mr. Forrest, Dr. Lunsford, I see little in the history of this case that would deter others from partaking of like acts. The policy of delay and obfuscation practiced by your lawyers in courts throughout this country has made it possible for your insurance company and you, the Aetna Casualty and Assurance Company and the A.H. Robins Corporation, to delay the payment of these claims for such a long period that the interest you earn in the interim covers the costs of these cases. You in essence, assuming you owe something at the time the harm came, pay nothing out of your pocket to settle these cases. What other corporate officials anywhere could possibly learn a lesson from this? The only lesson could be that it pays to delay compensating victims, and to intimidate, harass and shame your victims, the injured parties.

Mr. Forrest, Mr. Robins and Dr. Lunsford, you gentlemen have consistently denied any knowledge of the deeds of the company you control. You, Mr. Robins, Jr., I read your deposition. Many times you state that your management style was such as to delegate work and responsibility to other employees in matters involving the most important aspects of this nation's health.

Judge Frank Theis, who presided over the discovery of these cases during the Multi-District Litigation proceedings, noted this [phenomenon] in a recent opinion, he wrote, I quote:

> The project manager for Dalkon Shield explains that a particular question should have gone to the medical department. The medical department representative explains that the question was really the bailiwick of the quality control department. The quality control department representative explains that the project manager was the one with the authority to make a decision on that question.

Under these circumstances, Judge Theis noted, it is not at all unusual for the hard questions posed in

Dalkon Shield cases to be unanswerable by anyone from Robins.

Your company seeks and has sought to segment and fragment litigation of these cases nationwide. The Courts of this country are now burdened with more than 3,000 Dalkon Shield cases. The sheer number of claims and the dilatory tactics used by your company's attorneys clog court calendars and consume vast amounts of judicial and jury time. Your company settles those cases in which it finds itself in an uncomfortable position, a handy device for avoiding any proceeding which would give continuity or cohesiveness to this nationwide problem. The decision as to which cases to try rests almost solely at the whim and discretion of the A.H. Robins Company.

In order that no plaintiff or group of plaintiffs might assert a sustained assault upon your system, evasion, and avoidance, you have time after time demanded that able lawyers who have knowledge of the facts must, as a price of settling their cases, agree to never again take a Dalkon Shield case nor to help any less experienced lawyers with their cases against your company. Minnesota lawyers have filed cases in this jurisdiction for women from throughout the United States. The cases of these women have waited on the calendar of this Court for as many as three years.

Until such time as this settlement came about, the evidence that the women were to present was simply their own testimony and/or that of their doctor, usually taken by deposition, and then the generic evidence concerning the company's actions — which is as easy to produce in Minnesota as anywhere else. Yet your company's attorneys were persisting in asking that these cases be transferred to other jurisdictions and to other judges unfamiliar with the cases, there to wait at the bottom of the calendar for additional months and years before they could have their day in Court. Another of your callous legal tactics is to force women of little means to withstand the onslaught of your well financed nationwide team of attorneys, and to default if they cannot keep up with the pace. Your target, your worst tactics were reserved for the meek and the poor.

Now again I point out that Faegre & Benson and the local law firms do not come under any of the strictures of that which I have said. As far as I have been able to know and has been reported to me, they have acted honorably with the evidence that was available to them.

Despite your company's protestations, it is evident that these thousands of cases cannot be viewed in isolation, and that is one of the main reasons why I feel free to make this statement here today. If every Judge is terminated as soon as he catches on to what's going on, if you settle the case and flee the jurisdiction, that leaves no one to follow up to make any cohesiveness to this.

The multi-district litigation panel of the Federal District Court found these cases to have sufficient similarity on issues of law and fact to warrant their reference to a single Judge who, for varying periods of time, conducted discovery depositions and proceedings designed to devise an efficient method of handling these cases. Yet I find, as I previously indicated, from the report of the Masters — as late as this morning — that the Multi-District Litigation Unit was only given about a third of the documents, and the most relevant documents are in the hands of the lawyers for the defendant. So that is 12 years of delay.

In each of the thousands of cases, the focal point of the inquiry is the same, the conduct of your company, through its acts and omissions. Indeed as I speak here of when Judge, Judges being spun off from time to time, Judge Gerald Heaney of the Court of Appeals, I believe he said it, with the Eighth Circuit, recently urged Judges in Minnesota to work together to devise a coordinated system for dealing with all of their Dalkon Shield cases. These litigations must be viewed as a whole.

If a Judge were to wait until all the cases were over before he spoke out on the evils he sees inherent in the system and in the trial tactics, then no one would ever speak out. There is a time when measures must be taken, when steps must be taken to see that fair play and ethical standards apply to the disposition of all the cases that are [to] come [in] the future, regardless of what might have happened in the past. These litigations must be viewed as a whole.

Were these women to be gathered together with their injuries in one location, this matter would be denominated a disaster of the highest magnitude. The mere fact that these women are separated by geography blurs the total picture. Here we have thousands of victims, present and potential whose injuries arise from the same series of operative facts. You three gentlemen have made no effort whatsoever to locate them and bring them together to seek a common solution to their plight.

If this were a case in equity, I would order that your company make an effort to locate each and every woman who still wears this device, and to recall your product. I would order you now to take to the Food and Drug Administration a correct and proper report on what's happened with these devices. If I did that, they would order you to recall.

So while the governmental agencies are set up to protect the public, there is evidence here that you didn't tell the truth to the governmental agencies. I believe that evidence[;] I've made it — I've made judgment on it. These matters of which I speak are not matters about which I speculate. They are matters contained in the evidence that has gone before me in the briefs of counsel, in the admissions and in the documents — some of which I have seen and no lawyer has seen — but I haven't disclosed anything about them except my conclusion about the matters about which I [have heard spoken].

I do not have the power to order you to do this. I must therefore resort to moral persuasion and a personal appeal to each of you. Would you believe it, Gentlemen, I am not angry with you. I don't dislike you personally. I am not happy with some of the things you have done. I would really like to try to talk you into doing this.

It's just awful, and you can't get hung up in that corporate thing, you can't worry about whether or not the stocks are going to drop. You've got lives out there, people, women, wives, moms, and some who will never be moms. Can't you move in on this thing now? You are the people with the power to recall. You are the corporate conscience. Please, in the name of humanity, lift your eyes above the bottom line.

You, the men in charge, must surely — I know you have hearts and souls and consciences — and I am not a great "Bible pounder," but this almost takes you into a Biblical reference, you can only explain it in that way. If the thought of facing up to your transgressions is so unbearable to you — and I think it will be difficult for you —you might do as Roger Tuttle did and confess to your Maker and beg forgiveness and mend your ways.

The options are few. Either you go along stonewalling it, like you are going, or you face up to what you have done, and then you have to start thinking about how you might make amends for that.

Please, Gentlemen, give consideration to tracing down the victims and sparing them [the] agony that will surely be theirs. And I just want to say I love you. I am not mad at you.

Editor's Note: This is the text of the reprimand Judge Miles Lord delivered on February 29, 1984, to A.H. Robins corporate officers E. Claiborne Robins, Jr., William A. Forrest, Jr., and Dr. Carl D. Lunsford and their defense counsel in the consolidated cases under the title of *Gardiner v. A.H. Robins, Inc.*, Civil Nos. 84-5061-MN; 84-5062-MN. The statement was delivered five days after the parties had entered into a settlement agreement.

The text of the reprimand as annotated was submitted to the Eighth Circuit Court of Appeals following A.H. Robins' appeal of Judge Lord's entry of a "So Ordered" notation to the parties' settlement agreement. A.H. Robins claimed that the settlement of the cases was solely within the power of the parties to the agreement and that Judge Lord's notation created a legal prejudice to the company sufficient to warrant an exercise of appellate jurisdiction by the Eighth Circuit striking the notation. A.H. Robins and its three executives also filed misconduct complaints against Judge Lord for his "speech" in court.

In a November 2, 1984 ruling, the Eighth Circuit Court of Appeals declared that Judge Lord's entry of the notation on the parties' agreement was improper and "effectively deprived the parties of their unconditional right to a Rule 41(a)(1)(ii) dismissal by stipulation." *Gardiner* v. *A.H. Robins Co.*, 747 F.2d 1180, 1190 (8th Cir. 1984). The court of appeals also struck Judge Lord's reprimand from the district court's records of the consolidated cases. The court concluded that A.H. Robins' and the three Robins executives' due process rights had been violated because, according to the court, they had "received no adequate notice of the nature of the informal and personal charges...." *Id.* at 1191.

On December 26, 1984, the Judicial Council of the Eighth Circuit followed the recommendations of a five-judge investigative panel and dismissed the misconduct complaints against Judge Lord which had been filed by A.H. Robins and its three officers. The Judicial Council noted that the disciplinary complaints had become moot because the appropriate relief had been granted in the November 2 ruling. *In Re* A.H. Robins Co., Nos. JCP 84-001; JCP 84-002 at 2 (8th Cir. Judicial Council Dec. 26, 1984).

In late October 1984, eight months after Judge Lord's reprimand, the A.H. Robins Company announced that women still wearing the Dalkon Shield should have the devices removed at the expense of the company. The company also announced its intention to notify physicians and clinics, and to conduct a campaign to alert women.

The text is set forth as transcribed with minor editorial changes. The notes to the reprimand are set forth at the end of the statement.

■

The footnotes deleted from Judge Lord's reprimand contain a wealth of factual detail, references to depositions, and legal materials. Consult these footnotes to get a full sense of the ordeal of the Dalkon Shield litigation.

In 1985, Robins petitioned for bankruptcy under Chapter 11 of the United States Bankruptcy Code, claiming that its solvency was threatened by the civil litigation against the corporation. As part of its reorganization plan under the code, Robins was sold to American Home Products [hereinafter AHP] in 1988. Karen M. Hicks, in *Surviving the Dalkon Shield IUD: Women v. The Pharmaceutical Industry* (New York: Teacher's College Press, 1994) [hereinafter *Surviving*] describes how women injured by the Dalkon Shield organized to resist and contest the terms of the bankruptcy and to gain access to information about A.H. Robins. At page 10 of her book she notes that the Robins family successfully shielded its family and other business assets through the bankruptcy claim and gained, together with the former executives of Robins, the majority position as stockholders in AHP. Hicks lists the other implications of the deal for A.H. Robins: Robins' stock values increased fourfold when the proposed sale was announced; AHP received tax write-offs for buying a "distressed" company; E.C. Robins, Jr. was elected honorary president of the American Pharmaceutical Association in 1992; and, in 1991, experts who had testified on behalf of Robins published articles, which coincided with the commencement of civil trials by women who had refused to settle with the Trust Fund, claiming once again that the Dalkon Shield was safe: *ibid.* at 10, 47.

The bankruptcy plan provided total and permanent immunity against Dalkon Shield litigation to the Robins company, the family, and to all other third parties such as the insurer. On 6 November 1989 the U.S. Supreme Court approved the proposed trust of $2.5 billion from the assets reserved through the bankruptcy, to compensate approximately 2.3 million survivors of the Dalkon Shield. It rejected a challenge by 650 of the women, among them Canadians, to the adequacy of the plan: Terry Gilbert, "Ruling angers Dalkon victims. Settlement called 'pittance'" *Calgary Herald* (7 November 1989) A3: "Canadian victims had asked the Canadian government to get involved in the appeal of the bankruptcy organization plan, but they received no response from the Departments of Health or Justice." The Supreme Court also rejected claims against Robins' insurer on the basis that Aetna had received Chapter 11 immunity, which Hicks asserts, in *Surviving*, *supra* at 7, was a novel legal ruling.

Recall that Judge Lord made the following observation: "I dread to think what would have been the consequences if your victims had been men rather than women, women who seem through some strange quirk of our society's mores to be expected to suffer pain, suffering and humiliation." He also stated that "[i]f one poor, young man were by some act of his, without authority or consent, to inflict such damage upon one woman, he would be jailed for a good portion of the rest of his life." Do these observations help you make sense of the legal treatment of the consequences of the Dalkon Shield? For further analysis linking corporate criminality and gendered harms, see Hicks, *Surviving*, *supra* at 9–11 and chapter two, "Medical Violence Against Women"; Laureen Snider, *Bad Business*, *supra* at 54–57; Michael Levi, "Masculinities and white-collar crime" in Tim Newburn and Elizabeth Stanko, eds., *Just Boys Doing Business? Men, masculinities and crime* (London: Routledge, 1994) 234; and Walter DeKeseredy and Ronald Hinch, "Corporate Violence" in their book, *Woman Abuse. Sociological Perspectives* (Toronto: Thompson Educational Publishing, 1991) 97.

The Bhopal disaster in 1984 also raises significant questions about the appropriate legal response to large-scale death and injury caused by regulatory crime. By 1990, the leak of the toxic chemical methyl isocyanate from the Union Carbide Corporation's pesticide factory in Bhopal had killed 3,787 people and caused serious disabling injuries to 202,672: N.D. Jayaprakash, "Perilous Litigation: The Leak Disaster Case" *Economic and Political Weekly* (22 December 1990) 2761, as cited in Jamie Cassels, *The Uncertain Promise of Law: Lessons From Bhopal* (Toronto: University of Toronto Press, 1993) at 28. Charges of culpable homicide were laid in India against the United States chair of the corporation, Warren Anderson, and against 11 other corporate officers on the basis of alleged design flaws in the factory's systems and poor maintenance. These charges were not heard by any court but were instead dismissed by the Indian Supreme Court as part of its imposition of a $470-million settlement: Sanjoy Hazarika, "Bhopal Payments By Union Carbide Set At $470 Million" *The New York Times* (15 February 1989) A1. Details regarding the original criminal charges may be found in Upendra Baxi and Amita Dhanda, eds., *Valiant Victims and Lethal Litigation: The Bhopal Case* (Bombay: Indian Law Institute, 1990) at 639 ff.

The terms of the imposed "settlement" were widely protested in India by survivors, social action groups, and public figures: Cassels, *supra* at 27–32. In November 1989 Gandhi's government was voted out of office, and in January 1990 "the new Law Minister, Mr. Dinesh Goswami, announced that the government would support the demands of the victims for increased compensation and join in the effort to have the settlement overturned": *ibid.* at 27. Legal challenges to the original settlement were argued before the Supreme Court in 1990, and a final decision was rendered in October 1991. While this decision upheld the settlement in several key respects, the court added flexibility to its terms in order to meet the uncertainties of compensation needs. It also agreed that the criminal charges should not have been dismissed: *ibid.* at 29–32. Jamie Cassels, in "The Uncertain Promise of Law: Lessons from Bhopal" (1991) 29 Osgoode Hall L.J. 1 at 14 suggests that the government of India was also implicated in the tragedy as a major owner of the company and as administrator of health and safety laws. One might thus query whether the Indian government's interests and potential embarrassment contributed significantly to the paltry settlement: Sudhir K. Chopra, "Multinational Corporations in the Aftermath of Bhopal: The Need for a New Comprehensive Global Regime for Transnational Corporate Activity" (1994) 29 Val. U. L. Rev. 235.

In February 1992 charges of culpable homicide, maiming, and causing injury were resumed against three of Union Carbide's corporate executives, including Anderson. According to Christopher Thomas, "Corruption makes mockery of claims by Bhopal victims" *The [London] Times* (3 December 1994) Overseas News, Anderson "was arrested briefly on a visit to Bhopal soon after the accident, released on bail of 1,600 pounds and allowed to fly home."

Extradition proceedings were commenced in order to bring the men before the Indian courts: "Carbide seizure vowed" *The [Toronto] Globe and Mail* (3 February 1992) B2. However, U.S. legal experts said soon afterwards that extradition of Warren M. Anderson to India was unlikely, as Union Carbide claimed that when it "agreed" to try matters in India, it assumed that there would be no criminal trials: Andrew Blum, "Is criminal Bhopal case in store?" *The National Law Journal* (16 March 1992) 3. It appears that the Indian government is reluctant to pursue extradition due to concerns about scaring off foreign investment, and that the prosecution is probably permanently stalled: AP, "Bhopal disaster still haunts trim Carbide; Cloud remains despite turnaround" *Chicago Tribune* (11 December 1994) B14; Eric Weiner, "A Lasting Legacy of Bhopal's Leak" *Christian Science Monitor* (12 December 1994) 8.

C. CHALLENGES TO THE DEFINITION OF "CRIME"

Challenges to the definition of "crime" come in many forms: critiques of the legitimacy of the criminal law; efforts to create criteria by which to assess the appropriateness of criminalization or the failure to criminalize; law reform; *Charter* challenges to current criminal offences; and political protest and defiance. These forms of challenges will be discussed in turn.

In the following extract from Christine Boyle in *A Feminist Review of Criminal Law* [hereinafter *Feminist Review*], the author articulates the basis for the claim that the criminal law is illegitimate with respect to women. She also identifies criteria for criminalization, which were first articulated by the *Report of the Canadian Committee on Corrections* (Ottawa: Queen's Printer, 1969) at 11–17 and later adopted by the Law Reform Commission of Canada [hereinafter LRCC]: see generally *The Limits of Criminal Law: Obscenity: A test case* (Ottawa: Supply and Services, 1979) and *Our Criminal Law* (Ottawa: Supply and Services, 1976). She argues that the use of the criminal law against women is frequently inappropriate in light of these criteria.

A Feminist Review of Criminal Law[†]

Problems of Legitimacy in Criminal Law

The problems of the legitimacy of criminal law are based on two factors: the lawmaking process and the acts which are considered criminal offences.

The Lawmaking Process

The first factor that contributes to the illegitimacy of criminal law in our liberal, capitalistic democracies is the lawmaking process itself. Even before legislators address a certain issue, or when they begin to debate it, powerful lobbies and interest groups endeavour to influence their views. The members of their political parties, religious leaders, unions, police departments and lobbyists from large corporations attempt to persuade legislators to include measures that serve their interests and their power in the legislation to be passed.

Therefore, not only do male legislators determine among themselves what values should be protected, but it is under the influence of interest groups, the vast majority of which are composed of men, that fundamental issues are either placed on the agenda of legislative bodies (such as capital punishment, under pressure from police officers) or denied serious consideration (such as abortion, under pressure from religious leaders, among others).

. . . .

Grounds for Criminal Sanction

The second factor that contributes to the illegitimacy of criminal laws is the basis for qualifying certain acts as crimes. In some cases, laws deal with acts which are not harmful to others or to society, or in any case, not sufficiently harmful to merit criminal sanctions....

[Many legal theorists] recommend that we should not apply criminal laws to victimless crimes or to matters which are no longer the subject of a clear moral consensus. Similarly, the Law Reform Commission of Canada has proposed the decriminalization of obsolete crimes, of acts that cause no harm to the person and of minor offences against property.

In order for an act to be legitimately considered a crime, it should meet the following specific criteria:

(1) the act must cause serious harm to others;
(2) the act must violate fundamental values and cause real harm to the community;
(3) the application of criminal law must not harm persons or society, and must not violate fundamental rights; and
(4) there must be reason to believe that qualifying an act as an offence can lead to a solution to problems caused by crime.

In Canada, 80% of the charges laid against women in recent years do not meet these criteria. In fact, non-violent theft of small amounts of money or objects of little value account for over 40% of their offences. Twenty-five per cent of female offenders are convicted for violations of provincial liquor laws, 7% are convicted for the mere possession of marijuana and approximately 5% are charged with breaking bail, disturbing the peace, prostitution, public mischief and so on. It is obvious that there is nothing "criminal" about the majority of offences committed by women. Although it is true that the number of women charged with violent and serious offences has risen in Canada in recent years, these offences still account for only 5% to 10% of the entire phenomenon of female crime.

Is this to say that no form of constraint is justifiable for 80% of women charged with offences? The right to compel offenders to compensate the persons harmed, return their stolen property and help restore their well-being is completely justified. Civil and administrative measures appear entirely appropriate. Physical constraints or custodial sentences, however, are certainly not justifiable for women, no more so than for males, adult or juvenile, who are convicted of similar offences.

For the true crimes for which women are charged — robbery, breaking and entering, serious assault and homicide — the right to intervene can include physical constraint, but should not go so far as to include imprisonment when the crimes are completely situational and when the likelihood that they will be repeated is low. The rate of recidivism

---

[†] From Christine Boyle, "Interests of Women Which Should be Protected by the Criminal Law" in Christine Boyle et al., A Feminist Review of Criminal Law (Ottawa: Status of Women, 1985) at 3–11. Notes omitted. Source of Information: Status of Woman Canada. Reproduced with the permission of the Minister of Public Works and Government Services Canada, 2002.

among females convicted of homicide is almost zero. Such crimes are committed within family relationships, and special, emotionally charged relationships. In an effort to make examples of such offenders, the criminal system may impose severe sentences, but it is not at all certain that, in the case of women, exemplary sentences serve useful and correctional purposes.

Problems of Equality under Criminal Law

The treatment accorded to women under the criminal justice system is often unfair for three reasons.

(1) The most obvious reason is that penal institutions for women provide few of the services and programs that would facilitate their resocialization and that are available to men.
(2) The second reason is based on the fact that the majority of women who have brushes with the law are young mothers with young children. Their social status has a considerable effect on the way they experience imprisonment. Moreover, separation from their children, which becomes necessary since most penal institutions do not have child-care services, places a double burden on women. The payment of fines is also difficult for women who are single parents with low socio-economic and educational status.
(3) The third and most important reason is that the criminal justice system was created by men for men. Paternalism and sexism lead police officers, judges and counsel to treat women as children whom they are excusing, and to doubt their word when they come forward as victims.

Throughout this analysis, we refer to literature, facts and studies that address the problems of morality, legitimacy and equality faced by women under our present criminal law system.

. . . .

Interests of Women Which Should Be Protected by the Criminal Law

INTRODUCTION

In this chapter the interests which ought, by feminist standards, to be protected by the criminal law will be identified. Protection can be offered in various forms: in the retention or introduction of a substantive offence, in the absence of any offence interfering with a particular interest, in the formulation of a defence, or in the administration of the law. The focus here is on the contents and silences of the substantive law. The method involves a critique of interests presently protected.

IDENTIFICATION OF INTERESTS

It is important for women to engage in this analysis for a number of reasons. First, women may wish to criticize the inconsistency of criminal law, e.g. it purports to protect physical integrity and yet women are not always adequately protected. Secondly, we may draw analogies. Thus, if privacy is an interest worth protecting in some contexts, we may argue that it ought to be protected in others. Thirdly, an interests analysis gives us a theoretical framework in which to expand our discussion on particular issues and helps us gauge the results of law reform.

. . . .

[Some examples follow]

Property Interests

Property interests are protected by such offences as theft, fraud, mischief, currency offences and by the recognition of the defence of property as a justification. The operation of the patriarchal structure has ensured that women have relatively less access to property ownership than men (*i.e.* through the economic oppression of women and the whole institution of ascribed gender roles). Thus, it is largely male interests which are being protected by the criminal law here.

Women so far have tended to lobby for matrimonial law reform rather than use self-help to achieve a more equitable distribution of property. It is possible that at some point in the future the criminal law might be used to control such attempts to acquire property without the assistance of the law, but the literature has not focused on this as an area for concern.

When the concept of property is broadened, however, to include what has been termed the "new property" — including the right to social security, public housing and economic survival — a number of concerns for women emerge. *E.g.*, the law of fraud is used to protect the property of the State against welfare recipients. A conflict of interests arises if criminal law is used against women who "defraud" the

State while the State does not provide for women's basic needs. This raises concerns about the scope of the defence of necessity and the equal protection of the law.

While the criminal law cannot be enlisted to respond to all societal problems, the interests of men are better protected by the criminal law than those of women. The criminal law does not provide adequate protection for such economic interests as access to the workforce; a safe, non-sexist work environment; or protection from employment discrimination. Contrast the careful protection of traditional property interests (by and large for the benefit of men), with the minimal protection of the new property interests of women. What affects the economic well-being and security of both women and men? Is equal protection given to both? A broad-ranging inquiry is necessary to determine whether the selection of property interests worth protection is based on a double standard.

Protection of Life and Physical Safety

There are many offences in the *Criminal Code* protecting these interests, *e.g.* assault, sexual assault, homicide, kidnapping and abduction, arson, driving offences, neglect in childbirth, offences relating to firearms and to public order. These offences enhance our freedom of movement, as fear of physical attack impedes our willingness to move around our environment. This interest has been recognized in s. 7 of the *Canadian Charter of Rights and Freedoms*, and when combined with s. 28, the result is that women and men have a constitutional guarantee of equal liberty and security of the person. A minimum duty of the State is to ensure the maximum degree of physical safety for its citizens, since physical attack is probably the most intimate harm we can suffer.

Feminist analysis focuses on the *effectiveness* of the criminal law's protection, rather than questioning the norms themselves. However, substantive concerns arise when life/security protecting norms for men clash with the same norms for women. A major inquiry for any feminist review of the criminal law is whether women's lives and physical safety are given a high enough value. Abortion is a case in point. To the extent that criminalizing abortion creates physical danger for women, it can be argued that the criminal law selectively protects life and health in a gender-specific way. In other words, a choice has been made not to protect the lives and health of women, as a sex, in this context. Similarly, to the extent that the criminal law does not protect against health hazards in the work-place, it is selective in a way that is negative to women.

Privacy

Privacy is a more abstract interest. There may be very different perceptions of what privacy is and whether it has been invaded. The criminal law does purport to protect privacy, *e.g.* overtly in the wiretapping offences and indirectly in the failure to enforce domestic assault offences. The privacy interest can also be detected in decisions about what is *not* criminal, *e.g.* with respect to homosexual relations between two consenting adults in private. Silence also reveals when privacy is not perceived as an interest, *e.g.* with abortion and the failure to protect the reproductive control of women.

The criminal law will inevitably place a value on privacy, in its utterances, its enforcement decisions and its silences. A serious attempt should be made to give universal protection to the privacy interests of both women and men, in a way that is meaningful and positive to both sexes.

[The authors' discussion of the interests of freedom of expression, preservation of the state, the integrity of relationships and the status of marriage, and sensibilities, feelings and morality has been deleted.]

The *Feminist Review* prompts consideration of whether there are other groups in Canada who can argue that the criminal law is illegitimate with respect to them. For example, Snider, in *Bad Business*, supra at 8–9 (notes omitted), makes the following comment:

> [B]ecause the capitalist class virtually owned the political state until well into the 20th century, the characteristic acquisitive activities of this class were not sanctioned by criminal law, and thus were not formally "crimes." ... Because of this power to shape law to reflect its interests, criminal laws characteristically focused on acts that the poor and powerless were most likely to commit: robbery, vagrancy, and homelessness, for example, were all crimes.
> ...

[D]ominant classes at the turn of the century argued, publicly and vociferously, that certain behaviours were "morally neutral." These actions included paying wages too low to allow employees to maintain their health or dignity; forcing workers to labour in conditions that caused thousands of injuries and deaths; and buying legislatures through secret rebate deals.... These "facts" [the justifications provided by capital] were self-evident to those who benefited by this set of arrangements; thus, decades of struggle, resistance, and debate were necessary to challenge and surmount them. The eventual extension of the right to vote, awarded first to middle class males, then lower class males, and finally to women, was crucial in forcing governments to act against capital....†

Are there other bases for establishing illegitimacy, apart from exclusion from the franchise at the time of enactment of the *Criminal Code*?

The *Feminist Review* also provides an important insight about the development and application of so-called "objective" criteria for criminalization. It is by no means obvious what "harm" is, nor will there be widespread agreement across this country as to which kinds of "harms" are serious enough to warrant criminalization. For example, while allegedly adhering to the same criteria for criminalization, the LRCC recommended in *Crimes Against the Foetus* (Ottawa: Law Reform Commission of Canada, 1989) at 53–54, that a new offence of "foeticide" be created. It would have criminalized the intentional conduct of pregnant women, most abortions in the third trimester and even the negligent conduct of third parties who harm a foetus (e.g. vehicular foeticide). As Audrey Macklin states in "Law Reform Error: Retry or Abort?" (1993) 16 Dalhousie L.J. 395 at 397 [hereinafter "Law Reform Error"] (notes omitted), "*Crimes Against the Foetus* proceeded with hardly a moment's hesitation to the conclusion that the criminal law was the optimal means of dealing with the pressing social issue of abortion. Part of this orientation may be explained by the predilections of individual Commission members...."

As may be evident, therefore, our criteria for criminalization and their application are dependent upon the underlying values and assumptions that animate those criteria. Although the LRCC was created as an advisory body to government in 1971 in order to mediate the social and values conflicts of the 1960s, it has relied upon assertions of our "common sense" morality to underpin its law reform proposals in the area of criminal law. It is precisely this failure to debate, defend, or even articulate an underlying value structure that has attracted criticism of the LRCC from authors such as Ross Hastings and Ron Saunders, in "Ideology in Canada: The Case of the Working Paper on the General Part" (1982–83) 25 Crim. L.Q. 206. These authors argue at 218 that it has proceeded with systemic and technical revision of the *Criminal Code* without ever addressing the underlying interests and values, thus implicitly affirming the *status quo*: "the work of the LRCC is ideological not because it was intended to be — it is not a case of bad will — but because it has failed to come to grips with the shifting nature of the conflicts, and to articulate its relationship to the conflicts."

The Department of Justice has been involved in the LRCC's recodification project. Although the Attorneys General issued a Statement of Commitment to Gender Equality in 1991 (see Department of Justice, *Gender Equality in the Canadian Justice System*, 1992 at 35), which stated that "[l]egal theory, common-law, and statute law must be developed equally from both the male and female perspective," only after a White Paper legislative draft had been released by the Minister of Justice (*Proposals to amend the Criminal Code (general principles*, 28 June 1993) was the Status of Women Canada able to commission feminist commentary on five of the defences already drafted in the White Paper. As Macklin comments in "Law Reform Error," *supra* at 401:

> [R]ules for the intoxication defence are assessed without any reference to the real costs imposed by the preferred rule on, say, women who are sexually assaulted by drunken assailants. To the extent that the LRCC was able to pursue a goal of uniformity and consistency and represent its views as a consensus, it did so by creating an institutional legal ethos that exalted internal purity, formal equality and uniformity over other values, such as the responsiveness of law to the social context from which law emerges and into which it

---

† Excerpts from *Bad Business: Corporate Crime in Canada*, 1st ed., by Laureen Snider. Reproduced with permission of Nelson Thomson Learning, a division of Thomson Learning. Fax: (800) 730-2215.

speaks. In the process, it silenced all other perspectives.[†]

In contrast, consider the work of H. Archibald Kaiser, "Preventing Which Crime? A Relative Outsider's Perspective on the Orthodoxy of Criminality in the Canadian Reform Agenda" (1990) 33 Crim. L.Q. 61, which is explicitly premised upon articulated notions of harm. His reform agenda includes new offences, such as abuse or neglect of institutionalized persons, hoarding essential commodities, irresponsible plant closures, making excess profits, lying to the public while running for office, wrongful use of access to government, and export of domestically banned products, among others. Both Macklin, "Law Reform Error," *supra* and H. Archibald Kaiser, "New Directions for Canadian Criminal Law Reform: Ensuring an End to Complacency" (1993) 13 Windsor Y.B. Access Just. 264 argue for a law reform process that is based on citizens' input rather than lawyers' ideas about law reform. As Kaiser explains at 278–79 (notes omitted):

> There are reasons for having reservations about an extended consultative process. One would not want the kind of expression of public opinion which one hears on the worst radio talk shows, for example. This kind of uninformed, distant, irresponsible and technologically filtered mode of expression is antithetical to real democratic values.... The recent lessons that the Canadian state has learned in its Spicer Commission, the Constitutional consultations and the Royal Commission on Aboriginal Peoples should be especially relevant to the expansion of the criminal law reform process.... One has only to recall the revelations in the Spicer Commission Report of the great frustration of the Canadian people with the abysmal treatment of Aboriginal Nations to see that the people may be well ahead of the politicians and the experts.
>
> ...
>
> Beyond this general popularization, it would be easy to consult with specific groups that are usually ignored or silenced. Penitentiary inmates, parolees, probationers, wrongfully convicted individuals and victims of crime are seldom, if ever, heard on law reform matters. Each of these communities has obviously experienced Canadian criminal law in various ways and will have powerful insights on what the future should hold....[‡]

The definition of "crime" continues to be challenged and reformulated. For example, legislation has been used to prohibit certain forms of conduct for the first time; other behaviours continue without criminal sanction despite the harm they cause; some offences have been declared unconstitutional pursuant to *Charter* litigation; and some "crimes" are the subject of ongoing protest and, sometimes, public defiance.

A number of reforms with respect to the substantive definition of "crime" have taken place in the past two decades. Consider the following developments:

- Sexual assault by husbands upon wives within marriage became criminal for the first time in 1983 (*The Criminal Law Amendment Act*, S.C. 1980-81-82, c. 125, s. 6).

- The purchase of sexual services from children under 18 at home or abroad by Canadian men because a new offence in 1996: (*An Act to amend the Criminal Code (child prostitution, child sex tourism, child harassment and female genital mutilation)*.

- New sentencing penalties for "hate crimes" or offences motivated by hatred based on "race," religion, sex, age, disability, or sexual orientation were passed into law in 1995 (*An Act to amend the Criminal Code (sentencing) and other Acts in consequence thereof*, S.C. 1995, c. 22). For discussion, see *infra*, **Sentencing**. For an analysis of the efficacy of the current *Criminal Code* offences that criminalize advocating genocide and hate propaganda and discussion of the constitutional problems with these offences identified in recent prosecutions, see Bruce P. Elman, "Combatting Racist Speech: The Canadian Experience" (1994) 32 Alta. L.R. 623.

- Abortion clinic harassment was criminalized through legislation in British Columbia in 1995 (*Access to Abortion Services Act*, B.C.S. 1995, c. 35). In Ontario, in a 548-page decision, Judge

---

[†] Reproduced by permission of the author.
[‡] Reproduced with permission of author, H. Archibald Kaiser, Professor of Law and Assistant Professor of Psychiatry, Dalhousie University, teaching Criminal Law, Criminal Procedure and Mental Disability Law. He is also a barrister, with a limited private practice, dealing exclusively with problems faced by persons with a mental disability.

George Adams imposed a 20-metre protest ban at clinics and a 160-metre ban at doctors' homes through a criminal injunction, requested for the first time by the Attorney General of Ontario and directed at 18 named protestors: *Ontario (AG)* v. *Dieleman* (1994), 20 O.R. (3d) 229 (Gen. Div.).

It has been argued that other behaviours ought to be reframed as crimes in light of their consequences. Consider, for example, the following:

- Racism: see Patricia Williams, "Spirit Murdering the Messenger: The Discourse of Fingerpointing as the Law's Response to Racism" under **Policing**; and Donna Young, *The Handling of Race Discrimination Complaints at the Ontario Human Rights Commission* (Toronto, 1992) [unpublished], who describes the systemic racism embedded even in the human rights complaints process.
- Depriving adults and children of adequate levels of social assistance: see Michael Shapcott, "Slow death by poverty also a form of violence" *The Toronto Star* (9 January 1991) A21; CP, "Parents, children steal to meet basic needs in wake of Ontario cuts, social workers say" *The Ottawa Citizen* (13 April 1996) A5; Michael Valpy, "One is too many. Deaths of the homeless" *The [Toronto] Globe and Mail* (1 June 1996) D1, D2.
- Destruction of the earth's ozone layer: see "Shell: Worst global warmer" *The Sydney Morning Herald* (12 December 1995) 9: "Shell's operations in Nigeria are the biggest single cause of global warming, emitting far more pollution than Britain's 20 million homes put together."
- Involuntary sterilization of persons with mental disabilities: see CP, "'Thousands' sterilized in Alberta. Operations part of 'improving race', experts say" *The [Toronto] Globe and Mail* (21 June 1993) A4.
- The marketing, sale, or use of cars: see Ross Howard, "Suburbs not safe haven from danger, study finds. Cars claim more lives than downtown crime" *The [Toronto] Globe and Mail* (18 April 1996) A3, and Russell Jacoby, quoted in Prisoners Action Group, "Crime and Aggregate Social Harm" (1980) 3 Alternative Criminology J. 46:

Insofar as one can calculate in advance the number of dead and maimed for each weekend, each day, automobile accidents are more than accidents. They form part of the murderous necessity that keeps the coffers filled: private automobiles over public transportation, highways over railroads are not merely consumer choices; they are dictated by a social reality which in the drive towards surplus value has dictated the choices.

See also Poveda, *Re-Thinking White-Collar Crime*, supra, "The Campaign to Motorize America" at 22–24 for a description of the prosecution for conspiracy of GM, Standard Oil of California, Firestone Tire and Rubber, Phillips Petroleum, and Mack Manufacturing for a 14-year conspiracy, commencing in the mid-1930s, to destroy the public transportation system in the United States.

Numerous "crimes" have been challenged pursuant to the *Charter*, with the result that the behaviour may be "de-criminalized" unless and until the cases are either successfully appealed or the legislature re-drafts the legislation so that it conforms with the court's interpretation of the *Charter*. Consider the following cases:

- Section 159 of the *Criminal Code* was declared unconstitutional in *R.* v. *C.(M.)* (1995), 23 O.R. (3d) 629 (C.A.) because, by using a higher age of consent for sodomy than for other sexual acts, it discriminated on the basis of age, sexual orientation, and marital status in violation of s. 15 (right to equality before and under the law) of the *Charter*.
- Section 21(1)(ii) of *Family Benefits Schedule "B" Regulations*, N.S. Reg. 72/87, made pursuant to the *Family Benefits Act*, R.S.N.S. 1989, c. 158, was declared unconstitutional in a fraud prosecution under s. 380(1)(a) of the *Criminal Code* in *R.* v. *Rehberg* (1994), 111 D.L.R. (4th) 336 (N.S.S.C. (T.D.)). The court ruled that the section, which imposed an obligation to report cohabitation and disqualified a cohabiting applicant from receipt of benefits, violated ss. 7 and 15 of the *Charter* by putting an applicant at risk of imprisonment if convicted and discriminating against single mothers in poverty.
- Sections of the *Controlled Drugs and Substances Act* have been repeatedly challenged using *Charter*, s. 7. One such case, *R.* v. *Clay*, follows.

R. v. Clay†

[ROSENBERG J.A.:]

This is one of two appeals heard by this court concerning the constitutionality of the marijuana prohibition in the former *Narcotic Control Act*, R.S.C. 1985, c. N-1 and the *Controlled Drugs and Substances Act*, S.C. 1996, c. 19. The Crown appeal in *R. v. Parker* [(2000), 49 O.R. (3d) 481] concerns the medical use of marijuana. This appeal centres primarily on the use of the criminal law power to penalize the possession of marijuana.

The appellant owned a store called "The Great Canadian Hemporium". In addition to selling items such as hemp products, marijuana logos and pipes, the appellant sold small marijuana plant seedlings from his store. The appellant is an active advocate for the decriminalization of marijuana. The appellant does not require marijuana for any personal medical reason although he did sell marijuana cuttings from his store to persons who did.

An undercover police officer bought a small marijuana cutting at the store. The police also seized marijuana cuttings and a small amount of marijuana when they executed search warrants at the appellant's store and home. As a result, the police charged the appellant under the former *Narcotic Control Act* with possession of *cannabis sativa,* trafficking in cannabis sativa, possession of cannabis sativa for the purpose of trafficking and the unlawful cultivation of marijuana.

At trial, the appellant challenged the constitutionality of the cannabis prohibitions in the former *Narcotic Control Act* on the basis that: (a) these prohibitions violate his rights under s. 7 of the *Canadian Charter of Rights and Freedoms*; and (b) the regulation of marijuana is not within federal jurisdiction. He also argued that the Crown failed to prove that the substances seized from him were prohibited narcotics as defined by the Act.

McCart J. dismissed the appellant's constitutional challenge and found that the Crown had proven the offences against him. In reasons reported at (1997), 9 C.R. (5th) 349, McCart J. fully reviewed the evidence at trial and made findings of fact and law with which I essentially agree.

For the reasons that follow, I would dismiss the appellant's appeal. I will deal with the appellant's constitutional arguments first and then with whether the Crown proved that the seized substances were narcotics as defined by the Act.

THE CONSTITUTIONALITY OF THE PROHIBITION AGAINST THE POSSESSION AND TRAFFICKING OF MARIJUANA

1. The Appellant's Position

The focus of the appellant's attack on the marijuana prohibitions is on the alleged deleterious health effects of marijuana use and the alleged danger to the public. Briefly, he argues that the evidence shows that marijuana use is not associated with any significant harmful health effects and that it is the criminalization of marijuana, rather than its use, that poses the greater danger to the public. He argues that inclusion of marijuana in the Act violates s. 7 of the *Charter* because:

(i) it is a principle of fundamental justice that the criminal law be used with restraint and not employed unless there is a reasonable basis for finding that the prohibition is directed to harmful conduct;

(ii) the marijuana prohibition is overly broad as it does not include an exemption for the medical use of marijuana and it prohibits forms of cannabis that are not harmful or intoxicating;

(iii) the right to use intoxicants in the privacy of one's home is a fundamental aspect of personal autonomy and human dignity and is thus guaranteed by s. 7.

. . . .

2. The Trial Decision

The trial judge heard two weeks of evidence, including evidence from some of the leading experts on marijuana. He was also referred to government and scientific studies and the reports of various law reform bodies. On the basis of this evidence, the trial judge concluded that previous concerns about marijuana use are exaggerated, but that there are certain health and public dangers associated with its use. In my view, these findings are founded in the

---

† (2000), 49 O.R. (3d) 577 (C.A.). [Notes omitted.]

evidence. They are set out in full below from pp. 360–62:

> From an analysis of their evidence I am able to reach the following conclusions:
> 1. Consumption of marijuana is relatively harmless compared to the so-called hard drugs and including tobacco and alcohol;
> 2. There exists no hard evidence demonstrating any irreversible organic or mental damage from the consumption of marijuana;
> 3. That cannabis does cause alteration of mental functions and as such, it would not be prudent to drive a car while intoxicated;
> 4. There is no hard evidence that cannabis consumption induces psychoses;
> 5. Cannabis is not an addictive substance;
> 6. Marijuana is not criminogenic in that there is no evidence of a causal relationship between cannabis use and criminality;
> 7. That the consumption of marijuana probably does not lead to "hard drug" use for the vast majority of marijuana consumers, although there appears to be a statistical relationship between the use of marijuana and a variety of other psychoactive drugs;
> 8. Marijuana does not make people more aggressive or violent;
> 9. There have been no recorded deaths from the consumption of marijuana;
> 10. There is no evidence that marijuana causes amotivational syndrome;
> 11. Less than 1% of marijuana consumers are daily users;
> 12. Consumption in so-called "decriminalized states" does not increase out of proportion to states where there is no decriminalization;
> 13. Health related costs of cannabis use are negligible when compared to the costs attributable to tobacco and alcohol consumption.

Harmful Effects of Marijuana and the Need for More Research

Having said all of this, there was also general consensus among the experts who testified that the consumption of marijuana is not completely harmless. While marijuana may not cause schizophrenia, it may trigger it. Bronchial pulmonary damage is at risk of occurring with heavy use. However, to be fair, there is also general agreement among the experts who testified that moderate use of marijuana causes no physical or psychological harm. Field studies in Greece, Costa Rica and Jamaica generally supported the idea that marijuana was a relatively safe drug — not totally free from potential harm, but unlikely to create serious harm for most individual users or society.

The LeDain Commission found at least four major grounds for social concern: the probably harmful effect of cannabis on the maturing process in adolescence; the implications for safe driving arising from impairment of cognitive functions and psycho motor abilities, from the additive interaction of cannabis and alcohol and from the difficulties of recognizing or detecting cannabis intoxication; the possibility, suggested by reports in other countries and clinical observations on this continent, that the long term, heavy use of cannabis may result in a significant amount of mental deterioration and disorder; and the role played by cannabis in the development and spread of multi-drug use by stimulating a desire for drug experience and lowering inhibitions about drug experimentation. This report went on to state that it did not yet know enough about cannabis to speak with assurance as to what constitutes moderate as opposed to excessive use.

The *Report of the National Task Force on Cannabis*, Canberra, Australia, was delivered on September 30, 1994. This Task Force concluded, in general, that the findings on the health and psychological effects of cannabis suggest that cannabis use is not as dangerous as its opponents might believe, but that its use is not completely without risk, as some of its proponents would argue. As it is most commonly used, occasionally, cannabis presents only minor or subtle risks to the health of the individual. The potential for problems increases with regular heavy use. While the research findings on some potential risks remain equivocal, there is clearly sufficient evidence to conclude that cannabis use should be discouraged, particularly among youth.

Sometime prior to the *Canberra Report*, the Royal Commission into the non-medical use of drugs in South Australia was released. This Commission concluded that marijuana is not an addictive drug and "is comparatively harmless in moderate doses, although there are effects on skills such as those required for driving, and its effects may be greater if it is taken in combination with other drugs. It is almost certainly harmful to some extent in high doses. The summary of the scientific and medical evidence does not entirely resolve the policy questions, since further value judgments have to be made."

Finally, I would refer to a commentary by Dr. Harold Kalant [the Crown's expert witness] on three reports which appeared in 1982 respecting the potential health damaging consequences of chronic cannabis use. The one report is that of an expert group appointed by the Advisory Council on the misuse of drugs in the United Kingdom. The second is that resulting from a scientific meeting sponsored jointly by the Addiction Research Foundation of Ontario and the World Health Organization. The third is that of a committee set up by the Institute of Medicine, National Academy of Sciences, of the United

States of America. There was general agreement by the three groups after a review of essentially the same body of evidence. In brief, the verdict in each case has been that the available evidence is not nearly complete enough to permit an identification of the full range and frequency of occurrence of adverse effects from cannabis use, but that the practice can certainly not be considered harmless and innocent.

I can only conclude from a review of these reports and the other *viva voce* evidence which I heard that the jury is still out respecting the actual and potential harm from the consumption of marijuana. It is clear that further research should be carried out. While it is generally agreed that marijuana used in moderation is not a stepping stone to hard drugs, in that it does not usually lead to consumption of the so-called hard drugs, nevertheless approximately 1 in 7 or 8 marijuana users do graduate to cocaine and/or heroin.

. . . .

THE CONSTITUTIONAL ARGUMENT

1. Section 7 of the *Charter*

. . . .

(ii) The "harm" principle

This part of the appellant's s. 7 argument rests upon the risk of deprivation of liberty through the possibility of imprisonment upon conviction for the marijuana offences under the *Narcotic Control Act*. Drawing together a number of themes from various authorities, not all of them dealing with s. 7, Mr. Young, on behalf of the appellant, argues that s. 7 of the *Charter* precludes Parliament from interfering with the liberty of Canadians through a penal sanction unless there is a reasonable basis for finding that the conduct to which the prohibition is directed is harmful.

In this aspect of the case, the appellant particularly relies upon the well-known principle expressed by Lamer J. at the opening of his reasons in *Reference re s. 94(2) of the Motor Vehicle Act (British Columbia)*, [1985] 2 S.C.R. 486 at p. 492:

> *A law that has the potential to convict a person who has not really done anything wrong offends the principles of fundamental justice* and, if imprisonment is available as a penalty, such a law then violates a person's right to liberty under s. 7 of the *Charter of Rights and Freedoms (Constitution Act*, 1982, as enacted by the *Canada Act, 1982*, 1982 (U.K.), c. 11). (Emphasis added)

This principle has been employed to measure the constitutionality of the *mens rea* or fault requirements of criminal and *quasi*-criminal provisions. It has not previously been used by the courts to evaluate the wisdom of penalizing the underlying prohibited conduct.

The appellant also relies upon statements from the Law Reform Commission of Canada, the *Report of the Canadian Committee on Corrections (Ouimet Report)* and the Government of Canada itself in *The Criminal Law in Canadian Society*, which have all affirmed the principle of restraint as a fundamental basis for use of the criminal law and especially the use of the sanction of imprisonment.

In summary, the appellant seeks to derive a "harm principle" from these and other statements as a principle of fundamental justice. He rightly points out that his liberty interest is engaged since imprisonment was available for the marijuana offences under the *Narcotic Control Act* (as it still is under the *Controlled Drugs and Substances Act*). Accordingly, he can only be deprived of his liberty in accordance with the principles of fundamental justice. He argues that penal legislation that does not comply with the harm principle is not consistent with the principles of fundamental justice and therefore violates s. 7 of the *Charter*.

In *Rodriguez* v. *British Columbia (Attorney General)* [[1993] 3 S.C.R. 519] at p. 590, Sopinka J. cautioned that the court must be careful that the principles of fundamental justice do not become principles in the "eye of the beholder *only*". As he said at pp. 590–91:

> Principles of fundamental justice must not, however, be so broad as to be no more than vague generalizations about what our society considers to be ethical or moral. They must be capable of being identified with some precision and applied to situations in a manner which yields an understandable result.

The harm principle as a principle of fundamental justice evokes many of these concerns when it is taken out of the context from which it is derived. While it is a good basis for legislative policy, a helpful guide for the exercise of discretion by prosecutions and an important principle for judges in exercising discretion in sentencing, it is a difficult principle to translate into a means of measuring the constitutionality of legislation. For example, how much harm is sufficient to warrant legislative action? And, can the harm principle be applied outside the *mens rea* area in a manner that yields an understandable result?

In *R.* v. *Malmo-Levine* (2000), 74 C.R.R. (2d) 189 the British Columbia Court of Appeal was presented with virtually the same arguments made in this case. In a thoughtful treatment of this difficult question, Braidwood J.A., speaking for himself and Rowles J.A., concluded that the harm principle is a principle of fundamental justice within the meaning of s. 7. He concluded, however, that the marijuana prohibition in the former *Narcotic Control Act* is consistent with the principles of fundamental justice.

Braidwood J.A. described the harm principle at para. 138 as "whether the prohibited activities hold a 'reasoned apprehension of harm' to other individuals or society". He also held that the degree of harm must be neither insignificant nor trivial. He rejected a higher test suggested by Prowse J.A. in her dissenting reasons. She held at para. 177 that the harm must be of a serious, significant or substantial nature.

I am prepared to accept for the purpose of this appeal that a harm principle is a principle of fundamental justice in the terms suggested by Braidwood J.A. I do not agree with the higher test propounded by Prowse J.A. which, in my view, could lead to an unjustifiable intrusion into the legislative sphere. Moreover, the principle, as derived by Braidwood J.A., appears to be consistent with the argument made by the appellant in this court, which in turn was based on some of the language from *R.* v. *Butler*, [1992] 1 S.C.R. 452. In that case, Sopinka J., in applying s. 1 to the alleged violation of freedom of expression from the obscenity prohibition in the *Criminal Code*, held at p. 504 that a rational connection between the impugned measure and the objective of the legislation was made out if Parliament had a "reasoned apprehension of harm". Later he held at p. 505, in applying the minimal impairment test, that it was sufficient that the prohibited material "creates a risk of harm to society" and "that it is sufficient in this regard for Parliament to have a reasonable basis for concluding that harm will result and this requirement does not demand actual proof of harm".

Finally, it seems to me that the test, as articulated by Braidwood J.A., is consistent with Sopinka J.'s discussion in *Rodriguez* about the principles of fundamental justice. Sopinka J. held that in determining whether the legislation was consistent with the principles of fundamental justice, it was necessary to consider the state interest and at pp. 593–94 he referred to the reasons of McLachlin J. in *Cunningham* v. *Canada*, [1993] 2 S.C.R. 143 at pp. 151–52:

> The principles of fundamental justice are concerned not only with the interest of the person who claims his liberty has been limited, but with the protection of society. Fundamental justice requires that a *fair balance* be struck between these interests, both substantively and procedurally ... (Emphasis added)

In *Cunningham* at p. 151, McLachlin J. had also held that the "*Charter* does not protect against insignificant or 'trivial' limitations of rights".

Finally, the harm principle as articulated by Braidwood J.A. is not unlike a principle of fundamental justice described by Sopinka J. at pp. 594–95 of *Rodriguez*. He held that where the "deprivation of the right in question does little or nothing to enhance the state's interest (whatever it may be), it seems to me that a breach of fundamental justice will be made out, as the individual's rights will have been deprived for no valid purpose". Similarly, if the marijuana prohibition, which risks depriving the appellant of his liberty, does little or nothing to enhance the state's interests because there is no rational basis for finding that marijuana use is harmful, there is a breach of fundamental justice.

As Sopinka J. said at p. 596 of *Rodriguez*, the determination whether substantive legislation is consistent with the principles of fundamental justice requires "an analysis of our legislative and social policy ... to determine whether fundamental principles have evolved such that they conflict with the validity of the balancing of interests undertaken by Parliament." I need not engage in an extended discussion of this issue since I agree with the findings of McCart J. at trial and much of the analysis of Braidwood J.A. in *Malmo-Levine*.

In considering whether Parliament has struck a fair balance, the deleterious effects of the marijuana prohibition should not be underestimated. In addition to the possibility of imprisonment, the evidence at trial also demonstrated the broader adverse impact. As Braidwood J.A. noted at paras. 146–47 in *Malmo-Levine*, the continued criminalization of marijuana has led to a "palpable disrespect for the law among the million or so Canadians who continue to use the substance despite the risk of imprisonment". The marijuana law has fostered disrespect and distrust for narcotic laws generally. The marijuana prohibition has also resulted in the stigmatization of many thousands of Canadians who have been given a criminal record or a record of a finding of guilt by reason of their being charged with possession of marijuana. That charge and the resultant court proceedings are often their only interaction with the criminal justice system.

In considering the other side of the issue, the interests of the state, it has to be conceded that origins of the marijuana prohibition in Canada are not based in good public policy. While the objective was to protect Canadians from harm caused by marijuana use, the supposed evidence of that harm was based on racism and irrational, unproven and unfounded fears. The Crown does not suggest that the harms identified in the early part of the last century can justify the legislation. It does, however, identify a number of other harms that can justify a continuing state interest in the prohibition. As discussed earlier, I accept McCart J.'s findings that there is some harm associated with marijuana use. In my view, the evidence established that there is a reasoned apprehension of harm that is neither insignificant nor trivial. I do not see this as the "shifting purpose" argument, condemned by the Supreme Court of Canada in *R.* v. *Big M Drug Mart Ltd.*, [1985] 1 S.C.R. 295. The purpose of the legislation has remained the same; the evidence to support the purpose has shifted. In any event, in considering the purpose, it is necessary to consider the particular legislation at stake. While the impugned provisions have their origin in the *Opium and Narcotic Drug Act*, 1923, S.C. 1923, c. 22, the legislation involved in this challenge is the *Narcotic Control Act*, which was enacted in 1961 after Canada became a party to the United Nations *Single Convention on Narcotic Drugs, 1961*. Under that Convention and those that have followed, Canada was obligated to prohibit the scheduled drugs, including marijuana, except in narrow circumstances, such as for medical use.

The legislative situation in other western democracies, in general, reflects a similar approach to that currently existing in Canada. I canvass this issue more fully in *R.* v. *Parker*. It is sufficient for this appeal to note that, except for the medical use of marijuana, there is nothing approaching an international consensus that even the simple possession of marijuana should be legalized.

Mr. Young also pointed to studies showing that cigarette smoking is more dangerous to the smoker's health than marijuana smoking and that alcohol abuse is associated with violent crime whereas marijuana use is not. In my view, this is not an apt comparison. The fact that Parliament has been unable or unwilling to prohibit the use of other more dangerous substances does not preclude its intervention with respect to marijuana, provided Parliament had a rational basis for doing so.

To conclude, given the harms identified by the trial judge and the other objectives of the legislation, I do not agree that there is no rational basis for the marijuana prohibitions. In terms expressed by Sopinka J. in *Rodriguez*, the legislation is not arbitrary or unfair in that it is unrelated to the state's objectives and lacks a foundation in the legal traditions and societal beliefs that are said to be represented by the prohibitions.

. . . .

Appeal dismissed.

2

Colonization and the Imposition of Criminal Law

The imposition of Canadian criminal law on Aboriginal peoples highlights issues of colonization, sovereignty, and the role of law, and must be understood in historical context. Consider the situation of the Aboriginal peoples in the late nineteenth century:

- the decline of the fur trade
- the dislocation from their lands by "settlers"
- the making of treaties (Treaties 1 to 11 were made between 1871 and 1921)
- the Riel Rebellion by the Metis people (1869–1885)
- the subsequent trial and hanging of a number of people for their participation in that "rebellion," including the trial and execution of Louis Riel for treason
- the decimation by European epidemic diseases such as smallpox
- the destruction of wildlife and resources
- "enfranchisement" (which was tied to the abandonment of Indian status and to taxation, in exchange for an allotment of land and the right to vote)
- the substitution of imposed elections for traditional leadership and the definition of "electors" as "male Indians of the full age of 21 ..." (until 1951); thus, depending on the history of individual nations, the impact would have been to impose patriarchal systems of governance and sharply alter the pre-existing pattern of social relations between men and women
- the outlawing of practices of tradition, governance, and ceremony, such as the Potlatch (S.C. 1884, 47 Vict., c. 27, s. 3 (1884)) and the Sundance (S.C. 1895, 58 & 59 Vict., c. 35, s. 6 (1895))
- the institution of the "Pass System" in the 1880s
- the imposition of compulsory education for Aboriginal children in the 1880s, and the creation of residential schools (S.C. 1894, 47 Vict., c. 24)
- the prohibition preventing lawyers from representing an "Indian" or a band in an action against the government (until 1951)

For a more detailed history of the legislation, see: *The Historical Development of the Indian Act* (Ottawa: Treaties and Historical Research Centre, Indian and Northern Affairs, 1978) and Sharon Venne, *Indian Acts and Amendments: 1868–1975, An Indexed Collection* (Saskatoon: University of Saskatchewan Native Law Centre, 1981).

As the Royal Commission on Aboriginal Peoples describes in *Bridging the Cultural Divide: A Report on Aboriginal People and Criminal Justice in*

Canada (Ottawa: Canada Communication Group, 1996) [hereinafter, *Bridging the Cultural Divide*] at xi: "the legacy of these historical policies for today's generation of Aboriginal people is high rates of social disorganization, reflected in acts such as suicide and crime." In a larger sense, the legacy is a fundamental challenge to the ideological underpinnings and legitimacy of criminal law, given the historical question of sovereignty, the lack of democratic foundation to the laws, the impact of lack of knowledge with respect to the laws, and the process of law enforcement.

A. OUTLAWING THE POTLATCH AND THE SUN DANCE

In the articles that follow, Forrest LaViolette and Brian Titley examine the ideological, economic, and political impetus for the suppression of cultural practices, such as the Potlatch and the Sundance. They detail the role of Christian missionaries and churches in the assault on Aboriginal institutions and the elaboration of policy and law with respect to Aboriginal peoples.

As Associate Chief Judge Murray Sinclair of Manitoba describes (*infra*, **Aboriginal Peoples and Criminal Law**), many of those prosecuted under these laws were the traditional leaders, making the consequences particularly serious. Also, because these offences carried mandatory minimum sentences of imprisonment, they formed the basis for the incarceration of most of the Aboriginal people in jails such as Stony Mountain Penitentiary at the turn of the century.

The Struggle for Survival: Indian Cultures and the Protestant Ethic in British Columbia†

THE PROTESTANT ETHIC

Industry was the outstanding character trait required of all those who aspired to success. Idleness was condemned by Franklin and by generations after him as injurious to the person as well as a detriment to the well-being of society. Perseverance was another prized quality required for success and was outstandingly evident, it was said, among those who carefully and diligently saved their money until they amassed great wealth. Sobriety was on the list, as was also the stricture against "the pleasures of bad company" that not only caused one to waste money foolishly but also would lead one astray. Additional virtues that were stressed included punctuality and a ready willingness to perform extra services without extra pay or special recognition.

Leonard Reissman
Class in American Society, p. 17

[Prime Minister John A. MacDonald, responding to the appeals of church groups, made the following Proclamation in 1883:]

Certified Copy of a Report of a Committee of the Honorable Privy Council approved by His Excellency the Governor General in Council, on the 7th July, 1883.

On a report dated 19th of June, 1883, from the Superintendent General of Indian Affairs representing that strenuous measures should be adopted to put a stop to the heathenish custom known as the "Potlack" [*sic*] and which his department has endeavored through its Superintendent and Agents to suppress, but which still prevails to a large extent among [some] of the tribes in the Province, although some of the more civilized Indians recognize the desirability in their own interests of its being put an end to, and have petitioned the Government to adopt measures to this end.

---

† Excerpts from Forrest LaViolette, *The Struggle for Survival: Indian Cultures and the Protestant Ethic in British Columbia* (Toronto: University of Toronto Press, 1973) at 2, 38–39, 43, 57, 59, 61, 69–72, 74, 83–85. Reproduced by permission of the publisher.

The Minister quotes the following extract from a Report on the system as it prevails and the evils attendant thereon from the late Indian Reserve Commissioner Mr. G.W. Sproat.

The Potlach [sic] is the parent of numerous vices which eat out the heart of the people. It produces indigence, thriftlessness, and habits of roaming about which prevent home association and is inconsistent with all progress. A large amount of prostitution common among some of the Coast Tribes is directly caused by the "Potlack" [sic].

There followed six paragraphs of explanatory statements about the nature of the potlatch — the desire for distinction, the system of credit, the rivalry involved, the deprivation of families, and of course the fact that it was "directly opposed to the inculcation of industriousness or moral habits." The *Proclamation* then continued:

The Minister advised that the earliest possible measures should be taken with a view to suppress the heathenish and worse than useless custom; and pending legislation which may be had with this object in view at the next session of Parliament, he, the Minister, recommends that Your Excellency will be pleased to issue a Proclamation discountenancing the custom and requesting in her Majesty's name that Her Indian subjects abandon the same.

The Minister is of opinion that such a Proclamation from the well-known loyalty of the Indians generally and their reverence for Her Majesty the Queen will go far to induce them to abandon the heathenish custom of "Potlack" [sic].

The Committee concurs in the foregoing recommendations and they advise that a Dispatch based upon this minute when approved together with copies of the Proclamation be transmitted to the Lieutenant Governor of British Columbia with the request that he will use his best efforts for the suppression of the "Potlack," [sic] and for the circulation of His Excellency's Proclamation discountenancing the heathenish custom in question.

. . . .

On April 19, 1884, assent was given to amend the Indian Act, 1880; included in the revision was the first legislation in the *Statutes of Canada* to prohibit potlatching. Section 3, later revised, read as follows in its original statement:

3. Every Indian or other person who engages in or assists in celebrating the Indian festival known as the "Potlach" [sic] or in the Indian dance known as the "Tamanawas" is guilty of a misdemeanour, and shall be liable to imprisonment for a term of not more than six nor less than two months in any gaol or other place of confinement; and any Indian or other person who encourages, either directly or indirectly, an Indian or Indians to get up such a festival or dance, or to celebrate the same, or who shall assist in the celebration of same is guilty of a like offence, and shall be liable to the same punishment.

The Potlatch Law as it came to be called, and shall be so designated in the analysis following, remained on the statutes of Canada until the Indian Act was revised completely in 1951, *Statutes of Canada*, Chapter 29, proclaimed on September 4 of that year.

. . . .

In February, 1887, Sir John Macdonald received a petition for the repeal of the law.

We the undersigned Indians of the Cowichan agency beg respectfully to ask you to use your influence to have the clause of the Indian Act forbidding the "Potlach" [sic] and "Tamanawas" Dances repealed.

In asking this we would point out that these are two of our oldest customs, and by them we do not injure anyone.

We cannot read like white people and the dances are our winter amusements.

When our children grow up and are educated they perhaps will not wish to dance.

Some only of us dance now, and we do not wish to teach others, but when one is seized with the ("Quellish") dance he cannot help himself and we believe would die unless he danced. On Saturdays and Sundays we will not dance as this offends the Christian Indians.

The lands of our fathers are occupied by white men and we say nothing.

We have given up fighting with each other.

We have given up stealing and many old habits, but we want to be allowed to continue the "Potlach" [sic] and the Dance. We know the hearts of most of the Coast Indians are with us in this. We therefore ask you to have the law amended, that we may not be breaking it when we follow customs that are dear to us.

This petition had twenty-four marks and signatures at the bottom, and possibly there were others, for the original is mutilated.

. . . .

[The first arrest was in August 1889:]

About the first of August, 1889, a Kwakiutl known as Hemasak, a member of the Malimalillekulla band, was arrested by Mr. Pidcock, who was a justice of the peace as well as an Indian agent, and sentenced to serve six months in jail — the maximum sentence, two months being the minimum. The case was appealed.

. . . .

[Justice M.B. Begbie discharged Hemasak:]

Shortly before the hearing by Judge Begbie, the Indians in the Alert Bay area had prepared a typewritten statement of the case for Lieutenant-Governor Nelson. A good portion of it was a recital of complaints against the Indian agent Mr. Pidcock who had arrested Hemasak, claiming that the agent had broken down the door of his house. It was claimed that "Ha-Mer-cee-lue" [Hemasak] had been arrested because of his connection with a marriage between his niece and one of their men; the agent had been falsely informed by two of the Indians at Fort Rupert who had apparently been made constables. The two Indians were described as:

> ... walking about our village saying they have power to arrest us for almost anything that we do and making us live in dread all the time. It is our nature to fear the law. When we are imprisoned we feel it so that many die. Several of our families have left us in fear. We do not know where they have gone. They have done nothing that they know is against the Law. If Potlatching is unlawful, why do we not receive such notice ... [the Agent] has never said anything about it to us, in fact we very seldom see him and when he does come, he only counts the people or makes an arrest.... We are willing to give up all such doings but then we should be allowed something to help us live. Formerly we had plenty but now everything is being taken from us. Our rivers, our trees, our lands, even our fish are scarce among us, yet we are trying to live in peace and want to be friendly to all, but why should we be threatened with arrest all the time, when we do not know what is required of us. We beg protection that we may live in peace unless we break the law.

This petition was signed by a long list of Indians.

. . . .

[In January 1896, another arrest was made. Indian agent Devlin reported:]

> The Indian mentioned ... Bill Uslick ... is one of those Indians that is very hard to manage. He still wishes to keep up the old habits and customs, and would like to be a leader among the Indians of the neighborhood. The Potlatch given by Bill Uslick was simply a Potlatch. I am not aware that any human, or animal bodies, were mutilated, or anything of that kind occurred. There certainly was a great waste. He practically left himself destitute, having given everything away that he had in the world. I am of the opinion if he was brought before the Court and got a couple of months in prison, that it would have a good effect, and would deter others from following his example....

Upon receiving the file from the Commissioner, the Department of Indian Affairs indicated that if there was certainty of securing a conviction, then prosecution should be initiated, "unless he promises to obey the law in the future." All the Indians of the district were at the court, and the agent explained to them that every Indian who went to the potlatch was liable to the same punishment, but "as he was the principal offender I would only punish him this time, but should a repetition occur I would punish every Indian who was guilty. I feel certain the steps taken will have the effect of stopping the Potlatch in Chilliwack." On February 4 a newspaper, identity undetermined, carried this short statement concerning Uslick's potlatch — "An Indian recently left his wife to starve near Chilliwack and held a hiyu skookum potlatch for his friends. Indian Agent Devlin and Mr. Millard sentenced the unnatural husband to two months in jail."

The arrest and imprisonment of Uslick triggered a renewed and wider interest in the potlatch; newspapers printed letters and petitions about it for several months. Letters from Indians by then, however, indicated distinct changes in their arguments. For example, on February 24, 1896, the *Victoria Colonist* published a petition from the Nass River tribes to Mr. G.E. Courbould, a member of Parliament, and the clippings were sent to Ottawa by Mr. C.M. Tate, who had placed the formal charge against Mr. Lomas. The theme of the petition was that they saw a

> ... contradictory state of affairs adorning your civilization. Churches are numerous; the theatres are located in the various sections of the town; and saloons multiply in numbers; all of which are in conformity with your laws, consequently we wish to know whether the ministers of the gospel have annihilated the rights of white men in these pleasures leading to heaven and hell exactly in different directions. They have kindly forced us out, as we are "not in it."

The petition mentioned Christmas, "Fourth of July," and "24th of May" celebrations, where "money is spent in squandrous profusion with no benefits to the poor of your race," and compared European and Indian funeral rights:

> We see in your graveyards the white marble and granite monuments which cost money in testimony of your grief for your dead. When our people die we erect a large pole, call our people together, distribute our personal property with them in payment for their sympathy, and condolence; comfort to us in the sad hours of our affliction. This is what is called a potlach† — the privilege denied us. It is a chimera that under the British flag slavery does not exist.

A prominent missionary responded with a personal account of the iniquities of the potlach. Rev. Alfred H. Hall ... in the *Weekly Colonist* on March 19, 1896, was calculated to support the enforcement of the Potlatch Law. Dealing first with prostitution, he told of counting "thirty-two women in one month who embarked by the steamers to bring back the coveted blankets. In my time about fifty women under 25 years of age have died, all of whom have been sacrificed to maintain the potlach. Whenever the tribe ceased to potlatch the life of shame, which some of these women lead, practically ceases." Moreover, because of the potlach, tribes left their villages and remained away for three to five months, leaving the aged and infirm behind to their fate — "once in a deserted village I found an old woman frozen to death and as hard as a stone. I have been applied to for poison to put such out of the way, because their friends (?) wished to follow those who had gone to the potlach. There can be no real progress while this system flourishes...." The missionary praised the efforts of the Indian Department, however. "It is school versus potlach." He concluded that "the law which forbids the potlach is not against liberty but licence. It is to the interests of this province that we keep our Indians alive; they are worth preserving.... They occupy land the white man does not require. They love the white man, and their ultimate future must be absorption and assimilation to the whites."

. . . .

On April 1, 1896, the *Daily Colonist* published "The Nootka Chief Speaks." Chief Maquinna referred to the potlach system as a bank and drew a parallel to the white method of banking. He called attention to the Indian ways of supporting the aged and to the fact that the Indian agent "does not support the old and poor now." Furthermore, "they say it is the will of the Queen. This is not true. The Queen knows nothing about our potlach feasts. She must have been put up to make a law by people who know us." And then he pointed out a number of other white-native parallels:

> ... a white man told me one day that the white people have also sometimes masquerade balls and white women have feathers on their bonnets and the white chiefs give prizes for those who imitate best, birds or animals. And this is all good when white men do it but very bad when Indians do the same thing. The white chiefs should leave us alone; they have their games and we have ours....
>
> ... The potlach [*sic*] is not a pagan rite; the first Christians used to have their goods in common as a consequence must have given "potlaches" and now I am astonished that Christians persecute us and put us in jail for doing as the first Christians.

In the last paragraph Chief Maquinna said, "I am sorry to hear the news about the potlach [*sic*] and that my friends of the North were put in jail."

. . . .

[Franz Boas, a well-known anthropologist, wrote in a letter published in the *Vancouver Daily Province* on 6 March 1897:]

> It must be clearly understood that an Indian who invites all his friends and neighbors to a great potlach [*sic*], and apparently squanders all the accumulated results of long years of labor has two things in mind which we cannot but acknowledge as wise and worthy of praise. His first object is to pay his debts.... His second object is to invest the fruits of his labor so that the greatest benefit will accrue from them for his own benefit as well as for his children....

. . . .

[The prosecutions for Potlatch violations intensified in 1921. A brief summary follows:]

January, 1921. Two Kwakiutls, one Mrs. McDougall and one Munday, prosecuted for alleged potlatching in December, 1920; case dismissed for want of evidence.

---

† This was the spelling in the original materials.

May, 1921. Mr. E.K. DeBeck, lawyer for the Alert Bay Kwakiutls, instructed by his clients to petition Ottawa for revision of section 149 of the Indian Act.

December 9, 1921. Five Indians charged with potlatching at Kingcome Inlet, October 15, 1921; convicted.

December 15, 1921. Circular letter from Ottawa to all agents, regarding the increase in potlatching. Instructions reinstated.

January 20, 1922. Appeal of five Kwakiutl Indians convicted December 9 heard before Chief Justice Hunter of the Supreme Court of British Columbia; appeal dismissed.

January 22, 1922. Five Indians arrived at Oakalla Penitentiary.

February 16, 1922. Vancouver barrister wrote to Ottawa regarding revision of section 149; stated belief of Indians in the imminent revision of the section.

March, first week, 1922. Twenty-nine Kwakiutls tried; seventeen found guilty; sentence delayed until March 31, to provide defendants with an opportunity to accept or reject the plan of R.W. Ellis, a barrister, namely to sign an agreement for no more potlatching and to surrender potlatching paraphernalia, to be paid for by the National Museum, Ottawa.

March 4, 1922. Mr. DeBeck sent to Ottawa three formal petitions protesting against section 149; these were signed by almost all older members of the Kwakiutl group.

March 13, 1922. Petition from seventy Cloyoquot (west central coast of Vancouver Island; not Kwakiutl) Indians asking for continuance of potlatch.

March 31, 1922. Indians, tried earlier in the month, sentenced: one given six months, second offence; twelve given two months; four given suspended sentence, two for taking only minor roles, two for signing agreement.

April 19, 1922. Mrs. Dick Mountain and Billy Moon charged with potlatching; both guilty. Mrs. Mountain given suspended sentence; Moon given two months at Oakalla.

April 28, 1922. Questions in the House of Commons about Alert Bay cases by Mr. Leon Ladner, a member from British Columbia.

April 29, 1922. Questions of Mr. Ladner replied to by Minister of Interior who reported that there were fifty convictions and at that time four were serving sentences, of whom three were being considered for parole by the Department of Justice.

May 10, 1922. A letter to Ottawa by Mr. James A. Teit, an early resident of British Columbia, assistant to Franz Boas, and special agent of the Allied Tribes of British Columbia referred to section 149 as "standing injustice."

May 11, 1922. Mr. Leon Ladner, M.P., asked Indian Affairs for a change in section 149.

May 19, 1922. Amos Dawson charged with perjury in trial of January, 1921; sentenced to three months in Oakalla; Bob Harris sentenced to four months in Oakalla for perjury in trial of January, 1921.

June 19, 1922. Debate in the House of Commons.

July, 1922. The Deputy Superintendent-General of Indian Affairs visited Vancouver and interviewed Indians and others.

August, 1922. Potlatch question discussed at the annual meeting of Allied Indian Tribes; special committee appointed. Mr. Andrew Paull of the Squamish band, and Mr. James A. Teit constituted the committee.

August 30, 1922. Franz Boas lectured before the National Historical Society and discussed the potlatch; reported in *Victoria Colonist*.

February 16, 1923. Formal petition received in Ottawa for either a revision of section 149 or appointment of an investigating committee. Petition claimed that prosecutions were being carried on only at Alert Bay while there was still potlatching in other agencies; sentences were harsh treatment as conviction required jail sentence.

August 13, 1923. *Vancouver Daily Province* reported three of the ten of the Nakwato band, of Blunden Harbor, released from Oakalla because of clerical error. Convictions reported by Halliday in *Potlatch and Totem* but date unascertained.

August 30, 1923. Letter of Mr. Andrew Paull to Mr. Stewart, Superintendent-General of Indian Affairs, setting down the major points of Mr. Stewart's July interview with Indians.

May 14, 1923. Inventory and evaluation by Dr. E. Sapir of the potlatch paraphernalia surrendered and shipped to Ottawa; value: $1,415.

October 31, 1924. Law firm of Dickie and DeBeck sued Alert Bay Indians in Supreme Court of British Columbia for non-payment for professional services rendered; total unpaid: $3,370.57.

May 22, 1925. *Vancouver Daily Province* editorial, "The Potlatch Question."

[As LaViolette explains in a footnote:]

This summary statement is not based upon exhaustive examination of court records and is therefore undoubtedly somewhat incomplete. It has been compiled from the statements of William Halliday in *Potlatch and Totem*, newspaper reports and comments, notes in the file of Dr. Marius Barbeau, anthropologist then in Mines and Resources Branch, Ottawa, and several entries in the Ottawa Potlatch File, as well as *Hansard*.

Senseless Drumming and Dancing[†]

On the other hand, attempts to stamp out the dances of the prairie Indians have largely been ignored by historians and they will therefore be the principal consideration here. The prohibition of both dancing and potlatching came under the same clause of the Indian Act, and so some preliminary observations regarding developments in British Columbia will help to set the stage.

The decision to employ the powers of the Indian Act to prohibit native customs was first taken in response to protests by missionaries and agents against the perceived evils of the potlatch. In the potlatch ceremony of the Indians of the northwest Pacific coast, a host entertained guests and distributed goods following elaborate rituals and protocols. One of its principal purposes was to establish or confirm rank in what were complex hierarchical societies. Missionaries invariably failed to comprehend its significance. Blinded by a puritanism that equated enjoyment with evil, they denounced it as an orgy of drunkenness, debauchery, idleness, and idolatry. And, of course, the Victorian idea of progress, which encouraged the individual accumulation of material goods, was the direct antithesis of the values implicit in the potlatch.

The campaign against this integral component of west coast native culture brought a ready response from Ottawa. An amendment to the Indian Act in 1884 made the celebration of the potlatch and of the Tamanawas dance a misdemeanor subject to a prison sentence that could range from two to six months. Much to the annoyance of the missionaries, who had been most vociferous in demanding this course of action, the prohibition proved impossible to enforce. Some Indian agents refused to seek prosecutions because they believed that the forbidden customs were harmless. Others feared that repressive measures would precipitate an Indian uprising. The minimal police presence on the coast, the reluctance of the provincial authorities to co-operate, and the absence of jails and guard-houses were additional factors that rendered the legislation meaningless.

Alert Bay, in the Kwawkewlth agency, was the principal centre of potlatching. And the local agent, R.H. Pidcock, was one of the custom's most intransigent opponents. In 1889, acting on his powers as justice of the peace, he arrested an Indian named Hema-sak for engaging in a potlatch and sentenced him to six months' imprisonment. The case was subsequently appealed to the provincial supreme court. Chief Justice Sir Matthew Baillie Begbie, whom the Indians had come to know and respect over the years, ruled that the prisoner should be released on account of a technicality in the manner of his arrest. The chief justice also observed, however, that the law was vague and did not clearly define the acts that were forbidden. This opinion was brought to the attention of the federal deputy minister of justice who concluded that the clause in the Indian Act would probably have to be rephrased in order to make it effective.

Meanwhile on the prairies, missionaries and government officials were engaged in a similar struggle — the self-imposed burden of weaning the Indians from their "Heathenish customs" and transforming them into model Anglo-Canadian citizens. The sun dance of the Blackfoot and the thirst dance of the Crees were perceived as the major obstacles to progress in that part of the country. The two ceremonies were sufficiently similar in purpose and procedure that a description of one will largely suffice for the other.

The Indians of the Blackfoot confederacy (Blood, Peigan, and Blackfoot proper) held the sun dance during the months of June and July. It was designed "to propitiate the Sun and other lesser spirits." A woman of good character sponsored the event, having made a vow to do so previously, per-

---

[†] From Brian Titley, *A Narrow Vision: Duncan Campbell Scott and the Administration of Indian Affairs in Canada* (Vancouver: University of British Columbia Press, 1986) at 163–65, 166, 167–69, 177–78. Notes omitted. Reproduced by permission of the publisher.

haps in a time of need. In preparation, she began to collect buffalo tongues, which were cut into slabs, dried, boiled, and subsequently consumed as a sacred food during the dance. As part of the ritual, she was obliged to remain in her teepee abstaining from food for four days.

The men constructed the circular dance lodge with elaborate ceremonies, especially when they were selecting and raising the centre pole. Each tribe contained a number of different societies, and they took turns officiating at the sun dance. The songs and dances performed were often the exclusive property of the individual societies. Gifts were generously distributed to visitors.

The most controversial feature of the sun dance was the custom known as "the making of a brave." It was not necessarily performed by everyone who wished to become a brave, as has been generally believed, but rather by individuals who wanted to make a special sacrifice to the sun in the hope of receiving a favour. A man might go through the rite several times during his life. Clad in breech cloth and moccasins, his body plastered with white clay, and his head, wrists and ankles adorned with sage bush, he had his breasts pierced, sticks placed through openings, and the sticks fastened by rawhide thongs to the top of the centre pole. He danced in a backward motion until the flesh broke, and he was freed.

The thirst dance of the Crees was remarkably similar, except that it was sponsored by a man. For example, Fine Day, a leader of the Sweetgrass Cree and a warrior with a formidable reputation, held seven during his lifetime, in spite of official disapproval.

The sun dance and thirst dance were only two of a vast array of dances performed by the plains Indians. The smoking tipi dance, rain dance, prairie chicken dance, beer dance, grass dance — these are the names of a few. Most of them involved some form of gift-giving, which reflected the high regard in which generosity was held among these people. Prestige was acquired by giving goods away rather than by hoarding them. Similar values existed among the west coast tribes where they were associated with the potlatch. Among the plains Indians, however, the gift-giving did not take the form of a single ostentatious display of generosity. Instead, it was done constantly and in a more modest manner.

Government officials began to see dancing in a particularly dangerous light in the aftermath of the Rebellion of 1885. After visiting the sun dance of the Bloods in July 1889, Sam Steele, Superintendent of the North-West Mounted Police, wrote a report to his superiors urging that the festival be discouraged since it tended to revive old associations "too vividly":

> Old warriors take this occasion of relating their experience of former days, counting their scalps and giving the number of horses they were successful in stealing. This has a pernicious effect on the young men; it makes them unsettled and anxious to emulate the deeds of their forefathers.

. . . .

The advocates of repressive measures were undoubtedly relieved to read the revised version of Section 114 of the Indian Act which was adopted in the summer of 1895. The new wording offered a definition of what was forbidden and sought to extend the prohibition on the potlatch to the dances of the plains. Indian ceremonies involving the giving away of "money, goods or articles" or "the wounding or mutilation of the dead or living body of any human being or animal" became indictable offences liable to prison sentences ranging from two to six months. The wounding clause was aimed at "the making of a brave." It also applied to the dog feast and arm-biting rites of some coastal tribes. With the power of the law clearly behind them, officials hoped that Indian agents throughout the west would meet with more success in eradicating these unacceptable aspects of culture.

. . . .

[T]he law had sufficient teeth to allow for an occasional arrest to take place, and department officials believed that convictions served to discourage dancing in general. Wanduta, a member of the Oak River Sioux band of Griswold, Manitoba, was convicted of engaging in an illegal dance in January 1903 and sentenced to four months' imprisonment. Appeals for clemency on his behalf to Ottawa went unheeded. Commissioner Laird and Deputy Superintendent Pedley were adamant that the full sentence be served since Wanduta was said to be the ringleader of the "discontented Indians" and the prison term would undermine his activities.

In March 1903 an "agitator" named Etchease, of Muscowpetung's band, appeared on Piapot's reserve and started "circle dances," at which nothing was given away except a supper. *The Globe* reported that this was a "crafty effort" to evade the law. The local agent, W.M. Graham, became alarmed and took proceedings against Etchease. In spite of an able legal defence, the Indian was found guilty and sentenced to three months' imprisonment. In reporting the trial to headquarters, Assistant Commissioner J.A.J. McKenna observed that the conviction had put an end to dancing in the agency. He also pointed out that if such tough measures were adopted in all western agencies, the problem would soon disappear.

But the enthusiasm of some department officials for the mailed fist could sometimes backfire. This was certainly true in the case of Tapassing, a member of the Fishing Lakes band who was sentenced to two months' imprisonment with hard labour for dancing in January 1904. Upon the intervention of the NWMP at Regina, who had discovered that the prisoner was over ninety years old, feeble, and almost blind, the department consented to his release. The incident nonetheless found its way into the press with the *Winnipeg Telegram* proclaiming it under the following headline: "Injustice to Poor Old Indian — He had deserved better treatment from Canada."

Such embarrassing publicity was the predictable consequence of a misguided policy which was administered in a clumsy and uneven manner. Headquarters in Ottawa and, to a lesser extent, the commissioner's office in Winnipeg were often vague and evasive in the directions given to agents regarding the dancing prohibition. They were frequently advised to use their own discretion, which automatically meant that the degree of permissiveness varied from agency to agency.

Two of the most intransigent opponents of dancing among department officials in the west were W.M. Graham of the Qu'Apelle agency and J.A. Markle of the Blackfoot agency. They both believed that the Indians ought to become self-sufficient farmers and that agriculture and dancing were fundamentally incompatible. Their influence on the course of events was increased during the first decade of the new century when both were promoted to inspector.

Graham's advocacy of repressive measures won the enthusiastic support of Father J. Hugonard, principal of Qu'Appelle industrial school, and close collaborator in the forming of the File Hills colony. In November 1903, the Oblate priest wrote a lengthy letter to Laird describing in alarming terms the evil effects of dancing. He was particularly concerned at the ability of the dance to lure school graduates back to paganism — "the change from discipline and a regular life to unbridled licence and debauchery soon transform a promising youth into a shiftless unreliable Indian." If anyone thought otherwise, he ought to attend these events and see for himself the Indians "nearly nude, painted and decked out in feathers and beads, dancing like demented individuals and indulging in all kinds of debauchery." He pointed out that long absences from reserves to attend dances resulted in neglect or loss of crops and farm animals and reiterated the familiar argument that the custom was inimical to progress:

> I am convinced that Christianity and advancement, and paganism and indolence cannot flourish side by side; one or the other has to give way; paganism, dancing and indolence are most natural to the Indian, who has no thought for the morrow.

. . . .

The dance camps were sometimes the scenes of Indian politicking.... The forces of law and order, then, had their own reasons for taking an interest in the dances.

During 1921, police patrols at dance gatherings increased noticeably. On many occasions, they merely observed the proceedings; on others, they forcibly intervened, sending the participants back to their respective homes. With agents and police working closely together a number of prosecutions for violations of Section 149 took place. With summary procedure, convictions were relatively easy to secure. As a result several Indians found themselves languishing in jail for the heinous crime of holding "give away" dances.

Some Indian leaders reacted with understandable indignation at what they regarded as unwarranted interference with their customs and religion. Among the more eloquent condemnations of the policy of repression was that of Chief Thunderchild, the old Cree warrior who had once supported Big Bear in resisting the treaty process:

> according to its own understanding, its power is worthless ... why has the white man no respect for the religion that was given to us, when we respect the faith of other nations?

1921 and 1922 were the peak years of prosecution for violations of Section 149 on the prairies. On the west coast, the potlatch was being subjected to similar measures of repression at the same time. The jail terms, fines, and suspended sentences handed down were supposed to have a salutary effect on the Indians by convincing them of the folly of resisting the department.

■

The two great Kwakiutl Potlatches and the prosecutions of 45 participants described in *The Struggle for Survival* are depicted in the film *Potlatch: A Strict Law Bids Us Dance* by 'U'Mista Cultural Society (Alert Bay: 1975). See also: Tina Loo, "Dan Cranmer's Potlatch: Law as Coercion, Symbol, and Rhetoric in British Columbia, 1884–1951" in Tina Loo and Lorna McLean, eds., *Historical Perspectives on Law and Society in Canada* (Mississauga: Copp Clark Longman, 1994) 218. See also Douglas Cole and Ira Chaikin, *An Iron Hand Against the People: The Law Against the Potlatch on the Northwest Coast* (Seattle: Douglas & McIntyre, 1990).

More recently, claims are finally being heard for the return of articles seized, confiscated, and later placed in private and museum collections as a consequence of the criminal laws prohibiting the Potlatch. For example, many of the items seized by or surrendered to William Halliday in a coerced mitigation of sentence during the trials of the Kwakiutl Nation in 1922 were sent to the National Museum in Ottawa. Some of those items have only recently been repatriated, for example, to the U'Mista Society museum. Human skeletal remains obtained through the desecration of Aboriginal graves and burial sites remain in museums.

Consider the role of criminal law and the definition of crime in precluding these actions from being characterized as "theft" perpetrated by the colonizers against Aboriginal peoples. For a discussion of Aboriginal claims in the U.S.A. with respect to the appropriation of property by institutions, such as museums, see: Stephen Platzman, "Objects of Controversy: The Native American Right to Repatriation" (1992) 41 Am. Univ. L. Rev. 517.

Outlawing the Potlatch did more than drive a ceremonial and cultural practice underground. It effectively destroyed the people's traditional government — they used the Potlatch to make law, confer responsibilities and judge wrongdoing, and make amends for crimes against the community.

In their opening statement in *Delgamuukw* v. *B.C.*, [1991] 3 W.W.R. 97 (B.C.S.C.), rev'd [1993] 5 W.W.R. 97 (B.C.C.A.), rev'd [1997] 3 S.C.R. 1010, the Gitksan and Wet'suwet'en Chiefs forcefully explained the centrality of the Feast (or Potlatch) to their society:

> When today, as in the past, the hereditary chiefs of the Gitksan and Wet'suwet'en Houses gather in the Feast Hall, the events that unfold are at one and the same time political, legal, economic, social, spiritual, ceremonial and educational. The logistics of accumulating and borrowing to make ready for a Feast, and the process of paying debts in the course of the Feast have many dimensions; they are economic in that the Feast is the nexus of the management of credit and debt; they are social in that the Feast gives impetus to the ongoing network of reciprocity, and renews social contracts and alliances between kinship groups. The Feast is a legal forum for the witnessing of the transmission of chiefs' names, the public delineation of territorial and fishing sites and the confirmation of those territories and sites with the names of the hereditary chiefs. The public recognition of title and authority before an assembly of other chiefs affirms in the minds of all, the legitimacy of succession to the name and transmission of property rights. The Feast can also operate as a dispute resolution process and orders peaceful relationships both nationally, that is within and between Houses, and internationally with other neighbouring people.
>
> The Feast is charged with the power of the spirit world in the form of the crests used in the Feast and in songs and dances performed. Furthermore, the public and ceremonial emphasis upon giving, paying debts, recognizing and legitimizing the status and authority of the chiefs and the ownership of territories, and maintaining the etiquette of reciprocity — all of these aspects of feasting are highly educational. By means of their practice, their repetition and recombination through the course of the Feast, the essential values of the culture are both given expression and transmitted from generation to generation. [Source: Gisday Wa and Delgam Uukw, *The Spirit in the Land* (Gabriola, B.C.: Reflections, 1989) at 31.]

B. EARLY "MURDER" TRIALS

The early murder trials of Aboriginal people, in the late nineteenth and early twentieth centuries, can be seen as part of the assertion of control over Aboriginal peoples. As Cornelia Schuh suggests in "Justice on the Northern Frontier: Early Murder Trials of Native Accused" (1979–80) 22 Crim. L.Q. 74:

What these cases demonstrate quite clearly is that the criminal law seemed useful to the Canadian government in the furtherance of national and colonial objectives in the North. Arrest, trial and conviction of Inuit and Indians served to demonstrate to a wide radius the effective power of the white man. The cases described here occurred in areas where white penetration was accomplished quite peacefully. Where Canadian rule was established essentially by conquest, as took place further south in the Northwest Rebellion of 1885, the trials of native people accused of murder took on a more overtly colonial and political character. But the elements of political policy in the northern cases are nevertheless quite strong. They can be read between the lines of trial transcripts and in the correspondence of officialdom.

The northern patrols of the N.W.M.P. were part of Canada's efforts, during these years, to assert its sovereignty over the still disputed Arctic territories. This element was repeatedly stressed in the Commissioner's reports (and supported his regular requests for more funds, men and outposts). Anxieties about sovereignty and the violation of Canadian territory and customs regulations by American whalers lay behind the establishment of the new detachment at Herschel Island in 1903. The commanding officer's report speaks of the need, for national reasons rather than for considerations of revenue, to "protect all parts of our own national domain from poachers and smugglers." And the Commission's report declared that:

> ... the establishment of these outposts is of far-reaching importance. They stand for law and good order, and show that, no matter what the cost, nor how remote the region, the laws of Canada will be enforced, and the native population protected.

But the more immediately significant purpose of police activities and eventual trials was the symbolic assertion of control over native people that it represented. This holds true for parts of the northern land mass that were in no sense disputed territory, as well as the Arctic islands and coastal areas. North of the 60th parallel, the N.W.M.P. were (and for long years thereafter remained) the only effective or even visible arm of government. Police on patrol often were in the position of explaining their role to native communities who had not seen white men or been informed of Canadian rule before.

[As Schuh describes in a footnote:]

> Riel was the most famous but by no means the only native person to be tried and hanged after the rebellion. Department of Justice records contain an interesting series of files dealing with trials that arose out of the "Frog Lake Massacre." Eight native accused were convicted of murder, most of them on guilty pleas. None had counsel, and all eight, after commutation was refused, were executed at Battleford on November 27, 1885. (Public Archives, RG 13, vol. 1421, files 194–199). As John A. Macdonald wrote to Edgar C. Dewdney a week earlier, "the execution [on] the 27th of the Indians ought to convince the Red Man that the white man governs" (Edgar Dewdney Papers, Glenbow-Alberta Institute). The highly political nature of these proceedings becomes even clearer when they are compared with the contemporary case of Engana, the brother of the chief of a band which had remained loyal during the rebellion. He had counsel (and chose jury trial), and was convicted of murder in the fall of 1885 — like the eight discussed above (the murder took place on a reserve under extenuating circumstances not amounting to provocation; the victim was a fellow band-member). His sentence was commuted, partly, it is obvious, because of the "commendable" behavior of his band in the rebellion. One letter to the Secretary of State pointed out that "this conduct on their part would be graciously rewarded by an act of clemency towards their unfortunate relation, and I have no doubt would go a long way in maintaining their present good feeling towards the authorities" (Northwest Territories Lieutenant-Governor, October 9, 1885). Less than three years later he was released from prison at the recommendation of the Indian Commissioner (Public Archives, RG 13, vol. 1421, file 193).†

Cyril Greenland explains, in "The Last Public Execution in Canada: Eight Skeletons in the Closet of the Canadian Justice System" (1986) 29 Crim. L.Q. 415, that the political objective of the trials and the executions of the eight Aboriginal accused (Wandering Spirit, Itka, Man Without Blood, Round The Sky, Bad Arrow, Miserable Man, Iron Body, and Little Bear) at Battleford was "an act of genocide" (at 420) calculated to "teach the rebellious Indians an indelible lesson" (at 419). The executions took place unlawfully, in spite of an 1869

---

† Reproduced with the permission of the author and the publisher.

Act banning public hanging: H.E. Taschereau, *The Criminal Law Consolidation and Amendment Acts of 1869, 32–33 Vict., for the Dominion of Canada*, Vol. 2 (Toronto: Lovell, 1875), s. 109:

> Judgement of death to be executed on any prisoner after the coming into force of this Act, shall be carried into effect within the walls of the prison in which the offender is confined at the time of the execution.

Although the original plan was for a public hanging on the reserves, the venue was shifted to the stockade of the old fort because of fears that people would abandon the reserves if the hanging took place there. Greenland quotes (at 419) the account of one eyewitness, Charles Whitehead of the North-West Mounted Police, "A Day in Battleford, 'Reveille' in December and Horse's Wateringhole Mile Away — Public Execution of Eight Indians while Chanting a Death Song," (1919) Fifth Annual *Scarlet and Gold*:

> ... The scaffold consisted of a platform about twenty feet high with four heavy posts, one at each corner, and two higher posts in the centre with a cross-beam. This had the effect of giving an uninterrupted view from all sides of everything that went on, both on and under the scaffold. Hundreds of Indians from the many reserves surrounding Battleford were gathered to witness the execution. ...

For further historical background to these cases and the struggle for control of the North-West, see D'Arcy Jenish, *Indian Fall: The Last Great Days of the Plains Cree and the Blackfoot Confederacy* (Toronto: Viking, 1999).

By 1869, public executions were already ended in England. For a thoughtful analysis that traces the use of capital statutes, public executions, and the prerogative of mercy (for example, pardons and transportation to the colonies) in England, see: Douglas Hay, "Property, Authority and The Criminal Law" in Douglas Hay *et al.*, *Albion's Fatal Tree: Crime and Society in Eighteenth-Century England* (New York: Pantheon, 1975) 17.

Several bills have been introduced in the House of Commons and the Senate to vacate the conviction of Louis Riel and celebrate his contribution to the advancement and development of Confederation and to the rights and interests of Metis people specifically and Western Canadians generally. See, for example: Bill S-35, *An Act to honour Louis Riel and the Metis People*, 1st Sess., 37th Parl., 2001 (2nd reading 12 December 2001).

In another example of the characterization of armed resistance to colonization (or acts of war) as "murder," five Tsilhqot'n chiefs were hanged in 1864 in British Columbia for the killing of 13 members of a road-surveying crew working on unceded Tsilhqot'n territory. As Judge Sarich describes in *The Report on the Cariboo-Chilcotin Justice Inquiry* (Victoria: The Inquiry, 1993) at 26:

> In every community west of the Fraser River, there was still barely concealed anger and resentment about the trickery that led to the hanging of the Chilcotin Chiefs in 1864 at Quesnel. The village Chiefs spoke with passion about the desecration of their graves, the spread of smallpox that killed so many of their people, and the brutish conduct of Waddington's road builders.
>
> In accusatory tones the Chiefs also spoke about how their land was taken by government agencies, particularly those lands now used by the Canadian army as weapons proving ground. They railed as well against the many fenced ranches carved from what they considered their traditional lands, and the forced move of a whole village to accommodate a ranching enterprise.[†]

As the Royal Commission on Aboriginal Peoples report *Bridging the Cultural Divide* documents at length, at 7–11, there were many breaches of fundamental justice and fairness in the legal proceedings that led to the hanging. For example, Judge Sarich describes a continuing concern that the Chiefs were induced to "surrender" and give inculpatory statements on a promise of immunity by Magistrate Cox. Also, their court-appointed lawyer was described as a principal in a road-construction company that was also attempting to build a road through Tsilhqot'n territory. Responding to the report by Judge Sarich, B.C. Attorney-General Colin Gabelman said he would support the Tsilhqot'n demands for a pardon for the five chiefs: Deborah Wilson, "B.C. minister backs bid to pardon chiefs: Five hanged for murder 129 years ago" *The [Toronto] Globe and Mail* (30 October 1993) A2. For a discussion of those events and the context, see also: Edward Sleigh Hewlett, "The Chilcotin Uprising of 1864" (1973) 19 B.C. Studies 50. He describes an earlier smallpox epidemic in 1862–1863 in which two-thirds of the Tsilhquot'ns were wiped out, and the subse-

---

[†] Copyright © 2004 Province of British Columbia. All rights reserved. Reproduced with permission of the Province of British Columbia.

quent threats to bring a plague of sickness upon them.

While the application of criminal law in the "treason" and "murder" trials of those who resisted is perhaps the most visible and instrumental use of criminal law in colonization, there were a range of measures that effectively extended the reach of Anglo-Canadian law and undermined Aboriginal authority and institutions. To understand the role of criminal law vis à vis Aboriginal peoples requires a historically specific tracing of the processes of law-making and the imposition and enforcement of law. This interrogation also raises important questions about legitimacy and criminal law and the source of state and judicial authority with respect to Aboriginal peoples. Yet these jurisdictional questions have been relatively unexamined and unchallenged: Hamar Foster, "Forgotten Arguments: Aboriginal Title and Sovereignty in *Canada Jurisdiction Act* Cases" (1992) 21 Man. L.J. 343.

Apart from the role of criminal law in colonization, the prosecution of Aboriginal persons for murder and other offences challenged several of the premises of criminal law, including the idea that there was a community with shared assumptions and values; the requirement of *mens rea*; and the premise that because everyone is "presumed" to know the prohibitions of the criminal law, "ignorance of the law" is no defence. Consider, for example, the case of Jack Fiddler and Joseph Fiddler, who were charged with murder in 1907.

What does the excerpt below demonstrate about the court process? Who were the parties to the proceedings (the judge, the lawyers, the jury, the witnesses)? What evidence is there of the views of the different communities, the non-Aboriginal community and the Sucker clan? How were the actions of the accused and their belief system characterized?

Killing the Shamen[†]

In the fall of 1907, one of the most unusual cases in the history of Canadian jurisprudence commenced in Norway House, Manitoba. Charged with murder was old Jack Fiddler, a shaman and leader of the Sucker clan from the upper Severn River in what is now northwestern Ontario. Joseph Fiddler, Jack's younger brother, was also charged. Their alleged crime was the killing of a possessed woman who had turned into the dreaded windigo. The Canadian press emblazoned their headlines with reports of this so-called murder: "Chief and Medicine Men Choked Out The Evil Spirit"; "Barbarian Custom Among Indians"; "Strangler Chief"; "Devilish Indian Cruelty." Headlines like these ensured political exposure for all the participants in the trial, especially for the Commissioner of the Royal North West Mounted Police, Aylesworth Bowen Perry. The Commissioner viewed the R.N.W.M.P. as being mainly responsible for Canadian Indians. In the face of a wide range of duties assigned to the Mounties, Perry asserted, "It does seem that at times the most important reason for the existence of the Force is overlooked. If the Northwest Territories had no Indian population it would need no Mounted Police Force." The trial of these two shamen would appear to have been a justification of the Mounties' presence in an era when murder trials were a rarity. In 1907 there were only eight convictions for murder among Canada's population of five and one-half million people. Malicious injury to horses (136 convictions) was a far more common crime. It was very unusual, too, for native persons to be involved in any criminal activity. Among the 1,423 people incarcerated in Canadian penitentiaries, only 57 were classified as Indians and half-breeds. In 1907, old Jack Fiddler and his brother Joseph were the only Indians in Canada charged with murder. The trial, which lasted one day, brought the desired results against "this savage tribe." Then the headlines vanished and the Sucker clan of about one hundred and twenty-five natives were forgotten again in their unceded forests in the upper Severn.

What was to remain unnoticed in the public eye would be the duplicity of Aylesworth Bowen Perry and his cruel handling of this case. What would remain unnoticed was the effect this action would

---

[†] Reproduced with permission of Penumbra Press from *Killing the Shamen*, Thomas Fiddler & James R. Stevens, at Preface, 87–89, 91–95, 97–101, 103–11, 113, 115–18. Moonbeam, Ont.: Penumbra, 1985.

have upon the Sucker clan who were involved in a treaty just three years later. What remained unsaid were the qualities of the Sucker leader, Jack Fiddler. The Canadian public had been left with the distinct impression that the shaman had been a banal and devilish person. What also remained away from public scrutiny were several appeals for freedom for Joseph Fiddler who was left languishing in Stony Mountain Penitentiary.

In the summer of 1971, I went to the village of Sandy Lake in the upper Severn River country to meet Chief Thomas Fiddler, the grandson of the shaman Jack Fiddler. From the meetings that followed we began an investigation into deaths that the Commissioner of the Royal North West Mounted Police claimed were murder.

[On 15 June 1907, Mounties arrested Jack and Joseph Fiddler for murder and ordered them to accompany them to Norway House. Jack agreed to accompany them for his people's sake, to avoid military retaliation and to preserve good relations. A preliminary hearing was held at Norway House, and Jack and Joseph were kept in custody despite pleas for their return before winter. On 30 September 1907, Jack Fiddler walked away from his R.N.W.M.P. escort and strangled himself with his own assumption sash. The two men had been in custody for over three months.]

. . . .

What does the Sucker Band, to which you belong, do to anyone who is sick and cannot be cured?

At Norway House, the trees transform into patched yellow, rusted brown and rich golds. These, among green pines, turn in another changing of the season. The north wind speaks, winter coming above Lake Winnipeg.

On October 7, 1907, in the elapsing time of Joseph Fiddler, the western system of justice begins. Joseph, hunter among the Sucker family and uncle of Thomas Fiddler, stands in trial at nine o'clock in the morning. Everyone concerned is inside the council chamber at the HBC post. The judge is Commissioner Aylesworth Bowen Perry of the Royal North West Mounted Police who assumes his position under legislation called the stipendiary magistrate's court. The white men allow Perry to sit as a magistrate in a court where his men will give evidence. The crown prosecutor is D.W. McKerchar, a well known Winnipeg lawyer and prominent Liberal. Observing on behalf of the Indian Department is C. Crompton Calverley. Constable Daisy O'Neill is clerk for the court. James Kirkness, the outpost trader among the Sucker people, is interpreter. He will not be called to give any evidence during the trial: he who knows the prisoner better than any English speaker does not testify in Joseph's behalf. Superintendent W.H. Routledge, the acting sheriff of the Northwest Territories, is present. The court, as described by a Manitoba Free Press reporter at the trial has the "pomp and circumstance of a military tribunal combined with the powers of a civil court."

A jury of six men from the neighbourhood of Norway House will decide Joseph Fiddler's fate. Charles A. Wilkins is the foreman of those who try to determine justice.

The trial of Joseph Fiddler starts with the testimony of Constable William J. Cashman, who is asked if any white people live among the Sucker band to instruct them in the law. No one, is his answer. Cashman then points out the closest white people live over at Island Lake, is a distance of one hundred and twenty miles, by the winter trail, and two hundred miles by the rivers in summer. The only white people in the district are at Island Lake; William Campbell, the trader, and Mr. McKersie, a Methodist school teacher.

The next witness is Minowapawin — called Norman Rae by the traders. He is married to Joseph Fiddler's daughter. His father-in-law, Norman Rae says, is called Pesequan, but his nick-name is Chawanee or Sandy. Rae tells the court that he lives at Goose Lake, a branch of Sandy Lake, and that he belongs to the Crane clan. The Indian name of the woman who was killed was Wahsakapeequay, and she is the daughter-in-law of Joseph Fiddler. She had mated his son, Thomas.

Norman Rae was present one evening, in the time when berries were ripe, at the Sucker encampment near James Kirkness' HBC outpost on Narrows Lake when Joseph and his son, Thomas, arrived with Wahsakapeequay. Joseph and Thomas lifted the woman out of the canoe and carried her on two poles up to the longhouse lodging. "She was very sick then; she would not be quiet" and some of the women held her down on the ground to keep her under control. That night, Norman went off in the forests hunting and when he returned in the evening moon, Wahsakapeequay had been moved away from the longhouse and placed behind a clump of willows.

McKerchar, the Crown prosecutor, asks about the second night Wahsakapeequay was at the encampment.

2: Colonization and the Imposition of Criminal Law

McKerchar: Did you see her, where she had been taken to?

Norman Rae: I went over during the night and saw where she was taken to.

McKerchar: Was she still delirious?

Norman Rae: Yes.

McKerchar: Did she have to be held down when you saw her there?

Norman Rae: When I went there, nobody held her down, and the prisoner, Joseph, had a string — with the other man, the ogema, Jack Fiddler. The string was in their hands and the woman was lying there.

McKerchar: Was anyone holding her down?

Norman Rae: No.

McKerchar: She was just lying on the ground?

Norman Rae: She was lying on the ground but they had spread the cotton on the ground and laid the woman on it.

McKerchar: She was in that position when you first saw her at that time?

Norman Rae: Yes.

McKerchar: What happened then?

Norman Rae: Of the cotton she was lying on, they pulled up the end of it, and put it around her neck, and they got the string in one knot or noose, and strangled her.

McKerchar: Who was it that took the cord and strangled her?

Norman Rae: The ogema and prisoner, Joseph.

McKerchar: What became of it after that?

Norman Rae: When we got there, Joseph told me that I had to take the body over to the Company's place and bury it there.

McKerchar: What did you do?

Norman Rae: I dug the grave and after I had done the digging, I put birchbark in the bottom. Then I got sticks and put them across the body and more birchbark on top of the body. I put earth on it.

McKerchar: Was this a law of the band that was being carried out?

Norman Rae: This is the law from what I heard.

McKerchar: From whom did you hear it?

Norman Rae: I don't know — everybody said it.

McKerchar: Is it a matter of general conversation among the tribes?

Norman Rae: Yes.

McKerchar: Do you know anything about the white man's law?

Norman Rae: No.

McKerchar: Have you ever been taught to distinguish between what is right and wrong?

Norman Rae: I have never been taught.

McKerchar: Have you ever seen a white man before this time of coming out of Norway House?

Norman Rae: I have seen a white man come down sometimes to Island Lake.

McKerchar: Did any white man ever speak to you about right and wrong or did they have it translated to you?

Norman Rae: No. I never spoke to them at all.

McKerchar: Did you ever speak to them about anything else?

Norman Rae: No.

The questioning of Norman Rae goes on the rest of the morning and, soon after lunch, it becomes clear that the windigo died by strangulation, carried out by Jack Fiddler and Joseph while John Rae (Edward Rae's father) and Norman Rae held her arms.

Shortly after lunch, Angus Rae, Manawapait, a young hunter in the Sucker family who lives at the Trout Lakes, takes the stand to give evidence in the court. McKerchar, speaking from behind a droopy mustache proceeds to question Angus through Kirkness, the interpreter. McKerchar proceeds, trying to ascertain when, in time, Wasakapeequay was killed.

McKerchar: When did you see her last?

Angus Rae: Last summer.

McKerchar: This summer just gone by or the earlier summer?

Angus Rae: The summer before this.

McKerchar: At what time during that summer was it that you saw her last?

Angus Rae: About the middle of the summer.

McKerchar: Do you know the division of time into months and years?

Angus Rae: No.

McKerchar: Was it during the warmest part of the summer or was it when it was getting cool?

Angus Rae: It was not the hottest part of summer; it was a little cool.

McKerchar: Was it after the hottest weather had gone by or before it came?

Angus Rae: After the hottest of the summer had gone.

McKerchar: To what tribe did she belong?

Angus Rae: Sucker Tribe.

Then McKerchar pauses and decides to ask Angus about the second night Wasakapeequay was delirious, the night the windigo dies in the camp of ogema, Jack Fiddler.

McKerchar: When you went out there, where was the woman?

Angus Rae: When we went over there, she was lying by the campfire. Joseph Fiddler the prisoner, was there.

McKerchar: Anyone else?

Angus Rae: Norman and John Rae.

McKerchar: [Were] any of them talking when you got there?

Angus Rae: They were talking. Joseph and Jack Fiddler had a string in their hands.

McKerchar: What did they say?

Angus Rae: They were saying that they were going to strangle her and put her out of her misery.

McKerchar: Who said that?

Angus Rae: Jack Fiddler said it.

McKerchar: Who was Jack Fiddler talking to when he said this?

Angus Rae: He was talking to his brother, the prisoner, and to John Rae.

McKerchar: Did the prisoner say anything?

Angus Rae: Joseph says, "It's all right."

McKerchar: Did Jack Fiddler, the ogema, say anything else beyond that they were going to strangle her to put her out of her misery?

Angus Rae: No, he did not say anything else.

McKerchar: Nothing else while you were there?

Angus Rae: No, I did not hear him.

McKerchar: Did Joseph, the prisoner, say anything except that it was alright to put her out of her misery?

Angus Rae: He said: "It's all right." That is all he said.

There is a long quiet space in the court room. McKerchar is thinking about how he will proceed with his questioning. The jurymen along the far wall fidget nervously and whisper to each other. Kirkness takes a drink of water. Then McKerchar begins again, trying to discover the relationship of young Angus Rae to the ogema, Jack Fiddler.

McKerchar: Did you object to their putting her to death?

Angus Rae: No.

McKerchar: Did you say anything?

Angus Rae: I did not say anything. They were all older than I was and I did not say anything.

McKerchar: Would you be punished if you objected to anything that the ogema suggested?

Angus Rae: I do not know. They might.

McKerchar: Is a member of the band bound to obey the ogema, bound to do what the ogema says?

Angus Rae: Yes.

McKerchar: Is a member of the band bound to do what the ogema says?

Angus Rae: Yes. If the ogema tells me to do a thing I must do it.

McKerchar: What would happen to you if you did not do what the ogema told you?

Angus Rae: Something would happen to me.

McKerchar: Of what nature, of what kind?

Angus Rae: I do not know what would happen. Something would happen anyway.

Commissioner Perry: Good or bad?

Angus Rae: Bad.

McKerchar: From what source?

Angus Rae: I do not know what would happen. Something would be wrong.

McKerchar: Would it be bad medicine?

Angus Rae: I will be punished in some way but I do not know how.

McKerchar: By whom?

Angus Rae: I do not know by whom but I will be punished, however, some way.

McKerchar: Did either John Rae or Norman Rae make any objection to the putting of this woman to death?

Angus Rae: No, nobody made objection.

McKerchar: Was the woman lying quiet on the ground by the campfire?

Angus Rae: She was not quiet. She was lying on her back and rolling her head about and moving her hands.

McKerchar: Did she say anything?

Angus Rae: No, nothing; but she moaned sometimes.

McKerchar: Did she hear the ogema say that she would have to be put to death?

Angus Rae: I heard the ogema say it.

McKerchar: Did she hear it?

Angus Rae: She must have heard it but I do not think that she understood.

McKerchar: Did she say anything when the ogema stated that she would have to be put to death?

Angus Rae: She did not. She was not able to.

McKerchar: Did she make any sign or motion to indicate that she heard it?

Angus Rae: She was rolling about when the ogema was talking like that.

McKerchar: What was done with her then — after the ogema made this statement?

The court becomes silent again as Angus Rae thinks back to the night scene of over two winters ago when Wasakapeequay was destroyed to protect the people. Then, Angus asks for a piece of cord. When it is handed to him, Angus ties it into a noose, then pulls the cord quickly, tightening the cord to a knot. Then Angus starts to talk to Kirkness again.

Angus Rae: Before they put this string on, they put cotton around her neck.

McKerchar: Which one did it?

Angus Rae: Jack Fiddler put the cotton around.

McKerchar: Who put the string around?

Angus Rae: Both of them, Joseph and Jack Fiddler.

McKerchar: Was the woman lying still while they were putting the cotton and cord around her neck?

Angus Rae: No, she was not lying quiet.

McKerchar: What was she doing?

Angus Rae: She was moving her head. She was swinging her hands.

McKerchar: Did she move her hands to prevent the cotton from being put on her neck?

Angus Rae: She did not try to do anything like that.

McKerchar: Did she attempt to do anything to prevent it, or did she say anything?

Angus Rae: No.

McKerchar: Did she make any noise?

Angus Rae: She made the same noise she did before.

McKerchar: Did the ogema give direction to the prisoner, Joseph, as to how the cotton and cord should be put on?

Angus Rae: The ogema gave directions. He said: "We will put the cotton around so that the cord will not cut the flesh."

McKerchar: Do you know why the woman was put to death?

Angus Rae: My wife told me that people were saying that the woman was going to turn into a cannibal. The people in the wigwam were saying this.

McKerchar: Was it before or after the death that your wife told you this?

Angus Rae: Two days after the death.

The mention of windigo causes McKerchar to stop questioning. He looks back over the transcripts and asks some things to be read back to him. When he begins, he does not ask about windigo. He decides to find out how much Angus Rae knows about white men.

McKerchar: Did you ever see any white men before you were brought in here by the officers of the Royal North West Mounted Police?

Angus Rae: I saw a missionary once, at Sandy Lake.

McKerchar: Who was the missionary?

Angus Rae: Mr. Lowes.

McKerchar: How long was the missionary there at that time?

Angus Rae: I do not know how long he was there, I saw him for half a day anyway.

McKerchar: Did the missionary talk to your band at that time?

Angus Rae: Yes.

McKerchar: Did you understand what he was saying?

Angus Rae: No, I did not understand.

McKerchar: Was it translated to the band?

Angus Rae: Yes.

McKerchar: What was the missionary discussing? What was he talking about?

Angus Rae: I do not know what the missionary was talking about. I was not well at the time.

McKerchar: Do you know anything about the white man's laws?

Angus Rae: No.

McKerchar: Did you ever hear anything said about the white man's laws?

Angus Rae: No. The only thing we ever heard about the white man was that he sent the Indians off to hunt furs.

The courtroom falls into silence after Angus Rae's assessment of white men. McKerchar shuffles through his papers, rethinking the evidence before he proceeds. All this time, Joseph Fiddler has sat on a straight backed chair beside a guard. His face is impassive and he shows no emotion in his face or eyes during the testimony of Angus Rae. Then, McKerchar looks up from his papers and begins to investigate the nature of windigo killings.

McKerchar: What does the Sucker Band, to which you belong, do to anyone who is sick and cannot be cured?

Angus Rae: One time I went over to the other camp visiting and I saw a man killed. One time, I saw a man killed named David. After they killed him they burned the body.

McKerchar: What tribe did this?

Angus Rae: The same tribe.

McKerchar: What members of the Sucker tribe committed the killing in that case?

Angus Rae: The prisoner, Joseph, was there and three other men: James Meekis, Joseph Meekis and Elias Rae, my brother.

McKerchar: Was the ogema there?

Angus Rae: He was not there.

McKerchar: Who was put to death at that time?

Angus Rae: David Meekis.

McKerchar: Was he a brother of these other two that you have named?

Angus Rae: He was their brother.

McKerchar: Did you see David alive before this killing was committed?

Angus Rae: Yes, I saw David alive. When I went to bed at night David Meekis was alive.

McKerchar: What more?

Angus Rae: While I was sleeping I heard somebody yelling and I went out and saw the body being put on the fire.

McKerchar: Did you see these parties commit the killing?

Angus Rae: No.

McKerchar: Was David dead before he was put into the fire?

Angus Rae: David was dead before he was put into the fire.

McKerchar: Why was David put to death by these people?

Angus Rae: I do not know why he was put to death. I was not there long enough.

McKerchar: Was he sick?

Angus Rae: Yes.

McKerchar: Was he sick at night when you went to bed?

Angus Rae: Yes, he was very sick.

McKerchar: How was he acting?

Angus Rae: He was sitting up and making a big noise while he was breathing.

McKerchar: Was he out of his mind?

Angus Rae: He, he was delirious.

McKerchar: Was he dangerous or was he likely to cause any harm to the people in the wigwam?

Angus Rae: No, I don't think so.

McKerchar: Was he moving or still?

Angus Rae: He was moving.

McKerchar: Was he speaking?

Angus Rae: Yes, he was speaking.

McKerchar: Could you understand what he was saying?

Angus Rae: He was talking but we could not understand him.

McKerchar: When was this?

Angus Rae: I could not tell, but it was four or five years ago.

McKerchar: Do you know of any other cases of sick people being put to death besides these two?

Angus Rae: I saw another man fixed the same way long ago.

McKerchar: How old were you when this took place?

Angus Rae: I was very small at that time.

McKerchar: In what tribe was it?

Angus Rae: In the Crane tribe.

McKerchar: Who was put to death at that time?

Angus Rae: I did not see anyone put to death, but the body was burned when I saw it. I knew of it because I was told it was killing.

McKerchar: What was the name of the murdered man?

Angus Rae: Askamekeseecowiniew. (Peter Flett).

McKerchar: Where was it that you say this body burned?

Angus Rae: Pretty near the other end of Caribou Lake and close to the Little Grand Rapids.

McKerchar: Had this man been sick before he had been put to death?

Angus Rae: This man was very sick when somebody brought him and landed him in one side of the wigwam where I was.

McKerchar: Who put him to death?

Angus Rae: I saw James Meekis, and his brother, Lucas, and Joseph Meekis and John Rae.

McKerchar: Were they the parties who put this man to death?

Angus Rae: Yes. They were the parties. I did not see who killed the man but I saw the body.

McKerchar: Did you ever hear the ogema give any reason for having people put to death who were sick?

Angus Rae: When they are sick and so long in misery they put them out of their misery.

McKerchar: Did you hear the ogema say that?

Angus Rae: Yes.

McKerchar: You heard him?

Angus Rae: Yes.

McKerchar: What ogema?

Angus Rae: Jack Fiddler.

McKerchar: Give the exact words.

Angus Rae: Jack Fiddler said that when anyone was sick like that and is so miserable they might as well put them to an end.

McKerchar: Did you ever hear them giving any other reason for putting them to an end?

Angus Rae: No, I never heard him give any other reason.

McKerchar: Did you ever hear the ogema say that anyone who died out of his mind turned into a cannibal?

Angus Rae: Yes, that is what the ogema says.

McKerchar: Did you hear anyone else say that?

Angus Rae: Yes, I have heard men talking the same way.

McKerchar: What men?

Angus Rae: All the men talk the same way, among them my brother, John Rae.

McKerchar: Did you ever hear the prisoner, Joseph, say that?

Angus Rae: Yes. I heard the prisoner say that more than once.

McKerchar: What would be the likely result if she turned into a cannibal?

Angus Rae: I don't know.

McKerchar: Would anything happen to the band if she became a cannibal?

Angus Rae: Yes.

McKerchar: What would likely happen?

Angus Rae: She would kill people.

McKerchar: Would anything else happen to the band?

Angus Rae: Nothing else but that!

McKerchar: To get back to the time of the murder in question, was the woman likely to cause any harm to the people in camp when you saw her first, by reason of her out of mind state?

Angus Rae: I cannot tell.

McKerchar: Was she strong or weak?

Angus Rae: She was pretty strong and two women were holding her down.

McKerchar: Was she strong or weak at the time you saw her at the campfire?

Angus Rae: She was pretty weak when she was at the campfire.

McKerchar: Were any others sick just about that time?

Angus Rae: Another man was sick at that time.

McKerchar: Out of his mind?

Angus Rae: Yes.

Commissioner Perry: What did they do to the out of mind man?

Angus Rae: This man was brought to the wigwam of the Sucker Tribe and the wife of this man was telling Jack Fiddler to strangle the man. This was the wife of the sick man. The next morning I went out with my nets and my brother came down and I came up and he told me to come up quick. They were going to strangle a man; this man. And when I came I went up and I passed the wigwam where the sick man was. I went up right past the wigwam. I had a private job in the bush and my brother came to me. I came back to the wigwam; to where the wigwam was; the small wigwam. When I was going along with my brother, I saw a piece of string coming out from the wigwam and my brother told me to pull the string and I got the string and pulled it. And only then I knew that I had strangled a man.

It was Jack Fiddler who pulled on the line, the other side; the other end. After we had done I went back to my wigwam. I got frightened as I only knew then that I had done wrong. I had strangled a man. When I came back to the wigwam I saw the body wrapped up in a blanket. All the covering of the wigwam was pulled off and the body was lying exposed. I and my brother helped bury the man. We buried him four feet down. I did not make a coffin but I put in bark on top of the body. I laid cross pieces and put bark on that again and then I threw in the body. That is all.

McKerchar: After you pulled the string did you go in the wigwam?

Angus Rae: No.

McKerchar: Did you know who was pulling on the other end of the rope?

Angus Rae: Ogema, Jack Fiddler.

McKerchar: How did you know that?

Angus Rae: Joseph told me that it was the ogema at the other end. Joseph was in the wigwam.

McKerchar: How did you know the prisoner was in the wigwam?

Angus Rae: Joseph told me.

McKerchar: Which of your brothers told you to pull the string?

Angus Rae: John Rae.

McKerchar: Did he tell you what you were to pull the string for?

Angus Rae: No, he did not tell me right then, but my brother told me down on the bank to come up and help strangle a man.

McKerchar: How long after the woman was strangled did this take place? How many days? Ten days?

Angus Rae: More than that.

McKerchar: Twenty days?

Angus Rae: About that.

McKerchar: The summer was getting toward the end?

Angus Rae: Yes.

McKerchar: Why, when you were asked before did you not tell us about this other man being killed this way?

Angus Rae: I was leaving this till last because they were Crane tribes.

McKerchar: Whom?

Angus Rae: That man.

McKerchar: What was the name of that man?

Angus Rae: It was Menewascum.

McKerchar: Had he any English or nickname?

Angus Rae: Yes, nickname.

McKerchar: What was his nickname?

Angus Rae: It was Piiwaapik.

Angus Rae's testimony is a history of killing in at least fifteen years among the Sucker people. This is the end of Angus' testimony to a jury who sit in decision on whether Joseph Fiddler will drop from a scaffold at the end of a rope.

It is late in the afternoon but there is time for another witness, a man they say, who might offer an explanation to the supposed murder. He is Reverend Edward Paupanakiss, a Norway House Cree, who was in his youth, a hard drinking servant of the HBC.

McKerchar: What is your profession, Mr. Paupanakiss?

Paupanakiss: Indian missionary of the Methodist denomination.

McKerchar: You are a full-blooded Indian yourself?

Paupanakiss: Yes.

McKerchar: For how long have you been a missionary?

Paupanakiss: For 18 years since I was ordained. Before that I was a local preacher for 8 years.

McKerchar: Have you ever been in the Sandy Lake district?

Paupanakiss: Never, but I have been as far as Island Lake.

McKerchar: Did you ever meet the Sucker Tribe to whom the prisoner belongs?

Paupanakiss: Whenever I could, I met them at the post at Island Lake. I go there twice a year for seven years.

McKerchar: Have you ever met the prisoner there?

Paupanakiss: I never know him to meet him.

McKerchar: Did you ever meet the ogema, Jack Fiddler?

Paupanakiss: Yes, I met him.

McKerchar: Did you often meet him?

Paupanakiss: Three times I met him there.

McKerchar: Did you ever speak to the tribe when you were there?

Paupanakiss: Every chance I had. During the time they were there, they were calling for their summer outfit, we had service in the morning and evening. The longest they will stay there is 4 days and the shortest they will stay there is 2 days.

McKerchar: Did you meet them on each visit during these 7 years?

Paupanakiss: I could never meet them — only just when I went to Island Lake. I saw this tribe every summer for seven years, fourteen times altogether, and I used to hold service with them each time.

McKerchar: Did you speak to them in your native language?

Paupanakiss: A little. I used to ask them if they understood mine and they told me that they easily understood me. On each occasion I preached to them on religion. I told them it was not right to steal; that it was against the law; anything which the Book forbade, which the Bible forbade, was not right.

McKerchar: Did any of them ever express their beliefs?

Paupanakiss: The old ogema, Jack, with whom I had a long talk at Island Lake, stated that they believed their dreams.

McKerchar: What other beliefs did he express to you?

Paupanakiss: That that was their religion; their dreams are their religion.

McKerchar: Did he speak to you about delirious people turning into cannibals if they abide in their out of mind state?

Paupanakiss: I don't believe that he ever told me anything about it. I remember it from a very long time ago.

McKerchar: Have you any knowledge of their belief along that line gathered from members of the band?

Paupanakiss: No.

McKerchar: Where did you acquire that knowledge, from that band or from your general knowledge?

Paupanakiss: From when I was a boy I heard our own people; from our own people in our band; not from members of the Sucker Tribe.

McKerchar: What else took place at that conversation with Jack Fiddler excepting the long conversation on dreams?

Paupanakiss: That is all he said. That everything they dreamed was right for them; and that by virtue of their dreams and singing and conjuring in the tent that they would see meat, moose and deer. Jack Fiddler told me this. That is all that he told me.

Commissioner Perry: Did you tell them that it was wrong to take human life?

Paupanakiss: I do not remember that.

Commissioner Perry: Did you ever know of their tragedies which we have heard of this afternoon?

Paupanakiss: No.

Juryman Christian: Have you ever heard of them using poisonous medicines?

Paupanakiss: None that I have ever heard of.

Juryman Christian: I have heard it all over.

Paupanakiss: But when I go there, they never mention it.

McKerchar: When were you last at Island Lake?

Paupanakiss: In 1896.

Commissioner Perry: You have not been to Island Lake in eleven years?

Paupanakiss: No.

Paupanakiss could probably have added much more to the trial evidence had he been asked the proper questions, but his long absence from Island Lake precludes any further questioning. So, at six o'clock, the court adjourns for an hour for supper. At seven, it will be Joseph Fiddler's turn to take the stand if he so desires. When the court resumes, Joseph is asked if he will give evidence. He declines and asks that Crompton Calverley speak on his behalf. Calverley gives a short speech defending him on the grounds his actions were in accord with tribal custom.

Then McKerchar addresses the jury, asking for a conviction. He is followed by Commissioner Perry who speaks:

'As Mr. McKerchar has explained, murder is the intentional killing or taking of a human life. You have to consider the facts brought out. You have to find out whether the accused intended to kill the woman. . . . If you believe the facts of this evidence, Mrs. Thomas Fiddler came to her death through the hands of the accused. The law says that is murder. It evolves upon the accused to explain it [...] either by justification or in some way to reduce the crime to justifiable homicide or manslaughter. . . . To my mind the evidence is not clear on the customs of the Sucker Tribe.

The missionary, the Reverend Edward Paupanakiss, was unable to give us any evidence other than what he had been told by chief Jack, but he said nothing about the treatment of the insane and the hopelessly sick. He discussed dreams and conjuring, but not all the beliefs of the Sucker Indian, not the actual belief of Joseph, the prisoner, and Jack. . . .

The only thing we have is the evidence of Angus Rae, in which he says that the accused told him that if the woman was not killed she would become cannibal and therefore a menace to the band.

If you believe that you will have to accept it all. You will then believe this accused man was in the belief that if this delirious woman was not put out of her misery she would become a menace to the tribe by becoming a cannibal.

Does pagan belief justify murder? You have to answer that. You cannot find anything but that Joseph Fiddler killed this woman.

Was he justified in killing her because she might have turned into a cannibal? This might possibly be urged as a defence. The tribe was ignorant of the law of the land.

We questioned both witnesses as to that and the impression left on my mind is that they do know what the law forbids. . . .

As to the question of pagan belief, if you find that the accused is justified in killing because of his pagan belief where will it land us if we accept such a belief? What the law forbids no pagan belief can justify. The law says: "Thou shalt not kill." He cannot justify his act by pleading it.

However, you have a perfect right in spite of what I say, if you think that pagan belief would justify him, to say so, but consider first what the result would be. For as to his ignorance of the law that is a matter for executive clemency.

Before committing his case to you, I wish to say that you can give anyone of these three verdicts: Guilty, Not Guilty, or Guilty of Manslaughter.

I will now ask you to retire and to consider the verdict which you shall give.'

The six-man jury retires and after some study they return to the court and ask for two definitions: guilt of manslaughter, and death from the result of self-defense. The jury appears confused. Perry defines self-defense as a killing that results from immediate danger and manslaughter as intent and loss of self-control. Juryman Wright then asks Perry if they are restricted to only three verdicts. Perry states this is the case but they can add a recommendation to any of these three verdicts. Wright then proceeds with another question:

Juryman Wright: Why did they object to taking the woman into the wigwam where the rest of the family was?

The Commissioner: There is no evidence to that effect.

Juryman Wright: Was it ascertained the distance the woman was brought?

The Commissioner: It was not ascertained.

Foreman Wilkins: Could we ask that question now of the witness?

The Commissioner: No.

Foreman Wilkins: Then the jury cannot come to any decision!

The Commissioner: Kindly retire again, gentlemen, and consider your verdict.

When the jury returns, the foreman, Wilkins, [gives] the verdict: guilty of murder but with a recommendation for mercy, "on account of the prisoner's ignorance and superstition."

Joseph, who sits attentively through the trial, is asked if he has anything to say to the court who has passed the law upon him. Joseph stands up to speak to the court through James Kirkness, the translator.

'I did not know better. I am angry. I was in hopes I would be let off without being punished. I do not want my life to be taken away until my death comes. I wish that God had blest me. I have no wish to say any more.'

Commissioner Perry then passes the sentence of the westerners on Joseph, hunter of the Sucker people.

'. . . The law does not permit me to exhibit any mercy toward you. It is that he who commits murder shall be hanged.... I can hold out to you no hope that a pardon will be extended to you. You have been found guilty ... by a jury of six men who have given you a fair and impartial hearing.

The evidence which has been given before the court disclosed that this is not the only case in which human beings have been done to death by yourself and other members of the Sucker Band.

The law says that this must be. The object of punishing you is not to prevent a death so much as it is to be a warning to the other members of your tribe that human life is sacred and cannot be taken.

The sentence of the Court is upon you, the said Joseph Fiddler, an Indian, and known among the Indians as Pesequan, that you be taken to the place from whence you came, namely, the Royal North West Mounted Police Guard Room at Norway House in the Northwest Territories and that you be taken from between the hour of six o'clock in the forenoon and twelve of the clock of that day, to the place of execution, there, and that you be hanged by the neck until you are dead: and may God Almighty have mercy on your soul.'

Two weeks later, Commissioner Perry, having obtained the desired conviction, completely reverses his opinion on what have been the customs of the Sucker people. He is writing to the Minister of Justice in Ottawa on October 30, concurring with the jury's recommendation for mercy.

> The accused knew it was wrong to take life under ordinary circumstances. He believed, however, that insane persons were dangerous to the well being of his tribe and that unless they were strangled they would turn into cannibals.... It is clear that it has been the custom of the tribe from time immemorial to put to death members of their band, and other bands, who were thought by them to be insane or incurable.

In the following weeks, an Order in Council, based on Perry's recommendation, commutes Joseph Fiddler's sentence to life imprisonment and the Department of Justice drops any proceedings against Angus Rae, John Rae and the Meekis brothers.

In January, 1908, Joseph, now ill, is transferred to Stony Mountain where he is placed in the infirmary to somehow recover his health. Norman Rae returned to Island Lake and died shortly thereafter. James Kirkness left the Sandy Lake country, never to return. The HBC posts him to Poplar River on Lake Winnipeg. William, "Big Bill" Campbell is transferred to York Factory by the HBC at the conclusion of the trial.

. . . .

Indians Survived Without the Help of Any White Man

After clan leader Jack Fiddler and his brother, Joseph, were taken from their ancestral grounds by the R.N.W.M.P. in June, 1907, Robert Fiddler and James Meekis remain to lead the people through still trying times. The arrests of Jack and Joseph were not widely discussed in the years that followed. Forest clansmen preferred to forget this humiliation. After all, nothing could be done against the forces of westernization that were sweeping North America, and the less than bountiful forests made it difficult for clansmen to concentrate on anything but survival. The best that could be hoped for was that Joseph Fiddler would be returned to the clan and his family of two women, two daughters and two sons.

At Island Lake, February, 1908, the news was disturbing for the clans. Two red coat soldiers, R.N.W.M.P., have returned again, bringing back young Angus Rae. They will dog sled east on Island Lake, up the Sagawitchewan River and over the long portage down into the Bay River. Angus Rae is to be returned and the soldiers, Inspector E.A. Pelletier and Constable Cashman, want to talk to clan leader Robert Fiddler. He will endure insult from them. In the minds of these western men, Robert is an ignorant man.

The soldiers come with HBC servant, Donald Flett, for their interpreter. Angus, away from his people for eight months, guides the party to the HBC outpost on Narrows Lake.

At the outpost, set among the snowed in birches above the shore of Narrows Lake, Paul Fiddler, manages the trade goods. He is the first of the Sucker clansmen to learn commerce. At the post, his brother, Robert Fiddler, meets with Inspector Pelletier. Robert, "strikingly handsome" and powerful looking, is a man of about forty-four winters. For many years, Robert, along with his brother Adam, have been, in effect, leaders. But it is Robert Fiddler, the oldest brother that is hereditary clan leader. He will talk to Pelletier. Before this, Robert has spoken only to five white men.

Pelletier now speaks about this meeting. In his mind he sees the Suckers "as the worst band in the district. They are murderers, liars and very crooked."

He speaks his attitude in an insulting manner to one of the forest's most prestigious hunters: Robert Fiddler, son of Jack Fiddler, grandson of Porcupine Standing Sideways, a descendant of Yellow Sky, Long Fellow, Tinpot and Little Crane. He is clan leader in the forests that are unceded to the whites and their soldiers.

> I spoke to them about two hours explaining the law.... I told the chief that if he did not change his ways I would put another chief in his place ... that we were friends of the good Indians and that bad Indians need fear us as we were numerous....
>
> They were not to think that because they were living in an isolated place we would not hear of their doings....
>
> I said that I hoped that the next time I shook hands with him I would be able to say, "I shake hands with a good chief." Pelletier also warns the Suckers that Angus is now a friend of theirs and that if they molest him in any way they will feel very sorry for it.

After the soldiers leave, Thomas Fiddler tells how happy Angus Rae is to be returned to his people. "Angus went around shaking hands with everybody. It was winter, so Angus thought it was time to say 'Merry Christmas' to everybody. He said 'ahniken-Kismas' to all." Angus tried hard to speak English now. He told the people the way to say *today* is, "o'tay." Of course, Angus can't speak English but he heard a lot of people speaking English. When he heard the word, yesterday, he pronounces it "Keeask o-tay." But in Indian, o'tay means, heart, and keeask o-tay means, seagull's heart.

Thomas also tells about the effects of the imprisonment on Angus Rae. "He built a cellar under his lodging so that he can escape should the police ever come to take him away again. There will be a cellar in his lodgings for many winters to come. He will always fear the white man."

Outside of the isolated forests of the Sucker clan there is much discussion about the imprisoned Joseph Fiddler. Many of the northern fur traders are shocked by the outcome of the trial. Although no one says so, all the traders know the trial was farcical. Six months after Joseph is locked in Stony Mountain, many of the notable men from Norway House sign a letter that petitions for his complete pardon. These men are: William "Big Bill" Campbell — who reported the windigo killings; James Begg; James Garson and Henry T. Wright, who were three jurors in the trial; Crompton Calverly, Indian Agent at the trial; J.A. Louseley; Edward Paupanakiss; Thomas Ferrier and Alex Cunningham, all Methodist missionaries; Donald A. McIvor, a private trader with 31 years experience among the Indians; and Donald C. McTavish, A.A. Sinclair, E.J. Bivington, J.K. MacDonald, Donald Flett, John Taylor, all of the HBC.

In part, their petition for Joseph Fiddler reads:

> We have learned that the old man had been in the hospital nearly all the time since he reached Stony Mountain. He suffered from a very severe attack of pneumonia during the process of which no hope was entertained of his recovery. While he has partially recovered he is still in such a condition of health that he has almost no chance of living through another winter.
>
> We are not sure that you have had the opportunity of knowing that the entire band is in perfect sympathy with those, who because of possessing a little more nerve than the rest, are detailed to do the gruesome task. Their actions in this respect are the very opposite of what we call murder being undertaken sometimes at the earnest solicitations of one who has been delirious and regained consciousness for a time, when they would beg, even implore relatives to kill them, if they should relapse rather than leave them to run and risk of turning a wretched creature and a terror to men, never allowed to enter the Happy Hunting Ground. That condition is the hell of those Indians.
>
> Sir, we earnestly beg that you will do all in your power to secure his pardon.

From the Department of Justice in Ottawa, a copy of the petition was sent to Commissioner A. Bowen Perry in Regina for his recommendation. Perry's short and hard reply is: "While I agree largely with it, I am of the opinion that the prisoner should not be released too soon...."

Possibly Perry did not read, or care what one of the paragraphs said.

It was two years plus a day since Joseph Fiddler was arrested at Caribou Lake, when, in June, 1909, John Semmens of the Indian Department wrote to Colonel Irving, the Commanding Officer at Stony Mountain and offers to take Joseph Fiddler back to Island Lake in mid-July on the understanding that he will be released. To this request, A. Power, the Acting Deputy Minister of Justice in Ottawa, writes, "I beg to inform you that it is not the intention of the Department to release this man at present...." Then, on July 26th, 1909, Joseph Fiddler, pleading for his life, dictates a letter through an unknown translator to the Minister of Justice.

> To the Minister of Justice.
>
> Dear Sir — I desire to lay my case before you and ask that a pardon be granted me. I am fifty three years old and if I am confined here longer I will die, but I think if I can get back to where I belong I will live.
>
> I desire to ask you not to look upon me as a common murderer. I was the Chief of my tribe, we had much sickness, and the sick ones were getting bad spirits and their friends were afraid of them and sent for me to strangle them. This was *not* common killing, for we never strangle a well person, neither would we dare to shoot, or stab a sick person. It has always been the rule of our people to strangle sick ones who went mad.
>
> No one but the Chief of the tribe or one named by him could strangle anyone.
>
> If you let me go back to my place I will teach my family and people the white man's law. I am sick now and can't walk, but I think I will live if you let me go home.
>
> I will tell them how the white man lives. I wish you to consider that I am a poor Indian and don't know anything. I beg of you to remember your promise of last fall and send me back to my people before I die, and I will tell my people that the white man's Government always speaks true.

In the late summer winds a third letter of petition for Joseph Fiddler's pardon is sent to the Minister of Justice, by Archdeacon Robert Phair of Winnipeg. Phair points out that he has been a missionary among the Indians since 1865. He was, in fact, the Superintendent of Indian Missions in Ruperts Land for the Anglican Church of Canada; and asks:

... if action can be taken soon, he might get out to the end of Lake Winnipeg before he is too weak and the season too far advanced.

Hoping this message for the old man will be acceptable and result in his getting his liberty.

To Phair's request, comes an answer and freedom for Joseph Fiddler.

C.P. Telegram
September 4th, 1909

The Warden of the Manitoba Penitentiary
Stony Mountain, Manitoba

Governor General authorizes immediate release of Joseph Fiddler, alias Pesequan. Release accordingly. Letter confirming this message follows.

Thomas Mulvey
Under-Secretary of State Canada

To Under Secretary of State
September 5th, 1909

In reply I beg to state this convict died of consumption on September 1st at 8:15 a.m. after being in the penitentiary hospital for 18 months.

A. Irving Warden

Joseph Fiddler was gone to the spiritual world of the Sucker clansmen. Pardoned and released from prison by an Ottawa word paper. He had already been free for three days. The records concerning Joseph Fiddler's pardon contain no correspondence from Commissioner Perry authorizing approval. Presumably, he had not been consulted about the pardon. It is ironic that in 1909, the year that Joseph Fiddler died in Stony Mountain, Aylesworth Bowen Perry was made a Companion of the Order of St. Michael and St. George. For Perry, this British award for chivalry was a step toward knighthood.

As we sit and talk sadly about these days, Thomas tells about Joseph's family: of how they struggle to survive in the woods.

Thomas Fiddler: Joseph Fiddler, the man the Sucker people called Pesequan, had two wives. One of his wives was Charlotte Mamakeesik. I don't know the name of his other wife but they had five children. Charlotte had two sons, Thompson Quill, and Tommy Fiddler. The other woman had three children, two daughters, both called Mary, and another daughter named Jessie.

In this time, after the missionary came, the Sucker people were just taking English names. This was confusing and this is why Thompson Quill ended up with this name, not Fiddler. This is also why two of Joseph Fiddler's daughters were named Mary. They thought all white women were called Mary.

Now, when the white men took Jack and Joseph away in 1907 there was no treaty here, but there was a store. After Jimmy Kirkness left in 1907, two half-breeds looked after the store. When these guys left, Paul Fiddler looked after it but this store was very poor in equipment so often people went to Little Grand Rapids to trade. When the store on Narrows Lake closed, Paul Fiddler moved over to Island Lake. He never came back.

And when Joseph Fiddler never returned, Charlotte and the other woman had to raise their children alone.

It is true that Charlotte Mamakeesik was a very strong woman.

With only twine for nets and snares, and equipment, axes, hooks and ice chisels, they spent the winters roaming the lakes trying to survive. So these two women and Joseph's children caught fish from the open rivers at the outlet from Name Lake and at the inlet of the two other lakes. They built weirs in the rivers and caught fish there because the lakes were frozen solid. It was impossible to catch fish in lakes. They also caught fish along the river from Loud Beaver Lake.

In the summertime, they got twine from the store to make gill nets for fishing, and they camped on the shores of Caribou Lake. At the east [end] of Caribou Lake, they caught a lot of whitefish; it was their only way of surviving. At this place there is a small lake and a river running between it and another lake. It is called Owajosewayahink Lake. They fished at another lake right across Caribou Lake called Antamake Lake. This lake is filled with dark water so the whitefish in this lake are much darker in colour.

In the summer, Charlotte and her children would set up a wigwam. They would make a structure like a small wabinogamick. They used moss and spruce to cover the frame. At night, they built a fire inside that made smoke to drive out the mosquitoes. When the mosquitoes all left, they would close the door and put out the fire.

Now it happened that when they fished too long in one place, they wouldn't catch fish anymore. So they moved across a portage to another river where they caught whitefish.

Joseph's family just kept moving about these lakes and rivers. These women, Charlotte and Joseph's other wife and children were about the only ones who lived this way. It was the only way they could survive and raise their children.

■

In contrast to the rigid application of the law in *R. v. Fiddler*, in the recent case of *R. v. Jacko*, [1997] 1 C.N.L.R. 164 (Ont. Ct. Just. (Gen. Div.)), the accused was acquitted of manslaughter on the basis of contextual evidence. Evidence established that the victim was known and feared as a "Bearwalker" in the Ojibwe community. The defence argued that the accused acted in self-defence according to s. 34(2) of the *Criminal Code*. The trial judge considered evidence about native spirituality in assessing the reasonableness of the accused's apprehension and belief as to the danger that he was facing when the victim attacked him, and found the accused not guilty.

C. POISONING THE LAND

Now, consider a more contemporary issue confronting the Sucker people: the mercury poisoning of the Wabigoon River by the Reed pulp and paper mill at Dryden, and its effects on the Aboriginal peoples of White Dog and Grassy Narrows Indian reserves.

No Safe Place†

People have been poisoned by methyl mercury in Northwest Ontario. That's fact, just as it's fact that the economies of two Ojibway Indian communities have been destroyed in large measure by the consequences of mercury "spills" from a chemical and pulp mill at Dryden, Ontario, owned by the Reed Paper Company.

What's still at issue in Ontario is the degree of poisoning in any one individual. The 1,200 people at risk aren't consoled by suggestions they are just a little bit pregnant from the mating of the toxic heavy metal with delicate brain tissue. What's at issue, too, is the matter of how the industry and governments involved have responded to the hazard and to the needs of the people living in the target zone.

Mercury is only one element of the witches' brew of industrial pollution in our society. Asbestos, lead and uranium play havoc of a different sort but with similar tragic results. So do DDT, and PCBs, Dioxin and a galaxy of toxic, sometimes carcinogenic, chemicals. One recently published "partial list" of industrial substances-to-be-feared lists 300 separate elements and compounds. Northwest Ontario, too, is just one place on a map dotted with locations of mercury emissions. Forty American states and five Canadian provinces have banned fishing in some lakes and streams because of mercury contamination of fish beyond levels safe for human consumption.

But it's because there is, literally, no safe place any more, no place where people can comfortably believe themselves safe from the hazards of pollution, that we need to study the forces which create the problems — and which can delay, even prevent, solutions. And in Northwest Ontario almost all possible elements and interests are present: federal and provincial governments with their complex of departments, boards, agencies, divisions and branches; the factory of a huge, multinational conglomerate; an isolated society directly affected by the pollution; a social ambience in which the victims have become "an embarrassment" because other area residents fear panic and economic loss in a tourist-based economy; scrutiny and research (some say interference) by the international scientific community; dramatic and emotional (some say sensational and irresponsible) coverage by the world's mass media; a web of interlocking political, cultural, financial and social relationships impinging on every decision and policy.

We are said to differ from other species in our capacity to learn from experience. This is not just the conditioned reflex of the pet which, once burned, will never again touch the front burner. We are the sophisticated animal. We go on to learn why the burner was hot, to elaborate systems through which we can avoid future injury. But nothing in the experience of Northwest Ontario between 1969 and 1977

---

† From Warner Troyer, *No Safe Place* (Toronto: Clarke, Irwin & Co., 1977) at 3–6, 221–23.

suggests that we humans learn from observed experience, and act on the data our research yields.

The following are a few of the questions raised in this book. It's frightening that most of them are not different, fundamentally, from those to be asked in every major case of industrial pollution anywhere in the world:

Why were a whole series of federal and provincial studies and reports — medical and environmental — hidden from public view between 1970 and 1977?

Why are anglers still permitted to fish in the area and a handful of fishing camps and tourist lodges still allowed to operate there?

Why have 1,200 people whose livelihoods, culture, pride and bodies have been poisoned by industrially dumped mercury still not been adequately tested seven years after that poisoning was detected, still not been provided with proper alternate diet or alternate employment, still not been compensated or even told that compensation was a possibility?

Why in 1977 has the government of Ontario yet even to threaten to prosecute, fine or sue Reed Paper Company for dumping more than ten tons of mercury into the Wabigoon River between 1962 and 1970? This, though best scientific estimates are that the contaminated river systems will not be safe for upwards of fifty — possibly as many as 100 — years.

Why has no governmental agency sought compensation for costs incurred in responding to the problem? Costs to the tax-paying public are somewhere in at least the seven-figure range — none of it recovered?

Then there is the matter of mercury poisoning, Minamata Disease. Still a matter of passionate controversy seven years after the danger was first officially established, the case is, according to government, "not proved."

What is proved is that local Indians have alarmingly high mercury blood levels and that some area residents have neurological symptoms "consistent with" Minamata Disease.

What's acknowledged by every government agency and researcher is that the situation is sufficiently grave to warrant much more research aimed at getting definitive answers to the key questions: Has anyone got Minamata Disease? How badly? Has anyone died? Is anyone going to?

Data from suppressed government reports and files, the correlation of material already published, and the examination of scientific research ignored until now by government all lead to the irresistible conclusion that there are dozens, probably scores of people who now have the clinical signs and symptoms. A further probability is that a number of deaths in the communities have been mis-attributed to other causes when the real killer was mercury-contaminated fish.

There's abundant documentation of the pollution. Once again, however, much lies in unpublished and suppressed government reports and memos — some published for the first time in this book. What's been missing, since the problem surfaced in late 1969, has been any political or bureaucratic will to deal effectively with the dangers, either through strong action or preventive legislation.

From the formal discovery of the problem in 1969, through 1976, the bureaucratic posture was one of "no panic." By late 1976 both Ontario and federal employees and government-hired scientists were down-playing the mercury hazards, suggesting the Byzantine labyrinth of surveys and reports had answered most questions; not that they weren't in favour of more studies.

The extraordinary coincidence apparent to one studying these events was that every scientific researcher and physician outside the governments' services who looked at the problem reacted with alarm and demands for urgent action, while virtually every scientist, researcher and physician on the staffs of government departments and ministries, or contracted to do studies for them, was exuding comfort and complacence. Difficult to avoid recalling George Orwell's response to co-option: "A bought mind is a spoiled mind."

In 1973 a still-unpublished report by a federal task force said: "At present, the federal government's approach to the special problems of White Dog and Grassy Narrows [the Indian reserves affected] is fragmented and lacks cohesion.... The free flow of information and data on mercury in the environment with the Province of Ontario is impeded for reasons that are not clearly understood."

Northwest Ontario's mercury pollution illuminates how industries can ignore public safety, how governments fail those they are employed to protect, how fear of economic loss can immobilize populations, and how parliament and the press can miss alerting us to danger. If we can't extrapolate from Northwest Ontario, there'll be more diaries of despair, maybe in your neighbourhood, on your bedside table. Later we'll look at other jurisdictions, other industries and other poisons, and see that without constant vigilance and questioning there is no safe place for any of us.

. . . .

POLICING POLLUTION

On 26 November 1976 Reed was charged by Ontario's Environment Ministry with ten counts of causing "pollution dangerous to the environment and possibly hazardous to human health," at the Dryden plant. Reed, with Abitibi Paper Co. Limited (charged the same day), thus joined a very short list of companies charged under Ontario's 1971 Environmental Protection Act. Both firms were charged for failure to clean up pollution at their paper mills.

Ministerial orders for Reed to reduce its punishment of the Wabigoon River date from 3 December 1970. Yet in 1970 Reed was dumping 25 tons of suspended solid waste into the Wabigoon daily; in 1975 the daily average was 24.9 tons. (The Ministry "guideline" [voluntary] allowed daily loadings of 8 tons.) In 1970 Reed was dumping 24 tons of organic waste every day (voluntary "guideline" 5 tons). In 1975 Reed was fouling the Wabigoon with 46.2 tons of organic waste daily.

The 1970 order, delivered to Reed on 16 January 1971, required a clean-up by 31 October 1974. Reed asked for time — and got it — until 31 December 1976. In November 1976 the Ministry decided, and announced, that Reed couldn't have the required primary and secondary treatment facilities on stream by the deadline.

If the 1976 charges were proceeded with, *if* the company failed to get yet another extension, *if* the full weight of the law and the maximum penalties were brought to bear — a lot of "ifs" given the less than rigorous record of prosecutions in Ontario — Reed stood to face a fine of $200 daily after 1 January 1977, in the worst of all worlds. Extended over a full year the fines would total $73,000, probably not enough to fuel Robert Billingsley's executive jet on its regular trips to Atlanta. No one, though, in early 1977, was holding very large stakes on bets that the prosecutions would proceed either vigorously or expeditiously.

Moreover, on Wednesday, 5 January 1977, George Kerr told the *Toronto Star* in an interview that his ministry, "... had decided not to prosecute Reed for not meeting a pollution control order deadline of December 31, 1976." Emphasizing that his ministry was not "letting Reed off the hook," Mr. Kerr allowed that, "We've been aware for sometime that Reed couldn't possibly meet the deadline on time."

Adds the *Star* story: A Reed spokesman told the *Star* last month the installation of the treatment equipment had been delayed by a lengthy strike at the Dryden mill last year. Kerr said the government began negotiating a new clean-up deadline for Reed "some months ago, and take it from me, this time there'll be no extensions."

A CBC radio newscast of January 5 quoted an official of the Ministry of the Environment as saying the new deadline was to be three years from the 31 December 1976 cut-off date.

On 29 October 1976, Robert Billingsley, in a memo distributed to Reed employees, said: "Overall, this company has a strong commitment to environmental protection...." The quotations which follow are from Copy No. 20 of "The Ontario Pulp and Paper Industry" Alternative Policies for Pollution Abatement ... (prepared in 1973, printed in 1974, but never, as of November 1976, publicly distributed by the "Special Studies Section" of the Ministry of the Environment, although a "summary" version was revealed and published about sixty days after the original was made available to the author):

> Summary of Environment Effects if Mill [at Dryden] Meets Ministry of Environment [Ontario] Water Quality Objectives:
>> No improvement because river flow too small relative to mill discharge.
>
> Effects if Mill Closes Permanently:
>> Massive sludge deposits would continue to ... affect bottom flora and fauna for many years.... Accumulations of sludge and fibre are so extensive in the Wabigoon River that even closure ... would not result in short-term restoration of satisfactory water quality (pp. 281 and 287).
>>
>> ... there appear to be few additional benefits that could be gained by closing a mill which could not be achieved through some kind of currently available waste water treatment. *Except for the Wabigoon River, it would not be necessary to close any of the mills* listed in Table IV-5 in order to restore most of the potential uses which can be made of the respective receiving water systems. *Even in the case of Wabigoon, a restoration of water quality and water uses could be achieved without mill closure, but this would involve large capital expenditures for dredging or rerouting the river* (p. 306).
>>
>> In principle, the Ministry of the Environment is able to enforce its policy for pollution control by using the provisions for fines, stop orders and control orders that were established by the Ontario Water Resources Act.... In practice, the Ministry has been reluctant to utilize these powers of enforcement, preferring to seek the cooperation of the companies concerned. *This approach has met with only limited success in achieving effluent control by the pulp and paper industry* (p. 327).

In September 1976, in a "Summary and Update" of the same document:

The Present Approach Assessed. Continuation of the present policy has the advantage of being understood by Government and industry and it will avoid open conflicts between Ministry officials and industry representatives. However, it is essential to realize that, in the present economic and legal context, *companies have a powerful financial incentive to continue polluting the air and water.* Firms seek to minimize their costs wherever possible. Pulp and paper mills have traditionally been able to use the air, lakes and rivers to dispose of their wastes free of charge. Waste treatment, waste recovery and proper disposal techniques are generally very costly to companies even when half the costs are borne by government through the tax system. *Hence, it is in the companies' interests to resist incurring these costs, even when this may lead to prosecution and fines.* Between 1968 and the present, only twelve convictions under the Ontario Water Resources Act and five convictions under the Environmental Protection Act have been obtained against pulp and paper companies. The fines for water pollution averaged $812 per conviction: for air $1,400 per conviction. *Fines of this magnitude provide the companies with virtually no economic incentive to incur the much greater costs for pollution control.* This is especially the case in the pulp and paper industry since there have been no convictions for water pollution by these mills since 1971, and only two for air pollution, both in 1974.

Continuing the present policy approach is, therefore, unlikely to achieve the Ministry's abatement objectives over the next ten years. Furthermore, it is inequitable in that some mills have spent large sums of money on pollution abatement while *those who still pollute excessively have not been penalized.*

This situation will not be remedied by an even greater share of the costs of pollution control being shifted to the Government as has been proposed by representatives of the pulp and paper industry. *The primary deficiency lies in the lack of an adequate penalty to induce companies to abate their pollution to the desired levels.* (pp. 57–8)

■

A settlement agreed upon by the industry, the government, and the peoples of Grassy Narrows and White Dog was not reached until 1985, 15 years after the problem and the cause had been identified. Of the $17 million arrived at, 50 per cent was to be paid by the federal government, 25 per cent by the Ontario government, and only 25 per cent by Reed. For further information on the situation confronting White Dog and Grassy Narrows, see Peter Usher, "Choosing Your Poison: Differences of Opinion About the Destruction of a Native Community" *This Magazine* (December 1986–January 1987) 5 and Anastasia M. Shkilnyk, *A Poison Stronger Than Love* (New Haven: Yale University Press, 1985).

The Japanese case that alerted the world to the horrible injuries of mercury poisoning by industrial pollution was only settled in May 1996, 40 years after the Minamata injuries were reported to authorities: Stephen Strauss, "Settlement finally reached in Minamata mercury case: Hundreds died, thousands injured after eating tainted seafood" *The [Toronto] Globe and Mail* (23 May 1996) A11.

Despite disasters such as that caused by Reed Pulp and Paper, unsettled land claims, and outstanding treaty obligations, governments continue to make land available to corporations, as this excerpt from Chief Thomas Fiddler and James R. Stevens, *Killing the Shamen*, supra, at 199–202 demonstrates. (Thomas Fiddler is the grandson of Jack Fiddler, the Shaman of the Sucker clan who was charged with murder in 1907.)

Killing the Shamen (Continued)[†]

In 1976, the Province of Ontario gives a huge tract of land to a paper company, Reed International, the company responsible for polluting the Wabigoon and Winnipeg Rivers with mercury from its plant at

---

[†] Reproduced with permission of Penumbra Press from *Killing the Shamen*, Thomas Fiddler & James R. Stevens, at Preface, 199, 201–202. Moonbeam, Ont.: Penumbra, 1985.

Dryden, Ontario. A natural gas pipeline from the high arctic is planned to come across the clan folks land on its way to southern markets. There are vague plans for river diversions on the Albany River. In response to native peoples' outcries a *Royal Commission On The Northern Environment* is ordered by the Province of Ontario. These intrusions lead an elder from Big Trout Lake to lament:

. . . .

> *Jeremiah Sainnawap*: I always go along when the chiefs have meetings in the big cities. They often discuss our land. They are afraid that our land will someday be destroyed.
>
> The water is being polluted and the fish are being poisoned. Everything that grows is being threatened. We fear that there may be nothing left for our future generations to hunt and trap and live off the land.
>
> I believe the white people will take over our land. There are too many white people here now and too many of their works. The ways they travel are fast, just like the wind.
>
> The chiefs believe that the Indian people own the land. They were born on this land and so were their great-grand-fathers. The people will continue to be worried about the land.
>
> The white man wants everything. It is hard to say yes to him when what he wants is something that is precious to us.
>
> There is one thing we know. God made everything we see in the world — everything that grows — all living things. Only God can say "This is my land." He loves every being that lives on his land.

. . . .

Thomas Fiddler has his deep concerns also, especially about pulp and paper companies. When a lawyer for the *Royal Commission On The Northern Environment* asks Thomas Fiddler how he would view the cutting of trees if they can be regrown and jobs would be given to his people, he replied: "I have never seen anyone grow a forest. Now, I have a question for you. There is a lot of land in Canada that does not have trees. Why don't these companies plant trees and grow their forests there?"

This concern for his people and the land keeps Thomas Fiddler active, even in his eighties. In 1984, the Province of Ontario awards him with a Bicentennial Medal. At the convocation for this award, he is given the honorary title, Chief Emeritus. The Sucker leader stands proudly in wearing it.

> *Thomas Fiddler*: I think about a question that was asked of me. It was: What do I think of myself being an Anishinaapi — an Indian? Do I like being Indian? Do I enjoy living?
>
> I said, I believe Manitou made this light. I believe that Manitou made every Creature who lives on this earth. I also believe that Manitou made plants, and every vegetation that is growing on this earth; there are so many things with various and different shapes. There are so many things both above in the air and below in the water — and Manitou made these things. I really believe that Manitou thought about it when He began creating this world. To this we give greatest respect.
>
> I said I like my life because Manitou willed it that I be on this earth. Manitou willed it that I should be here and Manitou wants me to keep my life existing. If I destroyed my life early, I don't think Manitou would like this. If I keep my life long I think Manitou would like this. I believe that every human being should hold his life valuable and should value this earth. I believe this is what Manitou wants of us.
>
> I said, I am happy that I am an Indian.
>
> I said Manitou didn't make a mistake by not giving me a tongue to speak English. Manitou didn't make a mistake when He put the white men across the ocean.
>
> And Manitou didn't make a mistake when he made me an Indian.

■

More recently, Grassy Narrows First Nation members have been fighting to preserve their rights to hunt, trap, and fish in the Whiskey Jack Forest near Kenora. They argue that large-scale clear-cutting by Abitibi Consolidated Inc. is decimating animal populations that members of Grassy Narrows First Nations rely on for their livelihood: "Clearcutting the Ojibway way of life" *Sierra Legal Defence Fund Newsletter* (June 2000) 5.

In another example of the poisoning of Aboriginal lands, the Mathias Colom Cree Nation has blamed the federal government for building a school in 1980 on a contaminated site at Pukatawagan, Manitoba, where there had been spills of toxic chemicals and PCBs. In turn, the subsequent health and financial costs have resulted in inadequate and overcrowded housing conditions and, therefore, created new health problems: Rudy Platiel, "Indians blame polluted land for epidemic of hepatitis, TB: Federal government built school on hazardous-waste site" *The [Toronto] Globe and Mail* (23 November 1995) A3. For a discussion of community trauma in the wake of hydro development projects on Aboriginal land, see Martin Loney, "Social Problems, Community Trauma and Hydro Project Impacts" (1995) 15 Cdn. J. Native Stud. 231. As a recent inquiry concludes, "the environmental and social costs of hydro production are being off-loaded on the peoples of the north, while the balance of benefits accrue to society at large." The result is an ongoing "ecological, social and moral catastrophe" for northern Manitoba and its Aboriginal inhabitants: Interchurch Inquiry into Northern Hydro Development, *Let Justice Flow: Report of the Interchurch Inquiry into Northern Hydro Development*, Executive Summary (Winnipeg: Manitoba Aboriginal Rights Coalition, 2001).

The criminal law has also been used to enforce the dumping of toxic wastes on lands inhabited by Aboriginal communities. In August 1989, the Baie-Comeau police force provided escort against protesters for 180 tonnes of PCB-contaminated waste that were stored on Betsiamitel land after legal efforts to halt the dumping foundered: André Picard, "Riot squad clears way for PCBs" *The [Toronto] Globe and Mail* (30 August 1989) A1. Testimony from Aboriginal leaders before the Commission d'enquête sur les déchets dangereux identified the federal departments of Defence, Indian Affairs, and Northern Development as the worst polluters in northern Québec. These leaders have also identified specific legal structures that facilitate dumping, such as the Québec law that exempts northern land from public environmental review and that also excludes the by-products of mining and the pulp and paper industries from the definition of "hazardous waste": André Picard, "Pollution of Indian lands ignored, witnesses tell toxic waste inquiry" *The [Toronto] Globe and Mail* (9 May 1990) A20. Growing concerns about water safety in Aboriginal communities and elsewhere in Canada enlarge these concerns. See, for example: Kevin Dougherty, "Cree community more polluted than 'Love Canal': Study on ground water, environment finds high levels of arsenic, cyanide, lead, mercury" *The Ottawa Citizen* (23 October 2001) A9, discussing a study by Christopher Covel that implicated dumping of waste tailings by mines in northern Québec. The Ouje-Bougoumou Cree Nation is also concerned about the impact of forestry practices, such as clear-cutting, on their environment.

Consider whether the term "environmental racism" might aptly be used to describe the decision-making and legal processes that send hazardous waste to particular communities, enforce its deposit and storage against the wishes of the community, fail to police environmental pollution, and resist the costs of compensation and clean-up. See the discussion in Abell and Sheehy, *Proof, Defences, and Beyond*, **Broadening the Defences: Necessity, Self-Defence and Beyond**; and see Robert D. Bullard, ed., *Unequal Protection: Environmental Justice and Communities of Color* (San Francisco: Sierra Club, 1994); Richard Hofrichter, ed., *Toxic Struggles: The Theory and Practice of Environmental Justice* (Philadelphia: New Society, 1993).

D. THE APPROPRIATION OF LAND AND THE ROLE OF THE MILITARY

In this context, unresolved land claims, outstanding, unmet treaty obligations, and a failure to grapple with the demands of Aboriginal peoples have led to considerable frustration. In response to protests, the state has invoked criminal law and resorted to both police and military force.

A contested issue in many areas is the continuing assumption of military control over Aboriginal land: for example, the appropriation of land for military bases, the conversion of reserve land to land grants for returning non-Aboriginal veterans after World War II under the *Veterans' Land Act, 1942*, S.C. 1942, c. 33, s. 5(2), the lack of adequate compensation, the specific uses to which the land has subsequently been put (bombing, strafing, military waste), and the resultant interference and harm. A few representative examples follow.

- **The Tsilhqot'n**: As Judge Sarich describes in *Cariboo-Chilcotin Justice Inquiry* (British Columbia: 1993) at 26, the chiefs condemned the appropriation of their lands, particularly those appropriated for military use as a weapons proving ground.

- **Ipperwash**: In the summer of 1995, Chippewa protesters at Ipperwash Provincial Park protested the desecration of burial grounds and demanded the return of adjacent land that had been arbitrarily appropriated "temporarily" for use as a military training facility and base (Canadian Forces Detachment Ipperwash) in 1942 under the *War Measures Act*, R.S.C. 1927, c. 206 [hereinafter *War Measures Act*]. According to s. 6 of the *War Measures Act*, the appropriation power was only in force during war, invasion, or insurrection. See generally the Statement of Claim in *Maynard Donald George, Carolyn Joyce George, Perry Watson Neil George, Joan Marie Price, Pamela Rose George, Laverne Ralph George, and Reginald Ransford George, Jr. v. Michael D. Harris, Charles Harnick, Robert Runciman, Christopher Coles, Todd Colonelvain, Wade LaCroix, Larry Parks, John Wright, John Slade, John Graham, John McLean, John McGriff, Certain Unnamed Individuals, Thomas B. O'Grady, Her Majesty the Queen in Right of Ontario and Her Majesty the Queen in Right of Canada* Court File No. 96-CU-99569 (April 1996) (Ont. Ct. (Gen. Div.)) [hereinafter *George* v. *Harris*] (paragraphs 38–40, 44).

> The Plaintiffs allege that the appropriation and ongoing retention and use of the Camp Ipperwash lands by Canada contravened the First Nation's and the Plaintiffs' right of exclusive use and occupation as guaranteed at common law and by Treaty, including the provisions of Treaty No. 29, by the provisions of the *Indian Act*, R.S.C. 1927, C.98, s. 19, 34, 39 and 50, as amended by the provisions of the *Royal Proclamation of 1763*, and by the *Constitution Act, 1867* and the *Constitution Act, 1982*.
>
> Accordingly, the Plaintiffs allege that Order-in Council 2913 was null and void *ab initio*, and that Canada's occupation and use of the land at Camp Ipperwash since 1942 has constituted a continuing trespass, and a breach of the Plaintiffs' Aboriginal and Treaty Rights.
>
> The Plaintiffs allege that as a result of the appropriation in 1942 their father, Reginald Ransford George, Sr., then 16 years old, along with 11 other families, their buildings and chattels, were removed on Thanksgiving weekend in 1942 to make room for Camp Ipperwash, and the Plaintiffs allege that the families so removed and the First Nation were paid some compensation in or about 1942 and again in 1981, which compensation was incapable of, and not intended to, and failed to remedy their losses.
>
> ...
>
> [The First Nation made numerous requests for the return of the lands in the intervening years, without success.]
>
> In the summer of 1993, in frustration over their longstanding and fruitless efforts to have the Camp Ipperwash lands returned to the First Nation in an intact state, members and descendants of some of the Indian families who were removed in 1942 from the reserve lands which became Camp Ipperwash, and other First Nation members, commenced an occupation of Camp Ipperwash in protest. The group included individual First Nation members who had resided on the lands at Stony Point prior to 1942 and who had been serving in the Canadian forces overseas at the very time their lands were being appropriated by DND in 1942.

Finally, in July 1995, the military abandoned the base: Peter Moon, "A long story of occupation" *The [Toronto] Globe and Mail* (8 September 1995) A3; Peter Moon, "Natives prepare to claim park: Ontario unlikely to open Ipperwash" *The [Toronto] Globe and Mail* (9 April 1996) A1, A5. Negotiations for the settlement of this claim and the return of the land to the Kettle and Stony Point First Nation are ongoing. The killing of Anthony (Dudley) George by the Ontario Provincial Police in September 1995 and the lawsuit in *George* v. *Harris*, [1999] O.J. No. 639 (Ct. Just. (Gen. Div.)), online: QL, that seeks to establish liability on the part of the Premier, the Attorney-General and the Solicitor General of Ontario *are discussed infra*, **Policing**.

- **The Innu**: The Innu in Labrador have faced numerous criminal charges for their protest against low-level military flights over their territory, which began in the 1950s. See Daniel Ashini, "David Confronts Goliath: The Innu of Ungava versus the NATO Alliance" in Boyce Richardson, ed., *Drumbeat: Anger and Renewal in Indian Country* (Toronto: Summerhill Press, 1989) 43–70 and see discussion in Abell and Sheehy, *Proof, Defences, and Beyond*, **Colour of Right: Mistake of Fact, Mistake of Law, or Affirmative Defence?**

- **Primrose Lake Air Weapons Range**: In 1954, the Government of Canada established a 3-million acre bombing and gunnery range in northern Saskatchewan and Alberta on Aboriginal land, without consultation or adequate compensation or rehabilitation. Aboriginal people were not allowed to exercise their rights to hunt, trap, or fish within the area, which had previously provided 75 per cent of their livelihood. In 1996, the Indian Claims Commission concluded that the claim of the Canoe Lake Cree Nation in Saskatchewan and that of the Cold Lake First Nations in Alberta were valid ones, which should not have been rejected by the Government of Canada in 1975 and 1986.

The Commission found a clear breach of treaties (Treaty 6, 1876; and Treaty 10, 1906) and a breach of fiduciary obligations owed to the First Nations. See Indian Claims Commission, "Canoe Lake Cree Nation and Cold Lake First Nations Claims: Executive Summary" (Ottawa: Indian Claims Commission, 1996) at 3–5:

> Our investigation involved participating in a process that had never occurred before in connection with these land claims. We had the privilege of visiting these communities and listening to the narratives and disclosures of three generations who have experienced the devastation of exclusion from the air weapons range lands....
>
> It is more than 40 years since the air weapons range was established; this was the first chance these people had to express their feelings directly to anybody concerned about their claims. The people expressed their deep appreciation that an Indian Commission such as ours had been struck, after all these years, to travel to their community and listen.
>
> Their evidence can only be described as sincere and compelling. Their moving accounts of their plight were unchallenged and uncontradicted.
>
> We were struck by the totality of the destruction of these communities. After the First Nations were expelled from their traditional lands, their pride and independence were quickly displaced as they faced an inescapable cycle of poverty, and a degrading and almost total dependence on government. The result of this devastation was alcoholism and crippling social ills which the community is still struggling to overcome.
>
> ...
>
> ... [T]he creation of the air weapons range completely destroyed their independence. The result for these First Nations was an abrupt and complete termination of a centuries-old traditional lifestyle. The abruptness of the dispossession deprived them of the opportunity to adapt that a more gradual intrusion into their lifestyle would have given them.†

In conclusion, the Indian Claims Commission recommended that the Primrose Lake Air Weapons Range claims of the Cold Lake First Nations and the Canoe Lake Cree Nation be accepted for negotiation pursuant to the 1982 Specific Claims Policy of Canada, after they had been repeatedly rejected by successive governments for 30 years. That claim has now been partially settled (with the Canoe Lake Cree Nation). However, Metis claims with respect to the same area are unresolved. Thus, there are outstanding issues with respect to the interference with Aboriginal rights to hunt, trap, and fish in the area.

- **Transfer of reserve land to returning non-Aboriginal veterans**: In spite of their military service, Aboriginal veterans were refused the land grants made available to non-Aboriginal veterans: Fred Gaffen, *Forgotten Soldiers* (Penticton: Theytus, 1985). First Nations have challenged the adequacy of compensation and the breaches of fiduciary duties by the Crown. In *Blueberry River Indian Band* v. *Canada*, [1995] 4 S.C.R. 344, the Court recognized a fiduciary duty on the Crown with respect to the transfer of land to the Director of The Veterans' Land Act and allowed the claim by the Band for losses stemming from the failure of the Crown to reserve mineral rights.

E. TREATY RIGHTS AND SOVEREIGNTY

At the same time, Aboriginal peoples have successfully asserted their sovereignty with respect to one aspect of their relationship to land in the courts. In response to legal argument, the Supreme Court of Canada has declared quasi-criminal provincial laws prohibiting certain uses of park lands (e.g. cutting trees and making fires) and trafficking in wildlife without a license, to be unenforceable against treaty beneficiaries due to conflicts with Aboriginal treaty rights protected by s. 35(1) of the *Charter*: *R.* v. *Sioui*, [1990] 1 S.C.R. 1025; *R.* v. *Horseman*, [1990] 1 S.C.R. 901; *R.* v. *Sparrow*, [1990] 1 S.C.R. 1075; and *R.* v. *Sundown*, [1999] 1 S.C.R. 393. The Court has also recognized the treaty right to hunt for food on privately owned land that lies within the territory surrendered under the treaty and held that the geographical limitation on the existing hunting right should be based upon a concept of visible, incompatible land use: *R.* v. *Badger*, [1996] 1 S.C.R. 771. See also *Delgamuukw* v. *British Columbia*, [1997] 3 S.C.R. 1010, which recognized a constitutional basis for

---

† Reproduced with the permission of the Public Works and Government Services, 2002.

Aboriginal land claims in British Columbia. The lower court decision by Mr. Justice McEachern has been extensively criticized for racism: see Gisday Wa and Delgam Uukw, "A Travesty of Justice" in *The Spirit in the Land*, supra, at 96–97:

> ... This judge concludes, more or less, that prior to contact, native people in British Columbia [led] a life that was nasty, brutish and short and that it took European contact to make them culturally self-aware and to give them any sense of territoriality. In short, prior to contact, this judge thinks native people were little more than fairly bright animals.
>
> The tone this judge is attempting to set is that native people in B.C. have no rights, no real culture that could in any way be equated with what was imported from Europe, and certainly no say in what happens to their land. When the Europeans came, it was game over. If native people think they have been denied justice, too bad.... Perhaps he expects the native rights struggle in B.C. and Canada to magically end because of this decision. Instead, in his myopia, he has fuelled the causes of racism. Judgements of this kind foster only enmity. Aboriginal people will protect their rights and will force this agenda. The actuality, or threat of violent force by the state cannot keep people down. It has not worked in South Africa and it did not work last summer at Oka. Justice will be served in the end and this province may expect considerable unrest, protest, and direct political action if the government attempts to use this small, silly judgement to inform policy....†

A United Nations study by Miguel Alfonso Martinez concluded that Justice McEachern's ruling in *Delgamuukw* was proof that "deeply rooted Western ethnocentric criteria are still widely shared in present-day judiciary reasoning": Geoffrey York, "Land-claim ruling shows 'ethnocentric' bias, UN report says" *The [Toronto] Globe and Mail* (2 April 1993) A4. For further background to the case, see: Don Monet and Skanu'u (Ardythe Wilson), *Colonialism on Trial: Indigenous Land Rights and the Gitksan and Wet'suwet'en Sovereignty Case* (Philadelphia: New Society, 1992).

Hunting cases do not often compete with non-Aboriginal commercial interests. In contrast, fishing cases often do. Two recent B.C. cases have narrowly interpreted fishing rights by defining rivers adjacent to or running through a reserve as extra-territorial: *R. v. Lewis*, [1996] 1 S.C.R. 921; *R. v. Nikal*, [1996] 1 S.C.R. 1013. However, subsequent Aboriginal fishing cases have recognized specific limited commercial interests. See, for example, *R. v. N.T.C. Smokehouse*, [1996] 2 S.C.R. 672 and *R. v. Gladstone*, [1996] 2 S.C.R. 723. See also *R. v. Marshall*, [1999] 3 S.C.R. 456, a fishing rights case involving Donald Marshall, Jr. For a detailed examination of the implications of the *Marshall* case, see (2000) 23 Dalhousie L.J. (Forum on *R. v. Marshall*).

The determination as to whether the Aboriginal right to hunt or fish embraces a right to sell the game or fish has depended on historical evidence and evidence of any relevant treaties. Thus, the decisions to prosecute such cases result in considerable expense for the Aboriginal peoples involved. In spite of the rulings in *Sioui*, *Horseman*, and *Sparrow*, controversy continues about the ways in which state resources have been and are deployed to police Aboriginal hunting and fishing. See, for example, the discussion of "Operation Rainbow" (a five-year undercover operation) on Manitoulin Island, in Abell and Sheehy, *Proof, Defences, and Beyond*, **Entrapment**.

The difficulty of asserting Aboriginal claims with respect to hunting and fishing is compounded for Metis people. Two recent cases currently on appeal to the Supreme Court highlight the complexity of the definition of a people and the definition and test of Aboriginality: *R. v. Blais*, [1999] 2 W.W.R. 445 (Man. C.A.); *R. v. Powley* (2001), 53 O.R. (3d) 35 (C.A.).

The cases demonstrate that the forcible separation of Aboriginal peoples from their land continues and that struggles around colonization, appropriation of land, resettlement and relocation, and erosion of sovereignty and Aboriginal rights are current as well as historical issues. See, for example, the following discussions on: the Innu at Davis Inlet, infra, **Powers of Prosecution, Judicial Powers**; the Ipperwash and Gustafson Lake, *infra*, **Policing**; and the Lubicon Nation, in Abell and Sheehy, *Proof, Defences, and Beyond*, **Broadening the Defences: Necessity, Self-Defence and Conscience**.

---

† Reproduced by permission of Reflections Publisher, Gabriola, BC.

F. FURTHER EXAMPLES OF COLONIALISM

The previous examples deal with colonialism and Aboriginal peoples in Canada. However, the practices of colonialism within one territory, or with respect to one people, are clearly connected to other practices of colonialism and to the construction of race and racial hierarchy.

English criminal law and procedure were also imposed on the Canadien(ne)s of Québec, who had, prior to British conquest in 1759, been governed by French judicial institutions and forms of criminal law. The work of Douglas Hay assesses the reactions of the Canadien(ne)s to the rapid shift from French to English criminal law and the actual functioning of English criminal laws in the specific context of Québec. His research suggests that the Canadien(ne)s rarely appeared in the newly instituted criminal courts as either the accused or the accuser: Douglas Hay, "The Meanings of the Criminal Law in Quebec, 1765–1774" in A. Knafla, ed., *Crime and Criminal Justice in Europe and Canada* (Waterloo: Wilfrid Laurier University Press, 1985) 83–100. As he concludes, while the form of English law prevailed, the social meaning did not necessarily follow.

For another example of the ways in which criminal law and "treason" charges in particular were used to preserve colonial authority, see: Bev Boissery, *A Deep Sense of Wrong: The Treason Trials, and Transportation to New South Wales of Lower Canadian Rebels After the 1838 Rebellion* (Toronto: Dundurn, 1995). She describes the court martial, conviction, and subsequent transportation to Australia of 58 civilian Canadiens for treason in the aftermath of the 1837 and 1838 rebellions.

□

3

Aboriginal Peoples and Criminal Law

It has been apparent for some time that the criminal justice system treats Aboriginal peoples more harshly than non-Aboriginal people. Both police and prison statistics reflect this disparity. See, for example:

Rita M. Bienvenue and A. H. Latif, "Arrests, Disposition and Recidivism: A Comparison of Indians and Whites" (1974) 16 Can. J. Crim. & Corr. 105.

Trish Elliot, "Pot-shot Justice" New Internationalist (December 1985) 28.

John Hagan, "Criminal Justice and Native People: A Study of Incarceration in a Canadian Province" (1974) (special issue) Can. Rev. Soc. & Anthro. 220.

Jim Harding and Beryl Forgay, *Breaking Down The Walls: A Bibliography on the Pursuit of Aboriginal Justice* (Regina: Prairie Justice Research, 1991).

John Hylton, "The Native Offender in Saskatchewan: Some Implications for Crime Prevention Programming" (1982) 24 Can. J. Crim. 121.

Michael Jackson, "Locking up Natives in Canada" (1989) 23 U.B.C.L. Rev. 215.

Carol LaPrairie, "Aboriginal Women and Crime in Canada: Identifying the Issues" in Ellen Adelbeg and Claudia Currie, eds., *In Conflict with the Law* (Vancouver: Press Gang, 1993) 235.

Simon N. Verdun-Jones and Gregory K. Muirhead, "Natives in the Canadian Criminal Justice System: An Overview" (1979–80) 7/8 Crime & Just. 3.

In the 1980s, the issues facing Aboriginal peoples in the criminal justice system gained more prominence and surfaced as an area of broader concern for the bar, the judiciary, and the general public in the wake of the revelations about the treatment of Donald Marshall, Jr., a Mi'kmaq from Nova Scotia and the submissions to the *Royal Commission on the Donald Marshall, Jr. Prosecution: Digest of Findings and Recommendations* [hereinafter Marshall Commission]. Since the Marshall Commission, there have been numerous commissions of inquiry across the country and reports on the situation of Aboriginal peoples in the criminal justice system.

- **Nova Scotia**: T. Alexander Hickman, Lawrence A. Poitras, and Gregory T. Evans, *Royal Commission on the Donald Marshall, Jr. Prosecution: Digest of Findings and Recommendations* (Halifax: McCurdy's Printing and Typesetting Ltd., 1989).

- **Ontario**: *Report of the Osnaburgh/Windigo Tribal Council Justice Review Committee: Truth, Justice and First Nations* (Ontario (no city): The Committee, 1990).

- **Manitoba**: Judge A.C. Hamilton and Judge C. Murray Sinclair, *Report of the Aboriginal Justice Inquiry of Manitoba* [hereinafter *Aboriginal Justice Inquiry (Manitoba)*] (Winnipeg: Queen's Printer, 1991).

- **Alberta**: Task Force, *Justice on Trial: Report of the Task Force on the Criminal Justice System and its Impact on the Indian and Metis People of Alberta* (Edmonton: The Task Force, 1991).
- **Saskatchewan**: Judge Patricia Linn et al., *Report of the Saskatchewan Indian Justice Review Committee* (Saskatoon: The Committee, 1992); Judge Patricia Linn et al., *Report of the Saskatchewan Metis Justice Review Committee* (Saskatoon: The Committee, 1992).
- **Northwest Territories**: Katherine Peterson, *The Justice House: Report of the Special Advisor on Gender Equality to the Minister of Justice of the Northwest Territories* (Yellowknife: Govt. of the Northwest Territories, 1992);
- **Eastern Arctic (Nunavut)**: Inuit Justice Task Force, *Blazing the Trail to a Better Future: Inuit Justice Task Force Final Report* (Montréal: Makivik Corp., 1993)
- **British Columbia**: Judge Anthony Sarich, *Report on the Cariboo-Chilcotin Aboriginal Justice Inquiry* (Victoria: The Inquiry, 1993).
- **Québec**: Jean-Charles Coutu, *La justice pour les autochtones: Raport et recommendations du committée* (Québec: Committée, 1995)
- **Canada**: Royal Commission on Aboriginal Peoples, *Bridging the Cultural Divide: A Report on Aboriginal People and Criminal Justice in Canada* (Ottawa: Canada Communication Group, 1996); Law Reform Commission of Canada, *Report on Aboriginal Peoples and Criminal Justice: Equality, Respect and the Search for Justice* (Report 34) (Ottawa: The Commission, 1991); Canadian Bar Association, *Locking Up Natives in Canada* (Ottawa: Canadian Bar Association, 1988), an abbreviated version reprinted as Michael Jackson, "Locking up Natives in Canada" (1989) 23 U.B.C. L. Rev. 215.

The inquiries have documented the historical impact of colonization, exploitation of lands and resources, and the imposition of criminal law; the present-day perpetuation of those practices; the links between colonization and racism; the links between colonization and poverty, marginalization and cultural breakdown, and violence; differential patterns of enforcement within the criminal justice system; attitudes often permeated with racism, classism, English-language bias, and ethnocentrism; and the specific historical basis for separate justice systems for Aboriginal peoples.

As the Royal Commission on Aboriginal Peoples emphasizes in *Bridging the Cultural Divide* at 52:

> [L]ocating the root causes of Aboriginal crime in the history of colonialism, and understanding its continuing effects, points unambiguously to the critical need for a new relationship that rejects each and every assumption underlying colonial relationships between Aboriginal peoples and non-Aboriginal society.
>
> Locating the root causes of Aboriginal crime and other forms of social disorder in the history of colonialism has other important implications related to the nature of the interventions most likely to bring about significant changes and improvements in Aboriginal peoples' lives, rather than provide merely short-term palliative relief of the underlying problems.[†]

Support for judicial education and training to begin to address issues of bias has emerged, as the following presentation by Associate Chief Judge Murray Sinclair demonstrates. As you read the following excerpts, consider what is demonstrated about the continuing impact of colonization by the submissions, the reports, and other responses to the findings of the inquiries. Overall, individual instances of miscarriages of justice have been more readily acknowledged than systemic wrongs or the need for separate justice systems. The characterization of incidents as demonstrating "bias" or "racism" has been responded to defensively, by denial or explanation or by recharacterization of the incidents as anomalous on the part of individual police officers, lawyers, or judges. Thus, even when the law is invoked to invalidate racist or biased decision-making, the blandness and moderation of the language demonstrates the level at which racism is embedded in legal culture.

---

† From Canada, Royal Commission on Aboriginal Peoples, Bridging the Cultural Divide: A Report on Aboriginal People and Criminal Justice in Canada (Ottawa: Minister of Supply and Services, 1996). Reproduced with the permission of the Minister of Public Works and Government Services Canada, 2002 and Courtesy of the Privy Council Office.

A Presentation to the Western Workshop of the Western Judicial Education Centre[†]

Events of the past few years have given rise to the question whether the administration of justice in Canada — particularly the criminal justice and child welfare components of that system — must re-evaluate the manner in which it goes about its affairs.

The Report of the Royal Commission into the Prosecution of Donald Marshall, Jr. in Nova Scotia, the Inquiry into Policing on the Blood Reserve in Alberta, the trial of the Innu people in Labrador and Manitoba's Inquiry into the Administration of Justice and Aboriginal People have (or should have) given us pause to consider whether the time has arrived when we as judges or the administration over which we preside should perhaps rethink some of the basic assumptions with which we have been operating.

If nothing else, at least we should be acknowledging that, at best, the relationship between the administration of justice and aboriginal people is, if not already so, becoming severely strained. We who are involved in setting the direction for our courts in years to come must begin to determine how we can improve both our relations with aboriginal people generally, and the way we handle cases involving aboriginal people and aboriginal issues.

Statistics are very clear. Nationally, aboriginal people are over-represented in the courts and jails and prisons of our country to the tune of five or six times their presence in the population. In some parts of the country, aboriginal people are incarcerated at a rate of over ten times their presence in the population. In provincial systems, aboriginal women make up 70–90% of all women incarcerated. In Western Canada 40–70% of all men incarcerated are aboriginal.

In many Provinces, particularly in Western Canada, aboriginal people represent the single largest identifiable group of accused who will appear before us.

It would appear as well that with the greater growth rate among aboriginal people, there is a good chance that those numbers in our courts will increase. In Manitoba, approximately 45% of the aboriginal population are under the age of 15 and over 50% are under the age of 18. Those statistics would appear to hold true for most other provinces. The majority of youth in the youth courts of Western Canada is aboriginal.

Frankly, there is every possibility that, without significant steps being taken to alter the situation, the number of aboriginal accused, charged, and incarcerated will increase in the future rather than decrease.

IN HISTORY LIES KNOWLEDGE — IN KNOWLEDGE LIES THE ANSWER

In order to understand the present, one must have some regard for events which have occurred in the past, for in understanding the forces at play in past generations, we can more easily come to some conclusions about how to handle current problems.

When the Red Man and the White Man first met in this country, aboriginal people had among other things, quite satisfactory means of resolving serious social, political and legal problems without any outside help. Indian tribes still believe that they have that ability, but they point out that they have been denied the opportunity and the resources to do so for the past two or three generations.

The white man's justice system and other ways of doing things have been imposed upon Indian people, such that without the resources and the opportunities to exercise their responsibilities, some tribes and bands — not all — have lost the inclination to deal with what in the absence of the European settler governments, they would have necessarily and naturally done for themselves.

Even though aboriginal people see that the white man's way of doing things does not seem to be working for their people, some still cannot pick up the tools which have been left along the trails of their past in order to help themselves; instead the white man is expected to try to improve the way he is doing things and it is hoped that he does better.

Other tribes, on the other hand, assert that they, their traditions and customs are the best vehicle to resolve the serious dilemmas facing the administrations of justice in this country. They point out, quite forcefully, that the failures of the administra-

---

[†] By Murray Sinclair, Associate Chief Judge, Provincial Court of Manitoba, 14 May 1990 [unpublished]. Reproduced by permission of the author.

tion of justice stem from the inability of the justice system to properly take into account the customs, values, and traditions of the aboriginal people which they believe to be the cornerstone of any positive changes which the justice system is to have in their communities.

They point out that if the white man had never come to this land, Indian tribes would have continued to take care of their own problems and would have evolved naturally into modern times. As part of that natural evolution, they assert that they would have had well-established and more-effective court systems to deal with the kinds of problems that modern society faces.

That they were not allowed to do so is the white man's legacy.

"KINDNESS CAN KILL"

People have talked about the manner in which aboriginal people have been treated in this country as cultural genocide — a rather dramatic if not wholly accurate phrase. The phrase is intended to convey the concept that past government policies and efforts were aimed at "killing" the cultures of the various tribes. That is what genocide means — the killing of a people, and one is asked to conclude that cultural genocide is a killing of a culture.

Other writers have coined the term "ethnocide" to better capture the flavour of what went on, but the two phrases mean the same — that the culture of the people is to be done away with. The difference, if indeed there is one, is that the genocidist believes that the target group must be destroyed. The ethnocidist believes that the target group can or must be saved, and the inferior culture to which the members of the target group belong must be destroyed. In doing so, the target group can be saved from a life of barbarism or paganism or backwardness.

In using the term "genocide" it is hard to envision the possibility that the practitioner of the belief could be motivated by anything other than malice or evil or, at the very least, cold-heartedness.

With the ethnocidist, however, the motivation is not an evil one. Almost always, it is a belief that what the practitioner is in fact doing is in the best interests of the target group or race. The acts of ethnocide are perceived by both the practitioner and others as being acts of kindness. It is, we are told, unfortunately, a case of having to take strong medicine to overcome a terrible condition.

Past and present governments in Canada, both Federal and Provincial have practiced ethnocide. Past and present educational systems in our country have been practitioners of ethnocide. Past and present administrations of justice in our country have been practitioners of ethnocide.

Most, if not all, of the legal and political efforts and policies of the institutions of government, including those of the administrations of justice, insofar as Indian people are concerned, both in the past and to a certain extent in the present, have been motivated out of a genuine belief that what was being done, in the long run, was or is the best thing for the Indian — his gradual civilization.

There was and still is a generally unspoken belief in all that was done, that aboriginal people and their cultures beliefs and customs were just not capable of dealing with the complicated and complex social problems of the day: that western civilization with its emphasis on and respect for professional training and specialization still holds the answers and is a better road to travel on than the aboriginal one. Such a belief is part of the problem we face in coming to grips with the issue of the failure of the justice system for aboriginal people.

So long as we judges, and other administrators of justice, lack the willingness to look to aboriginal societies for some of the answers, the problems we face will be perpetuated. So long as we believe that the European-based Canadian legal system has the cure we will remain ineffective.

We must recognize and come to understand how the phenomenon of ethnocide or cultural genocide works, for we must protect our future decisions from it. There is no cure within its inherent premise — the superiority of one culture over another.

The sad truth is, as we are now discovering — and what Indian people have known all along — that the cure has only worsened the condition.

Many examples of government ethnocidal policies can be found in our history:

In the 1880's the Government of Canada enacted special amendments to the Indian Act of Canada at the request of the missionary societies who were mandated by the government of Canada to educate the Indians. These became known as the Potlatch and Sundance laws and they made it an offence for any Indian person to participate in any traditional Indian ceremony or to wear traditional Indian costume or dress. Many of the ones who were prosecuted under these laws were the traditional leaders of the tribe, who, upon conviction, were invariably sentenced to hard labour. The statistical evidence available (such as it is) for Stony Mountain Penitentiary in Manitoba at the turn of the century shows that most of the Indian people who were incarcerated at that time were sentenced under these laws.

In this way, as well, their influence within the tribe was reduced both by their removal from the community, and by the fact that the Government could show the Indians that they had the power to lock up their most influential leaders.

There is ample evidence from Canadian and Provincial Archives of ministerial and departmental directives issued both prior to and for some time after the turn of the century to prosecutors, justices and magistrates in Western Canada exhorting and, in some cases, demanding that they sentence Indian offenders harshly so as to make it clear to their fellow tribesmen that they must abide by the laws of Canada. We must bear in mind that at that time magistrates did not enjoy any type of judicial independence, holding office "at pleasure." In addition, most of the magistrates in the Northwest Territories (before the western provinces were created) were employees of the Federal Government, foremost among them being Indian agents and RCMP (NWMP) officers.

In the 1880's the Federal Government enacted amendments to the Indian Act in which Indian children were legally required to attend schools as established or directed by the Minister of Indian Affairs. This was some time before compulsory education existed for the rest of Canada. The only schools established by the Minister at that time were residential schools patterned on the Industrial school model then popular in the United States for Indian children and juvenile delinquents. Indian children were taken from their parents (and from their influence), the Minister was appointed their legal guardian and they were educated in schools run sometimes by the Department, but generally by missionary societies (thereby coincidentally facilitating the Christianization of the Indians — another ethnocidal belief I might add — that aboriginal people needed to be saved from their paganistic existence through Christianity).

At the same time the Department inaugurated what came to be called the "Pass System" whereby Indian people were not allowed to leave their reserve without written permission of the local Indian agent. The system was designed and requested by the Canadian military following the Saskatchewan Rebellion of 1885 in order to control Indian movement in Western Canada (then the Northwest Territories) and prevent another aboriginal insurgency. Though never legally mandated or sanctioned, the system was primarily used to prevent Indian parents from travelling to where their children were attending schools and interfering with them, or attempting to remove them. Not only could Indians not leave their reserves to see their children: the pass system was also sometimes invoked to prevent Indians from seeking employment outside of their reserves. There is considerable evidence that it was abused in many other ways to enhance the power of the local Indian agents over the lives of the Band members.

Enfranchisement laws were enacted allowing the Minister to remove the legal status of an Indian, if the Minister believed that the Indian should live "like a white man." Not only did these laws permit the Minister (without legal recourse) to strip an Indian of his special legal rights as an Indian, but they also allowed the Minister to enfranchise an entire Band.

In the 1890's the Minister was empowered by further amendment to the Indian Act to declare that the traditional leaders and chiefs of the Band no longer held any legal authority in the tribe and that only chiefs and councils elected under the supervision of the local Indian agent were allowed to represent the tribe. Also, the amendment required that any time the newly elected council wished to hold a council meeting they had to notify the Indian agent and the Indian agent was, automatically and by law, the chairman of the council meeting. Any legislation enacted by the tribe could be disallowed by the Minister, according to the same amendments. The amendments were interestingly and ironically entitled "The Indian Advancement Act."

Amendments to the Indian Act at around the same time made it an offence for a lawyer to represent an Indian or a band in an action against the Government unless the consent of the Minister of Indian Affairs was first obtained. Needless to say, many perfectly valid legal claims against the Government languished for decades — nobody ever got the Minister's permission.

The famous case of *St. Catherine's Milling* which decided the nature of the aboriginal title in Canada, was decided not only without aboriginal representation in the form of counsel, but also without any evidence from aboriginal people about how they understood their rights.

Finally, the Indian Act was amended at around this time to include a definition. "Person" was defined to mean "anyone other than an Indian" — the ultimate reflection of government thinking.

These are only a few examples of legislative or administrative initiatives that were believed, or at least asserted, to be acts of benevolence, designed to protect Indians (from what, it is hard to say) or to advance them along the road to civilization. In addition to those matters mentioned, the efforts of the provincial governments would be equally revealing although there is some evidence that provincial efforts were less benign.

These legislative and administrative efforts had several effects:

For the most part the children who were removed from their families and sent to residential schools suffered emotional and psychological harm which had differing degrees of impact upon their own coping and parenting skills. Often the result was a belief on their part that what was "Indian" was bad — their language ceremonies, beliefs, rituals, religion, their elders or other traditional Indian people (medicine people, etc) — so that when these children became adults, they sometimes carried on the culturally destructive attitudes and attacks of the missionary people with whom they had grown up.

In addition, they generally lacked the skills necessary to cope with reserve life. Hunting, fishing, trapping, hide tanning, food preparation, beadwork and other traditional pursuits that had formed an integral part of aboriginal lifestyle not simply for economic reasons but also for social ones, were activities which many did not know how to do and were not inclined to learn. Despite the promise of the residential school system, most who were sent there did not receive any training in any employment-related field beyond physical labour. Reliance upon government handouts or social assistance subsequently became commonplace. None had received instruction on how to raise children, so that when they had families, they experienced coping problems.

Because of the legal ban on Indian ceremonies and rituals, traditional Indian men and women were harassed and prosecuted. The public display which had always accompanied such practices became dangerous and so the practices went underground. They were never effectively wiped out — many Indian people still practiced their traditional ways and customs but they had to do so clandestinely. This reduced the effectiveness of those customs as tools of societal bonding for the number of those who could attend such ceremonial gatherings and teaching sessions — for that is what they were — was necessarily limited.

In addition, with the advent of Christianity among many of the tribes, some tribal members became agents for the "white man's churches" and the Indian agents who were bent on destroying such practices. They actively assisted in the discovery and destruction of ceremonial gathering places and symbols. This occasioned distrust between the older traditional people and the younger ones returning from the missionary schools, and further prevented the public transmission of the cultural values inherent to the tribes which the traditions and ceremonies were designed to promote.

Though they continued to be practiced by a number of tribal members, the utility of the tribe's religious beliefs and practices as a social tool was limited to older people and those who were outside the influence of the missionary societies.

In addition, the Christian churches could not replace what was lost, for in losing the right to publicly and regularly engage in their traditional practices, beliefs and customs, large numbers of Indian people lost contact with not only their religious rituals, but an entire lifestyle. While many Indian people did gravitate to Christianity, it did not gain as important a foothold in the lives of Indian tribes as what had been removed.

The enforcement of the kinds of laws about which I have spoken engendered a certain amount of distrust of the white man's laws and legal systems on the part of the Indians. One can well understand that.

For the most part, the inordinate numbers of aboriginal people we now see in the justice system did not begin to occur until the 1950's. In Manitoba, elders point out that the increase in police contacts and court appearances by aboriginal people coincides with the change in liquor laws allowing Indian people to drink in beer parlours — a "right" hitherto denied them in most provincial legislation. There is no doubt that there is a high incidence of alcohol-related crime among aboriginal people today, and that the beginning of the rise of those numbers starts at around the same time.

Until the mid-1950's, it would appear that aboriginal representation in our court system was about equivalent to their numbers in society — in other words, there was little if any evidence of over-representation. One must be careful of drawing conclusions from the relationship in time between the rise in aboriginal-justice system contacts and liquor law changes, however, for the rise in criminal charges also coincides with an increase in the numbers of RCMP officers in our province due to a new Federal-Provincial agreement, and with a policy by the Department of Indian Affairs to encourage the migration of Indian people from their reserves to cities. In Manitoba as it is with most provinces, most aboriginal people appear in urban courts.

It is fair to say that aboriginal people generally regarded the courts of our country as tools of oppression and not as vehicles of dispute resolution and positive influence. The vast majority of aboriginal contacts with the justice system even today involve appearances in our criminal courts as accused or as parents of a young person charged with an offence, or as parents in our family courts fighting some child welfare agency who wishes to remove their children from the home. Aboriginal people do not go to our court system for relief from their civil and domestic problems. We are not providing the same type of service to them that other members of society receive. Civil and family disputes are resolved informally or not at all. Interestingly, geography has nothing to do with it: aboriginal people in urban areas are just as unlikely to make claims for relief in our civil and family courts as are aboriginal people in remote isolated communities.

Interestingly, despite the early belief on the part of those involved in the administration of justice as to its educational utility, there was generally little effort, outside of larger remote communities, to establish courts on Indian reserves until the 1960's and 70's. Indian people charged with offences were generally transported or were required to travel on their own to larger urban centres for court appearances. Though perhaps cost effective, the absence of a connection between the community and the process of dispute resolution undoubtedly led to further misunderstanding, and perhaps even mystery. We encountered several elderly people in our hearings in remote communities in Manitoba, who asked us to find out what happened to their child who had been arrested and taken away years ago, and whom they'd not seen again.

The absence of traditional leadership, the removal of tribal institutions and the lack of appropriate replacement with Canadian models or institutions led almost inevitably, in some places, to situations bordering on social chaos. To list the kinds of things that can go on in communities in which there are few effective social controls would be too depressing, but I am sure that you can well imagine what it is I am alluding to.

In a strange sort of way, this state of affairs — an almost direct result of the ethnocidal policies mentioned — reinforced the unspoken belief that Indian people were inherently inferior. The result of the practice confirmed its premise — a true self-fulfilling prophecy.

Finally, there is one other effect which I want to mention — and there are undoubtedly others but I only wanted to mention a few so as to give a flavor of what it is that the system faces — and that is what one can call a collective social depression. The phenomenon arose because many of the victims came to believe what the system was telling them.

The fact that the Government of Canada was officially opposed to aspects of Indian culture so basic to their continued survival as a unique people, was the catalyst for a pervasive belief among the rest of Canadian society that it was best for all native people to assimilate and surrender their "Indianness." Any attempt on the part of Indian people to resist doing so was dealt with harshly.

All aboriginal people were affected by this belief, Metis, Indian and Inuit, for Canadian society could not and would not distinguish between the variety of aboriginal groups in society.

Some aboriginal people who were the object of such policies actually came to believe the propaganda. Others, even if they did not believe it, at least would have sensed the futility of resistance and thereby sought passivity. Resistance very easily led to punishment, and any person who felt inclined to speak out would have very quickly found out that discretion was the better part of valour. There was silence, for the most part, from Indian people to the oppression they were under, at least until very recently. Why that was so can be the subject of another discussion, but the fact is that from the perspective of aboriginal people, for the past few generations, all levels of government have essentially "had their way" with aboriginal people. If one were to try to describe the Indian attitude to what was going on, one could easily describe it as individual passive resistance — an unwillingness to be co-opted as part of the system.

SYSTEMIC DISCRIMINATION AND CULTURAL BIAS — HOW THEY WORK

In an article entitled Books Without Bias — Through Indian Eyes, one of the editors states:

> Educated people are likely to have acquired most of their attitudes towards Indians from the writings of anthropologists, for whom Native societies are considered worthy of study insofar as they have preserved aspects of pre-conquest cultures. For them, contemporary Indians are, by and large, degenerate survivors of a more glorious past. The idea that such people may have meaningful contributions to make to the literature, is one that is received with scorn. At the same time, to be educated is to somehow become less "Indian"; to be successful is to find oneself dismissed as no longer "authentic."

One of the major issues with which we will have to come face to face, is the extent to which systemic discrimination plays a part in the problem of over-representation of aboriginal people in the justice system and the role played by cultural bias.

It is trite to say that aboriginal people have unique cultures and histories. Part of the unique history of aboriginal people in this country is the way in which the relationship of aboriginal people to the criminal justice system evolved. Indian people in Canada were not always subject to the same criminal laws as were other Canadians. It is possible, therefore, that from time to time the question of the historical application of the criminal law to Indian people may arise and it may in fact become relevant in future litigation.

It is apparent from the historical evidence that Canadian lawmakers made liberal use of criminal and quasi-criminal laws to curtail traditional aboriginal rights and customs. This fact, combined with the fact that for most of the history of the white man and the Indian in Canada Indians were not subject to the white man's laws, can be important for us to come to an understanding about how and why cases come before us, and perhaps can give us some inkling about how best to resolve them.

For example, Indian hunters and fishermen have often found themselves in conflict with the laws of the country concerning the exercise by them of what they view to be their traditional right to hunt and fish. In some jurisdictions the primary contact between aboriginal people and the justice system will be as a result of charges under the Fisheries Act, Migratory Birds Convention Act or Provincial Wildlife Legislation. One author writing about native legal issues stated:

> It is fair to say that for whole communities of native people in Canada one of their main contacts with the justice system has been a seemingly endless series of petty charges under the Fisheries Act or the Wildlife Acts. This pattern shows that Canadian law makers have failed to obtain consensus among native people with respect to the moral seriousness or validity of these offences. Even a generation ago the inappropriateness of this particular use of the criminal system was recognized.

In some instances, aboriginal accused have persisted in exercising their traditional hunting practises in the full knowledge that they will likely be prosecuted, but in the belief that their "right" should enjoy a legal status greater than the legislation.

More recently, and somewhat related, is the fact that civil disobedience is seen by some aboriginal people as a justifiable means to confront governments over longstanding disputes.

To a large extent, one might think that there is little which we as judges can do to alter the facts which confront us. After all, we do not arrest and charge the aboriginal accused, nor do we prosecute or defend him or her. We would appear to be at the tail end of an unfortunate process and, while we may have strong influence within our sphere, our sphere is somewhat limited.

That isn't necessarily true.

Canadian jurisprudence eventually concluded, — not without some difficulty and some might say questionable legal maneuvering — that aboriginal people generally, and Canadian Indians specifically, were subject to the criminal laws of Canada. However, in the past twenty years or so judicial efforts to come to grips with aboriginal people and aboriginal issues nationally and internationally have been greater than at any time in the past. Cases recognizing aboriginal cultures as factors in mitigation of sentence begin in Saskatchewan in 1966. In Australia, they begin at about the same time.

THE ANUNGA RULE AND ABORIGINAL CONFESSIONS

Probably one of the more perplexing issues which will arise in the course of dealing with aboriginal accused has to do with the admissibility of confessions. The rules relating to the admissibility of statements by accused persons have been developed to provide protection to an accused so that only those statements which are given freely and voluntarily and with the full knowledge and appreciation of one's legal rights, including a full appreciation of the right not to give a statement, are admissible.

Despite these general safeguards, aboriginal people, particularly those in remote communities and those whose primary language is not English, appear to have special problems in exercising their right to remain silent and to refrain from incriminating themselves. Their statements appear to be particularly open to being misunderstood by police interrogators and when read out in court. Their vulnerability arises from the legal system's inability to break down the barriers to effective communication between aboriginal people and legal personnel, differences of language, etiquette, concepts of time and distance and so on. In an Australian case, *R* v. *Anunga and others*, Forster J., made the following statements:

> ... aboriginal people often do not understand English very well and that even if they do under-

stand the words, they may not understand the concepts which English phrases and sentences express. Even with the use of interpreters this problem is by no means solved. Police (terminology) and legal English some times is not translatable into the aboriginal languages at all and there are no separate aboriginal words for some simple words like "in," "at," "on," "by," "with," or "over," these being suffixes added to the word they qualify. Some words may translate literally into aboriginal language but mean something different. "Did you go into his house?" means to an English speaking person "Did you go into the building?" But to an aboriginal it may also mean, "Did you go within the fence surrounding the house?" English concepts of time, number and distance are imperfectly understood, if at all, by aboriginal people, many of ... whom cannot tell the time by a clock. One frequently hears the answer, "long time," which depending on the context may be minutes, hours, days, weeks or years. In case I may be misunderstood, I should also emphasize that I am not expressing the view that aboriginal people are any less intelligent than white people but simply that their concepts of certain things and the terms in which they are expressed may only be different to those of white people.

Another matter which needs to be understood is that most aboriginal people are basically courteous and polite and will answer questions by white people in the way in which they think the questioner wants. Even if they are not courteous and polite there is the same reaction when they are dealing with an authority figure such as a policeman. Indeed, their action is probably a combination of natural politeness and their attitude to someone in authority. Some aboriginal people find a standard caution quite bewildering, even if they understand that they do not have to answer questions, because, if they do not have to answer questions, then why are the questions being asked?

In recognition of the conflict between the cultures, Forster J. established a number of rules with which police authorities must comply in order to convince the court that the statement was indeed given freely and voluntarily. One would think that it is only a matter of time until similar principles are announced by a Canadian court.

Probably the single greatest impetus toward the establishment of judicial credibility among Canada's aboriginal population, however, is the pronouncement by the Supreme Court of Canada in the case of *R. v. Nowegijick* that rights afforded to Indians were to be given a "fair large and liberal interpretation" and that doubtful wording was to be resolved in favour of the Indians. As well, treaty provisions and other agreements between the Indians and Her Majesty were to be interpreted "as the Indians would have understood them." Such pronouncements encouraged aboriginal leaders to begin to look to the courts for redress of their grievances and protection of their unique rights — a direction theretofore never highly regarded by them.

We are only now beginning to realize the possibility that perhaps what is most wrong with the way that the administration of justice is dealing with aboriginal people is not the presence of overt discrimination, but the presence of accidental, or unconscious discrimination. Systemic discrimination is not a particularly well understood phenomenon — its utility and application has so far been confined to the field of employment law and practices. But even drawing upon the various legal analogies which arise from the field of employment law, one can come to some small understanding of what is meant by systemic discrimination.

I am often asked, what is systemic discrimination. The answer to that is not an easy one to grasp for it requires an acceptance of and a respect for "invisibility." Unlike racism or prejudice, or blatant discrimination, systemic discrimination is discrimination which arises from the application of "unseen forces" at play within or by an institution or system. The existence of the discrimination arises not because we can see or hear discrimination in action, but because it creates impacts, results, or effects which are clearly unfair or which disclose unfairness. Systemic discrimination has also been called "unconscious discrimination" or "unintentional discrimination" — primarily because we are usually unaware of what we are doing, and generally do not intend to discriminate.

Simply put, systemic discrimination is discrimination which arises from the adverse impact upon an identifiable group within society by the systematic application of supposedly neutral criteria. Discrimination is by definition, adverse selection.

A good example of systemic discrimination with which we are all familiar involves the height and weight restrictions employed by many police departments in past years for their recruits. Height and weight requirements are neither gender nor racially-based. However, the imposition of height and weight restrictions had the effect of eliminating most women and many visible minorities from applying. Neutral criteria, when applied, had an adverse impact upon particular groups. And while one could not argue with the wish of police forces to have members who could withstand the physical demands of the work, it was universally recognized that there were better ways of achieving the goal (i.e. physical durability) without utilizing standards which had an unfair impact. As well, the automatic usage within our courts of the Christian Bible when witnesses are called forward to testify requires that non-Christians or others who hold legitimate and different beliefs, state their objections publicly to so swearing. Placing the onus on such persons is both unnecessary and unfair.

Within the administration of justice, the statistical evidence of over-representation by aboriginal people in our institutions is a fair indication that the system's use of its criteria for client selection and method of treatment warrant review. Simply put, evidence of adverse impact, in the absence of any reasonable and proven alternative explanation, is proof of systemic discrimination.

In addition, where reference is made to criteria which supposedly cross all racial, cultural and gender-based lines, and there is still an adverse impact, it strikes me that it is quite fair to look behind the criteria and determine whether the use of the criteria in question is essential to obtain the desired result. In some employment cases, for example, the use of educational standards, if found to be systematically eliminating identifiable groups within society, may have to be eliminated, especially if it can be shown that the degree to which educational resources are provided to members of visible minority groups or men and women, differs.

In the United States, for example, in the mid-70s the Supreme Court ruled that an employer's requirement that all employee applicants had to meet a minimum educational standard before being hired was discriminatory against black people, as the evidence showed that educational opportunities and resources had been denied to black people in the state for years, and as a result the vast majority of black people would be unable to meet the standard. The educational standard itself was not essential for the performance of many of the tasks required of many of the employees, so it was not a bona fide occupational qualification. The application of a seemingly neutral criterion had an adverse impact on an identifiable minority group in society and, therefore, was discriminatory.

In the course of our Inquiry, we have been told — by non-aboriginal people I might add — that the problem which the justice system faces insofar as aboriginal people are concerned is not a problem stemming from race, but rather is a problem stemming from socio-economic circumstances. The justice system, we have been told, does not discriminate against persons because of their race, but rather, if there is any discrimination, then it is against people at the lower end of the social and economic scales. All poor people we are told, get the shaft — not just the Indians.

There may be a grain of truth to that but, personally, despite its appeal, I have some difficulty with that argument. If that argument holds true then theoretically, there should be some relationship between the proportion of aboriginal people in our institutions and the proportion of aboriginal people living in poverty. If aboriginal people represent 60% of our jail population in Manitoba, then they must, roughly at least, represent 60% of the poor population; if they represent 8–9% of the national prison population, then they must roughly represent 8–9% of the poor people in Canada — but they don't. In addition, aboriginal women represent over 70% of the population of the women's jail in Manitoba, yet we can be reasonably confident that they do not represent an equivalent percentage of women living in poverty in Manitoba. The fact is that, despite the high degree of poverty among Indian people, there are still a lot more poor white people than there are poor Indians. The justice system may indeed draw disproportionately from the impoverished and the desperate, but there appears to be an added factor for aboriginal people, and frankly I believe that it arises from the kinds of things I have been discussing.

It is, actually, rather surprising to note that there has been little attention given to the role of cultural or ethnic bias in the justice system.

There is no question but that there exists within all of us biases and influences of which we are all unaware, and which cause us to behave and think in certain ways, sometimes to the detriment of others in society. Your education in the public school system, universities, and law schools of this country was permeated with the ethnocidal beliefs about aboriginal people I have spoken about. Mine was too. The difference between us is that I had elders, and aunts and uncles and grandparents to whom I could turn to straighten me out because they knew the truth. You, unfortunately, didn't.

The information and research on gender bias tells us that it is bias which arises from our upbringing and develops subliminally — almost unconsciously. The predominance of men among the judiciary has fostered gender bias, we are told, and unless we as judges make an effort to recognize it, gender bias can go undetected. If we as judges do not take control of issues such as gender bias, and begin to change some of our patterns of thought and action which are reflective of it, then change will be forced upon us by outside interest groups.

The same is true for cultural or ethnic bias as well. We must begin to question whether we are able to deliver ourselves to the judicial process free from influences which are culturally in conflict with the aboriginal accused with whom we deal. Very little has been written in this area, but what little exists, suggests that we judges need to do more work.

I'd like to conclude this portion of my presentation by leaving you with something to think about.

It is important that the judiciary come to as full an understanding as is possible about the importance aboriginal people place on their culture and traditions. Sometimes the most difficult aspect of communicating the importance of aboriginal culture to other people lies in the fact that there is an almost insurmountable gulf in our relative experiences as peoples.

Professor Bruce Sealey who for years was a Professor of Education at the University of Manitoba, a Metis and a personal friend, also used to conduct cultural training sessions for the new recruits of the RCMP at the training depot in Regina, Saskatchewan. He told me that he used to begin his sessions with the following scenario in an effort to get the recruits to relate to the aboriginal situation in Canada. With thanks and acknowledgement to him for his ideas, allow me to do the same.

Imagine if you can, that Canada suddenly experienced a ten-fold increase in its population as a result of the increased immigration of millions of new people. California seems to be going through that scenario right now. It wouldn't be hard to imagine the clashes that would arise between the Newcomers and the original Canadians. If you can, imagine that the Newcomers came from a culture totally different from Canadian culture, and because of their superior numbers were not only able to continue to practice their cultural ways but were soon dominating cultural institutions such as television, radios, books, newspapers, etc.

As well, imagine if you can that these Newcomers believed totally in an entirely different way of landholding, with title to the land, for example, vesting in the group and no individual able to own any land individually.

In addition, their cultural influences would dominate the workplace, new holidays might have to be set aside to accommodate their religious holidays. Changes to our own ways of doing things might have to change if nobody showed up for work on Tuesdays for example, because that was their "day of rest" and in addition all Newcomers wanted to work on Sundays. Our own eating and sleeping patterns might have to be changed to accommodate their different work habits. They might soon take over the legislative and judicial functioning of the country and the result would be that the original Canadian people will have soon lost their position of relative importance in society. To say that there would be conflicts would be an understatement.

A very real threat would clearly seem to arise and that would be that the Newcomers' customs and beliefs could become constitutionally and legislatively the standard applied to all. The way of life of the original Canadian would be threatened.

Think, for just a moment, about how Canadians could legitimately respond to that. If rebellion is not seen as the only avenue of response, then other means suggest themselves.

One way to protect Canadian life and identity would be to ask for there to be guarantees in writing that the way of life of the original Canadian people would not be interfered with, that Canadians could be guaranteed the right to continue to be Canadians, that they would be guaranteed that right within defined territories, and that the Newcomers would not try to interfere with those rights or take away their land. If the Newcomers agreed, a deal could be signed.

If you as original Canadians are smart, then you would want some legal protection for those rights, and though the Newcomers assure you that legislative or constitutional provisions are unnecessary, you insist. So they are enacted.

So you've got your deal in writing protecting your landholdings and assurances that you will no be interfered with in your territories. You've got your legislative and constitutional protections for your deal, so everything seems okay.

But wait a minute!

Imagine that a few months after the deal is signed, the Newcomers pass a law saying that despite what is in the agreement you will still have to abide by their religious feasts and holidays and accommodate yourselves to them. In addition, the law states that any Canadian children born in the future must be educated in the Newcomers' schools by the Newcomers' teachers. They must, in addition, learn to speak "Newcomese" and dress in accordance with the Newcomers' fashions. In addition, the law states that if the newborn Canadian child marries a Newcomer then the Canadian child loses all rights under the deal signed earlier and must live as a Newcomer, and cannot live in Canadian territories.

So what do you do?

Well, like any good contemporary and right-thinking Canadian, and following Canadian cultural practices and traditions, you would have hire a lawyer to go to court and fight the law, right?

But the new law states that if you want to hire a lawyer, it has to be a lawyer approved by the Newcomer's lawyers society and it has to be one approved by the Newcomer's Minister of Canadian Affairs. With a combined air of fairness and confidence in the outcome, he approves of the one you wish to hire and off you go to court.

In court you find that the judge is a Newcomer. The jury (who are required to decide the case) consists entirely of Newcomers, the lawyers are all Newcomers (including yours) and the laws that govern the case, including the rules of procedure in the court, have been enacted by authorities controlled by the Newcomers.

Do you feel that you are going to get justice? Maybe you will, and then again, maybe you won't; but don't you feel just a little bit powerless in influencing — never mind predicting — the outcome? More importantly, don't you feel that the "playing field" is not level — that it has just become just a little bit tilted? If you do, and if you can accept that all of what I have described can be done quite legally, then you have an inkling of how aboriginal people in this country feel and how systemic discrimination can and does work. Maybe, if you can appreciate the fact that what has just occurred in your imagination is a daily occurrence in the vast majority of aboriginal communities of Canada, then you might also be able to appreciate why it is that aboriginal accused appear to be overly charged, overly incarcerated, plead guilty disproportionately, and appear to ignore or fail to respect (whatever your viewpoint) our court orders, sentences and processes. We have a lot of work to do.

There is no question in my mind but that one of the most significant causes of adverse impact upon aboriginal people by the justice system lies in the fact that to this point the culture of the justice system has been a white, middle-class male culture that has not yet learned how to recognize and overcome its own momentum and inertia.

CONCLUSION

The thrust of my presentation is to try to assist in overcoming the gulfs which exists between the judiciary and aboriginal people, and, I hope, to assist in some small way to formulate a process which can assist our courts and the aboriginal people of our provinces to establish lines of effective and meaningful communication. I hope that our courts can grow in ways that are the best for the administration of justice and result in a more effective system for all concerned.

There is no question but that the judiciary wants to be more effective as judges. Many of us feel a degree of frustration at the almost helpless feeling with which we leave our court settings in aboriginal communities or where, having had to render a decision concerning an aboriginal accused, we are just not certain we have received all of the relevant information or taken all of the right matters into proper consideration.

I know that the members of the judiciary in attendance here today will nod their heads in agreement when I say to the non-judiciary in attendance, that we as judges **do** care about the people who appear before us and we **do** care about the impact we are having on the communities we serve. As judges we like to go home at night and wake up in the morning thinking that we are making a difference and that we are having a positive impact on our society.

WHAT CAN WE BE DOING?

We know that there are problems with the way that aboriginal people are dealt with in the justice system, but you may well ask, what can we as judges be doing about it? Let me make a few suggestions.

Firstly, we need to establish ways and means for us to identify and eliminate cultural bias in the judicial process — at least to the extent that we can influence that bias. I have no doubt that we will be very influential when it comes to doing that on a general basis.

Secondly, let us begin to learn about the various tribes in our provinces and let us begin to communicate with them. Bridges between our courts and the aboriginal communities need to be built.

Thirdly, let us establish and maintain ongoing cross-cultural awareness that benefits both our judges and the aboriginal communities where our judges have influence. This means going to the land of the aboriginal people, seeing how their communities function and how we influence what goes on. In addition, we should attend, where possible, tribal gatherings and functions. Our judges must quite frankly learn the history, customs, and values of the tribes of our area in such a way that we never have to wonder what the community thinks of how we are doing our work, for we will feel like we are, at least, a small part of that community.

Fourthly, let us include the aboriginal community in our court processes. We do not need to engage in much elaborate thinking to do so. We can look to both common law and common sense for the authority to do so. England, as you might imagine, with its long history of expansionism and colonialism, had well-established forms of tribal involvement with the judicial process in its colonies in Africa, Australia and New Zealand. The involvement of the community can range from sentencing advisory panels to judicial functioning. One's limits are determined more by one's inclination than by anything else. Certainly sentencing practices which are community approved and sanctioned will have a greater impact upon the accused and the rest of the tribe than do our current isolationist practices. That is, after all, the real goal of what we are trying to achieve.

As part of that process, we should encourage the establishment of appropriate court sittings in as many aboriginal communities as seems to make the most sense. To the fullest extent possible, aboriginal people should have their legal issues dealt with in their own communities so that both the accused and the community derive the greatest benefit.

Finally, we should begin to acknowledge and sanction ways that the community itself can be performing some of the functions which are currently left to us. Recognizing that we are not necessarily the be all and end all of justice in the world of aboriginal people may be the most important step that we can take.

Thank you.

Royal Commission on the Donald Marshall, Jr. Prosecution: Digest of Findings and Recommendations[†]

The criminal justice system failed Donald Marshall, Jr. at virtually every turn from his arrest and wrongful conviction for murder in 1971 up to, and even beyond, his acquittal by the Court of Appeal in 1983. The tragedy of the failure is compounded by evidence that this miscarriage of justice could — and should — have been prevented, or at least corrected quickly, if those involved in the system had carried out their duties in a professional and/or competent manner. That they did not is due, in part at least, to the fact that Donald Marshall, Jr. is a Native.

These are the inescapable, and inescapably distressing, conclusions this Royal Commission has reached after sifting through 16,390 pages of transcript evidence given by 113 witnesses during 93 days of public hearings in Halifax and Sydney in 1987 and 1988; after examining 176 exhibits submitted in evidence during those hearings; after listening to two-and-one-half days of presentations by experts on the criminal justice system's treatment of Blacks and Natives and on the role of the office of Attorney General in that system; and after examining five volumes of research material prepared for the Royal Commission by leading academics and researchers.

The Royal Commission on the Donald Marshall, Jr. Prosecution was not established, however, just to determine whether one individual was the victim of a miscarriage of justice, or even to get to the bottom of how and why that miscarriage occurred. The Nova Scotia Government, which appointed this Royal Commission on October 28, 1986, also asked us to "make recommendations" to help prevent such tragedies from happening in the future.

As a result, our final Report contains not only findings of "fact" concerning the Marshall affair, but also specific recommendations dealing with everything from the role of police and Crown prosecutors in the criminal justice system, ways to ensure more equitable treatment of Blacks and Natives in the criminal justice system, and new mechanisms to deal with cases in which there are allegations of wrongful conviction.

. . . .

Shortly before midnight on May 28, 1971, Donald Marshall, Jr., a 17-year-old Micmac, and Sandy Seale, a 17-year-old Black, met by chance and were walking through Wentworth Park in Sydney when they met two other men, Roy Ebsary, 59, a former ship's cook, and James (Jimmy) MacNeil, 25, an unemployed labourer.

[†] T. Alexander Hickman, Lawrence A. Poitras, and Gregory T. Evans, *Royal Commission on the Donald Marshall, Jr. Prosecution: Digest of Findings and Recommendations* (Halifax: McCurdy's Printing and Typesetting Ltd., 1989) at 1–8.

Following a brief conversation, Marshall and/or Seale tried to "panhandle" Ebsary and MacNeil. That simple request — the kind most of us have encountered at one time or another — triggered a deadly over-reaction in the drunken and dangerous Ebsary. "This is for you, Black man," Ebsary said, and stabbed Seale in the stomach. He then lunged at Marshall, cutting him on the arm. Although Marshall's wound was superficial, Seale died less than a day later.

The Commissioners have found that Seale was not killed during the course of a robbery or attempted robbery. Seale, who came from a strict family and was expected home before his midnight curfew, had enough money to catch a bus home. We heard no evidence during our hearings to indicate that he had ever been involved in any criminal activity. Although Marshall had had a few brushes with the law, they were of a minor nature and did not involve theft. Roy Ebsary, on the other hand, had a reputation for violence and unpredictable behaviour, and had previously been convicted on a weapons charge involving a knife.

In our view, Seale and Marshall, who barely knew one another, would not have had the time or the inclination to plan a robbery in the few moments between their accidental meeting and the stabbing. According to the evidence we heard, they didn't even initiate the fateful conversation with MacNeil and Ebsary that ended in the stabbing.

The four Sydney police officers who initially responded to the report of the stabbing — Constables Leo Mroz, Howard Dean, Richard Walsh and Martin MacDonald — did not do a professional job. They did not cordon off the crime scene, search the area or question witnesses. In fact, none of the four officers dispatched to the scene even remained there to protect the area after Seale had been taken to the hospital. We found their conduct entirely inadequate, incompetent and unprofessional.

The same can be said of the subsequent police investigation directed by then Sergeant of Detectives John MacIntyre. MacIntyre very quickly decided that Marshall had stabbed Seale in the course of an argument, even though there was no evidence to support such a conclusion. MacIntyre discounted Marshall's version of events partly because he considered Marshall a troublemaker and partly because, in our view, he shared what we believe was a general sense in Sydney's White community at the time that Indians were not "worth" as much as Whites.

Regardless of the reasons for his conclusions, MacIntyre's investigation seemed designed to seek out only evidence to support his theory about the killing and to discount all evidence that challenged it.

The most damning evidence against Marshall came from two teenaged "eyewitnesses," Maynard Chant, a 14-year-old who was on probation in connection with a minor criminal offence, and John Pratico, a mentally unstable 16-year-old whose psychiatrist later testified that he was known to fantasize and invent stories to make himself the centre of attention.

Shortly after Seale died, both youths gave statements to MacIntyre. Chant, although he had seen nothing, generally corroborated Marshall's version of events, while Pratico claimed to have seen two men running away from the stabbing scene. A few days later, however, they both gave contradictory second statements to MacIntyre. Pratico claimed he had seen Marshall stab Seale during an argument. Chant said he had also heard the argument and seen the stabbing. He placed a "dark-haired fellow" — presumably Pratico — in the bushes near where the stabbing took place.

None of this, as we now know, was true. The information in these second statements came from Pratico and Chant accepting suggestions John MacIntyre made to them. His attempt to build a case against Marshall that conformed to his theory about what had happened went far beyond the bounds of acceptable police behaviour. MacIntyre took Pratico, an impressionable, unstable teenager, to a murder scene, offered the youth his own version of events and then persuaded Pratico to accept that version as the basis for what became Pratico's detailed and incriminating statement. MacIntyre then pressured Chant, who was on probation and frightened about being sent to jail, into not only corroborating Pratico's statement, but also into putting Pratico at the scene of the crime. MacIntyre's oppressive tactics in questioning these and other juvenile witnesses were totally unacceptable.

Largely because of the untrue statements MacIntyre had obtained, Donald Marshall, Jr. was charged on June 4, 1971 with murdering Sandy Seale.

While the perjured evidence of Chant and Pratico did prove damning in court, we have concluded [that] Marshall's wrongful conviction resulted as well from the failure of others — including both the Crown prosecutor and Marshall's own defence counsel — to discharge their professional obligations. The Crown prosecutor, Donald C. MacNeil, should have interviewed the witnesses who had given contradictory statements. He did not. He should also have disclosed the contents of those earlier inconsistent statements to the defence. He did not.

Marshall's defence counsel, for their part, failed to provide an adequate standard of professional representation to their client — C.M. (Moe) Rosenblum and Simon Khattar, who had access to whatever financial resources they required, conducted no independent investigation, interviewed no Crown witnesses and failed to ask for disclosure of the Crown's case against their client. Even though, prior to the trial, they were aware that some witnesses had provided earlier statements, they made no effort to obtain them.

During the course of the trial, the trial judge, Mr. Justice Louis Dubinsky, made several errors in law. The most serious of those was his misinterpretation of the *Canada Evidence Act* which prevented a thorough examination of Pratico's dramatic recanting of his statement against Marshall outside the courtroom. The cumulative effect of all of this was that Donald Marshall, Jr. was convicted and sentenced to life in prison.

Just ten days after Marshall's conviction, however, Jimmy MacNeil came forward to tell police that he had seen Ebsary stab Seale. At the request of the Sydney City Police Department and the Department of [the] Attorney General, the RCMP looked into MacNeil's allegations, but the officer in charge of that investigation, in his own words, "botched" it.

Inspector Alan Marshall did not demand to see the Sydney City Police Department's entire file on the Seale case, did not interview Ebsary, Marshall, Chant or Pratico, and did not even speak to Jimmy MacNeil, except briefly in connection with the taking of a polygraph test. Instead, he relied almost exclusively on the results of those polygraph tests, on what MacIntyre himself had told him about the case, and on his own innate faith in the workings of the criminal justice system. Based on an incompetent and incomplete investigation, Inspector Marshall filed a report that claimed to be "a thorough review of the case," and concluded that Marshall had stabbed Seale.

The fact that MacNeil had come forward with this new and potentially important information was not disclosed to Marshall's defence counsel nor to the Halifax Crown counsel assigned to handle Marshall's appeal of his conviction. As a result, this information was never presented to the Court of Appeal. If it had been, we believe it is all but inevitable that a new trial would have been ordered.

This, however, is not the only important issue that was not brought to the attention of the Court of Appeal. Neither Marshall's counsel nor Crown counsel raised the issue of the trial judge's erroneous rulings. And the Court of Appeal, which we believe had a duty to review the complete trial record to ensure that all relevant issues were argued, did not identify the significant errors. We believe that the trial judge's errors were so fundamental that the Court of Appeal would inevitably have ordered a new trial if it had been aware of those errors. Unfortunately, however, these issues were not raised by counsel or identified by the Court of Appeal and Marshall's appeal was denied.

Despite that, the case resurfaced on a number of occasions after the failure of the appeal. In 1974, for example, Roy Ebsary's daughter, Donna confided to a friend that she had seen her father washing what appeared to be blood from his knife on the night of the murder. When she and the friend went to the Sydney City Police Department with this information, however, they were told by one of the key officers in the original Marshall investigation, Detective William Urquhart, that the case was closed. We believe Urquhart had a duty to pass this information on to his superior officer who in turn would have had an obligation to pass it on to the Crown. The Crown, for its part, would have then had an obligation to provide it to Marshall's counsel, who could have pursued the matter further.

In the end, Marshall's innocence only became apparent as the result of an almost accidental series of coincidences. While in prison in 1981 Marshall learned that Ebsary had admitted killing Seale. On the basis of that information, Marshall's new lawyer, Stephen Aronson, following his own review of the matter, asked police in January 1982 to reopen the case.

Although the RCMP officers assigned to the reinvestigation, Staff Sergeant Harry Wheaton and Corporal James Carroll, were initially skeptical of Marshall's innocence, they did what Inspector Marshall had not done in 1971 — they conducted a painstaking, professional investigation. They not only interviewed all of the appropriate witnesses — including Maynard Chant, John Pratico, Roy Ebsary and Marshall himself — but they also gathered the physical evidence that indicated that Ebsary's knife had been used to stab Sandy Seale.

This is not to suggest that we believe everything about the 1982 investigation was handled well. We believe the RCMP officers should not have suggested to Marshall during their interview with him in Dorchester Penitentiary that Marshall had better tell them a story they could believe or they would leave and never return, or that they believed "there was something else going on in the park other than just a casual walk through the park to catch a bus."

That led Marshall who, it must be remembered, had spent 11 years in jail unsuccessfully protesting his innocence, to go along with what he already knew was Roy Ebsary's version of events — that the stabbing had occurred in the course of an attempted robbery. Marshall's statement, which we believe would not have been regarded as voluntary and therefore would not have been admitted into evidence in court if Marshall were on trial, was used to devastating effect against him during the later Court of Appeal Reference hearing. We have also concluded that Harry Wheaton, like John MacIntyre, became blinded by his own assumptions during the course of his investigation. Wheaton believed Marshall had been victimized by MacIntyre, who he considered an "unscrupulous" police officer. As a result, Wheaton incorrectly accused MacIntyre of deliberately concealing evidence and erroneously suggested that the Department of [the] Attorney General attempted to interfere in the RCMP investigation by restricting their efforts to interview key members of the Sydney City Police Department.

In fact, we believe the RCMP's own sensitivity to its relations with the Sydney City Police Department and the Department of Attorney General was at the heart of its failure to fully pursue the investigation of the Sydney City Police Department's role in the Marshall case.

Wheaton's credibility as a witness was further tarnished when, during his testimony, he made a number of unsolicited comments about matters that were unrelated to the work of this Commission and which cast unwarranted aspersions on the reputation of an individual.

Nonetheless, it is fair to say that the investigative work by Wheaton and Carroll did lead directly to Justice Minister Jean Chrétien's decision to refer the Marshall case to the Nova Scotia Court of Appeal for hearing and determination. While we believe that the Court of Appeal could have been an appropriate forum to examine why Marshall had been wrongfully convicted, we have also concluded that the decision to hold the Reference under what was then Section 617(b) [now Section 690(b)] of the *Criminal Code* instead of Section 617(c) [now Section 690(c)] precluded such a wide-ranging examination.

We find it regrettable that the federal Justice Minister was influenced in this decision by the views of the Chief Justice of Nova Scotia, Mr. Justice Ian MacKeigan, who expressed "real concern over whether [a reference under Section 617(b)] would work." As a result of this decision, Marshall was not only put in the position where he was required to prove his own innocence, but the issue placed before the Court was narrowed to the simple question of whether Marshall was guilty or innocent of the charges against him.

We have serious concerns with certain aspects of the Reference hearing and the decision itself.

Mr. Justice Leonard Pace, who was the Attorney General of Nova Scotia at the time of the original Marshall trial and appeal, should not have sat as a member of the panel hearing the Reference. (It is important to note that the Commission asked to question members of the Court of Appeal about this and other matters relating to the Reference hearing and decision, but they declined to testify before us on the grounds of judicial immunity. The courts upheld their refusal to testify, and so our comments about the Reference are based only on the information available to us from the court records and Chief Justice MacKeigan's letter of transmittal to the Justice Minister.)

While the Court did quash Marshall's conviction and enter a verdict of acquittal, it also inexplicably chose to blame Marshall for his wrongful conviction. We have concluded that the Court's conclusion in this regard represented a serious and fundamental error. The Court used the evidence before it — as well as information that was never admitted into evidence — to "convict" Marshall of a robbery with which he was never charged, and concluded, in our view erroneously, that Marshall had "admittedly" committed perjury. The Court's further suggestion that Marshall's "untruthfulness ... contributed in large measure to his conviction" was not sustained by the evidence before the Court.

At the same time, the Court did not deal with either the significant lack of disclosure by the Crown prior to Marshall's original trial, or the reasons for the perjured "eyewitness" testimony, nor did it deal with the trial judge's error in limiting the cross-examination of Pratico.

We have concluded that the Court's decision amounted to a defence of the criminal justice system at the expense of Donald Marshall, Jr. in spite of overwhelming evidence that the system itself had failed.

The Court of Appeal's gratuitous comments about Marshall's responsibility for his own conviction and its conclusion that any miscarriage of justice was more apparent [than] real played a critically important role in Marshall's negotiations with the Department of Attorney General for compensation for his wrongful conviction. The Supreme Court of Canada commented on this influence in the course of its 1989 decision on judicial immunity. Within the Department of Attorney General, the Marshall case was not handled with the care and respect for fairness that it demanded.

Much of the blame for this must rest with Deputy Attorney General Gordon Coles. He failed to recognize the unique and tragic aspects of the Marshall case, and effectively prevented his Department from treating Marshall with the appropriate respect [or] fairness.

When Coles did take action in the Marshall case, those actions were often inappropriate. For example, he should not have engaged in unilateral correspondence with counsel to the Campbell Commission, the Royal Commission which the Province had appointed to determine appropriate compensation for Marshall. Also, he should not have urged Crown prosecutor Frank Edwards to take no position with regard to Marshall's guilt or innocence when Edwards appeared before the Court of Appeal Reference hearing.

Although Edwards must be commended for his refusal to back down from his position that he would urge the Court to acquit Marshall, he too acted improperly in arguing that the criminal justice system was in no way responsible for Marshall's wrongful conviction at a time when he knew such a position was not supported by facts.

That argument, as we noted above, was adopted by the Court of Appeal and became an important factor in determining the amount of compensation paid Marshall. We believe that the Province's reliance on those comments — as well as the failure of senior officials within the Department of Attorney General to instruct their negotiator to treat the Marshall case as a unique situation rather than simply another civil dispute to be settled as cheaply as possible — made the compensation process itself flawed and unfair. We believe, as we stated earlier, that the Government should now reconsider the issue of compensation in light of the facts as we have found them.

Neither the Court of Appeal's decision nor the settlement of the compensation issue put to rest public concern about the Marshall case. Shortly after the Supreme Court of Canada turned down an appeal by Roy Ebsary — who had been convicted of manslaughter in 1985 after three trials — the Government of Nova Scotia appointed this Royal Commission in October 1986 to look into the matter and to make recommendations to the Governor in Council.

. . . .

In the process of investigating the specifics of [this] case, we were confronted with a number of more general but no less troubling questions. Was the original Sydney police investigation inadequate, incompetent and unprofessional because the police were inadequately trained? Because they were poorly managed? What should be the role of the Crown prosecutor, defence counsel, and officials in the Department of Attorney General in ensuring the "justness" of the criminal justice system? Should the Attorney General be responsible for both the provincial policing function and the administration of justice? Is the criminal justice system inherently biased against minorities and the poor? Should there be specific mechanisms in place to deal with allegations of wrongful conviction and imprisonment? We approached these issues from a number of different perspectives.

During our hearings, we examined the way in which the criminal justice system treated certain high profile individuals who were the subjects of criminal investigations. We compared their treatment with that accorded Donald Marshall, Jr. and used that examination as a basis to assess whether the system treats all citizens equally.

■

The recommendations of the Marshall Commission were extensive and dealt with such issues as:

- processes for the wrongfully convicted
- visible minorities in the criminal justice system
- Nova Scotia Micmacs and the criminal justice system
- Blacks in the criminal justice system
- administration of criminal justice
- police and policing
- prosecutorial independence

For a full summary of those recommendations, see *Royal Commission on the Donald Marshall, Jr. Prosecution: Digest of Findings and Recommendations*, which includes the individual briefs and submissions to the Commission.

Donald Marshall was incarcerated for fifteen years for a murder he did not commit. As even the Marshall Commission concludes, the miscarriage of justice should have been prevented or corrected at any one of numerous points in the criminal justice system. In the immediate aftermath of the release of the report, the main protagonists responded with expressions of remorse and contrition. For example, in "The Aftermath of the Marshall Commission: A Preliminary Opinion" (1990) 13 Dalhousie L. J. 364, Archibald Kaiser notes the following responses, among others:

Government of N.S.: Release of 58 page report (7 February 1990) accepting all recommendations of the Marshall Inquiry that are its responsibility and endorsing all others; request to Canadian Judicial Council to review conduct of the judges of the Nova Scotia Supreme Court, Appellate Division.

N.S. Barrister's Society: Promise to review conduct of lawyers condemned by the Inquiry; support for Indigenous Black and Micmac programs at Dalhousie [Law faculty]; changes to Bar Admissions course to deal with systemic racism.

RCMP: Expression of "sincere regret"; promise to establish community outreach such as a native advisory committee.

N.S. Legislature: Passed motion of sincere apology for "grievous injustice" to Mr. Marshall and his family.

Micmac community: Support for recommendations, but concern regarding the failure to recommend laying of charges against police, the failure to set guidelines for compensation, and the failure to criticize Ministers.

Black community: Call for inquiry into racism in the N.S. education system, for a Black and Micmac committee to monitor implementation of recommendations, for strengthening of anti-discrimination mechanisms, and for compensation for the family of Sandy Seale.

Donald Marshall and family: Request for re-examination of compensation issue.

However, as Kaiser argues, the analysis by the Commission and the initial responses have been framed in a theoretical vacuum. Also, the issues the case raises are not isolated. Instead, they must be contextualized and politicized. The Marshall case is about more than the avoidance of wrongful conviction and, thus, formalistic changes alone will not address the problems the case raises. These issues are highlighted by the subsequent response of the justice system.

In another critical analysis of the responses of the Canadian justice system to Donald Marshall, Jr.'s wrongful conviction, H. Archibald Kaiser comments on the extension of judicial immunity by the Supreme Court of Canada to Justice MacKeigan (formerly of the Nova Scotia Court of Appeal) so as to block his subpoena to testify before the Marshall Commission: "[T]he Supreme Court [in *MacKeigan* v. *Hickman* (1989), 61 D.L.R. (4th) 688] determined that the principle of judicial independence is so crucial that it requires judges to be immune from testifying with respect to the grounds for their decision and the reasons for the composition of a given panel of the court": "Legitimation and Relative Autonomy: The Donald Marshall, Jr. Case in Retrospect" (1990) 10 Windsor Y.B. Access Just. 171 at 187.

The final figure for the total cost of the Marshall Commission was released in 1990: $5.7 million, excluding Mr. Marshall, Jr.'s compensation. The amount paid to the Marshall family on 5 July 1990 was $715,679, in addition to $270,000 the province awarded to Donald Marshall, Jr., over half of which went to his lawyers. For a breakdown of the monies paid to the various lawyers and publishers, see "Final Marshall figures in" *Micmac News* (June 1990) 6. With this new package, Donald Marshall, Jr. will receive more than $1 million in annuities over the next 30 years: Indian and Northern Affairs Communication, Press Release (17 July 1990).

One result of the Marshall Commission was the instigation of an inquiry into the conduct of the five justices of the Nova Scotia Court of Appeal to ascertain whether they should be removed from office pursuant to s. 65(2)(a) to (d) of the *Judges Act* on the basis of misconduct, having failed in the execution of the office, or having been placed in a position incompatible with the due execution of that office. Prior to the inquiry, two of the five justices, Leonard Pace and Ian MacKeigan, resigned from office: Susan Allen, "Appeal justices leave N.S. Bench prior to judicial council hearings" *The Lawyers Weekly* (27 April 1990) 16.

During the course of the hearings, counsel for the remaining justices, Gordon Henderson of Ottawa, returned to the victim-blaming strategy that has characterized the response of the legal system to Mr. Marshall, Jr.'s wrongful conviction. He argued that "by lying [Marshall] set in motion a chain of events which helped to convict him"; that "They (Marshall and Seale) certainly weren't collecting money for the Salvation Army"; that "there was no doubt ... that they were planning a robbery"; and that "The Royal Commission was wrong to conclude that this was just innocent panhandling — that they were just two innocents in the park looking at the stars": Editorial, Brian Douglas, "Donald Marshall is blamed again. Has nothing changed?" *Micmac News* (June 1990) 30.

David Nahwegahbow, an Ottawa lawyer, responded to Mr. Henderson's arguments in a letter to the editor of *The Lawyers Weekly* (29 June 1990) 5: "[I]t is ... the responsibility of a lawyer to exercise some discretion and good judgment in the course of representing his [sic] clients." Concerns were also raised about whether Henderson was in a conflict of interest situation given that another lawyer at his firm had acted as agent to the Commission in litigation on whether the five justices could be compelled to testify at the inquiry: Douglas, "Donald Marshall is blamed again," *supra*. On 10 July 1990 after a three-hour closed-door session of the Canadian Judicial Council, Henderson withdrew from the case, although he maintained that he was not in a conflict of interest situation: Kevin Cox, "Judges' lawyer leaves probe of Marshall case" *The [Toronto] Globe and Mail* (11 July 1990) A5.

In October 1990, the Council "scathingly" condemned the five justices for committing serious legal error, using grossly inappropriate language, and for insensitivity to the injustice suffered by Mr. Marshall; they did not, however, remove them from the bench: Kevin Cox, "Marshall judges rebuked" *The [Toronto] Globe and Mail* (6 October 1990) A5.

Mary Ellen Turpel describes and criticizes this decision of the Inquiry Committee of the Canadian Judicial Council from her perspective as a First Nations woman: "The Judged and the Judging: Locating Innocence in a Fallen Legal World" (1991) 40 U.N.B.L.J. 281. She concludes that the legal system has been unrepentant in its response to both the injustice committed against Donald Marshall, Jr. and to the racism inflicted upon Aboriginal peoples through the criminal justice system. In addition, Joy Manette's edited collection, *Elusive Justice: Beyond the Marshall Inquiry* (Halifax: Fernwood, 1992) provides a critique of the way the Marshall Commission itself ignored the traditions, customs, and culture of the Micmac people.

Finally, alleging a lack of substantiation, RCMP investigators have declined to prosecute police chief McIntyre for his role in producing the false statements that implicated Donald Marshall, Jr.: CP, "RCMP won't charge ex-police chief who arrested Marshall" *The Ottawa Citizen* (27 October 1990) 4.

Thus, there has been a lack of penalty for anyone involved in the breaches of justice and professional conduct. Instead, the focus has been on formalistic changes. One of the formal changes has been the creation of an independent Director of Public Prosecutions and the *Public Prosecutions Act*, S.N.S. 1990, c. 21, discussed *infra*, **Powers of Prosecution**.

The Marshall Commission sparked calls for inquiries in other provinces, including Manitoba and Alberta. In April 1988, the Manitoba government, under Howard Pawley, established a Public Inquiry into the Administration of Justice and Aboriginal People. The Order-in-Council acknowledged that a Public Inquiry to investigate, report, and make recommendations about the relationship between the administration of justice and Aboriginal peoples was needed to respond to a number of concerns, such as:

> ... the death of J.J. Harper, the coverup of the rape of Betty Osborne ... [which] have raised concerns of systemic discrimination against aboriginal peoples in the administration of justice in Manitoba (Order-in-Council, No. 468, 13 April 1988).

The scope of the inquiry was broadly sketched, and the submissions made canvassed extensively the history and the present situation confronting Aboriginal peoples.

Submission to the Aboriginal Justice Inquiry†

> [We] have allowed ourselves to fall into the hands of a Government which only thinks of us to pillage us. Had [we] only understood what God did for us before Confederation, we should have been sorry to see it coming. And the half-breeds of the North-West would have made con-

---

† Excerpts from *The Struggle for Recognition*, edited by Samuel W. Corrigan and Lawrence J. Barkwell, pp. 151, 190–94 (Winnipeg, Man.: Pemmican Publication Inc., 1991). © The Manitoba Metis Federation. Reproduced by permission.

ditions of a nature to preserve for our children that liberty, that possession of the soil, without which there is no happiness for anyone; but fifteen years of suffering, impoverishment and underhand, malignant persecution have opened our eyes; and the sight of the abyss of demoralization into which the Dominion is daily plunging us deeper and deeper every day, has suddenly, by God's mercy as it were, stricken us with horror.

Louis Riel, March 1885

The plight of Metis and other aboriginal people in the criminal justice system has been well documented over the last three decades and thousands of pages of recommendations have been forth coming from the boards and commissions studying these social issues.

. . . .

The MMF justice committee members are appalled that the Attorney-General's report to the inquiry makes no attempt to analyze the status of aboriginal persons within the justice system. Having done no analysis, no substantive actions or initiatives are suggested. One would hope that they would at least be embarrassed to present the outcome figures they have produced (failure rates as high as 65% ...).

ASSESSMENT AND CONCLUSIONS

It has been the recurring theme of this submission that white people keep making decisions about and for aboriginal people. The Manitoba Metis Federation research and analysis of the impact of the justice system on the Metis is ultimately, a study of the social control of aboriginal people within the contemporary state.

. . . .

Even a cursory overview of Metis history in Manitoba reveals that natural resource development and other capitalist ventures have fueled the exploitive relationship between Canada and the Metis Nation. This set of uneven exchanges has resulted in the damaging underdevelopment that indigenous people now experience, whether they be rural resident or urban migrants. The unfair application of the law has also degraded the relationship.

. . . .

These same forces have shaped the "corrections industry" where non-native job creation is pursued at the expense of justice for indigenous people — its ostensible reason for existence. The image of regular airlifts of highly paid white professionals into isolated communities to dispense justice, followed by the subsequent airlift out, of aboriginal offenders to fill large urban institutions, is an image that the MMF finds distasteful.

. . . .

The MMF would argue, as have others, that semi-autonomous justice services delivered and controlled by Aboriginal groups are only appropriate when indigenous people can also participate in making rules which are to be enforced; and, when an aboriginal agency also has an advocacy role. MMF research has revealed that the integration of indigenous people into the imposed social control system has been a painfully slow process simply co-opting aboriginal people into an alien value system which has produced mostly negative results.

Racial stereotyping is only reinforced by the observed double standard with respect to lower pay, lower qualifications, and the lesser support structures and inadequate budgets, which are the hallmarks of the affirmative action type of programs implemented to date. Examples come to mind of Native Clan and Dakota Ojibway policing contracts, the RCMP Special Constable Program, the Provincial Court Communicator Program and the integration of probation and correction services.

. . . .

The racism that MMF has observed in the justice system resides in individuals and their lack of respect, sensitivity, and awareness of aboriginal peoples. This racism is perpetuated and exacerbated if not created by the dehumanizing and depersonalized institution of the dominant society police, court and correctional responsibilities.

. . . .

The annual reports of government which we reviewed are replete with numbers — numbers of people processed and numbers of dollars spent. It is a system managing numbers not social problems; there has been an almost complete abrogation of this responsibility by government agencies.

By labelling a problem as too complex, or related to what they wish to perceive as non-justice issues — poverty, alcoholism, low education, lack of jobs — the justice system cradles and nurtures a philosophy of despair. It becomes apparent that this system of so called justice cannot and will not be held responsible for either the improvement of offenders or the deteriorating situation. Furthermore, by not relating their programs to measures of effectiveness, they avoid responsibility for failure, they avoid questions as to relevancy and feed the syndrome of blaming the victim.

This situation cannot be allowed to continue in a civilized society. As Dr. Keith Jobson, Faculty of Law, University of Victoria, pointed out as early as 1977:

> The availability of a tax supported prosecution and court branch of the industry must not be allowed to continue as a magnet to draw to it cases that should properly be dealt with by alternative sanctioning systems.
>
> To this end, prosecutorial and police services should be reviewed to ensure that relatively non-serious cases are not put forward for entry into the crime industry or unnecessarily processed into the penal sector. Restraint, economy, and justice demand this at the front gate of the industry.

. . . .

It is obvious from the foregoing that the only reasonable, appropriate long term solution is to transfer authority in all matters of justice, corrections and child and family services to aboriginal people and aboriginal directed agencies where the advancement of their specific interests is at stake. It is only through this transfer that the vast economic windfall created by the "consumers" of the justice system can be eradicated and redirected toward amelioration of the factors identified by MMF. We, therefore, urge the Commission of Inquiry to recommend, and the respective governments to take the necessary actions and enact the necessary laws to ensure compliance with the fundamental principle that issues affecting aboriginal people predominantly should be controlled by aboriginal people predominantly.

We recognize, of course, that this will not be accomplished in the short to medium term. Both the federal and provincial governments have vested interests to protect. Within the structure we have developed, and on behalf of Metis people, we propose initiation and development of negotiated settlement of the transfer of control through the tripartite process that has been so successful in other areas.

. . . .

We believe that transfer could be effected without any substantial new monies and could be accomplished by transfer from existing budgets on a per capita formula. (Current per capita costs for all Justice (Provincial) services in Manitoba are currently in the vicinity of $120 per year.)

As we have said earlier, there are two recurring themes of this presentation. First, that the history of the "Justice" system in Manitoba reflects the ongoing reality of aboriginal people as premium payers and white people as general beneficiaries. This is most evident in the fact that white people perpetually make the decisions that directly [affect] aboriginal people.

Perhaps more importantly, however, the Commissioners and the Government will not be judged on how long it takes. You will not be judged on how "pretty" the report is, nor necessarily upon what words are spoken or recommendations given. You, as all players on the stage of history, will be judged upon actions and results. The only satisfactory action, the only appropriate result is transfer of appropriate responsibility. Without this, we will consider the exercise a failure. We have long known that the system, and some people within it, were biased against us ... your deliberations and the presentations at these hearings confirm this belief.... What we now expect, is correction of that iniquity.

∎

The Manitoba Metis Federation made extensive recommendations emphasizing the need for governments to negotiate in good faith with the various Aboriginal peoples of Canada and for Manitoba to transfer necessary power and authority (over lands, courts, and budgets for justice services). Among others, they identified the need for a Metis child and family services agency, a Metis-operated community constable program, Aboriginal control of the court communicator program, interpreters, a Metis-based Metis/Police Community Relations Officer, a system of appointment of Metis Magistrates, and an Aboriginal victim-witness assistance program. They also called for the creation of a criminal offence or quasi-criminal offence for any person in a position of authority who knowingly discriminates or commits any discriminatory act or makes any racist comments or statements.

The Manitoba Metis have also filed suit against the Attorneys General of Canada and Manitoba in pursuit of their land claims. The Attorney General of Canada brought a motion to strike out their action and was successful at the Manitoba Court of Appeal. However, in March 1990, the Supreme Court of Canada set aside the order striking out the claim: *Dumont* v. *Canada (AG)*, [1990] 1 S.C.R. 279. The case is now set to go to trial. For a brief overview of the historic claim of the Metis, see Appellant's Factum, *Dumont* v. *Canada (AG)*, *supra*.

In 1994, the Metis Nation of Saskatchewan also filed suit against the Attorney General of Canada and the Minister of Justice of Saskatchewan in pursuit of their land claim: *Morin* v. *Canada (AG)*. They allege that "they remain a landless people and that they continue to be economically and politically marginalized as a result" (paragraph 70, Statement of Claim) of the wrongful alienation of their land by the defendants and they assert an "inherent right of self-government" (paragraph 71, Statement of Claim).

The historical background to the claims of the Metis, particularly as related to the role of criminal law in their dispossession of their lands, is further described by Mike Brogden in "Law and Criminal Labels: The Case of the French Métis in Western Canada" (1990) 1 J. Human Justice 13. He traces the history of the use of criminal action and law enforcement to delegitimize opposition by the Metis. Arguing that criminal labels emerge within social and economic conflicts, he points to three major uses of criminal labels to segregate and marginalize Metis people: economic criminalization (e.g. illicit fur trade); political criminalization (e.g. to overrule Aboriginal law and policing, the construction of treason); and social criminalization (e.g. vagrancy). See also Paul Chartrand, "Aboriginal Rights: The Dispossession of the Metis" (1991) 29 Osgoode Hall L.J. 457.

In August 1991, after holding community hearings throughout Manitoba, including in many remote Aboriginal communities, Mr. Justice A. Hamilton, Associate Chief Justice (Family Division) of the Manitoba Court of Queen's Bench and Judge Murray Sinclair, Associate Chief Judge of the Manitoba Provincial Court, co-chairs of the Public Inquiry, released the *Report of the Aboriginal Justice Inquiry of Manitoba*. The comprehensive two-volume Report concluded at 1, 249:

> The justice system has failed Manitoba's Aboriginal peoples on a massive scale. ... It is not merely that the justice system has failed aboriginal people; justice has also been denied to them. For more than a century the rights of aboriginal people have been ignored and eroded. The result of this denial has been injustice of the most profound kind. Poverty and powerlessness have been the Canadian legacy to a people who once governed their own affairs in self-sufficiency.
>
> ...
>
> **In examining the court system in Manitoba, we are struck by the fact that there clearly exists a distinguishable, separate justice system for aboriginal people**. Indeed, the rhetoric that surrounds the equality of the justice system evaporates as one examines the way the courts deal with Aboriginal people. It is a system administered by non-Aboriginal people. The laws which the courts apply are alien to aboriginal people, the adversarial approach employed by the courts does not reflect Aboriginal values, and the sanctions these courts apply are ineffective in terms of deterring accused or others from further involvement. [Emphasis added]

The report recommended the creation of separate Aboriginal Justice Systems. See *Report of the Aboriginal Justice Inquiry of Manitoba*, volumes I and II (Winnipeg: Queen's Printer, 1991). See also the videotaped summary *The Justice Inquiry System and Aboriginal People* (a video summary of Vol. I). Refer back to the more general questions raised by the Marshall Commission. How does the focus or mandate of the *Aboriginal Justice Inquiry (Manitoba)* compare? At what stages in the criminal justice system did the Marshall and Manitoba inquiries identify systemic discrimination?

In 1999, after the NDP were re-elected, NDP Premier Gary Doer appointed Paul Chartrand and Wendy Whitecloud to the Aboriginal Justice Implementation Commission to review what recommendations could be implemented from the Aboriginal Justice Inquiry. Their report and the consultation papers are available online at <www.ajic.mb.ca/consult.html>. They made specific recommendations with respect to the over-representation of Aboriginal young offenders in remand and in custody generally, advocated more use of diversion and involvement of Aboriginal communities, and called for an Aboriginal employment strategy to ensure that Aboriginal people were employed in the justice system. They also provided detailed recommendations with respect to improving the quality of policing.

The Argument for Aboriginal Justice Systems[†]

- The federal and provincial governments recognize the right of Aboriginal people to establish their own justice systems as part of their inherent right to self-government.

  The federal and provincial governments assist Aboriginal people in the establishment of Aboriginal justice systems in their communities in a manner that best conforms to the traditions, cultures and wishes of those communities, and the rights of their people.

- Federal, provincial and Aboriginal First Nations governments commit themselves to the establishment of tribal courts in the near future as a first step toward the establishment of a fully functioning, Aboriginally controlled justice system which includes (but need not necessarily be limited to):
  - A policing service.
  - A prosecution branch.
  - A legal aid system.
  - A court system that includes:
    1. a youth court system;
    2. a family court system;
    3. a criminal court system;
    4. a civil court system;
    5. an appellate court system.
  - A probation service including a system of monitoring community service orders.
  - A mediation/counselling service.
  - A fine collection and maintenance enforcement system.
  - A community-based correctional system.
  - A parole system.

  The federal and provincial governments begin the process of establishing Aboriginal justice systems by enacting appropriate legislation.

  At the same time as legislation to begin the process of establishing Aboriginal justice systems is enacted, the federal and provincial governments acknowledge, by resolution of their respective legislative bodies, that Aboriginal justice systems must be protected constitutionally from federal and provincial legislative incursions and that such systems will ultimately be recognized as an aspect of the right of Aboriginal people to self-government and will not be dependent solely upon federal or provincial legislation for their existence.

  Aboriginal governments enact their own constitutions setting out, among other things, the principle of the separation of the judicial from the executive and legislative arms of each Aboriginal government so as to protect Aboriginal justice systems from interference and to provide security for their independence.

CREATING ABORIGINAL JUSTICE SYSTEMS

- Wherever possible, Aboriginal justice systems look toward the development of culturally appropriate rules and processes which have as their aim the establishment of a less formalistic approach to courtroom procedures so that Aboriginal litigants are able to gain a degree of comfort from the proceedings while not compromising the rights of an accused charged with a criminal offence.
- Where Indian and Metis communities are located side by side, the leaders of the two communities give serious consideration to establishing a jointly managed Aboriginal justice system which serves both communities.
- In establishing Aboriginal justice systems, the Aboriginal people of Manitoba consider using a regional model patterned on the Northwest Intertribal Court System in the state of Washington.
- Regional Aboriginal justice systems establish an independent and separate appeal process which makes use of either separate appeal judges or other judges of the Aboriginal system as judges of appeal.
- All people, Aboriginal and non-Aboriginal, within the geographical boundaries of a reserve or Aboriginal community, be subject to the jurisdiction of the Aboriginal justice system in place within that community.
- Aboriginal communities be entitled to enact their own criminal, civil and family laws and to have those laws enforced by their own justice systems. If they wish they should also have the right to adopt any federal or provincial law and to apply or enforce that as well.

[†] Judge A.C. Hamilton and Judge C. Murray Sinclair, *Report of the Aboriginal Justice Inquiry of Manitoba*, Vol. I (Winnipeg: Queen's Printer, 1991) at 733–35.

Aboriginal traditions and customs be the basis upon which Aboriginal laws and Aboriginal justice systems are built.
- The jurisdiction of Aboriginal courts within Aboriginal lands be clear and paramount, and that in appropriate cases Aboriginal courts be recognized as having jurisdiction over some matters arising in places other than the Aboriginal community, such as:
  - Child welfare cases in which the domicile of the child is the Aboriginal community over which the court has jurisdiction.
  - Cases in which a member of an Aboriginal community breaches the laws of his or her community, such as where a First Nation member hunts in a manner that is contrary to a First Nation law or regulation enacted by the government of that First Nation.
  - Cases in which an individual has breached a law of the Aboriginal community and has left the community to avoid detection or responsibility.
  - Civil matters in which the parties have agreed to submit the matter to an Aboriginal court for determination.
- The Manitoba Metis Federation and the government of Manitoba establish a forum of elected and technical representatives with a mandate to identify those Metis communities in the province where Metis justice systems can be established.

Metis communities that are identified as such by agreement of the Manitoba Metis Federation and the government of Manitoba be defined geographically through negotiations between the government of Manitoba and the Metis people of each community for the purpose of establishing a Metis justice system.

The presence of non-Aboriginal people within a Metis community should not prevent the community from being declared a Metis community, and the legitimate concerns of that minority should be respected.

If, and to the extent, that juries are a part of Aboriginal justice systems, jury selection processes be implemented which permit non-Aboriginal persons to sit on juries, provided they comply with appropriate residential criteria established by the community.
- Aboriginal judges be exempt from all civil liability in reference to actions or omissions while in the exercise of their judicial capacity.

Through appropriate Aboriginal legislation an Aboriginal Judicial Council be established to which any person can complain of judicial misconduct on the part of an Aboriginal judicial officer.

The same principles of judicial conduct be applied to Aboriginal judges as apply to other members of the judiciary.

THE CHARTER OF RIGHTS AND FREEDOMS

- First Nation governments draft a charter of rights and freedoms which reflects Aboriginal customs and values.

■

For another study that supports the argument for separate justice systems and likewise makes many recommendations with respect to Aboriginal people and criminal justice, see the 1988 Canadian Bar Association study authored by Michael Jackson, *Locking Up Natives in Canada*, supra. The recommendations include entrenching the Aboriginal right to self-determination and sovereignty and the development of separate Aboriginal justice systems, which includes the following: sentencing, the correctional process, Aboriginal spirituality in prison, correctional services geared to Aboriginal culture and communities, and affirmative action in terms of hiring Aboriginal persons into the correctional services. For a less far-reaching report, but one that confirms a number of the issues identified, see Law Reform Commission of Canada, *Report on Aboriginal Peoples and Criminal Justice: Equality, Respect and the Search for Justice* (Report 34) (Ottawa: LRCC, 1991).

By now, many reports have echoed the findings of systemic discrimination, bias, and over-representation of Aboriginal people at virtually every stage in the criminal justice process. There have been hundreds of recommendations for reform. According to the Alberta Task Force, *Justice on Trial*, supra (Volume III, at 4–7) the recommendations that recurred most frequently were those for:

- cross-cultural training for non-Aboriginal staff
- more Aboriginal staff
- more community-based programs in corrections

- more community-based alternatives in sentencing
- more specialized assistance to Aboriginal offenders
- more Aboriginal community involvement in planning, decision-making, and service delivery
- more Aboriginal advisory groups at all levels
- more recognition of Aboriginal culture and law in service delivery
- additional emphasis on crime prevention programs
- consideration to self-determination in planning and operation of the criminal justice system

Yet, in spite of the number of studies and commissions and the similarity of findings, there has been very little implementation of any of the recommendations and, as the Royal Commission on Aboriginal Peoples documents in *Bridging the Cultural Divide* at 284: "there has not been significant change in the day-to-day realities facing Aboriginal people in their involvement with the criminal justice system, except where Aboriginal initiatives have taken hold."

As the readings on **Colonization and the Imposition of Criminal Law** demonstrate, Anglo-Canadian criminal law was initially imposed on Aboriginal peoples. The law lacked legitimacy both in terms of the basis for its application and the way in which the law was enforced and applied, even when judged solely by Anglo-Canadian standards. Currently, the criminal process glaringly continues to fail to deliver on promises of justice, equality, and dignity, values that the legal system purports to enshrine. The challenge to that differential treatment of Aboriginal people has been substantiated over and over again. At the same time, claims are being made for the special status and rights to which Aboriginal nations are entitled historically on the basis of sovereignty, international law, treaties, and s. 35 of the *Charter*. Closely connected to this is the crucial need for a process of decolonization. Thus, the demands with respect to justice are necessarily situated within the struggle over self-determination.

Ironically, demands for separate justice systems provoke questions about the "justice" and "fairness" of differential justice and the feasibility of multijurisdictional sets of laws and legal systems. Yet, as the *Aboriginal Justice Inquiry (Manitoba)* concluded, there already exists a clearly distinguishable, separate justice system for Aboriginal people. Also, while there are unifying features, a multijurisdictional set of laws and legal systems already operates in terms of criminal and quasi-criminal law, as was discussed *supra*, **The Definition of Crime**.

Finally, separate jurisdiction over criminal law is already designated with respect to the military; for example: *National Defence Act*, R.S.C. 1985, c. N-5, s. 130. The Supreme Court has upheld the constitutionality of a separate system of military law, along with a distinct regime of service tribunals to apply this law, with respect to s. 11(d) of the *Charter*: *R. v. Généreux*, [1992] 1 S.C.R. 259.

The argument for the authority to create separate Aboriginal justice systems is based on the right of self-government as an existing Aboriginal and treaty right, as encompassed by the language of s. 35 of the *Charter*. Thus, according to the Royal Commission, the jurisdiction and rights rest with individual nations, although those rights might be exercised in cooperation with other nations at a community level. See, for example, *Bridging the Cultural Divide* at 54–76.

As Patricia Monture-Angus powerfully argues in "Myths and Revolution: Thoughts on Moving Justice Forward in Aboriginal Communities" in Patricia Monture-Angus, *Thunder in my Soul: A Mohawk Woman Speaks* (Halifax: Fernwood, 1995) at 251–52:

> When Aboriginal people assert jurisdiction in matters of so-called criminal justice (which is not by any means how I conceive what justice is), we hear in response that there is a single system of criminal laws in Canada. Non-Aboriginal people fear the results of Aboriginal Peoples asserting jurisdiction over criminal law matters. What should be heard is the simple plea of Aboriginal Peoples to have both the resources and the control to address the many problems that our communities now face. People must stop fearing the possible creation of many Aboriginal criminal codes. What Aboriginal people seek is the acceptance that there can be more than one valid and legitimate way to address disputes and wrong-doings. Aboriginal Peoples do not wish to displace anyone else's right to be governed by the legitimate and properly consented to laws of their nation. To do such a thing would amount to becoming oppressors ourselves. Our challenge is not a challenge to your right to be in your own unique way, but a simple desire to follow our own ways. The creation of written criminal codes that merely mimic the dominant system's solution of social order is not what I am talking about when I talk about Aboriginal justice systems. This idea of too many criminal codes is also a myth that is per-

petuated by those who have been unable to understand that there are many paths to follow to arrive at a just society.

In reality, there are already many criminal law authorities in Canada. Yes, Canada has a single federal criminal code. Canada also has a number of other federal statutes that create a vast number of offences. The federal criminal code also passes certain authority over to the provinces although this authority is not always expressly stated.... The administration of justice, that is to say the organization of the courts and the appointment of judges, is shared between federal and provincial authorities with provinces occupying the centre of this sphere. There exists both federal and provincial authority for policing. Canadians do not complain loudly about the separate criminal law jurisdiction held by the military. The Canadian system of justice is a very complicated system. I do not believe that word, unitary, describes it at all.

Canadians do not question the general workability of the civil and common law traditions in this country. Why is the recognition of a third tradition of law such an impossible and unworkable one? To suggest that there is a single, unitary system of criminal justice in the first place in Canada is to perpetuate a dangerous myth which acts to support only the existing, status quo arrangements. At the same time, this assertion of an existing unitary system forecloses the discussion about Aboriginal justice systems in a premature way.†

While the Royal Commission highlighted both the need to recognize the right of Aboriginal peoples to re-establish their own justice systems and the need for resources to exercise that right, the Commissioners also stressed the importance and inter-relatedness of reforms within the non-Aboriginal justice system (what others have described as "indigenization" of the current criminal justice system). They identified both goals as connected to the "decolonization of the Canadian justice system" (*Bridging the Cultural Divide* at 78). They stressed the importance of an "intercultural dialogue" (*Bridging the Cultural Divide* at 79) on justice reform at all governmental levels and of responses shaped according to the specific situations of particular communities. Their views echoed many of the submissions and recommendations to the Aboriginal Justice Inquiry of Manitoba and the Cariboo-Chilcotin Inquiry. As others have argued, there is not a clear dichotomy between reforms that support the establishment of separate justice systems and those that contribute to "indigenization" of the existing system. Instead, both reforms potentially constitute part of the process of decolonization and reassertion of control over sovereignty.

See, for example, Mary Ellen Turpel, "Reflections on Thinking Concretely About Criminal Justice Reform" in Richard Gosse, James Youngblood Henderson, Roger Carter, compilers, *Continuing Poundmaker and Riel's Quest: Presentations Made at a Conference on Aboriginal Peoples and Justice* (Saskatoon: Purich, 1994) 206 at 215.

At the same time, clear tension exists between Aboriginal visions and attempts to recuperate the present system with add-on Aboriginal input. For example, the disjuncture between understandings of what justice and peace mean and the goals of dispute resolution emerges forcefully in the work of Patricia Monture-Angus:

> ... The suggestion that alternative dispute resolution practices mirror Aboriginal reality is not a truth. Alternatives are merely that, small add-ons to the existing system — which stands ready with the full force of its adversarial and punishment-oriented values if the "nice" solution does not work. Aboriginal people and Aboriginal nations have been marginalized for long enough. I do not like or think appropriate the comparison between Aboriginal ways of resolving disputes and the movement known as alternative dispute resolution (sometimes fondly called ADR).
>
> My initial response to the comparison of Aboriginal experience with the goals of alternative dispute resolutions was actually pleasure. This joy was not long lived. The way in which disputes were (and sometimes are) resolved in Aboriginal communities does not correspond to any process that I have any knowledge about that exists within the current system....
>
> . . . .
>
> Peacemaking, not alternative dispute resolution, is an English word that captures the essence of Aboriginal systems of social order. Peacemaking is a complex process and is unique because the roles of policing, adjudicating and corrections are not necessarily fragmented.
>
> Peacemaking is both family-based and spiritual. An "offender" in the Navajo system is often described, "He acts as if he had no

---

† Reproduced by permission of Fernwood Publishing, Halifax, Nova Scotia.

relatives" [Philmer Bluehouse and James Zion, "Hozhooji Naat'aanii: The Navajo Justice and Harmony Ceremony" in (1994) 10:4 *Mediation Quarterly* ("Editorial," Special Issue) 327]. These two values bring a system of peacemaking into direct conflict with the values of western dispute resolution where objectivity and neutrality are omnipotent. Underlying any superficial resemblance between alternative dispute resolution and Aboriginal systems of dispute resolution are fundamental and often contradictory value systems. These differences are often masked under attempts to explain the Aboriginal system of dispute resolution in terms the mainstream system can easily understand. The result is dangerous and takes us further away from our goals.

It is not just non-Aboriginal people that fall into this language trap. It is the same trap that was the source of my initial pleasure at the inclusion of the Aboriginal ways in alternative dispute resolution discussions. Aboriginal justice must be seen to be a process, not a concept or an institution. Too frequently when conversations occur about Aboriginal justice systems we all begin by imagining Aboriginal police officers, courts or tribunals, Aboriginal jails filled with Aboriginal staff and inmates. This is **not** an Aboriginal justice system. I think it is misleading to talk about Aboriginal justice systems. I fear that it is also dangerous to have this discussion. Dangerous because indigenizing the existing system has been tried and has not yet provided a solution to the drastic over-representation of Aboriginal people in the Canadian system. Indigenization may alleviate some of the pain and confusion that a person who is brought before the Canadian system experiences, but it is only a partial solution. I have never been happy with less than all. [Sources omitted.]†

The Royal Commission canvassed the initiatives taken either to curb or mitigate the harshness of the criminal justice system vis-à-vis Aboriginal people, and to respond to their needs and experiences. The reforms include: Aboriginal policing; the appointment of Aboriginal justices of the peace and Aboriginal judges; Aboriginal court worker programs; cultural awareness training of non-Aboriginal participants in the justice system; Aboriginal courts established under the *Indian Act*, R.S.C. 1985, c. I-5, s. 107; diversion projects and alternative conflict resolution; sentencing circles and elders panels; initiatives with respect to young people in conflict with the law; and initiatives with respect to prisoners and in particular the contribution of Aboriginal spirituality to healing and the creation of healing lodges.

Some of these initiatives, such as the Hollow Water First Nation's Community Holistic Circle Healing Project, will be discussed *infra*, in the chapters on **Sentencing** and **Prisons**. For further details, see *Bridging the Cultural Divide*, Chapter 3.

---

† Reprinted by permission of Fernwood Publishing, Halifax, Nova Scotia.

4

Enforcement of the Law

We begin here to introduce the "distinction" between law on the books (e.g. in the statutes and in the cases) and law in action or practice. By the latter phrase, we refer to the actual operation of law, as implemented by police officers, lawyers (particularly Crown attorneys), and judges in their day-to-day work and to the lived experience of law, from the point of view of those "practised upon." "Law in practice" has rarely been the subject of legal education, although it has been documented and analyzed in other disciplines. This gap in legal education has occurred in part because law in practice is more difficult to describe and evaluate, because legal education is based on certain assumptions about law and learning, and partly because, until the passage of the *Charter*, there were limited remedies for the discordance between what the legal "rules" dictate and the outcomes of criminal law.

The most familiar critique of the inequities in the enforcement of the law have focused on the treatment of poor people. However, this analysis is rendered more complex by looking at the links between class and gender, the inter-relationship between class and race, and the impact of sexual orientation on patterns of law enforcement. More recently, attention has moved to examining the treatment of Aboriginal people as accused and as victims (e.g. the cases of Helen Betty Osborne, J.J. Harper, and Leo LaChance), as well as several well-known individual examples of miscarriages of justice (Donald Marshall, Jr., Wilson Nepoose, and David Milgaard). This chapter has important links with the earlier chapter, **The Definition of Crime**, and also raises issues discussed more fully in a later chapter, **Policing**, where we consider the role of the police in the differential enforcement of the law with respect to women, as victims/complainants of wife assault and sexual assault, and with respect to the use of lethal violence to apprehend African-Canadian and other racialized men.

A. CLASS

Crime and Class: Unequal Before the Law[†]

INTRODUCTION — CRIME, CLASS, AND CULTURE

Common knowledge and official statistics have led people to conclude that low status groups are more prone to committing criminal and delinquent acts than those of higher status. Why this might be the case and how the illegal conduct of poor people relative to wealthier folk may be exaggerated in official data is the subject of this article.

People examining the way in which official crime data are constructed often doubt the extent to which such reports represent actual illegal conduct. Instead, such data may be regarded as information about enforcement rather than criminality. Tepperman points out that the legal system in Canada is a vast machine which has the certification of crime as its task. He suggests that to begin with, one can take just about anyone for most of the criminal value of our criminals is added by the machine itself (1977: 26).

In the same vein, Box (1971: 21) concluded a chapter on the social construction of official statistics as follows:

> By conceiving official data as objects fit for study, we have been able to sustain the argument that the end product is not a valid indicator of a country's "real" extent or pattern of criminal activity. Its formulation and variation is determined by organizational, legal and social pressures, rather than by a rigorous attempt to measure criminal activity accurately.

In particular, Tepperman and Box agree that social class differences in crime rates must at least be qualified. After looking at such unofficial measures as self-report studies in comparison with official ones, Box notes that the unofficial data failed to reveal the significant inter-class differences implied in official statistics. Some have located differences but these have tended to be much smaller than those officially recorded (1971: 58–91).

Tepperman allows that Canadian official crime data have a variable and uncertain degree of validity. Definitive conclusions cannot be drawn regarding the reasons for differences in criminal convictions by social class, so one must tentatively conclude that some element of both class bias and differential motivation and opportunity for crime enter into making these differences (1977: 191).

The data may be both an indication of criminality and an indication of enforcement procedures which do not randomly select subjects for processing.

Very often sociologists attempting to offer explanations for criminality and delinquency have disregarded Tepperman's reminder and have centered on differential motivation and opportunity among working-class and, more particularly, poor people. Class bias is too often ignored, as are the social processes which create and sustain the invidious conditions of poverty (Watson, 1976). Instead, the culture of poverty often becomes an explanation for crime in many of the best known theories of sociologically oriented criminologists.

Literature on the sociology of crime and delinquency is replete with explanations which, in effect, blame the poor for problems of deviance, while ignoring the role of men of power.

. . . .

In sum, sociological explanations ... have often accepted the common sense notion that crime and delinquency are peculiarly lower-class problems. They have rarely, until recently, examined the social construction of crime data to determine its accuracy in locating deviance in the social structure. Taking the accuracy of official crime data for granted, criminologists have devoted a great deal of attention to the culture of poverty, expecting to find in it a theory of crime and delinquency. When structural inequality has been recognized, this has often meant examining how unfair competition exists in some anomalous fashion to pressure people to ignore commonly held standards of conduct or to develop and sustain their own deviant standards. Cultural explanations are often geared to blaming the poor even though the subcultural followers of Merton, and Merton himself, were cautiously critical of the actual opera-

---

[†] By William K. Greenaway in John Harp and John Hofley, eds., *Structured Inequality in Canada* (Scarborough: Prentice-Hall, 1980) 247 at 247–48, 251–55, 256–60, 262. Notes omitted. Reproduced by permission of publisher.

tion of liberal societies because of the failure of such systems to meet the ideals of meritocracy.

Subcultural explanations have failed to fulfill their intentions. The numerous criticisms of this approach all point to one central problem: "Most poor people do not become criminals and many well-to-do and rich people become crooks" (Hartung, 1965: 29).

Even if one could demonstrate that law violation is peculiarly or predominately a lower-class phenomenon and that cultural supports for such conduct do exist among lower-class people in a way in which they do not for others, one would still have to ask, why is this the case? Weak structural explanations like Merton's do not suffice. A more thorough structural analysis is needed.

In the remainder of this article attention is turned to an interpretation of crime and delinquency and its generation and certification by official agencies of state control, from a perspective which attempts to delve into the roots of our social, political, and economic order. Clearly, simple explanations for the apparent relationship between law violation and class are not possible. The relationship has to do with the mode of production, class conflict, the nature of the state and the law in Canada, the operation of legal systems and the enforcement of laws. It may also be dependent on social psychological factors at different class levels.

LAW AND DOMINANT INTERESTS

The law, as opposed to other instruments of social control, is a system of rules and sanctions generated and administered by the state. Any analysis of law violation should begin with an examination of the law itself. It has often been remarked in jest that the principal cause of crime is law! Too few sociologists have appreciated the serious implications of this statement. Many have taken law as "given" — a representation of generally held social goals or common cultural values (see, for example, Friedmann, 1959).

Others have conceived law to be the result of the interplay of a multitude of political pressure groups, all of whom exercise a share of power. Small (1978), for example, has analyzed the early development of Canadian narcotics legislation as an outgrowth of a number of social and cultural factors: imbedded and exaggerated ideas about the pharmacological effects of certain substances, racism (especially anti-Asiatic sentiments), and the reform efforts of identifiable groups of moral entrepreneurs. The dynamic of class, as conceived by Marx and elaborated elsewhere in this volume, is absent in Small's analysis, as it is in other liberal-pluralist interpretations.

A Marxist perspective sees the capitalist state and therefore its instrument, the law, as based on relationships of production. The state and the law are largely within the domain of the relatively few people who constitute its ruling class. The Marxist approach holds that rather than reflecting commonly held social values or emanating from the machinations of relatively autonomous and diverse pressure groups, the law in capitalist states pursues the interests of its dominant class. This perspective suggests that to ignore the larger social context in examining law violation among the poor, and to suggest that the conduct of the poor is unrelated to the conduct of the wealthy is an overly-restricted sociological view. The law quite clearly is not an outgrowth of relationships existing solely among the poor. Neither, therefore, is its violation.

The law and law enforcement practices and priorities are structured in a way people may see as natural or universal. The law may be based at times on a consensus which may or may not exist relatively independently of the influence of the media or educational institutions — powerful cultural tools in the hands of dominant groups. Yet laws and law enforcement are not natural, but instead are outgrowths of class relationships. A change in those relationships yields variations in law, a point we will now elaborate.

. . . .

Capitalism emerged out of feudalism. In feudalism the dominant class was the aristocracy, which owned the land and controlled those who were attached to land and to the aristocracy by bonds of fealty. Feudalism also comprised a small middle class of merchants, artisans and others who sometimes had a base in the free cities. As commerce and then industry developed, this middle class or *bourgeoisie* first entered into a struggle for social and economic power with the aristocracy and eventually came to supersede them. In contemporary capitalist systems, it is the bourgeoisie which is the dominant class and wage labor is the prevailing mode of production.

In the transition from feudalism to capitalism, a new legal philosophy which accompanied a broader liberal ideology gained force. While the new philosophy and the system of laws and law enforcement which grew out of it unquestionably brought benefits to both dominant and many non-dominant groups, the principal gain was, and still is, realized by the bourgeoisie: they gained dominance through the legitimized right to own, accumulate, control, and exploit private property. This dominance was reinforced by a philosophy which argued that feudal divisions and hereditary rights were no longer useful or rational. This liberal philosophy professed that societies should be conceived as a composite of individuals and that individual rights should replace the perquisites of nobility and the obligations of others. In other words, the bourgeoisie, not just the aristocracy, should be able to own, accumulate, control, and exploit property. Ironic as it may seem, the idea that we live in a society composed of individuals, not classes, thus became entrenched in the liberal ideology in the period in which the bourgeoisie *as a class* struggled to gain its hegemony.

. . . .

The ethic of individualism, behavioral diversity, and the existence of opportunities to make choices, however restrictive, obscures the process of social domination in capitalist societies.

With respect to the law, conduct which may be more probable among the lower classes or among powerless minorities is placed under restrictions of criminal law more frequently than deviant conduct, which is more typical of people at the other end of the social spectrum. Although the extraction of surplus value is consistent with some definitions of theft, appropriating for oneself part of the value produced by workers is not only excluded from the formal definition of theft in our society, but is viewed as natural, right, and even a socioeconomic necessity. Profit is perhaps capitalism's central freedom. Acquiring private property by shoplifting, on the other hand, is deemed illegitimate, even in circumstances where the pursuit of profit leads to marketing practices where people are exhorted daily to accumulate products they do not need, where such goods are displayed openly in an attempt to encourage impulse buying, and where, at the same time, the system creates unemployment and impoverishment. Most people, however, do not regard as arbitrary the restricted definition of theft or the placing of only certain violations of law in criminal codes, with its powerful sanctions, and other violations in less stigmatizing civil codes (Sutherland, 1945).

Anthony Platt (1969), a U.S. social researcher who analyzed the "invention of delinquency," has argued that the philosophy of the juvenile court and official definitions of delinquency were developed with specific reference to the conduct of lower-class, urban, immigrant children. Susan Houston (1978), examining some of the same developments in Canada, suggests that special delinquency processing agencies, along with compulsory schooling, were measures adopted to mold from the lower class a literate and disciplined work force. With such a developmental history, is it surprising that official delinquents are by and large recruited from the lower classes?

. . . .

Addressing a Winnipeg audience, Roland Penner, an attorney, a law professor and former chairman of Legal Aid Manitoba, asked people to use their imaginations:

> Let's suppose I became philosopher-king and I could make any changes I wanted. Suppose I decided that minor social control offences and crimes-without-victims were to be eliminated from the Criminal Code. Also suppose that minor property offenders were to be dealt with in the community rather than in jails. At the same time suppose that I made tax evasion, knowingly polluting the environment, false advertising, fraudulent bankruptcy, and price-fixing crimes which carried automatic jail terms. Now, let's introduce the proverbial "man from Mars" who always gets into stories like this one. He arrives and I take him on a tour of (the Provincial Jail near Winnipeg). What would he say? "You sure have a problem with your middle class white people, don't you?"

The point is that the law in capitalist societies is structured *a priori* on the basis of social class. It is structured in a way that determines at the outset that lower-class people will predominate among its violators, at least in the case of criminal law. Pretensions of equality before the law, that is, of fairness in legal *processing*, should not obscure this fact. As Anatole France once remarked, "The law in all its majestic equality, forbids the rich as well as the poor to sleep under bridges on rainy nights, to beg in the streets and to steal bread."

THE POOR IN THE LEGAL PROCESS

The criminal law may proscribe acts which are most likely or most advantageously committed by lower-class people while, as suggested by Sutherland (1945) in his work on white collar crime, many socially harmful acts — those more likely to be committed by the well-to-do — are covered by less brutal civil prohibitions and sanctions. Or, as Herman and Julia Schwendinger (1970: 148–49) argue, acts are not proscribed at all which may be regarded as "criminal" if one defines the word in terms other than existing law in capitalist countries. Such acts might be those relating to imperialism, racism and poverty itself (Schwendingers, 1970: 148):

> If the terms imperialism, racism, sexism and poverty are abbreviated signs for theories of social relationships or social systems which cause the systematic abrogation of basic rights, then imperialism, racism, sexism and poverty can be called crimes according to the logic of our argument.

Given that the structure of law itself may be an initial reason that official data contain a preponderance of lower-class violators, let us turn to other factors which add to such a result.

. . . .

When an individual today appears in court in Canada the person does not do so solely to account for a particular law violation. All aspects of past life as well as future possibilities are taken into account. This situation Edwin Schur (1969: 159) contends, "... allows the respectable (middle or upper class) citizen caught in criminal acts a degree of immunity not available to the supposedly less respectable (lower class) colleagues in crime." Throughout the justice system people are dealt with on the basis of the quality of their lives prior to the act and the projected quality of their futures, judged to a large degree by factors associated with social class. The so-called individualization of justice and the exercise of increasingly diversified forms of discretion in the legal system are contemporary characteristics of justice in Canada.

Investigating a number of studies done in Canada and elsewhere, Tepperman (1977: 159) concludes, "... the evidence suggests that wherever discretion is available it is used in ways ultimately damaging to poor people." Such is the case at virtually every level of the criminal or delinquency processing system.

Discretion in the legal system begins with the deployment of enforcement resources. For a variety of reasons, Box (1971: 177–90) suggests, police may be deployed to pay closest attention to lower-class areas. Differential deployment follows a choice of statutes to be enforced, since not all can be enforced with equal fervor. As well, there is a choice made of potential offenders. The police thus begin the process by which a number of people are selected for official processing from among those who might be included by virtue of their conduct relative to the law. The bureaucratically selected population of law violators become subjects of criminological study, and their characteristics, however related or unrelated to their criminal or delinquent conduct, may become the basis for scientific explanations. Buttressed by such authoritative theories and their own experience, the police look for law violators where they have found them before and where they "know" them to exist. As Box emphasizes, this "social construction of reality" takes on a reified existence. The situation is an example of the self-fulfilling prophecy and is reminiscent of the old vaudeville routine where a drunk is seen looking for a lost article beneath a burning street-light surrounded by darkness. Someone asks him what he is doing and he responds that he is trying to find his wallet. "Where did you lose it?" inquires the observer. "About 100 yards that way," he replies. "Well, then why are you looking for it here?" he is asked. "Because the light is better here!" is his slurred response. To a degree at least, crime and delinquency are "found" among the poor because that is where they are sought and the poor have little ability to resist intrusion.

The head of an RCMP Commission Fraud section once confided to the writer that a lead given to his group would not likely be followed up. The RCMP have too few personnel even to begin to investigate more than a very small portion of the cases which come to their attention. Compare this situation to the concentrated police patrols of lower-class neighborhoods.

Beyond initial deployment practices and decisions to concentrate attention on certain kinds of laws and to give scant attention to others, studies have indicated other ways in which discretion in the justice system operates to the disadvantage of the poor.

An example of the operation of police discretion with respect to juveniles is provided by Nease (1966) in a study conducted in Hamilton, Ontario. She examined official contact and referral in "high delinquency" as compared with other areas in the city. As an initial condition resulting in differential contact, she suggests that there is an over-dependence on the police in poor areas (142). This is similar to a later conclusion by Black and Reiss (1970) in the U.S. that people in poor areas more frequently resort to calling the police for relatively trivial matters. Such a finding does not explain subsequent differences in delinquency processing, however. Nease found that "... boys from economically disadvantaged neighborhoods are sent to juvenile courts more frequently than their fellow delinquents from the rest of the city" (141). Such decisions were apparently unrelated to the seriousness of offenses. In other words, the characteristics of an area seem to operate independently of age, religion, nationality, offense or past record to influence the police decision to refer a case to juvenile court rather than to release with a warning.

Having examined the Nease study in a class taught by the author, members of the Winnipeg Police Juvenile Division suggested the following explanation in terms of their own experience: police are reluctant to push a case any further along the official processing route than seems necessary. This is so for two reasons. The first stems from compassion and sometimes from knowledge of labeling research, which suggests that the further a juvenile penetrates into the official system, the more he or she is liable to develop a delinquent self-concept. The second reason for avoiding official channels is that it often involves the officer in a great deal of paperwork, court appearances and other bureaucratic burdens, which bring little personal or organizational reward. Why then should police more frequently push kids from poor areas along the official route? The Juvenile Officers suggest that it has to do with police ability to contact parents or other responsible adults, the perceived cooperativeness of the adults, and a general, subjective assessment of the adequacy of an alleged offender's home. In other words, the conditions of poverty, the attitudes that adults who are poor may, as a result of their own experience, develop toward official representatives of the state, and the subjective assessments of the police may add up to the creation of official delinquents for reasons independent of personal conduct.

Nease's (1966) study of Hamilton delinquents found that juvenile court decisions were less influenced by area than the police decision on whether or not to refer a case to juvenile court, possibly because the police act as a filter prior to the exercise of court discretion. Others have found that the filter continues to operate at the level of juvenile court decisions.

Haldane, Elliott and Whitehead (1972) examined cases passing through the Halifax Family Court. Their results indicate that receiving a "major disposition" is positively associated with "low social class, low income, broken home, unmarried parents, families judged to be unstable, a history of legal involvement on the part of the parent, and an overcrowded home" (240). Although differences in the statistical relationships occurred when offense category was held constant, discrimination — they used the more polite term, "particularism" — based on factors related to class remained. In fact, it was found that juveniles from low social class families were more likely to receive major dispositions for minor infractions than those from the higher social class (241).

In the processing of adult offenders, similar sorts of filtering occur to the disadvantage of lower-class people. Again, the process begins at the level of police contact. While delinquency legislation may be [agreeably] ambiguous to many, there is a general expectation, suggests Brian Grosman (1975) in his work on the police in Canada, that criminal law is mechanical and objective in its application. On the contrary, Grosman (1974: 90) says that much of what follows in the criminal process depends upon "... the individual policeman (sic) who engages in selective enforcement without any real guidance.... Obviously law enforcement neither means total enforcement nor equal enforcement when the law enforcement policy is made by individual policemen (sic)."

Discretion is also a major factor affecting outcomes at levels in the justice system beyond the police, as Grosman (1969) found in his study, *The Prosecutor: An Inquiry into the Exercise of Discretion*, an examination of Canadian court procedures. John Hogarth (1971), in a monumental study of decision-making in Ontario's courts, examined regularities of sentencing within very wide limits of discretion given to such courts to administer sanctions.

Precisely what influence social class has upon one's chances of arrest and conviction and how class influences functionaries' use of discretion is not clear in all instances. There is some evidence, however, that poor adults are at a disadvantage in the criminal justice system in ways similar to the demonstrated disadvantage of poor youngsters in the delinquency processing system.

Tepperman (1977: 161–65) reviewed a number of studies touching upon poverty, access to legal representation, and one's chances in court. He concluded that there is a difference in the chances of conviction between those who are remanded in custody and those who obtain an interim release. The difference remains when both obtain legal counsel. Likewise, custody tends to increase the chances that one will be imprisoned upon conviction. Tepperman (1977: 162) concludes, "These risks fall most heavily on poor people because they are least likely to be able to raise bail."

While it may not be absolutely certain that discretion always works to the disadvantage of lower-class defendants, investigation and processing of so-called white collar crimes is often conducted so as to keep high status law violators out of the courts. In her examination of legislation — municipal, provincial and federal — affecting corporate conduct in Canada,

Snider (1978) points out that procedures often dictate that past infractions be ignored if such violations are remedied or if future compliance is assured. Attrition rates for such offenses tend therefore to be much higher than rates for normal, that is, predominately lower-class, crimes. If someone burglarizes your house and is apprehended in circumstances which would clearly yield a conviction, it would not be common for the offender to be released by the police on the promise that stolen articles will be returned and that the offender will go straight. If someone steals from you by deliberately withholding your wages (Snider, 1978), then such is not the case.

Emphasizing the way in which high status law violators are kept out of the courts, Tepperman (1977: 163) cites a newspaper report of a Supreme Court of Canada case. A representative of the Department of Revenue frankly admitted that "tax evaders were not prosecuted if they could pay when caught." As C.B. Macpherson (1965: 7) said, "All are free, but some are freer than others." The statement could refer to the freedom to violate the law in Canada.

While most studies of judicial processing have centered on restricted bureaucratic practices, a study by Kellough (1977) takes a macrosociological view. She examined the effects which general political and economic conditions have upon patterns of incarceration. Her sociohistorical investigation covers a 29-year period in the Eastern Judicial District of Manitoba. Data indicate a fluctuation in rates of incarceration associated with general social conditions and such fluctuations are "... almost entirely made up by incarcerations of the most powerless groups for 'social control' offenses" (2). (Social control offenses include those related to alcohol, morality, offenses against public order, and vagrancy.)

Here is another important finding in Kellough's research: "... while only slight differences are found in the severity of sentence imposed, the lowest social classes are most apt to serve their full sentence" (2). The recent growth of parole authority and other conditional release procedures in Canada makes this finding all the more important. A study by Waller (1974) failed to discover a rational basis for parole board decision-making; this leaves open the question of whether parole boards merely grant privileges to those most like themselves in terms of education, lifestyle, and professed values.

If we combine studies which indicate that lower-class people are at a disadvantage in the legal process with evidence (Stebbins, 1971) that the farther one penetrates into the crime and delinquency processing system, the more difficult it is to escape from the "criminal role," one is at least suspicious that the system may be unwittingly exacerbating problems it ostensibly wishes to minimize. A more cynical interpretation (Liazos, 1974) suggests that minimizing crime is a goal superseded in capitalist systems by that of terrorizing lower-class people (who step out of their meagre "place"), thereby keeping their confreres in line.

If we take data from any stage in the legal process, lower-class people prevail, but to what extent this is due to the patterns of conduct of lower-class people we cannot truly estimate.

. . . .

CONCLUSION

. . . .

Surely no culture of poverty explanation is needed to explain the predominance of lower-class people in jails, police statistics, or other official records of crime and delinquency. Crime and delinquency are social products and, given the nature of Canadian political and economic organization, it should surprise no one that the status of criminal or delinquent is one which is, with few exceptions, reserved for those at the bottom of the social order.

Canadian criminologists have too often relied upon theories grounded in U.S. race and ethnic relations, urban settlement patterns, and an obscurantist liberal ideology. Subcultural explanations not only do not suffice as analytical tools, they tend to blame the poor for social problems which are more properly seen as being the result of the activities of the rich.

As pointed out recently by Morton, Snider and West (1978: 2), we have yet to produce a distinctive Canadian political economy of crime. Such an analysis would have to recognize the basis of such organization in the mode of economic production and the historical use of the law in Canada to preserve a social order conducive to dominant class interests.

■

Reuben Hasson's major study of the legal treatment of social security abuse provides an example of the differential enforcement of law based on class: "The Cruel War: Social Security Abuse in

Canada" (1981) 3 Can. Taxation 114. In contrasting the resources devoted to detecting and prosecuting "welfare fraud" as opposed to tax evasion and the stigma associated with each, he comments at 115 (notes omitted):

> [A] disturbing feature of the behaviour of politicians and propagandists who allege that social security abuse is epidemic is that they fail to generate the same or indeed any concern about tax evasion. This is so despite the fact that the sums estimated lost through tax evasion — $3 billion per annum — are far in excess of even the most extravagant estimates of all moneys lost through all social security schemes as a result of fraud. Yet, at a time when all levels of government were appointing more people to control social security abuse, the percentage of income tax returns audited decreased from 0.93 per cent in 1971 to 0.62 per cent in 1976. In the field of corporate audits, the number went down between 1974 and 1979 from 6.5 per cent to 4.6 per cent.†

The most recent trends in social security reform, 20 years after Hasson's article, have been to continue to depict "welfare fraud" in crisis proportions and to invest further in fraud detection rather than to ensure that benefit levels are adequate to support a healthy and non-degrading existence. This trend can be observed in several provinces, notably Ontario: Brigitte Kitchen, "'Common Sense' Assaults on Families" in Dianna Ralph, André Régimbald, and Nérée St.-Amand, eds., *Open for Business. Closed to People* (Halifax: Fernwood, 1997) 103 at 109–11.

Furthermore, even though current figures suggest that the "return" on every dollar spent in tax audits is extraordinary — $17 — the rate at which audits are undertaken has dropped further: Neil Brooks and Linda McQuaig, "OK Michael Wilson: Here's the Alternative" *This Magazine* (December 1989) 15 at 20. These authors note, at 19, that while corporations were audited at a rate of 7.4 per cent in 1973, only 1.8 per cent were audited in 1988. Deborah Jones, "Telling tales at tax time" *The [Toronto] Globe and Mail* (29 April 1995) D3, notes that in 1993, 73,000 audits yielded $3 billion in taxes (compared to 78,700 audits in 1976, according to Hasson, *supra*, at 115). For other examples of law enforcement decisions regarding "suite crime," see Jock Ferguson, "Police engulfed in fraud cases" *The [Toronto] Globe and Mail* (2 July 1993) A5: "Police in the Metro Toronto region are so swamped by white-collar crime that they are telling people they might never be able to investigate their complaints"; and Geoffrey York, "Won't file charges in diplomat travel scam, Crown says; Federal government recovers almost $500,000 from External Affairs officials after false claims made on airline tickets" *The [Toronto] Globe and Mail* (27 March 1993) A6.

It will be noted here that the comparison of the enforcement of welfare fraud with tax evasion raises not only class issues but also issues of gender for, as Dianne Martin demonstrates in her article, "Passing the Buck: Prosecution of Welfare Fraud; Preservation of Stereotypes" (1992) 12 Windsor Y.B. Access Just. 52 at 89–90, the prosecution of welfare fraud has an adverse impact upon women (38 out of 50 cases studied). As Martin argues, punitive attitudes towards social assistance recipients combined with the stereotypes associated with single mothers, particularly those with "boyfriends," already make this offence the subject of "particularly high reporting rates" by other citizens, suggesting that further investment in fraud detection is unnecessary (at 85).

Errlee Carruthers goes further, in "Prosecuting Women for Welfare Fraud in Ontario: Implications for Equality" (1995) 11 J. Law and Soc. 241 at 250: "The negative stereotype of the 'welfare cheat' is not gender neutral. With more and more frequency (and hostility) the image of the welfare cheat is that of the irresponsible single mother (often black) who refuses to get a man or a job...." She argues that the targeting of women on welfare with the new fraud detection schemes, the use of home visits as the investigatory method, the "spouse in the house" rule, and the role of prosecutorial discretion constitute violations of s. 15 of the *Charter*. For a successful legal challenge to the Ontario "spouse in the house" rule see: *Falkiner* v. *Ontario*, [2002] O.J. No. 1711 (C.A.), online: QL.

Another example of the intersection of class, gender, and race in the differential enforcement of the law can be found in the policing and prosecution of the offence of soliciting for the purpose of prostitution where "[t]he sale of sexual services becomes an option for women in a society that endorses sexual bargaining and offers women limited, under-valued employment opportunities": Frances Shaver, "Prostitution: A Women's Crime?"

---

† Reprinted by permission of the author and the publisher.

in Ellen Adelberg and Claudia Currie, eds., *In Conflict with the Law* (Vancouver: Press Gang Publishers, 1993) 153 at 165. Historically, the *Criminal Code* contained an offence that was sex-specific: s. 164(1)(c) made it an offence to be a "common prostitute or night walker ... found in a public place ... [who] failed to give a good account of herself." While this offence was challenged under the *Canadian Bill of Rights* for sex discrimination (*R. v. Viens* (1970), 10 C.R.N.S. 363 (Ont. Prov. Ct.) (offence declared inoperative) but compare *R. v. Lavoie*, [1971] 1 W.W.R. 690 (B.C. Co. Ct.) (offence upheld)), even its neutrally worded counterpart, the offence of soliciting for the purpose of prostitution in s. 195 of the *Criminal Code*, was at times interpreted as applying solely to women, relying on dictionary definitions and common understandings that equated prostitution with women: *R. v. Patterson* (1972), 19 C.R.N.S. 289 (Ont. Co. Ct.) (male acquitted) but see *R. v. DiPaola* (1978), 43 C.C.C. (2d) 199 (Ont. C.A.) (new trial directed for male acquittee). Although legislative amendments in 1983 ensured gender neutrality (S.C. 1980-81-82-83, c. 125, s. 13) and in 1985 extended the offence to include customers (S.C. 1985, c. 50, s. 1), Shaver argues at 155–57 and 163 that the enforcement of s. 213 is skewed against women (notes omitted):

> [W]omen represent only a small proportion of the individuals implicated. Conservative estimates based on the ratio of female to male prostitutes in Montreal in 1991 (4:1), and the average number of male clients they service each week (20 and 10, respectively) indicate that only 4 per cent of those involved (or potentially involved) in communicating for the purpose of prostitution are women. The remainder — a full 96 percent — are men, and, of those, the vast majority (99 percent) are clients. These figures stand in sharp contrast to those ... [that] indicate that fewer than 50 percent of those arrested in the last three years were male.
>
> ...
>
> First, male prostitutes were under-represented in the charge statistics in several cities. In 1989, in Calgary, where 18 percent of street prostitutes identified in head counts were male, only 12 percent of prostitution charges involved males. In Toronto, about 25 percent of the prostitutes counted were male but only 5 percent of the prostitution charges involved males. In Halifax the figures were 33 percent and 11 percent respectively, and in Vancouver they were 10 percent and 8 percent. Montreal was the exception: a slightly higher percentage of males were charged (27 percent) than appeared in the head counts.
>
> Second, more prostitutes than customers were charged in nine of the ten Canadian cities studied in 1989. The law was most equally applied in Toronto and London, where about one-half of the charges laid involved customers. In Winnipeg, Niagara Falls, Montreal, and Quebec City, only between 30 and 40 percent of charges involved customers, and in Vancouver, Calgary, and Halifax, customers represented 25 percent or fewer of the charges laid.[†]

Consider the case below, in which a challenge to the enforcement of law with respect to s. 213 in Halifax was pursued.

R. v. White[‡]

[ROSCOE, J.A.:]

The issue in this appeal is whether the equality rights of the appellants were breached as a result of the manner in which the Halifax Police Department enforced s. 213 of the *Criminal Code*....

The appellants were each charged in separate informations with communicating for the purposes of prostitution, Ms. White as an adult and S.L.B. as a young offender.

. . . .

At the trials of the appellants, it was submitted that their rights pursuant to s. 15 of the *Charter* had been infringed as a result of the methods of enforcement of the Halifax Police. Statistics showing that more females were charged under s. 213 during a specific period of time, including the offence dates herein, were submitted along with other extrinsic evi-

---

[†] Reproduced with permission of the author.
[‡] (1994), 136 N.S.R. (2d) 77 (C.A.).

dence consisting of reports on street prostitution. Judge Bremner's finding that the defence had not proven a violation of s. 15 was upheld on appeal to Justice Anderson who concluded that there was no error in law or fact by the trial judge. Judge Daley, finding no difference between the case of S.L.B and that of Ms. White, relied on Justice Anderson's decision and concluded there had been no breach of *Charter* rights.

The issue on appeal is whether the learned trial judges and summary appeal justice erred in law in failing to find a breach of the appellants' equality rights.

The argument of the appellants can be summarized as follows: The result of the exclusive use of the "decoy" system to enforce s. 213, is that the police charge more women than men with communication for the purpose of prostitution. Since as many men commit the offence as women, there is discrimination on the basis of gender.

The statistics presented at both trials indicate that from June 1, 1990 to November 30, 1991, of a total of 234 charges under s. 213(1)(c), 189 were laid against females and 45 against males. These numbers include adults and young offenders. In other words 80.77% of the total charged were female and 19.23% were male.

Constable William MacLeod of the Morality Section of the Halifax Police Department testified at both trials concerning the so-called "decoy" method of enforcing s. 213. He said that in Halifax there are two main areas where female street prostitutes frequent, and one area where male homosexual prostitution is practised. The "decoy" method consists of having one or more male police officers in plain clothes drive by one of the "strolls" in an unmarked vehicle and stop the vehicle. A female approaches the car, a conversation takes place and if sex for money is offered, she is arrested. Similar attempts to charge male prostitutes have not been successful according to Constable MacLeod because the targets of the enforcement are not as likely to approach unknown males and they are more cautious in their conversations. Additionally, there are only a couple of male prostitutes. When the police are attempting to enforce the section against customers as opposed to the prostitutes, they use female police officers who stand on a corner of a "stroll" and wait until they are approached by someone. Constable MacLeod testified that the police have as many female officers working as "decoys" as they do male officers, but that not as many charges result against customers as against prostitutes because of certain limitations. There are a number of reasons the female officer is less effective than her male colleague. One is that the real prostitutes often recognize the newcomer as a police officer and tip off potential customers. Also the female officer is often harassed by pimps, customers and prostitutes, making the role a dangerous one and requiring backup in the immediate area. Thirdly, the female "decoy" is limited in what she can say to a potential customer in order to avoid entrapment. She must wait until the male initiates the conversation and directs it to talk of sex for money. Constable MacLeod testified that there is no other effective method of enforcing s. 213.

The appellants' argument has a major flaw and that is that it is premised on the assumption that every time an offence is committed under s. 213(1)(c) there are two parties to the offence, usually a male and a female. It is clear from the evidence of Constable MacLeod that many solicitations are made by a prostitute before one is accepted by a customer. In the absence of evidence to the contrary, it can be inferred that many of these solicitations do not attract any answer from a potential customer that contravenes s. 213, and therefore the offence is committed more often by prostitutes than by customers. In other words, contrary to the argument of the appellants, the offence can be committed by one person acting unilaterally. There was no evidence that male customers regularly approach women who are not prostitutes and engage in conversation that is prohibited by the section. If the offence is committed more often by females than by men, it is not surprising that more females are charged. If the burden of s. 213 falls more heavily on females because the offence is committed more often by females, then the appellants have not met the burden of proving a breach of s. 15 of the *Charter*. There being no reversible errors in law by the Youth Court judge or the Summary Appeal Court judge, the appeals are accordingly dismissed.

■

Is the logic of this decision compelling? Are there any other ways of analyzing the data presented? Would additional information have strengthened the case for the accused?

Scholars have explored the ways in which other institutions also "police" certain groups and classes outside of the criminal justice system. See Dorothy Chunn, "Regulating the Poor in Ontario:

From Police Courts to Family Courts" in Tina Loo and Lorna McLean, eds., *Historical Perspectives on Law and Society in Canada* (Toronto: Copp Clark Longman Ltd., 1994) 184 for an account of the operation of family courts in the period 1890s–1940s in enforcing middle-class norms with respect to poor women.

B. SEXUAL ORIENTATION

Targeted law enforcement practices with respect to the gay community have a long history. In August 1977 a young boy, Emmanuel Jaques, was sexually assaulted and murdered in Toronto in what was described by the police and media as a "homosexual murder." See Yvonne Ng, *Ideology, Media and Moral Panics: An Analysis of the Jaques Murder* (M.A. Thesis, Centre of Criminology, University of Toronto, 1981) [unpublished] for a thorough description of the case.

The ensuing panic and public outrage was the setting within which the police then executed a massive raid and group arrest. On Thursday, 5 February 1981 at 11 p.m., approximately 300 officers were involved in a simultaneous raid on the four major Toronto gay baths. On that night, 336 men were arrested, representing the largest arrest in Canada since 1970 when 465 persons were jailed under the *War Measures Act* in that year, and a greater number than those arrested for any one-year period in Ontario from 1974 to 1980 for similar offences. The arrests were reportedly accompanied by physical and verbal abuse, damage to the premises, and posing for the media: Thomas S. Fleming, "The Bawdy House 'Boys': Some Notes on Media, Sporadic Moral Crusades, and Selective Law Enforcement" (1981) 3 Can. Crim. Forum 101.

In some cities, relations between police and gay and lesbian communities may have undergone changes through the work of activists in naming and in criminalizing bias crimes (see discussion, *infra*, **Sentencing**). However, these alliances have proven uneasy and fragile. Thus, even in the context of investigating a series of murders of gay men in Montréal, the police allegedly devoted resources to an undercover operation that, instead of looking for "bashers" in the locale, targeted "cruisers" and resulted in the arrest of a dozen gay men: André Picard, "Gays target of police, activist alleges" *The [Toronto] Globe and Mail* (13 May 1993) A2B.

A successful challenge to the enforcement of law was launched in *Little Sister's Book and Art Emporium* v. *Canada* (1996), 131 D.L.R. (4th) 486 (B.C.S.C.) wherein the plaintiffs identified the practices of Canada Customs in its administration of quasi-criminal legislation, the *Canada Customs Act* (S.C. 1986, c. 1 (2nd Supp.)) and Schedule VII of the *Customs Tariff* (S.C. 1987, c. 41 (3rd Supp.)) prohibitions on the importation of materials believed to be "obscene" under s. 163(8) of the *Criminal Code* into Canada, as violative of the *Charter*. The Supreme Court ruled on the case in 2000:

Little Sisters Book and Art Emporium v. Canada†

[BINNIE J.:]

After a trial of considerable complexity lasting two months, the trial judge in this case concluded not only that Customs officials had wrongly delayed, confiscated, destroyed, damaged, prohibited or misclassified materials imported by the appellant on numerous occasions, but that these errors were caused "by the systemic targeting of Little Sisters' importations in the [Vancouver] Customs Mail Center." Little Sisters is a lesbian and gay bookshop owned by the appellants James Eaton Deva and

---

† [2000] 2 S.C.R. 1120.

Guy Bruce Smythe, who say their equality rights as gay men have been violated by the government's action. The store carried a specialized inventory catering to the gay and lesbian community which consisted largely of books that included, but was not limited to, gay and lesbian literature, travel information, general interest periodicals, academic studies related to homosexuality, AIDS/HIV safe sex advisory material and gay and lesbian erotica. It was not in the nature of a "XXX Adult" store. It was and is a boutique carrying a fairly broad range of inventory of interest to a special clientele. It was considered something of a "community centre" for Vancouver's gay and lesbian population.

The appellants concede that much of the material imported by Little Sisters consisted of erotica but have denied throughout that anything it has imported is obscene. If the erotica had been manufactured in Canada, the government would have had no legal basis to suppress it short of a successful prosecution under s. 163 of the *Criminal Code*, R.S.C., 1985, c. C-46, in which the state would have the onus of establishing obscenity.

. . . .

FACTS

. . . .

Since its establishment in 1983, Little Sisters has imported 80 to 90 percent of its erotica from the United States. For the last 15 years it has been a reluctant participant in a running battle with Canada Customs. Its foreign suppliers typically insisted on payment within 30 days, yet administrative delays at Customs frequently held up shipments until months after they were paid for, and then, not infrequently, materials were seized or ordered returned to sender. In the usual course the appellants were given no reason for the seizure or return. Some of the suppliers refused to make further shipments.

In very detailed and comprehensive reasons, the trial judge made a number of key findings of fact in the appellants' favour. He identified very high error rates in determinations respecting Little Sisters' imports at all levels of the Customs review procedure. He held that "[s]uch high rates of error indicate more than mere differences of opinion and suggest systemic causes" ((1996), 18 B.C.L.R. (3d) 241, at para. 100). He identified several reasons for these high error rates, including the minimal resources given to Customs officials combined with inadequate training in obscenity law ranging from a few hours in the case of inspectors to a few days for higher ranks. Specifically, he found (at para. 116) that:

> Many publications, particularly books, are ruled obscene without adequate evidence. This highlights perhaps the most serious defect in the present administration of code 9956(a), that is, that classifying officers are neither adequately trained to make decisions on obscenity nor are they routinely provided with the time and the evidence necessary to make such decisions. There is no formal procedure for placing evidence of artistic or literary merit before the classifying officers. Consequently, many publications are prohibited entry into Canada that would likely not be found to be obscene if full evidence were considered by officers properly trained to weigh and evaluate that evidence.

. . . .

The trial judge found that the administration of the Customs scheme has a significantly differential impact on small or specialty publishers, importers and bookstores. He specifically found (at para. 105) that:

> Customs' administration of Code 9956(a) results in arbitrary consequences. Traditional bookstores do not have similar encounters with Canada Customs. Helen Hager, who operated a general-interest bookstore in Vancouver for many years, did not know that Customs inspected books for obscenity until she left that business and opened a store catering to women, in which she stocked some material for lesbians. She had two shipments from Inland [a book distributor] interrupted at the border and has never received two of the books in the shipment, nor any documents from Customs in relation to them.

. . . .

Seizure included not only magazines, videos and photographic essays, but books consisting entirely of text, including works by internationally acclaimed authors such as *The Man Sitting in the Corridor* by Marguerite Duras and *Querelle* by Jean Genet. Also seized were the award-winning novels *Trash* by Dorothy Allison and *The Young in One Another's Arms* by Jane Rule. Frequently AIDS/HIV safe-sex education literature was classified as prohibited. The Court record includes testimony from mainstream booksellers to the effect that no such problems were encountered in their importation of the same books. In fact, the President of Duthie's, a general bookstore chain in Vancouver, testified that an order she placed on behalf of the British Columbia Civil Liberties Association consisting of titles prohibited when sought to be imported by Little Sisters was inspected by Customs but released to Duthie's without difficulty. Duthie's Customs broker testified that its book shipments are examined solely for the purpose of determining GST payments. He thought that in the case of Duthie's there was generally no examination of titles for obscenity.

On the other hand the evidence showed that other small bookstores with specialized inventory or clientele comparable to Little Sisters' had encountered similar targeting. These included a scholarly bookstore "Pages" in Toronto carrying gay studies and HIV/AIDS literature as well as "The Toronto Women's Bookstore," a feminist bookstore. "Crosstown Traffic," a bookstore in Ottawa, was similarly affected. It appears that there was no such blanket surveillance of heterosexual erotica even in the case of so-called "adult" bookstores that sold nothing else.

Little Sisters complains that the frequent delay of shipments destined for its store, and the subsequent prohibition of some of the delayed items, have negatively impacted its business by, *inter alia*, disrupting planned book launches, causing loss of business to competitors stocking the same delayed or prohibited items, and items such as magazines, which depend for their shelf value on their timeliness. The case, however, is not about business losses. It is about the loss by a minority of the freedom to read and experience a broad range of writings and depictions, some of it claimed to be of high artistic value, by reason, they say, of bureaucratic refusal to release perfectly lawful material into the country.

Little Sisters identified 261 items that have been detained between 1984 and 1994, 77 of them on more than one occasion. Items sought to be imported by Little Sisters and subsequently delayed or prohibited included items that were previously ruled admissible when imported by Little Sisters. The trial judge noted (at para. 75) that a "striking example of this" is the collection of short stories entitled *Macho Sluts*, written by Pat Califia, a well-established author. It has been prohibited pursuant to s. 58 of the *Customs Act*, R.S.C., 1985, c. 1 (2nd Supp.) on four separate occasions since October 23, 1989, when it was re-determined under s. 63 to be admissible. The satire *Hothead Paisan* was prohibited when ordered by Little Sisters and, on one occasion, by The Women's Bookstore in Toronto, but was released to the latter bookstore without difficulties on subsequent orders. The trial judge noted another 35 publications that were prohibited after they had earlier been ruled admissible by Customs. Many items that have been prohibited when Little Sisters attempted to import them are found in the Vancouver Public Library including *Gay Ideas*, *Tom of Finland*, *The Men With the Pink Triangle*, *Dzeleron: Myths of the Northwest Coast*, *Gay Spirit* and *The Sexual Politics of Meat*. Customs officials were intrigued by the titles, apparently.

SCOPE OF THE CUSTOMS MANDATE

Customs officials testified that there are approximately 10.5 million entry transactions each year and that each day between 20,000 and 40,000 items of mail enter the Customs Mail Center in Vancouver. Much of this mail is of commercial value, and must be sorted and classified for tariff purposes. As part of this classification procedure, Parliament has charged the Customs authorities to intercept and exclude from this country obscene, hateful, treasonable or seditious goods.

. . . .

... In the wake of the decision in *Luscher* v. *Deputy Minister, Revenue Canada, Customs and Excise*, [1985] 1 F.C. 85 (C.A.), obscenity was defined by reference to s. 163 of the *Criminal Code*. As Parliament has prohibited only material that it has criminalized, Parliament apparently intended there to be a free flow of other materials across the border including sexually expressive material that appeals to minority tastes. The *Criminal Code* does not characterize "obscenity" based on sexual orientation and neither, it must be inferred, did Parliament intend Customs officials to do so.

. . . .

Nobody has a *Charter* right to import materials that are obscene within the meaning of s. 163 of the *Criminal Code*. The concern expressed by the trial judge was that much of the delayed or prohibited material did *not* qualify as obscene. The courts in British Columbia found that the appellants had established *Charter* violations. The real arguments are about the sources of the violations — whether they are located in the statutes themselves or only in their implementation — and what to do about them. This involves a consideration of how certain materials come to be classified as "obscene," and thus prohibited, and whether the appellants when contesting such a classification were fairly dealt with.

THE STATUTORY FRAMEWORK

Section 99 of the *Customs Act* authorizes Customs officers to examine imported goods and mail and to open packages that they reasonably suspect may contain goods referred to in the *Customs Tariff*, R.S.C., 1985, c. 41 (3rd Supp.). Mail is referred to Customs on a similar basis (*Canada Post Corporation Act*, R.S.C., 1985, c. C-10, s. 42)....

At the entry level, Customs inspectors determine the appropriate tariff classification (s. 58). At the relevant time, an item considered "obscene" and thus prohibited was subject to a re-determination upon request, by a specialized Customs unit and upon a further appeal subject to a further re-determination by the Deputy Minister....

. . . .

ANALYSIS

[The discussion of s. 2(b) of the *Charter* has been omitted.]

The Appellants' Claim that the Legislation Is Unconstitutionally Discriminatory Against the Gay and Lesbian Community

In addition to their free speech attack on the machinery of the Customs legislation, the individual appellants invoked their equality rights under s. 15(1) of the *Charter*. Their position is that the Customs legislation itself is the source of violations of s. 15(1) as well as s. 2(b) of the *Charter*, and they claim that they are entitled to a s. 52 nullification remedy based as much on infringement of their equality rights as on a denial of their right of free expression. It is therefore convenient, before addressing the *Morgentaler* issue, to determine whether their equality rights have been infringed and if so whether the source of the problem is the Customs legislation itself, as the appellants contend, or whether the problem described by the trial judge resulted from the unconstitutional conduct of Customs officials exercising powers under constitutional legislation.

The appellants argue that the legislative scheme operates with disproportionate and discriminatory effects on the gay and lesbian community and therefore contravenes s. 15(1) and is to that extent null and void.

A number of recent decisions in this Court have emphasized a "purposive" interpretation of s. 15(1) equality rights: *Law* v. *Canada (Minister of Employment and Immigration)*, [1999] 1 S.C.R. 497; *Corbiere* v. *Canada (Minister of Indian and Northern Affairs)*, [1999] 2 S.C.R. 203; *Granovsky* v. *Canada (Minister of Employment and Immigration)*, [2000] 1 S.C.R. 703, 2000 SCC 28; and *Lovelace* v. *Ontario*, [2000] 1 S.C.R. 950, 2000 SCC 37. These decisions were not available at the time this case was dealt with by the courts of British Columbia. It is now clearly established that the analysis proceeds in three stages with close regard to context. At the first stage the claimant must show that the law, program or activity imposes differential treatment between the claimant and others with whom the claimant may fairly claim equality. The second stage requires the claimant to demonstrate that this differentiation is based on one or more of the enumerated or analogous grounds. The third stage requires the claimant to establish that the differentiation amounts to a form of discrimination that has the effect of demeaning the claimant's human dignity. The "dignity" aspect of the test is designed to weed out trivial or other complaints that do not engage the purpose of the equality provision. In *Law, supra*, the Court stated, at para. 51:

> It may be said that the purpose of s. 15(1) is to prevent the violation of essential human dignity and freedom through the imposition of disadvantage, stereotyping, or political or social prejudice, and to promote a society in which all persons enjoy equal recognition at law as human beings or as members of Canadian society, equally capable and equally deserving of concern, respect and consideration.

The trial judge made strong findings of fact in support of the appellants' position, even though in the end he refused substantial relief on this ground.

Stage One: Differential Treatment

The trial judge found that shipments to gay and lesbian bookstores were subjected to delays and seizures that were not only unjustified but were disproportional to their share of imported material (paras. 105 and 251); that the appellants had imported publications seized notwithstanding the identical publications were freely available at other bookstores and in the Vancouver Public Library; and that these problems of differential treatment were systemic (para. 250). The trial judge found that "much *homosexual* erotica that has been prohibited as obscene is not, in fact, obscene" (para. 223 (emphasis added)). I will not repeat the findings in these respects set out earlier in these reasons. Contrary to the conclusion of the trial judge, however, the appellants contend that the source of this adverse treatment lies in the Customs legislation itself.

The appellants were seen as key players in the lesbian and gay community in Vancouver, and were targeted because homosexuality was too often equated with obscenity. While homosexuals are said to form less than 10 per cent of the Canadian population, up to 75 per cent of the material from time to time detained and examined for obscenity was directed to homosexual audiences. (The percentage varied of course.) The proportion of erotica produced for homosexual audiences detained and examined by Customs was, the trial judge found, "a proportion far in excess of the relative size of the group" (para. 251). There was evidence on which these findings could be made.

The trial judge identified Customs' relentless pursuit of depictions of anal sex in gay erotica as symptomatic of the Department's misplaced zeal. It appears that the Department of Justice accepted as correct the view of Borins J. (as he then was) in *R. v. Doug Rankine Co.* (1983), 36 C.R. (3d) 154 (Ont. Co. Ct.), quoted in 1985 by Wilson J. in *Towne Cinema, supra*, at p. 523, that the courts have taken the view that "[c]ontemporary community standards would also tolerate the distribution of films which consist of scenes of group sex, lesbianism, fellatio, cunnilingus, *and anal sex*" (p. 173 (emphasis added)). Despite this opinion of the Department of Justice, Customs officials continued to prohibit depictions of anal sex until Memorandum D9-1-1 was revised in September 1994 just prior to trial. The trial judge found (at para. 272) that Customs' refusal to abide by the Justice opinion deprived the gay community

> of representations of practices central to the values and culture of the minority group to which they belong. As well, as Professor Waugh pointed out, it constituted an embargo of "safe sex" guidelines within Canadian homosexual communities at a time, in the context of the AIDS epidemic, when such guidelines have been particularly important.

Significantly, the trial judge found that the failure of Customs to amend their manuals in this regard was no accident. He states (at para. 268):

> The decision not to amend was one deliberately taken, and no satisfactory explanation was offered by the federal Crown for the fact that Customs continued to prohibit depictions of anal penetration in the face of the jurisprudence I have referred to and the opinions received from the Department of Justice.

Taking the evidence as a whole, it was clearly open to the trial judge to find, as he did, that the appellants suffered differential treatment when compared to importers of heterosexually explicit material, let alone more general bookstores that carried at least some of the same titles as Little Sisters.

Stage Two: Enumerated and Analogous Grounds

The trial judge rejected the second stage of the appellants' analysis despite his view that the appellants had suffered adverse treatment because they were part of, and suppliers to, the lesbian and gay community. He concluded the differentiation was based on "real" characteristics and not the "stereotypical application of presumed group or personal characteristics." He thought it significant that both homosexuality and obscenity are defined in terms of sexual practices. He agreed that the differentiation was based on sexual orientation (second stage). He nevertheless found (at para. 135) no infringement because:

> Since homosexuals are defined by their homosexuality and their art and literature is permeated with representations of their sexual practices, it is inevitable that they will be disproportionately affected by a law proscribing the proliferation of obscene sexual representations.

There was no evidence to support the linkage thus made between the frequency and scale of sexual representations and the quite different issue of obscenity. A flourishing of sexual expression may have no connection whatsoever with harm-based obscenity. The trial judge himself protested against the detention of a "disturbing amount of homosexual art and literature that is arguably not obscene" (para. 252). Nevertheless he concluded that much of the imported material could be seen as degrading and dehumanizing and therefore prohibited "because it is obscene, not because it is homosexual" (para. 136).

In my view, the issue of discrimination arises with regard to material that was *not* obscene but was nevertheless detained, damaged, misclassified or without justification turned back at the border *because* it was destined for the gay and lesbian community. While sexual orientation is not mentioned explicitly in s. 15 of the *Charter*, it is clearly an analogous ground to the listed personal characteristics, as was held in *Egan* v. *Canada*, [1995] 2 S.C.R. 513;

Vriend v. *Alberta*, [1998] 1 S.C.R. 493, and *M.* v. *H.*, [1999] 2 S.C.R. 3.

Stage Three: Discrimination

There is no need here to review at length the "[contextual] factors which may be referred to by a s. 15(1) claimant in order to demonstrate that legislation has the effect of demeaning his or her dignity, as dignity is understood for the purpose of the *Charter* equality guarantee" (*Law*, supra, at para. 62). The Court held in *Vriend*, supra, that the gay and lesbian community has historically been the victim of disadvantage, stereotyping, prejudice and vulnerability. As discussed earlier, the community standard of tolerance of harm is a broad church that embraces respect for minority expression. It is antithetical to the remedial reasons underlying adoption of the community standard to single out a particular minority as being less worthy than others of protection and respect.

The appellants claim that only 14 charges of obscenity were laid in four years in British Columbia while approximately 35,000 prohibitions were imposed by Customs in the same period. We do not know how many of these charges relate to material imported by, amongst others, the appellants, or how many of the 14 charges (if any) resulted in convictions. Targeting is not necessarily unconstitutional. The Customs Department is obliged to use its limited resources in the most cost-effective way. This might include targeting shipments that, on the basis of experience or other information, are more likely than others to contain prohibited goods. The evidence here, however, did not justify the targeting of Little Sisters and the three other lesbian and gay bookstores. The Crown did not suggest that so-called XXX sex shops that specialize in hard core heterosexual material were subject to such blanket surveillance, even though, unlike in the case of Little Sisters, little if any of their stock is found routinely on display in the Vancouver Public Library. The appellants were entitled to the equal benefit of a fair and open Customs procedure, and because they imported gay and lesbian erotica, which was and is perfectly lawful, they were adversely affected in comparison to other individuals importing comparable publications of a heterosexual nature.

On a more general level, there was no evidence that homosexual erotica is proportionately more likely to be obscene than heterosexual erotica. It therefore cannot be said that there was any legitimate correspondence between the ground of alleged discrimination (sexual orientation) and the reality of the appellants' circumstances (importers of books and other publications including, but by no means limited to, gay and lesbian erotica).

As to the nature and importance of the interest affected, the trial judge himself concluded that access to homosexual erotica was central to gay and lesbian culture at para. 128:

> Because sexual practices are so integral to homosexual culture, any law proscribing representations of sexual practices will necessarily affect homosexuals to a greater extent than it will other groups in society, to whom representations of sexual practices are much less significant and for whom such representations play a relatively marginal role in art and literature.

There was ample evidence to support the trial judge's conclusion that the adverse treatment meted out by Canada Customs to the appellants and through them to Vancouver's gay and lesbian community violated the appellants' legitimate sense of self-worth and human dignity. The Customs treatment was high-handed and dismissive of the appellants' right to receive lawful expressive material which they had every right to import. When Customs officials prohibit and thereby censor lawful gay and lesbian erotica, they are making a statement about gay and lesbian culture, and the statement was reasonably interpreted by the appellants as demeaning gay and lesbian values. The message was that their concerns were less worthy of attention and respect than those of their heterosexual counterparts.

While here it is the interests of the gay and lesbian community that were targeted, other vulnerable groups may similarly be at risk from overzealous censorship. Little Sisters was targeted because it was considered "different." On a more general level, it seems to me fundamentally unacceptable that expression which is free within the country can become stigmatized and harassed by government officials simply because it crosses an international boundary, and is thereby brought within the bailiwick of the Customs department. The appellants' constitutional right to receive perfectly *lawful* gay and lesbian erotica should not be diminished by the fact their suppliers are, for the most part, located in the United States. Their freedom of expression does not stop at the border.

That having been said, there is nothing on the face of the Customs legislation, or in its necessary effects, which contemplates or encourages differential treatment based on sexual orientation. The definition of obscenity, as already discussed, operates without distinction between homosexual and heterosexual erotica. The differentiation was made here at the administrative level in the implementation of the Customs legislation.

. . . .

This Court has already recognized that the existence of prosecutorial discretion does not offend the principles of fundamental justice; see *R.* v. *Lyons*, [[1987] 2 S.C.R. 309], at p. 348; see also *R.* v. *Jones*, [1986] 2 S.C.R. 284, at pp. 303–4. The Court did add that if, in a particular case, it was established that a discretion was exercised for improper or arbitrary motives, a remedy under s. 24 of the *Charter* would lie, but no allegation of this kind has been made in the present case.

If Parliament is constitutionally able to confer broad powers on the police and Justice Department officials under the *Criminal Code* without establishing a specific institutional framework to deal with out-of-court *Charter*-sensitive activities, I fail to see how Parliament is nevertheless required to legislate special procedures to govern Customs officials.

In the case of the Customs legislation, Parliament contemplated that more detailed regulations may be necessary for the guidance of officials and others. It provided in s. 164(1)(j) of the *Customs Act*, to repeat, that the Governor in Council "may make regulations ... generally to carry out the purposes and provisions of this Act." Many of the systemic problems identified by the trial judge in the department's treatment of potentially obscene imports might have been dealt with by institutional arrangements implemented by regulation, but this was not done. However, the fact that a regulatory power lies unexercised provides no basis for attacking the validity of the statute that conferred it.

The specific provisions of the *Customs Act* relevant to the appellants are the tariff classification provision (s. 58) and the various rights to a re-determination (ss. 60, 63 and 71) and appeals to the courts (ss. 67 and 152). Parliament was entitled, I think, to expect that the Minister, with or without regulations under s. 164, would put in place the necessary detailed procedures, including procedures appropriate for processing constitutionally sensitive material.

The fact this issue arises in connection with the administration of a government department prompts two further comments. The first is that it is in the nature of government work that the power of the state is exercised and the *Charter* rights of the citizen may therefore be engaged. While there is evidence of actual abuse here, there is the *potential* for abuse in many areas, and a rule requiring Parliament to enact in each case special procedures for the protection of *Charter* rights would be unnecessarily rigid.

Secondly, the government needs neither a special statute nor special regulations to deal with its own employees. Customs officials are responsible to the Minister by virtue of their jobs. I have already held that *Customs Tariff* Code 9956 creates a constitutionally valid standard. In the administration of the department the Minister may supplement by directive the provisions of the *Customs Act* for its implementation. The public service responds to ministerial direction with no less alacrity than it responds to statute or regulation. In short, an importer's rights may be protected in fact by statute, regulation, ministerial direction or even departmental practice. What is crucial, at the end of the day, is that *Charter* rights are in fact respected. The modalities for achieving that objective will vary with the context. There is nothing unconstitutional about the option selected by Parliament in this case.

All of this is to say that there are various methods to ensure respect by the public service for the *Charter* rights of importers. Each method has its advantages and disadvantages. The fact Parliament opted for the more flexible routes of delegated regulation and ministerial directive is not, I think, a reason to invalidate the legislation itself.

Section 1 Justification

. . . .

It should be noted at the outset that the s. 15(1) infringements identified by the trial judge are incapable of s. 1 justification. Violative conduct by government officials that is not authorized by statute is not "prescribed by law" and cannot therefore be justified under s. 1. The equality rights issues therefore proceed directly to the remedy phase of the analysis. Limitations on free expression were, however, authorized by Parliament in the Customs legislation, and on that branch of the appeal consideration must be given to whether a border inspection regime in which the government assumes the burden of proving obscenity on a balance of probabilities is a reasonable limit prescribed by law that can be demonstrably justified in a free and democratic society.

. . . .

Remedy

In my view, the appellants have established that:

1. Section 152(3) of the *Customs Act* should not be construed and applied so as to place the

onus on an importer to establish that goods are not obscene within the meaning of s. 163(8) of the *Criminal Code*. The burden of proving obscenity rests on the Crown or other person who alleges it.

2. The rights of the appellants under s. 2(b) and s. 15(1) of the *Charter* have been infringed in the following respects:
   (a) They have been targeted as importers of obscene materials despite the absence of any evidence to suggest that gay and lesbian erotica is more likely to be obscene than heterosexual erotica, or that the appellants are likely offenders in this regard;
   (b) In consequence of the targeting, the appellants have suffered excessive and unnecessary prejudice in terms of delays, cost and other losses in having their goods cleared (if at all) through Canada Customs;
   (c) The reasons for this excessive and unnecessary prejudice include:
      (i) failure by Customs to devote a sufficient number of officials to carry out the review of the appellants' publications in a timely way;
      (ii) the inadequate training of the officials assigned to the task;
      (iii) the failure to place at the disposal of these officials proper guides and manuals, failure to update Memorandum D9-1-1 and its accompanying illustrative manual in a timely way, and the failure to develop workable procedures to deal with books consisting mostly or wholly of written text;
      (iv) failure to establish internal deadlines and related criteria for the expeditious review of expressive materials;
      (v) failure to incorporate into departmental guides and manuals relevant advice received from time to time from the Department of Justice;
      (vi) failure to provide the appellants in a timely way with notice of the basis for detention of publications, the opportunity to make meaningful submissions on a re-determination, and reasonable access to the disputed materials for that purpose; and
      (vii) failure to extend to the appellants the equal benefit of fair and expeditious treatment of their imported goods without discrimination based on sexual orientation.

It is apparent that this catalogue particularizes in greater detail the declaration issued by the trial judge, namely:

> THIS COURT DECLARES that Tariff Code 9956(a) of Schedule VII and s. 114 of the *Customs Tariff*, S.C. 1987, c. 41 (3rd Supplement) and ss. 58 and 71 of the *Customs Act*, S.C. 1986, c. 1 (2nd Supplement) have at times been construed and applied in a manner contrary to s. 2(b) and s. 15(1) of the *Canadian Charter of Rights and Freedoms*.

The Crown did not cross-appeal the grant of the declaration and neither in this Court nor in the British Columbia Court of Appeal did the appellants make submissions on whether or how a declaration under s. 24(1) of the *Charter* could be better framed to grant substantial relief. Their objective there as here was to get rid of the legislation altogether.

Having rejected that s. 52 argument, except as to the reverse onus provision, the remaining question is whether the Court should attempt to fashion a more structured s. 24(1) remedy. I conclude, with some hesitation, that it is not practicable to do so. The trial concluded on December 20, 1994. We are told that in the past six years, Customs has addressed the institutional and administrative problems encountered by the appellants. In the absence of more detailed information as to what precisely has been done, and the extent to which (if at all) it has remedied the situation, I am not prepared to endorse my colleague's conclusion that these measures are "not sufficient" (para. 262) and have offered "little comfort" (para. 265). Equally, however, we have not been informed by the appellants of the specific measures (short of declaring the legislation invalid or inoperative) that in the appellants' view would remedy any continuing problems.

The most detailed suggestion the appellants have made in the way of a s. 24(1) remedy is the following request:

> ... in the final alternative an injunction restraining Customs from applying and administering the *Customs Tariff*, S.C. 1987, c. 41 (3rd Supplement) s. 114, Schedule VII, Code 9956(a) and the *Customs Act*, S.C. 1986 (2nd Supp.), s. 58 and s. 71, as amended, permanently or until such time as

there is no risk that the unconstitutional administration will continue.

The first branch of the proposed injunction ("permanently") amounts to a s. 52 declaration of inoperability, which I do not consider justified. The second branch ("until such time") sets an unrealistic standard (*"no* risk"). If diluted to a call for constitutional behaviour, the result would add little to the general duty that falls on any government official to act in accordance with the Constitution, injunction or no injunction, and would scarcely advance the objectives of either clarity or enforceability. A more structured s. 24(1) remedy might well be helpful but it would serve the interests of none of the parties for this Court to issue a formal declaratory order based on six-year-old evidence supplemented by conflicting oral submissions and speculation on the current state of affairs. The views of the Court on the merits of the appellants' complaints as the situation stood at the end of 1994 are recorded in these reasons and those of my colleague Iacobucci J. These findings should provide the appellants with a solid platform from which to launch any further action in the Supreme Court of British Columbia should they consider that further action is necessary.

[The judgment of Iacobucci, Arbour, and LeBel JJ., dissenting in part, has been omitted. They would have found that the legislation violated s. 2(b) because it lacked any safeguards to prevent *Charter* violations.]

∎

C. RACISM

Racism may also be implicated in decisions regarding the enforcement of the law, as recent cases illustrate.

LEO LACHANCE

The killing in Prince Albert, Saskatchewan, of Leo LaChance, a Cree man, by Carney Nerland, a high profile member of the Aryan Nations, and the legal treatment of Nerland's crime provoked considerable controversy. On 28 January 1991, as Mr. LaChance was leaving Nerland's gun shop, Nerland fired two bullets into the floor of his shop before raising the gun and firing a third shot at the door that LaChance was pulling closed behind him. The shot entered LaChance's body. He staggered 35 metres before collapsing. Nerland did not call an ambulance, and refused an effort by a passerby to use his telephone for that purpose. The two witnesses in the store likewise made no effort to assist LaChance or to contact police; one of these witnesses was a provincial jail guard who was therefore also a sworn peace officer.

After LaChance died in the hospital and Nerland was arrested, he stated to the police, "If I'm convicted of shooting that Indian, I should get a medal and you should pin it on me." The police charged Nerland with manslaughter, although at the bail hearing Judge Tom Ferris expressed surprise that the charge had not been one of murder and that the Crown was not opposing the release of the accused: David Roberts, "Conviction of white supremacist brings little relief to prairie city" *The [Toronto] Globe and Mail* (21 May 1991) A1.

The Crown did not oppose Nerland's release on bail and also agreed to a four-year jail sentence on Nerland's guilty plea in spite of his apparent lack of remorse. Chief Allen Felix, speaking for the Prince Albert Tribal Council, called for a public inquiry. His remarks were reported in Maureen Marud, "P.A. Tribal Council seeks inquiry into justice system" *The [Saskatoon] Star-Phoenix* (4 May 1991) A3:

> We believe there were some shortcuts taken during this judicial process. Decisions were made too quickly, the investigation was not properly carried out, and overtones of racism and Aryan Nations involvement were never analyzed or taken into consideration.
>
> [Any inquiry should examine] to what extent does the Aryan Nation and its genocidal philosophy have support within the Prince Albert community and the various institutions of the criminal justice system.... [W]e cannot assume that the local authorities were not involved.†

The Nerland case was widely discussed in the media and provoked protest and criticism: Editorial, "Nerland's sentence too light for crime"

---

† Reproduced by permission of the author.

Prince Albert Daily Herald (16 April 1991) 4; Bill Doskoch, "Case frustrates natives" *[Regina] Leader Post* (4 May 1991) A8; Dana Wagg, "Supremacist gets four years: 'You'll have to pin a medal on me'" *[Edmonton] Windspeaker* (26 April 1991) 1; Ivan Morin, "Nerland sentence a mockery of justice system" *[Edmonton] Windspeaker* (10 May 1991) 5; Donella Hoffman, "White supremacist's manslaughter case needs review, says mayor" *The [Saskatoon] Star-Phoenix* (10 July 1991) A8. For a detailed description of the case by a journalist who wrote extensively on the events, see Connie Sampson, *Buried in Silence* (Edmonton: NeWest, 1995).

In response to the public outcry, the LaChance/Nerland Commission of Inquiry was convened pursuant to terms of reference that are reproduced in *Re Royal Canadian Mounted Police and Commission of Inquiry* (1992), 75 C.C.C. (3d) 419 at 420 (Sask. C.A.). In this case, the court held that the Commission could not compel the RCMP to disclose the name of a police informer involved in the facts under investigation on the grounds of protection of the public interest. After the Supreme Court of Canada refused to hear an appeal of the Court of Appeal ruling without giving reasons, the Prince Albert Tribal Council itself publicly identified the informant as Carney Nerland himself: CP, "Cree's killer named as police informant" *The [Toronto] Globe and Mail* (13 November 1992) A5.

The LaChance/Nerland Commission faulted the police and prosecutors for failing to consider that Nerland's racism may have motivated the offence, for failing to investigate Nerland's link with the Aryan Nations, for allowing Nerland to operate a gun shop given his threats of violence and his association with a hate group that promotes white supremacy through violent action, and for failing to investigate the evidence suggesting that in fact LaChance was inside, not outside, when shot. However, in spite of these findings, the Commission stated that all officials had acted in good faith and made only very minor recommendations for reform (that at least one officer fluent in Cree be on duty in Prince Albert at all times and that race relations training be instituted for officers): CP, "Report on LaChance case faults police, prosecutors" *The [Toronto] Globe and Mail* (20 November 1993) A7. Furthermore, as Aboriginal leaders pointed out, the issue of whether Nerland received special treatment in terms of the enforcement of the law was not addressed by the inquiry, as it seemed to accept at face value the police assertion that Nerland's status as an informant did not influence their investigation: David Roberts, "Racism not probed, native leaders say" *The [Toronto] Globe and Mail* (23 November 1993) A10. See LaChance/Nerland Commission of Inquiry, *Report of Commission of Inquiry into the Shooting Death of Leo LaChance: Relating to the January 1991 shooting death of Leo LaChance at Prince Albert, Saskatchewan and the consequent plea and sentence of Carney Milton Nerland for the crime of manslaughter* (Prince Albert: LaChance/Nerland Commission of Inquiry, 1993) (Commissioner E.N. (Ted) Hughes).

Nerland's involvement with the white supremacist group, Church of Jesus Christ Christian-Aryan Nations, had been documented by a Board of Inquiry Decision, *In the Matter of Section 2 of the Individual's Rights Protection Act, R.S.A. 1980, c. I-2; and In the Matter of The Public Inquiries Act, R.S.A. 1980, c. P-29 between Harvey Kane et al. v. Church of Jesus Christ Christian-Aryan Nations* (28 February 1992). That inquiry dealt with complaints about a white supremacist gathering (Aryan Fest) that was held in Alberta in September 1990. As the lengthy report documents at 37:

> Several persons at the Aryan Fest carried, and provocatively displayed, a variety of weapons.... [T]hese were not simple hunting rifles. Instead, the participants carried various types of military-style assault weapons. One masked man carried a rifle with an enlarged magazine and fixed bayonet.... Another uniformed man carried a shotgun and bandolier of shells.
>
> The assault weapons added to the atmosphere of hostility and intimidation. The video tapes show the weapons being handled in an aggressive way.
>
> Carney Nerland played a prominent role. He approached the gate and menacingly pumped his shotgun. He held it up over the gate to display it to the protestors and journalists. He said, "This is called Native birth control." At one point in his exchange with Mr. Sobolewski [an Auschwitz survivor] he said, "Why don't you come on private property and say that. We'll have to practice some birth control."
>
> Holding out his loaded, pistol-handled, pump action 12 gauge shotgun, Carney Nerland said, "A 12 gauge cuts a person right in half, it's just great for preventing further births. It's a way to customize the womb."

Charges of wilfully promoting hatred laid against other individual members of the Ku Klux Klan and the Church of Jesus Christ Christian-Aryan Nations in Manitoba were stayed by the

Crown due to questionable police evidence. There were also defence allegations of "entrapment" on the basis that the police helped one of the accused to select the hate material and copied it for him at the police station: David Roberts, "Manitoba Klan case collapses" *The [Toronto] Globe and Mail* (9 September 1992) A5. Saskatchewan Justice Minister Gary Lane, in anticipation of an election, announced his intention to undertake a general inquiry of "native justice" in the province, but without reviewing specific cases: Roberts, "Conviction of white supremacist," *supra*.

The questions raised about the link between police and Nerland and the use of such informants continue to ferment. For example, Nerland was released on parole into the police witness protection program in mid-December 1993, provoking further protest about police involvement in shielding Nerland from the full force of the criminal law: Chris Wattie, "Native leaders express outrage at white supremacist's parole" *The Ottawa Citizen* (16 December 1993) A5. Furthermore, revelations about the broader role of agencies such as the Canadian Security Intelligence Service in facilitating the crimes of white supremacist organizations have also kept the issue alive in the media and in public debates: Stephen Bindman, "CSIS denies looking the other way while racists broke law" *The Ottawa Citizen* (7 October 1994) A3; see also the discussion in Abell and Sheehy, *Proof, Defences, and Beyond*, **Entrapment**.

WILSON NEPOOSE

Another case that attracted calls for a public inquiry is that of Wilson Nepoose, a Cree man convicted in 1987 by an all-white jury. A key witness later claimed that she was intimidated by the RCMP The questionable aspects of this conviction include the facts that the key witness stated that the RCMP used intimidation to force her to incriminate Mr. Nepoose by testifying that she saw him with the victim the day she was killed; that the date this key witness testified to was, in fact, two days after the murder; and that the police failed to disclose this and other evidentiary inconsistencies to the defence lawyer. In 1991, Justice Minister Kim Campbell asked the Alberta Court of Appeal to re-open the case. The Court of Appeal appointed Justice Sinclair to hear the new evidence on the issues identified above, and he reported back in 1991: *Her Majesty the Queen versus Wilson W. Nepoose: Report of the Court of Appeal of Alberta by Mr. Justice W.R. Sinclair, Special Commissioner, appointed pursuant to s. 683 (1)(e)(ii) of the Criminal Code of Canada*.

On 10 March 1992 in reliance upon Justice Sinclair's report, the Alberta Court of Appeal ordered a new trial on the basis that there was a strong possibility that a miscarriage of justice had occurred: *R. v. Nepoose* (1992), 71 C.C.C. (3d) 419 (Alta. C.A.). The Crown declined to re-prosecute the case and instead announced its intention to enter a stay of proceedings. Nepoose had, by 1992, served five years of imprisonment. Both Nepoose's lawyer and a public petition called for a public inquiry into the case (CP, "Nepoose wins new trial after five years in jail" *The [Toronto] Globe and Mail* (10 March 1992) A5), but no response has been made by the government.

However, one of the police on the original investigation, Donald Zazulak, was subsequently convicted of perjury and demoted for lying to Justice Sinclair in 1991 about the notations referring to Nepoose, "slimeball" (written by another officer) and "yeah" (written by Zazulak) in the investigation report. Zazulak's conviction was affirmed by the Supreme Court of Canada, although Major, J. stated that the sentence ought to be mitigated by his "good but misguided motive" of protecting the reputation of the RCMP: *R. v. Zazulak*, [1994] 2 S.C.R. 5. Nepoose was apparently compensated under federal provincial guidelines discussed *infra*, **Civil Remedies**: see Kirk Makin, "A lawsuit nearly impossible to win" *The [Toronto] Globe and Mail* (16 November 1995) A8.

Not all cases receive the same media attention and prominence, but there are other examples where Aboriginal people have been unjustly targeted and convicted in the criminal law system. For example, in Manitoba, an Aboriginal man charged with murder remained in jail for 11 months before being released on the basis that his alleged "confession" could not possibly have been true given that he was in jail already at the time of the killing: David Roberts, "Manitoba officials drop double murder charges" *The [Toronto] Globe and Mail* (1 October 1991) A1.

Racially discriminatory enforcement of the law has been challenged in several cases. In *R. v. Bob* (1991), 3 C.R. (4th) 348 (Sask. C.A.), the accused were charged with the offence of keeping a common gaming house, contrary to s. 185(1) of the *Criminal Code*. They had refused to pay provincial licensing fees that would have made their charitable bingo lawful under s. 190(1)(a) of the *Criminal Code*, on the basis that as members of a band within the meaning of the *Indian Act*, R.S.C. 1985,

c. I-5, s. 87(1),(2), they were exempt from paying "taxation" with respect to personal property situated on a reservation. They argued, among other things, that the enforcement of the criminal law against them violated s. 15 of the *Charter*. The court stated (at 359) that the registrar had improperly applied the fee requirement to the accused and in denying them licenses upon their refusal to pay, had violated their s. 15 rights to equality before the law: "[T]he effect of his ruling was to require a group of people, the Indians, to give up a right before they could obtain a licence and be in a position to take advantage of s. 190 of the *Code*. No other group of individuals in our society was required to give up a right which they possessed in order to take [this] advantage." As a result, the court set aside the convictions and acquitted the accused.

D. MISCARRIAGES OF JUSTICE

While miscarriages of justice and wrongful convictions plague members of groups identified by class, sexual orientation, race and racism, other innocent individuals are caught up in the machinations of the criminal justice system. Several examples come to mind, in addition to the cases of Donald Marshall, Jr., *supra* **Aboriginal Peoples and Criminal Law** and Wilson Nepoose including the case of David Milgaard and Guy Paul Morin, discussed below. The cases of Wilbert Coffin, Thomas Sophonow, and Steven Truscott are discussed in Barrie Anderson and Dawn Anderson, *Manufacturing Guilt. Wrongful Convictions in Canada* (Halifax: Fernwood, 1998).

DAVID MILGAARD

After serving 22 years of a life sentence, Milgaard's 1970 conviction for the murder of Gail Miller was set aside by the Supreme Court of Canada: *Reference Re Milgaard*, [1992] 1 S.C.R. 866. The Court reviewed the conviction pursuant to s. 53 of the *Supreme Court Act*, and concluded (at 871, 873) that "new," credible evidence (recantation by a key witness, additional evidence regarding Milgaard's alleged confession, and a confession by another man) "could well affect a jury's assessment of the guilt or innocence of Milgaard. The continued conviction of Milgaard would result in a miscarriage of justice if an opportunity was not presented for a jury to consider the fresh evidence." Because the Court also could not find that Milgaard was innocent either beyond a reasonable doubt or on a preponderance of evidence, a new trial was ordered. The Saskatchewan Minister declined to re-prosecute.

The RCMP investigated whether the police were involved in criminal wrongdoing in terms of a cover-up of the Milgaard case and began to release their findings in fall 1994. After 18 months, in July 1995, 250 pages were released (and three volumes withheld), which concluded that there was no evidence of criminal wrongdoing in the original investigation and prosecution: M.J. Sawatsky (Assistant Officer-in-Charge), *The RCMP investigation into allegations of wrongdoing by the Saskatoon City Police and the Saskatchewan Department of the Attorney General (Saskatchewan Justice) in the investigation and prosecution of David Edgar Milgaard* (Regina: RCMP, 1994). Milgaard's lawyer commented: "This is a report for law enforcement, by law enforcement, on behalf of law enforcement for the benefit of law enforcement"; "[i]t has nothing to do with justice for David Milgaard": David Roberts, "Milgaard probe 'slanted rehash'" *The [Toronto] Globe and Mail* (13 July 1995) A5.

Because the government had refused to compensate Milgaard or to acknowledge wrongdoing, he launched a civil suit claiming conspiracy by the prosecutors and police in covering up evidence that would have exonerated him in 1970. In *Milgaard* v. *Kujawa*, [1994] 9 W.W.R. 305 (Sask. C.A.) the court ruled that Milgaard could proceed with claims of abuse of statutory powers against the Crown (for failing to disclose exculpatory evidence) and conspiracy against the police and Crown; it also stated that these types of claims should not be shielded by the doctrine of prosecutorial immunity as they essentially amount to a "fraud upon the law" (at 315). It noted as well that Milgaard had amended his statement of claim to include the tort of malicious prosecution, which is also exempt from the immunity doctrine.

Milgaard thereafter instigated another civil action, this one in defamation, against the Saskatchewan Minister of Justice, Robert Mitchell. When announcing his decision not to re-prosecute

Milgaard after the Supreme Court ruling, Mitchell stated that he still believed that Milgaard was properly convicted, that he "did it." Milgaard alleges that these words "were intended to convey to the Canadian public that [he] should be forever viewed as a murderer": Henry Hess, "Milgaard sues Saskatchewan Justice Minister" *The [Toronto] Globe and Mail* (5 May 1995) A3.

Milgaard was finally exonerated fully in 1997 when DNA test results proved that he was not Gail Miller's killer; these same results identified Larry Fisher as the perpetrator. The Saskatchewan government issued a formal apology in 1999 and, together with the federal government, agreed to a $10 million compensation award for Milgaard. A full inquiry into his wrongful conviction was announced in 2000, but as of 2002 has not yet commenced: Darren Bernhardt, "Gov't dragging its feet on wrongful conviction probe: Milgaard Justice department to wait until Larry Fisher case closed" *The Saskatoon Star-Phoenix* (12 February 2002).

GUY PAUL MORIN

Morin was arrested in 1985 for the murder of Christine Jessop, and was finally cleared of all charges in 1995. He had been acquitted by a jury in 1986 after spending ten months in jail, but the Crown successfully appealed based on errors committed at trial. He was re-tried in 1992, after years of being in the process, and convicted by a jury. He spent six months in jail before being released on bail pending appeal. During the appeal process, DNA testing was used to exonerate Morin, and in 1995, the appeal prosecutors asked the Ontario Court of Appeal to acquit Morin: Kirk Makin, "Crown to seek Morin's acquittal" *The [Toronto] Globe and Mail* (23 January 1995) A1, A3.

One clue to understanding the investigation of Morin, who was a neighbour of the deceased girl, was the perception that he was mentally ill (he allegedly suffered from schizophrenia). At his first trial, a decision by the defence to advance insanity as a defence may have fuelled the pursuit of the prosecution over the years: *ibid*. As one of the jurors in the 1992 conviction stated: "What is so frightening ... is that so many items of evidence can end up being knitted together against a wholly innocent man": *ibid*. at A3.

The Ontario government initially resisted calls for an inquiry into the many questions and problems already identified with respect to the police investigation, the forensic evidence, the prosecution's decisions, and the charge given by the judge to the jury, stating that [...] hinder a re-opening of the mu[...] Kirk Makin, in "What was misse[d ...]" *The [Toronto] Globe and Mail* ([...]) A6, gives a detailed description [of the] major weaknesses in the evidence and process. For example, one investigating officer admitted to having fabricated an entire notebook purporting to describe evidence collected at the scene. His prosecution for obstructing justice was stayed on the ground of his ill health (*R. v. Michalowsky* (12 November 1991), (Ont. Ct. (Gen. Div.)) [unreported]), but he nonetheless testified as a prosecution witness in the second trial. According to Makin, the police, the prosecutors, and the judge also highlighted for the jury the question of Morin's sanity at the second trial, even though he chose not to put it at issue in his defence.

While the government then promised both compensation and an inquiry in the future for Morin, more than a year later no action had been taken. Kirk Makin, in "Morin appeals to Premier for justice" *The [Toronto] Globe and Mail* (14 June 1996) A6, reported that Morin "is frustrated that most or all of the police officers and prosecutors who helped secure his conviction in July 1992 were subsequently promoted for their efforts." In June 1996, former Québec justice Fred Kaufman was appointed to head the inquiry.

The Morin Commission reported in 1998 in two volumes (The Honourable Fred Kaufman, *The Commission Proceedings Involving Guy Paul Morin: Report* (Toronto: Queen's Printer for Ontario, 1998), having examined both the factual and systemic issues that gave rise to the failure of Ontario's criminal justice system. The Commission granted standing to a number of interveners, including the Association in Defence of the Wrongfully Convicted, the Criminal Lawyer's Association, and the Law Union, to allow them to contribute to an informed analysis of the 57 systemic issues identified by Commission counsel. The Commission made 119 recommendations for change, many of which focused on the use of "jailhouse informants," the handling of forensic evidence, police investigative practices, and Crown disclosure. In the meantime, Morin agreed to a $1.25 million compensation package from the Ontario government and abandoned a malicious prosecution claim: Kirk Makin, "Ontario awards Morin compensation" *The [Toronto] Globe and Mail* (25 January 1997) A1.

BIRMINGHAM SIX; GUILDFORD FOUR; MAGUIRE SEVEN

In the U.K., numerous convictions, including those of the three above-named groups, for alleged I.R.A. bombing, have been challenged on the basis of police fabrication of evidence, police violence to secure "confessions," and prosecutorial failure to disclose evidence favourable to the accused. Like the Donald Marshall, Jr. and Milgaard cases, government officials and members of the judiciary in the U.K. consistently defended the integrity of the system and refused to reopen the cases until forced to do so by public campaigns. For example, in *McIlkenny* v. *Chief Constable of the West Midlands*, [1980] 1 Q.B. 283 at 383, an action claiming damages for assault by the Birmingham Six, Lord Denning opined:

> Just consider the course of events if this action were to proceed to trial.... If the six men fail it will mean that much time and money and worry will have been expended by many people for no good purpose. If the six men win, it will mean that the police were guilty of perjury, that they were guilty of violence and threats, that the confessions were involuntary and improperly admitted in evidence, and that the convictions were erroneous. That would mean that the Home Secretary would have to either recommend that they be pardoned or that he would have to remit the case to the Court of Appeal.... This is such an appalling vista that every sensible person in the land would say, "It cannot be right that these actions should go any further."

A measure of justice has ultimately been secured through the exoneration and release of the accused in these three cases, although the police officers in the Guildford Four case were acquitted of fabricating evidence: Reuters, "Police officers cleared in Guildford Four case" *The [Toronto] Globe and Mail* (20 May 1993) A7. However, there have been other, broader repercussions flowing from these miscarriages of justice, including the investigation into the conduct of several prominent Queen's Counsel who failed in their duties of disclosure and defence, the forced resignation of Lord Lane, the Chief Justice of the House of Lords, and a Royal Commission on Criminal Justice: John Mullin, "Police 'had names of real culprits 16 years ago'" *The [London] Guardian* (16 March 1991) 2; David Pallister, "Vital evidence kept from defence" *The [London] Guardian* (16 March 1991) 2; David Rose and John McGhie, "All-party campaign to oust Lord Lane" *The [London] Observer* (17 March 1991) 1; "Complete overhaul ordered of English justice system" *The [Toronto] Globe and Mail* (6 January 1992) A7; and Paul Koring, "Justice tarnished by tainted convictions" *The [Toronto] Globe and Mail* (9 March 1992) A1.

Perhaps not surprisingly, some judges continue to defend the integrity of convictions in spite of overwhelming evidence to the contrary. Consider, for example, the comments made by Lord Denning after the quashing of the convictions in the two cases. When asked "If they had hanged the Guildford Four, they would have hanged the wrong men?," he replied, "No, they'd probably have hanged the right men. Not proved against them, that's all." Of the Birmingham Six, he said: "We shouldn't have all these campaigns to get the Birmingham Six released if they'd been hanged. They'd have been forgotten, and the whole community would be satisfied." See Andrew Cuff, "Repentant Denning says he was misled" *The [London] Guardian* (17 August 1990) 9 and Joanna Coles, "A.N. Wilson stands by Spectator 'scoop' interview" *The [London] Guardian* (17 August 1990) 9.

For more detailed accounts of these and other miscarriages of justice, see Robert Kee, *Trial & Error* (London: Penguin Books, 1986) and John Horgan, "Book Review" *London Review of Books* (16 August 1990) 9, 10 of the following books: Paul Hill with Ronan Bennett, *Stolen Years: Before and After Guildford* (London, UK: Doubleday, 1990); Gerry Conlon, *Proved Innocent* (London: Hamish Hamilton, 1990); Gerry Adams, *Cage Eleven* (Dingle, Ireland: Brandon, 1990); Kevin Taylor and Keith Mumby, *The Poisoned Tree: The untold truth about the Police conspiracy to discredit John Stalker and destroy me* (London: Sidgwick, 1990); and Ann Maguire, *Miscarriage of Justice: An Irish Family's Story of Wrongful Conviction as IRA Terrorists* (Niwot, Colorado: Rhinehart-Roberts, 1994).

In England, as a result of recommendations made by the Royal Commission on Criminal Justice, a convicted person may request a remedy from the newly constituted Criminal Cases Review Commission under the *Criminal Appeal Act 1995* (U.K.), 1995, c. 35. Section 9 of the new law allows the commission to refer a conviction to a court where there is a "real possibility" that the conviction will not be upheld, if there is either fresh evidence or a new argument to be made, and if an appeal has already been determined or leave to appeal was refused. In "exceptional circumstances" the commission may make a reference even where the last two conditions are not met.

The new process has several advantages: the commission is independent from the prosecutorial branch of the government; it will receive more resources to investigate and determine alleged miscarriages of justice; it must provide written reasons to the applicant when a reference is refused (s. 14(6)); it can develop its own criteria for investigation and its own processes; upon hearing the reference the court may now allow the appeal if it thinks that the conviction "is unsafe" (s. 2(1)); and new evidence must now be received if it is "capable of belief," rather than "likely to be credible."

However, many limitations on the new process have also been identified: the commission remains dependent on the police for investigative services: Kate Malleson, "The Criminal Cases Review Commission: How Will It Work?" [1995] Crim. L. Rev. 929; there is no obligation on the commission to disclose to the accused the information collected during the investigation; there is no provision for legal aid for the applicant; the government has stated that the new process will not result in a substantial increase in references (*ibid.* at 933); and, with respect to the changes to the powers of the Court of Appeal, the government interprets these as simply codifying existing practices (*ibid.* at 935–36).

These low expectations of the new Commission have been surpassed: in its first two years of operation, the Criminal Cases Review Commission (CCRC) received 2,325 applications and by 1999 it had completed its review of 727 files and referred 43 cases to the Court of Appeal. Of these referrals, 13 cases had been heard and eight convictions quashed as a consequence: "Murderers, or wrongly convicted?" *The Guardian* (5 April 1999). By 2000, the CCRC had made its 100th referral to the Court of Appeal (Press release, CCRC, "Commission's 100th Case Referral" (16 October 2000)) and by February 2001, 40 convictions had been quashed at the Court of Appeal: Bob Woffinden, "Injustice Act needs changing" *The [London] Times* (20 February 2001).

LINDY CHAMBERLAIN

The Chamberlain case in Queensland, Australia (discussed in Abell and Sheehy, *Proof, Defences, and Beyond*, **Media and the Trial Process**), and numerous other cases (most notoriously the Tim Anderson prosecution) confirm that Australia has also produced its share of wrongful convictions: Paul Wilson, "Miscarriages of Justice in Serious Cases in Australia" in Kerry Carrington *et al.*, eds., *Travesty! Miscarriages of Justice* (Sydney: Fast Books, 1991) 1. In fact, officials in Australia have been forced to acknowledge that the practice of police fabrication of evidence is not "anomalous" but is in fact widespread (see, for example, *R. v. McKinney* (1991), 171 Comm. L.R. 468 (H.Ct.)).

The Royal Commission into the New South Wales Police Service "has put the far-ranging tragedy of wrongful convictions on the main stage of media and public scrutiny": Liz Gulliver, "Are you being FRAMED?" *Framed* (October 1995) 1. Gulliver reports: "Ex-Detective Sergeant Trevor Haken told the Royal Commission on October 9 [that] he had committed perjury on 'numerous occasions'. Other detectives knew he did it. It was 'part of being a detective ... giving false evidence was purely a matter of course'." So much evidence of police fabrication has emerged that the Attorney-General has promised to "fast-track" investigations into alleged wrongful convictions arising out of testimony before the commission, and has acknowledged that a new process is needed (outside of their equivalent to *Criminal Code* s. 690, discussed below) for those wrongly convicted based on fabricated evidence.

E. REMEDIES

A convicted person has several avenues through which to challenge the justice of a conviction: appeals; s. 690 applications; pardons; and civil remedies. Each will be briefly outlined below.

APPEALS

Both convictions and acquittals are subject to appeal pursuant to the *Criminal Code*. With respect to offences that are prosecuted by way of indictment (see **Introduction to Criminal Procedure**, *infra*), the following sections apply:

- s. 675(1)(a) An accused can appeal to the court of appeal: on a question of law alone; on a question of mixed law and fact, with leave from the court; or on any ground "sufficient" according to the court of appeal.

- s. 691 An accused may pursue a further appeal to the Supreme Court of Canada: on a question of law on which one of the judges at the court of appeal dissented; on a question of law where an acquittal was set aside by the court of appeal or where a co-accused's acquittal was set aside by the court of appeal; or on any question of law if leave is granted by the Supreme Court.
- s. 676(1)(a) The Attorney General can appeal (to a court of appeal) on question of law alone.
- s. 693: The Attorney General may pursue a further appeal to the Supreme Court of Canada: on a question of law on which one of the appellate judges dissented, or on any question of law, with leave from the Supreme Court.

The court has the following powers upon hearing appeals for offences prosecuted by way of indictment:

- s. 686 Under ss. (1)(a) it may allow an appeal against conviction where: (i) the verdict is unreasonable or cannot be supported by the evidence; (ii) the decision was wrong on a question of law; or (iii) on any ground, there was a miscarriage of justice.
- s. 686 Under ss. (1)(b) it may dismiss an appeal where: (i) the accused was properly convicted on another count of the indictment; (ii) there were no grounds for the appeal to succeed within (a); (iii) even if there was an error of law, there was no "substantial wrong or miscarriage of justice"; or (iv) even if there was a procedural irregularity, the accused suffered no prejudice.
- s. 686 Under ss. (4) on an appeal against acquittal, the court can order a new trial or enter a guilty verdict unless the decision had been rendered by a jury (the *"Morgentaler"* amendment, see discussion in Abell and Sheehy, *Proof, Defences, and Beyond*, **Trial Process, Necessity**). If a court substitutes a conviction, it can sentence the accused or remit the matter back for sentencing.
- s. 695(1) The powers of the Supreme Court of Canada include any powers exercisable by a court of appeal; it may make any order necessary to execute its judgment.

Offences prosecuted by way of summary conviction are subject to the following rules for appeal:

- s. 813(a),(b) Appeals by a convicted person or the Crown may be pursued, on any ground, to an "appeal court" as defined in s. 829 (the superior court of criminal jurisdiction for the province).
- s. 822 The court's powers on appeal include the power to order a new trial or to hear the appeal by way of trial *de novo*.
- s. 830(1) A summary appeal, based on the transcript or an agreed statement of facts, to an "appeal court" may be based on an alleged error of law, or on an excess of or failure to exercise jurisdiction.
- s. 839 A further appeal to a court of appeal is available, on any ground involving a question of law alone, with leave.

The powers of the court with respect to appeals for summary conviction offences are very broad, essentially permitting both appeal courts and courts of appeal to do anything that the original summary conviction court could have done: see ss. 834, 839(4).

Despite some of these wide powers, appeals are imperfect remedies for a number of reasons: legal aid may not be available since its dispensation is discretionary for appeals (see **Right to Counsel**, *infra*); findings of fact, and especially assessments of credibility, are difficult to review on appeal, except to the extent that they amount to a "miscarriage of justice"; the ability to introduce new evidence on appeal is greatly circumscribed (*R. v. Palmer*, [1980] 1 S.C.R. 759); the burden of proof on an accused on appeal is heavier than it is at trial (while at trial the accused need only raise a doubt as to possible innocence, on appeal under s. 686(1)(a)(i) the test is whether the court is satisfied that no properly instructed jury could reasonably have found the accused guilty); and, finally, an accused may not be entitled to release from imprisonment pending appeal (see **Judicial Interim Release**, *infra*). David Cole and Allan Manson, *Release from Imprisonment: The Law on Sentencing, Parole and Judicial Review* (Toronto: Carswell, 1990) and Allan Manson, "Answering Claims of Injustice" (1992), 12 C.R. (4th) 305 both give more detail on appeals, and at 311–15, Manson specifically addresses the problems noted above. For discussion of appeals against sentence, see **Sentencing**, *infra*.

EXTRA-JUDICIAL REVIEW

Section 690 of the *Criminal Code* gives the Minister of Justice the power to (a) send a case back to trial for a re-trial; (b) refer the case to a court of appeal for it to consider the case as if it were an appeal and to exercise the appropriate powers; or (c) request that a court of appeal render an opinion on specific issues arising from the case, leaving the final decision to the Minister of Justice. This section has received more attention recently, as it was under s. 690(b) that the convictions of Donald Marshall, Jr. and Wilson Nepoose were reviewed and quashed; David Milgaard applied under s. 690, but his case was referred to the Supreme Court of Canada under another statute (*Supreme Court Act*, R.S.C. 1985, c. S-26, s. 53), perhaps because his trial counsel was by then a member of the Saskatchewan Court of Appeal (see Manson, "Answering Claims of Injustice," *supra* at note 10).

As Manson argues, there are numerous problems with s. 690: the *Code* fails to legislate a process by which the Minister assesses and determines applications for s. 690 review, leaving the setting of criteria and their application to Justice staff; the staff rely on re-investigations by police forces, which may replicate the same problems that produced the original conviction; and, of the perhaps thirty applications per year, less than one is referred under s. 690 (*ibid.* at 308, note 11). Clayton Ruby, in "The Marshall and Milgaard cases show we need a court of last resort to right the system's wrongs" *The [Toronto] Globe and Mail* (7 April 1992) A18, argues that the current system of asking the federal Minister of Justice to review s. 690 applications violates principles of fairness:

> A crown prosecutor is put in charge of the "investigation." The prosecutor draws upon existing police forces where necessary, but there are no facilities for re-investigation. Where outside advice is sought, the standards applied and the reasons for the decision are kept secret. It is not surprising that almost all these applications fail.

Both Manson and Ruby argue that like the U.K., Canada should have learned, from the miscarriages of justice described above, that s. 690 is inadequate to the task. They advocate creation of a permanent structure of last resort, along the lines of the Criminal Cases Review Commission, to investigate miscarriages of justice and to advise the Minister.

In spite of the many criticisms of s. 690 and the proposals advanced to the federal government in response to its consultation paper (*Addressing Miscarriages of Justice: Reform Possibilities for Section 690 of the Criminal Code* (Ottawa: Department of Justice, 1998)) by groups such as the Association in Defence of the Wrongfully Convicted, The Innocence Project (Osgoode Hall Law School), the Canadian Bar Association, and the Canadian Association of Elizabeth Fry Societies to create a new legal structure to review wrongful convictions claims, the federal government has proposed, in Bill C-15, *Criminal Law Amendment Act, 2001* (First Reading: 14 March 2001; Second Reading: 26 September 2001) a very modest reform. If passed, the new s. 696 will extend ministerial review to summary conviction offences and articulate a standard of review requiring that the Minister be "satisfied that a miscarriage of justice likely occurred" before the case is referred to the Court of Appeal. The process of assessing applications will be governed by regulations made by the Governor in Council; the Minister will be required to provide annual reports; and the Minister will be required to take into account "new matters of significance that were not considered by the courts," "the relevance and reliability" of information connected with the application, and the fact that the process is not an appeal and a reference is an "extraordinary remedy."

Finally, the inherent limitations of the individualized process of s. 690 review should be noted. For example, the Canadian Association of Elizabeth Fry Societies, in its four-year lobby to the Minister of Justice to review the cases of women convicted of homicide with respect to a violent mate, argued that s. 690 was inadequate for the women because of lack of provision for access to legal aid, possible failure of individual reviews to reveal the systemic problems that women encounter in the criminal law system in dealing with violent men, and also to highlight the problems in the law of self-defence for such women: see Canadian Association of Elizabeth Fry Societies, "Battered Women's Defence Committee Update" (Ottawa: CAEFS, November 1994) at 6. Ultimately, the government gave terms of reference (reproduced in Abell and Sheehy, *Proof, Defences, and Beyond*, **Self-Defence**) to Judge Lynn Ratushny to review the women's cases, on terms that were not confined by s. 690.

Although in the end the Self-Defence Review did not result in the release from prison of any women, the process created by Judge Ratushny was unique and her recommendations for reform of the law of self-defence and prosecutorial practices regarding charging and plea bargaining with battered women who kill remain significant: see Elizabeth Sheehy, "Review of the Self-Defence Review" (2000) 12 C.J.W.L. 197.

PARDONS

The Royal Prerogative of Mercy, as recognized by ss. 749 and 751 of the *Criminal Code*, permits the Governor General in Council, usually on the recommendation of a Minister (the Solicitor General, most commonly) to grant a free or a conditional pardon to a convicted person. Guidelines issued by the Clemency and Pardons Division of the National Parole Board, "The Royal Prerogative of Mercy" (Ottawa: National Parole Board, 1991), suggest that a free pardon may be appropriate where "the innocence of a convicted person is clearly established" (at 3). A conditional pardon may be granted where the individual suffers a comparative hardship (e.g. where the law was later changed but the person cannot benefit from that change), or where the person suffers privation that is out of proportion to the offence committed. While a person granted a free pardon is relieved of all consequences flowing from conviction, a conditional pardon may accomplish different results, e.g. it may seal a criminal record, result in early release from imprisonment subject to conditions, alter the underlying sentence itself, remit any fines or other penalties, grant respite from execution of a sentence (or a new trial), and cancel or vary a prohibition order (e.g. against owning firearms).

The limitations of the pardon remedy may perhaps be obvious: the remedy is entirely discretionary, although Manson, *supra* (at 311) suggests that review pursuant to s. 7 of the *Charter* may be possible; the applicant bears the onus of proof with respect to an allegation of innocence; the guidelines stress that the pardon is for "exceptional" cases only; one would predict that the free pardon would be even rarer given that the investigative services of the police and prisons personnel are relied upon in assessing applications; and the guidelines stress that pardons are for individual hardships, not for systemic problems in the criminal justice system (at 2). For additional inadequacies of pardons, see the discussion of the application for a pardon on behalf of Louis Riel, *supra*, **Aboriginal Peoples and Criminal Law**.

CIVIL REMEDIES

A convicted person may also seek compensation for the wrongful prosecution or conviction. Criminal lawyers are often involved in negotiations around the compensation of their clients. There are several routes available. Some, like Susan Nelles, a Toronto nurse charged with the murder of four babies and discharged after a judge at the preliminary inquiry determined that there was not enough evidence to put her on trial (see Abell and Sheehy, *Proof, Defences, and Beyond*, **Trial Process**), may be able to secure an order-in-council acknowledging the wrong and granting them compensation (Kirk Makin, "A lawsuit nearly impossible to win" *The [Toronto] Globe and Mail* (16 November 1995) A8). This remedy was probably available to Nelles due to a number of circumstances unique to her case and the political environment at the time of the negotiations.

Others may apply for compensation through guidelines set out in a 1988 federal-provincial agreement. However, these guidelines have been widely criticized by lawyers, who state that the ceiling of $100,000 for non-monetary losses is "laughable," that they were designed to protect government pockets, not victims of the criminal justice system, and that they only apply to a narrow range of cases (where a free pardon is granted, where an accused is acquitted, or where new facts suggest a miscarriage of justice): Rudy Platiel, "One question on compensation: How much?" *The [Toronto] Globe and Mail* (24 June 1995) A6.

A civil action in malicious prosecution is often pursued simultaneously with other remedies, and, according to Clayton Ruby, may provide the incentive to the government to settle the case for amounts that exceed the guidelines (Platiel, *supra*). In *Nelles* v. *Ontario (AG)*, [1989] 2 S.C.R. 70, the Court ruled that agents of the government cannot shield themselves from liability for the tort of malicious prosecution based on the doctrine of "Crown immunity" where the prosecution was: initiated by the defendant; terminated in favour of the plaintiff; instituted without reasonable cause; and motivated by malice (at 211). As noted above with respect to the discussion of David Milgaard's case, this interpretation has also been applied to claims in tort based on conspiracy and deliberate breach of statutory duty.

However, it should be noted that such lawsuits carry risks as well. A plaintiff may be vulnerable to a counter-suit in defamation. See, for example, *Popowich* v. *Saskatchewan*, [1995] 3 W.W.R. 576 (Sask. Q.B.), in which three of the many defendants counterclaimed in defamation against an accused whose charges were stayed in the "Martensville" prosecutions and who later sued the police and prosecution for mishandling the case. Furthermore, the element of "malice" for proof of the tort is hard to establish and the government has vast resources available in defending these cases, making it impossible for some claimants to continue: see Makin, *supra*. On the other hand, Ruby states that many of these cases are settled out of court because the government does not want the allegations of incompetence or malice aired publicly: see Platiel, *supra*.

Finally, governments may appoint commissioners to assess whether a subsequently exonerated person is entitled to compensation, the legal basis underlying it, and the amount that ought to be awarded. For example, the Manitoba government appointed The Honourable Peter Cory as head of a commission of inquiry, pursuant to an Order in Council, into the wrongful conviction of Thomas Sophonow in order to identify what went wrong in terms of the conduct of the investigation and criminal proceedings against Sophonow, to make recommendations for change, and to advise as to the appropriate compensation. In addition to many recommendations regarding investigative practices involving identification and informant evidence, His Honour recommended the creation of a "completely independent entity ... which can effectively, efficiently and quickly review cases in which wrongful conviction is alleged." He found the tort basis for compensation to be very frail, given the difficulty of proving malice on the part of police and prosecutors, and instead grounded entitlement to compensation on the basis of the claimant's factual innocence, which he said was supported by the *International Covenant on Civil and Political Rights*, the 1988 Federal-Provincial Guidelines on compensation, and comparable Manitoba Guidelines (1986). He rejected, however, the $100,000 cap used by both sets of guidelines, and after itemizing Sophonow's losses (damage to liberty and reputation, loss of privacy, humiliation, danger of physical assaults, loss of enjoyment of life, continuing effects of imprisonment, resulting psychological damage from prison life and discipline, as well as pecuniary losses associated with future counselling needs and loss of income) recommended that Manitoba pay a sum of approximately $2.2 million: The Honourable Peter Cory, Commissioner, *The Inquiry Regarding Thomas Sophonow* (2001).

5
Sentencing

A. ISSUES IN SENTENCING

Sentencing is a critical moment in the criminal law process. For the person on trial, the sentence will shape his/her future by determining whether or not there is a criminal record; whether she or he will have to maintain regular contact with police or a probation officer; and, if a term of imprisonment is imposed, whether the person will lose a job, a home, and custody or contact with their children, in addition to personal freedom.

Sentencing is also pivotal for the public and for complainants/witnesses. Much attention is often focused on the sentence because it is both a visible and a powerful symbol of the judgment of the criminal law system, although opinions are shaped in particular ways by the media presentation of sentences: Julian Roberts, "Sentencing, Public Opinion and the News Media" (1995) 26 Revue général de droit 115. The Canadian Judicial Council finds that a high proportion of complaints from the public about judges emanate from sentences in sexual assault cases: Canadian Judicial Council, *Annual Report 1988–1989* (Ottawa: Canadian Judicial Council, 1988) at 12. See also Renate Mohr, "Sexual Assault Sentencing: Leaving Justice to Individual Conscience" in Julian Roberts and Renate Mohr, eds., *Confronting Sexual Assault: A Decade of Social and Legal Change* (Toronto: University of Toronto Press, 1994) 157.

Given the meaning of the sentence for the accused and others, the role of lawyers in sentencing cannot be overstated. Because 80 to 85 per cent of accused plead guilty without a trial, the bulk of the work of the criminal lawyer is to prepare the person for sentencing, strike bargains regarding sentence, make submissions as to sentence, and appeal sentences. A lawyer's ability to advise on likely sentencing outcomes must take into account the legal structure of sentencing as well as the impact of a conviction upon the client's life, such as their eligibility for social assistance.

The legal structure of sentencing is found first in the individual offences in the *Criminal Code*, which usually specify maximum sentences and occasionally contain minimum sentences. Second, legal structure is contained in the sentencing options set out in more general sections of the *Criminal Code*. Third, the sentencing options are to be selected based on a set of legal criteria: the purpose(s) (e.g. general deterrence, specific deterrence, punishment, and rehabilitation) that the judge decides should be served by a given sentence, and the factors identified by the judge as aggravating or mitigating the offence. Finally, the *Criminal Code* provides a legislative framework for the process of sentencing, including the nature of the materials admissible as evidence and the allocation of the burden of proof. Overall, the constraints provided by these structures are minimal, with the result that judicial discretion plays an important role in sentencing. These four components of the legal structure will be considered in turn, followed by an identification of the issues in sentencing that they raise.

MAXIMUM AND MINIMUM SENTENCES

Generally, offence definitions include a sentence maximum that can be imposed by the sentencing judge. Section 743 states that a maximum term of five years imprisonment can be imposed if an indictable offence fails to specify a maximum; s. 787(1) states that the maximum for a summary conviction offence where unspecified is a fine of $2,000 or six months imprisonment or both.

It can be argued that the values underlying the *Criminal Code* are signalled by the structure of maximum sentences. As you read the extract from Mary Crawford below, written in 1913, consider whether these sorts of comparisons can still be drawn with reference to the current *Criminal Code*. What values and priorities are reflected by this sentencing structure?

The Criminal Code Unfair to Women, Manitoba, 1913†

COMPARISONS OF PUNISHMENTS UNDER THE CRIMINAL CODE

Section 211. Seduction of girls between fourteen and sixteen previously chaste — two years' imprisonment, maximum sentence.
Compare *Section* 371: For stealing oysters, or oyster brood, liable to seven years' imprisonment, or a lesser term at discretion of magistrate.

Section 292. Indecent assault on female — two years' imprisonment, maximum sentence.
Compare *Section* 364: For stealing a post letter-bag, or a letter from a post-bag, or post-office, or any valuables from or out of a post letter, sentence liable to life imprisonment, or not less than three years.

Section 315. Abduction of girl under sixteen — sentence five years.
Compare *Section* 369: For cattle stealing — fourteen years, maximum sentence.

Section 213. For the seduction of ward, or employee, by her guardian or employer, said ward or employee being under twenty-one years, *two years*.
Compare *Section* 552: *For making counterfeit gold or silver coin, liable to imprisonment for life.*

Section 212. For seduction under promise of marriage by a male over twenty-one years of age, of a female previously chaste, and under the age of twenty-one years, maximum sentence, *two years*.
Compare *Section* 373: Liable to two years for stealing a tree, sapling or shrub of the value of twenty-five dollars, or of the value of five dollars, if growing in any park, pleasure-ground, garden, orchard, or in any ground adjoining or belonging to any dwelling-house.

Section 308. For bigamy, *seven years' imprisonment*.
Compare *Section* 384: Liable to fourteen years who steals anything in, or from any railway station or building, or from any vehicle of any kind on any railway.

Section 215. A parent or guardian procuring or a party to the defilement of a girl or woman over fourteen years of age, *five years' imprisonment*.
Compare *Section* 372: For stealing brass, woodwork, or lead, iron, copper, etc., fixed to any building, or on any building whatsoever, or anything made of metal used for a fence on public or private property or a burial ground, liable to *seven years' imprisonment*.

Section 216. Procuring a girl under twenty-one, and not of known immoral character, liable to *five years' imprisonment, with hard labor*.
Compare *Section* 379: For stealing from the person any chattel, money, or valuable security, liable to a sentence of *fourteen years' imprisonment*.

■

---

† Mary E. Crawford, "The Criminal Code Unfair to Women, Manitoba, 1913" in Mary E. Crawford, ed., *Legal Status of Women in Manitoba* (Winnipeg: Political Equality League of Manitoba, 1913) at 37.

Currently, the *Criminal Code* contains 29 offences that carry a mandatory minimum sentence. Although the Supreme Court of Canada in *R. v. Smith*, [1987] 1 S.C.R. 1045 declared the minimum seven year sentence of imprisonment for persons convicted of trafficking or importing narcotics to be unconstitutional pursuant to ss. 7 and 12 of the *Charter* using a very broad analysis, it has rejected every such challenge brought before it since that time: *R. v. Luxton*, [1990] 2 S.C.R. 711 (life imprisonment without parole eligibility for 25 years for first degree murder); *R. v. Milne*, [1987] 2 S.C.R. 512 and *R. v. Legons*, [1987] 2 S.C.R. 309 (indeterminate sentences for dangerous offenders); *R. v. Goltz*, [1991] 3 S.C.R. 485 (mandatory fine and seven days imprisonment for driving under suspension); and *R. v. Morrisey*, [2000] 2 S.C.R. 90 (unlawful act manslaughter using a firearm). The only argument left open by this jurisprudence is the possibility of arguing that the accused should be constitutionally exempted from the mandatory penalty, although this argument was soundly rejected on the facts in *R. v. Latimer*, [2001] 1 S.C.R. 3. A s. 15 challenge to a mandatory minimum sentence has yet to be litigated. For a special double issue devoted to the many legal and policy issues arising out of mandatory minimum sentencing in Canada, including their discriminatory impacts upon Aboriginal people, African-Canadians, and battered women, as well as the complicated issues arising for people with disabilities, see (2002) 39 Osgoode Hall L.J., nos. 2 & 3.

SENTENCING OPTIONS

The *Criminal Code* sets out the following options for the sentencing judge:

- **Alternative Measures:** Under s. 717, before the charges against the accused are heard and adjudicated, if the conditions set out in ss. (1) are met (e.g. the accused consents and accepts responsibility for the offence and there is sufficient evidence to justify prosecution of the accused, among other requirements), "alternative measures may be used to deal with [the] person" provided that "it is not inconsistent with the protection of society." In jurisdictions where programs are in place, community service or other terms may be agreed upon in resolution of the criminal charges. Although the charges against the accused can be pursued thereafter, ss. 4(a) requires the judge to dismiss the charges where the person complied wholly with the terms of the alternative measures, and gives the judge a discretion to dismiss them where the accused complied partially with the terms.

- **Absolute Discharge:** An absolute discharge, which is entered by the judge after a finding of guilt but before the conviction is registered, leaves the person without a conviction or criminal record for the purposes of employment. Section 730(1) is available for an accused other than a corporation, provided that the offence has no minimum sentence and the maximum sentence for the offence is not 14 years or more, if it is "in the best interest of the accused and not contrary to the public interest." As a matter of practice, an accused will not be given an absolute discharge more than once.

- **Conditional Discharge:** A conditional discharge is also governed by s. 730(1), but it attaches conditions in a probation order authorized by s. 731(2). The types of conditions that can be imposed are set out in s. 732.1. Note that the payment of a fine cannot be added as a condition: *R. v. Carroll* (1995), 38 C.R. (4th) 238 (B.C.C.A.). If the conditions are breached, the discharge can be revoked and the accused convicted and sentenced (ss. 733.1, 730(4)). If the conditions are fulfilled, the discharge will have the same effect as an absolute discharge in that the accused will not be convicted of the offence.

- **Suspended Sentence**: Under s. 731(1)(a), a suspended sentence is available where the offence does not provide for a minimum sentence, "having regard to the age and character of the offender, the nature of the offence and the circumstances surrounding its commission." The judge suspends the passing of sentence on terms prescribed in a probation order under s. 732.1. If the person breaches the terms, then a sentence will be imposed under s. 732.2(5)(d). If the person complies with the terms, the sentence will be complete upon the expiry of the prescribed period.

- **Fine**: Fines are available as a sentence under s. 734(1) for an accused other than a corporation where the offence does not have a minimum sentence. This punishment may also be added to any other disposition (but may not be available in combination with imprisonment and probation: T.W. Ferris, "The Legality of Imposing a Fine, Imprisonment and Probation at the Same Time" (1996) Crim. L.Q. 277). For a corporation a fine may be imposed under s. 735: any amount may be ordered with respect to an indictable offence and a maximum fine of $25,000 may be imposed for a summary conviction offence. The sentencing judge must be satisfied that the accused has the means to pay or discharge the fine (s. 734(2)) and must calculate a term of imprisonment in default of payment of the fine in accordance with s. 734(4), (5). See discussion *infra* under **Charter Implications**.

- **Restitution**: Pursuant to s. 738, restitution can be added to any other disposition, although it cannot stand alone as a penalty. The order can cover the cost of damaged or lost property, pecuniary losses associated with bodily harm (lost wages, etc.), and pecuniary costs suffered by the offender's family when victimized by the offender, such as moving costs, food, and shelter costs. Section 739 allows a restitution order for those other persons who suffered financial losses by relying on the accused's transaction.

- **Victim Fine Surcharge**: Section 737 provides for a mandatory additional punishment of a victim fine surcharge, in an amount not to exceed 15 per cent of any fine imposed or $10,000 (if no fine was imposed) or a lesser amount pursuant to regulations made by the Governor in Council, unless the offender "establishes" "undue hardship" to himself or herself or his or her family. This money goes into a fund earmarked to assist victims of crime.

- **Probation**: Under s. 731, probation can be added to a discharge, a fine, or to a sentence of imprisonment for less than two years. Section 732.1 sets out mandatory and optional terms for probation orders.

- **Conditional Sentence of Imprisonment**: This sentence, set out in s. 742.1, is available where the accused is convicted of an offence that has no minimum sentence, where a term of imprisonment of less than two years is imposed, and where the judge is "satisfied that serving the sentence in the community would not endanger the safety of the community." This option involves a judge sentencing the accused to serve a sentence in the community pursuant to a conditional sentence order under s. 742.3, which contains some mandatory terms of probation, as well as options that a judge can attach (ss. (2)) such as up to 240 hours of community service over a period not exceeding 18 months.

The Supreme Court has rendered several judgments giving guidance to the lower courts implementing this new sentencing option. In particular, in *R. v. Proulx*, [2000]1 S.C.R. 61, the Court confirmed that all offences, except those statutorily barred because they carry a mandatory sentence of imprisonment, can be punished by conditional imprisonment. Nor should the courts develop categories of offences for which this punishment is *prima facie* imposed or barred. Instead, in each case the judge must determine which sentencing goals should be pursued through the sentence. The Court went on to hold that the goals of deterrence and denunciation can be pursued through conditional imprisonment and, since this sentence is only available if the judge first determines that a jail sentence of less than two years is appropriate, that conditional imprisonment should normally involve rather serious restraints upon the offender's liberty such that condition like house arrest should be the norm, not the exception. Julian Roberts *et al.* have produced an empirical analysis of data from two provinces implementing conditional sentences prior to release of the *Proulx* decision: "Conditional Sentences of Imprisonment: An Empirical Analysis of Optional Conditions" (2000), 30 C.R. (4th) 113. They found that only 18 per cent of conditional sentences included curfews, and in Ontario only three per cent imposed house arrest. The impact of *Proulx* remains to be seen.

- **Imprisonment**: Imprisonment is available on terms specified for the offence (see above), or, in the case of indictable and summary conviction offences that fail to specify a sentence, up to five years and six months respectively. Under s. 732, if the sentence is for 90 days or less, the judge may order that it be served intermittently, having regard to "the availability of appropriate accommodation to ensure compliance with the sentence." Under s. 743.1(1), if the sentence is two years or more, it is to be served in a federal penitentiary; if the sentence is less, it is served in a prison or other provincial institution: s. 743.1(3). However, federal penitentiaries and provincial institutions may transfer inmates between them.

- **Indeterminate Sentence**: The prosecutor may apply under s. 753 of the *Criminal Code* to have the accused declared a dangerous offender, in which case the person is sentenced to an indeterminate sentence and will be entitled to periodic review by the Parole Board under s. 761 to ascertain whether parole should be granted.

The criteria in s. 753 include conviction of a serious personal injury offence and evidence "establishing" that the offender "constitutes a threat to the life, safety or physical or mental well-being of other persons." It should be noted that until 1977, "habitual criminals" could be incarcerated indefinitely (R.S.C. 1970, c. 34, ss. 687–95); in 1977, the law was changed so as to limit indeterminate sentences to dangerous offenders: *Criminal Law Amendment Act, 1977*, S.C. 1977, c. 53, ss. 14 and 15. Those incarcerated under the old legislation were not released automatically but had to apply for review. Thus, it was only in 1995 that one man, jailed for 28 years in federal institutions for 37 petty offences such as vagrancy, theft, and causing a disturbance, was finally released: Thomas Claridge, "Habitual criminal released after 28 years" *The [Toronto] Globe and Mail* (22 September 1995) A7.

It should also be noted that although the current legislation is much narrower than its predecessor, systemic discrimination plays a role in dangerous offender determinations. Consider, for example, the cases of Marlene Moore, Canada's first woman dangerous offender, acknowledged later by an Ontario judge to be a danger only to herself (she committed suicide in the Prison for Women in 1988: June Callwood, "Marlene Moore's death of 1,000 cuts" *The [Toronto] Globe and Mail* (13 December 1989) A8, discussed *infra*, **Prisons**) and Lisa Neve, Canada's second and only living woman dangerous offender (Wayne Renke, "Case Comment: Lisa Neve, Dangerous Offender" (1995) 33 Alta. L. Rev. 650). Her designation as a dangerous offender was subsequently over-turned: *R. v. Neve*, [1999] A.J. No. 753 (C.A.), online: QL. Compare the cases of Moore and Neve with the kinds of histories and issues that male offenders present: *R. v. Currie* (1995), 26 O.R. (3d) 444 (C.A.)), but see *R. v. R.E.G.*, [1996] A.J. No. 652 (Prov. Ct.), online: QL, where, for the first time, a man has been declared a dangerous offender for his persistently violent behaviour towards his wife and others, including her family, police, and shelter workers who attempted to protect her.

Finally, it should be noted that in some provinces, the effect of a dangerous offender application — detention — is achieved without resort to s. 753. In Ontario, for example, it appears that upon release from prison and without a s. 753 application, some offenders are then detained under mental health legislation in Penetanguishene, which is where those found not guilty on account of mental disorder are incarcerated: Kirk Makin, "Dangerous offenders sent to psychiatric hospitals" *The [Toronto] Globe and Mail* (10 May 1996) A4A. Other provinces such as Manitoba have responded with a process to notify the public upon the release of "high-risk" offenders: CP, "Tough high-risk-offender laws sought" *The [Toronto] Globe and Mail* (15 April 1996) A4.

- **Additional Orders:** A number of additional orders, which increase the punitive nature of a sentence, can be added to the above sentences. For example, there are provisions that impose prohibition orders (s. 446 (5),(6) (custody or control of an animal or bird), ss. 100, 103((6)(b) (firearms and ammunition) and ss. 259, 260 (operation of a motor vehicle, aircraft, vessel, or railway equipment)) that would affect a person's ability to pursue a livelihood, among other things. It should also be noted that for those convicted of second-degree murder, s. 743 of the *Criminal Code* allows the jury to make a recommendation to the judge as to the period of parole ineligibility (from 10 to 25 years) for the accused. There are "proceeds of crime" provisions in Part XXII.2 of the *Criminal Code* that permit the seizure and confiscation of the "proceeds of crime" for certain offences and in particular circumstances, such as where no conviction has been registered but the accused has absconded (see, for example, *R. v. Ping*, [1996] B.C.J. No. 1343 (S.C. (T.D.)), online: QL).

- **Other Sentences:** It should be noted that there are judges who attempt to create new forms of sentences for particular types of offences and offenders that pose particular problems of recidivism. For example, in the area of corporate criminality, numerous judges have sentenced corporate offenders to unusual sentences, some of which have been successfully appealed: see *infra*, **Corporate Criminality**. Another example is provided by an initiative in Toronto, whereby men charged with soliciting for the purpose of prostitution may be given an option of attending a "john school" and receiving a conditional discharge, or proceeding to trial: Gay Abbate, "Johns on the spot sent to school" *The*

[Toronto] *Globe and Mail* (8 January 1996) A5. Crowns request a $500 fine and a criminal record for men convicted after attending the school. Finally, many provinces have enacted new laws that permit the automatic suspension of the driving licenses of those who fail breathalyzer tests prior to adjudication. Thus far these schemes have survived constitutional challenge: *Buhlers* v. *British Columbia*, [1998] B.C.J. No. 495 (C.A.), leave to appeal denied [1999] S.C.C.A. No. 219, online: QL; *Horsefield* v. *Ontario* (1999), 44 O.R. (3d) 73 (C.A.); and *Gonzalez* v. *Alberta*, [2001] A.J. No. 1159 (Q.B.), online: QL.

PURPOSE OF SENTENCE; AGGRAVATING AND MITIGATING FACTORS

Judges generally select among sentencing options by reference to the purpose(s) to be served in sentencing a particular offender, such as specific deterrence, general deterrence, punishment, and rehabilitation. For general references in this area see:

Canadian Sentencing Commission, *Sentencing Reform: A Canadian Approach* (Ottawa: Minister of Supply and Services, 1986).

Herbert L. A. Hart, *Punishment and Responsibility* (Oxford: Clarenden Press, 1968).

Patrick Healy and Hélène Dumont, eds. *Dawn or Dusk in Sentencing?* (Montréal: Éditions Thémis, 1997).

Allan Manson, *Sentencing and Parole Policy in Canada* (Toronto: Emond-Montgomery, 2000).

Renate Mohr, "Sentencing as a Gendered Process" (1990) 32 Can. J. Crim. 479.

Julian Roberts and David Cole, eds. *Making Sense of Sentencing* (Toronto: University of Toronto Press, 1999).

Clayton Ruby, *Sentencing*, 5th ed. (Toronto: Butterworths, 1999).

Section 718 of the *Criminal Code* states that "[t]he fundamental purpose of sentencing is to contribute ... to respect for the law and maintenance of a just, peaceful and safe society by imposing just sanctions that have one or more of the following objectives...." In addition to deterrence, rehabilitation, and punishment, this section refers to the separation of offenders from society, where necessary, the provision of reparations to the victim or community, and the promotion of responsibility and acknowledgment of harm caused by offenders to complainants/victims.

Judges in each province have also developed common law principles that are used to match sentencing objectives to particular options. For example, in the *Carroll* case above, the court stated that although a discharge cannot be used to serve the objectives of specific deterrence or punishment, it can be employed to promote general deterrence.

Judges will also have regard to aggravating and mitigating factors in selecting a sentencing option and its precise content (for example, the amount of fine or the term of probation). Section 718.1 states that the sentence must be proportionate to the gravity of the offence and to the responsibility of the offender, which is gauged under 718.2 by reference to aggravating and mitigating factors that must be considered by the judge, although s. 718.3 also explicitly preserves judicial discretion in sentencing. Specific factors under s. 718.2 will be discussed *infra* under **Race and Racism** and **Study in Sentencing: Violence Against Women**. The impact of aggravating and mitigating factors is contested, as the discussions in **Cultural Conflicts? The Relevance of Culture to Sentencing** and **Circle Sentencing** indicate.

In addition, there is a body of common law that has emerged in each province that identifies other aggravating and mitigating factors. For example, a guilty plea will mitigate a sentence, and an accused's relevant criminal record, including a *Young Offenders Act* record (*R.* v. *Partridge* (1995), 167 N.B.R. (2d) 276 (C.A.)), will aggravate a sentence.

The courts have also refused to consider certain factors as aggravating factors. In *R.* v. *Kozy* (1990), 58 C.C.C. (3d) 500 (Ont. C.A.), the court stated that the accused's conduct at trial, which extended to perjury by fabricating a story to the effect that there had been no intercourse and that the complainant/victim of the sexual assault had tried to initiate sexual contact, could not be used in aggravation of his sentence although such false statements could be used as indicators of a lack of remorse and a need for rehabilitation.

Higher courts have told lower court judges that certain factors must not be taken into account in mitigation of a sentence. See *R.* v. *Hemlow* (1995), 147 N.S.R. (2d) 1 (S.C. (A.D.)) (sexual abuse of accused as a youth not a mitigating factor for a break and enter offence); *R.* v. *Glykis* (1995), 41 C.R. (4th) 310 (Ont. C.A.) (a breach of an accused's *Charter* right should not be used to mitigate sentence unless it lessened the seriousness of the offence or amounted to an additional "punishment" in itself); and *R.* v. *Debraga* (1995), 107 Man. R. (2d) 56 (C.A.) (accused's assertion that he would require protection from other inmates if sent to a federal penitentiary not an appropriate consideration for sentencing).

Some mitigating factors will also be quite contentious. See, for example, "Rapist praised by judge" *The [London] Guardian* (12 April 1991) 3 (sentence of three years mitigated by the fact that the rapist used a condom) and Meredith Carter and Beth Wilson, "Rape: Good and Bad Women and Judges" (1992) 17 Alt. L.J. 6 (mitigation of sentence on the basis that the victim worked as a prostitute).

PROCESS OF SENTENCING

The process of sentencing is somewhat circumscribed by the *Criminal Code*. Section 721 permits a judge to request the preparation of a pre-sentence report by a probation officer, containing information as set out in ss. (3) (e.g. offender's attitudes and willingness to make reparations, previous dispositions under the *Young Offenders Act* and previous findings of guilt). If facts become disputed at the sentencing hearing, under s. 724(3)(d) they must be proven on a balance of probabilities; factors that would aggravate the sentence, including prior convictions, must be proven beyond a reasonable doubt under ss. (3)(e).

Victim impact statements, if prepared pursuant to a program established by the Lieutenant Governor of the province, must be considered by the sentencing judge: s. 722. The language in s. 722(4) defining a "victim" as one "to whom harm was done or who suffered physical or emotional loss as a result of the commission of the offence" has been broadly interpreted in one recent case as including a police officer's fiancée, his patrol partner, and the chair of the local police-community organization: *R.* v. *Phillips* (1995), 26 O.R. (3d) 522 (Ct. Just. (Gen. Div.)).

Section 726 allows the offender to "speak to sentence" before the judge passes sentence. For the unrepresented accused, this opportunity may be relatively meaningless. A representative of the accused can, however, bring forward arguments in mitigation of sentence, focusing on, among other matters: the nature of the offence, the harm caused by the offence, any mitigating circumstances surrounding the offence (for example, intoxication, the influence of other people or stresses, the motivation of the accused), the accused's attitude towards the offence or victim (have any efforts at reparations been made?), the prospects of rehabilitation (past record of the accused, employment, education, family situation), the need for specific or general deterrence (e.g., for the offender or with respect to a perceived high rate of offending within a given community), the impact of the offence upon the victim, the legislative range of sentence, and judicial patterns of sentencing for similar offences.

Under s. 726.2 the judge must give written reasons for the sentence ordered, which is closely linked with an accused's ability to appeal a given sentence. For indictable offences, an appeal against sentence is available to the accused under s. 675(1)(b), and to the Attorney General under s. 676(1)(d) to the court of appeal, with leave. Under s. 687, the court of appeal has the power to vary the sentence or to dismiss the appeal. Although the *Criminal Code* does not expressly permit sentence appeals to the Supreme Court of Canada, the *Supreme Court Act*, R.S.C. 1985, c. S-26, s. 41(1) gives a broad discretion to the Supreme Court to hear any appeal on a question of law or law and fact, if the question "is of such a nature or significance as to warrant a decision by it." Thus, while the issue of whether a sentence is "fit" cannot be argued before the Supreme Court, the Court can determine the relevant principles for sentencing: see *R.* v. *C.A.M.*, [1996] 1 S.C.R. 500 where the Court decided an appeal regarding the application of the "totality principle" in sentencing to an offender with multiple convictions for sexual assault.

For summary conviction offences, under s. 813(a)(ii), (b)(ii), either party may appeal the sentence to an appeal court (defined in s. 812); a further appeal to the court of appeal is available to either party with leave on a question of law alone: s. 839(1)(a). Appeals regarding dangerous offender designations are available pursuant to s. 759.

The role of judicial discretion and the reliance upon individual factors in sentencing raise many issues. Disparity in sentences (case to case, judge to judge, court to court, and province to province) has frequently been presented as a serious concern (see, for example, the Canadian Sentencing Commission, *Sentencing Reform: A Canadian Approach*, supra at 71–77 and Bob Cox, "Criminal's guide to where to get caught" *The Ottawa Citizen* (26 November 1993) A1, where it is reported that on average, a man convicted of sexual assault in Edmonton serves 318 days in jail, while a man in Calgary serves an average of 90 days for sexual assault). Other problems identified include a lack of systemic knowledge of current practices or guidance from appellate courts and a lack of accountability on the part of the police and prosecutors regarding charging practices and judges regarding sentences: *Sentencing Reform: A Canadian Approach* at 71. Can you anticipate the resulting impact of sentencing practices upon diverse groups in Canada, such as Aboriginal peoples and poor people? In the sections that follow, a number of issues arising from these sentencing practices are discussed.

B. THE POLITICS OF SENTENCING

Recall that for Donald Zazulak, convicted of perjury for lying about notations in police records that suggested bias against wrongfully convicted Wilson Nepoose, his "good but misguided" motive for his offence was said to mitigate the sentence (**Enforcement of the Law**). Consider the circumstances in which an offender's motives will be characterized as "good."

In 1984, Juliet Belmas, Gerald Hannah, Ann Hanson, Douglas Stewart, and Brent Taylor, known as the "Squamish Five," were sentenced by the B.C. Supreme Court to sentences of 10 years, six years, life imprisonment, 20 years, and 22 years imprisonment, respectively, for their crimes of conspiracy to commit robbery, automobile theft, possession of stolen property, two counts of activating an explosive substance (at the Litton plant and at Dunsmuir hydro station), possession of explosives with intent to cause damage, possession of weapons for a dangerous purpose, and attempted arson (at the Red Hot Video store). The five young people, ranging from 21 to 30 years of age, had engaged in these crimes in pursuit of "Direct Action," a political agenda concerned with protection of the environment, opposition to pornography, the plight of the underprivileged in Western society, and the threat of nuclear destruction. They attempted to ensure that no one would be hurt in the explosions by taking precautions that included warning security at the Litton site. The total property damage caused by the crimes was approximately $8 million; at the Litton plant, 10 people were injured, and three experienced lasting impairment.

An article entitled "Politics and Sentencing: A Statement on the Squamish Five," (*This Magazine* (April 1985) 34) examined the sentences meted out to these offenders in the context of sentencing principles and by reference to the sentencing of offenders who have committed crimes with comparable outcomes. It argued that the sentences were unconscionably long in light of their youth, the sincere concerns that motivated them, their remorse at the human suffering they caused, and their lack of prior criminal records. It compared the sentences with those imposed on offenders in 1978 convicted of causing bodily harm, manslaughter, attempt murder, arson, and robbery, among other offences, and found that many received no prison sentence (52%, 12%, 8%, 41%, and 18%, respectively); the vast majority received sentences that were vastly less punitive than those received by the Squamish Five (81% received either no prison or less than seven years; 88% less than five years; 58% less than two years; 72% less than seven months; and 78% less than two years); and, with the exception of robbery, the sentences imposed on the Squamish Five exceeded the maximum sentence imposed on any offender convicted in 1978 for the four other crimes excluding robbery (longest sentences were five years, 14 years, 14 years, five years). Furthermore, the article pointed to examples of numerous brutal offences, such as a rapist who stabbed his victim 29 times, where the sentence imposed (15 years) was well below the sentences of three of the Squamish Five. Finally, it also pointed out how much conduct causing bodily harm and death remains either free of criminal sanction when it is committed against workers, consumers, and the environment, or is punished minimally by regulatory offences and small fines.

On appeal in this case, Clayton Ruby argued that the sentences imposed were excessive, the trial judge having failed to give adequate weight to the good motives behind the offences. The appeal court noted that "this is the first time that a Canadian appellate court has had to consider sentences imposed for serious crimes committed to achieve alleged political, sociological and ecological objectives": *R. v. Belmas* (1986), 27 C.C.C. (3d) 142 (B.C.C.A.) at 144. It rejected the defence argument on the basis that "the enormity of the crimes" dictated that primary emphasis should be placed on protection of the public and deterrence.

With respect to Ann Hansen, Chief Justice Nemetz emphasized that her statement from the dock affirmed her political beliefs although she expressed remorse for the injuries she caused: "A salient feature of her text was that legal channels are not available to remedy the wrongs she perceives to exist and that accordingly she had the right to take illegal action" (at 155). "These are not the words of a person who has abandoned the undertaking of further illegal acts in support of a philosophy which rejects the democratic process" (at 156). Similarly, because Brent Taylor had not renounced violence as a means to achieve political goals, his "good motive" appeal was dismissed. Juliet Belmas's appeal was successful (she had renounced violence) and her sentence was reduced to 15 years imprisonment; she was released on parole in May 1989.

The motivations of the Squamish Five arguably aggravated their crimes for the purposes of sentencing, since it is difficult to justify these extraordinary sentences through principle or precedent.

Their sentences cannot be explained simply by asserting that the crimes of the five were "politically motivated." As the Statement "Politics and Sentencing" noted, the offender who firebombed the Morgentaler Clinic in Toronto in 1984 was sentenced to two years less a day imprisonment. The sentences imposed on the Squamish Five suggest instead a particular understanding of what constitutes a "good" motive. This understanding is consonant with Ann Hansen's analysis in her book, *Direct Action: Memoirs of an Urban Guerrilla* (Toronto: Between the Lines, 2001), where she argues that their arrest, prosecution, and sentencing was followed by a campaign of police repression that included raids and arrests of political activists, increased monitoring and intelligence gathering, and criminalization of members of the left in Canada. For arguments that sentencing patterns reflect class interests, see Michael Mandel, "Democracy, Class and Canadian Sentencing Law" in Stephen Brickey and Elizabeth Comack, eds., *The Social Basis of Law: Critical Readings in the Sociology of Law* (Toronto: Garamond Press, 1986) 137 and Michael Levi, "Suite Justice: Sentencing for Fraud" [1989] Crim. L. Rev. 420.

C. CORPORATE CRIMINALITY

Corporations and corporate representatives present different issues at sentencing. For corporations themselves, there are limited sentencing options available to the judge. Corporations and their representatives may also be shielded from the impact of a given sentence by the law surrounding corporations. Finally, for these reasons and perhaps because there is little stigma attached to corporate criminality, corporations can present particular problems of recidivism.

R. v. Manchester Plastics[†]

[COSGROVE, D.C.J.:]

This judgment as to sentencing arises out of an appeal by the Crown against an acquittal of a charge under Section 14(1)(c) of the Occupational Health and Safety Act R.S.O. 1980 c. 321 against the respondent on the 30th of January of this year. In written reasons I found that I agreed with the appeal of the Crown and I set aside a finding of not guilty on both counts under the Act and conviction was registered under Section 14(1)(c) (I am reading from my judgment) "resulting from the respondent's failure to follow safe procedures to guard a potentially dangerous machine." I went on to say that

---

[†] [1989] O.J. No. 384 (Dist. Ct.), online: QL.

although I thought there was evidence to support another conviction under Section 14(1)(b), that it should be stayed because in effect the matter complained of was adequately dealt with under Section 14(1)(c).

In my view, the risk permitted by the failure to which I referred, was a risk of serious injury or death to anyone in that plant around that machine, whether they wore the hat of supervisor or management, or whether they were a worker. I would put the degree of risk as, if risks are low, moderate and high, I would put it at moderate risk that faced anyone in the vicinity of that machine, and I included the operator because I thought he, because of the particular circumstances, would conceivably have some problems.

There is other legislation which deals with the guarantee and concern of life of the individual and security of the individual. For example, the Canadian Charter of Rights and Freedoms, section 7 says:

> everyone has the right to life, liberty and security of the person

In the last few years a great amount of time, money and effort has been expended in looking at the plight or the rights of the individual under the Charter of Rights; we do that in the context of the individual versus the state, or government. The hazard is uncontrolled government.

This Act, The Occupational Health and Safety Act, by its words deals with the same thing, that is, concern about the welfare of the individual, vis-a-vis the hazards in the work place. In my view, this Act, The Occupational Health and Safety Act, although it's said that the Charter of Rights and Freedoms is the sovereign piece of legislation in Canada, this Act in some respects is more important than is the Charter. This Act should be called the Charter of Life and Limb, and its purpose is the protection not only of the workers but of management; of anyone who is in the working place. It is in my opinion a very important piece of legislation.

I asked for statistics from counsel to try to get some idea of the severity of the problem of hazards in the work place compared for example to hazards or injury on the highway. Counsel unfortunately were not able to give me any statistics on short notice. I can tell you that my source of information is from the Ottawa Citizen dated January 5, 1989; it reports that in the last year 300 people died in the work place in the Province of Ontario. It says that approximately 2,000 people per working day were injured in the Province. That compared to, for example, 1,200 people killed on the roads in Ontario during the same period. (I am reading from the Toronto Star March 4, 1989) with approximately half of the number of people injured on the roads as are injured in the workplace: approximately 122,000 people injured on the highways, whereas if I can believe the statistics that I have referred to, there are more people injured in the work place than there are on the highways. Finally, I have no answer to the last question I posed to counsel; how many people are injured in the home[. All] I can say is that I can recall seeing somewhere that there were more people injured at home than are injured anywhere else. That being said, the statistics I have are the ones which I have identified.

There is no doubt in my mind that the Government of the Province of Ontario in putting forth Bill 208 in the last sitting of the Provincial House, was concerned about injury and death in the work place. It is a Bill to amend the Occupational Health and Safety Act. I wanted to know whether there was an increase in the number of injuries or death. I wasn't able to get that information from anybody. I will deal with the figures that I have now.

300 people dead in a year in the work place are 300 too many; a quarter of a million injuries are a quarter of a million too many. They are scandalous.

The Province obviously wanted to improve the Act, with the amendments in Bill 208. It purports to change a number of things. Relevant to what is before the court is that it proposes to change the penalty from $25,000 maximum to $500,000, because, I suppose, if money is a deterrent you have to know whether you are dealing with Jim and Bob's Local Ironworks or whether you are dealing with General Motors. All things being relative, $25,000 or indeed $500,000 to some companies can be a spit in the bucket. If the increase is intended to be a deterrent; my sinking feeling is that the deterrent is not working and simple fines are too easy. They are not acting to solve the problem.

The other thing I observed as I thought about this sentencing, is that I can't understand why we have the large amount of deaths or accidents in the work place. We are presently going through a technological revolution. We live in the space age. We have technology that can do anything and probably do it very cheaply. Why can't we make safety in the work place more effective and do it cheaply?

I must say that I am encouraged by the evidence that I've heard today, that the Respondent has come forward with some technological answers to address the problems of safety on the machine in question.

When I listened to the case originally, I thought I was in the middle ages. A once-a-month inspection was totally inadequate in meeting safety concerns and potential risk in the Respondent's operation. In any event, if our concern as a community is the welfare of the individual, then surely technology can be used more effectively in the work place to protect the individual, to look after his life, his limbs, and his health.

That takes me finally to the Act and to what I am supposed to do as a Judge now having registered a conviction. Quite frankly I was surprised to find that the method that the Act uses to attempt to effect compliance with safety regulations is simply fine or jail; a fine up to $25,000 maximum or imprisonment for 12 months, are the only devices that are provided.

Why is that surprising? Well, because as a judge upon any other day of the week I deal with sentencing. Probably the majority of my time is dealing with matters which end up in sentencing. I have before me for example, the Report of the Canadian Sentencing Commission; I have the recent Report of the Standing Committee on Justice, and the Solicitor General, which have published huge reports on sentencing in Canada. Although the Reports deal with the Criminal Code and drug laws, both the recent Committee and the Commission Reports consider the issue of deterrence and attempted effective control of conduct. Similarly, both consider the objective of attempting to persuade people to respect law or to respect the rights of other individuals in the community.

Both reports consider and make recommendations respecting alternate sentencing programs on alternate ways in which persons who are convicted are dealt with in an attempt to persuade them to follow a remedial course of action.

I think of such examples, as the Community Service Program. As far as the Province of Ontario is concerned, I think of the Highway Traffic Act with the demerit point system; I understand new proposals are coming forward respecting the demerit program where in addition to simple demerit points there will be educational programs mandated in an attempt to educate offenders under the Highway Traffic Act.

I am convinced that there is a need of a Provincial review to apply what I already know, and which the judges who worked on the Sentencing Commission of Canada knew and recommended to the Government of Canada, that there are more effective ways of attempting to persuade people to change their conduct. It is not difficult, in my mind, to conclude that we should be applying alternative programs as a remedy in the provincial charter of life and limb (i.e. The Occupational Health Act). I think that some changes ought to be made to this Act, in an attempt to educate or to alter the conduct of people who are found in breach of the Act, or in an attempt to change their attitude to respect the law and to be more safety conscious.

Section 108 of the Provincial Offences Act provides as follows:

> Where a court exercises any of the powers conferred by Sections 100–107, it may make any order in addition that justice requires

Section 104 is the section under which I acted to overturn the acquittal and to register a conviction. With the additional jurisdiction under Section 108, I can make any additional order that justice requires.

In my view, justice requires that alternative measures be applied in this case in order to ensure safety consciousness on the part of the Respondent. In my view, from what I have heard of the facts in this case, were I hearing it in a criminal court I would be listening to argument about conditional discharge. I would be hearing argument that this is the first offence. I would be hearing an argument that this is not one of the most serious or blatant (as I've agreed) infractions of the Code or the Regulations. I would be hearing that the Company has already taken steps to mend [its] ways and to make certain safety improvements.

In my view, there are better ways than simply fining the Respondent or spending my time trying to decide whether it should be five to fifteen thousand or one to twenty-five hundred fine as a deterrent. I don't know enough about the Respondent. It could be making millions of dollars a year and a $25,000 fine could be meaningless.

I think I should attempt to find a more effective remedy. Section 108 says I can do anything that justice requires. I want to be satisfied that the Respondent, in fact, is more safety conscious and is going to continue to be safety conscious in the future.

In one sense I am introducing a Safety Training Program as an alternative to fines or imprisonment. Just as the Community Service Program is an alternative remedy, I am initiating a Safety Training Program. I am going to grant a conditional discharge to the Respondent upon conditions. (I appreciate under the Criminal Code the pertinent section doesn't apply to corporations but this isn't the Criminal Code; this is the Provincial Charter of Life and Limb which is designed to keep people alive and whole.)

The discharge will be conditional upon the following terms:

1. That the Respondent will apply new safety procedures comparable to those which are illustrated in Exhibit No. 1 in this sentencing, to all heavy equipment that it has in its plant, not just these big machines — the presses.
2. That its monthly tour of safety inspection, to which reference was made in the trial, will become a bi-monthly inspection.
3. That the Respondent introduce in its bi-monthly meetings, to which I have made reference, a procedure called a "Future Risk Analysis."

You will recall in my judgment in this case I indicated that Mr. Justice Goodman said that the test as to whether a company is doing all it ought reasonably do to avoid risk has to do with the issue of foreseeability; foreseeability is simply going through the procedure of planning, or of looking ahead.

This is a significant aspect of the law which ought to find practical application in the work place because it is a test that the superior courts have said is pertinent to what safety standards are expected in the work place.

Again, the third condition is that the Respondent introduce consideration of a "future risk test," and that it apply that against the various inspections that it makes in its bi-monthly report.

Finally, when the Respondent returns to this court at the end of twelve months to advise the court that it has complied with the three conditions which I have outlined, then I am satisfied that this is an appropriate case for a conditional discharge. I am satisfied that the hazard that was posed by the problem which resulted in the conviction in this case, will have been cured. I am satisfied that the Respondent ... [having adopted] this alternative process will do a lot more towards reducing the risk to all people who are in that plant (I repeat myself, not only the workers but supervisors and people who are part of management as well).

I was interested to hear that the Respondent has already taken steps to go a certain way to upgrading its concern about safety. Again, getting back to technology, I have seen news reports and television reports showing, for example, certain auto makers who hold small group get-togethers every day, every shift that they work to promote safety. Safety consciousness is introduced almost as a daily occurrence let alone a bi-weekly or bi-monthly occurrence.

Court: Mr. Dolezel, I am not sure if you work under the Ministry of the Attorney General or Labour or Solicitor General or who, can you help me?

Mr. Dolezel: Yes, Your Honour, we are members of the Ministry of the Attorney General, seconded to Ministry of Labour.

Court: Alright. I am going to ask that a copy of my sentencing be typed. I am going to ask if you would in your report back to your Ministry, report on what I have done here and ask that the Ministry consider amendments to the Act in order to promote and to look at the question of alternate ways of dealing with the issue of remedying breaches of the Act.

In addition, I am going to ask the Registrar of this court to forward, at the same time, copies of my judgment and sentencing to the Attorney General, to the Minister of Labour, and to the Solicitor General. I will respectfully recommend to those Ministers (because I don't know in which way they share responsibility in this area), that they conduct a study as to alternatives to jail or fine in the area of occupational health and safety in the Province. I will also respectfully suggest to them that they take as a starting point the work that has been done by the Canadian Sentencing Commission and by the Standing Committee of Justice to which I've referred (the Daubney report).

■

The companion decision by Cosgrove, C.J. overturning the acquittal in *Manchester Plastics* is discussed in Abell and Sheehy, *Proof, Defences, and Beyond*, **Mens Rea**. The legal basis for Cosgrove, C.J.'s sentence was disapproved of by the Ontario Court of Appeal in *R.* v. *Sztuke* (1993), 16 O.R. (3d) 559, where the court stated that the *Provincial Offences Act* made no provision for the granting of discharges for anyone other than a young person, and that this power could not be "read in" via s. 125 (then s. 108) of that act. On the other hand, the creative approach of designing probationary terms for a corporate violator of safety laws has been specifically adopted in *R.* v. *Van-Rob Stampings*, [1996] O.J. No. 2076 (Ct. Just. (Prov. Div.)), online: QL. In this case, in addition to a fine, the company was ordered to publicize the accident, its analysis of what went wrong, and its recommendations for short- and long-term steps to avoid such future accidents to all companies in the same industry.

What are the benefits and risks of efforts to devise new sentences? See, for example, the decision of Judge Bourassa in *R. v. Northwest Territories Power*, [1990] N.W.T.R. 115 (Terr. Ct.) (corporate executives ordered to publish an apology, accompanied by their own photographs, in the local paper), rev'd [1990] N.W.T.R. 125 (S.C.). Another recent example is provided by *R. v. Bata Industries* (1995), 25 O.R. (3d) 321 (C.A.), where the court reversed an order by the judge that the company not indemnify the two individual directors who were convicted and fined along with the corporation. Because the non-indemnification order was intended to preclude the individuals from being relieved of paying the fines, it was said to be outside of the scope of the law to attach the term to the corporate offender's probation order since it was not directed at the corporation's rehabilitation or deterrence. For further discussion of the sentencing issues for corporations see Andrew Roman, "Personal Liability of Directors and Officers of Corporations for Violations of Environmental Norms" (1993–94) 12 Nat. Banking L. Rev. 20.

In a sentencing decision regarding a conviction against a corporation under s. 61(1)(a) of the *Competition Act*, *R. v. Shell Canada Products* (1990), 75 C.R. (3d) 365 at 375, the Manitoba Court of Appeal made the following remarks:

> The Attorney General of Canada submits that the learned trial judge, in assessing the appropriate fine, should have applied a formula whereby the fine would be a percentage of Shell's earnings. Although there is ample support in the case law for the proposition that the wealth of a corporation should be taken into account, there is no support for the concept of a formula. Nor was I persuaded that there is sufficient merit in the concept to warrant its adoption.
>
> Nonetheless, when assessing a fine, regard must be had to the earnings of the company. The point was dealt with by Brooke J.A. in *R. v. Browning Arms Co. of Can. Ltd.* (1974), 18 C.C.C. (2d) 298, 15 C.P.R. (2d) 97 (Ont. C.A.). He said (at p. 299):
>
>> When considering the appropriate fine one must carefully characterize who it is who has committed the offence and the significance of a penalty to that person or corporation.
>
> Those words were spoken in dissent, but it is clear from the majority judgment, delivered by Arnup J.A., that the corporate earnings were important in the assessment of the fine. Arnup J.A. considered the amount of the fine with specific reference to the profits.
>
> The total fine in *Browning Arms Co.* represented 7 per cent of the anticipated profits from the company's Canadian operation for the year in which the offence was committed and well in excess of 10 per cent of the profit in each of the three previous years. I do not refer to these percentages to suggest that they should be similar in this case. The cases are quite different. I refer to the percentages only to indicate the relationship of the fine to profits in that case. It should not be as high in this case, but should it be as low as 0.1 per cent of earnings?
>
> It is an admitted fact that in each of the years 1986, 1987 and 1988 Shell earned in excess of $100,000,000 from its business as an oil producer. In the context of those earnings, a fine of $100,000 is but a slap on the wrist: it is inordinately low. Having regard to the circumstances of the offence and the significance of the penalty to the offender, I would increase the fine to one of $200,000.

Is this an appropriate method of assessing a sentence? Why or why not? What are the *Charter* implications of this approach?

D. RACE AND RACISM

A racist motivation for a crime generally acts as an aggravating factor in sentencing, as *R. v. Ingram* (1977), 35 C.C.C. (2d) 376 (Ont. C.A.) and *R. v. Lelas* (1990), 74 O.R. (2d) 552 (C.A.), two of the leading cases, have affirmed.

Bill C-41, S.C. 1995, c. 22 put into statutory law the principles set out in these cases. Section 718.2 deems it as an aggravating circumstance that the offence was motivated by "bias, prejudice, or hate based on the race, nationality, colour, religion, sex, age, mental or physical disability or sexual orientation of the victim."

In spite of the common law principles and s. 718.2, it is by no means straightforward that police, prosecutors, and judges will take seriously racially motivated violence. Reflect back to the evidence of racist motivation surrounding the killing of Leo LaChance by Carney Nerland (**Enforcement of the Law**) and consider whether this new law will be enforceable. The new law requires proof of the hate motive beyond a reasonable doubt; it also requires political will on the part of public and Crown attorneys. Given this, would it be more productive to draft new bias crimes rather than tinker with sentencing? See, for example, the argument in favour of new hate crimes made by Martha Shaffer, "Criminal Responses to Hate-Motivated Violence: Is Bill C-41 Tough Enough?" (1995) 41 McGill L.J. 199.

Consider, in this regard, the convictions and sentences imposed upon five young men who beat and kicked to death an elderly Sikh man, Nirmal Singh Gill, on the grounds of his Temple in Surrey, B.C. In *R. v. Miloszewski*, [1999] B.C.J. No. 2710 (Prov. Ct.), online: QL, the five young men were originally charged with murder with respect to this killing. At the conclusion of the preliminary inquiry, which lasted 25 days, they were all committed to stand trial on second degree murder charges. Thereafter, the Crown charged them with manslaughter, and they all entered guilty pleas to these charges. These pleas were accepted by the judge:

> After full consideration of all of the evidence, I am satisfied that the charge of manslaughter is the correct charge. In saying this I do not mean that the original charge of second degree murder was inappropriate. In the circumstances existing at the time it was laid, it was extremely appropriate. However, at the conclusion of the Preliminary Inquiry both Crown and Defence Counsel were in a position to fully assess the evidence and to decide how to proceed. In my view their decision was correct and the plea by all five accused to the charge of manslaughter is appropriate in fact and in law.

The sentencing hearing lasted 11 days. Its major focus was the question of whether the Crown had proven beyond a doubt that the killing was motivated by racial hatred, within the meaning of s. 718.2 of the *Code*. As you read the extract from this case, think about whether the law reform objectives behind this new law have been realized.

R. v. Miloszewski[†]

[STEWART, J.:]

I make the following findings of fact ...

1. That Mr. Gill as an Indo-Canadian is a person contemplated by section 718.2(a)(i) of the *Criminal Code*.

2. The accused are caucasian and are of a different racial, religious and ethnic origin from Mr. Gill.

3. That each of the accused was in January, 1998 a Neo-Nazi skinhead. I come to that conclusion after considering the following:
   - The 1998 edition of the Canadian Oxford Dictionary defines 'skinhead' as follows:
     > "a person, especially a youth, with shaven or close cropped hair worn as a symbol of anarchy, racism or non-conformity."
   - Corporal Rideout, the senior investigating officer in this case, defined a skinhead as a person with white supremacist beliefs who is against persons of other races or religious backgrounds. Most believe in a New World Order following the extermination of these religions and races. See transcript dated October 21, 1998 at page 1.
   - Corporal Rideout at pages 2 and 3 of the same transcript testified that skinheads wear military-style combat-boots or Doc [Marten] boots. They have Neo-Nazi beliefs. They may wear blue jeans cuffed at the bottom or grey, camouflage pants. They wear U.S. military flight-jackets referred to as "flights" with pins and insignias on the jackets displaying their particular ideology. At page 4 of the transcript Corporal Rideout stated that other than one faction of skinheads, in general skinheads advocate the use of violence.
   - Corporal Daley testified that one branch of Neo-Nazi skinheads advocates white supremacy:

[†] [1999] B.C.J. No. 2710 (Prov. Ct.), online: QL.

See Page 18 lines 39–40 of the transcript dated March 15, 1999.
- Each of the accused displayed the following attributes of a skinhead:
  - each of them had a shaved head at the time of the offence and on their arrest.
  - by their manner of dress with particular reference to flight jackets and to their foot wear.
  - the racist music they listened to.
  - each had a penchant for violence.
  - each described himself and the other accused as a skinhead, racist and white supremacist.
  - each of the Defence Counsel has conceded that their clients adhered to a racist philosophy abhorrent to most Canadians.
  - Mr. Synderek displayed a Nazi flag in his home.
  - they displayed with pride a Nazi flag at the party they attended on January 3, 1998 and Mr. Kluch and Mr. LeBlanc can be seen in photographs (Exhibit 38) giving the Nazi salute.

4. That prior to going to the Temple, each of the accused had consumed a large quantity of beer and alcohol. Their judgment may have been clouded but none of them was impaired to the point that he did not know what he was doing. During the time leading up the offence all of the accused were sufficiently alert to time, place and circumstance to avoid detection by the police on Scott Road and to hide from Corporal Bissonnette when he attended the parking lot at 3:18 a.m.

5. That the accused knew that the Temple was a place of religious worship and that it was on private property because they had to climb over or somehow get around the chain link fence that separates the Temple property from access by the general public.

6. I am skeptical of the defence submission that the accused left the party in order for Mr. Synderek and Mr. Kluch to buy cigarettes and snacks and for Mr. Miloszewski to go home. My doubts are based on the following:
   - There was no explanation as to why Mr. LeBlanc and Mr. Nikkel were in the car.
   - Despite being parked in close proximity to the 7 Eleven store, not one of the accused went into the store and there was no reasonable explanation as to why their stated reason for leaving the party was abandoned and no explanation as to why Mr. Miloszewski was not driven home.
   - The accused have asserted that they were afraid to be discovered by the police consuming beer and in particular that Mr. Kluch was driving while impaired. The concern about impaired driving would have been alleviated as soon as the car was parked. If they had any fear about encountering police with open alcohol in their possession, they could have left the beer in the car. If they wanted to avoid police attention, I question why they would risk a potential problem by trespassing on Temple property.
   - There has been no explanation as to why the five accused decided to vandalize cars parked at the Temple. As the Temple and its grounds are fenced so as to deny access to the general public, the inescapable conclusion is that the accused knew that the vehicles parked there would likely be owned by members of the Indo-Canadian community and they targeted cars in the Temple parking lot for that reason only, rather than vehicles more easily accessible on public thoroughfares.

   Based on the foregoing, I reject the Defence submission and find as a fact that the accused left the party with the intention of vandalizing cars owned by members of the Indo-Canadian community and parked on Temple grounds.

7. None of the accused attended the Temple with the intention of assaulting Mr. Gill or any member of the Indo-Canadian community.

8. Mr. Gill appeared on the scene suddenly and surprised Mr. Nikkel, Mr. Kluch and Mr. Miloszewski. At this time Mr. LeBlanc and Mr. Synderek were some distance away.

9. The accused submit that none of them knew the racial origin of the man they assaulted. I reject that assertion for the following reasons:
   - They knew they were in a fenced-off area that was a place of worship for members of the Indo-Canadian community.
   - It is reasonable to conclude, despite their consumption of alcohol, that at that time of night and in that place any person they would meet would likely be of Indo-Canadian origin.

- Visibility was good enough for Suzanne Czech to see the accused from her apartment some distance away. Furthermore, the lights on the lamp standards in the parking lot were illuminated and considering the fallen snow, visibility was good to a minimum of at least 50 meters.
- Mr. Gill spoke English with a very heavy accent and he said to Mr. Nikkel, Mr. Kluch, and Mr. Miloszewski: "What are you doing"? Or words to that effect (Exhibit 91). It is reasonable to conclude that these 3 accused heard Mr. Gill's accent.
- That it was Mr. Nikkel who began the assault on Mr. Gill and his reason for doing so, as stated to Mathew Gontier, was to join a racist group.
- Mr. Mileszowski admits (Exhibit 91) that he kicked Mr. Gill indiscriminately and that some of his blows landed on Mr. Gill's head.
- Mr. Nikkel admits (Exhibit 91) that some of his kicks struck Mr. Gill's head.
- Mr. Kluch admits (Exhibit 91) that he kicked Mr. Gill 4 to 6 times in the chest area and some of his kicks may have hit Mr. Gill in the head.
- The only evidence as to what Mr. LeBlanc did to Mr. Gill is found in Exhibit 91 and I find as a fact that he came from a distance of 50 to 100 meters away to deliver one kick to Mr. Gill's ribs while Mr. Gill was lying on the ground.
- Mr. Synderek admits (Exhibit 91) and in his testimony under oath before me that he put his foot on Mr. Gill's mouth. While he denies that he realized that Mr. Gill was Indo-Canadian, I am not convinced of that denial because he admits he could see that Mr. Gill had a beard, that he was approximately 45 years of age and that Mr. Gill was wearing a trench coat.
- When the ambulance personnel and police attended they found Mr. Gill lying on his back and were able to immediately identify him as Indo-Canadian.

10. I have a reasonable doubt as to whether the accused appreciated the religious significance of the bracelet taken from Mr. Gill's wrist and have discounted that as a factor to be considered under Section 718.2(a)(i). However, the theft of the bracelet by Mr. Kluch is an aggravating factor generally.

. . . .

I have considered as well the comments made by each of them as to their motivation in assaulting Mr. Gill. These comments were made by the accused over a period of some 4 months from shortly after the offence to shortly before their arrest in April, 1998. There appears to have been an element of exaggeration or bravado in the accuseds' statements as to the level of violence visited upon Mr. Gill and the quantity of blood which he lost. In some cases these exaggerated statements were made after the consumption of alcohol. However, after taking these factors into account, I find that there is nonetheless a very substantial level of consistency in the accuseds' comments as to the details of the assault regardless of whether the comments were made to each other, to uninvolved third parties or to police agents and undercover police officers. Taken together the accuseds' statements are consistent as to:

a) the unprovoked nature of the assault,
b) the basic mechanics of the assault as involving kicking, stomping and punching of Mr. Gill's head and torso,
c) their pride in their involvement in the assault and their status as skinheads,
d) their hateful descriptions of Mr. Gill, including the use of derogatory descriptions of his race, and laughter and excitement when recounting the assault,
e) their efforts to destroy evidence including boots, jackets, car mats and Mr. Kluch's car, and
f) their failure to characterize the assault on Mr. Gill as being any different from other past or contemplated racially motivated violence which was discussed, in some cases contemporaneously, with the assault on Mr. Gill.

I do not propose to exhaustively review the comments of each accused to witnesses and in intercepted communications, but set out below are some of their comments that are illustrative of their attitudes and motivations with respect to the offence.

With respect to Mr. Nikkel's motivation, Mathew Gontier, a witness called by the Crown at the Preliminary Inquiry, testified that Mr. Nikkel described the assault on Mr. Gill to him. Mr. Gontier testified that Mr. Nikkel demonstrated kicking and stomping motions. Mr. Gontier was then asked at pages 20 and 21 of the transcript dated October 14, 1998:

Q: And how is Lee acting while he's doing this?

A: Like happy kind of . . .

Q: Does he tell you why he did this?

A: To get recruited.

Q: And what does he tell you getting recruited is?

A: Joining the group

Q: And what does he tell you — or does he tell you how you get recruited into this group?

A: You beat up an [derogatory racist terms deleted].

In an intercepted communication on March 6, 1998 between Mr. Nikkel, Mr. Leroux and a friend, Ms. Roy, Mr. Nikkel says at page 9 of the transcript that the assault was "awesome" and ". . . I was just dying to you know, I gave him the first hit." At page 12 he says "yeah I was tryin' to see I was . . . see I can prove myself to the guys now. . .".

In the first of two intercepted communications between Mr. Nikkel and Mr. Leroux on March 13, 1998, Mr. Nikkel says at page 4 of the transcript "yeah, I'm the man. So you know I'm proud for what I did" then "Hundred percent, I'll do it again. (laughs) Over and over." In the second conversation at page 4, Mr. Nikkel talks about getting a rise [...] out of the beating and says "I live for that kind of shit". At page 5 he described Mr. Miloszewski jumping on Mr. Gill's head and characterized this action as 'hero worshiping'.

In an intercepted telephone call on March 8, 1998 between Mr. Nikkel and friend, Melissa, he says "...as you knew me when I, even when I went to Banting I was really racist ... well I'm even worse now. Like I'm fuckin' ten times worse now." To another friend, Adam, in the same telephone call, Mr. Nikkel says that he is a skinhead and at page 43 of the transcript says that "...the skinheads are just people that fuckin' hate every other race than their own...".

Mr. LeBlanc was circumspect in making comments to friends over the telephone with respect to the offence. However, I am satisfied that the following three excerpts from intercepted communications are an indirect discussion of the beating of Mr. Gill.

On January 18, 1998, Mr. LeBlanc had a conversation with Chris Bridges, a friend from the military who lived out of province. At page 5 of the transcript Mr. LeBlanc refers to being in "some fuckin sticky situation" and at page 6 states:

N: If it ever makes the news, you'll fuckin laugh your ass off, man.

C: Oh, is that right?

N: I mean, like . . . you'll be like, "Oh shit, that sucks but, it's kinda fuck funny (chuckles)".

Later, Mr. LeBlanc tells a friend on March 6, 1998 about a need to get a new flight jacket. When asked what happened to the old one, Mr. LeBlanc states at page 22 of the transcript "It's uh gone, casualty of war." In another conversation with Mr. Bridges on March 30, 1998, Mr. LeBlanc at page 6 of the transcript complains about discord with other skinhead groups and says:

NL: Basically what's been goin' on is fuckin' me and some other guys have been, being fuckin' real Skinheads and uh some of the other guys like the fuckin' Hammerskins and that are fuckin' feeling infringed upon because we're makin' them look like the couch potatoes that they are.

Later at page 9 of the transcript there is the following:

CB: What about that other crap?

NL: Oh, nothin' so far.

CB: Good.

NL: No no uh, n-nothin' comin' out of it. I mean, I don't know, it may eventually, whatever, I just don't fuckin' give a shit anymore.

CB: Yeah.

NL: Like whatever, if it happens it happens and it's fuckin', whatever. I done my good deed for the lifetime.

With respect to Mr. Kluch, in a conversation with Mr. Synderek on January 15, 1998, he referred to media reports that police were very close to arresting suspects. He said "I know, I'm not worried. I never did shit! Just uh . . . just uh . . . shitty, like, shitty, because . . . it'd be kinda neat if there was a Holy war over this and stuff."

In a conversation with an acquaintance, Lori-Lynn, on February 24, 1998, there is a discussion about 'Hindus' in Surrey and at page 17 of the transcript Mr. Kluch says "...I've grown up with them all my life, like I hate them too. But in Surrey, it's kind of our home turf you know." Later Mr. Kluch says at p.19 of the transcript "...Hitler's my mentor you know, like fuck, I love that guy man (chuckles)". He later says that he is a neo-nazi and all his friends are too. At pages 25–26 he says:

RK: But uh, but anyway uh, like I don't know like what's the white man supposed to do, just sit back and like I think violence is the only way to get 'em out of the country but you have to gain support and numbers before you can you know overthrow the government or whatnot, right.

In a later conversation with Mr. Nikkel and Mr. Leroux on March 13, 1998, Mr. Kluch states at page 5 of the transcript: "I hate the police and the government right." Mr. Kluch tells Mr. Synderek at page 1 of the transcript of a conversation on April 2, 1998, "Can't go wrong with a Hindu death cause it always . . . a fuckin message."

With respect to Mr. Gill's death, on April 11, 1998 at 1948 hours, Mr. Synderek told Mr. Leroux at page 1 of the transcript that this was "an accident at work". Later that day at 2156 hours, in the context of discussing Mr. Gill's death, there was the following conversation between Mr. Leroux, Mr. Synderek and Mr. Miloszewski from pages 9 and 10 of the transcript:

> S: Yeah, that was the first murder in the, in the year. In this year, the first one.
> L: Was it?
> S: (Laughs.) Yeah.
> L: Harsh. And you guys are the ones fuckin' got fuckin' name all over it.
> M: (Laughing.) The new years bash eh.
> L: (Laughing.) The new years bash. Was a good one eh.
> M: . . . new years resolution too. (Laughs.)
> L: (Laughs.) You'd kill a Hindu?
> M: (Laughs.)
> S: We got a good start.

In a conversation on April 11, 1998 at 2140 hours between these same three persons, Mr. Miloszewski at page 9 of the transcript spoke of how he and Mr. Synderek got together after finding out that Mr. Gill had died. He was laughing when he said, "We fuckin' had our first couple beer just to salute the death."

On April 17, 1998 police ran an undercover operation at the Sutton Place Hotel involving Mr. Kluch, Mr. Synderek and Mr. Miloszewski. These three accused made a number of statements revealing their motivation and attitude to the attack on Mr. Gill. At page 121 of the transcript Mr. Miloszewski said:

> M: Nothing to gain, but for me that first guy was an adrenaline rush, power, you know . . . feels.
> S: Yeah (inaudible) we hurt people before, but we have never . . .
> M: Gone to that extent.
> M: The first (inaudible) when I got drunk (inaudible) later, ah cool man. But at first just proud, you know power.

At page 122, Mr. Miloszewski and Mr. Synderek described their encounter with Mr. Gill to undercover officer 'B' as follows:

> S: Fuckin that guy was also just not another guy eh, was one of those guys who protect the Temple right, like in their religion he was one of the top.
> B: So you got one of the head guys there?
> S: Yeah (laughs)
> M: (inaudible) it was a fluke?
> B: What do you mean a fluke?
> M: We were, we were a little a little buzzed right, having little war games, running around, you know how it is (inaudible) right and like we stumbled on a Hindu walking to his little Temple.

At page 125, the undercover officer asked if the accused had been paid for killing Mr. Gill. Mr. Synderek replied, "No, we only do that for pleasure". Mr. Miloszewski added, "Our ... amounts that we got for it was uhm our own pride...." At page 209 of the transcript, Mr. Kluch said, "Some things are more important than money to me, and that's my race and that's why that was done." At page 199, Mr. Kluch was asked in reference to Mr. Gill's death, "How did you feel about that?" Mr. Kluch responded "Ah . . . ah . . . was personal, that was out of hate..."

None of these findings of fact can be viewed in isolation. Taken as a whole I conclude as follows:

- The accused were motivated by hatred to trespass on Temple grounds to damage vehicles owned by members of the Indo-Canadian community.
- When surprised by Mr. Gill, they were not provoked by him and none of the accused ran away which would have been easy for them to do.
- When he was attacked, Mr. Gill was on the ground and presented no threat to the accused. The only reason why Mr. Nikkel, Mr. Kluch and Mr. Miloszewski delivered so many vicious blows to Mr. Gill is that they knew he was Indo-Canadian.
- With reference to Mr. Synderek's testimony, when he and Mr. LeBlanc arrived on the scene Mr. Gill was no physical threat to them either. Mr. Synderek and Mr. LeBlanc came to the scene and participated because Mr. Gill was Indo-Canadian.

Hatred was defined by the Supreme Court of Canada in *R. v. Keegstra* (1991), 61 C.C.C. (3d) 1, where Dickson, C.J.C. stated at pages 59–60:

> Noting the purpose of s. 319(2), in my opinion the term "hatred" connotes emotion of an intense and extreme nature that is clearly associated with vilification and detestation. As Cory J. A. stated in *R. v. Andrews*, supra, at page 211: "Hatred is not a word of casual connotation. To promote hatred is to instil detestation, enmity, ill-will and malevolence in another. Clearly an expression must go a long way before it qualifies within the definition in [s. 319(2)]. Hatred is predicated on destruction, and hatred against identifiable groups therefore thrives on insensitivity, bigotry and destruction of both the target group and of the values of our society. Hatred in this sense is a most extreme emotion that belies reason; an emotion that, if exercised against members of an identifiable group, implies that those individuals are to be despised, scorned, denied respect and made subject to ill treatment on the basis of group affiliation."

Considering all of the above I am satisfied that the Crown has proven beyond any reasonable doubt that each of the accused was motivated by bias, prejudice or hate based on Mr. Gill's race, national or ethnic origin, colour or religion and has proven this as an aggravating factor pursuant to Section 718.2(a)(i) of the *Criminal Code*.

■

An appeal from sentence was dismissed: *R. v. Miloszewski (appeals by L.E.N. and Synderek)*, [2001] B.C.J. No. 2765 (C.A.), online: QL.

In *Miloszewski* the court declined to impose the maximum sentence upon the accused, because it is to be reserved for the worst offenders and the worst offences. Here, with the exception of one accused, none had a criminal record and, while the killing was recognized as horrible, it did not involve protracted brutality or torture. The court referred to several constitutional values in considering the appropriate sentence given the accuseds' racist motivations:

> These are views which are alien to a tolerant, multi-cultural and civilized society. However, it must be remembered that another cherished principle of our democracy is freedom of speech. Individuals have a constitutional right to say things which are distasteful and unpopular subject only to the reasonable limits prescribed by law as can be demonstrably justified in a free and democratic society.
>
> . . . .
>
> Finally, the sentences which I impose must not be disproportionate to other sentences imposed on similar offenders for similar offences. Repugnant and brutal as this crime was, it is not, unfortunately, unique to Canadian jurisprudence. For hundreds of years, a paramount principle of the Common Law has been equality before the law. This principle applies equally to the law abiding and to the law breaker. No one, not even the most repugnant criminal ought to be singled out for special or markedly different punishment. Every person in our society has the right to both a full and fair trial, and if convicted, to a full and fair sentencing process.

In light of the individual aggravating and mitigating circumstances, the time served in pre-trial custody (three years), and the law, three of the accused in *Miloszewski* were sentenced to 12 years imprisonment and two were sentenced to 15 years imprisonment. Why did the court invoke freedom of expression and equality in explaining the sentences? Compare these sentences and the reasoning with the sentences imposed on the Squamish Five.

The court identified *Ingram* and *Lelas* as the two leading authorities on the impact of racist motivation on sentencing, but went on to say that "Section 718.2(a)(i) ... is not simply a re-affirmation of an existing principle. It is a direction to the courts of this country, as expressed by Parliament, that a sentence ought to be increased if the offence was motivated by bias, prejudice or hate based on the enumerated factors." In their article, "Sentencing in Cases of Hate-Motivated Crime: An Analysis of Subparagraph 718.2(a)(i) of the *Criminal Code*" (2001) 27 Queen's L.J. 93 at 116–22, Julian V. Roberts and Andrew J.A. Hastings argue that in light of the difficulties of proving that a crime was motivated primarily by hate beyond a reasonable doubt, the law might better focus on whether the crime was racially aggravated, either due to the offender's hate motivation, or because the offender demonstrated immediately before, during or after the crime, hostility toward the victim based upon their race. What advantages would such a law reform offer? Roberts and

Hastings note that while one empirical study found that approximately 60,000 hate-motivated crimes are committed each year in Canada (Julian V. Roberts, *Disproportionate Harm: Hate Crime in Canada* (Ottawa: Department of Justice, 1995) at 28), a Victimization Survey revealed 273,000 such incidents (S. Besserer and C. Trainor, "Criminal Victimization in Canada" (1999) 20:10 Juristat 1) as reported by victims.

While racist motivation aggravates the seriousness of a crime, the race of an offender or of a victim is said to be legally irrelevant: *Ingram*, *supra*. However, there is some evidence from several jurisdictions that suggests that the offender's race tends to increase the severity of sentence, particularly where the offender is racialized and the victim is white: Monica A. Walker, "The Court Disposition of Young Males, by Race, in London in 1983" (1988) 28 Brit. J. Crim. 441; and Sheri Lynn Johnson, "Unconscious Racism and the Criminal Law" (1988) 73 Cornell L. Rev. 1016.

In *McCleskey* v. *Kemp*, 481 U.S. 279 (1987), the U.S. Supreme Court affirmed the constitutionality of the death penalty, in spite of overwhelming evidence that it is applied by jurors and judges in a racist fashion. Mr. Justice Brennan, in dissent, stated at 321:

> At some point in [his] case, Warren McCleskey doubtless asked his lawyer whether a jury was likely to sentence him to die. A candid reply to this question would have been disturbing. First, counsel would have to tell McCleskey that few of the details of the crime or of McCleskey's past criminal conduct were more important than the fact that his victim was white. Furthermore, counsel would feel bound to tell McCleskey that defendants charged with killing white victims in Georgia are 4.3 times as likely to be sentenced to death as defendants charged with killing blacks.... The story could be told in a variety of ways, but McCleskey could not fail to grasp its essential narrative line: there was a significant chance that race would play a prominent role in determining if he lived or died.

For further discussion of the implications of *McCleskey*, see Paul Brown, "Book Review: Analyzing Racial Bias Claims After *McCleskey*" (1995) 23 Am. J. Crim. L. 231 and Gregory Russell, *The Death Penalty and Racial Bias: Overturning Supreme Court Assumptions* (Westport, Ct.: Greenwood Press, 1994).

There is evidence that the use of the death penalty in Canada, from 1867 until its abolition in 1976, was discriminatory against African-Canadian, Aboriginal, and working class men. Carolyn Strange, in her article "The Lottery of Death: Capital Punishment, 1867–1976" (1996) 23 Man. L.J. 594 describes the legal context of the death penalty at that time. It was an automatic sentence for "capital" crimes, although juries could make a recommendation for mercy to the executive. The Department of Justice reviewed applications for mercy and had the power, originating in the "Royal Prerogative of Mercy," to commute the execution and substitute some term of imprisonment.

There were, however, no legislated standards for the exercise of the power to grant mercy. Attempts by the Special Joint Committee of the House and Senate to study "capital punishment, corporal punishment and lotteries" in its 1956 report were frustrated by the Department of Justice's assertions that its deliberations in post-conviction applications for relief from the death penalty "could neither be defined nor disclosed": *ibid.* at 595. Strange states that although "the most critical decisions in criminal justice were those least governed by rules," the Committee was prepared to accept this deviation from the "rule of law": Special Joint Committee of the House of Commons and the Senate, "Final Report on Capital Punishment" in *Debates of the Senate* (27 June 1956) 545e, as quoted in Strange at 595.

Strange describes the impact of this discretion in discussing the statistical and qualitative analyses of the capital case reviews conducted by the Department of Justice. She comments on the evidence that suggests that while Aboriginal convicted persons at times were spared execution based upon racist beliefs about Aboriginal people as "savage" or "pagan," this leniency was constrained by the type of offence committed and the identity of the victim: "[F]rom 1920 to 1957, Aboriginality contributed significantly to the likelihood of execution: Native condemned persons' risk of execution was 62 per cent (if their victims were also Native), but jumped to 96 per cent when victims were white" (at 605). She discusses the forces that led to the abolition of the death penalty in Canada in 1976, as well as those that ensure that the reintroduction of the death penalty remains on the public agenda as a possibility, in spite of the compelling evidence that its use has been "discriminatory [and] unprincipled."

Current available data in Canada suggests that racial biases in sentencing are not historical anomalies. The *Report of the Commission on Systemic Racism in the Ontario Criminal Justice System*

(Toronto: Queen's Printer for Ontario, 1995) discusses at 265–81 a study that found that Black men are disproportionately more likely to receive the harshest penalty available (imprisonment) than are white men, in spite of the fact that they are less likely to have a prior criminal record than their counterparts:

> **Direct and indirect racial discrimination**
>
> These detailed comparisons reveal notable differences between black and white convicted men:
>
> - Black convicted men were less likely than their white counterparts to have a criminal record, or a lengthy record, but those with a record were more likely than white convicted men to have a recent conviction.
> - Black convicted men were more likely than their white counterparts to have contested the charge, been detained before trial, and been prosecuted by indictment.
> - Black convicted men were more likely than their white counterparts to be described as unemployed.
>
> Some of these differences are consistent with harsher sentencing of the black men, some are inconsistent, and others raise the possibility that discrimination earlier in the criminal justice process was transmitted into sentencing. To clarify the relationship between these differences and racial discrimination at sentencing, we conducted multivariate analyses of the entire sentenced sample and the sub-sample of those sentenced for drug, bail violation and sexual assault offences. These analyses allowed us to see if racial differences in sentencing remained when all the other factors identified in the detailed comparisons were simultaneously taken into account.
>
> We found that —
>
> - within the entire sentenced sample, race did not account for any more of the disparity in sentences than was due to differences in pre-trial detention and employment status. This finding indicates that unemployment and detention before trial had an indirectly discriminatory influence on judges.
> - within the sub-sample, race had a small but statistically significant influence on sentencing decisions beyond the effects of other factors. This finding indicates that some black convicted men were sentenced to prison when white convicted men with the same personal and case characteristics were not sentenced to prison.
> - within the sub-sample, unemployment, detention before trial, not-guilty pleas, and prosecution by indictment were related to the likelihood of prison sentences. These findings indicate that apparently neutral factors, which are not directly related to race, indirectly contributed to higher incarceration rates for black than white convicted men.[†]

For other studies on this issue see Bruce P. Archibald, "Sentencing and Visible Minorities: Equality and Affirmative Action in the Criminal Justice System" (1989) 12 Dalhousie L.J. 377 and the Halifax study by Renner and Warner, *infra*, **Right to Counsel**.

E. CULTURAL CONFLICTS? THE RELEVANCE OF CULTURE TO SENTENCING

The cases and articles in the following section highlight issues of culture and their relevance to criminal justice in terms of the process of sentencing, the factors to be considered in sentencing, and the authority for decision-making with respect to sentencing. While the factors considered in sentencing (such as employment, education, prior criminal record, stability, and family circumstances) are seemingly "neutral" and "objective," they lend themselves to differential applications and in fact structure systemic bias on the basis of race and class. Thus, legal doctrine and legal process inform and shape the differential impact of sentencing. For an analysis of some of those factors, see Tim Quigley, "Some Issues in Sentencing of Aboriginal Offenders" in Richard Gosse, James Youngblood Henderson, and Roger Carter, compilers, *Continuing Poundmaker and Riel's Quest: Presenta-*

[†] © Queen's Printer for Ontario, 1995. Reproduced with permission.

tions Made at a Conference on Aboriginal Peoples and Justice (Saskatoon: Purich, 1994) 269 [hereinafter Continuing Poundmaker and Riel's Quest]. As the Aboriginal Justice Inquiry of Manitoba concluded, discrimination on the basis of socio-economic status "is no less racial discrimination: it is merely 'laundered' racial discrimination" (Volume 1 at 109) because it builds on the history of oppression of Aboriginal peoples that led to their current poverty.

The issues raised in this section form the background to the discussion in the next section of **Circle Sentencing and First Nation Initiatives**. In preparation for reading the appeal of R. v. Naqitarvik, screen the videotape recording of the sentencing hearing at the lower court level: "Arctic Bay: A Community and the Circuit Court" (1985), available from Margit Nance and Curt Taylor Griffiths, Simon Fraser University, Burnaby, B.C.

R. v. Naqitarvik†

[LAYCRAFT, C.J.N.W.T.:]

In this case the Crown appeals a sentence of 90 days' imprisonment to be served intermittently, followed by two years' probation for a major sexual assault on a 14-year-old girl at Arctic Bay, Northwest Territories. His Honour Judge Bourassa of the Territorial Court stated the ground for this disposition as being the existence at Arctic Bay of a system of traditional Inumarit Committee counselling which is a suitable alternative to the longer sentence of imprisonment which would ordinarily be imposed.

I have had the opportunity to consider the reasons for judgment of my brother Belzil. I agree with his summary of the facts of this offence but I regret that I am unable to concur in the conclusion which he has reached. I would allow the Crown's appeal and substantially increase the sentence.

Neither Belzil J.A. nor Judge Bourassa has treated this as a case, such as R. v. Fireman (1971), 4 C.C.C. (2d) 82, [1971] 3 O.R. 380, where a very unsophisticated person must be sentenced for an offence against the laws of a more complex society which has intruded upon his culture. In this view, they are, in my respectful opinion, correct. I shall review the personal attributes of the respondent later in these reasons, but he has had considerable contact with, and experience of, the way of life of Canadians outside his own remote community.

There is no doubt that for the last quarter century, much of northern Canada, particularly its more remote region, has been a land in transition. The traditional institutions and the old cultures of its people are being replaced or modified, in collision with influences from the south. But while the community of Arctic Bay is remote in distance from other parts of Canada, being situated on the northern coast of Baffin Island, it has many of the facilities of other towns and cities in other parts of Canada. Its people have been exposed for some time to the same laws and customs as other Canadians.

The witnesses in this case do not describe a culture markedly different than that in the rest of Canada. Rather the incident itself arose as the victim and her sister played music on a modern player for which there was an electric cord. The complaint of sexual assault was conveyed to the police by telephone and the victim was taken to a modern nursing station for examination and treatment. Both victim and accused have at least grade school education. A large and modern mine is in the vicinity and several of the witnesses, including the accused, had worked there at some time.

My brother Belzil has described in his reasons the traditional Inumarit Committee. It is a traditional governing body of the Inuit, consisting of the experienced elders of the community. Among its functions is the counselling of offenders. If required, that counselling was traditionally relentless and continuous until effective. The offender reformed or he was excluded from community life. In a harsh and hostile environment where the offender could no longer be part of community co-operation in hunting and other food gathering, that exclusion could have fatal consequences.

The present Inumarit Committee in Arctic Bay is not a direct successor to the traditional governing body described by the witnesses. The witness Koonoo Ipkirk, the chairperson of the committee, has lived

---

† (1988), 26 C.C.C. (3d) 193 (N.W.T.C.A.).

in Arctic Bay since childhood. She did not say when the traditional committee last existed but the present body was started in 1975. In that year six members were elected by the community. Since that time "anybody who wants to become a member becomes one." The ages of the members range "from 50 and up," and "a member should have more experience than other people."

Witnesses who spoke of relentless counselling by a committee of Inumarit standing in a circle around the offender were describing a tradition rather than the present situation in Arctic Bay. Ms. Ipkirk said that the present membership of the committee is six and that an individual member was assigned to counsel the respondent. That counselling is done much as it would be done in any other Canadian community. Indeed, one member of the committee, who gave evidence, brings to his assignments a sophisticated background in counselling; he was trained as a counsellor while serving with the Canadian Armed Forces in the United Kingdom and gained experience counselling underprivileged children in Liverpool, England.

The modern reincarnation in Arctic Bay of the traditional Inumarit Committee resembles the usual community counselling service rather than the traditional governing and counselling body of earlier times. I am unable to see, given its recent origin, the community which it serves, its methods of operation, and the absence of the traditional ultimate sanction on the offender, that it is a remnant of ancient culture. Its counselling service, admirable as it undoubtedly is, cannot, in my opinion, replace the sentence of imprisonment which is required in virtually all cases of major sexual assault.

In *R. v. Curley, Nagmalik and Issigaitok*, [1984] N.W.T.R. 281, McGillivary C.J.N.W.T. said [at 283]:

> We wish at this point to say something of cultural circumstances. There are people who suggest that members of an isolated community should be judged in and by that community and by the standards of that community. The judge did not accede to any such suggestion. There is one criminal law of Canada. What he said was that the accused were ignorant of that law and that ignorance is relevant to sentencing as a mitigating factor, just as deliberate flouting of the law is relevant as an aggravating factor. He recognized, and we recognize, that knowledge of the law is an evolving factor. This case will assist the community to better understand the law. A second factor in cultural consideration is that to take these accused out of their own community and imprison them in a totally foreign environment adds a harshness to a jail sentence that must be recognized.

In this case the accused committed a most serious offence. He attacked a 14-year-old girl, tied her hands behind her back and forced her to have sexual intercourse with him despite her shouted objections, her struggles, and her attempts to bite him as she attempted to defend herself. The respondent was her cousin and the trial judge found as fact that they had had consensual sexual intercourse previously.

The respondent had a criminal record, though it is unrelated to this offence. In March, 1982, he was sentenced to six months' imprisonment and two years' probation for six offences of breaking and entering. He actually served some five months of this sentence, presumably in the territorial correctional facility away from Arctic Bay. In June, 1984, he received a suspended sentence and probation for one year for possession of a narcotic. The present offence occurred on July 20, 1984, while he was on probation for the narcotics conviction.

There are a number of points to be made in mitigation of sentence. The respondent ceased the sexual assault when the victim's sister came into the room. He untied the girl's hands at her request. He tried to apologize to her within a few minutes and some time later made a full apology to her in public. There is considerable evidence that he is genuinely remorseful and the learned trial judge so found. Moreover, in the six-month interval before the imposition of the sentence now appealed, he had reacted to counselling in a very positive manner.

The respondent had a common law wife and child born in August, 1984. He "dropped out" of school in 1979 after completing grade 7. He has also attended a house maintenance course given at Frobisher Bay. He has worked at a nearby mine and has also been employed as a roofer by housing contractors in the area. He is described as a reliable employee.

There is little in the material before us to show the effect on the victim. She gave evidence briefly on the sentencing hearing when the respondent denied she had shouted during the attack and her evidence was accepted by Judge Bourassa. However, both counsel chose not to examine on the traumatic effect of the incident and no medical evidence was called. In *R. v. Sandercock* (1985), 22 C.C.C. (3d) 79 at p. 85, 48 C.R. (3d) 154, 62 A.R. 382 at p. 386, Kerans J.A. said on this aspect of sexual assault:

> The other aspect which creates a major sexual assault is the effect on the victim. Notwithstanding statements in some authorities to the con-

trary, the tradition is to assume, in the case of a rape for example, that the victim has suffered notable psychological or emotional harm aside entirely from any physical injury. Of course, once this assumption is brought into question, the Crown must prove it. Nevertheless, harm generally is inferred from the very nature of the assault. This harm includes not just the haunting fear of another attack, the painful struggle with a feeling that somehow the victim is to blame, and the sense of violation or outrage, but also a lingering sense of powerlessness. What we mean by this last is that, while we all are aware in an intellectual way about the fragility of normal existence, to experience a sudden and real threat to one's well-being, a threat so intense that one must beg to be spared, tends to destroy that sense of personal security which modern society strives to offer and humanity so obviously wants. It matters little in this respect whether that threat comes from a robber, a rapist, or any swaggering bully.

I follow *Sandercock* in using a sentence of imprisonment for three years as a starting point in cases of major sexual assault. No doubt some of the aggravating and mitigating factors mentioned in that case may be somewhat modified when applied to northern Canada. In particular one must have careful regard to the degree of sophistication of both the offender and the victim. Nevertheless, *Sandercock* offers a general guide-line of the starting point and of the various factors involved in upward or downward revision of that starting point in the light of aggravating or mitigating factors.

It is unfortunate that there has now been a considerable lapse of time since the offence was committed. The respondent has served the intermittent sentence of imprisonment imposed on him. Nevertheless, on a consideration of all the factors in this case, I consider the sentence to be wholly inadequate, though the mitigating factors justify a considerable reduction from the starting point. I would substitute for the sentence imposed in Territorial Court, a sentence of imprisonment for 18 months.

[Haddad, J.A. concurs with Laycraft, C.J.N.W.T.]

[BELZIL, J.A. (dissenting):]

This appeal raises important considerations in the imposition of sentence in a remote and isolated Inuit community for a serious offence committed there by a member of that community.

The Crown appeals a sentence of 90 days' imprisonment to be served intermittently at the local detachment of the R.C.M.P. at Arctic Bay on Baffin Island plus two years' probation and 100 hours of community work imposed upon the respondent by His Honour Judge R.M. Bourassa following a guilty plea on a charge of sexual assault under s. 246.1 of the *Criminal Code*.

The agreed statement of facts filed shows that on July 20, 1984, at approximately 1800 hours, the accused, who is 21 years of age, came to visit the complainant, who is 14 years of age, at her residence in Arctic Bay, Northwest Territories. Both the complainant and her sister were listening to tapes on a tape-recorder. Their father had left a short time previously, and both girls were alone in the residence. The accused wanted both girls to play the same music over and over. The complainant then took the tape-recorder and electric cord, leaving the living-room and walked into her bedroom. The accused followed the complainant to the bedroom and tried to take the tape-recorder and cord away from her, but she held on to them. The accused then started to touch the complainant's breast. When he did this, the complainant called for her sister. The accused then tied the victim's hands behind her back. The accused tried to kiss her, but she turned her head away. The accused then undid her pants and the victim bit him on the shoulder. The accused took down his pants. The victim tried to keep her legs together, but the accused forced them apart and entered her vagina with his penis. The victim all this time was shouting and trying to make a lot of noise. She was calling for her sister. Her sister came into the bedroom and told the accused to stop or she was going to call her grandfather. The victim kept asking for someone to untie her hands which the accused did. The complainant went and put her pants on and went to the bathroom where she stayed for some time crying. The victim went to her bedroom. The accused entered the bedroom and tried to apologize. The victim telephoned the police a short while later and was taken to the nursing station. The complainant and the accused are cousins.

In addition to these agreed facts, the learned trial judge accepted as unchallenged fact from the presentence report that the accused and the complainant had had sexual intercourse before and that the complainant had always consented until this occasion.

Judge Bourassa held a special sentencing hearing at Arctic Bay which attracted great community interest. About half the citizens of a community of some 400 people were in attendance throughout the 12 hours of evidence and submissions. In passing sentence at the end of this long hearing, Judge Bourassa delivered extensive oral reasons addressed as much to the community as to the accused. He pointed out the gravity of the offence and the long term of imprisonment which it would have attracted elsewhere in Canada. He discussed all the factors properly to be taken into account in imposing sentence. In arriving at the sentence which he imposed, he gave weight to the concerns of the community expressed to him by its elders known as the "Inumarit" and he took into account the unquestioned effectiveness of its traditional treatment of offenders.

It will be seen from the extracts of the evidence hereunder reproduced that the primary concern of the community had been and still is to maintain its harmony and cohesiveness, a concern undoubtedly traditionally considered crucial to the very survival of a small group in a harsh and isolated environment and now considered crucial to the survival of its cultural identity in the face of intrusion by a civilization foreign to it. Imprisonment, even banishment, were historically unknown as forms of punishment. Imprisonment is viewed not only as destructive of the accused himself but as containing the seed of disharmony and division and hence destructive of the community itself. The traditional method of handling an offender is forced confrontation by the elders even to the point of denying him food or other amenities until a willingness to change for the better is manifested, and this is followed by relentless counselling until the offender is considered rehabilitated. The treatment is shown by the evidence to have achieved what must be the ultimate purpose in all punishment for crime, that is to say, protection of the community and rehabilitation of the offender. It has had the added benefit of effecting reconciliation between victim and offender, a concept only now being advanced in our society by some criminologists.

I turn to an examination of the evidence before the learned sentencing judge, with the caution that this evidence comes to the transcript through untrained interpreters.

The trial judge first heard the testimony of Rebecca Williams. A native of Arctic Bay, social worker and probation officer of the community, she prepared a presentence report recommending against incarceration outside of the community. She testified that before preparing the report she had consulted with the Social Services Committee of Arctic Bay and also with the Inumarit and she explained to the court the status of these groups in the community.

The Social Services Committee comprises a group of persons elected by the community and confirmed by the Commissioner of the Territories to advise and assist in the care and rehabilitation of persons with social problems, including offenders.

Miss Williams then described the Inumarit:

Q. Who are the members of the Inumarit?

A. The Inumarit people are the age from fifty and up, and they form themselves in order to rectify some of the problems in the community that they can see or to be any assistance to anybody who is in need.

Q. Do you know how members of the Inumarit are chosen?

A. I am not really sure on that, but I can — I think it would be fair to say that you have to be a mature person. You have to have some experience in life in dealing with problems or anything, maybe hunting, sewing, anything that is traditional.

She was asked in cross-examination whether rape was always considered an offence with her people and how it was traditionally punished, and she said:

Q. ... Since my friend asked you questions about the historical facts of your people, can you tell me whether or not the sexual assault of a young lady while tying her up and then having forced sex with her was an accepted part of the ways of your people?

A. No, it is not accepted behavior.

Q. It never has been?

A. Not as far as I know.

Q. People who did that were punished by your people historically always?

A. The punishment would be getting the people for confrontation and counselling after that.

Q. Absolutely, and it was the elders who would sit in a circle — I'm sorry, go ahead. Translate what she said. It was the elders who stood together in a circle with the rapist, the assaulter, in the middle of the circle, and they confronted him, didn't they?

A. Yes.

Q. And hopefully that counselling would result in the community being a better place for everybody to live in?

A. Yes.

Q. And do you know what your people did if the counselling didn't work?

A. No, I don't.

Three members of the Inumarit testified through an interpreter. Each saw a slightly different role for the group. The Chairman, Ms. Koonoo Ipkirk said there were then six members, and that the age requirement was 50 years or up. She viewed their role as follows:

Q. Could you tell me what the role of the Inumarit is?
A. They have been helping people solve some problems.

Q. What kinds of problems does it deal with?
A. They were all different kinds of problems, like marriage problems and all those things, marriage problems and some other problems.

Q. Does Inumarit ever counsel people who have committed criminal offences?
A. Yes.

. . . .

Q. Could you describe the course of treatment or the course of counselling?
A. What they do is they talk to this particular person who was in trouble before and they should try to stay away from trouble they had before, and if they don't listen to them, they just go back to that person and talk to them again.

In cross-examination, she said:

Q. I would like to ask you some questions about your committee and what you know about the history of your people and this kind of committee. In your community are the stories and history and traditions passed down by the elders to the younger people?
A. Yes, they are.

Q. And it has always been a part of the history of your people that to do what Joanasie did was wrong?
A. She thinks so.

Q. In the old days when somebody did what Joanasie has done, what happened to him?
A. They talked with him. If it was the first time there would be less people, but if he did it again, there would be more people, and they would still talk with him.

Q. And if he did it again, there would be more people; is that right?
A. Yes.

Q. And the purpose of this counselling had two reasons. Well, it is two-fold. The first was to protect the community from the wrong, from the person who is doing the wrong, and the second was to change the person from being a bad person to a good person?
A. Yes.

Q. If a person didn't listen and just kept on doing one thing after another, doing something wrong all the time, didn't stop, what did the community do, if anything?
A. These elderly won't give up on this person. They just try to stop it, doing what he was doing over and over again. They just don't give in. They just keep trying.

Q. And that is the right way to be, isn't it?
A. Yes.

Q. And they kept trying for two reasons again, to protect the community and to try to get the person to change?
A. Yes.

Philip Qamanirq, the Mayor of Arctic Bay and vice-president of the Inumarit, saw as a primary role of the Inumarit the bridging of the conflict between the traditional ways and the law. I quote from his evidence:

Q. Do you live in Arctic Bay?
A. Yes.

Q. How long have you lived here?
A. He has been here most of his life.

Q. Are you a member of the Inumarit?
A. Yes.

Q. What is your position on the committee.
A. He would like to tell you his position in the committee. Even though they don't have any laws written down, like, they don't have laws that they should follow even though they don't have laws written down, they try to do what is best for the people. He is the youngest one from the committee. Because they don't have a law written down, the reason why he wants to stay as a member is he wants to get closer to more important people like the court. They want to cooperate with the judge and everything. What he could remember is the law we have to follow and the position they were not going well with each other, and they were, like, the law and the traditional way were against each other, so he wanted to become a member in order to cooperate.

Q. May I ask you another question? Could you describe the role of the Inumarit?

A. Yes. He knows that nobody else in this court is going to tell us the traditional way. He can talk a bit about it himself.

He also pointed out that the Inumarit handle more problems than the authorities:

Q. In your experience, has your committee been successful in helping the people with this counselling?

A. Those that the committee will deal with will be those who will not be dealt with here, let's say, in the court or by the R.C.M.P. If you drew a line on the other side, you will have those who have been dealt with by the courts and the R.C.M.P., and if you counted the numbers on the side that they deal with, the numbers would be larger than the people that the courts and the R.C.M.P. deal with.

Q. Have you counselled people who have committed criminal offences?

A. Explain yourself. Which offences do you mean? Offences against the Criminal Code or the offences against the laws that have been passed in the culture?

Speaking of the offence of rape and of the community's objection to imprisonment he said:

A. Throughout the years, in the past it has been stated that they should not have sex with those that they don't plan to get married with, and this act has been considered serious in the culture especially the part where this act has been forceful, but in the case of a person being charged and then being taken away to jail, what you will see then is a community that will start to get split. On one side you will have those who are glad that the person is gone, but on the other hand, you will have people who are sorry to see him go, and to prevent this, what the community is starting to do is to ask this committee to get involved more and more just to keep that unity among the community. As the committee gets involved and is starting to get recognized, they can do more and more. For example, the working relationship with the church, that is a body that can help religious problems. The other public feeling around here is that this is one body, the committee, that can get the whole backing of the community.

The third Inumarit witness, Lazarus Aola, was the member designated to counsel the present respondent. Convicted of incest in 1973, he had spent one month in jail and served two years' probation. As a former beneficiary of Inumarit treatment he now saw a constructive role for himself.

Q. Were you counselled by the Inumarit at any point?
A. Yes.
Q. When was that?
A. It started around 1975.
Q. Were you on probation also at that time?
A. Yes.
Q. Could you tell the court a bit about what the Inumarit counsel do?
A. One way he got involved was he didn't want to get into the same situation that he was in, and he wanted to be able to help others prevent him from doing the same act.
Q. Do you feel that the Inumarit assisted you.
A. Yes, a lot.
Q. Do you know Joanasie Naqitarvik?
A. Yes.
Q. Have you counselled him in your capacity as an Inumarit member?
A. Yes.
Q. Has he been responsive to counselling?
A. Yes.
Q. Could you tell the court how he has responded to counselling and give examples?
A. Even before he was asked to get involved he had been previously talking to Joanasie and then afterwards when he met with him he had found him to respond well to his questions and answers, and so on, and he is also thinking of the fact that he is still young, and that he is going to make mistakes but his conclusion is that he is not a lost soul.
Q. Have you noticed any changes in his life style?
A. For example, when he first met him he had stated that what he did was wrong, and he himself had done the same thing previously, and the counselling, this made the counselling session more successful, but on the one hand when they first got together, he noticed that Joanasie was sad, and after the incident happened, but after some sessions he had noticed that he has been more — he is happier since.
Q. Could you explain what you mean by your statement you had done the same thing previously?
A. Because he had committed a sexual offence as well, and the time he got involved with the Inumarit Committee, that is when he decided to help others

to help them, and also to prevent them from doing the same thing. The reason he is involved with Joanasie is not because of the person but because of the fact that because he is now able to help others, one day Joanasie will be able to help others who do the same thing.

I then turn to the reasons expressed by Judge Bourassa for imposing the light sentence which he did [summarized 14 W.C.B. 82]:

> Now, I have to say a few words about the community of Arctic Bay. I have been coming to Baffin Island for three years now, and I think I can say quite fairly that there is something here in Arctic Bay that is not found in very many other communities. I do not know exactly what it is, I do not know how it works. I only had a small description this afternoon from the testimony of the Inumarit members. But what is important to the court is that whatever control mechanism there is in this community, it has kept it crime-free. There are few other communities like Arctic Bay, but not many. Igloolik and Lake Harbour for example are two. In each of those communities, and Arctic Bay, it seems as though there are enough people that care, and are involved in such a way that people don't commit crimes. If all of the communities in the Northwest Territories were like Arctic Bay and Igloolik, we would not need any jails.
>
> It is obvious to me that what has been said in evidence today that the community is willing to act, the Inumarit is willing to act and social services are willing to act in this case is not an empty promise. It is true. It is a fact. It is proven in the past by the very absence of crime or disturbance. This special part of Arctic Bay is something that I would be very sad to see in any way taken away or diminished. The very things that the Inumarit are trying to do is what the court is trying to do: rehabilitating an offender, reconciling the offender, the victim and the community so that there is unity in the community and a programme of education. Can any of us really say that jails do that? For the person that responds, the Inumarit, the Social Services Committee and the whole community together can obviously heal; they can unite; they can reconcile, and they can reform.
>
> ...
>
> I am impressed with the Inumarit. They promise and appear in the past to have delivered more than what jails can do. I accept what they say without reservation because as I say for the last three years that I have been here we hardly ever come to Arctic Bay, because there is simply no trouble in this community.
>
> So the issue is, what do I do with this group of people in this community that is so eager to be involved and to take care of the problems within the community, and at the same time do what is right in the law. If the court can do something to help the community to continue to solve its own problems, to help those, whoever they are, and however they work to continue to keep Arctic Bay the good community that it is then I think the courts should do it. If whatever it is in Arctic Bay that keeps this community crime-free continues to function and work with respect to this man then everybody is served and the people in this community will be protected.

There is precedent for the imposition of a comparatively lesser sentence for serious offences in isolated communities of the North under the recognition of a very broad discretion by the trial judge in fixing sentence when particular local conditions warrant it. Judge Bourassa referred to the case of *R.* v. *Amauyak* (unreported) where Justice deWeerdt of the Supreme Court of the Northwest Territories imposed a suspended sentence for rape and careless use of a firearm. The respondent has referred us to the case of *R.* v. *King* in the British Columbia Court of Appeal (unreported) where a sentence of 21 days' imprisonment given to an accused for sexual assault upon his daughter was sustained. The discretion of a trial judge in imposing sentence is set out in s. 645(1) and (2) of the *Criminal Code*:

> 645(1) Where an enactment prescribes different degrees or kinds of punishment in respect of an offence, the punishment to be imposed is, subject to the limitations prescribed in the enactment, in the discretion of the court that convicts a person who commits the offence.
>
> (2) Where an enactment prescribes a punishment in respect of an offence, the punishment to be imposed is, subject to the limitations prescribed in the enactment, in the discretion of the court that convicts a person who commits the offence, but no punishment is a minimum punishment unless it is declared to be a minimum punishment.

This is the wide discretion spoken of by Macdonald J.A. for a five-man court of this jurisdiction in *R.* v. *Ayalik* (1960), 33 W.W.R. 377 at p. 378:

> However it should be noted that in the present case the learned trial judge had a distinct advantage over the members of the court for with his wide experience in the far-flung areas of the extensive jurisdiction of the trial division of this court he has knowledge of local conditions, ways of life, habits, customs and characteristics of the race of people of which the accused is a member.

It is clear from a study of the evidence adduced at trial that the learned trial judge gave weighty and anxious consideration to all of the circumstances of the case. We cannot say in reviewing his decision that he failed to take any circumstances into consideration or that he proceeded under any wrong principle.

As individual judges we may have imposed a different sentence than the one imposed by the learned trial judge, but as the discretion of a trial judge in imposing a sentence is a wide one we cannot say that the sentence he gave was a wrong one.

While this was said in an appeal by the accused against sentence, there is no reason why the same principle should not apply in this appeal by the Crown.

The trial judge properly took into account the special circumstances disclosed in evidence of a small isolated group striving to preserve its cultural heritage by maintaining its cultural unity, not for the purpose of blocking the imposition of criminal law but by gradually introducing it by bridging the gap between traditional law and the new law. The crime-free record of the community obviously satisfied the trial judge that this community was much more successful in this than had generally been the unfortunate case in too many communities of the far North.

I am unable to detect any error in principle in the reasons of the sentencing judge. The preservation of cultural heritage is given new recognition by the *Canadian Charter of Rights and Freedoms* and it was proper to take it into account. The trial judge weighed this and all other factors and imposed a sentence which in my view was fit in the circumstances disclosed by the evidence before him.

I would refuse the Crown leave to appeal.

Appeal allowed.

Locking Up Natives in Canada†

THE INUMARIT OF ARCTIC BAY, NORTHWEST TERRITORIES

The attempt to accommodate the Canadian criminal justice system to aboriginal communities has a long history in the Northwest Territories. Territorial judges of the stature of Mr. Justice Sissons and Mr. Justice Morrow, in taking justice to the far flung communities of the Northwest Territories on circuits covering many thousands of miles, have in the course of their judgments analyzed certain aspects of the indigenous and customary law of the Inuit and Dene. To some extent there has also been incorporation of this law in the context of family law, such as the recognition of the Inuit custom of adoption as being a legal adoption within the meaning of the *Child Welfare Ordinance*.

More recent attention has, however, focused on Inuit law in relation to criminal issues. A recent case which arose in the community of Arctic Bay before His Honour Judge Bourassa of the Territorial Court provides a unique opportunity to see an aboriginal justice system in operation and how a judge working within the context of the Canadian system sought to reach an accommodation between them.

As a case study, *R. v. Naqitarvik* is important because it raises some of the central issues with which we have to grapple in order to understand the meaning of justice in the context of native people.

. . . .

The approach taken by the majority of the Court of Appeal in this case quite clearly circumscribes the ability of a native community to reach an accommodation between its own and the larger Canadian justice system. In my view there are a number of serious flaws in the Court of Appeal's judgment which reflect some common misconceptions about the nature of change and continuity in native societies which must be addressed if we are to take seriously the task of accommodation of native community processes within the existing justice system.

The Court seizes upon the surface realities of the presence of electricity, telephones and the infrastructure of schools, nursing stations and police forces as evidence of the essential similarities between contemporary native communities and other small non-native communities. However, the surface similarities obscure far more than they reveal about

† By Michael Jackson, (1989) 23:2 U.B.C. L. Rev. 215 at 260–61, 265–68, 272–73. Reproduced by permission of the author.

Arctic Bay and hundreds of other native communities across the country. The links within these communities between the past and the present, the continuity of deeply held values of sharing and cooperation, the respect for elders and the importance of maintaining community coherence through consensus decision making, are not sign-posted or visible to outside eyes in the same way as the evidence of outside intrusion, in the form of telephones, nursing stations and mines. We have to work much harder to see and understand the inner structure of native communities.

The Court of Appeal judgment falls into the trap of seeing native communities as evolving from an earlier to a modern state of civilization, with the ineluctable conclusion that their old "traditional" ways will inevitably wither as they assume the values, institutions and trappings of our civilization. I have already alluded to this in the introductory comments and have suggested that it is part of the colonialist and superiorist stereotype with which many Canadians have typically viewed aboriginal peoples. There is also another part of this stereotyped thinking about native peoples which requires that if they wish to assert rights to aboriginality, they must demonstrate that their "traditional" practices and laws have remained intact and unchanged. The assumption behind this thinking is that native societies are inherently static and non-adaptive; hence, they provide a corollary to the assumption that necessarily any change will be in favour of the incorporation and adoption of non-native practices and laws.

The judgment of the Court of Appeal in *Naqitarvik* illustrates the combined effect of this thinking. The role of the Inumarit is seen as evolving from its "traditional" role as governing body of the Inuit to a specialized counselling service similar to that operating in any other small Canadian community. At the same time, because the membership of the Inumarit includes individuals who have experience in "modern" counselling and there have been changes in its methods and sanctions, it is no longer part of "traditional" culture. It is easy to understand the implications of this sort of reasoning. Essentially it denies native people the right to be contemporary, the right to develop their indigenous systems of government and decision making to cope with the realities of contemporary life, without acknowledging their own demise as distinctively native societies.

In the case of Arctic Bay we have an example of an Inuit community which over the past forty years has experienced major changes in their social and economic organization: from a life in which small hunting groups moved from camp to camp across the tundra, they now live within a central community while still spending a considerable part of the year on the land; their economy has become a mixed one where wage employment and transfer payment now provide supplements and, for some people, replacements for hunting, fishing and trapping. In the same way the old political processes have had new layers added to them in the form of community councils elected under territorial legislation; new religions have been introduced and incorporated into Inuit spiritual values; there has also been introduced a new language and an educational system modelled on the non-Inuit society's values.

The cumulative effect of these changes was reviewed by Mr. Justice Berger in the *Report of the Mackenzie Valley Pipeline Inquiry*. He noted that it seemed to many in government that the old way of life was disappearing and that it was appropriate that government policies be geared to helping native people make as rapid an adjustment as possible to a new economy, a new political system, a new way of seeing themselves in the world. However, the evidence placed before the Inquiry, not only by the Inuit but by the other native peoples of the North, made it clear that they were not prepared, as others were, to consign their way of life to the past. Instead they aspired to the development of their distinctive societies in ways which were consistent with their values, social structures and economic systems. What they sought was the acknowledgment by the larger society of their rights to control the scale and pace of development in the North so that it did not overwhelm them. It was during the 1970s that Inuit communities and other native communities across the country (with the benefit of a generation of young people who had been to the white man's schools and universities and had observed how Canadian political institutions functioned and the extent to which they diverged from those of aboriginal communities) started to develop initiatives which sought to make the old values and processes work in a modern context in order to provide the balance of continuity and change.

It is within this wider context that the formal introduction of the Inumarit Committee in Arctic Bay must be placed. The assumptions which underlie the role and responsibilities of the Inumarit are entirely different from those of a "counselling service." The elders in a native community are not seen as they typically are in the larger society, as those whose productive life has ended, but as the guardians of the society's history and the repository of its collective wisdom. There is respect accorded the elders which has no counterpart in a mere counselling service. The concern for the healing of collective wounds and of ensuring community cohesion is a mandate which private or state counselling services do not have. To equate the two is to fail to comprehend, as the Court of Appeal did, the respect afforded elders in Inuit society and the constructive ways in which that respect is channelled back by the elders in producing and maintaining social order. The implications of such lack of comprehension are equally self-evident in the judgment of the Court. A substantial sentence of imprisonment, judged by the community after due deliberation to be unnecessary from the perspective of the community, the victim and the accused, is imposed with the clear message to the community that our non-native elders, or at least some of them, know better than theirs as to what will contribute to a just and orderly society.

It is important to ask why the majority of the Court of Appeal in *Naqitarvik* felt that they could not respect the wishes of the community, as expressed through the Inumarit, to have the accused dealt with by the community and not be subjected to punishment by imprisonment far removed from the community. The Court does not clearly articulate this but it may be inferred from their reference to the *Sandercock* case that a substantial sentence of imprisonment is deemed to be necessary in order to further general deterrence and to reflect appropriately the denunciation of society for sexual assault. In making judgments about deterrence and denunciation, however, the Court is seeking to reflect Alberta or Canadian society in general. Clearly, it was not focusing on native communities. The judgments of Judge Bourassa and Mr. Justice Belzil did refocus the inquiry in this way and concluded that the intermittent sentence plus the community service order was adequate for general deterrence, and reflected the denunciation of the Inuit of Arctic Bay. At the same time, it was consistent with the reconciliation between the victim and the offender and the reintegration of the offender into the community.

. . . .

In a Canadian context where there is considerable mobility between native and non-native communities and where there has been a certain gravitational pull, particularly of young people, away from their communities to larger urban centres, there is likely to be a broad spectrum of cases in which it is more or less appropriate to permit a native community to have the decisive voice in determining the shape and extent of appropriate sanctions. Relevant factors would be the community's ability to exercise control and influence over an accused, which necessarily would involve the extent to which an accused was likely to respect the sanctions recommended by the community. Where, as in the case of Arctic Bay, the evidence shows that the community has such control and that the accused has this respect, and where the crime is one which is community based, I do not see any basis for the subordination of the community's views to a sentence policy conceived for a larger society, particularly where the application of that policy will have the effect of undermining the native community's cohesion and ability to resolve its own problems.

. . . .

In a Canadian context we have already seen how the Inumarit functions in Arctic Bay and the way in which the Territorial Court looks to their evidence as reflecting the considered views of the community. The Court, by hearing the evidence of the elders in front of the whole community and placing its [imprimatur] on what is the "voltgeist" of the community, serves to recognize and affirm the community's collective sentiments and judgments.

■

The preceding article by Michael Jackson seeks to address issues of culture and their relevance to criminal justice. Consider whether the issues of culture and gender are severable and the limits of analysis with reference to any single factor. Critically analyze the *Naqitarvik* decisions (both that of the lower court and that of the appeal court, majority and dissent) from the point of view of Pauktuutit, for example. Bear in mind:

- the aims and purposes of sentencing and the factors to be taken into account
- the aims and purposes of criminal law
- cultural and political issues, and in particular the relationship between Aboriginal communities and the Canadian criminal justice system
- gender issues, including the nature of the crime of sexual assault
- the circumstances of the accused
- the circumstances of the community, including the role of the Inumarit
- possible dispositions, and whose views and representations should be taken into account

The trial judge in both *R. v. Curley* (cited in *Naqitarvik*) and *R. v. Naqitarvik* was Judge Michel Bourassa. In December 1989, Judge Bourassa made several comments in an interview: Laurie Sarkadi, "Sexual Assaults in the North are often less violent" *The Edmonton Journal* (20 December 1989) A1, A2, which followed on another sentence given by Judge Bourassa of five days imprisonment and nine months probation to a former politician for repeatedly fondling a young girl. Judge Bourassa said (at A1):

> The majority of rapes in the Northwest Territories occur when the woman is drunk and passed out. A man comes along and sees a pair of hips and helps himself.
>
> That contrasts sharply to the cases I dealt with before (in southern Canada) of the dainty co-ed who gets jumped from behind.

A judicial inquiry was convened in response to the outcry from the public and from Northern women's groups. In *In The Matter of an Inquiry Pursuant to Section 13(2) of the Territorial Court Act, S.N.W.T. 1978 (2), c. 16* and *In The Matter of an Inquiry into the Conduct of Judge R.M. Bourassa*, Madam Justice Carole Conrad of the Alberta Court of Queen's Bench ruled that there was no "misbehaviour," "bias," or "inability to perform his duties properly" on the part of Bourassa: "Bourassa did not say that sexual assault is less violent in the North than in the South, but that rapes in southern Canada were frequently accompanied by more violence before the act of rape occurs," said Conrad. She found no evidence Bourassa was biased against women, Northerners, or people who are drunk, although his choice of phrases such as "pair of hips" and "dainty co-ed" was careless, she said.

Representatives of the Territorial Status of Women Council, Yellowknife Women's Society, and the Northwest Territories Representative on the National Action Committee on the Status of Women protested Justice Conrad's decision: "Women upset as N.W.T. judge exonerated" *The Toronto Star* (14 October 1990) A9.

Pauktuutit, the Inuit Women's Association, condemned Justice Conrad's decision and proceeded to research a court challenge to judicial decision-making in the Northwest Territories, alleging that sentencing practices (particularly, the factors taken into account as mitigation) violated Inuit women's constitutional rights under sections 7 and 15 of the *Charter*:

> In our view, allowing Judge Bourassa to remain on the bench brings the administration of justice in the NWT in question. The lenient sentences in rape and sexual assault cases handed down by Judge Bourassa from 1984 to 1989, as well as those by other northern judges, have done nothing to ensure the rights of Inuit women to personal security and equality under the law.
>
> ... We believe there is evidence of racial bias contrary to section 15 of the *Charter of Rights and Freedoms* when culture is considered as a factor in sentencing. In 1984, Judge Bourassa handed down a one-week sentence to three Inuit men who raped a mentally impaired 14-year-old Inuk girl. That girl had section 15 equality rights too! She was entitled to "equal benefit of the law," which includes protection, despite her mental disability. Judge Bourassa gave a six-month sentence in an incest case where there was violence for years by a father against his daughter. Another Inuk male received one month imprisonment for sexually attacking a sleeping victim.[†]

In conclusion, Pauktuutit called for a full, public inquiry to examine judicial appointment, discretion of Crown attorneys, policing, sentencing (particularly sexual assault and incest cases), victim participation in the justice system, and the role of culture in law enforcement decisions.

For further details regarding the cases mentioned in this statement, see Teressa Nahanee, "Sexual Assault of Inuit Females: A Commentary on 'Cultural Bias'" in Julian Roberts and Renate Mohr, eds., *Confronting Sexual Assault: A Decade of Legal and Social Change* (Toronto: University of Toronto Press, 1994) 192; and Pauktuutit Inuit Women's Association, *Inuit Women and Justice: Progress Report Number One* (Ottawa: Pauktuutit Inuit Women's Association, 1995) [hereinafter, *Inuit Women and Justice*]. The report highlights a number of issues facing the complainant/victim, including lack of awareness of the legal process, the role of the prosecutor, the lack of representation of the complainant/victim, the way in which sentencing factors and practices may exclude the complainant/victim, and the potential role of "victim impact statements" to provide evidence of the impact of violence on Inuit women and children. In reviewing *R. v. Avadluk*, [1989] N.W.T.R.

[†] "Pauktuutit Condemns Madam Justice Conrad's Decision on Judge Bourassa," A Statement by Mary Sillet, President of Pauktuutit, The Inuit Women's Association of Canada, October 29, 1990. Reproduced by permission of Pauktuutit Inuit Women's Association.

235; *R.* v. *Ekalun*, [1986] N.W.T.J. No. 40 (S.C.), online: QL; and *R.* v. *Qavavauq*, [1988] N.W.T.J. No. 44 (S.C.), online: QL, Pauktuutit also criticizes factors taken into account by the judiciary to mitigate sentence (at 9–10):

> [O]ften the judiciary takes into account, as a mitigating factor (information that can lessen the sentence), that there was no violence other than "the violence against a person which is inherent in a non-consensual act of intercourse." Since the victim did not resist due to her unconscious state, the court interprets the absence of struggle as being synonymous with an absence of violence. From our perspective, the identification of the absence of resistance as a mitigating factor when determining a sentence is but one example of how the criminal justice system, and the judicial process in particular, can victimize women.[†]

Pauktuutit has been particularly concerned about the role of the judiciary and the ways in which arguments about culture have been made. As Mary Sillett, Commissioner, Royal Commission on Aboriginal Peoples, stated in 1992:

> The northern judiciary has made child sexual assault among the Inuit acceptable in a way it is not permissible in Canadian society, or in fact in Inuit communities. Inuit women have said that this kind of sexual exploitation must stop, and it must be recognized that it is not part of Inuit sexual mores and practices. [Cited in *Inuit Women and Justice* at 18, endnote 29.]

In the years since *R.* v. *Naqitarvik*, community consultations, elders panels, and sentencing circles have become more common. Sentencing circles and diversion are possible within the existing discretion afforded by the criminal justice system, and that authority was recognized explicitly by the Bill C-41, S.C. 1995, c. 22 amendments to the *Criminal Code*. See, for example, s. 717 with respect to alternative measures. Also, s. 718.2(e) explicitly requires courts to consider non-carceral sanctions, with particular attention to the circumstances of Aboriginal offenders. In *R.* v. *Gladue*, the Supreme Court considered the impact of the new section.

R. v. Gladue[‡]

[CORY AND IACOBUCCI JJ.:]

On September 3, 1996, the new Part XXIII of the *Criminal Code*, R.S.C., 1985, c. C-46, pertaining to sentencing came into force. These provisions codify for the first time the fundamental purpose and principles of sentencing. This appeal is particularly concerned with the new s. 718.2(*e*). It provides that all available sanctions other than imprisonment that are reasonable in the circumstances should be considered for all offenders, with particular attention to the circumstances of aboriginal offenders. ...

FACTUAL BACKGROUND

The appellant, one of nine children, was born in McLennan, Alberta in 1976. Her mother, Marie Gladue, who was a Cree, left the family home in 1987 and died in a car accident in 1990. After 1987, the appellant and her siblings were raised by their father, Lloyd Chalifoux, a Metis. The appellant and the victim Reuben Beaver started to live together in 1993, when the appellant was 17 years old. Thereafter they had a daughter ... [and, in 1995, moved to Nanaimo where they lived] with the appellant's father and two of her siblings, Tara and Bianca Chalifoux, they lived in a townhouse complex. By September 1995, the appellant and Beaver were engaged to be married, and the appellant was five months pregnant with their second child, a boy, whom the appellant subsequently named Reuben Ambrose Beaver in honour of his father.

In the early evening of September 16, 1995, the appellant was celebrating her 19th birthday. She and Reuben Beaver, who was then 20, were drinking beer with some friends and family members in the townhouse complex. The appellant suspected that Beaver was having an affair with her older sister, Tara. During the course of the evening she voiced those suspicions to her friends. The appellant was

---

† *Ibid.*
‡ [1999] 1 S.C.R. 688. Sources omitted.

obviously angry with Beaver. She said, "the next time he fools around on me, I'll kill him"....

. . . .

The appellant and Beaver returned separately to their townhouse and they started to quarrel. During the argument, the appellant confronted him with his infidelity and he told her that she was fat and ugly and not as good as the others. ... [Subsequently, a neighbour was awakened by the loud quarrelling of Gladue and Beaver.]

[He] saw the appellant run toward Beaver with a large knife in her hand and, as she approached him, she told him that he had better run. [The neighbour] heard Beaver shriek in pain and saw him collapse in a pool of blood. ... [He then heard Gladue] say, "I got you, you fucking bastard." ... [He described the appellant] as jumping up and down.... [S]he did not appear to realize what she had done. At the time of the stabbing, the appellant had a blood-alcohol content of between 155 and 165 milligrams of alcohol in 100 millilitres of blood.

On June 3, 1996, the appellant was charged with second degree murder. On February 11, 1997, following a preliminary hearing and after a jury had been selected, the appellant entered a plea of guilty to manslaughter.

There was evidence which indicated that the appellant had stabbed Beaver before he fled from the apartment [with a paring knife]....

There was also evidence that Beaver had subjected the appellant to some physical abuse in June 1994, while the appellant was pregnant with their daughter Tanita. Beaver was convicted of assault, and was given a 15-day intermittent sentence with one year's probation. The neighbour, Mr. Gretchin, told police that the noises emanating from the appellant's and Beaver's apartment suggested a fight, stating: "It sounded like someone got hit and furniture was sliding, like someone pushed around" and "The fight lasted five to ten minutes, it was like a wrestling match." Bruises later observed on the appellant's arm and in the collarbone area were consistent with her having been in a physical altercation on the night of the stabbing. However, the trial judge found that the facts as presented before him did not warrant a finding that the appellant was a "battered or fearful wife".

The appellant's sentencing took place 17 months after the stabbing. Pending her trial, she was released on bail and lived with her father. She took counselling for alcohol and drug abuse at Tillicum Haus Native Friendship Centre in Nanaimo, and completed Grade 10 and was about to start Grade 11. After the stabbing, the appellant was diagnosed as suffering from a hyperthyroid condition, which was said to produce an exaggerated reaction to any emotional situation. The appellant underwent radiation therapy to destroy some of her thyroid glands, and at the time of sentencing she was taking thyroid supplements which regulated her condition. During the time she was on bail, the appellant pled guilty to having breached her bail on one occasion by consuming alcohol.

At the sentencing hearing, when asked if she had anything to say, the appellant stated that she was sorry about what happened, that she did not intend to do it, and that she was sorry to Beaver's family.

In his submissions on sentence at trial, the appellant's counsel did not raise the fact that the appellant was an aboriginal offender but, when asked by the trial judge whether in fact the appellant was an aboriginal person, replied that she was Cree. When asked by the trial judge whether the town of McLennan, Alberta, where the appellant grew up, was an aboriginal community, defence counsel responded: "it's just a regular community". No other submissions were made at the sentencing hearing on the issue of the appellant's aboriginal heritage. Defence counsel requested a suspended sentence or a conditional sentence of imprisonment. Crown counsel argued in favour of a sentence of between three and five years' imprisonment.

The appellant was sentenced to three years' imprisonment and to a ten-year weapons prohibition. Her appeal of the sentence to the British Columbia Court of Appeal was dismissed.

. . . .

JUDICIAL HISTORY

Supreme Court of British Columbia

... [T]he trial judge took into account several mitigating factors [including her youth, the lack of a previous criminal record other than for impaired driving, the presence of a supportive family, her two children, her attendance at school and the alcohol counselling she had undertaken]. The appellant was provoked by the deceased's insulting behaviour and remarks. At the time of the offence, the appellant had a hyperthyroid condition which caused her to overreact to emotional situations. The appellant showed some signs of remorse and entered a plea of guilty.

On the other hand, the trial judge identified several aggravating circumstances [including the gravity of the offence and the fact that the appellant had stabbed the deceased twice].... From the remarks she made before and after the stabbing it was very clear that the appellant intended to harm the deceased. Further, the appellant was not afraid of the deceased; indeed, she was the aggressor.

. . . .

The trial judge noted that both the appellant and the deceased were aboriginal, but stated that they were living in an urban area off-reserve and not "within the aboriginal community as such". He found that there were not any special circumstances arising from their aboriginal status that he should take into consideration. He stated that the offence was a very serious one, for which the appropriate sentence was three years' imprisonment with a ten-year weapons prohibition.

Court of Appeal for British Columbia (1997), 98 B.C.A.C. 120

The appellant appealed her sentence of three years' imprisonment, but not the ten-year weapons prohibition. She appealed on four grounds, only one of which is directly relevant, namely whether the trial judge failed to give appropriate consideration to the appellant's circumstances as an aboriginal offender. The appellant also sought to adduce fresh evidence at her appeal regarding her efforts since the killing to maintain links with her aboriginal heritage....

The Court of Appeal unanimously concluded that the trial judge had erred in concluding that s. 718.2(e) did not apply because the appellant was not living on a reserve. However, Esson J.A. (Prowse J.A. concurring) found no error in the trial judge's conclusion that, in this case, there was no basis for giving special consideration to the appellant's aboriginal background. Esson J.A. noted that the appellant's actions involved deliberation, motivation, and "an element of viciousness and persistence in the attack", and that the killing constituted a "near murder" (p. 138). He found that, on the facts presented in this case, it could not be said that the sentence, if a fit one for a non-aboriginal person, would not also be fit for an aboriginal person [and] ... concluded therefore that the trial judge did not err in not giving effect to the principle set out in s. 718.2(e)....

. . . .

[Rowles J.A., in dissent, was prepared to consider the context more broadly. She] agreed that the crime committed by the appellant was serious. The circumstances surrounding the offence were tragic for everyone, including the appellant's children. Yet, the circumstances of the offence included provocation, superimposed on an undiagnosed medical problem affecting the appellant's emotional stability. The offender was young and emotionally immature. She had an alcohol problem but no history of other criminal conduct or acts of violence. The success the appellant enjoyed while on bail awaiting trial showed that she was likely to be a good candidate for further rehabilitation. Rowles J.A. also referred favourably to the fresh evidence which showed that the appellant was taking steps to maintain links with her aboriginal heritage.

Rowles J.A. concluded that a sentence of three years' imprisonment was excessive. The principles of general deterrence and denunciation had to be reflected in the sentence, but the sentence could have been designed to advance the appellant's rehabilitation through a period of supervised probation. Rowles J.A. would have allowed the appeal and reduced the sentence to two years less a day to be followed by a three-year period of probation.

ISSUE

The issue in this appeal is the proper interpretation and application to be given to s. 718.2(e) of the *Criminal Code*....

. . . .

ANALYSIS

Introduction

As this Court has frequently stated, the proper construction of a statutory provision flows from reading the words of the provision in their grammatical and ordinary sense and in their entire context, harmoniously with the scheme of the statute as a whole, the purpose of the statute, and the intention of Parliament. The purpose of the statute and the intention of Parliament, in particular, are to be determined on the basis of intrinsic and admissible extrinsic sources regarding the Act's legislative history and the context of its enactment....

Also of importance in interpreting federal legislation is s. 12 of the federal *Interpretation Act*, which provides:

12. Every enactment is deemed remedial, and shall be given such fair, large and liberal construction and interpretation as best ensures the attainment of its objects.

The Wording of Section 718.2(e) and the Scheme of Part XXIII

. . . .

A core issue in this appeal is whether s. 718.2(*e*) should be understood as being remedial in nature, or whether s. 718.2(*e*), along with the other provisions of ss. 718 through 718.2, are simply a codification of *existing* sentencing principles....

Section 12 of the *Interpretation Act* deems the purpose of the enactment of the new Part XXIII of the *Criminal Code* to be remedial in nature, and requires that all of the provisions of Part XXIII, including s. 718.2(*e*), be given a fair, large and liberal construction and interpretation in order to attain that remedial objective....

In our view, s. 718.2(*e*) is *more* than simply a re-affirmation of existing sentencing principles. The remedial component of the provision consists not only in the fact that it codifies a principle of sentencing, but, far more importantly, in its direction to sentencing judges to undertake the process of sentencing aboriginal offenders differently, in order to endeavour to achieve a truly fit and proper sentence in the particular case. It should be said that the words of s. 718.2(*e*) do not alter the fundamental duty of the sentencing judge to impose a sentence that is fit for the offence and the offender. For example, as we will discuss below, it will generally be the case as a practical matter that particularly violent and serious offences will result in imprisonment for aboriginal offenders as often as for non-aboriginal offenders. What s. 718.2(*e*) does alter is the method of analysis which each sentencing judge must use in determining the nature of a fit sentence for an aboriginal offender. In our view, the scheme of Part XXIII of the *Criminal Code*, the context underlying the enactment of s. 718.2(*e*), and the legislative history of the provision all support an interpretation of s. 718.2(*e*) as having this important remedial purpose.

. . . .

The next question is the meaning to be attributed to the words "with particular attention to the circumstances of aboriginal offenders". The phrase cannot be an instruction for judges to pay "more" attention when sentencing aboriginal offenders. It would be unreasonable to assume that Parliament intended sentencing judges to prefer certain categories of offenders over others. Neither can the phrase be merely an instruction to a sentencing judge to consider the circumstances of aboriginal offenders just as she or he would consider the circumstances of any other offender. There would be no point in adding a special reference to aboriginal offenders if this was the case. Rather, the logical meaning to be derived from the special reference to the circumstances of aboriginal offenders, juxtaposed as it is against a general direction to consider "the circumstances" for all offenders, is that sentencing judges should pay particular attention to the circumstances of aboriginal offenders *because those circumstances are unique*, and different from those of non-aboriginal offenders. The fact that the reference to aboriginal offenders is contained in s. 718.2(*e*), in particular, dealing with restraint in the use of imprisonment, suggests that there is something different about aboriginal offenders which may specifically make imprisonment a less appropriate or less useful sanction.

. . . .

It is true that there is ample jurisprudence supporting the principle that prison should be used as a sanction of last resort. It is equally true, though, that the sentencing amendments which came into force in 1996 as the new Part XXIII have changed the range of available penal sanctions in a significant way. The availability of the conditional sentence of imprisonment, in particular, alters the sentencing landscape in a manner which gives an entirely new meaning to the principle that imprisonment should be resorted to only where no other sentencing option is reasonable in the circumstances. The creation of the conditional sentence suggests, on its face, a desire to lessen the use of incarceration. The general principle expressed in s. 718.2(*e*) must be construed and applied in this light.

Further support for the view that s. 718.2(*e*)'s expression of the principle of restraint in sentencing is remedial, rather than simply a codification, is provided by the articulation of the purpose of sentencing in s. 718.

. . . .

Clearly, s. 718 is, in part, a restatement of the basic sentencing aims, which are listed in paras. (*a*) through (*d*). What are new, though, are paras. (*e*) and (*f*), which along with para. (*d*) focus upon the restorative goals of repairing the harms suffered by individual victims and by the community as a whole, promoting a sense of responsibility and an acknowledgment of the harm caused on the part of the offender, and attempting to rehabilitate or heal the offender. The concept of restorative justice which underpins paras. (*d*), (*e*), and (*f*) is briefly discussed below, but as a general matter restorative justice involves some form of restitution and reintegration into the community. The need for offenders to take responsibility for their actions is central to the sentencing process. Restorative sentencing goals do not usually correlate with the use of prison as a sanction. In our view, Parliament's choice to include (*e*) and (*f*) alongside the traditional sentencing goals must be understood as evidencing an intention to expand the parameters of the sentencing analysis for all offenders. The principle of restraint expressed in s. 718.2(*e*) will necessarily be informed by this re-orientation.

. . . .

Legislative History

Support for the foregoing understanding of s. 718.2(*e*) as having the remedial purpose of restricting the use of prison for all offenders, and as having a particular remedial role with respect to aboriginal peoples, is provided by statements made by the Minister of Justice and others at the time that what was then Bill C-41 was before Parliament. ...

For instance, in introducing second reading of Bill C-41, Minister of Justice Allan Rock made the following statements regarding the remedial purpose of the bill:

> *Through this bill, Parliament provides the courts with clear guidelines....*
>
> ...
>
> The bill also defines various sentencing principles, for instance that the sentence must be proportionate to the gravity of the offence and the offender's degree of responsibility. *When appropriate, alternatives must be contemplated, especially in the case of Native offenders.*
>
> ...
>
> A general principle that runs throughout Bill C-41 is that jails should be reserved for those who should be there. *Alternatives should be put in place for those who commit offences but who do not need or merit incarceration.*
>
> ...
>
> Jails and prisons will be there for those who need them, for those who should be punished in that way or separated from society.... [T]*his bill creates an environment which encourages community sanctions and the rehabilitation of offenders together with reparation to victims and promoting in criminals a sense of accountability for what they have done.*
>
> It is not simply by being more harsh that we will achieve more effective criminal justice. We must use our scarce resources wisely. [Emphasis added [by Court].]

The Minister's statements were echoed by other Members of Parliament and by Senators during the debate over the bill....

In his subsequent testimony before the House of Commons Standing Committee on Justice and Legal Affairs, the Minister of Justice addressed the specific role the government hoped would be played by s. 718.2(*e*):

> [T]*he reason we referred specifically there to aboriginal persons is that they are sadly overrepresented in the prison populations of Canada.* I think it was the Manitoba justice inquiry that found that although aboriginal persons make up only 12% of the population of Manitoba, they comprise over 50% of the prison inmates. Nationally aboriginal persons represent about 2% of Canada's population, but they represent 10.6% of persons in prison. *Obviously there's a problem here.*
>
> What we're trying to do, particularly having regard to the initiatives in the aboriginal communities to achieve community justice, is to encourage courts to look at alternatives where it's consistent with the protection of the public — alternatives to jail — and not simply resort to that easy answer in every case. [Emphasis added [by Court].]

. . . .

The Context of the Enactment of Section 718.2(e)

Further guidance as to the scope and content of Parliament's remedial purpose in enacting s. 718.2(*e*) may be derived from the social context surrounding the enactment of the provision....

The parties and interveners agree that the purpose of s. 718.2(*e*) is to respond to the problem of overincarceration in Canada, and to respond, in particular, to the more acute problem of the disproportionate incarceration of aboriginal peoples....

. . . .

The Problem of Overincarceration in Canada

Canada is a world leader in many fields, particularly in the areas of progressive social policy and human rights. Unfortunately, our country is also distinguished as being a world leader in putting people in prison. Although the United States has by far the highest rate of incarceration among industrialized democracies, at over 600 inmates per 100,000 population, Canada's rate of approximately 130 inmates per 100,000 population places it second or third highest.... Moreover, the rate at which Canadian courts have been imprisoning offenders has risen sharply in recent years, although there has been a slight decline of late.... This record of incarceration rates obviously cannot instil a sense of pride.

[The Court went on to detail how the systematic overuse of the sanction of imprisonment and its lack of effectiveness has been broadly criticized in Canada by the Canadian Committee on Corrections, the Canadian Sentencing Commission, and the Standing Committee on Justice and the Solicitor General.]

. . . .

Thus, it may be seen that although imprisonment is intended to serve the traditional sentencing goals of separation, deterrence, denunciation, and rehabilitation, there is widespread consensus that imprisonment has not been successful in achieving some of these goals. Overincarceration is a long-standing problem that has been many times publicly acknowledged but never addressed in a systematic manner by Parliament. In recent years, compared to other countries, sentences of imprisonment in Canada have increased at an alarming rate....

The Overrepresentation of Aboriginal Canadians in Penal Institutions

If overreliance upon incarceration is a problem with the general population, it is of much greater concern in the sentencing of aboriginal Canadians. In the mid-1980s, aboriginal people were about 2 percent of the population of Canada, yet they made up 10 percent of the penitentiary population. In Manitoba and Saskatchewan, aboriginal people constituted something between 6 and 7 percent of the population, yet in Manitoba they represented 46 percent of the provincial admissions and in Saskatchewan 60 percent.... The situation has not improved in recent years. By 1997, aboriginal peoples constituted closer to 3 percent of the population of Canada and amounted to 12 percent of all federal inmates: Solicitor General of Canada, Consolidated Report, *Towards a Just, Peaceful and Safe Society: The Corrections and Conditional Release Act — Five Years Later* (1998), at pp. 142–55. The situation continues to be particularly worrisome in Manitoba, where in 1995–96 they made up 55 percent of admissions to provincial correctional facilities, and in Saskatchewan, where they made up 72 percent of admissions. A similar, albeit less drastic situation prevails in Alberta and British Columbia: Canadian Centre for Justice Statistics, *Adult Correctional Services in Canada, 1995–96* (1997), at p. 30.

This serious problem of aboriginal overrepresentation in Canadian prisons is well documented. Like the general problem of overincarceration itself, the excessive incarceration of aboriginal peoples has received the attention of a large number of commissions and inquiries: see, by way of example only, Canadian Corrections Association, *Indians and the Law* (1967); Law Reform Commission of Canada, *The Native Offender and the Law* (1974), prepared by D. A. Schmeiser; Public Inquiry into the Administration of Justice and Aboriginal People, *Report of the Aboriginal Justice Inquiry of Manitoba*, vol. 1, *The Justice System and Aboriginal People* (1991); Royal Commission on Aboriginal Peoples, *Bridging the Cultural Divide* (1996).

. . . .

[The Court cited with approval the work of Michael Jackson: "Locking Up Natives in Canada" (1988–89), 23 U.B.C. L. Rev. 215, who provides a disturbing account of the magnitude of the disproportion (at pp. 215–16):]

> Statistics about crime are often not well understood by the public and are subject to variable interpretation by the experts. *In the case of the statistics regarding the impact of the criminal justice system on native people the figures are so stark and appalling that the magnitude of the problem can be neither misunderstood nor interpreted away.* Native people come into contact with Canada's correctional system in numbers grossly disproportionate to their representation in the community. More than any other group in Canada they are subject to the damaging impacts of the criminal justice system's heaviest sanctions. Government figures — which reflect different definitions of "native" and which probably underestimate the number of prisoners who consider themselves native — show that almost 10% of the federal penitentiary population is native (including 13% of the federal women's prisoner population) compared to about 2% of the population nationally.... *Even more disturbing, the disproportionality is growing. In 1965 some 22% of the prisoners in Stony Mountain Penitentiary were native; in 1984 this proportion was 33%. It is realistic to expect that absent radical change, the problem will intensify due to the higher birth rate in native communities.*

Bad as this situation is within the federal system, it is even worse in a number of the western provincial correctional systems. ... A study reviewing admissions to Saskatchewan's correctional system in 1976–77 appropriately titled "Locking Up Indians in Saskatchewan", contains findings that should shock the conscience of everyone in Canada. In comparison to male non-natives, male treaty Indians were 25 times more likely to be admitted to a provincial correctional centre while non-status Indians or Métis were 8 times more likely to be admitted. If only the population over fifteen years of age is considered (the population eligible to be admitted to provincial correctional centres in Saskatchewan), then male treaty Indians were 37 times more likely to be admitted, while male non-status Indians were 12 times more likely to be admitted. For women the figures are even more extreme: a treaty Indian woman was 131 times more likely to be admitted and a non-status or Métis woman 28 times more likely than a non-native.

The Saskatchewan study brings home the implications of its findings by indicating that a treaty Indian boy turning 16 in 1976 had a 70% chance of at least one stay in prison by the age of 25 (that age range being the one with the highest risk of imprisonment). The corresponding figure for non-status or Métis was 34%. For a non-native Saskatchewan boy the figure was 8%. *Put another way, this means that in Saskatchewan, prison has become for young native men, the promise of a just society which high school and college represent for the rest of us. Placed in an historical context, the prison has become for many young native people the contemporary equivalent of what the Indian residential school represented for their parents.* [Emphasis added [by Court]; footnotes omitted.]

Not surprisingly, the excessive imprisonment of aboriginal people is only the tip of the iceberg insofar as the estrangement of the aboriginal peoples from the Canadian criminal justice system is concerned. Aboriginal people are overrepresented in virtually all aspects of the system. As this Court recently noted in *R. v. Williams*, [1998] 1 S.C.R. 1128, at para. 58, there is widespread bias against aboriginal people within Canada, and "[t]here is evidence that this widespread racism has translated into systemic discrimination in the criminal justice system".

Statements regarding the extent and severity of this problem are disturbingly common. In *Bridging the Cultural Divide*, supra, at p. 309, the Royal Commission on Aboriginal Peoples listed as its first "Major Findings and Conclusions" the following striking yet representative statement:

The Canadian criminal justice system has failed the Aboriginal peoples of Canada — First Nations, Inuit and Métis people, on-reserve and off-reserve, urban and rural — in all territorial and governmental jurisdictions. The principal reason for this crushing failure is the fundamentally different world views of Aboriginal and non-Aboriginal people with respect to such elemental issues as the substantive content of justice and the process of achieving justice.

To the same effect, the Aboriginal Justice Inquiry of Manitoba described the justice system in Manitoba as having failed aboriginal people on a "massive scale", referring particularly to the substantially different cultural values and experiences of aboriginal people: *The Justice System and Aboriginal People*, supra, at pp. 1 and 86.

These findings cry out for recognition of the magnitude and gravity of the problem, and for responses to alleviate it. The figures are stark and reflect what may fairly be termed a crisis in the Canadian criminal justice system. The drastic overrepresentation of aboriginal peoples within both the Canadian prison population and the criminal justice system reveals a sad and pressing social problem. It is reasonable to assume that Parliament, in singling out aboriginal offenders for distinct sentencing treatment in s. 718.2(*e*), intended to attempt to redress this social problem to some degree. The provision may properly be seen as Parliament's direction to members of the judiciary to inquire into the causes of the problem and to endeavour to remedy it, to the extent that a remedy is possible through the sentencing process.

It is clear that sentencing innovation by itself cannot remove the causes of aboriginal offending and the greater problem of aboriginal alienation from the criminal justice system. The unbalanced ratio of imprisonment for aboriginal offenders flows from a number of sources, including poverty, substance abuse, lack of education, and the lack of employment opportunities for aboriginal people. It arises also from bias against aboriginal people and from an unfortunate institutional approach that is more inclined to refuse bail and to impose more and longer prison terms for aboriginal offenders. There are many aspects of this sad situation which cannot be addressed in these reasons. What can and must be addressed, though, is the limited role that sentencing judges will play in remedying injustice against aboriginal peoples in Canada. Sentencing judges are among those decision-makers who have the power to influence the treatment of aboriginal offenders in the justice system. They determine most directly whether an aboriginal offender will go to jail, or whether other sentencing options may be employed which will play perhaps a stronger role in restoring a sense of balance to the offender, victim, and community, and in preventing future crime.

A Framework of Analysis for the Sentencing Judge

(What Are the "Circumstances of Aboriginal Offenders"?

How are sentencing judges to play their remedial role? The words of s. 718.2(e) instruct the sentencing judge to pay particular attention to the circumstances of aboriginal offenders, with the implication that those circumstances are significantly different from those of non-aboriginal offenders. The background considerations regarding the distinct situation of aboriginal peoples in Canada encompass a wide range of unique circumstances, including, most particularly:

(A) The unique systemic or background factors which may have played a part in bringing the particular aboriginal offender before the courts; and

(B) The types of sentencing procedures and sanctions which may be appropriate in the circumstances for the offender because of his or her particular aboriginal heritage or connection.

SYSTEMIC AND BACKGROUND FACTORS

The background factors which figure prominently in the causation of crime by aboriginal offenders are by now well known. Years of dislocation and economic development have translated, for many aboriginal peoples, into low incomes, high unemployment, lack of opportunities and options, lack or irrelevance of education, substance abuse, loneliness, and community fragmentation. These and other factors contribute to a higher incidence of crime and incarceration. [Professor Tim Quigley] describes the process whereby these various factors produce an overincarceration of aboriginal offenders, noting ... that "[t]he unemployed, transients, the poorly educated are all better candidates for imprisonment. When the social, political and economic aspects of our society place Aboriginal people disproportionately within the ranks of the latter, our society literally sentences more of them to jail."

It is true that systemic and background factors explain in part the incidence of crime and recidivism for non-aboriginal offenders as well. However, it must be recognized that the circumstances of aboriginal offenders differ from those of the majority because many aboriginal people are victims of systemic and direct discrimination, many suffer the legacy of dislocation, and many are substantially affected by poor social and economic conditions. Moreover, as has been emphasized repeatedly in studies and commission reports, aboriginal offenders are, as a result of these unique systemic and background factors, more adversely affected by incarceration and less likely to be "rehabilitated" thereby, because the internment milieu is often culturally inappropriate and regrettably discrimination towards them is so often rampant in penal institutions.

In this case, of course, we are dealing with factors that must be considered by a judge sentencing an aboriginal offender. While background and systemic factors will also be of importance for a judge in sentencing a non-aboriginal offender, the judge who is called upon to sentence an aboriginal offender must give attention to the unique background and systemic factors which may have played a part in bringing the particular offender before the courts. In cases where such factors have played a significant role, it is incumbent upon the sentencing judge to consider these factors in evaluating whether imprisonment would actually serve to deter, or to denounce crime in a sense that would be meaningful to the community of which the offender is a member. In many instances, more restorative sentencing principles will gain primary relevance precisely because the prevention of crime as well as individual and social healing cannot occur through other means.

APPROPRIATE SENTENCING PROCEDURES AND SANCTIONS

Closely related to the background and systemic factors which have contributed to an excessive aboriginal incarceration rate are the different conceptions of appropriate sentencing procedures and sanctions held by aboriginal people. A significant problem experienced by aboriginal people who come into contact with the criminal justice system is that the traditional sentencing ideals of deterrence, separation, and denunciation are often far removed from the understanding of sentencing held by these offenders and their community. The aims of restorative justice as now expressed in paras. (*d*), (*e*), and (*f*) of s. 718 of the *Criminal Code* apply to all offenders, and not only aboriginal offenders. However, most traditional aboriginal conceptions of sentencing place a *primary* emphasis upon the ideals of restorative justice. This tradition is extremely important to the analysis under s. 718.2(*e*).

The concept and principles of a restorative approach will necessarily have to be developed over time in the jurisprudence, as different issues and different conceptions of sentencing are addressed in their appropriate context. In general terms, restorative justice may be described as an approach to remedying crime in which it is understood that all things are interrelated and that crime disrupts the harmony which existed prior to its occurrence, or at least which it is felt should exist. The appropriateness of a particular sanction is largely determined by the needs of the victims, and the community, as well as the offender. The focus is on the human beings closely affected by the crime....

The existing overemphasis on incarceration in Canada may be partly due to the perception that a restorative approach is a more lenient approach to crime and that imprisonment constitutes the ultimate punishment. Yet in our view a sentence focussed on restorative justice is not necessarily a "lighter" punishment. Some proponents of restorative justice argue that when it is combined with probationary conditions it may in some circumstances impose a greater burden on the offender than a custodial sentence....

. . . .

In describing in general terms some of the basic tenets of traditional aboriginal sentencing approaches, we do not wish to imply that all aboriginal offenders, victims, and communities share an identical understanding of appropriate sentences for particular offences and offenders. Aboriginal communities stretch from coast to coast and from the border with the United States to the far north. Their customs and traditions and their concept of sentencing vary widely. What is important to recognize is that, for many if not most aboriginal offenders, the current concepts of sentencing are inappropriate because they have frequently not responded to the needs, experiences, and perspectives of aboriginal people or aboriginal communities.

... Sentencing judges should not conclude that the absence of alternatives specific to an aboriginal community eliminates their ability to impose a sanction that takes into account principles of restorative justice and the needs of the parties involved. Rather, the point is that one of the unique circumstances of aboriginal offenders is that community-based sanctions coincide with the aboriginal concept of sentencing and the needs of aboriginal people and communities. It is often the case that neither aboriginal offenders nor their communities are well served by incarcerating offenders, particularly for less serious or non-violent offences. Where these sanctions are reasonable in the circumstances, they should be implemented. In all instances, it is appropriate to attempt to craft the sentencing process and the sanctions imposed in accordance with the aboriginal perspective.

The Search for a Fit Sentence

The role of the judge who sentences an aboriginal offender is, as for every offender, to determine a fit sentence taking into account all the circumstances of the offence, the offender, the victims, and the community....

. . . .

... [T]he circumstances of aboriginal offenders are markedly different from those of other offenders, being characterized by unique systemic and background factors. Further, an aboriginal offender's community will frequently understand the nature of a just sanction in a manner significantly different from that of many non-aboriginal communities. In appropriate cases, some of the traditional sentencing objectives will be correspondingly less relevant in determining a sentence that is reasonable in the circumstances, and the goals of restorative justice will quite properly be given greater weight. Through its reform of the purpose of sentencing in s. 718, and through its specific directive to judges who sentence aboriginal offenders, Parliament has, more than ever before, empowered sentencing judges to craft sentences in a manner which is meaningful to aboriginal peoples.

In describing the effect of s. 718.2(*e*) in this way, we do not mean to suggest that, as a general practice, aboriginal offenders must always be sentenced in a manner which gives greatest weight to the principles of restorative justice, and less weight to goals such as deterrence, denunciation, and separation. It is unreasonable to assume that aboriginal peoples themselves do not believe in the importance of these latter goals, and even if they do not, that such goals must not predominate in appropriate cases. Clearly there are some serious offences and some offenders for which and for whom separation, denunciation, and deterrence are fundamentally relevant.

Yet, even where an offence is considered serious, the length of the term of imprisonment must be considered. In some circumstances the length of the sentence of an aboriginal offender may be less and in others the same as that of any other offender. Generally, the more violent and serious the offence the more likely it is as a practical reality that the terms of imprisonment for aboriginals and non-aboriginals will be close to each other or the same, even taking into account their different concepts of sentencing.

As with all sentencing decisions, the sentencing of aboriginal offenders must proceed on an individual (or a case-by-case) basis: For *this* offence, committed by *this* offender, harming *this* victim, in *this* community, what is the appropriate sanction under the *Criminal Code*? What understanding of criminal sanctions is held by the community? What is the nature of the relationship between the offender and his or her community? What combination of systemic or background factors contributed to this particular offender coming before the courts for this particular offence? How has the offender who is being sentenced been affected by, for example, substance abuse in the community, or poverty, or overt racism, or family or community breakdown? Would imprisonment effectively serve to deter or denounce crime in a sense that would be significant to the offender and community, or are crime prevention and other goals better achieved through healing? What sentencing options present themselves in these circumstances?

. . . .

The Duty of the Sentencing Judge

[The Court emphasized the duties of the judge when sentencing an Aboriginal offender.] This element of duty is a critical component of s. 718.2(*e*)....

... In all instances it will be necessary for the judge to take judicial notice of the systemic or background factors and the approach to sentencing which is relevant to aboriginal offenders. However, for each particular offence and offender it may be that some evidence will be required in order to assist the sentencing judge in arriving at a fit sentence. Where a particular offender does not wish such evidence to be adduced, the right to have particular attention paid to his or her circumstances as an aboriginal offender may be waived. Where there is no such waiver, it will be extremely helpful to the sentencing judge for counsel on both sides to adduce relevant evidence. Indeed, it is to be expected that counsel will fulfil their role and assist the sentencing judge in this way.

However, even where counsel do not adduce this evidence, where for example the offender is unrepresented, it is incumbent upon the sentencing judge to attempt to acquire information regarding the circumstances of the offender as an aboriginal person. Whether the offender resides in a rural area, on a reserve or in an urban centre the sentencing judge must be made aware of alternatives to incarceration that exist whether inside or outside the aboriginal community of the particular offender. The alternatives existing in metropolitan areas must, as a matter of course, also be explored. Clearly the presence of an aboriginal offender will require special attention in pre-sentence reports. Beyond the use of the pre-sentence report, the sentencing judge may and should in appropriate circumstances and where practicable request that witnesses be called who may testify as to reasonable alternatives.

Similarly, where a sentencing judge at the trial level has not engaged in the duty imposed by s. 718.2(*e*) as fully as required, it is incumbent upon a court of appeal in considering an appeal against sentence on this basis to consider any fresh evidence which is relevant and admissible on sentencing. In the same vein, it should be noted that, although s. 718.2(*e*) does not impose a statutory duty upon the sentencing judge to provide reasons, it will be much easier for a reviewing court to determine whether and how attention was paid to the circumstances of the offender as an aboriginal person if at least brief reasons are given.

The Issue of "Reverse Discrimination"

. . . .

There is no constitutional challenge to s. 718.2(*e*) in these proceedings, and accordingly we do not address specifically the applicability of s. 15 of the *Charter*. We would note, though, that the aim of s. 718.2(*e*) is to reduce the tragic overrepresentation of aboriginal people in prisons. It seeks to ameliorate the present situation and to deal with the particular offence and offender and community. The fact that a court is called upon to take into consideration the unique circumstances surrounding these different parties is not unfair to non-aboriginal people. Rather, the fundamental purpose of s. 718.2(*e*) is to treat aboriginal offenders fairly by taking into account their difference.

. . . .

Who Comes Within the Purview of Section 718.2(e)?

. . . .

The class of aboriginal people who come within the purview of the specific reference to the circumstances of aboriginal offenders in s. 718.2(*e*) must be, at least, all who come within the scope of s. 25 of the *Charter* and s. 35 of the *Constitution Act, 1982*. The numbers involved are significant. National census figures from 1996 show that an estimated 799,010 people were identified as aboriginal in 1996. Of this number, 529,040 were Indians (registered or non-registered), 204,115 Metis and 40,220 Inuit.

Section 718.2(*e*) applies to all aboriginal offenders wherever they reside, whether on- or off-reserve, in a large city or a rural area. Indeed it has been observed that many aboriginals living in urban areas are closely attached to their culture....

. . . .

Section 718.2(*e*) requires the sentencing judge to explore reasonable alternatives to incarceration in the case of all aboriginal offenders. Obviously, if an aboriginal community has a program or tradition of alternative sanctions, and support and supervision are available to the offender, it may be easier to find and impose an alternative sentence. However, even if community support is not available, every effort should be made in appropriate circumstances to find a sensitive and helpful alternative. For all purposes, the term "community" must be defined broadly so as to include any network of support and interaction that might be available in an urban centre. At the same time, the residence of the aboriginal offender in an urban centre that lacks any network of support does not relieve the sentencing judge of the obligation to try to find an alternative to imprisonment.

. . . .

WAS THERE AN ERROR MADE IN THIS CASE?

From the foregoing analysis it can be seen that the sentencing judge, who did not have the benefit of these reasons, fell into error....

The majority of the Court of Appeal, in dismissing the appellant's appeal, also does not appear to have considered many of the factors referred to above....

In most cases, errors such as those in the courts below would be sufficient to justify sending the matter back for a new sentencing hearing. It is difficult for this Court to determine a fit sentence for the appellant according to the suggested guidelines set out herein on the basis of the very limited evidence before us regarding the appellant's aboriginal background. However, as both the trial judge and all members of the Court of Appeal acknowledged, the offence in question is a most serious one, properly described by Esson J.A. as a "near murder". Moreover, the offence involved domestic violence and a breach of the trust inherent in a spousal relationship. That aggravating factor must be taken into account in the sentencing of the aboriginal appellant as it would be for any offender. For that offence by this offender a sentence of three years' imprisonment was not unreasonable.

More importantly, the appellant was granted day parole on August 13, 1997, after she had served six months in the Burnaby Correctional Centre for Women. She was directed to reside with her father, to take alcohol and substance abuse counselling and to comply with the requirements of the Electronic Monitoring Program. On February 25, 1998, the appellant was granted full parole with the same conditions as the ones applicable to her original release on day parole.

In this case, the results of the sentence with incarceration for six months and the subsequent controlled release were in the interests of both the appellant and society. In these circumstances, we do not consider that it would be in the interests of justice to order a new sentencing hearing in order to canvass the appellant's circumstances as an aboriginal offender.

Appeal dismissed.

Judge Mary Ellen Turpel-Lafond characterizes the Court's decision as a watershed in Canadian criminal law that clarifies the remedial nature of s. 718.2(e). "The *Gladue* decision has brought the notion of healing into the mainstream as a principle that a judge *must* weigh in every case involving an Aboriginal person in order to build a bridge between their unique personal and community background experiences and criminal justice" (at 35): Judge M.E. Turpel-Lafond, "Sentencing within a Restorative Justice Paradigm: Procedural Implications of *R. v. Gladue*" (1993) 43 Crim. L.Q. 34.

As Turpel argues, the impetus for change in C-41 was informed by years of work documenting and analyzing the criminal justice system in Canada and its impact on Aboriginal peoples. She cites specifically the influence of the Royal Commission on Aboriginal Peoples, the Manitoba Aboriginal Justice Inquiry, and the Law Reform Commission of Canada.

As a result of s. 718.2(e) and the decision in *Gladue*, according to Judge Turpel, it is now incumbent on both counsel and judges to make inquiries when the accused is Aboriginal and risks incarceration. She provides a checklist of questions that should be considered, including questions to explore the ancestry of the accused, the residence of the accused, circumstances that may have affected the accused (including substance abuse within the community, poverty, racism, family or community breakdown, unemployment, and dislocation, among others) (at 40). Lawyers should make detailed arguments about these issues and be prepared to address systemic inequalities, restorative justice, and available alternatives to incarceration. She suggests that the proof of some of these issues might be accomplished through the vehicle of "judicial notice." That possibility depends on judicial willingness. Yet questions of disproportionate impact have historically been controversial for the courts, as *R.D.S.* (reproduced *infra*, **Policing**), illustrates.

Realistically, the groundwork for these arguments continues to require considerable preparation. Without that preparation, courts will be unable to implement *Gladue* in practical terms. Given cutbacks in legal aid, there will be pressure on both judges and Crown prosecutors to ensure that this information forms part of the considerations for sentence. Ironically, *Gladue* highlights the impact that lack of evidence will have for an accused. Even the Supreme Court seemed prepared to skim over the glaring absence of evidence in *Gladue* and assert confidently the reasonableness of the sentence. The justices did so despite the vacuum of evidence on the accused's circumstances and context as an Aboriginal woman at the trial level, and the subsequent refusal by the Court of Appeal to allow fresh evidence by the defence on these precise points. They concluded that a new trial was not warranted.

If courts do not need to weigh such evidence to arrive at determinations of "reasonableness," what is the likely impact of the section? How did the Court arrive at its conclusion with respect to the standard of "reasonableness"? Is it different from the test for a non-Aboriginal offender? Think about, for example, the challenges posed for Jamie Gladue and her counsel to establish the impact of s. 718.2(e) in relation to her case. What were some of the factors that the Court identified as limiting the application of the section? What examinations of context were taken account of? As defence counsel put it in the leave application to the Supreme Court:

> [I]f the Applicant's personal circumstances are insufficient to give rise to special consideration against incarceration, it is difficult to think of an aboriginal background which would qualify. The Applicant suffered from the historical disadvantage of aboriginal people: poverty, limited education, unemployment, substance abuse, family violence and ill health.

How was the specific situation of Aboriginal women, and violence against Aboriginal women in particular, understood and analyzed? Jean Lash argues persuasively that violence against Aboriginal women is rendered invisible in the Court's decision: Jean Lash, "Case Comment: *R.* v. *Gladue*" (2000) 20:3 *Canadian Woman Studies* 85. The decision in *Gladue* highlights the over-incarceration of Aboriginal people generally and solidifies a shift towards a more contextualized understanding of the circumstances of an accused. However, the Court concentrated its analysis on the racialized rather than the gendered dimensions of those circumstances, and neglected the impact of the intersection of race and gender on those circumstances.

Nonetheless, *Gladue* is being interpreted by lower courts as mandating judges to carefully consider the circumstances of Aboriginal offenders, in light of the directive in s. 718.2(e). In *R.* v. *Sackanay* (2000), 47 O.R. (3d) 612, for example, the Ontario Court of Appeal allowed an appeal against sentence on the basis that the trial judge had not adequately considered the impact of the circumstances of the Aboriginal offender and the nexus between the two serious assaults for which he was convicted, "a nexus attributable to the appellant's consumption of drugs and alcohol, which in turn is related to the systemic disadvantages the appellant has suffered" (at 615). In *R.* v. *Carratt*, [1999] S.J. No. 626 (Q.B.), online: QL, Justice Klebuc chastized the Crown for the failure to provide any evidence as to the relevant circumstances and suggested a stay might be a remedy in a future case. The judgment sets out the expert evidence (for the defence) relied upon, including that of Ross Green (*Justice in Aboriginal Commu-*

nities: Sentencing Alternatives (Saskatoon: Purich Publishing, 1998)) and of Tim Quigley ("Some Issues in Sentencing of Aboriginal Offenders," in *Continuing Poundmaker and Riel's Quest, supra*, quoting the latter extensively as to the disproportionate rates of incarceration of Aboriginal people and the context of systemic discrimination. See also: *R. v. A.J.J.*, [1999] S.J. No. 917 (Prov. Ct.), online: QL (in which Judge Turpel-Lafond applied the reasoning of *Gladue* to a young offender's case).

Finally, the interplay between *Gladue*'s interpretation of s. 718.2 (e) and the analytical framework within which the option of conditional imprisonment is to be approached was considered by the Supreme Court of Canada in *R. v. Wells*, [2000] 1 S.C.R. 207. For extensive commentary on these two cases and their impact upon the over-incarceration of Aboriginal people, see: "Colloquy on *Empty Promises: Parliament, the Supreme Court, and the Sentencing of Aboriginal Offenders*" (2002) 65:1 Saskatchewan L. Rev.

F. CIRCLE SENTENCING AND FIRST NATION INITIATIVES

Sentencing circles do not fundamentally challenge the existing authority of the Anglo-Canadian system, nor do they explicitly challenge systemic bias. Nonetheless, consensual sentencing circles present challenges to the traditional adversarial role of the lawyer as advocate: Larry Chartrand, "The Appropriateness of the Lawyer as Advocate in Contemporary Aboriginal Justice Initiatives" (1995) 23 Alta. L. Rev. 874. Also, they force a consideration of cross-cultural issues that have been largely ignored by lawyers and judges. For a further discussion of the narrowness of the cultural vision of the current system, see Rupert Ross, *Dancing with a Ghost* (Markham: Octopus, 1992).

There are a number of limits on the scope of sentencing circles including the adversarial and individualistic model of the current criminal justice system, the sentencing circle requirement that an accused admit guilt within that context, and the jurisdiction of appellate courts to review decisions. An examination of sentencing initiatives highlights the tension between different concepts of justice and different analyses of the efficacy of the criminal justice system, the disjuncture between Anglo-Canadian and Aboriginal models of dispute resolution, and the competing interests within communities. Such an examination also prompts a challenge to envision healing or restorative goals rather than punitive goals, and raises difficult questions about the definition of community, the scope of such hearings, and the types of offences that are appropriately dealt with by sentencing circles.

The manner in which the authority of judges and sentencing panels has been exercised has been challenged: *R. v. Johnson* (1994), [1995] 2 C.N.L.R. 159 (Y. Terr. C.A.), and *R. v. Morin*, [1995] 4 C.N.L.R. 37 (Sask. C.A.). At the same time, the legitimacy of the Anglo-Canadian court system and judiciary is clearly open to challenge (on the basis of disparate impact, for example). As well, the current criminal justice mechanisms (such as jails) are obviously not working. This has forced or facilitated exploration of other avenues, such as returning responsibility to the community and re-envisioning the goals of sentencing and criminal justice (such as taking responsibility, healing, restorative justice, and reconciliation). In circle sentencing, the community is invited into the court, whereas normally the victim and community are marginalized and excluded except for individual testimony about, for example, the character of the accused.

One of the early reported cases of circle sentencing is *R. v. Moses*, decided by Judge Barry Stuart of the Yukon Territorial Court. In *Moses* (1992), 71 C.C.C. (3d) 347, Judge Stuart decided to hold a sentencing circle for an accused found guilty of carrying a weapon (a baseball bat) for the purpose of assaulting a constable, theft of clothes from someone's home, and breach of probation. Philip Moses was a 26-year-old member of the Na-cho Ny'ak Dun First Nation of Mayo, Yukon. He had a criminal record encompassing 43 convictions and jail terms totalling eight years. Judge Stuart's sentencing decision summarized Philip Moses's childhood, noting that "[a]nyone who reads Philip's personal history would simply not believe that someone could be subjected to such abuse and survive." The judge described the process that the circle underwent, the human waste occasioned by the processing of Aboriginal people through the criminal justice system, and the failure of sentences of imprisonment to change the lives of individual offenders or to shift dynamics within Aboriginal communities.

Instead, members of the circle, including Moses, crafted the terms of a rehabilitative sentence that included a suspended sentence with a two year probation order and a three part plan: the first part called upon Moses' family and community to integrate him back into their family and cultural practices, living on the trapline; the second part sent him to a two month residential program for Aboriginal people suffering alcoholism; the third part returned him to his community in Mayo where he was to receive life and employment skills and support to seek paid employment. At each stage a court review was to be held to monitor and fine-tune the program. Judge Stuart concluded his sentencing decision as follows: "In making the circle work, the Na-cho Ny'ak Dun First Nation took an important first step. Can we follow?"

Circle sentencing initiatives began in the Yukon and Northwest Territories. Similar initiatives are now in place in British Columbia, Saskatchewan, Manitoba, Ontario, Québec, and New Brunswick. For a review of the early developments with respect to community consultation and the use of sentencing circles, see: the Royal Commission on Aboriginal Peoples, *Bridging the Cultural Divide*: "Elders Panels and Sentencing Circles" at 109–16 and the references to a number of conference papers noted therein: Heino Lilles, "Tribal Justice: A New Beginning" (Whitehorse: 1991); and Barry Stuart, "Alternative Dispute Resolution in Action in Canada: Community Justice Circles" (Aylmer: 1995). See also: Pierre Allard, "Le cercle de consultation" *National* (October 1994) 32; and Marianne Nielsen, *Surviving in-Between: A Case Study of a Canadian Aboriginal-Operated Criminal Justice Organization* (Ph.D. Dissertation, University of Alberta, 1993) [unpublished].

CIRCLE SENTENCING CRITERIA

The cases have considered the legal basis for sentencing circles and the possible requirement of explicit guidelines; the criteria for determining the appropriateness of sentencing circles; and the limitations on the options available to sentencing circles. In some jurisdictions, guidelines for the use of sentencing circles have been developed by the court. For example, the Saskatchewan Provincial Court has developed seven criteria, as referred to by Judge Claude Fafard in *R.* v. *Joseyounen*, [1996] 1 C.N.L.R. 182 (Sask. Prov. Ct.) at 182:

> i. The accused must agree to go before a sentencing circle.
> ii. The accused must have deep roots in the community in which the sentencing circle is held and from which the participants are drawn.
> iii. That there are elders or respected non-political leaders willing to participate.
> iv. The victim is willing to participate and has been subjected to no coercion or pressure in so agreeing.
> v. The Court should try to determine beforehand, as best it can, if the victim is subject to battered spouse syndrome. If she is, then she should have counselling made available to her and be accompanied by a support team in the circle.
> vi. Disputed facts have been resolved in advance.
> vii. The case is one in which a court would be willing to take a calculated risk and depart from the usual range of sentencing.

In most jurisdictions, the criteria have been developed by the judges who are consulting with sentencing circles. It has been suggested that the absence of explicit guidelines makes the process vulnerable to challenge: Mr. Justice McEachern in *R.* v. *Johnson* (1994), [1995] 2 C.N.L.R. 159 (Y. Terr. C.A.) at 160:

> Sentencing circles are not prescribed by the *Criminal Code* of Canada. If the judges of a Court propose to use sentencing circles to assist them in some kinds of sentencing (and I do not suggest they should not), they should establish and publish rules under *Code*, s. 482(2) and *Interpretation Act*, R.S.C. c. I-21, s. 35 (which defines "province" to include the Yukon territory), so that both the Crown and the accused, and their counsel, will know the kinds of cases to be tried in this way, and precisely what they and their client may expect. It would be wrong, in my view, if the judges of a Court should follow different procedures on such a common question as sentencing which is an important component of every case where a conviction is entered.

This passage was cited with approval by Mr. Justice Sherstobitoff in *R.* v. *Morin* (Sask. C.A.), *infra*. Consider whether the promulgation of criteria is or should be required. Is that in itself a limit on judicial authority with respect to sentencing? Would that have the effect of further limiting community input and decision-making?

There is judicial agreement on a number of the criteria that make sentencing circles appropriate:

- the remorsefulness of the accused and an intention to rehabilitate himself or herself
- an identifiable community
- the desire of the community to become involved

Other criteria are contested:

- whether an accused who has pleaded not guilty and is subsequently found guilty (as was Moses), can also be found to have demonstrated remorse: *R. v. Taylor*, infra.
- whether the accused should be a fit candidate for a sentence of less than two years (so that options of suspended sentence, intermittent sentence, and probation are available): Contrast the majority and dissent in *R. v. Morin* (1995), 4 C.N.L.R. 37 (Sask. C.A.). Mr. Justice Bayda, in dissent, argued at 73 that to limit the availability of sentencing circles in that way "is tantamount to equating the incarceral component of a fit ordinary sentence with the incarceral component of a fit restorative sentence."
- whether the unwillingness of the victim to participate is determinative: *R. v. Severight* (1996), 137 Sask. R. 306 (C.A.). The Saskatchewan Court of Appeal upheld the trial judge's rejection of a sentencing circle where the non-Aboriginal victim was unwilling to participate.
- whether circle sentencing should be available for non-Aboriginal accused: *R. v. Munson*, [2001] S.J. No. 714 (Q.B.), online: QL (sentencing circle inappropriate for two non-Aboriginal Saskatoon police officers convicted of unlawful confinement of Darrell Night, who they had abandoned on a bitterly cold winter morning in a deserted area on the outskirts of the city).

ROLE OF APPELLATE COURTS

The interpretation of these criteria and the evidence required to satisfy them has been the subject of appeal. In *R. v. Morin*, [1994] 1 C.N.L.R. 150 (Sask. Q.B.), Mr. Justice Milliken granted the application for a sentencing circle on the basis of the "existence of a community who appeared to be interested in helping Morin change his life-style, and [an] ... indication from Morin that he desired to change his life-style" (at 150). He explicitly rejected a consideration of other criteria, such as whether the accused was living in an Aboriginal community, the type of offence and the violence involved, the criminal record of the accused, and the possibility that the accused might be sentenced to a term greater than two years imprisonment. The accused, who had a lengthy criminal record, was sentenced to 18 months imprisonment with 18 months probation for robbery with violence.

However, the Saskatchewan Court of Appeal overturned the sentence on the basis that the accused showed little remorse and demonstrated little potential for rehabilitation and added a sentence of 15 months (in addition to the time already served on remand, imprisonment, electronic monitoring, and probation): *R. v. Morin*, (Sask. C.A.), supra. The majority criticized the breadth of the criteria employed by Mr. Justice Milliken, which they said would apply to almost any case. In reviewing the fitness of the sentence, the majority and dissent differed on the significance of disparity of sentence. According to Mr. Justice Sherstobitoff (for the majority) at 49–52:

> [O]ne of the duties of the Court of Appeal is to prevent disparity of sentences. Disparity between the sentence imposed on Mr. Morin in this case and other sentences for like offences in like circumstances in other cases, and between Mr. Morin and his co-accused, is the Crown's main ground of appeal in this case....
>
> The sentencing judge and the Court of Appeal are bound by these principles of sentencing, since the law must be applied equally to everyone irrespective of race or culture....
>
> The very purpose of sentencing circles seems to be to fashion sentences that will differ in some mix or measure from those which the courts have up to now imposed in order to take into account Aboriginal culture and traditions, and in order to permit and to take into account direct community participation in both imposition and administration of the sentence. It also seems implicit in all discussions of sentencing circles that they will in many cases, if not most of them, recommend sentences imposing lesser terms of incarceration than would have been imposed by a judge alone and to substitute alternative sanctions, usually involving the community in the administration of those sanctions.
>
> . . . .
>
> Since the sentence imposed on Mr. Morin clearly falls outside of the established range, it must be set aside on account of disparity, unless it can be shown that there are, in this

particular case, reasons for putting rehabilitation ahead of the other factors considered in sentencing, or unless there are other extraordinary circumstances to justify departure from the normal range of sentences.

In contrast, Mr. Justice Bayda in dissent argued at 70–73:

> In the end the factors that a judge ought to consider at this stage of the proceedings are those that will enable him or her to answer this critical question: Is a fit sentence for **this** accused who has committed **this** offence better arrived at by using the restorative approach or the ordinary approach? In considering this question the judge will have to keep in mind that the sentence arrived at using the restorative approach will likely be quite different from the one arrived at using the ordinary approach.... [T]o assess the fitness of a restorative sentence by comparing its incarceration component with the incarceration component of a fit sentence using the ordinary approach is to engage in an exercise that is either flawed or irrelevant....
>
> The approach I suggest raises two concerns. The first brings to the fore the issue of disparity. What are we to do with a principle that mandates similar sentences for similar offences committed by individuals with similar personal circumstances? The second has regard for the likelihood that sentencing circles will be resorted to by First Nations people more frequently than non-First Nations people. Is this apt to produce one system of justice for First Nations people and one for everyone else? I answer these concerns by pointing to the shocking disparity in the composition of the prison populations of this province....

[He then cited the work of Tim Quigley, *supra* and the work of Lucia Zender, "Reparation and Retribution: Are They Reconcilable?" (1994) 57 Modern L. Rev. 228]

> Given that unhealthy scenario, the argument that the need to eliminate the disparity in sentencing as it is understood in the traditional sense must defer to the need to eliminate the disparity reflected in the composition of the prison population is compelling indeed.... [T]he perpetuation of entrenched attitudes in relation to sentencing in the guise of maintaining sentence parity is not in the interests of the administration of justice in this province or the well-being of our society.
>
> ... The nature and seriousness of the offence for which the accused is convicted is clearly a factor that the judge will need to take into account at this stage but it is only one factor, sometimes a determinative factor, but not necessarily a determinative factor (unless there is a prescribed minimum sentence). A hard and fast rule is tantamount to starting the process of a restorative sentence at the wrong end. It is tantamount to equating the incarceral component of a fit ordinary sentence with the incarceral component of a fit restorative sentence. Such a rule in my respectful view would have a serious emasculating effect on the underlying need for sentencing circles and would amount to offering the benefit of a sentencing circle to only those offenders who need it least. In cases involving First Nation offenders there would be justification for the contention that the courts were only paying lip service to the principle of sentencing circles rather than searching for "drastic steps."

There are as yet very few appellate decisions on sentencing circles: Luke McNamara, "Appellate Court Scrutiny of Circle Sentencing" (1999) 27 Man. L.J. 209 and "The Locus of Decision-Making Authority in Circle Sentencing: The Significance of Criteria and Guidelines" (2000) 18 Windsor Y.B. Access to Justice 60. However, in other areas, appellate courts often hesitate to disturb the findings of a trial judge precisely because that trial judge is better situated to assess testimony and credibility. Consider whether the willingness of an appellate court to supplant the findings of the court of first instance as to an accused's remorse and rehabilitative potential is troubling in that context.

To view the Alberta sentencing circle of Jarvis Spear Chief and a thoughtful discussion of the *Morin* case, including commentary by participants in the sentencing circles and the victims, see the video "Sentencing Circles: Traditional Justice Reborn" by Doug Cuthand and Vicki Hunter Covington, a production of the Alberta RCMP, 1995. For a video of a re-enactment of a Yukon circle sentencing case involving wife abuse, see: Vic Istchenko, "Circle Sentencing: A Yukon Experiment," Northern Native Broadcasting, 1992. Judge Barry Stuart was the presiding judge in the case.

In *R. v. Taylor*, [1996] 3 W.W.R. 88 (Sask. C.A.), rev'g (1995), 132 Sask. R. 221 (Q.B.), the Saskatchewan Court of Appeal overturned the decision by Mr. Justice Milliken (acting upon the recommendation of a sentencing circle) to adjourn proceedings for a year, release the accused from custody, and banish him to an island in Northern Saskatchewan for one year. They sent the case back for sentencing on the basis that the decision to adjourn amounted to a failure to exercise jurisdiction. Taylor had been convicted of sexual assault (s. 271), assault (s. 266) of his ex-girlfriend, and threatening to kill her should she report the occurrence (s. 264(1)(a)). Justice Milliken has said he was under pressure from members of the Provincial Court and the Saskatchewan Department of Justice not to proceed with a sentencing circle or, alternatively, to adopt many more restrictions: Peter Moon, "Urged not to use Cree justice, judge says: Saskatchewan government denies it tried to limit consultation in banishment case" *The [Toronto] Globe and Mail* (13 June 1995) A1. In particular, he referred to the contention by the Crown that a circle should not be held if the accused has pleaded not guilty and is subsequently found guilty; the question of whether a circle should be held if a victim chooses not to attend; and the argument by the Crown that a circle should not be held if one of the offences involved is a sexual offence or if the jail sentence to be imposed could be for more than two years (at 224):

> [T]he issue of having plead guilty or not guilty is irrelevant to the issue of sentencing [instead] what is relevant is whether the accused person wishes to change his lifestyle and whether there is a community which is willing to help him to do so. A circle provides an opportunity for members of a community to register support of an accused person who wants to change his lifestyle and still protect the community.
>
> Should a circle be held if a victim chooses not to attend or signifies that she does not wish a circle be held? There is no requirement under the Criminal Code that a presentence report cannot be ordered if a victim refuses to participate in the preparation of the report or if a victim does not want a presentence report to be made. What is the difference between a presentence report and a circle? The only difference appears to me to be that a presentence report is prepared by a probation officer in writing. The same persons who are at a circle are usually interviewed for a presentence report.
>
> If a victim does not wish to participate in a circle then his or her views may be given to the circle by Crown counsel, or by a third party, or by way of a victim impact statement.
>
> It must be remembered that the recommendation of a circle is not binding on the sentencing judge. The primary purpose of a circle ... is to help an accused person change lifestyles with community involvement. Therefore the presence or absence of the victim at a circle is not crucial for the having of a circle. A circle may well have healing effect on the victim and the accused but that is not the primary purpose of the circle.
>
> Should a circle be held if one of the [offences] involved is a sexual offence. The view was expressed to me by Crown counsel and members of the circle that because in this case Taylor had been found guilty of sexual assault, a circle should not be held, as by holding a circle the victim would be revictimized.
>
> Clearly, no one wants to revictimize a victim. A victim need not attend a circle if she feels she will be revictimized. A victim can make a victim impact statement which can be read to the circle or she can express her views to the Probation Officer preparing for a presentence report and a copy of the report can be read to the circle in this way the victim should not be revictimized. The judge at the commencement of the circle should make it clear that there will be no tolerance for any remarks which may have the [effect] of revictimizing the victim.

Justice Milliken resentenced Taylor in December 1995 to an additional term of 90 days in jail and three years probation, including a condition that he spend an additional six months in isolation. Morin had by then spent nine months in jail and six months in isolation. The Crown unsuccessfully appealed the latter sentence: *R. v. Taylor* (1997), 122 C.C.C. (3d) 376 (Sask. C.A.) Although the court split on a number of issues and criticized Justice Milliken for failing to sufficiently explore the question of remorse and for failing to seek input from the victim, ultimately the majority (Bayda C.J. and Jackson J.A.) upheld the process and decision of the sentencing circle.

CRITIQUE OF SENTENCING CIRCLES

Compare Mr. Justice Milliken's views on the primary goals of a sentencing circle to those of Judge Fafard in *Joseyounen*, *supra*, and those of Judge Stuart in *Moses*, *supra*. What is the impact on women and children who are victims of violence? Might it depend on the composition of the sentencing circle? As the Royal Commission notes, the question of who speaks for a "community" can be a contentious one, particularly if judges rather than communities select the representation. Joan Mercredi speaks forcefully of the difficulty in small isolated communities of overcoming power structures that may protect particular offenders and inhibit any possibility of healing: *Bridging the Cultural Divide* at 114.

While sentencing circles and elders panels provide the opportunity for input from Aboriginal communities, that input is circumscribed and comes very late in the criminal process. The cases have explicitly recognized that sentencing circles are bound by the *Criminal Code* guidelines and provisions, for example, with respect to minimum sentences and prohibitions on the possession of a firearm: *Johnson*, *supra*.

To address some of the limitations of sentencing circles, the Royal Commission describes how Aboriginal communities might be involved at other points in the criminal justice system (such as diversion, bail, plea discussion, trial, and sentencing). They cite Rupert Ross, "Managing the Merger: Justice-as-Healing in Aboriginal Communities" (Kenora, 1994) [unpublished]; Barry Stuart and Barbara Hume, "Alternative Dispute Resolution in Action in Canada: Community Justice Circles" (Toronto: Society of Professionals in Dispute Resolution, 1993).

Critics of sentencing circles have problematized both the role of the victim in the process and the limited importance attached to concerns about violence against women and children. Others have challenged the supposed "traditional" basis of sentencing circles, asserting that these circles grew out of existing systems and that the practice did not in fact exist within specific cultural traditions such as those of the Inuit: Mary Crnkovich, "The Role of the Victim in the Criminal Justice System: Circle Sentencing in Inuit Communities" (Ottawa: Canadian Institute for the Administration of Justice, 1995); Carol LaPrairie, "Altering Course: New Directions in Criminal Justice Sentencing Circles and Family Group Conferencing" (1995) 28 Aust. and N.Z. J. Crim. 100; and Carol LaPrairie, "Community Justice or Just Communities? Aboriginal Communities in Search of Justice" (1995) 37 Cdn. J. Criminology 521.

Mary Crnkovich, "The Role of the Victim in the Criminal Justice System: Circle Sentencing in Inuit Communities," *supra*, critically examines the first sentencing circle proceedings in Nunavik (Northern Québec), in 1993 before Judge Jean-Luc Dutil. She raises concerns about the assumption that sentencing circles are a traditional practice of the Inuit, the variability in the operation of sentencing circles, and the implication that any community is homogenous. She highlights the gap between traditional practices and values and the workings of sentencing circles and the existing system. She also argues that the sentencing circle in the case was given very little direction (at 16–17):

> It would appear that the group was being asked to help construct a sentence that would prevent the accused from repeating his crime, but this was not explicitly stated. Was the sentencing circle also being asked to develop a sentence that would reconcile the accused with the community or protect the victim? This is not clear, as the direction given to the group by the judge was put in the form of a question — "what are we going to do with this man?"
>
>> In the matter at hand, a person broke the law, that is the court's ground. After guilt is proven or found, there is sentencing. In this forum, it is up to each and everyone of us ... what can we do to help [the accused] get a fresh start ...
>
> In the absence of clear direction from the judge about the objective of this process, the participants may have limited their discussion and options to focusing only on what could be done to help the accused get "a fresh start" when other issues could also have been addressed. For example, I think it is also significant that the crime he pleaded guilty to was physical assault and the person he beat was his wife. From the information provided by the judge, the accused committed this offence while on probation for the same offence on the same victim and openly confessed in court while he had been convicted three times already for beating his wife, he had beat his wife at least 50 times without being charged.
>
> Most of the community members involved in the circle had very little knowledge of the judicial process and were no doubt unfamiliar with principles upon which sentencing practices are based. Without some explanation regarding this sentencing alternative, active and meaningful contribution on the part of all of the circle members was severely limited. Questions were never answered about why this special circle was being used instead of the regular court hearing; what power the circle had to create new sentencing options; what a sentence is supposed to do; or what the law says a judge's sentence could be for someone convicted of wife assault.[†]

She examines the lack of attention given to who should participate in the circle or to ques-

---

[†] The text was first presented at the Canadian Institute for the Administration of Justice Conference, "Public Perceptions of the Administration of Justice" held in Banff, Alberta, 11–14 October 1995 at 16–17. Notes omitted. Reproduced by permission of author and the publisher.

tions of power and equality in the "community," and she criticizes the lack of efforts to inform or consult the complainant/victim prior to the circle. Instead, the complainant/victim was only invited to participate after the circle was in place. While acknowledging the visible bias of the existing system and that alternative sentencing might be more productive than current remedies, she emphasizes the importance of scrutinizing the process to ensure that the interests and needs of women are considered and that women are not worse off than under the existing system. Instead, the strengths of women as survivors should be built upon. See also: Mary Crnkovich, "Report on a Sentencing Circle in Nunavik" in *Inuit Women and Justice: Progress Report Number One, supra* at 19.

The Role of the Victim in the Criminal Justice System: Circle Sentencing in Inuit Communities[†]

Those who are proponents of the circle suggest that each circle will be different depending upon the community and that there is a need for flexibility in structure and process. This informality, on one hand, is welcome for many who are alienated by the formality and rigours of courtroom procedures. On the other hand, without any guidelines or standards, the extent to which this process is fully understood by the community members is doubtful and leaves one to question how meaningful the participation of the victim can be. Having said this, the predictability and professed universalism of the existing system, regardless of its deficiencies and inequities, may be more appealing to victims because it is well known and experienced by many.

Again, there appears to be an underlying assumption being made that with respect to these alternatives [...] the interests of the victim are understood, acknowledged and considered as equally important as those of the accused by the participating community members.

Advocates of the circle sentencing approach often suggest victims can be afforded more of an opportunity to be heard and have a role in rehabilitating the accused through this alternative approach. This ignores the reality of many women who are victims of violence. Found within this assumption that all participants within the community are equal and share the same interests, is this view that the victim, like any other person within the circle, is free and able to speak out. Yet at the same time, it is well understood there are very few, if any support services available to women who are victims of violence to provide the necessary support and advocacy to participate.

To many judges, such as the judge in this case, such services or supports for victims would not [be] seen as essential pre-requisites to this approach, as they have assumed that the community and the victim share the same views and beliefs. Accordingly, by having community members around the victim, this would be perceived as sufficient in providing her with the necessary support. Furthermore, it would appear that it is not really necessary for the victim to fully participate by speaking. Her presence, in the view of the judge, is sufficient in demonstrating some form of reconciliation and possibly forgiveness, which is an important message for other members of the community.

In the Nunavik case, this circuit court judge was relatively unfamiliar with the community members, the power dynamics within the community, including family ties and political links within the community and he was definitely not privy to community gossip. This unfamiliarity coupled with this assumption of a homogenous community prevented the judge from even considering examining more deeply who the accused is within the community, how this relationship with the community may impact on the ability of other community members to participate freely, what status the victim has [in] the community. Failing to explore these issues, and at the same time making decisions on whether or not the case will go to circle, serves to perpetuate further barriers to women who are victims of domestic violence.

So much depends on who a particular community member is. If the community member is a relative of the accused, himself an abuser or simply not interested in this matter, he may find it very hard to understand the impacts of this crime on the victim

---

[†] *Ibid.* at 22–26, 31, 34–35. Reproduced by permission of author and the publisher.

and, more generally, the community. This assumption further silences many victims. The assumption that all members of the community share the same values and views on justice precludes the need to really hear from the victim, especially if she is uncertain about participating. In other words, this assumption may (and in the Nunavik case did) render the need for the victim to speak about the impact [of] the crime upon her inconsequential.

In the Nunavik sentencing circle discussions, the focus was primarily on the accused and what could be done to "help" him and what he would have to do himself to overcome the problem. The tone of the discussions was never adversarial or emotional. Everyone who spoke did so in a very straightforward manner. No Inuit observing the circle were asked to speak during the process, only the people sitting in the circle spoke.

Very little was said about the victim during the session, other than that she suffered a burden when her husband was not in the community to help her raise her children. Only the family violence worker raised the need for the victim to have her own outlet of support should her husband begin assaulting her again. The activities and lifestyle of the accused were discussed initially as "his problem," but as the proceedings progressed some members of the circle started talking about "their problem." This shift in focus implies that some degree of blame or responsibility for the abuse was being placed on the victim.

At no time during the circle discussion did the offender or others hear from the victim, in her own words, what the impact of the accused's actions had been on her or her family. The victim appeared to be very nervous in the circle and would only briefly speak when asked a question by the judge. The victim's participation is essential, according to advocates of circles, because her comments are significant and necessary to developing a sentence that will rehabilitate the accused. Yet in this case, it was evident the victim was not able to fully participate.

A further assumption by the judge was that the community all shared an interest, responsibility and willingness to address this particular issue of domestic assault. The judge appears to believe there is widespread acceptance within the community to take on the responsibility to address violence against women in their community. In his written decision on this case, he stated that "all participants in a consultation circle share a common purpose: to settle a problem that distresses a family and, consequently an entire community." Beyond this statement, there is no evidence available from any community members or political leaders that this in fact is the case.

Not unlike communities in the south, Inuit communities are struggling with the issue of domestic violence and are no further ahead in having all members, especially male community members, accept responsibility for male violence against women. To expect this of this community, especially when the judge himself recognizes "violence ... in the form of battery or assault committed by a man against his wife, consort, friend, casual companion is the most common crime," is simply unrealistic.

Inuit communities can be small and everyone may know everyone else. There are complex networks of kinship and relationships through marriage. With such complex and well known relations within a community, it is not surprising few in the community want to take on the responsibility of sending another community member, a possible blood relative or in-law, to jail. As stated earlier, the experience with jury trials in some Inuit communities in the Nunavut demonstrates people within the communities do not like to send people to jail. In fact, it is understood by many in these [particular] communities that if you are charged with a crime of violence against women, especially sexual assault, you should always elect to be tried by judge and jury. The underlying message in this story is that juries seldom convict Inuit men of sexually assaulting Inuit women. Many reasons are given, some defense counsel blame it upon a bad Crown counsel, others in the community say people on the juries [do] not want to be responsible for sending the person down south to jail. With this as the background information, one must seriously question whether or not alternatives such as community-based sentencing circles can protect the interests of victims while respecting the rights of the accused. It is not surprising Inuit women fear the use of these circles in cases involving violence against women.

It became evident in the manner the circle was conducted that there was an assumption made by the judge that the "community" and "victim" are one [and] the same, sharing the same values, interests and outcomes. The judge did not seem at all concerned with the very limited engagement the victim had with the group during the circle. The focus remained on the accused; the victim was just part of the larger public identified as the community.

This is an assumption that is perpetuated in the existing system to the extent that the Crown, while representing the "state" and "public interest," is often perceived and referred to as the victim's lawyer. The conflicts surrounding this perceived dual role of Crown has begun to be addressed in one community with the establishment of an independent Inuit women victims advocacy and support service.

With such underlying assumptions, it is not a surprise that the issue of what happens to those women who are victims of violence and cannot speak out in their community are ignored....

This is important to acknowledge because if "community" is understood to be the local geographic unit and the "collectivity" empowered by judges to participate in and, eventually, decide on the design and procedures of such sentencing alternatives, the end result will mean women may be further discriminated against and unable to speak out.

. . . .

The use of sentencing circles for cases involving violence against Inuit women and children may in fact be sending the wrong message to the community and most importantly to victims of violence. For those women and children who are victims of male violence, the Nunavik case may send the message that men who abuse women and children and who go through this process will not really have to be responsible or accountable for their actions and will not likely get the help they need to change their behaviour and attitudes. With this result, many women may weigh the value in reporting such crimes against very real and possible harms they may suffer as a result of sentencing circle decisions.

For example, in the case in Nunavik, a third time repeat offender for domestic assault is not incarcerated or required to seek specialized counselling as a result of the circle. Rather, he and his wife are required to attend weekly sessions with community volunteers who have no training in dealing with these issues, but will agree to be available to talk to the "couple" together about "their problem." The outcome in this circle ignored the real threats and harms that exist for women who are victims of abuse in remote Inuit communities. It also ignored the real needs of the offender. These needs of the offender and the threats and harms to the victim cannot be discounted when discussing alternatives to the existing system.

. . . .

In addition, a fairly good understanding has to be reached about the objectives of alternatives such as the sentencing circle. Consideration must be given to broadening the accepted general principles of sentencing. For example, if sexual assault and wife assault cases are eligible for this process, the sentencing alternative must be designed to deal with rehabilitation of the accused, but it must also deal with rehabilitation and protection of the victim and family, independently of what is decided for the accused.

In the Yukon case, *R. v. P. (J.A.)*, Lilles, CJTC., stated that the focus of the sentence for the sexual assaults that took place "should not be on the removal of the offender from the community but on healing both the victims and wrongdoer in the community." What is missing from this focus of "healing" is the assurance that the community is able to provide this service. Does it have the necessary human and financial resources to assist both the victim and the offender in healing, where they are willing to do so? Does the community have the necessary services, if the wrongdoer stays in the community, to ensure that the victim is protected from further assaults. Without such protection, it is unlikely the victims will ever "heal."

As in the Nunavik case, the crime of violence against women is often seen by the Court and others as a problem shared by the accused and victim. As such, it should be worked out by them together. To suggest that the only way in which to resolve the problem is to bring the victim and the accused together is problematic. The syndrome of abuse that the victim in this case suffered may require that she be allowed the necessary support and counselling apart from the man who is abusing her. To require that they work this out together imposes even greater abuse upon the victim. This type of situation, in my view, would not have arisen, if the victim had adequate advocacy and support services. Had these services been available, questions, well in advance of the circle could have been asked of the judge and others responsible for organizing and conducting the circle to determine whether this was something that should be taking place at all and if so, whether the victim was able to participate in it and under what conditions.

■

Consider the ways in which justice systems might ensure safety and justice for women and children, in response to the concerns raised in the previous section. Cases such as *Taylor, supra*, clearly challenge the adequacy of current responses; see also *R. v. Naappaluk* (1993), 25 C.R. (4th) 220 (Court of Québec), a wife assault case. As many of the judges recognize, the current criminal justice system is neither effective nor equitable, and the formulation of solutions is incomplete without a reconceptualization of goals. However, the analysis of the problems is also incomplete without more attention to the prevalence of violence against women and children. For example, in *Naappaluk*, Judge Dutil described the docket of cases he hears, and suggested that half the cases involve violence, such as assaults, sexual assaults, or death threats, and that many of them involve violence against women. For additional discussion of the importance of a gendered perspective on circle sentencing, see, for example: Rashmi Goel, "No Women at the Center: The Use of the Canadian Sentencing Circle in Domestic Violence Cases" (2000) 15 Wis. Women's L.J. 293.

Surprisingly, while identifying the problem of violence against women, the Royal Commission on Aboriginal Peoples did not integrate those concerns into the discussion of sentencing circles. Thus, the Royal Commission fails to grapple in a sufficient way with difficult issues of intersectionality. See: "Ensuring the Safety of Women and Children in Aboriginal Justice Systems," *Bridging the Cultural Divide* at 269–75.

What these examples underline is the need for a comprehensive approach that encompasses a broader consideration of justice and community and that extends beyond sentencing. The Royal Commission points to Hollow Water First Nation's Community Holistic Circle Healing Project as one of those successful initiatives. The Commission also emphasizes the importance of a number of factors in the development of such initiatives, including: the community-driven dimension, the fact that the programs are oriented towards healing rather than punishment, and that the individual initiatives lead towards the eventual exercise of Aboriginal self-government. Consider the distinctiveness of this initiative. Is there an awareness and response to issues of power and inequality within the community? How does the initiative respond to concerns about violence against women and children and the situation of the victim?

Hollow Water First Nation's Community Holistic Circle Healing Project[†]

HISTORY AND DEVELOPMENT

Community holistic circle healing (CHCH) deals with cases of sexual abuse in the northern Manitoba First Nation community of Hollow Water and in the surrounding Métis communities of Manigotagan, Aghaming, and Seymourville. CHCH has fashioned a unique response to the particular needs of people affected by this offence.

The idea behind CHCH took root first in the Ojibwa community of Hollow Water in 1984, when a group of residents and other people involved in providing social services to the community sought to grapple with the legacy of decades of alcoholism and family abuse, suicide and cultural loss. By 1987 a resource group had been formed, and based on their work — and the first trickle of what was to become a stream of disclosures — they became convinced that many of the community's problems could be traced to sexual abuse. The degree to which sexual abuse was a problem undermining the very fabric of the community was illustrated by the fact that the resource group believes that 75 per cent of the community have been victims of sexual abuse and 35 per cent are victimizers.

In 1988 members of the resource group travelled to Alkali Lake to learn about the successful efforts of that community to address the problems of alcohol abuse and sexual abuse. The resource group found the trip to Alkali Lake a moving and profound experience. Upon their return to Hollow Water, the group launched a number of initiatives, among them CHCH.

A sub-committee of the resource group, the assessment team, was responsible for the development of CHCH. Before any initiatives were undertaken specifically to respond to cases of sexual abuse, those interested in participating in the process went through a two-year training program. The pro-

---

† From Canada, Royal Commission on Aboriginal Peoples, *Bridging the Cultural Divide: A Report on Aboriginal People and Criminal Justice in Canada* (Ottawa: Minister of Supply and Services, 1996) at 159–67. Notes omitted. Reproduced with the permission of the Minister of Public Works and Government Services Canada, 2002 and Courtesy of the Privy Council Office.

gram included cultural awareness; alcohol and drug awareness; team building; networking; suicide intervention; family counselling; communications skills; nutrition; and human sexuality.

CHCH focuses on cases of sexual assault, as it is felt that the root problems of the community can be dealt with only when the issue of sexual abuse is addressed. At the same time, resource group members feel it is important that people realize that CHCH is not about addressing a particular problem; rather it is integral to the healing and development of the community.

. . . .

At its core, CHCH addresses sexual abuse by providing support, counselling and guidance to everyone affected by the crime, including the victim, the victim's family, the victimizer, and the victimizer's family.

The CHCH method of treating sexual abuse contains thirteen steps:

Step 1.	Disclosure
Step 2.	Protecting the Victim/Child
Step 3.	Confronting the Victimizer
Step 4.	Assisting the Spouse
Step 5.	Assisting the family(ies)/the Community
Step 6.	Meeting of the Assessment Team/RCMP/Crown
Step 7.	Victimizer Must Admit and Accept Responsibility
Step 8.	Preparation of the Victimizer
Step 9.	Preparation of the Victim
Step 10.	Preparation of All the Families
Step 11.	The Special Gathering
Step 12.	The Healing Contract Implemented
Step 13.	The Cleansing Ceremony

Progress through the entire 13 steps is estimated to take five years.

PROJECT OPERATION

[The circle healing project includes an assessment team which is responsible for a broad range of prevention and intervention activities and a management team, and also draws on volunteers and professionals from within the community.]

. . . .

... The key to all interventions is the protection, support and healing of the victim. Once a disclosure of sexual abuse has been made, the assessment team conducts a detailed interview with the victim. Steps are then taken immediately to protect the victim and to ensure her or his long-term safety. Only after these steps have been taken is the victimizer confronted. In most cases the victimizer is confronted before the RCMP is notified and charges are laid. The CHCH process is explained to the victimizer at this time. It is emphasized that if the victimizer wishes to enter CHCH he must accept responsibility for the offence and plead guilty in court. The agreement to plead guilty is important because it spares the victim the trauma of testifying in court. The victimizer has five days to decide whether to participate in CHCH. In some cases, victims do not wish to bring formal charges against the victimizer. While the absence of charges limits some of the things CHCH can do, workers nevertheless continue to assist the victim.

Following confrontation of the victimizer, the team meets with the victimizer's spouse to provide support. In her review of CHCH for the federal solicitor general, Theresa Lajeunesse describes the role of team members in dealing with victims, victimizers and their families:

> In some cases, the family of the victim and victimizer will be the same, in other cases they are different. In most cases, they will be from the same community. In all cases, the pain brought about by a disclosure will have a rippling effect throughout the community and members of both immediate and extended families will be affected. As with the victim and the victimizer, individual workers will work with members of all affected families. Often workers must deal with not only the sexual abuse, but past trauma which occurred in the lives of all the participants.

The non-Aboriginal criminal justice system puts the bulk of its energies into securing the conviction of the offender. In cases of sexual assault, it is now recognized that victims too have a legitimate claim on the services of the justice system. There is no comparison, however, between the way the non-Aboriginal justice system understands the impact of sexual assault and the way it is understood in Hollow Water. Rupert Ross describes the energies that go into creating a support network for all those involved:

> At all times, from the moment of disclosure through to the cleansing ceremony, team members have responsibility to work with, protect, support, teach and encourage a wide range of people. It is their view that since a great many

people are affected by each disclosure, all of them deserve assistance, and just as important, all of them must be involved in any process aimed at creating healthy dynamics and breaking the inter-generational chain of abuse. I watched them plan for a possible confrontation with a suspected victimizer, and the detailed dispersal of team members through the community to support those whom the disclosure would touch reminded me of a military operation in its logistical complexity.

CHCH has entered into a protocol with the Manitoba Crown attorney's office to govern the way their intervention is respected. Enough time is taken before sentencing to allow the assessment team to work with the victimizer. Generally, victimizers who plead guilty receive three years's probation. During those three years they are required to continue their work with CHCH. Failure to follow through with the program would result in a charge of breach of probation. No such charges have yet been brought against a victimizer. The three-year probation term is the maximum permitted by the *Criminal Code*. As noted earlier, in the opinion of CHCH staff, five years are required to see a person through the entire program.

An understanding of the process of healing is crucial to an understanding of this initiative in particular and of Aboriginal justice programs in general. With reference to CHCH, Rupert Ross describes the healing process in the following manner:

> This healing process is painful, for it involves stripping away all the excuses, justifications, angers and other defences of each abuser until, finally, confronted with a victim who has been made strong enough to expose his or her pain in their presence, the abuser actually feels the pain he or she created. Only then can the re-building begin, both for the abuser and the abused. The word "healing" seems such a soft word, but the process of healing within the Hollow Water program is anything but.

. . . .

Understanding the healing process at work in Hollow Water helps also to understand the position CHCH now takes on the incarceration of offenders. Initially, CHCH dealt with the sentencing process by providing a pre-sentence report for the court. By 1993, however, dissatisfaction with this role led CHCH to re-evaluate the need for incarceration in the cases they were handling.

. . . .

As we worked through the casework ... we came to realize two things:

- that as we both shared our own stories of victimization and learned from our experiences in assisting others in dealing with the pain of their victimization, it became very difficult to define "too serious." The quantity or quality of pain felt by the victim, the family/ies and the community did not seem to be directly connected to any specific acts of victimization. Attempts ... to define a particular victimization as "too serious" and another as "not too serious" ... were gross oversimplifications, and certainly not valid from an experiential point of view, and
- that promoting incarceration was based on, and motivated by, a mixture of feelings of anger, revenge, guilt and shame on our part, and around our personal victimization issues, rather than the healthy resolution of the victimization we were trying to address.

Thus our position on the use of incarceration has shifted. At the same time, we understand how the legal system continues to use and view incarceration — as punishment and deterrence for the victimizers ... and protection and safety for the victim(s) and community. What the legal system seems not to understand is the complexity of the issues involved in breaking the cycle of abuse that exists in our community.

The use of judgement and punishment actually works against the healing process. An already unbalanced person is moved further out of balance.

What the threat of incarceration does do is keep people from coming forward and taking responsibility for the hurt they are causing. It reinforces the silence, and therefore promotes, rather than breaks, the cycle of violence that exists. In reality, rather than making the community a safer place, the threat of jail places the community more at risk.

In order to break the cycle, we believe that victimizer accountability must be to, and support must come from, those most affected by the victimization — the victim, the family/ies, and the community. Removal of the victimizer from those who must and are best able to, hold him/her accountable, and to offer him/her support, adds complexity to already existing dynamics of guilt and shame. The healing process of all parties is therefore at best delayed, and most often actually deterred.

The legal system, based on principles of punishment and deterrence, as we see it, simply is not working. We cannot understand how the legal system doesn't see this ...

We do not see our present position on incarceration as either "an easy way out" for the victimizer, or as the victimizer "getting away." We see it rather as establishing a very clear line of accountability between the victimizer and his or her community. What follows from that line is a process that we believe is not only much more difficult for the victimizer, but also much more likely to heal the victimization, than doing time in jail could ever be.

Our children and the community can no longer afford the price the legal system is extracting in its attempts to provide justice in our community.

As a result of this shift in perspective, CHCH moved away from providing pre-sentence reports and looked at more community-based ways of providing justice in sexual abuse cases [such as sentencing circles].

. . . .

By June 1995, CHCH had dealt with 409 clients, including 94 victims (32 of whom have completed the healing program), 180 family members of victims (27 of whom have completed the healing program), 52 victimizers (4 of whom have successfully completed the program), and 83 family members of victimizers. Two victimizers have re-offended since entering the program.

NEXT STEPS

As with other justice initiatives, the continued funding of CHCH is still unsettled. Funding from the federal Aboriginal Justice Initiative, which has supported the program, is time-limited, and it is not clear where the funds will come from once this funding ceases. Given the intense, holistic approach taken by the project, the per-case cost can appear high for a community of approximately 1,500. But comparisons with the cost of other programs, completely miss the point. CHCH is a program without precedent in Canada — one that truly addresses the needs of all those affected by sexual abuse and attempts to find solutions that deal with the root causes of behaviour and prevent the cycle of abuse from continuing....

See also: Rupert Ross, "Duelling Paradigms?: Western Criminal Justice Versus Aboriginal Community Healing" in Continuing Poundmaker and Riel's Quest, supra; and Thérèse Lajeunesse, "Community Holistic Circle Healing, Hollow Water First Nation" (Ottawa: Solicitor General of Canada, 1993).

G. A STUDY IN SENTENCING: VIOLENCE AGAINST WOMEN

The following case of wife battering, R. v. Inwood, attracted considerable media attention both at trial and at sentencing. Legal argument at the appellate level (here the Ontario Court of Appeal) is set out in writing as a factum.

Consider the arguments made in the facta filed in the appeal of the sentencing decision in R. v. Inwood. How would you characterize the Crown's arguments? How did the defence respond to the public policy issues raised by the Crown factum? As you read the decision of the Ontario Court of Appeal in this case, assess which arguments from each factum appear to have convinced the court.

R. v. Inwood† (Appellant's Factum)

STATEMENT OF THE CASE

1. On September 2, 1988, in the Provincial Court (Criminal Division) at College Park, Toronto, the Respondent was found guilty of two offences by His Honour Judge E.G. Hachborn. The offences, both committed on September 13, 1987, were alleged in the same information. With respect to Count 1, the

---

† Filed at the Ontario Court of Appeal.

Respondent was found guilty of an assault upon his wife, Tanya Sidorova, which caused her bodily harm. With respect to Count 2, he was found not guilty of an assault causing bodily harm to his infant son, Michael ("Misha") Inwood, but guilty of the included offence of assault.

> *Reference*:
> Information, *Appeal Book*, pp. 11–14
> Reasons for Judgment, *Transcript*, Tab A, p. 18, 1.30–p. 19, 1.7

2. On September 20, 1988, after four days of submissions and evidence called on the sentencing, the learned trial judge suspended the passing of sentence in respect of Count 1, the assault causing bodily harm to the Respondent's wife, and placed the Respondent on probation for a period of three years. In respect of Count 2, the assault on the baby, the Respondent was sentenced to 30 days in jail, to be followed by the same probation as already ordered.

> *Reference*:
> Information, *Appeal Book*, pp. 11–14
> Reasons for Sentence, *Transcript*, Tab F, p. 194, 1.18–p. 195, 1.19.
> Probation Order, *Appeal Book*, pp. 21–22

3. Pursuant to what was then s. 605(1)(d) [now s. 676(1)(d)] of the *Criminal Code*, this is an application by the Attorney General of Ontario for leave to appeal, and if leave is granted, an appeal against both dispositions.

> *Reference*:
> Notice of Application for Leave to Appeal and Notice of Appeal, *Appeal Book*, pp. 1–3

SUMMARY OF THE FACTS

The Offences

4. The facts with respect to the offences have been summarized both in the reasons for judgment given by the learned Provincial Judge (Tab A of the Transcript) and in the Agreed Statement of Facts set out in the Supplementary Appeal Book.

5. To restate the facts even more concisely, the Respondent's assault upon his wife occurred on Sunday evening, September 13, 1987, at their apartment in Toronto, nine days after she and their 12-month old son had arrived from the Soviet Union. Earlier in the day, the Respondent had evidently been disturbed by the baby's crying. He told his wife to take the child away or he would kill him. After putting the baby in his room, the Respondent verbally abused his wife, told her he was going to throw her out of the house, and then slapped her face. After preventing her from using the phone to call the police, the Respondent told her that when he returned in two hours, he was going to kill her. In his absence, Ms. Sidorova called the police, but she declined the advice of the attending officers to go to a shelter.

6. The Respondent returned home that evening after consuming what he described as three-quarters of a bottle of whisky. He went into the baby's room and poured water over the sleeping child, causing him to shriek; the Respondent's explanation was that he did it to make the baby stop crying. When Ms. Sidorova picked up the baby, the Respondent threw water at both of them, following which he struck his wife about the face, arms and head as she held the child. He continued to beat her as she phoned the police.

7. After she put the child down, Ms. Sidorova testified that the Respondent continued to slap, punch, and kick her, knocking her down, dragging her by the hair, banging her head against the wall, and choking her before dragging her downstairs and pushing her out of the house. While the learned trial judge accepted that the complainant had "exaggerated," he found that she was fending off an attack which she might honestly have perceived as more extreme than it actually was, and that her evidence was credible as to the essential issue of whether she was assaulted. Judge Hachborn restricted his findings of bodily harm to those injuries which had been confirmed by the medical evidence: tenderness in the left occipital area, a bump and slight swelling of her nose, a swollen lip with lacerations inside, and bruising to both arms.

8. The police arrived to find Ms. Sidorova running from the house in an hysterical condition, screaming, "He is killing my baby." When the officers entered the apartment, it was in darkness. Misha was found lying in his crib, naked and soaking wet, and screaming loudly. The Respondent was found lying on his own bed. The trial judge regarded the red marks on the baby's back, buttocks and thighs as transient, and insufficient to constitute bodily harm. These marks had been caused by 7 or 8 slaps which the Respondent admitted he had administered to the baby to punish him for crying. The year-old baby was crying, Judge Hachborn found, because he was terrified, having been held by his mother while she was assaulted, and then dropped on the floor twice by the Respondent, causing an unintentional injury to the baby's forehead, before the Respondent

stripped the child and hit him. The learned trial judge found that the force used by the Respondent exceeded what was reasonable in the circumstances, and rejected the "correction" defence under s. 43 of the *Criminal Code* on which the defence had relied.

The Respondent's Circumstances

9. At the urging of defence counsel, the Court declined to order the pre-sentence report sought by the Crown. In submissions, however, reference was made to the Respondent's testimony concerning his background. The Respondent was 44 years old, having been born on March 1, 1944. He was raised and educated in the Toronto area, and had worked in the advertising business for a lengthy period.

Reference:
Submissions by defence counsel, *Transcript*, Tab B, p. 66, 11.5–14

10. The Respondent's criminal record at the time of sentencing consisted of convictions on March 1, 1988 for 8 counts of making false statements in unemployment insurance claims for which he was sentenced to a fine of $200 for each count, and probation for one year including restitution in the amount of $2,985. At the time he committed the assaults, the Respondent had received a summons in respect of the fraud charges, which dated back to 1982 and 1983, but was not subject to any bail order.

Reference:
Submissions of defence counsel, *Transcript*, Tab B, p. 87, 1.13–p. 88, 1.10; Tab C, p. 55, 11.7–12
Exhibit 31, *Appeal Book*, pp. 123–28

11. Reference was made by defence counsel to the amount of media coverage which the case had attracted, and which had adversely affected the Respondent's business and resulted in his "public humiliation." After the charges, the Respondent's income was drastically reduced. Since April 1988, the Respondent had been collecting welfare, and shortly after, he moved to a shared townhouse in Don Mills. The Crown referred to the Respondent's "rather checkered financial past," specifically pointing to the unemployment insurance fraud, and referred to the fact that Ms. Sidorova was also on welfare and was solely supporting the child without any help from the Respondent. Defence counsel submitted that "... Mr. Inwood has truly suffered enough with his unfortunate error on that day ..."

Reference:
Submissions by defence counsel, *Transcript*, Tab B, p. 66, 1.2–p. 68, 1.16; p. 76, 11.10–20; p. 77, 11.11–12
Submissions by the Crown, *Transcript*, Tab C, p. 15, 1.30–p. 16, 1.7; p. 107, 11.3–10

12. Medical evidence was called by the defence on sentencing. Dr. Beairsto, a family practitioner who gives counselling and psychotherapy, testified that he had seen the Respondent on a frequent basis during the year between the offences and the sentencing. He also stated that the Respondent attended the Addiction Research Foundation between September and December 1987. The Respondent was described by the doctor as a "classic alcoholic with a short fuse and full of frustration" who had been responding well to treatment. In addition to his taking antabuse, the Respondent had become more honest, tolerant, and aware of his "triggers" and "frustration points." The doctor's assessment was that he was "generally contrite" and anxious to re-establish contact with his son. While he did not consider the Respondent "cured," he thought he had made progress and that a repetition of the conduct was unlikely as long as he did not drink and remained in therapy.

Reference:
Evidence of Dr. Beairsto, Tab D, p. 164, 1.5–p. 165, 1.20; p. 166, 11.10–24; p. 176, 11.3–30; p. 180, 11.5–15

13. The Respondent was not regarded by the doctor as more manipulative than most other alcoholics. The assaultive behaviour was attributed to the history of "dysfunctional relationships" the Respondent had had with women which had bred anger and frustration, and it was observed that his relationship with his parents and family had also been "dysfunctional." With respect to the violence which occurred when the Respondent had not been drinking, the doctor referred to the phenomenon of the "dry drunk" who displays rage, anger and frustration even when sober.

Reference:
Evidence of Dr. Beairsto, Tab D, p. 171, 11.10–26; p. 173, 11.11–15; p. 174, 1.18–p. 175, 1.11

14. It was accepted at trial that there would be no reconciliation between the Respondent and his wife. Defence counsel in his argument related his statement that "they are enemies for the rest of their lives" and that Ms. Sidorova would not be returning to the Respondent to the issue of individual or specific deterrence. Mr. Greenspan also agreed with the Crown's suggestion that any probation order should include a condition that he have no contact with Ms. Sidorova except through counsel, and also that he have no contact with the child except in accordance with a family court order.

Reference:
Submissions by defence counsel, *Transcript*, Tab B, p. 49, 11.18–30; p. 49, 11.20–24

The Respondent's Character

15. The Crown asserted that the assault on Tanya Sidorova was not out of character for the Respondent, and that it was not an isolated incident. The defence expressly refused to admit or dispute that assertion. Stating his view that the general character of an accused was always in issue on sentencing, the learned trial judge permitted the Crown to make allegations concerning the Respondent's character and, since they were not accepted by the defence, to call evidence in support of those allegations. The evidence called by the Crown is summarized chronologically as follows.

Reference:
Submissions by Crown, *Transcript*, Tab B, p. 11, 11.25–27; p. 23, 11.14–27; p. 60, 11.27–28; Tab C, p. 16, 11.24–25; p. 89, 11.18–23; p. 93, 11.15–20; p. 100, 11.17–30
Submissions by defence counsel, *Transcript*, Tab B, p. 16, 11.9–15; p. 19, 11.15–22; Tab C, p. 51, 11.15–26
Ruling of the trial judge, *Transcript*, Tab C

16. Denise Loader testified that in 1969 or 1970 when she was 16 or 17 years old, she kept a horse at the same farm in North Toronto where the Respondent and his then wife, Dianne, also had a horse. With defence counsel agreeing that hearsay was admissible at that stage of the proceedings, she testified that the Respondent's wife, whom she had observed in a very distressed state, had told her that the Respondent had on two occasions "beaten her up." One day, the Respondent approached Ms. Loader, wanting to know what it was that his wife had told her. He did not appear to be under the influence of alcohol at the time. When she refused to tell him, fearing that he would beat his wife again, the Respondent grabbed the girl by the shirt and started shaking her very hard. The Respondent then struck her head with his hand and knocked her to the floor. When she was down, he kicked her on her side or stomach. The Respondent then pulled her up and told her that if she told anyone about this, he would kill her. Ms. Loader testified that she was terrified and made no complaint because she was afraid it would get back to the Respondent.

Reference:
Evidence of D. Loader, Tab D, p. 4, 1.7–p. 8, 1.15; p. 9, 11.18–21; p. 10, 11.7–21

17. Jackie MacMillan was involved in a relationship with the Respondent from December 1971 until October 1974, living with him both in Vancouver and the Toronto area. In her evidence she described a number of episodes of assaultive behaviour during that period. One of the more serious incidents was when the Respondent chased her after she tried to calm him down when he was kicking sick and dead calves. She took refuge in a car, and he proceeded to kick the car and then smash the front passenger window before she was able to escape. On another occasion, when she declined a sexual act sought by the Respondent, he grabbed her, shoved her outside although she was naked, and locked her out despite the cool fall night. At a different time, when the Respondent objected to her having stayed with a female friend while he was away overnight, he struck her near her ear, knocking her to the floor. The final incident that led to Ms. MacMillan's departure was when the Respondent, evidently angry because water for animals in a barn was frozen, grabbed her by the shoulders and shook her before she was able to get away. Ms. MacMillan testified that the Respondent drank very little when she knew him, and that alcohol was not a factor in the violence at that time.

Reference:
Evidence of J. MacMillan, Tab D, p. 144, 11.8–30; p. 147, 11.3–15; p. 148, 1.28–p. 150, 1.29; p. 152, 11.20–27; p. 155, 11.14–30; p. 156, 1.28–p. 157, 1.8

18. For a period of time in 1979, Pamela Stagg was engaged to marry the Respondent. She had met him at the advertising agency where they worked, and initially he was generous and treated her well. The Respondent, however, became very possessive and short-tempered, and they sought counselling together. After one such session, the Respondent became enraged by a trivial comment she made, and hit her on both sides of her face with an open hand. When she put up her hands to block the blows, he grabbed both her arms in one hand and continued to beat her. When she started to scream, he put his hand over her mouth and cut her gum. The Respondent then pushed her to the floor with sufficient force to cause a whiplash injury for which she received medical treatment. Her other injuries were lacerations and bruises.

Reference:
Evidence of P. Stagg, Tab D, p. 125, 1.7–p. 126, 1.18; p. 128, 1.4–p. 130, 1.23; p. 133, 1.25–p. 134, 1.17

19. Ms. Stagg testified that she laid a charge against the Respondent, although the justice of the peace told her that domestic assaults were clogging the courts and they did not want any more such charges. She eventually withdrew it, however, as a result of pressure from her friends and family. Attempts at reconciliation were made until October 1979, during which time the Respondent saw a psychiatrist who told Ms. Stagg that it was unlikely that the Respondent would repeat his conduct. In an effort to allay Ms. Stagg's fears, the Respondent told her that he had only beaten a woman once before, telling her that he had "beaten the shit out of his first wife" when he suspected her of infidelity. In the late stages of Ms. Stagg's relationship with the Respondent, he made threats to harm and "crucify" her on a regular basis.

Reference:
Evidence of P. Stagg, Tab D, p. 132, 1.25–p. 133, 1.18; p. 134, 1.20–p. 135, 1.25

20. Christine Smith dated the Respondent during the summer of 1981, and was subjected to various incidents of verbal and physical abuse. On a group vacation in the Caribbean, she suffered from severe sea sickness, which led the Respondent at a restaurant to call her a "fucking bitch," screaming that she was ignoring him and spoiling his trip. When back on board the boat, the Respondent had to be restrained when he "went for" her, and she was taken to stay elsewhere for her own safety. She was determined to terminate the relationship after they returned to Toronto, but the Respondent phoned her to arrange a meeting at his apartment to discuss his "problem," telling her that he was going to Alcoholics Anonymous and that "things were going to change."

Reference:
Evidence of C. Smith, Tab D, p. 27, 11.25–30; p. 33, 1.10–p. 34, 1.12; p. 37, 11.5–20

21. When the Respondent found her in his apartment for the arranged meeting, he accused her of trespassing and threatened to call the police. When she went to leave, he threw her over the sofa and threw her shoes over the balcony. He grabbed Ms. Smith by the arms and pushed her hard against the walls, and onto the sofa and chairs. While continuing to yell and scream at her, the Respondent threw her around for a period she estimated to have been about two hours, and he would not let her have her car keys to leave. There was no indication that the Respondent had been drinking on this occasion.

Reference:
Evidence of C. Smith, Tab D, p. 38, 1.5–p. 41, 1.5

22. After telling Ms. Smith that her problem was that she had not been spanked enough as a child, the Respondent put her over his knee and hit her hard with an open hand and then a closed fist. He then grabbed her and pushed her onto the bed where he straddled her and started to strangle her. She testified that he squeezed her neck so hard it was difficult to breathe. When she broke away, he grabbed her around the mouth with his hand. He let go when she bit into his hand as hard as she could. As she rolled off the bed he grabbed her wrist with enough force to break her watchband, slitting her wrist and causing it to bleed.

Reference:
Evidence of C. Smith, Tab D, p. 42, 1.15–p. 44, 1.25

23. The Respondent tore the phone out of the wall after stating that he wanted to phone the police to have Ms. Smith charged with assault. He caught up to her as she ran toward the front door. He then opened the door and "heaved" her out so that she "smashed" into the door of the apartment across the hall. An officer who attended retrieved her belongings from the Respondent's apartment; she found that the Respondent had poured orange juice and coffee on the things in her bag and torn up the contents of her wallet. Ms. Smith's injuries consisted of bruises to her neck, arms and buttocks, which lasted for about a week and a half. Although the police advised her to lay charges, she was concerned that the matter might reflect poorly on her judgment and affect her career prospects, and decided against doing so. Subsequent to the incident, the Respondent continued to harass her, calling her at all hours, as well as calling her parents and her employer, visiting her at work, and threatening to "get her."

Reference:
Evidence of C. Smith, Tab D, p. 45, 1.5–p. 47, 1.24; p. 48, 1.5–p. 51, 1.8; p. 53, 1.5–p. 54, 1.25
Evidence of D. Robitaille, Tab D, p. 105, 11.3–6

24. The final witness called by the Crown was Dianne Tilley, who testified that in the winter of 1986 she joined a club called Shipmates, which had been founded by the Respondent to arrange sailing outings. In addition to an $80 initiation fee, she paid $189 to Mr. Inwood towards a trip to Chesapeake Bay. When she was unable to contact the Respondent to confirm the travel arrangements, she caught up with him at his office to demand her money back. He rushed outside and she followed him. The Respondent angrily shouted obscenities at her and threatened to punch her in the face, raising his hand

to her. Frightened by his stance and his rage, she retreated.

Reference:
Evidence of D. Tilley, Tab D, p. 115, 11.12–22; p. 119, 1.20–p. 120, 1.30

The Positions of the Parties in Provincial Court

25. While defence counsel acknowledged the heightened public awareness of domestic violence and abuse of children, as well as the primary importance of deterrence in such cases, he referred to a number of considerations which, it was submitted, could properly be regarded as mitigating factors:

(a) the Respondent had been drinking, and alcohol played a role in the commission of the offences;
(b) the assault which occurred after a quarrel was of short duration and resulted in only "minimal" bodily harm to Ms. Sidorova;
(c) the Respondent had already suffered significant non-penal sanctions in terms of his public humiliation and business losses;
(d) the Respondent's wife was not the typical helpless "battered wife";
(e) there was no continuing relationship between the Respondent and his wife that would make specific deterrence a relevant consideration;
(f) the Respondent had taken steps to deal with his alcohol and anger control problems.

While the thrust of the defence submissions was to probation as the appropriate disposition, his review of the authorities led him to submit that if a custodial sentence was imposed, it should be of short duration.

Reference:
Submissions by defence counsel, *Transcript*, Tab B, p. 70, 11.12–21; p. 74, 11.5–6; p. 75, 11.7–8; Tab C, p. 34, 11.15–20; (a) Tab B, p. 50, 1.16, p. 76, 1.7; (b) Tab B, p. 55, 11.25–30; p. 72, 11.8–15, p. 90, 11.20–30; p. 92, 11.6–8; Tab C, p. 69, 11.10–25; p. 73, 11.20–21; (c) Tab B, p. 66, 1.2–p. 68, 1.16; p. 76, 1.10–p. 77, 1.12; (d) Tab B, p. 55, 11.5–20; p. 56, 11.14–26; p. 72, 1.29–p. 73, 1.19; (e) Tab B, p. 49, 11.19–30; (f) Tab E, p. 13, 1.22–p. 16, 1.25; Tab E, p. 23, 11.20–30; p. 20, 11.20–30

26. In submitting that a denunciatory sentence involving a "substantial period of incarceration" was required, the Crown identified a number of matters as relevant considerations:

(a) the recent increase in the maximum penalties for assault and assault causing bodily harm as indicative of Parliament's increased concern with offences of violence;
(b) the victims, one a helpless child and the other a completely dependent wife, were members of particularly vulnerable classes deserving special protection from the courts;
(c) the breach of trust inherent in the assault upon the child;
(d) the lack of remorse demonstrated by the Respondent;
(e) the absence of any provocation;
(f) the obvious trauma resulting from the offences being as significant as the actual physical injuries;
(g) the case involved multiple assaults against multiple victims;
(h) the fact that the assaults were not isolated acts out of character for the Respondent.

Reference:
Submissions by the Crown, *Transcript*, Tab C, p. 27, 11.10–20; (a) p. 5, 11.8–10; p. 5, 11.20–30; p. 6, 11.8–15; (c) p. 18, 11.7–10; (d) p. 22, 1.10–p. 23, 1.5; (e) p. 16, 11.13–14; (f) p. 21, 11.13–16; (g) p. 27, 11.8–9; (b) Tab B, p. 23, 11.14–18; Tab E, p. 35, 11.3–10

The Trial Judge's Reasons for Sentence

27. In brief reasons, Judge Hachborn accepted the evidence of the women called by the Crown on sentencing, and found that the accused's character was such that he was abusive to women. He described the Respondent in terms of a "sick mind" and a "twisted personality." At the same time, the learned trial judge made it clear that he was not sentencing the Respondent for the offences disclosed by the evidence of the women, and stated that he would not make the Respondent "a scapegoat for all battered women." In suspending sentence on the assault causing bodily harm to his wife, the trial judge did not include in the probation order any conditions concerning contact with either victim. The only jail term was 30 days for the assault on the baby, described as "helpless, defenceless" and "terrified by what was going on around him and by what was done to him by his father."

Reference:
Reasons for Sentence, *Transcript*, Tab F, p. 193, 1.7–p. 195, 1.18

ISSUES AND LAW

The Position of the Appellant

28. It is respectfully submitted that the non-custodial sentence imposed for the assault causing bodily harm to the Respondent's wife was not a fit sentence in that it failed to adequately reflect the gravity of the offence, the need for societal denunciation, and the primary importance of general and specific deterrence when dealing with such offences of violence, particularly where injury has resulted. Although the Crown at trial focussed on totality in her submission that a substantial custodial sentence was required, rather than submitting that each offence called for a consecutive jail term, it is respectfully submitted that for the assault causing bodily harm to his wife, the Respondent ought to have received a period of imprisonment to be served consecutively to the sentence imposed in respect of the second count.

29. It is further respectfully submitted that in the circumstances of the case the 30-day sentence imposed for the assault on the baby was unduly lenient and constituted an unfit sentence.

The Need for Guidance from the Court of Appeal

30. It is respectfully submitted that there is a discernible need for this Honourable Court to provide a clear authoritative statement of the relevant sentencing principles for the guidance of trial courts dealing with so-called "lesser" domestic assaults. It is conceded that the suspended sentence granted in this case by the learned trial judge was not an exceptional disposition. While sentences imposed in such cases are not frequently reported, it is accepted that fines, probation and even discharges are routinely granted in cases involving wife-battering.

> *Reference may be made to*:
> Spousal Assault in Ontario — 1986: Statistical Highlights, (Ontario Police Commission)
> Linda MacLeod, *Battered But Not Beaten ... Preventing Wife Battering in Canada* (Canadian Advisory Council on the Status of Women, 1987), p. 84
> *Canadian Sentencing Digest*, "assault" and "assault causing bodily harm" domestic violence cases (1987-present)
> K.L. Campbell, "Sentencing in Cases involving Domestic Violence" (December 1986)

31. While it has long been recognized that in ordinary circumstances a custodial sentence should be avoided where practicable in the case of a first offender, the Court of Appeal has repeatedly asserted that in cases of serious offences involving violence to the person, that principle must yield to the principle of general deterrence. This Honourable Court appears not to have specifically stated that that principle applies equally to domestic assaults.

> *Reference may be made to*:
> R. v. Trask (1974), 28 C.R.N.S. 321 (Ont. C.A.)
> R. v. Denault (1981), 20 C.R. (3d) 154 (Ont. C.A.)

32. It is also submitted that this Court has viewed general deterrence in its "widest sense":

> The sentence by emphasizing community disapproval of an act and branding it as reprehensible has a moral or educative effect and thereby affects the attitude of the public. One then hopes that a person with an attitude thus conditioned to regard conduct as reprehensible will not likely commit such an act.

There appears not to have been explicit recognition by the Court of Appeal that general deterrence in that sense has particular application to spousal violence.

> *Reference may be made to*:
> R. v. Ramdass (1982), 2 C.C.C. (3d) 247 (Ont. C.A., per Zuber J.A. at p. 249)

33. It is to be noted, however, that the Ontario Court of Appeal has asserted, albeit in the context of a very serious case that has perhaps enabled it to be readily distinguished from more commonplace domestic assaults, "the necessity of general deterrence in cases involving callous and repeated acts of violence against a vulnerable victim belonging to a class requiring this court's protection."

> *Reference may be made to*:
> R. v. Petrovic (1984), 13 C.C.C. (3d) 416, 41 C.R. (3d) 275, (Ont. C.A., per Lacourcière J.A. at p. 430 C.C.C., p. 291 C.R.)

34. Similarly, this Honourable Court has stated what, it is submitted, should be accepted as the governing principle in all cases of domestic violence, and not merely in those where permanent, life-threatening injuries have been inflicted:

> ... This court has a duty to make it clear that however unhappy a spouse may be about his or her marital life, and however great the marital stress may become, resorting to violence is not the answer. The sanctions for violence will be very severe.

Again, however, the extreme facts of that case, despite the general language used, may have led to its being considered of limited authority in less serious cases.

> *Reference may be made to*:
> R. v. *Glen* (1983), 1 O.A.C. 212 (Ont. C.A., per Howland C.J.O. at p. 214)

35. It is further submitted that the Court of Appeal has recently made observations of the frequency of sexual assaults, although no statistical or comparable materials had been presented, and affirmed the Court's sensitivity to public concern with such offences. The sentence of imprisonment for sexual assault in the case in question was substantially increased on the basis that although consideration had to be given to rehabilitation and individual deterrence, the sentence imposed at trial had failed to give sufficient weight to the element of general deterrence.

> *Reference may be made to*:
> R. v. *Glassford* (1988), 42 C.C.C. (3d) 259, 63 C.R. (3d) 209 (Ont. C.A., per Brooke J.A. at pp. 265–6 C.C.C., p. 215 C.R.)

36. In a different context, the Court of Appeal has made what amounted to a pronouncement of policy expressly intended to alter existing sentencing practices. In a case of criminal negligence causing death, this Court took the opportunity to assert as a matter of principle that the sentences for "the so-called lesser (drinking and driving) offences" should be increased:

> Increasing sentences for offences at the "lower end" would emphasize that it is the conduct of the accused, not just the consequences, that is the criminality punished ... The public should not have to wait until members of the public are killed before the courts' repudiation of the conduct that led to the killing is made clear.

> *Reference may be made to*:
> R. v. *McVeigh* (1985), 22 C.C.C. (3d) 145 C.R. (Ont. C.A., per MacKinnon A.C.J.O. at p. 150)
> R. v. *Gardner* (Ont. C.A., October 11, 1988, as yet unreported)

37. While most cases involving domestic violence which have reached this Court appear to have been very serious cases in which the violence had resulted in death or serious physical harm, it is submitted that the problem of spousal assault is so widespread and the concern of the public so great that a similar attack on the so-called "lesser" such offences is required to appropriately repudiate the conduct and to effect general deterrence. The result in this case demonstrates, it is submitted, the need for the initiative to be taken at the appellate level.

The Reality of Domestic Assault on Women

38. It was stated by defence counsel in Provincial Court that "we live in this era of heightened public awareness concerning the existence of domestic violence, wife abuse and violence towards children, and no right-thinking person can do other than to deplore that phenomenon," and that "the reality of our society is that conduct like this is a daily occurrence" (Tab B, p. 70, 11.13–18; p. 74, 11.5–6). The accuracy of his observation is borne out, it is submitted, by the literature on the subject.

39. The literature discloses that domestic violence occurs throughout Canada on a very wide scale at all socio-economic levels. In one study in 1981, it was estimated that one in ten Canadian women had been assaulted by a male partner. In 1985 the same researcher estimated that 600,000 battered women had sought outside help, and almost one million women were assaulted in Canada each year. A 1982 study of 61,000 Canadians interviewed about their experiences with crime and the criminal justice system revealed 11,000 incidents of assault and sexual assault to women by a spouse or former spouse, 7,000 resulting in injury, and 2,800 of which required medical treatment.

> *Reference may be made to*:
> L. MacLeod, *supra*, pp. 6–7, 16
> Holly Johnson, "Wife Assault: The Findings of a Crime Survey," (1987), 11 Perception, pp. 5–7

40. It has been observed that an assault on a woman by a partner invariably has more than physical consequences. The victims' psychological damage has been described in terms of low self-esteem, overwhelming guilt, extreme isolation, and resort to alcohol or drugs to deal with physical and emotional pain. Similarly, the research is beginning to document the likely long-term effect of wife-battering on the children who observe it. It has been stated that boys, in particular, exposed to domestic violence are likely to have adjustment difficulties, to manifest behaviour problems, and more likely to be violent in their own marital families as adults.

> *Reference may be made to*:
> MacLeod, *supra*, at p. 33
> Debra Pepler and Timothy Moore, "The Impact of Family Violence on Children's Adjustment," Preliminary Report to the Ministry of Community and Social Services (1988)

41. While spousal assault statistics for 1986 collected by the Ontario Police Commission showed 15,507 "occurrences," leading to 7,451 charges laid that

year, studies indicate a low rate of even reporting such offences. One researcher stated that only one in six wife assaults is reported. The major reasons given for the failure to report are the fear of revenge by the offender and the victim's state of dependency being such that the victim may perceive the consequences of removing the offender as worse than further violence.

Reference may be made to:
Donald G. Dutton, *The Domestic Assault of Women: Psychological and Criminal Justice Perspectives* (Toronto: Allyn and Bacon Inc., 1988)
H. Johnson, *supra* at pp. 6–7
Ontario Police Commission statistics, *supra*

42. It has been noted that in recent years the police and the Crown have adopted more vigorous enforcement and prosecutorial policies in the area of domestic violence. A careful study of the impact in London, Ontario of the policy of the police laying criminal charges in such cases since 1981 has found evidence that family violence is reduced both at the time of the police intervention and subsequent to it. However, the researchers also reported that "many police officers who take wife abuse as a serious crime are faced with judges who may give the impression that the matter is trivial in comparison to other crimes and make the officers feel that he or she is wasting the Court's time."

Reference may be made to:
L. MacLeod, *supra* at p. 82
Peter Jaffe, "The Impact of Police Charges in Incidents of Wife Abuse," (1986) 1 *Journal of Family Violence* 37

The Sentencing Principles Applicable to Domestic Assault

43. It is respectfully submitted that in cases of domestic assault, particularly where bodily harm has resulted, general deterrence should be the paramount consideration, and the sentence should be sufficient to repudiate and denounce the conduct effectively. It is accordingly submitted that custodial sentences ought normally to be imposed. As in the case of drinking and driving offences, it is submitted that the courts should increase sentences at the lower range of domestic violence cases and not wait for death or serious harm to occur.

44. It is further submitted that there should be clear recognition that violence within the family, given the relationship of dependency and trust which exists in that context, should be regarded as even more serious than violence between strangers. The social, economic and physical vulnerability of women is a feature of domestic violence, it is submitted, which particularly aggravates such offences. It is also submitted that the extent of the social problem, and the enormous suffering caused directly and indirectly to so many members of the community, further reinforce the need for a firm response from the criminal justice system.

Reference may be made to:
R. v. Petrovic, *supra*
R. v. Glen, *supra*
Publicover v. The Queen (N.S.S.C., App. Div., June 17, 1986, as yet unreported)
R. v. Landry (1981), 61 C.C.C. (2d) 317 (N.S.S.C., App. Div.)

45. Particularly in such cases as domestic violence where victims often appear reluctant to involve outsiders, it is respectfully submitted that sentences imposed by the courts must not be so low that other victims are demoralized by a perceived lack of concern by the justice system. The public must have confidence, it is submitted, that offenders whose conduct violates core values of the community will be held accountable and will incur sanctions which reflect the nature and extent of that violation.

Reference may be made to:
Report of the Canadian Sentencing Commission, *Sentencing Reform: A Canadian Approach* (1987), pp. 150–51

46. It is not, of course, submitted that rehabilitation and individual deterrence are not also significant considerations in dealing with particular cases. Normal mitigating factors such as the offender's remorse, or evidence that the offence was an isolated incident out of character for the offender remain, it is submitted, relevant considerations in the context of domestic violence. It should be observed, however, that the parties' reconciliation or permanent separation, while a factor, should be scrutinized closely. There is a risk of coercion by an accused in a position of power. Concern about recurrence may not be limited to protecting the victim already assaulted. Moreover, it is important that there be a "public" response in addition to any "private" resolution.

Reference may be made to:
R. v. R.P.T.; R. v. T.S. (1983), 7 C.C.C. (3d) 109, at p. 114 (Alta. C.A.)

Application of the Principles to the Case under Appeal

47. It is respectfully submitted that there were no special circumstances in this case to have warranted

a suspended sentence for the assault causing bodily harm to the Respondent's wife. It is submitted that a significant custodial sentence was required, given the following factors:

(a) the primary importance of general deterrence when dealing with offences of this nature;

(b) the assault was brutal and frightening, involving repeated blows which caused actual physical injury;

(c) the victim was a member of a particularly vulnerable class, whose peculiar social isolation and dependence as a new immigrant with no friends or resources made her even more vulnerable;

(d) the assault was committed, without any provocation, in the presence of a terrified child;

(e) the offence was not an impulsive isolated act which could be regarded as out of character; rather, it was entirely consistent with the character of the Respondent who, the trial judge accepted, was abusive to women;

(f) the Respondent's attitude towards the offence did not display any remorse;

(g) prior consequences of abusive conduct and prior efforts at rehabilitation had been insufficient to provide an effective individual deterrent.

48. It is also respectfully submitted that the learned trial judge erred in failing to make the mandatory order under s. 98(1) [now s. 100(1)] of the *Criminal Code*.

Reference may be made to:
R. v. *Broome* (1981), 63 C.C.C. (2d) 426, 24 C.R. (3d) 254 (Ont. C.A.)

49. It is submitted as well that the probation ordered by the learned trial judge ought to have included, on the consent of both counsel, conditions prohibiting contact with the Respondent's wife, as well as contact with the infant victim except in accordance with any family court order.

The Assault on the Child

50. It is further respectfully submitted that while the learned trial judge appeared to appreciate, and attempted to apply, the principles which have been stated by this Court to govern such offences involving violence to children, the 30-day sentence was inadequate as an expression of the community's abhorrence of the Respondent's conduct. The assault upon the baby involved repeated callous acts by a person of violent character against the completely defenceless infant and, it is submitted, called for a longer custodial term.

Reference may be made to:
R. v. *Cudmore* (1972), 5 C.C.C. (2d) 536 (Ont. C.A.)
R. v. *Poaps* (Ont. C.A., January 27, 1982, unreported)

51. It is finally respectfully submitted that the jail term imposed for the assault on the infant should properly be ordered to be served consecutively to any custodial sentence imposed for the assault causing bodily harm to the other victim. While the two offences were obviously related in terms of time and place, they involved different victims, separate applications of force, and distinct societal interests deserving protection.

Reference may be made to:
R. v. *Gummer* (1983), 38 C.R. (3d) 46 (Ont. C.A.)
R. v. *Prince* (1986), 30 C.C.C. (3d) 35 at p. 54 (S.C.C.)

ORDER REQUESTED

52. It is respectfully submitted that leave to appeal should be granted and the appeal allowed, with the imposition of substantial consecutive custodial sentences in respect of each offence, the addition of non-association conditions to the probation ordered, and the mandatory order prohibiting possession of firearms.

ALL OF WHICH is respectfully submitted by,

_____

DAVID A. FAIRGRIEVE

_____

DON STUART
Of Counsel for the Applicant/Appellant

R. v. Inwood[†] (Respondent's Factum)

RESPONSE TO APPELLANT'S ISSUES

Introduction

7. The Attorney General concedes that the sentences imposed in this case were within the range of sentences imposed for like offences by like offenders. However, the Appellant argues for a fundamental re-evaluation of the sentence range for domestic assault in much the same way that this honourable Court raised the "tariff" for serious offences involving drinking and driving in *Regina* v. *McVeigh* (1985), 22 C.C.C. (3d) 145 (Ont. C.A.).

It is respectfully submitted that this raises two core issues:

  i. Has the Appellant met the burden of proof that increased sentences for crimes of domestic violence are required.
  ii. If so, is the sentence imposed on the Respondent so low as to require intervention by this Honourable Court.

8. It is respectfully submitted that the Appellant puts its case for increased terms of imprisonment on the following basis:

(1) The paramount principle is general deterrence, the courts should increase sentences at the lower range of domestic violence cases and not wait for death or serious harm to occur. [Appellant's Factum para. 43]
(2) Victims and the police are demoralized by the low sentences imposed and will not report the offence or respond to it. [Appellant's Factum para. 41, 45]
(3) Domestic violence is more serious than assaults on strangers. [para. 44]
(4) Normal mitigating factors must be more closely scrutinized than in other cases. [Appellant's Factum para. 46]

9. It is respectfully submitted that the Appellant has failed to make out a case for heavier sentences of *imprisonment* on any of the bases alleged.

General Deterrence

9. [*sic*] It is respectfully submitted that in *Regina* v. *McVeigh, supra* the case for a change of sentencing policy was made out on the basis that lesser sentences and emphasis on individual deterrence and rehabilitation had not adequately dealt with the serious problem of death and injury caused by drinking and driving:

> Members of the public when they exercise their lawful right to use the highways of this province should not live in the fear that they may meet with a driver whose faculties are impaired by alcohol. It is true that many of those convicted of these crimes have never been convicted of other crimes and have good work and family records. It can be said on behalf of all such people that a light sentence would be in their best interests and be the most effective form of rehabilitation. *However, it is obvious that such an approach has not gone any length towards solving the problem*. In my opinion, these are the very ones who could be deterred by the prospect of a substantial sentence for drinking and driving if caught. General deterrence in these cases should be the predominant concern, and such deterrence is not realized by over-emphasizing that individual deterrence is seldom needed once tragedy has resulted from the driving. [emphasis added]

Regina v. *McVeigh, supra* at page 150

10. Superficially it may appear that a similar statement might be made about domestic violence in view of the evidence of its very high incidence. However, it is respectfully submitted that such an approach is overly simplistic and fails to come to grips with the real causes of the high incidence of domestic violence and the impact of the entire criminal justice structure. Put another way, the Courts should not too readily jump to the conclusion that they have failed in their duty to protect the public, including battered women, or that increased sentences of imprisonment would solve the problem. In fact, as will be demonstrated *infra*, a policy of increased use of imprisonment may have unintended consequences which are inconsistent with the protection of the public, especially the victim and her children.

[†] Filed at the Ontario Court of Appeal.

The High Incidence of Abuse and Confidence in the Criminal Justice System

11. The thrust of the empirical research referred to in the Appellant's Factum is on the battered woman. While there are cases of single assaults by husbands with violence never to recur, the problem of domestic violence and battered women is a problem of repeated assaults of increasing severity, what Dr. Lenore Walker refers to as the cycle theory of violence. While individual isolated assaults are to be deplored they are most likely a response to particular situations and therefore relatively unresponsive to theories of general deterrence and thus increased punitive sentences on others. Moreover, an attempt to focus on these isolated events would divert attention from the real problem which, as indicated above, is the problem of repeated and escalating violence.

> Walker, L.E., *The Battered Woman* (1979), (Harper and Row Publishers, New York) especially Chapter 3 "The Cycle Theory of Violence"

12. Therefore it is respectfully submitted that the focus of the discussion of the impact of general deterrence must be on deterring the repeated and escalating violence — breaking the cycle of domestic violence. It is the submission of the Appellant in its factum that the "courts should increase sentences at the lower range of domestic violence cases and not wait for death or serious harm to occur." However, as Dr. Walker and other researchers have demonstrated, cases of death or serious harm, except in rare instances, do not occur spontaneously. They are the product of attacks of ever increasing severity. Therefore, the case for increased punitive sentences for the "lower range of sentences" must be put on the basis that such sentences are necessary to break the cycle of violence.

13. It is respectfully submitted that to determine whether increased punitive sentences would deter the battering of women, the courts must understand why the violence continues. Obviously, an important reason why the violence continues is that it is not brought to the attention of the criminal justice system and/or the victim remains with the offender. However, it is respectfully submitted that it is unfair and misleading to state that non-punitive sentences have failed to deter domestic violence and it is respectfully submitted that there is no evidence that the problem of domestic violence would respond to increased use of punitive sentences, except in special cases involving incorrigible recidivists.

14. It is respectfully submitted that research has identified a number of factors which help to explain why the violence continues, why assaults are not reported and why women continue to reside with the offender despite his assaultive behaviour.

Some of the important factors which have been identified are:

(1) The criminal justice system screening process;
(2) Reluctance of victims to report what they consider to be a "private" matter;
(3) Lack of adequate alternatives to jail for offenders;
(4) Perceived ineffectiveness of the ability of the criminal justice system to protect the victim;
(5) Perceived lack of alternatives to remaining with the offender.

Each of these factors is discussed briefly below. The point is, however, that the criminal justice system can deal only with those offences and offenders which are brought to the courts. If there is a perception that courts have not contributed to a solution to the problem, this is because it sees only a relatively few examples of the problem. Put another way, while there is no evidence that the problem of domestic violence would respond to increased use of punitive sentences, there is abundant evidence of why other factors have contributed to the problem.

. . . .

Domestic Violence Is More Serious Than Violence on Strangers

30. The Appellant also puts its case for lengthier prison sentences on the basis that domestic violence is more serious than assaults on strangers. It is respectfully submitted that this is not a helpful approach to the problem. A single assault which causes bodily harm is equally grave in terms of physical harm whether inflicted by a stranger or a spouse. There are different dynamics which may make one offence more serious than another from a psychological view, depending on the particular victim. One reason, however, that courts have tended to treat assaults on strangers *more* seriously so that for example discharges are virtually never given in such cases, is the perception that unlike the case in domestic assault the victim had no defence. The perception was that an unprovoked attack by a stranger could never be foreseen and therefore steps [could not be] taken to avoid it. The perception was however that in cases of domestic violence the victim

knew her assailant and could usually avoid the attack and in any event since she knew her assailant somehow this made the offence less serious. The contribution made by the recent research on domestic violence is that in fact women are unable to avoid the assault even if it was foreseeable. Thus it is not a question of categorizing one assault as being more serious than another. Rather, it is a matter of not unfairly or improperly depreciating the seriousness of either.

31. It is respectfully submitted that this does not mean that cases of "wife *battering*" are not more serious than isolated attacks on strangers.

32. The Appellant in paragraphs 38 to 42 of the Appellant's Factum makes reference to statistics concerning domestic assault and "battered women" [paragraph 39]. In her study, Linda MacLeod defined "wife battering" as follows:

> The following definition of wife battering was developed by the author to better reflect the multifaceted nature of battering emphasized by shelter workers and battered women, and to incorporate the current state of our knowledge of the scope of wife battering.
>
>> Wife battering is the loss of dignity, control, and safety as well as the feeling of powerlessness and entrapment experienced by women who are the direct victims of *ongoing or repeated* physical, psychological, economic, sexual and/or verbal violence or who are subjected to *persistent* threats or the witnessing of such violence against their children, other relatives, friends, pets and/or cherished possessions, by their boyfriends, husbands, live-in lovers, ex-husbands or ex-lovers, whether male or female. The term "wife battering" will also be understood to encompass the ramifications of the violence for the woman, her children, her friends and relatives, and for society as a whole.
>
> This new definition reflects society's growing awareness of psychological violence as a central element of wife battering. *It is also emphasized in this definition, and will be repeatedly stressed throughout this book, that it is the persistence of the violence that establishes violence as battering. It is this persistence, the horror of living with the constant threat of violence, whether psychological, physical, sexual, verbal, or economic, which most debilitates the women who experience battering and which transforms so many Canadian households into prisons.* This is not to say that one single brutal assault by a man against his wife should not be taken seriously, and should not be dealt with expeditiously as a criminal assault. *However, until the violence is repeated, or until the woman is subjected to other forms of abuse by her husband or partner, this single incident will remain an assault — according to the definition just presented and used in this study — and not an example of battering. It bears noting, however, that episodes of physical violence are almost always preceded by a period of escalating psychological, verbal, or economic violence. Therefore, it is probable that such totally isolated events are rare.* [Italics added]

MacLeod, L. *supra*, at pages 16–17.

33. Much of the literature referred to by the Appellant and also referred to in this Factum must then be seen in its context. It is concerned with the serious social problem of persistent physical abuse over a period of time. The consequences of spousal abuse identified in the literature and referred to in paragraph 40 of the Appellant's Factum "psychological damage," "low self-esteem, overwhelming guilt, extreme isolation, and resort to alcohol or drugs to deal with physical and emotional pain" and long term effects on the couple's children are consequences of the persistent and prolonged abuse. This Honourable Court's decision in *Regina* v. *Petrovic* (1984), 13 C.C.C. (3d) 416 where the victim was led to suicide after callous and repeated acts of physical and verbal abuse over an extended period of time, is an example of this problem.

As Linda MacLeod noted: [page 44]

> It is after prolonged battering, as a result of the battering, that battered women begin to display certain similar psychological traits. After prolonged battering, women suffer from low self-esteem and isolation. They are emotionally dependent on the batterer, are compliant, feel guilty, and blame themselves for the violence, and yet demonstrate great loyalty to the batterer. Not only do they want the relationship to continue, they state that they are staying for the sake of the family. They believe the batterers' promises to change and they frequently believe that the violence would stop if only their partners would get the one lucky break they've always wanted.

34. It is respectfully submitted that [a] proper understanding of the distinct problem of battered women and the serious consequences of that conduct has important implications when considering the appropriateness of the sentence imposed in the Respondent's case.

35. It is respectfully submitted that the Respondent's case is not an example of wife battering. The complainant in this case, as do some other victims, following the initial incident left the Respondent, never to return. Whether or not this complainant could have gone on to become a battered wife is at this point speculative. What must be recognized

is that in this case the police intervention, arrest and subsequent court proceedings was an adequate solution to the particular problem. That is not to say that the courts and the sentences they impose do not have a role to play in cases of spousal abuse. The point is, and this case is an example, heavy sentences are neither the only answer nor necessarily the preferred option. On the other hand, as noted above, adoption of a policy of increased prison sentences in all cases of spousal assault could have unforeseen consequences inconsistent with the aims of preventing harm to the victims (spouses and children) of abuse and inconsistent with the legitimate aspirations of the victim.

> Martin, D. *Battered Wives*, 1976, San Francisco, Glide Publications, "The Victim — Why Does She Stay?" at page 75

36. As Linda MacLeod noted, faulty assumptions by well-intentioned persons concerning the nature of the relationship and the desires of the victim can have disastrous effects: [page 45]

> Unfortunately, as will be demonstrated in subsequent chapters, many of the services and initiatives which have been created for battered women and for their partners have been built on the assumption, either consciously or unconsciously, that the relationship is not worth saving and ignore or belittle the woman's hopes to save and rekindle it. The hope of the service-providers is most often to save or protect the woman as an individual or to help or change the batterer as an individual in some way. This well-intentioned, institutional hope often buries the woman's pleas for a different kind of help. It is this very basic discrepancy between the battered woman's hope and the hopes of the service-providers which renders so many of the initiatives taken inappropriate and frustrating for the women who are battered and which contribute to the burnout and despair of the sincere and hopeful people who try to help the women, their children, and their partners.
>
> MacLeod, L. *supra*, at page 45

37. To summarize, it is respectfully submitted that it is unfair and inequitable to depreciate assaults either on spouses or on strangers, especially when the result is serious bodily harm. Wife battering is more serious than an isolated assault on a stranger, or a single assault on a spouse, because it is the product of previous and persistent psychological and physical abuse. It is this pattern of previous abuse leading to the assault causing bodily harm which results in the serious consequences identified by researchers.

Normal Mitigating Factors Must Be Scrutinized More Closely

38. The Appellant also puts the case for more severe prison terms on the basis that factors such as remorse, reconciliation and permanent separation should be scrutinized carefully because of the risk of coercion. In other words the Appellant asserts that care must be taken in balancing against the need for general deterrence, statements by the offender that he will not repeat the offence and that therefore individual deterrence and rehabilitation have already been accomplished. However, it is respectfully submitted that there is no evidence that cases of domestic violence require special treatment in this respect. To the contrary, what evidence there is indicates that the fact of police intervention, court involvement and court mandated treatment are successful in the case of such offenders.

39. As regards treatment of men who batter, Linda MacLeod noted as follows: [at page 94]

> Even though not all programs accept court-mandated clients, most group leaders feel that counselling groups for men who batter can provide an effective sentencing alternative to imprisonment or fines. Some group leaders have made a conscious attempt to increase the number of referrals from the courts by informing judges of the existence of their program, and have organized workshops to help criminal justice, social service, and health service professionals develop better skills in working with men who batter.

She also notes that treatment is the preferred option from the victim's point of view: [at page 95]

> Research has repeatedly shown that most battered women want counselling for their husbands. Meredith and Conway, in a study of the needs of battered women, found that:
>
>> ... the most frequently expressed need [91% of the victims interviewed] was for professional help for their assailants. Such help can take the form of alcoholism treatment and/or counselling programs specifically for wife batterers ... Most victims do not want their assailant punished so much as they want the abuse to stop and they want their assailant helped.
>
> These conclusions are supported by the finding for the current study, reported in the previous chapter, that 81% of shelter workers felt that more battered women would want the police to lay charges if they knew that the man would be ordered to get special treatment.

40. It is respectfully submitted that research also indicates that non-punitive mechanisms such as peace bonds, easily accessible restraining orders, bail condi-

tions and other types of court orders are effective and usually respected by the offender. Further, merely holding the offender criminally accountable for the assault through prosecution has demonstrated a "remarkable reduction in recidivism" even if there is no conviction.

> Sonkin, D., Martin, D., Walker, L., *The Male Batterer, A Treatment Approach* (1985, New York, Springer Publishing Company) at pages 28–29
> Fleming, J.B.: *Stopping Wife Abuse* (1979, Anchor Books, New York) Chapter III, "The Legal System"

41. To summarize, it is respectfully submitted that there is no evidence that once the criminal justice system is involved through a police-laid information, "wife batterers" are any more or less amenable to treatment and individual deterrence than other offenders, and in fact availability of better treatment options may make rehabilitation of the offenders even more likely. In other cases, termination of the relationship is the only option, but it too is effective.

What Are the Proper Sentencing Principles

42. It is respectfully submitted that when the problems of spousal abuse, domestic violence and wife battering are properly understood it is possible to apply the appropriate sentencing principles bearing in mind the fundamental principle of sentencing which is the protection of the public.

43. It is respectfully submitted that single incidents of assault not part of a pattern of persistent and prolonged abuse of the victim, should be treated the same as an assault by a stranger. In such a case the court looks to the severity of the injuries, the length and nature of the attack, use of a weapon, permanent physical damage, involvement of other persons, psychological damage, whether the assault was provoked, the offender's prior criminal record, the prospects of rehabilitation, the impact of the offence on the offender and victim.

44. It is respectfully submitted that the case of the Respondent is such a case and therefore the proper considerations were:

 (i) the minor nature of the physical injuries;
 (ii) the brief duration of the attack (less than 10 minutes);
 (iii) the repeated blows to the face and arms;
 (iv) the lack of significant psychological harm;
 (v) the lack of any permanent physical damage;
 (vi) the lack of provocation by the victim;
 (vii) the Respondent's lack of prior criminal record [his subsequent record was for unrelated offences contrary to the Unemployment Insurance Act, 1971 not fraud as indicated in the Appellant's Factum];
 (viii) the Respondent's apparent lack of remorse;
 (ix) the Respondent's attendance for treatment to control his use of violence and alcohol abuse;
 (x) the Respondent appeared to have good prospects for rehabilitation according to Dr. Beairsto;
 (xi) the Respondent and the victim had both been reduced to seeking welfare as a consequence of the offence;
 (xii) the presence of the couple's child during the assault.

45. It is respectfully submitted that as offences move away from the single incidents of the type represented by the Respondent's case, and towards the wife-battering cases such as *Regina* v. *Petrovic, supra*, additional principles are important. Further, resort to lengthier jail sentences may be necessary as part of an appropriate sentence because the abuse has been more prolonged, the physical and psychological damage profound and the offender may be less amenable to treatment. As one researcher noted the Courts must take steps to better identify incorrigible offenders so that special sentencing for this group can be designed to reduce their recidivism.

> Dutton, D.G. "Domestic Assault of Women," *supra* at p. 142.

The Use to Be Made of the Evidence of Assaults on Other Women

46. In its Factum the Appellant seeks a greater sentence of imprisonment, *inter alia* on the basis that "the offence was not an impulsive isolated act which could be regarded as out of character; rather it was entirely consistent with the character of the Respondent who, the trial judge accepted, was abusive to women."

47. It is respectfully submitted that, assuming that the evidence of the prior incidents was properly admissible, and showed that the offence on this occasion was not "out of character" this could not justify an increased penalty. To the contrary, to so employ this evidence would be contrary to fundamental principles of justice by punishing him for offences for which he was neither charged nor convicted. This Honourable Court has already held that the sentencing court is not entitled to punish an accused for such past act. Rather such evidence has

a very limited function to assist the trial Judge in understanding the Respondent.

> *Regina* v. *Roud and Roud* (1981), 58 C.C.C. (2d) 226 (Ont. C.A.) at pages 241–2.

48. It is respectfully submitted that the evidence of other crimes was relevant only to questions of individual deterrence and rehabilitation. The evidence had no relevance where the Crown, as here, concedes that the sentence originally imposed was within the appropriate range but seeks a greater penalty on the basis of general deterrence.

> *Regina* v. *Roud and Roud, supra*
> *Regina* v. *M.B.* (1987), 36 C.C.C. (3d) 573 (Ont. C.A.)
> *Regina* v. *Luther* (1971), 5 C.C.C. (2d) 354 (Ont. C.A.)
> *Lees* v. *The Queen* (1979), 46 C.C.C. (2d) 385 (S.C.C.)

49. It is respectfully submitted that the learned Trial Judge took into account the evidence of past acts and that accordingly, the good character was not a mitigating factor. It was also apparent that as a matter of individual deterrence and rehabilitation a lengthy period of probation including mandatory treatment was required. It is respectfully submitted that the evidence of other crimes, if admissible, was therefore properly used by the learned Trial Judge.

50. The Appellant also seeks a greater sentence of imprisonment because "prior consequences of abusive conduct and prior efforts at rehabilitation had been insufficient to provide an effective individual deterrent."

51. It is respectfully submitted however, that aside from the rather vague evidence given by Pamela Stagg relating to a period of time about ten years earlier there was little evidence that any significant consequences had ensued from the assaultive behaviour or that significant efforts at rehabilitation had been undertaken and failed. Rather, it is respectfully submitted that the only reliable information was that the Respondent's year long treatment by Dr. Beairsto, which included treatment with antabuse, was the first significant efforts at rehabilitation for the Respondent, and the evidence was that this period of therapy was proving successful.

Whether the Sentence in This Case Is Inordinately Low

52. It is respectfully submitted that the sentence imposed in this case must be looked at as a whole. While it might have been more appropriate for the 30 day jail sentence to have been attached to the conviction for assault causing bodily harm, rather than the common assault conviction, the propriety of the sentences under appeal must be considered in their totality.

53. It is respectfully submitted that the important aspects of that sentence were the specific and general deterrent effect of a 30 day jail sentence imposed on [essentially] a first offender for assaults resulting in relatively minor injuries, and the provision for mandatory treatment as part of a three year probation order. The impact of the probation order was, of course, enhanced by the fact that it was attached to a suspended sentence. In the result the Respondent was not only under supervision for a three year period, but any breach of the order could lead to revocation of the suspended sentence and imposition of a jail term.

54. It is respectfully submitted that the sentences imposed in this case were not only within the range of sentences imposed for domestic assaults, but in fact were at the upper end of that range. The sentences in fact were more in accord with sentences imposed by courts in cases of assaults on strangers.

> *Regina* v. *Mills* (1984), 5 O.A.C. 79
> *Regina* v. *Newman* (1985), 10 O.A.C. 93
> *Regina* v. *Taylor* (August 5, 1982), unreported (Ont. C.A.)
> *Regina* v. *Banci and Boucher* (April 15, 1982), unreported (Ont. C.A.)
> *Regina* v. *Gibbs* (October 15, 1985), unreported (Ont. C.A.)
> *Regina* v. *Lewis* (May 26, 1983), unreported (Ont. C.A.)
> *Regina* v. *Sparks* (1985), 66 N.S.R. (2d) 253 (App. Div.)
> *Regina* v. *Durst* (1987), 79 N.S.R. (2d) 5 (App. Div.)
> *Regina* v. *Arsenault* (1981), 30 Nfld. & P.E.I.R. 489 (P.E.I. C.A.)
> *Regina* v. *Butler* (1984), 34 Sask. R. 292 (C.A.)
> *Regina* v. *Vuong and Nguyen* (1985), 35 Man. R. (2d) 315 (C.A.)
> *Regina* v. *Bottrell* (No. 2) (1981), 62 C.C.C. (2d) 45 (B.C.C.A.)

55. Further, it is respectfully submitted that the Respondent has already served the sentence of imprisonment and it would constitute a considerable hardship to reincarcerate him at this point, over three months since he was released from prison.

It is respectfully submitted that the total sentence imposed was fit and proper in the circumstances and reflects no error in principle.

ADDITIONAL ISSUES

The Respondent does not raise any additional issues.

ORDER REQUESTED

It is respectfully submitted that the appeal should be dismissed except for the making of an order under section 98 of the Criminal Code.

ALL OF WHICH is respectfully submitted,

MARC ROSENBERG, ESQ.
Of Counsel for the Respondent

R. v. Inwood†

[HOWLAND, C.J.O.:]

On September 2, 1988 the respondent (Inwood) was convicted of two offences, an assault upon his wife, Tanya Sidorova (Sidorova) which caused her bodily harm and an assault upon his infant son, Michael (Misha). While Inwood was charged with assault causing bodily harm on his son, he was convicted only of the lesser and included offence of assault. After a sentencing hearing the trial judge suspended sentence with respect to the assault causing bodily harm on Sidorova and placed Inwood on three years' probation. The probation order contained the condition that Inwood attend for treatment and/or assessment of alcohol abuse and violence toward women as may be required, according to a schedule to be determined by the probation officer. As to the assault on Misha, Inwood was sentenced to thirty days in jail to be followed by probation for three years on the same conditions.

. . . .

This court has acted on the principle that where there is a serious offence involving violence to the person then general and individual deterrence must be the paramount considerations in sentencing in order to protect the public. In my opinion, this principle is applicable not only to violence between strangers but also to domestic violence. Domestic assaults are not private matters, and spouses are entitled to protection from violence just as strangers are. This does not mean that in every instance of domestic violence a custodial term should be imposed, but that it should be normal where significant bodily harm has been inflicted, in order to repudiate and denounce such conduct. I am pointing out later that battered wives, where there are persistent or prolonged assaults, may require special consideration in determining the appropriate punishment.

In *R. v. Glen* (1983), 1 O.A.C. 212, in dealing with the appropriate sentence for a husband who had been convicted of attempted murder of his wife, this court recognized its responsibility at p. 214:

> The prime consideration in imposing the proper sentence for this offence is the protection of the public by general and individual deterrence. This court has a duty to make it clear that however unhappy a spouse may be about his or her marital life, and however great the marital stress may become, resorting to violence is not the answer. The sanctions for violence will be very severe.

In that case, the attack was a brutal one which made the wife's life barely tolerable, and almost brought it to an end. A sentence of seven years was imposed. The principle that spouses are entitled to protection from serious acts of violence must apply to all such acts, though the appropriate sentence will have to be commensurate with the gravity of the particular assault.

In considering the appropriate sentence for the offences committed by Inwood it is necessary to go to the heart of the matter and see exactly what the finding of the trial judge was. He did not accept the description of the assault given by Sidorova, as he found it to be exaggerated. One is left with an assault on Sidorova between 8:40 p.m. and 8:52 p.m. on September 13, 1987 which caused injuries to her which were not merely transitory or trifling in

---

† (1989), 32 O.A.C. 287.

nature. These included tenderness of an area of her head, a bump on the bridge of her nose and a slight swelling of the nose, a slightly swollen lower lip with lacerations inside, a small bruise at the right elbow and bruising of the inner upper arm. Fortunately, they healed quickly and there were no permanent injuries. It was conceded by counsel both for the Crown and for Inwood that the assault on Sidorova was more serious than the common assault committed on Misha, for which a custodial term of one month was imposed. In my opinion, the learned trial judge erred in failing to impose a custodial sentence on Inwood for the assault on his wife. Although of comparatively short duration, the violence to Sidorova was serious and merited more than a suspended sentence, and a lengthy term of probation in order to bring home to the public and to Inwood that such behaviour will not be tolerated. In all the circumstances, a custodial term of three months should have been imposed.

Inwood's rehabilitation was also an important matter to be considered in determining what was a fit and proper sentence. The three-year maximum term of probation was fit and proper. Due regard was given to Inwood's problem of alcohol abuse, and the need for counselling and therapy so that he could gain control over his anger and his abusive behaviour respecting women. He was required by the probation order to attend for treatment and/or assessment for alcohol abuse and violence towards women in accordance with a schedule to be determined by his probation officer.

The common assault on his helpless and terrified one-year-old baby was cowardly and reprehensible and such as to disgust any normal human being. It merited the custodial term which was imposed, even though the slapping caused only marks of a transitory nature.

I consider, however, that the assault on Sidorova and the assault on Misha could be treated as one incident, and the sentences should be concurrent. In considering the appropriate sentences I have not overlooked the fact that Inwood's conduct was such that he lost any public respect that he had, and his business suffered to the extent that he ended up on welfare.

I am fortified in my view as to what would be an appropriate sentence for Inwood's assault on his wife by the decision of the Appeal Division of the Supreme Court of Nova Scotia in *R. v. Publicover* (1986), 74 N.S.R. (2d) 23; 180 A.P.R. 23, released June 17, 1986. There, the appellant had pleaded guilty to a charge of assault causing bodily harm to his wife, and had been given an intermittent sentence of 80 days. The appellant on arriving home found his wife had a man visiting her. The appellant "went into a rage and basically was throwing her around and punching and kicked at her.... [H]e pinned her on the floor at one time and slapped her in the face and basically assaulted her ..." Her injuries comprised a contusion on the left ear, and bleeding in the left eardrum with some contusions around the left ear and left jaw, contusions of the left upper eyelid and on the right side of the neck, and right jaw, swelling over the left scalp area, contusions on her forearm and thumb, and soreness and mild swelling of her fingers. The injuries were not of a permanent nature. Macdonald J.A., in delivering the judgment of the court dismissing the appeal from sentence, stated at p. 24:

> ... In our opinion, there was absolutely no justification for this type of conduct and the actions of the appellant must be strictly sanctioned. Incidents of wife-beating appear to be more prevalent in our society than at one time believed. The courts have an obligation to show society's denunciation of such conduct by the imposition of sentences that primarily emphasize the element of general deterrence.

The court considered that the trial judge did not err in any respect in imposing the sentence that he did.

Counsel for the Crown sought a mid-range reformatory term which would be at least twelve months for the two assaults. They relied particularly on the decision of this court in *R. v. Petrovic* (1984), 4 O.A.C. 29; 13 C.C.C. (3d) 416, where a sentence of two years was imposed. In that case, the appellant, who had remarried his former wife after a separation of ten years, was convicted of assault causing bodily harm. He verbally abused his wife repeatedly at the apartment of friends for allegedly having had relationships with other men during their separation and divorce. While being driven home by a friend in the early hours of the morning, he assaulted his wife by pushing and slapping her across the mouth and nose with his hand, causing her nose to bleed. During a stormy ride, he continued to mishandle her. She attempted to jump out of the car, threatened to throw herself under the car and did get out and stand in the road. The trial judge found that she was in a suicidal state of mind and that the accused was aware of this fact. The appellant again repeatedly slapped his wife across the face when they reached their apartment causing her nose to continue to bleed. She asked to leave the apartment, purportedly on an errand, but he refused and continued his abuse. She had a swollen face and a bloody nose which were held to be neither transient nor trifling. Lacourciere, J.A., in delivering the judgment of the court, referred to the conduct of the appellant, at p. 429, as "callous and not an isolated impulsive act but part of a long-standing pattern of physical abuse." At p. 430, he referred to "the necessity of general deterrence in cases involving callous and repeated acts of violence against a vulnerable victim belonging to a class requiring this court's protection."

The facts in *Petrovic* are clearly distinguishable from the facts in this appeal. In *Petrovic*, there was a long-standing pattern of physical abuse which is typical of what is sometimes referred to as the "battered wife" syndrome. On the hearing of this appeal, we were referred to a considerable amount of literature respecting battered wives and the special considerations which may be pertinent to the punishment for such battering. Without attempting to characterize the distinctive features of "battered wife" cases a predominant characteristic is the persistent or repetitive and escalating nature of the violence. In my opinion, the case before this court is not a "battered wife" case in that sense. It might in time have developed into one if the relationship between Inwood and Sidorova had not terminated. Although the two assaults in question in this appeal were serious, they involved only one incident, the gravity of which did not approximate the gravity of the assault in *Petrovic*. It is a fundamental principle that the punishment must not exceed the gravity of the particular offences committed.

Having concluded that a three-month custodial term to be followed by a term of probation for three years would have been appropriate, one must now consider whether the respondent should be reincarcerated, bearing in mind that it is some months since he was released after serving the one month sentence imposed for the assault on Misha and that he has conducted himself properly during this period. Reincarceration in itself imposes a considerable additional hardship. The fresh evidence of Dr. Beairsto which was received in this appeal, discloses that Inwood is making steady progress in his rehabilitation, including reestablishing himself after suffering bankruptcy as a result of the adverse publicity from the charge. The hardship resulting from reincarceration for a comparatively short period of time would, in my opinion, be out of proportion to the deterrent effect such additional custodial sentence would have, and would be counter-productive so far as Inwood's rehabilitation is concerned.

Accordingly, leave to appeal sentence is granted but the appeal is dismissed, except that the probation order should be amended to include an additional condition that the respondent refrain from contact with Sidorova except through legal counsel, and have no contact with Misha except in accordance with an order of the Provincial Court (Family Division). Inwood's probation officer will comply with the requirements of s. 737(4) of the *Criminal Code*. There will be the usual mandatory order under s. 100 of the *Criminal Code* for a term of five years.

Order accordingly.

The Alberta Court of Appeal has taken a similar approach. In *R. v. Ollenberger* (1994), 29 C.R. (4th) 166 (Alta. C.A.), it ruled that the starting point for "domestic assaults" is the same sentence that would be imposed for an assault upon a stranger. In *R. v. Bonneteau* (1994), 93 C.C.C. (3d) 385 (Alta. C.A.), it went further and stated that the starting point sentence identified by reference to the sentence for a stranger assault should be aggravated by the breach of trust involved in assaulting a common-law wife.

However, in *R. v. McDonnell*, [1997] 1 S.C.R. 948, in a 5:4 decision, the Supreme Court held that while the provincial appellate courts can provide sentencing guidelines for the lower courts that include the "starting point" sentencing approach that originated in decisions of the Alberta Court of Appeal, they cannot categorize the failure to adhere to this approach as an error of law justifying appellate intervention. Instead, they must be able to identify an error in principle — either a failure to consider or over-emphasis of a relevant factor — or a "demonstrably unfit" sentence as a precondition to interfering with the sentencing judge's discretion.

The Nova Scotia Court of Appeal has, in a case called *R. v. Doyle* (1991), (1992), 108 N.S.R. (2d) 1 (S.C. (A.D.)), articulated important principles of sentencing for intimate femicide. Teressa Scassa, in her article "Sentencing Intimate Femicide: A Comment on *R. v. Doyle*" (1993) 16 Dalhousie L.J. 270 notes that the court in *Doyle* took judicial notice of the seriousness of wife assault, called for judges to show their "stern disapproval," and ruled that the context of an intimate relationship and the breach of trust involved must be treated as aggravating factors, such that the minimum period of parole ineligibility should be raised from 10 to 17 years.

Section 718.2 of the *Criminal Code* now designates abuse of the offender's spouse or child and abuse of a position of trust or authority as aggravating factors in sentence determinations. However, in spite of its pronouncements in *Inwood*, the Ontario Court of Appeal has yet to analyze the social facts and policy at issue in intimate femicide or to develop legal principles for sentencing attempted murder of wives. Thus, in *R. v. Edwards*; *R. v. Levo* (1996), 28 O.R. (3d) 54 at 57, the Ontario Court of Appeal refused leave to the Crown to introduce fresh evidence on appeal that "was directed towards a Crown submission that as a matter of policy th[e] court should announce a higher range of sentences for male persons convicted of the attempted murder of their wives, girl friends or other women with whom they have had an intimate relationship."

The proposed evidence discussed the use of escalating violence and murder by violent men whose partners were attempting to escape the relationship, and argued in favour of general deterrence and denunciation as sentencing objectives for attempted femicide. The proposition was rejected as "speculative": "it is simplistic to assume that the problems of domestic violence can be successfully attacked by increasing the sentencing tariffs" (at paragraph 41). This decision has been criticized by Isabel Grant and Debra Parks in a comment, "Sentencing for Domestic Attempted Murders: 'Special Interest Pleading?'" (1997) 9 C.J.W.L. 196, for failing to heed the serious concerns around the use of lethal violence against escaping women and for failing to account for the stark horror of the two attempts, both of which were committed in front of the women's children.

H. CHARTER IMPLICATIONS

As described above, under **Issues in Sentencing**, the *Charter* has been raised to challenge sentencing, most obviously with respect to mandatory minimum sentences. Section 15 has also been invoked, as the *Hebb* case illustrates.

R. v. Hebb†

[KELLY, J.:]

In August of 1987 Judith Ann Hebb was convicted of the theft of a package of cigarettes and was fined $500.00 and costs or thirty days in default. She was ordered to pay the fine before a specific date but was unable to pay it within that time and was granted two extensions of time by the court. She failed to make any fine payment within the designated time limits. After her last failure, the Provincial Court issued a warrant of committal to the effect that Ms. Hebb was committed to thirty days' imprisonment.

The warrant has not been executed and has been stayed by this court until this application to quash the warrant has been dealt with.

. . . .

In a general sense, the applicant is seeking two distinct remedies. The first is a declaration that parts of the legislative scheme contained in ss. 646 and 722(2) of the *Criminal Code* are of no force or effect. She would thus be seeking a declaration under s. 52(1) of the *Charter* that some or all of these sections are inconsistent with ss. 7, 9 and 15 of the *Charter*. Section 52(1) of the *Charter* is as follows:

> 52(1) The Constitution of Canada is the supreme law of Canada, and any law that is inconsistent with the provisions of the Constitution is, to the extent of the inconsistency, of no force or effect.

† (1989), 89 N.S.R. 137 (S.C.T.D.).

The second thrust of the applicant is that she is seeking an order under s. 24(1) of the *Charter* to quash her warrant of committal and granting her any relief appropriate because of the non-availability in Nova Scotia of a fine option program. She submits that this personal remedy should be granted her because of the infringement of her rights under ss. 7, 9 and 15 of the *Charter*. Section 24(1) of the *Charter* states as follows:

> 24(1) Anyone whose rights or freedoms, as guaranteed by this Charter, have been infringed or denied may apply to a court of competent jurisdiction to obtain such remedy as the court considers appropriate and just in the circumstances.
>
> ...

FACTS

Judith Ann Hebb is a thirty-five year old divorced lady who lives in a rooming house and whose only revenue is social assistance payments. Her monthly income from the time of her conviction to the time of this hearing was approximately $450.00 to $500.00 a month. From this amount she pays about $300.00 for rent and, as the balance is normally insufficient for her other expenses, she regularly takes many of her meals at a "soup kitchen" in Halifax.

Ms. Hebb is functionally illiterate, has no marketable job training skills, and has never been able to obtain employment.

She has a history of mental illnesses that have required treatment at the three local psychiatric facilities, most recently attending for such treatment in June of 1987. A medical report submitted to the court states as follows:

> This lady has a very lengthy history of psychiatric illness, with numerous admissions both to the Nova Scotia Hospital, to the Abbie Lane Memorial Hospital, and most recently to Camp Hill Hospital. She has been diagnosed as having a Bipolar Mood Disorder, mild mental retardation, and severe disturbance of personality. Her mood disorder has led at times to periods of severe illness, in which she becomes hyperactive, sleepless and engages in bizarre acts ...

and further in the same report:

> She has been more compliant than previously with her medication and her symptoms have been, for the most part, controlled. She continues to have major difficulties in the area of interpersonal relationships, and in her social circumstances. These result from problems relating to her level of intellectual functioning and the abnormalities of personality.

Ms. Hebb has continued treatment and is presently on medication to control her symptoms.

She was divorced in 1983 and has two children, aged eight and 13 years, who reside with their father in the metropolitan Halifax area but at an address that is unknown to her. She has not had contact with these children for the past few years.

Ms. Hebb's affidavit evidence indicates that she does not drink alcohol but smokes approximately a package of cigarettes a week. She apparently was in the process of obtaining cigarettes for herself when the theft was detected.

I make the following further findings from the evidence:

1. That Judith Ann Hebb is essentially unemployable and that there is no realistic prospect of her earning an income in excess of her most basic needs.
2. That during the relevant period, that is from the date of her conviction and sentence to the time of this hearing, she did not have the financial ability to pay the fine imposed upon her and it is highly probable that she will never have the financial resources with which to pay the fine.
3. That the nature of social assistance available in this province is such that she will not receive additional funding for the purpose of assisting her with the payment of the criminal fine.
4. Current statistics indicate that approximately 40% of people jailed in Nova Scotia provincial institutions were so committed for having defaulted on the payment of a fine. Of these admissions approximately two-thirds pay their fine and gain their release, normally the day of or the day after their committal. The other one-third serve their time in full for their default of payment of fine. The agreed statement of facts also indicates that on a review of two particular days, one in 1986 and one in 1988, 6.5% and 5.5% of all inmates in the province were fine defaulters.
5. There is no fine option program currently in place in Nova Scotia although a pilot project is planned in the near future for the Bridgewater area.

After making these findings of fact, the essential issue for the court to determine is whether a person sentenced to a fine and a period of time in jail in default of payment of that fine should be incarcerated if they do not pay that fine by reason of being impecunious and unable to pay the fine.

There are those in our society who, for reasons of principle or merely because of a stubborn nature, will refuse to pay a fine and accept incarceration in lieu of payment of such a fine. There are those as well who would seek to test or challenge the administrators of our judicial system and who fail to pay fines and hope that the bureaucracy somehow fumbles so that they are forgotten in the process. These are situations where a person can exercise a true choice as to whether they wish to pay the fine or suffer the consequence.

But no such choice exists for those who are unable to pay their fine because of a temporary financial limitation brought on by either misfortune or bad judgment on their part. As well, no such choice exists for those, such as the applicant in this matter, who are the walking wounded of our society, those who cannot now and are unlikely ever to be in a position to pay a fine of any amount in excess of a few dollars. Judith Ann Hebb comes before this court as a person without financial resources or any prospect of having sufficient resources to pay the fine which is assessed against her.

Parliament has accepted the concept that there should be an alternative method of sentence satisfaction for a person punished by a fine. This is the fine option program provided for in s. 646.1 of the *Criminal Code* and which has been implemented in a number of other jurisdictions in Canada but has yet to be introduced in Nova Scotia. In such a program a person works off a fine by earning credit for work performed, usually community service. It is argued by counsel for Ms. Hebb that the absence of such a program in this province while it is available in other jurisdictions results in her being treated differently than persons in those jurisdictions. They argue that the criminal law in that respect violates Ms. Hebb's rights to equality as guaranteed by s. 15 of the *Charter*.

In general, Ms. Hebb's counsel argue that her position is analogous to that of imprisonment for debt and submit that the courts should strike down any legislative scheme which is similar to the long ago discredited system of imprisonment for debt.

Before determining if any of Ms. Hebb's constitutional rights have been violated or if any legislation restricts her constitutionally protected rights, a review of the existing provisions of the *Criminal Code* which affect this application would be appropriate.

STATUTORY BACKGROUND

Code section 646

Ms. Hebb's original sentence was for a fine of $500.00 and thirty days in default of payment of that fine. I have no evidence whether Ms. Hebb's financial capacity to pay such a fine was considered at the time of the imposition of this sentence. The normal practice is for the court to determine whether the convicted person has the capacity to immediately pay the fine and, if not, to give them time to make such payment. Failing their making payment within such a period of time, and on application, the court may defer payment of the fine to a future date as provided by s. 646(4), (5), (6) and (11) of the *Criminal Code*.

Sections 646 and 722 of the *Criminal Code* deal generally with the use of a fine as one of the punishments for an offence. Sections 646(10) and 646(11) are of particular relevance in this matter but a full reading of the section is helpful to understand the legislative scheme within which these subsections are applied:

. . . .

Subsection (3) authorizes a term of imprisonment in default of payment of a fine imposed, which term can be for a very lengthy period depending on the nature of the offence. The maximum term of imprisonment that might have been imposed for default of Ms. Hebb's fine is two years.

Section (4) permits the sentencing court to defer payment of a fine if it is not satisfied that the convicted person has sufficient means to pay the fine immediately. It is noteworthy that the onus is on the court to make such an inquiry under this subsection. The subsection also directs the court to inquire of the convicted person whether he or she wishes time for payment or if they wish to discharge the fine by a fine option program if one has been established.

When a convicted person has been allowed time to make payment of their fine, they may return to the court pursuant to subs. (11) and apply for further time for payment. This was the situation in the present case where Ms. Hebb was twice granted for extension of time to make payment of her fine.

Subsection (10) provides that people of the age of 16 to 22 years who have been allowed time for the payment of their fines will not be imprisoned for failing to pay their fine unless "the court shall ... obtain and consider a report concerning the conduct and means to pay of the accused."

In Ms. Hebb's case, she does not fall within this age group and there is no indication that the court dealing with her matter considered any report regarding her "conduct and means to pay."

Section 722 authorizes the use of a fine and imprisonment in default where it is not otherwise specified in the *Criminal Code*.

. . . .

Charter s. 15(1) Consideration

Is There a Denial of "Equal Benefit of the Law"

In *Reference Re Family Benefits Act (N.S.) Section 5* (1986), 75 N.S.R. (2d) 338; 186 A.P.R. 338; 26 C.R. 336 (sub nom. *Re Family Benefits Act (N.S.)*) it was found that sections of the *Family Benefits Act* were inconsistent with s. 15(1) of the *Charter* because they discriminated in providing certain benefits to women but not to men. After a review of the state of the law on this subject, the per curiam judgment of the court stated at p. 351 N.S.R.:

. . . .

> It will be necessary under s. 15(1) of the *Charter* to establish that a challenged law not only treats a class unequally but also in a discriminatory manner. The burden of proof in the first instance of establishing that a law prima facie violates s. 15(1) will be on the person challenging the statute. We see no reason to distinguish in this regard between laws which fall within the listed classifications and those which discriminate on other grounds. No doubt it will be easier to establish a case under the listed classifications as laws classifying on some of those grounds will be inherently suspect. On the other hand, it may not be apparent that a law is discriminatory until the purpose and effect of the law is carefully examined.

. . . .

In *Re Family Benefits Act (N.S.)*, supra, the Nova Scotia Appeal Division also applied the constitutional interpretation provisions stated in *R.* v. *Big M Drug Mart Ltd.*, [1985] 1 S.C.R. 295; 58 N.R. 81; 60 A.R. 161; 18 C.C.C. (3d) 385; 18 D.L.R. (4th) 321; [1985] 3 W.W.R. 481; 13 C.R.R. 64. There it was specified that the approach to the definition of the *Charter* was to be a purposive one, and that the meaning was to be ascertained by the analysis of the purpose of the constitutional right or guarantee and further that the interpretation should be a "generous rather than a legalistic one, aimed at fulfilling the purpose of the guarantee and securing for individuals the full benefit of the *Charter's* protection." (page 344)

. . . .

It is therefore necessary to determine whether s. 646(10), which extends preferred treatment based on age, treats a class unequally and in a discriminatory manner.

In considering s. 646(10) of the *Criminal Code* it appears that its purpose is to provide a class of persons, those 16 to 22 years of age, with certain benefits based on age, a listed classification. It is clear that Parliament over the years has provided special criminal exemption and protection to the young. At the time of the implementation of s. 646(10) this special protection was afforded to those 16 years of age and younger. Since that date the *Young Offenders Act*, 1980–81–82–83, c. 110, has extended special criminal treatment to those aged 12 to 18 years. The *Young Offenders Act* creates a distinction in the type and degree of sentences available to be imposed on those under 18 when compared with sentences under the *Criminal Code* for those who are 18 years of age and older. That such protection should be afforded to the young in that age category is not disputed in this application.

Is it discriminatory to afford persons 18 to 22 years of age the protection of a review under s. 646(10) of the *Criminal Code* and not afford the same protection to someone 35 years of age? "Equality under the law" and "equal benefits of the law" requires that no special class of person be chosen for the imposition of special burdens nor for the receipt of special benefits. Here those over 22 are selected to be treated differently by the criminal law from those who are 21 years of age or younger.

. . . .

It would therefore appear that s. 646(10) was enacted to provide the protection of review to the young — that is, those in the age group of 16 to 22 years. Since 1959 the general federal legislative scheme for criminal enactments, voting and other general benefits appear to use the age of 18 as the "age of majority." Those over the age of 18 can vote and are considered adults in all respects and those under the age of 18 are considered "minors" who are entitled to special protections under the law through such legislation as the *Young Offenders Act*.

Other than that general information, no evidence was advanced to the court to indicate other "purposes" for the implementation of [s.] 646(10).

. . . .

Whatever the original purpose behind s. 646(10), its continued existence creates a class of individuals — those between the ages of 16 and 22 years, who are treated differently than those who are older. Although some of this class, those under the age of 18, are presumably not similarly situated to those more than 21 years of age, it is my opinion that those in the age group of 18 to 22 are similarly situated to the older class in relation to the purpose of the law. Under all of these circumstances, the difference in treatment between these two groups is discriminatory in the sense explained by the courts.

To adopt the words of MacDonald, J.A., in *R. v. Hardiman* (1987), 78 N.S.R. (2d) 55; 193 A.P.R. 55 (C.A.), this "... *unequal and unjustified application of substantive criminal law is on its face prima facie discriminatory within the meaning of s. 15 of the Charter*."

In my view the creation of a special class who are to receive special benefits under the criminal law creates a prima facie violation of a right under s. 15(1) to equal benefits of the law and is clearly discriminatory.

The unequal application of the criminal law is prima facie a breach of s. 15 and unconstitutional unless otherwise justified as a reasonable departure.

Charter s. 1 Consideration

Whether a departure from the s. 15(1) benefits of the *Charter* is reasonable and justifiable or not is a matter to be determined within the context of s. 1 of the *Charter*.

Section 1 of the *Charter* reads as follows:

> **1.** The Canadian Charter of Rights and Freedoms guarantees the rights and freedoms set out in it subject only to such reasonable limits prescribed by law as can be demonstrably justified in a free and democratic society.

The burden of proving that a distinction should be upheld under s. 1 is on the Crown as the party supporting the distinction (see *R. v. Oakes*, [1986] 1 S.C.R. 103; 65 N.R. 87; 14 O.A.C. 335; 50 C.R. (3d) 1; 26 D.L.R. (4th) 200; 24 C.C.C. (3d) 321). Here the Crown has not satisfactorily provided the court with evidence to support the imposition of a distinction between those under 22 years of age and those older. A rational basis has not been demonstrated for legislating that a 21 year old person should have a "report" or an inquiry into his or her means before incarceration for default and a person over that age should not have the benefit of such an important inquiry. Whether such distinction was justifiable in the past is not relevant to its present operation. Parliament has determined that those persons under the age of 18 years should have special protections of the law because of their age. There is absolutely no evidence to suggest that any such benefits should be extended to include those up to the age of 22.

I therefore find that the age specific phrase s. 646(10) of the *Criminal Code* is in contravention of s. 15(1) of the *Charter* and is not a reasonable limit on *Charter* rights justified in accordance with s. 1 of the *Charter*.

REMEDIES OPEN TO THE COURT

The court has two alternatives in dealing with s. 646(10) after determining that it is inconsistent with the *Charter* because it discriminates in providing restrictions on the benefits of the law based on age. The choices are to reject the whole subsection and thereby deny the review benefits to those in the 16 to 22 age category or to sever the constitutionally objectionable age references. If the latter choice was selected the courts would then be required to "obtain and consider a report concerning the conduct and means to pay of the accused" in every instance before a warrant committing a person to prison could be issued.

. . . .

Counsel for Ms. Hebb submit to the court that an appropriate remedy would be to sever the offending phrase from s. 646(10) so that that section is age-neutral and applies to all [...] persons or to make a declaration extending the benefits of s. 646(10) to the applicant personally or, alternatively, order a stay of the warrant of commitment of Ms. Hebb so long as she is not provided with the rights accorded to 16 to 22 year olds under s. 646(10).

The first consideration is whether the determination of unconstitutionality should result in a finding that the full s. 646(10) should be voided or whether the constitutionally objectionable age reference should be severed from that subsection.

. . . .

It is important that the courts not unjustifiably invade the domain which is properly that of the legislature. In following either of the alternatives above, the court will be interfering to some extent with the efforts of the legislators of the enactment. Where the result is the removing of a protection that is constitutionally encouraged — that is judicial consideration before incarceration — as opposed to the enlarging of such a protection, it is submitted that the court should favour a result that would expand the group of persons protected rather than remove that protection completely.

It is argued by the Crown that the words of the section make it clear that Parliament did not intend for this subsection to apply to all fine defaulters and to make it age-neutral would be undue interference into the arena of the legislators. I do not accept that such action in these circumstances is unjustifiable or inappropriate. Since the initial proclamation of this legislation, the *Constitution Act* has been implemented and the legislative authorities have specified in it the importance of basic constitutional rights. Section 15 of the *Charter* is legislative expression of their respect for equality and for equal benefits of the law and the court is not unjustifiably interfering into the legislative domain when it applies that *Charter* in such a way as to expand the benefits of the principles enunciated in the *Charter*. It would not be "appropriate and just in the circumstances" to deprive 18 to 22 year olds of such an important safeguard as the requirement of judicial review before incarceration.

It has been submitted that even the application of s. 646 may be effected in such a way that Ms. Hebb's constitutional rights will still be infringed. For example counsel for Ms. Hebb suggest that ss. 646(10) and (11) are both constitutionally flawed in that neither provision *prohibits* the jailing of the poor if they fail to pay fines with default provisions.

It has also been argued that the usefulness of the extension of the review right to Ms. Hebb is minimal because if the review results only in an extension of time for her to pay her fine, it is ineffectual in that she will never be capable of paying the fine. Thus, it is submitted, in "default hearings" an impecunious offender faces the continual repetition of the "default hearing." It is then argued that any remedy following a default hearing short of the cancellation of the warrant can only be a stopgap.

It is submitted in response to these arguments that a judge, upon being satisfied that he or she is dealing with a chronically poor offender, can simply decide not to issue the warrant without granting an extension to a date certain. This would remove the sword of Damocles from over the head of such an offender. Cannot the court grant an extension sine die? In such event, the onus will remain upon the Crown to take the initiative to move to a default hearing and it is unlikely that it will do so unless it is satisfied that there is some information tending to support a finding that the defaulter has the competence to pay the fine.

In any event, I cannot conclude that ss. 646 and 722 of the *Criminal Code* are incapable of being applied by our courts in a manner that does not offend the *Charter*. If Ms. Hebb and others who are similarly situated are afforded their constitutional procedural safeguards and protections in the application of ss. 646(10) and (11) by our courts, I cannot conclude that impecunious persons will necessarily be incarcerated.

CONCLUSION

Some things are so offensive to the rule of common sense and so offend our sense of propriety that there is no need for precedent of law to condemn them or requirement of scholastic constitutional principle to denounce them.

The *Charter* is a fresh but already treasured legacy that demands from our society those principles of fairness and justice which are inherent in the soul of a mature democracy.

Our Constitution enshrines a system of justice based upon a belief in the inherent dignity and worth of every individual. (See *R. v. Big M Drug Mart Ltd., supra*, page 47 *R. v. Oakes, supra*, at page 333 and *Reference Re Section 94(2) of the Motor Vehicle Act (B.C.)* (1985), 63 N.R. 266; 48 C.R. (3d) 289 (S.C.C.), at page 317.) That a person should be imprisoned only because of his or her inability to pay a fine is inconsistent with such a system.

I therefore conclude that the age-limiting phrase should be removed from s. 646(10) so as to make it age-neutral and it would thus be applied as reading as follows:

> 646(10) Where a person has been allowed time for payment of a fine, the court shall, before issuing a warrant committing the person to prison for default of payment of the fine, obtain and consider a report concerning the conduct and means to pay of the accused.

As there is not evidence that the court in the instant case "considered a report concerning the conduct and means to pay" of Ms. Hebb I grant her an order quashing the Warrant of Commitment.

The *Charter* analysis of s. 15 in this case should be read in light of *R.* v. *Turpin*, [1989] 1 S.C.R. 1296 at 1332 wherein the Court ruled that a s. 15 challenge requires discrimination, which is the imposition of benefits or burdens on individuals or groups, based on the grounds listed in s. 15 as well as "analogous" grounds: "A finding that there is discrimination will ... in most but not all cases, necessarily entail a search for disadvantage that exists apart from and independent of the particular legal distinction being challenged." In *Turpin*, an Ontario accused's argument that he was discriminated against because an Albertan would have had the option to be tried for murder by a judge alone rather than face a mandatory jury trial, was rejected. The Court found that provincial residency was not a ground analogous to the other prohibited grounds listed in s. 15; it also found that the legal distinction created did not either create or reinforce inequality of an accused not a resident of Alberta in the larger social, economic, or political context.

The Court has also moved away from the narrowness of the "similarly-situated test" for gauging discriminatory treatment in violation of s. 15 and seems willing to look at the context rather than searching for an exact comparison group: see *Weatherall* v. *Canada (AG)*, [1993] 2 S.C.R. 872, in which the Court found no s. 15 violation where male prisoners were subject to different search rules than female prisoners, discussed *infra* under **Prisons**. Case law also suggests that discriminatory intent is not required to show a s. 15 violation; rather discriminatory impact is sufficient: see *Bob* discussed *supra*, **Enforcement of the Law**.

Could Hebb succeed in her *Charter* challenge based on age distinction in light of these legal developments? What other s. 15 grounds might be argued? Consider how the imprisonment in default of payment of fines affects the poor: for example, a fine will have a different meaning for a woman living on welfare as opposed to a middle-class employed person, and it will have another meaning for a mother as well. Furthermore, consider the number of days (10) that the accused in *Bob* were ordered to serve in default of payment of a $500 fine, and ask whether such a system has an equal impact on the poor. Read the new *Criminal Code* provisions governing the setting of fines and days to be served in default of payment (ss. 734(5), 734.5, 734.6). Do they address the issues raised?

After the *Hebb* decision in March 1989, the Nova Scotia government introduced the "Hebb" bill, *An Act Respecting an Alternative Penalty to Fines*, S.N.S. 1989, c. 2, which requires offenders to file an affidavit outlining their financial circumstances in order to be considered for eligibility for community service in substitution for fines at sentencing.

Prince Edward Island has enacted legislation that precludes imprisonment in default of payment of a fine for a number of specific offences and that permits imprisonment in default only after all reasonable means of collection have failed and the judge has reason to believe that the accused can pay the fine: the *Summary Proceedings Act*, R.S.P.E.I. 1988, c. S-8 as amended by the *Summary Proceedings Act*, S.P.E.I. 1994, c. 58, ss. 2 and 6. Québec also prohibits imprisonment in default of payment of a fine except as otherwise provided by its penal code and for contempt: *Code of Penal Procedure*, R.S.Q., c. C-25.1, ss. 231, 333–48.

Ontario has not yet enacted such broad reforms, but Ontario's *Provincial Offences Act*, R.S.O. 1993, c. 31 (declared in force August 1994) provides alternative methods of enforcement (licence revocation), a formula for the number of days to be served in default of payment of fines, and a process to ensure that a hearing is held before imprisonment is ordered: s. 69. It also bars imprisonment for fine default for persons under 18 years of age and for several specific *Liquor License Act* offences: s. 69(20).

Several provinces have dealt with the issues raised by *Hebb* by following the example first set by Saskatchewan in 1975 (*The Summary Offences Procedure Act*, 1979, S.S. 1979, c. 70, s. 12) and the Yukon (*Fine Option Act*, R.S.Y. 1986, c. 66) of enacting fine option programs whereby the person can perform community service in lieu of paying a fine: *Summary Convictions Amendment Act*, S.M. 1989–90, c. 31, s. 21; *An Act to Amend the Provincial Offences Procedure Act*, R.S.N.B. 1990, c. 18, s. 46.

However, it is important to note that fine option programs do not resolve all of the issues. For example, although Saskatchewan was the first province in Canada to establish a fine option program (1975), nonetheless, a large proportion of women in the Saskatchewan Women's Correctional Centre in Pine Grove continue to be imprisoned for non-payment of fines. Also, this situation is aggravated by budget cutbacks to justice programs, such as fine option and diversion programs, as discussed *infra* under **Law and Order**. What are the ss. 15 and 28 implications of the circumstances described by Carrie Watkins below? Carrie Watkins in "Fine

Options Programs and Women in Conflict with the Law" (1989) 23 CAEFS News 6 reports:

> At the time of imposing a fine, most judges automatically order a period of incarceration to be served in default of fine payment. Statistics collected by the Elizabeth Fry Society of Saskatchewan in June 1986, reveal that 45% of the women incarcerated at the Pine Grove Correctional Centre in Prince Albert, Saskatchewan were serving sentences for the non-payment of fines.
>
> The implicit objective of imposing fines (i.e. to avoid incarcerating offenders) is at odds with its result: imprisonment of those offenders who are genuinely unable to pay their fines. The disposition is supposed to be the fine and the time in default a method by which to enforce its payment. But when offenders do not have the means to pay the fine, then the imposition of a fine is, in essence, a jail sentence and no amount of time to pay will ever result in the payment of the fine.
>
> ...
>
> The importance of the *Hebb* case lies in how it will impact upon women in conflict with the law, who, for most part are poor. Now that provincial governments may very well be forced to implement fine option programs (barring an appeal to the Supreme Court of Canada), it is hoped that women will no longer be imprisoned for fine default.
>
> But even if fine option programs were uniformly available across the country, many women would be unable to take advantage of them because of their inability to make suitable childcare arrangements. This is a legitimate concern. Again, the Pine Grove statistics are revealing in this regard: 58.5% of the inmates had at least one dependent child; 78% had more than 2 children (including non-dependent children).
>
> The Standing Committee, which tabled its report in August 1988, made two recommendations with respect to women and fine option programs: first, it urged governments to make fine option programs more widely available and, in the interim, to encourage the judiciary to use community service orders or other community sanctions in lieu of fines for economically disadvantaged female offenders; secondly, it recommended that those who are developing and funding community sanctions include appropriate provision of quality childcare so that all offenders may benefit from them.
>
> Clearly, the recommendation of the Committee must be taken into account when designing fine option programs. To date, however, the federal government has not tabled its response to the "Daubney Report" — after its chairperson, former M.P. David Daubney.†

In *R.* v. *Joe*, [1994] 3 W.W.R. 1 (Man. C.A.), the accused challenged the constitutionality of a fine option program under s. 20 when, upon defaulting under that program, administratively he could neither re-enter the program nor pay the unpaid fines (for parking tickets) in instalments and so was automatically issued a warrant of committal for over five months imprisonment. While not ruling on the constitutionality of the fine option program *per se*, the court held that imprisonment in default of payment of fines with respect to parking tickets violated ss. 7 and 12 of the *Charter*, and that the existence of the fine option program did not remedy the problem given that the program itself restrains the person's liberty, and given that default results in automatic committal, without the opportunity for a hearing.

Imprisonment in default of payment of fines also has a disproportionate impact upon Aboriginal peoples, as statistics regarding the incidence of poverty among Aboriginal peoples might suggest. In *R.* v. *Hill* (1990), (1991), 1 C.R. (4th) 45 (Ont. Ct. Just. (Gen. Div.)), warrants of committal were quashed on the basis that imprisonment should only be ordered as a last resort, particularly when the underlying offence is a liquor licensing offence. In reaching this conclusion, Judge Wright emphasized at 50–51 the context of the use of imprisonment in default:

- Between 1977–80 (prior to the implementation of the *Provincial Offences Act*), there were 15,000 arrests in the District of Kenora for public drunkenness. Virtually all were native people.
- 60 to 80 per cent of people sent to Kenora [District] Jail were there because of liquor offences.
- 64 per cent of fines for liquor offences in Kenora District were not paid. The provincial average was 25 per cent.

  ...

- 96 per cent of the sentenced offenders in the study had been jailed for fine default on liquor offences two or more times during the preceding year.
- Although native people constituted 44 per cent of the population of the District of

---

† Reproduced by permission of Canadian Association of Elizabeth Fry Societies, Ottawa, Ontario.

Kenora, 98 per cent of the fine defaulters were of native ancestry.
- Fine defaulters accounted for 71 per cent of the admissions to the Kenora District Jail.
- If all warrants of committal for default of fines under the *Liquor Licence Act* then outstanding were executed, the jail would have been filled four times over.

What sorts of *Charter* challenges might be raised to oppose imprisonment in default for an accused such as Hill?

6

Prisons and Parole

The issues facing accused persons clearly continue beyond sentencing into service of sentence in prison. Lawyers are therefore involved in a number of legal actions in this context. Some of the issues are:

- decisions by prison officials to transfer an inmate to a different institution
- availability of medical, psychological, or psychiatric treatment for prisoners
- prison conditions generally (e.g. overcrowding, visits, programs)
- freedom of religion
- prison discipline (e.g. solitary confinement, searches)
- injuries sustained by prisoners because of actions of guards or prison officials
- voting rights
- right to counsel
- differential treatment (e.g. on the basis of sexual orientation, gender, culture)

Judges will intervene in decisions made by prison authorities only if serious injustice has been committed. As Justice Dickson said in *Martineau* v. *Matsui Disciplinary Board*, [1980] 1 S.C.R. 602 at 630:

> It should be emphasized that it is not every breach of prison rules of procedure which will bring intervention by the courts. The very nature of a prison institution requires officers to make "on the spot" disciplinary decisions and the power of judicial review must be exercised with restraint. Interference will not be justified in the case of trivial or merely technical incidents. The question is not whether there has been a breach of the prison rules, but whether there has been a breach of the duty to act fairly in all of the circumstances. The rules are of some importance in determining this latter question, as an indication of the views of prison authorities as to the degree of procedural protection to be extended to inmates.

Yet these decisions shape the lives of prisoners substantially over the course of their sentences.

There are too many issues involved; to canvass all of them seems impractical. Only a few examples follow. Consider these in the context of the reality of prison conditions and the criminal justice system.

A. PUNISHMENT

Punishment in the context of prison may be formal, in that it may result from disciplining charges laid pursuant to the *Penitentiary Service Regulations*, C.R.C. 1978, c. 1251, as was the case in *Armstrong*, reproduced below. However, punishment can also be informal, as in the case of transfer or "administrative" segregating. For example, segregation may be imposed without formal charges or convictions in order to maintain "good order and discipline" or "in the best interest" of the prisoner (s. 40(1)(a),(b) of the above regulations). As is clear from the materials in this chapter, administrative segregation is frequently used with both punitive intent and effect.

DISCIPLINE

Armstrong v. Warkworth[†]

[TEITELBAUM, J.:]

This is an application for an order of certiorari made by the applicant, Terry Armstrong (Armstrong) to quash the convictions imposed by the Independent Chairperson of the Disciplinary Court at Warkworth Institution on August 16, 1988 and August 23, 1988.

. . . .

In support of the present application, Armstrong attached his own affidavit dated March 21, 1988, together with a transcript of the August 16 and August 23, 1988 hearings.

The relevant facts involved in this application can best be summarized as follows.

At the time of the application, Armstrong was an inmate at Millhaven Institution. At all material times upon which the present application is based, Armstrong was an inmate at Warkworth Institution, a medium security institution.

On July 5, 1988, Armstrong's cell, which he shared with another inmate, Ross, was searched. As a result of the search, Armstrong was charged pursuant to s. 39(1) of the *Penitentiary Service Regulations* "has contraband in his possession." The contraband was a cigarette paper containing cannabis. The charge was dealt with as an intermediary offence.

For the offence pursuant to s. 39(1), the hearing took place on August 16, 1988 before Howard Aziz in his capacity of Independent Chairperson (I.C.P.) of the Disciplinary Court of Warkworth Institution. There were present at this hearing Armstrong, the I.C.P., a Mr. Bouchard, the officer who brought forth the charge, a Mr. Haines and a Mr. Steenberg, both persons representing the Institution.

After the hearing, Armstrong was found guilty of the charge of being in possession of contraband and sentenced by the I.C.P. to "20 days OP (off privileges) and a $20.00 fine."

A second charge was brought against Armstrong. The second charge is made pursuant to s. 39(k) of the *Penitentiary Service Regulations* "doing an act calculated to prejudice the discipline or good order of the Institution."

The second charge states:

> At approximately 17:05 hours this on the 27th of July, while proceeding to supper, inmate Armstrong appeared to be disoriented. Subject was directed into the head office, into LU1 office and told to remove his sunglasses. He was very unsteady on this feet. His eyes were glassy, red and watery. Armstrong's speech was very slow, deliberate and slurred, had trouble forming his words. LU2 Flowers was notified. CX5 Eaves dispatched CX3 Kelly to escort Armstrong to 6 building. Armstrong's speech was still slurred and he staggered while being escorted to segregation. And this information to Mr. Hutchinson under 39k "does any act which is calculated to prejudice the good order of the Institution."

The hearing on this charge took place on August 23, 1988, before Mr. Aziz, the same Independent Chairperson (I.C.P.) who heard the July 5, 1988, charge of contraband. At this hearing were the applicant, Armstrong, the I.C.P., Mr. Hutchinson, the officer who brought forth the charge and two representatives of the Institution. The I.C.P. found Armstrong guilty of this charge and sentenced Armstrong to seven days' disassociation.

At the hearing before me, counsel for Armstrong spoke of a number of issues for which he is of the belief certiorari should issue for both decisions of the Independent Chairperson.

(a) The Independent Chairperson acted unfairly in denying Armstrong the right to counsel;
(b) The Independent Chairperson breached s. 11(d) of the Charter because he was not an independent and impartial tribunal;

[†] (1989), (1990), 28 F.T.R. 89 at 90–98 (T.D.).

(c) The Independent Chairperson had a bias against Armstrong's counsel and thus was biased against Armstrong;

(d) There is no evidence upon which the Independent Chairperson could have found Armstrong guilty of the charges, particularly s. 39(k) being so general as to be unfair;

(e) The Independent Chairperson failed, in the August 23, 1988, hearing to decide to refuse or allow a request by Armstrong to call a witness and thus he acted unfairly;

(f) The Independent Chairperson acted unfairly when he failed to follow the Commissioner's Directives (paragraph 33) in failing to ask Armstrong for his comments before passing sentence.

DENYING ARMSTRONG THE RIGHT TO COUNSEL

. . . .

In dealing with the issue of representation by counsel, one must refer to the case of *Re Howard and Presiding Officer of Inmate Disciplinary Court of Stoney Mountain Institution* (1985), 57 N.R. 280; 19 D.L.R. (4th) 502. The facts of the Howard case can be gleaned from the headnote on page 503 D.L.R.:

> The appellant was an inmate of a federal penitentiary, charged with disciplinary offences characterized as serious or flagrant offences contrary to s. 39 of the *Penitentiary Service Regulations*, C.R.C. 1978, c. 1251. *Prior to the hearing of the charges, the inmate had obtained counsel who appeared with him at the time of the hearing. After obtaining submissions, the presiding officer* of the inmate disciplinary court held that the inmate was not entitled to be represented by counsel. The inmate then applied for prohibition to the Federal Court, Trial Division, which application was dismissed. The inmate then launched an appeal but in the interim the [officer] proceeded with the hearing and the inmate was convicted and sentenced to forfeiture of 70 days of his earned remission. Prior to the hearing of the appeal, the inmate had served the sentence. On appeal by the inmate, held, the appeal should be allowed and a declaration issued that the appellant was entitled to counsel for the defence of the charges against him. (Italics is mine)

In this case, Thurlow, C.J., as he then was, states that there is no absolute right to counsel, the right to be represented by counsel is determined by the factual situation of the case:

> I am of the opinion that the enactment of s. 7 has not created *any absolute right to counsel in all such proceedings*. It is undoubtedly of the greatest importance to a person whose life, liberty or security of the person are at stake to have the opportunity to present his case as fully and adequately as possible. The advantages of having the assistance of counsel for that purpose are not in doubt. But what is required is an opportunity to present the case adequately and I do not think it can be affirmed that in no case can such an opportunity be afforded without also as part of it affording the right to representation by counsel at the hearing.
>
> Once that position is reached it appears to me that whether or not the person has a right to representation by counsel will depend on the circumstances of the particular case, its nature, its gravity, its complexity, the capacity of the inmate himself to understand the case and present his defence. The list is not exhaustive. (Italics is mine)

Mr. Justice MacGuigan, at pages 535 and 536 D.L.R. states:

> As I see it, s. 7 enhances the previous requirement of an adequate opportunity of answering a charge, but whether it necessitates representation by counsel in any set of circumstances can be determined only by a full analysis of the circumstances.
>
> Webster, J., in *R. v. Secretary of State for Home Department, Ex p. Tarrant*, [1984] 2 W.L.R. 613, at 635–637, enumerated six considerations to be taken into account in relation to the right to counsel:
>
> (1) the seriousness of the charge and of the potential penalty;
> (2) whether any points of law are likely to arise;
> (3) the capacity of a particular prisoner to present his own case;
> (4) procedural difficulties;
> (5) the need for reasonable speed in adjudication;
> (6) the need for fairness as between prisoners and as between prisoners and prison officers.

In the *Howard* case, there was a loss of earned remission. There was no loss of earned remission in the present case.

I am satisfied from my reading of the transcript of the August 16, 1988 hearing, where Armstrong requests counsel that the I.C.P. failed to give any consideration to the test to be applied before refusing the request. From the reading of the transcript, it is impossible to know why the I.C.P. immediately and, it seems, without any thought refused the request for counsel. Nevertheless I am satisfied he was right in his refusal. The charge is not of a serious nature, it was a charge of an intermediary offence. There was no loss of earned remission, only the sentence of "20 days OP (off privileges) and a fine of $20.00."

I am also satisfied that Armstrong never intended to have counsel present to defend him. It was only after being well into the hearing that he decided he would ask permission to be represented by counsel. I believe the I.C.P. wrong in first refusing the right of Armstrong to be represented by counsel and then asking what counsel would have to say but nevertheless Armstrong, if he had wanted to be represented by counsel, should have asked for an adjournment of the hearing in order to retain counsel or make his request for counsel at the commencement of the hearing. His request for counsel was only an afterthought. I am also satisfied from reading the transcript that Armstrong was able to defend himself. He knew enough to try to have the charge dismissed because of an error on the part of Bouchard whereby Bouchard called the cigarette paper containing cannabis a "butt toke" when the cigarette paper containing cannabis is not a "butt toke" (page 14, Motion Record).

I am satisfied that the writ of certiorari should not issue as a result of the I.C.P. refusing Armstrong the right to counsel for the August 16, 1988 hearing.

BREACH OF SECTION 11(D) OF CHARTER OF RIGHTS

> 11. Any person charged with an offence has the right
> (d) to be presumed innocent until proven guilty according to law in a fair and public hearing by an independent and impartial tribunal.

Counsel for Armstrong makes the submission that because representatives of the Institution were present at both the August 16 and August 23, 1988 hearings, and were permitted to ask questions, the hearing was not impartial nor did the I.C.P. act independently.

I do not share the view of counsel.

Section 38.1(3) of the *Penitentiary Service Regulations* specifically allows for the appointment of one or two officers of the Institution to assist the I.C.P. at the hearing. The asking of questions can certainly assist the I.C.P.

> 38.1(3) Where a hearing is conducted by a person appointed by the Minister under subs. (1), the institutional head shall designate one or two officers of the Service with major responsibilities within the institution, who had no direct involvement in the incident giving rise to the hearing, to assist that person during the hearing.

. . . .

I am satisfied that the presence of the representatives of the Institution at both hearings did not cause the tribunal to become partial nor did it cause the tribunal to lose its independency.

NO EVIDENCE TO FIND ARMSTRONG GUILTY

It is not for me, on an application for the issuance of a writ of certiorari, to place myself in the position of the I.C.P. holding the disciplinary hearing and state that I would not have found the inmate guilty on the evidence filed. I must find that a [principle] of natural justice was not followed by the I.C.P. in order to quash his decision. It would be a denial of natural justice to find an inmate guilty if no evidence is made to show the inmate guilty. In the present case, the I.C.P. was satisfied with the evidence produced by Bouchard in the first case and by Hutchinson in the second case to find Armstrong guilty.

. . . .

I agree with the submission of counsel for Armstrong that a charge under s. 39(k) of the *Penitentiary Service Regulations*, which states:

> 39. Every inmate is guilty of a disciplinary offence who
> (k) does any act that is calculated to prejudice the discipline or good order of the institution.

is very general. I do not agree with his submission that it is so general as to be unfair nor do I agree that the charge must or should be limited to *special circumstances*. I am satisfied that the authorities have a very difficult time trying to keep order amongst a large number of inmates. In order to do so, the authorities must be able to prevent an inmate or inmates from doing acts that could prejudice the discipline or good order of the institution. When an inmate, while proceeding to supper appears disoriented, is unsteady on his feet, whose eyes are glassy, red and watery and has slow, deliberate and slurred speech and has difficulty forming words, he has committed an act which he knows, being in a prison setting, would prejudice the discipline or the good order of the institution.

As I have stated the authorities of the institution must be given the right to charge inmates under this general section in order to maintain the discipline and good order of the institution. The charge is neither unfair nor illegal.

FAILURE IN AUGUST 23, 1988 HEARING TO ALLOW APPEARANCE OF WITNESS

Armstrong requested of the Independent Chairperson witnesses to prove his physical condition earlier in the day and to make proof that his cell had undergone fumigation. He was unable to make this proof through Mr. Hutchinson as Mr. Hutchinson stated he had no knowledge of this. As a result Armstrong requested the presence of Ron Grant who was the individual who did the fumigation of Armstrong's cell. To this request the I.C.P. replies "Ya" but never decides to allow Grant to be called or not to be called as a witness.

In cases where a witness or witnesses are readily available to be questioned and a request to have the witness testify is made by an inmate, the request should normally be granted if it is determined that what the witness would testify to could or would be a significant factor in determining the guilt or innocence of the inmate. In the present instance, I am of the opinion that if Ross were to have been called as a witness, his evidence would not have affected the outcome of the hearing.

. . . .

THE INDEPENDENT CHAIRPERSON ACTED UNFAIRLY IN NOT ASKING ARMSTRONG FOR HIS COMMENTS BEFORE PASSING SENTENCE

Paragraph 33 of the Commissioner's Directives states:

> At the request of the Chairperson, the officers may provide recommendations to the Chairperson on appropriate punishment. The inmate shall be given the opportunity to make submissions as to punishment before the punishment is imposed.

Section 38(4) of the *Penitentiary Service Regulations* states:

> 38(4) An inmate who is present at his hearing is entitled
> (a) to be informed of the nature of any consultation that takes place in his absence during the deliberations on the imposition of a punishment; and
> (b) to make submissions before the imposition of a punishment.

There is no doubt that the Independent Chairperson failed to give Armstrong the opportunity to make submissions as to his punishment before the punishment was imposed nor did he inform Armstrong of the nature of the consultation that took place in Armstrong's absence during the deliberations on the imposition of punishment. The respondents agree with the submission of Armstrong that the Commissioner's Directives have been held not to be law but a breach of these Directives is indicative of a breach of the duty to act fairly. Counsel for respondents submits that in neither hearing was there a breach of the Commissioner's Directives indicating a breach of the duty to act fairly.

I am satisfied that the failure of the I.C.P. to give Armstrong the opportunity to make submissions as to his punishment or the failure to inform Armstrong of the consultation in his absence does not indicate that *the hearing* that found Armstrong guilty of the ss. 39(i) and 39(k) charges to be unfair [italics in original]. The hearing can and should be considered as having two parts. The first part of the hearing is to determine the guilt or innocence of the inmate, the second deals only with the issue of punishment.

I am of the opinion that the failure of the I.C.P. to give Armstrong an opportunity to make submissions as to his punishment before it was imposed and the failure to inform on the consultation in his absence is a breach of duty on the part of the I.C.P. to act fairly.

The I.C.P. failed, on both charges, to give Armstrong the opportunity to make submissions as to his punishment. On both charges the I.C.P. failed to inform Armstrong of the nature of the consultation that took place in his absence dealing with the issue of punishment.

I therefore will issue an order quashing the punishment given to Armstrong on August 16, 1988 and August 23, 1988, for the s. 39(i) and (k) charges and will further order that, if it be so decided, to convoke Armstrong before the I.C.P. to be informed of the nature of the consultations that took place between the I.C.P. and the representatives of the Institution in the absence of Armstrong and to give Armstrong the opportunity to make submissions with regard to his punishment.

Application allowed in part.

TRANSFER

Transfer to another institution may be an additional form of punishment for inmates. However, in *Trono v. Gallant* (1989), 68 C.R. (3d) 174 (F.C.A.), the court held that transfer decisions made by prison officials are subject to the procedural fairness requirements of s. 7 of the *Charter*. In certain circumstances, a prisoner is therefore entitled to receive sufficient information and details regarding the reasons for the proposed transfer so that the allegations can be answered, although such denials of information may be justified where an informant's safety is at risk. An example of a case where the prisoner was successful in challenging a transfer decision is provided by *Williams v. Canada (Regional Transfer Board, Prairie Region)* (1993), 19 C.R. (4th) 151, where the Federal Court of Appeal reviewed an "administrative" segregation and transfer, imposed in response to the prisoner's alleged "obstructive behaviour" during a lockdown. It concluded that the denial of the right to counsel and the withholding of information from the prisoner should result in a reversal of the decision to transfer Williams to a maximum security prison.

In his book, *Justice Behind the Walls. Human Rights in Canadian Prisons* (Vancouver: Douglas and MacIntyre, 2002) [hereinafter *Justice Behind the Walls*], Michael Jackson reports that involuntary transfers are the greatest source of prisoner complaints to the office of the federal Correctional Investigator. "Involuntary administrative transfer" to and among maximum security institutions is widely used as a disciplinary measure and, according to Professor Jackson, "in a significant number of cases," is implemented based upon allegations and suspicion rather than formal charges and adjudication: see Sector 5, Chapter 1, "Involuntary Transfers: Greyhound Therapy Then and Now" at 436.

SEGREGATION

Segregation is another common disciplinary measure. Prisoners in the U.K. experienced a short-lived victory when the Court of Appeal ruled in *Weldon v. Home Office*, [1990] 3 All E.R. 672 that they retained "residual liberty" while incarcerated, thus entitling them to sue for false imprisonment when unjustifiably segregated. However, on appeal, the House of Lords rejected the argument, and instead ruled that prisoners lost all liberty upon incarceration and could only sue for false imprisonment when the officials were in "bad faith" or the conditions were "intolerable": *Hague v. Deputy Governor of Parkhurst Prison*; *Weldon v. Home Office*, [1991] 3 All E.R. 672.

In Canada, several courts have been willing to recognize false imprisonment claims by segregated prisoners: *Saint Jacques v. Canada* (1991), (1992), 45 F.T.R. 1; *Abbott v. Canada* (1993), 64 F.T.R. 81; and *Brandon v. Correctional Service of Canada* (1995), 105 F.T.R. 243 (punitive damages of $3,000, as well as $680 for nonphysical damages, plus legal costs of $1,000 awarded to the plaintiff). The court in *R. v. Hill*, [1997] B.C.J. No. 1255 (C.A.), online: QL, determined that false imprisonment would lie where the prison officials breached their statutory duty to review a segregation order on a timely basis.

The report by The Honourable Louise Arbour, Commissioner, *Commission of Inquiry into Certain Events at The Prison For Women in Kingston* (Ottawa: Public Works and Government Services Canada, 1996) [hereinafter *The Prison For Women*] at 139–40, 185–87 contains a discussion of the harmful effects of segregation, particularly long-term segregation, including "perceptual distortions such as hallucinations, affective disturbances such as massive anxiety, difficulties thinking, disturbances in thought content, problems with impulse control...," "damage in the form of cognitive impairment (e.g. concentration, memory, hallucinations) and emotional impairment (feelings of hopelessness, depression, rage and self-destructiveness)" (at 186–87). Justice Arbour made several recommendations with respect to the use of "administrative segregation," which, unlike "punitive segregation," has no maximum term or requirement of review. For some of her recommendations regarding segregation see *infra*, **Women in Prison**.

Michael Jackson's book *Justice Behind the Walls* documents the work of the Task Force on Administrative Segregation, 1996–97, convened by the federal government to respond to the recommendations of the Arbour Commission that independent adjudication and review processes be instituted for administrative segregation, or alternatively, that judicial supervision be put in place. The chapters in Sector 4 of his book examine the practices and effects of administrative segregation in Canadian prisons and document the resistance to reforms, such as independent adjudication, recommended by both the Arbour Commission and the Task Force. For further discussion of legal challenges to administrative segregation see Matthew Groves, "Administrative Segregation of Prisoners:

Powers, Principles of Review and Remedies" (1996) 20 Melbourne U. L. Rev. 639.

CRIMINAL PROSECUTION

When a prisoner's behaviour within prison violates not only internal disciplinary rules but also the *Criminal Code*, the prisoner may be vulnerable to several forms of punishment. In *R. v. Shubley*, the prisoner was first disciplined by five days of solitary confinement on a "special diet" by the jail superintendent (pursuant to Reg. 649 of *Ontario Ministry of Correctional Services Act*) for allegedly assaulting another prisoner, and was then charged under the *Criminal Code* with assault causing bodily harm. In its decision reported at [1990] 1 S.C.R. 3, the Court rejected a claim that such a prisoner had been subjected to "double jeopardy" in violation of *Charter* s. 11(h).

Madam Justice McLachlin, for the majority in *Shubley* (Justices Wilson and Cory dissenting), held that prison disciplinary proceedings were not "criminal proceedings," as their purpose was not to punish "crime" but to maintain "order." She also held that solitary confinement and the revocation of other privileges pursuant to Reg. 649 do not constitute "true penal consequences" because such measures affect only the conditions under which prisoners serve their sentences. The ambit of this decision seems to be very wide: the majority opinion suggested that none of the s. 11 rights will necessarily apply in the context of prison disciplinary proceedings because it would "make the task of those charged with maintaining order in our prisons immeasurably more difficult."

Further information about rights and remedies in the context of prison discipline can be found in A. Wayne MacKay, "Inmates' Rights: Lost in the Maze of Prison Bureaucracy" (1988) 11 Dalhousie L.J. 698; Michael Jackson, "Justice Behind the Walls — A Study of the Disciplinary Process in a Canadian Penitentiary" (1974) 12 Osgoode Hall L.J. 1; Michael Jackson, *Justice Behind the Walls*, *supra*, particularly the chapters in Sector 3 that deal with discipline; and Alan Mewett, "The Rights of the Institutionalized" in Ronald St. J. MacDonald and John P. Humphrey, eds., *The Practice of Freedom* (Toronto: Butterworths, 1979) 249.

B. PRISON CONDITIONS

Prison conditions in federal prisons, provincial jails and detention centres, and police holding cells vary widely across the country. The dangerousness of the conditions in many institutions is made manifest by deaths in custody through neglect, violence, suicide, illness, and riots. In Ontario, the conditions in provincial detention centres have been assessed as so appalling that judges have begun to reduce sentences to reflect the fact that pre-trial detention is extraordinarily punitive. For example, the Metro West Detention Centre is triple-bunking inmates in cells designed for one inmate, resulting in increased risks of tuberculosis for inmates: 53 have tested positive, and another 108 are waiting in general population to be tested. Inmates awaiting trial and sentencing are sleeping on the floors, eating their meals on the toilet, living in cells uncleaned for two months, and are untreated medically over lengthy periods of time. As a consequence of these conditions, Judge Joseph Kenkel sentenced a man convicted of theft of a car to one day of prison, counting his seven months in detention awaiting disposition as the equivalent of 24 months (instead of the usual formula of counting pre-trial custody at double time) because the conditions at Metro West were inhumane: *R. v. Krachor*, [2002] O.J. No. 2172 (Ct. Just.), online: QL.

In 1977, prisoners at Archambault prison staged a 110-day work strike to support their demands for more humane conditions.

OVERCROWDING

Prisoners have also protested conditions of overcrowding. *Mennes v. Canada* (1989), 23 F.T.R. 181 dismissed an application under ss. 12 and 15 of the *Charter* to stop double-bunking of inmates at the Kent Institution because of defects in the application. In so doing, the court directed that the institution co-operate with the inmates in terms of providing the support necessary to prepare appropriate legal documents: "the directing staff of the institution cannot lawfully plead shortage of staff as a ploy to try to thwart inmate's access to the court. It is worthwhile here to repeat that in the last analysis such access cannot be thwarted even if applications for relief have to be smuggled out of the prison or have to be made by outsiders on behalf of an inmate." The court also noted that the issue of double-bunking under the *Charter* "is a serious issue to be adjudicated" and "[i]t is in the interests of the adversaries here to see that the issue is properly presented to the court." This litigation is still in the courts: see *Sweet* v. *Canada*, [1999] F.C.J. No. 1539 (C.A.), online: QL.

The issue of overcrowding is of drastic proportions in many countries, and this condition of imprisonment seems particularly resistant to change. In 1985, prisoners in Brazil called attention to their situation by drawing up a list of who among them were to be killed by other prisoners; several prisoners were subsequently killed: Marco Vanucchi, "Changing prison" *New Internationalist* (December 1985) 275.

RIOTS

In *Justice Behind the Walls*, supra at 51, Michael Jackson describes the phenomenon of prison riots as the result of the "volatile mix of deteriorating prison conditions and rising prisoner expectations." He outlines three major riots that took place at the British Columbia Penitentiary, Laval Institution in Québec, and Millhaven Institution in Ontario, all within a few weeks in 1976. A Parliamentary subcommittee undertook a major inquiry in response: House of Commons Subcommittee on the Penitentiary System in Canada, *Report to Parliament* (Ottawa: Minister of Supply and Services, 1977) Chair: Mark MacGuigan. In spite of this work and the many recommendations made by the subcommittee, including its call for a halt to lawlessness within federal prison and adherence to the rule of law by prison officials, another major riot exploded in July 1982, this time at the Archambault Institution in Québec.

In April 1983, the internationally recognized human rights organization, Amnesty International (AI), went to Québec to investigate the treatment of inmates at Archambault following a riot in July 1982. In its report, *Amnesty International Report on Allegations of Ill-Treatment of Prisoners at Archambault Institution, Québec, Canada* (1983), [hereinafter *Report on Allegations of Ill-Treatment of Prisoners at Archambault*], AI recounted its methodology for investigation and evaluation of the evidence received, the allegations that AI believed were substantiated, and the government's response to the report. The Archambault riot occurred after two prisoners initiated an escape attempt, and then killed two guards before committing suicide. Several other guards were injured in the ensuing riot, which lasted until the following day. Thereafter, a number of actions were taken against prisoners at Archambault in the two weeks following the riots: prisoners were denied all access to lawyers, they were denied showers, even though tear gas had been used during the riot and Correctional Services regulations require that showers be available as soon as "practicable," and 18 prisoners were subjected to abuses in the segregation unit, including being held naked for up to three weeks without mattresses or covers, given clothing and bedding that had been urinated upon, given food that had been adulterated with spit or thrown on the floor or in the toilet, subjected to food and sleep deprivation, tear gassed in the mouth or through the food hole in the door to the cell, burned by cigarettes, beaten and assaulted, denied medical attention, and threatened with death.

The Reverend Clarke MacDonald, Moderator of the United Church of Canada on visits to Archambault, recounts the explanation offered by Michel Gilbert, Assistant Director for Security at Archambault:

> Unfortunately in isolating the inmates responsible for the riot by sending them to the hole, those guards seeking revenge had free access to the "guilty ones." "I was never," he affirmed, "ashamed of what went on in the hole until the period between July 25th and several weeks ago. The inmates probably had a rough time in the hole." He went on to indicate his opinion. "They were probably badly harassed, but it has been calm for the last two or three weeks. I cannot, however, verify any of these hypotheses. If I approach an area, guards 'warn' other guards of my whereabouts as I approach. The guards felt the score was 3 to 0 since no inmates were murdered, but had committed suicide, and some of the staff were, and still are, 'looking for revenge.'" Mr. Gilbert indicated that while he understood this desire for revenge, he rejected it as any kind of practical solution. [*Report on Allegations of Ill-Treatment of Prisoners of Archambault* at 15]

While the Director of the prison acknowledged that "regrettable acts" had been committed by guards, he claimed that he could not control the guards, whose actions he called "natural and normal ... in the face of the murderous violence of the prisoners....": *ibid.* at 14. There was no official government investigation of the guards' violence, nor was there any response to the AI report.

In July 1988, a class-action suit claiming $18.6 million against the former Director of Archambault was launched on behalf of 424 prisoners who claim that their human rights were violated in the aftermath of the 1982 riot: CP, "Class-action suit filed against ex-warden on prisoners' behalf" *The [Toronto] Globe and Mail* (22 July 1988) A4. The suit, *Kaplan* v. *Lasalle*, [1988] A.Q. No. 57 (C.A.), online: QL, was authorized by the Québec Court of Appeal as a class action against the Director, André Le Marier, although the claim against Robert Kaplan, the former Solicitor General of Canada, was dismissed because the Québec court did not have jurisdiction to hear the claim against him.

SEARCH AND SEIZURE

Prisoners have argued that their rights to privacy and bodily integrity protected under the *Charter* should be respected while in prison. There are cases in which prisoners' s. 8 *Charter* right to be protected against unreasonable search and seizure has been upheld: *R.* v. *Rodney* (1991), 65 C.C.C. (3d) 304 (B.C.S.C.) (a tape from a monitored telephone call was excluded as evidence).

However, it is not uncommon to see the same pattern of less rigorous *Charter* scrutiny that was applied in *Armstrong*, *supra* applied to s. 8 claims. For example, in *Weatherall* v. *Canada (AG)*, [1993] 2 S.C.R. 872, the Court refused to condemn frisk searching and unscheduled surveillance of male prisoners by female guards, even though such cross-sex searches are prohibited for male guards with respect to female prisoners. While the Court's rejection of the prisoner's s. 15 equality claim might be persuasive, in that it ruled that historical, biological, and sociological differences between men and women suggest that cross-sex searches are more threatening for women such that the equality rights of men are not violated by a different rule, it failed to give credence to the privacy interests of male prisoners: Amy Bartholomew, "'Achieving a Place for Women in a Man's World': Or, Feminism with No Class" (1993) 6 C.J.W.L. 465 at 477. See also *Everingham* v. *Ontario*, [1993] O.J. No. 55 (Ct. Just. (Gen. Div.)), online: QL (policy of opening mail in a maximum security psychiatric institution did not violate the *Charter*) and *Fieldhouse* v. *R.* (1994), (1995), 98 C.C.C. (3d) 207 (B.C.C.A.) (random urinanalysis program did not violate the *Charter*), discussed *infra*, **Search and Seizure**.

PHYSICAL SECURITY

The conditions under which people are imprisoned may in fact produce not only humiliation, but also injury and death. According to Statistics Canada, 189 Canadian prisoners died in 1999–2000 from neglect, suicide, and violence. The film by Nina Rosenblum, *Through the Wire* (Daedaleus Productions, 1990) documents the use of sensory deprivation and its deadly impact upon women who are "political prisoners" in the United States. See also Geoffrey York, "Warden affirms right to shackle some prisoners despite UN ban" *The [Toronto] Globe and Mail* (13 November 1989) A1 (prisoners shackled when appearing before federal Immigration and Refugee Appeal Board in spite of Canadian endorsement of Standard Minimum Rules for the Treatment of Prisoners, (UN Congress, 1955) and in spite of the fact that security guards accompany prisoners to the hearings).

Many prisoners in Canada live in fear of assault by other inmates and by guards: Stephen Bindman, "Inmates live in fear of guards and other inmates, survey shows" *The Ottawa Citizen* (6 June 1996) A4 (describing the results of a Corrections Canada survey that found that one in five of the 4,285 male prisoners surveyed had been assaulted in prison); Kirk Makin, "Inmates fear attacks; drug use common" *The [Toronto] Globe and Mail* (7 June 1996) A1, A5 (almost half of the men surveyed said they do not feel safe from other prisoners).

Consider the following examples: Alan Jeffries, "Widow of man killed in Halifax jail wins $500,000 from Nova Scotia" *The Ottawa Citizen* (18 May 1994) A4 (Donald Findlay was killed by other inmates within 90 minutes of arriving to serve a two-week sentence for dangerous driving); Mike Blanchfield, "Jail guard reinstated despite lying on report" *The Ottawa Citizen* (6 July 1993) A1 (an inquest into the murder by other prisoners of a 27-year-old prisoner, Michael Sienkiewicz, considered the evidence that a guard admitted falsifying his report to state that he had personally checked hourly on the prisoners).

Although in the cases described above charges of murder were laid and convictions secured against the other inmates, only once in Canadian history (discussed below) have guards been charged with killing a prisoner. See, for example, the following two deaths, where no charges were pursued: Phillip Day, "Guards accused of beating inmate just before death" *The Ottawa Citizen* (17 March 1990) A12; (mentally handicapped inmate serving indeterminate sentence for sexual assaults on children allegedly beaten by four guards minutes before his death); André Picard, "Police, coroner probe death in Quebec jail" *The [Toronto] Globe and Mail* (9 August 1993) A4 (Ernst Prophète, an African-Canadian, was detained for $1,724 in unpaid traffic tickets and beaten when he refused to comply with a strip-search during his admission to jail. Although he was unconscious when placed in his cell and never regained consciousness, his death was attributed to respiratory failure, not violence).

In the case of the death of African-Canadian prisoner Robert Gentles in Kingston Penitentiary in October 1994, after he had been subdued by six guards and maced in his cell, the Crown's office again decided not to lay charges. The family of the deceased laid charges of manslaughter and criminal negligence causing death, after learning that Gentles' body was discovered face down on a pillow on a bed in segregation. Apparently footprints were found on the sheets beside the body, and he had been held face down on the pillow for between two and one half and ten minutes after being maced: Lori MacLean, "6 guards charged in inmate's death" *The Ottawa Citizen* (20 September 1994) A3. The Crown later assumed control of the prosecution (see **Powers of Prosecution**, *infra*) and dismissed the charges (CP, "Charges against two guards dropped" *The [Toronto] Globe and Mail* (22 June 1995) A2), stating that there was insufficient evidence to proceed with the prosecution.

The Coroner's Inquest into the cause of Gentles's death commenced in 1998 and heard 134 days of testimony from 98 witnesses, including evidence linking the subculture among prison guards to their claimed memory loss and faulty recollections surrounding the death of Gentles. The verdict released in June 1999 attributed his death to accident, and made 74 recommendations for changes to prison practices regarding the use of mace, administrative segregation, and adherence to legal norms governing the use of force, among others: *Coroner's Inquest into the Death of Robert Gentles* (24 June 1999).

As is evidenced by the dearth of prosecutions for violence by guards, the criminal law system rarely acknowledges the dangerousness of prison conditions. See, for example *R. v. Carker No. 2*, [1967] S.C.R. 114 (denial of duress defence to a prisoner who participated in a riot in order to protect himself against retaliation by other prisoners) and *R. v. McKay* (1992), 13 C.R. (4th) 315 (B.C.C.A.) (denial of necessity defence to charges arising out of prison escape allegedly based on mistreatment in segregation, which included being hosed down and left in unheated cells in January and threatened with assault by two guards). Self-defence has, however, been successful in two prison cases: *R. v. Plain*, [1997] O.J. No. 4927 (Gen. Div.), online: QL, and *R. v. McConnell*, [1996] 1 S.C.R. 1075. These cases are discussed in Abell and Sheehy, *Proof, Defences, and Beyond*, under **Duress**, **Necessity**, and **Self-Defence**.

Finally, the risk of suicide is another consequence of imprisonment. Moira Farr reports that "people in prison or police custody, especially young people, are at significantly higher risk for suicide than the general population." Her article, "No Good Reason" 1 *This Magazine* (July/August 1998) 27 at 28, describes the legal response that ensued when three Calgary youths committed suicide in police custody in 1996–97. Further information on the risk of suicide in custody will be provided in the sections on **Women in Prison** and **Aboriginal Peoples**, which follow.

MEDICAL TREATMENT AND REHABILITATION

Some of the examples above suggest that medical treatment in prison is not assured, although the deaths of prisoners may be easily prevented with medical intervention. Consider, for example, Robert McLeod, "Prisoner killed by gangrene confined to cell, guard says" *The [Toronto] Globe and Mail* (24 March 1990) A16, where the official explanation was to the effect that the prisoner was in segregation for his own protection and that he had flooded his cell by blocking the sink and toilet. Consider as well *R. v. Downey*, [1989] O.J. No. 436 (Dist. Ct.), online: QL: the prisoner was released from prison where he was being held pending trial on the basis that having tested AIDS positive, Mr. Downey was subjected to verbal and physical abuse by both staff and other inmates, and was not provided with the appropriate medical treatment for AIDS-related illnesses, in violation of s. 12 of the *Charter*.

Prisoners express frustration and cynicism about the lack of appropriate rehabilitation services, arguing that they are set up to fail in society by being provided with meaningless certificates and credits, rather than university programs or even courses in computer repair or programming. The Auditor General of Canada has also criticized the Correctional Service for failing to assess the effectiveness of the programs provided, failing to allocate resources fairly among prisoners, and failing to follow up through parole programs. The Auditor General emphasized the crucial link between employment and rehabilitation, but noted that CORCAN, the prison industry, is the Correctional Service's most expensive rehabilitation program. CORCAN costs double what educational and vocational programs cost, yet over half of the offenders in CORCAN do not need the skills taught. More importantly, in terms of recidivism and long-term costs to society, "over 95 percent of the Service's employability resources are focused in the institutions, leaving very little to help offenders get a job once they return to the community. The Service does not have a coherent strategy to deal with offender employability." *Report of the Auditor General of Canada to the House of Commons* (Ottawa: Minister of Public Works and Government Services Canada, 1996) at 10–15.

DEMOCRATIC RIGHTS

Prisoners have recently been successful in arguing that the removal of the right to vote as part of the conditions of imprisonment violates s. 3 of the *Charter*: *Belczowski* v. *Canada* (1991), 42 F.T.R. 98, affirmed (1992), 90 D.L.R. (4th) 330 (F.C.A.). The Crown's s. 1 argument failed in this case because there was held to be insufficient proportionality between the objective of punishment and blanket disqualification, and because "punishment" is not the goal of imprisonment. In affirming the judgment of the Federal Court of Appeal, the Supreme Court simply gave an oral judgment, not considering it necessary to address the Crown's s. 1 arguments: [1993] 1 S.C.R. 438.

The government responded with new legislation denying the right to vote for offenders serving sentences of two years and over: *Canada Elections Act*, R.S.C. 1985, C. E-2, s. 51(e), as am. by S.C. 1993, C. 19, s. 23. This legislation was also declared unconstitutional in *Sauvé* v. *Canada (Chief Electoral Officer)*, [1996] 1 F.C. 857 (F.C.T.D.), but reversed on appeal: [2000] 2 F.C. 117 (C.A.). The appeal is currently before the Supreme Court of Canada.

CONJUGAL VISITS

Conjugal visits and privileges associated with the prisoner's "family" are an important part of that person's life line to their community and to their own "rehabilitation." In *Veysey* v. *Correctional Service of Canada* (1990), 29 F.T.R. 74, a prisoner argued that he was denied participation in the "Private Family Visiting Program" because a same-sex partner was not listed in the definitions of qualifying "family" members in the Correctional Services Canada booklet and in the Commissioner of Federal Prisons' Directive 770 outlining the program. Mr. Veysey argued that the denial of conjugal visits offended his s. 15 *Charter* right to equality. The court held as follows at 78–80:

> Most of the grounds enumerated in s. 15 of the Charter as prohibited grounds of discrimination connote the attribute of immutability, such as race, national or ethnic origin, colour, age. One's religion may be changed but with some difficulty; sex and mental or physical disability, with even greater difficulty. Presumably, sexual orientation would fit within one of these levels of immutability. Another characteristic common to the enumerated grounds is that the individuals or groups involved have been victimized and stigmatized throughout history because of prejudice, mostly based on fear or ignorance, as most prejudices are. This characteristic would also clearly apply to sexual orientation, or more precisely to those who have deviated from accepted sexual norms, at least in the eyes of the majority.
>
> Of course, the purpose of these proceedings is not to pass moral judgment on sexual orientation, but to decide whether or not the rights of the applicant have been violated under s. 15 of the Charter on the ground that he was excluded from the program because of his sexual orientation. Again, sexual orientation is not a prohibited ground listed under s. 15 but, in my view, it is an analogous ground recognized by the above provincial and territorial human rights acts, as well as the House of Commons Parliamentary Committee on Equality Rights. In my view, the applicant's rights have been violated.
>
> Having determined that his right to equality has been infringed as a result of discrimination based on an analogous ground under s. 15, I must now turn to s. 1 of the Charter and find whether the denial of his right falls within such reasonable limits prescribed by law as can be demonstrably justified in a free and democratic society.
>
> The first question to be resolved is whether the purpose of this differential treatment based on sexual orientation is to further a desirable social goal. Bearing in mind that a goal of the program is the preparation of inmates for their return to life in the community through the preservation of their most supportive relationships, this desirable goal is

not furthered by denying the applicant's access to his most supportive relationship. Obviously, the successful reintegration into the community of this inmate would be a benefit not only to him, but to the community as a whole.

. . .

The second justification criterion is the proportionality test of balancing the nature of the right affected with the extent of the infringement and the degree to which the limitation furthers a desirable social goal. It appears to me that the respondent can reduce any risk to the safety of the applicant merely by maintaining the confidentiality of the applicant's participation in the program, and for that matter, the confidentiality of the participation of any and all inmates. No evidence has been adduced to show that such an obvious precaution would present any particular difficulty to the administration and good order of the institution.

Consequently, the decision of the respondent denying the applicant's grievance is quashed and the Commissioner of the Correctional Service is ordered to reconsider the applicant's grievance in accordance with the provisions of s. 15 of the *Canadian Charter of Rights and Freedoms*. Costs of this motion to the applicant.

C. RACISM IN PRISON

In the *Report of the Commission on Systemic Racism in the Ontario Criminal Justice System* (Toronto: Queen's Printer for Ontario, 1995) [hereinafter *Report on Systemic Racism*], the Commission reported its findings as to the over-representation of Black persons in Ontario prison admissions at pp. 69–70:

> Ontario prison data show that over the six-year period from 1986/87 to 1992/93 —
> - The number of prisoners described as black admitted to Ontario prisons increased 204% while the number of white prisoners admitted increased 23%.
> - Black admissions to prisons serving the Metro Toronto area for drug trafficking/importing charges increased by several thousand percent. White admissions to the same prisons for drug trafficking/importing also increased, in some prisons by large percentages, but nowhere near as much as the growth in black admissions.
>
> Data from 1992/93 show that among total admission —
> - Both men and women described as black or Aboriginal are over-represented relative to their proportions in the provincial population, while those described as Asian, East Indian or Arab are under-represented.
> - Although many more black and Aboriginal men are in jail than black and Aboriginal women, women described as black or Aboriginal are more over-represented among prison admissions than are men described as black or Aboriginal.
>
> Data from 1992/93 on the offences leading to admission to prison show that —
> - Persons described as black are most over-represented among prisoners charged with drug offences, obstructing justice and weapons possession.
> - Persons described as black are most under-represented among prisoners charged with impaired driving offences.†

In attempting to explain these findings, the Commission referred to the discrimination in sentencing (discussed *supra* under **Sentencing**), the charging practices of police and Crown Attorneys, who are more likely to prosecute Black accused by way of indictment rather than by summary conviction (discussed *infra* under **Introduction to Criminal Procedure**), and the so-called "war on drugs" (discussed **Definition of Crime**, *supra*, **Judicial Interim Release**, *infra*, and by the Commission, *ibid.* at 81–84).

The *Report on Systemic Racism* also explored the ways in which racism is manifested in the context of prison through the maintenance of a hostile, racist environment, racial segregation of prisoners, and differential use of prison discipline. In its interim report, *Racism Behind Bars* (Toronto: Queen's Printer for Ontario, 1994) [hereinafter *Racism Behind Bars*] at 15–16, the Commission discussed its findings as to the frequency with

---

† © Queen's Printer for Ontario, 1995. Reproduced with permission.

which staff in Ontario prisons use racist language in their dealings with prisoners:

> Almost all staff and prisoners agree that blatant racist language "goes with the prison territory." Although prisoners differed in how serious they feel the problem to be, we were given at least one example of overtly racist name-calling in every adult prison we visited. We heard the same things in youth prisons, including "Phase I" institutions housing 12- to 15-year-old young offenders. Prisoners and COs [Correctional Officers] gave us the following examples of commonly-used racist names, particularly in prisons for adult males and male young offenders.
>
> ...
>
> We heard countless examples of COs using this type of language in their exchanges with prisoners. Black and white prisoners as well as COs agreed that COs routinely use these names when talking to or about black and other racial minority prisoners and sometimes when talking about their black colleagues.[†]

The list of racial epithets encountered by the Commission in its investigation has been omitted. *Racism Behind Bars* also examined the practices of racial stereotyping by staff as well as the denial of or contempt expressed by staff for the cultural identities of Black prisoners (at 19–27). It commented at 28: "We are concerned that so many senior officials said they did not know about the same racially hostile environment that their staff quite openly describe. We are troubled that some officials replicated, as facts, racially damaging stereotypes." *Racism Behind Bars* concluded at the same page: *"We have found no evidence that racist practices are necessary to maintain order in prisons.* On the contrary, the negative feelings, adversarial relationships, and hostility generated by such practices can only contribute to dissension, conflict, unrest, and instability." (italics in original)

With respect to racial segregation, the Commission reported in *Racism Behind Bars* at 41–43 that one institution, Hamilton-Wentworth Detention Centre, experienced a highly disproportionate transfer rate of Black prisoners on remand (80 per cent of such transfers to this institution are Black prisoners), resulting in a prison population that is disproportionately Black as compared to the surrounding population and to other institutions. After considering and refuting official efforts to explain this finding, the Commission noted the implications for Black prisoners, which include increased distance from their local communities and families, as well as decreased access to their lawyers. The Commission found as well that Black and other racial minority prisoners were over-represented in relatively high-security institutions (at 44), without adequate data in terms of offence patterns to explain this placement. They were also over-represented in the "worst" institutions and under-represented in the "best" ones (at 51), again without objective justification. After identifying the pattern of segregation in living areas within prisons as well, the Commission concluded as follows:

> The Commission is convinced that some prisons in Ontario tolerate and encourage racial segregation in the allocation of prisoners among living units....
>
> . . .
>
> Racial segregation in jails and detention centres clearly is a departure from the policies contained in the Initial Placement Report and suggests that judgments of admissions officers are shaped by assumptions based on "race" rather than indicators of security risk. It also appears that some admissions officers are influenced by prisoners' "choices." This idea of prisoners' choices is more complex than it might at first seem. Not only are many prisoners influenced by fears based on the hostility of prison environments for black and other racial minority prisoners, but it also appears that prison staff, by giving advice about the "reputations" of different areas of the prison, are able to manipulate prisoners' choices. Whatever the truth about the meaning and role of prisoners' choice in placement decisions, the result, as we have shown, is racial segregation in the initial allocation of prisoners among living units.
>
> However, admissions officers are not wholly responsible for placing prisoners. Crucial decisions about cell and corridor assignments are usually made by COs. It is these "low-visibility" decisions that seem to be most significant to the patterns we have described. While we were told that the most important factor in these assignments is bed space, it is clear that the patterns of segregation are not the result of the random distribution of prisoners. If prisoners had been assigned randomly based on available bed space, it is unlikely that so many COs and prisoners from different institutions would consistently view living areas in their prisons as racially segregated.

[†] © Queen's Printer for Ontario, 1995. Reproduced with permission.

Our findings are consistent with research in other jurisdictions with "racially" mixed populations. Studies in the United Kingdom and in the United States have found that racial segregation occurs in many prisons. Interestingly, the excuses given by prison staff and officials in these studies are quite similar to what we heard. For example, two American studies found that management and COs frequently use security concerns to rationalize segregated living areas, believing that integrated prisons are likely to lead to violent, interracial conflict. Similarly, "prisoner choice" is frequently cited as a reason for segregation, and the explanations for such choices are familiar: physical safety, psychological security, and shared interests.

In effect, the best case that prison authorities are able to make for racial segregation is that it improves relationships among prisoners, making the prison easier to manage. However, an important finding of many studies is that *the creation of segregated groups within prisons makes relations among prisoners worse, not better*. For example, one recent study concludes that racial segregation intensifies hostilities between racial groups and contributes to tensions in the prison. These consequences occur because racial segregation:
- Reduces opportunities for the development of relationships that cut across racial lines;
- Reinforces cohesion within groups and hostility among groups, contributing to a hardening of an "us against them" mentality; and
- Enforces social distance among prisoners from different communities, creating opportunities for misinformation and destructive rumours.

There is no evidence that racial segregation improves race relations within Ontario prisons. At best, it is a "band-aid solution" directed at the symptoms of racial tensions. At worst, racial segregation contributes to the hostile prison environments described in Chapter 2.

Racial segregation behind bars reflects a lack of leadership on the part of prison management. Ultimately, it is the failure of effective direction and control that permits correctional staff to allocate prisoners to living areas on the basis of "race." This practice must end. [italics in original]†

In the *Report on Systemic Racism*, the Commission reported on its findings with respect to differential treatment in terms of prison discipline at 312–13:

Policing discretion
- Taken as a whole, black prisoners were most over-represented and white prisoners most under-represented in misconduct reports for wilfully disobeying an order. By contrast, black prisoners were most under-represented and white prisoners most over-represented in misconduct reports for possession of banned substances — the misconduct known as "contraband."
- Black women were most over-represented and white women most under-represented in misconduct reports for issuing a "gross insult." By contrast, black women were most under-represented and white women most over-represented in misconduct reports for contraband.
- Among youths aged 16 and 17, black males were most over-represented and white males most under-represented in misconduct reports for wilfully disobeying an order. By contrast, black young males were most under-represented and white young males most over-represented in misconduct reports for committing or threatening assault.
- Black adult males were most over-represented and white adult males most under-represented in misconduct reports for committing or threatening assault. By contrast, black adult males were most under-represented and white adult males most over-represented in misconduct reports for contraband.

These trends indicate that black prisoners are more likely to be charged with misconduct involving interpretation of behaviour, in which correctional officers exercise a greater degree of subjective judgment. However, black prisoners are less likely to be charged with misconduct when the discretionary powers of correctional officers are limited by the need to show factual proof, such as possession of forbidden substances. The reverse is true for white prisoners.

Penalty discretion
- Taken as a whole, black prisoners were most over-represented and white prisoners most under-represented in the "closed confinement" or segregation category of punishment.
- Black women prisoners were most over-represented and white women prisoners were most under-represented in the segregation category. By contrast, black women

---

† © Queen's Printer for Ontario, 1995. Reproduced with permission.

were most under-represented and white women most over-represented among prisoners punished with a reprimand.
- Among 16- and 17-year-old youths, black males were most over-represented and white males most under-represented in the segregation category. By contrast, black males were most under-represented and white males most over-represented in punishment involving "changes in program or living accommodation."
- Black men were over-represented and white men under-represented in segregation penalties, but this was not the penalty with the greatest over-representation of black and under-representation of white prisoners. The category with the greatest disparity favouring white men was changes in program or living accommodation. Black men were most under-represented and white men most over-represented in punishments involving loss of remission.

Given these findings, it was clearly important to explore the relationship between the type of misconduct and penalty to see if over-representation of black prisoners in the segregation category of penalty simply reflected the nature of the offence charged or the combined effect of policing and punishment choices. This analysis shows a striking absence of a correlation between offence type and penalty, indicating complete randomness in the assignment of penalties to offences.

This finding strongly confirms the views of prisoners, OPSEU and individual correctional officers about disparities in the exercise of penalty discretion, at least if the nature of the offence is supposed to be the most important factor. As noted above, however, decision-makers are to take account of several factors when selecting penalties. Since they generally do not record the reasons for the penalty, or even the factors they took into account, the study was unable to identify any explanations for penalty choices.[†]

The Commission concluded its two reports with recommendations directed at eliminating segregation, establishing uniform criteria for placement and transfer decisions, reducing subjectivity and discretion in the disciplinary process, and identifying means by which racism in the prison environment could be eliminated.

D. WOMEN IN PRISON

The relatively small numbers of women offenders and the even fewer numbers of women serving federal sentences (most women are incarcerated in provincial institutions for minor offences) have provided some part of the explanation for the fact that, historically, there was only one federal Prison for Women (P4W). See generally, Ellen Adelberg and Claudia Currie, eds., *Too Few To Count* (Vancouver: Press Gang, 1987). P4W was located in Kingston, Ontario, which meant that women serving sentences of two years and up were removed to Kingston, thus losing contact with their partners, children, and communities. Because many women are sole support mothers, their children often end up in the child welfare systems. For Aboriginal women, the loss of access to family and community may be even more destructive. According to Joanne Mayhew, then imprisoned at P4W, "[t]he only reason men would go to Kingston Penitentiary is for really horrendous crimes.... Women who have committed much lesser crimes are dragged across the country (to the Prison for Women)," quoted in Linda Hossie, "Women charge discrimination at prison" *The [Toronto] Globe and Mail* (23 June 1990) A5.

There were other significant problems associated with P4W, according to Hossie's article:

Men who are classified minimum-security, or who gain that status through good behaviour, are sent to the wide range of minimum-security prisons throughout the country.... [A]bout 10 per cent of the 109 prisoners at P4W are legitimate maximum-security prisoners. Their situation, however, governs life for the rest, since the single alternative is P4W's minimum-security house nearby, which has room for only 11 women.

In addition, P4W offered a lesser range and lower quality of treatment, job training, and community programs than the comparable men's

---

[†] © Queen's Printer for Ontario, 1995. Reproduced with permission.

prisons. With respect to Ontario prisons, in which women constitute eight per cent of the population, Patti Starr states: "There are no meaningful opportunities to learn job skills — cleaning, laundry and dishwashing constituted the only work opportunities in most institutions. There isn't enough counselling since most of the funding is funnelled into the men's facilities.": Patti Starr, "'Afterthoughts' behind bars" *The Toronto Star* (26 November 1993) A23. Human rights complaints and *Charter* s. 15 claims have been launched on the basis of the disparities described above: one by Ms. Mayhew, and another by the Women's Legal Education and Action Fund (LEAF): see Hossie, *supra*.

The number of suicides and attempted suicides in P4W prompted the Canadian Association of Elizabeth Fry Societies (CAEFS) to expose the conditions of women's imprisonment and to initiate change. In the period of December 1988 to February 1991 there were six suicides and one attempted suicide (resulting in a coma) in P4W. Marlene Moore, Canada's first woman "dangerous offender" (discussed *supra* under **Sentencing**), was the first among these deaths. She died in December 1988 at the age of 31. There was evidence that she had attempted suicide the month before her death, and was left unattended in the prison hospital in spite of the fact that she had threatened suicide if she did not get relief from a painful, chronic bladder infection. For an account of the last weeks of Moore's life, see Anne Kershaw and Mary Lasovich, *Rock-a-Bye Baby: A Death Behind Bars* (Toronto: McClelland and Stewart, 1991) at 178–94.

CAEFS requested standing at the inquest into Moore's death to instigate recommendations "aimed at increasing the availability of psychiatric treatment for women and establishing a psychiatric wing within the Prison for Women": CP and Staff, "Court asked to rule on group's standing at jail-death inquest" *The [Toronto] Globe and Mail* (23 June 1989) A4. Although it was initially denied standing, in the face of an appeal, the Crown and the Chief Coroner dropped their opposition to the request for standing. See Kershaw and Lasovich, *ibid*. at 195–204 for an account of the advocacy and strategies used to secure standing. Unfortunately, the scope of inquiry pursued by the inquest was drastically limited by the coroner's rulings. As Dianne Martin, Moore's lawyer, stated of the resulting inquest report, *ibid*. at 224: "It's a tremendously false document about Marlene and about the Prison for Women."

Of the remaining five suicides and the one tragic attempt, all were Aboriginal women. In 1991, the Chief Coroner ordered that three inquests be held together to inquire into the circumstances that produced the deaths of Marie Le Douxe and Careen Daigneault, and the attempted suicide by Lorna Jones, (who died later, in the spring of 1992) and to ascertain whether common factors contributed to the suicides. The recommendations produced by the jury include some of the same ones made by CAEFS, in the Moore inquest, of establishing psychiatric services that are appropriate for women within P4W. The recommendations also focus on the need for culturally appropriate services, links to elders, the provision of access to spiritual practices, such as ceremonial sweats, as well as the closure of P4W by 1994 and the building of a Healing Lodge for Aboriginal women: *Verdict of Coroner's Jury* (17 December 1991) (Office of the Chief Coroner, Ministry of the Solicitor General for Ontario). For more context about the prison experience of Aboriginal women, see below, **Aboriginal Peoples**.

Since 1938, 15 government reports have identified serious problems in the provision of services for women at P4W, and nine federal task forces have recommended its closing: see Task Force on Federally Sentenced Women, *Creating Choices: Report of the Task Force on Federally Sentenced Women* (Ottawa: Correctional Service of Canada, 1990) for the most recent report. In 1990, the federal government announced that the prison would be closed in five years time, and that it would be replaced by five regional centres, a Healing Lodge for Aboriginal women, and increased numbers of halfway houses. The centres are to be within commuting distance by public transportation in large cities and accessible to existing services, such as rape crisis counsellors, women's groups, universities, and teaching hospitals.

Events at the Prison for Women in Kingston culminated in a Commission of Inquiry and a report by The Honourable Louise Arbour, Commissioner, *The Prison For Women*, *supra*. Madam Justice Arbour was appointed, by terms of reference dated 10 April 1995, P.C. 1995-608, to make findings of fact related to incidents that occurred within the P4W on 22 April 1994 and the response of the Correctional Service thereafter, as well as recommendations regarding improvements in the policies and practices of Corrections Canada in relation to those incidents and responses.

Commission of Inquiry into Certain Events at the Prison for Women in Kingston[†]

[Justice Arbour summarized the events as follows in a brief "overview chronology" at 25–26:]

On the evening of Friday, April 22, 1994, a brief but violent physical confrontation took place between six inmates at the Prison for Women and a number of the correctional staff. The six inmates were immediately placed in the Segregation Unit at the Prison for Women. Criminal charges were laid against them; and five of the six inmates ultimately pleaded guilty to offences connected to the incident.

Tension was very high at the prison — particularly in the Segregation Unit. In the subsequent days, behaviour in that unit was very agitated. On Sunday, April 24th, three inmates who had not been involved in the April 22nd incident, but who were already in segregation when the six were brought in, variously slashed, took a hostage, and attempted suicide.

On Tuesday, April 26, 1994, correctional staff demonstrated outside the Prison for Women demanding the transfer of the inmates that had been involved in the April 22nd incident.

On the evening of April 26, 1994, the Warden of the Prison for Women called in a male Institutional Emergency Response Team ("IERT") from Kingston Penitentiary to conduct a cell extraction and strip search of eight women in segregation: the six who had been involved in the April 22nd incident, and two others. As is customary when the IERT is deployed, the cell extractions and strip searches were videotaped. At the end of the lengthy procedure, which finished early in the morning of April 27th, the eight inmates were left in empty cells in the Segregation Unit wearing paper gowns, and in restraints and leg irons.

On the evening of Wednesday, April 27th, seven of the eight inmates were subjected to body cavity searches.

On Friday, May 6, 1994, five inmates, four of whom had been involved in the April 22nd incident, were transferred to a wing of the Regional Treatment Centre, a male psychiatric treatment facility within Kingston Penitentiary. Two of these women subsequently launched *habeas corpus* applications, and on July 12, 1994, they were ordered returned to the Prison for Women. Four inmates were returned to the Prison for Women between July 14th and 18th, 1994, while another was transferred to the Regional Prairies Centre.

The six women who had been involved in the April 22nd incident remained in segregation for many months. On December 1, 1994, the women's agreement to plead guilty to related criminal charges was publicly announced. They appeared in court and pleaded guilty to the agreed charges on December 22, 1994.

The women were released from segregation between December 7, 1994 and January 19, 1995. (One inmate was released from the prison during the period of her segregation. She was subsequently returned to the prison and was admitted directly to the Segregation Unit.)

On January 20, 1995, the Correctional Service released the report of a Board of Investigation which had been appointed by the Commissioner of the Correctional Service to look into the incident of April 22nd, subsequent events in the Segregation Unit and certain associated matters. The report was critical of certain aspects of the management of the Prison for Women generally. It gave little attention to the IERT attendance, and in fact mis-described the nature of the IERT's procedure. It did not deal extensively, and sometimes not at all, with many aspects of the response of the Correctional Service to the April 22nd incident and its aftermath.

On February 14, 1995, the Correctional Investigator made a special report to the Solicitor General which was severely critical of the Board of Investigation Report, the IERT attendance, and the conditions and duration of the segregation of the inmates involved.

On February 21, 1995, the Solicitor General tabled the Correctional Investigator's Special Report in the House of Commons and announced his intention to call for an independent inquiry into the matters described above. The same day, substantial

---

[†] The Honourable Louise Arbour, *Commission of Inquiry into Certain Events at the Prison For Women in Kingston* (Ottawa: Canada Communication Group-Publishing, 1996). Source of Information: Solicitor General Canada. Reproduced with the permission of the Minister of Public Works and Government Services Canada, 2002.

extracts of the video of the IERT attendance were shown on the CBC program, *Fifth Estate*.

On April 10, 1995, the Governor General in Council appointed this Commission of Inquiry pursuant to Part II of the *Inquiries Act*.

[Justice Arbour made detailed findings of fact in her report, and analyzed the events and actions in light of the relevant law and policy at 3–5, 11:]

In 1992, Parliament passed the *Corrections and Conditional Release Act*, S.C. 1992, c. 20 (*CCRA*) which replaced the *Penitentiary Act*, R.S.C. 1985, c. P-5 and the *Parole Act*, R.S.C. 1985, c. P-2. The *CCRA* and associated Regulations are the principal legislation governing the operations of the Correctional Service of Canada.

In addition to the law, the Correctional Service has established a detailed and complex set of policies. Pursuant to the *CCRA*, the Commissioner of the Correctional Service is authorized to designate as Commissioner's Directives (CD's) rules for the management of the Service and the carrying out of the *Act*. Commissioner's Directives must be accessible to correctional staff, inmates and the public. Judicial decisions have indicated that Commissioner's Directives have at least a higher status than policy and other rules, and that they constitute, as a minimum, a set of standards of fairness to which the Service must adhere. In some cases, the Commissioner's Directives restate the law and provide specific guidance as to how the law is to be implemented within the Correctional Service, and in other areas, they set policy and practice with respect to matters not specifically dealt with in the *CCRA* and Regulations. In addition to Commissioner's Directives, each region may issue Regional Instructions, which either repeat or elaborate on matters dealt with in Commissioner's Directives, or address regionally specific issues.

Each individual institution also issues a separate set of Standing Orders which often repeat or further elaborate on matters dealt with in the *CCRA*, the Regulations, the Commissioner's Directives, and the Regional Instructions. Standing Orders provide a specific set of rules applicable to the institution. Standing Orders are further elaborated in Post Orders which provide specific instructions for those staff members who occupy particular posts within the institution and outline the responsibilities assigned to that post. To varying degrees, Post Orders, like Standing Orders, either repeat or elaborate on already existing law and policy.

Notwithstanding their enormous volume, Commissioner's Directives, Regional Instructions, Standing Orders, and Post Orders do not exhaust the written policy documents used by the Correctional Service. In addition, there are memoranda and other more specific policy manuals which further elaborate on CSC's written policy. For example, manuals on Security, Contingency Planning, Case Management, Policies and Procedures, and the Conduct of Investigations are among innumerable written policies referred to during the course of this inquiry. The CSC also sets policy by virtue of the usual practice and procedure which it employs in a given situation.

In this report, references to the law include the *CCRA*, the Regulations, and any applicable judicial decisions. CSC policy means both explicit written policy (Commissioner's Directives, Regional Instructions, Standing Orders, Post Orders, Manuals and other written policies) and operational policy, which is the usual practices and procedures of the CSC.

The events examined by this Commission indicate some significant discrepancies between CSC's operational policy, its written policy, and the law. Indeed, it is evident that some very important, yet essentially simple, legal principles which govern crucial aspects of the operation of the Correctional Service have become lost in a myriad of elaborate policy and regulatory provisions. It is apparent that it is not well understood within the Correctional Service that the decision to follow the law (as opposed to policy) is not a matter of discretion.

When confronted with an apparent departure from law or policy, I have found it helpful to analyze the problem by addressing the following questions:

1. What is the law and/or policy applicable to the event?
2. Is the applicable law or policy appropriate?
3. Is the applicable law or policy known within the Correctional Service?
4. Is the applicable law or policy perceived within the Correctional Service to be appropriate?
5. If the applicable law or policy is not known, why is that so? Is it due to questions of complexity, issues of communication, understanding, acceptance or otherwise?
6. Was the law or policy complied with in this case?
7. If the law or policy was not complied with, was there an appropriate response on behalf of the Correctional Service?
8. If the law or policy was not complied with in this case, what should be done about it?

Throughout this report, my findings and conclusions reflect this framework of analysis.

. . . .

It is generally accepted in the international community that a set of minimum standards should apply to imprisonment. These standards are designed to ensure that the inmates are humanely treated, that their responsibility and dignity is maintained, and that they are prepared as much as reasonably possible for reintegration in their community at the end of their term of imprisonment. The standards which the international community has generally accepted are contained in the *United Nations Standard Minimum Rules for the Treatment of Prisoners*, which were first adopted in 1955. While Canada, and the Correctional Service in particular, are not obliged to conform to the specific terms of the UN Rules in the management of prisons, those rules are accepted as international norms and minimum standards, and departures from them generally only occur where there is a reasoned justification.

[Justice Arbour found that although the altercation of April 22 was serious from the point of view of the guards, it constituted neither an attempted murder nor an attempted escape. She identified a number of important departures from policy with respect to the decontamination procedures after the women were gassed, failure to prepare use of force reports, failure to comply with search procedures upon admission to segregation, and failure to facilitate investigation of the incident by police. Justice Arbour found a number of violations of law and policy in connection with the use of segregation in the period 22–26 April, the strip search of April 26–27, the body cavity searches of April 27, the transfers to the Regional Treatment Centre, the Board of Investigation's process and report, the use of segregation from April 26 to December and January 1995, and the complaint and grievance procedure.

Specifically, she found: denials of the right to be advised of the right to counsel and to a reasonable opportunity to contact counsel without delay; denials of the right to one hour of exercise per day; denials of many other basic, legal entitlements while in segregation (e.g. telephone calls, showers, the removal of garbage, etc.); illegal conduct of the strip-search; illegal body cavity searches; procedural irregularities in the transfers to the Regional Treatment Centre; numerous errors and omissions, some "extremely serious" (such as the "mis-description" of the strip-search, at 117) in the report of the events filed by the Board of Investigation; illegal and prolonged segregation of the women in "deplorable conditions"; and finally, with respect to the complaints procedure, "chronic untimeliness" and a mindset "that the admission of error is perceived as an admission of defeat by the Correctional Services" (at 162).

Justice Arbour frequently noted that the Correctional Service appeared to be unaware of its legal obligations and constraints. Consider, for example, her description at 81–83 of the legal position taken on the issue of the strip-searches:]

In its written submissions, the Correctional Service advances the proposition that the IERT did not proceed contrary to the law. More specifically, the Service does acknowledge that this is not a case where a strip search by a person of the opposite sex would be permitted under s. 49(4)(b) of the *CCRA* because a delay in obtaining the assistance of a person of the same sex as the inmate would result in danger to human life or safety, or loss or destruction of the evidence. It is common ground that it is only in such circumstances that a strip search by a person of the opposite sex is permissible under the law, and the evidence does not suggest that the IERT intervention could not have been delayed.

Rather, the Correctional Service takes the position that since a strip search as defined in s. 46 of the *CCRA* requires a "visual inspection of the naked body," there was no strip search conducted by the male IERT officers who did not conduct a "visual inspection" of the inmates, and were merely present during the search for security reasons. CSC concedes that the procedure followed by the IERT contravenes s. 46 of the Regulations which requires a strip search to be conducted in a private area, out of sight of every other person except for one staff member of the same sex as the person being searched. The argument advanced is, therefore, that the male IERT members were at most witnesses to the inspection, in contravention of the Regulation, but not performing the strip search, which would put them in contravention of the *Act*.

Whatever the proper legal characterization of what took place, upon viewing the videotape which records these events, no reasonable person could come to the conclusion that the male IERT members were merely witnessing the visual inspection of the naked inmates by a female staff member. Women were forced to take their clothes off, at the command of men and in their presence. They either took their clothes off themselves, had their clothes removed by a female officer with the assistance of a male officer, or, in one case, one inmate had her clothes cut and ripped off her by a male officer. In all these circumstances, either a strip search was conducted, and men participated in it, or if what was done was not "a strip search," then the men had no legal authority to compel the removal of the women's clothes in their presence. The least plausible option, in my opinion, is the suggestion that a strip search was performed by female officers, and that it was merely witnessed by men. Should this be the case, it would still be in contravention of the Regulations, and of CSC policy, and wrong.

In any event, what is particularly disturbing in watching the video is not only the men "witnessing" the naked inmates, it is the combination of the inevitable brutality of this type of intervention, combined with the necessary physical handling of individual women by several male IERT members, while each woman is completely naked for a period of time, and then very improperly covered by a paper gown or bib. When properly understood in its full context, these events raise a legal and moral question much more basic than merely whether it technically constituted a "strip search." It raises the question of whether the treatment of the inmates was cruel, inhumane, and degrading. I think that it was.

This seems to be once again a case where the law was not known by those who were asked to implement it. The assumption was, again, that an emergency, which this was perceived to be, overrides any other applicable legal requirement. Despite the evidence of many witnesses that they never turned their minds to it, it is clear to me that they knew, or should have known, that in all the circumstances of which they were aware, the IERT intervention would take place exactly as it did, and as it is depicted on the video. As for the IERT members themselves, it is more plausible that, since they had not been given instructions otherwise, they did not actually question their entitlement to perform a cell extraction at the Prison for Women in exactly the same manner as they perform it at Kingston Penitentiary. However, considering the extreme force that they are authorized and trained to apply, they should be particularly sensitive to the limits of their legal authority, and this should form part of their ongoing sophisticated training. I understand that it is not expected that a male IERT team will ever be required to intervene again in a prison for women. Any protocol or memorandum of understanding with local police forces, the RCMP, or any other security organization, should ensure that the persons required to apply force to women, particularly to search their person in any fashion, are apprised specifically of the limit of their authority.

[Justice Arbour commented at 197 on the need for lawyers specializing in corrections law arising from the failure to accord legal rights to prisoners:]

There are not many lawyers who specialize in correctional law. Many are based in Kingston, Ontario, where the Correctional Law Project of the Faculty of Law of Queens University also has had a long tradition of offering assistance to prisoners. The closure of the Prison for Women and the opening of the new regional facilities will deprive women of access to this base of expertise. I would recommend that bar associations and defence lawyers' organizations across the country who are engaging in continuing legal education consider offering more training to their members in correctional law. Aside from the rules governing the computation of sentences, as the proceedings of this Commission have illustrated, the law that essentially governs the treatment of prisoners is not unduly complex. It is merely unduly difficult to access for the uninitiated, and, unfortunately, also for those who should be aware of it. Indeed, the myriad of rules, directives, instructions and orders rest on a few well known principles of criminal procedure and administrative law, such as the duty to act fairly, the right to counsel and the concept of free and voluntary consent. The legal profession could make a valuable educational contribution in that regard. Improved access to legal principles should improve compliance and improved awareness by counsel should facilitate redress.

[Justice Arbour commented broadly upon the issues raised by her review in the Preface to her report and in her evaluation of Correctional Services' self-avowed objectives at xi–xii, 73–74, reproduced below. Following those remarks are some of the numerous recommendations with which she concluded the report, at 253–56.]

The incidents that gave rise to this inquiry could have gone largely unnoticed. Until the public viewing of a videotape which shed light on part of these events, and the release of a special report by the Correctional Investigator in the winter of 1995, the Correctional Service of Canada had essentially closed the book on these events.

This was perceived as, by far, not the most serious series of events to have taken place in a Canadian penitentiary. Sadly, that is probably true. At the Prison for Women, loss of life and self-mutilation are among the many tragedies that occur, and that are largely unknown to the Canadian public.

However, this inquiry was concerned not only with what happened at the Prison for Women in 1994, but with the response of the Correctional Service of Canada to these events. The shortcomings that have been revealed in the course of this inquiry are, in my opinion, of the most serious nature. Corrections is the least visible branch of the criminal justice system. Occasions such as this, where its functioning is brought under intense public scrutiny, are few and far between. This may explain the discomfort of Corrections officials in handling this level of public attention. The lack of public scrutiny is in stark contrast to accountability processes in the law enforcement and judicial branches of the criminal justice system. Through hundreds of criminal trials and appeals, systemic shortcomings and individual performances of police officers, prosecutors and judges are examined publicly in a robust adversarial fashion.

Anyone familiar with criminal law enforcement, and with the prosecutorial and trial processes, would identify the presumption of innocence as the principle that animates the many rights granted by law to a person charged with a criminal offence. The risk of convicting an innocent person is not one which we would assume lightly.

A fair criminal process produces reliable convictions and, as a result, the management of a custodial sentence does not have to be plagued with uncertainties about the legitimacy of the enterprise. However, even though the presumption of innocence is displaced by the conviction, in the imposition of punishment, all authority must still come from the law. Parliament authorizes the imposition of certain sentences; the courts impose them and corrections officials implement the court orders. A guilty verdict followed by a custodial sentence is not a grant of authority for the State to disregard the very values that the law, particularly criminal law, seeks to uphold and to vindicate, such as honesty, respect for the physical safety of others, respect for privacy and for human dignity. The administration of criminal justice does not end with the verdict and the imposition of a sentence. Corrections officials are held to the same standards of integrity and decency as their partners in the administration of criminal law.

My objective in bringing forward recommendations on various aspects of corrections that have been touched upon by this inquiry is to assist the correctional system in coming into the fold of two basic Canadian constitutional ideals, towards which the rest of the administration of criminal justice strives: the protection of individual rights and the entitlement to equality.

. . . .

In its Mission Statement, the Correctional Service of Canada commits itself to "openness," "integrity," and "accountability." An organization which was truly committed to these values would, it seems to me, be concerned about compliance with the law, and vigilant to correct any departures from the law; it would be responsive to outside criticism, and prepared to engage in honest self-criticism; it would be prepared to give a fair and honest account of its actions; and it would acknowledge error. In this case, the Correctional Service did little of this. Too often, the approach was to deny error, defend against criticism, and to react without a proper investigation of the truth.

This approach was demonstrated not only with respect to the events in issue, but in its dealings with the Commission, for example, on the question of documents.

Although the Commissioner has not, to my knowledge, made other statements to the press on this issue, I take his admissions at the hearings in December to be a retraction of all of the statements contained in his letter to The Whig-Standard.

It was patently inaccurate for the Commissioner to assert in his letter that the Correctional Service had not been given an opportunity to explain the late production of documents; the issue was raised frequently at the public hearings, at which the Correctional Service was ably represented by competent and diligent counsel. In any event, it has now had that opportunity.

The Commissioner took an inaccurate stance publicly, in defence of the Correctional Service, which he retracted only when personally confronted, in the course of his testimony, with yet another example of the problems in document disclosure that he had refused to acknowledge.

This precipitous, yet ill-informed and inaccurate defensive reaction, is reminiscent of the position taken by the Commissioner and the Correctional Service generally, with respect to the content of the videotape of the IERT intervention at the Prison for Women, until Mr. Edwards actually personally reviewed it.

In both instances, it would have been preferable for the head of the Correctional Service to inform himself accurately and to concede, in the case of the documents, the shortcomings of the Service and, in the case of the strip search, that wrong had been done.

The Commissioner was also defensive about the Board of Investigation process and the quality of its report, until confronted, in his evidence, with the specifics of the obvious failings of the report.

Similarly, the Correctional Service filed inaccurate and misleading evidence in defence of its position with the court, and prepared an inaccurate and defensive briefing note for the Solicitor General.

. . . .

The deplorable defensive culture that manifested itself during this inquiry has old, established roots within the Correctional Service, and there is nothing to suggest that it emerged at the initiative of the present Commissioner or his senior staff. They are, it would seem, simply entrenched in it.

I believe that it is also part of that corporate culture to close ranks, and that the defensive stance of senior managers was often motivated by a sense of loyalty to their subordinates. This otherwise admirable instinct should, however, always defer to the imperatives of scrupulous commitment to the truth which must be displayed by those entrusted with people's liberty.

. . . .

The Commissioner was asked during the course of his evidence to consider, given that the inmates' assertions about how they had been treated had now been shown to be true, whether they were due an apology. His response was that they were, but that they should also be asked to apologize for their behaviour on April 22nd.

The resolution of criminal charges against the inmates by their guilty pleas in December of 1994 closes that chapter. No further apology is required on their part, contrary to the Commissioner's suggestion. Their behaviour after April 22nd could have been the object of institutional charges. It was not. To the extent that they "misbehaved" during that period of time, their subsequent treatment in segregation was ample punishment. They have been held accountable for their actions.

As for their treatment by the IERT, their prolonged segregation, the inadequate segregation review and grievance process, I think that they should have received an apology. I also think that they are entitled to compensation. Counsel agreed that I should not address the issue of quantum.

. . . .

6. With respect to use of force and use of IERT's, I recommend:

(a) that male IERT's not be deployed again in an institution for women;

. . . .

(e) that the Correctional Service of Canada acknowledge that the following is a correct interpretation of the existing law, or that it seek modification of the existing law to accord with the following:
 (i) men may not strip search women. The only exception is where the delay in locating women to conduct the search would be dangerous to human life or safety, or might result in the loss of evidence. No man may witness the strip search of a woman, except as above.

(f) that inmates be given the right to counsel before expressing their consent to a body cavity search, and that inmates be advised of that right at the time their consent is sought;

(g) that body cavity searches only be performed in surroundings that are appropriate for consensual, non-emergency medical examination or intervention;

(h) that a body cavity search be performed only by a female physician, if the inmate so requests, and that the physician ensure, to her satisfaction, that the consent was not obtained as a result of inducement or coercion;

(i) that body cavity searches and strip searches performed in contravention of these recommendations be treated as having rendered the conditions of imprisonment harsher than that contemplated by the sentence, for the purposes of the remedies contemplated in the recommendation dealing with sanctions. (see recommendation 8(b) and (c))

. . . .

8. With respect to correctional issues more generally, I recommend:

(a) that the Department of Justice, at the initiative of the Solicitor General, examine legislative mechanisms by which to create sanctions for correctional interference with the integrity of a sentence;

(b) that such sanctions provide, in substance, that if illegalities, gross mismanagement or unfairness in the administration of a sentence renders the sentence harsher than that imposed by the court:
   (i) in the case of a non-mandatory sentence, a reduction of the period of imprisonment be granted, to reflect the fact that the punishment administered was more punitive than the one intended, should a court so find; and
   (ii) in the case of a mandatory sentence, the same factors be considered as militating towards earlier release;
(c) that the Correctional Service properly educate its employees with respect to the rights of incarcerated offenders and inform them of the Service's commitment to seeing that these rights are respected and enforced.

9. With respect to segregation, I recommend:

(a) that when administrative segregation is used, it be administered in compliance with the law and appropriately monitored;

. . . .

(d) that the practice of long-term confinement in administrative segregation be brought to an end;
(e) that, in order to so achieve, a time limit be imposed along the following lines:
   (i) if the existing statutory pre-conditions for administrative segregation are met, an inmate be segregated for a maximum of three days, as directed by the institutional head, in response to an immediate incident;
   (ii) after three days, a documented review take place, if further detention in segregation is contemplated;
   (iii) the administrative review specify what further period of segregation, if any, is authorized, up to a maximum of 30 days, no more than twice in a calendar year, with the effect that an inmate not be made to spend more than 60 non-consecutive days in segregation in a year;
   (iv) after 30 days, or if the total days served in segregation during that year already approaches 60, the institution be made to consider and apply other options, such as transfer, placement in a mental health unit, or other forms of intensive supervision, but involving interaction with the general population;
   (v) if these options proved unavailable, or if the Correctional Service is of the view that a longer period segregation was required, the Service be required to apply to a court for a determination of the necessity of further segregation;
   (vi) that upon being seized of such application, the court be required to consider all the components of the sentence, including its duration, so as to make an order consistent with the original intent of the sentence, and the present circumstances of the offender;
(f) failing a willingness to put segregation under judicial supervision, I would recommend:
   (i) that segregation decisions be made at an institutional level subject to confirmation within five days by an independent adjudicator;
   (ii) that the independent adjudicator be a lawyer, and that he or she be required to give reasons for a decision to maintain segregation;
   (iii) that segregation reviews be conducted every 30 days, before a different adjudicator each time, who should also be a lawyer, and who should also be required to give reasons for his or her decision to maintain segregation;
(g) that failure to comply with any of the above provisions be treated as having rendered the conditions of imprisonment harsher than that contemplated by the sentence, for the purposes of the remedy contemplated in recommendation 8(b) and (c).

■

For the video whose release instigated the appointment of the Commission of Inquiry, and which documents the significant role played by outside organizations such as the CAEFS in ensuring that the issue was brought under public scrutiny, see CBC, *Fifth Estate* (21 February 1995).

Further discussion of the issue of strip-searching can be found in Amanda George, "Strip Searches: Sexual Assault by the State" (1993) 18 Alternative L.J. 31. For the submissions to the Commission by CAEFS, see CAEFS, *Phase II Submission of the Canadian Association of Elizabeth Fry Societies to the Commission of Inquiry into Certain Events at the Prison for Women in Kingston* (Ottawa: CAEFS, 1996).

Immediately upon the release of Justice Arbour's report, John Edwards resigned from his post as Commissioner of Corrections: Jeff Sallot, "Corrections system head resigns: Prison service operates without concern for rule of law, human rights, report declares" *The [Toronto] Globe and Mail* (2 April 1996) A1, A4. Solicitor General Herb Gray apologized to the women and stated that the government was considering the issue of compensation: *ibid.* He also gave a press release dated 4 June 1996 in which he stated that the government accepted some of the recommendations, including the appointment of a Deputy Commissioner of Women's Corrections, granting the right to counsel before body cavity searches, ensuring privacy for women in bathrooms and for dressing and undressing, developing new policies for non-violent intervention for crisis intervention, and desisting from using men to strip-search women prisoners. The recommendations regarding the creation of sanctions for staff and officials who violate the law and the institution of judicial review for administrative segregation decisions are apparently "under review." It has since been reported that guards in federal prisons are "just livid" about the report (Kirk Makin, "Hard time" *The [Toronto] Globe and Mail* (20 April 1996) D1, D2), which hostility may have repercussions for the conditions under which inmates live.

The Arbour Commission's Report has been described as a "remarkable document" that ought to be viewed as a "blueprint for change": Alan Manson, "Scrutiny from the Outside: The Arbour Commission, the Prison for Women and the Correctional Service of Canada" (1996) 1 Can. Crim. L. Rev. 321 at 321. Yet, with the exception of the appointment of a Deputy Commissioner for Women's Corrections responsible for overseeing federally sentenced women, very few of the recommendations have been implemented: Kelly Hannah-Moffat and Margaret Shaw, "Introduction" in Hannah-Moffat and Shaw, eds. *An Ideal Prison? Critical Essays on Women's Imprisonment in Canada* (Halifax: Fernwood, 2000) 11 at 24 [hereinafter *An Ideal Prison?*].

The Prison for Women closed in 2000 as regional women's prisons had been opened to implement the vision behind *Creating Choices* of replacing static security with dynamic security and providing women with minimum security conditions of imprisonment. However, Corrections changed course in 1996, citing escapes and an inmate's death soon after the opening of the Edmonton institution as the impetus for its decision to divert maximum security women from the regional institutions, as well as some women with severe mental health problems, and place them in segregated units in men's prisons. Security at the regional women's prisons was increased to medium security; static security measures were implemented; and Aboriginal women classified as maximum security were denied access to the newly opened Healing Lodge. Corrections plans to move maximum security women into separate units with "enhanced security" within the regional women's prisons as they are completed. Kelly Hannah-Moffat's book, *Punishment in Disguise. Penal Governance and Federal Imprisonment of Women in Canada* (Toronto: University of Toronto Press, 2001) at 183 states that although the new prisons were intended to rectify the problem that women at P4W served their sentences under conditions of high security regardless of their classification, this problem has now been replicated: "minimum security women do not have access to living units outside the fence, as is the case in men's minimum-security prisons."

In the meantime, Kim Pate, Executive Director of the Canadian Association of Elizabeth Fry Societies, reports that the incidents that sparked the Arbour Commission have been all been repeated in the new regional prisons: Kim Pate, "50 Years of Canada's International Commitment to Human Rights: Millstones in Correcting Corrections for Federally Sentenced Women" (2000) 20:3 Can. Woman Stud. 44 at 44–45. She identifies strip searches of women and women being stripped, shackled and chained to beds and body boards in segregation as well as the denial of access to minimum security conditions as ongoing human rights problems in the new women's prisons. As well, the experience of women housed in men's prisons and those subjected to segregation suggest that little has changed since the Arbour Commission reported: Nahlah Ayed and Sue Bailey, "Some women face months in segregation without services" *The National Post* (20 February 2001) online. For reports by Amnesty International that document and condemn the rape and sexual assault of women in prisons by male guards and the shackling of pregnant women during childbirth in U.S. prisons, see *Abuse of Women in Custody–Sexual Misconduct and Shackling of Pregnant Women* (2001) and *"Not Part of My Sentence": Violations of Human Rights of Women in Custody* (1999).

E. ABORIGINAL PEOPLES

Recall that the rate of incarceration of Aboriginal peoples is extremely high in relation to their representation in the population of Canada (see Judge Murray Sinclair, **Aboriginal Peoples and the Criminal Law** and the *Gladue* decision, **Sentencing**). The impact of incarceration is also particularly severe for Aboriginal prisoners: they will be even more isolated from their communities, families, culture, and spirituality, as the excerpt from *Killing the Shamen*, **Colonization and the Imposition of the Criminal Law**, and the cases in **Sentencing** on sexual assault in the North demonstrate.

Aboriginal inmates may have greater difficulty in "negotiating" the prison system themselves or through lawyers, and they may be subjected to further discrimination and abuse while in prison: Geoffrey York, "Native prisoners complain of discrimination" *The [Toronto] Globe and Mail* (13 April 1989) A4 (Mr. Antoine was at first denied leave to visit his dying father because he refused to sign a document which alleged that his father was an alcoholic; Mr. Antoine was then shackled for his attendance at the funeral). Other problems include a denial of access to elders, restricted access to spiritual practices, and parole on terms that prevent parolees from returning to their home reserves. See, for example, "Native inmates' demands get action" *Winnipeg Free Press* (16 July 1990) 3 (Manitoba Human Rights Commission considering claims of Aboriginal inmates at Headingley Correctional Institute for entitlement to burn sweetgrass, wear headbands, and construct a sweatlodge as part of their spiritual practice).

For Aboriginal women, their isolation and the consequences of imprisonment can be devastating, as Fran Sugar and Lana Fox, in "Nistum Peyako Seht'wawin Iskwewak: Breaking Chains" (1989–90) 3 C.J.W.L. 465, makes plain. Their article includes testimonials from 39 Aboriginal women that were incorporated into the report of the Task Force on Federally Sentenced Women. The experiences of these women were shaped by childhood violence, violence by the state, and isolation, loss, and violence within prison, including strip searches, macing, and slashing.

Of the eight women whose strip-searches at P4W were investigated by Justice Arbour, five were Aboriginal women. Consider the symbolism and the psychological impact of these searches upon the women. In her report, Justice Arbour commended the Ministry of the Solicitor General for the opening of the first Healing Lodge for federally sentenced women in Maple Creek, Saskatchewan, Okimaw Ohci, but noted that it has the capacity to house approximately 30 women, only half the population of federally sentenced Aboriginal women. She therefore recommended another Healing Lodge for the east and made numerous specific recommendations as to the provision of culturally appropriate services for Aboriginal women prisoners, including formalizing and facilitating access to Elders and Aboriginal counsellors, the recruitment of Aboriginal staff and contract workers, the provision of culturally sensitive training for staff, and increased resort to s. 81(3) of the *Corrections and Conditional Release Act*, which permits the placement of Aboriginal women in the care and custody of Aboriginal communities: *The Prison For Women, supra* at 254–55.

Herb Gray, then Solicitor General of Canada, declined to commit to a Healing Lodge in Eastern Canada. The promise of the Healing Lodge has been blunted as well by the decision to bar maximum security women from the Lodge, as these are the women who arguably need it most, including the very Aboriginal women who were the subject of Justice Arbour's Inquiry. Furthermore, according to Patricia Monture-Angus, Healing Lodges "are institutions, no matter how much Aboriginal culture inspires their contour, shape and form": "Aboriginal Women and Correctional Practice. Reflections on the Task Force on Federally Sentenced Women" in *An Ideal Prison?, supra* at 52, 53.

R. v. Daniels[†]

[WEDGE J.:]

Now as we've heard several times, the application alleges that the rights under ss. 7, 12, 15 and 28 of the *Canadian Charter of Rights and Freedoms* of women of native ancestry from the prairies region in general, and Carol Daniels in particular, sentenced to penitentiary terms, will be violated if they must serve any part of that term in the women's prison in Kingston, Ontario.

I'll begin with the rights under s. 15, and that's discrimination on the basis of sexual gender. Now the Crown has made that one very easy for me. I think it has conceded that women have been discriminated against in the federal penal system. Because the numbers of women are so few — (The total number as of April, 1990 was 130. I'm not exactly sure of the number. There's no evidence as to exactly how many of those are of native ancestry, but I understand the majority, as men's prisons also.) The numbers are so few in comparison with the large male population; various federal governments, although aware of this, have not considered that they were worth the financial cost of equal treatment. Other programs have had high priority. I'm not saying those programs are not necessary, but they have been priorized.

Prison for Women has been the subject of studies and commissions for over 50 years, and I shall not repeat the whole sad history. In 1982 the Human Rights Commission listed nine areas in which women were treated unequally from men, of course to the detriment of the women.

In April of this year a widely publicized report [*Creating Choice*], which has been referred to many times during this hearing, commissioned by the federal Department of Corrections was handed down. The Deputy Commissioner of Correctional Programs in Corrections Canada was co-chairman of the task force. The report presents a plan for the future to be fully implemented by 1993–94. The first of their recommendations, most relevant to this application, is that five regional penal institutions for women will be built across Canada, one region being the prairie region. Two, that a native spiritual healing lodge [will be] established in this region, that is, the prairie region, to meet the spiritual and cultural needs of aboriginal women, as they are referred to in the report. And three — I quote this from page 155 of the report:

> The plan presented by this Task Force finally closes the prison for women and brings women closer to their families, culture and communities.

. . . .

There is a quote on page 38 of the report from a recent Daubney Report, one of the latest of a series of reports about the plight of federal women prisoners:

> Imprisoned native women are triply disadvantaged: they suffer the pains of incarceration common to all prisoners; in addition, they experience both the pains native prisoners feel as a result of their cultural dislocation and those which women prisoners experience as a result of being incarcerated far from home and family.

The Task Force admitted on page 118 of the report that one of the central issues it faced with respect to aboriginal women was the discrimination within discrimination that is experienced by this group of federal women.

We heard the evidence of the witness, Joan Lavallee, a native elder and spiritual counsellor, who has worked with women prisoners for years and has had some personal knowledge of conditions at the women's prison. She had visited there many times. She described the high security, fortress like buildings, the dearth of programs which are available in men's prisons, and in particular the isolation, despair and hopelessness of native women far from home and children, extended family, exiled to an alien culture. All of this confirms the findings and contents of the Task Force report.

I am very satisfied that women of native ancestry from the prairie region in general, and Carol Daniels in particular, will be discriminated against if they must serve any time in the Prison for Women in Kingston. These potential discriminations arise out of s. 731 of the *Criminal Code*, which requires that women who are sentenced to more than two years must serve their time in a federal penitentiary, and s. 15 of the *Penitentiary Act*, R.S.C. 1985, c. P.-5 which gives the Commissioner discretion to direct

---

[†] [1990] 4 C.N.L.R. 51 (Sask. Q.B.).

where a prisoner must serve her sentence, and the various regulations and directions under that Act.

The Crown has not attempted to justify the violations under s. 1 of the Charter.

I should mention s. 15(2) which in essence, makes provision for certain affirmative action programs. I think I can ignore it as sentencing native women to a women's prison is certainly no affirmative action to their benefit.

Section 28 of the Charter provides that:

> 28. Notwithstanding anything in this Charter, the rights and freedoms referred to in it are guaranteed equally to male and female persons.

In these circumstances, it would be illogical to suggest that these women should suffer the discriminatory treatment and be denied relief because men are subject to the same exercise of the Commissioner's discretion. There is no basis for comparison.

Federal penitentiaries for men have superior programs. They're stretched across the width of the country. Female prisoners are not similarly treated to male prisoners.

There was no attempt at justification under this section (if in fact you can justify under that section).

Sections 7 and 12 of the Charter. I also find that sentencing native women from this region to the Prison for Women would violate their rights under ss. 7 and 12.

Section 7 guarantees the life and security of everyone to whom it applies, including Carol Daniels and her peers. There was evidence before me that two native women recently committed suicide in the prison, and another did the same shortly after her release.

Women like Carol Daniels who commit serious offences must be punished for their crimes by imprisonment, even for life, but the high risk of death by suicide in a far away, "medieval, castle-like prison," is in my opinion unacceptable in a free and democratic society.

Section 12 was considered by the Supreme Court in the *Smith* case, which I mentioned this morning [*R. v. Smith*, [1987] 1 S.C.R. 1045, 40 D.L.R. (4th) 435, 34 C.C.C. (3d) 97, 58 C.R. (3d) 193]. Mr. Justice McIntyre described cruel and unusual punishment as a compendious expression of a norm. Punishment may be cruel and unusual because it's disproportionate to the gravity of the offence, which is not the case here, Carol's crime was one of the very gravest, or because it inflicts unnecessary pain or degradation.

Mr. Justice McIntyre said on page 205 [C.R.] of the report which I have:

> How then is this compendious expression of a norm to be defined? There is no problem of definition or recognition of cruel and unusual treatment or punishment at the extreme limit of the application, but of course the day has passed when the barbarous punishments of earlier days were a threat to those convicted of crime. In my view in its modern application the meaning of "cruel and unusual treatment or punishment" must be drawn "from the evolving standards of decency that mark the progress of a maturing society."

And on page 204 [C.R.]:

> There are conditions associated with the service of sentences of imprisonment which may become subject to scrutiny under the provisions of s. 12 of the Charter, not only on the basis of disproportionality or excess but also concerning the nature or quality of the treatment. Solitary confinement as practiced in certain circumstances affords an example.

Now there are other examples. I am going to skip down to the bottom:

> ... and imprisonment at locations far distant from home, family and friends, a condition amounting to virtual exile which is particularly relevant to women, since there is only one federal penitentiary for women in Canada. I offer no opinion as to what a court would decide in respect of any one of these examples of treatment should a challenge be made. I merely note there exists a field for the exercise of s. 12 scrutiny in modern penal practice. It has not become obsolete.

It also seems implicit in this case and others that s. 12 confers an absolute right and may not be saved by s. 1 of the Charter, but in any event, the Crown has not attempted a justification.

. . . .

But in Saskatchewan there is an alternative. Arrangements have been made through federal-provincial agreements and I'm satisfied that they could be made again at Pinegrove. Annette Neustaidler, who by the way is the first female Director at Pinegrove and since 1967, described new programs which are in effect there. Life skills, work placement, literacy and more. Frequent family visits are allowed. A native elder visits regularly. Arrangements are in place for women who give birth during imprisonment, as will probably be the case with Carol Daniels, to be with their babies during the daytime hours. And I understand that was Joan Lavallee that understood that in her studies and knowledge that in some of the provincial prisons in Alberta and Manitoba that these programs were also being put in force.

Now because of these federal provincial agreements, some federally sentenced women are now serving their sentences in Pinegrove. During the three years in which Miss Neustaidler has been Director, nine women from there have been transferred to Kingston.

Mr. Rollo, the Crown's witness this morning, says that sentences being served in Pinegrove are in the two to five-year range, not life with a ten-year minimum eligibility for parole with release that can happen here. Usually the last two years of a long sentence are all served at Pinegrove.

. . . .

[An interchange ensued regarding the appropriate sentence.]

THE COURT: All right. Stand up, Ms. Daniels. I sentence you to life imprisonment, without eligibility for parole for ten years. You may sit down.

As a result, you'll notice I didn't say in a federal penitentiary in that sentence. I just said life imprisonment as a result of my decision here today.

I may need help with this order, Mr. White, unless you think the one I am about to suggest is appropriate or you may submit a draft for my approval.

There will be an order pursuant to s. 52(1) of the *Constitution Act* declaring that s. 731 of the *Criminal Code*, s. 15 of the *Penitentiary Act*, and any other sections or regulations or directions under that Act, which may from this date on, cause Carol Daniels or other women of native ancestry from the prairie provinces to be incarcerated in the Kingston Prison for Women, are of no force or effect to the extent that they are inconsistent with the rights of these women under ss. 7, 12, 15(1) and 28 of the Charter.

. . . .

THE COURT: There will be a remedy under s. 24(1) of the Charter which will be afforded Carol Daniels in order to protect her from anticipated breaches of her Charter rights, and that is that there will be an order endorsed on the Warrant of Committal concerning Carol Daniels, that Carol Daniels is not to serve any part of her sentence in the Prison for Women in Kingston, Ontario.

■

The ruling in *Daniels* was reversed by the Saskatchewan Court of Appeal in *R. v. Daniels*, [1991] 5 W.W.R. 340 on the basis that the relevant legislation (the *Prisons and Reformatories Act*, s. 5, and the *Penitentiary Act*, s. 3) permitted the Commissioner of Corrections to designate provincial institutions as "penitentiaries," and thus the legislative scheme itself did not violate s. 15. The trial judge's powers were held to cease upon sentencing, and did not extend to anticipated acts or defaults in the "administration" of the sentence by the Commissioner; these can only be challenged through a federal court action.

The Koori peoples (Aboriginal peoples) of Australia also experience shockingly high rates of incarceration and the consequent isolation and risk of death in custody. In 1987, the Royal Commission into Aboriginal Deaths in Custody was established to investigate 99 deaths of Koori prisoners that occurred from 1 January 1980 to 31 May 1989. The total number of deaths in custody during this period exceeded 400.

The Commission determined that a Koori was 10 times more likely to die in prison than a non-Koori and 20 times more likely to die while in police custody: Royal Commission into Aboriginal Deaths in Custody, *National Report* (Canberra: Austr. Govt. Pub. Service, 1991) 3.5.3. It stated that "an examination of the lives of the 99 shows that facts associated in every case with their Aboriginality played a significant and in most cases dominant role in their being in custody and dying in custody": *Overview and Recommendations*, 1.

However, the Commission failed to find that even one of these deaths was "the product of deliberate brutality or violence by police or prison officials": *National Report*, 1.1.3; 1.2.2. The conclusion that these deaths were not "culpable" has been challenged: Leannine Purdy, "Royal Commissions and Omissions" (1992) 17 Alternative L.J. 32. See also Kate Kerley and Chris Cuneen, "Deaths in Custody in Australia: The Untold Story of Aboriginal and Torres Strait Islander Women" (1996) 8 C.J.W.L., 531.

The Commission made extensive recommendations regarding the policing and incarceration of Koori people in Australia, and some of these have already found their way into law: Desmond

Sweeney, "Police Questioning of Aboriginal Suspects for Commonwealth Offences: New Laws" (1992) 2:54 Aborig. L. Bull. 10. The recommendations aimed at reducing the over-imprisonment of Koori people have been thwarted by the adoption of mandatory minimum sentencing laws in two states: Megan Hoey and Martin Flynn, "Deaths in Custody. The Royal Commission: 10 Years on" (2001) 26:4 Alt. L.J. 196.

This discussion should not close without reference to the broader debates about the use of imprisonment. According to the Canadian Centre for Justice Statistics, Canada in 1994–95 had the second highest rate of incarceration (after the United States) in the industrialized world, imprisoning 151 per 100,000 adults: CAEFS, "National Elizabeth Fry Week: Alternatives to Incarceration" (6 May 1996). Abolition of imprisonment, particularly for non-violent offenders, has been urged on numerous grounds: civil rights, the reduction of future violence by those who have served lengthy terms of incarceration, as well as the economic and cost-effectiveness of imprisonment. For argument in support of abolition, see Ruth Morris, *Penal Abolition: The Practical Choice* (Toronto: Canadian Scholars Press, 1995); Jim Consedine, *Restorative Justice: Healing the Effects of Crime* (Lyttleton: New Zealand: Ploughshares, 1995); Prisoners Action Group, "Submission to the Royal Commission into New South Wales Prisons: Abolition" (1980) 3 Alternative Criminology J. 1; CP, "Swift action for justice system urged to avoid financial crisis" *The [Toronto] Globe and Mail* (4 December 1995) A4; Claire Culhane, *Barred From Prison: A Personal Account* (Vancouver: Pulp Press, 1979); and Claire Culhane, *No Longer Barred from Prison: Social Injustice in Canada* (Toronto: University of Toronto Press, 1991). Culhane was a social activist who battled with Canadian prison officials on behalf of prisoner's rights over many years until her death in 1996: "Ms. Culhane was as fearless as she was indefatigable. Temporarily banned from Canadian prisons several years ago, she happily trespassed and invited the authorities to risk arresting a white-haired grandmother." Kirk Makin, "Lives Lived" *The [Toronto] Globe and Mail* (2 May 1996) A20.

At the same time, provincial governments and corrections officials are increasingly considering the privatization of Canadian prisons as a cost-cutting measure. Privatization presents serious risks of further emphasis on law and order solutions to crime, reduced governmental accountability, limited access to law and human rights, and an increased corporate control of the criminal justice agenda. Carl Wilson reports in "Renting Out the Big House. Could private prisons shake up our failing jails?" *This Magazine* (October 1995) 19 at 20, that Ontario, Nova Scotia, New Brunswick, and Alberta considered privatization. He notes: "Critics in Britain and Australia have complained of prison companies campaigning for longer sentences and tougher policing, in order to increase 'client base.' "The government of New Brunswick has backed down from its plan to allow Wackenhut Corrections Corporation to operate the youth jail that it is contracted to build: CP, "Florida company to build N.B. prison" *The [Toronto] Globe and Mail* (21 June 1996) A2, but Ontario forged ahead.

Ontario opened Canada's first privately run prison in 2001, a "superjail" for 1200 maximum security men in Penetanguishene. Ohio senator Robert F. Hagan, who was responsible for the district in which a private prison failed in a spectacular manner, wrote to then Premier Mike Harris and urged him not to privatize. He called Ohio's experience with privatization "wholly regrettable," and said that it was consistent with similar problems of under-staffing, inexperienced staff, escapes, and violence reported by other privately-run U.S. prisons: Patti Ryan, "Making Crime Pay" *The National* (October 2001) 14 at 20. For example, one study out of George Washington University examining California jails found an escape rate that was 30 per cent higher in privately run prisons, and several U.S. studies (from the U.S. General Accounting Office and the Oklahoma Corrections Department) show that they are more costly to run than prisons run by the government (*ibid.* at 16). In "Correctional Renewal Without the Frills: The Politics of 'Get Tough' Punishment in Ontario" in Joe Hermer and Janet Mosher, eds. *Disorderly People: Law and the Politics of Exclusion in Ontario* (Halifax: Fernwood, 2002) 105 at 120, Dawn Moore and Kelly Hannah-Moffat argue that the privatization of Penetanguishene advances the new-right agenda of reducing the welfare state: "We in Ontario are being brought back to a myth of corrections, an emotional tale in which vengeance and frugality breed safety and reduce criminality. We know that what happens in fairy tales never occurs in reality."

F. PAROLE

Parole offers the possibility of both discretionary and mandatory release from prison before the expiration of the sentence. According to Mary Campbell, "Sentencing and Conditional Release," in *Making Sense of Sentencing*, supra at 242, parole serves several important functions in a criminal justice system: it can mitigate the harmful effects of institutionalization; provide incentives for co-operation by prisoners; facilitate a gradual and successful re-integration into the community; and reduce recidivism by former inmates. Paroled offenders remain under the authority of the National Parole Board [hereinafter NPB] until warrant expiry, which is, in the case of persons convicted of murder, the remainder of their lives. If the terms of release are breached they are re-incarcerated, they can also be re-incarcerated upon a determination by their parole supervision that it is necessary or reasonable to prevent a breach of condition or to protect society.

Parole is governed by the *Corrections and Conditional Release Act*, R.S.C. 1992, c. C-20 [hereinafter *CCRA*] and the *Criminal Code*. It is administered by the NPB for all federally sentenced prisoners. With respect to provincially sentenced prisoners, the *CCRA* delegates the NPB's authority to the provinces, but only Ontario and Québec have their own parole boards, leaving the NPB with the responsibility of making parole decisions with respect to most provincially sentenced inmates, albeit in accordance with the criteria set out in provincial parole legislation. For further details regarding the division of authority in this area see Sandra G. Leonard, "Conditional Release from Imprisonment" in *Making Sense of Sentencing*, supra at 259.

The *CCRA* represents the most comprehensive changes to parole since 1959, replacing both the *Parole Act* and the *Penitentiaries Act*. Part I of the new act is corrections legislation governing the mandate and operations of prisons. Part II redefines the parole system and the operation of the National Parole Board, and Part III creates a new Office of the Correctional Investigator, or ombud for federal prisoners.

The act includes some of the following features:

- New powers are granted to sentencing judges with respect to offences listed in schedules to the act (generally offences of actual or potential violence, offences involving children, and other offences such as trafficking in drugs) to increase the custody portion of the accused's sentence so that eligibility for full parole is delayed until at least one-half of the sentence has been served (see *Criminal Code*, s. 743.6). Under the prior act most prisoners would have been entitled to consideration for parole after service of one-third of the sentence.

- Accelerated parole review has been established for first-time federally sentenced offenders, except those convicted of offences listed in the schedules (murder, a life sentence, or other listed office) to the act.

- The system of earned remission has been abolished (up to 15 days per month could be earned for "good behaviour" under the prior system) and replaced by automatic statutory release after service of two-thirds of the sentence.

- Detention until warrant expiry for the full sentence ("gating") can be imposed by the NPB for listed offences where it is satisfied that the offender is likely to commit a violent offence or one involving a serious drug if released.

- Drastically reduced availability of day parole has been instituted for all those incarcerated. Under the prior act a prisoner would be eligible for day parole after service of one-sixth of the sentence; it will now be available only after six months have been served or during the last six months of sentence, whichever period is longer.

- Victims of offenders will now be allowed to attend parole hearings at the discretion of the National Parole Board, and will be able to make submissions to the Board.

Parole eligibility for murder is governed by the *Criminal Code*: for first degree murder offenders are, subject to s. 745.6, ineligible for parole until at least 25 years of the mandatory life sentence have been served (s. 745(a)); in the case of second degree murder, parole ineligibility is at least 10 years (s. 745(b)), and a judge may, after hearing the advice of the jury, increase the period of ineligibility beyond 10 years up to a maximum of 25 years (s. 745.4). For a detailed discussion of the law of parole for people convicted of murder see Julian V. Roberts and David P. Cole, "Sentencing and Early Release Arrangements for Offenders Convicted of Murder" in *Making Sense of Sentencing*, supra at 277.

The impetus for these major changes to the law of parole appears to have been created by groups such as Victims of Violence and the climate of fear generated by several horrific murders committed by parolees. "[W]hat is certain is that over all, the changes will translate into longer sentences for many future prisoners convicted of serious offences": Timothy Appleby, "Stricter parole law proclaimed quietly" *The [Toronto] Globe and Mail* (November 1992) A1, A6.

The new legislation has had a significant impact upon the parole process and the debates around parole. A recent study of the "grant rate" found that 58 per cent of those who applied for day parole last year succeeded, as compared to 65 per cent in 1993–94; the comparable figures for full parole are 31 per cent compared to 37 per cent: Kirk Makin, "Delayed jail releases exceed prediction" *The [Toronto] Globe and Mail* (14 February 1996) A5. Prosecutors in Alberta are now requesting longer parole in eligibility terms for violent offenders (Brian Laghi, "Alberta to free up jail space; keep violent criminals in longer" *The [Toronto] Globe and Mail* (9 April 1996) A4) and Toronto police are lobbying for reforms that would make it easier for them to arrest parole violators (Henry Hess, "Toronto police board seeks tougher parole enforcement" *The [Toronto] Globe and Mail* (24 September 1993) A2C. In addition, even though the legislative authority for "gating" was said to be targeted at approximately 50 prisoners, as of 1995–96, 484 prisoners had been detained, and in 1998–99 233 prisoners were detained: Allan Manson et al., *Sentencing and Penal Policy in Canada. Cases, Materials and Commentary* (Toronto: Emond Montgomery, 2000) at 705. Another study reports that although judges are exercising their new authority to lengthen parole ineligibility in only 4 per cent of the cases before them, this group of offenders is less likely to be granted parole once eligible and twice as likely to be gated once on statutory release: Julian Roberts, "Corrections and Conditional Release Act: Five Years Later" (1998) 13:2 Justice Report 8 at 8, 9.

It should be noted that the impact of systemic discrimination emerges in parole determinations. Whether attributable to systemic discrimination in law enforcement, the nature of the conviction, the weighting of aggravating and mitigating factors at sentencing, or the variables used to determine parole, such as "risk assessment," Aboriginal offenders are less likely to apply for full parole (47.7 per cent of eligible Aboriginal prisoners and 73.5 per cent of eligible non-Aboriginal offenders) and less likely to receive it (29.3 per cent of Aboriginal applicants and 38.7 per cent of non-Aboriginal applicants): Andrew Welsh and James R.P. Ogloff, "Full parole and the aboriginal experience: Accounting for the racial discrepancies in release rates" (2000) 42 Can. J. Crim. 469 at 483–84.

Consider as well the impact of the requirement for parole that an inmate accept responsibility for the crime and express remorse. Will it have a disproportionate impact upon certain groups of people? For example, in *The Report of the Commission on Systemic Racism in the Ontario Criminal Justice System* (Toronto: Queen's Printer for Ontario, 1995), although the Commission was unable to compare outcomes for white and Black parole applicants, it noted that there are information and communication barriers for Black applicants, and that stereotypes also resurface in the parole process, to the detriment of Black applicants: "For example, a black female prisoner who denied having a drug problem was repeatedly asked what programs she had entered to address her drug addiction" (*ibid.* at 325). What will be the impact of this condition for parole for battered women who have killed violent mates? See Abell and Sheehy, *Proof, Defences, and Beyond*, **Self-Defence**.

Furthermore, members of visible minority communities may be more likely to be wrongly convicted, as was discussed *supra* under **Enforcement of the Law**. For example, Donald Marshall, Jr. was also denied parole on the basis that he refused to accept responsibility for the death of Sandy Seale. Peter Hill, "The unwritten rule of parole" *New Law Journal* (12 April 1996) 510 at 512, comments on the remorse requirement as follows:

> [I]s it right to demand that a man incriminate himself before he can qualify for parole? Having convicted him of a crime, must we force him to agree he is guilty before we will even think of letting him out of prison? If this is the full meaning of a prison sentence, why do judges not make it clear when they pronounce judgment? If we acknowledge, as we must, that there are some cases of miscarriage of justice, must we grant to those who protest their innocence less right of parole than we grant to convicts who happily admit their guilt?
>
> If we do, then we may soon find ourselves supporting the view that the innocent must suffer whilst the guilty go free.

7

Law and Order

Law and Order and the Canadian State[†]

Beginning in the 1970s and the 1980s, expenditure by Canadian governments on law and order increased dramatically. See, for example, Ian Taylor, *Crime, Capitalism and Community* (Toronto: Butterworths, 1983) at 141–42. Criminal justice budgets continued to escalate until the early 1990s, with a large proportion of those budgets going to policing and prisons. According to Statistics Canada, justice costs tripled between 1975 and 1987, while the "crime rate" increased 32 per cent. "The breakdown of costs (totalling $7.7 billion) indicates that in 1990, each Canadian spent $179 on adult corrections; $15 on incarcerating young offenders; $13 on legal aid; and $25 on running the court system": Ann Blood, "Particulars" *The Lawyers Weekly* (24 May 1991) 4.

Spending on criminal justice starkly contrasts with spending on other programs. For example, as Mary Ellen Turpel points out, in Saskatchewan in 1992–93, approximately $81 million (74 per cent of the criminal justice budget) was spent on Aboriginal people's interaction with the criminal justice system. In contrast, less than $200,000 was available to First Nations in Saskatchewan for justice projects: Mary Ellen Turpel, "Reflections on Thinking Concretely about Criminal Justice Reform" in Richard Gosse, James Youngblood Henderson, and Roger Carter, compilers, *Continuing Poundmaker and Riel's Quest: Presentations Made at a Conference on Aboriginal Peoples and Justice* (Saskatoon: Purich, 1994) at 214. Undoubtedly, only a fraction of that was available to autonomous Aboriginal women's organizations.

In recent years the federal government has withdrawn billions of dollars of transfer payments for social programs, abdicated responsibility to the provinces, and defunded social programs and the NGO sector. In 1990, the federal government imposed a ceiling on the Canada Assistance Plan (CAP) funding for Alberta, British Columbia, and Ontario. That freeze on CAP payments was followed by the complete abandonment of CAP and the substitution of the Canada Health and Social Transfer (CHST) in 1995.

There have been a number of important shifts in labour, poverty, criminal justice, equity, and legal services across the country. Many groups are facing cuts to benefits and social programs and political struggle over earlier gains. When combined with an erosion of legal victories in the

---

[†] Jennie Abell, "Law and Order and the Canadian State."

courts, these cuts are further exacerbated by the narrowing availability of legal aid and a new set of laws ranged against poor people.

These issues intersect and are contained within a larger political context of structural adjustment in Canada and the ensuing dislocation and deepening poverty for women and children, the widening gap between rich and poor, and a growing racialization of that gap. This context includes increasing conservatism and broad cuts to the public sector and to social justice programs, the abandonment of commitments to equity, the denial or reframing of "poverty" (for example, the denial that poverty exists and the debates about the definition of a "poverty line"), the restriction of entitlement to social assistance, cuts to welfare rates and the criminalization of new categories of people by a new regime of law. Criminalization proceeds amid appeals for "law and order" and moves towards the privatization of policing, prisons and law enforcement, and the privatization of essential social programs such as education and health. For a more detailed discussion of these issues, see: Jennie Abell, *Structural Adjustment and the New Poor Laws: Gender, Poverty and Violence and Canada's International Commitments* (Ottawa: Feminist Alliance for International Action, 2002).

Cuts to equity programs have been drastic, and the language of equity and social justice has been abandoned. Meanwhile, the relationship between police and Aboriginal peoples has deteriorated further, and there have been repeated calls for inquiries into systemic racism and for disciplinary actions against a number of police officers. Despite the wide-ranging documentation of racism and injustices against Aboriginal people, individual instance of miscarriages of justice have been more readily acknowledged than systemic wrongs, as the discussion of *R.* v. *Munson* (involving police officers who abandoned an Aboriginal man on the outskirts of Saskatoon), **Sentencing**, supra, demonstrates.

Prisoners, whose rights have been somewhat enlarged under the *Charter*, and whose long-standing grievances were substantiated by the *Report of the Commission on Systemic Racism in the Ontario Criminal Justice System* (Toronto: Queen's Printer for Ontario, 1995) and, in the case of women, by the *Commission of Inquiry into Certain Events at The Prison For Women* (Ottawa: Canada Communication Group, 1996) are left with virtually no access to legal representation, because of the cutbacks. At the same time, law and order lobbies are challenging the rights of those convicted of criminal offences to rehabilitation and reentry into society. Vigilantes are insisting on the publication of information about released prisoners and promoting their harassment. Characterizations of "dangerousness" and the current classification and "security" system within prisons, and their brutal effect on the sentences of women and, more particularly, Aboriginal women and women with disabilities, remain relatively unchallenged except by prisoners' advocates.

Despite some contradictory initiatives at the federal level — for example, the creation of Okimaw Ohci Healing Lodge and the closure of the Prison for Women (P4W) — conditions for women prisoners continue to be the subject of criticism. Women have been moved from P4W to men's prisons and, increasingly, face segregation as they are housed in men's penitentiaries. The lack of access to programs continues to violate women's equality rights. Earlier this year, the Correctional Investigator of Canada described the conditions under which women were held as "brutal" and "discriminatory" generally, and particularly under-resourced in the area of mental health services: Sue Bailey and Nahlah Ayed, CP, "Female inmates in men's jails suffer, report says" *The [Toronto] Globe and Mail* (9 February 2001) A3. The callous disregard for the rights of women prisoners is mirrored by the failure of the Solicitor-General or the Minister of Justice to act on many of the recommendations with respect to federally sentenced women made by Judge Lynn Ratushny in the *Self-Defence Review: First Interim Report — Women in Custody* and by Justice Arbour in the *Commission of Inquiry into Certain Events at the Prison For Women in Kingston*.

Women prisoners are now challenging, once again, the conditions of their detention and the lack of access to programs. Discrimination on the basis of race and disability continues with respect to the disproportionate segregation and designation of women as "maximum security." The recent complaint by the Canadian Association of Elizabeth Fry Societies to the Canadian Human Rights Commission, highlights these grievances and requests the Commission to undertake a broad-systemic review (per s. 61(2) of the *Canadian Human Rights Act*) into the discrimination against federally sentenced women. The complaint was supported by a broad range of organizations, including the Aboriginal Women's Action Network, Assembly of First Nations, National Association of Friendship Centres, Federation of Saskatchewan Nations, Strength in Sisterhood, DisAbled Women's Network Canada,

National Action Committee on the Status of Women, National Association of Women and the Law, Canadian Association of Sexual Assault Centres, Canadian Research Institute for the Advancement of Women, FAFIA, and by the Canadian Bar Association and Amnesty International: Canadian Association of Elizabeth Fry Societies, "Complaint Regarding the Discriminatory Treatment of Federally Sentenced Women by the Government of Canada" (Letter to Michelle Falardeau-Ramsay, Chief Commissioner, Canadian Human Rights Commission, 8 March 2001).

Youth face the militarization of prisons as "boot camps" are created and more punitive regimes are implemented. Young women are additionally disadvantaged by the lack of provision of gender-sensitive and safe spaces, disadvantages that are compounded for specific groups of girls (for example, Aboriginal girls, racialized girls, lesbian girls, disabled girls).

Diversion programs, mediation programs, and bail-supervision programs in Ontario and elsewhere have been targeted for cuts. Parole rates have been declining despite a decline in recidivism: Graeme Smith, "Fewer inmates get parole in Ontario" *The [Toronto] Globe and Mail* (20 November 2001) A10. The result will be more people incarcerated in already overcrowded jails and increasing discrimination against accused persons on economic grounds. Conditional sentencing and sentencing alternatives return the obligation to the communities, often without adequate resources and without a gendered analysis. For example, support for Aboriginal justice alternatives is being undermined fiscally as the evidence mounts that demonstrates the need for it. One of the criticisms of alternative sentencing and community responsibility has been the failure to provide adequate funding and resources to First Nations communities to accompany the downloading of responsibility. Another criticism from within First Nations communities has been the failure of alternative sentencing to sufficiently attend to women's needs, discussed *supra*, **Sentencing**.

In various provinces, the moves to offload responsibility have included moves to privatize and "militarize" prison, a discounting of rehabilitation and the consequent de-funding of halfway houses and counselling programs, a denial of state responsibility for victims of violence and the de-funding of battered women's shelters and transition houses, and massive cuts to welfare. The cuts have been accompanied by strategies of disentitlement and ideological justifications for the abdication of responsibility.

Critics of the moves to privatize prisons in New Brunswick, Nova Scotia, Ontario, and Alberta argue that it will be in the interest of prison companies to campaign for longer sentences and heavier policing and to discount rehabilitation and parole: Carl Wilson, "Renting Out the Big House: Could Private Prisons Shake Up our Failing Jails" *This Magazine* (October 1995) 19. Canada already has one of the highest rates of incarceration in the world (topped only by the U.S. and Russia), and prisons are badly over-crowded. Segregation is widely used, and Canadian prisoners are held in segregation for longer periods than are deemed lawful elsewhere. Now, that problem is compounded for women housed in men's institutions. Added to the rights violations faced by women prisoners generally, Aboriginal women continue to be confronted by extreme inequalities, including their disproportionate incarceration and their disproportionate labelling as "dangerous."

The cuts in many provinces have had a devastating impact on legal aid, on legal clinics, on the courts, on access to justice and, ultimately, on the evolution of law. Madam Justice Arbour, for example, has referred to "an alarming increase [in unrepresented litigants] throughout the country in all kinds of matters, not just in criminal matters ... [which] puts an enormous strain on the system that it's not designed to operate with." As she says, "If there is no time or no money [to fully scrutinize and prepare cases], I think your entire jurisprudence and therefore the legal system is impoverished....": Kirk Makin, "Crisis in legal aid dire, Arbour warns" *The [Toronto] Globe and Mail* (2 March 2002) A1. Crown attorneys are also under considerable pressure. The cuts seem likely to have a more severe effect on women, for example, in terms of the incapacity to pursue cases involving domestic violence against women. It is not yet clear how severely the cuts will impact on policing and prison budgets, nor which programs will be affected, but it seems likely that equity programs will be sacrificed.

Critics have argued that, even from an economic analysis, slashing social programs and "getting tough on crime" is a dubious strategy. Dehumanizing prisoners, for example with chain gang labour, is likely to increase rage and violence and crime. Rehabilitative programs and community service programs are considerably less costly than jails and more effective. Also, cuts to social programs and increased poverty and hopelessness contribute to prison riots: Justice E.N. (Ted) Hughes, *Report of the independent review of the circumstances surrounding the April 25–26, 1996 riot at the Headingley Correctional Institution* (Winnipeg: Manitoba Justice, 1996). In the case of women prisoners, the desperate conditions have led to abuse and self-inflicted violence: Task Force on Federally Sentenced Women, *Creating Choices: Report of the Task Force on Federally Sentenced Women* (Ottawa: Correctional Service of Canada, 1990).

Proponents of increases to law and order budgets and increased powers for police argue that crime and consequent fear or panic about safety are increasing. Those claims continue to be made, in spite of the evidence from Statistics Canada that violent crime, murder rates, and youth crime have declined each year since 1993: Doug Fischer, "Fall in rate of violent crime confounds public perception" *The [Toronto] Globe and Mail* (3 August 1995) A1; Jeff Sallot, "Drop in violent crime doesn't reduce fear" *The [Toronto] Globe and Mail* (4 August 1995) A17. See also: Canadian Centre for Justice Statistics, *The Juristat Reader: A Statistical Overview of the Canadian Justice System* (Toronto: Thompson, 1999), which documents, at 117, a decrease in police-reported crime (5%, leading to the lowest rate since 1980); decrease in violent crime (1.1%); decrease in almost all violent offences; decline in rate of youths charged with both property (12%) and violent offences (2%) (overall decline of 7%); and a decrease in the rates of violent crime in 16 of the 25 metropolitan areas. The most recent statistics confirm the trend of declining crime rates (1%), but point to a slight increase in violent crimes (3%), which some observers attribute to higher reporting levels: CP, "Overall crime dropping, but violence on the rise" *The Toronto Star* (19 July 2001).

Statistical evidence also does not support claims of increased violent crimes by women, nor claims of higher levels of violence among women, despite the excessive media coverage of high-profile cases: Michele Landsberg, "Misogynists misrepresent 'violent' women" *The Toronto Star* (14 August 1999). The character and level of anxiety about crime varies, and studies have challenged many assumptions about the fear of crime.

The unwarranted fear is shaped and fed by proponents of increases to police budgets and to police powers. For example, the Metro Toronto Police Association responded to the news that staffing levels had fallen to the lowest level since the early 1970s with an advertisement, underneath a picture of a hooded gunman:

> Go ahead, call the cops.
> There's more of us than them.
> FACT In the last ten years,
> - violent crimes INCREASED by 75%
> - assaults INCREASED by 97%
> - armed robberies INCREASED by 164%

(Reproduced in Henry Hess, "Police under double-barrelled gun: Budget cuts and shift to community policing could be deadly for Toronto officers, who already face lowest staffing levels in more than 20 years" *The [Toronto] Globe and Mail* (29 December 1995) A5).

Fear about rising crime has also prompted a greater willingness to consider more invasive policing techniques and databases on offenders, suspects, complainants, and potential victims: for example, of DNA. These proposed powers have very serious consequences for the privacy and equality rights of both suspects and complainants. They extend the state's surveillance powers dramatically, powers that are then vulnerable to differential application on the basis of class and race, for example. The *DNA Identification Act*, S.C. 1998, c. 37 came into force in June 2000 and its constitutionality and applicability (authorizing the taking of a bodily sample from an offender with respect to an offence committed *before* June 2000) was upheld in *R. v. Briggs* (2001), 55 O.R. (3d) 417 (C.A.). Critics have argued that a DNA databank is unlikely to enhance the effectiveness of the policing and prosecution of violent crime against women, yet the databank would draw considerable financial resources from more essential programs such as women's survivor and advocacy organizations: Fiona Miller, "The DNA Bank: A Feminist Critique" (Toronto: Feminist Alliance on New Reproductive and Genetic Technologies, 1996). For example, Miller refers to RCMP costs of $6 million annually for DNA casework, $5.8 million to develop the forensic laboratory, and further costs of $2.2 million in Ontario to double the current capacity of the DNA testing unit. For a further discussion of these concerns, see also: Michael Grange, "Police back plan to use DNA bank in crime fight" *The [Toronto] Globe and Mail* (20 January 1997) A1.

One of the insidious aspects of the DNA databank that Fiona Miller identifies is the growing practice of gathering DNA material from complainants and potential victims. This coincides with other moves to gather identification information on potential victims, for example, children: "New ID program launched for newborns" *The [Toronto] Globe and Mail* (9 April 1996) A7 (describing a program to be used at 58 Ontario hospitals that would gather photos, footprint and vital statistics of babies and *even their mother's thumbprint*). Other programs have advocated the fingerprinting of children so that they can potentially be identified if they are subsequently victims of some horrific crime. For an example of one of these clinics, or "fingerprinting events," as they are referred to, see: Linda Denley, "Operation Child Print" *The Ottawa Citizen* (16 January 1999) C8.

Connected to the increased surveillance proposed to combat crime, the elision of reliance on welfare with criminality is used to bolster more invasive scrutiny and surveillance of welfare recipients. Advocates of the fingerprinting of welfare recipients seem totally unconcerned about privacy issues, both for welfare recipients and for all citizens: Paul Bobier, "Chipping Away at Privacy: Will every detail of your personal life end up some day on easily accessible micro-chips?" (May 2001) *Briarpatch* 23–24. For example, Metro Toronto Council, in voting to investigate the possibility of replacing the current security system at Metro Hall with finger-scanning, suggested that the system should be used for identification nation-wide.

Solutions to crime are articulated in law and order terms. There have been calls for tougher laws to control high-risk offenders and, even, potential offenders. The *Young Offenders Act*, R.S.C. 1985, c. Y-1 has increasingly been the subject of controversy, and new legislation has now been passed without any countervailing attention to the social problems confronting young people, such as increasing suicide rates, cuts to education, and increasing unemployment: *Bill C-7: The Youth Criminal Justice Act* (Royal Assent: 19 February 2002). Québec has consistently been the only significant opponent of moves to "get tough," arguing that the focus should be on youth rehabilitation. They plan a Court Challenge to the new legislation: Mark Bourrie, "Liberals ram through youth crime bill: Feds ignore Ontario proposals to toughen bill for some offences" *Law Times* (11 February 2002) 1. In contrast, Ontario has characterized the new federal legislation as mere "slaps on the wrists," and has called instead for increased jail sentences and automatic raising to adult court for young offenders charged with serious crimes: Canada NewsWire, "Ottawa misses another opportunity to get tough on youth crime" (5 February 2001); Theresa Boyle, "Crime commission hits road to challenge 'timid' proposal: Ontario planning hearings on Ottawa's youth justice bill" *The Toronto Star* (11 August 2001); CP, "Ontario plans hearings on new Young Offenders Act" *The Toronto Star* (10 August 2001).

Responses to complainants/victims are also both shaped and sold in law and order terms: Simone Chiose, "Nobody's Victim: The families of murdered children want life insurance and the Reform Party is selling it to them on a law-and-order platter" *This Magazine* (December/January 1995) 15; Sean Fine, "Victims of escapees strike back" *The [Toronto] Globe and Mail* (4 March 1995) D3. The law and order response to victims obliterates gender and race. So, for example, "victim assistance" programs may be provided, but feminist resources to counsel survivors are under-resourced as victims' services are depoliticized and defunded. New legislation addresses the needs of victims generally for protection and participation, without any specific recognition of the situation of, for example, women as survivors of male violence: *Bill C-79: An Act to amend the Criminal Code (victims of crime) and another Act in consequence* (Assented to 17 June 1999).

New laws resurrect the criminalization of vagrancy and poverty. While vagrancy is no longer a *Criminal Code* offence, the definition and enforcement of criminal law and quasi-criminal legislation clearly penalizes poor people. There has been an increasing criminalization of activities associated with homelessness (such as begging, trespass, and squeegy-ing) and with poverty (fingerprinting of welfare recipients and the deployment of resources to police welfare fraud) in many parts of the country, what Abell has described as a system of "new poor laws" (a return to surveillance, regulation, containment, and labelling of poor people as undeserving): Jennie Abell, *Structural Adjustment and the New Poor Laws: Gender, Poverty and Violence and Canada's International Commitments*, supra. As a particularly appalling systematic attack on poor people, the shifts in Ontario stand out in terms of criminalization of poor people and cuts to benefits and programs. For a thoughtful discussion of the form that attack has taken, see: Joe Hermer and Janet Mosher, eds. *Disorderly People: Law and the Politics of Exclusion in Ontario* (Halifax: Fernwood, 2002) [hereinafter *Disorderly People*]. Recall the earlier discussion of *R. v. Banks*, supra, **Definition of Crime**.

The creation of "new criminals" and the consequent need for representation combines with less access to legal services for certain accused, and increasingly limited access for complainants to compound the difficulties facing such groups as: poor women and children, homeless people, youth, Aboriginal people, prisoners, victims of racist violence, and immigrants. Court cuts further exacerbate the disadvantage encountered on the basis of disability and language.

Recent events in Ontario, British Columbia, and Québec raise further troubling questions about the state's authority to define "emergencies" and threats to security and prompt an examination of the use of military and police powers against civilians to quell political demonstrations: The Globe and Mail, "Protesters accuse Toronto police of brutality" The [Toronto] Globe and Mail (11 October 1995) A3; James Rusk, "Opposition asks why OPP charged public-service picket lines at legislature; Metro police criticize fellow officers" The [Toronto] Globe and Mail (20 March 1996) A5; James Rusk, "Ontario to hold inquiry into riot squad's actions: Investigation expected to avert lengthy debate over clash between police and public-service pickets" The [Toronto] Globe and Mail (21 March 1996) A5A. For example, in Ontario, the charges of "intimidating the legislature," under s. 51 of the Criminal Code, laid against student demonstrators in Ontario, underscore the breadth of the state's legal arsenal. Bob Shenton traces the history of the intimidation law back to the 1795 English Treasonable Practices Bill, incorporated into Canadian law in 1868, making it a felony to "intimidate, or to put any force or constraint upon any Legislative Council, Legislative Assembly, or House of Assembly." As he argues, the "temporary" law has been resurrected to quell unrest and intimidate political opposition: Bob Shenton, "Intimidating a legislature? Where did that come from?" The [Toronto] Globe and Mail (16 February 1996) A21. The charges were withdrawn in March 1996 due to a flaw in the indictment.

Also, at the Asia-Pacific Economic Cooperation (APEC) meetings in Vancouver in 1997, the Free Trade Area of the Americas (FTAA) meetings in Québec in 2001, and the G20 meetings in Ottawa in 2002, police use of force and government responsibility have been condemned, although the limits to police complaints processes mean there has been insufficient scrutiny of police practices or accountability: Gay Abbate, "Mounties assailed for APEC bungling: Widespread incompetence led to violence at summit, says report by former judge" The [Toronto] Globe and Mail (9 August 2001); Ted Hughes, Commission for Public Complaints Against for RCMP (Canada: 2001); W. Wesley Pue, ed., Pepper in Our Eyes: The APEC Affair (Vancouver: UBC Press, 2000). There are by now many accounts from protesters and civil libertarians, critiquing the use of force (including tear gas) against civilians and the pattern of arrests. See, for example, generally, Briarpatch (June 2001); Brendan Myers, "A protester's story of what really happened at Quebec City" CCPA Monitor (June 2001) 26–29; Peter Zimonjic, "Police grilled over G20 conduct" The Ottawa Citizen (22 February 2002) B3.

In Stuart Hall et al., Policing the Crisis: Mugging, the State, and Law and Order (London: MacMillan, 1978), the phenomenon of mugging, its emergence as a "frightening new strain of crime," and the social construction of a "moral panic" are examined. The authors suggest that this response must be understood in terms of its context and specific historic moment: the "crisis of hegemony" in Britain in the 1970s, a sense of concern about the loss of the "British way of life," and generally the particular structures, beliefs, and ideologies that predispose society at particular moments. They examine the role of the media in its interpretation and construction of the problem, but also examine the receptivity of the general public to certain kinds of explanations and easy "solutions" rather than engaging with the complexity and contradictions.

This discussion resonates with contemporary examples in Britain and in Canada. For example, in Britain, so-called "super courts" are being set up to fast-track the prosecution of young offenders and "regain the initiative against spiralling lawlessness on the street": Kamal Ahmed, "Fast-track justice for teenagers" The [London] Observer (5 May 2002). In Ontario, moves against youth have been characterized as demonizing them: Dianne Martin, "Demonizing Youth, Marketing Fear: The New Politics of Crime" in Disorderly People, supra at 91.

Consider how particular crimes and groups of offenders are discussed and constructed. Can you think of other examples of "moral panics"? The extract that follows provides one example of the relationship between the state, the police, and the media in the construction of a national "moral panic" or crisis, and the impact of the invocation of the label of "terrorism" on fundamental rights and freedoms.

Democracy and Terror: October 1970[†]

The FLQ had emerged in the 1960s, a turbulent decade in the province of Quebec. On March 8, 1963, Molotov cocktails had been thrown through the windows of three federal armouries in Montreal. Throughout the rest of the decade, bombings of federal armouries and Anglophone institutions in Quebec continued. Many persons were injured, and some were killed. Military equipment, dynamite, and ammunition were stolen. On February 13, 1968, a bomb planted by the FLQ at the Montreal Stock Exchange injured 27 persons. Then came more explosions during May and June, 1970.

Some of the persons responsible for these bombings had been arrested, convicted and sentenced to prison. The FLQ regarded them as political prisoners and proclaimed their intention of resorting to kidnapping and assassination to free them.

. . . .

On Monday morning, October 5, the FLQ kidnapped James Cross, the British trade commissioner in Montreal.

. . . .

At noon that day, the kidnappers telephoned a radio station and said to look for a message in a locker at the University of Quebec in Montreal. The message said that Cross was being held by the Liberation cell of the FLQ. It went on to set out the conditions for Cross's release: the FLQ manifesto had to be published in all newspapers and on French-language television; 23 "political prisoners" convicted of or facing trial for acts of terrorism must be freed and given safe passage to Algeria or Cuba; the federal government had to take back into its employ 450 truck drivers the post office had recently dismissed; half a million dollars worth of gold bullion was to be delivered to the FLQ; and the search for the kidnappers must be called off. The key demand was for the release of the "political prisoners."

. . . .

From the beginning, Prime Minister Trudeau asserted that there could be no compromise. But not everyone agreed with him. Claude Ryan, then publisher of *Le Devoir* and a figure of immense intellectual authority in Quebec, suggested that the government should be prepared to release some of the prisoners in question to save Cross's life. The federal government made one concession: the FLQ manifesto was read over the radio and television network of Radio Canada, the French-language service of the Canadian Broadcasting Corporation, on Thursday evening.

. . . .

Exchanges of imprisoned terrorists for captives had taken place in other countries. But Ottawa and Quebec City held firm. The kidnapping of Pierre Laporte followed. But though this second kidnapping was a response by the FLQ to Choquette's refusal to release the "political prisoners," it was not an articulated response. Laporte was carried off by the Chenier cell of the FLQ, but this cell had no contact with the Liberation cell, which had kidnapped Cross.

. . . .

The kidnapping of Laporte, a powerful member of the Quebec cabinet, was quite a different matter from the kidnapping of Cross, a foreign diplomat. With this second kidnapping, a crisis which had seemed manageable became a crisis the consequences of which could not be foreseen. It might have been possible to resolve the Cross kidnapping in a calm and detached fashion, but the kidnapping of Laporte engaged the anguished attention of virtually every politician in Ottawa and Quebec City. Laporte's kidnapping affected them far more closely than had Cross's, and it threw into disarray the machinery of crisis management that Ottawa and Quebec City had established to deal with the Cross kidnapping. This time the two governments had to decide what to do with the life of one of their own at stake.

On Sunday night, Premier Bourassa received a letter in which Laporte, addressing him as "Mon cher Robert," urged him to release the "political prisoners."

. . . .

[†] From Thomas Berger, *Fragile Freedoms: Human Rights and Dissent in Canada* (Toronto: Clarke, Irwin & Co., 1981) at 191–92, 194–204, 206–9. Reproduced by permission of the author.

Bourassa replied that same night by a radio broadcast. The government of the province, he said, was prepared "to set up mechanisms that would guarantee, as Mr. Laporte says it will, that the release of political prisoners will surely result in the safe release of the hostages." Bourassa's statement was tantamount to a promise to release the prisoners that he had now called "political," and he may have been going further than the federal government was prepared to go.

. . . .

In any event, Trudeau was uncompromising. On Tuesday, October 13, the CBC broadcast an interview with him, now famous, in which he declared that the federal government could never allow "a parallel power" to dictate to the duly elected government of Canada.

. . . .

Claude Ryan and René Lévesque, the leader of the Parti Québécois, gathered a group of prominent Quebecers, who issued a statement on Wednesday evening, October 14, calling upon Bourassa to free the "political prisoners" in exchange for Cross and Laporte. They claimed that the federal government's ascendancy over the provincial government and Trudeau's over Bourassa "risks reducing Quebec and its government to tragic impotence."

. . . .

Bourassa quickly abandoned the conciliatory line he had taken on Sunday night. On Wednesday, he asked that the Canadian armed forces be sent into the province of Quebec. The armed forces, which had already begun to guard prominent figures in Ottawa, now moved into Quebec to provide protection for public figures and public buildings in Quebec City and in Montreal.

On Thursday, October 15, at 9:00 pm, Bourassa broadcast an offer of safe passage out of Canada for the kidnappers of both Cross and Laporte, once they had released their captives, but he offered no other concessions. He said that he must have an answer to this offer by 3:00 am the next day. No one expected an answer, and none came. At 4:00 am on Friday, October 16, the federal government invoked the War Measures Act. At the same time, under the authority of the Act, it proclaimed the Public Order Regulations, 1970.

The federal government's official reason for invoking the War Measures Act rested on two letters to Prime Minister Trudeau, one written by Mayor Jean Drapeau of Montreal, the other by Premier Bourassa. Both letters were sent during the early hours of Friday, October 16, and both letters requested extraordinary measures.

. . . .

Under the War Measures Act, the federal cabinet may assume extraordinary powers in time of "war, invasion or insurrection, real or apprehended." The Act was invoked in 1914, following its enactment during the First World War, and again, in 1939, at the outbreak of the Second World War. In 1970, the federal government invoked the War Measures Act for the first time without the excuse of war. The proclamation of October 16 read:

> Whereas the War Measures Act provides that the issue of a proclamation under the authority of the Governor-in-Council shall be conclusive evidence that insurrection, real or apprehended, exists and has existed for any period of time therein stated and of its continuance, until by the issue of a further proclamation it is declared that the insurrection no longer exists.
>
> And whereas there is in contemporary Canadian society an element or group known as Le Front de Libération du Québec who advocate and resort to the use of force and the commission of criminal offences including murder, threat of murder and kidnapping as a means of or as an aid in accomplishing a governmental change within Canada and whose activities have given rise to a state of apprehended insurrection within the Province of Quebec.
>
> Now Know Ye that We, by and with the advice of our Privy Council for Canada, do by this Our Proclamation proclaim and declare that apprehended insurrection exists and has existed as and from the fifteenth day of October, one thousand nine hundred and seventy.

The War Measures Act gives the cabinet authority to pass whatever regulations it deems necessary for the "security, defence, peace, order and welfare of Canada," including such measures as censorship, arrest, detention, and deportation. The cabinet proceeded to do just that, approving the Public Order Regulations, 1970, at the same time that the War Measures Act was invoked.

The Public Order Regulations banned the FLQ. Section 3 of the Regulations provided that,

> The group of persons or association known as Le Front de Libération du Québec and any

successor group or successor association of the said Le Front de Libération du Québec, or any group of persons or association that advocates the use of force or the commission of crime as a means of or an aid in accomplishing governmental change within Canada is declared to be an unlawful association.

The Regulations also provided that to be a member or an officer of the FLQ was an offence, and attendance at an FLQ meeting was *prima facie* evidence of membership. The owner, lessee, agent or superintendent of any premises who allowed them to be used for meetings of the FLQ was guilty of an offence.

A series of provisions conferred on the police enhanced powers of arrest. Under the Criminal Code, a police officer may, on reasonable and probable grounds, arrest a person he or she believes has committed or is about to commit an indictable offence. But, under the Regulations, a police officer was given the power to arrest anyone he or she had "reason to suspect" had committed or was about to commit a crime. Similarly, with regard to police powers of search and seizure. Ordinarily a police officer may enter premises and seize property only with a search warrant, which must be obtained from a judicial officer. The Public Order Regulations gave police officers the right to search and to seize whenever and wherever they had "reason to suspect," without their having to obtain a warrant from a judicial officer. Professor D.A. Schmeiser has said the Regulations had the effect of obviating the requirement that police officers act reasonably.

Another series of provisions abrogated due process of law, by limiting the citizen's right to *habeas corpus,* the right to bail, and the right to counsel. Under the Criminal Code, an arrested person must be brought before a justice of the peace within 24 hours, and the Crown must be ready at that time to prefer a charge. Under the new Regulations, the Crown did not have to charge an arrested person until seven days after his arrest and the attorney-general could, before seven days passed, order the accused to be detained for a further 21 days. This power effectively disposed of the right of *habeas corpus* as we know it. A person arrested under the Criminal Code may apply to be released on bail. Under the Regulations, a prisoner could apply for bail only with the consent of the provincial attorney-general. The Regulations also permitted a prisoner to be held incommunicado, thereby denying him the right to counsel.

What, in the face of the War Measures Act and the Public Order Regulations, 1970, had become of The Canadian Bill of Rights? The Canadian Bill of Rights had been enacted in 1960 specifically to prohibit (among other things) arbitrary detention and denial of bail without just cause. These provisions had no application during the October Crisis because The Canadian Bill of Rights itself provides that it is to be inoperative in a case where the War Measures Act has been proclaimed.

On Saturday, October 17, the day after the War Measures Act had been invoked, Pierre Laporte was murdered. That evening, his body was found in an abandoned car at St. Hubert airport. James Cross was still in the hands of his captors.

The War Measures Act had been proclaimed to deal with the insurrection that was said to be imminent. The Act did not assist the police to find the kidnappers. The Act did give the police the power to intern, and this extraordinary power was used to arrest and detain hundreds of persons associated with a broad range of political dissent in the province of Quebec.

The Quebec provincial police began to take persons into custody at dawn on the morning that the federal government proclaimed the War Measures Act. Those arrested did not know of the proclamation. They were unaware that during the night their right to due process of law had been taken away while they slept. The War Measures proclamation declared that the activities of the FLQ had "given rise to a state of apprehended insurrection within Quebec." But the proclamation was not limited to Quebec: it applied throughout Canada. The same extraordinary powers were conferred on the police in every province, and the police of Halifax, Toronto, Vancouver and other cities made arrests.

On October 16, the prime minister addressed the nation on television. The government, Trudeau said, intended to "root out the cancer of an armed, revolutionary movement." Public support for the government's assumption of extraordinary powers was tremendous. Everyone seemed to be swept along by what was perceived to be the government's firmness in a confrontation with terrorists who sought the forcible overthrow of Canada's institutions.

. . . .

Perhaps the most exaggerated reaction to the crisis came in British Columbia. The provincial government there, carried along by the prevailing hysteria — indeed, swimming strongly with the current — passed an order-in-council on November 2, 1970, that declared "as public policy that no person teaching or instructing our youth in educational institutions receiving Government support shall continue in the employment of the educational institution if they advocate the policies of Le Front de Libération du Québec, or the overthrow of democratically elected governments by violent means." The language of this order-in-council illustrates the way the morbid excitement of a crisis can spread and lead to the abrogation of civil liberties, even in places far removed from the threat. For who could say what the policies of the FLQ were? Clearly, they opposed Anglophone domination of the Quebec economy. They wanted to achieve independence for Quebec. Surely teachers should have been allowed to discuss the crisis, and these goals of the FLQ — goals shared by many Quebecers — and revolutionary politics, without having to be fearful of being denounced as an ally of the FLQ? It is bad enough that the *Alliance des Professeurs de Montréal* felt obliged to warn its members that any attempt to discuss the FLQ's manifesto in relation to contemporary events might result in loss of employment. It is ludicrous that teachers in British Columbia should have found themselves in the same situation.

Was there any evidence at all that an insurrection in Quebec was imminent? Two men had been kidnapped — by two different groups who might or might not be closely linked. Public figures in Quebec, who had been making inflammatory speeches for years, were still making inflammatory speeches. There had been meetings. Students had publicly demonstrated their support for the FLQ, but it was not the first time that students in Quebec or elsewhere had supported radical or dubious causes. Did this kind of evidence justify a state of siege?

. . . .

The difficulty the federal government had in persisting in its contention that an insurrection, imminent on October 16, was still about to occur began to be felt. On November 2, 1970, the federal government introduced in Parliament new legislation, the Public Order (Temporary Measures) Act, 1970. The new legislation, assented to on December 3, revoked the proclamation of the War Measures Act. But extraordinary measures were to remain in force. The preamble to the new legislation said that public order in Canada was still endangered by the FLQ. Under this new Act, a person arrested had to be brought before a justice within three days, rather than seven; and the attorney-general of a province could extend a period of arrest to a maximum of seven days, rather than 21. But even when a prisoner had appeared before a justice of the peace, the attorney-general's consent was still required for anyone thus detained to be released on bail. There was a special provision in the Act that it was to override the provisions of the Canadian Bill of Rights prohibiting arbitrary detention or imprisonment and denial of bail without just cause. (The new legislation expired on April 30, 1971, and with it the extraordinary measures called forth by the October Crisis lapsed.)

. . . .

Where Trudeau and his advisors can be called to account is in the proclamation of the War Measures Act without sufficient cause, in the stringency of the measures taken under the authority of the Act, and in the perpetuation of those measures by the enactment of the Public Order (Temporary Measures) Act. On the strength of powers conferred by these measures, the police in Quebec detained hundreds of their fellow citizens who constituted no threat to the province or to Canada, who had not committed criminal acts of any kind, and who were not in any way connected with FLQ. On proclamation of the War Measures Act on October 16, 1970, the Quebec provincial police and the Montreal city police arrested hundreds of persons; they were subjected to interrogation, many of their homes were searched, sometimes repeatedly. Four hundred and ninety-seven persons were arrested in Quebec. Of all those arrested, only 62 persons were ever charged. Of this number, only 18, less than one-third, were convicted. The ones who were convicted were, of course, primarily those responsible for the kidnappings and the murder of Pierre Laporte. Only two of these convictions were for offences under the Public Order Regulations and the Public Order Act. Two convictions out of nearly 500 arrests is not by any standards a great haul of insurrectionists. Over 450 persons were either never charged or were acquitted. The conclusion is inescapable that these arrests were made arbitrarily, and that the interrogation of all these people did not reveal any evidence that an insurrection was imminent. The whole exercise reveals how unwise it is to have such extraordinary power easily available to any government.

■

Law and Order and the Canadian State (Continued)[†]

Although all the information upon which the government acted is not available, it is now widely acknowledged that the "apprehended insurrection" was exaggerated, the abrogation of civil liberties was unjustified, and the existing criminal law powers would have adequately responded to the situation. Herbert Marx, in "The 'Apprehended Insurrection' of October 1970 and the Judicial Function" (1972) 7 U.B.C. L. Rev. 55, criticizes the Québec courts for failing to question the existence of an "apprehended insurrection" within the meaning of the *War Measures Act* in considering several legal challenges to its invocation. Historical context for the enactment and periodic resort to the *War Measures Act* in 1970 is provided by F. Murray Greenwood in "The Drafting and Passage of the War Measures Act in 1914 and 1927: Object Lessons in the Need for Vigilance" in W. Wesley Pue and Barry Wright, eds., *Canadian Perspectives on Law and Society: Issues in Legal History* (Ottawa: Carleton University Press, 1988) 29. For additional readings on the events of October 1970 and the situation in Québec, see Aubrey Golden and Ron Haggart, *Rumours of War* (Toronto: James Lorimer & Co., 1971); and Denis Smith, *Bleeding Hearts, Bleeding Country: Canada and the Québec Crisis* (Edmonton: Hurtig, 1971).

One example of the use of the *War Measures Act* prior to the October Crisis of 1970 was its invocation during the Second World War as against, among others, Japanese Canadians. These persons were removed from their homes, interred in camps, and stripped of their property: Ann Gomer Sunahara, *The Politics of Racism. The Uprooting of Japanese Canadians During the Second World War* (Toronto: James Lorimer and Co., 1981). In September 1988, the federal government announced that it would compensate Japanese Canadians with a settlement that included $21,000 to each person interned, $12 million to the community itself, and $24 million for a Race Relations Foundation to fight racism. An account of the struggle to gain redress has been published by Maryka Omatsu, *Bittersweet Passage. Redress and the Japanese Canadian Experience* (Toronto: Between the Lines, 1992). Other groups, such as Ukrainian Canadians and Mennonites, were also interred as "enemy aliens" during the two world wars: James Carruthers, "The Great War and Canada's Enemy Alien Policy" (1978) 4 Queen's L.J. 43; Lubomyr Luciuk, *A Time for Atonement: Canada's First National Internment Operations and the Ukrainian Canadians 1914–1920* (Kingston: Limestone Press, 1988). For a thoughtful evocation of the effects of those laws and policies on the Mennonites, who were pacifists, see: Rudy Wiebe, *Peace Shall Destroy Many* (Toronto: McClelland and Stewart, 1962).

Another example of the use of the *War Measures Act* was to appropriate Aboriginal land, discussed *supra*, **Colonization and the Imposition of Criminal Law**. For an analysis of some of the uses of the *War Measures Act* from its enactment in 1914 until 1970, see: Patricia Peppin, "Emergency Legislation and Rights in Canada: The *War Measures Act* and Civil Liberties" (1993) 18 Queen's L.J. 129.

The *Emergencies Act*, S.C. 1988, c. 29, s. 80, assented to July 21, 1988, consolidated in R.S.C. 1985, c. 22, replaced the *War Measures Act*, but civil libertarians have criticized the scope of that act and the *National Defence Act* (which was invoked to bring in the military to Oka): David South, "Taking Measure of the Emergency Act" *This Magazine* (August 1992) 38.

In response to the events of September 2001, Justice Minister Anne McLellan introduced *Bill C-36: an Act to amend the Criminal Code, the Official Secrets Act, the Canada Evidence Act, the Proceeds of Crime (Money Laundering) Act and other Acts, and to enact measures respecting the registration of charities, in order to combat terrorism* (Assented to 18 December 2001). The new anti-terrorism legislation has been criticized for its breadth, its invulnerability to scrutiny, and the absence of a "sunset clause" by a wide range of organizations including the Canadian Bar Association: Mark Bourrie, "Tough anti-terrorism legislation called a threat to civil liberties" *Law Times* (22 October 2001) 1. As Eric Rice, President of the Canadian Bar Association argued, Bill C-36 shifts the relationship between security and freedom and endangers the rule of law. Also, the lack of clarity in the definition of "terrorism" potentially encompasses "many legitimate activities that disrupt social order, for example, the recent ille-

---

[†] Jennie Abell, "Law and Order and the Canadian State."

gal nurses' and truckers' strikes, anti-globalization marches and demonstrations by First Nations": Eric Rice, "Speaking Notes to the Special Senate Committee on Bill C-36" (24 October 2001), available online: <http://www.cba.org>. Other concerns have been raised with respect to investigative hearings, preventative arrests, privacy invasions, restricted freedom of the press and access to information, and the challenge these pose to fundamental rights. A further over-arching concern is the potential for abuse and differential treatment of specific communities within Canada. Despite the minor amendments, many of these concerns continue: Malcolm Rogge, "Rule of Force v. Rule of Law: The Global Lock-down on Civil Liberties" *Canadian Dimension* (December 2001).

The measures resonate with recent new legislation and political moves in a number of countries, including Great Britain and the U.S.A. In the U.S.A., for example, the *USA Patriot Act* grants police increased surveillance and search powers and the *White House Military Order On Detention, Treatment and Trial Of Certain Non-Citizens In the War Against Terrorism* provides the authority to submit non-citizens to trial before secret military commissions. In the United Kingdom the *Anti-Terrorism, Crime and Security Bill* (Assented to 13 December 2001) also provides for increased police powers, including potential indefinite detention without charge in the case of those suspected of being international terrorists: Michael Zander, "The Anti-terrorism Bill — what happened?" (2001) 151 *New Law Journal* 1880.

At the same time in Canada, police powers have been strengthened by new legislation further immunizing police and other law enforcement agents who commit criminal offences where such crimes are deemed necessary to assist designated officers in law enforcement. Prior approval for the commission of crimes will not always be required: *An Act to amend the Criminal Code (organized crime and law enforcement) and to make consequential amendments to other Acts* (Assented to 18 December, 2001). Critics worry that these measures undermine the rule of law, are anti-democratic, and unconstitutional as infringing sections 7, 8, 9, and 15 of the *Charter*. The breadth of the statute leaves considerable discretion to law enforcement officers, something that potentially leads to differential enforcement of the law and vulnerability to police brutality, for example: Elizabeth Sheehy, "Twelve Good Reasons To Oppose Granting Criminal Immunity To Police" 20:1 *Jurisfemme* (Winter 2001) 19.

Blind Justice[†]

Close your eyes and think of three criminals in as many seconds. The first images that come into your mind will do. Done it? There is a strong likelihood that most of us thought of the same kind of people. Your selection might look something like this: there is a rioter (black, hurling bricks at crouching police); a "hustler" (a roving thief, light-fingered and expert at robbery with violence); and there is a terrorist (his face hidden by the tell-tale black and white kerchief of the Palestine Liberation Organisation or a similar group, his fanaticism revealed by his wild gestures with an unwieldy — Russian made — rifle).

These archetypal criminals occur in our imaginations for a reason. Our imaginations — at least as far as crime is concerned — have been hijacked. The media — and here I'm including thrillers and detective stories, *James Bond* movies and TV cop shows as much as the news — has developed the "crime problem" to the point where fiction dominates fact. We see criminals only in terms of stereotypes. Our vision of criminals prowling the streets and looking for trouble is as media-derived — and so as predictably scripted — as a comedy-show or a detergent advertisement.

Britain's recent riots provide a good example of how our understanding of what is going on is distorted. Night after night our televisions have shown buildings buckling to reveal interiors blazing as disturbances occurred on the streets of Birmingham, Liverpool and Tottenham. We demand drama from the news, and here it was delivered. Yet the meanings of these pictures are not found in the riot-torn streets, but are *made* by those who write the scripts and edit the sequences in which the images appear. Those participating in the riots are depicted as merely criminals, and crime is reduced to something

---

[†] By Amanda Root from *New Internationalist* (December 1985) 7 at 7–11. Reproduced with permission from New Internationalist, Dec/85.

that exists outside politics: a nasty but inevitable feature of all societies, rich and poor, communist or capitalist. The news presents a taken-for-granted consensus that the law exists to protect us — it is depicted as if it was neutral.

Yet the agents of that law — the police — are clearly not impartial. The riots in Brixton were sparked off by the shooting of a black woman in the back when she was in her nightdress (leaving her paralysed for life), and the riots in Tottenham followed the death of another black woman, who died from a heart-attack whilst police searched her home. These incidents are exceptional only in their tragic outcomes: black people in London and other big cities report constant, and often violent harassment from the police. However, the popular press refuses to document black Londoners' experiences of racist policing. And it was left to the establishment journal *The Economist* to substantiate accusations of police racism, by pointing out that the police were making comments like "There's nothing like a bit of coon-bashing" during the riot.

[Root contrasts a number of international examples which are not generally portrayed as "crimes," ranging from the terrorism of South Africa's apartheid regime, to the negligence of Union Carbide at Bhopal, to France's explosion of the Greenpeace ship, "Rainbow Warrior." She then highlights the gap between the fear of crime and the risk of crime, and the impact of race and poverty on that reality.]

. . . .

As things stand, more and more money is spent on the police (to combat "enemies within" such as striking miners, airport controllers and peace protestors) and the army (to counter such "evil empires" as the Sandinistas, the Filipino freedom fighters and the Russians). If this money was used to alleviate poverty in ways that empowered the poor, rather than fostered their passivity, then the resulting change in political consciousness in inner-city areas would virtually eliminate "street" crime. Such expenditure would also enable the financing of alternatives to prison, which is a major breeding-ground of career criminality.

Greater numbers of police often exacerbate the very problems that they are trying to cure. By arresting petty offenders, they feed people into a criminal justice system that teaches them how to be professional criminals; either by association or via the not-so-tender mercies of an employment market which rarely accommodates people with criminal records.

Neither can we expect that the current "toughening up" of sentencing by the courts will help deter criminals. The sad fact is that America is one of *the* most crime-ridden societies *and* that it has one of the world's highest rates of imprisonment. Similarly, it is clear that the courts amplify rather than reduce already existing social prejudices against women and black people.

. . . .

[We] have to be eternally vigilant: asking, whenever we hear the word criminal being bandied about, who has the power to decide which meanings are given to the term and which are silenced. As we sit on a time-bomb of "law and order" repressiveness, we should remember the words of Angela Davis that "The real criminals in this society are not all the people who populate the prisons across the State, but those who have stolen the wealth of the world from the people."

■

Another account of the ways in which racism shapes "law and order" campaigns and spurs vigilantism and white violence can be found in the work of Angela Davis, "Rape, Racism and the Myth of the Black Rapist," *Women, Race and Class* (New York: Random House, 1981) 172.

Now consider the standpoint from which the preceding article by Amanda Root is written. Patricia Williams in "Spirit-Murdering the Messenger: The Discourse of Finger-Pointing as the Law's Response to Racism," under **Policing**, suggests that African-Americans' *experience* of white violence and criminality shapes images of criminality that diverge from the accounts provided by the dominant culture through the media. For example, as bell hooks writes in "Representations of Whiteness," *Black Looks. Race and Representation* (Toronto: Between the Lines, 1992) 165 at 170: "Returning to memories of growing up in the social circumstances created by racial apartheid, to all black spaces on the edge of town, I reinhabit a location where black folks associate whiteness with the terrible, the terrifying, the terrorizing."

Another consequence of rhetoric around "street crime" is a willingness to characterize vigilantes and those who "take the law into their own hands" as heroes. The most notorious example of this phenomenon is that of Bernhard Goetz. A grand jury refused to indict this accused vigilante on four counts of attempted murder and four counts of assault. He was, however, indicted on charges of illegally possessing three guns, one used in the shooting. Ultimately, he was sentenced to one year on a gun possession charge: Reuter and AP, "Jury refuses to indict N.Y. subway gunman on shooting charges" *The [Toronto] Globe and Mail* (26 January 1985) 1. Patricia Williams discusses the *Goetz* case in her article "Spirit-Murdering the Messenger: The Discourse of Fingerpointing as the Law's Response to Racism," *infra*,

Policing. In April 1996, a jury ordered Bernhard Goetz to pay $43 million to Darrell Cabey, one of the four young African-American men shot by Goetz 12 years earlier: AP, "Goetz told to pay victim $43-million" *The [Toronto] Globe and Mail* (24 April 1996) A8. However, there is little prospect of any money actually being paid out to Cabey, because of Goetz's limited resources.

The articles that follow draw links between the law and order rhetoric of the state, the social construction of "masculinity" and "femininity," and the incidence of "violent self-help," with reference to the examples of Bernhard Goetz, Marc Lépine, and Kanehsatake.

The Rambo Spirit[†]

Three days before Christmas in New York City last year, a self-employed electronics specialist named Bernhard Hugo Goetz took a .38 pistol out of his waistband and fired at least ten rounds at four young black men who had sidled up to him on the 7th Avenue subway train and asked him for five dollars. "I have five dollars for each of you," Goetz was reported to have said just before he began firing. After shooting the youths — the last of whom implored him not to and was hit in the back as he fled — Goetz reportedly had a few words with a conductor and then escaped from the train.

The New York City Police Department quickly set up a hotline for tips as to the identity and whereabouts of the assailant. Much to the surprise of the police, the overwhelming majority of the calls to the hotline expressed support for the "subway vigilante." After all, people argued, he was the victim. These kids had long-handled screwdrivers in their pockets. Each had a police record. They came looking for trouble and they got it. Some of the callers went so far as to suggest that the vigilante, whoever he was, should be the next Mayor of New York.

About ten days after the shooting, Bernhard Goetz turned himself in, claiming publicly that his actions were justified. A lot of New Yorkers — and Americans around the country — agreed. According to radio talk show hosts, rarely had any issue sparked so much rage and emotion or tapped so deep a nerve in their audiences as Goetz' response to the fear of crime that people live with every day. More than one private citizen volunteered to pay Goetz' $50,000 bail. The *New York Post*, a tabloid owned by Australian Rupert Murdoch and read primarily by working-class residents of New York, editorialised that "far from being a manifestation of 'insanity' or 'madness', the universal rejoicing in New York over the gunman's success is a sign of moral health." That opinion was apparently held by the Grand Jury which heard the case: the jurors decided that Goetz acted in self-defense and recommended no indictment.

For many Americans Goetz' action was a brief release from the intense frustration, sense of powerlessness and fear they have come to feel in relation to urban crime. People experienced a momentary, cathartic hope that justice could be swift and that determined individuals could bring order where governmental authority had so totally failed.

"Taking the law into one's own hands" is a very American tradition. In reality, there are two different traditions that get rolled into one: the lone avenger, and the self-protective community. The roots of this vigilante spirit run deep — historically, culturally and psychologically. They are part of the American worldview. In situations where Americans feel frightened, confused and threatened by a breakdown of their social order and way of life, the vigilante impulse often takes hold. At times, as in the case of neighbors banding together to watch out for

---

[†] By Richard Kazis from *New Internationalist* (December 1985) 12 at 12–13. Reproduced with permission from New Internationalist, Dec/85.

each other's safety or to defend their neighborhood against a wave of arson, this impulse can be very positive. Often, though, as in the case of Bernhard Goetz, vigilante self-help turns ugly, motivated by race hatred and bigotry, as people lash out violently against the "outsiders" they fear.

The mythology of the lone avenging angel, doing battle against corrupt authority and against overwhelming threats to traditional social values and relations, is a staple of Hollywood films and American culture. Clint Eastwood's Dirty Harry is that kind of cop. So is Gene Hackman's Popeye Doyle in *The French Connection*. The most recent film of this genre is Michael Cimino's *Year of the Dragon*, which plays on the racist currents of vigilantism by pitting a cop who breaks all conventions in the name of higher values against the lawlessness of New York's Chinatown.

The lone avenger is not always a cop. This past summer's box office blockbuster, Sylvester "Rocky" Stallone's *Rambo — First Blood Part II* is a slick variation on the lone vigilante theme. The film, which has already grossed over $150 million and has been lauded publicly by Ronald Reagan, is the story of one man's fight against corrupt American military and political leaders and against wave upon wave of determined communist soldiers in his effort to free American GIs still being held prisoner in Vietnam. Violent, racist, a morality tale of one individual "taking the law into his own hands" and taking action — *Rambo* has tapped a rich lode of xenophobic pro-vigilante sentiment.

The vision of vigilantism that is in the back of every American's mind is not primarily a vision of the city, "the urban wilderness" of today. Nor is it a vision of the Third World, that dangerous, lawless threat to US stability, as it is portrayed in films such as *Rambo*. Rather, vigilantism and the romanticism associated with it harken back to the days of the American frontier, the Wild West. The gunfighter who stoically does "what a man has to do," the posse that forms to ride out into the valley to capture lawless cattle rustlers — these are the heroic images that are part of our national mythology and that have been enshrined in Hollywood Westerns.

The frontier is the source of America's affinity with what one student of vigilantism calls "violent self-help." But America has obviously changed since the frontier days and, as the nation has changed, so has vigilante activity. Typical targets of early frontier vigilantism were horse thieves, counterfeiters and murderers. By the late 1800s, however, the frontier had been tamed; the West had been won. America had become an industrial nation of urban dwellers, immigrants and free blacks. In this new America, increasingly fragmented along class, race and ethnic lines, the impulse to "take the law into one's own hands" did not disappear. It simply found new targets — primarily among blacks, Catholics, Jews, labor and political activists and proponents of civil liberties.

In America, despite our nostalgia for frontier justice, vigilantism in the past century has primarily been a vehicle for intolerance. Between 1882 and 1951 over 4700 Americans were killed by unorganized lynch mobs. The overwhelming majority of these lynchings took place in Southern states; well over 80 per cent of the victims were black. As late as 1955 a 14-year-old black boy in Mississippi was lynched by an angry white mob for whistling at a white woman.

Today, vigilantism by individuals and by organized groups seems to be on the rise. The peaceful form of organized crime patrols such as the somewhat controversial Guardian Angels group which began in New York and spread to other cities, or more indigenous Neighborhood Watch groups which exist in every major American city, grew rapidly in the 1960s and 1970s. According to one estimate, more than 8500 unpaid volunteers served on Tenant Safety Patrols in New York City's public housing projects in the early 1970s.

While there are some signs that neighborhood patrols may have peaked in popularity and may not be growing as quickly as they did in the previous decade, organized violent vigilantism — much of it indistinguishable from terrorism — is clearly on the rise. Last spring authorities broke up a ring of fundamentalist anti-abortion activists who had firebombed a number of abortion clinics across the US. Members of the Jewish Defense League have been connected, though never charged, with bombings of the offices of Arab-American and anti-Israel organizations.

Perhaps most frightening of all is the growth of openly violent, racist and anti-Semitic vigilante groups in the Midwest and West. The Aryan Nations is a newly-formed alliance of a number of smaller groups that includes elements of the American Nazi Party, the Ku Klux Klan and less well-known organizations such as the Silent Brotherhood. Although very small — with a core of perhaps only 500 activists — these groups have robbed banks and gunned down a liberal, Jewish radio talk show host in Denver. In December 1984, a few weeks before the New York City subway shooting, members of one of these groups engaged in a deadly shootout with federal marshals in rural Washington state. These groups take self-reliance to the extreme. Some believe that, because it is controlled by a Zionist conspiracy, the US government is immoral and its laws void. One group, the Posse Comitatus, recognizes no law above the county level.

Clearly there is no connection between organized terror groups like the Posse and an individual like Bernhard Goetz flailing out violently from frustration with urban crime. There is no *direct* connection, that is. However, their shared sense that it is legitimate to use violence and to mete out their own justice, their rejection of the claim that legitimate authorities are providing adequate protection, and their intense fear of residents of this country who are not like them have similar roots. And they have a similar effect: in this world where we must rely on each other so much of the time, the translation of the frontier ethic into a freedom to exact extralegal, violent "justice" can only result in a deeper rending of the social fabric.

Urban crime is real. Moreover, these are difficult times across the nation, as our economic preeminence in the world has been challenged and our fears that the world is out of control seem confirmed daily. Americans are confused about our place in the world as a nation, as members of very different social groups and as individuals. Under these conditions, which no Rambo or Dirty Harry can reverse, it should come as no surprise if vigilantism and its extensions into terrorism continue.

The communal commitment to peaceful social control that is reflected in the neighborhood watch groups and community anti-crime initiatives is a hopeful development emerging from the lessons of the frontier. But when the response turns to violent revenge against real or perceived aggressors, the end of social control gives way to social conflict. US Attorney General William Saxbe concluded more than a decade ago that because of the negative ways crime causes us to change our lives and our relations to others, there is no graver threat to individual security and social life than the breakdown of the socially agreed-upon system of law and justice. Today, vigilantism remains more a reflection of than a solution to this problem.

∎

The Men's Club: Rambo Ain't Heavy, He's My Brother†

. . . .

At the moment of this writing, any reasonable Canadian male intelligence is struggling with the ghost of Marc Lepine and the Montreal massacre. At best, we can translate this moment of moral crisis into a moment of clarity when actions, attitudes, institutions and their underlying ideologies become transparent. But these moments are dangerous. Cultivated and responded to, they can threaten our closely held definitions of our selves and our society. We (that is to say, men) assume that the moral vertigo we experienced on hearing of the death of the fourteen women in Montreal was a natural response to what we perceived as a senseless, incomprehensible act. I think, however, that it was precisely the reverse; it was our visceral recognition of the horrible familiarity of the act that in fact made Lepine's behavior so disturbing. The events in Montreal weren't incomprehensible — quite the opposite. Men knew exactly what was going on.

Lepine was simultaneously a wild card, highly unique and individualized in his madness, and a manifestation of a collective set of fears and dreads. He represented a tortured, inappropriate, archaic definition of masculinity as it attempts to deal with the frustration and limitations of its own loss of power.

Masculinity is not, of course, a single unchanging quality. Its inherently conservative nature conceives of itself as springing from some eternal source, but it is in actuality a constantly shifting dialogue of cultural models interacting with supposedly fixed normative psychological structures. If we do imagine masculinity as changing, we tend to see it as evolving in positive terms — the non-swishing gay male, for example, or the caring single father. But the truth is that it is within the realm of extreme representations of violence that some of the more radical transformations of masculinity have occurred.

The fact is that some current cinematic reactions can be seen as a disguised response to the stresses

---

† By John Scott, *Canadian Art* (Spring 1990) 17.

placed on the male psyche by the analysis and social transformations engendered by feminism. Some of the new media constructs and narratives are so extreme as to make chauvinism seem like a golden period of romantic restraint. With every revealing exposure of the means by which repressive structures have functioned against women and those who are technically women — children, immigrants, the powerless — a counter version of caricatured masculinity has surfaced.

Not long ago, film provided us with a pure, polarized emblem of masculinity in the person of John Wayne. During the latter part of his film career he seemed continually bathed in a nostalgic, rosy, twilight glow, acting as the custodian of righteous violence at a time when clear notions of honor, courage and the qualities of traditional manhood were beginning to fade. Realism — the need to transcend one-dimensional characterization — generated new cinematic models. And one of the unpleasant side-effects of dismantling the traditional concept of masculinity, with its rigid structure, has been that some of the worst aspects of masculinity are no longer held in check. In recent years, many filmmakers have pushed the envelope, constructing more and more extreme representations of violence perpetrated by heroes who are, as they dispense justice, more filled with sadism than with heroic resolve.

Within the new set of masculine heroes there are crucial differences. Clint Eastwood's Dirty Harry or Mel Gibson's Mad Max embody specific meanings, reinforce certain mythologies and organize certain fantasies. But there is something especially creepy about Sylvester Stallone's immensely and internationally popular Rambo, particularly when one acknowledges the sickening regularity with which individuals who flip out in a manner similar to Lepine's have identified with his character. This identification differs from the rest of the violence-dispensing pantheon. An analysis of those differences and their specific appeal might be useful in dealing with or possibly preventing more mindless outbreaks of violence.

Rambo, or rather a proto-Rambo, actually first appeared in the mid-'70s in Martin Scorsese's film *Taxi Driver*. In it, Scorsese constructed an articulately inarticulate voice-over narration from the diaries of the hopelessly isolated potential political assassin, Travis Bickle. Scorsese's depiction was culturally resonant enough to send a lot of not particularly disturbed or unintelligent males off into mirrored soliloquies ("You talkin' to me?") full of nebulous aggression.

Bickle, like Rambo, is inexorably drawn into a paroxysm of violence, but the difference is that in *Taxi Driver*, we have an adult consciousness (Scorsese's) interpreting the interior monologue of an emotional adolescent who is struggling to deal with a complex social reality and a horrific military history. In the Rambo movies, on the other hand, we have an adolescent consciousness (that animates a hyper-masculinated body) responding to a set of complex stresses by falling into the pure narcissism of the violent poseur while playing out a military combat tantrum (the Kill Spasm). In fact, the camera spends so much time focusing on Rambo in sado-masochistic, phallocentric delirium as to surpass its lingering gaze directed at any mainstream female sex symbol/film star. By so doing, the filmic experience moves us closer to the body/image time of pornographic movies, which presents us with a horrible possibility: Rambo-identification by disturbed individuals may simply be a last-ditch effort to be seen.

We have to understand that we are protected in large part from media-generated violence by our own — and filmmakers' — internalized system of censorship. Most male film characters who successfully use violence are in fact agents of authority — good sons if perhaps slightly rebellious, wise fathers if momentarily mistaken or overly rigorous — and are thus compelled to stay within a preordained set of social norms. But Rambo is, as Stallone has described him, "America's lost child," an orphan, a fatherless son irreversibly transformed by political necessity and military training before being abandoned, unloved, in an environment that necessitates emotional responses from someone in whom all emotion has been deliberately repressed. There is an inevitability to Rambo's seeking out of an apocalyptic combat situation so demanding and intense as to obliterate his unbearable interior feelings.

Anyone who has played with one of the dazzling array of combat video games knows this experience, the jumped-up but limited hyper-consciousness necessitated by the constant waves of attacking images. The result is a totally focused consciousness that is too busy engaging in survival/slaughter to experience the complexities of moral choice or the painful contingencies of feeling. Awareness is present only as a command centre for the robot/military body completely purged of the biological, the feminine. This apocalyptic burst of violence that obliterates feeling, along with the momentary disruption of the organization of power, are exactly what makes Rambo so popular.

Contemporary society is such that it demands men act and feel in ways that could be construed, under a limited definition, as feminine, or at least that men acknowledge that they interact with the reality of a growing female power in the world. At the same time, the rigid yet restraining structures of traditional masculinity are being dismantled. In effect, new beings are being created as a result of these complex and conflicting feelings, beings who, lacking the restraining image-identification of the old-model definition of a man, are filled with extreme nihilism and a real potential for violence.

It seems to me that what men need is to summon up the courage and strength to accept Marc Lepine as a brother, a sibling, who was raised in the same toxic cultural environment and with whom we share a number of internalized values, beliefs, desires and fears. Lepine was not a free-floating cloud of pure radical evil but the extreme end of a line that runs through us all.

■

Consider the ways in which violence against women is constructed. The different approaches to violence against women and the underlying ideological assumptions are exemplified in the reactions to the murder of 14 women students in Montréal in December 1989 and in the media treatment of the killings. Momentarily in the wake of the horror, perhaps as the ordinary explanations did not suffice, feminists were given space to analyze what had happened and connections were made to broader issues of misogyny and male violence against women: Lee Lakeman, "Women, Violence and the Montréal Massacre" *This Magazine* (March 1990) 20, and Louise Malette and Marie Chalouh, eds., *Polytechnique, 6 décembre* (Montréal: Editions du Remue-ménage, 1990). Just as quickly, that interlude was over and malestream voices prevailed, characterizing the act as the aberrant and random act of a madman and linking it to other isolated incidents of mass murder, not the much more routine violence against women.

Grim evidence that Lépine's actions and the hate behind them are not anomalous was provided to the Commission of Inquiry into the Deployment of Canadian Forces to Somalia. Apparently, a well-advertised Marc Lépine memorial dinner was held in a junior officers' mess at Canadian Forces Base Petawawa in 1991. A 14-shot salute was fired from a rifle similar to the one used by Lépine in 1989: CP, "Polytechnique killer honored by soldiers, inquiry is told: Army denies dinner celebration took place" *The [Montreal] Gazette* (3 November 1995) A6; CP, "Search on for proof of dinner honouring Lépine: Army commander accepts request from Somalia inquiry after allegation by former soldier" *The [Toronto] Globe and Mail* (10 November 1995) A7A.

In June 1991, a report on violence against women prepared by five women MPs was released. The four Progressive Conservative members of the seven-member Health and Welfare Committee of the House of Commons refused to endorse the report because they found the title, "The War Against Women," too inflammatory or too feminist: "Tories vs. women" *The Toronto Star* (21 June 1991) A22.

Now consider the social construction of "violence," "peace," "terrorism," "protest," and the characterization of Aboriginal peoples and their struggle. A reinforced perception of Aboriginal peoples as violent and law-breaking may be displacing the focus on the systemic racism and violence against Aboriginal peoples that the Marshall Commission and the Manitoba Aboriginal Justice Inquiry have made manifest. Consider, for example, the comments of Québec Premier Robert Bourassa on the Kanehsatake (Oka) dispute, quoted in André Picard, "Bourassa urges warriors to surrender: Premier questions support from Native leaders for besieged 'criminals'" *The [Toronto] Globe and Mail* (8 September 1990) A1:

> Mr. Bourassa painted the 20 or so Warriors holed up in a drug and alcohol treatment centre in Kanehsatake, and surrounded by 400 soldiers, as a ragtag bunch of thugs and criminals. He said those interested in justice for native people should distance themselves from the group. "These are not necessarily the greatest defenders of native causes ... *why would native leaders want to protect criminals*, many of who[m] are not natives and not Canadians?" ... He said the "do-gooders" [referring to a coalition of groups including the National Action Committee on the Status of Women, the Canadian Labour Congress, the Canadian Peace Alliance, and Greenpeace, among others] who criticized his calling the military "need to be reminded that tens of thousands of people could not earn their daily bread" because of the blockade of the Mercier Bridge. The Premier also invited them to visit

the "ransacked homes of Oka" before passing judgment on politicians. [emphasis added]

For two films that examine the Kanehsatake (Oka) dispute, see Alanis Obomsawin, "Kanehsatake: 270 Years of Resistance" (Montréal: N.F.B., 1993); and *Rocks at Whiskey Trench* (Montréal: N.F.B., 1997).

As Lee Maracle points out in "Peace" *The [Ottawa] Womanist* (Fall 1990) 9, the words "violence" and "peace" are susceptible to different interpretations:

> Thousands of citizens have decried violence in the resistance struggle of our people. Violence. "Organized, unjust and unwarranted attacks." We have never organized ourselves to attack anyone, unjustly or otherwise. Ours is a peaceful struggle, but it is not a passive one.

She discusses peace and violence as follows:

> *Peace.* "Tranquillity, freedom from strife, freedom from warring conditions, freedom of the mind from annoyance." We have not had peace for some 281,614 days since Columbus first came here. Worse, our homeland has not experienced peace since this country's inception.
>
> *Violence.* "Organized, unwarranted, unjust exertion of force." We know what that is, beginning in the grand banks of Newfoundland with the slaughter of the cod fish and the Beothucks, to the great lakes and the slaughter of the salmon, sturgeon — the main source of food for the Six Nations people — and the reduction of the Huron to a small band in Ontario; the massacre of millions of beaver, mink, and Anishnawbeg people from Sudbury to Winnipeg, the slaughter of the buffalo and the death of Cree Nation to the war against the Manitoba Nation and the dispersal of the Metis and Native people throughout the northern prairies, to the burning of our great forests in B.C. and the contamination of our rivers with toxic waste from pulp mills, saw mills and the very recent cutting of our forests — we know about organized violence.

In this context, consider the following article by Boyce Richardson. For additional background on the situation of the Algonquins, see Boyce Richardson, *Blockade: Algonquins Defend the Forest* (Ottawa: N.F.B., 1990); Jean-Maurice Matchewan, "Mitchikanibikonginik Algonquins of Barriere Lake: Our Long Battle to Create a Sustainable Future" in Boyce Richardson, ed., *Drumbeat: Anger and Renewal in Indian Country* (Toronto: Summerhill, 1989) 139.

The Media's Hypocrisy and Oka[†]

I have been writing about native affairs in Canada, off and on, since 1968. During many of these 22 years, it has often been difficult to find publishers for what I wrote, because for the most part natives are regarded as peripheral to the central affairs of the nation.

This notion that Indians are irrelevant has begun to change in the last three months because of the action of Elijah Harper in scuttling the Meech Lake accord. Probably not since the last stand of Tecumseh in 1814 has any native person been able to influence so decisively a major concern of mainstream Canada. The dignity, modesty and intelligence with which this task was carried out certainly transformed many people's view of native Canadians.

More recently the armed standoff at Oka has catapulted native people into the headlines as nothing else within living memory. The argument over the Oka land has been around since at least 1840, and has never changed. In spite of losing many cases in the white man's courts, the Mohawks of Kanesatake have never altered their view that the land is theirs.

Nobody has ever taken much notice of them. I wrote something about the issue five or six years ago, but it never found a publisher. No interest. Just a few months ago one Kanesatake leader asked if I was interested in making a film about their problem. Since neither they nor I had any money, and could not think of anyone who would be interested in putting up money for such a film, it was never made.

Now, of course, countless thousands of feet of film have been shot about the Oka situation. On some days, metropolitan media have devoted four, even five, newspaper pages and whole television programs to the subject.

[†] By Boyce Richardson, *The Ottawa Citizen* (1 September 1990) B7. Reproduced by permission of the author.

One thing has brought about this change. When the Oka people took up guns to defend their land, the media immediately re-defined the issue. [Overnight] it was transformed from a boring debate no one would want to read about, to a matter of primary interest to every reader and viewer.

This is not, of course, a new phenomenon. In 1966 a group of researchers at Keele University in England studied media coverage before, during and after a large anti-nuclear demonstration. They concluded that long before the event the media defined the context within which they would view it. The story they were looking for was the possibility of violence at the demonstration.

Similarly, a few years ago a superb American film was made about media coverage of black riots in Miami, where, again, a subject considered by the media to be of minimal interest was transformed overnight into a top story. A ghetto dweller told the filmmaker it didn't matter what people said about their conditions, nobody took any notice. But if he were to walk out of the room into the middle of the street and start shooting, there would be 200 reporters paying attention the next day.

This is what happened in Oka. This definition of an issue as news is entirely the work of the media and no one else. It is a decision made by editors, presumably. Its motive is to make exciting programs, sell lively newspapers and to make money.

But the media twist the knife further. Having dictated that only violence will attract their attention, they then denounce the use of violence, in an effort, usually successful, to undermine the credibility of the minority group and its claims. We have seen this at Oka, too, with the columnists, writers and editors of the *Montréal Gazette* leading the charge.

This method of defining news obscures the issue that gave rise to the violence. Media people would deny this is done deliberately, but it serves a social purpose: it marginalizes protest. As a result, it creates immense problems for all groups opposed to the status quo, not just for native people.

Some may feel this is an exaggerated view of media behaviour. But compare the media excitement over Oka with the relative indifference shown towards another native group whose issue is very much larger. The Algonquin of Barriere Lake have used peaceful methods of protest for more than two years, without getting major media coverage.

They have always lived about 200 miles north of Ottawa and have always depended for their substance and their way of life, on a forest that is now being cut down around them. Their rights in this forest have never been dealt with. They are suffering because our society violated [a] 1763 undertaking that Indian lands would be occupied only by consent. Today, in a policy notable for its moderation and good sense, the Algonquins are trying to get the Canadian and Quebec governments to collaborate with them in creating a conservation strategy that will lead to a sustainable future economy for their traditional lands.

What is happening to them is a monstrous violation of their rights. As well, they are arguing for all of us for an ecologically sane future. Unable to get anywhere in face of incredible government duplicity, they have maintained peaceful blockades of logging roads and have been met with arrests, injunctions, police intimidation, and criminal charges. They have even been described by a judge in one recent court decision (which, of course, they lost) as infidels.

Their blockades have been covered sporadically by the local media, but I cannot recall any supportive editorials. It is not exaggeration to say that they have been left alone to carry on their struggle in obscurity without any help or moral support.

It has been virtually impossible to obtain national publicity for their issue, even though it is of central importance to all Canadians. Just to describe my own experience, I have had articles returned by two metropolitan dailies and a program I made for the CBC's *Sunday Morning* was never broadcast for reasons that were never stated. The National Film Board has been sitting for months on a nearly-completed film about the Algonquin. No urgency at all about this grave human rights and ecological issue, right in our own backyard.

Could it be that this has something to do with the fact that the Algonquins are mounting a challenge to the all-powerful forest industry? Or is it just that they have not taken up guns to defend themselves? Last September when their whole community was peacefully defying a court injunction ordering them to dismantle their blockade (an act of non-violent civil disobedience in the tradition of Thoreau), they asked CBC TV in Toronto to send a crew, but were given the answer, "if something happens, let us know."

Since there had already been arrests, confrontation, and civil disobedience, that "something" could be only one thing: violence, perhaps death. If they could arrange that, the Algonquins of Barriere Lake would be guaranteed blanket coverage. Of course, then, they would be denounced as extremists.

When the Algonquins came to camp in Ottawa recently, I felt I should march with them, just to show moral support for their cause. I got a lot out of it; they are decent and gentle people, whom it is a privilege and a pleasure to know. But, at another level, I felt somewhat diminished by the experience. For it was obvious we were simply trying to attract the attention of the media, playing the foolish game that the media imposes on all advocates of change. The media will cover such events, report demonstrations, take pictures, ad infinitum, but they will hardly ever subject the issue to serious analysis, or — heaven forbid — take a principled position of support for a just and moral cause.

As I write this, there is the threat of another round of confrontation between the Algonquins and the logging companies. Since the media have recently been falling over themselves talking about the need to redress the injustices done to native people, it will be interesting to see if they support the Algonquins in their just struggle — or simply stick to their disastrous present policy of treating violence as the only news worth bothering about.

8

Introduction to Criminal Procedure

The preceding chapters have examined the broader issues of the definition of "crime," the use of criminal law in colonization, and systemic patterns of enforcement and non-enforcement of criminal law. They have also focused on the outcome of the imposition of criminal law: sentencing, imprisonment, parole, and the intensification of "law and order" campaigns.

The following chapters examine specific components of the criminal process by which people are brought before the courts, including the classification of offences, search and seizure, arrest, access to counsel, judicial interim release, and prosecutorial powers. In Abell and Sheehy, *Proof, Defences, and Beyond*, we return to some of the other procedural issues that arise during the course of the prosecution and defence, such as the burden of proof, disclosure, plea bargaining, jury selection, and the role of the media.

Although the term "procedure" heads this chapter, it is important to recognize that the dichotomy between substantive and procedural criminal law is elusive. First, the *Criminal Code* is the primary source of all criminal law, and it encompasses both substance and process. Second, *Charter* litigation has enlarged the scope for legal argument and accelerated the development of criminal procedure, giving it as much "substance," legal significance and influence in terms of actual trial outcomes. Third, and most significant, "procedure" as a description commonly suggests narrow, technical, and relatively fixed "rules" that govern the prosecution process and are completely distinct from the definition of crimes and the substance of the law of criminal responsibility. In fact, procedure and substance constantly shape each other.

Several examples should illustrate the breakdown of this "distinction." The chapter on **Compelling the Accused's Appearance in Court** sets out the statutory provisions that circumscribe powers of arrest for police. In the cases of *Biron* and *Moore*, *infra* the Supreme Court of Canada gave such expanded interpretations of these powers, in accordance with actual police practices, that the substantive definitions of the two offences with which Biron and Moore were charged, obstruction of a police officer and resisting arrest, were also enlarged. Under the chapter heading **Search and Seizure**, it can be seen that the exclusion of evidence obtained in violation of the *Charter* has an impact upon the Crown's ability to prove the substantive elements of an offence.

CLASSIFICATION OF OFFENCES

All offences in the *Criminal Code* are designated as summary conviction, indictable, or hybrid (that is, triable as summary or indictable at the election and discretion of the Crown).

The classification of an offence has implications in terms of: powers of arrest; investigatory powers (such as fingerprinting); judicial interim release; right to select mode of trial (judge alone or judge and jury); right to select place of trial (before a justice of the peace (JP), a provincial court judge, or a judge of the "superior court of criminal jurisdiction," defined variously for each province and territory in s. 2 of the *Criminal Code*); and the sentencing options available to the judge or justice. The *Charter* may also have a bearing on the implications of classification of offences, although s. 11(f) of the *Charter* does not guarantee a right to a jury trial for offences under military law, and only guarantees access to a jury trial for offences that carry a maximum sentence of five years imprisonment or more. A hybrid offence is treated as an indictable offence until the election is made (s. 34(1)(a) of the *Interpretation Act*, R.S.C. 1985, c. I-21).

The Crown prosecutor will usually declare her election at the first appearance of the accused before the court. Can you speculate as to what kinds of factors will influence the Crown's decision in this regard? See also the findings of the *Report on Systemic Racism in the Ontario Criminal Justice System* (Toronto: Queen's Printer for Ontario, 1995) at 192. The Commission reports findings from the period 1989–90 that Crowns are more likely to elect to proceed summarily against white than against Black accused: for all offences, 37 per cent of charges against whites versus 31 per cent of those against Blacks; for assault on a police officer, 29 per cent of charges against whites versus 12 per cent of those against Blacks; and for drug charges, 65 per cent of charges against whites versus 46 per cent of those against Blacks.

SUMMARY CONVICTION OFFENCES

Offences fall within this category by virtue of statutory designation, or Crown election in the case of a hybrid. In addition to certain *Criminal Code* offences, this category includes provincial offences, municipal by-laws, and specific federal offences.

Summary conviction offences found in federal legislation are governed by Part 27 of the *Code*. They are commenced by the swearing of an "information" (a sworn allegation that a named person has committed a criminal offence) by either a private citizen or, more typically, a police officer, before a justice of the peace, who then issues some form of document (a warrant of arrest, for example, or an appearance notice) to compel the appearance of the accused before a court of law: ss. 788, 789. The accused is tried on this "information" and receives a "summary" trial (a fast trial, in that there is no preliminary inquiry) before a JP or a provincial court judge: s. 785(1). Under s. 787(1), the maximum sentence available for a summary conviction offence is up to $2,000 fine, imprisonment of up to six months, or both, unless the offence specifies another penalty. Note that as a result of the new legislation (*An Act to amend the Criminal Code and other Acts (miscellaneous matters)*, S.C. 1994, c. 44), the following offences have a maximum sentence of 18 months instead of six months when prosecuted summarily: ss. 264.1(a), 267, 269, and 271.

SECTION 553 OFFENCES

Section 553 lists the specific offences to which it applies. Most of the listed offences are indictables, but some are hybrids. For these offences, the accused is not entitled to the usual safeguards associated with indictables of a preliminary inquiry and a trial by jury. The accused charged with a s. 553 offence is given a summary trial before a provincial court judge sitting alone *unless* the judge declines to hear the case and, instead, allows the accused to elect the mode of trial: s. 555.

SECTION 469 OFFENCES

Section 469 also lists the specific offences to which it applies. All of the listed offences are indictables, such as murder, which means that trial will ordinarily be preceded by a preliminary inquiry. Persons accused of s. 469 offences do not, however, have an option as to mode of trial: they must be tried before a jury and a judge of the "superior court of criminal jurisdiction," *unless* both the accused and the Attorney General (AG) consent (s. 473), or the accused loses the right to a jury trial by failing to appear in court when ordered to do so: s. 475.

OTHER INDICTABLE OFFENCES

Indictable offences (either by statute or Crown election) that do not fall within either s. 553 or s. 469 are governed by s. 536. Once the accused has been "arraigned" (the charge is read to the accused, who must plead either "guilty" or "not guilty"), the accused is then given the choice of: (a) a summary trial without preliminary inquiry before a provincial court judge alone (no indictment need be prepared); (b) trial before a judge alone, preceded by a preliminary inquiry; or (c) trial before a judge and jury, again preceded by a preliminary inquiry. If the accused elects either (b) or (c), an indictment will be prepared, a preliminary inquiry will be held in provincial court (unless waived by the accused), and the trial will be held in the "superior court of criminal jurisdiction." An accused who fails to elect is deemed to have elected trial by judge and jury; in certain cases the AG can impose this mode of trial upon an unwilling accused: s. 568.

An accused who has elected or who has been deemed to have elected a mode of trial has rights to re-elect either unilaterally or with the consent of the Crown (depending on when the accused wishes to re-elect) pursuant to s. 561.

CHARTER RIGHTS

The cases and materials in the preceding chapters have touched on a number of *Charter* rights, including s. 2(b) (freedom of expression); s. 3 (right to vote); s. 7 (right to life, liberty and security of the person and the right not to be deprived thereof except in accordance with principles of fundamental justice); s. 10(c) (right to have the validity of a detention determined by way of *habeas corpus*); s. 12 (right not to be subjected to cruel and unusual punishment); s. 15 (right to equality before and under the law); s. 25 (no derogation of Aboriginal treaty rights or rights acquired by land claims agreements); and s. 28 (rights in the *Charter* guaranteed equally to women and men). Many of these *Charter* sections will resurface in the remaining chapters, as these are issues and arguments that have an ongoing relevance.

The chapters that follow address a number of *Charter* rights in more detail: s. 7 (see above); s. 8 (right to be secure against unreasonable search and seizure); s. 9 (right not to be arbitrarily detained or imprisoned); s. 10(a),(b) (right to be informed promptly of the reasons for an arrest or detention, and the right to be informed of and to retain and instruct counsel without delay); s. 11(d) (right to be presumed innocent until proven guilty in a fair and public hearing by an independent and impartial tribunal); and s. 11(e) (right not to be denied reasonable bail without just cause).

These are not, however, the only *Charter* issues that might arise in a criminal trial. For example, additional arguments can be pursued with respect to s. 2(a),(c) or (d) (freedom of conscience or religion, freedom of peaceful assembly, and freedom of association); s. 11 (rights to be informed of the specific charge against one, to be tried within a reasonable time (discussed in Abell and Sheehy, *Proof, Defences, and Beyond*, **Trial Process**), the right to be presumed innocent until proven guilty according to law by a fair and impartial tribunal (discussed *ibid.*, **Burden of Proof**), the right not to be compelled to testify against oneself in one's own prosecution, the right not to be found guilty of an offence unless it was an offence at the time of the act or omission, the right against "double jeopardy," and the right to the lesser punishment if the sentence has changed between the time of commission and sentencing); s. 13 (right against self-incrimination); s. 14 (right to an interpreter for those who do not speak the language used in the proceedings and for those who are deaf); and s. 27 (interpretation of the *Charter* must proceed in a manner consistent with the preservation and enhancement of the multicultural heritage of Canada). Furthermore, ss. 530, 530.1 of the *Criminal Code* also bear on the accused's right to translation and to conduct a defence in either official language of Canada: see *R.* v. *Simard* (1995), 27 O.R. (3d) 116 (C.A.).

The classification of offences and the accompanying criminal procedures may have serious implications for the quality of "justice" that an accused can expect. Thus, the work of a number of scholars has documented the differences between the "summary" justice dispensed by the lower courts and the kinds of trials that take place in the higher courts: Doreen McBarnet, *Conviction: Law, the State and the Construction of Justice* (London: Macmillan, 1981); Pat Carlen, *Magistrates' Justice* (Oxford: Martin Robertson, 1976); and Richard Ericson, "The Decline of Innocence" (1994) 28 U.B.C.L. Rev. 367. Are *Charter* arguments advanced in all levels of court likely to encounter the same reception?

In reading the following chapters, consider the impact of the issues from the earlier chapters. For example, how does the definition of what is "criminal" affect the exercise of police powers of search and arrest? What is the impact of the criminal process, for example judicial interim release, upon identifiable groups such as Aboriginal peoples? Which groups are empowered by criminal laws and structures, such as the power to initiate private prosecutions and the judicial power to cite for contempt?

□

9

Policing

The materials in this chapter discuss:

- the role of the police
- police methods
- systemic bias in policing
- policing the police: legal responses
- police resistance

A. THE ROLE OF THE POLICE

The Police: Solutions to or Sources of Crime?†

[In this chapter of his book, Augustine Brannigan describes the nature of police work (law enforcement, order maintenance, and social work; reactive versus proactive), the role conflicts faced by officers, and a unique police culture (high levels of cohesiveness; social isolation; suspicion of the public; feelings of powerlessness; and problems of social status). He argues that police culture combined with the ambiguities of their status and their work, as well as the futility of much police work, together produce police deviance and criminality.]

POLICE RESPONSES: DEVIANT OCCUPATIONAL BEHAVIOUR

Beside[s] exploiting their roles to take graft (e.g. to avoid gambling joints or to ignore cars illegally parked in front of classy restaurants) and in addition to the frequent reliance on physical force to produce confessions and to dole out revenge (see Hagan, 1977: 148–150), the police appear to routinely trample over the rights of accused people. Mr. Justice Donald Morand's 1976 Royal Commission into Metropolitan Toronto Police Practices found "a sense of

---

† From Augustine Brannigan, *Crimes, Courts and Corrections: An Introduction to Crime and Social Control in Canada* (Toronto: Holt, Rinehart and Winston of Canada, 1984) at 57–59, 61–66. © 1984. Reproduced with permission of Nelson Thomson Learning, a division of Thomson Learning. Fax 800-730-2215.

alienation from the public.... Some police officers believe that they are the only remaining barrier between the public who hired them and the anti-social persons who break society's laws." This alienation from the public appears to lead some officers to believe that their job is "not only to investigate crimes but to act as judge and jury" as well. Lorne Tepperman (1977: 28) argued that it was "largely this alienation from the public" that led to the kinds of abuses of power documented in a controversial 1970 study by the Canadian Civil Liberties Education Trust.

Justice Morand found that excessive force was used by police in 6 of 17 cases studied by him. Tepperman recounts some of the findings (1977: 28–29):

> In the most grisly case, Mr. Justice Morand came to believe the allegation by one victim that two police constables had, in a police station and overheard by other police constables, placed a claw-like device on his nose and on his penis with the intention of intimidating him. In subsequent investigations of these and other allegations, Mr. Morand was disturbed at the extent to which he found "the evidence of police officers mistaken, shaded, deliberately misleading, changed to suit the circumstances and sometimes entirely and deliberately false." Besides the occurrences of brutality carried out, apparently, by a few police against a few citizens, other police officers aware of such occurrences did not try to stop them and these incidences were covered up by both those directly involved and by other police when these allegations were investigated. It is impossible to tell how much these cover-ups account for the discrepancy between the findings of the Canadian Civil Liberties Education Trust study and the rarity of public acknowledgement of police brutality, but the Morand commission opens the door to further investigations along these lines.

The Morand commission was unprecedented in Canadian police history in encouraging public discussion and recognition of the problem of police deviance. Unfortunately, the later McDonald Commission on RCMP wrongdoings and the Quebec Keable Inquiry into the RCMP confirmed the propensity for lawlessness in Canadian policing. Similarly, admissions of police lying and police brutality were videotaped by Neil Proverbs in a sensational 1982 Toronto case (*Globe and Mail*, Nov. 4, 5, 6 and 9, 1982). In the Proverbs case, two senior police officers were recorded as saying that they frequently lied in the courts, altered notebooks to suit the requirements of prosecution and framed individuals with planted evidence. Though they later retracted such claims when the tapes were brought to court, similar incidents had already been documented by Justice Morand.

The most recent report on the Toronto police confirms that the unnecessary use of force by the Toronto police is a substantial problem. Richard Henshel (1983: 10) reports that "for a ten month period from mid-1978 to early 1979 there was almost a killing a month, mostly of members of minority groups. Widespread protest erupted in Toronto's ethnic communities, culminating in September of 1979 in the passage by Toronto City Council of a resolution of non-confidence in the Metropolitan Toronto Police Commission." Henshel (1983: 98–101), working in conjunction with the Citizens' Independent Review of Police Activities, reviewed the complaint procedures in Toronto and concluded that alteration of evidence by the police was common, that complaints to the police department of physical abuse were inadequately processed, that penalties to officers were inconsequential and that certain elements of the police service, specifically the hold-up squad, tortured suspects to get confessions. This last observation was already familiar to several criminal lawyers and has been brought to the attention of Amnesty International. It is an empirical question whether the situation in Toronto is unique and whether or not it is applicable elsewhere.

POLICE DEPLOYMENT AND THE CRIME RATE

Police violence and police disregard of due process are an ironic source of criminal activity in our society. However, critics of police work argue that normative police behaviour, not just infrequent cases of abuse, in a curious way is the greatest contributor to crime statistics. The kernel of this observation is that there is a relationship between the amount of crime reported to Statistics Canada in the Uniform Crime Reports and the organization of police work. Because of their great discretionary power and the conflicting demands of the role, police exercise a great control over how much criminal activity actually gets certified in the official records. For example, Piliavin and Briar (1964) suggested that the police decision to arrest juvenile offenders was not based simply on the offense having been committed. The juvenile's demeanour or show of respect for the police, as well as any exhibition of contrition or show of remorse or sorrow, determined whether the case was brought to court. Piliavin and Briar point out that these informal conditions of arrest probably resulted in a racial slanting of the arrest statistics. Since American urban black males demonstrate a demeanour that provokes the police (or is lacking in shows of deference and contriteness), they are arrested disproportionately to white kids involved in the same kinds of behaviours. This has an application to the Canadian scene in that Indian, Inuit and Métis people frequently find themselves at odds with the police in urban areas where their dress, personal hygiene, physical characteristics and location in rundown sections of the city make them especially vulnerable to police suspicion (Hagan, 1977: 151).

POLICE DEPLOYMENT AS CRIME: THE RCMP SECURITY SERVICE SCANDAL

In 1976 former RCMP Constable Robert Samson gave testimony during his own trial for planting a bomb at a private residence in Montreal that he had done much worse things for the RCMP, including breaking into the office of a radical news service, the Agence de Press Libre du Québec and stealing documents. Subsequent investigation uncovered a host of crimes, wrongdoings and unauthorized activities committed by members of the RCMP security service. These included:

a. Operation Ham: a break-in at the offices of the Parti Québecois in January 1973 to remove and photocopy membership lists and financial information.
b. Over 400 break-ins, unauthorized by search warrants but with the knowledge of senior officers from 1970 to 1976, mostly in British Columbia by the Criminal Investigations Branch.
c. Investigation of New Democratic Party "Waffle Wing" members on the premise that the party had been penetrated by political subversives; this operation was authorized by senior Mounties with knowledge of the Privy Council Office.
d. Surveillance of federal Members of Parliament as well as persons seeking every kind of political office in Canada.
e. Unlawful opening of the mails contrary to the Post Office Act over a period from 1950 to 1976 and undertaken with probable government knowledge.
f. Unlawful destruction of property by burning a barn in May, 1972 at St. Anne de la Rochelle, Quebec, in order to prevent a suspected meeting of terrorists.
g. In December, 1971 in Montreal, the Security Service issued a false communiqué with the forged signature of a Quebec radical with the expectation that the communiqué would excite political extremists to violence.
h. From 1970 across Canada the Mounties gathered evidence from confidential medical files in an attempt to identify information that might discredit radicals. This was done in Ontario with knowledge of the provincial government.
i. In the early 1970s, Security Service members kidnapped and unlawfully detained members of radical groups in attempts to intimidate them and turn them into police informers.
j. For undisclosed reasons, members of the RCMP stole a case of dynamite and some electronic detonators on the night of April 27th, 1972 from the yard of a construction company after smashing the padlock. (See *Toronto Globe and Mail*, June 5, 1978; also see Henshel, 1979).

Since much of the RCMP behaviour had occurred in Quebec and since the Parti Québecois government had been the object of some of the RCMP "inquiries," the first commission to investigate the RCMP scandal was initiated under the direction of Jean K. Keable in Quebec. Michael Mandel (1983b: 3) reports that the federal Commission under the Direction of Mr. Justice D.C. McDonald was initiated in part by the RCMP itself in an effort to limit or contain the Keable Inquiry. Indeed, with the federal McDonald Commission of Inquiry into Certain Activities of the RCMP, the federal government could attempt to block the progress of Keable's inquiry while indicating its willingness to clear the air through its own Commission. Also, by having a Commission of Inquiry in place it was thought that criminal charges against individual Mounties could be postponed until the Commission completed its work. Subsequently the federal government lamented the fact that so much time had elapsed between the crimes in the early and mid 1970s and the completion of the inquiry in 1981, that evidence would be difficult to establish. Predictably, in fall 1982, the Solicitor General of Canada announced that the federal government planned no prosecutions arising from the McDonald Commission. This decision was made secretly by the Justice Department in summer 1982 (Mandel, 1983b: 1) and was confirmed in the summer of 1983 (McGuigan, 1983).

In the meanwhile the McDonald Commission had omitted the details of the most serious

RCMP crimes on the grounds that their publication would prejudice subsequent criminal trials of individual RCMP members (McDonald Commission, Third Report, 1981: 517–520). And so between them, Solicitor General Kaplan and Commissioner McDonald kept the RCMP's dirtiest laundry out of the public domain and out of the courts. Criminal prosecutions proceeded only in Quebec.

Nonetheless, the basic conclusion of the McDonald Commission was that there had been a breakdown in the rule of law in the RCMP Security Service in the early 1970s. In other words, in undertaking to uphold the laws of Canada, members of the RCMP had put themselves above the law and had committed a series of acts that, if undertaken by any other citizens, would have resulted in substantial periods of incarceration. These activities were, after all, not on the order of the highway patrolman who speeds to catch a speeding motorist. These were crimes of arson, breaking and entering, theft, contravening the Post Office Act, kidnapping and forcible detention and invasion of privacy. Despite this, few RCMP officers have been charged. In fact the government of Ontario blocked private prosecutions of Mounties brought by the victims by staying the proceedings (*Re Dowson and the Queen, 1982*). Of those charged and convicted, most have faced reduced charges and all have received non-jail sentences. Jean-Paul Brodeur (1981: 131ff) who was a consultant for two years with the Quebec's Keable inquiry, reported that internal records of the illegal RCMP activities were rewritten for submission to external agents. For example, the original report of the APLQ break in referred to "illegal entry," "theft," and "crime." The redrafted report substituted the terms "entry without warrant" and "removal of documents." The Mounties likewise tried to suppress the idea that their behaviour was illegal in the dynamite theft by characterizing the event as an "unauthorized seizure of dynamite" (Brodeur, 1981: 133). In both cases there was an attempt to create the impression that the search warrants would have automatically been extended and that seizure of private property would have been permissible if authorized.

Probably the most significant implication of the re-description of these crimes was that when Mounties ultimately did face criminal prosecutions for these activities, they faced charges on the downgraded offenses contained in their own revised reports. Specifically, the breaking, entering and theft committed by three policemen (one each from the RCMP, the Sûreté du Québec and the Montreal Police Force) at the APLQ resulted in charges of contravening a federal statute contrary to S. 115 of the Criminal Code by failing to obtain a search warrant. Where break, enter and theft carried a 14-year maximum penalty, S. 115 carries a maximum of two years. The low minimum attached to S. 115 allowed the accused policemen to qualify for the most lenient sentence upon conviction: an absolute discharge. The discharge wipes out evidence of a criminal record and allows people who have been convicted of crimes to be held as something other than criminals, and to keep their jobs as law enforcement officers. What is ironic is that this disposition was possible only because the charge was virtually dictated by the accused via the revised RCMP reports (Mandel, 1983b: 2). Judges have consistently awarded this type of penalty to convicted RCMP criminals.

From its inception the McDonald Commission was charged with bias. In 1978 the Law Union of Ontario, an association of progressive lawyers and legal workers, through lawyer Paul Copeland tried to arrange a court order to prevent the three Commissioners from sitting on the Inquiry. They pointed out that all three had strong affiliations with the Liberal Party. Mr. Justice David McDonald had been appointed to the bench in Alberta by a Liberal government and had been a devoted Liberal Party supporter, having once served as president of the Alberta Liberal Party. Donald Rickard was known to be a friend and business associate of the Solicitor General, Francis Fox, the Minister in charge of the RCMP. The third Commissioner, Guy Gilbert, was a loyal Quebec Liberal who "flamboyantly stated his confidence in the RCMP and the patriotic importance of protecting the image of the Liberal Party in Quebec since the election of the PQ, and whose annual donation of money to the Liberals continued throughout the Commission's deliberations" (Mandel, 1983b: 4). Critics of the Commission pointed out that since the extent of ministerial knowledge of illegal activities would be an important issue in the inquiry, it was imperative that the Commissioners be above any suspicion of protecting their Liberal colleagues in the federal cabinet. The order of prohibition sought by Copeland on behalf of the Law Union failed. The Ontario Court of Appeal argued that a Royal Commission, because it was not a judicial inquiry settling claims between two parties, could not be subject to review on the basis of bias (*Re Copeland and McDonald et al, 1979*). In other words, there is no bar in law against the government's stacking of a Royal Commission since in principle the purpose of such an inquiry is to investigate facts and advise governments and not to determine liability or guilt.

The final reports of the Commission ran to several volumes and covered several thousand pages. All the ministers of the Crown were exonerated of any direct involvement in the unauthorized activities. After much pulling of teeth, the Commission received cabinet minutes that suggested that the Prime Minister knew of illegalities committed by the RCMP but did not know the type of illegalities. Likewise one-time Solicitor General Warren Allmand "suspected" illegalities. Jean-Pierre Goyer, George McIllraith and Francis Fox knew of certain activities but did not know they were illegal. As Mandel (1983b: 4) points out, "this novel defence of ignorance of the law must have come as a pleasant surprise to all these legally trained Ministers." In the end the breakdown in the rule of law was found to have been limited to the RCMP and government ministers were on the whole cleared of responsibility. This was the section of the report best received by the government.

The reports of the Commission cover several major areas. First, they deal with the role of the security service within the RCMP and recommend that it be replaced by a civilian service. Secondly, they deal with the legal questions that arise from police illegalities and possible police defences in such cases. On the whole they dismiss defences of mistake of law, mistake of fact, lofty motives, necessity, duress, "just following orders" and the like. In the final volume they deal with specific wrongdoings and they suggest remedies. We shall deal with the areas covered in the final volume.

The wrongdoings fell into three different categories. First, there were cases "not requiring further action." These involved RCMP misrepresentations to the government of RCMP surveillance of radicals on university campuses, attempts by the RCMP to control information given to the 1966 Royal Commission on Security, attempts to recruit informers, failure to inform the Solicitor General of illegal acts, misleading the Solicitor General regarding the policy on mail interception, misrepresentation of its investigation of the Royal American shows in Western Canada to provincial and federal officials, the theft and subsequent destruction of private property during the surveillance of a foreign agent, and the misrepresentation to the Solicitor General of information about financial support given to the defector, Igor Gouzenko, from 1946 to 1962. For the most part, the Commission found that the failures of communication between the Force and various government officials were not purposefully deceptive, arose for unaccountable reasons or were inconsequential. Accordingly, the Commission recommended that no action be taken against individual Mounties.

The second type of activity reviewed by the Commission was one for which the Commissioners recommended internal disciplinary action. First, the Commission dealt with a case in which one particular officer felt that RCMP use of information from the National Revenue Department was probably unlawful; the officer refused to seek a legal opinion about the practice because of his expectation that it would make the unlawfulness explicit and hence would undermine the Force's reliance on revenue files, contrary to the Income Tax Act. As the Commissioners commented, this showed "a complete disrespect for the law and the legal process" (Third Report, 1981: 349). This attitude permeated other areas. For example, the second circumstance studied by McDonald involved the illegal use of master keys for automobiles. Master keys were developed by General Motors to allow dealers access to all GM products. Because of the illicit use of such keys, the Criminal Code in 1970 required that anyone possessing a master key have a provincial license. From 1970 to 1978, the RCMP used such master keys in criminal investigations to secretly search vehicles for evidence. This practice was only brought under control in 1978.

The third area requiring disciplinary action involved the destruction of the files relating to "Operation Checkmate." This operation involved the use of illegal activities to discredit, impede, deter or undermine political radicals. According to the Mountie who destroyed the files, they were "very sensitive" and "very explosive" and if brought to public attention would have brought the Security Service into disrepute. The Commissioners commented that in their opinion, "the explanation given by Mr. Yawarski for recommending in 1974 the destruction of the Checkmate files ... amounts to nothing less than an intention to reduce the possibility of the Government of Canada learning of acts which he himself had come to consider to have been 'wrong'" (Third Report, 1981: 367). Had Operation Checkmate involved illegal acts, the destruction of the records would amount to obstruction of justice. The RCMP's obstruction of justice by misinforming agencies of the federal and provincial government and the amazing gaps in memory of senior RCMP officers were on the whole the subject of little comment by the Commissioners (see for example, Third Report, 1981: 374–75).

The third area of inquiry in the final report dealt with "cases referred for possible prosecution and disciplinary action." These included breaches of the confidentiality of the National Revenue files, the Unemployment Insurance Commission files, breaches of the Post Office Act, unlawful attempts to recruit informers, breaking and entering, theft and invasion of privacy. The Commission did not publish its chapters on these cases because of possible criminal charges against those involved. In fact several such charges have been laid in Quebec at the suggestion of the Keable Inquiry, though no one has been jailed or fined as a result.

What has been the federal government's response to the McDonald Commission? At the level of individual Mounties, it has shown no interest in prosecution. In fact after receiving the final Commission reports in January 1981, it delayed publication for eight months and commissioned two legal opinions, which challenged McDonald's conclusions about RCMP crimes. These were released simultaneously with the publication of the Royal Commission in an attempt to discredit the conclusions of its own hand picked Commissioners (Mandel, 1983b: 7). The opinion of the government seems to be that whatever the police need to do in order to do their job is *ipso facto* legal. In other words, the end of law enforcement justifies any means. A consequence of this would be that anyone victimized in the course of police work has no protection and no redress under the criminal law. This is of course both morally reprehensible and legally incorrect. Nonetheless, the same mentality was at work in 1983 and 1984 in the preparation of the new security service. The Government is implementing the recommendation to create a civilian security service, but it is also making provisions both to legalize the sorts of crimes that gave rise to the McDonald and Keable inquiries and to loosen the new agency's public accountability. This would not be quite so distressing if such an agency were directed solely at foreign spies and subversives. However, the history of the RCMP in the area of national security reveals that the Mounties have maintained files on tens of thousands of Canadians, have targeted legitimate political organizations like the Parti Québecois and the NDP as well as members of the peace movement, Jehovah's Witnesses, progressive union leaders and those political elements that are trying to democratize social life and increase government accountability (see Mann and Lee, 1979: 107–121). This suggests that it would be politically regressive to model the new security service on an agency in which a totalitarian attitude towards the political left has been combined in the past with a pervasive breakdown in the rule of law.

SUMARY

The role of the police in a democratic society is precarious. We require the maintenance of order and coercive law enforcement as well as various social services. We require the exercise of discretion yet demand a fair and even application of law. This contributes to the ambiguities attributed to and the contradictory expectations that are held by the police. They are required to proceed in the face of situations marked by structural limitations in controlling crime as well as social futility in dealing with the problems of those in crisis and without hope. These factors contribute to a distinctive occupational subculture characterized by cohesiveness, isolation, suspicion, feelings of powerlessness and misgivings about status and worth. This subculture in turn may foster certain deviant responses, including a vigilante attitude among certain officers. Yet, when the police themselves become a source of deviance, accountability to the public is fraught with problems. The police control the investigation of complaints against police. The police exercise the discretion to discipline internally or to lay charges. If charges are laid, as in the RCMP break-in at the APLQ, the police control which charges they or their associates will face. The success of commissions of inquiry into police practices are mixed. They create bad publicity but the extent to which external publicity changes internal practices is an open question. For example, the aftermath of the McDonald Commission has seen attempts to normalize and legitimate police crimes. Civil rights is one of the major areas in the justice system that appears to limit or countervail the illegitimate elements of social control. In theory, the legal rights of the citizen offset the overzealous conduct of police. ...

∎

For a more recent account of police deviance see the Report of the Poitras Commission, which reported on the conduct of the Sureté de Québec (SQ) in 1999 in a 1700-page report that made 175 recommendations for change. The Commission found that the SQ "routinely breaks the law during criminal investigations," and criticized the understandings within the SQ of loyalty, integrity, and equality: "Any criticism of the organization or its practices made by a member seems suspect:" "Quebec police routinely break law: inquiry" *The Ottawa Citizen* (29 January 1999) A4.

In Los Angeles, the "Ramparts" trials have revealed the biggest police corruption scandal in the city's history involving the city's anti-gang unit: "Officers convicted in L.A. scandal" *The Toronto Star* (16 November 2000) A26. The convictions of three officers for obstruction of justice and filing false reports resulted from the first trial, among many, of officers involved in the unit, who are accused of assaulting and framing hundreds of innocent people, mostly Spanish-speaking immigrants. By the fall of 2000, some 100 convictions had been overturned, and dozens of officers had been put under investigation.

In light of these events, consider the passage of s. 25.1 of the *Criminal Code* (discussed *supra*, **Law and Order**), which will provide designated officers with immunity from criminal responsibility for most crimes committed in furtherance of law enforcement. What impact will this law have on police deviance and criminality?

B. POLICE METHODS

As the article by Brannigan suggests and as the findings of the McDonald Commission attest, police methods include a range of practices, some of them dangerous, and others illegal. While acknowledging the unique difficulties and dangers inherent in police work, consider the arguments for confronting police practices.

Some of the following methods have been challenged; others have been relatively immune to public scrutiny and restraint:

- **Police "construction" of a case against a suspect**: Several authors have documented the ways in which evidence is collected and shaped by police, in light of their interest in "solving" a case. See, for example, Mike McConville, Andrew Sanders, and Roger Leng, *The Case for the Prosecution: Police Suspects and the Construction of Criminality* (London: Routledge, 1993). In some of the cases discussed *supra* under **Enforcement of the Law**, miscarriages of justice were attributed by judges and commissioners to the manner in which police selectively sought evidence to support their initial theories of guilt. Both the Morin Commission and the Sophonow Inquiry, discussed *supra*, **Enforcement of the Law**, attributed the wrongful convictions they examined to what is called "tunnel vision," whereby police determine the identity of the suspect and pursue evidence in support of the theory, regardless of the emergence of exculpatory or contradictory evidence. For an argument that none of the remedies of exclusion of evidence, criminal prosecution, civil litigation, internal discipline, civilian complaints, improved internal or judicial supervision, or training can curb police investigative malpractice in light of police culture, see John Arnold Epp, "Penetrating Police Investigative Practice Post-*Morin*" (1997) 31 U.B.C. L. Rev. 95. He argues that changes to police culture must instead come from within, and suggests the enactment of an investigation code with a unique enforcement scheme implemented through an investigation review department.

  See also Alan Jeffers, "RCMP spy file rife with racism, documents show" *The Ottawa Citizen* (11 April 1994) A3, in which files from the 1960s constructed African-Canadian men involved in political activism through the Black Panthers organization as "hoodlums," "layabouts, thieves and drunks," which in turn would have made these men vulnerable to future criminalization.

- **Interrogation techniques**: Testimony and confessions produced through police interrogation can be challenged on the basis that they were involuntary, which is a difficult allegation to sustain, as is illustrated by the prolonged efforts of the Birmingham Six and the Guildford Four, discussed under **Enforcement of the Law**. See also *R. v. Paternak* (1995), 33 Alta. L.R. (3d) 71 (C.A.), where the standard was set at a high level: "the influence must be so overbearing that it can be said that the detainee has lost *any* meaningfully independent ability to choose to remain silent, and has become a mere tool in the hands of the police" (at 79) [italics in original].

  However, consider whether involuntariness should be the only test of the reliability of alleged "confessions"? See, for example, David Roberts, "Cleaning up the precinct house" *The [Toronto] Globe and Mail* (29 May 1993) D2 (referring to four cases in which charges were later dropped by Winnipeg police when "confessions" were later proved impossible).

- **Entrapment techniques**: Police may be involved in efforts to detect crime by using undercover police, by using informants, and sometimes by participating themselves in illegal activities. See, for example, the *White* case, discussed *supra* under **Enforcement of the Law**, and the materials in Abell and Sheehy, *Proof, Defences, and Beyond*, **Entrapment**. Consider the following controversial examples: allegations that surfaced in 1994 that a paid informant for CSIS was a co-founder and leading member of the Heritage Front (see Abell and Sheehy, *Proof, Defences, and Beyond*, **Entrapment**); and a 1993 case in which a Québec judge threw out charges of being found in a bawdy house laid against six women dancers based on the conduct of the officers who allegedly posed as clients, fondled the women, and urged them to perform sexual acts (see Abell and Sheehy, *Proof, Defences, and Beyond*, **Entrapment**).

  As Brannigan points out, even though police illegality does not have either statutory authorization or common law immunity, courts are reluctant to give effect to that illegality. For example, in Rudy Platiel, "Mercredi to tell UN about sting operation" *The [Toronto] Globe and Mail* (17 January 1996) A5, officers in "Operation Rainbow," a massive undercover operation involving 67 undercover officers in Ontario that resulted in 236 charges against 35 people, mostly Aboriginal, committed offences themselves under the same act to encourage violations. Although defence motions for a stay of proceedings based on abuse of process have thus far failed (see discussion *supra* under **Aboriginal Peoples and Criminal Law** and in Abell and Sheehy, *Proof, Defences, and Beyond*, **Entrapment**), a stay was granted to an accused charged following an undercover operation in Saskatchewan. In *R. v. Wolfe*, [1995] 10 W.W.R. 44 (Sask. C.A.), the court condemned the officer who had acted in violation of the Band's by-law and in violation of a treaty agreement with the Crown by bringing alcohol into a reserve and offering it to the accused: "all this amounts to an affront to fair play and decency which is disproportionate to the societal interest in the effective prosecution of criminal cases" (at 68).

- **High speed chases**: Civilian injuries and deaths through high speed chases have been the subject of coroner's inquests, criminal charges, and tort actions. See, for example, Dave Rodgers, "Set mandatory pursuit policy, jury urges" *The Ottawa Citizen* (30 September 1995) C1 (coroner's jury made 21 recommendations with respect to changes to the *Police Services Act*, R.S.O. 1990, c. P-15, to make the policy on guidelines for high speed chases mandatory and enforceable). In 1989, Ontario created guidelines in response to its reputation as the province with the worst record in terms of numbers of high speed chases and civilian deaths and injuries: Zuhair Kashmeri, "Ontario police have bloodiest record" *The [Toronto] Globe and Mail* (3 January 1985) A1 and Timothy Appleby, "Ontario unveils regulations governing police chases" *The [Toronto] Globe and Mail* (7 December 1989) A15. These rules were revised in 1999: Jennifer Lewington, "Police applaud new rules for high-speed chases" *The [Toronto] Globe and Mail* (2 April 1999) A11. The RCMP revised its high-speed chase policy in 2001: Joanne Laucius and Graham Hughes, "RCMP quietly brings in new pursuit policy" *The Ottawa Citizen* (20 November 2001) E1.

  Police have at times been charged and convicted of offences arising out of such chases. For example, see *R. v. Brennan* (1989), 75 C.R. (3d) 38 (Ont. C.A.) (conviction for failure to stop at a stop sign); *R. v. Boucher*, [1994] A.Q. No. 650 (C.A.), online: QL (conviction for assault causing bodily harm and negligent use of a firearm when the officer fired at the car to stop the driver at the conclusion of a chase).

- **Use of dogs**: Police dogs have also been responsible for civilian injuries. See, for instance, Clare Powell, "Violent use of police dogs is widespread in Regina" *Briarpatch* (October 1982) 3. For a recent example see *C. (T.L.) v. Vancouver (City)*, [1996] 2 W.W.R. 529 (B.C.S.C.), where a 14-year-old caught in the act of theft from a car was bitten three times by "Police Dog Brutus" (as well as kicked in the face by an officer) while being arrested. The boy sued successfully in tort for battery based on the excessive use of force and the failure to use reasonableness in containing the "weapon" posed by the dog.

- **Use of force**: Police use of force has been challenged through coroner's inquests, criminal charges, public inquiries, and tort actions. For an example of successful prosecution of a police officer who violently assaulted an African-Canadian citizen who was standing in front of his own home and refused the officer's request that he identify himself, see *R. v. Dunn*, [1992] O.J. No. 685 (Ct. Just. (Gen. Div.)), (aff'd [1994] O.J. No. 279 (C.A.), online: QL). See also *R. v. Groot* (1998), 41 O.R. (3d) 280 (C.A.). Discussion of the specific use of guns by police against members of the African-Canadian and Aboriginal communities will be pursued *infra* under **Racism**.

The use of force by police riot squads in response to mass citizens' protests has resulted in numerous challenges and inquiries. See, for example, the work of the RCMP Public Complaints Commission of Inquiry headed by Ted Hughes, Q.C., convened in response to the conduct of the police towards protesters at the Asia Pacific Economic Cooperation summit on the U.B.C. campus in 1997 (interim report by Hughes and final report by Shirley Heafey: Jim Bronskill, "RCMP should apologize for APEC: report" *The Ottawa Citizen* (17 March 2002) A4)) and that of a Commission of Inquiry headed by retired Supreme Court of Canada justice Willard Estey to inquire into the use of violence by the OPP in response to a mass demonstration at the Ontario Legislature in 1996.

More recently, the Citizens Panel on Policing and the Community heard and received submissions from some 60 individuals who witnessed the acts of the Ottawa police during the G20 protest in November 2001. Many individuals reported arrests and police violence through dogs, rubber bullets, and physical force against peaceful protesters. Although some of those arrested had their charges withdrawn (Jake Rupert, "Charges dropped against G20 protesters" *The Ottawa Citizen* (23 November 2001) C6), the request of 20 citizens seeking an inquiry by the Police Services Board into the actions of police was denied. The Citizens Panel was convened in order to address the concerns: *Overview Report of the Citizens Panel on Policing and the Community* (Chair: Marion Dewar) (Ottawa: 9 May 2002).

- **Racial profiling:** The use of race as a proxy for investigative detention has been documented in both the U.S. and in Canada. The U.S. Commission on Civil Rights has found that the N.Y. police department "widely uses" racial profiling to stop and question Hispanics and African-Americans, contributing to racial tensions that escalate into tragic police shootings, such as the killing of an unarmed man, Amadou Diallo, by 41 bullets fired by four officers: *Police Practices and Civil Rights in New York City* (Washington, D.C.: U.S. Commission on Civil Rights, 2000).

Similar practices of racial profiling by Customs Canada have been documented by the African Canadian Legal Clinic (Royson James, "Black passengers targeted in airport searches?" *The Toronto Star* (29 November 1998) A1 (African-Canadians arriving from Jamaica eight times more likely to be searched than whites)). A human rights complaint to this effect by Selwyn Pieters against Customs has resulted in a settlement whose terms include financial compensation, a commitment to instituting anti-racism training, and the collection of race- and sex-based statistics on Customs searches: John Saunders, "Customs bows to irate traveller" *The [Toronto] Globe and Mail* (6 February 2002) A1. Canadian criminal courts have also begun to come to terms with racial profiling in the context of criminal prosecution, as the materials that follow will illustrate.

C. SYSTEMIC BIAS IN POLICING

Examples of differential patterns in law enforcement vis-à-vis particular groups, on the basis of racism, sexism, and homophobia, follow.

RACISM

Across the country, reports and inquiries have further substantiated the allegations made by many Aboriginal and African-Canadian people of their experience of racism under the criminal law. Refer to the numerous reports cited *supra* under **Aboriginal Peoples and Criminal Law**. Some of these reports, such as the Marshall Inquiry, also pointed to the harsh treatment of Black Nova Scotians by the police and the courts. Despite this voluminous evidence, there has been a tendency to characterize what happened to Donald Marshall, Jr. as an individual failure of the justice system rather than as symptomatic of the underlying systemic problem of racism.

In addition to the reports on the racism experienced by Aboriginal peoples, consider the following studies that focus on the experience of Black and other racialized people: *Report of the Commission on Systemic Racism in the Ontario Criminal Justice System* (Toronto: Queen's Printer for Ontario, 1995) [hereinafter *Report on Systemic Racism*]; Ontario, *Task Force on Race Relations and Policy* (Toronto: Task Force, 1989); Stephen Lewis, *Report on Race Relations in Ontario* (Toronto: Queen's Printer for Ontario, 1992); and Québec, *Human Rights Commission Inquiry in Relations between Police and Visible Minorities* (Montréal: Ministry of Communications of Québec, 1988). For a more comprehensive bibliography, see Catherine Mathews and L. Lewis, *Racism in the Criminal Justice System: A Bibliography* (Toronto: Centre of Criminology, 1995).

Spirit-Murdering the Messenger: The Discourse of Fingerpointing as the Law's Response to Racism†

WINDOWS AND MIRRORS

Buzzers are big in New York City. Favored particularly by smaller stores and boutiques, merchants throughout the city have installed them as screening devices to reduce the incidence of robbery. When the buzzer sounds, if the face at the door looks "desirable," the door is unlocked. If the face is that of an "undesirable," the door stays locked. Predictably, the issue of undesirability has revealed itself to be primarily a racial determination. Although the buzzer system was controversial at first, even civil rights organizations have backed down in the face of arguments that the system is a "necessary evil," that it is a "mere inconvenience" compared to the risks of being murdered, that discrimination is not as bad as assault, and that in any event, it is not *all* blacks who are barred, just "17-year-old black males wearing running shoes and hooded sweatshirts."

Two Saturdays before Christmas, I saw a sweater that I wanted to purchase for my mother. I pressed my brown face to the store window and my finger to the buzzer, seeking admittance. A narrow-eyed white youth who looked barely seventeen, wearing tennis sneakers and feasting on bubble gum, glared at me, evaluating me for signs that would pit me against the limits of his social understanding. After about five seconds, he mouthed, "We're closed," and blew pink rubber at me. It was one o'clock in the afternoon. There were several white people in the store who appeared to be shopping for things for *their* mothers.

I was enraged. At that moment I literally wanted to break all of the windows in the store and *take* lots of sweaters for my mother. In the flicker of his judgmental grey eyes, that saleschild had reduced my brightly sentimental, joy-to-the-world, pre-Christmas spree to a shambles. He had snuffed my sense of humanitarian catholicity, and there was nothing I could do to snuff his, without simply making a spectacle of myself.

I am still struck by the structure of power that drove me into such a blizzard of rage. There was almost nothing I could do, short of physically intruding upon him, that would humiliate him the way he humiliated me. No words, no gestures, no prejudices of my own would make a bit of difference to him. His refusal to let me into the store was an outward manifestation of his never having let someone like me into the realm of his reality. He had no connection, no compassion, no remorse, no reference to me, and no desire to acknowledge me even at the estranged level of arm's length transactor. He saw me only as one who would take his money and therefore could not conceive that I was there to give him money.

In this weird ontological imbalance, I realized that buying something in that store was like bestowing a gift: the gift of my commerce. In the wake of my outrage, I wanted to take back the gift of my appreciation, which my peering in the window must have appeared to be. I wanted to take it back in the form of unappreciation, disrespect, and defilement. I wanted to work so hard at wishing he could feel what I felt that he would never again mistake my *hatred* for some sort of plaintive wish to be included. I was quite willing to disenfranchise myself in the

---

† By Patricia Williams, (1987) 42:1 U. Miami L. Rev. 127 at 127–56. Reproduced with permission of the publisher. Notes omitted.

heat of my need to revoke the flattery of my purchasing power. I was willing to boycott this particular store, random white-owned businesses, and anyone who blew bubble gum in my face again.

My rage was admittedly diffuse, even self-destructive, but it was symmetrical. The perhaps loose-ended but utter propriety of that rage is no doubt lost not just to the young man who barred me, but to those who appreciate my being barred only as an abstract precaution, and who approve of those who would bar, even as they deny that *they* would bar *me*.

The violence of my desire to have burst into that store is probably quite apparent to the reader. I wonder if the violence and the exclusionary hatred are equally apparent in the repeated public urging that blacks put themselves in the shoes of white store owners, and that, in effect, blacks look into the mirror of frightened white faces to the reality of their undesirability; and that then blacks would "just as surely conclude that [they] would not let [themselves] in under similar circumstances."

This article will consider how the rhetoric of increased privatization, in response to racial issues, functions as the rationalizing agent of public unaccountability, and ultimately irresponsibility. My emphasis will be more on the process of exclusion than on reiterating the substantive literature of silenced voices, a body as great as the history of this nation. I will analyze the language of lawmakers, officials, and the public in order to present racial discrimination — so pervasive yet so hard to prosecute, so active yet so unactionable — in a new light. My concern is the need for new tools with which to confront issues such as discriminatory prosecution, prejudice as a silent force in jury reallocation of the burden of proof, the adequacy of an evidentiary system in which relevance and materiality are subjective reflections of self-interested values, private assumptions about race and class, and right and wrong as forces in the allocation and distribution of the resources for survival. To this end, I will examine two cases: the death of Eleanor Bumpurs, an elderly black woman shot by police in the Bronx, and the beating of three black men by white teenagers in the Howard Beach section of Queens.

The second purpose of this article is to examine racism as a crime, an offense so deeply painful and assaultive as to constitute something I call "spirit-murder." Society is only beginning to recognize that racism is as devastating, as costly, and as psychically obliterating as robbery or assault; indeed they are often the same. Racism resembles other offenses against humanity whose structures are so deeply embedded in culture as to prove extremely resistant to being recognized as forms of oppression. It can be as difficult to prove as child abuse or rape, where the victim is forced to convince others that he or she was not at fault, or that the perpetrator was not just "playing around." As in rape cases, victims of racism must prove that they did not distort the circumstances, misunderstand the intent, or even enjoy it.

CRIMES WITHOUT PASSION

Eleanor Bumpurs and the Language of Lawmakers

On October 29, 1984, Eleanor Bumpurs, a 270-pound, arthritic, sixty-seven year old woman, was shot to death while resisting eviction from her apartment in the Bronx. She was $98.85, or one month, behind in her rent. New York City Mayor Ed Koch and Police Commissioner Benjamin Ward described the struggle preceding her demise as involving two officers with plastic shields, one officer with a restraining hook, another officer with a shotgun, and at least one supervising officer. All of the officers also carried service revolvers. According to Commissioner Ward, during the course of the attempted eviction Mrs. Bumpurs escaped from the restraining hook twice and wielded a knife that Commissioner Ward says was "bent" on one of the plastic shields. At some point, Officer Stephen Sullivan, the officer positioned farthest away from her, aimed and fired his shotgun. It is alleged that the blast removed half of her hand, so that, according to the Bronx District Attorney's Office, "[I]t was anatomically impossible for her to hold the knife." The officer pumped his gun and shot again, making his mark completely the second time around.

In the two and one-half year wake of this terrible incident, controversy raged as to whether Mrs. Bumpurs ought to have brandished a knife and whether the officer ought to have fired his gun. In February 1987, a New York Supreme Court justice found Officer Sullivan not guilty of manslaughter. The case centered on a very narrow issue of language pitted against circumstance. District Attorney Mario Merola described the case as follows: "*Obviously*, one shot would have been justified. But if that shot took off part of her hand and rendered her defenseless, whether there was any need for a second shot, which killed her, that's the whole issue of whether you have reasonable force or excessive force." My intention in the following analysis is to underscore the significant task facing judges and lawyers in undoing institutional descriptions of what is "obvious" and what is not, and in resisting the general predigestion of evidence for jury consumption.

Shortly after Mr. Merola's statement, Officer Sullivan's attorney, Bruce Smiry, expressed eagerness to try the case before a jury. Following the heavily publicized attack in Howard Beach, however, he favored a bench trial. In explaining his decision to request a nonjury trial, he stated:

> I think a judge will be much more likely than a jury to understand the defense that the shooting was justified.... The average lay person might find it difficult to understand why the police were there in the first place, and why a shotgun was employed.... Because of the climate now in the city, I don't want people perceiving this as a racial case.

Since 1984, Mayor Koch, Commissioner Ward, and a host of other city officials repeatedly have described the shooting of Mrs. Bumpurs as completely legal. At the same time, Commissioner Ward has admitted publicly that Mrs. Bumpurs should not have died. Mayor Koch admitted that her death was the result of "a chain of mistakes and circumstances" that came together in the worst possible way, with the worst possible circumstances. Commissioner Ward admitted that the officers could have waited for Mrs. Bumpurs to calm down, and that they could have used teargas or mace instead of gunfire. According to Commissioner Ward, however, these observations are made with hindsight. As to whether this shooting of a black woman by a white police officer had racial overtones, he stated that he had "no evidence of racism." Commissioner Ward pointed out that he is sworn to uphold the law, which is "inconsistent with treating blacks differently," and that the shooting was legal because it was within the code of police ethics. Finally, city officials have resisted criticism of the police department's handling of the incident by remarking that "outsiders" do not know all of the facts and do not understand the pressure under which officers labor.

The root of the word "legal" is the Latin word *lex*, which means law in a fairly concrete sense — law as we understand it when we refer to written law, codes, and systems of obedience. The word *lex* does not include the more abstract, ethical dimension of law that contemplates the purposes of rules and their effective implementation. This latter meaning is contained in the Latin word *jus*, from which we derive the word "justice." This semantic distinction is not insignificant. The word of law, whether statutory or judicial, is a subcategory of the underlying social motives and beliefs from which it is born. It is the technical embodiment of attempts to order society according to a consensus of ideals. When society loses sight of those ideals and grants obeisance to words alone, law becomes sterile and formalistic: *lex* is applied without *jus* and is therefore unjust. The result is compliance with the letter of the law, but not the spirit. A sort of punitive literalism ensues that leads to a high degree of thoughtless conformity. This literalism has, as one of its primary underlying values, order — whose ultimate goal may be justice, but whose immediate end is the ordering of behavior. Living solely by the letter of the law means living without spirit; one can do anything as long as it comports with the law in a technical sense. The cynicism or rebelliousness that infects one's spirit, and the enthusiasm or dissatisfaction with which one conforms is unimportant. Furthermore, this compliance is arbitrary; it is inconsistent with the will of the conformer. The law becomes a battleground of wills. The extent to which technical legalism obfuscates and undermines the human motivations that generate our justice system is the real extent to which we as human beings are disenfranchised.

Cultural needs and ideals change with the momentum of time; redefining our laws in keeping with the spirit of cultural flux keeps society alive and humane. In the Bumpurs case, the words of the law called for nonlethal alternatives first, but allowed some officer discretion in determining which situations are so immediately life endangering as to require the use of deadly force. This discretionary area was presumably the basis for the claim that Officer Sullivan acted legally. The law as written permitted shooting in general, and therefore, by extension of the city's interpretation of this law, it would be impossible for a police officer ever to shoot someone in a specifically objectionable way.

If our laws are thus piano-wired on the exclusive validity of literalism, if they are picked clean of their spirit, then society risks heightened irresponsibility for the consequences of abominable actions. Accordingly, Jonathan Swift's description of lawyers weirdly and ironically comes to life: "[T]here was a Society of Men among us, bred up from their Youth in the Art of proving by words multiplied for the Purpose, that White is Black and Black is White, according as they are paid. To this Society all the rest of the People are Slaves." We also risk subjecting ourselves to such absurdly empty rhetoric as Commissioner Ward's comments to the effect that both Mrs. Bumpurs' death and racism were unfortunate, while stating "but the law says...." Commissioner Ward's sentiments might as well read: "The law says ... and therefore the death was unfortunate but irremediable; the law says ... and therefore there is little that can be done about racism." The law thus becomes a shield behind which to avoid responsibility for the human repercussions of both governmental and publicly harmful private activity.

A related issue is the degree to which much of the criticism of the police department's handling of this case was devalued as "noisy" or excessively emotional. It is as though passionate protest were a separate crime, a rudeness of such dimension as to defeat altogether any legitimacy of content. We as lawyers are taught from the moment we enter law school to temper our emotionalism and quash our idealism. We are taught that heartfelt instincts subvert the law and defeat the security of a well-ordered civilization, whereas faithful adherence to the word of law, to stare decisis and clearly stated authority, would as a matter of course lead to a bright, clear world like the Land of Oz, in which those heartfelt instincts would be preserved. Form is exalted over substance, and cool rationales over heated feelings. But we should not be ruled exclusively by the cool formality of language or by emotions. We must be ruled by our complete selves, by the intellectual and emotional content of our words. Governmental representatives must hear the full range of legitimate concerns, no matter how indelicately expressed or painful they may be to hear.

But undue literalism is only one type of sleight of tongue in the attainment of meaningless dialogue. Mayor Koch, Commissioner Ward, and Officer Sullivan's defense attorneys have used overgeneralization as an effective rhetorical complement to their avoidance of the issues. For example, allegations that the killing was illegal and unnecessary, and should therefore be prosecuted, were met with responses such as, "The laws permit police officers to shoot people." "As long as police officers have guns, there will be unfortunate deaths." "The conviction rate in cases like this is very low." The observation that teargas would have been an effective alternative to shooting Mrs. Bumpurs drew the dismissive reply that "there were lots of things they *could* have done."

Privatization of response as a justification for public irresponsibility is a version of the same game. Honed to perfection by President Reagan, this version holds up the private self as indistinguishable from the public "duty and power laden" self. Public officials respond to commentary by the public and the media as though it were meant to hurt private, vulnerable feelings. Trying to hold a public official accountable while not hurting his feelings is a skill the acquisition of which would consume time better spent on almost any conceivable task. Thus, when Commissioner Ward was asked if the internal review board planned to discipline Officer Sullivan, many seemed disposed to accept his response that while he was personally very sorry she had died, he could not understand why the media was focusing on him so much. "How many other police commissioners," he asked repeatedly, "have gotten as much attention as I have?"

Finally, a most cruel form of semantic slipperiness infused Mrs. Bumpurs' death from the beginning. It is called victim responsibility. It is the least responsive form of dialogue, yet apparently the easiest to accept as legitimate.

All these words, from Commissioner Ward, from the Mayor's office, from the media, and from the public generally, have rumbled and resounded with the *sounds* of discourse. We want to believe that their symmetrical, pleasing structure is the equivalent of discourse. If we are not careful, we will hypnotize ourselves into believing that it *is* discourse.

Howard Beach and the "Private Property" of Neighborhood

In the early morning hours of December 20, 1986, three young black men left their stalled car on Cross Bay Parkway, in the New York City borough of Queens, and went to look for help. They walked into the neighborhood of Howard Beach, entered a pizzeria, ordered pizzas, and sat down to eat. An anonymous caller to the police reported their presence as "black troublemakers." A patrol car came, found no trouble, and left. After the young men had eaten, they left the pizzeria and were immediately surrounded by a group of eight to ten white teenagers who taunted them with racial epithets. The white youths chased the black men for about three miles, catching them at several points and beating them severely. One of the black men died as a result of being struck by a car as he tried to flee across a highway. Another suffered permanent blindness in one eye.

In the extremely heated public controversy that ensued, as much attention centered on the community of Howard Beach as on the assailants themselves. A veritable Greek chorus formed, comprised of the defendants' lawyers and resident after resident after resident of Howard Beach, all repeating and repeating and repeating that the mere presence of three black men in that part of town at that time of night was reason enough to drive them out. "They had to be starting trouble." "We're a strictly white neighborhood." "What were they doing here in the first place?"

Although the immensely segregationist instincts behind such statements may be fairly evident, it is worth making explicit some of the presuppositions behind such ululations.

Everyone who lives here is white.
No black could live here.
No one here has a black friend.
No white would employ a black here.
No black is permitted to shop here.
No black is ever up to any good.

These presuppositions themselves are premised on lethal philosophies of life.

"It's Better to Be Safe Than Sorry"
"Are we supposed to stand around and do nothing while these blacks come into our area and rob us?" one woman asked a reporter in the wake of the Howard Beach attack. A twenty year old, who had lived in Howard Beach all of his life, said, "We ain't racial.... We just don't want to get robbed." The hidden implication of these statements is that to be safe is not to be sorry, and that to be safe is to be white and to be sorry is to be associated with blacks. Safety and sorrow, which are inherently alterable and random, are linked to inalterable essences. The expectation that uncertain conditions are really immutable is a formula for frustration; it is a belief that feeds a sense of powerlessness. The rigid determinism of placing in the disjunctive things that are not in fact disjunctive is a set up for betrayal by the very nature of reality. The national repetition that white neighborhoods are safe and blacks bring sorrow is an incantation of powerlessness. And, as with the upside-down logic of all irrational incantations, it imports a concept of white safety that almost necessarily endangers the lives as well as the rights of blacks.

It is also an incantation of innocence and guilt, much related to incantations that affirmative action programs allow presumably "guilty" blacks to displace "innocent" whites. (Even assuming that "innocent whites" were being displaced by blacks, does that make blacks less innocent in the pursuit of education and jobs? If anything, are not blacks *more* innocent in the scheme of discrimination?) In fact, in the wake of the Howard Beach incident, the police and the press rushed to serve the public's interest in the victims' unsavory "guilty" dispositions. They overlook the fact that racial slurs and attacks "objectif[y] people — the incident could have happened to any black person who was there at that time and place. This is the crucial aspect of the Howard Beach affair that is now being muddied in the media. Bringing up [defendants' past arrest records] is another way of saying, 'He was criminal who deserved it.'" Thus, the game of victim responsibility described above is itself a slave to society's stereotypes of good and evil.

It does no good, however, to turn race issues into contests for some Holy Grail of innocence. In my youth, segregation and antimiscegenation laws were still on the books in many states. During the lifetimes of my parents and grandparents, and for several hundred years before them, laws prohibited blacks from owning property, voting, and learning to read or write. Blacks were, by constitutional mandate, outlawed from the hopeful, loving expectations that being treated as a whole, rather than three-fifths of a human being can bring. When every resource of a wealthy nation is put to such destructive ends, it will take more than a few generations to mop up the mess.

We have all inherited that legacy, whether new to this world or new to this country. It survives as powerfully and invisibly reinforcing structures of thought, language, and law. Thus, generalized notions of innocence and guilt have little place in the struggle for transcendence; there is no blame among the living for the dimension of this historic crime, this national tragedy. There is, however, responsibility for never forgetting one another's histories, and for making real the psychic obliteration which lives on as a factor in shaping relations, not just between blacks and whites, or blacks and blacks, but also between whites and whites. Whites must consider how much this history has projected onto blacks the blame for all criminality, and for all of society's ills. It has become the means for keeping white criminality invisible.

"Discrimination Doesn't Hurt As Much As Being Assaulted" or "A Prejudiced Society Is Better Than a Violent Society"
The attempt to split bias from violence has been this society's most enduring and fatal rationalization. Prejudice does hurt, however, just as the absence of prejudice can nourish and shelter. Discrimination can repel and vilify, ostracize and alienate. White people who do not believe this should try telling everyone they meet that one of their ancestors was black. I had a friend in college who having lived her life as a blonde, grey eyed white person, discovered that she was one-sixteenth black. She began to externalize all the unconscious baggage that "black" bore for her:

the self-hatred that is racism. She did not think of herself as a racist (nor had I) but she literally wanted to jump out of her skin, shed her flesh, and start life over again. She confided in me that she felt "fouled" and "betrayed." She also asked me if I had ever felt this way. Her question dredged from some deep corner of my suppressed memory the recollection of feeling precisely that, when at the age of three or so, some white playmates explained to me that God had mixed mud with the pure clay of life in order to make me.

In the Vietnamese language, "the word 'I' (toi) ... means 'your servant'; there is no 'I' as such. When you talk to someone, you establish a relationship." Such a concept of "self" is a way of experiencing the other, ritualistically sharing the other's essence, and cherishing it. In our culture, seeing and feeling the dimension of harm that results from separating self from "other" requires more work. Very little in our language or our culture encourages or reinforces any attempt to look at others as part of ourselves. With the imperviously divided symmetry of the marketplace, social costs to blacks are simply not seen as costs to whites, just as blacks do not share in the advances whites may enjoy.

This structure of thought is complicated by the fact that the distancing does not stop with the separation of the white self from the black other. In addition, the cultural domination of blacks by whites means that the black self is placed at a distance even from itself, as in the example of blacks being asked to put themselves in the position of the white shopkeepers who view them. So blacks are conditioned from infancy to see in themselves only what others who despise them see.

It is true that conforming to what others see in us is every child's way of becoming socialized. It is what makes children in our society seem so gullible, so impressionable, so "impolitely" honest, so blindly loyal, and so charming to the ones they imitate. Yet this conformity also describes a way of being that relinquishes the power of independent ethical choice. Although such a relinquishment can have quite desirable social consequences, it also presumes a fairly homogeneous social context in which values are shared and enforced collectively. Thus, it is no wonder that western anthropologists and ethnographers, for whom adulthood is manifested by the exercise of independent ethical judgment, so frequently denounce tribal cultures or other collectivist ethics as "childlike."

By contrast, our culture constructs some, but not all, selves to be the servants of others. Thus, some "I's" are defined as "your servant," some as "your master." The struggle for the self becomes not a true mirroring of self-in-other, but rather a hierarchically-inspired series of distortions, where some serve without ever being served, some master without ever being mastered, and almost everyone hides from this vernacular domination by clinging to the legally official definition of "I" as meaning "your equal."

In such an environment, relinquishing the power of individual ethical judgment to a collective ideal risks psychic violence, an obliteration of the self through domination by an all powerful other. In such an environment, it is essential at some stage that the self be permitted to retreat into itself and make its own decisions with self-love and self-confidence. What links child abuse, the mistreatment of women, and racism is the massive external intrusion into psyche that dominating powers impose to keep the self from ever fully seeing itself. Because the self's power resides in another, little faith is placed in the true self, that is, in one's own experiential knowledge. Consequently, the power of children, women and blacks is actually reduced to the "intuitive," rather than the real; social life is necessarily based primarily on the imaginary. Furthermore, because it is difficult to affirm constantly with the other the congruence of the self's imagining what the other is *really* thinking of the self, and because even that correlative effort is usually kept within very limited family, neighborhood, religious, or racial boundaries, encounters cease to be social and become presumptuous, random, and disconnected.

This peculiarly distancing standpoint allows dramas, particularly racial ones like Howard Beach, to unfold in scenarios weirdly unrelated to the incidents that generated them. At one end of the spectrum is a laissez faire response that privatizes the self in order to remain unassailably justified. At the other end is a pattern that generalizes individual or particular others into terrifyingly uncontrollable "domains" of public wilderness, against which proscriptive barriers must be built to protect the eternally innocent self.

PRIVATIZING INNOCENCE

The prototypical scenario of the privatized response is as follows:

Cain: Abel's part of town is tough turf.

Abel: It upsets me when you say that; you have never been to my part of town. As a matter of fact, my part of town is a leading supplier of milk and honey.

Cain: The news that I'm upsetting you is too upsetting for me to handle. You were wrong to tell me of your upset because now I'm terribly upset.

Abel: I felt threatened first. Listen to me. Take your distress as a measure of my own and empathize with it. Don't ask me to recant and apologize in order to carry this conversation further.

This type of discourse is problematic because Cain's challenge in calling Abel's turf "tough" is transformed into a discussion of the care with which *Abel* challenges that statement. While there is certainly an obligation to be careful in addressing others the obligation to protect the feelings of those others gets put above the need to protect one's own. The self becomes subservient to the other, with no reciprocity, and the other becomes a whimsical master. Abel's feelings are deflected in deference to Cain's, and Abel bears the double burden of raising his issue properly *and* of being responsible for its impact on Cain. Cain is rendered unaccountable for as long as this deflection continues because all the fault is assigned to Abel. Morality and responsiveness thus become dichotomized as Abel drowns in responsibility for valuative quality control, while Cain rests on the higher ground of a value neutral zone.

Caught in conversations like this, blacks as well as whites will feel keenly and pressingly circumscribed. Perhaps most people never intend to be racist, oppressive, or insulting. Nevertheless, by describing zones of vulnerability and by setting up fences of rigidified politeness, the unintentional exile of individuals as well as races may be quietly accomplished.

PUBLICIZING GUILT

Another scenario of distancing self from the responsibility for racism is the invention of some great public wilderness of others. In the context of Howard Beach, the specter against which the self must barricade itself is violent: seventeen year old, black males wearing running shoes and hooded sweatshirts. It is this fear of the uncontrollable, overwhelming other that animates many of the more vengefully racist comments from Howard Beach, such as, "We're a strictly white neighborhood.... They had to be starting trouble."

These statements set up angry, excluding boundaries. They also imply that the *failure* to protect and avenge is bad policy, bad statesmanship, and an embarrassment. They raise the stakes beyond the unexpressed rage arising from the incident itself. Like the Cain and Abel example, the need to avenge becomes a separate issue of protocol and etiquette — not a loss of a piece of the self, which is the real cost of *real* tragedies, but a loss of self-regard. By self-regard, I do not mean self-concept as in self-esteem; I mean that view of the self that is attained by the self stepping outside the self to regard and evaluate the self. It is a process in which the self is watched by an imaginary other, a self-projection of the opinions of real others, where "I" means "your master" and where the designated other's refusal to be dominated is felt as personally assaultive. Thus, the failure to avenge is felt as a loss of self-regard. It is a psychological metaphor for whatever trauma or original assault that constitutes the real loss to the self. It is therefore more abstract, more illusory, more constructed, and more invented. Potentially, therefore, it is less powerful than "real" assault, in that with effort it can be unlearned as a source of vulnerability. This is the real message of the attempt to distinguish between prejudice and violence: names, as in the old "sticks and stones" ditty, although undeniably and powerfully influential, can be learned or undone as motivation for future destructive action. As long as they are *not* unlearned, however, the exclusionary power of such free-floating emotions makes its way into the gestalt of prosecutorial and jury decisions and into what the law sees as crime, or as justified, provoked or excusable. Law becomes described and enforced in the spirit of our prejudices.

The Evidentiary Rules of Legitimating Turf Wars

The following passage is a description of the arraignment of three of the white teenagers who were involved in the Howard Beach beatings:

> The three defense lawyers also tried to cast doubt on [the prosecutor's] account of the attack. The lawyers questioned why the victims walked all the way to the pizza parlor if, as they said, their mission was to summon help for their car, which broke down three miles away.... At the arraignment, the lawyers said the victims passed two all-night gas stations and several other pizza shops before they reached the one they entered.
>
> A check yesterday of area restaurants, motels and gas stations listed in the Queens street directory found two eating establishments, a gas station and a motel that all said they were open and had working pay phones on Friday night.
>
> A spokesman for the New York Telephone Company, Jim Crosson, said there are six outdoor pay telephones ... on the way to the pizzeria.

In the first place, lawyers must wonder what relevance this has. Does the answer to any of the issues the defense raised serve to prove that these black men assaulted, robbed, threatened or molested these white men? Does it even prove that the white men *reasonably* feared such a fate? The investigation into the number of phone booths per mile does not reveal why the white men would fear the black men's presence. Instead, it is relevant to prove that there is *no* reason a black man should walk or just wander around the community of Howard Beach. This is not semantic detail; it is central to understanding burdensomeness of proof in such cases. It is this unconscious restructuring of burdens of proof into burdens of white over black that permits people who say and who believe that they are not racist to commit and condone crimes of genocidal magnitude. It is easy to rationalize this as linguistically technical, or as society's sorrow. As one of my students said, "I'm so tired of hearing the blacks say that society's done them wrong." Yet these gyrations kill with their razor-toothed presumption. Lawyers are the modern wizards and medicine people who must define this innocent murderousness as crime.

Additionally, investigations into "closer" alternatives eclipse the possibility of other explanation. They assume that the young men were not headed for the subway (which was in fact in the same direction as the pizzeria), and further, that black people must have documented reasons for excursioning into white neighborhoods and out of the neighborhoods to which they are supposedly consigned.

It is interesting to contrast the implicit requirement of documentation imposed on blacks walking down public streets in Howard Beach with the implicit license of the white officers who burst into the private space of Mrs. Bumpurs' apartment. In the Bumpurs case, lawmakers consistently dismissed the availability of less intrusive options as presumption and idle hindsight. This dismissal ignored the fact that police officers have an actual burden of employing the least harmful alternatives. In the context of Howard Beach, however, such an analysis invents and imposes a burden on nonresidents to stay out of strange neighborhoods. It implies harm in the presence of those who do not specifically "own" something there. Both analyses skirt the propriety and necessity of public sector responsibility. Both redefine public accountability in privatized terms. Whether those privatized terms act to restrict or expand accountability is dichotomized according to the race of the actors.

Finally, this factualized hypothesizing was part of a news story, not an editorial. "News," in other words, was reduced to hypothesis based on silent premises: they should have used the first phone they encountered; they should have eaten at the first "eating establishment;" they should have gone into a gas station and asked for help; surely they should have had the cash and credit cards to do any of the above or else not travel in strange neighborhoods. In elevating these to relevant issues, however, *The New York Times* did no more than mirror what was happening in the courtroom.

The Appropriation of Psychic Property

In an ill-fated trip to the neighborhood of Jamaica, in the borough of Queens, Mayor Koch attempted to soothe tensions by asking a congregation of black churchgoers to understand the disgruntlement of Howard Beach residents about the interracial march by 1400 protesters through "their" streets. He asked them how they would feel if 1400 white people took to the streets of the predominantly black neighborhood of Jamaica. This remark, from the chief executive of New York City, accepts and even advocates a remarkable degree of possessiveness about public streets. This possessiveness, moreover, is racially rather than geographically bounded. In effect, Koch was pleading for the acceptance of the privatization of public space. This is the de facto equivalent of segregation. It is exclusion in the guise of deep-moated private property "interests" and "values." In such a characterization, the public nature of the object of discussion, the street, is lost.

Mayor Koch's question suggests that 1400 black people took to the streets of Howard Beach. In fact, the crowd was integrated — blacks, browns, and whites, residents and nonresidents of Howard Beach. Apparently, crowds in New York are subject to the unwritten equivalent of Louisiana's race statutes (which provide that 1/72 black ancestry renders a person black) and to the Ku Klux Klan's "contamination by association" standard ("blacks and white-blacks" was how one resident of Forsythe County, Georgia described an interracial crowd of protesters there).

On the other hand, if Mayor Koch intended to direct attention to the inconvenience, noise, and pollution of such a crowd in those small streets, then I am sympathetic. My sympathy is insignificant, however, compared to my recognition of the necessity and propriety of the protestors' spontaneous, demonstrative, peaceful outpouring of rage, sorrow, and pain.

If, however, Mayor Koch intended to ask blacks to imagine 1400 angry white people descending on a black community, then I agree, I would be frightened. This image would also conjure up visions of 1400 hooded white people burning crosses, 1400

Nazis marching through Skokie, and 1400 cavalry men riding into American Indian lands. These visions would inspire great fear in me, because of the possibility of grave harm to the residents. But there is a difference, and that is why the purpose of the march is so important. That is why it is so important to distinguish mass protests of violence from organized hate groups that openly threaten violence. By failing to make this distinction, Mayor Koch created the manipulative specter of unspecified mobs sweeping through homes in pursuit of vague and diffusely dangerous ends. From this perspective, he appealed to thoughtlessness, to the pseudoconsolation of hunkering down and bunkering up against the approaching hoards, to a glacially overgeneralized view of the unneighborhooded "public" world.

Moreover, the Mayor's comments reveal that he is ignorant of the degree to which the black people have welcomed, endured, and suffered white marchers through their streets. White people have always felt free to cruise through black communities and to treat them possessively. Most black neighborhoods have existed only as long as whites have permitted them to exist. Blacks have been this society's perpetual tenants, sharecroppers, and lessees. Blacks went from being owned by others, to having everything around them owned by others. In a civilization that values private property above all else, this effectuates a devaluation of humanity, a removal of blacks not just from the market, but from the pseudospiritual circle of psychic and civic communion. As illustrated in the microcosm of my experience at the store, this limbo of disownedness keeps blacks beyond the pale of those who are entitled to receive the survival gifts of commerce, the property of life, liberty, and happiness, whose fruits our culture places in the marketplace. In this way, blacks are positioned analogically to the rest of society, exactly as they were during slavery or Jim Crow.

There is a subtler level to the enactment of this dispossession. The following story may illustrate more fully what I mean: Not long ago, when I first moved back to New York after some twenty years, I decided to go on a walking tour of Harlem. The tour, which took place on Easter Sunday, was sponsored by the New York Arts Society, and except for myself, was attended exclusively by young, white, urban, professional, real estate speculators. They were pleasant looking, with babies strapped to their backs and balloons in their hands. They all seemed like very nice people.

Halfway through the tour, the guide asked the group if they wanted to "go inside some churches." The guide added, "It'll make the tour a little longer, but we'll probably get to see some services going on ... Easter Sunday in Harlem is quite a show." A casual discussion ensued about the time that this excursion might take.

What astonished me was that no one had asked the people in the churches if they minded being stared at like living museums. I wondered what would happen if a group of blue-jeaned blacks were to walk uninvited into a synagogue on Passover or St. Anthony's of Padua in the middle of High Mass. Just to peer, not pray. My overwhelming instinct is that such activity would be seen as disrespectful.

Apparently, the disrespect was invisible to this well-educated, affable group of people. They deflected my observations with comments such as, "We just want to look"; "No one will mind"; "There's no harm intended." As well intentioned as they were, I was left with the impression that no one existed for them whom their intentions could not govern. Despite the lack of apparent malice in their demeanor, it seemed to me that to live so noninteractively is a liability as much as a luxury. To live imperviously to one's impact on others is a fragile privilege, which depends ultimately on the inability of others to make their displeasure known.

THE GIFT OF INTELLIGENT RAGE

Owning the Self in a Disowned World

Reflecting on Howard Beach brought to mind a news story from my fragmentary grammar school recollections of the 1960's: a white man acting out of racial motives killed a black man who was working for some civil rights organization or cause. The man was stabbed thirty-nine times, a number which prompted a radio commentator to observe that the point was not just murder, but something beyond.

What indeed was the point, if not murder? I wondered what it was that would not die, which could not be killed by the fourth, fifth, or even tenth knife blow; what sort of thing that would not die with the body but lived on in the mind of the murderer. Perhaps, as psychologists have argued, what the murderer was trying to kill was a part of his own mind's image, a part of himself and not a real other. After all, statistically and corporeally, blacks as a group are poor, powerless, and a minority. It is in the minds of whites that blacks become large, threatening, powerful, uncontrollable, ubiquitous, and supernatural.

There are certain societies that define the limits of life and death very differently than our own. For example, death may occur long before the body ceases to function, and under the proper circumstances, life may continue for some time after the body is carried to its grave. These non-body-bound, uncompartmentalized ideas recognize the power of spirit, or what we in our secularized society might describe as the dynamism of self as reinterpreted by the perceptions of other. These ideas comprehend the fact that a part of ourselves is beyond the control of pure physical will and resides in the sanctuary of those around us. A fundamental part of ourselves and of our dignity is dependent upon the uncontrollable, powerful, external observers who constitute society. Surely a part of socialization ought to include a sense of caring responsibility for the images of others that are reposited within us.

Taking the example of the man who was stabbed thirty-nine times out of the context of our compartmentalized legal system, and considering it in the hypothetical framework of a legal system that encompasses and recognizes morality, religion, and psychology, I am moved to see this act as not merely body murder but spirit-murder as well. I see it as spirit-murder, only one of whose manifestations is racism — cultural obliteration, prostitution, abandonment of the elderly and the homeless, and genocide are some of its other guises. I see spirit-murder as no less than the equivalent of body murder.

One of the reasons that I fear what I call spirit-murder, or disregard for others whose lives qualitatively depend on our regard, is that its product is a system of formalized distortions of thought. It produces social structures centered around fear and hate; it provides a tumorous outlet for feelings elsewhere unexpressed. For example, when Bernhard Goetz shot four black teenagers in a New York City subway, an acquaintance of mine said that she could understand his fear because it is a "fact" that blacks commit most crimes. What impressed me, beyond the factual *in*accuracy of this statement, was the reduction of Goetz' crime to "his fear," which I translate to mean *her* fear. The four teenage victims became all blacks everywhere, and "most crimes" clearly meant that most *blacks* commit crimes.

In the process of devaluing its image of black people, the general white population seems to have been socialized to blind itself to the horrors inflicted by white people. One of the clearest examples of the mechanics of this socialized blindness is the degree to which the public and the media in New York repeatedly and relentlessly bestialized Goetz' victims. Images of the urban jungle, of young black men filling the role of "wild animals," were favorite journalistic constructions. Young white urban professionals were mythologized, usually wrapped in the rhetorical apparel of lambs or sheep, as the tender, toothsome prey. The corollary to such imagery is that the fate of those domesticated white innocents is to be slaughtered in confrontation, the dimensions of which thus become meaninglessly and tragically sacrificial. Locked into such a reification, no act of the sheep against the wolves can ever be seen as violent in its own right, because active sheep are so *inherently* uncharacteristic, so brave, so irresistibly and triumphantly parabolic. Thus, when prosecutor Gregory Waples cast Goetz as a "hunter" in his final summation, juror Michael Axelrod said that Waples "was insulting my intelligence. There was nothing to justify that sort of [characterization]. Goetz wasn't a hunter."

Furthermore, most white people do not seem to feel as criminal the dehumanizing cultural images of sterile, mindless white womanhood and expressionless, bored but righteous, assembly line white manhood. For example, although it is difficult to document in any scientific way, I think many whites do not expect other whites to rape, rob, or kill them. They are surprised when it happens. Perhaps they blind themselves to the warning signals of approaching assault. Some do not even recognize it when it does happen; they apologize for the assailant, think it must have been their fault; *they* misperceived the other's intent.[82]

The following vignette may better illustrate what I mean:

> A lone black man was riding in an elevator in a busy downtown department store. The elevator stopped on the third floor and a crowd of noisy white high school students got on. The black man took out a gun and shot as many of them as he could before the doors opened on the first floor ... the rest fled for their lives. The black man later explained to the police that he could tell from the students' "body language," from their "shiny eyes and big smiles," that they wanted to "play with him, like a cat plays with a mouse." Furthermore, the black man explained, one of the youths had tried to panhandle money from him and another asked him, "How are you?" "That's a meaningless thing," he said in his confession, "but in certain circumstances, that can be a real threat." He added that a similar greeting had preceded the vicious beating of his father, a black civil rights lawyer in Mississippi, some time before. He confessed that he intended to murder the high school students.

My guess is that most white Americans would view the severe contextual misapprehensions of the black gunman as a form of serious insanity. Although degrees of sympathy might vary, I suspect that the social consensus would be nearly unanimous that he presents a danger to himself and to others and should therefore be institutionalized or imprisoned. The above story is, however, with minor character alteration, consistent with a videotaped confession by Bernhard Goetz. Nevertheless, the public overwhelmingly presumed Goetz innocent. Most accounts did *not* propose that he be institutionalized, but pointed instead to the failure of public institutions to engage in *more* such punitive activities. Bernhard Goetz' defense blatantly reflected this consensus in its claim, not that Goetz was temporarily insane, but rather that he acted *reasonably* under the circumstances. It is reflected as well in the degree to which the public devoured, ex post facto, stories about the deviant behavior of the victims in this case. Goetz became a cited authority and favorite interviewee on the subject of crime in New York. "Criminals," he declared, must realize that being shot is a "risk they are going to have to take." I can think of no better example of the degree to which criminality has become lodged in a concept of the black "other."

If Americans are subject to such utter emotional devastation, it is no wonder that the urge to act as a victimizer is so irresistible; it appears to be the only right thing, the only defensible thing to do. It is no wonder that society has created in blacks a class of ready-made, prepackaged victims. To discount as much violence as we do in this society must mean that we have a very angry population suppressing explosive rage. Most white Americans, at least those in urban areas, have seen the angry, muttering "lunatic" black person who beats the air with his fists and curses aloud. Most people cross the street to avoid him; they don't choose him to satisfy their need to know the time of day. Yet for generations, and particularly in the wake of the foaming public response to incidents like Howard Beach, the Goetz shooting, and Forsythe County, that is precisely how white America has looked to many black Americans.

For these reasons, I think we need to elevate what I call spirit-murder to the conceptual, if not punitive level of a capital moral offense. We need to see it as a cultural cancer; we need to open our eyes to the spiritual genocide it is wreaking on blacks, whites, and the abandoned and abused of all races and ages. We need to eradicate its numbing pathology before it wipes out what precious little humanity we have left.

Mirrors and Windows

The night after the Bumpurs story became public, I dreamed about a black woman who was denied entry to a restaurant because of her color. In response, she climbed over the building. The next time she found a building in her way, she climbed over it, and the next time and the next and the next. In time, she became famous, as she roamed the world, traveling in determined straight lines, wordlessly scaling whatever lay in her path, including skyscrapers. Well-meaning white people came to marvel at her and gathered in crowds to watch and applaud. She never acknowledged their presence, but went about her business in unsmiling silence. The white people grew angry and condemned her for failing to appreciate their praise and rejecting their gift of fame. I stood somewhere on the periphery of this dream and wondered what unspoken rule, what deadened curiosity kept anyone from ever asking why.

Upon waking, I asked myself a progression of "why's" about the Bumpurs death. My life experiences had prepared me better to comprehend and sympathize with the animating force behind the outraged, dispossessed knifewielding of Mrs. Bumpurs.[89] What I found more difficult to focus on was the "why," the animus that inspired such fear, and such impatient contempt in a police officer that the presence of six other heavily armed men could not allay his need to kill a sick old lady fighting off hallucinations with a knife. It seemed to me a fear embellished by something beyond Mrs. Bumpurs herself; something about her enlarged to fill the void between her physical, limited presence and the "immediate threat and endangerment to life" that filled the beholding eyes of the officer. Why was the sight of a knife-wielding woman so fearfully offensive to a shotgun-wielding policeman that he felt that blowing her to pieces was the only recourse, the only way to preserve his physical integrity? What offensive spirit of his past experience raised her presence to the level of a physical menace beyond real dimensions? What spirit of prejudgment and of prejudice provided him with such a powerful hallucinogen?

However slippery these questions may be on a legal or conscious level, unresponsiveness to them does not make these issues go away. Failure to resolve the dilemma of racial violence merely displaces its power. The legacy of killing finds its way into cultural expectations, archetypes, and "isms." The echoes of both dead and deadly others acquire a hallucinatory quality; their voices speak of an unwanted past, but also reflect for us images of the future. Today's world condemns those voices as superstitious and paranoid. Neglected, they speak from the shadows of such inattention, in garbles and growls, in the tongues of the damned and the insane. The superstitious listen, and perhaps in the silence of their attention, they hear and understand. So-called enlightened others who fail to listen to the voices of demonic selves, made invisibly uncivilized, simply make them larger, more barbarously enraged, until the nearsightedness of looking glass existence is smashed in upon by the terrible dispossession of dreams too long deferred.

[NOTE: The footnotes have been deleted from this article, but they should be consulted in the original version for details of statements quoted in local and national papers, examples of "everyday" racism, and the critical and literary theory from which Patricia Williams constructs her argument. We reproduce, by way of example, footnotes 82 and 89:]

[82] In a now famous videotape, Bernhard Goetz described to police in New Hampshire his intention to inflict as much harm as he could. He detailed his wish to see his victims dead; said that if he had to do it over again, he'd do the same or worse, and expressed a retrospective desire to gouge their eyes out. Yet in finding him "not guilty" of each of twelve counts of attempted murder, assault and reckless endangerment, the jury entirely discounted this confession. "We felt he said a lot of things he was unsure about. He had nine days of thinking about what happened and reading the newspapers, and combined with the guilt, we felt that he may have gotten confused. His own confusion coupled with his feelings of guilt might have forced him to make statements that were not accurate." *N.Y. Times*, April 30, 1987, at B6, col. 2.

[89] I know few blacks who have not had some encounter with police intimidation. My earliest remembrance of such an instance was when I was about nine and my sister was about seven. My family was driving to Georgia to see my father's relatives. Two highway patrolmen stopped our car on a deserted stretch of highway in South Carolina. They were attracted to the Massachusetts license plate, and they wanted to know what "y'all" were doing in those parts. They inquired about the weather in Boston, they fondled my father's driver's license with great curiosity and they admired the lines of the car. They were extremely polite, their conversation a model of southern hospitality and propriety. Throughout the entire fifteen or twenty minutes of our detention, one officer questioned my mother and father in soothing, honeyed tones: the other held a double-barrelled shotgun through the rear window, pointed at my sister and me. If he had "accidentally" shot us both, our deaths would have been, like that of Eleanor Bumpurs, entirely legal in the state of South Carolina.

■

The issues raised by the preceding article continue. In February 1999, Amadou Diallo died as a result of police gunfire when, in response to their request for identification, he attempted to pull out his wallet. Their defence of mistaken belief in the need to use self-defensive violence was accepted by the jury, and the four officers were acquitted in early 2000 of all charges, even though among them they fired 41 bullets at the deceased: Salman Rushdie, "Anyone can make 41 deadly mistakes" *The Toronto Globe and Mail* (11 March 2000) A15. On the other hand, Officer Justin Volpe of the Bronx pleaded guilty to violating the civil rights of Bronx resident Abner Louima by sodomizing him with a broken broomstick. He was sentenced to 30 years in prison: Brian Milner, "New York officer gets 30 years for torture" *The Toronto Globe and Mail* (14 December 1999) A9. For further readings see Stephen L. Carter, "When Victims Happen to be Black" (1988) 97 Yale L.J. 439.

In the U.K., the murder of Stephen Lawrence in London in 1993 by five or six white youths, the incompetent police investigation, and the failed prosecution, which resulted in acquittal of the prime suspects, were the subject of an inquiry: Sir William Macpherson of Cluny, *The Stephen Lawrence Inquiry: A Report* (London: Secretary of State for the Home Department, 1999). The Inquiry concluded that racism fuelled the murder of Lawrence, and that the police investigation "was marred by a combination of professional incompetence, institutional racism and a failure of leadership by senior officials" (at 317). Among the many recommendations by the Inquiry is one that a racist incident be classified by police as one perceived as racist by the victim or any other person, and another that would require recording and monitoring of all "stop and search" police interventions, including the self-identified ethnicity of the person stopped.

Read a choice of articles in the next section. Think about the issues raised in light of the article by Patricia Williams and earlier readings, for example, on Aboriginal peoples. Are there other examples of racism and discrimination not raised in the materials? How does Williams' analysis assist in understanding the relationship between criminal law and racism? What role could the criminal law play?

Alberta

An inquiry into relations between the RCMP, the Lethbridge City Police, and the Blackfoot Confederacy heard testimony about the inadequate investigation of five sudden deaths; police prejudice, brutality, and racism; and the consequent distrust and suspicion of police by Blood Indian people. In one case, Norbert Fox, a Blood Indian man, testified that he had to investigate his wife's teenage son's disappearance himself, due to lack of concern by the police. The investigating officer, Constable Douglas Webber, testified that he had erred in listing the death as suicide-related. See CP, "Natives got 'runaround', inquiry told" *The [Toronto] Globe and Mail* (16 May 1989) A5.

In another case reported in Matthew Fisher, "Indian distrusted police too much to give evidence, probe told" *The [Toronto] Globe and Mail* (12 July 1989) A5, Jordan Head, a Blood Indian man, testified that he did not volunteer evidence to the police that his cousin might have been murdered because he distrusted them so much:

> Because of the bad feelings going on between natives and police, I didn't think anything would be done ... I think there have always been bad feelings between natives and police because of the way they've been treated in the city. Whatever natives have to say isn't considered.

More recently, Connie Jacobs and her nine-year-old son Ty were shot and killed on the lands of the Samson Cree Nation south of Calgary in March 1998 by an RCMP officer who had been called by social service workers attempting to remove six children she was caring for. Constable Dave Voller reported that she fired at him using a high-powered rifle. Alberta's Attorney General's department and former judge Allan Cawsey both reviewed the evidence and recommended that no charges be laid against the officer: Alanna Mitchell, "Mountie who killed native woman faces no charges" *The [Toronto] Globe and Mail* (22 October 1998) A3.

Manitoba

Early on the morning of 9 March 1988 John Joseph Harper, executive director of the Island Lake Tribal Council, was walking alone down a Winnipeg street. He was stopped by Constable Robert Cross, who was searching for a suspect in a car theft. Constable Cross' gun went off and shot Mr. Harper in the chest, killing him within minutes. A brief police investigation exonerated Constable Cross. At the subsequent inquest there were many troubling revelations and unanswered questions, and evidence that contradicted police testimony about the incident:

- The suspect had been described as about 22 years old, whereas Mr. Harper was 36 years old. Also, shortly before stopping Mr. Harper, the officer had been told that a suspect was already in custody.
- The gun was not dusted for fingerprints.
- Four witnesses testified that they saw the police with their guns drawn, whereas the police testified that their guns remained in their holsters.

The shooting, the cursory investigation, and the unanswered questions prompted calls from Aboriginal leaders for a provincial inquiry. As Stirling Ranville, executive director of the Indian and Metis Friendship Centre of Winnipeg said, as quoted in Geoffrey York, "Native leader's death raises questions: Inquest ruling will not end bitterness" *The [Toronto] Globe and Mail* (26 May 1988) A4:

> If they're allowed to get away with this — and they will — it could set a precedent. Whenever I'm waved down by a police car now, I get cold inside. I'm afraid because I could get shot.

In September 1992, the Manitoba Law Enforcement Agency made a disciplinary ruling against Constable Robert Cross for using excessive force and abuse of authority in firing his service revolver when he killed J.J. Harper, but it did not recommend that criminal charges be laid. Cross was demoted to the rank of fourth-class constable as punishment for this disciplinary offence: "Officer demoted over Harper's shooting" *The [Toronto] Globe and Mail* (4 November 1992) A2. The Harper family has agreed on a compensation package from the City of Winnipeg: "Harper family compensated" *The Lawyers Weekly* (19 January 1993) A4.

Another case that provoked considerable criticism of the criminal justice system was the brutal rape and murder of Helen Betty Osborne, a young Cree woman, in The Pas in 1971. Although several people in the town knew the identity of the four men (Lee Colgan, Jim Houghton, Dwayne Johnston, Norman Manger) involved, they remained silent. Indeed, although a sheriff heard one of the men confess, he, too, remained silent for eight years. The RCMP acknowledged that their investigation was badly flawed. For example, they did not search the vehicle of one of the men until seven months later. However, they denied that the identity of the four men was known to them within days of the murder. There were allegations of racism and also of threats and cover-ups, allegations that implicated lawyers, court officials, police officers, and townspeople. There was criticism of a jury selection system that could produce an all-white jury for the trial in 1987.

For more detail on the inaction of the RCMP and other law enforcement officers, altered evidence, and what has been called "the conspiracy of silence" in the Osborne case, see *Report of the Aboriginal Justice Inquiry of Manitoba, Volume 2: The Deaths of Helen Betty Osborne and John Joseph Harper*. See also Lisa Priest, *Conspiracy of Silence* (Toronto: McClelland and Stewart Inc., 1989). Priest's book is the basis for a docudrama of the same name. This docudrama has been criticized, among a number of other dramatized accounts of crimes, in Karen Mazurkewich, "Snuff TV" *Canadian Dimension* (July–August 1992) 5. She argues: "The stories are used to help isolate events and illustrate how the legal system comes to terms with extraordinary circumstances." Consider how the media portrayal differs from the account of the Aboriginal Justice Inquiry of Manitoba.

Other examples of racism in the criminal justice system came out in testimony before the Aboriginal Justice Inquiry of Manitoba. Witnesses described incidents of police harassment and brutality on the basis of race. Chief Emery Stagg described being stopped because of dirty tail-lights and license plate:

> As soon as I stopped, the police officer ordered me to "come out with your hands up" through the patrol car loud-speaker.... When I got out I was told to put my hands on the roof of the car. Then the officer came towards me with his hand on his gun holster and told me to put my wallet on the roof of the car.... I am convinced that if I had made a sudden movement for some reason, I would have been shot.

Chief Stagg was never charged with any offence: see Geoffrey York, "RCMP often harass Indians, chief tells Manitoba justice probe" *The [Toronto] Globe and Mail* (9 February 1989) A9. Witnesses also described harsher penalties being imposed on Aboriginal people, inadequate representation by legal counsel, and the expansion of prison facilities contrasted with the lack of alternatives for rehabilitation.

In another incident, Debra Redhead had been assaulted by her mate, but left unattended, while seven months pregnant, in a police cell on the Shamattawa reserve, where she died. Police stated that they believed that she was drunk and that she had been causing a disturbance, although her mother, who was employed at the station, described her daughter's injuries as profound and obvious: CP, "Autopsy finds pregnant native died in jail of head injuries" *The Ottawa Citizen* (27 July 1994) A5.

Québec

In Québec, police shootings involving African-Canadian men have also provoked calls for civilian review and for the laying of criminal charges:

ANTHONY GRIFFIN: Shot and killed by Montréal police Constable Allan Gosset, Montréal, 11 November 1987. See CP, "Constable's acquittal in Montreal shooting angers black leader" *The [Toronto] Globe and Mail* (8 June 1988) A1; Patricia Poirier, "Killed teen, Montreal policeman to be rehired" *The [Toronto] Globe and Mail* (3 October 1989) A8.

Allen Gosset's acquittal was successfully challenged on the basis of an erroneous jury instruction. He was ordered to undergo a retrial: *R. v. Gosset* (1991), 6 C.R. (4th) 239 (Que. C.A.), aff'd [1993] 3 S.C.R. 76. He was acquitted for a second time, in spite of evidence by his partner that Griffin had already halted when Gosset shot him: "Youth shot by officer had halted, says witness" *The Ottawa Citizen* (24 March 1994) A3; James Mennie, "Ex-police officer cleared in teen's death" *The Ottawa Citizen* (9 April 1994) A3.

PRESLEY LESLIE: Shot and killed by Montréal police, April 1990. See CP, "Inquest told police officers fired 8 shots to subdue, kill man in Montreal bar brawl" *The Ottawa Citizen* (6 June 1990) A10. The Coroner ruled that Leslie fired the first shot: "Dan Philip, president of the Black Coalition of Quebec, immediately called for a full public inquiry into the shooting": Eddie Collister, "Leslie fired first shot, coroner rules" *The [Montréal] Gazette* (7 August 1990) A3.

MARCELLUS FRANCOIS: Shot and killed by Montréal police Sergeant Michel Tremblay, 3 July 1991, while sitting unarmed in a car: Patricia Poirier, "Police shooting galvanizes Montreal blacks" *The [Toronto] Globe and Mail* (6 July 1991) A3.

The coroner's report documented a "totally unacceptable" level of racism within the Montréal Urban Community Police, which amounted to an institutional failure to protect the lives and security of citizens: Patricia Poirier, "'Cry for help has been heard': Report condemning racism in Montreal police force buoys black community" *The [Toronto] Globe and Mail* (8 May 1992) A1. A report by a retired judge of the Québec Court of Appeal, Albert Malouf, released in 1994, also examined the killing of Francois and concluded that the police were "poorly co-ordinated, badly equipped and undertrained." He made 42 recommendations for change: CP, "Montreal police incompetent, poorly trained, report says" *The Ottawa Citizen* (6 July 1994) A4.

OSMOND FLETCHER: Shot and killed, Montréal, 14 November 1991. Fletcher died in a shooting incident that police described as suicide. Earlier he had given an interview to a CBC TV reporter concerning police harassment of himself and other African-Canadian: Patricia Poirier, "Montreal shooting labelled suicide" *The [Toronto] Globe and Mail* (15 November 1991) A1.

TREVOR KELLY: Shot and killed by two members of the Sûreté du Québec, on 1 January 1993, approximately one hour after an argument with the same officers in his home: André Picard, "Police visited man before shooting" *The [Toronto] Globe and Mail* (5 January 1993) A3. A police investigation found that the officers had "no choice": CP, "Montréal police officer cleared in fatal shooting of black man" *Calgary Herald* (4 February 1993) A3. The Black Coalition of Québec and Kelly's sister filed a complaint with the Québec police ethics committee after the exoneration of the officers: Carolyn Adolph, "Black leader complains to ethics panel" *The [Montréal] Gazette* (5 February 1993) A3.

Additional criticism has been levied against the police for the shooting and killing of a Metis man, Jeffrey Fortin, and a Salvadorean refugee. Most recently, a man identified by the media as Peruvian was shot under shocking circumstances.

UNIDENTIFIED SALVADOREAN MAN: Shot and killed by Montréal Urban Community police officer, 22 November 1990: Patricia Poirier, "Police shooting called self-defence: No charges expected in death of shoplifter who stole $10" *The [Toronto] Globe and Mail* (24 November 1990) A6.

JEFFREY FORTIN: Shot and killed by a Sûreté du Québec officer, 15 June 1991: Patricia Poirier, "Pulling the trigger too often" *The [Toronto] Globe and Mail* (17 July 1991) A3; Patricia Poirier, "600 in Montreal march for action in police killings: Fatal shooting of three black people called a national embarrassment" *The [Toronto] Globe and Mail* (27 July 1991) A4.

MARTIN OMAR SUAZO: Martin Suazo, 23, was shot in the head by police on 31 May 1995, as he lay on a Montréal city street after being stopped on suspicion of shoplifting. The officer claimed that the gun fired accidentally. The inquest into Suazo's death featured a publication ban ordered by the coroner, and an order to the police to turn over the written reports of all officers on the scene: see Staff, "Inquiry into recent deaths" *The [Toronto] Globe and Mail* (17 June 1995) A3; André Picard, "Inquest raises issue of how police gaffes probed" *The [Toronto] Globe and Mail* (27 February 1996) A2. The publication ban was quashed by the Québec Court of Appeal: *The [Montreal] Gazette* v. *Québec (Coroner)*, [1996] A.Q. No. 765 (Sup. Ct.), online: QL; the order to turn over the police reports from officers at the scene was held to be *ultra vires* the coroner: *Garneau* v. *Québec (Coroner)*, [1996] A.Q. No. 307 (Sup. Ct.), online: QL.

In January 1993, a provincial task force report on race relations between Montréal police and minorities was released: Estanislao Oziewicz, "Better training on racism urged for Montreal police" *The Lawyers Weekly* (19 January 1993) A4. In another report, Québec coroner Pierre Trahan has ruled that four shooting deaths caused by Québec police in the period between November 1990 and November 1991, including those of Jorge Alberto Reyes Chavarria, the "unidentified Salvadorean man," and Jeffrey Fortin, the Metis man, were not culpable. While commenting that police required better crisis training, he suggested that the deaths do "not indicate that police officers are trigger-happy, but [are] a reflection of the rising crime rate in society and widespread drug use by criminals": André Picard, "Coroner absolves police in four fatal shootings" *The [Toronto] Globe and Mail* (23 April 1993) A3.

Finally, police have been criticized for their role at Kanehsatake and Oka in the summer of 1990. In particular, their inaction as 500 people threw stones at cars carrying Aboriginal women and children on the Mercier bridge was characterized as racist. See André Picard, "Stoning of autos, police inaction disturbs critics: As windshields were smashed, message conveyed was 'racism is acceptable'" *The [Toronto] Globe and Mail* (30 August 1990) A5; Michele Landsberg, "Sûreté on racist rampage" *The Toronto Star* (21 September 1990) B1.

Other abuses (such as the denial of access to Québec Human Rights Commission officials who were investigating reports of rights abuses by the police and intimidation of journalists) are chronicled in the "Minutes of Proceedings and Evidence of the Standing Committee on Aboriginal Affairs pursuant to its Order of Reference dated October 22, 1990, consideration of the events at Kanehsatake and Kahnawake during the Summer of 1990" (February 1991). See also Monique Rochon and Pierre Lepage, "Oka-Kanehsatake — Été 1990, Le Choc Collectif: Rapport de la Commission des droits de la personne du Québec" (April 1991).

The military presence was compared to the excessive use of military force in October 1970 in Québec under the *War Measures Act*: Elizabeth Payne, "Mohawks' treatment queried: Civil libertarians consider standoff October crisis of '90s" *The [Toronto] Globe and Mail* (28 September 1990) A3. The Red Cross was required to go behind the lines of an armed conflict in Canada for the first time since 1885, which was, ironically, during the Riel Rebellion: Geoffrey York, "Red Cross repeats role played in Riel Rebellion: Emergency food, medical supplies taken behind lines during armed conflict" *The [Toronto] Globe and Mail* (20 July 1990) A4. For a further discussion of the situation, see: Beverly Nelson, "Oka and After" (July/August/September 1991) 25 Socialist Studies Bull. 7. Beverly Nelson was the Station Manager for CKHQ, Mohawk Radio, at Kanehsatake.

Five years later, a coroner's report on the death of the police officer killed at Oka has concluded that there was no need for the provincial police intervention that sparked the Oka crisis. While not pinning the blame on the Québec police, who did not have enough information to assess the situation, the coroner stated that the provincial minister of security underestimated the risk of intervention and should have sought more opinions, and that the federal minister of Indian Affairs let the situation worsen by refusing to listen to a delegation of longhouse members who had attempted to meet with him in Ottawa: CP, "No need for police action, coroner's report on Oka says" *The Ottawa Citizen* (12 August 1995) A2.

Nova Scotia

As Kevin Cox reported in "N.S. justice system victimizes blacks, Marshall probe told" *The [Toronto] Globe and Mail* (26 November 1988) A9:

> Graham Jarvis, a black Nova Scotian, bled to death near a highway on June 8, 1985, while the white man who shot him watched from his house. The man who fired the shot was acquitted and the judge was reported to have said later: "You know what happens when those black guys start drinking."

In a lengthy brief to the Royal Commission on the Donald Marshall, Jr. Prosecution, the Black United Front reported on a number of cases, including the Jarvis case, which involved racism in the enforcement of criminal law by police, prosecutors, judges, and juries. Cox, *ibid.*, reported:

> For shooting and killing black Graham Jarvis, white ... was investigated by all-white police officers, tried by a white prosecutor in front of a white judge and an all-white jury in a predominantly white community while being defended by a white lawyer. He was acquitted.

A compelling literary account of the murder of an African-Canadian man and the exoneration of his white killer by the Nova Scotia justice system has been published by George Elliot Clarke, "The Martyrdom of Othello Clemence" in his book of poems, *Whylah Falls* (Winlaw, B.C.: Polestar Press, 1990). This poem is a fictionalization of a case that might well be the Jarvis case. As Clarke says, "These poems are fact presented as fiction. There was no other way to tell the truth save to disguise it as a story."

In his monograph *Racial Discrimination in Canada: The Black Experience* (Ottawa: Canadian Historical Association, 1985), James W. St. G. Walker debunks the "North Star" myth, which holds that slavery and racism were phenomena of the United States, alien to Canada. He argues that without a historical perspective on racism in Canada, those who attempt to resolve current conflicts reinforce racism by attributing the problems to rising numbers of African-Canadians, cultural conflicts posed by immigrant populations, or economic recession. He points out the importance of historical analysis for understanding current conflicts, and argues that although many groups have encountered discrimination in Canada, the African-Canadian experience is "particularly instructive": discrimination against African-Canadians was uncomplicated by special legislative status, language barrier, or differences in dress, food, or religion. Instead, it was based solely on grounds of "colour," as understood at different historical junctures.

Exploring the different meanings attributed historically to "colour," he notes that the first enslaved African was brought to Québec in 1628, and that until 1783 almost all Africans in Canada were enslaved. He argues that although their place in the social hierarchy as "slaves" was shared by some Aboriginal people, with British conquest, slavery became almost exclusively a condition of people of African descent. Stereotypes regarding African Canadians were fostered by slavery, and the negative associations were perpetuated in Canada even after 1783 because the British Empire practised enslavement until 1834, and the United States until 1865.

Walker chronicles events that reinforced the negative images of African-Canadians and drew the "colour line" so that they were relegated to unskilled labour and service roles as immigrants in Canada. He surveys the various laws and practices that were used to curtail immigration by people of African descent and to segregate them in Canada not only in employment but also in housing, education, worship, and services: "Locked in poverty, denied the means of self-improvement, and dependent on white charity, the blacks suffered from an image of helplessness and lack of industry that reinforced white stereotypes" (at 10).

He also describes the resistance of African-Canadians to segregation, including the struggle of railway porters in the 1920s for access to promotion, the challenge to the practices of the National Selective Service during the Second World War, as well as the collective actions launched by the Nova Scotia Association for the Advancement of Coloured People, starting in 1945, against many practices of segregation in Nova Scotia. He reviews events and studies in the 1970s and 1980s, as discrimination surfaced more publicly through hate groups, and argues that for the first time, racism had to be acknowledged by Canadians as part of their culture.

What role does this historical account have in shaping legal analysis and argument? For further readings see James W. St. G. Walker, *The West Indians in Canada* (Ottawa: Canadian Historical Society, 1984); Robin Winks, *Blacks in Canada* (New Haven, Conn.: Yale University Press, 1971); Daniel G. Hill, *The Freedom-Seekers: Blacks in Early Canada* (Agincourt: Book Society of Canada, 1981) and the essays organized under the chapter heading, "Historical Racism: The Canadian Past" in Ormond McKague, ed., *Racism in Canada* (Saskatoon: Fifth House Publishers, 1991) at 15. For other Canadian books explicating the legal history of racism in Canada, see James W. St. G. Walker, *"Race," Rights and the Law in the Supreme Court of Canada* (Toronto: The Osgoode Society, 1997) and Constance Backhouse, *Colour-Coded. A Legal History of Racism in Canada, 1900–1950* (Toronto: The Osgoode Society, 1999).

In 1989 the Parent-Student Association of Preston, Nova Scotia, received partial funding from the Court Challenges Program for a systemic discrimination case against the RCMP In the following case, *R. v. Thompson*, the Association challenged the way in which the RCMP investigated and eventually laid charges against African-Canadian students who were involved in racial fights at a high school in Nova Scotia in January 1989. Specifically, the Association argued that the RCMP violated s. 15 of the *Charter* in the exercise of their discretion to investigate and charge. The Association alleged that: the RCMP did not make efforts to interview African-Canadian students, that a disproportionate number of African-Canadian students were charged; the charges laid against the African-Canadian students were more serious than those laid against white students; and while charges were dropped with respect to most of the white students, they were pursued against most of the African-Canadian students.

The result of the first level of court hearing is reproduced below.

R. v. Thompson[†]

[POTTS, J.:]

I'll deal first with the decision in the matter of the Queen and John Thompson, Steven Fraser and Marvin Smith.

The applicants, John Thompson, Steven Fraser and Marvin Smith seek a permanent stay or dismissal of the charges against them on the basis that their constitutional rights as guaranteed by Section 15 and Section 7 of *The Charter of Rights and Free-*

[†] (23 March 1990), (N.S. Prov. Ct.) [unreported].

doms have been infringed. I propose to deal mainly with the arguments advanced with respect to the Section 15 matter since it is my view that a finding with respect to that matter would, of necessity, result in a similar finding in regards to Section 7. That is to say that a ruling as to whether or not the [applicant's] rights to life, liberty and security of the person in accordance with the principles of fundamental justice have been denied depends on whether or not the investigation was racially discriminatory and if it was, then the principles of fundamental justice obviously have been violated. Section 15 of *The Charter* states:

> Every individual is equal before and under the law and has the right to the equal protection and equal benefit of the law without discrimination and, in particular, without discrimination based on race ...

The particular law in question in these proceedings is the Criminal Code of Canada which is racially neutral. Thus the applicants argue not that the law itself violates Section 15 or their rights under Section 15, but rather that their rights were violated by the manner in which the law was administered or applied by law enforcement authorities. It is clear that the protection afforded by Section 15 includes equality in the administration or application of the law and it is equally clear that the issue of intention is not relevant in determining whether or not discrimination exists.

Mr. Justice MacIntyre, in *Andrews vs. The Law Society of British Columbia*, 1989, 56 DLR 4th, at page 1, a decision of the Supreme Court of Canada, defined discrimination as follows:

> I would say that discrimination may be described as the distinction, whether intentional or not, but based on grounds relating to personal characteristics of the individual or group which has the effect of imposing burdens, obligations, or disadvantages on such individuals not imposed on others or which withholds or limits access to opportunities, benefits and advantages available to other members of society.

The applicants carry the burden of establishing that their rights had been violated and that burden is on a balance of probabilities. It is not sufficient that the applicants establish that the investigation was sloppy or incomplete but rather must establish that it was, whether intentionally or not, racially discriminatory. The applicants argue that if it was impossible for the R.C.M.P. to contact the numerous black witnesses who filed affidavits and gave *viva voce* evidence before the Court, their motion must fail. With respect, that is an oversimplification of the issue. It must rather be established that the blacks were treated differently than the whites by the R.C.M.P. in their investigation or by the Crown in their prosecution and that such differential treatment resulted in the blacks being unfairly and adversely affected.

During the course of the hearing of this application, evidence was heard concerning virtually all aspects of the investigation and prosecution of the incidents at Cole Harbour High School. This included evidence not only with respect to the incidents of January 10, 1989 with which the applicants are charged, but also with respect to the initial incident of January 9th and the subsequent incident of January 11, 1989. Even though all the incidents occurred at Cole Harbour High and are similar in other respects, they are not by any means identical, either in terms of the facts themselves or the way in which the investigation commenced and proceeded. It is important for the purpose of this application to examine the facts relative to the investigation of the events of January 9th and 11th to determine if there is a pattern suggesting that the investigation, as a whole, was racially discriminatory.

The investigation of the incident of January 9, 1989 was commenced by the R.C.M.P. as a result of a complaint made by Jason Cannon, a white student, when he personally attended at the Cole Harbour Detachment of the R.C.M.P. on January 10, 1989. Subsequently, Wendy Archer and Mary Jewers, both white students, came forward and gave statements to the R.C.M.P. concerning this incident. Additional statements were then obtained from Michelle Ferrar, Lori Dauphinee, Roger Lachappelle and Otis Steele and charges were laid against Jason Cannon, Roger Lachappelle, Darren Simmonds and Otis Steele. The applicants have consistently argued that the R.C.M.P. conducted a thorough and comprehensive investigation of what they call the "white side of things" while virtually ignoring the blacks. But do the facts, at least as they exist with respect to the January 9th incident, support such a conclusion?

Clearly, the statements obtained with respect to the January 9th incident reveal the names of other potential witnesses and some of whom may have been potential accused. The names referred to in those statements include Raymond Naugle, Kathleen Gould, Tanya Kidney, Paul Connor, Sterling Steeves, Adrian Pomeroy, Reid Thompson, John Thompson and Javarro Smith. Of that group, four were apparently white students and three were black. It is true that no effort was made to interview the black students contained in this list but similarly, no effort was made to interview the white students either. Further, it is to be noted that the names provided are contained in the statements of the white students and the statement of Otis Steele essentially describes acts committed by Jason Cannon and Roger Lachappelle, both of whom were charged. Ultimately, Jason Cannon and Darren Simmonds were acquitted after trial and Otis Steele and Roger Lachappelle had their charges dismissed for want of prosecution.

Obviously, an exhaustive investigation of the incident would have involved locating and interviewing every potential witness known to the R.C.M.P. The police, in retrospect and with the benefit of hindsight and after having had their investigation probed under a microscope, probably wished they had done so. But their failure to do so did not result in an investigation which can be described as racially discriminatory.

I next turn to the facts relating to the investigation of the incidents of January 11, 1989 and what was the evidence relied upon by the police to substantiate charges against Deon Provo, Jason Downey and Dwayne Saulnier. Examination of the Crown files indicates that the police relied, with respect to the Provo matter, heavily on the evidence afforded by the MITV tape which they seized. There were no doubt, as evidenced by the [affidavits] filed on behalf of the applicants as well as the tape itself, many witnesses to the event, none of whom the police interviewed or attempted to interview. Given the evidence that the police had, they were entitled to rely on that evidence and conclude their investigation. Although ideally every criminal investigation would be exhaustive, the reality of financial resources and manpower make that ideal an impossibility. It must be remembered that, for the most part, the police were investigating summary offences, the least serious in the Criminal Code, and could not be expected to investigate with the same thoroughness as one might expect were the charges more serious. The fact that the R.C.M.P. did not pursue the investigation beyond the seizure of the MITV tape does not lead me to the conclusion that the investigation was probably discriminatory. Similarly in the case involving Jason Downey and Dwayne Saulnier, the police relied essentially on the evidence afforded by a CBC news tape. Jason Downey was not included as a witness against Mr. Saulnier and vice-versa and charges against both were dismissed for want of prosecution. The only distinction with respect to the two was that Mr. Saulnier was interviewed by the R.C.M.P. and Mr. Downey was not. That fact, standing alone, does not establish that the R.C.M.P. conducted a thorough investigation of the white side of things and further does not establish that the investigation was racially discriminatory.

Essentially then, the applicant must establish that the investigation of the events of January 10, 1989 was racially discriminatory and thus resulted in a violation of their Section 15 and Section 7 rights. Once again, the evidence is overwhelming that there were numerous witnesses to the events of January 10, 1989, both black and white. Further, that only eight statements were obtained from the R.C.M.P. concerning these events — seven of them from white students and one from a black student. The applicants again argue that this constituted a complete investigation of the white side of the story while blacks were ignored.

The investigation of this incident commenced when Constable Curley was advised by Mr. MacNeil, Principal of the school, that the incident had occurred and that an injured party had been taken to hospital. Constable Curley, as would be expected, attended at the hospital and questioned a number of people, eight in total, including a black female who advised him that she hadn't seen anyone fighting. Subsequently, Constable Curley provided the names of those people along with eight other names to Constables Slawson and Taylor. The name of the black girl was not included on the list passed on by Constable Curley. The evidence establishes that efforts were made to contact all of the people on the list by telephone on the evening of January the 10th. What were the results of those telephone calls? Mary Jewers and Lori Dauphinee, both white students, and apparently at the urgings of their parents, came to the Cole Harbour Detachment of the R.C.M.P. and gave statements. Wendy Archer, also apparently at the urging of her mother, came to the detachment and gave a statement. Michelle Ferrar agreed to meet with the R.C.M.P. the following morning and indicated at that time that she might be prepared to give a statement later that day and later that afternoon, the police attended at her home and Miss Ferrar gave a statement. Apparently quite by chance, Shelley McMaster and Tina Ferrar were also at the Ferrar residence that day and of the two, only one, Miss McMaster, agreed to give a statement. The police also visited the home of Scott Walker, the party who had been injured and treated at the hospital, and obtained a statement. The evidence establishes that the police were unsuccessful in reaching any of the blacks with the exception of Otis Steele who later cooperated with the police and gave a statement concerning the January 9th incident. Later, however, on January 11th, the police made contact with Myles Smith and obtained a statement from him. The only other statement was given by Craig Sheridan who was brought forward by Muriel Tupper. There is no evidence that the police made any effort to obtain statements from other whites questioned at the hospital. Other names including Ted Noble, Tracey Way, Doug Spencer or Felicia Berringer, beyond the initial telephone calls. It is true that the police could have made efforts to obtain names and addresses of witnesses at the scene on January 10th and failed to do so. In this respect, however, the blacks were dealt with in exactly the same way as the white students. There was no effort ... no real effort by the R.C.M.P. to obtain names and addresses of white students at the scene any more than there was an effort made by the R.C.M.P. to obtain names and addresses of blacks. The police also asked the assistance of Miss Tupper, Vice Principal of the school, to have witnesses come forward which resulted in them obtaining only one statement.

Many of the black students who filed [affidavits] and gave sworn evidence in this proceeding complained of having had criminal acts committed against them. Obviously there is no obligation on those individuals to come forward and make complaints to the police. The police, however, do not conduct investigations in a vacuum. They respond, for the most part, to complaints and do not go out looking to find offences to investigate. No doubt, if more witnesses had come forward or been discovered and located, more charges would have been laid against both whites and blacks.

The applicants argue that the way in which the investigation was conducted resulted in a disadvantage or adverse [effect] to the blacks which did not result in the same way to the whites. But let us examine for a moment the effect of the investigation on the white students. Of the seven whites who agreed to give statements concerning the January the 10th incident, five were charged, two of which went to trial and were acquitted and the charges against the others were dismissed for want of prosecution. Of the six blacks charged, two were dismissed for want of prosecution, one was acquitted, leaving the remaining three applicants for trial. With the exception of Myles Smith who, in his statement, made allegations against Michelle Ferrar, not one black student complained at the time of any offence having been committed by others against them. Myles Smith alleged that Miss Ferrar had assaulted him and she was not charged with that offence. On the other hand, Miss Ferrar made the same allegation against Mr. Smith and he was not charged with the offence of assault either. Michelle Ferrar was acquitted after trial and the charge against Myles Smith was dismissed for want of prosecution. The whites, in large measure, were charged essentially because they incriminated themselves in their own statements.

It is blatantly obvious that the prosecution of both blacks and whites might have been more successful had more investigation been done and no doubt many of the blacks who testified before this Court and others would willingly have given statements to the police if they had been approached. In this respect, I am not satisfied, despite their evidence, that all of them would have been cooperative in giving statements in the same way that not all of the whites were cooperative in so doing. It is, however, in my view, overstating the case to say that the investigation was one-sided and it is not appropriate to suggest that a racially unbiased investigation would have required that the same number of blacks as whites be interviewed. In my view, virtually the same opportunities were afforded to both groups and the rights of the defendants under Section 15 and of necessity under Section 7 have not been infringed and the application must fail.

∎

Subsequent to this conviction, the Attorney General's office acknowledged that Steven Fraser had been wrongly convicted since he had never in fact been charged with causing a disturbance. His conviction was then quashed by Judge Fran Potts. The Attorney General refused either to apologize or to provide compensation to Mr. Fraser: Kevin Cox, "Family furious at refusal to apologize: N.S. black community also angered by way justice system handled man's wrongful conviction" *The [Toronto] Globe and Mail* (17 July 1990) A3.

The appeal by the remaining two accused from conviction was dismissed in *R.* v. *Smith* (1991), 109 N.S.R. (2d) 394 (Co. Ct.), aff'd [1993] N.S.J. No. 124 (C.A.), online: QL, where the court held that the facts as found by the trial judge were supported by the evidence and that no error in application of the law had been committed. However, it should be noted that *Charter* claims regarding s. 15 violations on the grounds of systemic racism in the administration of criminal justice are not mere theoretical possibilities, as the cases surveyed above under **Enforcement of the Law**, **Sentencing**, and **Prisons and Parole** demonstrate.

Finally, the judgment in *R. v. Thompson* reproduced above refers to police reliance upon MITV video evidence for their investigation of the Cole Harbour incident. How might systemic racism shape the production of such news accounts? What are the implications for police "investigation" of crime? See, for example, Kathy Laster, "A justified omission?" (1989) 14 Legal Services Bull. 258 at 258: "Aboriginal groups argued at the Human Rights Inquiry into Racist Violence that their 'number one enemy' was the media."

In the case that follows, consider the different ways in which a judge's individual experience, the "reasonable person" test, and social context evidence play a role in the critical credibility contests between police witnesses and accused persons who are racialized.

R. v. R.D.S.†

[L'HEUREUX-DUBÉ and McLACHLIN JJ.:]

INTRODUCTION

We have read the reasons of our colleague, Justice Cory, and while we agree that this appeal must be allowed, we differ substantially from him in how we reach that outcome. As a result, we find it necessary to write brief concurring reasons.

We endorse Cory J.'s comments on judging in a multicultural society, the importance of perspective and social context in judicial decision-making, and the presumption of judicial integrity. However, we approach the test for reasonable apprehension of bias and its application to the case at bar somewhat differently from our colleague.

In our view, the test for reasonable apprehension of bias established in the jurisprudence is reflective of the reality that while judges can never be neutral, in the sense of purely objective, they can and must strive for impartiality. It therefore recognizes as inevitable and appropriate that the differing experiences of judges assist them in their decision-making process and will be reflected in their judgments, so long as those experiences are relevant to the cases, are not based on inappropriate stereotypes, and do not prevent a fair and just determination of the cases based on the facts in evidence.

We find that on the basis of these principles, there is no reasonable apprehension of bias in the case at bar. Like Cory J. we would, therefore, overturn the findings by the Nova Scotia Supreme Court (Trial Division) and the majority of the Nova Scotia Court of Appeal that a reasonable apprehension of bias arises in this case, and restore the acquittal of R.D.S. This said, we disagree with Cory J.'s position that the comments of Judge Sparks were unfortunate, unnecessary, or close to the line. Rather, we find them to reflect an entirely appropriate recognition of the facts in evidence in this case and of the context within which this case arose — a context known to Judge Sparks and to any well-informed member of the community.

THE TEST FOR REASONABLE APPREHENSION OF BIAS

The test for reasonable apprehension of bias is that set out by de Grandpré J. in *Committee for Justice and Liberty v. National Energy Board*, [1978] 1 S.C.R. 369. Though he wrote dissenting reasons, de Grandpré J.'s articulation of the test for bias was adopted by the majority of the Court, and has been consistently endorsed by this Court in the intervening two decades: see, for example, *Valente v. The Queen*, [1985] 2 S.C.R. 673; *R. v. Lippé*, [1991] 2 S.C.R. 114; *Ruffo v. Conseil de la magistrature*, [1995] 4 S.C.R. 267. De Grandpré J. stated, at pp. 394–95:

> ... the apprehension of bias must be a reasonable one, held by reasonable and right-minded persons, applying themselves to the question and obtaining thereon the required information.... [T]hat test is "what would an informed person, viewing the matter realistically and practically — and having thought the matter through — conclude. Would he

---

† [1997] 3 S.C.R. 484 at 501–517, 531–548.

think that it is more likely than not that [the decision-maker], whether consciously or unconsciously, would not decide fairly."

The grounds for this apprehension must, however, be substantial and I ... refus[e] to accept the suggestion that the test be related to the "very sensitive or scrupulous conscience".

As Cory J. notes ... the scope and stringency of the duty of fairness articulated by de Grandpré depends largely on the role and function of the tribunal in question. Although judicial proceedings will generally be bound by the requirements of natural justice to a greater degree than will hearings before administrative tribunals, judicial decision-makers, by virtue of their positions, have nonetheless been granted considerable deference by appellate courts inquiring into the apprehension of bias. This is because judges "are assumed to be [people] of conscience and intellectual discipline, capable of judging a particular controversy fairly on the basis of its own circumstances": *United States* v. *Morgan*, 313 U.S. 409 (1941), at p. 421. The presumption of impartiality carries considerable weight, for as Blackstone opined at p. 361 in *Commentaries on the Laws of England*, Book III, cited at footnote 49 in Richard F. Devlin, "We Can't Go On Together with Suspicious Minds: Judicial Bias and Racialized Perspective in R. v. R.D.S." (1995), 18 Dalhousie L.J. 408, at p. 417, "the law will not suppose a possibility of bias or favour in a judge, who is already sworn to administer impartial justice, and whose authority greatly depends upon that presumption and idea". Thus, reviewing courts have been hesitant to make a finding of bias or to perceive a reasonable apprehension of bias on the part of a judge, in the absence of convincing evidence to that effect: *R.* v. *Smith & Whiteway Fisheries Ltd.* (1994), 133 N.S.R. (2d) 50 (C.A.), at pp. 60–61.

Notwithstanding the strong presumption of impartiality that applies to judges, they will nevertheless be held to certain stringent standards regarding bias — "a reasonable apprehension that the judge might not act in an entirely impartial manner is ground for disqualification": *Blanchette* v. *C.I.S. Ltd.*, [1973] S.C.R. 833, at pp. 842–43.

In order to apply this test, it is necessary to distinguish between the impartiality which is required of all judges, and the concept of judicial neutrality. The distinction we would draw is that reflected in the insightful words of Benjamin N. Cardozo in *The Nature of the Judicial Process* (1921), at pp. 12–13 and 167, where he affirmed the importance of impartiality, while at the same time recognizing the fallacy of judicial neutrality:

> There is in each of us a stream of tendency, whether you choose to call it philosophy or not, which gives coherence and direction to thought and action. Judges cannot escape that current any more than other mortals. All their lives, forces which they do not recognize and cannot name, have been tugging at them — inherited instincts, traditional beliefs, acquired convictions; and the resultant is an outlook on life, a conception of social needs.... In this mental background every problem finds its setting. We may try to see things as objectively as we please. None the less, we can never see them with any eyes except our own.
>
> ...
>
> Deep below consciousness are other forces, the likes and the dislikes, the predilections and the prejudices, the complex of instincts and emotions and habits and convictions, which make the [person], whether he [or she] be litigant or judge.

Cardozo recognized that objectivity was an impossibility because judges, like all other humans, operate from their own perspectives. As the Canadian Judicial Council noted in *Commentaries on Judicial Conduct* (1991), at p. 12, "[t]here is no human being who is not the product of every social experience, every process of education, and every human contact". What is possible and desirable, they note, is impartiality:

> ...the wisdom required of a judge is to recognize, consciously allow for, and perhaps to question, all the baggage of past attitudes and sympathies that fellow citizens are free to carry, untested, to the grave.
>
> True impartiality does not require that the judge have no sympathies or opinions; it requires that the judge nevertheless be free to entertain and act upon different points of view with an open mind.

THE REASONABLE PERSON

The presence or absence of an apprehension of bias is evaluated through the eyes of the reasonable, informed, practical and realistic person who considers the matter in some detail (*Committee for Justice and Liberty*, supra). The person postulated is not a "very sensitive or scrupulous" person, but rather a right-minded person familiar with the circumstances of the case.

It follows that one must consider the reasonable person's knowledge and understanding of the judicial process and the nature of judging as well as of the community in which the alleged crime occurred.

The Nature of Judging

As discussed above, judges in a bilingual, multi-racial and multicultural society will undoubtedly approach the task of judging from their varied perspectives. They will certainly have been shaped by, and have gained insight from, their different experiences, and cannot be expected to divorce themselves from these experiences on the occasion of their appointment to the bench. In fact, such a transformation would deny society the benefit of the valuable knowledge gained by the judiciary while they were members of the Bar. As well, it would preclude the achievement of a diversity of backgrounds in the judiciary. The reasonable person does not expect that judges will function as neutral ciphers; however, the reasonable person does demand that judges achieve impartiality in their judging.

It is apparent, and a reasonable person would expect, that triers of fact will be properly influenced in their deliberations by their individual perspectives on the world in which the events in dispute in the courtroom took place. Indeed, judges must rely on their background knowledge in fulfilling their adjudicative function. As David M. Paciocco and Lee Stuesser write in their book *The Law of Evidence* (1996), at p. 277:

> *In general, the trier of fact is entitled simply to apply common sense and human experience in determining whether evidence is credible and in deciding what use, if any, to make of it in coming to its finding of fact.* [Emphasis in original.]

At the same time, where the matter is one of identifying and applying the law to the findings of fact, it must be the law that governs and not a judge's individual beliefs that may conflict with the law. Further, notwithstanding that their own insights into human nature will properly play a role in making findings of credibility or factual determinations, judges must make those determinations only after being equally open to, and considering the views of, all parties before them. The reasonable person, through whose eyes the apprehension of bias is assessed, expects judges to undertake an open-minded, carefully considered, and dispassionately deliberate investigation of the complicated reality of each case before them.

It is axiomatic that all cases litigated before judges are, to a greater or lesser degree, complex. There is more to a case than who did what to whom, and the questions of fact and law to be determined in any given case do not arise in a vacuum. Rather, they are the consequence of numerous factors, influenced by the innumerable forces which impact on them in a particular context. Judges, acting as finders of fact, must inquire into those forces. In short, they must be aware of the context in which the alleged crime occurred.

Judicial inquiry into the factual, social and psychological context within which litigation arises is not unusual. Rather, a conscious, contextual inquiry has become an accepted step towards judicial impartiality. In that regard, Professor Jennifer Nedelsky's "Embodied Diversity and the Challenges to Law" (1997), 42 McGill L.J. 91, at p. 107, offers the following comment:

> What makes it possible for us to genuinely judge, to move beyond our private [idiosyncrasies] and preferences, is our capacity to achieve an "enlargement of mind". We do this by taking different perspectives into account. This is the path out of the blindness of our subjective private conditions. The more views we are able to take into account, the less likely we are to be locked into one perspective.... It is the capacity for "enlargement of mind" that makes autonomous, impartial judgment possible.

Judicial inquiry into context provides the requisite background for the interpretation and the application of the law. For example, in a case involving alleged police misconduct in denying an accused's right to counsel, this Court inquired not simply into whether the accused had been read their *Charter* rights, but also used a contextual approach to ensure that the purpose of the constitutionally protected right was fulfilled: *R. v. Bartle*, [1994] 3 S.C.R. 173. The Court, placing itself in the position of the accused, asked how the accused would have experienced and responded to arrest and detention. Against this background, the Court went on to determine what was required to make the right to counsel truly meaningful. This inquiry provided the Court with a larger picture, which was in turn conducive to a more just determination of the case.

An understanding of the context or background essential to judging may be gained from testimony from expert witnesses in order to put the case in context: *R. v. Lavallee*, [1990] 1 S.C.R. 852, *R. v. Parks* (1993), 15 O.R. (3d) 324 (C.A.), and *Moge v. Moge*, [1992] 3 S.C.R. 813, from academic studies properly placed before the Court; and from the judge's personal understanding and experience of the society in which the judge lives and works. This process of enlargement is not only consistent with impartiality; it may also be seen as its essential precondition.

A reasonable person far from being troubled by this process, would see it as an important aid to judicial impartiality.

The Nature of the Community

The reasonable person, identified by de Grandpré J. in *Committee for Justice and Liberty, supra*, is an informed and right-minded member of the community, a community which, in Canada, supports the fundamental principles entrenched in the Constitution by the Canadian *Charter of Rights and Freedoms*. Those fundamental principles include the principles of equality set out in s. 15 of the Charter and endorsed in nation-wide quasi-constitutional provincial and federal human rights legislation. The reasonable person must be taken to be aware of the history of discrimination faced by disadvantaged groups in Canadian society protected by the *Charter*'s equality provisions. These are matters of which judicial notice may be taken. In *Parks, supra*, at p. 342, Doherty J.A., did just this, stating:

> Racism, and in particular anti-black racism, is a part of our community's psyche. A significant segment of our community holds overtly racist views. A much larger segment subconsciously operates on the basis of negative racial stereotypes. Furthermore, our institutions, including the criminal justice system, reflect and perpetuate those negative stereotypes.

The reasonable person is not only a member of the Canadian community, but also, more specifically, is a member of the local communities in which the case at issue arose (in this case, the Nova Scotian and Halifax communities). Such a person must be taken to possess knowledge of the local population and its racial dynamics, including the existence in the community of a history of widespread and systemic discrimination against black and aboriginal people, and high profile clashes between the police and the visible minority population over policing issues: *Royal Commission on the Donald Marshall Jr. Prosecution* (1989); *R. v. Smith* (1991), 109 N.S.R. (2d) 394 (Co. Ct.). The reasonable person must thus be deemed to be cognizant of the existence of racism in Halifax, Nova Scotia. It follows that judges may take notice of actual racism known to exist in a particular society. Judges have done so with respect to racism in Nova Scotia. In *Nova Scotia (Minister of Community Services) v. S.M.S.* (1992), 110 N.S.R. (2d) 91 (Fam. Ct.), it was stated at p. 108:

> [Racism] is a pernicious reality. The issue of racism existing in Nova Scotia has been well documented in the *Marshall Inquiry Report* (*sub. nom. Royal Commission on the Donald Marshall, Jr., Prosecution*). A person would have to be stupid, complacent or ignorant not to acknowledge its presence, not only individually, but also systemically and institutionally.

We conclude that the reasonable person contemplated by de Grandpré J., and endorsed by Canadian courts is a person who approaches the question of whether there exists a reasonable apprehension of bias with a complex and contextualized understanding of the issues in the case. The reasonable person understands the impossibility of judicial neutrality, but demands judicial impartiality. The reasonable person is cognizant of the racial dynamics in the local community, and, as a member of the Canadian community, is supportive of the principles of equality.

Before concluding that there exists a reasonable apprehension of bias in the conduct of a judge, the reasonable person would require some clear evidence that the judge in question had improperly used his or her perspective in the decision-making process; this flows from the presumption of impartiality of the judiciary. There must be some indication that the judge was not approaching the case with an open mind fair to all parties. Awareness of the context within which a case occurred would not constitute such evidence; on the contrary, such awareness is consistent with the highest tradition of judicial impartiality.

APPLICATION OF THE TEST TO THE FACTS

In assessing whether a reasonable person would perceive the comments of Judge Sparks to give rise to a reasonable apprehension of bias, it is important to bear in mind that the impugned reasons were delivered orally. As Professor Devlin puts it in "We Can't Go On Together with Suspicious Minds: Judicial Bias and Racialized Perspective in R. v. R.D.S.", *supra*, at p. 414:

> Trial judges have a heavy workload that allows little time for meticulously thought-through reasoning. This is particularly true when decisions are delivered orally immediately after counsel have finished their arguments.

(See also *R. v. Burns*, [1994] 1 S.C.R. 656, at p. 664.)

It follows that for the purposes of this appeal, the oral reasons issued by Judge Sparks should be read in their entirety, and the impugned passages should be construed in light of the whole of the trial proceedings and in light of all other portions of the judgment.

Judge Sparks was faced with contradictory testimony from the only two witnesses, the appellant R.D.S., and Constable Stienburg. Both testified as to the events that occurred and were subjected to cross-examination. As trier of fact, Judge Sparks was required to assess their testimony, and to determine whether or not, on the evidence before her, she had a reasonable doubt as to the guilt of the appellant R.D.S. It is evident in the transcript that Judge Sparks proceeded to do just that.

Judge Sparks briefly summarized the contradictory evidence offered by the two witnesses, and then made several observations about credibility. She noted that R.D.S. testified quite candidly, and with considerable detail. She remarked that contrary to the testimony of Constable Stienburg, it was the evidence of R.D.S. that when he arrived on the scene on his bike, his cousin was handcuffed and not struggling in any way. She found the level of detail that R.D.S. provided to have "a ring of truth", and found him to be "a rather honest young boy". In the end, while Judge Sparks specifically noted that she did not accept all the evidence given by R.D.S., she nevertheless found him to have raised a reasonable doubt by raising queries in her mind as to what actually occurred.

It is important to note that having already found R.D.S. to be credible, and having accepted a sufficient portion of his evidence to leave her with a reasonable doubt as to his guilt, Judge Sparks necessarily disbelieved at least a portion of the conflicting evidence of Constable Stienburg. At that point, Judge Sparks made reference to the submissions of the Crown that "there's absolutely no reason to attack the credibility of the officer", and then addressed herself to why there might, in fact, be a reason to attack the credibility of the officer in this case. It is in this context that Judge Sparks made the statements which have prompted this appeal:

> The Crown says, well, why would the officer say that events occurred the way in which he has relayed them to the Court this morning. I am not saying that the Constable has misled the court, although police officers have been known to do that in the past. I am not saying that the officer overreacted, but certainly police officers do overreact, particularly when they are dealing with non-white groups. That to me indicates a state of mind right there that is questionable. I believe that probably the situation in this particular case is the case of a young police officer who overreacted. I do accept the evidence of [R.D.S.] that he was told to shut up or he would be under arrest. It seems to be in keeping with the prevalent attitude of the day.
> At any rate, based upon my comments and based upon all the evidence before the court I have no other choice but to acquit.

These remarks do not support the conclusion that Judge Sparks found Constable Stienburg to have lied. In fact, Judge Sparks did quite the opposite. She noted firstly, that she was *not* saying Constable Stienburg had misled the court, although that could be an explanation for his evidence. She then went on to remark that she was *not* saying that Constable Stienburg had overreacted, though she was alive to that possibility given that it had happened with police officers in the past, and in particular, it had happened when police officers were dealing with non-white groups. Finally, Judge Sparks concluded that, though she was not willing to say that Constable Stienburg did overreact, it was her belief that he *probably* overreacted. And, in support of that finding, she noted that she accepted the evidence of R.D.S. that "he was told to shut up or he would be under arrest".

At no time did Judge Sparks rule that the probable overreaction by Constable Stienburg was motivated by racism. Rather, she tied her finding of probable overreaction to the evidence that Constable Stienburg had threatened to arrest the appellant R.D.S. for speaking to his cousin. At the same time, there was evidence capable of supporting a finding of racially motivated overreaction. At an earlier point in the proceedings, she had accepted the evidence that the other youth arrested that day, was handcuffed and thus secured when R.D.S. approached. This constitutes evidence which could lead one to question why it was necessary for both boys to be placed in choke holds by Constable Stienburg, purportedly to secure them. In the face of such evidence, we respectfully disagree with the views of our colleagues Cory and Major JJ. that there was no evidence on which Judge Sparks could have found "racially motivated" overreaction by the police officer.

While it seems clear that Judge Sparks *did not in fact* relate the officer's probable overreaction to the race of the appellant R.D.S., it should be noted that if Judge Sparks *had* chosen to attribute the behaviour of Constable Stienburg to the racial dynamics of the situation, she would not necessarily have erred. As a member of the community, it was open to her to take into account the well-known presence of racism in that community and to evaluate the evidence as to what occurred against that background.

That Judge Sparks recognized that police officers *sometimes* overreact when dealing with non-white groups simply demonstrates that in making her determination in this case, she was alive to the well-known racial dynamics that may exist in interactions between police officers and visible minorities. As found by Freeman J.A. in his dissenting judgment at the Court of Appeal (1995), 145 N.S.R. (2d) 284, at p. 294:

> The case was racially charged, a classic confrontation between a white police officer representing the power of the state and a black youth charged with an offence. Judge Sparks was under a duty to be sensitive to the nuances and implications, and to rely on her own common sense which is necessarily informed by her own experience and understanding.

Given these facts, the question is whether a reasonable and right-minded person, informed of the circumstances of this case, and knowledgeable about the local community and about Canadian *Charter* values, would perceive that the reasons of Judge Sparks would give rise to a reasonable apprehension of bias. In our view, they would not. The clear evidence of prejudgment required to sustain a reasonable apprehension of bias is nowhere to be found.

Judge Sparks' oral reasons show that she approached the case with an open mind, used her experience and knowledge of the community to achieve an understanding of the reality of the case, and applied the fundamental principle of proof beyond a reasonable doubt. Her comments were based entirely on the case before her, were made after a consideration of the conflicting testimony of the two witnesses and in response to the Crown's submissions, and were entirely supported by the evidence. In alerting herself to the racial dynamic in the case, she was simply engaging in the process of contextualized judging which, in our view, was entirely proper and conducive to a fair and just resolution of the case before her.

CONCLUSION

In the result, we agree with Cory J. as to the disposition of this case. We would allow the appeal, overturn the findings of the Nova Scotia Supreme Court (Trial Division) and the majority of the Nova Scotia Court of Appeal, and restore the acquittal of the appellant R.D.S.

[The judgment of Cory and Iacobucci JJ. was delivered by CORY J.:]

In this appeal, it must be determined whether a reasonable apprehension of bias arises from comments made by the trial judge in providing her reasons for acquitting the accused.

FACTS

R.D.S. is an African-Canadian youth. When he was 15 years of age he was charged with three offences: unlawfully assaulting Constable Donald Stienburg; unlawfully assaulting Constable Stienburg with the intention of preventing the arrest of N.R.; and unlawfully resisting Constable Stienburg in the lawful execution of his duty.

The Crown proceeded with the charges by way of summary conviction. There were only two witnesses at the trial: R.D.S. himself and Constable Stienburg. Their accounts of the relevant events differed widely. The credibility of these witnesses would determine the outcome of the charges.

Constable Stienburg's Evidence

Constable Stienburg testified that he was in his police cruiser with his partner when a radio transmission alerted them that other officers were in pursuit of a stolen van. In the car was a "ride-along", Leslie Lane, who was unable to testify at the trial. The occupants of the stolen van were described as "non-white" youths. When Constable Stienburg and his partner arrived at the designated area they saw two black youths running across the street in front of them. Constable Stienburg detained one of the individuals, N.R., while his partner pursued the other. He testified that there were a number of other people standing around at the time.

N.R. was detained outside the police car since the "ride along" was in the back seat. While Constable Stienburg was standing by the side of the road with N.R., the accused, R.D.S., came towards Constable Stienburg on his bicycle. Constable Stienburg testified that R.D.S. ran into his legs, and while still on the bicycle, yelled at him and pushed him. R.D.S. was then arrested for interfering with the arrest of N.R., and Constable Stienburg called for back-up. Constable Stienburg stated that he put both R.D.S. and N.R. in "a neck restraint". When R.D.S. was finally brought to the police station, he was read his rights, and charged with the three offences.

In cross-examination, it was suggested to Constable Stienburg that R.D.S. had been overcharged. It was pointed out that R.D.S. had no prior record and it was suggested, although not particularly clearly, that R.D.S. had been singled out because he was black.

Testimony of R.D.S.

R.D.S. testified that he remembered that the weather on the particular day was misty and humid. While riding his bike from his grandmother's to his mother's house he saw the police car and the crowd standing beside it. A friend told him that his cousin N.R. had been arrested. R.D.S. approached the crowd, and stopped his bike when he saw N.R. and the officer. R.D.S. then tried to talk to N.R. to ask him what had happened and to find out if he should tell N.R.'s mother. Constable Stienburg told him: "Shut up, shut up, or you'll be under arrest too". When R.D.S. continued to ask N.R. if he should call his mother, Constable Stienburg arrested R.D.S. and put him in a choke hold. R.D.S. indicated that he could not breathe, and that he heard a woman tell the officer to "Let that kid go . . . ." He also heard her ask for his phone number. He could not talk so N.R. gave the number to her. R.D.S. indicated that the crowd standing around were all "little kids" under the age of 12. He denied that he ran into anyone or that he intended to run into anyone on his bike. He also testified that his hands remained on the handlebars, and he did not push the officer.

In cross-examination, he indicated that the reason he approached the crowd was because he was "being nosey". He remembered that N.R. was handcuffed when he arrived. Both R.D.S. and N.R. were placed in a choke hold at the same time. He repeated his denial that he touched the officer either with his bicycle or his hands. He also denied that he said anything to Constable Stienburg prior to his arrest. He indicated that all his questions were directed to N.R.

History of Proceedings

In Youth Court, Judge Sparks weighed the evidence of the two witnesses and determined that R.D.S. should be acquitted. In her oral reasons, she made comments which were challenged as raising a reasonable apprehension of bias. They are the subject of this appeal. After the reasons had been given and an appeal to the Nova Scotia Supreme Court (Trial Division) had been filed by the Crown, Judge Sparks issued supplementary reasons which outlined in greater detail her impressions of the credibility of both witnesses and the context in which her comments were made.

In the Trial Division, Glube C.J.S.C., sitting as summary conviction appeal judge, allowed the Crown's appeal. She held in oral reasons that a new trial was warranted on the basis that the remarks of Judge Sparks gave rise to a reasonable apprehension of bias. This decision was upheld in the Nova Scotia Court of Appeal by Flinn J.A. and Pugsley J.A., Freeman J.A. dissenting.

JUDGMENS BELOW

Youth Court

In her oral reasons, Judge Sparks reviewed the details of Constable Stienburg's testimony, and noted that R.D.S.'s evidence was directly opposed to it. In describing R.D.S.'s testimony, she observed that she was impressed with his clear recollection of the weather conditions on that day, and his candour in pointing out that he was simply being nosey in approaching the crowd. She also noted that his description of being placed in the choke hold was vivid. R.D.S. stated clearly that when he was placed in the choke hold, he could not speak and had difficulty breathing. In fact, he was unable to respond when a woman asked him for his phone number so she could notify his mother.

The Youth Court Judge paid particular attention to R.D.S.'s testimony that N.R. was handcuffed when R.D.S. arrived on the scene. This aspect of R.D.S.'s testimony suggested that N.R. was not a threat to the officer. Significantly, Constable Stienburg did not mention that N.R. was handcuffed, and gave the court the distinct impression that he had difficulty restraining N.R. In Judge Sparks' view, R.D.S.'s testimony that N.R. was handcuffed had "a ring of truth" to it, which raised questions in her mind about the divergence between R.D.S.'s evidence and the evidence of Constable Stienburg on this point.

In general, Judge Sparks described R.D.S's demeanour as "positive", even though he was not particularly articulate. She found him to be a "rather honest young boy". In particular, she was struck by his openness in acknowledging his own "nosiness" and by his surprise at the hostility of the police officer. Judge Sparks indicated that she was not saying that she accepted everything that R.D.S. said, but noted that "certainly he has raised a doubt in my mind". She still had queries about "what actually transpired on the afternoon of October the 17th". As a result, she concluded that the Crown had not discharged its evidentiary burden to prove all the elements of the offence beyond a reasonable doubt.

She concluded her reasons with the controversial remarks that gave rise to this appeal. ...

[These remarks were reproduced in the preceding judgment. Justice Cory then reviewed the lower court decisions of the Nova Scotia Supreme Court Trial Division and the Court of Appeal before proceeding to his analysis of the claim of reasonable apprehension of bias. He noted, first, that the right to trial by an impartial tribunal has been expressly enshrined in ss. 7 and 11(d) of the Canadian *Charter of Rights and Freedoms*. He went on to articulate the test from *Committee for Justice and Liberty*, referred to in the preceding judgment.]

. . . .

This test has been adopted and applied for the past two decades. It contains a two-fold objective element: the person considering the alleged bias must be reasonable, and the apprehension of bias itself must also be reasonable in the circumstances of the case. ... Further the reasonable person must be an *informed* person, with knowledge of all the relevant circumstances, including "the traditions of integrity and impartiality that form a part of the background and apprised also of the fact that impartiality is one of the duties the judges swear to uphold": *R.* v. *Elrick*, [1983] O.J. No. 515 (H.C.), at para. 14. ... To that I would add that the reasonable person should also be taken to be aware of the social reality that forms the background to a particular case, such as societal awareness and acknowledgement of the prevalence of racism or gender bias in a particular community.

. . . .

Judicial Integrity and the Importance of Judicial Impartiality

. . . .

The requirement for neutrality does not require judges to discount the very life experiences that may so well qualify them to preside over disputes. It has been observed that the duty to be impartial does not mean that a judge does not, or cannot bring to the bench many existing sympathies, antipathies or attitudes. There is no human being who is not the product of every social experience, every process of education, and every human contact with those with whom we share the planet. Indeed, even if it were possible, a judge free of this heritage of past experience would probably lack the very qualities of humanity required of a judge. Rather, the wisdom required of a judge is to recognize, consciously allow for, and perhaps to question, all the baggage of past attitudes and sympathies that fellow citizens are free to carry, untested, to the grave.

. . . .

It is obvious that good judges will have a wealth of personal and professional experience, that they will apply with sensitivity and compassion to the cases that they must hear. The sound belief behind the encouragement of greater diversity in judicial appointments was that women and visible minorities would bring an important perspective to the difficult task of judging. See for example the discussion by the Honourable Maryka Omatsu, "The Fiction of Judicial Impartiality" (1997), 9 C.J.W.L. 1. See also Devlin, *supra*, at pp. 408–9.

Regardless of their background, gender, ethnic origin or race, all judges owe a fundamental duty to the community to render impartial decisions and to appear impartial. It follows that judges must strive to ensure that no word or action during the course of the trial or in delivering judgment might leave the reasonable, informed person with the impression that an issue was predetermined or that a question was decided on the basis of stereotypical assumptions or generalizations.

Should Judges Refer to Aspects of Social Context in Making Decisions?

It is the submission of the appellant and interveners that judges should be able to refer to social context in making their judgments. It is argued that they should be able to refer to power imbalances between the sexes or between races, as well as to other aspects of social reality. The response to that submission is that each case must be assessed in light of its particular facts and circumstances. Whether or not the use of references to social context is appropriate in the circumstances and whether a reasonable apprehension of bias arises from particular statements will depend on the facts of the case.

At the outset, I would note that this appeal was not put forward by the appellant as engaging the principles of judicial notice. Rather it was the appellant's contention that the references to social context by Judge Sparks simply made use of her background, experience and knowledge of social conditions to assist her in the analysis of the persons involved in the case. One of the interveners did argue that the principles of judicial notice apply in this case. However, since the appellant did not put forward this position, it would be inappropriate to consider the question as to whether the existence of anti-black racism in society is a proper subject for judicial notice.

Certainly judges may, on the basis of expert evidence adduced, refer to relevant social conditions in reasons for judgment. In some circumstances, those references are necessary, so that the law may evolve in a manner which reflects social reality. For example, in *R.* v. *Lavallee*, [1990] 1 S.C.R. 852, expert evidence of the psychological experiences of battered women was used to inform the standard of reasonableness to be applied when self-defence is invoked by women who have been victims of domestic violence.

In *Lavallee*, the references to social context were based on expert evidence and were used solely to develop the relevant legal principle. In an individual case, however, it is still the responsibility of the woman putting forward the defence to establish that the general principles about women's experiences of domestic violence actually apply. The trier of fact still retains the important task of determining whether the evidence of a battered woman of her experiences in the particular case is in fact believable — in other words, whether the generalizations about social reality apply to the individual female accused. See *Lavallee, supra*, at p. 891.

Similarly, judges have recently made use of expert evidence of social conditions in order to develop the appropriate legal framework to be utilized for ensuring juror impartiality. In *Parks, supra*, Doherty J.A. referred to a body of studies and reports documenting the prevalence of anti-black racism in the Metropolitan Toronto area. On the basis of his conclusions, at p. 338, that anti-black racism is a "grim reality" in that community he developed a legal framework permitting jurors to be challenged for cause on the basis of racial preconceptions. This legal framework is applicable in circumstances where a realistic possibility exists that such preconceptions might threaten juror impartiality.

Other cases have applied and extended these principles on the basis of expert knowledge of the social context existing in the particular community, or in the particular relationships between parties to the case. See, for example, *R.* v. *Wilson* (1996), 29 O.R. (3d) 97 (C.A.); *R.* v. *Glasgow* (1996), 93 O.A.C. 67.

In *Parks* and *Lavallee*, for instance, the expert evidence of social context was used to develop principles of general application in certain kinds of cases. These principles are legal in nature, and are structured to ensure that the role of the trier of fact in a particular case is not abrogated or usurped. It is clear therefore that references to social context based upon expert evidence are sometimes permissible and helpful, and that they do not automatically give rise to suspicions of judicial bias. However, there is a very significant difference between cases such as *Lavallee* and *Parks* in which social context is used to ensure that the law evolves in keeping with changes in social reality and cases, such as this one, where social context is apparently being used to assist in determining an issue of credibility.

Use of Social Context in Assessing Credibility

It is, of course, true that the assessment of the credibility of a witness is more of an "art than a science". The task of assessing credibility can be particularly daunting where a judge must assess the credibility of two witnesses whose testimony is diametrically opposed. ... It is the highly individualistic nature of a determination of credibility, and its dependence on intangibles such as demeanour and the manner of testifying, that leads to the well-established principle that appellate courts will generally defer to the trial judge's factual findings, particularly those pertaining to credibility....

However, it is also the individualistic nature of a determination of credibility that requires the judge, as trier of fact, to be particularly careful to be and to appear to be neutral. This obligation requires the judge to walk a delicate line. On one hand, the judge is obviously permitted to use common sense and wisdom gained from personal experience in observing and judging the trustworthiness of a particular witness on the basis of factors such as testimony and demeanour. On the other hand, the judge must avoid judging the credibility of the witness on the basis of generalizations or upon matters that were not in evidence.

When making findings of credibility it is obviously preferable for a judge to avoid making any comment that might suggest that the determination of credibility is based on generalizations rather than on the specific demonstrations of truthfulness or untruthfulness that have come from the particular witness during the trial. It is true that judges do not have to remain passive, or to divest themselves of all their experience which assists them in their judicial fact finding. ...Yet judges have wide authority and their public utterances are closely scrutinized. Neither the parties nor the informed and reasonable observer should be led to believe by the comments of the judge that decisions are indeed being made based on generalizations.

At the commencement of their testimony all witnesses should be treated equally without regard to their race, religion, nationality, gender, occupation or other characteristics. It is only after an individual witness has been tested and assessed that findings of credibility can be made. Obviously the evidence of a policeman, or any other category of witness, cannot be automatically preferred to that of accused persons, any more than the testimony of blue eyed witnesses can be preferred to those with gray eyes. That must be the general rule. In particular, any judicial indication that police evidence is always to be preferred to that of a black accused person would lead the reasonable and knowledgeable observer to conclude that there was a reasonable apprehension of bias.

In some circumstances it may be acceptable for a judge to acknowledge that racism in society might be, for example, the motive for the overreaction of a police officer. This may be necessary in order to refute a submission that invites the judge as trier of fact to presume truthfulness or untruthfulness of a category of witnesses, or to adopt some other form of stereotypical thinking. Yet it would not be acceptable for a judge to go further and suggest that all police officers should therefore not be believed or should be viewed with suspicion where they are dealing with accused persons who are members of a different race. Similarly, it is dangerous for a judge to suggest that a particular person overreacted because of racism unless there is evidence adduced to sustain this finding. It would be equally inappropriate to suggest that female complainants, in sexual assault cases, ought to be believed more readily than male accused persons solely because of the history of sexual violence by men against women.

If there is no evidence linking the generalization to the particular witness, these situations might leave the judge open to allegations of bias on the basis that the credibility of the individual witness was prejudged according to stereotypical generalizations. This does not mean that the particular generalization — that police officers have historically discriminated against visible minorities or that women have historically been abused by men — is not true, or is without foundation. The difficulty is that reasonable and informed people may *perceive* that the judge has used this information as a basis for assessing credibility instead of making a genuine evaluation of the evidence of the particular witness' credibility. As a general rule, judges should avoid placing themselves in this position.

To state the general proposition that judges should avoid making comments based on generalizations when assessing the credibility of individual witnesses does not lead automatically to a conclusion that when a judge does so, a reasonable apprehension of bias arises. In some limited circumstances, the comments may be appropriate. Furthermore, no matter how unfortunate individual comments appear in isolation, the comments must be examined in context, through the eyes of the reasonable and informed person who is taken to know all the relevant circumstances of the case, including the presumption of judicial integrity, and the underlying social context.

. . . .

Application of These Principles to the Facts

Did Judge Sparks' comments give rise to a reasonable apprehension of bias? In order to answer that question, the nature of the Crown's allegation against Judge Sparks must be clearly understood. At the outset, it must be emphasized that it is obviously not appropriate to allege bias against Judge Sparks simply because she is black and raised the prospect of racial discrimination. Further, exactly the same high threshold for demonstrating reasonable apprehension of bias must be applied to Judge Sparks in the same manner it would be to all judges. She benefits from the presumption of judicial integrity that is accorded to all who swear the judicial oath of office. The Crown bears the onus of displacing this presumption with "cogent evidence".

Similarly, her finding that she could not accept the evidence of Constable Stienburg cannot raise a reasonable apprehension of bias. Neither Constable Stienburg nor any other police officer has an automatic right to be believed, any more than does the accused R.D.S. or any other accused. Police officers cannot expect to be immune from a finding that their testimony is not credible on some occasions. The basic function of a trial judge to determine issues of credibility and make findings of fact would be rendered meaningless if the credibility of police officers were to be accepted without question whenever their evidence diverged from that given by another witness. An unfavourable finding relating to the credibility of Constable Stienburg could only give rise to an apprehension of bias if it could reasonably be perceived to have been made on the basis of stereotypical generalizations, or ... on the basis of "wrongful or inappropriate" opinions not justified in the evidence.

. . . .

A reading of Judge Sparks' reasons indicates that before she made the challenged comments, she had a reasonable doubt as to the veracity of the officer's testimony and had found R.D.S. to be a credible witness. She gave convincing reasons for these findings. It is clear that Judge Sparks was well aware that the burden rested on the Crown to prove all the elements of the offence beyond a reasonable doubt, and she applied that burden. None of the bases for reaching these initial conclusions on credibility was based on generalizations or stereotypes. Her reasons for rejecting or accepting testimony could be applied to any witness, regardless of race or gender.

Did Judge Sparks' subsequent comments about race taint her findings of credibility? ...

. . . .

The statement that police officers have been known to mislead the court, or to overreact is not in itself offensive. Police officers are subject to the same human frailties that affect and shape the actions of everyone. The remarks become more troubling, however, when it is stated that police officers do overreact in dealing with non-white groups.

The history of anti-black racism in Nova Scotia was documented recently by the Royal Commission on the Donald Marshall Jr. Prosecution (1989). It suggests that there is a realistic possibility that the actions taken by the police in their relations with visible minorities demonstrate both prejudice and discrimination. I do not propose to review and comment upon the vast body of sociological literature referred to by the parties. It was not in evidence at trial. In the circumstances it will suffice to say that they indicate that racial tension exists at least to some degree between police officers and visible minorities. Further, in some cases, racism may have been exhibited by police officers in arresting young black males.

However, there was *no* evidence before Judge Sparks that would suggest that anti-black bias influenced *this particular police officer's reactions*. Thus, although it may be incontrovertible that there is a history of racial tension between police officers and visible minorities, there was no evidence to link that generalization to the actions of Constable Stienburg. The reference to the fact that police officers may overreact in dealing with non-white groups may therefore be perfectly supportable, but it is nonetheless unfortunate in the circumstances of this case because of its potential to associate Judge Sparks' findings with the generalization, rather than the specific evidence. This effect is reinforced by the statement "[t]hat to me indicates a state of mind right there that is questionable" which immediately follows her observation.

There is a further troubling comment. After accepting R.D.S.'s evidence that he was told to shut up, Judge Sparks added that "[i]t seems to be in keeping with the prevalent attitude of the day". Again, this comment may create a perception that the findings of credibility have been made on the basis of generalizations, rather than the conduct of the particular police officer. Indeed these comments standing alone come very close to indicating that Judge Sparks predetermined the issue of credibility of Constable Stienburg on the basis of her general perception of racist police attitudes, rather than on the basis of his demeanour and the substance of his testimony.

The remarks are worrisome and come very close to the line. Yet, however troubling these comments are when read individually, it is vital to note that the comments were not made in isolation. It is necessary to read all of the comments in the context of the whole proceeding, with an awareness of all the circumstances that a reasonable observer would be deemed to know.

The reasonable and informed observer at the trial would be aware that the Crown had made the submission to Judge Sparks that "there's absolutely no reason to attack the credibility of the officer". She had already made a finding that she preferred the evidence of R.D.S. to that of Constable Stienburg. She gave reasons for these findings that could appropriately be made based on the evidence adduced. A reasonable and informed person hearing her subsequent remarks would conclude that she was exploring the possible reasons why Constable Stienburg had a different perception of events than R.D.S. Specifically, she was rebutting the unfounded suggestion of the Crown that a police officer by virtue of his occupation should be more readily believed than the accused. Although her remarks were inappropriate they did not give rise to a reasonable apprehension of bias.

A reasonable and informed person observing the entire trial and hearing the reasons would be aware that Judge Sparks did not conclude that Constable Stienburg misled the court or overreacted on the basis of the racial dynamics of the situation. This is clear from her observation "I am not saying that the

Constable has misled the court" and "I am not saying that the officer overreacted". Although she went on to suggest that she believed he probably did overreact, she did not say that he did so because he was discriminating against R.D.S. on the basis of race. She links her findings that Constable Stienburg overreacted to the statement made to R.D.S.: "Shut up, shut up, or you'll be under arrest too".

Judge Sparks suggested that Constable Stienburg overreacted on *some* basis. Although she noted that he was young, she was careful not to make a final determination as to the reason for his overreaction. In fact, it was not necessary for her to resolve the question as to why the officer might have overreacted. The reasonable and informed observer would know that the Crown at all times bore the onus of proving the offence beyond a reasonable doubt. It was obvious that Judge Sparks had a reasonable doubt on the evidence. As long as she had a reasonable doubt regarding the veracity of the officer's testimony, R.D.S. was entitled to an acquittal. Judge Sparks' remarks could reasonably be taken as demonstrating her recognition that the Crown was required to *prove* its case, and that it was not entitled to use presumptions of credibility to satisfy its obligation.

Judge Sparks accepted the evidence of R.D.S. that he was told to shut up or he would be under arrest because that was the "prevalent attitude of the day". This comment is particularly unfortunate because of its potential to associate her findings of credibility with generalizations. However, it is ambiguous. It is not clear whether it refers to a prevalent attitude of anti-black racism, or the attitude that prevailed on the day in question. I accept that it refers to the specific day of the incident.

Finally, she concluded that "[a]t any rate", on the basis of her comments and all the evidence in the case, she was obliged to acquit. A reasonable, informed person reading the concluding statement would perceive that she has reached her determination that R.D.S. should be acquitted on the basis of all the evidence presented. The perception that her impugned remarks were made in response to the Crown's suggestion that she should automatically believe the police officer is reinforced by her use of the words "[a]t any rate".

A high standard must be met before a finding of reasonable apprehension of bias can be made. Troubling as Judge Sparks' remarks may be, the Crown has not satisfied its onus to provide the cogent evidence needed to impugn the impartiality of Judge Sparks. Although her comments, viewed in isolation, were unfortunate and unnecessary, a reasonable, informed person, aware of all the circumstances, would not conclude that they gave rise to a reasonable apprehension of bias. Her remarks, viewed in their context, do not give rise to a perception that she prejudged the issue of credibility on the basis of generalizations, and they do not taint her earlier findings of credibility.

Both Glube C.J.S.C. and the majority of the Court of Appeal correctly articulated the test to be applied when a reasonable apprehension of bias is alleged. However, in applying the test to the facts and circumstances of this case they failed to consider the impugned comments in context and to take into account the high threshold that must be met in order to find that a reasonable apprehension of bias has been established.

CONCLUSION

In the result the judgments of the Court of Appeal and of Glube C.J.S.C. are set aside and the decision of Judge Sparks dismissing the charges against R.D.S. is restored. I must add that since writing these reasons I have had the opportunity of reading those of Major J. It is readily apparent that we are in agreement as to the nature of bias and the test to be applied in order to determine whether the words or actions of a trial judge raise a reasonable apprehension of bias. The differences in our reasons [lie] in the application of the principles and test we both rely upon to the words of the trial judge in this case. The principles and the test we have both put forward and relied upon are different from and incompatible with those set out by Justices L'Heureux-Dubé and McLachlin.

[The reasons of Lamer C.J. and Sopinka and Major JJ. were delivered by MAJOR J. (dissenting). He would have found that Judge Sparks' remarks gave rise to a reasonable apprehension of bias such that the acquittal should have been set aside.] ■

Consider the impact of *R.D.S.* upon the effort by defence lawyers to challenge practices of racial profiling, discussed below with the materials from Ontario.

Ontario

Synopsis: Law Union of Ontario Presentation to Task Force on Race Relations and Policing[†]

The Law Union of Ontario, a 300 member organization of lawyers, law students and legal workers, has called on the Lewis Race Relations and Policing Task Force to recommend sweeping changes in police management and training programmes, the establishment of a province-wide civilian controlled police complaints commission and the reform of Federal and Provincial laws that presently allow the use of deadly force to stop escaping suspects.

Law Union spokesman Jack Gemmell told Lewis and his fellow task force members that uncontrolled police violence represents a serious threat to all Canadians. "Police spokesmen" he said "have tried to portray the outcry and concern surrounding the shooting of Wade Lawson and Lester Donaldson as solely the product of politically motivated black activists. I want to assure saddened parents that they do not stand alone. Many Canadians of all walks of life share their concern and grief about these unnecessary deaths. Now is the time for serious reform of the policing practices in this province to prevent this from happening again."

Gemmell said the veiled racist comments of police spokesmen have done tremendous disservice to the police in this province. "These comments reinforce racist attitudes in the worst police officers and slander those hard-working officers who never have seen the need to draw their gun let alone shoot anyone and who don't think the colour of a person's skin should affect how they treat them."

He further said that the Law Union was appalled by the failure of some members of the Metropolitan Toronto Police Commission, in particular Chairman June Rowlands, to condemn the police association for its statements. "The Chairman has failed to show real moral leadership when the community needed it. She should resign," he said.

The Law Union decried the rise of a police culture that isolates police officers from the community and the people they serve and that looks to the technologies of violence rather than human understanding in dealing with society's problems. "Any officer who relies on his bullets rather than his brains shouldn't be on the street," Gemmell said.

The Law Union called on the Task Force to investigate the growing multinational "police-industrial complex" that promotes the sale of increasingly violent police armaments and the need for their use.

The Law Union recommended several steps which would alleviate the crisis which it said we now face:

1. The Law Union calls for the establishment of an independent province-wide civilian controlled police complaints commission with wide-ranging powers. In Metropolitan Toronto the Office of the Public Complaints Commissioner, although inadequate, keeps a bad situation from getting worse. It is disastrous that even such minimal protection is missing for the rest of the province.

2. The Law Union demands new approaches to police management and new training programmes in police departments, coupled with cuts in budgetary items which emphasize hardware and violence. Police commissions should take a more active role in setting policy and providing leadership rather than being apologists for police misconduct. The Law Union believes that more could be done about preventing crime by beefing up drug abuse programs, insuring proper housing and providing jobs for all Canadians.

3. The Law Union wants the reform of the Federal and Provincial laws which allow a police officer to kill an escaping person suspected of even a minor offence. Maximum respect for human life and property and the minimum use of necessary force should be the guiding principles. At present Section 25 of the *Criminal Code* allows an arresting officer to use as much force as is necessary to prevent the escape of a suspect, unless the escape can be prevented by reasonable means in a less violent manner. There are no limitations on the use of force likely to cause death or serious injury nor any weighing whether the force is proportional to the offence and the dangerousness of the offender.

[†] 6 February 1989. Reprinted with permission of the Law Union of Ontario.

4. The Law Union urges that any prosecutions of police officers be conducted by private lawyers, known for their independence from the police.

The Law Union called for immediate action on these recommendations before more people are killed or seriously injured.

20 YEARS OF POLICE MISCONDUCT

The Late 1960's

Prior to the 1960's, the Toronto police functioned as a basically British, paramilitary police force. The bulk of new recruits were in fact, from British police forces, supplementing poorly educated but very large Anglo Canadian males, many of them veterans of World War II, many of them members of the Orange Lodge.

In the late 1960's this stolid police mind-set ran head on into a rebellious youth movement, anti-war immigrants from the US and non-Anglo immigrants from around the world. The visible flashpoints were beatings of "flower children" in Yorkville and [cavalry] charges against anti-war demonstrators and later in the decade, against Eastern European immigrants opposing the visit of a Soviet official. In all these cases, officers were careful to remove their number badges.

The Early 1970's

The Toronto police had always maintained a "Red" squad and other specialized squads to deal with anyone outside of the police defined "mainstream." Not finding "Reds under every bed," the police focused more and more on other dissident groups such as labour unions (the brutal Artistic Woodworking Strike), leading edge artists (seizing paintings and arresting performers) and radical thinkers (the siege of Rochdale College).

Out on the street, the police began a systematic confrontation of long haired youths, minorities and gays (who were starting to emerge publicly). The police, in effect, had declared war on these groups.

The Late 1970's

The police excesses of the early 1970's turned the latter part of the decade into the "police inquiry" period.

The *Maloney Report* of 1975 recommended setting up a Commissioner of Public Complaints to help curb the tide of police abuse. A year later, the *Morand Report*, investigating newspaper revelations, highlighted several cases of police brutality. It too called for a public complaints process, better supervision and training and better leadership from the Chief of Police. In 1977 the *Robarts Report* recommended that control of the Toronto police be transferred from the Province to Metro Council, to make the police more accountable. Also in 1977 the *Pitman Report* on Racism in Metro, focused on the police as a major problem. It called for cross cultural training, affirmative hiring practices and psychological testing of officers.

What was the police response to all this? Buddy Evans, a Black man, was killed by a police bullet as he allegedly threatened an officer with his own billy club. No charges were laid and a subsequent inquest raised more questions than it answered.

Shortly after the Evans case, Albert Johnson, a Black immigrant was shot to death in his own home. Massive public demonstrations by the Black community drew attention to the case and two officers were charged with manslaughter. (They were subsequently acquitted.)

The decade ended with revelations that the internal Police Association Newsletter regularly published racist, sexist, homophobic and anti-semitic articles and "humour."

The Early 1980's

The community fought back. The racist and bigoted drivel, published by the Police Association, resulted in the formation of a community based *Working Group on Minority Police Relations*. Despite its innocuous label, it aggressively badgered the police administration and raised issues in the media. Within a year it transformed itself into the *Citizens Independent Review of Police Activities* (CIPRA) ... an even fiercer advocate of police reform. The catalyst was the largest police raid in Toronto history. Over 350 officers raided four Gay steambaths, arresting and humiliating 300 people. Within days, 5,000 people marched down Yonge St. and surrounded 52 Division, effectively shutting it down, the same way the black community shut down 31 Division over the Albert Johnson killing. Throughout this period, the Gay community responded with well organized demonstrations every time the police moved on a Gay bar or bath. The protest leaders were targeted for police harassment. They were soon joined by leaders of the Peace Movement who had their phones tapped and mailing lists seized.

Under intense public pressure, the Province established the *Office of the Commissioner of Public Complaints*. The only groups, aside from the Provincial and Metro governments, to support the creation of the new office were the Police Commission and the Police Association. Community organizations viewed it as a worthless window dressing exercise. At the end of its first 3 years, 2009 complaints had been laid with the Commission, of which 76 resulted in disciplinary action, 74 of which were cautions or counselling.

As the community at large challenged police misconduct, so did the criminal bar. A group of lawyers stumbled onto a pattern of allegations from their clients, which would not go away. The allegations were that the Hold Up Squad systematically tortured prisoners to extract confessions. A compilation of cases revealed the use of the same techniques by the same officers, in case after case. The allegations were so widespread and pervasive that Amnesty International called for an inquiry. The resulting publicity forced the police to curb their excesses.

The early 1980's ended with the police adopting a policy of "high profile" policing. This was a euphemism for rousting Black kids in the Regent Park, Alexandra Park and [Jane Finch] neighbourhoods. It was a prelude to the current intensified confrontation.

The Late 1980's

At the beginning of this period, a major re-arming of the police began. First oversized batons were issued to Metro police. This resulted in a dramatic upsurge in incidents where people were beaten by the new toys. The Police Commission publicly threatened to take them away unless the beatings stopped. Undeterred by the baton episode, the police re-equipped themselves with new open, quick draw holsters. Next on the list were assault rifles and Uzi submachine guns. It is worth noting that the first time an Uzi was used in action, an OPP officer accidentally killed another OPP officer. The second time one was used, the OPP blew away the wrong man. The 1980's are the "Power" decade for the police. More power in the holster and under the hood. In one year, 1600 high speed chases left 7 Ontarians dead, 130 injured and $800,000 in property damage. This lack of discipline was mirrored in increases in sexual misconduct and liquor and drug abuse while on duty.

The late 1980's is shaping up as a rerun of the late 1970's. Once again two Black men are killed by the police under questionable circumstances. Once again manslaughter charges are laid in both cases. Again the province establishes a Task Force. Predictably, senior police officials come forward with racist comments. The head of the Police Association goes one step further and suggests that the Black community may be laying itself open for punitive measures. Shortly thereafter Metro and Peel police burst in on a church service and dragged out 5 Black youths who were later determined to not be the suspects being sought. Church officials indicated that while the Peel officers were polite, the Metro officers were rough and verbally abusive.

The 1990's?

To prevent a rerun of the 1980's, the community will have to intensify the pressure for police reform. Politicians at all levels of government must show courage in standing up to the police establishment and putting it firmly under civilian control.

■

A number of police shootings of African-Canadian men and women in Ontario have provoked calls for civilian review and for the laying of criminal charges:

ALBERT JOHNSON: Shot and killed by police on 26 August 1979. In *Johnson v. Adamson* (1982), 34 O.R. (2d) 236 (C.A.), the family of Albert Johnson was successful at the interim stage of a tort suit against the Metro Board of Commissioners of Police and its Chief for, among other things, failing "to take reasonable steps to deal with racism in 14 Division," failing "to take reasonable steps to investigate the complaints by Albert Johnson of police harassment," and failing "to take reasonable steps to train constables regarding non-violent arrest and first aid." What are the advantages and disadvantages of resorting to the tort system instead of the criminal law?

Officers Inglis and Cargnelli were acquitted on charges of involuntary manslaughter: H.J. Glasbeek, "A Report on Attorney-General's Files, Prosecutions and Coroners' Inquests Arising out of Police Shootings in Ontario" (Toronto, 1993), [unpublished] Johnson case analysis at 21 [hereinafter *Police Shootings*]. A third officer, Dicks, was not charged: *ibid.* at 22. The decision not to charge the officers with second-degree murder, as originally contemplated, made it virtually impossible to examine the issue of racism in the shooting during the criminal prosecution, since manslaughter is not an intentional crime, and the rules of evidence therefore exclude as irrelevant evidence of racist motivation or intention: *ibid*. at 11.

LESTER DONALDSON: Shot and injured by police, Toronto, April 1988; shot and killed by Metro Police Constable Deviney, Toronto, 9 August 1988. See Timothy Appleby, "Brutality charges: History repeats itself in York shooting for victim, police officer, even street" *The [Toronto] Globe and Mail* (13 August 1988) A1, A2; Timothy Appleby, "Police officer charged with manslaughter in Toronto shooting" *The [Toronto] Globe and Mail* (12 January 1989) A4; Timothy Appleby, Donn Downey, and Deborah Wilson, "Police protest against manslaughter charge" *The [Toronto] Globe and Mail* (13 January 1989) A1, A14; and *R. v. Deviney* (1990), 1 O.R. (3d) 69 (Ct. Just. (Gen. Div.)) (unsuccessful attempt to argue that his prosecution was "selective" and, therefore, an abuse of process). Officer Deviney was acquitted by a jury of the manslaughter charges on 13 November 1990: CP, "Policeman cleared in fatal shooting" *The Ottawa Citizen* (14 November 1990) A5.

In August 1992, an inquest into Mr. Donaldson's killing commenced. The coroner denied standing to both the Black Action Defence Committee and the Urban Alliance on Race Relations for Metropolitan Toronto to participate in the inquest on the basis that there was no evidence that "race" played a part in Mr. Donaldson's death. This ruling was affirmed in *Re Black Action Defence Committee and Huxter, Coroner*; *Re Urban Alliance on Race Relations for Metropolitan Toronto (Justice) and Huxter* (1993), (1992), 11 O.R. (3d) 641 (Ct. Just. (Gen. Div.)), although the court did decide to grant standing to the Alliance to testify as to appropriate cross-cultural training as it relates to dealing with the mentally ill. After several more legal challenges to the scope of the inquest (e.g. *Re Booth et al. and Huxter* (1994), 16 O.R. (3d) 528 (Ct. Just. (Gen. Div.))), the inquest concluded and 85 recommendations were made in 1994.

EARL EDWARDS: Shot by Ontario Provincial Police (OPP) Constable Amo Giek, Ottawa, 18 November 1988. See Warren Kinsella, Mohammed Adam, and John Kessel, "Solicitor General orders probe of police shooting" *The Ottawa Citizen* (19 November 1988) A22; Spectrum, "Following November shooting: Civil suit filed vs. OPP" *The [Ottawa] Spectrum* (15 April 1989) 1.

WADE LAWSON: Shot and killed by plainclothes Peel Regional police Constables Darren Longpre and Anthony Melaragni, Mississauga, 8 December 1988. See CP, "Police cite self-defence in killing of youth, 17" *The [Toronto] Globe and Mail* (10 December 1988) A10; Lesley Simpson, "Police version of youth's death called cover-up by his friends" *The [Toronto] Globe and Mail* (26 December 1988) A18.

In early January 1989, charges were laid against the officers. Judge Draper, who presided over the preliminary inquest and the actual trial of Constables Longpre and Melaragni, ordered that the charge be upped from manslaughter to murder (*Police Shootings*, *supra*, Lawson case analysis at 12 and 13). This decision was appealed to the Ontario Court of Appeal, which denied the appeal. Leave was then sought, but denied, to appeal to the Supreme Court: *ibid.* A civil action was commenced by the estate of Wade Lawson and his family for damages arising from his death: Paul Copeland, "Wade Lawson: A Litigation Update" *Law Union News* (Fall 1990) 8.

After several reported decisions regarding questions of law in the prosecution of the two officers (see *R. v. Melaragni* (1992), 76 C.C.C. (3d) 78 (Ont. Ct. Just. (Gen. Div.)); *R. v. Melaragni* (1992), 75 C.C.C. (3d) 546 (Ont. Ct. Just. (Gen. Div.)), they were acquitted by an all-white jury of all charges: Farrell Crook, "Officers cleared in fatal shooting of teenager in car" *The Toronto Star* (9 April 1992) A1, A32. In spite of protest rallies and demonstrations against the acquittal, the AG decided not to appeal the verdict: Martin Mittelstaedt and Lila Sarick, "Lawson verdict won't be appealed, Hampton says" *The [Toronto] Globe and Mail* (9 May 1992) A1, A2.

SOPHIA COOK: Shot and rendered paralyzed by Metro Toronto Constable Cameron Durham in October 1989 while sitting in a car: Timothy Appleby, "Woman shot by police paralyzed, lawyer says" *The [Toronto] Globe and Mail* (3 October 1989) A9. The constable was charged with the offence of careless use of a firearm; his lawyer argued successfully for a stay of proceedings based on an argument that the *Criminal Code* section was unconstitutional under s. 7 of the *Charter*: *R. v. Durham* (1991), 66 C.C.C. (3d) 66 (Ont. Ct. Just. (Gen. Div.)), rev'd (1992), 10 O.R. (3d) 596 (C.A.).

MARLON NEIL: Shot by Metro Toronto Constable Brian Rapson, Scarborough, 14 May 1990. See: Mike Trickey, "Toronto officer charged with attempted murder: Probe reveals black teenager was shot twice" *The Ottawa Citizen* (2 June 1990)

A4. Brian Rapson was discharged at the preliminary inquiry with respect to the attempted murder charge, and the AG then preferred an indictment against him: Lisa Priest, "Ontario reinstates murder-bid charge against constable" *The Toronto Star* (7 May 1991) A1. Rapson was subsequently acquitted by a jury: *Police Shootings*, supra, Neil case analysis.

VINCENT GARDNER: Shot by Nepean Constable John Monette, Ottawa, 26 September 1991: Jochen Kessel, "Condition of police-shooting victim deteriorating, lawyer says" *The Ottawa Citizen* (24 October 1991) C6. Gardner died seven weeks later.

The police had been executing a major drug raid on the home where Gardner was shot, believing it to be a trafficking centre, based partly on the fact that African-Canadian men ("Rastafarians") frequented the home. In fact, the home was being used for rehearsals by a Reggae band. Only a minuscule quantity of marijuana (half a gram) was found in the house, on the person of Guntley Lewis. However, even this charge (of simple possession) was thrown out by Judge Dianne Nicholas, who ruled that the police acted on incomplete information in carrying out the raid, and that they committed serious and flagrant breaches of the *Charter* rights of the 13 men on the premises: *R. v. Lewis*, [1992] O.J. No. 2971 (Ct. Just. (Prov. Div.)), online: QL.

In July 1992, the province concluded a seven-month investigation into the killing of Mr. Gardner. Without making the findings public, Constable John Monette was charged with manslaughter, criminal negligence causing death, and aggravated assault. In late 1993, Monette was acquitted by the jury of all charges. For a description and analysis of the trial, see *Police Shootings*, supra, Gardner case analysis.

Ottawa police chief Flanagan decided that no disciplinary charges were necessary with respect to the four officers involved in the "raid," but also asked Glenda Simms, president of the Canadian Advisory Council on the Status of Women, to head a civilian review of procedures. In her report, *Beyond Fear* (Ottawa: Prepared for the Ottawa Police Services, 1993) [unpublished], Simms concluded that "racist relationships" influenced the police actions; thereafter, disciplinary charges were laid against three of the officers. The decision to hold a disciplinary hearing by the Police Services Board was appealed by the officers: Staff, "Officers appeal decision to hold disciplinary hearing" *The Ottawa Citizen* (21 May 1994) A2.

The Gardner family filed complaints against the officers with the Public Complaints Commission. Those hearings commenced in 1994. It considered as well the complaint that Police Chief Wayne Phillips of the Nepean Police seconded Staff Sgt. Murray Gordon to help Constable John Monette's defence team at a cost of $49,209 to taxpayers. In its report released in July 1994, the Board criticized the Chief's actions and recommended provincial guidelines to prohibit secondment in these circumstances: Peter Hum and Carolyn Abraham, "Board blasts Nepean's police chief" *The Ottawa Citizen* (26 July 1994) A1, A2.

It was later revealed, in a Grievance Settlement Board hearing, that the investigator from the Ontario Police Complaints Commissioner's office, Archie Hurge, was pulled from the Gardner investigation "because he was a 'loose cannon' who could no longer be controlled," the Commission's lawyer stated. Hurge's lawyer alleged that Hurge was hired as a "safe black" before he was yanked from the investigation: Charles Rusnell, "Investigator hired as a 'safe black' lawyer tells hearing" *The Ottawa Citizen* (9 November 1994) B8.

The family of Vincent Gardner finally settled tort claims against the police for the wrongful death of Vincent Gardner. They will receive $100,000, a $10,000 scholarship in Vincent Gardner's name, and $45,000 in legal fees. In return the police were not obliged to admit liability and the disciplinary hearings against the officers involved were suspended: CP, "Ottawa regional police pay $170,000 for shooting" *The [Montreal] Gazette* (11 July 1995) A9. The family had little alternative to negotiating a settlement, since they had been denied fully funded legal representation. See infra, **Right to Counsel**.

ROYAN BAGNAUT: Shot and injured by Toronto Police, 3 November 1991: *Report on Systemic Racism* at 378. Constable Douglas Lines was charged with unlawful discharge of a firearm, intent to wound, and careless use of a firearm. The Crown in *R. v. Lines*, [1993] O.J. No. 3284 (Ct. Just. (Gen. Div.)), online: QL, was successful in having the "fleeing felon rule," s. 25(4) of the *Criminal Code*, struck down under the *Charter*). See infra, **Policing the Police: Legal Responses**.

JONATHAN HOWELL: Shot, sustaining brain injury, by Toronto Police, 9 November 1991. After a three-day preliminary inquiry, a Toronto judge ruled that Detective Constable Carl Sokolowski was to stand trial on charges of careless use of a firearm: "Police officer to stand trial in death of black youth"

The Ottawa Citizen (13 September 1992) A6. Sokolowski was subsequently found guilty of careless use of a firearm: "Toronto police officer convicted in shooting" *The Ottawa Citizen* (11 July 1994) A3; *R. v. Sokolowski*, [1994] O.J. No. 728 (Ct. Just. (Gen. Div.)), aff'd [1995] O.J. No. 3737 (C.A.), online: QL.

RAYMOND LAWRENCE: Shot and killed by Metro Toronto Police Constable Robert Rice, 2 May 1992: Scott Feschuk and James MacGowan, "Blacks urge chief to resign" *The [Toronto] Globe and Mail* (4 May 1992) A1, A11. The Special Investigations Unit (SIU) investigation of the shooting, which exonerated Constable Rice, was "slipshod at best," and relied too heavily upon the Metro Police Force's own investigation: *Police Shootings*, supra, Lawrence case analysis at 29–33. The coroner's inquest determined that "race" was not a factor in the Lawrence shooting: see Gay Abbate, "Race not a factor in police shooting, jury concludes at Lawrence inquest" *The [Toronto] Globe and Mail* (6 November 1993) A16; but see *Police Shootings*, supra, Lawrence case analysis at 11–13, 33–34 and 37–39.

IAN COLEY: Shot and killed in Toronto area by police on 20 April 1993. Coley reportedly shot at the officers while being chased after being stopped by the officers in a car believed to be stolen: "Gun found near where police killed black man" *The Ottawa Citizen* (21 April 1993) A3; Gay Abbate, "SIU finds officer justified in fatal shooting" *The [Toronto] Globe and Mail* (9 July 1994) A8. No charges were laid, and a coroner's inquest recommended that the term "non-white" be eliminated from police jargon, since "some officers use the term 'non-white' in a manner that can be misconstrued as offensive": Philip Mascoll, "Son's death forgotten by jurors, mom says" *The [Toronto] Globe and Mail* (19 August 1995) A4.

ALBERT MOSES: Shot and killed by police in Toronto on 29 September 1994. Five months after the shooting the Special Investigations Unit (SIU) investigation was still stalled because Constable Jeffrey Vance, the officer who shot Albert Moses, refused to speak to the SIU Constable Vance's refusal meant that a coroner's inquest could not be called because the SIU investigation could not be closed, and Albert Moses' family could not make a determination as to whether or not to launch civil proceedings because of inadequate information: Rosie DiManno, "Officer's silence stalls case" *The Toronto Star* (5 March 1995) A6. Despite provincial legislation that prohibits the police force from conducting an investigation parallel to the SIU, when the SIU showed up to interview officers who were outside Albert Moses' room at the time of the shooting, they were already being interviewed by Metro Toronto Homicide officers: *ibid.*

WAYNE WILLIAMS: Shot and killed by Constables Kenneth Harrison and Gordon Hayford, 11 June 1996. The constables refused to speak to the SIU, but did so five weeks after the shooting once the parents of Williams initiated an action in the General Division Court of Ontario to compel them to do so. The parents have also commenced a $1-million civil suit. See Ijeoma Ross, "Slain man's parents want police to talk" *The [Toronto] Globe and Mail* (18 July 1996) A7A; Phinjo Gombu, "2 officers in shooting talk to SIU" *The Toronto Star* (20 July 1996) A5.

Other African-Canadians have been shot by police in Ontario since 1996. For example, Hugh Dawson was shot six times and killed by Toronto police in spring 1997 while allegedly trying to disarm an officer during a drug bust. Apparently the officers refused to co-operate with the SIU: Gabriella Pedicelli, *When Police Kill. Police Use of Force in Montreal and Toronto* (Montréal: Véhicule Press, 1998) at 130.

Aboriginal spokespersons, such as Marlene Pierre, have also criticized police racism in Ontario and suggested that there are two kinds of justice, "one for the white man and one for us." See CP, "Police racism review: Natives blast justice system" *The Ottawa Citizen* (18 February 1989) A16.

STANLEY SHINGEBIS: Beaten by OPP officer, Thunder Bay, March 1987. Stanley Shingebis was beaten when he was arrested for public drunkenness, a charge for which he was subsequently acquitted. He was left a quadriplegic as a result of the beating.

EUGENE MIGWANS: Removed from hospital by OPP and taken into custody where he died, Manitoulin Island, 5 August 1990. See Don Umpherson, "Ojibway taken from hospital died in cell" *The Toronto Star* (22 February 1991) A12.

VINCENT WASSIGIJIK: Died in a holding cell of OPP, Little Current, July 1989. See Special, "Police handling of intoxicated probed" *The [Toronto] Globe and Mail* (20 February 1990) A10.

DUDLEY GEORGE: Shot and killed in September 1995, when the OPP sent a heavily armed tactical squad of more than 250 officers into Ipperwash

Provincial Park in response to occupation of the park by Chippewa protestors. See *R. v. Deane*, *infra*; see also discussion *supra*, **Colonization and the Imposition of Criminal Law**.

In other cases, police have failed to respond adequately to a victim's needs. The charge has been made that they have responded differently based on the race of the victim.

MINNIE SUTHERLAND: Hull/Ottawa, January 1989. In a tragic case in Hull, both Hull and Ottawa police who were called to the scene of an accident assumed that Minnie Sutherland, a Cree woman, was simply drunk and not in need of medical attention. When she was finally taken to the hospital (after first being taken to a detoxification centre) doctors were not told she had been hit by a car. She died 10 days later as a result of a skull fracture. See Kim Goggins, "Racism questioned in Sutherland case" *The [Ottawa] Centretown News* (2 February 1989) 4; Katherine Scott, "Witness, police accounts differ" *The [Ottawa] Centretown News* (2 February 1989) 4; Lori Kennedy, "Sutherland worked with underprivileged" *The [Ottawa] Centretown News* (2 February 1989) 5; Gregory Ip, "Nurses aiding woman ordered to move car, coroner's inquest told" *The [Toronto] Globe and Mail* (23 February 1989) A10; Mike Blanchfield, "Police ignored pleas for ambulance, inquest told" *The Ottawa Citizen* (24 February 1989) A1; Gregory Ip, "Procedure not followed with victim of accident, constable tells inquest" *The [Toronto] Globe and Mail* (28 February 1989) A18; Julia Bennett, "Call for police sensitivity course not enough, native groups warn" *The [Toronto] Globe and Mail* (3 March 1989) A13; George Kalogerakis, "Family of native woman launches suit against Hull" *The Ottawa Citizen* (29 June 1990) C3.

MAY NOOTCHTAI: Toronto, October 1988. See Rudy Platiel, "Probe into native justice sought at demonstration for slain Indian" *The [Toronto] Globe and Mail* (15 February 1989) A5.

For additional examples, see also: Timothy Appleby, "Natives' stories of police abuse shock race panel" *The [Toronto] Globe and Mail* (20 February 1989) A1.

The Ontario government appointed a commission of inquiry into racism and the criminal justice system in October 1992 in response to the concerns raised about the police killings noted above. The Commission had a very broad mandate, and was to inquire into matters such as "the extent to which the exercise of discretion, at important decision-making points in the criminal justice system, has an adverse impact on racial minorities" and "how the criminal justice system should respond to future charges of criminal conduct against justice system officials and personnel involving racial minority victims." Its report, *Report on Systemic Racism*, *supra*, examined many issues that have already been canvassed in prior chapters.

One of the issues addressed by the report was the legal treatment of police killings of African-Canadian men in Ontario. The Commission employed Harry Glasbeek to analyze the police files for eight of the men (Evans, Johnson, Neil, Lawson, Donaldson, Savoury, Lawrence, and Gardener) and to determine whether racism was responsible for the outcomes. Portions of the introduction to his report, *Police Shootings*, *supra*, are reproduced below.

A Report on Attorney-General's Files, Prosecutions and Coroners' Inquests Arising Out of Police Shootings in Ontario to the Commission on Systemic Racism in Ontario Criminal Justice System, 1993[†]

The Problematic: If a police officer shoots a black person, supposedly when acting in the line of duty, and such a police officer is convicted of a serious crime, this does not prove that she acted in a racist way unless the nature of the charge, and the evidence adduced in support of it, permits this conclusion. This will rarely, if ever, be the case. Such a conviction will also, therefore, not prove that the

---

[†] By H.J. Glasbeek, Toronto, 1993, [unpublished] at 8–14, 17–24, 29–30, 35–37. Notes omitted. Reproduced by permission of the author.

police force and/or the method of policing was racist. Similarly, if such a police officer is acquitted, it will not prove that the police officer's conduct was not racist, nor that the police force and/or its operation was not racist. Conversely, an acquittal will not prove that other components of the criminal justice system — jurors, judges, prosecutors — behaved in a racist manner.

To determine the weight of the allegation of racism in the criminal justice system when the issue is raised by police shootings and the way in which the shooters are dealt with by the system, it is therefore necessary to assess the concrete conduct of the functionaries and the institutions in each of the separate components of the criminal justice system. This is what I did on the basis of the files of police shootings made available to me through the offices of the Attorney-General.

My task, then, was to go through the dossiers to determine whether or not the internal deliberations and the way in which decisions were reached, as well as the decisions themselves, were racist in any way. Here I must draw attention to a problem which arose out of this mode of analysis.

While the various component parts of the criminal justice system work together to form an integrated whole, each of these parts is given specific goals to achieve. The functionaries of each such component part, therefore, necessarily keep themselves at some arm's length from their counterparts in other segments of the system. There are, of course, large overlaps in their functions and daily activities. For example, at the political level the ministers responsible belong to the party in government and are cabinet colleagues. Necessarily, there also is a good deal of co-ordination and symbiosis between the various component parts. For example, the state prosecutorial offices (the Attorney-General's department) and the police work together on a daily basis; similarly, but more attenuatedly, the coroner's office works closely with the Attorney-General's office and with the police. Yet, the compartmentalization of functions and goals is real. A complex framework emerges.

Each component, in large part to justify and legitimate its actions, has developed standard operating procedures to attain its specific goals. Each component's decisions eventually are to meld with those made by the other component parts of the system in order to attain the overall objective of this combined decision-making. This imposes a specialized discipline of decision-making on the functionaries of each component; in particular, this compartmentalization means that the discretion necessary to carry out the specific tasks given to a component's functionaries is boundarized by the limited goals of each of the particular components of the criminal justice system. It is this which reinforces the notion that the functionaries have the kind of autonomy which gives their particular segment of the criminal justice system a relatively independent role to play within it, one which does not have to be subjugated to the needs or the scrutiny of any of the other component parts. This fragmented, structured approach to decision-making makes systemic racism in the criminal justice system, if it exists, very hard to prove.

Findings: The described structure mandated the way in which I had to conduct the study. The deliberations and decisions made had to be assessed from within the setting of differently operating logics. Given the bureaucratic standardization of the exercise of discretion over time, it was to be expected that such of the deliberations and decisions which might be characterized as racist because of their **ultimately** unfavourable impact on racially different groups and interests, would be justifiable by reference to rational and professional criteria which made sense when viewed from the perspective of the internal operation of a particular component. Indeed, for the most part, this is what the analyses of the ways in which decisions to lay charges and the way in which prosecutions were conducted in the cases I examined tended to show. But, this does not lead to the satisfactory conclusion that the criminal justice system is not racist in nature.

The whole is not just the sum of its parts. The final impact of a large number of discrete, internally justifiable, decisions may be that the end result is one which is different in character to each, or to some, of the separate decisions which combined to make-up the final one. I believe that this is what happens in the operation of the criminal justice system: for the most part, the individual, independent decisions can be defended rationally, yet the outcomes of the criminal justice system may be racist in effect.

The analyses of the files I read do raise serious concerns about the way in which the system operates. In particular:

(a) The criminal justice system, particularly the criminal **trial's** processes, is systemically biased against permitting attempts to uncover socially constructed discrimination on the basis of race.
(b) Some of the rules governing criminal law and the **trial** system favour the police officers when they are accused to such an extent that

their racially different victims begin to look as if they are on trial.

(c) Inasmuch as there is systemic racism in our polity, the criminal **trial** processes perpetuate this by making it difficult to confront the issue, even when the race of the victim plays a crucial, if unarticulated, role in the trial.

(d) The impact of the criminal **trial** may be racist as a result of (b) and (c) even though no overtly racist practices are condoned by the process.

(e) The **coroner's** inquest potentially is more open to have the issue of systemic racism addressed, but its functionaries have shown themselves very unwilling to do so. This reinforces the notion that there is a residual establishment view that the criminal justice system and its associated institutions should not be used to this end. The backlash has created positive pressures for a changed approach to inquests.

(f) The criminal justice system, as presently constituted, may not be the cause of whatever systemic racism does exist. Certainly, it is not the conscious desire of the various criminal justice institutions and functionaries to promote racism. But, **the criminal justice system may have the problem of socially constructed racism, inasmuch as it exists, built into its core. It cannot be counted on, therefore, to solve such a problem by tinkering with it, by internally reforming it. For the criminal justice system to be part of the solution it will require radical restructuring.**

A Request: These overall findings are derived from my interpretation of the analyses of each of the files I read. What needs to be remembered is that I read each dossier to determine whether or not the decisions to lay charges, how to prosecute and/or to run a trial or a coroner's inquest, could be said to have racist overtones. That is, I looked at each of the components' behaviour from within their own sets of norms and practices. Then, at the end, I looked to see whether, from an external perspective, the effects of all these decisions might be said to be racist.

The bulk of this study, therefore, presents the analysis of each file as I read it. As the period in which these episodes occurred is relatively short, the cases are quite similar in their essentials and as the options (nature of charges available, possible fora — trial, coroner's inquest) also are limited, there is some apparent repetition. It is that contextualized repetition which, in large part, substantiates my conclusion that there is a pattern which allows the argument to be made that the effect of the normal operation of the criminal justice system is to hide the issue of racism and, thereby, to perpetuate it, or worse. The strength of my conclusion, then, rests heavily on the analysis of each of the dossiers and the final threading together of the separate interpretations.

The next section of this introduction sets out some of the more salient, specific findings I made. Nonetheless, I ask that this summary be treated as skeletal only and that each separate dossier's analysis be read to see the context in which the findings were made: the credibility of the arguments I offer rests on the detailed analysis....

Summary of Some Specific Findings and Arguments

(i) The establishment of the criminal justice system, as well as the political elites, including the media, start off from the assumption that the criminal justice system, governed as it is by the Rule of Law, administered by responsible career professionals — Crown lawyers, judges, coroners — and the time-honoured jury system, is a neutral system. Equality before, according to and under the law, are considered the norm. Law is assumed not to be racist. People are. The shooting of a black person by a police officer acting in the line of duty is viewed from this perspective by the powers-that-be.

. . . .

(v) Of all the functionaries in the criminal justice system, the members of the judiciary are the least responsive to arguments that they should be seen to bend over to avoid allegations of apprehension of bias in the system. The judges — in part because of their prestige, in part because they are furthest removed from the daily political pressures, in part because their own success as professionals in the legal system is due to their belief in, and adherence to, its claims of neutrality — show their faith in all aspects of the criminal justice system, from policing to the probity of the Crown and the coroners' decisions, even if this means that they have to marginalize the claims of victims and minorities. This is shown in their charges to the juries, their rulings on evidence, their legal approach to claims that bias was shown by the Crown or by a coroner. Characteristically, they ward-off any possible claims that they — the judges — may be biassed by telling jurors that the judges' personal opinions (while based on long experience) may be ignored by them and by dealing with legal claims of bias in legal institutions by splintering such claims into discrete isolated items, ignoring the possibility that the total effect may demonstrate bias, even if the individual decisions which made up the whole are justifiable.

(vi) There also has been something of a learning curve in respect of the dangers to the status quo which inhere in the criminal prosecution of a police officer involved in a shooting. Whereas the police, for obvious reasons, are opposed to such prosecutions, from the overall political perspective, and more importantly from the vantage point of the Attorney-General, it is gradually becoming clear that criminal prosecutions, in and of themselves, do not open up the question of systemic racist police violence to public scrutiny. Nor are they likely to lead to many convictions. The criminal trial of a police officer does not endanger the system very much. More dangerous are the political events before and after the trial. Indeed, the nature of the stratagem of those who seek to prove racism in the criminal justice system by exerting pressure to have police officers convicted of serious criminal charges is such that they are likely to be able to get more mileage out of an acquittal than out of a conviction.[1] In sum, this kind of politics, **legalized politics**, has built-in contradictions.

(vii) A vigorous prosecution and a well-run trial enhance the political standing of those who claim that there is a working Rule of Law which eschews racism and that arm's length investigations and professional prosecutions are its faithful servants. The reasons that there is little opportunity to address racism in a criminal trial or that a conviction of a police officer of a charge arising out of a shooting in the line of duty will be a rarity, stem from the operation of this self-same Rule of Law which frowns on racism. In particular:

(a) It is our legal-political view that the liberty of the individual to act freely as she wishes must be left as unconstrained as possible by the state. Any substantive or procedural law which constrains such liberty should be read as narrowly as possible. Most importantly, when a person is alleged to have violated one of these constraints, she is presumed innocent until proven guilty.

(b) The burden of proof on the Crown to show wrongful intent — which is what those who allege racism want to prove — is very heavy.

(c) The criminal trial begins by treating the police officer-victim confrontation as it does any encounter between two individuals. The fact that one was white, the other black, one a member of the power structure, the other one of its objects, is ignored. This has untoward effects.

It has become conventional wisdom that it is better for the Crown and trial judges to be soft, rather than harsh, on the accused. The understanding is that the state has massive coercive powers which ought to be exercised with restraint. But, where the accused is a centrally placed state agent, as a police officer is, treating the police officer as just another accused, with all the privileges of an accused and entitled to all the give there is in the system, results are likely to be distorting.

(d) Because the accused police officer will claim that s/he was executing her duty and/or a moment of crisis created danger when the shooting took place, the normal justifications and defences available to accused persons are given more scope than they usually are. Further, while some of the provisions of the Criminal Code which provide these defences are notionally available to all citizens, they have more application in police violence cases than in any other. The legal justifications for police violence are cast in elliptical language. Over time, this language has been given increasingly police-protecting readings by the judiciary. Trial judges have a good deal of discretion when reading the law. While this discretion may yield different interpretations on a case-by-case basis, from a police officer-as-accused perspective, the general thrust has been to broaden the scope of the defences available to police officers.

(e) The rules relied upon by the police-as-accused to attack a victim's character are directly related to the rules of relevance and credibility which, in the run-of-the-mill case, are used by the Crown to obtain convictions. When police officers are accused, this sword of the Crown may become a shield for the defence. Rules such as the character evidence rule have an unusual effect when conviction-free police officers are accused of having committed a crime against a person with a bad record: the accused police officer obtains an advantage. This is not the product of the intrinsic unfairness of the rules or their biassed application. It is, rather, an indication of the dubious utility of the ordinary criminal process as a means by which to discipline deviant police officers: the ordinary application of otherwise acceptable rules will nearly always have a police-favouring effect. If the victim is a member of a racial minority community, there will be a racist effect, as the race of the victim is likely to help "taint" his character and behaviour. This pro-police officer racist effect will be exacerbated if the jurors are non-representative, that is, if for instance they are all-white and the victim was a black (particularly a black young male) bad actor.

(f) There is no obvious way in which alleged racist biasses in the policing system can be made legal and/or evidentiary issue in the criminal trial process, except by allegations that they are related directly to the role a particular accused's bias may have played in her/his alleged wrongdoing. This is a most unlikely possibility. If the victim belongs to a racial minority, her/his very appearance — especially if s/he has a tainted past — may raise the issue of race subliminally. It then may have the opposite effect, that is, it may cause decision-makers with (consciously or sub-consciously held) racist views to support a police officer who may have acted within a systematically racist set of parameters.

(g) Judges are used to seeing the police officers as accusers and, therefore, more credible witnesses than the accused.

(h) In these kinds of cases the Crown frequently has to rely on police officers as witnesses. They were the ones on the scene; they were the ones who conducted most of the investigation. They are likely to be very sympathetic to their accused comrade. The Crown will find it instinctively difficult, and strategically awkward, to try and treat these witnesses as possibly adverse to its own case, thereby weakening its case in an unusual way.

(i) When police officers are accused, they have access to vast resources. They are supported by their unions, a police association. Very well-known lawyers will be hired. Their prestige cannot help but have a positive impact on the trial judge. The defence may — not improperly — find it a little easier to present its theory favourably and to have its views on the admissibility of evidence treated sympathetically. Politically more significant is the fact that the police association's need to have a trial focus on the narrow issue of guilt or innocence is on all-fours with the accused's objectives. Moreover, this coincides with the goals of the police forces' governing bodies, that is, with the view of the police officers' employers. In short, when a criminal trial is sought to be used to bring out the racism of police officers and/or the systemic racism of policing, the logic of the adversary system works towards the avoidance of the canvassing of these issues, notionally because such a widening of the process is unfair to the accused. This potential unfairness is what the fine defence lawyers provided to the accuseds stress as they argue, on the one hand, for precise charges and, on the other, greater than normal latitude to damn the character of the victim. This suits the politics of all those who want to limit any inquiry into **systemic** racism.

(j) Those who want the trial to address the question of racism have to rely on the state's institutions. For these activist groups to participate in the process for these purposes it is incumbent on them to accept the starting premise that the system's legal functionaries are professional neutrals. But, this presents them with problems.

First, the best way for professional lawyers to live up to their own ideals is to avoid asking themselves, and to prevent others within the system from asking, questions about systemic biasses in the policing system, about the appropriateness of the law's definitions of offences and defences and, most importantly, about the possibility that discrimination might result by treating different kinds of witnesses and accused persons as if they were endowed with the same legally significant attributes and standing. By eschewing any conscious consideration of these questions, these legal professionals can hang on to their belief that the criminal justice system — based on the Rule of Law — will operate fairly and neutrally.

Thus, those who wish to use the criminal justice process to expose socially constructed racism have to rely on professionals whose very raison d'être demands that they discard the possibility of its existence and/or its influence on the criminal justice system's rules and operations. Unlike the police, the minority communities' views, then, are not congruent with those who carry their flags in the criminal trial system. It is only in the coroner's inquest situation that they have the potential to have their case presented in full — by themselves.

Second, because political activists around racial issues need to rely on the professionals in the system and on the probity of the system to validate their claims, their questioning of the system's operations may be characterized as extremist, dangerously radical and trouble-fomenting behaviour. Their political agenda may be harmed: appealing to the system while contemporaneously denouncing it gives their political work a sense of incoherence. Again, the lack of congruence of goals between those whose job it is to prosecute police officers and those groups which want to prove embedded racism by means of such prosecutions, is brought out.

. . . .

Inasmuch as the question is whether or not systemic racism inheres in the criminal justice system, it may be the wrong question. The criminal justice system exists to protect the status quo. That status quo supposedly rests on a shared consensus in respect of political, economic, social and moral goals. People who do not respect that status quo may have to be re-educated or removed. It is the police's function (true to the police's history as a para-military force) to uphold the consensus.

The police finds that it has been allocated the task of policing a consensus in communities where it is not so obviously shared. A transliteration occurs: the maintenance of order is seen to be an appropriate discharge of the policing function, as order notionally reflects the shared consensus. It is in this context that the police sees itself as the thin blue line which defends the status quo from the guerilla war (or worse) being fought by those who apparently reject the tenets of a freely chosen social contract. A culture of solidarity, of brothers (and a few sisters)-in-arms is developed to wage this war. The hierarchical, army type organization of police forces, their loyalty one to another (their predisposition to lie on each other's behalf is well-documented in criminological scholarship) all reinforce the idea that the police are the thin blue line which stands between chaos and order as our fragile and precious-supposed-consensus comes under attack. Indeed, the need for the police to bend soft-on-crime civil libertarian rules becomes acceptable, certainly to the police (known as the Dirty Harry syndrome in contemporary criminological work). All of this is fed by the moral panics created by opportunistic politicians, sensationalizing media and special interest groups. Thus it is no accident that governments declare "wars" on prostitution, drugs, etc. The police's prestige is enhanced by the pressing need to wage these "wars."

. . . .

Radical restructuring is impossible without changes in the existing power/class relations. Yet, it should be possible to explore the use of the existing ideological constructs to ask for changes which are more than reform of the existing institutions which maintain the same goals. Again, I am mindful of the fact that it is not my brief to offer these kinds of proposals. I do so only to the extent that the analyses of the incidents and events which I looked at — and which follow immediately — suggest at least one useful avenue of attack.

My findings show that investigations, prosecutions and judging are likely to be done with probity (especially if some internal reforms are instituted), yet without addressing fundamental issues. That is, efforts at changing facets of these activities will yield limited benefits. It may be worthwhile, therefore, to address the front-line activities which give rise to the unaddressed issues: policing. The idea would be to democratize policing.

Community-based controls would be a way in which the questions of what kinds of disorder ought to be the focus of repressive attention as well as the level of repression they warrant being used, might be addressed from a different perspective than they are now. But I do not want to overstate the potential of this approach. My own analysis of the files I read suggests that dominant groups — including the police hierarchy — might find it very easy to co-opt any community-based-input into the governance of the police, thus merely providing continued legitimacy for the status quo. Indeed, given existing power/class relations this is the most likely outcome of this stratagem....

The point is a simple one: the analyses which follow indicate that the criminal justice system's components other than the police, operating with propriety, according to their own rules, administered with integrity and honesty by committed and loyal professionals, support what turns out to be the unequal, repressive treatment of poorer and racially different people by the police. This is likely to continue if the police are merely re-educated and sensitized, as opposed to being given a new direction and sets of mandates. The task is enormous: growing inequality inevitably leads to more evidence of disorder, to more street crime committed by the powerless/property-less/ethnically different, and, therefore, to more calls for tougher police action. The Commission faces daunting problems.

---

[1] Although this remains to be proved: there was no conviction in any of the cases which I had to read.

Based on Glasbeek's analysis of the eight files, the Commissioners made a number of recommendations with respect to the SIU, discussed *infra* under **Policing the Police: Legal Responses**, and recommended changes to the coroner's inquest process. They also concluded that the police practice of releasing selective information to the media regarding police killings of African-Canadian men reinforces negative stereotypes of African-Canadians, fuels debates and distrust, and "casts doubt on the system's ability to scrutinize police conduct objectively and to address community concerns that police engage in racist violence" (at 380).

Consider the related role of the media in reporting the response of the African-Canadian community to the numerous acquittals of police charged with the shooting of African-Canadian men. See, for example, Banu Helvacioglu, "Wild in the Streets?" *This Magazine* (July–August 1992) 5 (analysis of the media coverage of the so-called Toronto "rampage" after the L.A. riots and the announcement of the jury acquittal of the Metro officers who shot and killed Wade Lawson in May 1992). As Dionne Brand commented with respect to columnist Michael Valpy's statement in *The [Toronto] Globe and Mail* on 4 May 1993 to the effect that "we" will never know what set off the "rampage": "He failed to notice ten years without a single conviction of a police officer ... [and] the image on national television of the white officer acquitted in the Lester Donaldson killing, a victory cigar in his mouth, triumph over and disdain for Black people on his face, smiling for the cameras."

In September 1997, Dudley George became the only Aboriginal person killed in a land claims dispute by a Canadian police officer in the twentieth century: Peter Edwards, *One Dead Indian. The Premier, the Police, and the Ipperwash Crisis* (Toronto: Stoddart Publishing, 2001) at 16. The officer who shot him, Kenneth Deane, himself became one of the first police to be convicted of homicide committed against a racialized person in the line of duty. Edwards' book (at 256) describes the history behind the land claim at Camp Ipperwash and the marshalling of enormous police resources in response to the occupation carried out by approximately two dozen Aboriginal protesters. Over 250 officers were employed in the operation over a 27-day period, at a total cost of $2.12 million. George was the only casualty, but Cecil George was severely beaten by OPP officers, almost to the point of death. Sixty-two charges were laid against the Aboriginal people involved; 45 were withdrawn by the Crown; and most of the remaining charges resulted in acquittals, with the exception of charges against Warren George, who drove a car into police in an effort to rescue Cecil: Edwards at 228; *R. v. George* (2000), 49 O.R. (3d) 144 (C.A.).

As you read the judgment below, consider what made conviction in this case possible when so many other prosecutions have failed.

R. v. Deane[†]

[FRASER PROV. J. (orally):]

The accused is charged that on or about the 6th day of September 1995 at the Township of Bosanquet [he] did by criminal negligence discharge a firearm, causing the death of Anthony O'Brien Dudley George, contrary to Section 220 of the *Criminal Code of Canada*.

To briefly summarize the facts: Beside Ipperwash Provincial Park [is] Camp Ipperwash [which] was once occupied by the Department of National Defence. The issue of title to both Camp Ipperwash and Ipperwash Provincial Park remains in dispute.

In 1993 a group from the Kettle and Stoney Point First Nations Reserve, occupied a portion of Camp Ipperwash and established a residence on the national defence site. In July 1995, the Department of National Defence and the Canadian military physically withdrew from the entire camp. On September 4th of 1995 the adjacent park, Ipperwash Provincial Park, was occupied by approximately 24 aboriginal men, women and children. Adjacent to the park is a sand covered roadway which permits access to the beach area bordering Lake Huron.

By the evening of September 6th, 1995, there was a build-up of O.P.P. officers at a site approximately one half kilometre west of the park. A tactical operation centre [TOC] had been set up at that location.

The accused is a member of the Tactics and Rescue Unit which are often referred to as the T.R.U. team of the Ontario Provincial Police. At the material time he was on duty and had the rank of acting Sergeant. On September 6th, 1995, the accused was deployed as a member of the immediate action plan. The T.R.U. team had the responsibility of providing cover for a 32 person crowd management unit of the O.P.P.

At approximately 10:45 p.m., the crowd management unit, which will be called at times the C.M.U., started marching in a cordon up the road towards the natives from the tactical operation centre. The C.M.U. marched in a cordon up East Parkway Drive towards the sand covered roadway. By the time that the C.M.U. had arrived at the intersection of East Parkway Drive and Army Camp Road, all the native occupiers were on the far side of the fence bordering the Provincial Park property. The fence separates the Provincial Park from the sand covered roadway.

The T.R.U. team had moved ahead of the C.M.U. to secure the site. At one point the C.M.U. was advised to split into two groups and to stay low to the ground due to the possible sighting of a firearm. Once it was determined that the object being carried by a native was not a firearm, the C.M.U. continued down the East Parkway Drive.

The C.M.U. had a mission or purpose to secure the public road allowance area adjacent to Ipperwash Provincial Park. At one point the C.M.U. arrived at a fence bordering the park. The C.M.U. told the natives to get out of the park. The natives shone spotlights on the officers. They threw sticks, some of which were fire lit. They threw stones and rocks at the C.M.U. As one of the occupiers was allegedly being beaten by some of the C.M.U. members, at least 15 of the native occupiers came over the fence and began to fight with the C.M.U. in an attempt to rescue him.

Almost simultaneously a large yellow school bus left the park, hit a garbage dumpster on the way out and drove in the direction of the officers, forcing them to scatter and retreat. A car followed the path taken by the bus. The car hit several C.M.U. officers while others took evasive action. As the bus and car reversed, a number of officers fired at both vehicles.

The natives began to retreat and seek cover when the gunfire began. Dudley George was the only person injured by gunfire. He was heard yelling out words to the effect that he had been hit. He was helped to a car by two of his colleagues and was taken to Strathroy General Hospital where he was pronounced dead at 2:00 a.m., on September 7, 1995.

Doctor Michael Shkrum, a pathologist performed an autopsy on September 8th, 1995. He determined that a bullet entered the left clavicle area, resulting in extensive bleeding and complications arising from the bleeding.

It was determined that the bullet which caused the death of Dudley George was fired from a police issue semi-automatic, Hoeckler and Koch, nine millimetre carbine registered to the accused.

The accused was subsequently charged with the offence before the Court.

Both counsels agreed that the essential issue in its narrowest focus for the Court to determine today is whether the Crown has been able to prove beyond

---

[†] [1997] O.J. No. 3057 (Ct. Just. (Prov. Div.)), online: QL.

a reasonable doubt that the accused, at the time that he shot Dudley George did not have an honest and reasonable belief that Dudley George was scanning the crowd management unit with a rifle.

To summarize the Crown's position, it is that Dudley George was unarmed. That the accused knew that Dudley George was unarmed. That the accused knew that there never were any muzzle flashes. That there was no physical evidence of any officer being shot at and that the accused is only justified in discharging his weapon if he is shooting to stop a threat to other team members or is shooting in self-defence.

I'll now summarize the Crown evidence. The Crown presented nine witnesses including the S.I.U. identification officer and the pathologist, Doctor Shkrum as well as Inspector John Carson in reply.

Other than the three witnesses I have just mentioned, the remaining six were natives who were actually at the scene on September 6th.

Those six witnesses testified to the fact that the confrontation initially involved yelling and name calling by the natives as the C.M.U. moved them into the park. They testified that initially there was no physical contact between the natives and the C.M.U. until one native Cecil Bernard George also known as Slippery, became embroiled in a confrontation with at least eight C.M.U. officers. Witnesses testified that he was beaten and kicked by at least eight of the C.M.U. members.

At least 15 native men armed with clubs, sticks and bats began to fight with the C.M.U. They also threw bricks, rocks and stones, sticks, as well as fire lit sticks and bats at the officers.

The natives testified that they were attempting to rescue Slippery, but he was eventually taken into police custody and placed in a van.

The women and children shone lights on the police, both flashlights and spotlights.

As the police were subduing Slippery, a school bus came out of the gate and onto the roadway scattering the officers and forcing them to retreat in a westerly direction down East Parkway Drive. The bus was followed by a car. As the bus and car reversed after dispersing the officers, the sound of gunfire was heard. We have heard testimony that there were three distinct shots, then after a short lull, a rapid burst of gunfire.

Some natives testified that they froze upon hearing the gunfire. Others began to run towards the park.

The Court heard testimony that eventually all of the natives headed for the park and several of the Crown witnesses encountered Dudley George as they moved towards the park.

One witness Isaac Doxtator testified he heard someone say "I think I'm hit." As he looked over he saw the individual walking backwards. He walked over to the man who was holding his chest walking in a crouched over fashion. ...[H]e later learned that it was Dudley George who had his hands folded across his chest. Dudley George was helped into a car and taken to hospital according to the witnesses.

All of the six Crown witnesses at the scene testified that no natives had any weapon that evening, that Dudley George had no weapon and that there were no weapons found near him at the time of his collapse.

Elwood George testified that he believed at some time during the evening he saw Dudley George with a stick in his hands. He further testified that as he was going towards the park gate after hearing the gunfire, he heard Dudley who may have been some 20 feet from the gate say that he was hit. Elwood George was about 15 feet away from Dudley George at the time. He went over to Dudley George, who he noted was moving more slowly than usual. It was his testimony that Dudley George walked another 10 feet before collapsing.

On cross-examination Elwood George testified that he was one of the people yelling for the bus to come out from the park to "get the cops off our ass".

During his cross-examination Isaac Doxtator testified that he stepped aside as the bus was coming out of the gate, otherwise the bus might have run him over; that when he heard the second burst of gunfire he crouched down.

Stacey George testified that he saw the bus split the officers into two groups; that once the bus began to reverse and then came to a stop, the shooting started.

It was the testimony of Charles George that as he was heading for the park after the gunfire had ceased he heard someone say "I think I'm hit." He turned around and saw Dudley fall over. He went over to Dudley George, who was holding his chest, turned him over and noticed that he was all bloody.

Kevin Simon was one of the Crown witnesses who was also at the scene. It was his testimony that he saw eight police C.M.U. officers in a circle clubbing Slippery. That he heard people yelling "they got Slippery, they got Slippery." He heard Slippery's sister say "you got to do something." The people then started to go through the gate and over the fence. He heard someone yell "get the bus." He said that he was scared but he didn't want to see Slippery beaten to death and he waited for the bus to come out and then walked beside the bus after it hit the dumpster. That he saw the police backing up as the bus came out and that he stopped near the sign at the intersection of East Parkway Drive and Army Camp Road, a location depicted in exhibits 9-13, 9-14. This gave Mr. Simon a different perspective from some of the other witnesses. He testified that he maintained that position until he heard Dudley George's cry that he had been hit. From that vantage point he testified that he saw the car turn to where the police were standing off to the side of the road. So he described the veering action of the car as it headed towards the officers and that the car in fact backed the police into the ditch. He did not see Slippery disappear and surmised that it must have been as the bus was arriving. He added that as the car backed up, he heard a quick two or three shots, three distinct volleys, and then "they all just started shooting" in his words. "It was like everybody shot at once." And I quote now "I took a quick look and could see the people like ducking trying to get out of the way or running for cover and the dirt was just kicking up around people's feet." He went on to say the police started splitting up after the bus came out. "I could see them all around. The cops were everywhere around." He saw the car reverse, noted that the bus was having a harder time. It was stopping and going and as it was doing so the shooting essentially stopped. He then heard someone yell that Dudley was shot. He saw someone lying on the ground. People were yelling orders to the bus and they were yelling things at the police as well. It was at that point that Kevin finally left his vantage point and went to Dudley George. Before he could get there he noted that the bus was coming back out, but the bus again hit a dumpster and Mr. Simon was forced to walk around the bus to get to Dudley George. By the time he got to Mr. George he could not move. His hands were up around his chest area according to Mr. Simon and there was blood all around his chest.

The pathologist, Doctor Michael Shkrum testified that the bullet, the mortal wound entered the clavicle of Dudley George at an angle. The bullet come from above. The clavicle was fractured completely. The left lung punctured. The left eighth and ninth ribs were fractured. The ninth completely fractured and a number of blood vessels were torn. There was an accumulation of 1000 cc.'s or one litre of blood in the left chest cavity. The bullet in his view followed a straight path into the body. The deceased would likely have been bent and twisted to the right. He testified he had no idea what Dudley George was doing with his hands at the time of the shooting. That could not be discerned from the post mortem. He acknowledged that a leg abrasion found on the deceased may have been the result of a grazing from a projectile. When questioned regarding the impact of the fractured clavicle he testified that it would impair movement of the arm. It would be painful to move the arm as a result of that injury. He also testified that Dudley George could have been ambulatory for up to several minutes after sustaining his injuries.

Dealing now with the defence position, it is that the accused shot an armed man who was scanning several C.M.U. officers with a long arm or rifle. That the accused had seen muzzle flashes a short time earlier. Muzzle flashes which he believed were aimed in his direction. The one and only reason that the accused fired his weapon at Dudley George was to stop an armed aggressor from harming an exposed police officer. That the accused had a duty to shoot to stop the threat from gunfire, if he honestly and reasonably believed that any member of the team faced a threat of deadly fire.

The first defence witness was the accused Ken Deane. He was questioned initially as to his specific training in the recognition of threats from weapons. He testified he was trained to find objects with the naked eye and to give discerning characteristics about those objects. Further that after the bus had raced past his position his attention was drawn to the sand covered roadway area where he saw a large vehicle leave that area. Then he saw two distinct muzzle flashes from the sandy embankment area. He then discharged four rounds from his carbine. He described the muzzle flashes as threatening fire. As the car reversed, Sergeant Deane testified that the accused walked forward on the lake side of East Parkway Drive, quoting now "as I walked forward I saw one individual leave this area and cross Army Camp Road and hide down by these three posts at the intersection. This individual left the three posts, the intersection area and half-walked and ran onto the roadway."

He was asked "what did you see?"

Answer: "As this individual left the P2 position and went to the P3 position I observed him shoulder a rifle in a half crouched position, scan our position, scan the crowd management unit's position with this rifle."

The question asked in-chief: "What did you do?"

Answer: "I discharged three rounds from my carbine."

Question: "Why?"

Answer: "To stop the threat of being shot at."

Question: "What did you see happen?"

Answer: "I saw this individual falter. He immediately went down on one knee and then immediately got back up. As he got back up he turned slightly towards the sand covered roadway and then immediately turned back towards the P2 position. As he turned towards the P2 position the rifle that he had, he threw it into this area somewhere. At that point the bus that had raced through our ranks was now reversing back through."

Next question: "Did you shoot at it?"

Answer: "At the bus? No I did not."

Question: "Why?"

Answer: "I did not deem it was a threat to me or the members."

Question: "What happened then?"

Answer: "The bus entered the sand covered roadway. I saw two individuals from the sand covered roadway area walk out and assist the individual that I had shot at."

Question: "What did you then do?"

Answer: "I just simply watched these individuals help the person that I had shot, back into the park area."

Question: "Did you pursue that individual?"

Answer: "No I did not."

Question: "Did you go to try and encounter him in any way?"

Answer: "No I did not."

Question: "What did you do?"

Answer: "I immediately turned to my right and I spoke to Officer George Hebblethwaite and asked him to do a head count or a physical check on his members to see if they were injured or hurt."

During cross-examination Sergeant Deane testified that he was equipped with a Motorola head-set, a walkie talkie plus the head-set which had an open mike which could be activated by flicking a switch.

He testified that he did not advise over the communication system that he had seen muzzle flashes because he did not have time to activate the communication system.

He was then questioned by Mr. Scott on this point.

Question: "You're telling us, can you walk and activate your communications system?"

Answer: "Yes I can."

Question: "And you walked 20 meters?"

Answer: "I would say I walked that within seconds."

Question: "Well how long does it take to say 'T.R.U. team, muzzle flashes, danger from sandy berm?'"

Answer: "At the time I did not have time to do that. I saw the muzzle flashes. I saw the car leave the area and strike the crowd management unit members. I was moving forward at this time. I still had both hands on my weapon and basically timing, I did not have time to activate my communication system."

Question: "Well you would agree with me that you still consider these muzzle flashes a threat?"

Answer: "Yes I do."

Question: "I mean notwithstanding the fact that, correct on this point, you never actually identified a target with respect to those muzzle flashes, right?"

Answer: "No I did not."

The next question: "You didn't know whether you knocked out this potential threat, correct?"

Answer: "No I did not."

Question: "Because you never, to this day, ever saw what was behind those muzzle flashes?"

Answer: "No I did not."

The next question: "All right so you're telling us that notwithstanding the fact you had time to move 20 meters and notwithstanding the fact that you never shot at those muzzle flashes again, you never got on your head set to warn your fellow officers about this potential threat, is that right?"

Answer: "Yes that's right."

A little bit further down is the question: "Did you tell Staff Sergeant Skinner when you got back to the TOC, the TOC centre that there were muzzle flashes out in the sand berm?"

Answer: "Yes I did."

Question: "You did?"

Answer: "Yes. As soon as the crowd management unit had formed up and started to go back down East Parkway Drive, we had accounted for all our members."

Question: "Okay."

Answer: "The crowd management unit and the T.R.U. team members, and it was at that time I advised Staff Sergeant Skinner of the events."

Question: "Was this face to face or over the communications?"

Answer: "No this was over the communication system."

Later on Mr. Scott poses the following question. "All I want to know right now is this. Did you get on the communication system and say there is a man scanning our officers with a firearm."

Answer: "No I did not."

Question: "You didn't think that that was important?"

Answer: "At the time it was important. I just did not have the time to get onto the com system and advise our members of that fact."

Question: "Well did you get on the com system after you shot him and said, 'I just shot a man, he may still be dangerous out on the roadway'?"

Answer: "I believe I said that at the time to Staff Skinner that a bus had come through our position, a car had come into our position striking members and also there is one individual down and we required an ambulance."

Question: "Did you say anything over the communication system about a rifle?"

Answer: "That I cannot recall."

Question: "Did you say over the communication system there's a rifle in the ditch which may be a threat to us in the future if a native got a hold of that?"

Answer: "I do not believe I said that no."

Next question by Mr. Scott: "Sorry, tell me, I missed again, repeat what if you would please what you did say with respect to the man that you shot over the communication's system?"

Answer: "I told Staff Sergeant Skinner that there was an individual down and we would require an ambulance at that area."

Question: "But you didn't say to him I just saw a man with a rifle?"

Answer: "I do not believe I said that. I cannot recall that."

Question: "Don't you think that would be an important thing to say over the communication system there was a man with a long arm who is trying to shoot our officers?"

Answer: "Yes that is important. I do not believe I said that. I do not recall that."

Later in cross-examination Sergeant Deane testified that he did tell Staff Sergeant Skinner about the muzzle flashes, about firing upon the muzzle flashes and further that he told him about the shooting of an individual. He was later then questioned by the Crown Attorney with regard to the first person that he told about shooting an individual. We have the following exchange.

Question by Mr. Scott: "And you told us that you told Sergeant Skinner (a) that there were muzzle flashes, and (b) that you shot and perhaps killed somebody in this operation, correct?"

Answer: "I'm not, I told him there were muzzle flashes. I told him that I had returned fire on the muzzle flashes. I further told him that I had shot an individual that had been scanning our position with a rifle. This individual faltered, fell to the ground and got back up again and then was assisted back into the park."

Question: "Is that the first time that you ever told anybody?"

Answer: "I don't think I had mentioned that on the way back from the sand covered roadway."

Question: "Pardon me?"

Answer: "I would have told Sergeant Skinner and only him. He would have been the first person."

Question: "So you didn't tell any of your colleagues that you walked back along East Parkway Drive to the TOC centre?"

Answer: "That I had shot an individual?"

Question: "Yes."

Answer: "I believe I asked one constable, Provincial Constable Beauchesne, if he had seen the individual on the roadway."

Question: "Right."

Answer: "That I had shot at, and he said no."

Still on the communication system, the Crown asked the following question.

"Okay you never, you said over the walkie talkie system that you saw muzzle flashes and that you never said over the walkie talkie system that there was a man with a long arm out on the roadway, and you never said you shot a man with a long arm over the walkie talkie system."

Answer: "Not that I can recall, no."

Sergeant Deane also testified that there were no police officers shot that evening. A question from the Crown Attorney: "All right well you'd agree with me because you were involved in kind of a head count later on that no police officer was shot, right, that evening?"

Answer: "No."

Question: "There's no item, no shield, no vehicle, no nothing that would suggest that the natives shot any weapons that evening that you're aware of?"

Answer: "At that area, no."

Question: "Any area that evening?"

Answer: "No."

Question: "All right now and you'd agree with me you didn't shoot Dudley George because of anything that happened on that bus, correct?"

Answer: "Yes that's correct."

Question: "All right so there's no relationship? Notwithstanding whether this person was trying to shoot a police officer which obviously if they did is one of the most serious things that ever could be done? You're not saying today under oath that the reason you shot the person on the roadway has anything to do with what that bus did or what anybody on that bus did?"

Answer: "No it has nothing to do with that."

Sergeant Deane also testified that the shooting of Dudley George is not in any way related to what the car did to the C.M.U. members. Later on in his testimony he described the rifle that he saw in Dudley George's hands. It had a long metal barrel and a wooden butt stock. He saw Dudley George's right hand up at the trigger group but he could not see his finger on the trigger. He testified also that he did not have time to use his weapon's lighting device on Dudley George before he shot him and that he saw Dudley George scanning in the direction of at least nine officers. On this point he was questioned in the following manner by Mr. Scott.

Question: "You say you shot him as quickly as you could?"

Answer: "Yes."

Question: "But you would agree with me that at the time that he was scanning officers he could have easily had mortally wounded one of your fellow officers?"

Answer: "If they were present there, yes. If they could have been down in the ditch area, he might not have seen them. I'm not positive, I'm not sure."

Question: "We don't know what he saw, but we do know that he's scanning very much in the direction that your officers were before you had an opportunity, to, you're telling, pull the trigger?"

Answer: "Yes. As soon as he came up and started to scan, that's when I shot."

Question: "But not sooner even though he was a threat to those officers in those few seconds before?"

Answer: "Yes. His scan as I said was very quick."

Question: "All right and you never had an opportunity to shout out anything?"

Answer: "No I did not."

Question: "And you never heard anybody shout anything to you?"

Answer: "No I did not."

Question: "Did any other officer light him up?"

The answer: "Not that I recall no."

The accused agreed with the Crown's suggestion that his notes do not mention that Dudley George was leaning over at the time that he was shot. The Crown later on asked: "When you were looking at Dudley George through your sights or shortly after you shot him, did it ever strike you that it was an act of incredible stupidity for a shooter to leave a protected area to go out on that roadway and scan up to 30 or 40 police officers who were all armed?"

Answer: "It never occurred to me. I never thought about."

Question: "Well you'd agree with me from a tactical perspective if you want to kill somebody you're much better off back in a protected area than you are in the middle of a roadway with 30 to 50 armed police officers?"

Answer: "Yes."

Next question: "I mean it's almost an act of suicide isn't it to go out there?"

Answer: "I would not say it was suicide. I never thought about that theory at all."

Sergeant Deane described how Dudley George went down to one knee after being hit, how he got up right away, turned to his right, stopped, turned back to his left, came to an area on the sand grass shoulder on the south side of the intersection of East Parkway Drive and Army Camp Road and threw the rifle.

Sergeant Deane was not sure whether the rifle went across the fence into the grass covered field or whether it landed on the east side of the fence in the sand/grass shoulder area. The path taken by Dudley George was marked on exhibit 26(c) by the accused as is the approximate location of the rifle, and the position of Constables Klym and Beauchesne in the grass covered field to the west of the area where the rifle was thrown.

Sergeant Deane then indicated on exhibit 26(c) that Dudley George crossed the intersection of East Parkway Drive and Army Camp Road, heading towards the sand covered roadway where he received help from two individuals. He further testified that 10 to 15 seconds after he shot Dudley George he spoke to Sergeant Hebblethwaite but he did not tell Sergeant Hebblethwaite that he shot a man with a long arm.

I'll just refer to the following exchange. Questions and answers from the Crown. First question on this point posed by Mr. Scott.

"What is the time lapse between the time you shoot Dudley George and the time you had the conversation with Sergeant Hebblethwaite?"

Answer: "Probably 15 seconds, 10, 15 seconds, I'm not sure."

Question: "So you didn't tell him that you had just shot and possibly killed a man?"

Answer: "No I did not."

Question: "Now your job as a T.R.U. team member is to provide support, you told us, correct?"

Answer: "Yes."

Question: "And part of your job in providing support is disarming aggressors, correct?"

Answer: "Yes."

Question: "Now in this case you had in your view effectively disarmed Dudley George, correct?"

Answer: "I had stopped the threat, yes."

Question: "You had stopped the threat but you'd agree with me that the rifle was still out there?"

Answer: "Yes."

Question: "Well did you make any attempt to get the rifle?"

Answer: "No I did not."

Question: "Did you, if so by that you're telling us that you personally did not attempt to retrieve the rifle?"

Answer: "I did not, no I did not."

Question: "You made no attempt to communicate to Klym and Beauchesne who were what, within, far west of that circle, just to give you the benefit of the doubt here, they were approximately 20 meters from the rifle, correct?"

Answer: "Yes."

Question: "And you knew that at the time or at least you thought at the time?"

Answer: "I thought they would be yes."

Question: "You could have turned on your headset and said Constables Klym and Beauchesne, whatever their first names are, there's a rifle within 20 meters of you, to get it right away because if you don't some other native might pick it up and shoot us?"

Answer: "At the time I felt it was prudent to make sure all our officers were accounted for."

Question: "Well wouldn't you agree with me that the best way to deal with a threat of a firearm is for you to have possession of the firearm?"

Answer: "Yes."

Question: "And you had that possibility in this case?"

Answer: "Yes."

Question: "And you didn't do it?"

Answer: "No I did not."

Question: "Is there any reason why you didn't?"

Answer: "No as I have said I felt it prudent to take care of my members to make sure they were accounted for."

Question: "Isn't the best way to take care of your members to make sure there's no firearms in the hands of the aggressors?"

Answer: "If we could do that yes."

Question: "Well you could have, right?"

Answer: "I'm sure I could have, but at the time I felt it was not prudent to rush back into that area to grab that firearm."

Question: "Why not?"

Answer: "I did not know what was still inside the park."

Next question "Well sir I think you told us earlier there's like no natives in the whole area at this point, correct?"

Answer: "Yes."

Question: "So did you perceive there to be a threat to your person if you'd attempted to get the rifle?"

Answer: "Basically I felt it necessary to make sure my members were accounted for. I did not think of the rifle at that time. No I did not."

Question: "All right so let me get this straight then. It's not like you thought about it and rejected the idea, you just never thought about it?"

Answer: "No I did not, no."

Question: "You didn't think about it?"

Answer: "No I did not."

A little later on in this series of questions the Crown asked the following.

"Looking back on it now wouldn't you agree with me that what would have been the best thing to do to either personally have got the rifle or to have sought the assistance of Constables Klym and Beauchesne to get the rifle?"

Answer: "I'm not positive I would have done that no."

Question: "Why not?"

Answer: "I still did not feel it was prudent."

Question: "Why not?"

Answer: "As I stated I wanted to take care of my members. I did not think of the rifle."

Question: "And also you'd agree with me that if you or one of the officers had got the rifle it would be of significant evidentiary value if there was ever a court case, right?"

Answer: "Yes."

As Sergeant Deane described the process of the head count carried out by Sergeant Hebblethwaite the Crown Attorney continued to question the accused about the rifle.

Question: "All right would you continue to look out in the direction of the rifle out of some concern that another native might get the rifle and try to shoot you?"

Answer: "At the time no. I was more concerned with the park area. We just trained our observations on the park."

Question: "But you never saw any firearms in the park?"

Answer: "I was still looking at the park."

Question: "But you never saw any firearms there, right?"

Answer: "At that point no."

Question: "Well you never saw any firearms in the park period?"

Answer: "No I did not."

Question: "And you knew there was a rifle, you're telling us, at the southeast intersection of Army Camp Road and East Parkway Drive?"

Answer: "Yes."
Question: "But you just left it there?"
Answer: "Yes we did."
Question: "You didn't have any concern that another aggressive native might grab that rifle and do exactly what you just told us Dudley George would do, just did to you?"
Answer: "It could have happened. I did not concern myself. I did not think about it to tell you the truth."
Question: "It couldn't be because there never was a rifle?"
Answer: "No it could not."

Later the Crown Attorney put the Crown position to Sergeant Deane for his response. Sergeant Deane agreed that the natives were acting aggressively that evening. The Crown suggested that the lighting in the park area was bad on the night in question.

This is the question: "Well I'm going to suggest to you that the lighting in the whole area of East Parkway Road at the time that you shot Dudley was bad? You couldn't really see into the darkness of that area, is that fair?"

Answer: "Actually the lighting, it was a dark night yes, but we could see in close proximity, yes we could."

The Crown made another suggestion that the accused shot in the general direction of Dudley George and that that is how Dudley George received the bullet in his chest. Answer to that question was as follows.

"The individual now known as Dudley George was facing me. You are correct in that he was scanning our position crouched over armed with a rifle."

Next question by the Crown "All right but I'm going to suggest to you that he never had a rifle. What is your answer to that?"

Answer: "He did have a rifle."

On re-examination by defence counsel the accused was questioned regarding his attendance on September 8th, 1995 at an interview with investigators from the O.P.P. and the S.I.U. He confirmed that during that tape recorded interview he described the fact that he had seen muzzle flashes, he described the fact that he had returned fire. He described where he had first seen Dudley George. He described where Dudley George had come from, what he had done and described seeing Dudley George scanning the police with a weapon.

The next defence witness was Sergeant George Hebblethwaite who is a 20 year veteran of the Ontario Provincial Police and had been a member of the emergency response teams since 1993. He testified that the C.M.U. does not engage a crowd knowing that there are firearms. ... During this time Sergeant Hebblethwaite and Staff Sergeant Lacroix were repeatedly telling the C.M.U. to wait. The people were advancing on them swinging sticks and poles, very menacingly, very threateningly. He believed contact was imminent. The C.M.U. was then given the "go" command. Some of his officers were taking slams against their shields with objects such as pipes and sticks and poles. He saw some of the hands-free officers struggling with a person on the ground. He did not see any clubbing or kicking of the person while looking in that direction. He testified that he and Staff Sergeant Lacroix yelled over to the hands-free officers to just get the man out of there. He did not believe that it was the time or place to be trying to put handcuffs on the individual. He believed the person was then removed, although he did not actually see it. But he told the prisoner vans to move back down the East Parkway Drive, to facilitate the reversal of the C.M.U. down that road. Even as they reversed direction and went back down East Parkway Drive, objects were still being thrown at them. At that point the school bus appeared.

Sergeant Hebblethwaite testified he drew his service pistol. He did not fire because of safety concerns. He recalls the bus sounding as if it was in a gear that was too low for its speed. He put his pistol back in its holster. He then saw the headlights of the car. He saw the car come down the centre of the East Parkway Drive and then veer sharply just to the right of Sergeant Hebblethwaite and the car then struck three officers. He saw one officer laying down on the hood of the car bent over at the waist. Another officer bounced off the car. A third member was laying down just off of the right front corner of the car thrown on the ground. He then re-drew his weapon but did not have a clear shot. The car reversed and then stopped. He believed that the car was going to make another run at the officers. He then raised his weapon intending to fire, at which time he saw an intense white light. He then heard two or three gunshots at the same moment. He fired four rounds from his pistol at the car to try to disable the driver. He testified then that all manner of shots started. He could hear multiple gun shots from multiple weapons. There was then a very brief lull in the gun fire according to his recollection. Then he heard a burst of two or three more shots coming from a position to his forward. He then saw a male person in the apex area of the road just after he heard the shots. Quoting directly from Sergeant Hebblethwaite's testimony now: "I saw this person holding an object which I perceived to be a pole or a stick and I saw this person turning or spinning in a clockwise fashion back towards the park, turning as he stood. My first thought was this person has been shot. He went down hard on his right knee as he turned but he was up almost as quickly as he went down." Sergeant Hebblethwaite was asked by Mr. Peel to describe how the object was being held. He gave the following answer: "Well it was similar to the way other objects had been held prior to this event as far as the contact. The aggressors that had come out of the park and had attacked us with their clubs and poles earlier. It was in a higher fashion such as this. (He described it for the Court.) And when the person turned and fell down to their knee they got up but not in a totally erect fashion. They were bent over some, and the person was up, as I said, just about as quickly as they hit the ground with their knee and I dismissed the thought that they had been shot." Then he saw the car move back. The bus was also reversing. He heard more gun fire. He then yelled for a head count.

It was his testimony that he wasn't sure at that point if the event was over just yet. There was a lot of yelling and screaming from the persons that had come over the fence from the park, that the C.M.U. then re-grouped into cordon formation. He saw the T.R.U. unit flanking them on either side as they illuminated areas ahead of the C.M.U. with their flashlights which were attached to their rifles. The C.M.U. then still facing east, reversed down East Parkway Drive in a westerly direction.

On cross-examination Sergeant Hebblethwaite testified that he did not see any muzzle flashes beyond his own. He was then asked a number of questions by the Crown regarding the person that he saw fall....

He testified further that he did not perceive the pole or the stick held by the man on the road to be a threat. He did not see where the man went after he got up, facing the park.

On this point he stated: "He was faced in the direction of the park and a step, maybe two, don't know. I only looked at him for the briefest of time."

He was not sure if the man still had the stick in his hand when he got up. Sergeant Hebblethwaite confirmed that there were no police issued equipment that appeared to have been damaged due to bullets, that he never saw a firearm in the hands of the natives that evening.

The next witness was Constable Beauchesne. He testified that he has over six years with the T.R.U. team, that he had training as a lead scout. In 1991 he and Sergeant Deane and others received a commissioner's citation for a problem at Grassy Narrows Reserve in which an O.P.P. officer had been shot and killed in that incident, and another officer wounded.

And that further there was a three day search through the woods in pursuit of the suspect and another officer was shot during that effort. Constable Beauchesne's team was involved in the final track and the arrest of that person.

On September 6th, 1995 he was part of the four man alpha team. He was partnered with Constable Klym on the south side of East Parkway Drive. Sergeant Deane and Constable O'Halloran were on the north side. He was equipped with a radio and Constable Beauchesne was equipped with a radio and a head set as well as night vision equipment. He understood his duty was to provide an advanced eye and cover for the C.M.U. against a potential firearms threat and incendiary devices.

He testified as he scanned with his night vision he saw two men, one of whom appeared to have something in his hand. The two men squatted and kept looking in the direction of Constables Beauchesne and Klym. He determined that the object was not a firearm and passed along this information to the technical operation centre. He later saw one of the original men squatting with what appeared to be a long gun in his hand. He communicated that information as well and then moved a little further forward to try to confirm whether it was in fact a firearm or not. The C.M.U. had been told to split and take to the sides of the road until they received further instruction. After moving 20 to 30 meters up the road Constable Beauchesne determined that the object was not a firearm and he communicated that information to the technical operation centre.

He testified that he then moved up to the grassy dune area with Constable Klym as the C.M.U. moved forward. And from the grassy dune area he was provided a very good observation point. As the C.M.U. moved forward and backwards and then forward again, he was looking for people with guns or threats to the C.M.U. He added that he was looking carefully at what people were carrying, making an assessment person by person. When the C.M.U. moved back onto the pavement Constable Beauchesne moved back with them on their south flank. So he would then be south, slightly east of the C.M.U. according to his recollection, just before the bus appeared. He was within a couple of meters of the start of a bush line, to quote: "maybe five meters and I could almost reach out and touch the fence." He recalled that as the bus accelerated down the East Parkway Drive a couple of C.M.U. officers ended up coming over the fence where Constable Beauchesne was. He considered shooting at the bus driver, but concluded that it was too late to stop the bus's actions. He then saw the car approach and hit several C.M.U. officers. He then decided that if the car took another run at the officers he would shoot the driver to stop him. He saw the car start to move forward and he shot twice in the direction of the driver. The car stopped and started slowly backing down the road. He then heard other shots. He testified further that when the bus and the car appeared to no longer be a threat he looked around. He then hopped the fence and went over to Sergeant Deane to ask if anyone needed assistance on that side of the road. It was at that point that Sergeant Deane then mentioned, quote: "Did you see the guy with the gun?"...

Constable Beauchesne testified that he never saw a gun or a firearm in the hands of any native that evening. He did not see any Molotov cocktails that evening. He was then questioned by the Crown Attorney regarding the conversation with Sergeant Deane after the bus and car went back into the park. "Okay and tell us exactly what he said to you?"

Answer: "He, we exchanged some information and one of the things he said was 'did you see the guy with the gun?'"

Question: "Yeah, what else did he say? Sorry let me ask you this. That's a question to you, correct?"

Answer: "Yes."

Question: "What did you say back?"

Answer: "No."

Question: "What did he say next?"

Answer: "I don't recall in terms of — that was one of the parts of the conversation. We were trying to form the team up, confirm that the sierra teams were there. That was exchanged do we have our people? Was there anybody hurt."

Next question: "Let me get this straight, he says to you, 'did you see the guy with the gun?' Then you say, 'no' and then you move on to do a head count, is that right?"

Answer: "Now this, in terms of the timing that may have been the first information shared or that may have been the last information shared or in the middle. I really couldn't tell you."

Question: "Well all right let's go back. I want to hear everything he said to you about the guy with the gun. Have you told us everything that he said to you at that point about the guy with the gun?"

Answer: "As far as I can remember that's basically what he said to me about the guy with the gun. That was it."

Question: "Pardon me?"

Answer: "That was it. That was pretty well it in its entirety."

Question: "What happened after, [...] you said 'no', what happened next?"

Answer: "Well I went back to my side of the road and waited for the unit to form up and we covered them as they went back down the road."

Question: "Let me get this straight sir. Your job was to look for people with guns, right?"

Answer: "Yes sir."

Question: "Sergeant Deane from your perspective is a reliable source, correct?"

Answer: "Yes."

Question: "He says to you, 'did you see the guy with the gun?' You're telling that today under oath, right?"

Answer: "Yes."

Question: "You say 'no' 'cause you never saw a guy with a gun right?'"

Answer: "That's right."

Question: "In your head, in your mind when he said to you, 'did you see the guy with the gun', did you think that he saw 'a guy with a gun?'"

Answer: "Yes."

Question: "Well tell the court why you didn't follow up on this?"

Answer: "We were in the process of getting everybody together, organizing the team and covering withdrawal. He put it to me in the past tense. It wasn't an immediate threat at that time. It was him sharing information with me."

Question: "Well how did you know it wasn't an immediate threat?"

Answer: "Because [...] his behaviour would have been much different, I imagine, if it was an immediate threat. He was speaking in the past tense. There was no point to say, 'there's a guy with a gun.' This was, 'did you see a guy with the gun.'"

Question: "Did you ask him, when did you see the guy with the gun?"

Answer: "No."

Question: "Did you ask him, is the guy you saw with the gun out on the roadway?"

Answer: "No."

Question: "Did you ask him did the guy with the gun, might he shoot me, did you ask him that?"

Answer: "No."

Further on he was asked the question: "Well did you put in your notes anywhere that Sergeant Deane might have seen somebody with a gun?"

Answer: "No."

Next question: "Well sir, the entire, your whole raison d'etre for being there is to look for somebody with a gun, is that right?"

Answer: "Yes sir."

Question: "You receive reliable information that somebody is out there with a gun, right?"

Answer: "Yes."

Question: "And you don't do anything with it?"

Answer: "The information didn't, other than being shared, the information was already out there that there was a concern about firearms. Obviously Sergeant Deane was confirming that he had seen somebody with a firearm."

Question: "Right."

Answer: "It did not change the way we were going to be behaving or responding from that point. We were in the process of withdrawing."

Question: "Okay, well you're standing in the roadway with Sergeant Deane at the time he tells you this, right?"

Answer: "Yes."

Question: "And there's what, 30, 40 C.M.U. members behind you?"

Answer: "Yes."

Question: "And if there was someone with a gun, and did you even ask him, do you think it was a sub-machine gun or just a single shot rifle. Did you ask him that?"

Answer: "No sir."

Question: "Okay, so you didn't ask him where this person was who you say had the gun, right. So you didn't know where he was, correct?"

Answer: "No."

Question: "You didn't ask him when he saw the person with the gun, so it might have been less than five seconds before he made the statement, correct?"

Answer: "His demeanor, this was an exchange of information. I trust that in this exchange that if it was a threat or an immediate threat then his demeanor would have been different and his way of relating information would have been different."

A little bit later on the Crown continues to pursue this line with the following question.

"So let me get this straight [...] in your view natives with guns are armed aggressors, correct?"

Answer: "A native with a gun would be considered a high threat, yes."

Question: "To you personally, correct?"

Answer: "To anybody out there. To certainly all the police officers out there."

Question: "And you made absolutely and utterly no follow up inquiries with respect to that question asked of you by Sergeant Deane, is that correct?"

Answer: "That is correct."

Question: "All right. Including, you never, did you ask Sergeant Deane, well did the guy with the gun shoot anybody?"

Answer: "No sir, I didn't ask that."

Question: "Did you ask Sergeant Deane if he shot the guy with the gun?"

Answer: "No sir."

Question: "Why didn't you ask him that?"

Answer: "Because we weren't debriefing the occurrence at that time."

Question: "Sir we're not debriefing at this point, we're in a situation where you're trying to protect yourself and the other officers, you're in the middle of this operation still. Isn't that right?"

Answer: "That's right."

Question: "Wouldn't it have been of interest to you to find out whether or not this armed aggressor had been shot by Sergeant Deane?"

Answer: "It would be nice to know. I'm making assumptions during this exchange that the way he put the statement to me, it was in the past tense. I did not take his actions as indicative of an immediate threat and since we were in the process of withdrawing, I also made the assumption that the man with the gun would have been down towards the park, so my area of threat or concern would obviously be in that direction. There was nothing that he said that would indicate any change in the plans that we were in the process of following through on and that is withdrawal."

Question: "But you don't know any of this sir. You never asked Sergeant Deane where this man with the gun went, right?"

Answer: "No, I didn't."

Question: "And for all you know he was just around the corner, or just behind a tree with a gun trained out on the roadway, right?"

Answer: "The way it was said to me led me to believe that it wasn't an immediate threat. If there was any indication that he was in our midst or off to the side then, yes, I would have had a concern."

Question: "Well I mean one [way] you could have found out whether or not it was an immediate threat was to ask Sergeant Deane if he shot the guy with the gun, isn't that right?"

Answer: "That's right."

Question: "But you didn't do that, did you?"

Answer: "No I didn't."

The next witness for the defence that I will comment on is Staff Sergeant Kent Skinner. He testified that he was the leader of the T.R.U. team at Ipperwash that night. He was operating from the tactical operation centre. He testified to the importance of securing the scene after the First Nation's protestors had gone back into the park following the shooting.

He was asked this question by Mr. Peel. "During the time of what I'm calling [...] the unit assembling and looking for injured people, would you expect him," and the reference is to Sergeant Deane, "would you expect him to go on the channel and start to advise you of the history of what had happened?"

Answer: "No sir."

Question: "Why?"

Answer: "He has other duties at that time sir, to insure the security of his fellow officers and the C.M.U. members."

A further question: "From what you knew of the scene did you still assess that your T.R.U. team members still had to protect the crowd management unit until it was back to the T.O.C. centre?"

Answer by Staff Sergeant Skinner: "Oh absolutely yes sir, yes."

On cross-examination Staff Sergeant Skinner was questioned about his meeting with Sergeant Deane at the tactical operation centre.

Question: "If we move to the next point then in time, once Officer Deane was back, did you have conversation with him?"

Answer: "Yes."

Question: "What do you recall him telling you?"

Answer: "Sergeant Deane told me when he came back, he told me he had discharged his weapon at an armed individual. That he saw that person fall down. His first reaction, he told me, was to want to go forward to assist but realized he could not because of the situation. He told me that person was then carried back in the park."

Later on Sergeant Skinner testified that he had no recollection of Sergeant Deane saying anything over the communication system that he saw muzzle flashes and that he had no note of any reference to muzzle flashes. He also testified that he recalled being told by Sergeant Deane that he had shot an armed person and agreed that he did not include that point in his notes.

Staff Sergeant Skinner was questioned by Mr. Scott regarding the rifle that Sergeant Deane saw.

Question: "Tell me Sergeant, tell me when Sergeant Deane told you about shooting this armed individual? Did you ask him about the rifle of the armed individual?"

Answer: "No."

Question: "Did you ask Sergeant Deane if the rifle was still out in the ... theatre of operation, is that the correct term?"

Answer: "It serves its purpose but no I didn't ask him that."

Question: "Okay, well, did that cause you any concern, that there could be [one] out there in the hands of natives who could use it".

Answer: "I was already aware that there were weapons out in the hands of natives because there had been an exchange of gunfire."

Question: "Right, but this was a rifle, that, well okay we'll go back sir, did Sergeant Deane tell you what the native that he shot at did with the rifle?"

Answer: "Not that I recall, no."

Question: "So for all you know he held onto the rifle when he went back to the park?"

Answer: "I don't know."

Question: "You just don't know?"

Answer: "No."

Question: "You don't recall him saying to you he threw the rifle in the ditch?"

Answer: "No I don't."

Question: "I guess there's no point in really discussing with him whether there's a possibility of retrieving the rifle because he never told you where the rifle was, right?"

Answer: "That's what I recall."

. . . .

The defence evidence just summarized requires the Court to accept the following points. First, that Dudley George left an area of safety to go to an open area on the roadway. Secondly, that the accused either was unable to or chose not to use his sure light flashlight device or laser light features before or after Dudley George was shot. That immediately after seeing Dudley George assisted back into the park, he turned to his right and spoke to Sergeant Hebblethwaite with regard to the head count. Further, that Sergeant Deane walked 20 meters but did not have time to get the message over the communication system, re: the muzzle flashes or danger from the sand berm. Further, that Sergeant Deane watched Dudley George move from the position where he was shot to a location in closer proximity to the C.M.U. still carrying the rifle in his hand and still, according to Doctor Spitz's evidence, with the ability to fire a rifle. And, not knowing how seriously he had injured Dudley George, [he] did not fire his weapon again to keep Dudley George from posing any further threat. Further, that Dudley George having just sustained a bullet wound to his chest, which fractured his clavicle completely, punctured his left lung, partially fractured his left eighth rib, completely fractured his left ninth rib, tore a number of blood vessels, that he established as his next priority, the disposal of the weapon he was allegedly carrying. Furthermore, that having made this decision, Dudley

George moved towards the police officers to dispose of the rifle, rather than heading immediately towards the park where his friends and relatives were. Further, that Dudley George, having sustained the injuries described above, was able to throw the rifle into the field or ditch. Further, that Dudley George threw the rifle into an area where Constable Klym and Constable Beauchesne happened to be. Also, that after the threat was over, he sent a message over the communication system, but that message did not include any reference to shooting a man with a rifle, or the rifle having been thrown in the ditch. Also, that someone with the responsibility to insure the security of his fellow officers and the C.M.U. members would not warn them about the rifle. The Court would also have to accept that Constable Beauchesne, having been involved in the Grassy Narrows incident, which resulted in the death of one O.P.P. officer and the wounding of two other officers, having been involved in tracking a suspect through the woods until he was arrested, having received a commissioner's citation for his efforts, was nevertheless not the least bit concerned when Sergeant Deane asked him if he had seen the guy with the gun. Also, that Constable Beauchesne, who gave the impression to the Court of being an intelligent, highly competent member of this elite team, suddenly became disinterested in the subject of a native with a gun because of some telepathic message given to him by Sergeant Deane. Further, that Sergeant Deane chose not to say anything to Sergeant Hebblethwaite about the individual on the roadway with the gun, even though he spoke to Sergeant Hebblethwaite no more than 15 seconds after he saw Dudley George being helped into the park. Further, that Sergeant Deane decided to save this question for his meeting a short time later with Constable Beauchesne.

Counsel agreed that this case was fact driven, and that there was no need for a lengthy discourse on the law as it relates to criminal negligence causing death.

I am therefore going to make reference only to one case which is often cited in matters where credibility may be an issue. In the decision of *R. v. (D)(W)* (1991), 63 C.C.C. (3d) 397, a decision of the Supreme Court of Canada, the Court confirmed that even in cases where the credibility of the witnesses plays a determining part in the judge's verdict, the issue is, as always, whether the Crown's case had been proved beyond a reasonable doubt.

If the accused is believed, I must acquit him. If I do not believe the accused I may still be left with a reasonable doubt as a result of the accused's testimony. Even if the accused's testimony does not raise a reasonable doubt, I must decide whether I am left without a reasonable doubt on the basis of the evidence that I do accept.

These are the findings that the Court is prepared to make at this time. I found Sergeant Hebblethwaite to be a helpful witness, a credible witness before the Court. I will not make a lot of reference to the exhibits except to say that when exhibits 26(a), (b) and (c) which were prepared by Sergeant Deane are put together with exhibit 27 which was prepared by Sergeant Hebblethwaite, what we find is that Sergeant Hebblethwaite is no more than a few meters behind Sergeant Deane when Dudley George is shot.

It follows from that that Sergeant Hebblethwaite was further away from Dudley George than was Sergeant Deane, yet he had no difficulty distinguishing what he recognized to be a pole or a stick. I also find that Dudley George was in Sergeant Hebblethwaite's line of vision. I accept Sergeant Hebblethwaite's testimony in this regard and that this fact would have been unknown to Sergeant Deane at the time of the shooting. I find that Sergeant Hebblethwaite did not see any muzzle flashes other than his own. And that Sergeant Hebblethwaite did not see any firearms in the hands of any native protestors that evening.

There were no Crown witnesses or defence witnesses that saw any weapons in the hands of the First Nations people except for Sergeant Deane and except for Constable Chris Cossett. And at this point, perhaps, I will comment on the testimony of Constable Cossett. The Crown called his testimony amusing, which is one word. I might choose others. Rather than scrutinize Constable Cossett's testimony for any grains of truth that might fall out, I have dismissed it entirely as being clearly fabricated and implausible.

I accept Sergeant Hebblethwaite's evidence that he saw a man turned in the direction of the park after he got up from his one knee, that he was bent at the waist and facing the park, before Sergeant Hebblethwaite turned his attention elsewhere.

In the Court's view this is not a situation of honest but mistaken belief. The accused has maintained throughout that Dudley George was armed. And the accused was able to even describe some of the features of the rifle that he saw Dudley George holding.

I find that Anthony O'Brien (Dudley) George did not have any firearms on his person when he was shot. I find that the accused Kenneth Deane knew that Anthony O'Brien Dudley George did not have any firearms on his person when he shot him. That the story of the rifle and the muzzle flash was concocted *ex post facto* in an ill fated attempt to disguise the fact that an unarmed man had been shot.

The accused testified that the Court heard essentially the same version of events that was given to the Ontario Provincial Police and the Special Investigations Unit in September 1995.

I find, sir, that you were not honest in presenting this version of events to the Ontario Provincial Police investigators. You were not honest in presenting this version of events to the Special Investigations Unit of the Province of Ontario. You were not honest in maintaining this ruse while testifying before this Court. I have considered all of the evidence presented in this case, and on the basis of the evidence that I have accepted, I find you, Kenneth Deane, guilty as charged.

■

Deane was sentenced to a conditional sentence of imprisonment ([1997] O.J. No. 3578 (Ct. Just. (Prov. Div.)), online: QL, a sentence that is no longer available for this offence when committed with a gun, since it now carries a mandatory minimum sentence of four years' imprisonment. His appeal from conviction and the cross-appeal against sentence were dismissed by the Court of Appeal: [2000] O.J. No. 403, online: QL. Civil litigation by George's family against then Premier Harris, some members of his Cabinet and the province of Ontario is ongoing: *George* v. *Harris*, *supra*.

Aboriginal Peoples and Criminal Law.

The use of racial profiling by police has been exposed in several recent cases. Cases such as *Dunn*, mentioned *supra* under **Use of force**, are strongly suggestive of racial profiling. In *Dunn*, the victim of the police assault had been asked to identify himself, while standing in front of his own home at night and having just taken out the garbage, on the basis that the officer believed that he was committing the offence of trespass at night. In *Brown* v. *Durham Regional Police Force* (1998), 43 O.R. (3d) 223 (C.A.) the court ruled that police may use their powers under the highway traffic laws to detain and investigate (profile) members of a motorcycle gang for additional purposes outside of that legislation, as long as these are "proper purposes." In that case, the court said that maintaining the public peace, investigating criminal activity, and intelligence gathering were legitimate purposes that did not detract from the validity of police stops of all gang members en route to a meeting, purportedly to check their documents and vehicle fitness. The court made clear, however, that "if only people of colour were stopped at a checkpoint, the inference could be made that the stop was discriminatory and, therefore, improper." As you read the decision below, think about the other ways in which the defence's argument could be framed using s. 15 of the *Charter*.

R. v. Brown†

[TRAFFORD J.:]

Introduction

On November 1, 1999, Decovan Brown, the appellant, was arrested under s. 253 of the *Criminal Code* for driving a motor vehicle on the Don Valley Parkway in Toronto, having consumed alcohol in such a quantity that its concentration in his blood exceeded the [prescribed] limit. Before he was stopped by the arresting officer, he was driving at a speed slightly in excess of the posted limit in the area. Traffic was moderate at the time. Speeding is common on this freeway. The motor vehicle driven was an expensive one, a Ford Expedition. The appellant is a young black man. At the time of the incident, he was wearing a baseball cap and an athletic suit. He was polite and courteous to the police throughout the investigation of the incident, including when he gave samples of his breath.

At trial the counsel for the defendant made an application under s. 24 of the *Canadian Charter of Rights and Freedom* for an order excluding the results of the breathalyzer tests on the basis of a violation of s. 9 of the *Charter*. It was alleged by the

† (2002), 57 O.R. (3d) 615 at 617–24 (Sup. Ct.).

defence that Mr. Brown was arbitrarily stopped by the investigating officer because of racial profiling rather than for driving at a speed slightly in excess of the posted speed limit. The arrest, in the submission of the defence, was based on the stereotypical assumption that young black men who are driving expensive motor vehicles obtained them by crime or are implicated in recent criminal activity. The defence had a significant amount of evidence to support the application. The evidence included an attack on the credibility of the arresting officer that was arguably substantiated, in part, by reliable independent evidence, and the testimony of the defendant. He was presented to the court as a respectable man who had no prior criminal record and played with the Toronto Raptors of the National Basketball Association.

The learned trial judge dismissed the application without calling upon the Crown Attorney for submissions. A conviction was entered.

This is an appeal against conviction.

Having read the transcript as a whole and considered the submissions of counsel, I am satisfied that it is appropriate to allow the appeal and to order a new trial. These are the reasons leading to this conclusion.

The Nature of the Appeal

The appellant raises a number of issues for the consideration of this court. The learned trial judge misconceived the nature of the practice of racial profiling and the evidence required to establish it. He conducted the trial in a manner giving rise to a reasonable apprehension of bias. He appeared to prejudge the issues of the case. He interjected in support of Crown witnesses. His comments about the application constituted an unwarranted deprecation of defence counsel and his role. Looking at the trial as a whole, in the submission of the appellant, the appearances of justice were undermined because of the inappropriate conduct of the learned trial judge. The appeal should be allowed and the appellant should be acquitted.

The Position of the Respondent Crown

The respondent submits that, when the whole of the proceedings are considered, including the extensive submissions by defence counsel, there were no actions by the learned trial judge that would raise a reasonable apprehension of bias. Nor was there actual bias in this case. Through two days of evidence he showed an appreciation of the facts, the issues and the applicable case law. He engaged in limited, but proper and relevant, dialogue with counsel and the witnesses to clarify questions and evidence given. He attempted to identify the issues pursued by the defence and the evidence directed to them. He ensured that he understood them. Extensive cross-examination of the Crown witnesses was permitted. The learned trial judge did not interfere with the proceedings, misapprehend the issues or belittle either the appellant or the defence counsel. The result was not unreasonable. He was entitled on all the evidence before him to dismiss the application and to find the appellant guilty of the offence charged. It is not for this court to analyze the evidence and to review the record at trial as if this appeal was a trial *de novo*. The appeal, in the submission of the Crown Attorney, should be dismissed.

The Legal Principles Governing the Appeal

Let me begin, then, with a brief review of the legal principles governing the determination of the appeal.

In what circumstances may there be a finding that the conduct of a judge has raised a reasonable apprehension of bias?

Impartiality can be described as a state of mind in which the adjudicator is disinterested in the outcome and is open to persuasion by the evidence and submissions of both parties. In contrast, bias denotes a state of mind that is, in some way, predisposed to a particular result or is closed with regard to particular issues. See *R. v. S.(R.D.)*, [1997] 118 C.C.C. (3d) 353 at 387–88 (S.C.C.) *per* Cory J.

When it is alleged that a decision-maker is not impartial, the test that must be applied is whether the particular conduct gives rise to a reasonable apprehension of bias. Actual bias need not be established. See *S.(R.D.)*, *supra*, at p. 389 *per* Cory J. The test for bias contains a twofold objective element — the person considering the alleged bias must be reasonable and the apprehension of bias itself must also be reasonable in the circumstances of the case. The reasonable person must be an informed person with knowledge of all the relevant circumstances, including the traditions of integrity and impartiality in the judiciary and the duties of judges to uphold them. The reasonable person knows the social reality that forms the background to a particular case such as societal awareness and acknowledgement of the prevalence of racism in a particular community. See *S.(R.D.)*, *supra*, at p. 390 *per* Cory J.

The test for reasonable apprehension of bias is reflective of the reality that while judges can never be neutral, in the sense of pure objectivity, they can and must strive for impartiality. See *S.(R.D.)*, *supra*, at p. 367 *per* L'Heureux-Dubé and McLachlin JJ. The presence or absence of an apprehension of bias, as evaluated through the eyes of the reasonable, informed, practical and realistic person who considers the matter in some detail, is not determined by a very sensitive or scrupulous person but rather by a right-minded person familiar with the circumstances of the case. The reasonable person's knowledge and understanding of the judicial process and the nature of judging, as well as of the community in which the alleged crime occurred, must be considered. Judges in a multiracial and multicultural society will approach the task of judging from their varied perspectives and with an apparent awareness of the sensitivity of the community to the issues raised by the case. See *S.(R.D.)*, *supra*, at pp. 369–370 *per* L'Heureux-Dubé and McLachlin JJ.

Although the threshold for a finding of real or perceived bias is high, courts should be held to the highest standards of impartiality. See *S.(R.D.)*, *supra*, at p. 391 *per* Cory J. There is a presumption that judges will carry out their oath of office. See *S.(R.D.)*, *supra*, at p. 392 *per* Cory J. This presumption can be displaced with cogent evidence demonstrating that something the judge has done gives rise to a reasonable apprehension of bias. Cogent evidence is required. See *S.(R.D.)*, *supra*, at p. 392 *per* Cory J. Suspicion is not enough. The threshold is high because such a finding, as advocated in this appeal, calls into question not only the personal integrity of the trial judge but the integrity of the entire administration of justice. However, as was stated by Cory J. in *R. v. S.(R.D.)*, *supra*, at p. 392:

> It is right and proper that judges be held to the highest standards of impartiality since they will have to determine the most fundamentally important rights of the parties appearing before them. This is true whether the legal dispute arises between citizen and citizen or between the citizen and the state. Every comment that a judge makes from the bench is weighed and evaluated by the community as well as the parties. Judges must be conscious of this constant weighing and make every effort to achieve neutrality and fairness in carrying out their duties. This must be a cardinal rule of judicial conduct.

An appellate court reviewing the impugned conduct must do so in light of the whole trial and contextually.

. . . .

The Analysis of the Trial as a Whole

Before looking at specific aspects of the trial, it is important to appreciate that the application under s. 24 of the *Charter* was based upon an allegation that the arrest of Mr. Brown resulted from racial profiling. This is a sensitive issue to a multicultural community such as Toronto. The application was not frivolous, vexatious or otherwise devoid of legal merit. The defence had a significant amount of evidence to support the application. It included an attack on the credibility of the arresting officer and the reliability of his evidence that was arguably substantiated, in part, by reliable independent evidence. The independent evidence included a videotape of the arresting officer presenting the appellant to the senior officer at the station that arguably showed a second set of notes as alleged by the defence. The arresting officer denied their existence. Only one set of notes was disclosed to the Crown Attorney and the defence. Only one set of notes was used by him in court. There was also a computerized printout that arguably proved the arresting officer began a licence check on the Ford Expedition before he stopped the appellant and obtained, after he had stopped him, information that it was not reported stolen. By then, in the submission of the defence, the arresting officer knew the basis for stopping the appellant was incorrect and had to do something to justify stopping him. This attack on the credibility of the arresting officer was complemented by the testimony of the appellant. If his testimony was accepted by the learned trial judge, it, like the videotape, could have proven the second set of notes and led inferentially to a conclusion that the only basis for stopping him in the circumstances of the case was a stereotypical assumption concerning young black men driving expensive motor vehicles. The approach of the defence was a simple one — to attack the credibility of the arresting officer for the purposes of convincing the learned trial judge to reject his evidence on material points and to invite the court to accept the testimony of Mr. Brown as credible and reliable evidence proving inferentially the subconscious racial stereotyping leading to the arrest. While the learned trial judge eventually knew and appreciated the essential nature of the application, he did not show such an understanding at all material times throughout the trial. The discretionary power given to a trial judge to call upon the defence at the beginning of an application under s. 24 of the *Charter* to summarize the anticipated evidence was not used in this case. See *R.* v. *Kutynec* (1992), 70 C.C.C. (3d) 289 at 301 (Ont. C.A.) for an elaboration of these principles.

Racism is a part of our culture and justice system. In *R.* v. *Parks* (1994), 84 C.C.C. (3d) 353 at 369 (Ont. C.A.) Doherty J.A. said:

> Racism, and in particular anti-black racism, is part of our community's psyche. A significant segment of our community holds overtly racist views. A much larger segment subconsciously operates on the basis of negative racial stereotypes. Furthermore, our institutions, including the criminal justice system, reflect and perpetuate those negative stereotypes. These elements combine to infect our society as a whole with the evil of racism. Blacks are among the primary victims of that evil.

It is helpful to emphasize that racism, whether it be conscious or subconscious, will rarely, if ever, be proven directly. If it is to be proven in court, it will be proven most often through circumstantial evidence.

In my opinion, judges must be particularly vigilant in their efforts to impartially determine applications like this one. Ample scope must be given to counsel attempting to prove such an allegation. Interjections by trial judges in cases like this one to clarify evidence, to further the dialogue with counsel during submissions and to otherwise control the trial process must be undertaken with a keen sensitivity for the requirements of impartiality, the appearances of justice and the undeniable value of imposing just and appropriate sanctions against racism in the administration of justice where it is proven. A judge hearing any such application must be scrupulously aware of the need to maintain the public confidence in the ability of the courts to hear and determine such applications fairly. As was said by Cory J. in *R.* v. *S.(R.D.), supra,* at p. 385:

> Canada is not an insular, homogeneous society. It is enriched by the presence and contributions of citizens of many different races, nationalities and ethnic origins. The multicultural nature of Canadian society has been recognized in s. 27 of the *Charter.* Section 27 provides that the Charter itself is to be interpreted in a manner that is consistent with the preservation and enhancement of the multicultural heritage of Canadians. Yet our judges must be particularly sensitive to the need not only to be fair but also to appear to all reasonable observers to be fair to all Canadians of every race, religion, nationality and ethnic origin. This is a far more difficult task in Canada than it would be in a homogeneous society. Remarks which would pass unnoticed in other societies could well raise a reasonable apprehension of bias in Canada.

Let me make a number of comments about specific aspects of the conduct of the learned trial judge in this case.

First, as the application was clearly one of arguable merit, the remarks made on sentencing, namely:

> ... I do not know whether my tone this afternoon might have displayed my distaste for the matters that were raised during the course of the trial ... you might extend an apology to the officer because I am satisfied the allegations were completely unwarranted. But that is my own assessment. You are not required to share it and I will leave it to you to do what you think is right in that regard ...

were completely inappropriate. In my view, they create an appearance of a mindset throughout the trial inconsistent with the duty to be impartial. No defendant need apologize to anyone for an application brought at trial by a competent defence counsel where the application is of arguable merit, even if it does not succeed. For a trial judge to regard the presentation of such an application as distasteful is a significant departure from his/her obligation to ensure the appearances of justice and the essential fairness of the trial. It is materially inconsistent with the duty of a judge to hear and determine the application with an open mind. Similar observations by this court would be appropriate if the learned trial judge had accepted the defence position on the application and suggested to the police officer that he apologize to the defendant.

Second, while dialogue with counsel during submissions can, and oftentimes does, move the trial to an orderly conclusion by defining the issues to be determined and inviting counsel to make concise submissions on them, that is not what occurred in this case. Here, the learned judge entered into the following dialogue with the defence counsel during his submissions:

> *MR. SKURKA:* What I would ask to be permitted, is to give you the building blocks of the position I'm taking, that's all.
>
> *THE COURT:* I could be anxious if you did because ...
>
> *MR. SKURKA:* Thank you.
>
> *THE COURT:* ... and I think ... if you want me to be frank with you so you know what my concerns are.
>
> *MR. SKURKA:* I do want you to be frank.
>
> *THE COURT:* But it does concern me that you have made such serious allegations, really

quite nasty, malicious, potentially, accusations based on, it seems to me, nothing and you are going to have to persuade me that there is some appropriate basis on which to make this kind of accusation about an alleged racist motivation on the part of the officer. I did not understand your client to say that he had any difficulty with the officers in the dealings that he had with them. He agreed that the officer's evidence concerning the conversation they had was accurate. We saw the videotape. There did not seem to be any particular tension or hostility between the two when they were at the police station.

This remark arguably showed a failure to appreciate material aspects of the evidence at a late stage in the trial. It also arguably showed a failure to appreciate that racial profiling can be a subconscious factor impacting on the exercise of a discretionary power in a multicultural society. Granted, the learned trial judge invited defence counsel to persuade him of the merit of his position. This invitation, however, was a hollow one as the appearances of this dialogue in the context of the trial as a whole are reasonably open to the interpretation that he had determined the merit of the application before counsel was heard on it and that he did not understand the practice of racial profiling. This interpretation of these remarks is consistent with the inappropriate remarks he made while sentencing the appellant.

Third, several remarks made by the learned trial judge during the cross-examination of the arresting officer on material aspects of the application, viewed in the context of the trial as a whole, appeared to show a failure to understand the importance of the evidence, a tendency to prejudge the merit of the application or an inclination to assist the officer at critical stages of the cross-examination. Interjections leading to these appearances occurred during the cross-examination of the arresting officer on a number of important themes — the driver was believed to be a black man as soon as the arresting officer's attention was directed to the Ford Expedition, the existence of a second set of notes that was destroyed and not disclosed to the defence and the time when the appellant was pulled over in relation to the computerized check done by the arresting officer to see, *inter alia*, if the licence was reported stolen. Despite saying that he had not made up his mind and would listen to the application, the comments of the learned trial judge that "... it is a very serious allegation ... and if it is based on the kind of questions you are asking now, I find it a little troubling ...", viewed reasonably, created the appearances of a very different mindset at these and other critical stages of the trial.

Fourth, in the context of these points, the remarks of the judge admonishing the defence counsel for the tone of his voice in the cross-examination of the arresting officer and the references to the amount of time being taken to present the application take on a different meaning than might first be apparent. By themselves, they would not be sufficient to allow the appeal. In the context of the trial as a whole, they added to the appearances of injustice in this case.

Looking at these themes, in the context of the trial as a whole, I am satisfied that there is a reasonable apprehension of bias in this case. This is not a case of a trial judge being biased. This analysis on appeal is not a substitution of my view of the merit of the application for the view of the learned trial judge. The result he arrived at was not unreasonable. However, this is a case where a reasonable person who is aware of the prevalence of racism in our community, the nature of the application and the traditions of integrity and impartiality in the judiciary would, after looking at the trial as a whole, reasonably apprehend a bias on the part of the learned trial judge.

Conclusion

Accordingly, the appeal is allowed and a new trial is ordered.

■

For another case in which the evidence suggests the possibility of "racial profiling" wherein the trial judge was held to have improperly assessed the issues around credibility, see *R.* v. *Richards*, [1999] O.J. No. 1420 (C.A.), online: QL. In that case, while denying that the accused's skin colour was the real impetus for deciding to stop Richards and ask him to produce his licence, the officer "conceded that he checked the vehicle licence while waiting outside the service station and found that it was registered in an "Oriental" name. Further, ... the officer called for "back-up" before stopping the vehicle and his notes indicate the skin colour of the driver and the occupants." See also *R.* v. *Law*, [2002] S.C.J. No. 10, online: QL, where an opportunity to raise the issue of racial profiling was lost.

In this case, Moncton police had, without a warrant, opened a safe belonging to the accused, removed documents, and copied them for a tax violation investigation. While the Court upheld the accused's acquittal on the basis of a s. 8 *Charter* violation, no mention was made by counsel or the Court of the fact that the officer was maintaining a file called "Asian crimes." See the Annotation on this case by Christine Boyle (2002), 48 C.R. (5th) 201 at 202–03.

Saskatchewan

The deaths of several Aboriginal men whose bodies were found frozen in the outskirts of Regina has led to a larger investigation. Lawrence Wegner and Rodney Naistus died in February 2000; they were found without jackets or shoes in a field outside the city. A third man, Darrell Knight, almost died on 28 January 2000 when two officers drove him to the same field, and left him there in –22 degree weather without a jacket. He survived because a night watchman at a powerhouse let him in. His allegations resulted in a trial and conviction of the two officers for unlawful confinement. For discussion of the sentence see **Sentencing**, *supra*. The death of a fourth Aboriginal man, Lloyd Joseph Dustyhorn, from hypothermia hours after his release from police custody in January 2002 is under reinvestigation. An RCMP task force has been convened to determine whether there are links between these deaths and the crime committed against Knight: David Roberts, "RCMP to face snags in probe of native deaths" *The [Toronto] Globe and Mail* (19 February 2000) A3.

Now, turning to issues of racism and policing in the context of the United States, consider the role of video evidence in challenging the denial of racism.

United States

In March 1991, African-American motorist Rodney King was beaten by Los Angeles police officers. The videotaping of that beating might have focused attention on police racism and police brutality; yet many responses at the time to the incident tended to support the police actions. In April 1992, a jury including no African-American jurors acquitted the four white Los Angeles police officers of 10 counts in the beating of Rodney King. That acquittal sparked the biggest civil disturbance in recent U.S. history. Troops were sent in by President George Bush (4500 Marines and federal law enforcement officials) and by California Governor Pete Wilson (6000 National Guards). See Murray Campbell, "Calm creeps back to Los Angeles" *The [Toronto] Globe and Mail* (2 May 1992) A1.

The acquittal and the riots provoked considerable discussion about the role and composition of juries, and about the causes of racism and violence. Maya Angelou wrote, in "The Arc of the Moral Universe is Long, But It Bends Towards Justice" (1991) 8 New Perspectives Q. 36 at 36, that the man who captured the images on video "is an embryonic historian. He, like the photographers at Selma, helped keep our plight in view; helped us to fight our invisibility." The video is important, argues Angelou at 37, because without it "we might have been able to deny our bestiality, but seeing it allowed us to face our barbarism and run from it...." Thus, the Rodney King debacle also resonated with the images preserved by video footage of police brutality against civil rights activists through the 1960s and 1970s in *Eyes on the Prize* (PBS video). Further background information on King's beating and the conduct of the Los Angeles Police Department can be found in the report, *The Independent Commission on the L.A.P.D.* (Los Angeles: R.R. Donnelly Int'l. Printing Services, 1991) (Chair: Warren Christopher).

The officers who assaulted Rodney King were re-tried under federal criminal laws that punish intentional violations of civil rights: Murray Campbell, "Trials and tribulations of a city under pressure" *The [Toronto] Globe and Mail* (2 February 1993) A1, A2. The same defence strategy that was used at the assault trial was again used, that of repeated showing of the video in slow motion, with a running commentary characterizing the victim's movements during the prolonged beating as possible efforts to get up and lunge at the officers (there were 28 officers in all within 25 metres of the assault). The defence strategy also relied on the "thin blue line defence," which holds that all that stands between order and chaos are the police: David Brown, "Postcard from LA LA land" (1992) 17 Alternative L. J. 274. Can you see links between Bernhard Goetz's defence (discussed under **Law and Order**, *supra*) and that of the L.A. officers?

On 24 April 1993 the jury in the second trial returned a verdict finding two of the officers guilty of intentionally violating Mr. King's civil rights, and the two other officers not guilty. Analyses comparing the two trials and their outcomes focus on the facts that: prosecutors in the second trial learned from errors committed by the state prosecutors; Mr. King took the stand to testify in the second trial; the federal prosecutors buttressed the video evidence with eyewitness evidence; the jury was given the opportunity to acquit two of the officers; the jury in the second trial was racially diverse; and the jury was aware of the possible implications of a second acquittal: Tom Matthews *et al.*, "Looking Past the Verdict" *Newsweek* (26 April 1993) 20 at 26.

Community leaders have been quick to point out that the two convictions do not solve the problems of violent policing signalled by the assault on Mr. King, nor the issues of differential treatment within the criminal trial process. Derrick Bell, in his article, "Racism Will Always Be With Us" (1991) 8 New Perspectives Q. 44, shows the importance of standpoint when considering the significance of the beating of Rodney King, noting at 45 that African-Americans saw it as "a graphic comment on the quality of their citizenship." While few whites would advocate police violence against African-Americans, most are willing to make "compromises" if the police assert that this is the only way that they can do their job. Bell argues, therefore, that racism is a permanent feature of American society, and "[i]t is the failure to develop a realistic perspective on the problem that stymies progress and makes setbacks very discouraging" (at 49). By way of illustration, he discusses the famous decision of the United States Supreme Court that ordered desegregation of U.S. schools, "with all deliberate speed," (*Brown v. Board of Education*, 347 U.S. 483 (1954)) as one produced by international pressures created by communism, not by any willingness to acknowledge responsibility for the practice of segregation or to make meaningful changes in access to education for African-Americans: "36 years after *Brown* the schools are resegregated and black children continue to receive an inferior education in substandard facilities" (at 46).

Since the trial of the officers who assaulted Rodney King, numerous events support Bell's reflections regarding the permanence of racism. For example, another African-American motorist was beaten to death by seven police officers soon after the L.A. riots, this time in Detroit (AP, "Motorist beaten to death" *The [Toronto] Globe and Mail* (7 November 1992) A2); a New York white police officer accidentally shot an African-American plainclothes officer four times (Peter Pringle, "Officers' 'friendly fire' heightens racial tension among New York police" *The Ottawa Citizen* (26 August 1994) A10); a Kentucky grand jury refused to indict a white officer who shot and killed an unarmed African-American teenager who was surrendering (NYT, "Officer in Kentucky is Cleared in Killing Of Black Teenager" *The New York Times (International)* (5 February 1995) 12); and an African-American plainclothes officer who repeatedly tried to identify herself was beaten by as many as 20 police officers, who mistook her for a suspect (NYT, "Black Officer Complains Of Beating in Philadelphia" *The New York Times* (13 February 1995) A7).

In February 1992, another home video, this time in Vancouver, captured police violence by the Vancouver Emergency Response Team directed against a Chinese man. As Timothy Appleby reported in "Officer's kick at suspect captured by camera" *The [Toronto] Globe and Mail* (24 February 1992) A5:

> In black face masks and military-style fatigues, four police officers are standing over Feng Hua Zhang. Two others stand by, weapons drawn, seemingly nonchalant. First comes the punch, a right-handed blow to the body. Then the kick, a hard one, which appears to strike Mr. Zhang's head as he lies face down in the alley after being tear-gassed and dragged out of his basement apartment....
>
> According to the formal complaint he filed, Mr. Zhang was in his apartment when he looked up to see a masked man standing in his doorway and holding a rifle. Thinking he was being robbed, Mr. Zhang fled to his bedroom, locked the door and hid in a closet.
>
> There was a bang, the sound of tear gas being fired through a living room window. Mr. Zhang's roommate, Wai Shuen Wong, was taken out in handcuffs and then the police came for Mr. Zhang. They shot the bedroom door lock and yelled questions at him, which he apparently couldn't understand. [He speaks only Cantonese.]
>
> Both men were treated in hospital for cuts, bruises and tear gas inhalation.

There were no charges laid, and the police said they were acting on the basis of a tip about guns and drugs.

SEXISM

Systemic sexism has also been raised as a legal issue in the context of policing.

Doe v. Metropolitan Toronto Commissioners of Police[†]

[MACFARLAND J.:]

Jane Doe was raped and otherwise sexually assaulted at knifepoint in her own bed in the early morning hours of August 24, 1986 by a stranger subsequently identified as Paul Douglas Callow. Ms. Doe then lived in a second-floor apartment at 88 Wellesley Street East, in the City of Toronto; her apartment had a balcony which was used by the rapist to gain access to her premises. At the time, Ms. Doe was the fifth known victim of Callow who would become known as "the balcony rapist".

Ms. Doe brings a suit against the Metropolitan Toronto Police Force (hereafter referred to as MTPF) on two bases; firstly she suggests that the MTPF conducted a negligent investigation in relation to the balcony rapist and failed to warn women whom they knew to be potential targets of Callow of the fact that they were at risk. She says, as the result of such conduct, Callow was not apprehended as early as he might otherwise have been and she was denied the opportunity, had she known the risk she faced, to take any specific measures to protect herself from attack. Secondly, she said that the MTPF being a public body having the statutory duty to protect the public from criminal activity, must exercise that duty in accordance with the *Canadian Charter of Rights and Freedoms* and may not act in a way that is discriminatory because of gender. She says the police must act constitutionally, they did not do so in this case and as the result, her rights under ss. 15 and 7 of the *Charter* have been breached. She seeks damages against the MTPF under both heads of her claim.

The trial of this action took place over approximately eight weeks; some 30 witnesses were called and voluminous documentary evidence filed. Counsel have filed lengthy written argument and had two days in which to give an oral outline of their written submissions.

OVERVIEW

It is necessary when considering claims under s. 15 of the *Charter* that they be considered in relation to the larger social, political and legal context. In the words of La Forest J. in *Eldridge* v. *British Columbia (Attorney General)*, [1997] 3 S.C.R. 624 at p. 668, 151 D.L.R. (4th) 577:

> As Wilson J. held in *Turpin*, the determination of whether a law is discriminatory is a contextual exercise. It is important, she explained, at p. 1331, "to look not only at the impugned legislation ... but also to the larger social, political and legal context".

In this respect the plaintiff called Dr. Peter Jaffe, well experienced in the topic of male violence against women, to give evidence in relation to the social and political context in which the plaintiff's discrimination claim is made.

In his evidence Dr. Jaffe cited a number of surveys and studies which have concluded that a very large number of Canadian women have been sexually assaulted by Canadian men. This social phenomenon is not new and has been known for many years.

The evidence establishes beyond peradventure that among adults, the perpetrators of sexual violence are overwhelmingly male and the victims overwhelmingly female. It is not disputed that this fact was known to the MTPF in 1986.

As Dr. Jaffe explained, sexual violence is a form of violence; it is an act of power and control rather than a sexual act. It has to do with the perpetrator's desire to terrorize, to dominate, to control, to humiliate; it is an act of hostility and aggression. Rape has nothing to do with sex, everything to do with anger and power.

It is accepted that one of the consequences of the pervasiveness of male sexual violence in our society is that most women fear sexual assault and in many ways govern their conduct because of that fear. In this way male sexual violence operates as a method of social control over women. For example, women are likely to avoid activities which they perceive may put them at risk of male sexual violence. They will, for example, avoid going out alone in the evening. As plaintiff's counsel put it in written submissions: "The sexual victimization of women is one of the ways that men create and perpetuate the power imbalance of the male-dominated gender hierarchy that characterizes our society."

It is also proved, on the evidence, that the majority of sexual assaults committed against women

---

[†] (1998), 39 O.R. (3d) 487 (Ont. Ct. (Gen. Div.)) 487 at 489–522.

are not reported to police, a fact of which the MTPF was also aware in 1986. The evidence establishes, to my satisfaction, that a reason many sexual assault victims do not report to police is because they have concern about the attitudes of the police or courts to this type of incident and this fact has been recognized by the Supreme Court of Canada: see *R. v. Osolin*, [1993] 4 S.C.R. 595 at p. 628, 109 D.L.R. (4th) 478, where Madam Justice L'Heureux-Dubé said in part:

> One of the most powerful disincentives to reporting sexual assaults is women's fear of further victimization at the hands of the criminal justice system; as I discussed in *Seaboyer, supra*, at p. 650, almost half of unreported incidents may be traced to this perception on the part of sexual assault victims. With good reason, women have come to believe that their reports will not be taken seriously by police and that the trial process itself will be yet another experience of trauma.

For those women who do report the fact that they have been sexually assaulted, the police constitute their first contact with the criminal justice system. At this preliminary stage, the police can and do act as a filtering system for sexual assault cases. If, for example, an investigating officer determines that a particular complaint is "unfounded", it likely will not proceed further in the justice system. Studies exist which show that, generally, the "unfounded" rate for crimes of assault is lower than for crimes of sexual assault.

One of the reasons suggested for the higher "unfounded" rate in relation to sexual assaults is the widespread adherence among investigating police officers to rape mythology, that is, the belief in certain false assumptions, usually based in sexist stereotyping, about women who report being raped. The fact that these stereotypical beliefs are widely held in society is a factor to be considered in relation to the larger social and political context in which this aspect of the plaintiff's claim must be analyzed.

Dr. Jaffe in his evidence gave a number of examples of common rape myths:

- that women lie about being raped;
- that women are not reliable reporters of events;
- that women are prone to exaggerate;
- that women falsely report having been raped to get attention.

In general, in matters relating to rape and sexual assault women tend to report things which have no basis in fact. There exists the belief that the report is false, grossly exaggerated or is done for another purpose such as attention seeking, essentially that women either precipitated or falsely reported rapes. The literature documents in far more detail and provides more examples of commonly held rape myths involving the attribution of stereotypical characteristics to survivors of rape and other serious sexual assaults.

The existence of rape myths is not something new; their existence and widely held belief among members of society in general has been well-known at least since the early 1970s when rape trauma began to be studied in a serious way. Certainly those persons engaged in the various fields of endeavour that would cause them to come into contact with survivors of sexual assault would have been aware of the Rape Trauma Syndrome and Rape Mythology from as early as the mid-1970s.

All of the investigative police personnel called to give evidence in this proceeding were aware of these matters in 1986 and earlier.

Every police officer who testified in this proceeding repeated the mantra that sexual assault was a very serious crime second only to homicide.

Problems Within the MTPF Concerning the Investigation of Sexual Assaults

It is important to keep in mind that the events giving rise to this lawsuit occurred in 1986 — now some 12 years ago.

In 1975 four members of the MTPF prepared a detailed report for the then Chief of Police, Harold Adamson; that report was entitled "Report of the Police Committee on Rape" and is dated July 30, 1975. The stated purpose of the report was to:

> look into the rape problem in our jurisdiction with a view to:
> (a) preparing a response to the Brief prepared by the Rape Crisis Centre for Alderman Dorothy Thomas; and
> (b) assessing the feasibility and/or advisability of forming a Special Squad for the investigation of sexual assaults.

This document is an important one in understanding the state of the police knowledge at the time. The four main categories of the report were: Statistical Analysis for the years 1970–1974, Victim Survey, Quality of Investigations and Training Programs.

It was learned from the analysis that of the 907 rapes reported in this five-year period only 37.5 per cent of them were found to be "confirmed" rapes. The recommendation is made by the authors of the report:

That the police explore some means of subtracting false rape reports from statistics before publishing them for the information of the community.

The authors then go on to observe:

The fact that so many occurrences are shown to be unconfirmed does not relieve the Police of their obligation to thoroughly investigate all reported rapes but a question does arise. On what basis is the decision made to categorize a report as founded or unfounded? From reading many occurrences, it would appear that the decision may be an arbitrary one made by the investigator without benefit of consultation with or confirmation from supervisory personnel or unit commanders. In that case, the personality, attitudes and experience of the investigating officer become a matter of concern not only for the victim but for the reputation of the Police and their stated desire to produce top quality investigation and case preparation. Stated simply — are all unconfirmed rapes really unconfirmed or should some of them, given proper investigation, be listed as confirmed? The question arises because the figures are so dramatically different e.g. only 37.5% of reported rapes confirmed as such during the years 1970–1974.

Recommendation: That experienced investigators take responsibility for rape investigations and that their decisions be subject to scrutiny and confirmation by senior investigative and supervisory personnel so that all reported rapes are properly investigated and categorized for statistical purposes.

Recommendation: That supervisors take into account the attitudes, personality and experience of an investigator to whom they assign rape investigations.

While discussing the investigator and the quality of investigation, is it possible that the number of rapists charged and convicted might increase if the above recommendations were implemented and the victims scrupulously and sensitively assisted through the investigative and court processes? Charges are not possible in some cases for a number of reasons, but should the Police be satisfied to lay charges in only 38.7% of confirmed rape cases as is indicated during the period 1970–1974?

Concern is expressed here that reported rapes should be categorized properly as confirmed or not.

A sampling of the comments of some of the victims who were interviewed for the report is interesting for the concerns expressed back in 1975 for example:

3. The majority remarked about the number of police officers involved in their cases — initially, during questioning, and during subsequent investigation.
4. Many commented that they were not kept informed of the status of the case, including final disposition.
5. Most were embarrassed to discuss the intimacies of the act with investigators and some of these felt that the male officers were embarrassed as well.
6. The majority expressed the opinion that they would have preferred relating to a mature, experienced female officer. They said that if a woman was not available, they would prefer to speak to an older, mature male (NOT a young policeman or policewoman).
7. Most expressed a desire to have a relative or friend present during the interview. Many who made such requests were refused.
8. Many wondered if the same investigators could not be in charge of the whole case, so that they could relate the facts only once.
9. Many women would prefer that police inform them and explain the reasons for looking into their past, particularly if they intended to interview former boy friends, neighbours, family, etc.
10. Most would appreciate more privacy at police stations. They were of the opinion that everyone wanted to see or talk to them. They would remind police officers that they are not victims by choice.
11. The court procedure was not always explained to witnesses.

The authors also noted that:

In our anxiety to produce results measured in arrests and convictions, the importance of treating complainants with respect, sympathy and understanding has not received the attention it deserves in field and college training programs.

And the recommendation made:

That Procedure 40, Rules and Regulations, be amended to reflect the importance of providing discreet sympathetic handling of the rape victim in addition to the mechanics of the investigation.

The authors acknowledged that their inquiries demonstrated that while most investigations were "excellent . . . some are shoddy and incomplete and decisions not to prosecute are made for obscure and flimsy reasons". They go on to observe that generally experienced investigators do a better job than those without personal experience themselves and/or without the availability of anyone else with experience to give them guidance and advice. It was recommended that competent, experienced investigators be made available for rape investigations and that supervisors take into account the attitude, personality and experience of an officer to whom they assign a rape investigator; that suitable controls and supervision be put in place over the progress of investigations and decisions being made by having an "independent" and supervisory reader of the occurrence reports among others.

The report indicated that while existing training programs were adequate it conceded greater emphasis should be placed on the needs of the victim. It is suggested that supervisory personnel be required to seek out those not doing a satisfactory job and ensure that such persons either come up to an acceptable standard of proficiency, or if such persons are unable to do so, that they be placed in positions where they will not "become an embarrassment to the Force". It was agreed greater emphasis should and would be placed on the treatment of victims of sexual assault.

As indicated above these observations are indicative of the awareness of the MTPF of some of the concerns of members of the public and of some of the shortcomings of the force in relation to the investigation of rape in 1975.

The next significant study in which the MTPF were directly involved was the Report of the Task Force on Public Violence against Women and Children. As stated in the introduction of the preliminary report of that group there had been a number of brutal rapes and murders in Toronto during the summer of 1982. In response to the public concern and outrage they generated, the Metropolitan Toronto Chairman at the time, Paul Godfrey, requested the Metropolitan Toronto Board of Commissioners of Police to establish a Task Force to examine the various issues raised and the Task Force on Public Violence against Women and Children was created. The MTPF had representatives on the Task Force and on several of its subcommittees. The preliminary report of the Task Force was published in July 1983. Among the recommendations and observations made by the Task Force in that preliminary document were the following:

- police officers are human beings, some will be more suitable than others to investigate sexual assault cases.
- training at Police College should include and emphasize rape trauma syndrome; training should be ongoing.
- a specialized sexual assault investigation team should be created.
- that crime prevention should be made a higher priority of the MTPF.

- there should be a publicity campaign by MTPF to increase public awareness of crime prevention programs and increase the public's participation in such programs.
- MTPF should encourage the media to alert the public to crime problems and means of crime prevention.
- police officers should receive additional training to scrutinize them to the special needs of women ... victims of violence.
- courses should be made immediately available at the Police College and in the form of video presentations in each police station.
- historically, sexual assaults have had a very low rate of reportage.

One of the reasons cited for non-reporting by victims was the victim's fear of not being believed and the Task Force recommended in this respect that police officers investigating these crimes be specially trained to be aware of and sensitive to the needs of these victims.

Linked to the recommendation that a specialized squad be created for the investigation of such crimes was the recognition of the need for co-ordination of sexual assault investigation on a Metro-wide basis.

In September 1983 the MTPF responded to the preliminary report of the Task Force intending to specifically focus on the recommendations directed at the MTPF. They agreed with each and every one of the observations and recommendations noted above. The MTPF reported that a course outline and proposed syllabus had been developed for "Sexual Assault and Child Abuse Investigative Techniques" to deal with victims of sexual assault and their unique problems. The course would be a week long, would include guest lecturers from various professions dealing with sexual assault victims and would start in October of "this year" — i.e., October of 1983.

Virtually all of the recommendations and observations contained in the Task Force's Preliminary Report are contained in the final report of that group delivered in March 1984. The only exception relates to the formation of a specialist squad. In the final report the committee preferred specialized training generally for all police officers rather than for a single specialized squad.

Again the Task Force noted that historically sexual assaults have a low rate of reportage and the need for the co-ordination of sexual assault investigations on a Metro-wide basis.

MTPF responded to the final report of the Task Force and there are three responses filed in evidence — the first bears the front page notation "Operational Planning, June 1984", the second "March 1986" and the third "Family and Youth Services

September, 1986". The second and third responses appear to be the same but they differ from the first response to the Final Report. Again the recommendations are accepted and the progress on implementation of those recommendations to date is set out.

It would appear then from the written material emanating from the MTPF to the public that by March 1984, MTPF not only knew and understood the importance and the necessity of the training of all officers in relation to the investigation of sexual assaults,

- that officers be taught and understand the Rape Trauma Syndrome and Rape Mythology.
- such courses be held both at College and every station across Metro.
- that victims of sexual assault be treated sensitively and respectfully.
- that officers who by their personality or otherwise were unsuited for the investigation of sexual assaults would be assigned elsewhere.
- that officers assigned to the investigation of sexual assaults would be supervised by senior experienced officers who would be required to read and sign off on occurrence reports filed.
- that the force become more focused on crime prevention and work with the media to inform the community of crime problems and crime prevention techniques.
- that there was a pressing need for the co-ordinating of all sexual assault investigations across Metro Toronto.

but that they had begun to implement the recommendations in all training programs, some of which would eventually reach all officers.

The office of the Sexual Assault Co-ordinator was created in direct response to the recommendations of the Task Force on Public Violence against Women and Children — or the Godfrey Task Force as it became known. Its function in a very general sense was to look into the sexual abuse of adults generally, to catalogue and categorize all aspects of these crimes, to act as a liaison with other agencies both internal and external to the force and to train police officers.

The purpose was obviously for the assistance of the officers engaged in investigating these types of crimes. Detective Sgt. Margo Boyd detailed the function and provided a history of the development of this office. She described the difficulties encountered in 1985 in trying to computerize the information.

On the evidence it would appear that one of the major difficulties faced by this office, if not the major difficulty, was that it appeared to have little credibility with the officers who were investigating these crimes. Detective Sgt. Boyd reported that when Bill Cameron telephoned her in relation to this investigation, she was pleased that "we had some credibility . . . that investigators were calling for help".

In September 1986 Ms. Boyd authored a report which her immediate superior passed up the chain of command. That report clearly set out the problems the MTPF was still having as of that date. Ms. Boyd confirmed in her evidence that these problems were not new as of the date of this report — September 29, 1986 — but had been ongoing to her knowledge from early 1985. There was some effort made to address these problems by a training blitz over the summer of 1985 but the problems continued into 1986 and thereafter.

Detective Sgt. Boyd's report which Inspector Dennis of the Family and Youth Services sent on to Supt. Maywood of Investigation Services was a hard-hitting document. The problems were clearly stated and set out. Inspector Dennis remarked in his covering memorandum:

> this police force is not meeting the needs of sexual assault victims.
>
> the MTPF has committed to improving the method to which we respond to sex assault victims. Although the Police Force has agreed, the officers in the field are not meeting that commitment.
>
> the monitoring of these (sexual assault) investigations has revealed that there is less adherence to the procedures, less investigation into the occurrences, less resources being utilized and a lack of understanding and support being given to the victim.

He concludes the covering memorandum with the following:

> The object of this report is not to identify individual mistakes as it should be pointed out that the problems being discussed have been seen *in every division in each district.* (Emphasis added)

The author of the report made the following observations which are important I think in the context of this action:

> Victims' response to sexual assault is varied. When the victim becomes overly concerned with the control she now must regain in her life, she could be described as "over reactive" and at times "obstructive". Many trained sexual assault investigators can handle this situation. However, we are finding that certain "trained" officers are unable to deal with the victims' "response". This is reflected usually in a complaint from either the victim or hospital personnel in terms of the

"treatment" the victim received from the police officer.

Certain victims' statements and synopsis as shown by the occurrence reports are not accurate and a proper analysis based on the information on the synopsis is not possible. The reasons for the inaccuracies are questionable.

"Trained" sexual assault investigators are ignoring important factors dealing with forensic evidence collection. ... in many cases the Identification Bureau is not notified to attend.

The "supplementary reports" to an original sexual assault occurrence are not being submitted and we cannot determine if any follow-up at all by the investigating officer has taken place.

Victims of serious sexual assaults are not being "called back" by anyone involved with the investigation. The victim has then initiated a telephone call to the police unit concerned and in essence been "brushed off".

The victim has now become not only a victim of a criminal assault, but the victim of "our" poor investigative follow-up.

Occurrence Reports reflect the investigator's belief or disbelief of the victim's complaint.

In reported incidents, the investigator disbelieves the victim but cannot advise as to what investigation he has done in support or to refute the victim's story. This is reflected by noted discrepancies, cautions of public mischief and polygraph threats.

Occurrences can be cleared based on judgments of character and comments on victim's behaviour and not as established by investigation or lack of forensic evidence.

It is observed that although the Godfrey Task Force recommended the establishment of a Sexual Assault Co-ordinator and the training of specialized sexual assault co-ordinators — and although the Force responded to both recommendations the incidents, which are the subject of the report, demonstrate that "we have some trained field personnel that have done a poor job of not only investigating a criminal sexual assault but have also done a poor job of dealing with the victim!"

Suggested reasons for the poor investigative qualities were:

(a) individual personality of the officer;
(b) lack of officer's ability to co-ordinate his time and caseload to incorporate follow-up investigation and victim "feed back".

It was observed that "inappropriate" personnel were sent to be trained as sexual assault specialists and rather than the "cream of the crop" being sent — officers were sent on the basis of who was available. Not all investigating officers responded favourably to the Sexual Assault Co-ordinator.

These shortcomings in relation to sexual assault investigations were not new and the officers in the upper ranks of the MTPF were well aware of them.

In his May 8, 1986 memorandum to the then Chief of Police, Jack Marks, in relation to the Toronto Sexual Assault Research Project, Inspector Dennis outlined these same difficulties which had been identified.

Detective Sgt. Boyd annexed to her report a "random" selection of occurrence reports to demonstrate the problems which she outlined in her report.

I found it unsettling that in at least one-half of this random selection the "motive" ascribed to the offence is that of "sexual gratification" which to me belies a very basic misunderstanding of this crime on the part of the investigators involved. As Dr. Jaffe stated, there is nothing sexual about rape; it is an act of violence.

Detective Sgt. Boyd details in notes annexed to the actual occurrences some of the problems revealed in the occurrence report attached.

For example:

1. police officer's absolute refusal to even file an occurrence report.
2. a victim reporting the fact she'd been sexually assaulted was yelled at so loudly by the Desk Sgt. that the S/Sgt on duty came to investigate the noise at the front desk; victim was never informed she would be required to go to court and avoided the service of a subpoena fearing her attacker would return and kill her — subpoena served by plain clothes officers who confined the victim in an elevator and chased her down a hallway for the purpose.
3. first officers on scene advised her to go to Women's College Hospital and C.I.B. personnel told her there was no point in doing so; no photos of injuries and marks left from binding; no call back for three months.
4. victim could neither hear nor speak; C.I.B. officer assigned because of ability to "sign" began by saying he did not believe the victim and refused to sign saying she (the victim) could lip read well enough; cautioned her with public mischief charge; accused her of having intercourse with a boyfriend and reporting sexual assault.
5. judgments and comments about her demeanour "did not appear to be upset at all"; disbelief of her report.
6. comments about the victim's behaviour i.e. she drinks to the point of oblivion; incon-

sistencies in report indicating victim not assaulted — disbelief of victim.
7. opinion of officer — "it would appear to me from talking to her, this young man is only fulfilling a fantasy of hers".
8. doctor not spoken to and forensic opinions ignored — all evidence consistent with victim's report, none inconsistent; victim cautioned with public mischief and advised to take polygraph; although hysterical and sobbing every time officer spoke to her, this was an act "put on".

(I have not included here those reports in relation to the seven-year-old male).

The last group of reports selected by Det. Sgt. Boyd for inclusion in the report were prepared by Police Constable Ian Moyer and by now Staff Sgt. Stephen M. Duggan in relation to the sexual assault of B.K. B.K. was the second known victim of the balcony rapist. Ms. Boyd noted:

9. entire occurrence slanted towards the opinion the victim is lying and she is disbelieved; discrepancies questioned and pointed out; public mischief discussed; comments regarding [victim's] lack of emotion; opinions and speculation on [victim's] behaviour and reasons for reporting a fictitious rape; "the story about an intruder having sexual relations with her is not plausible at this time."

In spite of the problems noted in the 1975 MTPF's own report on rape, the recommendations of the Godfrey Task Force and the reports from the Sexual Assault Co-ordinator's office — the problems in relation to the investigation of sexual assault by the MTPF continued in 1985 and 1986. While public pronouncements were made to the effect that steps had been taken to implement the various recommendations made, the reality was that the *status quo* remained unchanged. Whatever the changes were that may have been implemented they were clearly ineffective.

As Inspector Jean Boyd would note to Chief Marks in 1987:

The bottom line is we are going to get roasted very soon if we don't get our act together. *Over three years have passed since the recommendations were tabled and we are not very much further ahead* except that Margo does a considerable amount of in-house and community speaking. WAVA has identified and it is accepted that more intensive training is required. (Emphasis added)

With this background I move now to consider the specific investigation in issue.

The Specific Investigation

I am told that much of the MTPF documentation in relation to the investigation of the balcony rapist has been destroyed. All that remains are the occurrence reports and the officers' memo books for the most part. Additional documentation which was kept by officers working on the case while the investigation was active have been destroyed. While most of the officers were still in possession of their individual memo books, Staff Sgt. Duggan, who investigated the B.K. rape, was not; his memo books for this period were destroyed. So that it is perfectly clear, I should say there is no evidence that there was any deliberate destruction of records on the part of the MTPF. I point this out simply to record that by reason thereof the police were somewhat hampered in giving their evidence.

It is necessary in order to fully understand the investigation of the Jane Doe assault to also have reference to the investigations into the four other related assaults beginning with that of P.A. on December 31, 1985; B.K. on January 10, 1986; R.P. on June 25, 1986 and F.D. on July 25, 1986. Each of these women were victims of Paul Douglas Callow.

All of the attacks were within the geographical confines of what was known as 52 Division with the exception of the first attack which occurred within 51 Division of the MTPF. All were within very close proximity to the intersection of Church and Wellesley Streets in Toronto in an area known as the Church/Wellesley area.

P.A.

P.A., at the time she was attacked, lived in apartment 301 at 437 Jarvis Street, Toronto. In the early morning hours of December 31, 1985 she was raped and otherwise sexually assaulted at knifepoint in her own bed by a stranger who was subsequently identified as Paul Douglas Callow. The knife used during the attack had been taken from her own kitchen drawer. During the attack her head was covered so that she was unable to see her attacker who continued to speak to her conversationally throughout the attack. The locking mechanism on the balcony door of her apartment was broken and the door could not be locked. After the attack when P.A. left her bedroom she noted that the balcony door was open and as she reported to the police, assumed this was how her attacker had gained entrance to her apartment. P.A. told police she had ensured the front door to her apartment was locked before retiring that evening. It was through the front door that her attacker fled following the incident.

Immediately following the attack, and after notifying police, P.A. called her boyfriend "Gerry" who lived in the apartment next door to her in apartment 302. Gerry's apartment balcony was immediately beside P.A.'s apartment balcony.

The investigating officer who arrived at the scene noted in his occurrence report as follows:

> *Note:* the only way onto the #301 balcony is by way of #302 (practicably).

And later:

> It is the writer's opinion that the only way to gain entrance was from the balcony of #302. The occupant I.D. as Gerry _____ 09 Oct. 48 who was with her at the time of arrival of police matches the general description given by the victim and will be spoken to at a later time today by 51 investigators.

As is evident from the occurrence reports filed as well as from P.A.'s letters of complaint following the arrest of Callow, from the very outset the investigating officer insisted to P.A. that the assailant was her boyfriend. She denied it and when she pointed out to police that the description of her attacker did not match her boyfriend's, it was suggested she was protecting her boyfriend. She described her attacker, as the officer recorded it, as follows:

> *Suspect*: The complainant described the attacker as male, white, approximately 6' tall "built like Gerry, maybe thinner" 150 lbs. Dark fine shaggy hair to the collar, unshaven but not as full as a beard. The male was wearing a dark leather jacket with a light-coloured sweater and dress shirt underneath. The male was also wearing dark pants "not jeans but something finer like a dress pant". The complainant also stated the male had a soft spoken voice "kind of sexy and sweet" also a dark belt.

Shockingly, on the very day she had been assaulted, a police officer telephoned her while she was in the shower. She was asked why it had taken so long for her to answer the phone and when she explained that she had been in the shower — remarked that he should have been there.

She was asked invasive personal questions about the number of men she was seeing at the time. Police seemed preoccupied with P.A.'s personal sexual habits.

P.A. was not kept informed of the status of the investigation; what she learned was as the result of her own inquiry.

B.K.

B.K. lived in apartment 202 at 60 Gloucester Street, Toronto when she was raped in her bed in the early hours of January 10, 1986. Her attacker, who would later be identified as Paul Douglas Callow, wore a towel about his head with a hole cut into it which allowed him to see; he also held a knife, which had come from B.K.'s kitchen, to her face. Again the attacker apparently gained entrance to B.K.'s apartment by the balcony; there were no signs of forced entry to the front door. During the assault her attacker spoke conversationally to her. Before leaving her apartment, her attacker cut her telephone line.

P.C. Moyer in his occurrence report completed that same day noted that B.K.:

> ... was calm and relaxed and related the details of the story easily without emotion. These observations made by the investigating officer at the scene and at the hospital do not negate the possibility that a rape occurred but they do tend to shed some doubt on the credibility of the victim's story.

and further:

> Area of occurrence searched by Grummet and Dixon for weapon and towel negative results. Apartment was immaculate and looked undisturbed, with the exception of the blood from the victim's cut there is no evidence that anything happened in the apartment — no sign of forced entry.

and later:

> Victim was interviewed by Sgts. Duggan and P.C. Giancola at length and it is evident that this occurrence may be cleared with a public mischief charge once forensic examination complete.
>
> Investigation should be held back until results complete.

All of the foregoing observations were recorded by P.C. Moyer on the day of the attack — January 10, 1986. There is no apparent follow-up investigation until April 21, 1986 when we have the first supplementary report prepared by Staff Sgt. Duggan.

It is obvious from the subsequent occurrence reports that Staff Sgt. Duggan did not believe B.K.'s version of the events. In his report dated April 25, 1986 he opines as to a possible motive why B.K. would report a fictitious rape. I found the reasons he cited for disbelieving B.K.'s account of the events of January 10, 1986 to be simplistic, superficial, irrelevant and generally uninformed.

He concludes she was seeing a man other than her stated boyfriend at the time; that there were no signs of forced entry to the front door of her apartment; that she was too calm in reporting the incident; that it was impossible, within the given time-frame of the attack, for her attacker to have taken one of her towels and cut a hole in it as B.K. described, and noted that she had a matching set of towels without any missing; that her stated boyfriend at the time stopped seeing her because of her moods and tendency to fantasize; that she had given the boyfriend venereal disease and suggested this must go to show her possible sexual activities; that she was an only child with some contact with her mother, no immediate friends and keeps to herself. In conclusion he says that he does not doubt B.K. had sexual intercourse "during the incident" but is "positive" she knows who her attacker is — he then goes on to theorize a possible motive for reporting a fictitious rape.

As Det. Sgt. Boyd observed when commenting on these occurrence reports in relation to the B.K. attack they are "slanted toward the opinion the victim is lying" and she is disbelieved for no legitimate or substantiated reason.

Staff Sgt. Duggan had taken the sexual assault investigators' course in March 1986; only a month before he completed the April 1986 occurrence reports; one can only conclude that the course was ineffective in influencing his views in relation to the crime of sexual assault.

R.P.

She was raped and otherwise sexually assaulted at knifepoint in her own bed in the early morning hours of June 25, 1986 by an unknown assailant who covered his face with one of her shirts. At the time she lived alone at apartment 307 — 60 Gloucester Street in the same building as B.K. on the floor above. She was the third known victim of the balcony rapist who would be identified as Paul Douglas Callow. During the attack he tied her hands behind her back. Like the assailant in B.K.'s attack he initially indicated he wanted money. He spoke to her conversationally as he had to P.A. and B.K. After the attack he left by the front door of her apartment.

The description she provided of her attacker to police is recorded as follows:

> Male white late 20's — 5'10" 150 lbs light build dark shoulder length greasy straight hair. Days growth dark stubble, thin face around jaw, wearing blue jeans with a dark belt with a silver colour large buckle in the shape of a horseshoe. Solid black sleeveless t-shirt.

Although the officer at the scene noted that the windows leading to the balcony were open and without screens, it was also noted that although R.P. reported locking her front door by engaging all three locks on it before retiring on the evening of her attack, entry could have been gained via the front door without too much difficulty and without leaving signs of forced entry.

It is of interest to note that in a small article which appeared in the Toronto Star newspaper on the day of R.P.'s attack, it was noted:

> For the second time in 6 months a tenant in a Gloucester Street apartment building has been raped by a man who climbed the side of the building to get through a balcony window.
>
> Metro police suspect the same man committed the rape last January of a woman who lived on the second floor.
>
> This morning at 3 a.m., a 24-year old tenant of the third floor was awakened by a man in her bedroom brandishing a cheese cutter he had taken from the kitchen.
>
> She suffered a cut hand when she tried to fight him off.

It would appear that by June 25, 1986 MTPF had made at least a tentative link between the B.K. and R.P. rapes.

F.D.

F.D. was also attacked in her own bed, in her apartment #206 at 89 Isabella Street, Toronto. Her assailant was armed with a butcher knife, taken from F.D.'s apartment. He tied her hands behind her back and raped and otherwise sexually assaulted her. Ms. F.D. was the fourth known victim of Paul Douglas Callow. Her attacker had gained access to her apartment through a balcony window and left through the front door. Ms. F.D. was unable to describe her attacker because he covered her head during the attack. She did tell police he had long hair because she had been able to feel it, a gruff voice and was unshaven. Again the rapist spoke to F.D. conversationally during the assault and asked if she had any money or gold.

In his supplementary occurrence report dated July 25, 1986 Sgt. Bill Cameron recorded the following notation:

> This occurrence may be related to two similar ones that happened at 60 Gloucester Street in January and June of this year.

F.D. discovered that Callow had taken some of her jewellery and a camera from her apartment and provided Mr. Cameron with a description of those items.

By memorandum in writing dated July 29, 1988 Sgt. Jim Hughes of the 52 C.I.B. office reported to his superior, Staff Sgt. Hein, in relation to the F.D. rape as follows:

> The following steps have been taken with regards to sexual assaults in the Gloucester/Isabella area:
> 1. 172's have been obtained from the Crime Analyst.
> 2. Provincial Alert with the M.O. of the suspect has been sent out on the chance he has had past police contact.
> 3. Officers in Zone 2 have been advised of the occurrences. Since investigators believe the suspect may live in the area they have been encouraged to increase the 172's, especially in the early morning hours.
> 4. A key to the victim's apartment at 89 Isabella has been obtained for "occasional use" as an observation post.
> 5. Special attention has been given the area by Sgts. Hughes and Petruzzellis during their 7pm to 3am shifts both Monday and Tuesday. Sgt. Cameron is carrying this on throughout this night shift.
>
> Unfortunately the time period between assaults makes constant surveillance of this area a difficult procedure both to man and to justify. The investigators do not wish to scare off the suspect if he in fact lives in the area by overwhelming police presence.
>
> The writer feels that building superintendents should be contacted and that they advise "trusted tenants", especially single women to be aware of the occurrences and advise police of any person who they feel may be suspect.

Sergeant Hughes' suggestion that "trusted tenants" in apartment buildings in the area be made aware of the occurrences was not acted upon.

Sergeant Cameron testified that he did not agree with Sgt. Hughes' suggestion that "trusted tenants" be warned or alerted to the sexual assaults. By this time he says, they (meaning the police) had come to believe that the assailant they sought lived in the area. As he explained, he feared such a course as Hughes had suggested may alert the suspect and cause him to leave the area. Sergeant Cameron suggested they had no idea who their suspect was — he could have been a superintendent of a building, a "trusted tenant" or a husband or boyfriend of a "trusted tenant".

Sergeant Cameron explained the only certainty was that the suspect would attack again and continue to do so until he was stopped. He reasoned that if their suspect left the "small area" around Church and Wellesley and moved to Greater Metropolitan Toronto he could continue to attack victims for "who knew how long" before he was detected.

Additionally, he explained that he was aware of the substantial media coverage that had been given in the latter part of June in relation to the investigation of the "Annex Rapist" who had been attacking women in the Bloor/Avenue Road area earlier that same summer.

Sergeant Cameron said he had been told by members of the task force assigned to that investigation that Dawson Davidson, identified as the Annex Rapist, had fled the city and gone to Vancouver because of the extensive media coverage in that case.

Sergeant Cameron and the officers who investigated Dawson Davidson that same summer were part of the same office and worked within feet of one another. Shortly after his arrival in Vancouver Dawson Davidson raped another woman and Sergeant Cameron explained he did not want that to happen in this case and for this reason he said he wanted this investigation to be low-key by comparison and without extensive media coverage.

Sergeant Cameron believes, through inquiries he made of the Sexual Assault Co-ordinator, Det. Sgt. Boyd, he learned of the P.A. occurrence and had spoken to her by on or about August 5, 1986.

As of August 3, 1986 Sgt. Cameron was assisted in the investigation by Det. Sgt. Derry who, in his own words, took charge of the paper side of the investigation.

I am persuaded on the evidence that Messrs. Cameron and Derry were aware by August 7, 1986 that P.A., B.K., R.P. and F.D. had most probably all been attacked by the same man. It is conclusively established that they had this knowledge by August 16, 1986 when Sgt. Cameron filed a supplementary occurrence report recording the fact.

The 52 C.I.B. office is an extremely busy one and was particularly so in the summer of 1986. The police officers assigned to that office had extremely heavy caseloads and almost overwhelming responsibilities. Sergeant Cameron and Det. Sgt. Derry were no exceptions.

In August of 1986 they were both necessarily spending a significant amount of their time preparing for the trial of a fraud investigation of which they had been in charge. A review of their memo books at the time details the substantial time commitment required by that case.

Between the "Two Toes" case (as the fraud case was known) their days off and vacation times — there was little time left, I find, available to be devoted to the detailed, plodding, necessary detective work involved in the investigation of this series of sexual assaults.

They and the MTPF knew in early August 1986 that there was most likely a serial rapist attacking women who lived alone in second- and third-floor apartments with climbable balconies in the Church/Wellesley area who would most certainly attack again.

Yet for all intents and purposes — prior to August 24, 1986 — only Sgts. Cameron and Derry were assigned to the investigation. Even when they were otherwise unavailable no one else was specifically assigned to take up this investigation on their behalf.

The contrast between this investigation and that conducted into the Annex Rapist earlier the same summer is extreme. In that case, a task force was created to conduct the investigation with a number of officers assisting Det. Sgt. Reilly and his partner, Glen Sinclair, who were in charge of that investigation. There was significant media coverage whereby in addition to the information contained in the majors, the MTPF gave interviews to the press detailing those occurrences.

In that case the area of the attacks was searched and the neighbourhoods canvassed. Those doing the canvass were *not* instructed not to reveal the fact that they were investigating sexual assaults.

As Det. Sgt. Reilly explained, they were desperate; they had nothing to go on and the violence of the attacks was escalating. The police feared the next victim may be killed. He felt a duty to protect the women living in this area who faced a very specific threat of attack by this predator. It would be not only inappropriate but neglectful were he simply to sit back at his desk and wait for a break.

As it turned out in that case, a tenant who moved into the premises vacated by Dawson Davidson (the Annex Rapist), found a wallet which he had apparently left behind. That tenant turned the wallet over to the landlord who contacted the secretary of the wallet's owner who in turn called police. The wallet belonged to one of Dawson Davidson's victims. This was the lucky break police needed and Davidson was arrested shortly later in Vancouver. The fact of Davidson's arrest was also publicized in local papers.

There was discussion among the officers in the 52 CIB office in July 1986 to the effect that the media coverage and the obvious increased police presence in the Annex area had caused Dawson Davidson to leave Toronto. There was also evidence which suggested his departure was caused by neither.

In any event Sgts. Cameron and Derry were, I find, influenced by the discussion they heard among their fellow officers and determined that their investigation would, by comparison, be low-key.

I am satisfied that the only significant difference in the two investigations was the nature of the attacks themselves or as it has been characterized in submissions the "high level of violence" in the case of the Annex Rapist and the comparatively "low level of violence" in the case of the Balcony Rapist. The urgency that appeared to drive the investigation of the Annex Rapist was noticeably absent in the investigation of the Balcony Rapist to at least after August 29, 1986 and after Callow attacked his fifth known victim, the plaintiff, Jane Doe.

Jane Doe

Jane Doe lived at apartment 206, 88 Wellesley Street East when she was attacked in the early hours of August 24, 1986 by Paul Douglas Callow. As he had with other victims, Callow covered Ms. Doe's eyes with a pillow case, threatened her with the knife he had in his possession and spoke conversationally with her during the attack. He raped her and otherwise sexually assaulted her before leaving her apartment via the front door. Entrance to Ms. Doe's apartment had been gained by means of a balcony window which she had left slightly ajar for ventilation. For the duration of the attack Callow disguised his own appearance by covering his face.

Ms. Doe was interviewed at length by a number of police officers immediately following the occurrence at her apartment and at Women's College Hospital where she was taken for examination and completion of the customary rape kit.

Sergeant Cameron's notes for August 24, 1986 indicate, in considerable detail, that he interviewed Ms. Doe on the evening of August 24, 1986 without Det. Sgt. Derry. His notes and those of Det. Sgt. Derry indicated that they both met with Ms. Doe at her apartment on the evening of August 27, 1986.

Ms. Doe's recollection of these events is that she did not meet Sgt. Cameron until the evening of August 27, 1986 when she agreed to meet him at her apartment. She had not met Sgt. Cameron before then and had a friend with her, Mr. Maurice Arcand. She denies that Det. Sgt. Derry was at that meeting on August 27, 1986. She says she only met him after August 27. Mr. Arcand testified and essentially his version of these events corroborates Ms. Doe's.

I do not think a great deal turns on these differences in the testimony of the various witnesses.

I accept that Sgt. Cameron told Ms. Doe that he believed she had been raped by a serial rapist and that four other women had been similarly attacked. While he may not have used the word "cyclical" I find it reasonable that he indicated there was a pattern of sorts to the attacks and accept that he likely indicated in Ms. Doe's case that the rapist had struck a day early. The R.P. and F.D. attacks (the third and fourth), had taken place on the 25th day of the month and Ms. Doe was attacked on the 24th day of the month. That the officers in charge of this investigation believed that the suspect was likely to attack around the 25th of the month is borne out by the arrangements later made for a stakeout of the area to be carried out five days before and after September 25, 1986. I accept that Ms. Doe was told all victims lived on second and third floors and entry had been via balconies.

Ms. Doe expressed shock that women in the neighbourhood had not been warned that a serial rapist was in their midst. Sergeant Cameron indicated, I find, that it was not the practice to issue warnings in such cases because women would become hysterical or panic (I do not see any real difference which word he used, the meaning is the same), the rapist would flee and the investigation would be compromised. Of course it was not true that it was not the policy of the MTPF to issue warnings in such cases because it had been done in the Dawson Davidson case — just months earlier and in the very same division.

When Ms. Doe indicated that if the police were not prepared to warn area women she would. She was told that if she did, she may be considered to be interfering in a police investigation and she could be charged for doing so.

Ms. Doe testified that when she found the green dress that had been slashed, in her closet some time later, both Sgts. Cameron and Derry attended at her apartment on that occasion. The officers record these events as having occurred on August 27, 1986. The officers made their notes more or less contemporaneously with the events described therein. Ms. Doe's evidence essentially is that when she first spoke to Sgt. Cameron he was alone and that meeting was not until August 27, 1986. In this respect I accept the officer's evidence that Sgt. Cameron attended on Ms. Doe the evening of August 27, 1986 and was alone at the time — perhaps that is the meeting at which Mr. Arcand was present. I think Ms. Doe is simply mistaken on the dates and understandably so. This was an extremely traumatic time for her.

As for Mr. Arcand, his notes of the meeting with Sgt. Cameron and Ms. Doe were, he says, made the next day. He recorded his notes electronically. He could not recall if he ever showed the notes to Ms. Doe after they were prepared and he only gave them to her lawyer in 1996. While the word "hysterical" appears in his note — immediately after it he wrote "or words to that effect". In his evidence he said he was sure the word "hysterical" was used by Sgt. Cameron; he could offer no meaningful reason why his notes included the words in relation to it "or words to that effect". He could not recall any discussion about a white wool scarf with two holes having been cut in it — although he agreed it could have occurred and he did not recall it. He did recall the slashed green dress having been discussed on the evening Sgt. Cameron was there yet his notes do not record the fact. I am left in some doubt about when Mr. Arcand was present and what he heard.

By memorandum dated August 27, 1986 Sgts. Cameron and Derry for the first time requested the assistance of other officers and this, for the purpose of conducting a canvass of local apartment buildings. They requested that all apartments on the first, second and third floors of each building be checked. The additional officers were to be instructed to tell tenants only that there had been a number of break and enters in the area and specifically instructed *not* to mention the sexual assaults. They were to note any single females living in the apartments canvassed.

Later in a memorandum dated September 7, 1986 Sgt. Derry indicated to Staff Sgt. Bukowski as follows:

It is important that the officers check each apartment in order to establish the hair colour of the women and receive information from the people interviewed regarding prowlers etc.

On that same day Sgt. Cameron by memorandum detailed to Inspector Cowling, the officer in charge of 52 C.I.B. office, his request for manpower and equipment necessary for a stakeout to be carried out the five days before and after September 25, 1986. The operation is detailed as follows:

The operation would run as follows:
1. Using the streets as boundaries each group of apartments would be covered by two, three or four men.
2. Each group of men would have at least one unmarked car at their disposal in the event

there is an attack and they have to move quickly.
3. Vans would be used as stationary observation points within the area.
4. The uniform cars would stay just outside of their designated area and would be used to seal off the area around the location of any attack and stop all persons on foot or in vehicles. They will be assisted by some of the old clothes men.
5. The remainder of the old clothes men would then enter the area of attack and search on foot for any suspect that may be hiding.
6. The radio room would be advised in advance of this operation and would be required to assist in sealing off the area.
7. Sergeants Cameron and Derry would be present and take charge of the scene and direct the operation for those ten days.
8. Attached hereto is a map indicating the area of concern. Further recording will be made to the map upon completion of the canvassing detail.

Respectfully submitted

William Cameron Sgt. 2887
Kim Derry Sgt. 3373

Sergeant Derry in a memorandum to Inspector Cowling dated September 7, 1986 again detailed the request for foot patrol and beat officers to canvass the first three floors of the apartment buildings identified by him and Sgt. Cameron to obtain the apartment numbers with single females and their description. This original request to the staff sergeant had apparently been cancelled. He noted:

> If any chance at identifying possible targets through this method is not carried out, then the possibility of narrowing the surveillance cannot be done.

Once again the staff sergeants were advised that the officers conducting the canvass were "not to mention anything about sexual assaults which have occurred in the area but to advise people contacted that this is a crime prevention program and that single women are victims of break and enters and theft". Officers were to obtain the names and addresses of single women and note their hair colour.

The stakeout proceeded as planned. Unmarked vehicles were used and those participating were informed the only time the cover would be broken was in the event they observed someone attempting to climb a balcony in which event the person was to be stopped. The stakeout did not produce any useful information except that for all the covertness of the operation, crime in the area of the stakeout was almost entirely eliminated for its duration. Obviously the criminal element was aware of the police presence.

It has been suggested that the women who occupied these apartments were being used as "bait". The police adamantly denied the suggestion which they say implies that they knew who would, and when an attack would occur, when in fact they had no idea who would, where, or even if an attack would occur. I can only conclude on the evidence that the police believed it to be a virtual certainty that there would be another attack and that it would be made against one of the women their canvass had identified as a potential target and in view of the fact that the last three victims had been attacked on the 24th or 25th of the month that the attack would likely take place during that general time period in the month — the entire stakeout operation was premised on the assumption of these factors.

The police were there to wait and watch for an attack to occur. The women were given no warning and were thereby precluded from taking any steps to protect themselves against such an attack. Unbeknownst to them they were left completely vulnerable. When all of these circumstances are taken and considered together, it certainly suggests to me that the women were being used — without their knowledge or consent — as "bait" to attract a predator whose specific identity then was unknown to the police, but whose general and characteristic identity most certainly was.

The break in the investigation came when probation officer Debbie Alton contacted P.C. Gary Ellis of the 52 C.I.B. office to check a criminal record for her. Police Constable Ellis had arrested one, Paul Douglas Callow, on June 6, 1986 for assaulting his wife Jackie. Not being a "sexual" assault, the Sexual Assault Co-ordinator's office was not aware of this information. To me it is indicative that the MTPF as a whole did not understand the fundamental — that sexual assault is not about sex, it is about violence and anger against women. Had the force co-ordinated efforts to keep track of any and all acts of violence against women, they may have *been* aware of Callow's existence much sooner than they were. On September 24, 1986 Ms. Alton was preparing a pre-sentence report on Callow. Ms. Alton told P.C. Ellis that Callow had not been truthful with her about his previous criminal record and requested that he check it out for her. Callow's wife had told Ms. Alton that her husband had been convicted for rape in Vancouver which involved Callow "doing a break and enter then finding a woman sleeping and then raping her". According to the supplementary occurrence report prepared by P.C. Ellis, Callow's wife had indicated that her husband "has a sex problem (wants it all the time), booze problem and drug problem and he is still doing break and enters". Jackie Callow lived at 33 Maitland Street in the Church/Wellesley area and indicated her husband was in the area frequently and that she recently had problems with him.

Subsequent investigation would reveal that Paul Douglas Callow had, in May 1981, raped an elderly woman who resided in a fifth-floor apartment at 220 Wellesley Street East. The circumstances of that rape — for which Callow was arrested by the MTPF [—] were hauntingly similar to the *modus operandi* employed by him in the five rapes with which this action is concerned. Charges were not proceeded with in that case because of the age and health of the victim.

Police at the time felt reasonably confident however that Callow was responsible for that rape and noted that the *modus operandi* was similar to that used by Callow in the Vancouver rape in 1978 for which he was convicted and sentenced to four years imprisonment.

Surprisingly, P.C. Ellis took it upon himself to contact Jackie Callow directly and speak to her about her husband. I say surprisingly because of Sgts. Cameron and Derry's evidence in relation to the "low key" approach they wished to take in this investigation in order that the offender not be tipped off or displaced.

. . . .

In any event Callow was soon after put under constant surveillance and arrested October 3, 1986. He ultimately confessed to having committed all five rapes. After the commencement of the preliminary inquiry he pled guilty and was sentenced in total to a period of incarceration of 20 years.

CONCLUSIONS

Competency of the Investigation

It is suggested that the investigation into the balcony rapist was slipshod and incompetent. The plaintiff has criticized the documentary productions of the defendant and suggested they are incomplete. Professor Hodgson testified that every step in an investigation should be recorded on supplementary occurrence reports. In this way he said anyone picking up the file could be reasonably informed on the status of the investigation. While that may be the ideal I accept that it is not the reality. Often steps taken and information gathered were recorded on supplementary reports but often they were not. Officers differ in their manner and method of note and record-keeping. I accept that there were numerous documents created in relation to this investigation which unfortunately were destroyed before the litigation was commenced.

I am not persuaded on the evidence that Callow would have been identified and apprehended any earlier because of documentary deficiencies.

I am satisfied that the officers ultimately assigned to this investigation had too many other urgent assignments ongoing at the same time which prevented them from devoting the necessary attention which this investigation required. At the critical time much of their energy and attention was directed to other matters — often for days at a time. They had no back-up, no one else directly responsible for this investigation when they were otherwise engaged.

While it is true that there was no evidence called in relation to what other demands there may have been on the MTPF for manpower at this time, one must bear in mind that it is the evidence of the police that sexual assault is a very serious crime second only to homicide and then consider the resources made available in the Annex Rapist investigation in his same division only a month or two before.

While the plaintiff submits that I must infer that Callow would have been apprehended sooner had greater resources been devoted to this investigation earlier on the theory — the sooner a job is started the sooner it is finished — I cannot agree [...]. While one may say in that event Callow might have been apprehended sooner, it is to my mind equally probable that he might not have been.

I am compelled, however, to conclude that the only difference between the Annex Rapist investigation and this investigation was the level of violence in addition to the rape itself. Dawson Davidson also physically beat many of his victims in addition to sexually assaulting them.

As this is the only real distinguishing factor between the two investigations I must conclude that it was this factor — the lack of additional violence — which resulted in this investigation being essentially on the back burner in so far as resources were concerned. The sense of urgency which drove the Dawson Davidson investigation was markedly absent from this investigation. I can only conclude because Callow's victims were "merely raped" by a "gentleman rapist" — according to the Oliver Zink Rape Cookbook definition — this case did not have the urgency of the other.

Decision Not to Warn

As I have said, Sgts. Cameron and Derry determined that this investigation would be "low key" compared to the investigation conducted into the "Annex Rapist" and no warning would be given to the women they knew to be at risk for fear of displacing the rapist leaving him free to re-offend elsewhere undetected.

I am not persuaded that their professed reason for not warning women is the real reason no warning was issued.

Firstly, there is evidence that the Annex Rapist, Dawson Davidson, did not flee to Vancouver because of the media attention paid to his crimes and/or the obvious increased police presence in the neighbourhood. Indeed, much of the coverage occurred after Davidson had already left Toronto.

Additionally P.C. Gary Ellis, who had assisted in the Dawson Davidson investigation at one point, actually telephoned Callow's ex-wife directly when he learned of Callow's existence and record from probation officer Alton. Police Constable Ellis worked out of the same 52 Division as Sgts. Cameron and Derry and would have, presumably, been aware of any discussions in relation to the fear of displacing Callow — by media attention or knocking on his door for the purpose of giving a warning about sexual assaults — yet he phoned directly to Callow's wife without even hesitating it seems.

There was, I find, no "policy" not to issue warnings to potential victims in these cases — clearly warnings had been given in the Dawson Davidson Annex Rapist investigation — warnings [that] incidentally all defence expert witnesses agreed were appropriate in the circumstances.

I find that the real reason a warning was not given in the circumstances of this case was because Sgts. Cameron and Derry believed that women living in the area would become hysterical and panic and their investigation would thereby be jeopardized. In addition, they were not motivated by any sense of urgency because Callow's attacks were not seen as "violent" as Dawson Davidson's by comparison had been.

I am satisfied on the evidence that a meaningful warning could and should have been given to the women who were at particular risk. That warning could have been by way of a canvass of their apartments, by a media blitz — by holding widely publicized public meetings or any one or combination of these methods. Such warning should have alerted the particular women at risk, and advised them of suggested precautions they might take to protect themselves. The defence experts, with the exception of Mr. Piers, agreed that a warning could have been given without compromising the investigation on the facts of the case.

Even the experienced defence expert witnesses Det. Inspector Kevin Rossmo and former FBI special agent McCrary agreed that as Det. Inspector Rossmo said:

> The police have a responsibility to release a balanced volume of information to protect the community. ... where that balance is will depend on the particular facts of the case.

In my view it has been conceded in this case clearly and unequivocally by the Chief of Police at the time, Jack Marks, that no warning was given in this case and one ought to have been. His public response to the proposals of the group known as Women against Violence against Women in the aftermath of this investigation presented to the Board of Commissioners of Police could not in my view be any clearer when he said:

> I would concede that for a variety of reasons unique to the Church/Wellesley investigation, no press release in the nature of a general warning was issued and acknowledged that one should have been. This is not only a matter for concern and regret, but action has already been taken to prevent a similar breakdown from occurring in the future. Specifically, the Sexual Assault Co-ordinator who monitors all of these offences has been directed to ensure that members of the public are informed about such matters which may affect their safety. These warnings will be directed toward all potential victims with special attention given to members of the public who have been identified as most at risk, e.g. as in the case at hand, women living in high-rise buildings in the downtown area would be targeted as a high risk group and requiring extra efforts to bring the potential risk to their attention.

I accept and agree entirely with these remarks.

I must confess I was taken aback at the suggestion of Det. Sgt. Robin Breen who authored these remarks for the Chief when he suggested, I think, that in effect what it says is not what it says. The remarks were not intended to mean that the police felt a warning ought to have been given but rather were merely an invitation to get this group — known as WAVAW — to the discussion table.

His evidence was pure double-talk as far as I am concerned and simply made no sense.

It seems the MTPF has been trying to back away from these words of their then Chief ever since they were stated. The Chief's statement was an appropriate one in the circumstances and it is to his credit in my view, that he made the statement when and as he did.

There are three other factors which have influenced my decision that a warning ought to have been given.

1. the fact that Sgts. Cameron and Derry thought it appropriate to warn S.G. and M.L., that they may be potential targets of the balcony rapist after they reported break-ins to their apartments in their absence.
2. the fact that Dawson Davidson had been arrested in July 1986 received considerable publicity. Women living in the general vicinity may have felt some relief knowing that a serial rapist had been apprehended and let down their guard somewhat completely unaware that another serial rapist was on the loose in their neighbourhood.
3. the fact that Sgt. Hughes in his memo to his superior Staff Sgt. Hein — both of 52 Division — dated July 29, 1986 thought that building superintendents should have been contacted and told to advise "trusted tenants" especially single women to be aware of the occurrences and to advise police of any person they felt may be suspect.

I am satisfied on Ms. Doe's evidence that if she had been aware a serial rapist was in her neighbourhood raping women whose apartments he accessed via their balconies she would have taken steps to protect herself and that most probably those steps would have prevented her from being raped.

Section 57 of the *Police Act*, R.S.O. 1980, c. 381 (the governing statute at the time these events occurred), provides:

> 57. ... members of police forces ... are charged with the duty of preserving the peace, preventing robberies and other crimes ...

The police are statutorily obligated to prevent crime and at common law they owe a duty to protect life and property. As Schroeder J.A. stated in *Schacht* v. *R.*, [1973] 1 O.R. 221 at pp. 231–32, 30 D.L.R. (3d) 641:

> The duties which I would lay upon them stem not only from the relevant statutes to which reference has been made, but from the common law, which recognizes the existence of a broad conventional or customary duty in the established constabulary as an arm of the State to protect the life, limb and property of the subject.

In my view, the police failed utterly in their duty to protect these women and the plaintiff in particular from the serial rapist the police knew to be in their midst by failing to warn so that they may have had the opportunity to take steps to protect themselves.

It is no answer for the police to say women are always at risk and as an urban adult living in downtown Toronto they have an obligation to look out for themselves. Women generally do, every day of their lives, conduct themselves and their lives in such a way as to avoid the general pervasive threat of male violence which exists in our society. Here police were aware of a specific threat or risk to a specific group of women and they did nothing to warn those women of the danger they were in, nor did they take any measures to protect them.

Discrimination

The plaintiff's argument is not simply that she has been discriminated against, because she is a woman, by individual officers in the investigation of her specific complaint, but that systemic discrimination existed within the MTPF in 1986 which impacted adversely on all women and, specifically, those who were survivors of sexual assault who came into contact with the MTPF — a class of persons of which the plaintiff was one. She says, in effect, the sexist stereotypical views held by the MTPF informed the investigation of this serial rapist and caused that investigation to be conducted incompetently and in such a way that the plaintiff has been denied the equal protection and equal benefit of law guaranteed to her by s. 15(1) of the *Charter*.

The MTPF has since at least 1975 been aware of the problems it has in relation to the investigation of sexual assaults.

Among those problems:

- survivors of sexual assault are not treated sensitively;
- lack of effective training for officers engaged in the investigation of sexual assault including a lack of understanding of rape trauma syndrome and the needs of survivors;
- lack of co-ordination of sexual assault investigations;
- some officers not suited by personality/attitude to investigation of sexual assault;
- too many investigators coming into contact with victims;
- lack of experienced investigators investigating sexual assault;
- lack of supervision of those conducting sexual assault investigations.

The force has conceded in public documents as well as in internal documents at least since 1975, that it has difficulties in these areas, that it will take immediate steps to remedy these shortcomings — yet the problems continued through to 1987 and beyond.

It seemed in that period that the public and persons who had brought their concerns in these areas to the attention of police were being publicly assured the problems would be eliminated, yet within the force the *status quo* remained pretty much as it had always been.

Every police officer who testified agreed that sexual assault is a serious crime, second only to homicide. Yet, I cannot help but ask rhetorically — do they really believe that especially when one reviews their record in this area? It seems to me it was, as the plaintiff suggests, largely an effort in impression management rather than an indication of any genuine commitment for change.

Former Chief of Police, Jack Marks, said that he would not have stood for problems like those outlined above continuing in the homicide squad for example. He said, assuming he were aware of the problems, that he would "root them out" and "correct" them — yet these problems were allowed to continue over at least the better part of two decades in relation to the investigation of sexual assaults. Although the MTPF say they took the crime of sexual assault seriously in 1985–86 I must conclude, on the evidence before me, that they did not.

The rape trauma syndrome was clearly not understood by too many officers who were charged with the responsibility of investigating sexual assaults — others, including even some who had taken the sexual assault investigators course, adhered to rape myths. Examples can clearly be seen in this investigation — for example, Sgt. Duggan's occurrence reports in relation to the B.K. investigation — clearly "slanted toward disbelieving the victim", to quote Margo Pulford. It is obvious to anyone that Sgt. Duggan was strongly influenced by the fact that a bowl of potato chips on the bed where the rape occurred apparently remained undisturbed. He concluded there had been no struggle and hence no forced sexual intercourse. His denial in this regard is simply incredible in the face of his own written record. Other examples are set out above as quoted from Det. Sgt. Boyd's report and her comment that these problems existed in every station in every division in the force.

The protocol established by the force, AP No. 22, as it was designated, for the investigation of sexual assaults was often not followed and when it was not there is no evidence that any senior officer or supervisor followed up.

The problems continued and because among adults, women are overwhelmingly the victims of sexual assault, they are and were disproportionately impacted by the resulting poor quality of investigation. The result is that women are discriminated against and their right to equal protection and benefit of the law is thereby compromised as the result.

In my view the conduct of this investigation and the failure to warn in particular, was motivated and informed by the adherence to rape myths as well as sexist stereotypical reasoning about rape, about women and about women who are raped. The plaintiff therefore has been discriminated against by reason of her gender and as the result the plaintiff's rights to equal protection and equal benefit of the law were compromised.

Security of the Person

I am satisfied that the defendants deprived the plaintiff of her right to security of the person by subjecting her to the very real risk of attack by a serial rapist — a risk of which they were aware but about which they quite deliberately failed to inform the plaintiff or any women living in the Church/Wellesley area at the time save only S.G. and M.L. and where in the face of that knowledge and their belief that the rapist would certainly attack again, they additionally failed to take any steps to protect the plaintiff or other women like her. Clearly the rape of the plaintiff constituted a deprivation of her security of the person. As Madam Justice Wilson stated in *Singh* v. *Canada (Minister of Employment & Immigration)*, [1985] 1 S.C.R. 177 at p. 207, 17 D.L.R. (4th) 422:

> ... "security of the person" must encompass freedom from the threat of physical punishment or suffering as well as freedom from such punishment itself.

As I have indicated, because the defendants exercised their discretion in the investigation of this case in a discriminatory and negligent way as I have detailed above, their exercise of discretion was thereby contrary to the principle of fundamental justice.

Section 1 of the *Charter* has no application in circumstances because the conduct of police in issue here is not "prescribed by law" within the meaning the jurisprudence has ascribed to that phrase.

Here the plaintiff's *Charter* rights have been infringed by police conduct — not a legislative enactment or a common law rule.

In any event the defendants made no effort in evidence to satisfy the requirements of s. 1 and *demonstrate* a s. 1 defence — they simply denied the plaintiff's rights which were infringed. I have found differently.

In view of my findings the plaintiff is entitled under s. 24 to a remedy.

[The analysis of Jane Doe's negligence claim has been omitted. The court held that the police had breached a legal duty to warn her as a member of a discrete and identifiable group of women at risk from the rapist, based upon sex discriminatory beliefs about women, thus incurring liability in negligence as well as pursuant to the *Charter*. Her damages for both claims were assessed at approximately $225,000.]

■

In the wake of the *Jane Doe* decision, the City of Toronto charged its Auditor with the task of accounting for Metro Toronto Police practices in handling sexual assault investigations, as condemned by Justice MacFarland in her ruling. The report, Jeffrey Griffiths, *Review of the Investigation of Sexual Assaults. Toronto Police Services* (Toronto: Toronto Audit Services, 1999) (known in the media as the *Jane Doe Safety Audit*), made 57 recommendations for systemic change in light of the results of its social audit. The Auditor's review of occurrence reports found, for example, that certain of these were incomplete, contained unsupported conclusions, and used inappropriate language (at 52). Despite the fact that this report received the Special Project Excellence in Local Government Audits award for 1999 from the U.S.-based National Association of Local Government Auditors, Metro Police has balked at implementing several of the recommendations, including a key one that women's advocates be included on a steering committee to oversee implementation of the report: Jane Doe, "Breaking faith" *eye* (23 May 2002) online.

In another botched investigation, a 1996 judicial probe released findings regarding the police failure to follow several leads that would have identified Paul Bernardo as a dangerous threat to women before he killed two young women, Kristen French and Leslie Mahaffy. As well, Judge Archie Campbell was asked to consider why further investigation of the death of Bernardo's sister-in-law, Tammy Homolka, was not pursued by police and whether rivalries led to a failure to share information between two investigating teams, among other things. In his report, Campbell noted that about 12 leads that would have led to Bernardo were not followed up. Among those 12 leads was evidence from women who had been followed by Bernardo and had felt quite threatened by him. One such woman had reported his car once she spotted him again. Sadly, the police did not pursue her complaint, and missed an opportunity that may have prevented the death of one of the victims. Another of those 12 leads was a tip from an officer who had taken a report from a former girlfriend of Bernardo and who noted Bernardo's sexually violent behaviour. See *Bernardo Investigation Review: Report of Mr. Justice Archie Campbell* (Toronto: Ministry of the Solicitor General and Correctional Services, 1996).

Consider what a feminist analysis of the police treatment of this evidence, the "balcony rapist" investigation, and some of the other incidents of police sexism would have added to Judge Campbell's report and recommendations. See Martin Dionne, "The Voices of Women Not Heard: The *Bernardo Investigation Review: Report of Mr. Justice Archie Campbell*" (1997) 9 C.J.W.L. 394 as well as several litigation efforts: Caroline Mallan, "Seven victims of Bernardo file lawsuits against police" *The Toronto Star* (24 December 1996) A4; Harold Levy, "Rape victims can sue RCMP" *The Toronto Star* (12 January 2002) B2. See also CP, "Ex-hooker prods Mounties for answers in Olson case" *The Ottawa Citizen* (12 September 1994) A5. According to this report, Clifford Olson was released from custody without charges of sexual assault because of alleged inconsistencies in the victim/witness's statement. At the time of this assault, he had already killed one of the 11 children he went on to kill. See also Joan Smith's discussion of the police assumptions and errors in the Peter Sutcliffe investigation in "There's Only One Yorkshire Ripper" in *Misogynies* (New York: Random House, 1989) 144, and Warren Goulding's account of the indifference with which the deaths of four Aboriginal women were treated in *Just Another Indian. A Serial Killer and Canada's Indifference* (Calgary: Fifth House, 2001).

HOMOPHOBIA

As Thomas Fleming described in the article, "The Bawdy House 'Boys': Some Notes on Media, Sporadic Moral Crusades, and Selective Law Enforcement," supra, police have dealt more harshly with gay men (than with straight men) where gay men are alleged to be violating the law. However, the differential policing and differential enforcement of law have another dimension. Where gay men and lesbians are victims of violence, that violence and the homophobia and lesbophobia underlying it are often downplayed or excused. Thus, the assailants are treated more leniently precisely because their crimes are crimes against gay men or lesbians.

Cynthia Petersen describes in chilling terms both the prevalence of homophobic violence and the lack of any sufficient response by the justice system in the following article.

A Queer Response to Bashing: Legislating Against Hate[†]

On 19 March 1989, gay A.I.D.S. activist Joe Rose was murdered during an unprovoked assault which occurred on a city bus outside a Montreal subway station. A gang of 15 or more youths boarded the bus, taunted him with shouts of "faggot," then stabbed him to death with scissors and hunting and kitchen knives. Montreal police treated the crime as part of a juvenile gang problem rather than part of a pattern of heterosexist violence.

. . . .

Police and prosecutors frequently refuse to acknowledge the heterosexist nature of assaults, even when the victims survive to speak of their experience.

. . . .

Fear of mistreatment by the police also contributes to the reluctance to report heterosexist crimes. It is not unusual for complaints to be dismissed by law enforcement agents. Of the 90 queer-bashing cases referred to Toronto police by the Church Street Community Centre in 1990, only 45 were declared to be *bona fide* assaults. Trivialization is not the only concern. Official responses typically range from indifference to brutality. Police officers frequently engage in heterosexist violence themselves. Police activity in lesbian and gay communities has primarily consisted of harassment rather than protection. The legacy of police harassment in Canada was recently revived by violent confrontations with the Montreal lesbian and gay community. In the early morning of 15 July 1990 Montreal police officers harassed lesbians and gay men gathered outside a private residence in the city. They used billyclubs to disperse the group and made eight arrests. A subsequent peaceful demonstration to protest the police conduct was broken up by officers in riot gear who struck and choked demonstrators with their clubs. Forty-eight protesters were arrested. At least eight officers were not wearing name tags as required by police regulations. At least six officers wore latex surgical gloves, signifying their A.I.D.S.-phobia and either their ignorance of the methods of H.I.V. transmission or their intention to injure demonstrators to the point of drawing blood.

Lesbian and gay activists in cities across North America are currently engaged in efforts to sensitize police to the needs of our communities. While these efforts are commendable, their success has yet to be demonstrated, and at present community relations with the police remain strained at best. It seems counterproductive to rely on the legal system without first having implemented fundamental reforms to the criminal justice process.

■

Charges of homophobia and racism have been levied against the police department in Milwaukee in another case that has attracted national and international attention: the Jeffrey Dahmer serial murder case. There have been news conferences, marches, and rallies against the police. The out-

---

[†] By Cynthia Petersen, (1991) 16 Queen's L.J. 237 at 246–47, 250. Reproduced by permission of the author.

rage focused on the revelation of a complaint made by an African-American woman to 911 emergency operations and police officers on 27 May 1991, about an obviously injured young Laotian boy, two months before Dahmer was arrested. Although the police went to Dahmer's apartment that night, they dismissed the situation as a domestic dispute involving two homosexuals, despite the boy's obvious injuries and his youth. Two months later, the 14-year-old boy was identified as one of 17 men and boys that Dahmer had killed.

As Rev. LeHarve Buck, a neighbourhood organizer, said:

> If you're not an Anglo-Saxon white male, you're treated differently by the police in this city. The police have a picture of what a good citizen looks like. If you don't fit that description, you're not a good citizen and you're not worth serving. [Don Terry, "Angry Milwaukee turns against police" *The [Toronto] Globe and Mail* (3 August 1991) A9.]

Chief Arreola, the first minority police chief in the city's history, moved quickly to suspend three of the officers and to launch an investigation. The police union reacted in anger, suggesting that they might push for the resignation of the chief because of his failure to support his officers.

Excerpts from the transcript of the 911 call to the police follow:

> Woman: "OK. Hi. I am on 25th and State. And there's this young man. He's butt-naked and he has been beaten up. He is very bruised. He can't stand. He is ... butt-naked. He has no clothes on. He is really hurt. And I, you know, ain't got no coat on. But I just seen him. He needs some help...."

[An officer reported back, after investigating]

> Officer: "Intoxicated Asian, naked male. Was returned to his sober boyfriend."

[When indicating the squad was ready for new duties]

> Officer: "10-4. It will be a minute. My partner is going to get deloused at the station."

[Laughter is heard on the tape]

Excerpts from a later call asking about the outcome of the investigation:

> Woman: "... what happened? I mean my daughter and my niece witnessed what was going on. Was anything done about the situation? Do you need their names or information or anything from them."
>
> Officer: "No, not at all."
>
> Woman: "You don't?"
>
> Officer: "Nope. It's an intoxicated boyfriend of another boyfriend."
>
> Woman: "Well, how old was this child?"
>
> Officer: "It wasn't a child, it was an adult."
>
> Woman: "Are you sure?"
>
> Officer: "Yup."
>
> Woman: "Are you positive? Because this child doesn't even speak English. My daughter had, you know, dealt with him before, seeing him on the street. You know, catching earthworms...."
>
> Officer: "Ma'am. Ma'am. Like I explained to you. It is all taken care of. It's as positive as I can be. OK. I can't do anything about somebody's sexual preferences in life."
>
> Woman: "Well, no I am not saying anything about that, but it appeared to have been a child. This is my concern."
>
> Officer: "No. No. He's not."
>
> Woman: "He's not a child?"
>
> Officer: "No he's not. OK? ..."
>
> [AP, "Transcript shows police failed to share woman's concern" *The [Toronto] Globe and Mail* (3 August 1991) A7.]

The estate of the victim is in the process of suing the police for deliberately ignoring citizen complaints about the child's endangered situation, returning him to the custody of Dahmer, and denial of equal protection on the grounds of race and sexual orientation. The suit survived a motion to dismiss and was ordered on to trial: *Estate of Sinthasomphone* v. *Milwaukee*, 878 F. Supp. 147 (Dist. Ct. E. Wisc. 1995).

D. POLICING THE POLICE: LEGAL RESPONSES

Several responses of the legal system to the practices of policing have already been referred to, including the possibility of *Criminal Code* charges against police officers; internal disciplinary charges under the relevant provincial or territorial legislation; exclusion of the evidence against the accused if *Charter* violations have been proven; stay of proceedings if an abuse of process can be proven; coroner's inquests; public inquiries or investigations; and tort suits. What are the advantages and limitations of these various legal strategies?

There have also been several other responses to some of the issues raised in this chapter. Consider the following:

- *Charter* challenges to the relevant legislation: in *R. v. Lines*, *supra*, a prosecution against a police officer for criminal negligence causing bodily harm, unlawful discharge of a firearm, and careless use of a firearm, the court declared s. 25(4) of the *Criminal Code*, which then provided legal immunity for the use of deadly force by police against "fleeing felons," as violative of s. 7 of the *Charter* and not saved by s. 1. Interestingly, it was the Crown who challenged the validity of this section; the court ruled that its judgment would be suspended for six months to allow the government to respond. See now s. 25(4) of the *Criminal Code*.

- Special investigation units for allegation of police criminality: for example, Ontario in 1990 established a Special Investigations Unit (SIU) to look into cases where death or serious injury is caused by a police officer, so as to avoid conflicts of interest and the tendencies toward police solidarity described by Brannigan. However, both Clayton Ruby and the *Report on Systemic Racism* have documented numerous problems in practice with the SIU: Clayton Ruby, "Clayton Ruby believes the process by which we investigate the police isn't working" *The [Toronto] Globe and Mail* (4 May 1993) A20.

  The *Report on Systemic Racism*, *supra* at 382–84 made numerous recommendations based on the refusal of some officers to co-operate with the mandate of the SIU. Some of the Commission's recommendations, such as requiring that officers who have witnessed a colleague kill or injure someone co-operate with the SIU investigators, were replicated in a report commissioned by the Ontario government from former justice George Adams. The SIU was reported to have told police that they have nothing to fear from the SIU because, for example, in 1997 only five charges resulted from 150 investigations: James Rusk, "Ontario minister calls for shakeup of police agency" *The [Toronto] Globe and Mail* (13 August 1998) A5.

- Civilian complaints offices: some provinces and cities have established complaints offices, outside the structure of police departments, which have some degree of power to impose a resolution on citizen complaints. For example, in Ontario, pursuant to the *Police Act*, R.S.O. 1990, c. P-15, s. 77, all complaints made to police were forwarded on to the Office of the Police Complaints Commissioner, which then reviewed the department chief's response to the complaint and provided an avenue for review of that response should the citizen wish. Research by Tammy Landau, *Public Complaints Against the Police: A View from Complainants* (Toronto: Centre of Criminology, University of Toronto, 1994) found very serious shortcomings in this particular model, including that the Commissioner's office relied on the investigation of the complaint by the original department, since it rarely invoked its power to initiate a complaint or pursue its own investigation. Without an independent investigation, it was rarely in a position to order an investigation before a Board of Inquiry "in the public interest"; thus, the vast majority of complaints were concluded without further action from the Commissioner's office (at 76). She also notes that, from the viewpoint of citizens who have been wronged by police, the office has little credibility, because it is still recognized that, essentially, the police investigate themselves. In 1997 the Ontario government abolished the Public Complaints Commission. All complaints are instead handled by the respective chief of police, with a possibility of a review by the Ontario Civilian Commission on Police Services: *The Police Services Amendment Act*, S.O. 1997, c. 8, s. 35. Under the new structure, less than one per cent of Ottawa police decisions on public complaints are overruled: Don Campbell, "Panel rarely overrules police complaints" *The Ottawa Citizen* (26 April 2002) C1.

E. POLICE RESISTANCE

Police responses to efforts to curb their powers or to make them legally accountable have been numerous:

- Strikes and protests have been used by police when their members have been charged with killing citizens (see the actions reported under the Donaldson shooting, *supra*) and when new laws aimed at police have been introduced. Thus, in Ontario, police protested the new public complaints process by staging a 12-day work slowdown: André Picard, "Boycott demeans police, complaints arbitrator says" *The [Toronto] Globe and Mail* (7 October 1988) A4 (in the first case since the work action, an individual officer whose behaviour was before the commission boycotted the hearing). Again in Ontario, when a new regulation was put in place after the killing of Raymond Lawrence, requiring the filing of a report every time an officer draws a gun in public, police engaged in "work to rule": "Proposed gun law threatens lives, chief says" *The Toronto Star* (25 June 1992) A6; Gay Abbate, "Judge orders police to end their protest" *The [Toronto] Globe and Mail* (7 November 1992) A1.

- Harassment, intimidation, and criminal charges have at times been used against citizens who pursue complaints or who have resisted police intervention in some form. For example, Landau, *supra* discovered a disturbing rate of withdrawal of complaints (19 per cent) and a number of incidences of efforts by police to get citizens to withdraw their complaints by coercion, harassment, or the pursuit of criminal charges against them (at 69–73). See also the cases discussed *infra* under **Compelling the Accused's Appearance in Court** and CP, "Charges against man dropped as judge accuses Toronto police of lying and fabricating evidence" *The Ottawa Citizen* (26 April 1989) E1, where Justice Ted Matlow dropped charges against Donohue Morgan. Morgan claimed he had been harassed over five years by police, had commenced a civil action against them, and was then charged with multiple offences and told they would be dropped if he withdrew his civil action. Finally, consider the case of Winnipeg lawyer Harvey Pollock, whose charges of sexual assault were dropped after a public inquiry found that he had been framed by police as "payback" for his role as lawyer for the J.J. Harper family: David Roberts, "Cleaning up the precinct house," *supra*.

- Tort suits in defamation have been filed in response to criminal charges and even human rights claims against police. For example, a successful counterclaim for $15,000 by Hull police against Rolanda Coe was accepted by a judge in Hull in October 1995: "For the record: Why judge rejected charges of police racism" *The Ottawa Citizen* (19 October 1995) A15. Coe had sued the police for discrimination and use of excessive force under the Québec civil code for arresting her violently in Hull in 1991 and jailing her overnight. Although charges against Coe had been withdrawn, the judge hearing the subsequent lawsuit disbelieved her evidence, which he found contradictory and improbable, discounted her witnesses because they had criminal records, and accepted the testimony of the officers, whose credibility was said to be linked to the fact that they were college graduates in police training and had experience as police from eight to 10 years. Further, Québec Superior Court Judge Orville Frenette stated: "Just because they are police doesn't mean they should not be regarded as credible witnesses ... because it would be obvious if they were protecting one another": quoted in *The Ottawa Citizen*, *ibid*. The damages for defamation were based on the allegations in the lawsuit as well as statements Coe had made to the media and in public meetings about her arrest, including her argument that had she been a white woman she never would have been arrested. Consider the impact of power and standpoint on such determinations of credibility. See, for example, the discussion of Judge Corrine Sparks, *infra*, **Powers of Prosecution**.

  See also *Kenora Police Service* v. *Savino*, [1995] O.J. No. 486 (Ct. Just. (Gen. Div.)), online: QL. For another defamation suit by police, this time against two defence lawyers who were responding to media questions about whether the police search of their young client, an African-Canadian high school student, was indicative of racism, see *Campbell* v. *Jones*, [2001] N.S.J. No. 373 (Sup. Ct.), online: QL.

- Harassment and isolation of other police officers who have broken ranks and testified against police: Kevin Marron, "Ostracized policeman is granted discharge" *The [Toronto] Globe and Mail* (28 November 1988) A19 (police sergeant Kenneth Knowles exposed corruption within the vice squad in Hamilton and became the "pariah" of the Hamilton force); Jill Mahoney, "Breaking the silence" *The [Toronto] Globe and Mail* (11 December 1999) A16 (two officers who made allegations of corruption among Edmonton police say that their careers are in tatters).

- Challenges to the authority of judges who attempt to "police the police." For example, Justice Matlow, mentioned above in connection with the Donahue Morgan case, has encountered police claims that he is biased against police. Four years after he dismissed charges against Morgan and recommended that an OPP investigation be pursued with an eye to laying charges against the officers, the judge was refused access to the full report by the OPP, which had found no wrongdoing by police. He pursued legal avenues to force disclosure of the report, only to face legal wrangling by the OPP which, upon losing an unrelated civil case in Justice Matlow's court, then challenged him (unsuccessfully) for bias: see Michael Valpy, "Answers from the OPP prove hard to get" *The [Toronto] Globe and Mail* (24 March 1993) A2; Monique Conrod, "Ont. justice refuses to disqualify himself for anti-police bias" *The Lawyer's Weekly* (9 April 1993) 2.

□

10

Search and Seizure

Search and seizure may take place at any point in a criminal investigation. At law, a search is broadly conceptualized to include physical searches of the person or place, visual and olfactory inspections such as "perimeter searches" (*R. v. Plant*, [1993] 3 S.C.R. 281) and "knock and sniff" tactics (*R. v. Evans*, [1996] 1 S.C.R. 8), wiretaps, use of video cameras, and the taking of bodily samples, including blood and DNA.

Search and seizure is governed by the *Criminal Code*, other federal laws such as the *Controlled Drugs and Substances Act*, ss. 8 and 24 of the *Charter*, and the common law. Generally, for a search and seizure to comply with s. 8 of the *Charter*, it must be authorized by law, the law itself must be reasonable, and the search must be carried out in a reasonable manner: *R. v. Collins*, [1987] 1 S.C.R. 265.

A. AUTHORIZED BY LAW

Searches by police may be undertaken with the authority of a warrant, issued by a judge or justice, under s. 487 of the *Criminal Code* or through some other legislation that provides for a warrant or warrant-like process. Other sections of the *Criminal Code* provide for warrants to seize bodily substances and for specific investigative techniques, such as DNA warrants.

Searches may also be pursued without a warrant. Warrantless searches may be authorized by legislation or by virtue of a common law rule. The common law permits warrantless searches as an incident of a valid arrest with respect to the person arrested and the place where the person was arrested, including their car. The common law also permits search without warrant where the person has consented, but the courts may regard a citizen's alleged "consent" with some skepticism.

In *R. v. Dedman*, [1985] 2 S.C.R. 2 at 29, it was said: "Because of the intimidating nature of police action and uncertainty as to the extent of police powers, compliance in such circumstances cannot be regarded as voluntary in any meaningful sense." An accused's consent will not be said to be valid, for example, where the accused is misled as to the nature of the investigation: *R. v. Borden*, [1994] 3 S.C.R. 145. Consent must be proven by the Crown on a balance of probabilities: *R. v. Young* (1997), 34 O.R. (3d) 177 (C.A.).

The common law also recognizes the "plain view" doctrine, permitting warrantless seizures where the officer is lawfully on the premises, the article is immediately obvious, and the discovery is inadvertent (*Law, supra*). Finally, the police have common law powers to enter premises (*R. v. Godoy*, [1999] 1 S.C.R. 311) and stop vehicles

(*Dedman*, *supra*, and *R.* v. *Hufsky*, [1988] 1 S.C.R. 621) without warrants in order to respond to 911 emergency calls and to uphold public safety on the roads. Combined with the plain view doctrine, these interventions can produce lawful warrantless seizures, but not, for example, where officers must actually open a gym bag sitting on the front seat of a car to find the drugs claimed to be "in plain view": *R.* v. *Mellenthin*, [1992] 3 S.C.R. 615.

If a search is not authorized by law, it is *prima facie* unreasonable and a violation of s. 8 of the *Charter*. Thus, for example, in *R.* v. *Wong*, [1990] 3 S.C.R. 36, police use of video surveillance in a hotel room without a warrant was said to violate s. 8, although the majority of the Court did not exclude the evidence under s. 24(2) because the police were said to have acted in good faith.

Police failure to conform to the law authorizing the search can also negate that legal authority, rendering the search "warrantless." For example, the courts have begun to articulate constitutional standards for adjudication of reasonable cause to justify issuance of a search warrant. Informants' tips may be sufficient to provide the constitutionally required standard of "reasonable probability" when the information is specific, includes the basis for the information, and comes from a "reliable informer": *R.* v. *Debot*, [1989] 2 S.C.R. 1140; *R.* v. *Tesfai* (1995), 148 N.S.R. (2d) 87 (S.C.). However, the police cannot use illegal means to secure evidence to suggest reasonable cause. In *R.* v. *Kokesch*, [1990] 3 S.C.R. 3, the police had made an illegal entry onto the accused's property, and had thereby obtained the "reasonable grounds" to obtain a search warrant to search for marijuana. The Court held that the warrant was invalid, and that the evidence acquired should be excluded pursuant to s. 24(2) because the trespass was blatantly illegal (e.g. no "good faith" on the part of the police) and because the value of "privacy" should be upheld.

In *R.* v. *Gray* (1993), 81 C.C.C. (3d) 174 (Man. C.A.), evidence was excluded from trial based on: the practice of the police of presenting draft informations to the magistrate, who either signed them or assisted in re-drafting them; the officer's inability to recall whether the magistrate had assisted with respect to the warrant in question; and the fact that the information in this case failed to disclose sufficient grounds to justify issuance of a warrant. In contrast, in *R.* v. *Tooze*, [1995] O.J. No. 2947 (Ct. Just. (Prov. Div.)), online: QL, evidence obtained pursuant to a warrant that was executed the day before it was authorized was admitted into trial, even though the court classified the error as a serious defect. See also *Plant*, *supra*, in which the accused was unsuccessful in challenging the validity of a warrant. The Court agreed that an earlier warrantless, "perimeter" search of the accused's property violated s. 8 of the *Charter*, and did not fit within the terms of s. 10 of the *Narcotic Control Act*; thus the information thereby obtained could not support the warrant. However, its issuance could be supported by an anonymous tip and computerized electricity records, which were said not to invoke a reasonable expectation of privacy under s. 8.

B. LAW MUST BE REASONABLE

Laws authorizing searches and seizures may be challenged as "unreasonable" in reliance upon s. 8 of the *Charter*. *Hunter* v. *Southam* was the first case in which the Supreme Court began to flesh out the meaning to be given to s. 8.

Hunter v. Southam[†]

[DICKSON J.:]

The Constitution of Canada, which includes the *Canadian Charter of Rights and Freedoms*, is the supreme law of Canada. Any law inconsistent with the provisions of the Constitution is, to the extent of the inconsistency, of no force or effect. Section 52(1) of the *Constitution Act, 1982* so mandates. The con-

---

† [1984] 2 S.C.R. 145.

stitutional question posed in this appeal is whether s. 10(3), and by implication s. 10(1), of the *Combines Investigation Act*, R.S.C. 1970, c. C-23 (the "Act"), are inconsistent with s. 8 of the Charter by reason of authorizing unreasonable searches and seizures and are therefore of no force and effect.

BACKGROUND

Section 10(1) and (3) of the *Combines Investigation Act* provide:

> 10(1) Subject to subsection (3), in any inquiry under this Act the Director [of Investigation and Research of the Combines Investigation Branch] or any representative authorized by him may enter any premises on which the Director believes there may be evidence relevant to the matters being inquired into and may examine any thing on the premises and may copy or take away for further examination or copying any book, paper, record or other document that in the opinion of the Director or his authorized representative, as the case may be, may afford such evidence.
>
> ...
>
> (3) Before exercising the power conferred by subsection (1), the Director or his representative shall produce a certificate from a member of the [Restrictive Trade Practices] Commission, which may be granted on the *ex parte* application of the Director, authorizing the exercise of such power.

On April 13, 1982, in the course of an inquiry under the Act, the appellant Lawson A.W. Hunter, Director of Investigation and Research of the Combines Investigation Branch, authorized the other appellants, Messrs. Milton, Murphy, McAlpine and Marrocco, all combines investigation officers, to exercise his authority under s. 10 of the Act to enter and examine documents and other things at the business premises of the Edmonton Journal, a division of the respondent corporation, Southam Inc.

On April 16, 1982, in fulfilment of the requirement in s. 10(3) of the Act, Dr. Frank Roseman, a member of the Restrictive Trade Practices Commission (the "R.T.P.C."), certified his authorization of this exercise of the director's powers.

On April 17, 1982, the *Constitution Act, 1982*, incorporating the *Canadian Charter of Rights and Freedoms*, was proclaimed. Section 8 of the Charter provides:

> 8. Everyone has the right to be secure against unreasonable search or seizure.

On April 19, 1982, the officers presented their certified authorization at the premises of the Edmonton Journal. The English version of this certificate reads as follows:

> In the matter of the Combines Investigation Act and section 33 and section 34(1)(c) thereof
>
> and
>
> in the matter of an Inquiry relating to the Production, Distribution and Supply of Newspapers and Related Products in Edmonton
>
> To:
>
> M.J. Milton
> M.L. Murphy
> J.A. McAlpine
> A.P. Marrocco
>
> being my representatives under section 10 of the Combines Investigation Act
>
> You are hereby authorized to enter upon the premises hereinafter mentioned, on which I believe there may be evidence relevant to this inquiry, and examine anything therein and copy or take away for copying any book, paper record or other document that in your opinion may afford such evidence.
>
> The premises referred to herein are those occupied by or on behalf of
>
> Southam Inc.
> 10006-101 Street
> Edmonton, Alberta
>
> and elsewhere in Canada
>
> This authorization is not valid after May 31, 1982.
>
> Dated in Hull, in the Province of Quebec this 13th day of April 1982.
>
> Lawson A.W. Hunter
> Director of Investigation and Research
> Combines Investigation Act
>
> I hereby certify that the above exercise of powers is authorized pursuant to Section 10 of the Combines Investigation Act.
>
> Dated in Ottawa, in the Province of Ontario, this 16th day of April, 1982.
>
> Frank Roseman, Member,
> Restrictive Trade Practices Commission

The authorization has a breath-taking sweep; it is tantamount to a licence to roam at large on the premises of Southam Inc. at the stated address "and elsewhere in Canada."

On April 20th the officers commenced the search. They said they wished to search every file of Southam Inc. at 10006-101 St., Edmonton, except files in the news-room but including all files of J. Patrick O'Callaghan, publisher of the Edmonton

Journal. They declined to give the name of any person whose complaint had initiated the inquiry, or to say under which section of the Act the inquiry had been begun. They also declined to give more specific information as to the subject-matter of the inquiry than that contained in the authorization to search.

At noon on April 20th, Southam Inc. served upon the officers of the Combines Investigation Branch a notice of motion for an interim injunction. The application was heard by Cavanagh J., who held that although Southam had raised a serious question as to whether the search was in violation of s. 8 of the Charter, the balance of convenience militated in favour of denying the interlocutory injunction pending trial of the matter. At the hearing, the appellants maintained, unsuccessfully, that the Director of Investigation and Research, and his authorized representatives, acting pursuant to s. 10 of the Act were a "federal board, commission or other tribunal" within s. 2(g) of the *Federal Court Act*, R.S.C. 1970, c. 10 (2nd Supp.), and that the Federal Court, not the provincial courts of Alberta, had jurisdiction [see 68 C.C.C. (2d) 356, 136 D.L.R. (3d) 133, 65 C.P.R. (2d) 80].

Southam appealed to the Alberta Court of Appeal. The appellants also appealed, from that part of the judgment which held that the Alberta Court of Queen's Bench had jurisdiction. As an interim provision the Court of Appeal ordered that the documents taken from the premises of the Edmonton Journal be sealed pending resolution of the appeal. After hearing the parties, the court held that the case was a proper one to have been treated at first instance as an application for summary judgment on the issues of (1) whether the Alberta courts or the Federal Court had jurisdiction to make the orders requested, and (2) whether s. 10 of the Act was in whole or in part inconsistent with the provisions of the Constitution. The court therefore directed that the appeal itself be heard on this basis. At the subsequent hearing, the judgment of this Court in *A.-G. Can. et al. v. Law Society of British Columbia et al.* (1982), 137 D.L.R. (3d) 1, 66 C.P.R. (2d) 1 *sub nom. Jabour v. Law Society of British Columbia et al.*, [1982] 2 S.C.R. 307, having by then been delivered, the present appellants abandoned their challenge to the jurisdiction of the Alberta courts and addressed their arguments solely to the substantive issue of the constitutionality of s. 10 of the Act. A unanimous five-judge panel of the Alberta Court of Appeal, speaking through Prowse J.A., held that s. 10(3), and, by implication s. 10(1), of the Act, were inconsistent with the provisions of s. 8 of the Charter and therefore of no force or effect. It is from this ruling that the present appellants bring their appeal before this Court.

THE POSITIONS OF THE PARTIES

The Respondent Southam Inc.

In alleging that s. 10(1) and (3) of the *Combines Investigation Act* are inconsistent with the right to be secure against unreasonable search and seizure, Southam Inc. relies heavily on the historic protections afforded by common law and by statute as defining the correct standard of reasonableness for purposes of s. 8 of the Charter. This was essentially the approach taken by Prowse J.A. when he said [3 C.C.C. (3d) 497 at p. 503, 147 D.L.R. (3d) 420 at p. 426, 72 C.P.R. (2d) 145 at p. 150]:

> The roots of the right to be secure are embedded in the common law and safeguards according that right are found in common law, in statutes subsequently enacted, and in decisions of the courts made as the society in which we live has evolved. The expression of the right in a constitutional document reminds us of those roots and the tradition associated with the right. One would be presumptuous to assume that we have attained the zenith of our development as a civilization and that the right accorded an individual is frozen for eternity. Section 8, however, requires us to be ever mindful of some of the criteria that have been applied in the past in securing the right.

Applying this approach, Prowse J.A. concluded — correctly in Southam Inc.'s submission — that, absent exceptional circumstances, the provisions of s. 443 [now s. 487] of the *Criminal Code*, which extends to investigations of *Criminal Code* offences the procedural safeguards the common law required for entries and searches for stolen goods, constitute the minimal prerequisites for reasonable searches and seizures in connection with the investigation of any criminal offence, including possible violations of the *Combines Investigation Act.* Prowse J.A. summarized these procedural safeguards in the following propositions [at p. 506 C.C.C., p. 429 D.L.R., p. 153 C.P.R.]:

> (a) the power to authorize a search and seizure is given to an impartial and independent person (at common law a justice) who is bound to act judicially in discharging that function;
> (b) that evidence must satisfy the justice that the person seeking the authority has reasonable ground to suspect that an offence had been committed;

(c) that evidence must satisfy the justice that the person seeking the authority has reasonable grounds to believe, at common law, that stolen property may be on the premises or, under s. 443(1)(b), that something that will afford evidence of an offence may be recovered[;] and

(d) there must be evidence on oath before him.

Southam Inc. contends that s. 10(1) and (3) fail to provide any of these safeguards. In its submission, the approval by a member of [the] R.T.P.C. of the director's decision to authorize search and seizure is not approval by an independent arbiter or neutral and impartial person. It argues further that s. 10(1) and (3) do not require that the R.T.P.C. member be satisfied that the director has reasonable grounds to suspect an offence has been committed or to believe there may be evidence at the place at which the director wishes to search, nor does it require evidence under oath about these matters. In fact, Southam Inc. contends, as these subsections have been judicially interpreted in cases such as *Re Petrofina Canada Ltd. and Chairman, Restrictive Trade Practices Com'n et al.* (1979), 107 D.L.R. (3d) 319, 46 C.P.R. (2d) 1, [1980] 2 F.C. 386, they *prevent* the R.T.P.C. member from ascertaining or passing judgment on anything except that there is, *de facto*, an inquiry in progress under the Act, an interpretation which, in Southam's submission, constitutes the R.T.P.C. member as merely a "rubber stamp" for the director's decision to authorize a search. For all these reasons, Southam submits, giving effect to s. 10(1) and (3) could yield no other result than an unreasonable search and seizure.

The Appellants

The appellants take a different view. In their submission the constitutionality of s. 10 ought to be considered on the basis of whether its provisions *could be* applied consistently with the Charter. It is their contention that they can. In their view, approval by the R.T.P.C. member *does* constitute authorization by a neutral and impartial arbiter. They deny there is any reasonable apprehension of bias attaching to him or to his function in approving the director's authorizations to enter and search premises. As to the further requirements cited by Prowse J.A. and amplified on by Southam Inc., the appellants implicitly deny that an easy parallel can be drawn between the offences set out in the *Criminal Code* and those created by the *Combines Investigation Act* so as to justify invoking the procedural safeguards in s. 443 as the proper standard of reasonableness for searches and seizures by the authorities in connection with these latter offences. In their submission combines offences require specialized techniques for their detection and suppression. They say that for such offences, as compared to most other criminal offences, there is inherently less basis for certainty and specificity, both as to the commission of an offence and as to the existence of specific physical evidence in relation to such offence. In this context, they contend, s. 10 does not authorize "unreasonable" search and seizure. Further, the appellants argue, the wording of s. 10 does not prevent the R.T.P.C. member in appropriate cases from requiring, for instance, evidence under oath before he approves the director's authorization. In any event, they maintain, it cannot be said that s. 10 is incapable of being applied in a manner which does not offend the Constitution, and it ought not, therefore, to be struck down. At most, it ought to be read down as to include any necessary procedural safeguards. In support, they cite the decision of Van Camp J. in *R. v. Metropolitan Toronto Pharmacists' Ass'n* (unreported, Ont. H.C.J., May 4, 1983) [summarized 10 W.C.B. 367].

"UNREASONABLE" SEARCH OR SEIZURE

At the outset it is important to note that the issue in this appeal concerns the constitutional validity of a statute authorizing a search and seizure. It does not concern the reasonableness or otherwise of the manner in which the appellants carried out their statutory authority. It is not the conduct of the appellants, but rather the legislation under which they acted, to which attention must be directed.

As is clear from the arguments of the parties as well as from the judgment of Prowse J.A., the crux of this case is the meaning to be given to the term "unreasonable" in the s. 8 guarantee of freedom from unreasonable search or seizure. The guarantee is vague and open. The American courts have had the advantage of a number of specific prerequisites articulated in the Fourth Amendment to the United States Constitution, as well as a history of colonial opposition to certain Crown investigatory practices from which to draw out the nature of the interests protected by that Amendment and the kinds of conduct it proscribes. There is none of this in s. 8. There is no specificity in the section beyond the bare guarantee of freedom from "unreasonable" search and seizure; nor is there any particular historical, political or philosophic context capable of providing an obvious gloss on the meaning of the guarantee.

It is clear that the meaning of "unreasonable" cannot be determined by recourse to a dictionary, nor for that manner, by reference to the rules of statutory construction. The task of expounding a constitution is crucially different from that of construing a statute. A statute defines present rights and obligations. It is easily enacted and as easily repealed. A constitution, by contrast, is drafted with an eye to the future. Its function is to provide a continuing framework for the legitimate exercise of governmental power and, when joined by a Bill or a Charter of rights, for the unremitting protection of individual rights and liberties. Once enacted, its provisions cannot easily be repealed or amended. It must, therefore, be capable of growth and development over time to meet new social, political and historical realities often unimagined by its framers. The judiciary is the guardian of the Constitution and must, in interpreting its provisions, bear these considerations in mind. Professor Paul Freund expressed this idea aptly when he admonished the American courts "not to read the provisions of the Constitution like a last will and testament lest it become one."

The need for a broad perspective in approaching constitutional documents is a familiar theme in Canadian constitutional jurisprudence. It is contained in Viscount Sankey's classic formulation in *Re s. 24 of B.N.A. Act*; *Edwards v. A.-G. Can.*, [1930] 1 D.L.R. 98 at pp. 106-7, [1930] A.C. 124 at pp. 136-7, [1929] 3 W.W.R. 479, cited and applied in countless Canadian cases:

> The B.N.A. Act planted in Canada a living tree capable of growth and expansion within its natural limits. The object of the Act was to grant a Constitution to Canada.
>
> ...
>
> Their Lordships do not conceive it to be the duty of this Board — it is certainly not their desire — to cut down the provisions of the Act by a narrow and technical construction, but rather to give it a large and liberal interpretation....

More recently, in *Minister of Home Affairs et al. v. Fisher et al.*, [1980] A.C. 319 at p. 329, dealing with the Bermudian Constitution, Lord Wilberforce reiterated that a constitution is a document "*sui generis*, calling for principles of interpretation of its own, suitable to its character," and that as such, a constitution incorporating a *Bill of Rights* calls for [at p. 328]: "a generous interpretation avoiding what has been called 'the austerity of tabulated legalism' suitable to give to individuals the full measure of the fundamental rights and freedoms referred to". Such a broad, purposive analysis, which interprets specific provisions of a constitutional document in the light of its larger objects, is also consonant with the classical principles of American constitutional construction enunciated by Chief Justice Marshall in *M'Culloch v. State of Maryland* (1819), 17 U.S. (4 Wheaton) 316. It is, as well, the approach I intend to take in the present case.

I begin with the obvious. The *Canadian Charter of Rights and Freedoms* is a purposive document. Its purpose is to guarantee and to protect, within the limits of reason, the enjoyment of the rights and freedoms it enshrines. It is intended to constrain governmental action inconsistent with those rights and freedoms; it is not in itself an authorization for governmental action. In the present case this means, as Prowse J.A. pointed out, that in guaranteeing the right to be secure from unreasonable searches and seizures, s. 8 acts as a limitation on whatever powers of search and seizure the federal or provincial governments already and otherwise possess. It does not in itself confer any powers, even of "reasonable" search and seizure, on these governments. This leads, in my view, to the further conclusion that an assessment of the constitutionality of a search and seizure, or of a statute authorizing a search or seizure, must focus on its "reasonable" or "unreasonable" impact on the subject of the search or the seizure, and not simply on its rationality in furthering some valid government objective.

Since the proper approach to the interpretation of the *Canadian Charter of Rights and Freedoms* is a purposive one, before it is possible to assess the reasonableness or unreasonableness of the impact of a search or of a statute authorizing a search, it is first necessary to specify the purpose underlying s. 8: in other words, to delineate the nature of the interests it is meant to protect.

Historically, the common law protections with regard to governmental searches and seizures were based on the right to enjoy property and were linked to the law of trespass. It was on this basis that in the great case of *Entick v. Carrington* (1765), 19 State Tr. 1029, the court refused to countenance a search purportedly authorized by the Executive, to discover evidence that might link the plaintiff to certain seditious libels. Lord Camden prefaced his discussion of the rights in question by saying, at p. 1066:

> The great end, for which men entered into society, was to preserve their property. That right is preserved sacred and incommunicable in all instances where it has not been taken away or

abridged by some public law for the good of the whole.

The defendants argued that their oaths as King's messengers required them to conduct the search in question and ought to prevail over the plaintiff's property rights. Lord Camden rejected this contention, at p. 1067:

> Our law holds the property of every man so sacred, that no man can set his foot upon his neighbour's close without his leave: if he does he is a trespasser though he does no damage at all; if he will tread upon his neighbour's ground, he must justify it by law.

Lord Camden could find no exception from this principle for the benefit of King's messengers. He held that neither the intrusions nor the purported authorizations were supportable on the basis of the existing law. That law would only have countenanced such an entry if the search were for stolen goods and if authorized by a justice on the basis of evidence upon oath that there was "strong cause" to believe the goods were concealed in the place sought to be searched. In view of the lack of proper legal authorization for the governmental intrusion, the plaintiff was protected from the intended search and seizure by the ordinary law of trespass.

In my view, the interests protected by s. 8 are of a wider ambit than those enunciated in *Entick v. Carrington*. Section 8 is an entrenched constitutional provision. It is not therefore vulnerable to encroachment by legislative enactments in the same way as common law protections. There is, further, nothing in the language of the section to restrict it to the protection of property or to associate it with the law of trespass. It guarantees a broad and general right to be secure from unreasonable search and seizure.

The Fourth Amendment, of the United States Constitution, also guarantees a broad right. It provides:

AMENDMENT IV

The right of the people to be secure in their persons, houses, papers, and effects, against unreasonable searches and seizures, shall not be violated, and no warrants shall issue but upon probable cause, supported by oath or affirmation, and particularly describing the place to be searched, and the persons or things to be seized.

Construing this provision in *Katz v. United States* (1967), 389 U.S. 347, Stewart J., delivering the majority opinion of the United States Supreme Court, declared at p. 351 that "the Fourth Amendment protects people, not places." Justice Stewart rejected any necessary connection between that Amendment and the notion of trespass. With respect, I believe this approach is equally appropriate in construing the protections in s. 8 of the *Canadian Charter of Rights and Freedoms*.

In *Katz*, Stewart J. discussed the notion of a right to privacy, which he described at p. 350 as "the right to be let alone by other people." Although Stewart J. was careful not to identify the Fourth Amendment exclusively with the protection of this right, nor to see the Amendment as the only provision in the *Bill of Rights* relevant to its interpretation, it is clear that this notion played a prominent role in his construction of the nature and the limits of the American constitutional protection against unreasonable search and seizure. In the Alberta Court of Appeal, Prowse J.A. took a similar approach to s. 8, which he described [at p. 503 C.C.C., p. 426 D.L.R., p. 150 C.P.R.] as dealing "with one aspect of what has been referred to as a right of privacy which is the right to be secure against encroachment upon the citizens' reasonable expectation of privacy in a free and democratic society."

Like the Supreme Court of the United States, I would be wary of foreclosing the possibility that the right to be secure against unreasonable search and seizure might protect interests beyond the right of privacy, but for purposes of the present appeal I am satisfied that its protections go at least that far. The guarantee of security from *unreasonable* search and seizure only protects a *reasonable* expectation. This limitation on the right guaranteed by s. 8, whether it is expressed negatively as freedom from "unreasonable" search and seizure, or positively as an entitlement to a "reasonable" expectation of privacy, indicates that an assessment must be made as to whether in a particular situation the public's interest in being left alone by government must give way to the government's interest in intruding on the individual's privacy in order to advance its goals, notably those of law enforcement.

The question that remains, and the one upon which the present appeal hinges, is how this assessment is to be made. When is it to be made, by whom and on what basis? Here again, I think the proper approach is a purposive one.

When Is the Balance of Interests to Be Assessed?

If the issue to be resolved in assessing the constitutionality of searches under s. 10 were whether *in fact* the governmental interest in carrying out a given search outweighed that of the individual in resisting the governmental intrusion upon his privacy, then it would be appropriate to determine the balance of the competing interests *after* the search had been conducted. Such a *post facto* analysis would, however, be seriously at odds with the purpose of s. 8. That purpose is, as I have said, to protect individuals from unjustified State intrusions upon their privacy. That purpose requires a means of *preventing* unjustified searches before they happen, not simply of determining, after the fact, whether they ought to have occurred in the first place. This, in my view, can only be accomplished by a system of *prior authorization*, not one of subsequent validation.

A requirement of prior authorization, usually in the form of a valid warrant, has been a consistent prerequisite for a valid search and seizure both at common law and under most statutes. Such a requirement puts the onus on the State to demonstrate the superiority of its interests to that of the individual. As such it accords with the apparent intention of the Charter to prefer, where feasible, the right of the individual to be free from State interference to the interests of the State in advancing its purposes through such interference.

I recognize that it may not be reasonable in every instance to insist on prior authorization in order to validate governmental intrusions upon individuals' expectations of privacy. Nevertheless, where it is feasible to obtain prior authorization, I would hold that such authorization is a pre-condition for a valid search and seizure.

Here also, the decision in *Katz, supra*, is relevant. In *United States v. Rabinowitz* (1950), 339 U.S. 56, the Supreme Court of the United States had held that a search without warrant was not *ipso facto* unreasonable. Seventeen years later, however, in *Katz*, Stewart J. concluded that a warrantless search was *prima facie* "unreasonable" under the Fourth Amendment. The terms of the Fourth Amendment are not identical to those of s. 8 and American decisions can be transplanted to the Canadian context only with the greatest caution. Nevertheless, I would in the present instance respectfully adopt Stewart J.'s formulation as equally applicable to the concept of "unreasonableness" under s. 8, and would require the party seeking to justify a warrantless search to rebut this presumption of unreasonableness.

In the present case the appellants make no argument that it is unfeasible or unnecessary to obtain prior authorization for the searches contemplated by the *Combines Investigation Act* and, in my view, no such argument could be made. I would therefore conclude that in the absence of a valid procedure for prior authorization searches conducted under the Act would be unreasonable. In the event, s. 10(3) *does* purport to establish a requirement for prior authorization, specifying, as it does, that searches and seizures conducted under s. 10(1) must be authorized by a member of the R.T.P.C. The question then becomes whether s. 10(3) provides for an acceptable prior authorization procedure.

Who Must Grant the Authorization?

The purpose of a requirement of prior authorization is to provide an opportunity, before the event, for the conflicting interests of the State and the individual to be assessed, so that the individual's right to privacy will be breached only where the appropriate standard has been met, and the interests of the State are thus demonstrably superior. For such an authorization procedure to be meaningful it is necessary for the person authorizing the search to be able to assess the evidence as to whether that standard has been met, in an entirely neutral and impartial manner. At common law the power to issue a search warrant was reserved for a justice. In the recent English case of *Inland Revenue Com'rs et al. v. Rossminster Ltd.*, [1980] 1 All E.R. 80 at p. 87, Viscount Dilhorne suggested that the power to authorize administrative searches and seizures be given to "a more senior judge." While it may be wise, in view of the sensitivity of the task, to assign the decision whether an authorization should be issued to a judicial officer, I agree with Prowse J.A. that this is not a necessary pre-condition for safeguarding the right enshrined in s. 8. The person performing this function need not be a judge, but he must at a minimum be capable of acting judicially.

In *Minister of National Revenue v. Coopers and Lybrand* (1978), 92 D.L.R. (3d) 1, [1979] 1 S.C.R. 495, 78 D.T.C. 6528, this Court had occasion to discuss the difference between an administrative and a judicial function in the authorization of a search and seizure. The *Income Tax Act*, 1970-71-72 (Can.), c. 63, as amended, confers upon the Minister a number of powers including, in s. 231(4), the power under certain conditions to authorize the entry and search of buildings. At p. 10 D.L.R., p. 507 S.C.R., the court described the Minister's powers as "fundamentally administrative," going on to explain:

> The power he exercises under s. 231(4) is properly characterized as investigatory, rather than adjudicatory. He will collect material and advice from many sources. In deciding whether to exercise the right [to authorize entry and search], he will be governed by many considerations, dominant among which is the public interest and his

duty as an executive officer of the Government to administer the Act to the best of his ability. The decision to seek authority to enter and search will be guided by public policy and expediency, having regard to all the circumstances.

The court contrasted these powers with the judicial powers which s. 231(4) conferred on a judge of the superior or county court to approve the Minister's authorization.

Under the scheme envisaged by s. 10 of the *Combines Investigation Act* it is clear that the director exercises administrative powers analogous to those of the Minister under s. 231(4) of the *Income Tax Act*. They too are investigatory rather than adjudicatory, with his decision to seek approval for an authorization to enter and search premises equally guided by considerations of expediency and public policy. But what of the member of the R.T.P.C. whom s. 10(3) empowers to approve the director's authorization? Is his function investigatory or adjudicatory? In the Alberta Court of Appeal Prowse J.A. carefully reviewed the respective powers of the director and the commission and concluded that the Act was not entirely successful in separating the role of the director as investigator and prosecutor from that of the commission as adjudicator. In his view [at p. 508 C.C.C., p. 431 D.L.R., p. 155 C.P.R.] circumstances may arise under the Act where "the director is acting as investigator and prosecutor and the commission is acting as investigator and judge with respect to breaches of the Act." Southam Inc. summarizes and enlarges upon Prowse J.A.'s analysis, producing the following list of investigatory functions bestowed upon the commission or one of its members by the Act:

(i) the power in s. 47 to instruct the Director to commence a s. 8 inquiry;
(ii) the power to cause evidence to be gathered pursuant to ss. 9, 10, 12 and 17;
(iii) the power to issue a s. 17 order;
(iv) the power under ss. 17, 22(2)(b) to seek further or better evidence after the Commission has commenced a hearing;
(v) the power under s. 22(2)(b) after commencing a hearing and receiving evidence to direct the Director to make further inquiry and, in effect, to go back to the investigatory stage;
(vi) the power under s. 22(2)(c) to compel the Director to turn over to the R.T.P.C. copies of all books, papers, records or other documents obtained by the Director in such further inquiry;
(vii) the power under s. 27.1 to order the Director to give evidence before any other federal board, commission or other tribunal;
(viii) the power under s. 45.1 to seek production of statistics for evidence in an inquiry;
(ix) the power to deliver to the Director all books, papers, records of other documents produced on a s. 17 hearing;
(x) the power under s. 13 to request the appointment and instruction of counsel to assist in the inquiry.

In my view, investing the commission or its members with significant investigatory functions has the result of vitiating the ability of a member of the commission to act in a judicial capacity when authorizing a search or seizure under s. 10(3). This is not, of course, a matter of impugning the honesty or good faith of the commission or its members. It is rather a conclusion that the administrative nature of the commission's investigatory duties (with its quite proper reference points in considerations of public policy and effective enforcement of the Act) ill accords with the neutrality and detachment necessary to assess whether the evidence reveals that the point has been reached where the interests of the individual must constitutionally give way to those of the State. A member of the R.T.P.C. passing on the appropriateness of a proposed search under the *Combines Investigation Act* is caught by the maxim *nemo judex in sua causa*. He simply cannot be the impartial arbiter necessary to grant an effective authorization.

On this basis alone I would conclude that the prior authorization mandated by s. 10(3) of the *Combines Investigation Act* is inadequate to satisfy the requirements of s. 8 of the Charter and consequently a search carried out under the authority of s. 10(1) and (3) is an unreasonable one. Since, however, the Alberta Court of Appeal found other, perhaps even more serious defects in these provisions I pass on to consider whether even if s. 10(3) did specify a truly neutral and detached arbiter to authorize searches it would nevertheless remain inconsistent with s. 8 of the Charter.

On What Basis Must the Balance of Interests Be Assessed?

Section 10 is terse in the extreme on the subject of criteria for issuing an authorization for entry, search and seizure. Section 10(3) merely states that an R.T.P.C. member may grant an authorization *ex parte*. The only explicit criteria for granting such an authorization are those mentioned in s. 10(1), namely: (1) that an inquiry under the Act must be in progress, and (2) that the director must believe that the premises may contain relevant evidence.

In cases argued before passage of the *Canadian Charter of Rights and Freedoms* the courts took a narrow view of what s. 10 required or permitted the R.T.P.C. member to consider when asked to authorize search and seizure. In *Re Petrofina Canada Ltd. and Chairman, Restrictive Trade Practices Com'n et al.* (1979), 107 D.L.R. (3d) 319, 46 C.P.R. (2d) 1, [1980] 2 F.C. 386, the applicant challenged authorizations under ss. 9(2) and 10(3) of the Act on the grounds, *inter alia*, that the members who gave their authorizations did not show that they had before them sufficient information to enable them to determine the legality of the inquiry then in progress or the reasonableness of the director's belief that circumstances warranted the exercise of his powers. The Federal Court of Appeal rejected the relevance of such considerations to the members' decisions, at p. 322 D.L.R., p. 4 C.P.R., p. 391 F.C.:

> In making the decisions that ss. 9 and 10 require them to make, the members must act judicially ... However, that duty to act judicially applies only to the decisions that the members are required to make under ss. 9(2) and 10(3). Under those provisions, the members are neither required nor authorized to determine the legality of the Director's decision to hold an inquiry; they are merely required to ascertain that there is, *de facto*, an inquiry in progress under the Act. The members are not required or authorized, either, to pass judgment on the reasonableness of the motives prompting the Director to exercise his powers under ss. 9 and 10. As the members did not have to make decisions on those two points, they cannot, in my opinion, be blamed for not having required information on those points.

As Prowse J.A. pointed out, if the powers of a commission member are as the Federal Court of Appeal found them to be, then it follows that the decision of the director in the course of an inquiry to exercise his powers of entry, search and seizure is effectively unreviewable. The extent of the privacy of the individual would be left to the discretion of the director. A provision authorizing such an unreviewable power would clearly be inconsistent with s. 8 of the Charter.

Assuming, *arguendo*, that the Federal Court of Appeal was wrong, and the member *is* authorized, or even required, to satisfy himself as to (1) the legality of the inquiry, and (2) the reasonableness of the director's belief that there may be evidence relevant to the matters being inquired into, would that remove the inconsistency with s. 8?

To read s. 10(1) and (3) as simply *allowing* the authorizing party to satisfy himself on these questions, without requiring him to do so, would in my view be clearly inadequate. Such an amorphous standard cannot provide a meaningful criterion for securing the right guaranteed by s. 8. The location of the constitutional balance between a justifiable expectation of privacy and the legitimate needs of the State cannot depend on the subjective appreciation of individual adjudicators. Some objective standard must be established.

Requiring the authorizing party to satisfy himself as to the legality of the inquiry and the reasonableness of the director's belief in the possible existence of relevant evidence, would have the advantage of substituting an objective standard for an amorphous one, but would, in my view, still be inadequate. The problem is with the stipulation of a reasonable belief that evidence *may* be uncovered in the search. Here again it is useful, in my view, to adopt a purposive approach. The purpose of an objective criterion for granting prior authorization to conduct a search or seizure is to provide a consistent standard for identifying the point at which the interests of the State in such intrusions come to prevail over the interests of the individual in resisting them. To associate it with an applicant's reasonable belief that relevant evidence *may* be uncovered by the search, would be to define the proper standard as the *possibility* of finding evidence. This is a very low standard which would validate intrusion on the basis of suspicion, and authorize fishing expeditions of considerable latitude. It would tip the balance strongly in favour of the State and limit the right of the individual to resist to only the most egregious intrusions. I do not believe that this is a proper standard for securing the right to be free from unreasonable search and seizure.

Anglo-Canadian legal and political traditions point to a higher standard. The common law required evidence on oath which gave "strong reason to believe" that stolen goods were concealed in the place to be searched before a warrant would issue. Section 443 of the *Criminal Code* authorizes a warrant only where there has been information upon oath that there is "reasonable ground to believe" that there is evidence of an offence in the place to be searched. The American *Bill of Rights* provides that "no warrants shall issue but upon probable cause, supported by oath or affirmation...." The phrasing is slightly different but the standard in each of these formulations is identical. The State's interest in detecting and preventing crime begins to prevail over the individual's interest in being left alone at the point where credibly-based probability replaces suspicion. History has confirmed the appropriateness of this requirement as the threshold for subordinating the expectation of privacy to the needs of law enforcement. Where the State's interest is not simply law enforcement as, for instance, where State security is involved, or where the individual's interest is not simply his expectation of privacy as, for instance, when the search threatens his bodily integrity, the relevant standard might well be a different one. That is not the situation in the present case. In cases like the present, reasonable and probable grounds, established upon oath, to believe that an offence has been committed and that there is evidence to be found at the place of the search, constitutes the minimum standard, consistent with s. 8 of the Charter, for authorizing search and seizure. In so far as s. 10(1) and (3) of the *Combines Investigation Act* do not embody such a requirement, I would hold them to be further inconsistent with s. 8.

READING IN AND READING DOWN

The appellants submit that even if s. 10(1) and (3) do not specify a standard consistent with s. 8 for authorizing entry, search and seizure, they should not be struck down as inconsistent with the Charter, but rather that the appropriate standard should be read into these provisions. An analogy is drawn to the case of *McKay v. The Queen* (1965), 53 D.L.R. (2d) 532, [1965] S.C.R. 798, in which this Court held that a local ordinance regulating the use of property by prohibiting the erection of unauthorized signs, though apparently without limits, could not have been intended unconstitutionally to encroach on federal competence over elections, and should therefore be "read down" so as not to apply to election signs. In the present case, the overt inconsistency with s. 8 manifested by the lack of a neutral and detached arbiter renders the appellants' submissions on reading in appropriate standards for issuing a warrant purely academic. Even if this were not the case, however, I would be disinclined to give effect to these submissions. While the courts are guardians of the Constitution and of individuals' rights under it, it is the Legislature's responsibility to enact legislation that embodies appropriate safeguards to comply with the Constitution's requirements. It should not fall to the courts to fill in the details that will render legislative lacunae constitutional. Without appropriate safeguards legislation authorizing search and seizure is inconsistent with s. 8 of the Charter. As I have said, any law inconsistent with the provisions of the Constitution is, to the extent of the inconsistency, of no force or effect. I would hold s. 10(1) and (3) of the *Combines Investigation Act* to be inconsistent with the Charter and of no force and effect, as much for their failure to specify an appropriate standard for issuance of warrants as for their designation of an improper arbiter to issue them.

SECTION 1

Section 1 of the Charter provides:

> 1. The *Canadian Charter of Rights and Freedoms* guarantees the rights and freedoms set out in it subject only to such reasonable limits prescribed by law as can be demonstrably justified in a free and democratic society.

The phrase "demonstrably justified" puts the onus of justifying a limitation on a right or freedom set out in the Charter on the party seeking to limit. In the present case the appellants have made no submissions capable of supporting a claim that even if searches under s. 10(1) and (3) are "unreasonable" within the meaning of s. 8, they are nevertheless a reasonable limit, demonstrably justified in a free and democratic society, on the right set out in s. 8. It is, therefore, not necessary in this case to consider the relationship between s. 8 and s. 1. I leave to another day the difficult question of the relationship between those two sections and, more particularly, what further balancing of interests, if any, may be contemplated by s. 1, beyond that envisaged by s. 8.

CONCLUSION

. . . .

... I would dismiss the appeal with costs to the respondent.

Appeal dismissed.

■

Andrew Petter, in his article, "The Politics of the Charter" (1986) 8 Sup. Ct. L. Rev. 473, argues that *Charter* litigation is predominantly the preserve of the wealthy and the privileged, and that therefore the indeterminate nature of the "rights" articulated in the *Charter* means that judicial interpretations will be shaped in the context of corporate litigation: "over time, the disproportionate attention that (corporate) interests command will shape the court's perception of the purpose of rights and, hence, will influence the court's interpretation of their meaning and scope." He uses *Hunter* v. *Southam Inc.* to illustrate his analysis.

The Politics of the Charter†

One area in which institutional barriers and judicial attitudes have already combined to influence the nature of rights under the Charter relates to corporations. Of the first nine Charter cases to be decided by the Supreme Court, two concerned the rights of corporations. In *Big M Drug Mart*, a corporation invoked the Charter guarantee of freedom of religion to successfully defend itself against charges under section 4 of the federal *Lord's Day Act* for conducting business on a Sunday. In *Southam*, a corporation brought a successful action to strike down search and seizure provisions of the *Combines Investigation Act* on the basis that those provisions violated its right to be free from "unreasonable search and seizure."

More disturbing than the results of these cases are the assumptions made by the Court in reaching these results. In both cases, the Court speaks in the abstract about rights and freedoms under the Charter being *human* rights. In *Southam*, Dickson C.J. refers throughout his judgment to the purpose of the Charter being to protect "the public's interest" and "the right of the individual." In *Big M*, the Chief Justice refers to freedom being "founded in respect for the inherent dignity and the inviolable rights of the human person." In light of these sentiments, one might expect the Supreme Court to look with skepticism upon Charter claims brought before it by non-human entities such as corporations. Yet, as *Southam* in particular demonstrates, this has not been the case.

Nowhere in his reasons in *Southam* does Dickson C.J. even consider whether the rights enjoyed by corporations under section 8 of the Charter might be different from those enjoyed by human beings. This is especially disquieting given that the Chief Justice goes out of his way in the judgment to identify the right to be free from unreasonable search or seizure as a privacy right rather than a property right. A corporation, after all, is an artificial entity whose function is economic in nature. While the privacy interests of human beings relate to their needs for psychological and bodily security, in addition to economic security, the privacy interests of corporations do not. Thus, while Dickson C.J. insists that section 8 is a privacy right and not a property right, his application of it to a corporation renders the distinction he purports to make illusory. To grant a corporation a privacy right is to grant it a property right pure and simple. It was for this reason that the United States Supreme Court held in *Bellis v. United States* that "a substantial claim of privacy or confidentiality cannot often be maintained with respect to the financial records of an organized collective entity."

Furthermore, the powers and capacities of corporations flow from legislation. These powers and capacities permit corporations to accumulate capital in ways not available to individuals and protect from personal liability their shareholders, officers and directors. To accept uncritically that these entities should be entitled to the same degree of privacy from the state as human beings is to disregard the fact that the extraordinary powers they wield are themselves a product of state action, and require commensurate constitutional authority in government to guard against their abuse.

Indeed, surely it is bizarre that corporations should be granted *any* protection under the Charter. Why should an artificial entity whose powers flow from the state and whose function is economic be entitled to share in rights founded in respect for "the human person"? I do not mean to suggest by this that the shareholders, directors, officers (or, for that matter, the clients or employees) of a corporation should be denied a right of privacy under the Charter. But it is one thing to suggest that a search of corporate records might affect the privacy interests of an individual who is associated with a corporation; it is quite another to suggest that such a search affects the privacy interests of the corporation itself. The effect of giving corporations a right of

---

† By Andrew Petter, (1986) 8 Sup. Ct L. Rev 473 at 490–92, 493, 495, 496–98. Reproduced by permission of the author.

privacy is to place in the hands of those who own and manage corporations the right to invoke special constitutional protection with respect to corporate property independent of any privacy interests that they as individuals might enjoy in that property. Perhaps such a right could be defended if the relationship of all shareholders and directors to all corporations were the same; but clearly this is not the case. The privacy interest of a shareholder or director of a closely held company with respect to corporate records is likely to be vastly different from the privacy interest of a shareholder or director of a widely-held conglomerate. To evaluate the privacy interest in each case on the basis that they are both corporations and thus both entitled to equivalent degrees of privacy is to disregard the underlying human values at stake. Furthermore, to treat corporations as having privacy interests of their own is to give corporations preferred status over unincorporated businesses whose owners must presumably found their rights to privacy under the Charter solely on the basis of the nature of their personal interests in the business.

To Canadian judges, many of whom served corporations in private practice and who are used to treating them like any other litigant, the suggestion that corporations should not be accorded "human" status under the Charter must sound peculiar.

. . . .

One of the concerns often expressed by those who oppose entrenched charters of rights is that such charters can be used to undermine the ability of the state to control the use and abuse of private economic power. Underlying this concern is a belief that a charter of rights embodies a theory that favours a minimal state, and that the courts will reinforce this theory by interpreting freedom under the Charter solely in terms of freedom from state intervention.

. . . .

The early Charter decisions of the Supreme Court provide strong evidence that the Supreme Court embraces a wholly negative conception of freedom: a conception which views government solely as an inhibitor of freedom and which discounts the interests of individuals who depend upon the state to guarantee their freedom.

. . . .

In his decision, Dickson C.J., writing for a unanimous Court, concludes that these provisions violate the "right to be secure from unreasonable search and seizure" guaranteed by section 8 of the Charter.

. . . .

The first thing worth noting about this analysis is that it discounts entirely a role for the state in promoting rights and freedoms. In balancing the rights of the individual against the interests of the state, the Chief Justice characterizes the state's interest under the *Combines Investigation Act* as being "simply law enforcement." There is no reference in his judgment to the underlying purpose of that enforcement or to the interests that it serves. There is no consideration of the possibility that the actions of the state might be understood and justified in terms of the freedom that such actions bestow upon other individuals. These omissions are particularly noteworthy given the nature of the *Combines Investigation Act*. The Act is not aimed at protecting interests that are peculiar to the state nor is it, like most criminal statutes, aimed at activities that can be considered morally reprehensible. Its purpose is to promote freedom in the marketplace. In particular, it is to protect the interests of small entrepreneurs and consumers who might otherwise be subject to coercion at the hands of private economic interests powerful enough to undermine competitive market forces.

It is ironic that, in the context of a judgment that claims, above all, to be "purposive," the Chief Justice's consideration of the state's interest in enacting the *Combines Investigation Act*, and of the freedom that Act bestows upon others, should be so dismally "purposeless." Nowhere does he consider the public interest served by the *Combines Investigation Act*, nor does he consider how that public interest might be undermined by requiring a judicialized warrant procedure or, more significantly, by making proof that an offence has been committed a precondition to a "reasonable" search and seizure by the state. The only explanation that adequately accounts for this "purposeless" approach to assessing the interests of the state is that the Court subscribes to the "anarchical fallacy" to which MacDonald refers. The judgment reflects a hostility to state action of any character and an unwillingness to give weight to the correlative rights of those who rely upon state action for protection of their freedom.

. . . .

In these ways, the judgment in *Southam* takes some dangerous steps down the road of negative freedom. By ignoring the possibility that government action might facilitate individual freedom and by placing the onus upon government to justify the reasonableness of its searches, the Court jeopardizes the interests of the less powerful in society who depend upon government action to provide and protect their rights and freedoms.

The ultimate irony of the *Southam* case, however, only becomes apparent when the judgment is looked upon as a whole. The consequence of the Court's failure to distinguish between the privacy interests of corporations and those of human beings is to protect the right of artificial entities to wield economic powers granted to them by the state. At the same time, its adherence to a wholly negative notion of freedom is to curb the ability of the state to control those powers in the name of individual entrepreneurs and consumers. The result is a decision that sides against the interests of individuals and of competitive markets, the two touchstones of classical liberal thought.

■

What contextual information or evidence would have assisted the federal government in defending the legislation at issue in *Hunter* v. *Southam* against the s. 8 challenge or in making out a s. 1 argument? Legislation such as the *Combines Investigation Act* is aimed at preserving the viability of a free market economy by preventing unfair competition and monopolies. What is the significance of such an objective to the s. 1 analysis? Would it be relevant to know more about the investigative tools that are needed to police large corporate take-overs that violate the law? Should the fact that this investigation involved the press render the analysis more complex and the legislative objective more compelling? Do you need to know more about the concentration of newspaper ownership in Canada? See Canada, *Special Senate Committee on Mass Media* (Ottawa: Queen's Printer, 1970); Canada, *Royal Commission on Newspapers: Report* (Ottawa: Minister of Supply and Services, 1981); Jennifer Chen and Gary Graves, "Media Ownership in Canada" *CBC Backgrounder* (August 2001) online.

Petter's analysis of the public policy issues raised by *Hunter* v. *Southam* is prescient of later cases, such as *R.* v. *Wholesale Travel*, *supra*, wherein the majority of the Court applied ss. 7 and 11(d) of the *Charter* to a corporation, and *RJR-Macdonald* v. *Canada (AG)*, [1995] 3 S.C.R. 199, which held that sections of the *Tobacco Products Control Act*, R.S.C. 1988, c. 20 banning the advertisement of cigarettes were in violation of a corporation's s. 2(b) right to freedom of expression. Duff Conacher, Co-Ordinator for Democracy Watch, criticized the *RJR-Macdonald* case for failing to distinguish between individual and corporate rights in his Letter to the Editor, "Corporations are not people" *The [Toronto] Globe and Mail* (4 October 1995) A23:

> Corporations have been very successful in obtaining many rights from the state, mainly in the form of legislative benefits that make them distinctly inhuman. Unlike people, corporations can switch heads, merge with other bodies, be bought and sold and live forever. They can't be interrogated or jailed for their crimes, and they can use bankruptcy to avoid financial obligations, such as compensation to victims of their crimes. Indeed, the main reason a corporation is created is to protect individual officers of the corporation from responsibilities they would face as citizens, as several tobacco liability cases in the U.S. have revealed.
>
> When the courts extend to corporations constitutional protection equal to individuals, they add to the legislative benefits corporations already enjoy and create Frankensteins with inhuman powers who are often unaccountable to law enforcers, workers, consumers and taxpayers. To correct this problem and prevent any further expansion of corporate constitutional rights, Canadian governments should respond to the tobacco ad ruling by amending the Constitution to make it clear that our Charter is intended to be a Charter of Human Rights and Freedoms.[†]

Arguments like those advanced by Petter have clearly been influential in some of the Court's other s. 8 jurisprudence, as the extract below from *Thomson Newspapers* illustrates. The Court in this case was considering the constitutionality of s. 17 of the *Combines Investigation Act*, which provided for orders to compel the production of documents and records as part of an ongoing investigation.

---

† Reproduced by permission of Duff Conacher, Coordinator, Democracy Watch (www.dwatch.ca).

Thomson Newspapers v. Canada[†]

[LAFOREST, J.:]

What, in my view, is determinative is the nature of the conduct addressed by the legislation and the purposes for which it is designed to regulate that conduct. There can be little doubt that the conduct prohibited by the Act is far removed from what is the typical concern of the criminal law system, *i.e.*, the "underlining [of] crucial *social* values" (emphasis added) where "[t]he sort of things prohibited — acts of violence, dishonesty and so on — are acts violating common sense standards of humanity" which we regard as meriting disapprobation and punishment: see Law Reform Commission of Canada, Report No. 3, "Our Criminal Law" (1976), at pp. 3, 5, and 7....

. . . .

At bottom, the Act is really aimed at the regulation of the economy and business, with a view to the preservation of the competitive conditions which are crucial to the operation of a free market economy. This goal has obvious implications for Canada's material prosperity. It also has broad political overtones in that it is aimed at preventing concentration of power, of critical importance in the present case as it involves control of the press. It must be remembered that private organizations can be just as oppressive as the state when they gain such a dominant position within their sphere of operations that they can effectively force their will upon others.

The conduct regulated or prohibited by the Act is not conduct which is by its very nature morally or socially reprehensible. It is instead conduct we wish to discourage because of our desire to maintain an economic system which is at once productive and consistent with our values of individual liberty. It is, in short, not conduct which would be generally regarded as by its very nature criminal and worthy of criminal sanction. It is conduct which is only criminal in the sense that it is, in fact, prohibited by law. One's view of whether it should be so proscribed is likely to be functional or utilitarian, in the sense that it will be based on an assessment of the desirability of the economic goals to which combines legislation is directed or its potential effectiveness in achieving those goals. It is conduct which is made criminal for strictly instrumental reasons.

. . . .

To recapitulate, the relevance of the regulatory character of the offences defined in the Act is that conviction for their violation does not really entail, and is not intended to entail, the kind of moral reprimand and stigma that undoubtedly accompanies conviction for the traditional "real" or "true" crimes. It follows that investigation for purposes of the Act does not cast the kind of suspicion that can affect one's standing in the community and that, as was explained above, entitles the citizen to a relatively high degree of respect for his or her privacy on the part of investigating authorities. This does not, of course, mean that those subject to investigation under the Act have no, or no significant, expectation of privacy in respect of such investigations. The decision of this court in *Hunter v. Southam Inc.*, *supra*, makes clear that they do. But it does suggest that the degree of privacy that can reasonably be expected within the investigative scope of the Act is akin to that which can be expected by those subject to other administrative and regulatory legislation, rather than to that which can legitimately be expected by those subject to police investigation for what I have called "real" or "true" crimes.

■

Challenges to the constitutionality of laws authorizing warrantless searches have had some success with respect to provisions under the former *Narcotic Control Act* and under the *Criminal Code*. See, for example, *R. v. Grant*, [1993] 3 S.C.R. 223 where the Court held that s. 10 of the act, which permitted warrantless searches of all places except dwelling houses where the officer had reasonable grounds to believe a narcotic would be found, violated s. 8 for its failure to require "prior authorization." Rather than strike s. 10 down, however, the Court "read it down" so that this power is

---

[†] [1990] 1 S.C.R. 509, 510, 516–517.

only available where "exigent circumstances" exist such that seeking a warrant is impractical because of the imminent danger of the loss, destruction, or removal of the evidence. See the *Controlled Drugs and Substances Act*, s. 11(7).

In other contexts, such as searches pursuant to *Customs Act* powers and random urinalysis programs for prisoners authorized by legislation, the courts have backed away from a robust application of *Hunter* v. *Southam* on the basis of a lessened expectation of privacy for the individual and increased state interests on the other side of the equation. In *R.* v. *Simmons*, [1988] 2 S.C.R. 495, provisions that authorized customs agents, on "reasonable suspicion," to search travellers survived s. 8 scrutiny because border searches engaged a lesser expectation of privacy and heightened state interest in terms of the national interest of sovereign states to protect borders and collect tariff revenues. In *Fieldhouse*, *supra*, **Prisons and Parole**, a B.C. statute requiring prisoners to urinate under surveillance within a period of time after a demand, and face disciplinary sanctions for refusal, did not violate s. 8 because prisoners have a lesser reasonable expectation of privacy and the state interest in maintaining order is compelling. For a critical commentary on this case see Allan Manson, "Fieldhouse and the Diminution of Charter Scrutiny" (1995), 33 C.R. (4th) 358.

Charter challenges on the basis that a common law rule authorizing search and seizure is not reasonable are also possible. What are the particular difficulties that arise when such an argument is advanced? Consider *M.R.M.* below, and identify the legal and structural obstacles facing counsel for the accused high school student.

R. v. M.R.M.[†]

[CORY J.:]

Teachers and those in charge of our schools are entrusted with the care and education of our children. It is difficult to imagine a more important trust or duty. To ensure the safety of the students and to provide them with the orderly environment so necessary to encourage learning, reasonable rules of conduct must be in place and enforced at schools. Does the nature of the obligations and duties entrusted to schools justify searches of students? To what extent are students entitled to an expectation of privacy while they are on school premises? These questions must be considered in this appeal.

. . . .

FACTUAL BACKGROUND

The search at issue in this case was conducted by Mr. Cadue, the vice-principal of a junior high school. Mr. Cadue was responsible for enforcing school policies, which included a policy that any student found in possession of drugs or alcohol on school property would be suspended. If the vice-principal concluded that a criminal matter was involved, he was to call the RCMP.

Mr. Cadue testified that he had been told by several students that the appellant was selling drugs on school property. He said he had reason to believe this information because the students knew the appellant well and one of them had, on an earlier occasion, given him information which had proven to be correct. On this day, a school dance was to be held and Mr. Cadue was responsible for its supervision. Earlier in the day he had been told by one of the informants that he believed the appellant would be carrying drugs that evening.

When Mr. Cadue saw the appellant arrive at the dance, he called the RCMP to request that an officer attend at the school. He then approached the appellant and his friend and asked them to come to his office. He asked each of the students if they were in possession of drugs and advised them that he was going to search them. The RCMP officer, Constable Siepierski, then arrived, dressed in plain clothes. He spoke briefly with Mr. Cadue outside the room, then entered, identified himself to the two boys and sat down. He did not say anything while Mr. Cadue spoke to the students and searched them. The appellant turned out his pockets and at the request of Mr. Cadue, pulled up his pant legs. The vice-principal noticed a bulge in the appellant's sock and removed a cellophane bag. He gave the bag to

---

[†] [1998] 3 S.C.R. 393 at 401–33.

Constable Siepierski who identified the contents as marijuana. The Constable then advised the appellant that he was under arrest for possession of a narcotic and read to him the police caution and his right to counsel. The Constable also advised him that he had the right to contact a parent or adult. The appellant attempted unsuccessfully to reach his mother by phone and stated that he did not wish to contact anyone else. Constable Siepierski and the appellant then went to the appellant's locker and searched it but nothing was found there.

At trial, the judge concluded that the search had violated the appellant's rights under the *Charter* and excluded the evidence found in the search. The Crown did not offer any further evidence, and the charge against the appellant was dismissed. The Court of Appeal allowed the Crown's appeal and ordered a new trial. Thereafter, leave to appeal to this Court was granted.

RELEVANT STATUTORY PROVISIONS

. . . .

Education Act, R.S.N.S. 1989, c. 136

> 54 It is the duty of a teacher in a public school to
>
> ...
>
> (b) maintain proper order and discipline in the school or room in his charge and report to the principal or other person in charge of the school the conduct of any pupil who is persistently defiant or disobedient;
>
> ...
>
> (g) give constant attention to the health and comfort of the pupils, to the cleanliness, temperature, and ventilation of the school rooms, and to the aesthetic condition of the rooms, grounds and buildings;

Education Act, General Regulations, N.S. Reg. 226/84

> 3 ...
>
> (7) A principal is responsible to the school board through the superintendent of schools and is responsible for:
>
> (a) supervising and administering the educational program in the school as directed by the school board through the superintendent;
> (b) implementing and co-ordinating a curriculum;
> (c) supervising and evaluating staff and programs;
> (d) developing effective communication with parents.
>
> ...
>
> (9) A vice-principal is responsible for:

> (a) assisting the principal in carrying out his duties as directed by the school board or the principal;
> (b) assuming the duties of the principal in his absence.

. . . .

ANALYSIS

Application of the *Charter*

Application of the Charter *to Public School Authorities*

At the outset it must be determined whether the *Charter* applies to the actions of the vice-principal. The courts below assumed that it does, as have other courts in similar circumstances (e.g., *J.M.G.* (1986), 56 O.R. (2d) 705 (C.A.)). The respondent in this appeal did not dispute that the *Charter* should apply, arguing only that the *Charter* analysis should take into account the school context. The appellant submitted that the *Charter* applies because the school board, schools and their employees are part of the apparatus of government, according to the test set out by this Court in *McKinney* v. *University of Guelph*, [1990] 3 S.C.R. 229. It was suggested that schools and schools boards are analogous to the community college which was found to be part of government in *Douglas/Kwantlen Faculty Assn.* v. *Douglas College*, [1990] 3 S.C.R. 570. The alternative submission was that because the actions of the vice-principal were taken under the authority of the *Education Act*, R.S.N.S. 1989, c. 136, the *Charter* applies, following *Eldridge* v. *British Columbia (Attorney General)*, [1997] 3 S.C.R. 624.

In light of the concession made by the respondent it would be inappropriate to discuss and determine finally which of the alternative submissions should be applied. Rather it would be best to assume simply, for the purposes of this case, that schools constitute part of government and as a result the *Charter* applies to the actions of the vice-principal.

Was the Vice-Principal Acting as an Agent of the Police?

The trial judge in this case also found that the vice-principal was acting as an agent of the police. This finding, if accepted, would not only provide an alternative basis for the application of the *Charter* but would also affect the analysis of the alleged violations. The appellant submits that the finding of the trial judge on this issue should not be disturbed. Generally, a finding such as this would not be interfered with by an appellate court. However, in this case, the evidence adduced cannot support that finding and it should not be accepted.

It is clear that Mr. Cadue cooperated with the police. He was aware that if drugs were found it would be a criminal matter as well as a matter of school discipline, and that it was the policy of the school to contact the police in such a case. He called the police before beginning the search and permitted an officer to observe as he conducted the search. When the marijuana was found, it was handed over to Constable Siepierski, who arrested the appellant and conducted a further search of the appellant's locker.

The mere fact that there was cooperation between the vice-principal and the police and that an officer was present during the search is not sufficient to indicate that the vice-principal was acting as an agent of the police. The trial judge stated that there was an "agreed strategy" between Mr. Cadue and Constable Siepierski that resulted in Mr. Cadue's acting as a police agent. With respect, there is no evidence to support this conclusion. There is no evidence of an agreement or of police instructions to Mr. Cadue that could create an agency relationship.

The issue as to whether an individual is acting as an agent of the police was considered by this Court in *R. v. Broyles*, [1991] 3 S.C.R. 595. While that case involved a police informer, the essential elements of the test applied in that case are equally applicable to the case at bar. There it was said at p. 608:

> Only if the relationship between the informer and the state is such that the exchange between the informer and the accused is materially different from what it would have been had there been no such relationship should the informer be considered a state agent for the purposes of the exchange.... [W]ould the exchange between the accused and the informer have taken place, in the form and manner in which it did take place, but for the intervention of the state or its agents?

Applying the test to this case, it must be determined whether the search of the appellant would have taken place, in the form and in the manner in which it did, but for the involvement of the police. The evidence, in my opinion, demonstrates that it would have taken place and was not materially different than it would have been if there had been no police involvement. Although Mr. Cadue knew that criminal charges might result, the primary motive for the search was the enforcement of school discipline, for which he was responsible. There is nothing in the evidence to suggest that the vice-principal initiated the search or conducted it differently because of police intervention. It is thus apparent that the vice-principal was not acting as an agent of the police.

This conclusion is not determinative with respect to the application of s. 8 since the *Charter* applies, in any event, to the actions taken by Mr. Cadue. However, the finding that he was not an agent of the police will affect the analysis of the alleged violation of the appellant's *Charter* rights.

Were the Rights of the Appellant Under Section 8 of the *Charter* Violated?

Reasonable Expectation of Privacy

Did the appellant have, in the circumstances presented, a reasonable expectation of privacy, and if he did, what was the extent of that expectation? The appellant must first establish that in the circumstances he did have a reasonable expectation of privacy. This is apparent because if there is *no* reasonable expectation of privacy held by an accused with respect to the relevant place, there can be no violation of s. 8 (see, e.g. *R. v. Edwards*, [1996] 1 S.C.R. 128; *Schreiber v. Canada (Attorney General)*, [1998] 1 S.C.R. 841). The need for privacy "can vary with the nature of the matter sought to be protected, the circumstances in which and the place where state intrusion occurs, and the purposes of the intrusion" (*R. v. Colarusso*, [1994] 1 S.C.R. 20, at p. 53). A reasonable expectation of privacy is to be determined in light of the totality of circumstances (*Colarusso*; *Edwards*, at para. 31; *R. v. Wong*, [1990] 3 S.C.R. 36, at p. 62). The factors to be considered in assessing the circumstances may include the accused's presence at the time of the search, possession or control of the property or place searched, ownership of the property or place, historical use of the property or item, ability to regulate access, existence of a subjective expectation of privacy, and the objective reasonableness of the expectation (*Edwards*, at para. 45).

Here the search was of the appellant's person. In the circumstances it is obvious that some of the factors referred to in *Edwards* are not applicable. However, the existence of a subjective expectation of privacy and the objective reasonableness of that expectation remain important. It is also necessary to consider the context in which the search took place. Here the appellant was a student at the school, attending a school function held on school property. The search was carried out by the school authority responsible for supervision of that function. Considering all these factors, did the appellant have a reasonable expectation of privacy with respect to his person and the items he carried on his person? In my view he did. A student attending school would have a subjective expectation that his privacy, at least with respect to his body, would be respected. In light of the heightened privacy interest that has historically been recognized in one's person, a subjective expectation of privacy in that respect is reasonable. I do not think that this expectation is rendered unreasonable merely by virtue of a student's presence in a school. It follows that the appellant did have a reasonable expectation of privacy in that regard, with the result that s. 8 is engaged.

However, the reasonable expectation of privacy, although it exists, may be diminished in some circumstances, and this will influence the analysis of s. 8 and a consideration of what constitutes an unreasonable search or seizure. For example, it has been found that individuals have a lesser expectation of privacy at border crossings, because they know they may be subject to questioning and searches to enforce customs laws (see *Simmons*, [1988] 2 S.C.R. 485). It was because of this lesser expectation of privacy, that a customs search did not have to meet the standards in *Hunter* v. *Southam Inc.*, [1984] 2 S.C.R. 145, in order to be reasonable. Similarly, the reasonable expectation of privacy of a student in attendance at a school is certainly less than it would be in other circumstances. Students know that their teachers and other school authorities are responsible for providing a safe environment and maintaining order and discipline in the school. They must know that this may sometimes require searches of students and their personal effects and the seizure of prohibited items. It would not be reasonable for a student to expect to be free from such searches. A student's reasonable expectation of privacy in the school environment is therefore significantly diminished.

In some cases a court may be required to determine with greater precision whether and to what extent a student has a reasonable expectation of privacy in the location of the search. In the case of locker searches, for example, courts have engaged in more detailed factual analyses to determine the degree of control that school authorities maintain over the lockers and the effect that this may have on the reasonable expectation of privacy and the reasonableness of the search (see, e.g.... *State in Interest of T.L.O.* v. *Engerud*, 94 N.J. 331 (1983), aff'd 469 U.S. 325 (1985)). Here there was a search of the appellant's locker. However, since no evidence was found there, the lawfulness of that search is not in issue. For the purposes of these reasons the findings that the appellant did have a reasonable expectation of privacy with respect to his person, but that he would have reasonably expected a lesser degree of privacy in a school environment, will suffice. They may be taken into account in defining the standard to be applied to the search of the appellant.

Standard to Be Applied to Searches by School Authorities

IS A DIFFERENT STANDARD REQUIRED?

Teachers and principals are placed in a position of trust that carries with it onerous responsibilities. When children attend school or school functions, it is they who must care for the children's safety and well-being. It is they who must carry out the fundamentally important task of teaching children so that they can function in our society and [fulfill] their potential. In order to teach, school officials must provide an atmosphere that encourages learning. During the school day they must protect and teach our children. In no small way, teachers and principals are responsible for the future of the country.

It is essential that our children be taught and that they learn. Yet, without an orderly environment learning will be difficult if not impossible. In recent years, problems which threaten the safety of students and the fundamentally important task of teaching have increased in their numbers and gravity. The possession of illicit drugs and dangerous weapons in the schools has increased to the extent that they challenge the ability of school officials to fulfill their responsibility to maintain a safe and orderly environment. Current conditions make it necessary to provide teachers and school administrators with the flexibility required to deal with discipline problems in schools. They must be able to act quickly and effectively to ensure the safety of students and to prevent serious violations of school rules.

One of the ways in which school authorities may be required to react reasonably to discipline problems is by conducting searches of students and to seize prohibited items. Possession of items which are prohibited by school policy may, in some cases, also constitute or provide evidence of a criminal offence. As a result items found in a search by a school authority may be sought to be used as evidence in a criminal trial. The question then arises whether evidence found by a teacher or principal should potentially be excluded because the search would have been unreasonable if it had been conducted by police.

The United States Supreme Court considered this question in *T.L.O.*, *supra*. In that case, the assistant vice-principal of a high school searched the purse of a student suspected of smoking in the school lavatory, contrary to school rules. The student had denied that she even smoked, and the assistant vice-principal searched her purse, apparently to ascertain the truth of this claim. He found a package of cigarettes, and upon removing them, saw a package of cigarette rolling papers in the purse. This made him suspect drug use, and so he proceeded to make a thorough search of the purse. He found some marijuana, a pipe, plastic bags, a fairly substantial amount of money, a list of students who owed the student money, and letters implicating her in marijuana trafficking. Delinquency charges were brought against the student and a motion was brought to suppress the evidence found in her purse.

It was held that the Fourth Amendment's prohibition of unreasonable searches and seizures does apply to searches carried out by public school officials. It was also found, at pp. 338–39, that students in schools may claim a legitimate expectation of privacy. However, in the opinion of the majority, "[a]gainst the child's interest in privacy must be set the substantial interest of teachers and administrators in maintaining discipline in the classroom and on school grounds" (p. 339). Therefore, the Court held, at p. 340, that the school setting "requires some easing of the restrictions to which searches by public authorities are ordinarily subject". In particular, the warrant requirement is "unsuited to the school environment", and thus school officials need not obtain a warrant before searching a student who is under their authority (*idem*). In addition, it found that the school setting "also requires some modification of the level of suspicion of illicit activity needed to justify a search" (*idem*).

The Court noted that "'probable cause' is not an irreducible requirement of a valid search" and that it had not hesitated in the past to adopt a lesser standard when it would best serve the public interest. Consequently, the Court articulated the following test to be used in determining whether a search by a school official was reasonable (at pp. 341–43):

> We join the majority of courts that have examined this issue in concluding that the accommodation of the privacy interests of schoolchildren with the substantial need of teachers and administrators for freedom to maintain order in the schools does not require strict adherence to the requirement that searches be based on probable cause to believe that the subject of the search has violated or is violating the law. Rather, the legality of a search of a student should depend simply on the reasonableness, under all the circumstances, of the search. Determining the reasonableness of any search involves a two-fold inquiry: first, one must consider "whether the ... action was justified at its inception," *Terry* v. *Ohio*, 392 U.S., at 20, 88 S.Ct., at 1879; second, one must determine whether the search as actually conducted "was reasonably related in scope to the circumstances which justified the interference in the first place," *ibid*. Under ordinary circumstances, a search of a student by a teacher or other school official will be "justified at its inception" when there are reasonable grounds for suspecting that the search will turn up evidence that the student has violated or is violating either the law or the rules of the school. Such a search will be permissible in its scope when the measures adopted are reasonably related to the objectives of the search and not excessively intrusive in light of the age and sex of the student and the nature of the infraction.
>
> ... By focusing attention on the question of reasonableness, the standard will spare teachers and school administrators the necessity of schooling themselves in the niceties of probable cause and permit them to regulate their conduct according to the dictates of reason and common sense.

Applying this test, the majority of the Court found that the search conducted by the assistant vice-principal was not unreasonable.

The Ontario Court of Appeal in *J.M.G.*, *supra*, adopted the test articulated by the U.S. Supreme Court in *T.L.O.* In that case, a school principal, acting on information received from a teacher, brought a student to his office, searched him and found a small packet of marijuana hidden in his sock or pant leg. He then called a police officer, with whom he had spoken earlier. The officer came and arrested the student for possession of a narcotic. The Ontario Court of Appeal applied the test from *T.L.O.* and found that the search was justified at its inception (at p. 709). Once he had received information that a student was concealing drugs on a particular part of his person, it was not unreasonable for the principal to require the student to remove his socks to prove or disprove the allegation. The search was "reasonably related to the desirable objective of maintaining proper order and discipline" (*idem*). The Court also found that the search was not excessively intrusive (*idem*). It was noted that in Canada the law generally requires a warrant or other prior authorization. However, the Court thought that the relationship between the principal and student was different from that between a police officer and a citizen, and that "society as a whole has an interest in the maintenance of a proper educational environment, which clearly involves being able to enforce school discipline efficiently and effectively" (at p. 710). It was therefore held to be "neither feasible nor desirable" that prior authorization be required in the case of a principal searching a student (at p. 711).

The Court of Appeal in this case followed *J.M.G.* and applied the *T.L.O.* test. The test established in *T.L.O.* dispenses not only with the warrant requirement but also with the need for probable cause, imposing instead a generalized standard of reasonableness in all the circumstances. However it must be observed that this test has been subject to criticism in the United States (see, e.g., J.M. Sanchez, "Expelling the Fourth Amendment from American Schools: Students' Rights Six Years After *T.L.O.*" (1992), 21 *J. L. & Education* 381; Thomas C. Fischer, "From *Tinker* to *TLO*; Are Civil Rights for Students 'Flunking' in School?" (1993), 22 *J. L. & Education* 409). Nonetheless in my view the test set out in *T.L.O.* can be applied in the elementary and secondary school setting in Canada. Significantly the same result reached in *T.L.O.* can be obtained by applying principles to be derived from decisions of this Court which have considered the *Charter*.

In Canada, the need to establish the existence of reasonable and probable grounds for the search provide the required minimum constitutional guarantee of reasonableness in all but a few very limited exceptions. Nonetheless, the question remains, should this standard be required in the school setting?

WHAT STANDARD SHOULD BE APPLIED?

The general rule, established by this Court in *Hunter, supra,* is that in order to be reasonable, a search requires prior authorization, usually in the form of a warrant, from a neutral arbiter (at pp. 160–62). According to this rule, a search conducted without prior authorization is *prima facie* unreasonable. However, the Court recognized in *Hunter*, at p. 161, that "it may not be reasonable in every instance to insist on prior authorization". Prior authorization is a precondition for a reasonable search where it is feasible to obtain it (*idem*). Further it was acknowledged that it might be appropriate to dispense with the warrant requirement in situations where it is not feasible to obtain prior authorization.

In my opinion the search of a student by a school authority is just such a situation where it would not be feasible to require that a warrant or any other prior authorization be obtained for the search. To require a warrant would clearly be impractical and unworkable in the school environment. Teachers and administrators must be able to respond quickly and effectively to problems that arise in their school. When a school official conducts a search of or seizure from a student, a warrant is not required. The absence of a warrant in these circumstances will not lead to a presumption that the search was unreasonable.

The other basic principle enunciated in the *Hunter* decision was that a reasonable search must be based on reasonable and probable grounds. It was held, at p. 167, that "[t]he state's interest in detecting and preventing crime begins to prevail over the individual's interest in being left alone at the point where credibly-based probability replaces suspicion". Therefore, "reasonable and probable grounds ... to believe that an offence has been committed and that there is evidence to be found at the place of the search, constitutes the minimum standard, consistent with s. 8 of the *Charter*, for authorizing search and seizure" (p. 168). The requirement of reasonable and probable grounds has been maintained subject only to very limited exceptions (e.g., search incident to arrest; see *Cloutier* v. *Langlois*, [1990] 1 S.C.R. 158).

Yet teachers and principals must be able to act quickly to protect their students and to provide the orderly atmosphere required for learning. If a teacher were told that a student was carrying a dangerous weapon or sharing a dangerous prohibited drug the parents of all the other students at the school would expect the teacher to search that student. The role of teachers is such that they must have the power to search. Indeed students should be aware that they must comply with school regulations and as a result that they will be subject to reasonable searches. It follows that their expectation of privacy will be lessened while they attend school or a school function. This reduced expectation of privacy coupled with the need to protect students and provide a positive atmosphere for learning clearly indicate that a more lenient and flexible approach should be taken to searches conducted by teachers and principals than would apply to searches conducted by the police.

A search by school officials of a student under their authority may be undertaken if there are reasonable grounds to believe that a school rule has been or is being violated, and that evidence of the violation will be found in the location or on the person of the student searched. Searches undertaken in situations where the health and safety of students is involved may well require different considerations. All the circumstances surrounding a search must be taken into account in determining if the search is reasonable.

School authorities must be accorded a reasonable degree of discretion and flexibility to enable them to ensure the safety of their students and to enforce school regulations. Ordinarily, school authorities will be in the best position to evaluate the information they receive. As a result of their training, background and experience, they will be in the best possible position to assess both the propensity and credibility of their students and to relate the information they receive to the situation existing in their particular school. For these reasons, courts should recognize the preferred position of school authorities to determine whether reasonable grounds existed for the search.

A teacher or principal should not be required to obtain a warrant to search a student and thus the absence of a warrant in these circumstances will not create a presumption that the search was unreasonable. A search of a student will be properly instituted in those circumstances where the teacher or principal conducting the search has reasonable grounds to believe that a school rule has been violated and the evidence of the breach will be found on the student. These grounds may well be provided by information received from just one student that the school authority considers credible. Alternatively the reasonable grounds may be based upon information from more than one student or from observations of teachers or principals, or from a combination of these pieces of information which considered together the relevant authority believes to be credible. This approach to reasonable grounds in the school environment will permit school authorities to deal speedily and effectively with breaches of school regulations and disciplinary problems, which is so essential to providing a safe and positive environment for learning. Yet it will provide for the reasonable protection of students' rights. ...

. . . .

THE SEARCH MUST BE REASONABLE

If it is to be reasonable the search must be conducted reasonably and must be authorized by a statutory provision which is itself reasonable. There is no specific authorization to search provided in the *Education Act*, R.S.N.S. 1989, or its regulations. Nonetheless, the responsibility placed upon teachers, and principals to maintain proper order and discipline in the school and to attend to the health and comfort of students by necessary implication authorizes searches of students. See s. 54(b) and Regulation 3(7) and (9). Teachers must be able to search students if they are to fulfil the statutory duties imposed upon them. It is reasonable, if not essential to provide teachers and principals with this authorization to search. It is now necessary to consider the circumstances in which the search itself may be considered to be reasonable.

The search conducted by school authorities must itself be reasonable and appropriate in light of the circumstances presented and the nature of the suspected breach of school regulations. The permissible extent of the search will vary with the gravity of the infraction that is suspected. For example, it may be reasonable for a teacher to take immediate action and undertake whatever search is required where there are reasonable grounds to believe that a student is carrying a gun or some other dangerous weapon. The existence of an immediate threat to the students' safety will justify swift, thorough and extensive searches. That same type of search might not be justified where, for example, a student is reasonably believed to have gum which is prohibited by school regulations in his or her pocket. The reasonableness of a search by teachers or principals in response to information received must be reviewed and considered in the context of all the circumstances presented including their responsibility for students' safety.

The circumstances to be considered should also include the age and gender of the student. For example, a search of the person of a female student by a male teacher may well be inappropriate and unreasonable. Every search should be conducted in as sensitive a manner as possible and take into account the age and sex of the student. It should not be forgotten that the manner in which students are treated in these situations will determine their respect for the rights of others in the future.

. . . .

WHEN AND TO WHOM DOES THIS STANDARD APPLY?

This modified standard for reasonable searches should apply to searches of students on school property conducted by teachers or school officials within the scope of their responsibility and authority to maintain order, discipline and safety within the school. This standard will not apply to any actions taken which are beyond the scope of the authority of teachers or principals.

Further a different situation arises if the school authorities are acting as agents of the police. The application of the test set out in *Broyles, supra*, will determine whether the person conducting the search was a police agent. It will have to be determined whether the search would have taken place, in the form and in the manner in which it did, but for the involvement of the police. The usual standard, requiring prior authorization in the form of a warrant which is based upon information which provides reasonable and probable grounds, will continue to apply to police and their agents in their activities within a school. The modified standard for school authorities is required to allow them the necessary latitude to carry out their responsibilities to maintain a safe and orderly school environment. There is no reason, however, why police should not be required to comply with the usual standards, merely because the person they wish to search is in attendance at an elementary or secondary school. Since the usual standard continues to apply to police actions, it must also apply to any agent of the police. There would obviously be a potential for abuse, were that not the case.

Application to This Case

Was the search conducted in this case unreasonable? In my view it was not. As a result, there was no infringement of the appellant's rights under s. 8 of the *Charter*.

First, for the reasons set out earlier I am satisfied that Mr. Cadue was not acting as an agent of the police. The mere fact that there was some cooperation between the vice-principal and the police, since both knew that criminal charges might result, is not sufficient to establish an agency relationship. Quite simply, there is no evidence of any agreement between Mr. Cadue and Constable Siepierski, nor is there anything to indicate that Mr. Cadue was acting under the instructions of the police. He brought the appellant to his office and initiated the search with the primary purpose of fulfilling his duty to maintain order and discipline in the school. The search was conducted within the scope of his authority as vice-principal to enforce discipline. That he knew that criminal proceedings might also result if drugs were found does not alter the situation. The search would have taken place in the same form and manner regardless of any police involvement. Therefore the vice-principal was not acting as a police agent and as a result the modified standard applicable to school authorities should govern the consideration of his search.

Nor can it be said that the police officer himself carried out the search and that the usual higher standard should therefore apply. The police officer was present when the search took place, but took no active part whatsoever in the search. His presence was merely passive, up until the point when the drugs were found and given to him, and the arrest was made. If the police officer had in some manner, taken an active role in the search, the application of different considerations would be required. However that is not the situation presented in this case.

It was further argued that the mere presence of the police officer was sufficient to conclude that the officer was in fact the authority carrying out the search. That contention flies in the face of the evidence and cannot be accepted. The officer was at all times completely passive. It cannot be forgotten that on occasion a secondary school student may be larger and more powerful than the teacher who must in the interests of the safety of other students conduct the search. No doubt in these circumstances, if financial resources permitted it, a security officer might be employed by the school and would, unless violence was threatened, be present and sit passively in the office. His presence would not affect the validity of the search. There should be no difference if it is a police constable who is present as long as that constable remains passive during the search. In this case the student in his testimony expressed the opinion that Mr. Cadue was the "boss", that it was his school. This serves to confirm that in the eyes of the accused the Constable took no part in the search.

As a result, the test applicable to searches conducted by teachers applies to the search carried out by Mr. Cadue of the appellant's person. The absence of a warrant, therefore, does not mean that the search was *prima facie* unreasonable. Two additional matters need to be considered. First, it must be determined whether the vice-principal had reasonable grounds to believe that a school rule had been or was being violated, and that evidence of this violation would be found on the appellant's person. Second, it must be decided whether the search was conducted in a reasonable manner.

Mr. Cadue had received information from several students indicating that the appellant possessed marijuana and was trafficking in it on the school grounds. He thought that this information was reliable because these students knew the appellant well. One of the students had given him accurate information on a previous occasion. None of this information had been corroborated by his own observations, but this corroboration will not always be necessary.

In this case the information came from a number of sources which the vice-principal had reason to believe were credible. On the day of the search, he had received specific information that the appellant would be carrying drugs that evening. This would have provided him with reasonable grounds to believe that he would find marijuana, a prohibited substance, if he searched the appellant's person at that time. Taking into account all of these factors, the requirement of the existence of reasonable grounds was satisfied in this case.

The search undertaken by Mr. Cadue was conducted reasonably. It took place in the relative privacy of the principal's office. The search conducted was appropriate to the offence of possession of a prohibited substance Mr. Cadue reasonably believed was in the possession of M.R.M. The search was minimally intrusive and was carried out in an appropriately sensitive manner.

In summary, the search was by inference authorized by the provisions of the Nova Scotia *Education Act*. A provision to search students in appropriate circumstances is reasonable in the school environment. As a student M.R.M. would have a reduced expectation of privacy. Mr. Cadue had reasonable grounds to believe M.R.M. was in breach of school regulations and that a search would reveal evidence of that breach. The search was conducted in a reasonable and sensitive manner. Taking into account all the circumstances I am satisfied that the search was not unreasonable and in the circumstances there was no violation of M.R.M.'s s. 8 rights. In meeting these requirements the search as well meets all the conditions of the test set out in *T.L.O.* It should be noted that this case deals only with a search of students in an elementary or secondary school. No consideration has been given to searches made in a college or university setting.

Were the Rights of the Appellant Under Section 10(b) of the *Charter* Violated?

The appellant further submits that he was detained when Mr. Cadue took him to his office, and since he was not informed of his right to counsel at that time, his rights under s. 10(b) of the *Charter* were also violated. I cannot accept this submission.

The appellant testified that he felt he had no choice but to follow the vice-principal to his office and remain there. There is no doubt that he felt that he was under some measure of compulsion. Within the school students must often feel compelled to obey school rules and the instructions of their teachers and principals. Students may often be told by teachers to go to a certain location and to wait there for further instructions. Yet the school environment requires that this be done. It does not mean that the students were detained within the meaning of s. 10(b).

Detention has been defined to include a "deprivation of liberty by physical constraint" or "when a police officer or other agent of the state assumes control over the movement of a person by a demand or direction which may have significant legal consequence and which prevents or impedes access to counsel" (*R. v. Therens*, [1985] 1 S.C.R. 613, at p. 642). Even if the compelled attendance of a student at a principal's office or some other form of restraint by a school authority could be understood as falling within the strict terms of the definition of "detention" set out in *Therens*, it should not be considered as "detention" for the purposes of s. 10(b). In my view that section was not meant to apply to relations between students and teachers, but rather to relations between individuals and the state, usually focused upon the investigation of a criminal offence. The right to counsel provided in s. 10(b) was designed to address the vulnerable position of an individual who has been detained by the coercive power of the state in the course of a criminal investigation, and is thus deprived of his or her liberty and placed at risk of making self-incriminating statements (*R. v. Bartle*, [1994] 3 S.C.R. 173, at p. 191). Its application in the school context is inappropriate and would lead to absurd results. As a result, there was no detention for *Charter* purposes in this case, and thus no violation of s. 10(b) can be found.

Once again, it must be stated that if the vice-principal had been acting as an agent of the police, or if the police officer himself had taken any active role in detaining the appellant, it might well be that the appellant was detained within the meaning of s. 10(b). However, on the facts presented in this case, the appellant was not detained prior to his arrest by Constable Siepierski. He was properly cautioned and instructed as to his right to counsel at the time of the arrest. Therefore, I find that there was no violation of the appellant's s. 10(b) rights.

DISPOSITION

In the result the appeal is dismissed.

[Justice Major dissented on the basis that he believed that there was evidence of an agency relationship between police and the vice principal.

He concluded that the warrantless search was unreasonable since the evidence available did not satisfy the more stringent standard of reasonableness required for police and their agents. He would have excluded the evidence as conscriptive, and restored the acquittal of M.R.M.]

■

M.R.M. raises the important issue of the application of the *Charter* to persons other than police. Section 52 of the *Charter* indicates that it applies to government, and in *M.R.M.* it was conceded that the administration of public schools is sufficiently tied to the government to bind school officials to *Charter* norms. Another case, *R. v. Lerke* (1986), 43 Alta. L.R. (2d) 1 (C.A.), has held that when a tavern employee relies upon the *Code* provision that authorizes a citizen's arrest (discussed *infra*, **Compelling the Accused's Appearance**) and then searches as an incident of arrest, the person is effectively exercising a government function such that the *Charter* constraint that searches must be "reasonable" applies. On the other hand, in *R. v. Spindell* (1996), 149 N.S.R. (2d) 208 (S.C.), a doctor who reported to police statements made by a patient he was treating was said to have acted as a private citizen such that the obtention of the evidence did not constitute a s. 7 or 8 violation. In *M.R.M.*, the further distinction was made such that even if the *Charter* applies because the teacher or Vice Principal is carrying out a government function, if they are not an "agent of the state," a lesser standard of *Charter* scrutiny will apply.

After the decision in *M.R.M.* was released, 19 boys at a Windsor high school were strip searched by the gym teacher and the Vice Principal in an effort to locate $90 that was reported missing. Nine of them sought legal advice, claiming damages against the Ontario government as well as the school and teachers involved: Margaret Philip, "Ontario high-school students to sue over strip search incident" *The [Toronto] Globe and Mail* (23 January 1999) A3. At Trent University, eight women involved in a three day sit-in were strip searched by officers in riot gear: "Trent mulling resolutions condemning police, school" *The [Toronto] Globe and Mail* (14 March 2001) A17. As you read the *Golden* decision below, consider whether the *Charter* constraints imposed upon the common law governing strip searches set out by the Court will be applicable to the school and university context.

R. v. Golden†

[IACOBUCCI and ARBOUR JJ.:]

INTRODUCTION

The constitutional right to privacy requires that unjustified searches by the state be prevented. Accordingly, our Court has held that prior authorization, where feasible, is a precondition for a valid search and seizure (*Hunter v. Southam Inc.*, [1984] 2 S.C.R. 145). At the same time, the power to search "incident to arrest" has developed as a long-standing exception to this customary rule. As a concept that has evolved at common law, the search incident to arrest power has been framed by nebulous parameters.

This Court has, however, taken important steps toward defining the nature and scope of this power within Canadian law. As a result, it has been established that this search power may include the authority to fingerprint or conduct a "frisk" search of an arrested individual (see respectively *R. v. Beare*, [1988] 2 S.C.R. 387; and *Cloutier v. Langlois*, [1990] 1 S.C.R. 158). It may also authorize the search of a motor vehicle driven by an arrested person (*R. v. Caslake*, [1998] 1 S.C.R. 51). On the other hand, it does not entitle law enforcement authorities to conduct more invasive searches of the person, with a view to obtaining bodily samples as evidence (*R. v. Stillman*, [1997] 1 S.C.R. 607).

---

† [2001] S.C.J. No. 81, online: QL.

. . . .

For the reasons that follow, we are of the opinion that the common law search incident to arrest power does include the power to strip. ...

FACTUAL BACKGROUND

On January 18, 1997, in an effort to detect illegal drug activity in an area where trafficking was known to occur, officers from the Metropolitan Toronto Police Force set up an observation post in an unoccupied building across from a Subway sandwich shop that was approximately 70 feet away. From this vantage point and through the use of a telescope, one of the officers manning the observation post, Constable Theriault, observed the appellant, a black male, who was in the shop. Constable Theriault testified that he had a clear view into the shop and saw two transactions in which persons entered the shop and received a substance from the appellant. The officer testified that he saw the appellant take the substance from the palm of his hand with his thumb and forefinger, and that the substance was white. He further testified that, given the place where this transaction occurred, the manner in which it took place, and the colour of the substance, he believed the substance was cocaine.

After the second transaction, Constable Theriault communicated with the four other police officers involved in the operation who were not stationed at the observation post: the "take-down" members of the team. He gave them descriptions of the persons involved, including the appellant. Given what he had witnessed, Constable Theriault believed the appellant was trafficking in drugs, and he instructed the take-down officers to arrest the appellant.

When the take-down occurred, the officers entered the shop and arrested the appellant for trafficking in cocaine. Two other individuals in the shop were also arrested. During the arrests, the police found what they believed to be crack cocaine under the table where one of the suspects was arrested. Constable Ryan, one of the two officers who first entered the shop and the officer who arrested the appellant, also observed the appellant crushing what appeared to be crack cocaine between his fingers.

Following the arrests, Constable Ryan conducted a "pat down" search of the appellant and looked in his pockets. He did not find any weapons or narcotics. This officer then decided to conduct a visual inspection of the appellant's underwear and buttocks. Constable Ryan obtained from the shop's employee the key to a door leading to the basement where public washrooms were located. On the landing at the top of the stairwell, Constable Ryan undid Mr. Golden's pants and pulled back the appellant's pants and long underwear. Looking inside the appellant's underwear, he saw a clear plastic wrap protruding from between the appellant's buttocks, as well as a white substance within the wrap. Constable Ryan testified that when he tried to retrieve the plastic wrap, the appellant "hip-checked" and scratched him, so that he lost his balance and almost fell down the flight of fourteen stairs. Constable Ryan subsequently pushed the appellant into the stairwell, face-first.

Concerned that the landing was not a safe place to continue the search, Constables Ryan and Powell escorted the appellant to a seating booth at the back of the shop. Patrons remaining inside were asked to leave, and the front door was locked. However, the two other arrested suspects, five officers, and the shop's employee remained inside.

The officers forced the appellant to bend over a table. At this point, the appellant's pants were lowered to his knees and his underwear was pulled down. His buttocks and genitalia thus were completely exposed. According to the evidence, the partitions between the booths in the shop were high enough to block the view from the outside of the part of the shop where the search was conducted. The employee of the shop testified that passersby would not have been able to see what was taking place inside, but someone, "if ... look[ing] carefully by the side of the window", would have been able to see the appellant's leg.

Inside the shop, the officers tried to seize the package from the appellant's buttocks, but were unsuccessful, given that the appellant continued to clench his muscles very tightly. Following these attempts, the appellant accidentally defecated. The package, however, did not dislodge. Constable Powell then retrieved a pair of rubber dishwashing gloves from the shop's employee, put them on and again tried to remove the package. According to the testimony of the shop's employee, these gloves were used for cleaning the shop's washrooms and toilets. By this point, the appellant was face-down on the floor, with Constable Ryan holding down his feet. The officers instructed the appellant to "let it out" and to "relax". Finally, Constable Powell was able to remove the package once the appellant unclenched his muscles. It contained 10.1 grams of crack cocaine, with a street value of between $500 and $2,000.

The appellant's pants were pulled up and he was placed under arrest for possession of a narcotic for the purpose of trafficking, and for police assault.

The appellant was then brought to 51 Division, located about a two-minute drive from the Subway shop. He was strip searched again at the police station, fingerprinted and detained pending a bail hearing.

On a voir dire hearing, the appellant applied to have the evidence obtained from the search excluded under ss. 8 and 24 of the *Charter*. The application was denied, and the evidence was admitted. The appellant was found guilty by a jury of possession of a narcotic for the purpose of trafficking, but acquitted on the police assault charge. He was sentenced to fourteen months imprisonment, which he had served by the time this case was before our Court. The Court of Appeal for Ontario dismissed the appellant's appeal from his conviction and sentence.

. . . .

ANALYSIS

Introduction

This Court has held that a search will be reasonable within the meaning of s. 8 of the *Charter* where (1) it is authorized by law; (2) the law itself is reasonable; and (3) the search is conducted in a reasonable manner (*R. v. Collins*, [1987] 1 S.C.R. 265; *R. v. Debot*, [1989] 2 S.C.R. 1140; *Cloutier*, supra; *Stillman*, supra, at p. 633; *Caslake*, supra). Applying this analytical framework to the present case, the Court must address the following questions:

1. Was the search authorized by law?
2. Is the law itself reasonable?
3. Was the search conducted in [a] reasonable manner?

If these questions are answered in the affirmative, there will be no s. 8 violation ... Conversely, if any of the questions is answered in the negative, then the strip search will violate s. 8 and it will be necessary to consider whether the evidence obtained as a result of the search should be excluded pursuant to s. 24(2) of the *Charter*. Applying this analytical framework to the present case, the first question is whether the common law of search incident to arrest authorizes the police to conduct strip searches. If it does, the next question is whether the common law is reasonable. If the strip search was authorized by law and the law is reasonable, the final question is whether the strip search of the appellant was conducted in a reasonable manner.

This Court has emphasized on many occasions the need to strike the appropriate balance between the privacy interests of the accused on the one hand and the realities and difficulties of law enforcement on the other hand... . Similarly, in the present case, an appropriate balance must be achieved between the interest of citizens to be free from unjustified, excessive and humiliating strip searches upon arrest, and the interests of the police and of society in ensuring that persons who are arrested are not armed with weapons that they may use against the police, themselves or others, and in finding and preserving relevant evidence.

The appellant submits that the term "strip search" is properly defined as follows: the removal or rearrangement of some or all of the clothing of a person so as to permit a visual inspection of a person's private areas, namely genitals, buttocks, breasts (in the case of a female), or undergarments. This definition in essence reflects the definition of a strip search that has been adopted in various statutory materials and policy manuals in Canada and other jurisdictions (see for example Toronto Police Service, *Policy & Procedure Manual: Search of Persons. Arrest & Release* at p. 3; *Crimes Act 1914* (Austl.), Part 1AA, c. 3C, s. 1 "strip search"; *Cal. Penal Code* s. 4030 (West 1984); *Col. Rev. Stat. Ann.* s. 16-3-405 (West 1982); *Wash. Rev. Code Ann.* s. 10.79.070(1) (West 1983). In our view, this definition accurately captures the meaning of the term "strip search" and we adopt it for the purpose of these reasons. This definition distinguishes strip searches from less intrusive "frisk" or "pat down" searches, which do not involve the removal of clothing, and from more intrusive body cavity searches, which involve a physical inspection of the detainee's genital or anal regions. While the mouth is a body cavity, it is not encompassed by the term "body cavity search". Searches of the mouth do not involve the same privacy concerns, although they may raise other health concerns for both the detainee and for those conducting the search.

Applying this definition of strip search to the facts, the appellant was subjected to three strip searches in the present case. The first strip search occurred in the stairwell when Constable Ryan undid the appellant's trousers, pulled back the long underwear the appellant was wearing and looked down the long underwear at the appellant's buttocks. The second strip search occurred in the back of the restaurant at which point the appellant's pants and underwear were pulled down to his knees while the officers tried to seize the package from between the appellant's buttocks. This second strip search also involved the police officers using rubber dish gloves to forcibly remove the package containing the cocaine from between the appellant's buttocks. This physical contact with the appellant's buttocks in the course of the second strip search places this search farther along on the spectrum of intrusiveness than the first search, although on the evidence it falls short of being a body cavity search. The third strip search occurred at the police station.

Did the Court of Appeal for Ontario err in concluding that the strip search of the appellant did not violate s. 8 of the Charter?

Does the Common Law "Search Incident to Arrest" Power Include the Power to Strip Search?

It is clear that the common law in Canada recognizes the power of police to search a lawfully arrested person for the purpose of seizing weapons or evidence that may be in his possession (*Cloutier, supra*, at pp. 180–81). What is not clear, however, and what must be decided in this case, is the scope of this power to search incident to arrest. Specifically, does the common law authorize strip searches and, if it does, are there any restrictions at common law on the power to conduct such searches? [Discussion of the law of the U.K. and the U.S. has been omitted.]

. . . .

CANADA

In contrast with searches of the person incident to arrest, there is a plethora of legislative provisions dealing with searches of premises. In addition to s. 487 of the *Criminal Code*, R.S.C. 1985, c. C-46, which provides that reasonable grounds are required before a justice may issue a warrant authorizing the search of a "building, receptacle or place", there are many other provisions in the administrative and regulatory context governing the search of premises (see for example *Competition Act*, R.S.C. 1985, c. C-34, s. 15 ... The Law Reform Commission of Canada in its *Working Paper on Police Powers, supra*, at p. 20 remarked on this situation as follows:

> The restricted availability of powers of personal search in this context [the criminal law context], however, is due less to a heightened respect for personal integrity on the part of Anglo-Canadian lawmakers than to the historical association of the warrant with searches of private dwellings. Indeed, the development over the last three centuries of the warrant, with its safeguards against unjustified entry into private domains, has been accompanied by the accrual of relatively discretionary warrantless powers to search persons.

Thus, searches of the person incident to arrest fall to be governed by the common law.

There are relatively few reported pre-*Charter* cases in Canada dealing with the lawfulness of searches of the person carried out as an incident to arrest. The lack of case authority on this issue is not surprising given the lack of effective remedies for unlawful searches, whether strip searches or other types of personal searches. Prior to the advent of s. 8 of the *Charter*, the only possible remedy for an unlawful strip search would have been a tort action for assault, battery or false imprisonment. The cost of bringing such an action, the low amount of damages potentially recoverable and the ineffectiveness of civil actions as a remedy when real evidence was seized through an unlawful search likely explains the dearth of case law. Recent cases illustrate that damage awards in tort for unlawful strip searches remain low, and the costs of bringing a civil action would far exceed the nominal damages awarded: *Nurse* v. *Canada* (1997), 132 F.T.R. 131; *Blouin* v. *Canada* (1991), 51 F.T.R. 194.

. . . .

In the post-*Charter* era, there are many examples of cases dealing with personal searches in general, and strip searches in particular, carried out as an incident to arrest. The greater number of strip search cases is at least in part due to the greater availability of remedies with the advent of the *Charter*, particularly the possibility of excluding evidence under s. 24(2) of the *Charter* as a remedy for unlawful searches. However, the cases also suggest a disturbing trend towards strip searching detained persons as a matter of routine police policy, regardless of the particular circumstances surrounding the arrest.

While the constitutionality of strip searches incident to arrest has not previously been addressed by this Court, this Court has addressed the constitutionality of a strip search and "bedpan vigil" of a person detained at airport customs carried out pursuant to s. 98 of the *Customs Act*, R.S.C. 1985, c.1 (2nd Supp.). In *R.* v. *Simmons*, [1988] 2 S.C.R. 495, and *R.* v. *Monney*, [1999] 1 S.C.R. 652, this Court concluded that strip searches of travellers carried out under the customs legislation did not violate s. 8 of the *Charter*. However, this Court also made it clear that its conclusion that s. 8 was not violated in the circumstances was based upon the "unique factual circumstance" that border crossings present. The unique nature of the border crossing context was described as follows in the following passage from Iacobucci J.'s reasons in *Monney*, at para. 42, quoting from the majority reasons of Gonthier J. in *R. v. Jacques*, [1996] 3 S.C.R. 312, at para. 18:

> The unique context that border crossings present was recognized by this Court in *R. v. Simmons*, [1988] 2 S.C.R. 495. Dickson C.J., writing for the majority, said (at p. 528):
>> National self-protection becomes a compelling component in the calculus.
>> I accept the proposition advanced by the Crown that the degree of personal privacy reasonably expected at customs is lower than in most other situations. People do not expect to be able to cross international borders free from scrutiny. It is commonly accepted that sovereign states have the right to control both who and what enters their boundaries.

Given the unique context of border crossing searches, the reasoning in the customs cases is not directly applicable in the present case. While this Court has never pronounced on the lawfulness of strip searches conducted as an incident to arrest prior to the present appeal, it has made comments in obiter concerning such searches in the cases of *Beare*, supra, and *Cloutier*, supra. The *Beare* case was concerned with the constitutionality of legislation that provided for the fingerprinting of individuals charged but not convicted of an indictable offence. In the course of concluding that the legislation was not in violation of the *Charter*, La Forest J. made the following comments, at pp. 403–404:

> As an incident to a lawful arrest, a peace officer has a right to search the person arrested and to take any property the officer reasonably believes is connected with the offence charged, or any weapon found upon such person; see *R. v. Morrison* (1987),20 O.A.C. 230. This authority is based on the need to disarm an accused and to discover evidence. In the course of custodial arrest an accused may be stripped. Of particular relevance, height, weight and natural or artificial marks on the body, such as birth marks or tattoo marks, may be used for purposes of identification; see *Adair v. M'Garry*, [1933] S.L.T. 482 (J.).

In *Cloutier*, supra, this Court considered the common law power of search incident to arrest for the first time. The case involved a "frisk" or "pat" search of a motorist stopped for a traffic violation. L'Heureux-Dubé J., writing for the Court, surveyed the British, American and Canadian case authorities and concluded at pp. 180–81 that:

> [I]t seems beyond question that the common law as recognized and developed in Canada holds that the police have a power to search a lawfully arrested person and to seize anything in his or her possession or immediate surroundings to guarantee the safety of the police and the accused, prevent the prisoner's escape or provide evidence against him.

She noted, however, that while the existence of such a common law power is accepted, there is uncertainty as to the scope of the power. ...

Since *Cloutier*, this Court has addressed the constitutionality of the seizure of bodily samples at common law in *Stillman*, supra. Cory J., speaking for the majority, held that the seizure of bodily samples, namely hair samples, buccal swabs and teeth impressions, was not authorized by the common law power to search incident to arrest. Such a serious interference with a person's bodily integrity required statutory authorization and could not be justified under the common law power to search incident to arrest. Cory J. distinguished the situation in *Stillman* from other cases, such as *Cloutier*, supra, where searches incident to arrest had been found not to infringe the *Charter* on the basis that "completely different concerns arise where the search and seizure infringes upon a person's bodily integrity, which may constitute the ultimate affront to human dignity" (*Stillman*, supra, at para. 39).

At the appellate and trial court levels in Canada, strip searches and even body cavity searches have been held to be lawful at common law as an incident to arrest. At the appellate level, the only court in Canada that has addressed whether strip searches incident to arrest are constitutional is the Ontario Court of Appeal. In *R. v. Morrison* (1987), 35 C.C.C. (3d) 437, the Court of Appeal concluded that a strip search of a female detainee arrested for theft and possession of stolen goods and cash did not violate s. 8 of the *Charter* and that the evidence discovered in the search, namely marijuana, was therefore admissible. At p. 442 of *Morrison*, Dubin J.A. expressed the principles applicable to such searches as follows:

> As incident to a lawful arrest, a peace officer has the right to search the person arrested and take from his person any property which he reasonably believes is connected with the offence charged, or may be used as evidence against the person arrested, or any weapon or instrument found upon the person arrested, but he need not have reasonable grounds to believe that either such weapons or evidence will be found. It is the fact that the search of the person is made as incident to a lawful arrest which gives the peace officer the authority to search the person arrested.

In two subsequent cases, the Ontario Court of Appeal held that strip searches did violate s. 8. In *R. v. Ferguson* (1990), 1 C.R. (4th) 53, the accused was observed for several hours at a house where police suspected drug trafficking took place. The police later stopped the accused's vehicle, searched his vehicle and checked his name on C.E.P.I.C. They then noticed a bulge in the accused's pants, and discovered, after undoing his pants, that he was concealing a bag containing cocaine. The Court of Appeal ruled that the search violated s. 8 because it was conducted on the basis of mere suspicion, rather than reasonable and probable grounds. Although the violation of s. 8 was found primarily on the basis that there was a lack of reasonable and probable grounds, the court also noted the intrusive method of the search. The court held that the s. 8 violation was serious and that the evidence should therefore be excluded under s. 24(2) and an acquittal entered.

In *R. v. Flintoff* (1998), 16 C.R. (5th) 248 (Ont. C.A.), the accused was arrested for impaired driving and taken to the police station for a breathalyzer test. Prior to the breathalyzer test, the accused was strip searched as part of the routine policy of the police department and not on the basis of any circumstances related to the particular case. After the strip search, the appellant was taken to the breathalyzer room and failed the test. The Ontario Court of Appeal concluded that it was unreasonable to strip search the appellant and that the breach of s. 8 was serious. Accordingly, the court held that the breathalyzer evidence should be excluded and the decision of the trial judge dismissing the charge restored.

At the trial level, there are numerous examples of cases involving strip searches performed as an incident to arrest. In some cases, the courts have concluded that the strip searches did not constitute a s. 8 violation, while in other cases similar searches have been held to violate s. 8. In *R. v. Stott*, [1997] O.J. No. 5449 (QL) (Prov. Div.), a strip search of an individual arrested for impaired driving carried out as a matter of routine police policy was held not to violate s. 8. Similarly, in *R. v. K.D.S.* (1990), 65 Man. R. (2d) 301 (Q.B.), the strip search of a young offender at the police station as part of normal police procedure following his arrest for possession of a stolen licence plate was held not to be a violation of s. 8. Strip searches accompanied by the threat of a subsequent body cavity search as an incident to arrest have also been found not to infringe s. 8: *R. v. Miller*, [1993] B.C.J. No. 1613 (QL)(S.C.). On the other hand, a (QL)(S.C.) routine strip search of a female accused arrested for theft and possession of stolen property was held not to be authorized by the common law of search incident to arrest in *R. v. King*, [1999] O.J. No. 565 (QL) (Gen. Div.). Also, in *R. v. Kalin*, [1987] B.C.J. No. 2580 (QL) (Co.Ct.), a routine strip search conducted at the police station following an arrest for impaired driving was held to be unreasonable under s. 8 of the *Charter*. As these cases illustrate, there is inconsistency in the lower court decisions as to when strip searches are reasonable and when they are unreasonable under s. 8.

THE PRECONDITIONS OF A LAWFUL STRIP SEARCH INCIDENT TO ARREST AT COMMON LAW

The appellant's position is that, given the negative impact of a strip search on an individual's privacy interests and psychological well-being, s. 8 should demand that at least probable cause be required to authorize strip searches and, absent exigent circumstances, a warrant. The intervener African Canadian Legal Clinic (ACLC) agrees with the appellant that probable cause and a warrant requirement should be required for strip searches to be constitutional under s. 8 of the *Charter*. The ACLC says that given the negative stereotyping of African Canadians by police and the large number of African Canadians who are stopped and searched by police, a public process of obtaining a warrant is required to reduce the danger of racist stereotyping by individual police officers, who are more likely than a neutral arbiter to conclude that a strip search of a black person is appropriate. The intervener Aboriginal Legal Services of Toronto (ALST) also advocates a regime of prior authorization for strip searches and submits that the common law does not authorize warrantless strip searches except in the most exceptional circumstances, such as where there is an immediate threat to the safety of police and the public or a threat of immediate destruction of evidence. For its part, the intervener Canadian Civil Liberties Association proposes three limits on strip searches incident to arrest: (1) strip searches should be prohibited when less intrusive investigative steps are available; (2) police must have reasonable grounds to conduct strip searches, and (3) prior authorization in the form of a warrant should be required except in rare exigent circumstances.

The respondent's position is that the common law authorizes strip searches and is reasonable within the meaning of s. 8. The respondent says that the restrictions on searches outlined by this Court in *Cloutier, supra,* and *Stillman, supra,* are adequate to ensure that strip searches incident to arrest meet the requirements of s. 8. The interveners Attorney General for Ontario and the Canadian Association of Chiefs of Police both agree with the respondent that the common law authorizes strip searches and is reasonable.

While the respondent and the interveners for the Crown sought to downplay the intrusiveness of strip searches, in our view it is unquestionable that they represent a significant invasion of privacy and are often a humiliating, degrading and traumatic experience for individuals subject to them. Clearly, the negative effects of a strip search can be minimized by the way in which they are carried out, but even the most sensitively conducted strip search is highly intrusive. Furthermore, we believe it is important to note the submissions of the ACLC and the ALST that African Canadians and Aboriginal people are overrepresented in the criminal justice system and are therefore likely to represent a disproportionate number of those who are arrested by police and subjected to personal searches, including strip searches (*Report of the Aboriginal Justice Inquiry of Manitoba* (1991), Vol. 1, at p. 107; *The Cawsey Report: Justice on Trial: Report of the Task Force on the Criminal Justice System and its Impact on the Indian and Metis People of Alberta* (1991), Vol. II, at 2.48 to 2.50; Royal Commission on Aboriginal Peoples, *Bridging the Cultural Divide* (1996) at 33–39; Commission on Systemic Racism in the Ontario Criminal Justice System, *Report of the Commission on Systemic Racism in the Ontario Criminal Justice System* (1995)). As a result, it is necessary to develop an appropriate framework governing strip searches in order to prevent unnecessary and unjustified strip searches before they occur.

The law is clear in Canada that warrantless searches are *prima facie* unreasonable under s. 8 of the *Charter* (*Hunter, supra*). Where a search is carried out without prior authorization in the form of a warrant, the burden is on the party seeking to justify the warrantless search to prove that it was not unreasonable (*Hunter*, at pp. 160–61). Searches of the person incident to arrest are an established exception to the general rule that warrantless searches are *prima facie* unreasonable. In considering the constitutionality of strip searches carried out as an incident to arrest, it is still important to bear in mind that warrantless searches are the exception and not the norm in Canadian law. While characterized as an exception to the normal rule that a search warrant is required for a lawful search, however, warrantless personal searches incident to arrest are an exception whose importance should not be underestimated....

. . . .

While the common law authorities ... support the general proposition that a warrantless search conducted incident to arrest is permitted under the common law, the scope of this common law search power is less clear: *Caslake, supra*, at paras. 14–15. Thus, the task in the present case is to delineate the scope of the common law power as it pertains to warrantless strip searches carried out as an incident to lawful arrest in a way that is consistent with the *Charter* right to be protected against unreasonable search and seizure. As Lamer C.J. stated in *Caslake*, because there are no clear limits on the power to search incident to arrest it is "the courts' responsibility to set boundaries which allow the state to pursue its legitimate interests, while vigorously protecting individuals' right to privacy" (*Caslake, supra*, at para. 15). It is important to note that the discussion below relates only to the permissible scope of strip searches incident to arrest, as defined in these reasons. For greater clarity, if it appears during the course of a strip search that the detainee is concealing a weapon or evidence inside a body cavity, and the detainee refuses to co-operate, then in order to obtain the object in question the police officer must likely exceed the realm of the strip search and enter the realm of the body cavity search. More intrusive searches of the person such as this involve a higher degree of infringement of personal dignity and privacy as well as additional medical concerns and, accordingly, a higher degree of justification will be required before such a search can be carried out. In addition, more intrusive searches will be subject to greater constraints as to the manner in which they may be reasonably performed.

As noted by Dickson C.J. in *Simmons, supra*, the different types of searches raise different constitutional considerations: the more intrusive the search, the greater the degree of justification and constitutional protection that is appropriate: *Simmons*, at p. 517. The party seeking to uphold the validity of a warrantless personal search will face a lower burden in the case of a quick pat or frisk search than in the case of a highly invasive body cavity search.

Given that the purpose of s. 8 of the *Charter* is to protect individuals from unjustified state intrusions upon their privacy, it is necessary to have a means of preventing unjustified searches before they occur, rather than simply determining after the fact whether the search should have occurred (*Hunter, supra*, at p. 160). The importance of preventing unjustified searches before they occur is particularly acute in the context of strip searches, which involve a significant and very direct interference with personal privacy. Furthermore, strip searches can be humiliating, embarrassing and degrading for those who are subject to them, and any post facto remedies for unjustified strip searches cannot erase the arrestee's experience of being strip searched. Thus, the need to prevent unjustified searches before they occur is more acute in the case of strip searches than it is in the context of less intrusive personal searches, such as pat or frisk searches. As was pointed out in *Flintoff, supra,* at p. 257, "[s]trip-searching is one of the most intrusive manners of searching, and also one of the most extreme exercises of police power".

Strip searches are thus inherently humiliating and degrading for detainees regardless of the manner in which they are carried out and for this reason they cannot be carried out simply as a matter of routine policy. The adjectives used by individuals to describe their experience of being strip searched give some sense of how a strip search, even one that is carried out in a reasonable manner, can affect detainees: "humiliating", "degrading", "demeaning", "upsetting", and "devastating" (see *King, supra, R. v. Christopher,* [1994] O.J. No. 3120 (QL) (Gen. Div.); J.S. Lyons, Toronto Police Services Board Review. "The Search of Persons Policy — The Search of Persons — A Position Paper" (April 12, 1999)). Some commentators have gone as far as to describe strip searches as "visual rape" (Paul Shuldiner, "Visual Rape: A Look at the Dubious Legality of Strip Searches" (1979), 13 J. Marshall L. Rev. 273). Women and minorities in particular may have a real fear of strip searches and may experience such a search as equivalent to a sexual assault (*Lyons, supra,* at p. 4). The psychological effects of strip searches may also be particularly traumatic for individuals who have previously been subject to abuse (*Commission of Inquiry into Certain Events at the Prison for Women in Kingston* (1996), at pp. 86–89). Routine strip searches may also be distasteful and difficult for the police officers conducting them (*Lyons, supra,* at pp. 5–6).

In order for a strip search to be justified as an incident to arrest, it is of course necessary that the arrest itself be lawful. In the present case, there is no question that the arrest was lawful. While the appellant disputes the lawfulness of arrest, the trial judge and the Court of Appeal concluded that there were reasonable and probable grounds for making the arrest, and we see no reason to dispute this conclusion. Thus, the first requirement of a valid search incident to arrest was met in this case.

The second requirement before a strip search incident to arrest may be performed is that the search must be incident to the arrest. What this means is that the search must be related to the reasons for the arrest itself. As expressed by Lamer C.J. in *Caslake, supra,* at para. 17, a search "is only justifiable if the purpose of the search is related to the purpose of the arrest". In the present case, the strip search was related to the purpose of the arrest. The arrest was for drug trafficking and the purpose of the search was to discover illegal drugs secreted on the appellant's person. Had the appellant been arrested for a different reason, such as for a traffic violation, the common law would not have conferred on the police the authority to conduct a strip search for drugs, even if the police had knowledge of previous involvement in drug related offences, since the reason for the search would have been unrelated to the purpose of the arrest. In the circumstances of the present case, we conclude that the search was conducted incident to the arrest.

The reasonableness of a search for evidence is governed by the need to preserve the evidence and to prevent its disposal by the arrestee. Where arresting officers suspect that evidence may have been secreted on areas of the body that can only be exposed by a strip search, the risk of disposal must be reasonably assessed in the circumstances. For instance, in the present case, it was suggested that the appellant might have dropped the drugs on the sidewalk or in the police cruiser on the way to the station and that it was therefore necessary to search him in the field. As we discuss below, however, the risk of his disposing of the evidence on the way to the police station was low and, had the evidence been dropped in the police cruiser on the way to the station, circumstantial evidence could easily link it back to the accused.

In addition to searching for evidence related to the reason for the arrest, the common law also authorizes police to search for weapons as an incident to arrest for the purpose of ensuring the safety of the police, the detainee and other persons. However, a "frisk" or "pat down" search at the point of arrest will generally suffice for the purposes of determining if the accused has secreted weapons on his person. Only if the frisk search reveals a possible weapon secreted on the detainee's person or if the particular circumstances of the case raise the risk that a weapon is concealed on the detainee's person will a strip search be justified. Whether searching for evidence or for weapons, the mere possibility that an individual may be concealing evidence or weapons upon his person is not sufficient to justify a strip search.

The requirement that the strip search be for evidence related to the grounds for the arrest or for weapons reflects the twin rationales for the common law power of search incident to arrest. Strip searches cannot be carried out as a matter of routine police department policy applicable to all arrestees, whether they are arrested for impaired driving, public drunkenness, shoplifting or trafficking in narcotics. The fact that a strip search is conducted as a matter of routine policy and is carried out in a reasonable manner does not render the search reasonable within the meaning of s. 8 of the *Charter*. A strip search will always be unreasonable if it is carried out abusively or for the purpose of humiliating or punishing the arrestee. Yet a "routine" strip search carried out in good faith and without violence will also violate s. 8 where there is no compelling reason for performing a strip search in the circumstances of the arrest.

It may be useful to distinguish between strip searches immediately incidental to arrest, and searches related to safety issues in a custodial setting. We acknowledge the reality that where individuals are going to be entering the prison population, there is a greater need to ensure that they are not concealing weapons or illegal drugs on their persons prior to their entry into the prison environment. However, this is not the situation in the present case. The type of searching that may be appropriate before an individual is integrated into the prison population cannot be used as a means of justifying extensive strip searches on the street or routine strip searches of individuals who are detained briefly by police, such as intoxicated individuals held overnight in police cells: *R.* v. *Toulouse*, [1994] O.J. No. 2746 (QL) (Prov. Div.).

The difference between the prison context and the short term detention context is expressed well by Duncan J. in the recent case of *R.* v. *Coulter*, [2000] O.J. No. 3452 (QL) (C.J.), at paras. 26–27, which involved a routine strip search carried out incident to an arrest and short term detention in police cells for impaired driving. Duncan J. noted that whereas strip searching could be justified when introducing an individual into the prison population to prevent the individual from bringing contraband or weapons into prison, different considerations arise where the individual is only being held for a short time in police cells and will not be mingling with the general prison population. While we recognize that police officers have legitimate concerns that short term detainees may conceal weapons that they could use to harm themselves or police officers, these concerns must be addressed on a case by case basis and cannot justify routine strip searches of all arrestees.

The fact that the police have reasonable and probable grounds to carry out an arrest does not confer upon them the automatic authority to carry out a strip search, even where the strip search meets the definition of being "incident to lawful arrest" as discussed above. Rather, additional grounds pertaining to the purpose of the strip search are required. In *Cloutier*, supra, this Court concluded that a common law search incident to arrest does not require additional grounds beyond the reasonable and probable grounds necessary to justify the lawfulness of the arrest itself: *Cloutier*, supra, at pp. 185–86. However, this conclusion was reached in the context of a "frisk" search, which involved a minimal invasion of the detainee's privacy and personal integrity. In contrast, a strip search is a much more intrusive search and, accordingly, a higher degree of justification is required in order to support the higher degree of interference with individual freedom and dignity. In order to meet the constitutional standard of reasonableness that will justify a strip search, the police must establish that they have reasonable and probable grounds for concluding that a strip search is necessary in the particular circumstances of the arrest.

In light of the serious infringement of privacy and personal dignity that is an inevitable consequence of a strip search, such searches are only constitutionally valid at common law where they are conducted as an incident to a lawful arrest for the purpose of discovering weapons in the detainee's possession or evidence related to the reason for the arrest. In addition, the police must establish reasonable and probable grounds justifying the strip search in addition to reasonable and probable grounds justifying the arrest. Where these preconditions to conducting a strip search incident to arrest are met, it is also necessary that the strip search be conducted in a manner that does not infringe s. 8 of the *Charter*.

Parliament could require that strip searches be authorized by warrants or telewarrants, which would heighten compliance with the *Charter*. At a minimum, if there is no prior judicial authorization for the strip search, several factors should be considered by the authorities in deciding whether, and if so how, to conduct such a procedure.

In this connection, we find the guidelines contained in the English legislation, [*Police and Criminal Evidence Act 1984* (U.K.), c. 60 ("P.A.C.E.")] concerning the conduct of strip searches to be in accordance with the constitutional requirements of s. 8 of the *Charter*. The following questions, which draw upon the common law principles as well as the statutory requirements set out in the English legislation, provide a framework for the police in deciding how best to conduct a strip search incident to arrest in compliance with the *Charter*:

1. Can the strip search be conducted at the police station and, if not, why not?
2. Will the strip search be conducted in a manner that ensures the health and safety of all involved?
3. Will the strip search be authorized by a police officer acting in a supervisory capacity?
4. Has it been ensured that the police officer(s) carrying out the strip search are of the same gender as the individual being searched?
5. Will the number of police officers involved in the search be no more than is reasonably necessary in the circumstances?
6. What is the minimum of force necessary to conduct the strip search?
7. Will the strip search be carried out in a private area such that no one other than the individuals engaged in the search can observe the search?
8. Will the strip search be conducted as quickly as possible and in a way that ensures that the person is not completely undressed at any one time?
9. Will the strip search involve only a visual inspection of the arrestee's genital and anal areas without any physical contact?
10. If the visual inspection reveals the presence of a weapon or evidence in a body cavity (not including the mouth), will the detainee be given the option of removing the object himself or of having the object removed by a trained medical professional?
11. Will a proper record be kept of the reasons for and the manner in which the strip search was conducted?

Strip searches should generally only be conducted at the police station except where there are exigent circumstances requiring that the detainee be searched prior to being transported to the police station. Such exigent circumstances will only be established where the police have reasonable and probable grounds to believe that it is necessary to conduct the search in the field rather than at the police station. Strip searches conducted in the field could only be justified where there is a demonstrated necessity and urgency to search for weapons or objects that could be used to threaten the safety of the accused, the arresting officers or other individuals. The police would also have to show why it would have been unsafe to wait and conduct the strip search at the police station rather than in the field. Strip searches conducted in the field represent a much greater invasion of privacy and pose a greater threat to the detainee's bodily integrity and, for this reason, field strip searches can only be justified in exigent circumstances.

Having said all this, we believe that legislative intervention could be an important addition to the guidance set out in these reasons concerning the conduct of strip searches incident to arrest. Clear legislative prescription as to when and how strip searches should be conducted would be of assistance to the police and to the courts.

If the Common Law Power to Search Incident to Arrest Permits a Strip Search, Is the Common Law Unreasonable?

Given our conclusion that the common law does permit a strip search to be conducted as an incident to a lawful arrest, the question is whether the common law is unreasonable in this respect within the meaning of s. 8 of the *Charter*. In our view, as interpreted above, the common law power to search incident to arrest conforms with the constitutional protection against unreasonable search and seizure contained in s. 8 of the *Charter*. The common law rule as delineated above governs the conduct of strip searches incident to arrest and ensures that such searches are only carried out where the police establish reasonable and probable grounds for a strip search for the purpose of discovering weapons or seizing evidence related to the offence for which the detainee was arrested. Furthermore, the factors set out above ensure that when strip searches are carried out as an incident to arrest, they are conducted in a manner that interferes with the privacy and dignity of the person being searched as little as possible. Attention to these issues will also ensure that the proper balance is struck between the privacy interests of the person being searched and the interests of the police and of the public in preserving relevant evidence and ensuring the safety of police officers, detained persons and the public. We conclude therefore that the common law of search incident to arrest, which permits strip searches, does not violate s. 8 of the *Charter*.

Was the Strip Search Conducted in This Case Carried Out in a Reasonable Manner?

In light of the constitutional requirements set out above for a valid strip search incident to arrest, we are of the view that the search at issue in this appeal was unreasonable, and violated the appellant's rights guaranteed under s. 8 of the *Charter*. In this respect, it is critical to underscore that where the reasonableness of a strip search is challenged, it is the Crown that bears the onus of proving its legality. It thus must convince the court on a balance of probabilities that either (1) reasonable and probable grounds, as well as exigent circumstances existed, and therefore, a strip search "in the field" was warranted and was conducted in a reasonable manner; or (2) that reasonable grounds existed, that the strip search was carried out at a police station, and conducted in a reasonable manner. Because strip searches are of such an invasive character, they must be considered prima facie unreasonable. It is up to the state to rebut this presumption because it is in the best position to know and explain why the search took place, and why it was conducted in the manner and circumstances that it did. This onus rests upon the Crown in any case involving a strip search, as defined in these reasons.

In the present case, the Crown sought to distinguish the first part of the search in the stairwell from the subsequent efforts to seize the plastic wrap from the appellant's buttocks after he was brought back into the Subway shop. We are unwilling to accept such a distinction. The search in the stairwell, whereupon the police pulled back the appellant's pants and underwear in order to visually examine his buttock area, cannot be looked at in isolation. Rather, it must be assessed within the complete context of the events that took place after the appellant's arrest. According to the definition adopted in these reasons, the first part of the search in the stairwell was a strip search, although it was clearly of a less intrusive character than the subsequent search in the restaurant. This visual inspection of the appellant's buttocks, in and of itself, interfered with his privacy, dignity, and integrity. The Crown's burden of proof in regard to this first part of the search is thus the same as that required to justify the subsequent search and seizure that took place in the shop. However, as discussed above, the more intrusive the search, the greater will be the degree of justification required and the greater the constraints as to the way it may be conducted.

In this appeal, the Crown has failed to prove that the strip search of the appellant was carried out in a reasonable manner. More specifically, the evidence adduced at trial fell far short of establishing that a situation of exigency existed so as to warrant a strip search outside of the police station. The Crown asserted that this search was necessitated by Constable Ryan's observance of the appellant crushing what appeared to be crack cocaine between his fingers just after his arrest. In addition, this officer testified that he had made at least twelve narcotics-related arrests in his experience as a police officer, in which he discovered cocaine secreted by arrested persons in their buttocks or groin area. The Crown argued that these circumstances gave rise to reasonable and probable grounds for believing that the appellant was concealing evidence on his person. Further, it was submitted that exigency arose from the risk that this evidence might be lost or destroyed if police waited to conduct the strip search until the appellant was transported to a police station.

We find these submissions unpersuasive for the following reasons. First, Constable Theriault, the officer stationed at the observation post, testified that 51 Division police station was located on the corner of Dundas and Regent streets, a two-minute drive away from the shop where the strip search of the appellant took place. This fact alleviated any sense of exigency in this case. In our view, it seems highly improbable that the appellant, who was handcuffed, could have somehow surreptitiously ridded himself of the evidence concealed on his person during the very brief time it would have taken police to relocate him to 51 Division. Had he succeeded in dropping the evidence on the sidewalk or in the police cruiser, it is difficult to conceive that he would have been able to do so unobserved, given the number of officers involved in his arrest. Furthermore, the circumstances surrounding the discovery of any drugs dropped close to the appellant would have provided strong circumstantial evidence of the appellant's connection to the evidence. As such, we conclude that this case was not one involving an urgent and necessary need to conduct a strip search "in the field" for the purpose of preserving evidence.

The trial judge made no findings as to whether there were reasonable and probable grounds to conduct a strip search; he relied on the grounds for the arrest. As mentioned, Constable Ryan testified that in his experience, he had made at least a dozen drug arrests in which an arrested individual was concealing evidence in his private areas. At the same time, this officer also testified on cross-examination that he had arrested well over 200 persons dealing in crack cocaine. If these individuals were all strip searched, which is not evident in the record, he admitted to having found evidence hidden in an individual's private parts in merely five percent of drug arrests. If only a few of these individuals were strip searched, it raises the question: which ones and why? Constable Ryan thus knew that the chances of discovering evidence as a result of strip searching the appellant were quite slim.

Other than Constable Ryan's personal experience, the arresting officers had no reasonable and probable basis for conducting the strip search in the restaurant. No information was given to them by Constable Theriault that the appellant had reached into his pants to remove any substances, nor had they ever witnessed such conduct themselves. There was no bulging or protrusion in the appellant's buttock area to suggest that he was concealing evidence. In the result, the decision to strip search was premised largely on a single officer's hunch, arising from a handful of personal experiences. These circumstances, coupled with the absence of exigency discussed above, compel us to conclude that the police officers' decision to strip search the appellant in the restaurant was unreasonable.

Having so concluded, we should note, however, that there was some evidence suggesting the possibility of concealment of narcotics. The appellant was arrested for trafficking after police observed him engage in two transactions involving what they believed was a narcotic substance. Further, the arresting officers found what they thought was crack cocaine under the table where another suspect was arrested. Constable Ryan also observed the appellant crushing a substance that looked like crack cocaine between his fingers during the arrest. Finally, Constable Ryan did have some experience, albeit in relatively few cases, with drug arrests involving suspects who secreted evidence in their groin or buttock areas.

Taken together, these circumstances would have been sufficient to create reasonable and probable grounds to conduct a strip search of the appellant at the police station. However, by deciding to carry out the strip search in a public restaurant rather than the nearby station house, without appropriate safeguards in place, the police failed to meet a condition essential to the validity of such an intrusive, warrantless search. There were no reasonable and probable grounds to believe that this strip search had to be conducted with such urgency.

In addition, the manner in which the strip search was conducted in the restaurant did not comply with the requirements of reasonableness contained in s. 8 of the *Charter*. The appellant was not given the opportunity to remove his own clothing, a measure that might have reduced the sense of panic he clearly experienced. Rather, Constable Ryan pulled back the appellant's pants and underwear during the initial part of the search in the stairwell. He and Constable Powell then lowered the appellant's pants and underwear after the appellant was brought back into the main area of the restaurant. Also, the strip search was conducted without notice to, or authorization from, a senior officer. The decision to search the appellant was made unilaterally by the arresting officers, in particular, by Constable Ryan. Finally, the search was carried out in a manner that may have jeopardized the appellant's health and safety.

Where the circumstances of a search require the seizure of material located in or near a body cavity, the individual being searched should be given the opportunity to remove the material himself or the advice and assistance of a trained medical professional should be sought to ensure that the material can be safely removed. In this case, the plastic wrap was located between the appellant's buttocks. The police had no way of knowing whether it was physically lodged inside him in such a way that it could not be safely retrieved without medical intervention. Nevertheless, the arresting officers undertook to remove the package themselves, through physical coercion and forceful probing and tugging at the package, and by instructing the appellant to "let it out" and to "relax". The risk this presented to the appellant's health was made more acute by the fact that after the appellant accidentally defecated, Constable Powell retrieved a pair of rubber gloves that had been used for cleaning the shop's washrooms and toilets to continue in his attempts at dislodging the package. The entire episode created as well unsanitary conditions in a public restaurant, which would have been avoided had the search been conducted in a less precipitous manner.

The relevance of the appellant's resistance to the search also merits comment. At the *voir dire* hearing, McNeely J. held that had the appellant "relaxed and not attempted to retain the substance", the search would have been shorter and less intrusive. The respondent endorsed McNeely J.'s reasoning, relying on the British Columbia Court of Appeal's decision in *R. v. Garcia-Guiterrez* (1991), 5 C.R. (4th) 1. In that case, police observed the accused reach into his mouth, remove something and give it to another person, who gave the accused money in return. After arresting the accused for possession of cocaine for the purpose of trafficking, an officer grabbed his throat to prevent him from swallowing and breathing, and instructed him to open his mouth. The accused refused and a second officer punched him in the stomach. A majority of the Court of Appeal held that the search was reasonable, as it was found necessary to preserve the evidence. In this regard, Macdonald J.A. held (at para. 17) that the accused was "in complete control" of the violence inflicted upon him, since, had he simply opened his mouth, the police would have ceased applying physical force.

We particularly disagree with the suggestion that an arrested person's non-cooperation and resistance necessarily entitles police to engage in behaviour that disregards or compromises his or her physical and psychological integrity and safety. If the general approach articulated in this case is not followed, such that the search is unreasonable, there is no requirement that anyone cooperate with the violation of his or her *Charter* rights. Any application of force or violence must be both necessary and proportional in the specific circumstances. In this case, the appellant's refusal to relinquish the evidence does not justify or mitigate the fact that he was strip searched in a public place, and in a manner that showed considerable disregard for his dignity and his physical integrity, despite the absence of reasonable and probable grounds or exigent circumstances.

In light of the foregoing reasons, we conclude that the manner in which the strip search in this case was conducted was unreasonable. It therefore amounted to a breach of the appellant's constitutional guarantees under s. 8 of the *Charter*.

If the strip search of the appellant violated s. 8 of the *Charter*, would the admission of the evidence bring the administration of justice into disrepute under s. 24(2) of the *Charter*?

Seeing as the appellant has already served his 14-month sentence in full, and because the courts below did not engage in a s. 24(2) analysis, we believe it is neither necessary nor useful for this Court to determine whether the evidence deriving from the illegal strip search should have been excluded at trial, and if so, whether a new trial should be ordered. In these circumstances, examining and ruling on s. 24(2) of the *Charter* would be a mere theoretical exercise.

In preference to this analysis, our disposition rests on the premise that the courts below erred in finding the strip search of the appellant reasonable in the circumstances and consistent with s. 8 of the *Charter* and consequently erred in allowing the impugned evidence to be admitted. These errors provide a sufficient basis for our conclusion that this appeal must be allowed; in light of all the circumstances mentioned above, we conclude that an acquittal is the proper result.

DISPOSITION

For all of the foregoing reasons, the appeal is allowed, and the judgment of the Ontario Court of Appeal is set aside. The appellant's conviction is thus overturned and an acquittal is entered.

[Four justices dissented on the basis that no additional grounds should be required for a strip search. Although they would have found that the second strip search of Golden violated s. 8 because of the manner in which it was carried out, they would not have excluded the evidence under s. 24(2).]

C. SEARCH MUST BE REASONABLE

Even when authorized by a law that has survived a *Charter* challenge to its "reasonableness," pursuant to s. 8, a search must also be executed in a reasonable way.

R. v. Gogol[†]

[FAIRGRIEVE J.:]

The primary issue raised by this *Charter* application concerns the permissible treatment of an occupant of premises being searched pursuant to a search warrant.

The accused is charged with possession of marijuana, contrary to s. 3(1) of the *Narcotic Control*

[†] [1994] O.J. No. 61. (Div. Ct.), online: QL.

Act. The Crown has elected to proceed by way of summary conviction, so that this is a court of competent jurisdiction so far as granting remedies under the *Charter* is concerned. Pursuant to s. 24(2), Ms. Gogol seeks the exclusion of the evidence that half a gram of marijuana was found amongst her undergarments in a dresser drawer by one of the police officers who executed a search warrant at her residence during the early morning hours of February 8, 1992. The search warrant was one of an estimated 28 search warrants executed simultaneously at various premises in relation to an investigation into what was alleged to be a major conspiracy to traffic in cocaine.

The applicant alleges that the officers violated her rights under s. 8, s. 9, s. 10 and, in the event that the foregoing sections did not fully cover the situation, s. 7 of the *Charter* as well. Mr. Layefsky made clear, however, that the thrust of his application was that despite being authorized by a valid search warrant, the search was carried out in an unreasonable manner, and that his client's rights under s. 8 were thereby violated. The other *Charter* infringements, it was argued, occurred as incidents to that unreasonable search. To put it in a nutshell, Ms. Gogol alleges that during the search, she was unlawfully detained, her rights consequent upon that detention were disregarded, she was subjected to unwarranted physical and verbal abuse, and her property was needlessly and intentionally damaged or destroyed.

. . . . .

The Probable Facts

One of the major difficulties with this application has been the dubious quality of much of the evidence that was called. At the risk of offending both sides, I have to say that neither the accused nor the police officers who testified on the voir dire struck me as completely credible witnesses. They were, of course, the only persons present during the search and in a position to relate what occurred in the course of conducting it. The evidence was unsatisfactory in many respects, in my view, and both sets of testimony suffered from certain frailties and inherent implausibilities. I am compelled to find that the complete truth of the matter was simply not disclosed by the evidence that was given. That, perhaps, is not a unique occurrence, but it does complicate the process of making the findings of fact necessary to a proper determination of this application. In *Collins, supra* at pp. 13–14 C.C.C., Lamer J. referred to the consequences of a court's inability to determine the facts:

> The appellant, in my view, bears the burden of persuading the court that her *Charter* rights or freedoms have been infringed or denied.... The standard of persuasion required is only the civil standard of the balance of probabilities and, because of this, the allocation of the burden of persuasion means only that, in a case where the evidence does not establish whether or not the appellant's rights were infringed, the court must conclude that they were not.

With respect to Ms. Gogol's credibility, both her demeanour as a witness and the improbable nature of much of her evidence gave rise to serious concerns. When testifying, she inexplicably shifted on occasion, and not always at the most appropriate times, from a calm, reasoned recitation of her recollection of the events that occurred many months ago, to angry and emotional outbursts that included breaking down in tears. Her weeping was not very convincing, however, since she seemed to be more interested in watching the reaction of others than genuinely overcome by emotion. Although I have tried not to view her demeanour too cynically, recognizing that different people do react in different ways, the impression I was left with was that she was not always testifying with sincerity and candour. At other times, I think that she was simply mistaken in her evidence. For example, she testified that the other officers repeatedly called Cst. Lee "Psycho" during the course of the search. In fact, Cst. Lee's nickname is "Ug", as in "Ug Lee", and I am quite sure that he was never called "Psycho" by anyone. Nothing turned on this particularly, except that I think it indicated a tendency on the part of the accused to allow her apparent antipathy towards Cst. Lee to colour her evidence, leaving it less accurate and reliable than it might otherwise have been.

I also think that in addition to embellishing and exaggerating her account of the events when testifying, in some instances Ms. Gogol completely fabricated evidence. For example, having had the opportunity to observe both the accused and Cst. Karen Terejko, I reject outright Ms. Gogol's evidence that after the policewoman had taken her to use the toilet, still handcuffed according to the accused, the officer stated, "What do you expect me to do, wipe your fucking ass?" Even making allowances for the possibility that Cst. Terejko's politeness and dignified appearance in the courtroom might not be an absolutely reliable indicator of how she acts in other situations, the conduct attributed to her by Ms. Gogol seemed so inconsistent with the officer's deportment and apparently respectable character that I think it can safely be rejected. I believe Cst. Terejko's evidence that the accused's handcuffs were removed prior to taking her to the bathroom, and that no such statement was made by her. Moreover, I do not think that this was the subject of any honest mistake on the part of the accused, but a deliberate attempt to mislead the court.

Similarly, despite Cst. Lee's deficiencies as a witness, I do not believe the accused's evidence that he made all of the highly unlikely statements to which she testified. For example, at one time, according to Ms. Gogol's evidence, Cst. Lee said to her, spitting and spraying as he spoke, "You're lucky I don't take my [...] out and [...] all over you". At the conclusion of the search, Ms. Gogol testified that Cst. Lee said to her, "If you tell anybody what went on here, I'll come back, I'll put a bullet in your head. If not you, I'll get that big black [racist expletive] son of yours, and if not him, I'll get your dog". The vulgar language and the crude sentiments were the product of the accused's efforts to portray her treatment in a more shocking way, I believe, and I do not accept that Cst. Lee's conduct was even remotely violent or hostile to her as her evidence alleged.

My conclusion is that, feeling aggrieved at the way she was treated by the officers, Ms. Gogol considered that she had licence to embellish her evidence to dramatize her complaints, probably in the mistaken belief that they would then appear more compelling. It is unfortunate that she could not have felt greater confidence in simply telling the truth.

As already stated, the four officers who took part in the execution of the search warrant testified on the voir dire. The evidence of all of them, I think it fair to say, was characterized by uncertainty, vagueness and a lack of recall concerning matters that, in the normal course, one would have expected to have been remembered with some precision and clarity. While Ms. Gogol's residence in a public housing complex at 543 Dundas Street West had three floors, including a basement, it was described as a small townhouse. It would be remarkable, in my view, that an officer in one room could be as oblivious as was claimed to what was said or done by another officer in a different room. When questioned concerning the alleged racial and sexual comments and other threats Ms. Gogol testified were made by Cst. Lee, Cst. Terejko framed her answers in terms of not recalling such conduct, rather than as firm denials that it occurred. When confronted again with the suggestion that Cst. Lee had been abusive to the accused, Cst. Terejko's response was that she was not in a position to agree or disagree, stating that she did not see or hear what the other officer did. Cst. Page similarly testified that he was primarily engaged in searching a bedroom upstairs, so that he could not say whether Cst. Lee had been abusive. Although I can readily accept that each officer concentrated on the part of the search to which he or she had been assigned, and he or she did not interfere with the conduct of the others, I have considerable difficulty believing that all of the officers would not have been in a position to clearly confirm or deny the allegations made by Ms. Gogol.

In particular, Cst. Olsen, the officer in charge of the search, was an obviously intelligent and articulate witness. His notes and recollection, however, were sketchy and of limited assistance in piecing together the chronology. Cst. Lee, the officer against whom the most serious allegations were made, neglected to bring his notebook to court, suggesting that he may have misplaced it when he moved. He further explained that his notes would not have assisted him in any event, since they did little more than record the time the officers arrived at the accused's residence. It did not appear that any of the officers gave much thought to the fairly predictable prospect that at some point they would be asked to provide a detailed account of how the search was conducted.

I am in the position, then, of having to make factual findings on the basis of what I consider to be generally unsatisfactory and unreliable evidence. If this were the trial proper, I would simply state that the conflicting evidence in many areas left me in a state of doubt, precluding findings with the requisite degree of certainty concerning those matters. As it is, even with the standard of proof simply a balance of probabilities, I have considerable difficulty resolving many of the factual disputes. I intend, therefore, to make only those findings as to the probable facts that are necessary to dispose of this application.

One fact that can be stated with certainty is that Ms. Gogol was handcuffed shortly after she was awakened by the police at 3:00 a.m. and taken downstairs to the kitchen-dining area of her residence. Her evidence concerning this was confirmed by the evidence of the four officers, all of whom testified to having seen her in handcuffs. Precisely how and why she came to be handcuffed, however, was not so clear.

Ms. Gogol's evidence was that she was handcuffed as soon as she was brought downstairs. She testified that she was handcuffed initially with her hands in front. According to her evidence, however, after the red-haired officer, obviously referring to Cst. Lee, said that she looked "too comfortable", Cst. Terejko handcuffed both her hands behind her back. Ms. Gogol testified that she was made to sit on the floor, and then repeatedly ordered to get up and down from the floor to a chair over a period of two hours. During this period, she testified, Cst. Lee verbally abused her, repeatedly calling her "[racist expletive] lover" and making other racist comments, as well as throwing foodstuffs and various items from the kitchen at her.

While I would have thought that the handcuffing of an elderly woman for a prolonged period in these circumstances would have been a relatively memorable occurrence, the police officers' evidence turned out not to be very helpful to determining exactly how and why it happened. Two of the officers denied responsibility for having handcuffed her, without knowing who had done so. The most that Cst. Olsen conceded was that he probably was the one who [had] done so, but he was not sure. At one point in his cross-examination, Cst. Lee testified that he might have been the one, but it appeared to be speculation on his part, not a specific recollection. What was apparent from the evidence, however, was that none of the officers considered that confining Ms. Gogol in this way for a protracted period was a matter of any particular importance or concern.

Cst. Olsen was uncertain about the sequence of events. In his evidence in chief, he testified that he recalled that Ms. Gogol was handcuffed "probably about halfway through the search", which lasted about two and a half hours from the arrival of the police at 3:00 a.m. until their departure at 5:35 a.m. In cross-examination, however, he testified that he believed she was handcuffed around 3:15 or 3:20 a.m., i.e., an hour earlier than he had previously stated. Cst. Olsen testified that he believed that he had been the officer who had handcuffed the accused, but that it might have also have been Cst. Page or Cst. Terejko, both of whom denied having done so. In cross-examination, Cst. Olsen repeated that he could not recall specifically who had handcuffed her, although "possibly" it was himself. He went on to state that he was not sure whether he (Cst. Olsen) had handcuffed her to prevent her from interfering with the search, or whether it was Cst. Page who handcuffed her when he arrested the accused for the marijuana offence, although he further testified that the handcuffing was not part of that arrest. I will refer shortly to Cst. Page's evidence that he never did arrest the accused, and that his only involvement was to remove the handcuffs.

Cst. Olsen conceded that there was nothing in his notebook about Ms. Gogol's having been handcuffed or about any interference by her with the search. So far as the reason for handcuffing her is concerned, Cst. Olsen testified that

> [s]he kept fumbling with the documents, etc., so I believe it was myself, but she ended up getting handcuffed to the chair so that she wouldn't continue to disrupt the search. With only four of us there ... we couldn't keep an eye on her to keep her from fumbling around with the articles we were conducting the search for.

He testified that it was "normal procedure" to restrain persons during the course of a search if they interfered by getting in the way or handling property the police were attempting to seize. In cross-examination, Cst. Olsen agreed that Ms. Gogol had not destroyed any evidence, that she had merely moved some papers and keys, but that he "didn't want it to get to that level". It was somewhat difficult to reconcile Cst. Olsen's alleged concern that the accused might interfere in that way with the description of the accused elsewhere in his evidence as "friendly" and "co-operative" and "apologetic" when the officers' disgust with the state of her premises was apparent. Cst. Olsen's recollection was that Ms. Gogol was handcuffed by one hand to the chair at the table on which the documents being examined were placed, and that she remained handcuffed to the chair until the officers left. It was not entirely clear why, even assuming that the accused had been restrained in the way described by the officer, leaving her with a hand free in the area where items were placed would prevent the kind of interference allegedly anticipated by the officer.

Cst. Olsen's evidence was that Cst. Page informed the accused of her arrest for possession of marijuana at 3:20 a.m., and although it was not in his notes and he did not actually listen to what was being said, that Cst. Page advised her of "her rights" at that time. Cst. Page's evidence, on the other hand, was that it was at 5:00 a.m. that he came downstairs and told Ms. Gogol, whom he found already in handcuffs, that she would be charged with the marijuana offence. Cst. Page testified that he advised her of her right to counsel at that time, i.e., an hour and 40 minutes later than Cst. Olsen had stated. Cst. Page also testified that he was "a little bit mildly surprised that she was handcuffed", not being aware of when, why or by whom she had been handcuffed. He believed, he testified, that she had been handcuffed with both hands behind her back, and that she was "visibly shaking a little". Cst. Page further testified that he removed the handcuffs at that time, took a statement from her concerning some money that had been found, and then at 5:35

a.m., when the police left, issued her with an appearance notice.

Cst. Terejko testified that almost immediately after the arrival of the police, she escorted Ms. Gogol downstairs and left her there. In contrast to the description of the other officers, she stated that the accused was "very unco-operative" at that point. The policewoman then returned upstairs, according to her evidence, where she spent 45 minutes or an hour searching. When she then went downstairs, she found the accused handcuffed either, she testified, with both bands behind her back or to the chair. She did not know who had handcuffed her. Cst. Terejko testified that she took off the handcuffs to allow the accused to use the toilet, when in the sequence of events that occurred was left unclear, as were the circumstances surrounding the replacement of the handcuffs which presumably occurred when Cst. Terejko brought Ms. Gogol back downstairs. The accused's own evidence, as already stated, was that she was made to use the toilet while her hands were still cuffed behind her back.

Cst. Lee, the last officer to give evidence, testified that the accused was brought downstairs about five or ten minutes after the search commenced, and although she was just beside the kitchen area that he spent about an hour and a half searching, he was never alone with her. How this could be, when Cst. Olsen was evidently searching the basement and Cst. Page and Cst. Terejko were searching the bedrooms upstairs, was not altogether clear. Cst. Lee initially described Ms. Gogol as "basically co-operative", stating that he did not think she was obstructing in any way, but that she kept getting up to see what the officers were looking at. At another point in his evidence, Cst. Lee testified that she gradually calmed down and, by the end of the search, she was "no problem at all".

In cross-examination, Cst. Lee agreed that Ms. Gogol had been handcuffed with one arm to a chair about half an hour after the search commenced. He could not recall who had handcuffed her, but stated that it had definitely not been him. Cst. Lee explained that handcuffing people is a "routine thing" when executing a search warrant, not something he would have noted in his notebook, although he later stated, oddly I thought, that he probably would have made a note of whether she was handcuffed by one hand or two. At a later point in his cross-examination, without any apparent concern about contradicting his prior denial that he had handcuffed Ms. Gogol, Cst. Lee testified that he might have done so, but did not recall.

Similarly, despite Cst. Lee's evidence in chief that Ms. Gogol had not been obstructing the search in any way, in cross-examination, he testified that she was "sort of grabbing at things ... and just generally getting in the way", saying things like "it's private" or "put that down". He went on to say that he thought someone, though who he was not sure, had told her that if she did not stay sitting down, she would be handcuffed. Later in his cross-examination, Cst. Lee agreed that he might have been the one who issued the warning, and then that he was "probably" one of the people who did so. He then testified that although Ms. Gogol was "basically cooperative", she was also "obstructing" and had to be controlled. He added as well that if they had not placed some kind of restraint on her, "she could have just walked out the door", and that one of the primary reasons for handcuffing her was to prevent her from leaving.

Cst. Lee's recollection was that the accused had probably been released from the handcuffs about half an hour before the conclusion of the search and the departure of the police at around 5:35 a.m. He was clear in his evidence that the handcuffing was not related to the discovery of the marijuana and had no connection to that alleged offence. With respect to what was said to Ms. Gogol when she was handcuffed, although Cst. Lee testified that they explained the search to her, he did not suggest that the handcuffing was accompanied by any information concerning any rights she might then have had.

From all of this inconsistent and unconvincing evidence, I can at least make certain limited findings on a balance of probabilities. I am satisfied that the accused was placed in handcuffs shortly after the police arrived and she was taken downstairs, and that the handcuffs were not finally removed until Cst. Page did so at 5:00 a.m. Given the accused's evidence that she was handcuffed with both hands behind her back, Cst. Page's belief that that was the case, and Cst. Terejko's uncertainty about it, I think that she was probably restrained in that way. It follows that I think that the evidence of Cst. Olsen and Cst. Lee that she was handcuffed to the chair by one arm only is probably wrong, although, despite the absence of evidence that such was the case, I cannot rule out the possibility that Ms. Gogol was handcuffed in different ways at different times.

Having regard to the conflict between the evidence of the accused that it was Cst. Terejko who had handcuffed her and the uncertain evidence of Cst. Olsen and Cst. Lee, the two officers who conceded the possibility that he might have been responsible for it, I cannot definitely say which officer placed the handcuffs on Ms. Gogol. I am able to find, however, again on a balance of probabilities, that the reason for handcuffing her was to keep her in one place where she could be watched either by Cst. Lee in the kitchen or by Cst. Olsen when he was searching the living room. Her confinement in this way prevented her from leaving, as stated by Cst. Lee, and prevented her from interfering with the conduct of the search. The evidence, in my view, does not support a conclusion that she did in fact obstruct the search in any way, but does suggest that the handcuffing was designed, as a pre-emptive measure, to prevent her from doing so had she been inclined to interfere, and to ease the officers' task by allowing them to conduct their search without having to concern themselves with any potential interference. I accept Cst. Lee's evidence that he regarded handcuffing people as "a routine thing that happens when you conduct a search warrant" and that he personally had handcuffed "plenty, lots" while executing search warrants.

On the basis of the evidence of both the accused and the police officers, I am satisfied that Ms. Gogol was kept in handcuffs by the table for a period of at least an hour and a half, from shortly after 3:00 a.m. until about 5:00 a.m., apart perhaps from being taken to the bathroom at some point during that time. The handcuffing, I find, was not accompanied by any explanation of the reason why it was done, at least partly due to the difficulty the officer, whoever that might have been, would have had in articulating the justification for it. I also accept that when Ms. Gogol was handcuffed, she was not informed of any right to counsel or provided with a reasonable opportunity to exercise any such right had she wanted to do so. The only reference to her constitutional rights, I believe, came at about 5:00 a.m. when Cst. Page removed her handcuffs, and proceeded with the taking of a statement from her.

I am also satisfied, on a balance of probabilities, that the search was accompanied by unnecessary damage to the accused's property. While I would be reluctant to make that finding based solely on the accused's evidence, there was other evidence supporting her allegations in this regard. I accept the evidenced of Mr. Rebeiro, a former assistant bank manager and a friend of the accused's son, that he was requested by Ms. Gogol to take photographs of her premises the day following the search, and that the photographs filed as exhibits accurately portray the condition of Ms. Gogol's house at that time. Mr. Rebeiro described the place as having been "demolished", with broken glass everywhere and a great deal of damage that had not been observed by him when he had visited her residence previously.

Despite the officers' denials of responsibility for the damage, I think it more likely that they caused it than that the accused inflicted it herself for purposes of supporting her complaints against the police. The latter appeared to be the only alternative explanation to account for the damage. Specifically, I am satisfied that Ms. Gogol did not smash the glass door of her microwave oven, or rip apart the expensive stereo speakers, breaking their cones, or break the dresser mirror in the bedroom upstairs. I find that the police officers probably caused this damage during the course of the search, and it would be impossible to find that this kind of damage was done accidentally.

I make no findings concerning certain other accusations made by the accused, including her unconfirmed and inherently improbable testimony that it was only three days after the search that she was able to clean up the rotting meat that had beep removed from her basement freezer during the search, or that 25 garbage bags full of broken dishes, glasses and other items had to be thrown away as a result of the damage caused by the officers.

The officers' evidence was essentially that the accused's residence was left by them in about the same condition it had been in when they arrived, apart from the usual incidents to a search that would include such things as up-ended dresser drawers with their contents dumped on the floor or the contents of kitchen cupboards emptied onto the counter. Although Ms. Gogol was understandably upset at having to clean up the mess which was admittedly left by the officers, the more significant complaint she made concerned the alleged wanton destruction and damaging of her possessions.

The attitude of the officers appeared to be that because the accused already lived in dirty and untidy premises, the state they left the house in or their treatment of her property when they were there were not considered anything to be particularly concerned about....

The impression I was left with was that because of the seriousness of the narcotics offences under investigation that had led to the search warrant, the officers considered that the search could be conducted zealously, with little regard for Ms. Gogol's sensibilities or the need to avoid damage to her property. While I am reluctant to find that apparently reasonable and otherwise responsible police officers would deliberately damage another person's property, I am driven to the conclusion that that probably occurred here.

With respect to the very serious allegations that Cst. Lee directed repeated racist and abusive comments at the accused, I can make no specific finding. I might add, however, that I was inclined to believe the evidence of Maureen Forestall which tended to support Ms. Gogol's evidence in this regard. Ms. Forestall, employed by a marketing manager and the sister of a Metro Toronto police officer, testified that her own residence on Marion St. had been searched the same night and that she had been arrested. She was permitted to take her 3-year old son, evidently the accused's grandson, to Ms. Gogol's house to see if he could be left there. She was met at the door, she testified, by Cst. Lee, referred to as the red-haired officer with a bandanna, and that he told her to take her son to the Children's Aid where he would be better off than living with drug dealers. Ms. Forestall further testified that when she encountered the same officer at the police station later the same night, he called her a "[racist expletive] fucker" and similar names. Ms. Jaffe attacked the credibility of the witness by pointing to the fact that Ms. Forestall herself faced narcotics charges and that she had a personal interest in assisting Ms. Gogol. Ms. Forestall's evidence was not shaken in cross-examination, however, and she struck me as a generally credible witness. At the same time, despite my suspicions that what Ms. Gogol alleges in this regard may be true, I cannot say with any confidence that the racist statements and other verbal abuse she attributed to Cst. Lee probably occurred as she described. Bearing in mind the onus on the applicant, I am obliged to reject those particular complaints.

Were there *Charter* violations?

. . . .

There is no issue here concerning the validity of the search warrant or that there was a lawful search authorized by it. What is alleged is that the search was carried out in an unreasonable manner, in violation of s. 8, and that in the process of conducting the search, other constitutional rights of the accused were infringed.

As I have found, Ms. Gogol was handcuffed, probably with both hands behind her back, for a protracted period of time, probably approaching two hours. The restraint and confinement of the accused in this way clearly constituted a detention, as that term was explained by the Supreme Court of Canada in *R.* v. *Therens* (1985), 18 C.C.C. (3d) 481. It was not suggested that she had been arrested for obstructing the police officers in the execution of their duty by interfering with the search, and no one alleged that she had committed any offence of that kind for which she might have been arrested. It was also conceded that the handcuffing had nothing to do with the alleged possession of marijuana offence, for which she was given an appearance notice.

The justification for the handcuffing in the minds of the officers, although I appreciate it was nowhere expressly stated in this way, was that it was a preventive measure to preclude Ms. Gogol's interference with the examination of documents or other items placed by the police in the area where she had been brought. While it may be that from the officers' perspective, her mere presence there was a nuisance, it is difficult to ignore the evidence that she was co-operative or to elevate a vague description of her getting up and "fumbling" with items to any reasonable basis for believing that she would actually obstruct the search.

The other explanation for the detention offered by Cst. Lee was that she might have left the premises had she not been restrained. That the police had the authority in the circumstances to prevent her from leaving, if she had wanted to do so, appeared to have been simply assumed by the officers. Given that it was the middle of the night, that Ms. Gogol was dressed only in a dressing gown, and that there was no evidence of any indication by her that she wanted to leave, even assuming that she was not free to go if she wished, it is difficult to find on this ground any reasonable justification for the handcuffing and physical restraint of the accused.

The evidence of all of the witnesses was that this detention of Ms. Gogol was not accompanied by any compliance with s. 10 of the *Charter*. She was not informed of the reasons for her detention, as required by s. 10(a). This failure to inform her of the reasons reflected, I think, the absence of any valid articulable grounds for her detention. Similarly, there was no compliance with s. 10(b) of the *Charter* upon her detention. Ironically, according to the evidence I accept, reference was made to her right to counsel only when the handcuffs were removed at 5:00 a.m., effectively terminating that detention.

In Hutchison and Morton, *Search and Seizure Law in Canada* (1991), at p. 17-9, the learned authors provide the following summary of the common law concerning the treatment of occupants of premises being searched:

> Generally, peace officers have no special authority over persons found in premises being searched pursuant to a search warrant. Absent an arrest, persons found on premises being searched are not subject to a search by executing

officers. Occupants are entitled, in general, to leave the premises being searched.

According to Messrs. Hutchison and Morton, the only exception to this general rule of "non-molestation of occupants" is stated by the Ontario Court of Appeal in *Levitz* v. *Ryan* (1972), 9 C.C.C. (2d) 182, where the Court held that occupants may be restrained so far as is necessary to accomplish the search contemplated by the search warrant.

In *Levitz* v. *Ryan*, two R.C.M.P. officers with a writ of assistance issued under what was then s. 10 of the *Narcotic Control Act*, R.S.C. 1970, c. N-1, entered the plaintiff's Yorkville apartment to search for narcotics. Mr. Levitz was required to accompany one officer while he searched the kitchen and bedroom, and the other officer detained two visitors in the living room. Arnup J.A., at p. 183, stated that "... [i]t is quite clear that until the search was over none of the three occupants of the apartment would have been allowed to leave by the officers and indeed [Cst.] Alford testified that for the time being they were under arrest". The entire search took about 20 minutes. At p. 191, His Lordship dealt with the submission that the officers had no right to detain the three occupants of the premises while the search was being conducted:

> I was told that no Canadian cases bear upon the question of the right of officers conducting a search under a writ of assistance to "freeze" the premises and its occupants (this language is mine). The leading case in the United States is *Harbison* v. *Chicago R.I. & P.R Co. et al.* (1931), 37 S.W. Rep. 2d 609, a judgment of the Supreme Court of Missouri relied on by the trial judge herein. In that ease, where a person's home was being searched for liquor, and the person was first prevented from going to another unattended, the Court said at p. 164:
>> We regard a reasonable surveillance of a party whose premises are being searched as a necessary part of the search authorized by the search warrant. To hold otherwise would afford such party an opportunity to secrete or destroy the thing searched for and thus effectively defeat the purpose of the search.
>
> While there appear to be no more recent American cases, I was told that the case is cited and has been cited since 1931, in various editions of digests, etc., as being the law on the point.
>
> I regard the reasons given in this case as being convincing and as formulating a principle which ought to be adopted in this country. To have permitted any of the three occupants to leave the premises while the search was still incomplete might well have defeated the entire purpose of the search. Similarly, to permit the answering of telephone calls might in some cases permit the destruction by the caller of evidence which could become part of the investigation. It is to be observed that the *Harbison* rule refers to "reasonable surveillances"; it is not intended to apply, and I do not intend to apply it, to cases where the detention of occupants of premises under search is in the circumstances unreasonable and incapable of being regarded as a "necessary part of the search authorized".

. . . .

Applying Arnup J.A.'s dictum, and recognizing that the ultimate burden to establish a *Charter* infringement is on the accused, it is impossible to characterize Ms. Gogol's detention by being handcuffed as either "reasonable" or a "necessary part of the search authorized". The search being conducted at the accused's residence was one of a series of simultaneous searches of various premises. When the police arrived at 3:00 a.m., Ms. Gogol was found alone in her house, sleeping in her bed. None of the officers testified that her detention was a result of any concern that she might secrete or destroy evidence, thereby frustrating their search. Neither did they suggest that she had to be prevented from alerting others to the search in case evidence elsewhere might be destroyed. There was no basis, moreover, for regarding her as a dangerous or violent person who had to be restrained for the protection of the officers or anyone else. She was detained, I find, merely because her getting up from the chair or making comments about the documents being examined at the dining table were annoying to the officers, and it was simply more convenient for them to restrain her by placing her in handcuffs. This amounted, in my view, to an arbitrary detention of the kind proscribed by s. 9 of the *Charter*.

In any event, once she was detained, s. 10 of the *Charter* guaranteed her certain rights. The evidence does not establish that she was promptly informed of the reason for her detention, or that she was informed of her right to counsel and given an opportunity to exercise that right if she had chosen to do so. No attempt was made by the Crown to justify the failure to comply with s. 10.

Moreover, once the finding has been made that it is probable that one or more police officers gratuitously damaged the accused's property, it is impossible to say that the search was carried out in a reasonable manner. Smashing the glass door of a microwave oven or breaking the cones of the stereo speakers cannot be viewed as reasonable conduct. Coupled with the unnecessary force used to restrain the accused, it is apparent that s. 8 of the *Charter* was violated.

. . . .

In this case, the unreasonable manner of conducting the search encompassed the use of unnecessary force against Ms. Gogol and the unwarranted destruction of her property. Section 8 was accordingly violated. The accused's rights under ss. 9 and 10, I am satisfied, were also infringed during the execution of the search warrant.

Should the Evidence Be Excluded?

In applying s. 24(2), the court is obliged to consider "all the circumstances" to determine whether the evidence should be excluded. *Collins*, *supra*, continues to be the most instructive authority concerning the factors to be taken into account when examining whether admission of the evidence, in this case the finding of the marijuana in the accused's drawer, would bring the administration of justice into disrepute.

It is clear that the seized marijuana is what is regarded as "real evidence" which existed independently of any *Charter* violation, and that it would inevitably have been discovered during the course of the search. It cannot be said, then, that its admission would affect the fairness of the trial, as that admittedly ambiguous term has been used in the case law.

The seriousness of the *Charter* infringement has to be assessed. In my view, the violations here are extremely serious. It is outrageous, I think, that police officers would regard a search warrant as sufficient authority to handcuff an elderly woman and detain her for a protracted period either to prevent her from leaving her home or as an unjustified preemptive measure to prevent the mere possibility that a "basically co-operative person", as she was described in the evidence, might interfere with the search. It is more than a little alarming that Cst. Lee would testify that handcuffing occupants while premises are searched is a "routine thing" barely worthy of note. Equally shocking, I think, is the notion that in 1992 police officers could think that a person could be detained in this way without any consideration of the need to comply with s. 10 of the *Charter*. The court should not permit a search warrant to be misconstrued by police officers as a warrant for the arrest of the occupants of the premises, or as authority to disregard the rights that any other person under arrest would have.

It is also unacceptable that the search warrant would apparently be regarded as a licence to ignore the property rights of the occupant of the premises, permitting what were essentially acts of vandalism. The attitude displayed by the officers here appeared to be one of complete indifference to the legal requirements of reason and restraint when conducting the search. Implicit in the officers' evidence was an assumption that because of the gravity of the alleged offences being investigated, and because of the distaste they had for the accused's residence and her standards of housekeeping, there was no need to treat her property with care or respect. A wilful failure to appreciate the limits of their powers and the obligation to treat members of the public with courtesy and fairness cannot be condoned by the court. None of the reprehensible police conduct here occurred in circumstances of urgency or necessity. It can only be described, in my view, as a wilful and flagrant violation of Ms. Gogol's rights.

The approach taken by the Supreme Court of Canada in *R. v. Genest* (1989), 45 C.C.C. (3d) 385, is instructive, I think, of the principles to be applied here. In his analysis of s. 24(2) under the heading of "seriousness of the *Charter* violation", Dickson C.J.C., at p. 406, stated that "[b]ecause of the greater infringement of the individual's interests caused by the extensive power to search a dwelling-house, some officer must be accountable for the way the search is carried out". In this case, Cst. Olsen, the officer in charge of the search, would presumably be that person, but his evidence gave no indication that he recognized that he had any such responsibility. At pp. 408–9, the Chief Justice further stated:

> The greater the departure from the standards of behaviour required by the common law and the *Charter*, the heavier the onus on the police to show why they thought it necessary to use force in the process of an arrest or search. The evidence to justify such behaviour must be apparent in the record, and must have been available to the police at the time they chose their course of conduct. The Crown cannot rely on *ex post facto* justifications.
>
> ...
>
> While the purpose of s. 24(2) is not to deter police misconduct, the courts should be reluctant to admit evidence that shows signs of being obtained by an abuse of common law and *Charter* rights by the police.

The third set of factors outlined by Lamer J. in *Collins* requires consideration of the effect that the exclusion of the evidence would have on the reputation of the administration of justice. I assume that exclusion of the impugned evidence in this case will mean the acquittal of the accused, but the charge is a minor one and the *Charter* violations very serious.

In *R. v. Young* (1993), 12 O.R. (3d) 529 (Ont. C.A.), Carthy J.A. considered a situation involving an illegal arrest, an illegal search, and a violation of the accused's right to counsel. In rejecting the Crown's submission that the real evidence obtained in that case should nonetheless be admitted, His Lordship stated at pp. 536–7:

> There can be no question that the violations of the *Charter* were very serious. No one of them was a technical oversight or a mere error of judgment but, most importantly, the number of violations combined to form "a larger pattern of disregard for the appellant's *Charter* rights": see *R. v. Greffe*, [1990] 1 S.C.R. 755 at p. 795.
>
> In terms of the effect upon the administration of justice, someone might characterize the conduct of the police in this case as misdirected, but nonetheless reflecting a keen attention to their perceived roles in investigating a crime in pursuit of "getting their man". The appellant is in truth guilty of the offences in question and should be punished. To exclude the evidence is to that extent a disservice to the administration of justice.
>
> That characterization is, in my view, more than offset in this case by the necessity to assure that the courts do not condone conduct which represents a real threat to all persons, whether innocent or guilty, from wilful abuse of police powers. ... Once this assumption of innocence is inserted, the police conduct appears arrogant, oppressive and high-handed. ...

In my view, the conduct of the police officers in this case should be characterized in exactly that way. I do not see any reason to reach a conclusion here that differs from that stated by Carthy J.A. in *Young*.

Taking all of the circumstances into account, I am obliged to grant the accused's application. The evidence concerning the finding of the marijuana will accordingly be excluded from the trial.

∎

There are a number of other cases where a s. 8 argument has succeeded in circumstances where the manner of search is suggestive of racially-based hostility. The accused in *R. v. Lewis* (Ont. Ct. Just. (Prov. Div.)), *supra*, was successful in having evidence of half a gram of marijuana excluded even though, as a guest in someone else's home, he was unable to challenge the validity of the search warrant. On the facts, another man in the house, Vincent Gardner, had just been shot by police (see **Policing,** *supra*), and the police then strip-searched all of the remaining men found on the premises. Judge Dianne Nicholas ruled that the search was unreasonable under s. 8 on the basis of the number of officers involved (12), the failure to advise the men of their right to counsel, the fact that they were strip-searched, which was said to be very intrusive, and the use of unnecessary force, given that most of the men were handcuffed.

Most recently, the Supreme Court of Canada has ordered a new trial on the basis that a trial judge had failed to resolve the factual issues raised by the accused's argument. In *R. v. McCarthy*, [1996] S.C.J. No. 74, online: QL, the accused computer technician alleged that he was handcuffed during the search of his apartment, taunted with racist epithets, and terrorized by a mock execution. McCarthy was granted a new trial on the basis that these defence allegations went unchallenged by police, yet the trial judge had failed to rule in favour of the accused. For other cases where the manner of search has been challenged, see *R. v. Burton* (1993), 16 O.R. (3d) 660 (C.A.) (although police had grounds for a warrantless search of the accused and his car, the evidence was properly excluded on the basis that the police firing of a weapon and conducting a strip-search of the accused in public rendered the manner of execution "unreasonable") and *R. v. Hamilton*, [2000] O.J. No. 2722 (Ct. Just.), online: QL, where the arrest and subsequent search were ruled unlawful, in part due to use of excessive force (pepper spray).

Looking back on *Gogol* and the above examples, consider whether a s. 15 challenge would be a productive legal strategy. It is striking that in these cases and in the racial profiling case law that is emerging, no argument has yet been advanced using s. 15 of the *Charter*. Her Honour Judge Donna Hackett, in her article, "Finding and Following 'The Road Less Travelled:' Judicial Neutrality and the Protection and Enforcement of Equality Rights in Criminal Trial Courts" (1998) 10 C.J.W.L. 129, recounts that in her experience of hearing 21,000 criminal cases, s. 15 had not been raised even once by counsel for the defence or the Crown. She consulted her judicial colleagues and found the same result: from 1985–98, they had judged roughly 120,000 cases without ever hearing equality issues raised by counsel. She attributes this astonishing gap to three causes: while equality and the rule of law are widely accepted, they are taken for granted because many Canadians do not appreciate the disadvantage experienced by others; the historic development of the law has been based upon precedent and custom, rather than upon constitutional principles such as equality; and many lawyers have not been trained in equality rights as part of their legal education. She provides many examples of commonplace trial issues that raise significant s. 15 issues that need to be taken on by criminal lawyers.

D. SECTION 24(2): WHEN IS EVIDENCE EXCLUDED?

R. v. Collins[†]

[LAMER, J.:]

The appellant, Ruby Collins, was seated in a pub in the town of Gibsons when she was suddenly seized by the throat and pulled down to the floor by a man who said to her "police officer." The police officer, then noticing that she had her hand clenched around an object, instructed her to let go of the object. As it turned out, she had a green balloon containing heroin.

It is common knowledge that drug traffickers often keep their drugs in balloons or condoms in their mouths so that they may, when approached by the narcotics control agent, swallow the drugs without harm and recoup them subsequently. The "throat-hold" is used to prevent them from swallowing the drugs.

The issue is whether the evidence obtained under these circumstances is to be excluded under s. 24(2) of the Charter.

THE FACTS

Constables Rodine and Woods of the R.C.M.P. drug squad at Vancouver attended at Gibsons to assist the Gibsons detachment in dealing with a "heroin problem." They commenced a surveillance at 11:00 a.m. at the Ritz Motel. Ruby Collins and her husband Richard were observed moving their belongings from one room to another and going to and from a car parked in front of their room. The officers ceased their surveillance at noon.

At 2:50 p.m., the officers entered the Cedars Pub, where they observed Ruby Collins seated at a table with two other people. Richard Collins and another person joined the first group at 3:35 p.m. At 3:50 p.m., Richard Collins and one of the others left the pub, and the officers followed them. They arrested Richard Collins and the other man at a nearby trailer court. Richard Collins was searched and was found to be in possession of heroin.

The officers returned to the pub at 4:15 p.m. They observed Ruby Collins sitting with another woman at a different table. Constable Woods went directly to Ruby Collins. He testified:

> A: As I approached I quickened my pace. I then grabbed ahold of Mrs. Collins. At that time my impression was that she'd be under arrest. I grabbed her by the throat to prevent her from swallowing any evidence that may be there. In the process we had gone to the floor, taken her off the chair. We had gone to the floor. I observed her at that time move her hand away from her body. I observed a green item in that hand. It was clenched and just a piece of it was showing out. I asked her to open her hand and leave the item on the floor which she did and I subsequently seized a green balloon which had a knot on the top of it. I then picked Mrs. Collins from the floor, handcuffed her, and removed her outside.
>
> Q: Did you say anything to her at the time you seized her by the throat?
>
> A: Police officer. I stated that I was a police officer at that time.

The force used by Constable Woods was "considerable."

[†] [1987] 1 S.C.R. 265.

LEGISLATION

The search of Ruby Collins was purportedly authorized by s. 10(1) of the *Narcotic Control Act*, R.S.C. 1970, c. N-1, as amended, as that section read prior to the amendments of December, 1985....

. . . .

JURISDICTION

The trial judge's decision to exclude or not to exclude under s. 24(2) of the *Charter* is a question of law from which an appeal will generally lie: see *R. v. Therens* (1985), 18 C.C.C. (3d) 481, 18 D.L.R. (4th) 655, [1985] 1 S.C.R. 613, *per* Le Dain J. at p. 513 C.C.C., p. 687 D.L.R., p. 653 S.C.R....

THE LAW

The appellant seeks the exclusion of evidence that she was in possession of heroin, alleging that the heroin was discovered pursuant to a search which was unreasonable under s. 8 of the *Charter*. This court in *Therens, supra,* held that evidence cannot be excluded as a remedy under s. 24(1) of the *Charter*, but must meet the test of exclusion under s. 24(2). At first glance, the wording of s. 24 leads one to conclude that there are three prerequisites to the exclusion of evidence under s. 24(2) of the *Charter*.

(1) that the applicant's rights or freedoms, as guaranteed by the *Charter*, have been infringed or denied;
(2) that the evidence was obtained in a manner that infringed or denied any rights or freedoms guaranteed by the *Charter*, and
(3) that, having regard to all the circumstances, the admission of the evidence in the proceedings would bring the administration of justice into disrepute.

. . . .

THE REASONABLENESS OF THE SEARCH

The appellant, in my view, bears the burden of persuading the court that her *Charter* rights or freedoms have been infringed or denied.

. . . .

The appellant also bears the initial burden of presenting evidence. The standard of persuasion required is only the civil standard of the balance of probabilities, and, because of this, the allocation of the burden of persuasion means only that, in a case where the evidence does not establish whether or not the appellant's rights were infringed, the court must conclude that they were not.

. . . .

As a result, once the appellant has demonstrated that the search was a warrantless one, the Crown has the burden of showing that the search was, on a balance of probabilities, reasonable.

A search will be reasonable if it is authorized by law, if the law itself is reasonable and if the manner in which the search was carried out is reasonable. In this case, the Crown argued that the search was carried out under s. 10(1) of the *Narcotic Control Act.* As the appellant has not challenged the constitutionality of s. 10(1) of the Act, the issues that remain to be decided here are whether the search was unreasonable because the officer did not come within s. 10 of the Act, or whether, while being within s. 10, he carried out the search in a manner that made the search unreasonable.

For the search to be lawful under s. 10, the Crown must establish that the officer believed on reasonable grounds that there was a narcotic in the place where the person searched was found. The nature of the belief will also determine whether the manner in which the search was carried out was reasonable. For example, if a police officer is told by a reliable source that there are persons in possession of drugs in a certain place, the officer may, depending on the circumstances and the nature and precision of the information given by that source, search persons found in that place under s. 10, but surely, without very specific information, a seizure by the throat, as in this case, would be unreasonable. Of course, if he is lawfully searching a person whom he believes on reasonable grounds to be a "drug handler," then the "throat-hold" would not be unreasonable.

. . . .

However, before ordering a new trial, we must decide whether we agree with the trial judge and the Court of Appeal that the evidence of the heroin would be admissible regardless of the constable's grounds for the search, for there then would be no point in a new trial and we should dismiss the appeal. As a result, I must determine whether I would exclude the evidence under s. 24(2) on the assumption that Constable Woods testifies that he had not received any further information, thereby leaving matters in that regard as they stand at present on the record.

BRINGING THE ADMINISTRATION OF JUSTICE INTO DISREPUTE

On the record as it now stands, the appellant has established that the search was unreasonable and violated her rights under s. 8 of the *Charter*.

. . . .

[The question] is whether *the admission of the evidence* would bring the administration of justice into disrepute that is the applicable test. Misconduct by the police in the investigatory process often has some effect on the repute of the administration of justice, but s. 24(2) is not a remedy for police misconduct, requiring the exclusion of the evidence if, because of this misconduct, the administration of justice was brought into disrepute. Section 24(2) could well have been drafted in that way, but it was not. Rather, the [drafters] of the *Charter* decided to focus on the admission of the evidence in the proceedings, and the purpose of s. 24(2) is to prevent having the administration of justice brought into *further disrepute* by the admission of the evidence in the proceedings. This further disrepute will result from the admission of evidence that would deprive the accused for a fair hearing, or from judicial condonation of unacceptable conduct by the investigatory and prosecutorial agencies. It will also be necessary to consider any disrepute that may result from the exclusion of the evidence. It would be inconsistent with the purpose of s. 24(2) to exclude evidence if its exclusion would bring the administration of justice into greater disrepute than would its admission. Finally, it must be emphasized that even though the inquiry under s. 24(2) will necessarily focus on the specific prosecution, it is the long-term consequences of regular admission or exclusion of this type of evidence on the repute of the administration of justice which must be considered: see on this point Gibson, *ibid*, p. 245.

The concept of disrepute necessarily involves some element of community views, and the determination of disrepute thus requires the judge to refer to what he conceives to be the views of the community at large. This does not mean that evidence of the public's perception of the repute of the administration of justice, which Professor Gibson suggested could be presented in the form of public opinion polls (*supra*, pp. 236–47), will be determinative of the issue: see *Therens, supra,* pp. 653–4. The position is different with respect to obscenity, for example, where the court must assess the level of tolerance of the community, whether or not it is reasonable, and may consider public opinion polls: *R. v. Prairie Schooner News Ltd. and Powers* (1970), 1 C.C.C. (2d) 251 at p. 266, 12 Crim. L.Q. 462 at p. 477, 75 W.W.R. 585 at p. 599 (Man. C.A.), cited in *Towne Cinema Theatres Ltd. v. The Queen* (1985) 18 C.C.C. (3d) 193 at pp. 208–9, 18 D.L.R. (4th) 1 at p. 17, 1 S.C.R. 494 at p. 513. It would be unwise, in my respectful view, to adopt a similar attitude with respect to the *Charter*. Members of the public generally become conscious of the importance of protecting the rights and freedoms of accused only when they are in some way brought closer to the system either personally or through the experience of friends or family. Professor Gibson recognized the danger of leaving the exclusion of evidence to uninformed members of the public when he stated at p. 246: "The ultimate determination must be with the courts, because they provide what is often the only effective shelter for individuals and unpopular minorities from the shifting winds of public passion." The *Charter* is designed to protect the accused from the majority, so the enforcement of the *Charter* must not be left to that majority.

The approach I adopt may be put figuratively in terms of the reasonable person test proposed by Professor Yves-Marie Morissette in his article "The Exclusion of Evidence under the Canadian Charter of Rights and Freedoms: What to Do and What Not to Do," 29 McGill L.J. 521 at p. 538 (1984). In applying s. 24(2), he suggested that the relevant question is: "Would the admission of the evidence bring the administration of justice into disrepute in the eyes of the reasonable man, dispassionate and fully apprised of the circumstances of the case?" The reasonable person is usually the average person in the community, but only when that community's current mood is reasonable.

... The factors that the courts have most frequently considered include:

- what kind of evidence was obtained?
- what *Charter* right was infringed?
- was the *Charter* violation serious or was it of a merely technical nature?
- was it deliberate, wilful or flagrant, or was it inadvertent or committed in good faith?
- did it occur in circumstances of urgency or necessity?

- were there other investigatory techniques available?
- would the evidence have been obtained in any event?
- is the offence serious?
- is the evidence essential to substantiate the charge?
- are other remedies available?

I do not wish to be seen as approving this as an exhaustive list of the relevant factors, and I would like to make some general comments as regards these factors.

As a matter of personal preference, I find it useful to group the factors according to the way in which they affect the repute of the administration of justice. Certain of the factors listed are relevant in determining the effect of the admission of the evidence on the fairness of the trial. The trial is a key part of the administration of justice, and the fairness of Canadian trials is a major source of the repute of the system and is now a right guaranteed by s. 11(d) of the *Charter*. If the admission of the evidence in some way affects the fairness of the trial, then the admission of the evidence would *tend* to bring the administration of justice into disrepute and, subject to a consideration of the other factors, the evidence generally should be excluded.

It is clear to me, that the factors relevant to this determination will include the nature of the evidence obtained as a result of the violation and the nature of the right violated and not so much the manner in which the right was violated. Real evidence that was obtained in a manner that violated the *Charter* will rarely operate unfairly for that reason alone. The real evidence existed irrespective of the violation of the *Charter* and its use does not render the trial unfair. However, the situation is very different with respect to cases where, after a violation of the *Charter*, the accused is conscripted against himself through a confession or other evidence emanating from him. The use of such evidence would render the trial unfair, for it did not exist prior to the violation and it strikes at one of the fundamental tenets of a fair trial, the right against self-incrimination. Such evidence will generally arise in the context of an infringement of the right to counsel. Our decisions in *R. v. Therens* (1985), 18 C.C.C. (3d) 481, 18 D.L.R. (4th) 655, [1985] 1 S.C.R. 613, and *Clarkson v. The Queen* (1986), 25 C.C.C. (3d) 207, 26 D.L.R. (4th) 493, [1986] 1 S.C.R. 383, are illustrative of this. The use of self-incriminating evidence obtained following a denial of the right to counsel will, generally, go to the very fairness of the trial and should generally be excluded. Several Courts of Appeal have also emphasized this distinction between pre-existing real evidence and self-incriminatory evidence created following a breach of the *Charter*: see *R. v. Dumas* (1985), 23 C.C.C. (3d) 366, 41 Alta. L.R. (2d) 348, 66 A.R. 137 (Alta. C.A.); *R. v. Strachan* (1986), 24 C.C.C. (3d) 205, 25 D.L.R. (4th) 567, 49 C.R. (3d) 289 (B.C.C.A.), and *R. v. Dairy Supplies Ltd.*, Man. C.A. (January 13, 1987), unreported [since reported [1987] 2 W.W.R. 661, 44 Man. R. (2d) 275]. It may also be relevant, in certain circumstances, that the evidence would have been obtained in any event without the violation of the *Charter*.

There are other factors which are relevant to the seriousness of the *Charter* violation and thus to the disrepute that will result from judicial acceptance of evidence obtained through that violation. As Le Dain J. wrote in *Therens, supra*, at p. 512 C.C.C., p. 686 D.L.R., p. 652 S.C.R.:

> The relative seriousness of the constitutional violation has been assessed in the light of whether it was committed in good faith, or was inadvertent or of a merely technical nature, or whether it was deliberate, wilful or flagrant. Another relevant consideration is whether the action which constituted the constitutional violation was motivated by urgency or necessity to prevent the loss or destruction of the evidence.

I should add, that the availability of other investigatory techniques and the fact that the evidence could have been obtained without the violation of the *Charter* tend to render the *Charter* violation more serious. We are considering the actual conduct of the authorities and the evidence must not be admitted on the basis that they could have proceeded otherwise and obtained the evidence properly. In fact, their failure to proceed properly when that option was open to them tends to indicate a blatant disregard for the *Charter*, which is a factor supporting the exclusion of the evidence.

The final relevant group of factors consists of those that relate to the effect of excluding the evidence. The question under s. 24(2) is whether the system's repute will be better served by the admission or the exclusion of the evidence, and it is thus necessary to consider any disrepute that may result from the exclusion of the evidence. In my view, the administration of justice would be brought into disrepute by the exclusion of evidence essential to substantiate the charge, and thus the acquittal of the accused, because of a trivial breach of the *Charter*. Such disrepute would be greater if the offence was more serious. I would thus agree with Professor Morissette that evidence is more likely to be excluded if the offence is less serious (*supra*, pp. 529–31). I hasten to add, however, that if the admission of the evidence would result in an unfair trial, the seriousness of the offence could not render that evidence admissible. If any relevance is to be given to the seriousness of the offence in the context of the fairness of the trial, it operates in the opposite sense: the more serious the offence, the more damaging to the system's repute would be an unfair trial.

Finally, a factor which, in my view, is irrelevant is the availability of other remedies. Once it has been decided that the administration of justice would be brought into disrepute by the admission of the evidence, the disrepute will not be lessened by the existence of some ancillary remedy: see Gibson, *supra*, at p. 261.

. . . .

CONCLUSION

As discussed above, we must determine in this case whether the evidence should be excluded on the record as it stands at present.

The evidence obtained as a result of the search was real evidence, and, while prejudicial to the accused as evidence tendered by the Crown usually is, there is nothing to suggest that its use at the trial would render the trial unfair. In addition, it is true that the cost of excluding the evidence would be high: someone who was found guilty at trial of a relatively serious offence will evade conviction. Such a result could bring the administration of justice into disrepute. However, the administration of justice would be brought into greater disrepute, at least in my respectful view, if this court did not exclude the evidence and dissociate itself from the conduct of the police in this case which, always on the assumption that the officer merely had suspicions, was a flagrant and serious violation of the rights of an individual. Indeed, we cannot accept that police officers take flying tackles at people and seize them by the throat when they do not have reasonable and probable grounds to believe that those people are either dangerous or handlers of drugs. Of course, matters might well be clarified in this case if and when the police officer is offered at a new trial an opportunity to explain the grounds, if any, that he had for doing what he did. But if the police officer does not then disclose additional grounds for his behaviour, the evidence must be excluded.

I would allow the appeal and order a new trial.

■

Since *Collins*, the Court has begun to consider s. 24(2) applications using three broad headings: the fairness of the trial; the seriousness of the *Charter* breach; and the effect of exclusion upon the repute of the criminal justice system. The main consideration with respect to the fairness of the trial is the question of whether the evidence can be characterized as conscriptive or real, and in this regard, the conscriptive category has been enlarged to include any evidence whereby the accused was forced to provide evidence against her or himself, such as confessions or bodily samples, as well as real evidence derived from conscriptive evidence (*R. v. Burlingham*, *infra*, **Right to Counsel**), unless the Crown can prove on a balance of probabilities that it would have been obtained in any event (*R. v. Bartle*, *infra*, **Right to Counsel**). As well, another line of jurisprudence has directed the exclusion of real evidence where it would not and could not have been obtained without a *Charter* violation (*Simpson*, *supra*; *Mellenthin*, *supra*). Under the heading of seriousness of the violation, the court will look at whether someone's bodily integrity has been violated, whether circumstances of urgency render the violation less serious, and whether the police acted in good faith. Finally, the effect of exclusion on the criminal justice system must be assessed, having regard to the seriousness of the offence and the other evidence available to the Crown.

Even with this legal structure, s. 24(2) analyses tend to be quite fact specific. For example, it is difficult to predict how a court will assess the police claim to "good faith" belief regarding the legality of their conduct in the context of s. 24(2), adjudications. Compare, for example, the following cases. In *R. v. Sieben*, [1987] 1 S.C.R. 295, the Court declared that writs of assistance, blanket search warrants under s. 10(1)(a), and (3) of the *Narcotic Control Act* were invalid pursuant to s. 8 of the *Charter*. However, evidence gathered using the invalidated writs was not excluded under s. 24(2) in part because the officers entertained a good faith belief that the writs were valid, even though there was widespread legal analysis suggesting otherwise. In contrast, in *R. v. Pohoretsky*, [1987] 1 S.C.R. 945, the Court excluded a blood sample obtained prior to the introduction of the

Code provisions authorizing the extraction of blood samples in certain circumstances from an unconscious accident victim. Even though there were "reasonable grounds" to believe that the accused was intoxicated, the sample was excluded because "there [was] no suggestion that the police acted inadvertently or in good faith." In *Wong, supra*, where there was also no legislation purporting to authorize video surveillance, recall that the Court was prepared to find "good faith" on the part of the police. Can these cases be reconciled?

11

Compelling the Accused's Appearance in Court

A. ARREST

INTRODUCTION TO POWERS OF ARREST

Generally speaking, the legislative policy is to initiate the criminal process in the least intrusive fashion possible, providing that these less restrictive methods are sufficient to guarantee that the accused will respect the process.

The arrest aims to inform the accused unequivocally that the criminal process has commenced and ensures that she or he will be brought before the court to answer the charges. If the accused is arrested and not released on bail, she or he will be brought from incarceration directly to court to be arraigned. Arrest is the most drastic means of commencing the process, and the policy is that it should be used as a last resort (s. 507(4)). According to the Court in *R.* v. *Whitfield*, [1970] S.C.R. 46: "Arrest consists of the actual seizure or touching of a person's body with a view to his detention. The mere pronouncing of words of arrest is not an arrest, unless the person sought to be arrested submits to the process and goes with the arresting officer."

Police officers who observe a crime or who identify a suspect have several options. They may:

1. *Issue an appearance notice*: Under s. 496, an officer may issue an appearance notice for s. 553 offences, hybrids, and summary conviction offences. Under other sections, officers may also have the accused sign a recognizance or promise to appear (ss. 498 and 499). The contents of this notice are set out in s. 507, and the notice must be signed by the accused and a duplicate left with her or him. In order to commence the actual trial process an information must be laid and sworn before a justice of the peace before the date set for the accused's appearance in court (s. 505).

2. *Swear an information and apply for a summons or a warrant of arrest*: The officer may appear before a justice of the peace and swear out an information on oath (Form 2, *Criminal Code*). Under s. 504 or s. 788 (summary conviction offences) the party laying the information (it need not be a police officer) must allege reasonable grounds to believe that the accused has committed a named offence. The justice may hear witnesses and, if a case is made out, may issue either a summons (similar to an appearance notice — s. 509) or a warrant for the arrest of the accused if there are reasonable and probable

grounds to believe that it is necessary in the public interest to issue a warrant for the arrest of the accused (s. 507). See ss. 507, 508, 511 (contents of warrant) and 514 (execution of warrant).

3. *Arrest without warrant*: The general powers of arrest without warrant are set out in ss. 494 (for all persons) and 495 (for police officers).

Although s. 495(2) limits police powers to arrest without a warrant in certain circumstances, the Law Reform Commission of Canada has, in *Arrest* (Ottawa: LRCC, 1985), Working Paper 41 at 50–51 noted the illusory nature of the "duty not to arrest" given ss. 495(3):

> The direction not to arrest is deprived of any real potential for enforcement by subsection [495(3)] which in general provides that a police officer who arrests when he or she need not, in relation to one of these less serious offences, is nevertheless within the execution of his or her duty, as long as there exist grounds for arrest in accordance with the broad general powers for arrest without warrant described above. There may remain a possibility for civil suit against a police officer who arrests contrary to the statutory direction ... but it is cold comfort to a person who can be successfully charged with assaulting a peace officer in the execution of his duty, that he might have grounds to recover nominal damages in a civil action against the officer. Subsection [495(3)] almost turns subsection [495(2)] into a charade and no analogous provision must be allowed to appear in a reformed law of arrest.[†]

Similarly, police have considerable latitude over the decision not to arrest, absent any specific legislative provisions or directions from the Attorneys General.

RESISTING ARREST AND OBSTRUCTION

Section 495 (then s. 450) has been given a very wide reading by the Supreme Court of Canada in *R. v. Biron*. Law enforcement has been identified as a paramount policy concern, and the citizen's ability to challenge or resist police action has been significantly circumscribed, since it will be difficult to establish that an arrest was unlawful.

R. v. Biron[‡]

[MARTLAND, J.:]

This is an appeal, by leave of this Court, from the judgment of the Court of Appeal of the Province of Quebec, which, by a majority of two to one, allowed the appeal of the respondent, hereinafter referred to as "Biron," from his conviction on a charge of resisting a peace officer, contrary to what is now s. 118(*a*).

The charge related to resistance to an officer of the Montreal police force, Constable Dorion.

The facts which gave rise to this charge were as follows:

The Montreal police made an authorized raid on a Montreal bar on October 24, 1970. The raid was in search of illegal firearms and liquor. Biron was at the bar while the raid was taking place. He had been drinking. He refused to co-operate with the police, verbally abusing them and refusing to give his name.

Biron was arrested inside the restaurant by Constable Maisonneuve. He was led outside by Constable Gauthier for questioning. He was handed over by Constable Gauthier to Constables Dorion and Marquis, who took him to a police car. Subsequently, Constable Dorion tried to take him to the police wagon. Biron protested his arrest at this point and a scuffle with Constable Dorion occurred.

Biron was charged with creating a disturbance in a public place by shouting, contrary to s. 171(*a*)(i) of the *Code* (then s. 160(*a*)(i)). He was also charged with resisting a peace officer, as previously mentioned.

Section 171(*a*)(i) provides as follows:

---

† Source of Information: Department of Justice. Reproduced with the permission of the Minister of Public Works and Government Services Canada, 2002.
‡ [1976] 2 S.C.R. 56.

171. Every one who
(a) not being in a dwelling-house causes a disturbance in or near a public place,
  (i) by fighting, screaming, shouting, swearing, singing or using insulting or obscene language,

  ...

is guilty of an offence punishable on summary conviction.

Biron was convicted of both offences before a Judge of the Municipal Court. A trial *de novo* was held in respect of the s. 171(a)(i) offence. He was acquitted of "creating a disturbance by shouting" on the ground that there was no evidence he had been shouting as was alleged in the information.

Biron appealed the s. 118 (a) conviction to the Quebec Court of Appeal. By a two to one majority, the appeal was allowed and Biron was acquitted.

The question in issue is as to whether the charge against Biron of resisting Dorion in the execution of his duty must fail because of his successful appeal from his conviction under s. 171(a)(i) for causing a disturbance.

It is contended on behalf of Biron that he could not be so convicted because he was not under lawful arrest, and so was entitled to resist Dorion's efforts to take him to the patrol wagon. It is argued that he had not been lawfully arrested because Maisonneuve's right to arrest him for a summary conviction offence had to be based on s. 450(1)(b) [rep. & sub. R.S.C. 1970, c. 2 (2nd Supp.), s. 5] of the *Code* which provides that:

450(1) A peace officer may arrest without warrant

  ...

(b) a person whom he finds committing a criminal offence,

It is submitted by the respondent that Maisonneuve did not find him committing a criminal offence because he was acquitted on the charge laid against him. Reliance is placed on the judgment of the Court of Appeal for Saskatchewan in *A.-G. Sask.* v. *Pritchard* (1961), 130 C.C.C. 61, 35 C.R. 150, 34 W.W.R. 458.

Paragraph (a) of s. 450(1) permits a peace officer to arrest without a warrant:

(a) a person who has committed an indictable offence or who, on reasonable and probable grounds, he believes has committed or is about to commit an indictable offence,

This paragraph, limited in its application to indictable offences, deals with the situation in which an offence has already been committed or is expected to be committed. The peace officer is not present at its commission. He may have to rely upon information received from others. The paragraph therefore enables him to act on his belief, if based on reasonable and probable grounds.

Paragraph (b) applies in relation to any criminal offence and it deals with the situation in which the peace officer himself finds an offence being committed. His power to arrest is based upon his own observation. Because it is based on his own discovery of an offence actually being committed there is no reason to refer to a belief based upon reasonable and probable grounds.

If the reasoning in the *Pritchard* case is sound, the validity of an arrest under s. 450(1)(b) can only be determined after the trial of the person arrested and after the determination of any subsequent appeals. My view is that the validity of an arrest under this paragraph must be determined in relation to the circumstances which were apparent to the peace officer at the time the arrest was made.

This was the view of the Court of Appeal in England in *Wiltshire* v. *Barrett*, [1965] 2 All E.R. 271, when interpreting a provision of the *Road Traffic Act*, 1960 (U.K.) c. 16. Section 6(1) of that Act made it an offence for a person who, when driving or attempting to drive a motor vehicle on a road or other public place, is unfit to drive through drink or drugs.

Subsection (4) of s. 6 provided:

6(4) A police constable may arrest without warrant a person committing an offence under this section.

The case was a civil action for assault and wrongful arrest. The plaintiff's car had been overtaken and stopped by the police. A constable sought to arrest the plaintiff, who resisted by remaining in his car. He was removed after a struggle and taken to the police station. He was examined by the police doctor, who concluded that he was not unfit to drive. He was then released. No further action was taken against him. Subsequently he sued the police constable who had arrested him.

Lord Denning, M.R., said, at pp. 273–4:

Counsel for the plaintiff submitted that this section only empowered a constable to arrest a person who was actually committing an offence under the section; and, accordingly, that the constable was only justified if he could prove that the person was *in fact guilty*; whereas counsel for the defendant submitted that a constable was entitled to arrest any person who was *apparently* committing an offence; and, accordingly, the constable was justified so long as it *appeared to him* that the man was unfit through drink, even though the man should afterwards be found to be *not guilty*. This question has to be answered by examining the contents of this particular statute; see *Barnard* v. *Gorman*, [1941] 3 All E.R. 45 at pp. 50, 51; [1941] A.C. 378 at p. 387.... [T]his statute is concerned with the safety of all of Her Majesty's subjects who use the roads in this country. It is of the first importance that any person, who is unfit to drive through drink, should not be allowed to drive on the road; and that the police should have power to stop him from driving any further. The most effective way to do it is by arresting him then and there. The police have to act at once, on the facts *as they appear* on the spot; and they should be justified by the facts as they appear to them at the time and not on any ex post facto analysis of the situation. Their conduct should not be condemned as unlawful simply because a jury afterwards acquit the driver....

. . . .

It was said that this section expressly empowered arrest on reasonable suspicion. If Parliament intended a like power under s. 6, surely they would have expressed it in like language. But I think that different considerations apply. Section 217 deals with offences where the power of arrest may be exercised some time after the offence has been committed. It may be based, not on the constable's own observation, but on information received from others; whereas s. 6 deals with offences where the power of arrest is to be exercised at the very time when a person is committing the offence, or very soon afterwards. So much so that the constable acts on his own observation. Naturally enough there is a difference in language.

My conclusion is that, on the true construction of s. 6(4), a constable is justified in arresting the driver of a motor car if the driver was *apparently committing* an offence under the section.

In my opinion, this reasoning can properly be applied to the interpretation of s. 450(1)(*b*). It is true that the *Wiltshire* case was a civil action for damages, but it necessitated the judicial interpretation of a statutory provision which is substantially the same. There being no English equivalent of s. 25 of the *Criminal Code* to provide the constable with protection from suit, he could only escape from civil liability for damages if he could establish that he was entitled to make the arrest. His power to arrest without warrant arose in respect of "a person committing an offence under this section." The Court held that he was justified in making the arrest if the person arrested was apparently committing the offence.

In the *Wiltshire* case the statutory provision involved the power to arrest without a warrant a person unfit to drive because of drink or drugs and the Court referred to the public importance of an arrest being promptly made in such circumstances. Paragraph (*b*) of s. 450(1) deals with the power to arrest without a warrant a person found committing any criminal offence. It is certainly of public importance that the peace officer should be able to exercise this power promptly.

If the words "committing a criminal offence" are to be construed in the manner indicated in the *Pritchard* case, para. (*b*) becomes impossible to apply. The power of arrest which that paragraph gives has to be exercised promptly, yet, strictly speaking, it is impossible to say that an offence is committed until the party arrested has been found guilty by the Courts. If this is the way in which this provision is to be construed, no peace officer can ever decide, when making an arrest without a warrant, that the person arrested is "committing a criminal offence." In my opinion the wording used in para. (*b*), which is over simplified, means that the power to arrest without a warrant is given where the peace officer himself finds a situation in which a person is apparently committing an offence.

In the present case, Constable Maisonneuve observed an apparent offence being committed by Biron. That he was justified in so thinking is shown by the fact that, at trial, Biron was convicted of the offence of causing a disturbance, and that his appeal from conviction resulted from the fact that the information charged only causing a disturbance "by shouting," which "shouting" the Judge on appeal found was not established by the evidence.

In my opinion, the arrest of Biron by Maisonneuve was lawful, and, consequently, the resistance offered by Biron to Dorion constituted an offence.

[LASKIN, C.J.C. (dissenting):]

. . . .

The issues in this appeal have a background that must be explained. The accused was charged with two offences following a raid by the police on certain restaurant premises in which he was arrested. The arrest was made by Constable Maisonneuve, and another constable, one Gauthier, led the accused to a police car for interrogation. Then he was taken to a police wagon by Constable Dorion, who had a grip on the accused, and by another constable. The accused offered resistance, causing Dorion to fall, but the accused also fell, sustaining severe facial injuries. The two charges laid against the accused were (1) causing a disturbance in or near a public place by shouting in the restaurant, contrary to what is now s. 171(*a*)(i) of the *Criminal Code*; and (2) resisting a peace officer, Dorion, in the execution of his duty, the resistance being offered in front of the restaurant, contrary to what is now s. 118(*a*) of the *Criminal Code*.

Whether the accused was guilty of an offence under s. 118(*a*) depends in this case on whether he was under lawful arrest. I do not question, despite the contentions of counsel for the respondent accused, that the accused offered resistance to Dorion; it was not, however, suggested that it was of such a character as to amount in itself to the use of excessive force. There was, however, but one arrest, that effected by Maisonneuve in the restaurant; there was no suggestion of any release and rearrest. The issue turns therefore on its lawfulness. We are not concerned in this case with a constable's own responsibility or liability for effecting an allegedly unlawful arrest. It is to that that provisions such as s. 25 of the *Criminal Code* are addressed. I would find it astonishing that a provision concerned with a constable's criminal or other responsibility, and which immunizes him in specified circumstances in respect of an arrest that he has made, should become the vehicle for providing a basis upon which an accused may himself be convicted of resisting the arrest. To do that is to turn a protective provision, a shield for the constable into a sword against an accused by treating the protection as an expansion of the powers of arrest given by what is now s. 450 [rep. & sub. R.S.C. 1970, c. 2 (2nd Supp.), s. 5], of the *Criminal Code*.

The particular provision of s. 450, which is of relevance here is s-s. (1)(*b*), authorizing a peace officer to arrest without a warrant "a person whom he finds committing a criminal offence." Maisonneuve arrested the accused without a warrant and the charge laid in respect of that arrest was causing a disturbance by shouting under the now s. 171(*a*). It turns out that no such offence was committed at the time and place, and the arrest therefor was, *qua* the accused, unlawful. So far as the constable was concerned, his unlawful conduct was protected under s. 25. I repeat that the protection of the constable did not make the arrest lawful *qua* the accused. There are some cases which seem so to say. *R.* v. *Shore* (1960), 129 C.C.C. 70, and *R.* v. *Dand*, [1965] 4 C.C.C. 366, 53 W.W.R. 302, both judgments of the British Columbia Court of Appeal, are in that class.

The *Shore* case can stand on the finding that the police officer who made the arrest was empowered so to do under the provincial liquor statute, which authorized an arrest without warrant of a person found intoxicated in a public place. The reference in that case to s. 25 of the *Criminal Code*, in the bare narrative of its terms, seems to have been gratuitous but, if not, and if in context it was relied upon to support the power of arrest, I would regard the *Shore* case to be wrongly decided. The *Dand* case indicates that this last-mentioned view of the *Shore* case is the one that the British Columbia Court of Appeal took, and hence I hold the *Dand* case should similarly be overruled.

It seems to me that the British Columbia Court of Appeal later dissociated itself from the *Shore* and *Dand* cases by its decisions in *R.* v. *Klat*, [1969] 2 C.C.C. 129, 5 C.R.N.S. 136, 66 W.W.R. 339, and *R.* v. *Cottam and Cottam*, [1970] 1 C.C.C. 117, 7 C.R.N.S. 179, 69 W.W.R. 76, but, having regard to my opinion that those first-mentioned cases were wrongly decided on the point under discussion, I need not embark upon any close examination of the *Klat* and *Cottam* cases to see whether relevant distinctions are open. In the *Klat* case, reliance was placed upon the judgment of the Saskatchewan Court of Appeal in *A.-G. Sask.* v. *Pritchard* (1961), 130 C.C.C. 61, 35 C.R. 150, 34 W.W.R. 458, and I am of the opinion that Culliton, C.J.S., stated the law correctly, as it applies here, in the last paragraph of his reasons as follows (at pp. 65–6 C.C.C., p. 154 C.R.):

> While a Peace Officer has no right to arrest without a warrant a person he finds committing an offence unless an offence was in fact committed, nevertheless, even if the officer was in error in so arresting, if he acted on reasonable and probable grounds, he is given protection under s. 25 of the *Code*.

In short, the position of a person accused of an offence founded upon an allegedly lawful arrest which turns out to have been unlawful is one thing; the position of the arresting officer as a possible accused in a criminal prosecution or as a defendant in a civil suit arising out of the arrest is an entirely different thing: see *Frey* v. *Fedoruk* (1950), 97 C.C.C. 1, [1950] 3 D.L.R. 513, [1950] S.C.R. 517.

The reasoning and judgment of the English Court of Appeal in *Wiltshire* v. *Barrett*, [1965] 2 All E.R. 271, have no application to this case. It was a civil action for damages against a constable for assault and wrongful arrest, not a criminal prosecution, as here, against an accused person for resisting a peace officer in the execution of his duty. The *Wiltshire* case involved a provision of the English *Road Traffic Act, 1960*, which prohibited a person, on pain of fine or imprisonment, from driving or attempting to drive a motor vehicle on a road or other public place when he was unfit to drive through drink or drugs. This prohibition, in s. 6(1), was fortified by s. 6(4) which empowered a police constable to arrest without warrant a person committing the aforesaid offence. There was no such provision in the *Road Traffic Act, 1960* as s. 25 of the *Criminal Code*, which provides justification for a police constable when acting on reasonable and probable grounds. Hence, when the issue arose in *Wiltshire* as to protection of the constable from civil suit if he overstepped the literal command of s. 6(4), the Court there looked to statutory purpose and context and interpreted "committing" in s. 6(4) to mean "apparently committing," so as to make it immaterial whether the arrested person be found not guilty of the offence for which he was arrested without warrant. As Lord Denning put it (at p. 275 of the report) it is enough if the arrested person reasonably appeared to the constable to be committing an offence under the Act.

The position taken in *Wiltshire*, in the context of principle which I support, is well put by Salmon, L.J. (at p. 281 of [1965] 2 All E.R.), as follows:

> The first point raised by counsel for the plaintiff is one of importance and some difficulty. He contends that, in order for the arrest to be lawful, the person arrested must in fact be guilty of the offence; no matter how drunk he may appear to have been when arrested, he has an irrefutable claim for damages for false imprisonment if he is subsequently acquitted of being unfit to drive through drink. This argument is founded on the language of s. 6(4) of the Road Traffic Act, 1960. It is in this subsection that the power to arrest must be found, for the offence in question is a misdemeanor and not a felony and, accordingly, there is no common law power of arrest without warrant. The subsection reads: "A police constable may arrest without warrant a person committing an offence under this section." Clearly on a literal construction of these words there is much force in the contention of counsel for the plaintiff. He relies on the well established principle that any statute which impinges on the liberty of the subject should be strictly construed against the Crown; see *Bowditch* v. *Balchin* (1850), 5 Exch. 378. I agree that it is of great importance that nothing should be done which could in any way weaken that general principle. Moreover, if the legislature intends to give a police constable power to arrest without warrant on reasonable suspicion, it should do so in plain and unambiguous language which anyone can understand; see *Ledwith* v. *Roberts*, [1936] 3 All E.R. at p. 593. It is our duty to apply those principles and to give the language of this subsection its natural meaning if possible, but none the less in the end to give it its appropriate construction according to its context and the subject-matter with which it deals: ... I entirely agree with my lords that these considerations lead irresistibly to our construing the word "committing" as "apparently committing." This must have been the intention of Parliament. I reach this conclusion for the same reasons as my lords, which are the same as those which commended themselves to this court construing similar language in a similar Act in *Trebeck* v. *Croudace*, [1918] 1 K.B. 158. The very nature of the offence requires this construction.

This passage indicates how far removed the *Wiltshire* case [is] from the present one, how different is a civil suit against a constable charged with enforcing road traffic legislation, from a criminal prosecution against an accused person for resisting an unlawful arrest in respect of which the constable is given express protection from criminal and civil liability if he acted on reasonable and probable grounds: see also *R.* v. *Dean* [1966] 3 C.C.C. 228, 1 O.R. 592, 47 C.R. 311.

There is a further point that merits emphasis. If the word "apparently" is to be read into s. 450(1)(*b*), logical consistency, if not also ordinary canons of construction, demand that the word be read into s. 449(1)(*a*) [s. 449 rep. & sub. *idem.*] which empowers any person to arrest without warrant a person whom he "finds committing" an indictable offence. Moreover, it is plain to me, on grounds of context in aid of construction, that when s. 449(1)(*a*) is read with s. 499(1)(*b*), the former could not possibly embrace arrest without warrant on apparency or on reasonable and probable grounds. Further, reasonable and probable grounds for an arrest without warrant govern s. 450(1)(*a*) and s. 450(1)(*c*) but the words are excluded from s. 450(1)(*b*), and I see no textual or policy justification for reading them or the equivalent term "apparently" into s. 450(1)(*b*).

Of course, as Kaufman, J.A., points out in his reasons, a constable's lot is a heavy and even unenviable one when he has to make an on-the-spot decision as to an arrest. But he may be overzealous as well as mistaken, and it may be too that when a charge or charges come to be laid, the Crown attorney or other advising counsel may mistake the grounds and thus lay a charge which does not support the arrest. We cannot go on a guessing expedition out of regret for an innocent mistake or a wrong-headed assessment. Far more important, however, is the social and legal, and indeed political, principle upon which our criminal law is based, namely, the right of an individual to be left alone, to be free of private or public restraint, save as the law provides otherwise. Only to the extent to which it so provides can a person be detained or his freedom of movement arrested.

The position as it relates to resistance to unlawful arrest was established at common law as early as 1709 in *R. v. Tooley et al.* (1709), 2 Ld. Raym. 1296, 92 E.R. 349, and has been reaffirmed time and again: see, for example, *R. v. Curvan* (1826), 1 Mood. 131, 168 E.R. 1213; *R. v. Wilson*, [1955] 1 All E.R. 744, at p. 745, referring also to the qualification of the use of excessive force in resisting. It has been part of our criminal law from the beginning and is reflected in the provisions of the *Criminal Code*, which has sought to balance the competing interests in freedom and order by giving the peace officer protection in specified circumstances where he has exceeded his authority to make an arrest. Our law has not, as I understand it, deprived the citizen of his right to resist unlawful arrest. His resistance may be at his own risk if the arrest proves to be lawful, but so too must the police officer accept the risk of having effected [an unlawful] arrest. Of course, even if the resisted arrest is unlawful, the person resisting may still become culpable if he uses excessive force.

■

After *Biron*, when can you lawfully resist arrest by a police officer? What action is open to a citizen who thinks they are being unlawfully arrested? What might a third-party witness or lawyer do? In *Carr v. Gauthier* (1992), 97 D.L.R. (4th) 651 (Alta. Q.B.), the plaintiff (a lawyer) entered a police car, without permission, to advise his son, who had been unlawfully arrested (as it was subsequently determined). The court held that the client's *Charter* right to retain and instruct counsel forthwith did not create a corollary or derivative right in the counsel retained to provide that service. Additionally, the false arrest of the client did not afford a defence to the lawyer for a charge of obstruction.

In *R. v. Moore*, [1979] 1 S.C.R. 195, the Supreme Court of Canada further expanded the police statutory powers under s. 495 (then s. 450). The Court held that the police have the right to arrest and charge under s. 129 for failure to give one's name and address when asked, if the officer has witnessed the commission of even a provincial summary conviction offence. Note that nowhere in the *Criminal Code* or provincial legislation was there stipulated a duty on the part of citizens to give such information to an officer if not under arrest: Alan Grant, "*Moore v. The Queen*: A Substantive, Procedural and Administrative Nightmare" (1979) 17 Osgoode Hall L.J. 459. For one of the most far-reaching applications of *Moore* see *R. v. Pati* (1991), 118 Alta. R. 78 (Prov. Ct.), wherein the accused was arrested without a warrant for refusing to give his name and address where he was apparently violating a municipal by-law regulating noise.

In contrast, in *R. v. Waugh*, [1995] O.J. No. 3068, online: QL, the Ontario Court of Justice (General Division) held that there was no obligation on the accused to identify himself to a police officer with respect to an *Airport Traffic Regulation* offence, and thus acquitted the accused of obstruction. In *R. v. Smith*, [1996] O.J. No. 988 (Ont. Ct. Just. (Prov. Div.)), online: QL, the court held that there was no power to arrest an accused for failing to identify himself under the *Trespass to Property Act* (Ontario), and thus the accused was acquitted of assault with intent to resist arrest.

The Court in *R. v. Macooh* (1993), 16 C.R.R. (2d) 1 (S.C.C.) has expanded the powers of warrantless arrest further by holding that a police officer in "hot pursuit" of someone found committing a provincial offence may enter a private dwelling house to effect the arrest. In *R. v. Godoy, supra*, the Court held that police have the right to enter forcibly a dwelling house to respond to a 911 if entry is necessary to ensure that the distressed caller receives the needed assistance. The subsequent arrest of the accused was valid in law because the officers heard the woman's crying, noted her injured condition, and recorded her statement, thus establishing reasonable and probable grounds to effect a warrantless arrest. In *R. v. Feeney*, [1997] 2 S.C.R. 13, however, the Court held that police cannot enter a dwelling house to effect a warrantless arrest unless they are in hot pursuit. It was also stated that even when holding a warrant for arrest, officers must also obtain judicial authorization to enter a dwelling house and must announce entry prior to entering with force. See now ss. 529, 529.1 of the *Code*, as well as s. 529.3, which permits warrantless entry to arrest to prevent imminent bodily harm or death or the imminent loss or destruction of evidence related to an indictable offence, if it is not practicable to request authorization by reason of exigent circumstances.

Judicial interpretations have tended to expand these statutory arrest powers on the policy grounds that wider powers are necessary to protect public safety and to immunize police from the repercussions of errors in judgment (see also *M.R.M.*, *supra*, **Search and Seizure**, for comparable expansive interpretation). Do you agree? In addition to the immunity provided by s. 25 to officers, an accused who resists police action is vulnerable to being charged under s. 129 or s. 270 (obstruction of a peace officer or assault on a peace officer). For a case in which an obstruction charge failed because the court found no basis for the arrest and thus held that the police officer was not acting in the execution of duty, see: *R.* v. *Terrigno* (1995), 175 A.R. 100 (Prov. Ct.). Only if the arrest is subsequently characterized as unlawful may the police officer's actions not be protected by s. 25, and an action for false imprisonment or trespass possibly succeed.

THE *CHARTER* AND ARREST: SS. 9 AND 10

The *Charter* prohibits arbitrary detention, which includes arrest in this context. An accused can, therefore, argue that, for example, her warrantless arrest was unlawful pursuant to s. 495(1)(a) because it was based solely upon a hunch rather than reasonable grounds, rendering it arbitrary within the meaning of s. 9: *R.* v. *Duguay* (1985), 46 C.C.C. (3d)1 (Ont. C.A.). Note that the Ontario Court of Appeal has also held that a s. 495 arrest does not become "unlawful" simply because the police have failed to fulfill the duty not to arrest in s. 495(2); a lawful arrest made in contravention of that duty can only be characterized as arbitrary if it is "capricious, despotic or unjustifiable": *R.* v. *Cayer* (1988), 28 O.A.C. 105. Why might such an argument be difficult to make successfully?

Once detained or arrested, an accused under s. 10(a) has the right to be informed of the reasons therefor and, under s. 10(b), the right to retain and instruct counsel without delay and to be advised of that right. Section 10(c) guarantees the right to test the lawfulness of arrest or detention by way of *habeas corpus*.

B. DETENTION

INTRODUCTION TO POWERS OF DETENTION

Police powers to detain, short of arrest, have begun to be defined through *Charter* litigation. These powers may be implicit or explicit in legislation, or they may be recognized through the common law. In *Therens*, set out below, the Court began to define the parameters of "detention," which in turn shapes the application of ss. 9 and 10 of the *Charter*.

The case raised the issue of whether a demand by a police officer pursuant to s. 235(1) (now s. 254 of the *Code*) to accompany the officer to the police station for the purpose of providing a breathalyzer sample amounts to a "detention" within s. 10 of the *Charter* so as to trigger the rights provided in that section, such as the right to counsel.

Le Dain J.'s opinion, although a dissent on other issues, provided the majority interpretation on this point. Is Estey J.'s "reasoning" satisfactory? What about the result? For further discussion, see Don Stuart, "Four Springboards from the Supreme Court of Canada: *Hunter*, *Therens*, *Motor Vehicle Reference* and *Oakes* — Asserting Basic Values of Our Criminal Justice System" (1987) 12 Queen's L.J. 133.

R. v. Therens[†]

[LE DAIN, J.:]

The purpose of s. 10 of the *Charter* is to ensure that in certain situations a person is made aware of the right to counsel and is permitted to retain and instruct counsel without delay. The situations specified by s. 10 — arrest and detention — are obviously not the only ones in which a person may reasonably require the assistance of counsel, but they are situations in which the restraint of liberty might otherwise effectively prevent access to counsel or induce a person to assume that he or she is unable to retain and instruct counsel. In its use of the word "detention," s. 10 of the *Charter* is directed to a restraint of liberty other than arrest in which a person may reasonably require the assistance of counsel but might be prevented or impeded from retaining and instructing counsel without delay but for the constitutional guarantee.

In addition to the case of deprivation of liberty by physical constraint, there is, in my opinion, a detention within s. 10 of the *Charter* when a police officer or other agent of the State assumes control over the movement of a person by a demand or direction which may have significant legal consequence and which prevents or impedes access to counsel.

. . . .

... There can be no doubt that there must be some form of compulsion or coercion to constitute an interference with liberty or freedom of action that amounts to a detention within the meaning of s. 10 of the *Charter*. The issue, as I see it, is whether that compulsion need be of a physical character, or whether it may also be a compulsion of a psychological or mental nature which inhibits the will as effectively as the application, or threat of application, of physical force. The issue is whether a person who is the subject of a demand or direction by a police officer or other agent of the State may reasonably regard himself or herself as free to refuse to comply.

A refusal to comply with a s. 235(1) demand without reasonable excuse is, under s. 235(2), a criminal offence. It is not realistic to speak of a person who is liable to arrest and prosecution for refusal to comply with a demand which a peace officer is empowered by statute to make as being free to refuse to comply. The criminal liability for refusal to comply constitutes effective compulsion. This psychological compulsion or coercion effected by the consequence of a refusal to comply with a s. 235(1) demand appears to be what Laskin J. (as he then was) had in mind in *Hogan* v. *The Queen* (1974), 18 C.C.C. (2d) 65 at p. 74, 48 D.L.R. (3d) 427 at p. 436, [1975] 2 S.C.R. 574 at p. 587, where he said:

> There is no doubt, therefore, that the accused was "detained" within the meaning of s. 2(c)(ii) of the *Canadian Bill of Rights*; he risked prosecution under s. 235(2) if, without reasonable excuse, he refused the demand which involved accompanying the peace officer to fulfil it.

Any criminal liability for failure to comply with a demand or direction of a police officer must be sufficient to make compliance involuntary. This would be true, for example, of compliance where refusal to comply would amount to a wilful obstruction of a police officer in the execution of his or her duty, contrary to s. 118 of the *Criminal Code*.

Although it is not strictly necessary for purposes of this case, I would go further. In my opinion, it is not realistic, as a general rule, to regard compliance with a demand or direction by a police officer as truly voluntary, in the sense that the citizen feels that he or she has the choice to obey or not, even where there is in fact a lack of statutory or common law authority for the demand or direction and therefore an absence of criminal liability for failure to comply with it. Most citizens are not aware of the precise legal limits of police authority. Rather than risk the application of physical force or prosecution for wilful obstruction, the reasonable person is likely to err on the side of caution, assume lawful authority and comply with the demand. The element of psychological compulsion, in the form of a reasonable perception of suspension of freedom of choice, is enough to make the restraint of liberty involuntary. Detention may be effected without the application or threat of application of physical restraint if the person concerned submits or acquiesces in the deprivation of liberty and reasonably believes that the choice to do otherwise does not exist.

For these reasons I am of the opinion that the s. 235(1) demand to accompany the police officer to a police station and to submit to a breathalyzer test

[†] [1985] 1 S.C.R. 613.

resulted in the detention of the respondent within the meaning of s. 10 of the *Charter*.

The respondent was accordingly entitled at the time of his detention to be informed of his right to retain and instruct counsel without delay, and there was an infringement or denial of this right....

[Estey J.'s judgment provided the majority opinion on the question of exclusion of the results of the breathalyzer under s. 24(2). Without any supporting reasoning or evidence, he stated at 125:]

... Here the police authority has flagrantly violated a *Charter* right without any statutory authority for so doing. Such an overt violation as occurred here must, in my view, result in the rejection of evidence thereby obtained. We are here dealing only with direct evidence or evidence thereby obtained directly and I leave to another day any consideration of evidence thereby indirectly obtained. To do otherwise than reject this evidence on the facts and circumstances in this appeal would be to invite police officers to disregard *Charter* rights of the citizen and to do so with an assurance of impunity. If s. 10(*b*) of the *Charter of Rights* can be offended without any statutory authority for the police conduct here in question and without the loss of admissibility of evidence obtained by such a breach then s. 10(*b*) would be stripped of any meaning and would have no place in the catalogue of "legal rights" found in the *Charter*.

The violation by the police authority of a fundamental *Charter* right, which transpired here, will render this evidence inadmissible. Admitting this evidence under these circumstances would clearly "bring the administration of justice into disrepute." I am strongly of the view that it would be most improvident for this Court to expatiate, in these early days of life with the *Charter of Rights*, upon the meaning of the expression "administration of justice" and particularly its outer limits. There will no doubt be, over the years to come, a gradual build-up in delineation and definition of the words used in the *Charter* in s. 24(2).

■

R. v. Grafe†

[KREVER, J.:]

At approximately 6:40 p.m. on 1st May 1986, Constables Kalan and Waite, on routine patrol in their cruiser, were driving along King Street in the downtown area of the city of Kitchener. It was daylight. The respondent and another person were walking on the sidewalk on King Street. After passing the respondent, Constable Kalan, the driver of the cruiser, looked in the rear-view mirror and noticed, in his words, that these two persons "continually stared at the cruiser, watched it travel down the road." Constable Kalan turned the car around and, as he drove towards the respondent and the other person, he noticed that they were continuing to watch the cruiser as it approached. This behaviour seemed to Constable Kalan "something not quite kosher," and he concluded that the two persons were acting suspiciously. When Constable Kalan drew the pair to the attention of Constable Waite, she too, because of their staring, concluded that they were acting in a suspicious manner.

What occurred next is not entirely clear. According to Constable Kalan, he pulled the cruiser over, got out of the vehicle, went over to the two persons, who were then standing on the sidewalk on King Street, and asked them for their names. The respondent responded that his name was Peter Grafe, born 25th July 1965, with an address of 111 Hoffman Street, apartment 5. In cross-examination Constable Kalan repeated that it was his recollection that the first verbal contact with the respondent occurred after the officers had got out of the cruiser, but agreed that it was possible that one of the officers had said something to the two persons from the vehicle.

It was Constable Waite's evidence that she and Constable Kalan pulled up beside the two persons in the cruiser and got out of the car, and Constable Waite then "asked them for their information." In cross-examination, Constable Waite agreed that it was possible that, prior to getting out of the car, she rolled down the window and said something to the respondent and the other person.

The respondent, who testified on the voir dire or on what his counsel characterized as "a s. 24(1) [of the *Canadian Charter of Rights and Freedoms*]

---

† (1987), 22 O.A.C. 280.

application," gave quite a different version of the occurrence. It was his evidence that, after the officers stopped the vehicle on King Street, Constable Waite rolled down her window, and, speaking to the respondent and his companion, said, "Youse guys, would you please come over here?" The other person gave Constable Waite his name and the respondent gave her the name of his brother, Peter Grafe. At no time, according to the respondent, did either officer get out of their car, and no conversation occurred between the two persons and Constable Kalan. In repeating his version of the event [in] the cross-examination, the respondent agreed that the "officer politely asked [him] to come over and [he] went over and spoke to her."

On 1st May 1986 there was outstanding a warrant authorizing the arrest of the respondent in respect of an unpaid fine in the amount of $103, resulting from a conviction on an earlier occasion for trespassing. In the light of the misidentification by the respondent in using his brother's name, a computer search by Constable Kalan did not of course, reveal the existence of the outstanding warrant. Later in the evening, however, Constable Kalan discovered the true state of affairs, located the respondent and arrested him on the strength of the outstanding warrant. The propriety of that arrest is not an issue in this appeal. Arising out of this later involvement with the police was the respondent's statement to Constable Kalan, to which no objection is or was taken, that his reason for identifying himself as his brother earlier in the evening was that he had thought he had an outstanding fine. As a result, the personation charge was laid.

Before turning to the legal issue involved in this appeal, two other references to the evidence must be made. In his cross-examination of Constable Kalan, counsel for the respondent elicited the evidence that after the first discussion with the respondent and his companion, during which the respondent misidentified himself, he permitted the two to go their way, and that, had the respondent and the other person run away on being approached by the officers, he would have done nothing, because, to use his words, "I had nothing to — nothing that I could hold them with or to detain them on." Finally, although, as I have indicated, the respondent testified on the "s. 24(1) application," at no time did he suggest that in the first discussion with the police officers he felt under restraint or compulsion or that he was being detained.

. . . .

Was the respondent "detained" when first approached by Constables Kalan and Waite? It will be observed that the trial judge was of the view that the resolution of the respondent's Charter rights did not depend on the determination of the question whether the police officers summoned the respondent to the cruiser or whether they approached him on foot before requesting him to identify himself. Whether it can be said that a person has been detained on any given occasion depends on the circumstances at that time. There is no simple test. The criteria to which courts have referred include demand or direction as opposed to request, language used and tone of voice, compulsion, including psychological compulsion, and, it seems to me, place of contact.

. . . .

In this case, the trial judge concluded that the respondent had "perceived that there was a compulsion to answer the question that was put to him." Since the respondent did not testify that that was so, that conclusion must have been an inference which the trial judge drew. I do not draw the same inference. In any event, the evidence does not support a finding that the respondent reasonably believed that he was detained. His conversation with the police occurred on the sidewalk of a downtown city street in daylight. The respondent was not required to sit in the back seat of the cruiser. On the respondent's own evidence, the police officers treated him politely and used language of courtesy. The discussion was of short duration and the respondent left when it ended. The police officers could do nothing if the respondent had refused to talk to them, because, again in Constable Kalan's words, "I had nothing to — nothing I could hold them with or detain them on." In the light of the reasoning and result in *R.* v. *Moran,* [released August 27, 1987], where the inconvenience to the accused was considerably greater than that experienced by the respondent, it is impossible to characterize the respondent's condition during the conversation as one of detention.

The *Charter* does not seek to insulate all members of society from all contact with constituted authority no matter how trivial the contact may be. When one considers the full range of contacts in modern society between state and citizen, that which took place between the respondent and Constables Kalan and Waite on the first occasion cannot be characterized otherwise than as innocuous. Its occurrence was not an invasion of any of the respondent's *Charter* rights. Accordingly, the evidence should not have been excluded.

At the conclusion of the voir dire, because of his decision to exclude the evidence, the trial judge ordered that the respondent be acquitted. Thus, because of the ruling in his favour, the respondent was not given an opportunity to present evidence or make submissions with respect to the personation issue, the offence with which he was charged. The testimony which he gave was testimony on the voir dire only. He should now be given that opportunity.

I would allow the appeal, set aside the acquittal and remit the case to the trial judge for a determination on the merits in accordance with these reasons.

■

In *Grafe*, the Ontario Court of Appeal found no "detention" on the facts. Given that the accused in *Moore* was convicted of obstructing an officer for refusing to give his name and address, is the above analysis convincing?

Several cases have elaborated upon the meaning of "detention" in s. 10(b). In *R. v. Yorke* (1990), 37 O.A.C. 253, the Ontario Court of Appeal held that an accused who reluctantly agrees to accompany police officers to the station for questioning regarding an offence is **not necessarily** "detained" such that s. 10(b) rights are triggered. The court identified three factors that should be considered in making the determination, including whether the manner of asking the accused to attend at the station was such as to create an apprehension of detention, whether the police in fact regarded the accused as a suspect at the time of the questioning, and whether the accused had any reason to believe that she or he was being detained.

R. v. Shafie (1989), 31 O.A.C. 362 considered the effect of actions by persons other than police: "[A]ctions that, at the hands of the police or other governmental agents, would be a detention, do not amount to detention within the meaning of s. 10(b) of the *Charter* when done by private or non-governmental persons." Thus, interrogation by the accused's employer's private investigator did not amount to detention and did not, consequently, give rise to the right to counsel. A statement made by the accused, albeit while under psychological coercion, was admissible.

Are there other situations in which civilians often perform the initial detention and interrogation? Consider the impact of *Shafie* in shoplifting situations where a store detective may complete the initial interrogation. Reconsider the Vice Principal's actions in *M.R.M.*, supra, **Search and Seizure**. Compare *Shafie* with *R. v. Lerke*, supra, **Search and Seizure** and *R. v. Wilson* (1994), 29 C.R. (4th) 302 (B.C. Sup. Ct.). In the latter case, Shabbits J. held that violent actions by a security guard in arresting an accused shoplifter gave rise to *Charter* rights. The significance of these rulings is that the right to counsel does not emerge until there has been an arrest or detention.

THE *CHARTER* AND INVESTIGATIVE DETENTION: SS. 9 AND 10

Legislation may itself authorize detentions that are "arbitrary." For example, in *R. v. Hufsky*, supra, the Supreme Court held that a highway traffic law that authorizes random roadside stops by police violated s. 9 of the *Charter*, but went on to uphold it under s. 1 as a reasonable limit. In *R. v. Fosseneuve* (1995), 104 Man. R. (2d) 272 (Q.B.), the court held that s. 495(2) of the *Criminal Code* violates s. 9 to the extent that it permits warrantless arrests "in the public interest." It read this language out of s. 495(2) in order the preserve the rest of the section.

Detentions based in common law are also vulnerable to *Charter* challenge. In *R. v. Simpson* (1993), 12 O.R. (3d) 182 (C.A.), the court recognized that the police have the common law power, as derived from their duties imposed by the relevant *Police Act*, to detain individuals for investigative purposes short of arrest if the detention involves a justifiable use of their powers. The criteria were said to be that the officer must be acting in the execution of his or her duty; it must be necessary to interfere with individual liberty in order to execute that duty; the duty must be important in terms of the public good; and regard must be had to the nature and degree of interference with the person's liberty. The court went on to hold that when the person is being detained in an adversarial context whereby the officer suspects criminal activity on their part, the officer can only invoke these powers with "articulable cause": "objectively discernible facts which give the detaining officer reasonable cause to suspect that the detainee is criminally implicated in the activity under investigation." Justice Doherty, for the court, stated that a hunch based on intuition is inadequate in law, no matter how accurate, because hunches may be simply guesses and they can easily mask discriminatory conduct based on race, age, sexual orientation, or sex.

On the facts in this case, the detention of the accused was not supported by articulable cause, because the stop of the accused's vehicle was based solely on the fact that the driver was seen leaving a house that had been identified, at some unknown time, by another officer, as a "crack house." The information about the house had not been verified; there was no basis on which to assess its reliability; the officer knew nothing about the driver; and no other observations provided any additional evidence. The detention thus violated s. 9 of the *Charter*, and the drugs obtained through a search were excluded under s. 24(2). See also *R. v. Lott* (1998), 57 C.R.R. (2d) 88 (Sask. Q.B.), where the court ruled that the accused was arbitrarily detained when the police approached his car because it was parked in a high-crime area where prostitution was common, and only subsequently detected his intoxication.

Investigative detention may trigger other police powers, such as the right to search as an incident of detention, and *Charter* rights, such as the right to counsel under s. 10(b). In *R. v. Ferris*, [1998] B.C.J. No. 1415 (C.A.), online: QL, for example, the court held that when an officer stops a vehicle whose plates were reported as stolen, and where the driver flees the scene, the officer is entitled to perform a frisk search of the two passengers while they are handcuffed and to open a waist pack worn by one of them. This right to search was confined to a search for weapons as an incident of investigative detention, and was said to be contingent on the circumstances of the detention. In *R. v. Power*, [2001] N.J. No. 267 (C.A.), online: QL, the court held that when police are using their powers of investigative detention to stop a motorist whose car crossed the centre line while driving, they cannot justify a search of the person and the vehicle when there was no basis to suspect that a weapon might be present. A similar conclusion was reached in *R. v. Johnson* (2000), 74 C.C.C. (2d) 70 (B.C.C.A.) with respect to officers who opened two pillowcases that the accused had been carrying over his shoulder as he walked down the street, after they briefly interrogated him as to the contents of the pillowcases. In both of these latter cases, while the detention was lawful, the searches constituted s. 8 violations.

Several of the investigative detention cases have also held that *Charter* rights are triggered by investigative detention. In *Power, supra*, the trial judge had also found a violation of s. 10(a), as the accused had not been told the reason for his detention. In *Young, supra*, **Search and Seizure**, and in *Peck*, reproduced below, a s. 10(b) violation was found as well.

THE *CHARTER*, ARREST AND DETENTION: S. 15?

Systemic biases emerge in the exercise of the discretionary powers of detention and arrest. Section 495 leaves considerable latitude to the police in terms of arrest, and investigative detention is also a broad power. Arrest may pose specific risks for women, particularly those who are responsible for the care of dependent children: Sandra Lilburn, "Arresting Moments. Identifying risks for women and children from the time of police arrest" (2001) 26:3 Alternative L.J. 115. In the policing of wife assault, arrest and detention are notoriously underutilized. Litigation such as Tracey Thurman's suit below has sought to demonstrate that police failure to respond to wife battering is an issue of constitutional dimensions, implicating a denial of equal protection of the law.

Thurman v. City of Torrington†

[BLUMENFELD, S.D.J.:]

The plaintiffs have brought this action pursuant to 42 U.S.C. §§ 1983, 1985, 1986 and 1988, as well as the fifth, ninth, and fourteenth amendments to the Constitution, alleging that their constitutional rights were violated by the nonperformance or malperformance of official duties by the defendant

---

† 595 F. Supp. 1521. (D. Conn. 1984).

police officers. In addition, the plaintiffs seek to hold liable the defendant City of Torrington (hereinafter, the "City"). The defendant City has filed a motion to dismiss the plaintiffs' complaint, or various claims therein, pursuant to Rule 12(b) of the Federal Rules of Civil Procedure.

On a motion to dismiss, the sole issue is whether under the facts alleged in the plaintiff's complaint it appears to a certainty that the plaintiff is entitled to no relief. *Holmes* v. *Silver Cross Hospital of Joliet, Illinois*, 340 F. Supp. 125 (N.D. Ill. 1972). A complaint should not be dismissed unless it appears that the plaintiff could prove no set of facts in support of her claim which would entitle her to relief. *U.S. Steel Corp.* v. *Multistate Tax Commission*, 367 F. Supp. 107 (S.D.N.Y. 1973). Furthermore, it is well settled that for purposes of a motion to dismiss, the well pleaded material allegations of the complaint are taken as true. 2A *Moore's Federal Practice* 2267, ¶ 12.08 n. 3. Accordingly, the material facts of this case are as follows:

Between early October 1982 and June 10, 1983, the plaintiff, Tracey Thurman, a woman living in the City of Torrington, and others on her behalf, notified the defendant City through the defendant police officers of the City of repeated threats upon her life and the life of her child, the plaintiff Charles J. Thurman, Jr., made by her estranged husband, Charles Thurman. Attempts to file complaints by plaintiff Tracey Thurman against her estranged husband in response to his threats of death and maiming were ignored or rejected by the named defendants and the defendant City.

An abbreviated chronology of the plaintiff's attempted and actual notifications of the threats made against her and her son by her estranged husband to the defendant City and police officers is appropriate for consideration of this motion.

In October 1982, Charles Thurman attacked plaintiff Tracey Thurman at the home of Judy Bentley and Richard St. Hilaire in the City of Torrington. Mr. St. Hilaire and Ms. Bentley made a formal complaint of the attack to one of the unnamed defendant police officers and requested efforts to keep the plaintiff's husband, Charles Thurman, off their property.

On or about November 5, 1982, Charles Thurman returned to the St. Hilaire-Bentley residence and using physical force took the plaintiff Charles J. Thurman, Jr. from said residence. Plaintiff Tracey Thurman and Mr. St. Hilaire went to Torrington police headquarters to make a formal complaint. At that point, unnamed defendant police officers of the City of Torrington refused to accept a complaint from Mr. St. Hilaire even as to trespassing.

On or about November 9, 1982, Charles Thurman screamed threats at Tracey while she was sitting in her car. Defendant police officer Neil Gemelli stood on the street watching Charles Thurman scream threats at Tracey until Charles Thurman broke the windshield of plaintiff Tracey Thurman's car while she was inside the vehicle. Charles Thurman was arrested after he broke the windshield, and on the next day, November 10, 1982, he was convicted of breach of peace. He received a suspended sentence of six months and a two-year "conditional discharge," during which he was ordered to stay completely away from the plaintiff Tracey Thurman and the Bentley-St. Hilaire residence and to commit no further crimes. The court imposing probation informed the defendants of this sentence.

On December 31, 1982, while plaintiff Tracey Thurman was at the Bentley-St. Hilaire residence, Charles Thurman returned to said residence and once again threatened her. She called the Torrington Police Department. One of the unnamed police officer defendants took the call, and, although informed of the violation of the conditional discharge, made no attempt to ascertain Charles Thurman's whereabouts or to arrest him.

Between January 1, 1983 and May 4, 1983, numerous telephone complaints to the Torrington Police Department were taken by various unnamed police officers, in which repeated threats of violence to the plaintiffs by Charles Thurman were reported and his arrest on account of the threats and violation of the terms of his probation was requested.

On May 4 and 5, 1983, the plaintiff Tracey Thurman and Ms. Bentley reported to the Torrington Police Department that Charles Thurman had said that he would shoot the plaintiffs. Defendant police officer Storrs took the written complaint of plaintiff Tracey Thurman who was seeking an arrest warrant for her husband because of his death threat and violation of his "conditional discharge." Defendant Storrs refused to take the complaint of Ms. Bentley. Plaintiff Tracey Thurman was told to return three weeks later on June 1, 1983 when defendant Storrs or some other person connected with the police department of the defendant City would seek a warrant for the arrest of her husband.

On May 6, 1983, Tracey filed an application for a restraining order against Charles Thurman in the Litchfield Superior Court. That day, the court issued an ex parte restraining order forbidding Charles Thurman from assaulting, threatening, and harassing

Tracey Thurman. The defendant City was informed of this order.

On May 27, 1983, Tracey Thurman requested police protection in order to get to the Torrington Police Department, and she requested a warrant for her husband's arrest upon her arrival at headquarters after being taken there by one of the unnamed defendant police officers. She was told that she would have to wait until after the Memorial Day holiday weekend and was advised to call on Tuesday, May 31, to pursue the warrant request.

On May 31, 1983, Tracey Thurman appeared once again at the Torrington Police Department to pursue the warrant request. She was then advised by one of the unnamed defendant police officers that defendant Schapp was the only policeman who could help her and that he was on vacation. She was told that she would have to wait until he returned. That same day, Tracey's brother-in-law, Joseph Kocsis, called the Torrington Police Department to protest the lack of action taken on Tracey's complaint. Although Mr. Kocsis was advised that Charles Thurman would be arrested on June 8, 1983, no such arrest took place.

On June 10, 1983, Charles Thurman appeared at the Bentley-St. Hilaire residence in the early afternoon and demanded to speak to Tracey. Tracey, remaining indoors, called the defendant police department asking that Charles be picked up for violation of his probation. After about 15 minutes, Tracey went outside to speak to her husband in an effort to persuade him not to take or hurt Charles Jr. Soon thereafter, Charles began to stab Tracey repeatedly in the chest, neck and throat.

Approximately 25 minutes after Tracey's call to the Torrington Police Department and after her stabbing, a single police officer, the defendant Petrovits, arrived on the scene. Upon the arrival of Officer Petrovits at the scene of the stabbing, Charles Thurman was holding a bloody knife. Charles then dropped the knife and, in the presence of Petrovits, kicked the plaintiff Tracey Thurman in the head and ran into the Bentley-St. Hilaire residence. Charles returned from within the residence holding the plaintiff Charles Thurman, Jr. and dropped the child on his wounded mother. Charles then kicked Tracey in the head a second time. Soon thereafter, defendants DeAngelo, Nukirk, and Columbia arrived on the scene but still permitted Charles Thurman to wander about the crowd and to continue to threaten Tracey. Finally, upon approaching Tracey once again, this time while she was lying on a stretcher, Charles Thurman was arrested and taken into custody.

It is also alleged that at all times mentioned above, except for approximately two weeks following his conviction and sentencing on November 10, 1982, Charles Thurman resided in Torrington and worked there as a counterman and short order cook at Skie's Diner. There he served many members of the Torrington Police Department including some of the named and unnamed defendants in this case. In the course of his employment Charles Thurman boasted to the defendant police officer patrons that he intended to "get" his wife and that he intended to kill her.

. . . .

In the instant case, the plaintiffs allege that the defendants use an administrative classification that manifests itself in discriminatory treatment violative of the equal protection clause. Police protection in the City of Torrington, they argue, is fully provided to persons abused by someone with whom the victim has no domestic relationship. But the Torrington police have consistently afforded lesser protection, plaintiffs allege, when the victim is (1) a woman abused or assaulted by a spouse or boyfriend, or (2) a child abused by a father or stepfather. The issue to be decided, then, is whether the plaintiffs have properly alleged a violation of the equal protection clause of the fourteenth amendment.

Police action is subject to the equal protection clause and section 1983 whether in the form of commission of violative acts or omission to perform required acts pursuant to the police officer's duty to protect. *Smith* v. *Ross*, 482 F.2d 33, 36–37 (6th Cir. 1973) ("law enforcement officer can be liable under § 1983 when by his inaction he fails to perform a statutorily imposed duty to enforce the laws equally and fairly, and thereby denies equal protection."); *Byrd* v. *Brishke*, 466 F.2d 6, 11 (7th Cir. 1972) (police officer liable under section 1983 for failing to prevent beating of plaintiff by other officers); *Azar* v. *Conley*, 456 F.2d 1382, 1387 (6th Cir. 1972). See also *Cooper* v. *Molko*, 512 F. Supp. 563, 567 (N.D. Cal. 1981), and *Huey* v. *Barloga*, 277 F. Supp. 864, 872–73 (N.D. Ill. 1967) (failure of city officials and police officers to perform their duty of taking reasonable measures to protect personal safety of persons whom they know may be attacked is a denial of equal protection of the laws and is actionable under section 1983). City officials and police officers are under an affirmative duty to preserve law and order, and to protect the personal safety of persons in the community. *Id.* at 872. This duty applies equally to women whose personal safety is threatened by individuals with whom they have or have had a domestic relationship as well as to all other persons whose personal safety is threatened, including women not involved in domestic relationships. If officials have notice of the possibility of attacks on women in domestic relationships or other persons, they are under an affirmative duty to take reasonable measures to protect the personal safety of such persons in the community. Failure to perform this duty would constitute a denial of equal protection of the laws.

Although the plaintiffs point to no law which on its face discriminates against victims abused by someone with whom they have a domestic relationship, the plaintiffs have alleged that there is an administrative classification used to implement the law in a discriminatory fashion. It is well settled that the equal protection clause is applicable not only to discriminatory legislative action, but also to discriminatory governmental action in administration and enforcement of the law. ... Here the plaintiffs were threatened with assault in violation of Connecticut law. Over the course of eight months the police failed to afford the plaintiffs protection against such assaults, and failed to take action to arrest the perpetrator of these assaults. The plaintiffs have alleged that this failure to act was pursuant to a pattern or practice of affording inadequate protection, or no protection at all, to women who have complained of having been abused by their husbands or others with whom they have had close relations. Amended Complaint, ¶ 13. Such a practice is tantamount to an administrative classification used to implement the law in a discriminatory fashion.

If the City wishes to discriminate against women who are the victims of domestic violence, it must articulate an important governmental interest for doing so.

. . . .

A man is not allowed to physically abuse or endanger a woman merely because he is her husband. [Concomitantly], a police officer may not knowingly refrain from interference in such violence, and may not "automatically decline to make an arrest simply because the assaulter and his victim are married to each other." *Bruno* v. *Codd*, 90 Misc.2d 1047, 1049, 396 N.Y.S.2d 974, 976 (1976), *rev'd on other grounds*, 64 App. Div.2d 502, 407 N.Y.S.2d 165 (1978), *aff'd*, 47 N.Y.2d 582, 419 N.Y.S.2d 901, 393 N.E.2d 976 (1979). Such inaction on the part of the officer is a denial of the equal protection of the laws.

In addition, any notion that defendants' practice can be justified as a means of promoting domestic harmony by refraining from interference in marital disputes, has no place in the case at hand. Rather than evidencing a desire to work out her problems with her husband privately, Tracey pleaded with the police to offer her a least some measure of protection. Further, she sought and received a restraining order to keep her husband at a distance. Finally, it is important to recall here the Supreme Court's dictum in *Reed* v. *Reed*, 404 U.S. at 77, 92 S.Ct. at 254, that "whatever may be said as to the positive values of avoiding intrafamily controversy, the choice in this context may not lawfully be mandated solely on the basis of sex." Accordingly, the defendant City of Torrington's motion to dismiss the plaintiff Tracey Thurman's complaint on the basis of failure to allege violation of a constitutional right is denied.

. . . .

HAVE THE PLAINTIFFS PROPERLY ALLEGED A CUSTOM OR POLICY ON THE PART OF THE CITY OF TORRINGTON?

The Plaintiffs have alleged in paragraph 13 of their complaint as follows:

> During the period of time described herein, and for a long time prior thereto, the defendant City of Torrington acting through its Police Department, condoned a pattern or practice of affording inadequate protection, or no protection at all, to women who have complained of having been abused by their husbands or others with whom they have had close relations. Said pattern, custom or policy, well known to the individual defendants, was the basis on which they ignored said numerous complaints and reports of threats to the plaintiffs with impunity.

While a municipality is not liable for the constitutional torts of its employees on a *respondeat superior* theory, a municipality may be sued for damages under section 1983 when "the action that is alleged to be unconstitutional implements or executes a policy statement, ordinance, regulation, or decision officially adopted and promulgated by the body's officers" or is "visited pursuant to governmental 'custom' even though such a custom has not received formal approval through the body's official decision-making channels." *Monell* v. *New York City Department of Social Services*, 436 U.S. 658, 690, 98 S.Ct. 2018, 2035, 56 L.Ed.2d 611 (1978).

Some degree of specificity is required in the pleading of a custom or policy on the part of a municipality. Mere conclusory allegations devoid of factual content will not suffice. See *Schramm v. Krischell*, 84 F.R.D. 294 (D. Conn. 1979). As this court has pointed out, a plaintiff must typically point to facts outside his own case to support his allegation of a policy on the part of a municipality. *Appletree v. City of Hartford*, 555 F. Supp. 224, 228 (D. Conn. 1983).

In the instant case, however, the plaintiff Tracey Thurman has specifically alleged in her statement of facts a series of acts and omissions on the part of the defendant police officers and police department that took place over the course of eight months. From this particularized pleading a pattern emerges that evidences deliberate indifference on the part of the police department to the complaints of the plaintiff Tracey Thurman and to its duty to protect her. Such an ongoing pattern of deliberate indifference raises an inference of "custom" or "policy" on the part of the municipality. ... Furthermore, this pattern of inaction climaxed on June 10, 1983 in an incident so brutal that under the law of the Second Circuit that "single brutal incident may be sufficient to suggest a link between a violation of constitutional rights and a pattern of police misconduct." *Owens v. Haas*, 601 F.2d 1242, 1246 (2d Cir.), *cert. denied*, 444 U.S. 980, 100 S.Ct. 483, 62 L.Ed.2d 407 (1979). Finally, a complaint of this sort will survive dismissal if it alleges a policy or custom of condoning police misconduct that violates constitutional rights and alleges "that the City's pattern of inaction caused the plaintiffs any compensable injury." *Batista v. Rodriguez*, 702 F.2d 393, 397–98 (2d Cir. 1983); *Escalera v. New York City Housing Authority*, 425 F.2d 853, 857 (2d Cir.), *cert. denied*, 400 U.S. 853, 91 S.Ct. 54, 27 L.Ed.2d 91 (1970) ("an action, especially under the Civil Rights Act, should not be dismissed at the pleadings stage unless it appears to a certainty that plaintiffs are entitled to no relief under any state of the facts, which could be proved in support of their claims"). Accordingly, defendant City of Torrington's motion to dismiss the [plaintiffs'] claims against it, on the ground that the plaintiffs failed to properly allege a custom or policy on the part of the municipality, is denied.

CONCLUSION

For the reasons stated above, the City's motion to dismiss the complaint for failure to allege the deprivation of a constitutional right is denied; the City's motion to dismiss the claims of Charles Thurman, Jr. is granted; the City's motion to dismiss the claims against it for failure to properly allege a "custom" or "policy" on the part of the City is denied; the City's motion to dismiss the claims against the unidentified police officers for lack of jurisdiction due to improper service is denied without prejudice to its renewal at a later date; and, finally, the City's motion to dismiss the sixth count of the complaint is granted.

∎

Tracey Thurman sustained a broken neck as a result of the attack, and was left partially paralyzed. She received a $2 million settlement in the suit: CP, "Arrests help cut family violence, policemen told" *The Ottawa Citizen* (26 October 1987) D7.

In June 2002, a suit by the family of Maria Teresa Macias against the Sonoma County Sheriff's Department for denial of Macias' right to equal protection of the law was settled, with a damage award of approximately $1 million. In spite of the legal ruling and settlement in *Thurman*, the police in this case failed, on 20 occasions within the three month period before her death, to respond to requests for assistance and to enforce a restraining order against her estranged husband when he repeatedly threatened the lives of Macias and her three children. The lawsuit alleged discrimination against her as a woman, a Latina, and a victim of domestic violence. The suit survived a nonsuit application in *Estate of Maria Teresa Macias v. Ihde*, 219 F. 3d 1018 (9th Cir. 2000). Her killer, Avelino Macias, was never arrested once, in spite of a decade of violence against his wife and children, his refusal to obey a restraining order, and his commission of stalking, rape, threatening to kill, and harassment of Macias and her children.

The *Thurman* and *Macias* cases in the United States provide examples that are reproduced in police responses to wife assault around the world. In one Australian study, an effort was made to find out what kind of attitudes and beliefs shape the exercise of police discretion to arrest and charge in cases of wife assault. In Graham Williams, "Women and cops" *The Sydney Morning Herald* (5 July 1989) 17, it was reported that 55 per cent of the 500 officers surveyed said that they did not want to be involved in matters of domestic violence (approximately 35 per cent of the calls) because it involved "social work," not "police work." Two-thirds of the respondents said that violence was normal or typical in intimate relationships, one in four said that the wife's behaviour was the most important catalyst for male violence, and 17 per cent said that violence was normal (some said "biologically imperative") male behaviour. The article also reported that:

> Police attitudes as to why women stay in violent relationships are also highly revealing: 22 per cent said that women stay because they "enjoy the violence"; 18 per cent said "emotional dependency"; 16 per cent [said] "financial dependency"; and 14 per cent [said] because of sex.

Graham Williams, in another article entitled "Police 'support' wife bashing" *The Sydney Morning Herald* (7 September 1989) 1, reported that in an analysis of 56 cases of domestic violence involving injury:

> [Police] arrested only 20 (36 per cent) of the 55 male culprits and arrested the sole female offender who fatally shot her male partner after having frequently sought police protection from his violence.... A third of the men were charged with drunkenness, not with assault.... The police also advised 22 of the other injured women (40 per cent) to seek a private legal remedy....

In Delta, B.C., George Rigakos has studied the police response to calls from women to enforce peace bonds that have been issued by judges sitting in criminal court where the man is still there upon police arrival, the woman wants him arrested, and police are governed by an internal mandatory arrest policy for domestic violence when there are grounds to believe that an offence has been committed. He found, remarkably, that even in these conditions, police arrest in only 35 per cent of the incidents. Rigakos argues that this resistance to legal reform is embedded in police subculture, which views battered women as responsible for their mates' violence, manipulative and cunning, and unlikely to be co-operative witnesses, in spite of statistics to the contrary: "The Politics of Protection: Battered Women, Protection Orders, and Police Subculture" in Kevin D. Bonnycastle and George S. Rigakos, eds. *Unsettling Truths. Battered Women, Policy, Politics, and Contemporary Research in Canada* (Vancouver: Collective Press, 1998) 82.

There are, unfortunately, many examples of the failure of police to respond and take threats of violence seriously in Canada: Shelley Page, "Sherri Lee Guy abandoned when her life was at risk" *The Ottawa Citizen* (5 May 1995) C1. Sheila Amero, a Nova Scotia woman, sued the Dartmouth police for failing to protect her. Although police had been called to the scene, they released the attacker (her boyfriend) despite Amero's objections. He returned and viciously attacked her with a knife; she nearly died as a result: CP, "Woman suing police" *The [Toronto] Globe and Mail* (5 September 1995) A4.

On the other hand, the over-use of both detention and arrest against racialized people has been described by several sources. For example, in "Arrests, Disposition and Recidivism: A Comparison of Indians and Whites" (1974) 16 Can. J. Crim. & Corr. 105, Rita Bienvenue and A. H. Latif examine data from the city of Winnipeg for the period of one year — that is, 1969 — and conclude that Aboriginal men and women are over-represented in terms of total charges and arrests for all types of crime except drug and traffic offences. They suggest that police discrimination on the basis of race, class, and geographic location may explain the statistics. What explanation can you offer for the rates of arrest of Aboriginal people, drawing on the materials presented in this volume? For further discussion of arrest patterns, see Charles Reasons, "Crime and the American Indian" in Howard Bahr, ed., *Native Indians Today* (New York: Harper and Row, 1972) 319–26.

The Commission on Systemic Racism in the Ontario Criminal Justice System also found that Blacks were over-represented in arrest statistics. For example, the Commission describes the way in which the "war on drugs" strategy has produced racial inequalities in arrest and imprisonment: "Comment on the growth of racial inequality in admissions" in *Report of the Commission on Systemic Racism in the Ontario Criminal Justice System* (Toronto: Queen's Printer, 1995) at 81–84. For a recent example of racism, see: Michael Grange, "Prisoners' rights activist arrested in drug-squad error: Ex-boxer once wrongly held for 19 years angered by police action" *The [Toronto] Globe and Mail* (13 April 1996) A10A. In that case, Rubin (Hurricane) Carter did not fit the description of the person sought by police. He was in his 60s, while the officers were looking for an African-Canadian man in his 30s; he wore glasses, whereas the suspect did not; and his clothing was a different colour and style.

The use of racial profiling to guide investigative detention has been the subject of constitutional litigation in the U.S., whereby violation of the guarantee of equal protection is alleged. In June 1998, the first-ever claim for monetary damages was filed by the American Civil Liberties Union on behalf of 11 named plaintiffs and hundreds of others as a class action suit against Maryland state police, arguing that racial profiling is used to stop motorists on the I-95: Civil Action No. CCB-98-1098, filed in the U.S. District Court for the District of Maryland. In Canada issues of racial profiling have thus far been argued as s. 9 *Charter* challenges. As you read the case that follows, consider whether s. 15 could also ground such a challenge.

R. v. Peck[†]

[TRAFFORD J.:]

INTRODUCTION

On November 18, 1998, Dwayne Peck, the defendant, was arrested by Constable Murphy of the Toronto Police Services for, *inter alia*, possession of cocaine for the purposes of trafficking in the vicinity of O'Keefe Lane in the City of Toronto. ...

This is an application under s. 24 of the *Charter* for an order excluding the evidence seized from the defendant for violations of s. 8, s. 9 and s. 10(b) of the *Charter*. ...

THE CIRCUMSTANCES OF THE CASE AS FOUND BY THE COURT

What, then, are the circumstances of this case?

On November 18, 1998 the defendant drove from Brampton with two female friends, Natasha Prince and Chanele Henry, to the Eaton Centre. They intended to go to a store called "World of Shoes". The defendant and his friends are young black people apparently in their early 20s. They were well-dressed, clean and neat in their appearance. The defendant proceeded north off Dundas Street West on O'Keefe Lane to find a parking space. The vehicle was parked shortly before 5:00 p.m. The three of them then walked southbound through O'Keefe Lane towards the Eaton Centre. It is situated on the south side of Dundas Street West near Yonge Street. The lane was more or less dark at the time. There was some random indirect lighting of the lane from a parking structure in the area and from lights near exits from adjacent buildings.

O'Keefe Lane is located near the intersection of Yonge Street and Dundas Street in downtown Toronto. The laneway itself was notorious for the buying, selling and use of narcotics. Street level drug activity was commonplace in the lane. Dealers and users lurked in doorways. Often times they were dressed in a shabby way. Literally hundreds of arrests for drug offences have been made in the area by the Toronto Police Service over the years. Consequently, it was properly the object of undercover investigations by "old clothes" officers. Such officers are dressed not in ordinary police uniforms, but rather in casual attire consistent with the clothing worn by those in the drug culture and otherwise to facilitate an effective investigation of crimes committed by them. All such officers carry with them badges identifying themselves as members of the Toronto Police Services.

However, there was also an abundance of legitimate activity by legitimate persons in and around O'Keefe Lane. There are lots of retail businesses. Wholesale jewellers were there too. Street vendors were common in the area at large. Some people parked illegally in the lane. It was also a shortcut from Ryerson Polytechnic University to Dundas Street West. Generally, the lane and its immediate vicinity were also very busy with legitimate activity throughout the normal working day.

After the defendant and his friends drove northbound through O'Keefe Lane and before they walked southbound towards the Eaton Centre, Constable Murphy, Constable Niezen and Constable Laing arrested two other persons for drug crimes. They were placed in handcuffs. Constable Murphy and Constable Niezen had custody of one of them

---

[†] [2001] O.J. No. 4581 (Sup. Ct.), online: QL.

near the rear of 319 Yonge Street. Constable Laing had custody of the other one near the rear of 325 Yonge Street. 319 Yonge Street and 325 Yonge Street were approximately 20 feet from one another. All of these officers were awaiting the arrival of a cruiser to take their prisoners to 52 Division. All of the officers were dressed in "old clothes". These were the circumstances as the defendant, Ms. Prince and Ms. Henry approached Dundas Street West from the north.

As they passed Constable Laing, Mr. Peck noticed Constable Murphy and the other persons near 319 Yonge Street. While he noticed Constable Murphy and Constable Laing, he placed no significance on them or their presence in the area because he did not know they were police officers. They were dressed like others involved in the drug activity of the area. Nor did he notice the handcuffs on either of their prisoners. Nor did he place any significance on the position of their hands in relation to their bodies. The darkness in the area did not permit more precise observations. Mr. Peck was merely walking with two female friends towards "World of Shoes" in the Eaton Centre. He had nothing in his hands as he passed Constable Laing and Constable Murphy. His hands did move randomly in relation to his body and, at times, were in the immediate vicinity of the pockets of the pants he was wearing as he proceeded past Constable Laing. Neither he nor his friends quickened their pace as they passed Constable Murphy.

It was in those circumstances that Constable Murphy formed a belief that Mr. Peck may be a drug dealer passing through O'Keefe Lane. Consequently, he quickly moved southbound so as to be able to confront Mr. Peck and said "Police". Constable Murphy did not produce his badge identifying himself as a member of the Toronto Police Service. Mr. Peck and the women with him were confused by these circumstances because Constable Murphy, not being uniformed, did not appear to be a policeman. Immediately after saying "Police" in an authoritative tone, Constable Murphy said "What do you have in your pocket?" relying on a movement of Mr. Peck's hands near his body and, in particular, near the pocket of the pants he was wearing. Mr. Peck replied "Nothing". Constable Murphy suspected he had drugs in his pocket. He decided to detain Mr. Peck until he found what was in his pocket. There were no other questions asked of Mr. Peck of an investigative nature. As Constable Murphy reached for Mr. Peck, Mr. Peck pushed him aside, turned around and began to run northbound through O'Keefe Lane. Constable Murphy took up pursuit

and tackled him. An altercation followed. This led to the intervention of Constable Laing to assist in gaining control of Mr. Peck. Constable Laing used an asp to assist in the apprehension and arrest of the defendant. A bag containing a large piece of crack cocaine was seized from him together with an amount of cash and a cell phone.

THE CREDIBILITY OF THE OFFICERS

It is necessary in this case to comment on the credibility of Constable Murphy and Constable Laing. A brief summary of their evidence is helpful in this context.

Constable Murphy testified that he saw Mr. Peck proceeding southbound in O'Keefe Lane at a distance of approximately 30 yards. The lane was dark with some random lighting provided indirectly from buildings in the area. He could see the top of a plastic bag in his left hand. Mr. Peck apparently saw Constable Murphy as he approached him. Mr. Peck quickly closed his hand on the bag and put it into his pocket when he was about 10 feet away. Constable Murphy told Constable Niezen what he had seen. As Mr. Peck passed Constable Murphy, he quickened his pace. Constable Murphy suspected he had drugs in his pocket. Therefore, he positioned himself to confront Mr. Peck before he arrived at Dundas Street West at its intersection with O'Keefe Lane. At no time did he produce his badge identifying himself as a member of the Toronto Police Service.

Constable Laing testified that he had no recollection of the quickening of the pace described by Constable Murphy and made no note of it. He also testified it was "... his impression ... he saw ..." Mr. Peck look towards Constable Murphy and Constable Niezen. There was, he claimed, a movement of the left hand consistent with the placement of an item into the left pocket. He did not see anything in Mr. Peck's hand.

Having assessed the credibility of Constable Murphy and the reliability of his testimony in the context of the evidence as a whole, I reject its material aspects. In my opinion, it is not likely that a person with normal vision could see a portion of a plastic bag in the hand of a person 30 yards distant in a dark laneway. It is important to recall that Constable Murphy did not testify that he believed he saw such a bag. Rather he testified that he saw such a bag. Consequently, I reject that testimony as false. This circumstance was a material part of the foundation of his investigation of the defendant. Moreover, I prefer the evidence of Constable Laing on the issue of the quickening of the pace of the defendant as he passed Constable Laing. I reject Constable Murphy's evidence on this point as well. He is at least unreliable on this point. Insofar as he described the defendant, at a distance of approximately 10 feet, closing his hand on the bag and putting it into his pocket, I reject his evidence as false. If, as I have found, there was no plastic bag in the hand of the defendant at a distance of 30 yards and if, as I have found, he did not quicken his pace when he looked in the direction of Constable Murphy, apparently because he did not perceive him to be a policeman, there is no logical basis to find such an act by the defendant as described by Constable Murphy. Nor is there any logical basis for an honest but reasonable mistake by Constable Murphy in describing this act as he did. Again, it must be noted that his evidence was categorical on this point, namely, that Mr. Peck quickly closed his hand on the bag and put it into his pocket. Constable Niezen was not called to confirm a remark made to him by Constable Murphy at the time, namely, that he had told Constable Niezen what he had just seen. His evidence on this point is, accordingly, rejected as false.

This assessment of his credibility and the facts as found by the court leave a simple factual matrix before the court. A young black man in his early 20s was walking through a darkened laneway in downtown Toronto with two female friends towards the Eaton Centre. They were neat, clean and well-dressed in their appearance. The laneway was notorious for drug activity. Three members of the Toronto Police Services were assigned to the lane as "old clothes" officers to investigate any such activity on November 18, 1998. It was around 5:00 p.m. The overall area of Yonge Street and Dundas Street including O'Keefe Lane was also then being used lawfully by many other people. Thus, it will be readily appreciated that the notoriety of the area and the race of the defendant are the dominant circumstances in this case. It is in those circumstances that I conclude that Constable Murphy consciously relied on the race of the defendant as an important factor in deciding to stop him for questioning.

THE LEGAL SIGNIFICANCE OF THE FACTS AS FOUND BY THE COURT

What, then, is the legal significance of the facts as found by the court?

In my opinion, the defendant was "detained" from the moment Constable Murphy said, in an authoritative tone "... Police ... What do you have in your pocket?". This was a demand or direction made to the defendant in circumstances that might have legal significance for him and which, in themselves, prevented him from obtaining legal advice he was entitled to at the time. See *R.* v. *Therens* (1985), 18 C.C.C. (3d) 481 (S.C.C.)... . There was no attempt to comply with s. 10 of the *Charter*. While Constable Murphy believed Mr. Peck had illegal drugs on him, the belief was not based on circumstances that, objectively viewed, provided reasonable grounds to suspect he was involved in criminal activity. There was no basis for an investigative detention in this case. See *R.* v. *Simpson* (1993), 79 C.C.C. (3d) 482 (Ont. C.A.) at pp. 500–503 ... *Brown et al.* v. *The Regional Municipality of Durham Police* (1999), 43 O.R. (3d) 223 (Ont. C.A.)... . The presence of a reasonably well-dressed young black man, Mr. Peck, with two female friends who are similarly well-dressed, Ms. Prince and Ms. Henry, in an area notorious for street level drug activity around 5:00 p.m. on November 18, 1998 does not meet such criteria. The random movement of the arm of Mr. Peck in the vicinity of the pocket as he walked past Constable Murphy does not, in itself or contextually, provide such grounds. The reputation of the area in itself is not sufficient to do so. The overall area around O'Keefe Lane was, in any event, a diverse commercial area characterized by the racial and cultural diversity of downtown Toronto. Nor, I say most emphatically, does the race of a person and, in particular, a young black male person, provide such a basis by itself or in the context of the other circumstances as found by the court. Stereotypical assumptions linking young black men and the illegal use of narcotics do not provide a lawful basis to detain or arrest them. See *R.* v. *Simpson*, *supra*, where Doherty, J.A. observed that "... subjectively based assessments can too easily mask discriminatory conduct based on such irrelevant factors as the detainee's sex, colour, age, ethnic origin or sexual orientation ...".

Regrettably, I am satisfied that the race of the defendant and his appearance was a factor that consciously led to the belief of Constable Murphy. There was, accordingly, no lawful basis for Constable Murphy to position himself so as to impede the progress of Mr. Peck, Ms. Prince and Ms. Henry towards "World of Shoes".

Moreover, in these same circumstances, the question put to Mr. Peck by Constable Murphy after he had identified himself by saying "Police", namely,

"What do you have in your pocket?" was an element of a warrantless search conducted without consent. The defendant felt compelled to answer the question in circumstances where there were no reasonable grounds to suspect he was implicated in criminal activity. It was, therefore, an unreasonable search in contravention of s. 8 of the *Charter*. See *R.* v. *Mellenthin*, [1992] 3 S.C.R. 615 at para. 15–18.... The answer given by the defendant, namely, "Nothing", and the attempted flight immediately afterwards may not be relied upon as additional circumstances to be marshalled on the issue of probable cause. See *R.* v. *Kokesch* (1990), 61 C.C.C. (3d) 207 (S.C.C.). The subsequent arrest and search purportedly incidental to it that led to the actual seizure of the crack cocaine, cash and cell phone were also unlawful. It must be remembered that the actual seizure of the crack cocaine does not provide an *ex post facto* justification for the investigative misconduct in this, or any other, case. See *Hunter* v. *Southam Inc.* (1984), 14 C.C.C. (3d) 97 at 109 (S.C.C.), *R.* v. *Greffe* (1990), 55 C.C.C. (3d) 161 at 187–188 ... (S.C.C.) and *R.* v. *Kokesch*, *supra* at p. 228.

In all of the circumstances of the case, the admission of the evidence at trial would bring the administration of justice into disrepute. The breaches of s. 8, s. 9 and s. 10 of the *Charter*, looked at as a whole, were serious ones. The values embraced by those sections are of fundamental importance to a free and democratic society. Stopping people merely on the basis of a "hunch" is a serious departure from the standards we demand of, and expect from, our police officers. Stereotypical assumptions, including those concerning young black men and narcotics, have no proper place in a properly conducted investigation. The inherent worth and dignity of all people regardless of their race or ethnic origin must be respected by the police at all times during the investigation of even the most heinous crimes. While the tradition in Canadian policing is compatible with these considerations, I am satisfied Constable Murphy consciously departed from it in this case. Having regard to all of the circumstances, the admission of the items seized from the defendant on November 18, 1998 would bring the administration of justice into disrepute.

CONCLUSION

Accordingly, all of the evidence seized is inadmissible at trial.

12

Right to Counsel

Right to counsel issues emerge at two points in the criminal process: upon arrest or detention, and at trial. Even if an arrest or detention is lawful or justified (under s. 1), the right to counsel (s. 10(b)) emerges in the face of any detention. The questions that arise are:

- what that right to counsel encompasses
- when and how must the police inform the accused of the right to counsel
- what must the accused do to assert the right to counsel
- when can the accused be taken to have abandoned or waived her or his right to counsel
- when is it reasonable to limit the right to counsel under s. 1
- what are the consequences of any *Charter* violation (s. 24)

Section 10(b) imposes informational and implementational obligations on the police: *Brydges*, *Prosper*, *infra*. Subsequent issues of waiver and diligence arise with respect to the conduct of the accused, although, as the cases indicate, a valid waiver will be a rarity: *Leclair*, *Bartle*, *infra*. The denial of the right to counsel (including the right to be informed of the availability of counsel) may result in the exclusion of evidence obtained (e.g. confessions, identification evidence, breathalyzer and body samples).

Fair trial issues (ss. 7 and 11) may arise as a result of evidence improperly obtained and admitted, or as a result of lack of representation at trial. From a practical point of view, an impecunious accused is limited to the provisions of specific provincial/territorial legal aid plans, except where the courts enlarge those obligations via ss. 7 and 11.

The coverage provided by individual legal aid plans varies dramatically across the country, with respect to the types of cases handled, the model for the delivery of legal services (judicare, whereby lawyers are asked to accept certificates issued by a legal aid plan; duty counsel services; or clinics staffed by salaried lawyers), and the availability of "choice" of counsel. The discrepancy is reflected in the gross disparities in per capita expenditures for legal aid. Thus, although criminal law is a federal responsibility, provincial decisions about justice spending create different patterns of access to representation across the country. See generally: National Council of Welfare, *Legal Aid and the Poor* (Ottawa: Supply and Services Canada, 1995). The issues challenged by accused persons using the *Charter* include the denial of legal aid by the relevant provincial plan, the restriction on the type of coverage provided (e.g. elections, preparation time, and appeals), and the limits on the choice of counsel.

A. RIGHT TO COUNSEL UPON ARREST OR DETENTION

R. v. Leclair[†]

[BEETZ, J.:]

. . . .

THE FACTS

A break and enter occurred on 18th July 1983 into a dwelling-house in Sault Ste. Marie. The owners were not home at the time. A boarder was, but he was asleep and did not witness anything. However, two houses up the street there was a group, including four young people, one of whom heard the sound of breaking glass. Upon noticing two figures at the home broken into, she yelled, and the three others chased the perpetrators. It was around 10:00 p.m. The perpetrators were not caught, and they escaped in various directions.

About 2 ½ hours later the police stopped a vehicle on a nearby street. Inside the car were four persons, including the two appellants. When asked their names, the appellants gave false identities, which they shortly thereafter corrected. Nothing was found after a search was conducted of the car and the occupants. The three boys, one aged 16 and two aged 17, were arrested and charged with break and enter.

All three were advised of their right to counsel. The appellants each tried to telephone their respective counsel, but received no answer. It was now around 2:00 a.m. The appellant Leclair was asked if he wanted to call another lawyer and he said "No." He was placed in a police cell. The appellant Ross was also taken to the cells. The police officer's notes did not indicate that the appellant Ross was asked if he wanted to call other counsel.

In the middle of the night, the officers went to a nearby pinball arcade and found seven people, of similar age to the accused, who could participate in a line-up. The four young witnesses were then taken to the police station and the line-up was held at 3:00 a.m. Neither of the appellants was advised that they were under no obligation to participate. At trial the appellant Ross asked that the line-up evidence be excluded under s. 24(2) of the Canadian Charter of Rights and Freedoms because it was obtained in a manner that infringed or denied his right under s. 10(*b*) of the Charter and because the admission of this evidence in the proceedings would bring the administration of justice into disrepute.

1. Were the appellants given a reasonable and effective opportunity to retain and instruct counsel?
2. If not, was the line-up evidence obtained under the particular circumstances of this case to be excluded under s. 24(2)?

ANALYSIS

A Reasonable and Effective Opportunity to Retain and Instruct Counsel

The appellants were obviously detained, and that they had the right to retain and instruct counsel is not in dispute. Moreover, the police complied initially with s. 10(*b*) and advised Ross and Leclair of their right to retain and instruct counsel without delay. As this court held in *R. v. Manninen*, [1987] 1 S.C.R. 1233, 58 C.R. (3d) 97, 34 C.C.C. (3d) 385, 41 D.L.R. (4th) 301, 21 O.A.C. 192, 76 N.R. 198, s. 10(*b*) imposes at least two duties on the police in addition to the duty to inform detainees of their rights. The first is that the police must give the accused or detained person who so wishes a *reasonable* opportunity to exercise the right to retain and instruct counsel without delay. The second is that the police must refrain from attempting to elicit evidence from the detainee until the detainee has had a reasonable opportunity to retain and instruct counsel. I am of the view that in this case the police fulfilled neither duty.

*The First Duty: Affording
a Reasonable Opportunity*

Having been informed of their right to counsel and having clearly indicated their desire to assert that right, both appellants were permitted to telephone lawyers of their choice but were unable to make contact with them. This is hardly surprising, since the calls were made at approximately 2:00 a.m. In the circumstances, it was highly unlikely that they would be able to contact their counsel before normal office opening hours.

[†] [1989] 1 S.C.R. 3.

At this juncture, I would underline the fact that the appellant Leclair was asked if he wanted to call another lawyer, and his answer was "No." The Crown's submission was that by giving this answer Leclair waived his right to counsel. I do not agree. Leclair had clearly indicated that he wished to contact *his* lawyer. The mere fact that he did not want to call *another* lawyer cannot fairly be viewed as a waiver of his right to retain counsel. Quite the contrary: he merely asserted his right to counsel and to counsel of his choice. Although an accused or detained person has the right to choose counsel, it must be noted that, as this court said in *R. v. Tremblay*, [1987] 2 S.C.R. 435, 60 C.R. (3d) 59, 2 M.V.R. (2d) 289, 37 C.C.C. (3d) 565, 45 D.L.R. (4th) 445, 32 C.R.R. 381, 25 O.A.C. 93, 79 N.R. 153, a detainee must be reasonably diligent in the exercise of these rights, and if he is not, the correlative duties imposed on the police and set out in *Manninen*, supra, are suspended. Reasonable diligence in the exercise of the right to choose one's counsel depends upon the context facing the accused or detained person. On being arrested, for example, the detained person is faced with an immediate need for legal advice and must exercise reasonable diligence accordingly. By contrast, when seeking the best lawyer to conduct a trial, the accused person faces no such immediacy. Nevertheless, accused or detained persons have a right to choose their counsel and it is only if the lawyer chosen cannot be available within a reasonable time that the detainee or the accused should be expected to exercise the right to counsel by calling another lawyer.

Moreover, once the appellant asserted his right to instruct counsel, and absent a clear indication that he had changed his mind, it was unreasonable for the police to proceed as if Leclair had waived his right to counsel....

. . . .

Since the evidence reveals that Leclair asserted his right to counsel, the burden of establishing an unequivocal waiver is on the Crown. Here, the Crown has failed to discharge the onus.

In the case of the appellant Ross, there is no evidence that the police even asked whether he wanted to call another lawyer. Once Ross had tried and failed to reach his lawyer, it would appear that the police assumed that their obligation to provide a reasonable opportunity to retain counsel was at an end. One can reasonably infer that they also misconstrued the nature of their obligation as concerned the appellant Leclair. Obviously, there was no urgency or other reason justifying that the police proceed forthwith, and it cannot be said that the appellants had a real opportunity to retain and instruct counsel. This therefore leads us to consider the second duty.

The Second Duty: Refraining from Taking Further Steps

Having seen that the appellants got no answer to their telephone calls, the police officers placed them in police cells, and a few minutes later the appellants were told to participate in a line-up, which they did.

The police were mistaken to follow such a procedure. As this court held in *Manninen*, supra, the police have at least a duty to cease questioning or otherwise attempting to elicit evidence from the detainee until he has had a reasonable opportunity to retain and instruct counsel. In my view, the right to counsel also means that, once an accused or detained person has asserted that right, the police cannot in any way compel the detainee or accused person to make a decision or participate in a process which could ultimately have an adverse effect in the conduct of an eventual trial until that person has had a reasonable opportunity to exercise that right. In the case at bar, it cannot be said that the appellants had a real opportunity to retain and instruct counsel before the line-up was held. Nor can it be said that there was any urgency or other compelling reason which justified proceeding with the line-up so precipitously.

The Crown urged upon us that it was necessary to hold the line-up immediately, while the memories of the witnesses were fresh and undisturbed. I cannot accept this submission. While it may be desirable to hold a line-up as soon as possible, this concern must generally yield to the right of the suspect to retain counsel, which right must, of course, be exercised with reasonable diligence. Here, the line-up was held with utmost, indeed highly unusual, dispatch. There is nothing to suggest that the line-up could not have been held a few hours later, after the appellants had again attempted to contact their lawyers during normal business hours.

The respondent also submitted that there was no violation of the right to counsel because the appellants did not have the right to have their lawyers present during the line-up. This submission is without merit. Even if the appellants could not have their lawyers present during the line-up, this does not imply that counsel is of no assistance to a suspect. Identification evidence obtained through a line-up is usually strong evidence susceptible of influencing trial deliberations. The question as to whether a suspect has a positive right to refuse to participate in a line-up has not been decided in our law.... However, it is clear that there is no legal obligation to participate in a line-up.... Since there is no such legal obligation, it is clear that counsel has an important role in advising a client about participating voluntarily in a line-up.... This case illustrates that, while an accused or detained person has no obligation to participate in a line-up, failure to do so can have legal consequences respecting the evidence that might be admitted at trial. In the case at bar, had the appellants been allowed access to their lawyers, they could have been advised that they were under no statutory obligation to participate in the line-up, although failure to do so might have certain prejudicial consequences. They could have been advised, for example, not to participate unless they were given a photograph of the line-up, or not to participate if the others in the line-up were obviously older than themselves. In short, they could have been told how a well-run line-up is conducted, even though there is no statutory framework governing the line-up process. It was this advice, not the presence of their lawyers at the line-up, of which the appellants were deprived.

Furthermore, that the accused did not refuse to participate in the line-up cannot by itself amount to a waiver of the right to counsel. The very purpose of the right to counsel is to ensure that those who are accused or detained are advised of their legal rights and how to exercise them when dealing with the authorities. It would contradict this purpose to conclude that a detained or accused person has waived the right to counsel simply by submitting, before being instructed by counsel, to precisely those attempts to secure the detainee's participation from which the police should refrain....

The Exclusion of Evidence under s. 24(2)

This court recently decided in *R. v. Strachan*, No. 19749, 15th December 1988 [now reported 67 C.R. (3d) 87, [1989] 1 W.W.R. 385 [B.C.]], that for the purposes of s. 24(2) evidence was "obtained in a manner that infringed or denied ... rights" guaranteed by the Charter if the violation of one of those rights precedes the discovery of evidence, and if that discovery of evidence was not too remote from the violation. In this case the violation of the right to counsel was immediately prior to the discovery of evidence through the line-up. There is no question of remoteness; in fact, there was even a direct link between the violation of the right to counsel and the evidence obtained. As such, what remains to be determined is whether the line-up evidence should be excluded under s. 24(2) of the Charter. Evidence must be excluded under s. 24(2) if, having regard to all the circumstances, it is established that it would (in the sense that it could) bring the administration of justice into disrepute to admit the evidence.

In *R. v. Collins*, [1987] 1 S.C.R. 265, 56 C.R. (3d) 193, [1987] 3 W.W.R. 689, 13 B.C.L.R. (2d) 1, 33 C.C.C. (3d) 1, 38 D.L.R. (4th) 508, 28 C.R.R. 122, 74 N.R. 276, a majority of this court found it useful to identify three groups of factors which must be balanced by the court in determining whether the admission of the evidence into the proceedings would bring the administration of justice into disrepute. The first category of factors relates to the fairness of the trial process, the second relates to the seriousness of the Charter violation and the third relates to the effect of excluding the evidence and, more particularly, to the question as to whether the reputation of the system will be better served by the admission or the exclusion of the evidence.

In this case, there can be no doubt as to the importance of the line-up evidence. As the majority of this court held in *Collins*, among the factors relevant to determining the effect of the admission of the evidence on the fairness of the trial is the nature of the evidence obtained as a result of the violation. Any evidence obtained, after a violation of the Charter, by conscripting the accused against himself through a confession or other evidence emanating from him would tend to render the trial process unfair.

. . . .

A person's identity is pre-existing "real evidence" inasmuch as a person's physical characteristics exist irrespective of any Charter violation or of any steps taken by the police.

However, the identification evidence obtained through a line-up is not simply pre-existing "real evidence" in this sense. The purpose of a line-up is twofold. First, a line-up is designed to identify the detainee as the author of the crime. But second, and most important to the discussion here, the procedure of a line-up is designed to reinforce the credibility of identification evidence. In this sense the object of the line-up is to construct evidence that the accused was picked out from among a similar group of people by a witness who was not prompted in any way to make that choice, and to settle the memory of the witness for the purpose of the trial. When participating in a line-up, the accused is participating in the construction of credible inculpating evidence. Obviously, this piece of evidence could not be obtained without the accused's participation in its construction, since the evidence of a line-up held without the presence of the accused is irrelevant to the Crown's case. Thus, while the accused does not participate in the creation of "real evidence" of identity, the accused does participate in the creation of credible line-up evidence. An accused who is told to participate in a line-up before having had a reasonable opportunity to communicate with counsel is conscripted against himself, since he is used as a means for creating evidence for the purposes of the trial.... In my view, the use of such evidence goes to the fairness of the trial process.

The nature of the Charter violation is also relevant, given that we are confronted with a serious breach of rights. The appellants clearly asserted their right to counsel and there was no urgency of any kind to explain the behaviour of the police. Nothing prevented them from holding the line-up later in the day. Nor is this a case of a good faith error in police conduct.

. . . .

Furthermore, in this case the appellants were young, 16 and 17 years old, and we can reasonably presume that they were not aware of their rights.

. . . .

I am therefore of the opinion that, having regard to all the circumstances, the appellants have established that the admission of the line-up evidence into the proceedings would bring the administration of justice into disrepute. Accordingly, the evidence should have been excluded and a new trial should be ordered.

I would accordingly allow the appeal and order a new trial.

∎

As *Leclair* illustrates, the courts have interpreted s. 10(b) as a central *Charter* right and have therefore attempted to give substance to the right to be informed of one's entitlement to contact counsel and the right to actually make the telephone call.

Furthermore, the courts have held that generally the police must wait until an intoxicated accused is sufficiently sober to understand the import of this *Charter* right before proceeding to question an accused in custody. For example, in *R. v. Clarkson*, [1986] S.C.R. 383, the Court excluded statements made by an intoxicated accused because her waiver of her s. 10(b) rights was not truly voluntary, given that she could not pass the "awareness of the consequences" test. In another case, *R. v. Evans*, [1991] 1 S.C.R. 869, the Supreme Court held that the right to counsel imposes an obligation on the police to ensure that the accused understands that right. This obligation may be greater where the accused's capacity to understand that right is reduced. Additionally, Madam Justice McLachlin, writing for the majority at 893, held that police must re-inform the accused of the right to counsel "when there is a fundamental and discrete change in the purpose of the investigation, one involving a different and unrelated offence or a significantly more serious offence than that contemplated at the time of the [first] warning."

The emphasis on the primacy of the right to contact counsel should lead the courts to regard police allegations regarding "implied waiver" of the right to counsel very sceptically. For example, such an argument by police was rejected in *R. v. Laplante* (1987), 48 D.L.R. (4th) 615 (Sask. C.A.), where the accused asked on several occasions to use the telephone to see whether his wife had retained counsel. The court held that it was implicit that he was asserting his right to counsel and that, in any event, doubt should be resolved in favour of the accused. In *R. v. Coutereille* (1995), 33 C.R.R. (2d) D-1 (B.C.C.A.), the police were bound to refrain from taking any further statements from an accused (who had stated that he wanted to talk with a lawyer) until an opportunity to speak with counsel had been provided, in the absence of any subsequent explicit waiver by the accused.

On the other hand, the courts have not been consistent in presuming against waiver. Compare the following two cases. In *R. v. Smith*, [1989] 2 S.C.R. 368, the Court held that the accused's s. 10(b) *Charter* rights had not been infringed when he made incriminating statements to the police, whereas the accused in *R. v. Black*, *supra*, under **Search and Seizure**, was said not to have waived her rights. Smith was said to have failed to be diligent in exercising his right to counsel, even though afforded a "reasonable opportunity" to contact a lawyer. His conduct in answering police questions was said to amount to a "waiver" of his s. 10(b) right. Black was said not to have waived her right by answering police questions because the police had failed to afford her a reasonable opportunity to reach her lawyer, and they should have waited until the morning before attempting to interview the accused. See, also, *R. v. Shaw* (1995), 68 B.C.A.C. 314, in which the court deemed the accused to have understood the jeopardy he faced, and held that a second warning was not required. The original warning had been given when the accused was facing a possession of marijuana charge. Police then questioned the accused with respect to the more serious charge of possession for the purposes of trafficking.

R. v. Brydges†

[LAMER, J.:]

The accused, a resident of Alberta, was arrested in Manitoba in connection with a murder which took place in Edmonton. He was charged with second degree murder and informed without delay of his right to retain and instruct counsel. Upon arrival at the police station, the accused was placed in an interview room and, at the beginning of the interrogation, given a second opportunity to call a lawyer. The accused asked the investigating officer if they had Legal Aid in Manitoba because he could not afford a private lawyer. The officer, who was from Edmonton, answered that he imagined that they had such a system in Manitoba. The officer then asked the accused if he felt there was a reason for him to want to talk to a lawyer. The accused answered "Not right now, no". During the interrogation which followed, the accused made a number of statements. He later interrupted the questioning and requested a Legal Aid lawyer. The Legal Aid lawyer contacted by the police advised the accused not to say anything more and the interrogation ended. At trial, the judge found that, at the beginning of the interrogation, the accused essentially requested the assistance of counsel but that he was unsure if he could afford one. Because the police did not assist the accused in exercising his right to counsel by determining the availability of Legal Aid at that time, the trial judge held that the accused's rights under s. 10(b) of the *Canadian Charter of Rights and Freedoms* were violated, and the accused's statements were excluded pursuant to s. 24(2) of the *Charter*. As a result, the accused was acquitted. A majority of the Court of Appeal set aside the acquittal and ordered a new trial.

. . . .

ANALYSIS

Section 10(b) of the *Charter* reads as follows:

> **10.** Everyone has the right on arrest or detention
>
> ...
>
> (b) to retain and instruct counsel without delay and to be informed of that right;

This Court has on numerous occasions stated that the proper approach to interpreting the meaning of the rights and freedoms guaranteed by the *Charter* is to adopt a purposive analysis: *Hunter* v. *Southam Inc.*, [1984] 2 S.C.R. 145, and *R.* v. *Big M Drug Mart Ltd.*, [1985] 1 S.C.R. 295. In respect of s. 10 of the *Charter*, this Court has made clear that the right to counsel is, to cite the words of Wilson J. in *Clarkson, supra*, at p. 394, aimed "at fostering the principles of adjudicative fairness", one of which is "the concern for fair treatment of an accused person". It is of note that the right to counsel is triggered "on arrest or detention". Fair treatment of an accused person who has been arrested or detained necessarily implies that he be given a reasonable opportunity to exercise the right to counsel because the detainee is in the control of the police, and as such is not at liberty to exercise the privileges that he otherwise would be free to pursue. There is a duty then, on the police to facilitate contact with counsel because, as I stated in *R.* v. *Manninen*, [1987] 1 S.C.R. 1233, at pp. 1242–43:

---

† [1990] 1 S.C.R. 190.

The purpose of the right to counsel is to allow the detainee not only to be informed of his rights and obligations under the law but, equally if not more important, to obtain advice as to how to exercise those rights.... For the right to counsel to be effective, the detainee must have access to this advice before he is questioned or otherwise required to provide evidence.

As a result, s. 10(*b*) of the *Charter* imposes at least two duties on the police in addition to the duty to inform the detainee of his rights. First the police must give the accused or detained person a reasonable opportunity to exercise the right to retain and instruct counsel, and second, the police must refrain from questioning or attempting to elicit evidence from the detainee until the detainee has had that reasonable opportunity. The second duty includes a bar on the police from compelling the detainee to make a decision or participate in a process which could ultimately have an adverse effect in the conduct of an eventual trial until the person has had a reasonable opportunity to exercise the right to counsel: *R. v. Ross*, [1989] 1 S.C.R. 3, at p. 12.

It is the case, however, that the rights set out in the *Charter* are not absolute. Indeed, this Court has held that the right to retain and instruct counsel must be exercised diligently by the detainee. If the detainee is not diligent, then the correlative duties on the police are suspended: *R. v. Tremblay*, [1987] 2 S.C.R. 435.

. . . .

A detainee may, either explicitly or implicitly, waive his right to retain and instruct counsel, although the standard will be very high where the alleged waiver is implicit. A majority of this Court in *Clarkson, supra*, concluded as follows in respect of a waiver of the right to counsel at pp. 394–95, a passage that has been cited with approval in subsequent cases dealing with s. 10(*b*):

> ... it is evident that any alleged waiver of this right by an accused must be carefully considered and that the accused's awareness of the consequences of what he or she is saying is crucial. Indeed, this Court stated with respect to the waiver of statutory procedural guarantees in *Korponay* v. *Attorney General of Canada*, [1982] 1 S.C.R. 41, at p. 49, that any waiver "... is dependent upon it being *clear and unequivocal that the person is waiving the procedural safeguard and is doing so with full knowledge of the rights the procedure was enacted to protect and of the effect the waiver will have on those rights in the process*". [Emphasis in original.]

This then, briefly stated, is a summary of the principles developed thus far by this Court in respect of the scope of s. 10(*b*) of the *Charter*.

In applying these principles to the case at bar, I must once again state that I accept the findings of fact made by the trial judge. The learned trial judge concluded that the appellant was essentially requesting the assistance of counsel, but felt that his inability to afford a lawyer was an impediment to the exercise of his right to retain one. As I noted above, the trial judge had the unique advantage of hearing from witnesses on the *voir dire*, and more importantly, listened to the tape recording of the interrogation of the accused. In light of these circumstances, I am of the view that the learned trial judge's findings should not be disturbed. The majority of the Court of Appeal took a different view. McClung J.A. held that the appellant waived his right to retain and instruct counsel when he responded "Not right now, no" to the query about whether there was a reason for him to want to talk to a lawyer. McClung J.A. stated that the appellant "elected to go it alone and continued to do so until the intensity of his interrogation led him to believe that it was time to request counsel" (p. 334). The extract referred to by the majority of the Court of Appeal must, however, be read having regard to the entire context of the interrogation. The comment referred to takes place immediately after the appellant requested information about Legal Aid, and expressed his concern about being able to afford a lawyer. In that context, the appellant specifically stated that "the main thing" was that he was unable to afford counsel. The trial judge found that this amounted to a request for counsel. The appellant, however, was left with the mistaken impression that his inability to afford a lawyer prevented him from exercising his right to counsel. I agree with Harradence J.A. in dissent that in this context the appellant did not understand the full meaning of his right to counsel. In this respect, it can hardly be said that the appellant was in a position to carefully consider the consequences of waiving that which he did not understand. I am therefore of the view that the appellant, given the standard for waiver set out by this Court in *Clarkson* and subsequent cases, did not waive his right to retain and instruct counsel.

Once the appellant in effect requested the assistance of counsel it was incumbent on the police officer to facilitate contact with counsel by giving the appellant a reasonable opportunity to exercise his right to counsel. On the specific facts of this case, the Court is faced with the following question: when an accused expresses a concern that his inability to afford a lawyer is an impediment to the exercise of the right to counsel, is there a duty on the police to inform him of the existence of duty counsel and the ability to apply for Legal Aid? In my view there is. I say this because imposing this duty on the police in these circumstances is consistent with the purpose underlying the right to retain and instruct counsel. A detainee is advised of the right to retain and instruct counsel without delay because it is upon arrest or detention that an accused is in *immediate need of legal advice*. As I stated in *Manninen, supra*, at p. 1243, one of the main functions of counsel at this early stage of detention is to confirm the existence of the right to remain silent and to advise the detainee about how to exercise that right. It is not always the case that immediately upon detention an accused will be concerned about retaining the lawyer that will eventually represent him at a trial, if there is one. Rather, one of the important reasons for retaining legal advice without delay upon being detained is linked to the protection of the right against self-incrimination. This is precisely the reason that there is a duty on the police to cease questioning the detainee until he has had a reasonable opportunity to retain and instruct counsel.

On the facts of the case at bar, it is clear that the advice the appellant received from the Legal Aid lawyer he spoke to was to the effect that, and this was a situation which is not always the case, he should rest on his right not to make any more statements until he spoke to a lawyer in Edmonton. In retrospect, had the appellant been informed of the availability of duty counsel or Legal Aid at the time that he first raised a concern about affordability, the subsequent interrogation may never have taken place. In this regard I refer to the case of *R. v. Parks* (1988), 33 C.R.R. 1, an oral judgment by Watt J. of the Ontario High Court. In that case, the accused entered a police station and reported that he had killed two people. He was bleeding profusely from both hands and was taken to hospital so that he could be tended to. The accused was advised of his right to retain and instruct counsel and that he had a right to remain silent. The police then conducted two taped interviews with the accused. In the second interview, in response to the police officer's questions, the accused indicated that he had a lawyer but that he did not want the officer to contact the lawyer because he could not afford to pay him. The second interview continued despite the accused asserting that he had nothing further to say. The officer, although he was aware of the existence of the Ontario Legal Aid Plan and the availability of duty counsel, did not advise the accused of these. The accused testified that had he received the advice of counsel, he might not have continued with the second interview.

. . . .

The case at bar is one, like *Parks*, where the accused was clearly interested in obtaining counsel, but mistakenly believed that his right to retain a lawyer was contingent on affordability. The failure of the police to inform the appellant of the existence of Legal Aid or duty counsel at the time that he first indicated a concern about his ability to pay a lawyer, was a restriction on the appellant's right to counsel, in so far as the appellant was left with an erroneous impression of the nature and extent of his s. 10(*b*) rights. As a result, I would conclude, along with the trial judge and Harradence J.A. in dissent at the Court of Appeal, that the appellant's s. 10(*b*) rights were violated.

. . . .

In respect of the exclusion of the statements under s. 24(2) of the *Charter*, I would note that the majority of the Court of Appeal erred in concluding that the appellant needed to demonstrate a causal link between the *Charter* infringement and the evidence obtained thereby. This Court has clearly established in *R. v. Strachan*, [1988] 2 S.C.R. 980, that a requirement of strict causation is not appropriate under s. 24(2). Rather, s. 24(2) is implicated as long as a *Charter* violation occurred in the course of obtaining the evidence. In the case at bar there is no doubt that the statements were obtained in the course of the violation of s. 10(*b*) of the *Charter*. As regards the test set out to determine whether the admission of evidence obtained in violation of the *Charter* would bring the administration of justice into disrepute, I note the following. First, the nature of the evidence obtained was conscripted or self-incriminatory evidence whose admission would normally render a trial unfair. The fairness of the trial would be adversely affected since, in the words of Wilson J. in *R. v. Black*, [1989] 2 S.C.R. 138, at p. 160, "the admission of the statement would infringe on the appellant's right against self-incrimination, a right which could have been protected had the appellant had an opportunity to consult counsel." Second, in terms of the seriousness of the violation, although it cannot be said that the conduct of the officer was flagrant or blatant, it was a serious error not to inform the appellant of the existence of Legal Aid or duty counsel especially when the appellant explicitly raised the issue, and in light of the fact that such information was readily at hand. Finally, in balancing the admission of the evidence against the exclusion of the evidence, I note that the Crown concedes that the statements at most represent evidence of consciousness of guilt and admissions of recent possession of property stolen from the home of the victim. In addition, this Court has repeatedly held that the mere fact that an accused is charged with a serious offence provides no justification for admitting the evidence where there has been a serious *Charter* violation and the admission of the evidence would affect the fundamental fairness of the trial: see *Black, supra*, at p. 160, and also *Manninen, supra*, at p. 1246. I would conclude, therefore, that the evidence obtained as a result of the s. 10(*b*) violation was properly excluded by the trial judge.

Although my reasons thus far are sufficient to dispose of this appeal in favour of the appellant, I feel compelled to make certain comments on the broader question raised by Watt J. in *Parks, supra*, namely whether it should be part of the information component of the constitutional guarantee under s. 10(*b*) that accused persons should be told as a matter of routine *in all cases* of arrest or detention of the existence and availability of duty counsel and Legal Aid plans. In my view, it is consistent with the purpose underlying s. 10((*b*) of the *Charter* to impose that duty on the police in all cases of detention. I find it necessary to address this issue because otherwise, among other reasons, there is an element of uncertainty facing law enforcement officials as a result of the disposition of this appeal. Although in a case like *Parks* or the case at bar, it is clear that the accused expressed a concern about the inability to afford counsel acting as an impediment to the exercise of the right to counsel, that will not be the case in all situations. For example, there may be cases where the detainee does not explicitly ask for or about Legal Aid, but still expresses a concern about affordability of counsel. Additionally, there may be cases where a detainee says nothing about his inability to afford counsel because he believes it is a forgone conclusion that unless he can afford a lawyer, there is no other way to exercise the right to retain and instruct counsel. Thus, police officers would be put in the difficult position of having to judge, on the spot, whether a person has expressed concerns about affordability or whether there should be further inquiries made of a detainee who does not express concerns about affordability but whom the police officer suspects may be indigent and in need of duty counsel or Legal Aid. In fact, it is most often the indigent and the disadvantaged in our society that are not as aware of the schemes that the State has set up on their behalf. In this respect I quote from the landmark decision of the United States Supreme Court in *Miranda* v. *Arizona*, 384 U.S. 436 (1966), at p. 473:

> The warning of a right to counsel would be hollow if not couched in terms that would convey to the indigent — the person most often subjected to interrogation — the knowledge that he too has a right to have counsel present. As with the warnings of the right to remain silent and of the general right to counsel, only by effective and express explanation to the indigent of this right can there be assurance that he was truly in a position to exercise it.

In my view then, these policy concerns in respect of making police officers' duties under the *Charter* clear and of ensuring that all detainees are made aware of the existence of duty counsel and Legal Aid, complement each other, and support the view that information about the existence and availability of duty counsel and Legal Aid plans should be part of the standard s. 10(*b*) caution upon arrest or detention.

I also find support for my view in the nature of Legal Aid plans and delivery systems in Canada. Between 1967 and 1976 every province and territory in Canada has set up a Legal Aid plan. The responsibility for the provision of Legal Aid is divided between the federal government under its authority in matters of criminal law, and the provincial governments under their authority for the administration of justice and for property and civil rights. This joint responsibility for Legal Aid has been confirmed in agreements since 1972 when the federal Department of Justice began cost-sharing Legal Aid for criminal cases. The Legal Aid plans of each province vary somewhat with each province establishing its own financial conditions to be met by applicants, provided that the test is flexible so that the applicant need not be required to hire a private lawyer if in doing so the applicant would have to contract major debts or sell modest assets. Different systems are used to deliver Legal Aid. Judicare systems, in which services are delivered on a fee-for-service basis through private law firms and staff systems, in which professionals are employed directly by the plan are two types of systems that exist in Canada. The systems operate either independently, or as in Manitoba [...] are combined. Legal Aid in criminal matters extends to any eligible person who is charged with any indictable offence against an act of Parliament, and at the discretion of the province, to any eligible person charged with a federal summary conviction offence. The province has the responsibility to take reasonable measures to see that a lawyer is made available to the eligible person without delay.

In addition to the provisions set up for Legal Aid, each province also has, in one form or other, a system of duty counsel for adults and youths in criminal proceedings. As I noted above duty counsel are intended to provide with immediate but temporary advice and assistance those persons who cannot afford a lawyer or those who do not know a lawyer. Indeed, knowledge of the existence and availability of duty counsel is perhaps of primary importance since financial status is generally not considered as a pre-condition to obtaining the services of duty counsel. In fact, it is often duty counsel that is in a position to inform the detainee about making an application for Legal Aid, or his options if he is not eligible. As Wilkins, op. cit., states in his book at p. 137, "[d]uty counsel is prepared to act during any stage of the cases before the court and on behalf of any unrepresented person. However, an important part of his function is to refer the accused to the certificate aspect of the program". This is in addition to the other functions of duty counsel which include advising the detainee of his rights and taking such steps as are necessary to protect his rights such as representing him on an application for remand or on a bail application. (For a more complete account of Legal Aid and duty counsel services, see *Legal Aid in Canada 1985* (1986) published by the Canadian Centre for Justice Statistics.)

This brief overview of Legal Aid and duty counsel systems reveals the extent of Canada's recognition of the importance of the right to counsel for *all* persons detained in connection with criminal offences.... All of this is to reinforce the view that the right to retain and instruct counsel, in modern Canadian society, has come to mean more than the right to retain a lawyer privately. It now also means the right to have access to counsel free of charge where the accused meets certain financial criteria set up by the provincial Legal Aid plan, and the right to have access to immediate, although temporary, advice from duty counsel irrespective of financial status. These considerations, therefore, lead me to the conclusion that as part of the information component of s. 10(*b*) of the *Charter*, a detainee should be informed of the existence and availability of the applicable systems of duty counsel and Legal Aid in the jurisdiction, in order to give the detainee a full understanding of the right to retain and instruct counsel.

. . . .

As I noted above, in *Ross, supra*, this Court held that detained persons have a right to retain the counsel of their choice, and it is only if the lawyer chosen is not available within a reasonable time that the detainee should be expected to exercise the right by calling another lawyer. It may appear to some, as it does to me, that the additional duty imposed on the police combined with the increasing presence of duty counsel services, irrespective of a means test, may well have an effect on the consideration of what constitutes "reasonable diligence" of a detainee in pursuing the right to counsel. The purposive approach which leads us to the conclusion that a detainee has the right to be informed of the availability of Legal Aid and of duty counsel also raises questions as to how long the police must wait for counsel of the detainee's choice to become available.... [The Court returned to these implementational questions in *Prosper, infra*.]

I wish to also point out that the issue of whether there is a constitutional right to have the assistance or representation of counsel is not before the Court. This issue normally arises when an accused cannot bring himself within the provincial Legal Aid plan and duty counsel cannot, as they usually cannot, furnish a full defence. A consideration of this issue goes beyond an examination of s. 10 of the *Charter*, to ss. 7 and 11(*d*). That matter will have to be decided when the facts of the case raise the issue and the matter is fully argued before the Court.

Before concluding, it is my view that in light of the imposition of the additional duty on the police as part of the information component of the s. 10(*b*) caution, a transition period is appropriate. This transition period is needed to enable the police to properly discharge their new burden, more specifically to take into account the reality that police officers often use printed cards from which they read the caution given to detainees. In my view a period of thirty days from the date of this judgment is sufficient time for the police forces to react, and to prepare new cautions. I note, in passing, that the imposition of a transition period is not unusual. In *Mills* v. *The Queen*, [1986] 1 S.C.R. 863, for example, I stated that a transitional period was appropriate in the context of the application of the principles developed under s. 11(*b*) of the *Charter*. In addition, in *Reference re Manitoba Language Rights*, [1985] 1 S.C.R. 721, this Court established a period of temporary validity for the Acts of the Manitoba Legislature, in order to allow for the translation, re-enactment, printing and publishing of previously unilingual legislation.

I would, accordingly, allow the appeal and restore the acquittal of the appellant at trial.

Brydges added two elements to the informational requirements of s. 10(b). Police are now required to inform a detainee about access to legal aid and about access to temporary legal advice. This latter category has since been referred to as "Brydges duty counsel" (*Prosper*, *infra* at 257):

> Duty counsel in this context refers to the provision of immediate and free preliminary legal advice by qualified personnel, whether staff lawyers from Legal Aid offices, lawyers from the private bar, lawyers specifically hired for the purpose of fielding calls from detainees, or otherwise.

In light of *Brydges*, a number of provinces responded by establishing 24-hour duty counsel services. Consider the financial repercussions of these rulings.

In a series of cases released in 1994, the Supreme Court returned to a consideration of *Brydges* and the obligation of police to disclose available duty counsel systems under the information component of s. 10(b). In *R. v. Prosper*, [1994] 3 S.C.R. 236, the Court suggested that in provinces where a "Brydges duty counsel" was not available (Nova Scotia: *Prosper*, and Prince Edward Island: *R. v. Matheson*, [1994] 3 S.C.R. 328), police should "hold off" until counsel becomes available. Thus, according to the majority, the availability or unavailability of duty counsel services affects the length of the "holding-off" period, even though the Court recognized that there was no constitutionally imposed obligation on governments to ensure that free and immediate preliminary legal advice is available upon arrest or detention. In jurisdictions that provide some system of free preliminary legal advice, police are also obliged to inform detainees of the existence of these services and how to access them (e.g. by reading out the toll-free number): *R. v. Bartle*, [1994] 3 S.C.R. 173; *R. v. Pozniak*, [1994] 3 S.C.R. 310.

Once the court has determined that there is a breach of s. 10(b), the remaining issue is the assessment of whether the breach goes to the fairness of the trial, whether there is any justification (e.g. urgency), and whether the evidence should be excluded under s. 24(2): the nature of the evidence (real or conscripted), the seriousness of the violation of the right to counsel, and the effect of excluding the evidence.

In *Prosper*, breathalyzer evidence was excluded. The accused had indicated that he wanted to contact a lawyer. He was given a list of legal aid lawyers, whom he attempted to telephone. Unfortunately, only one of them was available outside regular office hours. Chief Justice Lamer, writing for the majority, held that the s. 10(b) violation was not saved by any "urgency" or compelling circumstances. In dissent, Madam Justice L'Heureux-Dubé considered the practical effect of the majority position, and held that the police should not be required to "hold off." To insist on that would be to:

> effectively [ring] ... the death knell of the breathalyser as a device to help take drunk drivers off the roads in provinces that do not have 24-hour duty counsel service programs or their equivalent.... To suggest that provinces which do not provide services which they are not constitutionally required to provide will be penalized in their means of promoting safety on their roads is to me unacceptable. [*Prosper* at 290]

She would have held that if there was a violation of s. 10(b), the evidence should not be excluded, on the basis of her characterization of the evidence as "real" rather than "conscripted," and on the basis that the accused would have had no choice but to comply with the demand, even had he had access to counsel's advice.

In *Bartle*, the breathalyzer evidence and a self-incriminating statement were also excluded. While the Ontario police officer mentioned the availability of legal aid, he did not read the section from the caution card that referred to a toll-free number for duty counsel. Chief Justice Lamer referred to the expansion of the availability of 24-hour duty counsel in reaction to *Brydges*, citing Kathryn Moore, "Police Implementation of Supreme Court of Canada Charter Decisions: An Empirical Study" (1992) 30 Osgoode Hall L.J. 547:

> One of the clauses which was added to the standard caution in Ontario and which received the most publicity was: "You also have the right to free advice from a Legal Aid lawyer." In addition, the 24-hour, 1-800 Legal Aid number for duty counsel was printed on all police caution cards. Initially, however, it appears that police in Ontario were not providing, as a matter of routine, detainees with the 1-800 number printed on their cautioncards. This is clear not only from the case at bar and from its companion case, *Pozniak*, but also from the set of six cases (which include this case and *Pozniak*) which were heard at the same time by the Ontario Court of Appeal, as well as from several lower court decisions in Ontario.... [In response], Ontario's Solicitor

General advised provincial police forces to ... include the 1-800 Legal Aid number already printed on their caution cards....

It also appears that the more fully people are advised of their rights under s. 10(b), the more likely they are to exercise these rights [citing Prairie Research Associates, *Duty Counsel Systems: Summary Report* (April 1993)]. [*Bartle* at 200]

In contrast to *Bartle* and *Pozniak*, in another case centred around the obligation to inform a detainee of available duty counsel systems under the information requirement of s. 10(b), *R. v. Harper*, [1994] 3 S.C.R. 343, the Court held that, despite the violation of s. 10(b), the accused would have acted the same way regardless. Thus, although the accused was told there was legal aid but given no specifics about duty counsel, the admission of the evidence was said not to taint the fairness of the trial. The majority referred to the accused's "almost irresistible desire to confess" (at 354). In contrast to the other four cases which dealt with breathalyzer samples, *Harper* involved self-incriminating statements in the context of a charge of assault causing bodily harm on his wife. Are there different interests at stake in insisting on s. 10(b) rights with respect to breathalyzer samples as opposed to confessions? What should the social policy be?

B. RIGHT TO COUNSEL AT TRIAL

The right to counsel includes the right to counsel of choice. This right is practically limited by counsel's competence and willingness to accept the retainer. It is also limited by a requirement that counsel be available within a reasonable period of time and be free of a conflict of interest: *R. v. McCallem* (1999), 43 O.R. (3d) 56 (C.A.).

In the pre-*Charter* case of *Re Ewing and Kearney v. R.* (1974), 18 C.C.C. (2d) 356 (B.C.C.A.), the B.C. Court of Appeal rejected the argument that the unavailability of legal aid necessarily interfered with the accused's *Bill of Rights* s. 2 right to "retain and instruct counsel without delay," or with his right to a fair trial, and thus refused to recognize a substantive right to counsel. In another early case, *Re Kennedy and the Queen et al.* (1984), 15 C.C.C. (3d) 60 (N.B.Q.B.), the trial judge denied the accused's application for judicial review of a refusal by legal aid officers to grant a certificate to cover the cost of a preliminary hearing in a break and enter case. Referring to the authority granted under the New Brunswick *Legal Aid Act* to the provincial Barristers' Society to determine whether or not the right to legal assistance should be financed out of public funds, Dickson J. held:

> There is no suggestion here that that authority has been exercised in any arbitrary fashion. It would, in my view, be impertinent for a court to supplant its discretion for that of the Society. I find that in so far as the applicant seeks a reversal of the refusal to issue a legal aid certificate, the application must fail.
>
> . . .
>
> It is still open to the applicant to apply to the trial judge at the outset of trial for appointment of counsel to act on his behalf if he is still unrepresented. That the inherent authority exists cannot be in doubt, but it is nevertheless not an authority which will be freely exercised, particularly since the advent of a legal aid programme. I express no opinion as to what the outcome of such an application might be, other than to say that an accused, having been given the opportunity to be represented by counsel in another appropriate forum, should not take it for granted that he will be afforded the right to counsel at trial. I do not particularly envy the responsibility of a trial judge in ensuring a fair trial where an accused does not have counsel. At the same time it may prove an advantage to him to appear even without counsel. *To achieve acquittal if he is innocent certainly is not an insurmountable object. I may say that in 20 years' experience as a trial judge I have never seen an innocent accused found guilty.* It would be surprising if that precedent were to be broken in this or any other similar instance. [Emphasis added.]

The right to counsel has not been thus far interpreted to impose many obligations upon trial judges conducting trials for unrepresented accuseds. For example, while an accused who is unrepresented must be informed by the trial judge that counsel would provide a distinct advantage, the trial judge need not take any steps in this regard if it is "patent" that the accused wishes to represent herself or himself: *R. v. McGibbon*

(1988), 31 O.A.C. 10. Furthermore, although the trial judge in such a situation is obliged to provide reasonable assistance to the accused so that any available defences are brought out with "full force and effect," the judge is not obliged to act as advocate by performing functions like reviewing the transcript from the preliminary inquiry for inconsistent statements.

The provinces administer legal aid using different models of service delivery: certificates, whereby accused persons receive a certificate from legal aid and then attempt to find counsel who will accept the terms of the certificate (hourly rates; maximum hours for certain matters; capping of fees for work such as *Charter* applications); duty counsel programs, whereby lawyers are paid to provide summary advice and assistance to unrepresented persons appearing in the criminal courts, and 24-hour advice lines, such as those already discussed; and clinics, whereby staff lawyers represent persons entitled to legal aid. Most provinces use a mix of these models.

Legal aid is allocated using both financial eligibility criteria and another set of criteria focused on the consequences of conviction if the accused is unrepresented. The main factor will be whether the accused faces a likelihood of jail, but some provincial schemes also look at other consequences, such as loss of livelihood, deportation, and loss of custody of children.

CERTIFICATES

Since the advent of the *Charter*, there have been a number of challenges that asserted that the right to counsel comprehends the right to funded counsel. Thus, where various provincial/territorial legal aid plans have denied funding for representation, accuseds have sought to compel the funding of that representation. Challenges with respect to legal aid funding have focused broadly on the right to counsel and specific issues arising from this right, such as the limits placed on choice of counsel by the tariffs set by legal aid schemes; the limits placed on the conduct of the defence (hours of preparation, restrictions on election of mode of trial); and the limits placed on the availability of counsel on appeal. Sections 7 and 11 of the *Charter* are invoked.

The *Rain* decision that follows is representative of the kinds of arguments, evidence, and precedents that will be considered when an accused advances a *Charter* claim of entitlement to funded counsel.

R. v. Rain[†]

[SULATYCKY J.A.:]

The Crown appeals from the judgment of a summary conviction appeal justice dismissing an appeal from the stay of proceedings against the respondent, Muriel Mary Rain, until funded legal counsel is provided. ...

. . . .

FACTS

On April 27, 1993, the respondent, Ms. Rain, was charged with two offences under the *Criminal Code*: unlawful operation of a motor vehicle while impaired, contrary to s. 253(a) and failing to comply with a demand for a breath sample, contrary to s. 254(5).

The Crown proceeded summarily on the charges. Ms. Rain appeared in Provincial Court in Glenevis, Alberta on May 20, 1993. She pleaded not guilty to the impaired driving charge and guilty to refusing to give a breathalyzer sample. The judge refused to take the guilty plea and suggested that she talk to one of the lawyers present. Later she pleaded not guilty to the refusal charge. She said she was going to get a lawyer through legal aid and a trial date was set allowing Ms. Rain time to contact the Legal Aid Society.

On June 17, 1993, the day set for trial which was estimated to take one hour, the court was informed that Ms. Rain had been denied coverage by Legal Aid because this was her first offence. The Provincial Court judge referred Ms. Rain back to Legal Aid and directed that failing the appointment

---

[†] (1998), 223 A.R. 359 (C.A.).

of counsel by Legal Aid, counsel would be appointed by the court at legal aid rates.

The Crown's application for an order in the nature of certiorari to quash the provincial court order was denied on December 13, 1993: *R. v. Rain (M. M.)* (1993), 147 A.R. 150.

An appeal to this court on November 14, 1994, was allowed, granted certiorari, quashed the provincial court order and returned the matter to the Provincial Court on the ground that both the Provincial Court judge and Court of Queen's Bench justice had erred in deciding the merits of the case without a proper factual record before them: *R. v. Rain (M. M.)* (1994), 157 A.R. 385.

At p. 390 (A.R.), this court also indicated the type of evidence which would be useful for applications of this sort could include the financial circumstances of the accused, the accused's educational background, what the accused knows of the charge, what particulars the accused has obtained from the Crown, what efforts were made to obtain Legal Aid, the reasons for Legal Aid's denial, whether the accused has any other access to a lawyer or agent capable of giving her an effective defence to the charge and any other matter which would help the accused make her argument that she cannot fairly meet the charge without counsel. This court (while questioning whether ordering the expenditure of public funds was an appropriate *Charter* remedy) also said that, before making a precedent-creating order of the kind here, it was necessary to have information on the cost to the government of such precedent.

Ms. Rain re-applied unsuccessfully for legal aid. Then, on March 20, 1995, after giving notice to the Crown, she applied in Provincial Court for an order appointing counsel. Ms. Rain was represented by counsel, who appeared *pro bono publico*. In support of the application, the court heard evidence from Ms. Rain; Wanda Fish, Northern Director of the Legal Aid Society of Alberta, and Peter Bruce Gunn, a lawyer who was qualified as a expert in the area of defence of impaired driving and related offences. Ms. Rain also entered into evidence a letter from Alan Wood, Regional Vice-President of the Insurance Bureau of Canada. The Crown's evidence consisted of the Law Society of Alberta's new Code of Conduct.

Ms. Rain's evidence included the facts that she had dropped out of high school in grade 12 and that because of her children, she had minimal job experience. Her last employment was running a hot lunch program on the Alexis Reserve. At the time of her testimony, she was unemployed.

Ms. Fish gave evidence of the terms of the agreement between the federal and provincial governments and the Law Society of Alberta for the provision of legal aid. Pursuant to those terms, the Legal Aid Society does not provide counsel for summary conviction matters unless a conviction would affect the accused's means of earning a livelihood, there is a chance of incarceration or the applicant has unusual needs such as illiteracy or some sort of mental or physical impediment. Following those terms, Ms. Rain was denied coverage. She also had exhausted all possible appeals.

Ms. Fish also testified that the budget for the Legal Aid Society was approximately $27,000,000, but had been subject to budget cuts. This did not affect coverage.

Mr. Gunn gave his expert opinion that impaired driving charges are the most litigated and technically difficult in the *Criminal Code*. In every case the *Charter of Rights* is a live issue.

With respect to the complexity of the case, after obtaining a waiver of privilege, Mr. Gunn testified that Ms. Rain had told him she was not the driver of the motor vehicle but had been pushed into the driver's seat. Because there were other witnesses, in his opinion, that aspect of the case may be dealt with fairly easily. The refusal to provide a breathalyser sample, he thought, raised different difficulties about whether there was a valid demand and whether the failure to provide her with a list of legal aid lawyers would be a defence to her refusal.

He further gave evidence that the typical penalty for a first offence is a fine of about $600. Although incarceration usually resulted from a failure to pay, he testified that the judges are "pretty good" if a person is incapable of paying the fine. They generally lower the fine when a person's circumstances make payment difficult and under the available fine option programs, there are ways of working off the fine in place of serving any default time.

In this case, there was no evidence that Ms. Rain, who was unemployed at the time of trial, could not participate in a fine options program.

Mr. Gunn was allowed to give his opinion on matters unrelated to his expertise in the defence of impaired driving and related charges, including the answer to the ultimate question before the learned Provincial Court judge. When asked if in his opinion it was possible for the respondent to be provided with a fair trial in the absence of counsel, he replied: "She wouldn't have a hope." No explanation or foundation for this opinion was given, but Mr. Gunn's evidence as a whole throws some light on the reasons for it.

Although not qualified as an expert in the execution of judicial functions, Mr. Gunn gave evidence and opinion on how judges discharge their duties. He was asked if it was not right that when an unrepresented accused recounted to a judge his version of events, similarly to the way he would recount them to an interviewing lawyer, (aside from credibility issues) and the facts are the foundation for a defence, the judge would take that into account. His anecdotal reply was as follows:

> No, sir, I disagree with you absolutely. I sat — when I articled back in 1969, I sat for a month with my uncle on the bench believe it or not. He was a Provincial Court judge in Cape Breton. We had a more relaxed atmosphere there. And I drove back to Sydney with him one time, and a fellow had come before him that morning on a speeding charge between Sydney and Glace Bay. There is a point to the story, believe it.
>
> There was an unusual section in the Nova Scotia *Highway Traffic Act*. It said that the speed limit on all roads in Nova Scotia was 60 miles an hour except where the speed should be reduced because of other circumstances, and a speed sign reducing it was *prima facie*, only *prima facie* evidence that that was a reasonable speed and anything above it would be unreasonable. There was one stretch of road between Sydney and Glace Bay that's totally empty, and for some particular reason they put up a 40 mile an hour speed sign there. That was the spot where the guy had been stopped doing 50.
>
> He did not know the rule that if you could show it wasn't reasonable, then it's not a speeding ticket, and my uncle was actually known as being one of the softer judges in the Maritimes, and we were driving back to Sydney, and I was very annoyed at him because he had convicted this fellow, and I had said to him, why didn't you acquit. Here we're driving on the road, there is nothing. He said, if he had raised it, I would have acquitted. It is not my job to be advocate, it is my job to adjudicate because — and it struck me like a slap in the face, and it's something I've never forgotten, sir. The judge is supposed to be an adjudicator. He can't become one of the litigants. If he does, he loses every possibility of being an adjudicator.

In the next question posed to Mr. Gunn, Crown counsel attempted to be more particular by referring to the specifics of this case and concluded by asking: "...as long as she can explain what happened to her, then those relevant issues come to the attention of the judge, and the judge will interpret them according to law; isn't that right?"

Mr. Gunn replied: "No, sir, that's fantasy land. With all due respect, that is not reality. That is not the way courts work, and if you honestly believe that that's how every trial takes place, I don't know where you've been, and I'm sorry, but that — that's just plum stupid."

This cynical view of the way judges function appears to be the foundation for Mr. Gunn's opinion that without counsel the respondent "wouldn't have a hope" of a fair trial.

In response to questions from the court, Mr. Gunn also gave evidence about the attitude of the general public to alcohol related drinking driving offences. He testified that such conduct is no longer socially acceptable. He said that it is now looked upon as a crime, not as merely wild behaviour.

The letter of Mr. Wood outlined the insurance implications of a conviction for impaired driving. These included that, following conviction for impaired driving, insurance coverage likely would only be available through a high risk insurer at a significantly higher premium.

On March 21, 1995, the Provincial Court judge ruled that Ms. Rain's right to a fair trial would be violated if funded counsel were not appointed to act for her. The judge ordered the appointment of counsel to be funded at the Legal Aid rate: *R. v. Rain*, [1995] 6 W.W.R. 137. Subsequently, on April 12, 1995, he acknowledged that he did not have jurisdiction to order the Crown or any other body to fund counsel or to compel *pro bono* work and therefore, ordered that the proceedings against Ms. Rain be stayed until she was provided with funded counsel: *R. v. Rain* [1995] 6 W.W.R. 146.

The Crown's appeal to a Summary Conviction Appeal Justice was dismissed on October 25, 1996: *R. v. Rain*, [1997] 2 W.W.R. 38.

ANALYSIS

Whether the *Charter* Guarantees Funded Counsel

Leave to appeal was granted, first, on the issue of whether Ms. Rain's rights under ss. 7 and 11(d) of the *Charter* would be infringed by virtue of the unavailability of funded counsel for her trial.

. . . .

[Sections 7 and 11(d) of the *Charter*], on their face, do not provide for funded counsel. Both this court in *R v. Robinson* (1990), 51 C.C.C. (3d) 452 and the Ontario Court of Appeal in *R. v. Rowbotham* (1988), 41 C.C.C. (3d) 1, among others, have held a general right to funded defence counsel cannot be inferred.

In *Robinson* and in *Deutsch v. Law Society of Upper Canada Legal Aid Fund* (1985), 48 C.R. (3d) 166 (Ont. Div. Ct.) (considered in *Rowbotham*), the courts were provided with the 1981 minutes of the Special Joint Committee of the Senate and the House of Commons on the Constitution of Canada respecting its recommendations on the *Charter*. The minutes showed that a proposed amendment would have enlarged s. 10 of the *Charter* to include a constitutional right to be provided with counsel for those with insufficient means to pay for counsel and if the interests of justice so required. The proposal was rejected. This court agreed with the conclusion of Craig J. in *Deutsch v. Law Society of Upper Canada Legal Aid Fund, supra*, that the minutes demonstrate that the *Charter* was not drafted to guarantee an unfettered right to funded counsel.

Although the *Charter* does not unqualifiedly provide for funded counsel, such a right may be inferred in rare circumstances. In *Deutsch v. Law Society of Upper Canada Legal Aid Fund, supra*, Craig J. explained those circumstances as follows:

> In conclusion as to this issue, under the common law the accused has a right to a fair trial and the trial judge is bound to ensure that an accused person receives a fair trial. Here the accused faces possible imprisonment. Pursuant to s. 7 of the *Charter*, the accused has an entrenched right not to be deprived of his liberty except in accordance with the principles of fundamental justice. Also, pursuant to s. 11(d), he has an entrenched right to a "fair and public hearing". The right to fundamental justice and a fair and public hearing includes the right to a fair trial. There may be rare cases where legal aid is denied to an accused person facing trial, but, where the trial judge is satisfied that, because of the seriousness and complexity of the case, the accused cannot receive a fair trial without counsel, in such a case it seems to follow that there is an entrenched right to funded counsel under the *Charter*.

In *Rowbotham, supra*, the Ontario Court of Appeal noted that, even prior to the *Charter*, the province of Ontario had enacted a comprehensive legal aid plan. In Alberta, the Legal Aid Society of Alberta was incorporated in 1973, also prior to the *Charter*. The objective of these legal aid plans is to provide the assistance of counsel to a person charged with a serious crime but who lacks the means to pay for such assistance.

The court in *Rowbotham* at p. 66 was of the opinion that, at the advent of the *Charter*, because legal aid systems were in force in the provinces, "those who framed the *Charter* did not expressly constitutionalize the right of an indigent accused to be provided with counsel, because they considered that, generally speaking, the provincial legal aid systems were adequate to provide counsel for persons charged with serious crimes who lacked the means to employ counsel." The court held, however, that where representation of the accused by counsel is essential to a fair trial and the case does not fall within provincial legal aid plans, sections 7 and 11(d) of the *Charter* require funded counsel to be provided if the accused wishes counsel but cannot pay a lawyer.

The Ontario Court of Appeal in *Rowbotham* referred to the portion of the judgment of Craig J. in *Deutsch v. Law Society of Upper Canada Legal Aid Fund, supra*, quoted above and also to a similar view expressed by McDonald J. in *Panacui v. Legal Aid Society of Alberta*, [1988] 1 W.W.R. 60 (Alta. Q.B.). Neither view was specifically adopted.

In *Robinson, supra*, this court had the opportunity to consider the views of McDonald J. in *Panacui, supra* where he stated at p. 67 that, in view of the interests protected by ss. 7 and 11(d) of the *Charter*, "a person charged with an offence that is serious and complex, when he cannot afford to retain counsel, is constitutionally entitled to have counsel provided to assist him at the expense of the state."

This court did not adopt that opinion. It referred to it only to point out that "keyed as it is to prosecutions for serious and complex offences" it does not extend previous authorities.

The authorities establish that funded counsel is not a right in every case, but in some circumstances, where the assistance of counsel is essential in order to assure a fair trial, the *Charter* requires the provision of funded counsel.

When Is the Assistance of Counsel Essential to a Fair Trial?

Representation by a lawyer is not a pre-requisite for a fair trial. A person is entitled to represent himself or herself and when he or she does so, there are other means which are intended to protect the right to a fair trial, the foremost being the duty of every trial judge to ensure that all persons receive a fair trial.

The *Criminal Code* recognizes the accused's right to self-representation at trial, for example, in ss. 651(2), (3) and (4) which sets out the accused's right to reply to the summing up by the prosecutor where the accused is not defended by counsel. Thus, an accused cannot be compelled to have counsel if he or she is unwilling: *Vescio* v. *The King*, [1949] S.C.R. 139 (S.C.C.), cited in *Robinson, supra* and elsewhere.

Whether an accused is represented by counsel or not the basic duty of a trial judge is to ensure that he or she receives a fair trial. It is true that the duty of a trial judge to preserve the accused's right to a fair trial does not go as far as providing the same assistance as would be given by counsel. The Quebec Court of Appeal has agreed with the Ontario Court of Appeal that the scope of the assistance a trial judge can give to an accused is limited to what is reasonable and cannot and does not extend at each stage of the trial to provision of the kind of advice that counsel could be expected to provide if the accused were represented by counsel: *R.* v. *Taubler* (1987), 20 O.A.C. 64 (C.A.) as quoted in *R.* v. *Sechon* (1995), 104 C.C.C. (3d) 554 (Que. C.A.) at p. 559.

The Ontario Court of Appeal in *R.* v. *McGibbon* (1988), 45 C.C.C. (3d) 334 at p. 347 described the duty of the trial judge when an accused is unrepresented by counsel as including the provision of reasonable assistance to the accused in the presentation of evidence and in putting any defences before the court and to guide the accused in such a way that his or her defence is brought out with its full force and effect.

Undoubtedly the trial judge's burden of assuring a fair trial appears heavier when an accused is unrepresented. But the nature of the duty imposed on the trial judge is not changed merely because an accused is represented by counsel. Judges who cede any aspect of that duty to counsel may be found in error. For example where the accused is represented by counsel who does not object to the admission of inadmissible evidence, it is still the duty of the trial judge to exclude it in order to ensure a fair trial: *R.* v. *D.(L.E.)* (1989), 50 C.C.C. (3d) 142 at 161 (S.C.C.) as quoted in *R.* v. *Lafontaine and Lafontaine*, [1998] A.Q. no. 1285 (Q.L.) (Que. S.C.).

Even though a criminal trial is an adversarial process and the judge is the adjudicator, the judge has ample latitude to participate in the examination of witnesses when necessary to ensure fairness. That applies whether the accused has counsel or not. In *R.* v. *Valley* (1986), 26 C.C.C. 207 (Ont. C.A.), (in which case accused had counsel at trial) at page 230 Martin J.A. described this aspect of the judge's role as follows:

The judge, however, is not required to remain silent. He may question witnesses to clear up ambiguities, explore some matter which the answers of a witness have left vague or, indeed, he may put questions which should have been put to bring out some relevant matter, but which have been omitted.... Further, I do not doubt that the judge has a duty to intervene to clear the innocent.

The trial judge is not the lone guardian of the right to a fair trial. That right can be protected retrospectively as well. As suggested in *Robinson, supra*, upon appeal, a court is in the position to determine if the conduct of the trial without counsel breached the accused's right to a fair trial. For examples of appellate scrutiny of the fairness of a trial without counsel see *R.* v. *Hardy*, (1991) 7 C.R.R. (2d) 382 (Alta. C.A.) and *R.* v. *Jones* (1994), 154 A.R. 118 (Q.B.).

In *Jones, supra*, Veit J. ordered a new trial because the trial judge failed to provide the unrepresented accused with basic information about the trial process. Certainly the type of information which was not provided would have been furnished by counsel if one had been available to the accused. But it was not the absence of counsel which caused the unfairness, rather, it was the failure of the trial judge to ensure trial fairness by properly providing information to the accused.

In most cases where representation by counsel is necessary for a fair trial, an indigent accused will receive assistance through the legal aid program. When legal aid is denied and exceptional circumstances make it probable that the trial judge cannot discharge the duty to ensure a fair trial then the appointment of counsel becomes necessary. What sort of cases are exceptional was discussed in *Rowbotham*.

The Guidelines Set Out in *Rowbotham*

In *Rowbotham*, the accused was one of 12 charged in a large-scale conspiracy to traffic in marijuana and hashish. The trial took more than one year although the particular accused's involvement was a small part of the overall case. Because she had full-time employment, the accused was denied legal aid. The trial judge was of the opinion that she had not proved she could not afford to retain counsel. She was unrepresented throughout the trial which resulted in her being sentenced to two years less one day imprisonment.

On appeal, the Ontario Court of Appeal considered *Deutsch* v. *Law Society of Upper Canada Legal Aid Fund, supra*, which involved an accused who faced charges under the *Income Tax Act* and separately, charges under the *Criminal Code* for fraud and possession of stolen property. He was refused legal aid because of doubts that he required financial assistance. In dismissing his application for judicial review, Craig J. observed that the accused might seek the appointment of funded counsel as an application under the *Charter*. Although he recognized there was no right to funded counsel under the *Charter*, he also pointed out that under both the common law and the *Charter*, the accused has a right to a fair trial from which could be inferred the right to counsel.

The Ontario Court of Appeal also considered *Panacui* v. *Legal Aid Society of Alberta*, *supra*, in which the accused faced charges of kidnapping, three counts of attempted murder, a number of robbery counts, escaping lawful custody and firearms offences. He was granted legal aid but he wanted the counsel to be one of his choice and not the counsel appointed to represent him. McDonald J., after reviewing ss. 7, 10(b) and 11(d) of the *Charter* and the role of counsel in protecting a person's liberty, concluded at p. 67:

> In my view, the foregoing statement of the purposes and interests which ss. 7, 10(b) and 11(d) are meant to protect when the issue is the scope and extent of the right to counsel, lead me irresistibly to the conclusion that a person charged with an offence that is serious and complex, when he cannot afford to retain counsel, is constitutionally entitled to have counsel provided to assist him at the expense of the state.

In *Rowbotham*, the court stated at p. 67 that for the purpose of the appeal before it, it was necessary "to consider only the right of an accused charged with a serious offence who lacks the means to employ a lawyer, to be provided with funded counsel at his or her trial".

The trial judge in this case applied *Re White* (1976), 32 C.C.C. (2d) 478 (Alta. S.C.-T.D.), a pre-*Charter* case which also set out the requirement that the charge be serious and complex.

Subsequent cases have regarded *Rowbotham* as setting out guidelines to determine when a case is so exceptional that funded counsel is necessary to assure a fair trial. Ontario cases sometimes describe applications for funded counsel for an indigent accused as *Rowbotham* applications. See, for example, *R.* v. *Belanger*, unreported, July 4, 1997 (Ont. Prov. Div.) and *R.* v. *Duong and Lam*, unreported, May 31, 1996 (Ont. Gen. Div.).

The test which has evolved from *Rowbotham* has two aspects which must be considered. One is the accused's circumstances. It must be determined if the accused can afford to retain counsel and if the accused has the education, experience and other abilities to conduct his or her own defence. The other is the nature of the charge or charges. Regard must be had to the seriousness of the offence, the complexity of the case and the length of trial. The central concern throughout is the fairness of the trial.

Cases Considering the Need for Counsel at Trial

As noted above, the authorities which have inferred the right to counsel have involved serious and complex offences in lengthy trials. In *Rowbotham*, the court considered the assistance of counsel necessary when the accused faced charges as part of a year-long trial for conspiracy to import narcotics. In *Panacui* v. *Legal Aid Society of Alberta*, the accused faced numerous charges including kidnapping, murder, robbery, escape from lawful custody and firearms offences.

More recently, in *R.* v. *Duong and Lam*, *supra*, two accused were charged with conspiring to commit insurance fraud arising from claims using stolen vehicles. The Ontario General Division court found that although the facts were simple, the complexity of the law of conspiracy and the anticipated trial time of six weeks, on balance, made representation by counsel essential to a fair trial. The accused had not proved, however, that he lacked the means to employ counsel and therefore, his application for funded counsel was dismissed.

Counsel on this appeal have cited many cases in which courts have applied *Rowbotham*. The authorities indicate that even where there are charges of some complexity and seriousness, depending upon the circumstances, counsel may not be necessary for a fair trial.

The Court of Queen's Bench of this province held in *R.* v. *Svidal and James* (1990), 107 A.R. 241, that the two accused, who were charged with three counts of fraud totalling in excess of $20 million, would not be denied their rights to a fair trial when they had been refused legal aid because they refused to provide a mortgage to the Legal Aid Society on the houses which were in the names of their wives and because their situation of impecuniosity resulted from having transferred all their assets to their wives. The issue of counsel was not appealed to this court: (1991), 120 A.R. 333.

The Quebec Court of Appeal in *Sechon*, *supra*, dismissed the appeal from a conviction for two counts of mischief by making a false statement to the police. The accused was without the assistance of counsel because she had been denied coverage by legal aid. The trial had lasted two or three hours and turned primarily on the issue of credibility. The court found that the absence of counsel did not deny the right to a fair trial.

In *R. v. Baig* (1990), 58 C.C.C. (3d) 156; leave to appeal denied (1991), 60 C.C.C. (3d) vi (S.C.C.), the British Columbia Court of Appeal held that a well-educated accused appealing five convictions for the unauthorized practice of medicine did not require the assistance of counsel in order to protect his rights. Although the appeal involved a *Charter* issue, it was not particularly complex and the appellant was not facing imprisonment.

In *Mireau v. Canada* (1991), 96 Sask. R. 197, the Saskatchewan Court of Queen's Bench held that a conviction arising from a sit-in demonstration and pursuit of two civil complaints under the provincial human rights legislation did not result in the violation of *Charter* rights if the applicant was not provided the assistance of funded counsel.

In *R. v. Satov*, [1996] O.J. No. 2500 (Q.L.), the accused was charged with common assault in a domestic situation. Even though the Ontario provincial division court recognized concerns for the delicacy of the situation, it held the accused's lack of legal representation would not breach his right to a fair trial.

In *R. v. Lafontaine and Lafontaine, supra*, the Quebec Superior Court held that the two accused, who were charged with indecent acts and being found in a bawdy house, did not have an exceptional case although the Crown's evidence would include photographs and film.

With the exception of *R. v. Hill* (1996), 34 C.R.R. (2d) 344 (Ont. Prov. Div.), courts in other provinces have held that persons charged with impaired driving and related offences would not have their *Charter* rights infringed if not provided with funded counsel.

In *Hill*, the accused was charged with driving over the legal limit of alcohol after failing the roadside screening tests. The accused, who was on welfare, could not afford the services of either a lawyer or toxicologist, who could give the opinion that if the accused's evidence of his consumption was correct, he could not have been over the legal limit. Because this was his first offence and the Crown was not seeking incarceration as a penalty, the accused was not provided with legal aid. The Ontario Court provincial division judge followed the decision of the Queen's Bench justice from which this appeal is taken and found that the accused would be unable to obtain a fair trial without state-funded counsel.

Subsequent Ontario cases have not followed the decision in *Hill*. For example, in *R. v. Belanger, supra*, the accused was charged with impaired driving and having a blood-alcohol level over 80 mgs. The Crown elected to proceed summarily and indicated it would seek a monetary penalty rather than incarceration. No evidence was adduced to show that a conviction would impair the ability of the accused to earn a livelihood. The evidence was that she was a full-time student in receipt of student loans. The court quoted the statements at p. 353 in *Hill*, holding that not every indigent accused charged with an "over 80" offence and where "evidence to the contrary" is argued will be provided with state-funded counsel. Rather, "it will be an unusual case where the absence of counsel will so fundamentally alter the trial process as to render it unfair." The judge in *Belanger* found in that case, which did not involve property damage or bodily harm, the charges were not complex or serious when compared to those faced in *Rowbotham*.

Prior to *Hill*, the Ontario Court Provincial Division in *R. v. Badertscher*, [1996] O.J. No. 4528 (Q.L.) considered the application of an accused who had numerous previous charges and had defended himself on an earlier impaired driving charge. The court found no particular level of complexity to the charges of operating a motor vehicle while impaired by alcohol and failing to comply with a demand for samples of breath. There was evidence that the accused was detained, taken to an accident scene and interviewed without being advised of his right under s. 10(b) of the *Charter*. On the basis of the evidence before the court, it held at para. 22 that the right to a fair trial would not be infringed if the trial proceeded without the presence of legal counsel.

In *R. v. Krzak* [1996] O.J. No. 3096 (Q.L.), the Ontario Provincial Division court held that the accused, charged for the first time with impaired driving and having over 80 mgs. of alcohol in his system, had not discharged the onus to establish sufficient seriousness and complexity to meet the test in *Rowbotham*. The trial judge was not prepared to find that every charge of "over 80 mgs." involves some complexity.

In *R. v. Metallic and LePage*, unreported, November 10, 1997 (Que. S.C.), the accused was charged with driving with blood-alcohol over 80 mgs. and obstructing a police officer. The trial was estimated to require no more than three hours but there was no other evidence regarding the complexity of the case. In *R. v. Cabot and St. Pierre*, unreported,

November 10, 1997 (Que. S.C.), the two accused were charged with impaired driving and having blood-alcohol over 80 mgs. The Crown had declared that it was not seeking a penalty of imprisonment. There was no other evidence suggesting the trial would be lengthy or involve complexity or some other particularly unusual circumstances. Both applications for funded counsel were heard before Tremblay J. After considering *Rowbotham*, *Sechon* and *Badertscher*, he found in both cases there was little complexity to the charges and therefore, did not warrant the appointment of funded counsel.

The determination of whether representation by counsel is essential to a fair trial must be made on a case-by-case consideration. As pointed out by Tremblay J. in *R. v. Metallic and LePage*, and in *R. v. Cabot and St. Pierre*, it would be possible for exactly the same offence, to have an accused, who is university educated with numerous previous offences, who would not be appointed a lawyer, while an illiterate accused could obtain one.

The Decisions in This Case

In each case, the onus is upon the accused to present evidence to present evidence to persuade the court on the balance of probabilities that his or her *Charter* rights were infringed: *R. v. Collins*, [1987] 1 S.C.R. 265... .

The learned Provincial Court Judge concluded in this case that the offences with which Ms. Rain was charged were complex and serious and that therefore she required counsel if her *Charter* right to a fair trial was to be ensured. He placed significant reliance on the evidence of Mr. Gunn, saying:

> [T]he Court notes and accepts his evidence on the following matters:
> 1. On the issue of complexity of alcohol related drinking and driving charges, Mr. Gunn gave his opinion that this area is the most litigated and technically difficult area in the *Criminal Code*.
> 2. If Ms. Rain had the assistance of competent counsel, Mr. Gunn advised that there are areas of obvious and potential defence including *Charter* issues, and he assessed her chances of success at trial at 50/50.
> 3. Mr. Gunn states that without counsel at trial, and I quote, "she wouldn't have a hope".
> 4. Mr. Gunn reviewed the impact of convictions for alcohol related driving charges including fines, loss of driving privileges, financial hardships including insurance costs, and the escalating social stigma which goes with such convictions.

The learned Provincial Court Judge, relying on the evidence of Mr. Gunn found that the charges facing the accused were complex. He then considered the question of seriousness as follows:

> Viewed from the subjective viewpoint of the accused, a finding of guilt leads to substantial penalties. The fines are substantial, the loss of driving privileges are at the very least inconvenient and often lead to a loss of employment. Insurance costs are very substantial, and the condemnation of family, friends, and business associates and the general community is a heavy burden.
>
> Viewed objectively by the community at large and the courts, there is no doubt alcohol related drinking driving charges are viewed very seriously. We note most recently again the concern and statistics set out in the decision of Mr. Justice Cory in the *Bernshaw* case in the Supreme Court of Canada. So clearly the alcohol related driving charges facing the accused are serious, *but are they serious enough to warrant appointment of Court ordered counsel* (emphasis added).
>
> One of the considerations Mr. Justice McDonald set out is whether the accused faces incarceration. In the present case, incarceration is a possibility on a first offence, but the Crown is not seeking incarceration, and hence it is not a reasonable probability. Legal aid has decided that as a matter of policy not to extend coverage for first offence if the Crown proceeds summarily and incarceration is not a probability.
>
> This court holds that once this court has found the offences facing an indigent accused to be complex and serious, and the court so finds in the present case, then it follows from the adoption of the reasons of Justice Smith that jurisdiction to grant the requested order has been established, and this court may grant such an order.

It should be noted that the Learned Provincial Court Judge abruptly concluded his consideration of the importance of probability of incarceration upon conviction in determining "seriousness" in this case. His reasons for doing so may be surmised as: (1) He considered that the possibility of incarceration was enough, or, (2) He considered that the possibility of incarceration becomes irrelevant when it is determined that the charges are "serious" having regard to other considerations. The latter interpretation is unlikely since his discussion of the issue of incarceration was opened by asking whether the charges are serious enough to warrant the appointment of court ordered counsel. He apparently recognized that the question of incarceration remained essential, even though he had already determined without regard to that factor that the charges were "serious". Since he did not answer that question the reasonable interpretation is that the learned Provincial Court judge decided that the possibility of incarceration was enough.

Having concluded that the charges were complex and serious without attention to the issue of imprisonment, the learned Provincial Court judge then went on to consider whether the appointment of counsel should be denied

> by reason of one or a combination of the following considerations:
> 1. There is an agency which may be capable of representing the accused; namely, Student Legal Services....
> 2. That defence counsel should undertake cases such as the accused faces on a *pro bono* basis...
> 3. The judge must ensure that an unrepresented accused has a fair trial, and accordingly, it is all right to deny counsel to an accused because the judge will take care of the interests of the accused.

He gave reasons why, in his opinion, none of the three considerations were reasonable alternatives to funded counsel. He concluded his consideration of the judge's role as follows: "This Court finds that the obligation of the trial judge to ensure a fair trial cannot and should not prevail over the need for counsel where an accused is facing a serious and complex matter."

When the Crown refused to pay for counsel as ordered by the learned Provincial Court judge, he made an order staying the charges against Ms. Rain in the absence of funded counsel.

The Crown appealed. The learned Summary Conviction Appeal Justice was of the opinion that there had been no error of law leading to the order under appeal. In assessing the trial court's conclusion on the seriousness issue, he said:

> [The learned Provincial Court judge] found that the charges facing the Respondent are serious. He relied on evidence of the seriousness with which the offences are viewed in the community and the severity of the consequences that flow from a conviction. He found that, in the Respondent's case, incarceration was a possibility but not a "reasonable probability". Mr. Gunn stated that it is "almost invariably the case" that there is prison time in default of fine payment for these offences. Thus, there is a possibility that the respondent may face incarceration as a consequence of conviction on these charges. In pre-trial applications, judges should not attempt to predict the outcome of a proceeding. Their role is not to weigh the evidence and decide whether it satisfies the "beyond a reasonable doubt" standard. Thus [the learned Provincial Court judge] correctly found, in my view, that these charges are serious, despite the Crown's assurance that it would not seek incarceration as a penalty. Incarceration is a possibility: that is enough.

With respect, it is an error of law to conclude that the possibility of incarceration is enough to satisfy the requirement of "seriousness", in the assessment of need for counsel in cases such as this. If the possibility of incarceration was enough every offence in the *Criminal Code* and virtually every violation of most Alberta statutes would fall into the "serious" category. That is because s. 787(2) of the *Criminal Code* and s. 7(2) of the *Provincial Offences Procedure Act*, S.A c. P-21.5 provide general authority for imposing imprisonment in default of payment of any fine.

The practical result of the position taken by the learned Summary Conviction Appeal Justice is to remove from consideration the question of "seriousness" in applications such as the one leading to this appeal. Such result is a radical and unwarranted departure from the jurisprudence both under common law and under the *Charter*.

As already noted the law prior to the *Charter* was as stated in *Re White*, *supra*. In that case McDonald J. classified an offence as "serious in that a conviction may result in imprisonment". This Court in *Robinson*, *supra*, noted that the decision of McDonald J. in *Panacui*, *supra*, in which the *Charter* was invoked "keyed as it is to prosecutions for serious and complex offences ... is not in practical discord with the case authorities ... including *Re White*." The decision of this court in *Robinson*, *supra*, limits the right to funded counsel to those indigent accused who face "serious and complex criminal offences". If the possibility of incarceration was enough to satisfy the requirement of "seriousness" then the constant use of the word "serious" by this and many other courts in the context of applications such as this one would be redundant and meaningless. That is because as noted every criminal charge by definition would be "serious" since every one carries the theoretical possibility of imprisonment.

The requirement that an offence be found "serious in that a conviction may result in imprisonment" must be based on more than theoretical possibility. At the very least it must be founded on a reasonable probability that a trial judge, correctly applying all relevant sentencing principles and considering all relevant circumstances, would not be in error by imposing a sentence of imprisonment, and that any monetary penalty correctly imposed would be beyond the means of the accused to pay and that the only alternative to payment was imprisonment in default. In the latter respect the availability of fine option programs is a necessary consideration. The learned Summary Conviction Appeal Justice disregarded the availability of such a program to Ms. Rain, although the reasons for the order under appeal drew attention to the program.

Since the learned Summary Conviction Appeal Justice erred in upholding the order under appeal, it follows that the learned Provincial Court Judge also erred in that he incorrectly considered the question of incarceration in determining whether the charges against Ms. Rain were "serious".

The decision of the learned Provincial Court judge is also in error in another fundamental way, namely, because he accepted and relied upon the opinion of Mr. Gunn, that without the assistance of counsel, Ms. Rain "wouldn't have a hope" of a fair trial.

The fairness of the trial is the ultimate question for the trial judge to decide. Leaving aside the debatable appropriateness of allowing expert evidence on the ultimate question, there is a clear requirement that a judge disregard evidence of a witness who does not have expertise in a given area. McLachlin J. in *R.* v. *Marquard* (1994), 85 C.C.C. (3d) 193 (S.C.C.), at p. 225 said:

> Important as the initial qualification of an expert witness may be, it would be overly technical to reject expert evidence simply because the witness ventures an opinion beyond the area of expertise in which he or she has been qualified. As a practical matter, it is for opposing counsel to object if the witness goes beyond the proper limits of his or her expertise. The objection to the witness' expertise may be made at the stage of initial qualification, or during the witness' evidence if it becomes apparent the witness is going beyond the area in which he or she was qualified to give expert opinion. In the absence of objection, a technical failure to qualify a witness who clearly has expertise in the area will not mean that the witness' evidence should be struck. However, if the witness is not shown to have possessed expertise to testify in the area, his or her evidence must be disregarded and the jury so instructed.

Mr. Gunn was not tendered, nor ruled qualified as an expert in curial decision-making or any similar field. His opinion that Ms. Rain "wouldn't have a hope" of a fair trial in the absence of counsel was not arrived at in the studied manner necessary to qualify him to express it as an expert opinion in court. Except for the anecdote concerning his uncle there was no evidence that Mr. Gunn had ever observed a criminal trial in which the accused was unrepresented by counsel. He testified that he had handled thousands of cases in court. But, *ipso facto*, those were not cases in which the accused was unrepresented. Further, there was nothing in the evidence from which to infer that Mr. Gunn, on his numerous appearances in courts, took the time to observe the conduct of trials other than those in which he was involved. On the contrary, he gave evidence that he was a time-conscious practitioner, not given to devoting any time to anything but the essentials of his busy practice. He said that he spends about six minutes in his client interviews. If the client wants to tell him a long story about what happened, he generally passes the client to another lawyer who might take an average of 45 minutes for the interview.

There was no foundation in the evidence for accepting the opinion of Mr. Gunn on the potential fairness of the trial. The learned Provincial Court judge was bound to disregard that evidence. He did the contrary and accepted it.

I cannot say that the adoption by the learned Provincial Court judge of the invalid opinion on the potential fairness of the trial had no effect on his decision. In fact it appears to have fundamentally influenced it.

Mr. Gunn's opinion, lacking empirical support, is based on his cynical view that it is unrealistic to expect judges to participate to the fullest extent permissible in order to discharge their duty to ensure a fair trial. That is an unacceptable premise from which to assess the potential for an unfair trial in any given case. If it were the appropriate starting point it would effectively establish a presumption of trial unfairness.

In considering whether a charge is so serious and complex that court-ordered counsel is required the basic premise must be that the trial judge will do everything appropriate to ensure a fair trial. Counsel should be ordered only in cases where, notwithstanding the fullest use of the trial judge's authority, the complexity or length, and the seriousness of the case alter the trial process so as to make it unfair.

Likely misled by Mr. Gunn's faulty premise, the learned Provincial Court judge found that the charges were complex and serious and that without counsel there would be trial unfairness. Only then did he consider the role of the trial judge. The duty of the trial judge to ensure a fair trial and everything which that entails must be considered in deciding whether a charge is so complex and serious as to warrant court-ordered counsel. With respect, once it is found that there is a probability of an unfair trial in the absence of counsel, consideration of the role of the trial judge will have been exhausted. All that remains to be considered is whether there may be an adequate alternative to court-ordered counsel such as Student Legal Services or pro bono counsel. To consider the possibility of the trial judge being that alternative, as did the learned Provincial Court judge, indicates an error in principle by misplacing consideration of a fundamental element of trial fairness — the duty of the trial judge to ensure it.

Had the Learned Provincial Court judge correctly approached the assessment of whether the charges faced by Ms. Rain were serious and complex thus rendering probable an unfair trial in the absence of counsel he could not have come to the conclusion that he did, at least on the issue of seriousness. As the learned Provincial Court judge found, there was no reasonable probability that Ms. Rain would be incarcerated upon conviction. The Crown was not seeking imprisonment, such penalty would be well beyond the usual penalty of a fine of $600 and therefore demonstrably unfit, and imprisonment in default of payment of any fine could be avoided through the available fine option program. There was no evidence that participation in the fine option program would work an unnecessary hardship on Ms. Rain.

Further, the learned Provincial Court judge did not consider the impact specifically on Ms. Rain of a conviction for one or both charges she was facing. He noted correctly that applications of this type are to be considered according to their particular circumstances. But he generalized in finding that conviction leads to substantial fines, the inconvenience or worse of lost driving privileges, increased insurance costs and the condemnation of family, friends, business associates and the general community.

As already noted there was evidence of the availability of a fine option program permitting Ms. Rain to avoid imprisonment in default of payment of any fine imposed, and also to avoid the financial hardship of a fine. There was no evidence that Ms. Rain required a car for employment or other reasons. Indeed, she was unemployed. While higher insurance premiums may be relevant if one has and needs a car, there was no evidence of that in this case. In short there was no specific evidence to support the finding that the charges against Ms. Rain were serious. Consequently, the trial judge's finding on this point were made in the absence of any evidence and he could not reasonably conclude that the absence of counsel would probably result in an unfair trial.

We need not consider, since the point was not argued, whether the learned Provincial Court judge erred by ordering funded counsel absent evidence that counsel who had been appearing *pro bono publico* for Ms. Rain would abandon her prior to trial. Such action would have been unexpected in view of the honourable history of the bar and the rules of the Law Society. In our view, under these circumstances no stay should have been imposed prior to trial.

Lastly, we also note that there was no evidence before the learned Provincial Court judge of cost projections, or even approximations, which would flow from the inflation of any right to state-funded counsel in trials. This court, when this matter was first before it, had said that such evidence was necessary. That was overlooked by the learned Provincial Court judge. So [too] was the admonition of this court in *Robinson*, *supra*, that the courts are not the best qualified, if they are qualified at all, agencies to determine spending priorities for public funds in this area. Arguments can be compellingly made that such spending by government should be directed to compensation of victims or rehabilitation programs for offenders. These issues are, of course, political and not justiciable.

CONCLUSION

In this case, the respondent has not proved that the lack of funded counsel would impair her right to a fair trial. Therefore, the learned Provincial Court judge erred by finding the Respondent's right under ss. 7 and 11(d) of the *Charter of Rights and Freedoms* would be infringed. Consequently, the learned Summary Conviction Appeal Justice erred by finding that the learned Provincial Court judge did not err.

The appeal on the first ground is allowed. As a consequence, the second ground of appeal (the correctness of the order staying the proceedings) need not be considered.

It is now more than five years since Ms. Rain was charged. She has not yet been tried. The delay is not her fault. Although she failed to appear when first scheduled in Provincial Court and a warrant was issued, she did appear later that day.

On the trial day Ms. Rain appeared and the court was advised that she had been rejected for legal aid. The court's own motion on that day started the chain of legal proceedings recounted above as a result of which [...] Ms. Rain and her right to be tried within a reasonable time have become hostages to other imperatives.

It appears that the learned Provincial Court judge was advised that there were interests at stake in this matter other than Ms. Rain's rights. He noted in his judgment that "[d]efence counsel in particular seems to view this as a test case which will open up the area of summary conviction alcohol related first offence driving charges for the appointed of funded defence counsel". The Crown has participated in this test, at least latterly, by funding Ms. Rain's counsel at both levels of appeal.

Now that it has been determined that the reasons for the stay order under appeal display an error in principle the ordinary course is for this matter to go back for trial. That will invite an application for another stay because of violation of the right to be tried within a reasonable time as guaranteed under s. 11(b) of the *Charter*.

The circumstances of this case include Ms. Rain's desire to dispose of this matter speedily by entering an early guilty plea, the refusal of the judge to accept that plea, the time consumed in appeals from the first order of the learned Provincial Court judge, the inexplicable return of the matter to the judge who had previously decided the very issue involved, the further time involved in the second set of appeals, and the time taken to render this judgment. Were this matter to now go to trial, Ms. Rain would be justified in feeling that she had been merely a pawn in what to her would appear a strange and bewildering contest. When she testified on March 20, 1995 she said that she did not know much about what was going on with her case and that she was "really confused." The prejudice to Ms. Rain caused by the delays was transparent at that time. Much more has transpired since. Her right to trial within a reasonable time demands respect. In the circumstances I conclude that the ends of justice require that we decline to vary the stay imposed by the learned Provincial Court judge notwithstanding that his reasons for imposing it were in error.

■

The responsibility of judges who conduct trials concerning unrepresented accused is a serious one. In *R.* v. *Tran* (2001), 55 O.R. (3d) 161 (C.A.), the accused was forced to proceed to trial without counsel on numerous serious charges, including impaired driving causing death, and was convicted. A new trial was ordered on appeal because Tran did not have a translator, and the trial judge failed to provide the significant degree of assistance and vigilance needed to avoid an unfair trial in all of the circumstances.

See also *R.* v. *R.H.B.* (1999), 131 B.C.A.C. 199, where the judge failed to make inquiries as to the accused's level of understanding and failed to inform him of the elements of the offence, the burden of proof, the right to cross-examine, the purpose of cross-examination, and the decision as to whether to call evidence in defence. A new trial was ordered.

YOUNG PERSONS

Young persons are in a special category in terms of access to funded counsel by reason of ss. 25(4),(5) of the *Youth Criminal Justice Act*, S.C. 2002, c. 1 [*YCJA*]. What is the policy behind this section? Consider also the decision of the Ontario Court of Appeal in *R.* v. *J.H.*, [1999] O.J. No. 3894, online: QL, which held that where a legal aid certificate is denied to a young person on the basis that their parents are assessed as having the means to retain counsel on their behalf, a judge should not direct the appointment of counsel until satisfied, having conducted an independent inquiry reviewing the reasons for denial of a certificate and the parents' willingness to assist, that the young person is "unable" to retain counsel within the meaning of the *YCJA*.

PRISONERS

It will be recalled from the *Armstrong* case, *supra*, **Prisons and Parole**, that prisoners have a more attenuated right to counsel within the regime of prison. While they are not necessarily precluded from provincial legal aid schemes, their requests for funding for internal disciplinary charges or appeals in the criminal courts may have a lesser priority in terms of funding. In *Winters* v. *Legal Services Society*, [1999] 3 S.C.R. 160, the Court reviewed B.C.'s provincial legal aid statute, and found that the prisoner had a statutory right to legal aid because the statute provided coverage for defendants in criminal proceedings that could lead to imprisonment. Here Winters faced disciplinary charges for assaulting another inmate, with a possible consequence of solitary confinement. The Court held, however, that the level of services to be provided remained in the legal aid society's discretion, consistent with the level of services that a reasonable person of average means would purchase. It emphasized that this level of services may not, in fact, include representation at a hearing.

DUTY COUNSEL SERVICES

Many provinces provide duty counsel services in court for unrepresented accused. In Ontario, duty counsel in criminal court can assist with judicial interim release, guilty pleas, and sentencing hearings, among other matters: *Legal Aid Services Act Regulations*, O. Reg. 106/99, s. 24(3). However, the lack of duty counsel services *per se* will not violate an accused's right to a fair trial, without more: *R. v. Ford* (2001), 52 O.R. (3d) 142 (Sup. Ct.).

CLINIC SERVICES

Clinics may be issue-specific, such as clinics for immigrant communities or for tenants. They may be run by law schools, relying upon students and staff lawyers, or may be run as independent clinics. What might be the strengths of clinics that serve the needs of groups such as Aboriginal persons? In Nova Scotia, the bulk of criminal legal aid is delivered through a clinic system rather than through individual certificates. Cases such as *White* (**Enforcement of the Law**), *Hebb* (**Sentencing**), and *Thompson* (**Policing**) might not have been litigated without a clinic program.

The article that follows raises many important issues about the significance of representation, delivery of legal aid, and access to justice.

The Standard of Social Justice Applied to an Evaluation of Criminal Cases Appearing Before the Halifax Courts[†]

The Law Reform Commission of Canada emphasizes that the criminal justice process should be the means to a socially "just" resolution of the conflict between the legitimate interest of the public in being protected against criminal behaviour and the rights and freedoms of the individual. The standard of social justice, however, can be conceptualized from both a socio-political and a technical perspective.

The socio-political perspective requires that social regulation, as institutionalized by written laws, should apply equally to all persons regardless of wealth, race, or social status. Hence, by the spirit of social justice, it is equally wrong for an executive to pad an expense account as for an employee to steal merchandise. And, if detected, the consequences should be no less serious or difficult for one to bear than the other.

In contrast, the technical perspective requires that the administration of the regulatory power of the State be fair and uniform. Hence, by the letter of social justice, both the executive and employee should face the same probability of surveillance, arrest, and prosecution, and they both should be subjected to similar procedures and standards before the law.

In this study we were concerned with applying both components of social justice to the operation of the criminal courts. Of particular interest were questions such as, who appeared before the courts? For what reasons? And, once before the courts, how were they treated?

While there have been empirical studies which have examined the American criminal process in the context of social justice, little comparable information exists for Canadian courts. One author concluded that "... We have no base judicial statistics in Canada on which to assess the performance of the legal system. We tend to live in ignorance of the human consequences of what the law does, substituting myth for what is often unpleasant fact." This paper applies a standard of social justice to the research findings obtained from the observation of 1,033 criminal cases appearing before the Halifax Courts.

. . . .

METHOD

Research Setting

The study was restricted to *Criminal Code* cases heard by the three magistrate courts and two county

---

[†] By K. Edward Renner and Alan H. Warner, (1981) 1 Windsor Y.B. Access Just. 62 at 63–65, 68–73, 75–80. Tables omitted. Reproduced by permission of the authors.

courts in Halifax. All persons charged under the *Criminal Code* first appear in magistrate's court for arraignment. Summary charges are processed in the magistrate's court. Defendants charged with indictable offences may elect to remain before the magistrate court or elect to be tried by a judge alone (county court) or by a judge and jury. All *Criminal Code* charges handled by the courts, during three separate periods of observation, were included in the data sample with the exception of driving offences. The defendant was the basic unit for data collection and the charge bearing the most severe penalty was selected when individuals were convicted on more than one offence.

Variables

Data were collected on eight defendant variables (age, employment status, marital status, sex, educational level, residence, race, and appearance), on four factors relevant to the court process (type and severity of charge, presence and type of counsel, frequency and time of prior convictions, and number of charges), and information on pleas, verdict, and sentence.

Sample

The data were collected on three occasions. The largest section of the sample included all non-driving, criminal code cases (N = 477) processed through the five courts during a fifteen week period in the summer of 1977. Three observers collected data each day on standardized forms through court observation and use of court records. A second set of cases (N = 251) was obtained by trained university students over an eight week period during the spring term of 1977. For both samples the observers rotated through the courts on a systematic basis. The final section of the case sample (N = 305) was collected from the county court records which were extensive enough to provide all of the required information for the subsequent analysis with the exception of race and appearance. All county court cases completed from January through September, 1977 were included in the sample.

Procedure

An instruction manual was developed over a six month trial period. No data were included in the analysis from this period. A copy of the instruction manual was provided to observers who were trained in the use of the forms through practice sessions in the court and a series of seminars in which coding discrepancies between raters were discussed and clarified. Periodically, two observers sat in different places and recorded data independently. Inter-observer agreement was over 98% for all information collected on the 144 cases in which two observers were present simultaneously in the same court. Information on each individual case was numerically coded and punched on computer cards. The tables and statistics were compiled using standard SPSS programs.

RESULTS

Eight defendant variables (age, marital status, sex, employment status, residence, educational level, race and appearances) plus legal information on the charge and on the defendant's prior record were examined to determine the characteristics of 1,033 persons who faced non-driving, criminal code offences. In addition, these defendant and offence characteristics were examined with respect to the presence of counsel and to the decisions rendered by the court.

Characteristics of Defendants Who Appeared Before the Court

Persons charged with non-driving, criminal code offences were typically white (83%), young (45% under 21), single (83%), male (88%) and frequently unemployed (49%). A sizeable portion had previous criminal records (45%). In addition, a majority of the persons with records (53%) had been convicted of another offence within the previous year.

Three of the defendant variables (educational level, race, and appearance) could only be evaluated for a specific portion of the cases. The defendant's educational level was defined as the highest grade level completed in the formal educational system and was typically available only for persons who had presentence reports. This restriction limited the sample to most county court cases (251) and a small number of magistrate cases (63). These defendants were poorly educated; a majority (61%) with no more than a ninth grade education. Race and appearance were available only for the cases with an observer present which excluded most county cases from the sample. Black persons accounted for 15% of the defendants, but less than 2% of the population. One third (32%) of the accused were poorly dressed, most informal in appearance (57%) and only a small percentage were well dressed (11%).

The basic descriptive frequencies are provided in Table 1 [omitted].

The majority of the defendants lived in the City of Halifax (62%). A disproportionate number of these cases (28%) came from the lowest socio-economic ward in Halifax with a rate of 130 defendants per 10,000 residents, which was more than twice the rate of any other ward. Wards with the highest proportions of low income housing had a high defendant/resident ratio; the ward which contained the largest proportion of upper and middle income housing had the lowest defendant/resident ratio.

Patterns of defendant's characteristics varied with the specific types of charges. Break and enter, and theft over $200 had a high proportion of defendants with low income and marginal social characteristics relative to the rest of the offences. These defendants were more frequently under 26 years of age (83%, 196), had not reached tenth grade (75%, 101), single (91%, 213), unemployed (56%, 107), and more likely to have criminal records (67%, 149) relative to defendants who faced other types of charges. In contrast, defendants charged with assault were more frequently over 25 years of age (45%, 42), employed (55%, 33), and married (37%, 33) relative to other persons.

. . . .

The Influence of Lawyers on the Court Process

The most prominent variable which distinguished represented from unrepresented cases was the nature of the charge. Most defendants charged with indictable offences had lawyers (90%) while a majority of persons facing summary charges were unrepresented (59%). Thus, in the next section, the evaluation of the importance of counsel is restricted to summary cases given the small number of unrepresented defendants facing indictable charges.

Absence of Counsel

Persons who pleaded guilty were less likely to have a lawyer (34%) than defendants who pleaded not guilty (61%). First offenders were more frequently unrepresented (67%) than second offenders (49%) or defendants with multiple records (46%). These differences were due to the fact that Legal Aid was typically not available to poor first offenders, charged with a summary offence. Thus, type of charge, plea, and prior record all had to be controlled to explore further whether there were differences in the personal characteristics of represented and unrepresented defendants. Only summary cases for first offenders who pleaded guilty were frequent enough to control for all three variables and still provide a sizeable case sample. Unrepresented first offenders were more frequently unemployed (no lawyer: 37%, 41; lawyer: 23%, 12; $\chi^2 = 12.7$, df = 2, $p = .002$), casual in appearance (no lawyer: 29%, 46; lawyer: 18%, 10; $\chi^2 = 23.2$, df = 2, $p < .001$), and faced minor summary charges (no lawyer: 38%, 70; lawyer: 23%, 17; $\chi^2 = 5.8$, df = 2, $p = .05$).

There were no significant differences in the conviction rates for represented and unrepresented defendants who pleaded not guilty to summary charges. Sentencing patterns, however, differed for represented and unrepresented defendants when the important legal variables of plea and prior record were controlled. Represented first offenders who pleaded guilty to summary charges were more likely to receive a discharge or a suspended sentence (64%) than persons without a lawyer (20%).... This finding remained significant when the sample was broken down by severity of charge into minor, property, and person categories.

Type of Counsel

The socio-economic characteristics of the defendants were correlated with the type of counsel. Having a private lawyer was associated with being of good appearance, older in age, white, and employed; clients represented by Legal Aid were young, non-white, and unemployed ($p < .01$). Legal Aid clients were more likely than clients of private lawyers to have a previous record and multiple charges, but, as noted earlier, because of personnel limitations Legal Aid was largely available to the poor only for an indictable but not a summary charge. Five Legal Aid lawyers handled 56% of all represented defendants facing indictable charges, the remaining 44% were handled by all the private [lawyers] combined.

Private lawyers were more successful in obtaining favourable trial verdicts for their clients than Legal Aid lawyers. Privately represented defendants were found guilty in 54% of their trials while Legal Aid defendants were found guilty in 72%.... The percentage of Legal Aid clients convicted was higher than that for private clients at each of six levels of charge severity.

For summary offences, but not indictable offences, Legal Aid defendants more frequently received punitive sentences than privately represented defendants, even when prior record was controlled. Privately represented first offenders were more likely to receive a discharge (50%) than Legal Aid first offenders (15%).... In addition, Legal Aid defendants with criminal records were more frequently incarcerated (58%) than similar privately represented defendants (27%)....

Factors Which Determine the Court's Decision

As would be expected, both type of charge and prior record were strongly related ($p < .001$) to sentencing patterns: persons who faced summary charges were more likely to receive discharges (15%) or fines (63%) than defendants convicted of indictable offences (discharges: 3%; fines: 12%). Defendants convicted of indictable offences were more frequently incarcerated (55%) than summary defendants (12%). For summary offences first offenders were frequently discharged (21%) and rarely incarcerated (1%) while defendants with records were frequently incarcerated (36%) and rarely discharged (2%). For indictable charges, the rate of imprisonment for defendants with records (68%) was more than twice the percentage for first offenders (31%). Thus, the legal factors of charge and record had to be controlled before examining the relationship between defendant characteristics and sentencing patterns.

Employment Status

Unemployed defendants were typically sentenced more severely than employed persons ($p < .05$). Employed first offenders, convicted of summary offences, more frequently received discharges (27%) than unemployed first offenders (8%). Unemployed defendants with criminal records were more frequently incarcerated for both summary (42%) and indictable (78%) charges than employed past offenders (summary: 20%; indictable: 51%).

Age

The 21–25 year old group tended to receive more severe types of sentences ($p < .01$). When convicted of summary charges they were more frequently fined relative to other age groups. For indictable charges, both first offenders and persons with criminal records who were 21–25 years old had the highest rates of imprisonment relative to other age groups.

Race

Sentencing patterns were significantly associated with the defendant's race, even when restricted to first offenders convicted of summary charges. White defendants received discharges in 23% of these cases, while a black first offender never received a discharge.... The number of black defendants for other combinations of prior record and type of charge was too small to allow meaningful statistical evaluation of the severity of sentence.

. . . .

DISCUSSION

A clear pattern runs through the data; it is poor and socially marginal persons who appear most frequently in court. When they appear for a summary first offence they are usually unrepresented leaving them at a disadvantage. When they appear for a subsequent offence or a serious charge they are likely to be represented by Legal Aid rather than a private lawyer. In both cases the poor and marginal person is more likely to be treated harshly by the court. Low social class, the nature of the representation, and judicial judgment all combine to the selective disadvantage of the poor, raising socio-political and technical issues of social justice, with clear implications for reform within the judicial process.

. . . .

Technical Issues of Social Justice

Selective Representation

Given the economic and social characteristics of defendants, and the nature of the court process, most defendants find themselves in a difficult situation of needing a lawyer but not having the necessary money to retain counsel. Public defender and legal aid systems are designed to provide this assistance. However, the criteria for qualifying for such assistance are strict, and even when assistance is provided, there are serious questions about its effectiveness. Such is certainly the case in Nova Scotia as shown by our data and apparently so in other provinces with alternative legal aid or public defender programs. Without a lawyer the potential advantages of plea bargaining are effectively closed to many, although the process is a seldom acknowledged reality in Canada. If the Halifax data are at all typical, we may well suspect that the judicial structure and process is itself a source of injustice. Some change is needed either in terms of the availability of legal assistance or in terms of the court process which makes legal representation so essential.

Selective Justice

Of even greater concern than the implicit bias of both impact and representation, is direct bias. In theory, crimes are punished equally, but in practice the actual penalty and its effective impact seem to depend, not on the nature of the crime, but on the person who commits it. It may be that the poor, the unemployed and the undereducated defendant is a poor risk and deserves harsh treatment, but that conclusion may also result from a court system that denies representation on economic grounds and then punishes for being poor.

Even when the sentence is the same, its actual effect may be different. For some, payment of a fine means reaching into one's pocket, for others it is a difficult if not impossible task. At the time of our research, one half of the persons serving time in the County Correction Institution were there for nonpayment of fines. One significant variable explaining a fine rather than a suspended sentence or discharge is the inability to retain counsel or to qualify for legal assistance. The standard of justice should be a social concept which requires the evaluation of current practices in light of their actual consequences. The presumed advantages of technical justice provided by the adversary system are nonfunctional if some are less defensible than others.

. . . .

There is no reason for the courts to be defensive about the results of our study. The data provide the basis for dealing with important questions and issues of justice in a problematic manner. There is, however, reason for concern that the courts to date have shown little interest in such information and resist the collection of such data. The study was carried out by community psychologists in response to citizen complaints from the poor district over perceived unequal treatment, rather than by the court itself or by a law class. We have called this legal resistance to examining the consequences of the legal process a "selective ignorance" and we regard the lack of a social criterion as a standard of justice as a major conceptual issue of judicial reform.

Justice as an ideal is not sufficient if in practice it is not provided.

. . . .

In contrast, an emphasis on the actual outcome of the judicial process requires the addition of new analytical components to the legal process which look to the social consequences of the procedures as the ultimate criterion. From this view the legal process is a means, not an end, in itself. As long as the concept of justice is restricted to legality and technical procedures there will never be the need to step beyond the current level of selective ignorance and significant judicial reform will never take place. Only when the consequences of current judicial practices are examined will it be possible for the court to see itself as a source of technical and socio-political injustice and therefore institute appropriate reform.

∎

C. SYSTEMIC BARRIERS TO ACCESS TO COUNSEL: SECTION 15?

The lack of representation or the quality of that representation exacerbates the disadvantage faced by specific accused, as the previous article by K. Edward Renner and Alan H. Warner demonstrates. There are numerous other areas in which state-funded counsel is not provided; for example, for coroners' inquests. See the discussion of Vincent Gardner's case *supra*, **Policing**. Gardner's family was forced to abandon their complaint against the police because they were denied full legal aid coverage: Jennie Abell, "Access to Legal Assistance and Representation and Rights of the Complainant/Witness/Victim" in Abell and Sheehy, *Proof, Defences, and Beyond* at 397 [hereinafter Abell, "Access to Legal Assistance"].

Consider possible explanations for the hostility accorded to the accused represented by "legal aid lawyers" or those funded by "taxpayers' money."

Consider, in this regard, the role of law in regulating access to "effective assistance of counsel," as guaranteed by the *Charter* s. 7. In *R. v. B.(L.C.)* (1996), 27 O.R. (3d) 686 (C.A.), the court held that the burden on the accused was to establish "the factual basis to support a finding that counsel provided ineffective or incompetent representation [and that] prejudice [resulted] as a consequence of counsel's incompetence" (paragraph 57). Counsel (who was funded by legal aid) admitted that he did not interview the accused while he was in custody because "I don't do jails" (702–3):

> It is clear from a review of defence counsel's evidence that his decision not to "do jails" had an economic, not a philosophic, basis.... [H]e had a high volume, "resolution-oriented" legal aid practice.... He said that he processed 500 to 600 criminal clients each year. Most would

be legal aid clients. About 50% of them plead guilty.... [T]his would work out to 250 to 300 guilty pleas and an equal number of trials each year.

[B]ecause of his schedule, defence counsel did not have the time, or make the time, to meet with his clients other than in court.... [I]t seems to me that the fact that defence counsel was working on a block-fee legal aid case, where his profit margin would have been adversely affected by extra transactions such as detention centre visits, may have had more to do with his decision not to "do jails" than he cares to admit.

... Nonetheless,... I am unable to conclude that there is a reasonable probability that the result would have been different had defence counsel acted as the appellant submits he should have acted.

Both lack of representation and representation by "legal aid lawyers" may be compounded by existing biases (class, race, ethnocentrism, linguistic, anti-union): Jennie Abell, "Legal Aid in Saskatchewan: Rhetoric and Reality, 1974–82" in Jim Harding, ed., *Social Policy and Social Justice: The Blakeney Years in Saskatchewan* 173 (Waterloo: Wilfrid Laurier University Press, 1995) 173. Also, legal aid guidelines differentially impact on particular groups in society, such as women. For example, consider the limitation of coverage to cases involving imprisonment, discussed *supra*. Might there be other, more "serious," issues than imprisonment? Some feminists have argued that this is a male standard that unduly discounts areas of service of importance to women: Jennie Abell, *ibid.*; Jennie Abell, "Ideology and the Emergence of Legal Aid in Saskatchewan" (1993) 16 Dalhousie L.J. 125. See also: Aboriginal Justice Inquiry of Manitoba, *Report of the Aboriginal Justice Inquiry of Manitoba, Volume 1: The Justice System and Aboriginal People* (Winnipeg: Queen's Printer, 1991) at 366–67, discussing the impact of the lack of representation of summary conviction matters on the creation of criminal records for Aboriginal accused.

Although no substantive right to counsel exists, the "constitutionalization" of legal aid is achieved by judicial decision-making. The decisions entrench existing interpretations of the "seriousness" of criminal charges and the priority attached to cases where imprisonment is a risk. They effectively limit legislative choices and usurp the legislative function to define priorities. In the context of budget cuts, this further erodes representation in already underserved areas by displacing limited resources and reallocating them to "serious" criminal charges: Abell, "Access to Legal Assistance," *supra*. One example of the effect of this prioritization is that defendants in complex criminal trials will be provided with funded representation at the expense of other accused who may actually be poorer. For example, Nova Scotia Legal Aid funded the defence of Gerald Philips in his appeal to the Supreme Court opposing a new trial on charges he caused the deaths of 26 Westray miners. He earned $6,000 a month as a mining consultant, but he argued that he had already spent $800,000 on lawyers, and thus required assistance: "Nova Scotia to pay bill of Westray mine official" *The Ottawa Citizen* (8 June 1996) A3. See also *D.Z., supra*.

The characterization of "serious" goes relatively unexamined because the understanding also mirrors a construction of seriousness that has been entrenched for some time (through the federal funding formula, for example). Thus, when provinces contemplate cuts in justice spending, they often adopt similar priorities. Also, funding to specialized legal services clinics has been reduced: Julius Melnitzer, "Funding cuts hamper efforts of African Canadian Legal Clinic" *Law Times* (22–28 April 1996) 4. Instead, much of the debate centres on the tariff structure for lawyers, and reinforces the importance of criminal defences in complicated trials.

The availability of legal aid and the guidelines concerning its application impact on victims as well as on the accused. The representation of victims has been a controversial issue in criminal law: Abell, "Access to Legal Assistance," *supra*. Thus, decisions made by the Women's Division of the University of Ottawa Student Legal Aid Clinic (to not represent men accused of violence against women) and the reaction by the Defence Counsel Association of Ottawa (to complain to the Law Society of Ontario alleging unprofessional conduct) raise questions and issues about what the feminist practice of law means, the relationship between activism and law, and the constraints and barriers impeding a radical redefinition of lawyering. This discussion in turn raises questions about the role and place of critical legal education in identifying deficiencies of the present approaches; the contribution of feminist scholarship in legal education and legal activism; the nature and goals of legal services and clinics, both historically and contemporaneously; and the needs of clients and the ways in which those are assessed and addressed. For an examination of the various stages of that particular dispute: the identification of the problems encountered in the criminal justice system by victims of violence; the decision to move to address those gaps; the consequent decision to no longer represent men charged with acts of violence against women with whom they were in relationships; the articulation of a policy reflecting that decision; the reaction of both the professional and the lay communities to that decision; the form that reaction took; the way in which the issues were framed in the subsequent debate; the forum chosen; and the outcome, see Jennie Abell, "Women, Violence and the Criminal Law: 'It's the Fundamentals of Being a Lawyer that are at Stake Here'" (1992) 17 Queen's L.J. 147. Ultimately, the actions of the student clinic were vindicated by the Law Society.

Many of the barriers to effective representation by counsel described above — those faced by legal aid clients, prisoners, Aboriginal peoples, African-Canadians, and battered women — could be articulated in terms of a denial of equality rights, particularly because they raise systemic issues and generate disparate impacts. In one significant case decided by the Supreme Court of Canada, *New Brunswick v. G. (J.)*, [1999] 3 S.C.R. 46, the Court decided that the provincial government was constitutionally obligated to provide an indigent mother with access to state-funded counsel because the litigation put her at risk of permanently losing custody of her children to the state, which was framed as an infringement on her security of the person within the meaning of s. 7 of the *Charter*. Three of the justices, Justices L'Heureux-Dubé, McLachlin, and Gonthier, also articulated the implications for an equality analysis were the woman to go unrepresented, because women and, particularly, single mothers and racialized mothers are disproportionately the subject of child protection proceedings. They argued that s. 7 must thus be interpreted through the lens of s. 15. Why might these justices have integrated s. 15 into the s. 7 argument and refrained from finding a s. 15 violation on its own?

Cartoon from Wasserman — Published by Los Angeles Times Syndicate. © Tribune Media Services, Inc. All Rights Reserved. Reproduced with permission.

13

Judicial Interim Release

The availability of release pending trial (or appeal) once charged is of great significance to the accused person. Susan Armstrong, Mary Jane Mossman, and Ronald Sackville in *Essays on Law and Poverty: Bail and Social Security* (Canberra: Australian Government, 1977) suggest some of the reasons release is significant, in that a person held in custody before trial is more likely to plead guilty, more likely to be found guilty, and more likely to be sentenced to jail if convicted. They criticize the brevity of bail hearings, given the serious consequences to the accused of imprisonment both in terms of the eventual outcome of proceedings and in terms of other costs, such as emotional trauma, loss of family support, loss of job or education, and financial loss. They suggest that the consequences for women may be particularly serious, since "[p]re-trial imprisonment may separate mothers from their children for long periods."

While the monograph describes pre-trial detention for accused persons in Australia and England, firsthand observations of the process and results in remand court may suggest that accused persons in Canada face similar processes and consequences. One example that is suggestive of "assembly line" justice in bail applications was reported by Catherine Buckie, "Judge orders 23 simultaneous bail hearings" *The [Montreal] Gazette* (4 October 1990) A6 (simultaneous hearings conducted with respect to charges of obstruction, participation in a riot, and weapons possession charges in the Kanehsatake stand-off between Mohawks and the Sûreté du Québec).

The *Code* underwent significant reform in 1970, which was intended to reduce the number of people held in detention prior to trial. The new sections deal with release by the arresting officer and the officer in charge of the station (ss. 497, 498, and 499). If not released by one of the officers, the accused must be brought before a justice of the peace "without unreasonable delay," in accordance with s. 503. Section 515 governs the interim release hearing, the available orders, and the burden of proof. Detention may be justified on primary (to ensure attendance in court), secondary (protection of safety of the public), or tertiary (public confidence in the administration of criminal justice) grounds. Note the reverse onus in ss. 515(6) and 522. Other provisions govern review of release orders, and the arrest and punishment of accused who violate the terms of their release.

Despite the reforms and their goal of reducing detention prior to trial, many problems continue. Consider the impact of our system of judicial interim release upon Aboriginal peoples in Canada as outlined in the following extract from *Report of the Aboriginal Justice Inquiry of Manitoba*, Vol. I by Judge A.C. Hamilton and Judge C. Murray Sinclair.

Report of the Aboriginal Justice Inquiry of Manitoba[†]

We believe that our justice system imprisons far too many people who have been found guilty of crimes. This is a serious problem and we deal with it in detail in Chapter 10. It is perhaps even more disturbing to discover the degree to which our system incarcerates individuals who have not been convicted of any crime. In some of the institutions we visited, many of the inmates, sometimes as many as 30%, were being held in custody pending consideration of their cases by the courts. Studies demonstrate that Manitoba makes excessive use of pre-trial detention and that this policy weighs adversely against Aboriginal people.

According to statistics in the 1988–89 *Annual Report* of the Manitoba Department of the Attorney General, considerably more persons are taken into pre-trial detention than are sentenced to jail. This suggests that many of those pre-trial detentions were unnecessary, that either the court found the individuals to be not guilty or found that incarceration was not appropriate for them.

In 1988 there were 15,138 admissions at the Winnipeg Remand Centre and 2,658 temporary detentions at the Manitoba Youth Centre, for a total of 17,796 pre-trial detentions. The statistics do not reveal how many pre-trial detentions there were at the other jails in the province. There were less than 10,000 adults sentenced to jails in the province, including federal institutions. There were, at most, approximately 1,300 youth sentenced to jail in the province in 1988.

These figures suggest there were more than one and one-half times as many pre-trial admissions for adults as there were sentences to jail.

The figure of 1,300 for sentenced youth includes 600 youth admitted to institutions other than the Manitoba Youth Centre and Agassiz Youth Centre. It is not clear whether these youth were being held in pre-trial detention or were sentenced to those institutions. The figure also includes 460 youth sentenced to open custody, which is not supposed to be considered the same as jail, but, in practice, Manitoba open custody is very similar to closed custody (24-hour lockup). Even using the figure of 1,300, this suggests there were more than two times as many pre-trial detentions for youth as there were youth sentenced to jail.

For women, there were 1,819 admissions to the Winnipeg Remand Centre, but only 628 women admitted to the other jails in the province. This suggests there were three times as many pre-trial admissions for women as there were sentences to jail.

According to the Canadian Centre for Justice Statistics, in 1988–89 only 33% of the individuals in provincial custody in Manitoba had been sentenced to a term of imprisonment after being found guilty of a crime, while 66% were in custody awaiting further court appearances, trial or sentencing (these individuals are usually referred to as being held on remand). Quebec was the only other province in which the number of individuals being held on remand exceeded the number of individuals who had been sentenced to a term of imprisonment. In Saskatchewan 63% of the individuals in provincial custody were sentenced; in Alberta the figure is 68%. The raw figures are equally disturbing. In 1988–89, 10,083 people were admitted to Manitoba's provincial correctional institutions on remand; the comparable figures for Saskatchewan, Alberta and British Columbia were, respectively, 4,464; 9,679; and 4,772.

Some jurisdictions have dealt with these problems by establishing bail supervision programs. Under these programs, people who cannot find anyone to post bail for them, but otherwise qualify for release, are released on condition that they regularly report to designated officials. These programs are now available in Ontario, British Columbia and Saskatchewan. To date, the Manitoba government has shown little commitment to developing alternatives to pre-trial detention. We believe the time has come to do so. Such programs for Aboriginal accused should operate in remote communities and urban centres, and should come under the direction of Aboriginal people.

Local communities must be equipped with short-term custody facilities. Accused individuals should be held in these facilities and a bail hearing should be arranged in the community before a local judicial officer.

In remote communities and in urban centres, there is also a need to develop new criteria for determining whether an individual should be released. These must take into account, among other things,

---

[†] Judge A.C. Hamilton and Judge C. Murray Sinclair, *Report of the Aboriginal Justice Inquiry of Manitoba*, Vol. I. (Winnipeg: Queen's Printer, 1991) at 360–61.

the strength of the Aboriginal community's network of extended families and this network's ability to provide pre-trial supervision.

The excessive use of pre-trial detention is another reason we recommend the establishment of time limits on prosecutions.

We believe an Aboriginal justice system will be able to deal effectively with many of the problems of pre-trial custody in remote communities. Such a system would be able to deal with the question of detention and supervision in the community where the offence took place.

WE RECOMMEND THAT

- Bail hearings be conducted in the community where the offence was committed.
- The Manitoba government establish a bail supervision program to provide pre-trial supervision to accused persons as an alternative to detention.
- Inappropriate bail conditions, such as requiring cash deposits or financial guarantees from low-income people, that militate against Aboriginal people obtaining bail, no longer be applied.

■

The findings of the *Report of the Commission on Systemic Racism in the Ontario Criminal Justice System* (Toronto: Queen's Printer, 1995) [hereinafter, *Report on Systemic Racism*] disclose similar, disturbing patterns in decisions by police and by judges (at 143, 145–6):

> This study of pre-trial detention of white and black persons charged with the same offence types reveals evidence of differential treatment across the entire sample.... [B]lack accused were less likely than white accused to be released by the police and more likely to be detained after a bail hearing.
>
> ...
>
> However closely we scrutinize the data, the findings disclose distinct and legally unjustifiable differences in release decisions for black and white accused, across the sample as a whole for some specific offences in particular. The conclusion is inescapable: some black men imprisoned before trial would not have been jailed if they had been white, and some white men freed before their trials would have been detained had they been black.
>
> In effect, these findings are evidence of the state exercising discretion as if it has more compelling reasons to imprison black adult males before their trials than white adult males charged with the same offences. This bias may reflect explicit beliefs that black men cannot be trusted to appear for trial, or are more dangerous or criminal than white men. But it could also arise from more implicit and subtle assumptions, since important characteristics of the release process are likely to promote stereotypical decision-making.
>
> As presently organized, the bail system demands fast decisions, sometimes made within minutes, and it expects both the police and bail justices to make predictions based on vague criteria and information that is often inadequate. These features obviously do not compel decision-makers to rely on racial or other stereotypes, nor in any way excuse such reliance. But they establish conditions in which reliance on stereotypes, perhaps subconsciously, may make decisions easier. For example, a justice who assumes that police testimony about drug charges is seldom mistaken and that most black males charged with drug offences sell drugs for profit may quickly conclude at a bail hearing that a specific black male accused is likely to offend before trial. By drawing on such assumptions, the justice avoids the more difficult task of attempting to predict the likely behaviour of that individual.
>
> However, our findings do not reveal racial bias in the exercise of discretion for each offence type in the study. Instead, they show clear variations in release decisions within the range of offence types selected. This finding poses the question of the extent to which bail decisions about persons charged with other offence types would reveal racial bias in the exercise of discretion. The racial bias against black men documented in this study also raises questions about the treatment of accused from other racialized communities, as well as the treatment of black women and black youth.
>
> The answers to these questions lie in future research. Clearly, however, action to eliminate the systemic conditions that permit unjust pre-trial imprisonment of racialized accused should not wait until more is known. It should begin immediately.[†]

---

† © Queen's Printer for Ontario, 1995. Reproduced with permission.

The report references the perceptions of defence lawyers, which confirm these conclusions about racial bias in detention decisions (at 119–20).

The Law Reform Commission of Canada has, in a Minister's Reference on *Aboriginal Peoples and Criminal Justice* (Ottawa: LRCC, 1991) at 101–2, made recommendations regarding bail reform. The LRCC suggests, among other reforms, that police officers should be required to release persons arrested for *any* crime unless specific grounds for detention are satisfied, that bail laws should direct justices to assess the reasonableness of a proposed bail condition by reference to factors such as the accused's cultural background and "the special requirements of traditional Aboriginal pursuits," that greater leniency be used regarding the requirements of sureties, and that resort to cash deposits by both accused persons and sureties be permitted.

The *Charter* has begun to have an impact upon the law of judicial interim release. For example, in *R. v. Morales*, [1992] 3 S.C.R. 711, the Court held that s. 515(10)(b) of the *Code*, which then permitted the detention of an accused pending trial on the grounds that it was in the "public interest," is unconstitutionally vague and thus offended s. 11(e) of the *Charter*, which guarantees the right not to be "denied reasonable bail without just cause." However, that portion of s. 515(10)(b) which, alternatively, permits the detention of the accused "for the protection or safety of the public," was upheld as constitutionally valid.

Another decision released at the same time held that the reversed onus of proof at bail hearings contained in s. 515(6)(d) for drug trafficking offences — which, in effect, requires the accused to show cause why their detention is not justified, does not offend s. 11(e), because the special circumstances of traffickers, in terms of access to money and avenues to flee the country, require special bail rules, constituting "just cause" within the meaning of the *Charter* section. In the same case, an argument under s. 11(d) was also rejected, on the basis that the presumption of innocence has no application at the bail stage, where guilt or innocence is not the subject of the inquiry: *R. v. Pearson*, [1992] 3 S.C.R. 665. However, the *Report on Systemic Racism* specifically criticized the decision in *Pearson* (at 155–59), arguing that (at 157–58) "the practical effect of presuming detention for persons charged with trafficking is to imprison small-scale offenders," thus contributing to (at 158) "racial inequality in the imprisonment of untried accused."

Parliament responded to *Morales* by enacting a new basis for detention in s. 515(10)(c), which, as *Hall* illustrates, has thus far survived *Charter* challenged.

R. v. Hall[†]

[OSBORNE A.C.J.O.:]

OVERVIEW

The appellant was charged with first degree murder and sought to be released from custody pending his trial. His application for bail was heard by the Honourable Mr. Justice Bolan who was satisfied that the appellant's detention was not necessary to ensure his attendance in court or for the protection or safety of the public. However, relying on s. 515(10)(c) of the *Criminal Code*, R.S.C. 1985, c. C-46, he concluded that the appellant's detention was necessary in order to maintain confidence in the administration of justice. He thus dismissed the appellant's application for bail. In doing so, he considered the strength of the Crown's case, and the gravity of the offence, including the circumstances of its commission. He also referred to fear that had been expressed by the general Sault Ste. Marie community.

Following Bolan J.'s decision denying the appellant bail, the appellant commenced *habeas corpus* proceedings and an application for his release pursuant to s. 24(1) of the *Charter* and s. 52 of the *Constitution Act*, 1982. In his application he sought to have s. 515(10)(c) of the *Criminal Code* declared unconstitutional. The Honourable Mr. Justice Caputo dismissed the appellant's application. He concluded that s. 515(10)(c) does not contravene s. 11(e) of the *Charter* and is not vague or overbroad. This

---

[†] (2000), 50 O.R. (3d) 257 at (C.A.).

appeal is from Caputo J.'s order and raises the issue of the constitutionality of that part of s. 515(10)(c) which provides for the detention of an accused person in circumstances where the judge before whom a bail application is heard concludes that detention is necessary "in order to maintain confidence in the administration of justice" (s. 515(10)(c)).

FACTUAL BACKGROUND

The body of Peggy Jo Barkley-Dube was found on the morning of May 3, 1999 on the kitchen floor of her home in a residential area of Sault Ste. Marie. Ms. Dube was pronounced dead at the scene. The cause of her death was determined to be a massive haemorrhage due to a number of lacerations. The forensic pathologist who conducted the autopsy noted 37 separate slashing type wounds to Ms. Dube's hands, forearms, shoulder, neck and face. Her neck had been cut completely through to the vertebrae. There was medical evidence that the person who assaulted Ms. Dube had intended to cut her head off.

The appellant, a close acquaintance and second cousin of the deceased's husband, was arrested on June 4, 1999 and charged with the first degree murder of Ms. Dube. He has been in custody since then.

The circumstantial evidence against the appellant as set out at his June 16, 1999 bail hearing included the following:

- a number of areas in the deceased's home, including the basement, contained traces of the appellant's blood;
- several footprint impressions, all from the same type of running shoe, containing the deceased's blood were found in the dining room and kitchen of the deceased's residence. According to two experts, some of the footprints had been left by the appellant's shoes which were discovered under a table in the back corner of the basement workshop area used by the appellant in his parents' home;
- a surveillance video from a local convenience store showed the appellant on the night of the homicide, wearing white running shoes with black marking on the toes and soles that matched the markings on running shoes seized from his parents' home;
- the appellant admitted to the police that he had been in the convenience store on the night of the homicide, but said that he had been wearing black running shoes.

At the time of his arrest, the appellant was 27 years old, married with two children. He was employed in the delicatessen department of a local grocery store. He was about to start new employment in Ottawa. There was evidence at the bail hearing that the appellant is a loving husband and father, with no history of violence, mental illness or psychological problems. He has no criminal record.

The deceased's death received considerable media attention in Sault Ste. Marie. The evidence disclosed that there was great public concern about the brutal homicide. The police officer in charge of the investigation testified that there was a general sense of fear in Sault Ste. Marie that the person who had committed such a heinous crime could be at large. The deceased's father testified that his wife and three other daughters were petrified and fearful since the murder.

SECTION 515(10)(c)

In *R. v. Morales*, [1992] 3 S.C.R. 711, the Supreme Court of Canada held that the "public interest" component of what was then s. 515(10)(b) of the *Criminal Code* did not represent a constitutional basis upon which to detain accused persons pending their trial because the "public interest" ground for detention was impermissibly vague and overbroad.

After *Morales*, until June 1997, the denial of bail could only be justified on the basis that the accused's detention was necessary to ensure that the accused would attend court when required to do so, or to protect the public.

On April 25, 1997, Parliament responded to *Morales* by revisiting the grounds upon which an accused could be denied bail pending trial. At that time Parliament passed the *Criminal Law Improvement Act*, 1997, S.C. 1997, c. 18, an omnibus Act that amended a number of sections of the *Criminal Code* and related legislation. It introduced s. 515(10)(c) to replace the unconstitutional "public interest" ground for detention. ...

. . . .

While it took approximately five years after *Morales* for s. 515(10)(c) to be brought into effect, this was not because the issue was of little importance to legislators. The provision was originally before Parliament at its 1994–95 sitting, in response to proposals at the Uniform Law Conference ("ULC") of 1993, less than a year after *Morales*. At the 1993 ULC, the delegations from three provinces (Saskatchewan, Quebec and Ontario) independently proposed amendments to the *Criminal Code* bail provisions that would add public confidence in the administration of justice as a ground for denying bail. Saskatchewan and Quebec withdrew their proposals in favour of Ontario's, which recommended that an amendment be made to the *Criminal Code* adding a new ground for denying bail: namely, that releasing the accused, in light of the gravity of the offence and the strength of the Crown's case, would tend to bring the administration of justice into disrepute. Ultimately, this proposal was withdrawn and replaced by the following proposal, which was carried unanimously:

> That Federal Justice study expeditiously the secondary ground as applied to bail decisions in light of the decision in *Pearson* and *Morales* so that recommendations could be made for legislation.

What eventually became s. 515(10)(c) was included in an omnibus bill (C-118). The bill received first reading, but Parliament was prorogued and as a result the bill died. However, when Parliament resumed, the provision was re-introduced as part of Bill C-17, and, as I have said, was duly enacted as part of the *Criminal Law Improvement Act*.

THE APPELLANT'S BAIL APPLICATION

Bolan J. found that the appellant's detention was not necessary to secure his attendance in court or for the protection and safety of the public. However, he concluded that the appellant's detention was necessary in order to maintain confidence in the administration of justice and, relying on s. 515(10)(c), he dismissed the appellant's application. As I have noted, he specifically referred to fears and concerns that had been expressed by members in the general Sault Ste. Marie community, the gravity of the offence, the apparent strength of the Crown's case and the horrific circumstances of the homicide. He felt that the strongest evidence against the appellant came from an expert who said that the footprints in the victim's blood came from a pair of shoes owned by the appellant and found in the appellant's father's residence.

The Appellant's Application for *Habeas Corpus* and Relief under s. 24(1) of the *Charter*

On August 31, 1999, the appellant applied for *habeas corpus* and relief pursuant to s. 24(1) of the *Charter*. He also sought a declaration that s. 515(10)(c) of the *Criminal Code* violated s. 11(e) of the *Charter* and was therefore of no force and effect. The appellant raised two issues. First, he submitted that s. 515(10)(c) provides for the denial of bail without "just cause" contrary to s. 11(e) of the *Charter*, as that constitutional right was defined by the Supreme Court of Canada and, second, that s. 515(10)(c) is impermissibly vague and overbroad and thus provides for the denial of bail without just cause, again contrary to s. 11(e) of the *Charter*.

Caputo J. ... held that s. 515(10)(c) of the *Criminal Code* was not vague or overbroad and thus complies with the "just cause" requirement for the denial of bail in s. 11(e) of the *Charter*. He relied on *R. v. Pearson*, [1992] 3 S.C.R. 665 and *R. v. Morales*, *supra*, where Lamer C.J.C. held that the restriction on the basic entitlement to bail is constitutionally valid if the following conditions are met:

- Bail is denied only in a narrow set of circumstances.
- The denial of bail is necessary for the proper functioning of the bail system and is not undertaken for any purpose extraneous to the bail system.

Caputo J. concluded that s. 515(10)(c) satisfied the above two part test for just cause as established in *Pearson* and *Morales*.

In reaching this conclusion, Caputo J. relied on the British Columbia Court of Appeal's decision in *R. v. MacDougal* (1999), 138 C.C.C. (3d) 38, the first direct challenge to Parliament's 1997 response to the Supreme Court of Canada judgment in *Pearson* and *Morales*. In *MacDougal*, Hall J.A. concluded that s. 515(10)(c) was not vague or overbroad. He stated that by delineating a list of relevant factors to be considered in s. 515(10)(c), Parliament had provided sufficient direction to afford guidance for informed legal debate.

Caputo J. went on to hold that s. 515(10)(c) satisfied the second *Morales* test since it provided for the denial of bail for a purpose related to the promotion and proper functioning of the bail system. He concluded that maintaining confidence in the administration of justice is necessary to the proper functioning of the bail system which is an integral component of the criminal justice system. He relied on Cory J.'s observations in *MacKeigan* v. *Hickman*, [1989] 2 S.C.R. 796 at p. 846, that "without public confidence, the courts cannot effectively fulfil their role in society". He also relied on Le Dain J.'s statement in *Valente* v. *R.*, [1985] 2 S.C.R. 673 at p. 689, that "without that [public] confidence, the system cannot command the respect and acceptance that are essential to its effective operation." Finally, he concluded that the rule of law depends on a credible justice system which includes bail.

The appellant appealed to this court pursuant to s. 784(3) of the *Criminal Code* from the order dismissing his application for *habeas corpus* and relief under s. 24(1) of the *Charter*. The constitutional issue which this court must address is whether that part of s. 515(10)(c), on which Bolan J., the bail judge, relied in denying bail, meets the constitutional standard for the denial of bail set out in s. 11(e) of the *Charter*.

The broad constitutional issue has two distinct, albeit related, components. First, whether s. 515(10)(c) meets the "just cause", constitutionally mandated standard for the denial of bail and second, whether s. 515(10)(c) is vague or overbroad and thus unconstitutional on that basis.

Statutory Charter Provisions

[The court then reviewed ss. 11(e) of the *Charter*.]

. . . .

Section 515(10) of the *Criminal Code* sets out a system of pre-trial release under which an accused must normally be granted bail. There are three statutorily prescribed grounds set out in s. 515(10) under which pre-trial detention of an accused may be justified. ...

The third ground for detention is in issue on this appeal. As noted, it provides for detention if "any other just cause" is shown. Any other just cause in s. 515(10)(c) may include the need to maintain confidence in the administration of justice.

The Positions of the Appellant, Respondent and Intervenors

The appellant's position on the issue of the permissible scope of "just cause" is that there can be "just cause" for pre-trial detention consistent with s. 11(e) of the *Charter* only if detention is necessary to ensure the accused's attendance in court or to protect the public. The appellant relies on *Pearson* and *Morales* to support this submission which is central to his position on the "just cause" issue. The appellant contends that limiting the grounds for detention to the grounds set out in s. 515(10)(a) and (b) is the only way to ensure that the basis for pre-trial detention could promote the proper functioning of the bail system, the first of the two controlling principles established by Lamer C.J.C. in *Pearson* and *Morales*. The appellant also submits that s. 515(10)(c) "is a transparent attempt to revive the public interest component of the former s. 515(10)(b) that was struck down in *Morales* as unconstitutional." As part of this submission, the appellant contends that *Morales* determined that maintaining confidence in the administration of justice did not provide a constitutional basis upon which to deny trial bail.

The appellant also takes issue with Caputo J.'s conclusion that maintaining confidence in the administration of justice was necessary to the proper functioning of the bail system, which he found to be an integral component of the broader criminal justice system. The appellant takes it further in submitting that s. 515(10)(c) permits detention based on factors "at odds not only with the proper functioning of the bail system but with the presumption of innocence itself." Apart from the just cause issue, the appellant contends that the basis for the denial of bail set out in s. 515(10)(c) is vague and overbroad and thus unconstitutional.

In his vagueness submission, the appellant contends that by authorizing the denial of bail for an accused "on any other just cause being shown," s. 515(10)(c) does not provide for the denial of bail only in a narrow set of circumstances. However, Caputo J. correctly noted that the phrase "any other just cause," in s. 515(10)(c) was not used as a basis for Bolan J.'s finding of just cause to detain the appellant. At para. 56, Caputo J. said:

> In any event, in this case "any other just cause" was not resorted to as a basis for finding just cause to detain. I will leave it to a higher authority to determine whether if [sic] the offending words "any other just cause are too vague," the section would be read down. If necessary, I would do so.

Since Bolan J., in dismissing the appellant's application for release pending his trial, did not resort to "any other just cause" in s. 515(10)(c) as a basis for detaining the accused, I do not think the constitutionality of this part of s. 515(10)(c) should be addressed on this appeal. ...

. . . .

The intervenor, the Criminal Lawyers' Association (Ontario) ("CLA"), supports the appellant's submissions on the "just cause" part of the required constitutional analysis. In summary form, the CLA's position is that to the extent that s. 515(10)(c) authorizes the denial of bail to an accused who satisfies the criteria set out in s. 515(10)(a) and (b) (as the appellant did), s. 515(10)(c) is inconsistent with

s. 11(e) of the *Charter*. The CLA also supports the appellant's submission that s. 515(10)(c) is vague and overbroad. Both the appellant and the CLA submit that the s. 515(10)(c) limitation on an accused's rights to bail cannot be justified under s. 1 of the *Charter*.

The respondent Attorney General of Ontario ("Ontario") submits that Caputo J. was correct in holding that s. 515(10)(c) of the *Criminal Code* complies with the "just cause" requirement for the denial of bail in s. 11(e) of the *Charter* since it provides for the denial of bail for a purpose related to the proper functioning of the bail system and limits the denial of bail to a "narrow set of circumstances". Ontario contends that neither the *Charter* nor the Supreme Court of Canada's decision in *Morales* have the effect of limiting "just cause" to the primary and secondary grounds for detention set out in s. 515(10)(a) and (b) of the *Criminal Code* and that that part of s. 515(10)(c) on which Bolan J. relied in denying bail is neither vague nor overbroad.

The Attorney General of Canada ("Canada"), also an intervenor, supports the position of Ontario that Caputo J. did not err in dismissing the appellant's challenge to the constitutionality of the legislation in question. Like Ontario, Canada submits that the Supreme Court of Canada's decisions in *Pearson* and *Morales* do not preclude Parliament from enacting legislation that imposes a basis for pre-trial detention beyond the traditional primary and secondary grounds (s. 515(10)(a) and (b)). Canada submits that s. 515(10)(c) does not infringe the just cause requirement of s. 11(e) of the *Charter* and provides the court with a structured discretion that is capable of judicial interpretation. Therefore, Canada submits that the section is neither vague nor overbroad.

ANALYSIS

Does s. 515(10)(c) Provide for the Denial of Bail without Just Cause?

In *Pearson* and *Morales*, the Supreme Court considered the context and application of s. 11(e) of the *Charter*. The Court held in *Pearson*, at p. 693 S.C.R., p. 143, and confirmed in *Morales* at p. 726 S.C.R., that "there will be just cause for denial of bail if the denial can occur only in a narrow set of circumstances and if the denial is necessary to promote the proper functioning of the bail system." For reasons that follow, I think that s. 515(10)(c) limits the denial of bail to a "narrow set of circumstances" and provides for the denial of bail for a purpose related to the proper functioning of the bail system. Accordingly, in my opinion, Caputo J. did not err in holding that s. 515(10)(c) of the *Criminal Code* complies with the "just cause" requirement for the denial of bail set out in s. 11(e) of the *Charter*.

The Meaning of "Just Cause" in s. 11(e) of the *Charter*

Section 11(e) of the *Charter* guarantees that reasonable bail is not to be denied "without just cause". In my opinion, in using this manifestly general language, the drafters of the *Charter* intended to leave it open to Parliament to develop grounds which could justify detention beyond the first and second grounds, now set out in s. 515(10)(a) and (b), provided, of course, that any further basis for detention met the "just cause" constitutional standard in s. 11(e) of the *Charter*. This is consistent with the perception of the *Charter* being a broad constitutional instrument, sometimes described as a "living tree".

It seems to me that had the drafters of the *Charter* intended to limit the grounds for detention to the first and second grounds (s. 515(10)(a) and (b)), the *Charter* would have said so. Instead, the drafters of the *Charter* used broader language, to provide that an accused had the right "not to be denied reasonable bail without just cause."

Furthermore, I see nothing in either *Pearson* or *Morales* that would freeze the bases for the denial of bail to the first and second grounds — to secure the accused's attendance in court and the need to protect the public. In making what I view as intentionally general statements on the scope of "just cause", Lamer C.J.C. in *Morales* conspicuously did not say that no ground for detention beyond the primary and secondary grounds could meet the constitutional "just cause" standard. Instead, he made the broad pronouncement that to meet the "just cause" constitutional standard, the denial of bail must occur in a narrow set of circumstances and must be necessary to promote the proper functioning of the bail system and not undertaken for any purpose extraneous to the bail system.

In my view, had Lamer C.J.C. concluded in *Morales* that the s. 11(e) *Charter* "just cause" requirement meant that an accused could be denied bail only when it was necessary to secure his attendance at trial (s. 515(10)(a)) or to protect the public (s. 515(10)(b)), he would have said so, or at least responded to Gonthier J.'s dissenting reasons which rejected the notion that there could only be a constitutionally valid denial of bail if the court found detention was necessary to secure the accused's attendance in court or to protect the public. He emphasized, in considering the "public interest" ground for detention, the importance of there being room for the development of grounds for denying bail. He said, at pp. 122–123:

> Also important is the consideration that the criterion of necessity in the public interest is capable of encompassing circumstances which have not been foreseen or, indeed, which may be unforeseeable, yet when they occur, albeit rarely, they obviously make the detention necessary and undoubtedly provide just cause for denying bail within the meaning of s. 11(e) of the *Charter*. The courts must be able to deal with such circumstances. The good governance of society and the rule of law itself require that Parliament be allowed to provide for social peace and order even in unforeseen circumstances. The appropriate instrument for doing this is through the administration of justice by the courts and allowing them a measure of discretion which they are bound to exercise judicially, that is, for reasons that are relevant, within the limits provided by law and in accordance with the *Charter*.

As a general proposition, I think that it is consistent with both the *Charter* and Lamer C.J.C.'s majority reasons in *Morales*, that the list of grounds which may constitute "just cause" are not frozen, that is limited to the primary and secondary grounds for the denial of bail set out in s. 515(10)(a) and (b).

With the advent of the *Charter*, the administration of justice has inevitably, and I think rightly, been exposed to an increased public scrutiny. To operate effectively, the administration of justice must have the confidence of a reasonably informed public, which accepts the presumption of innocence and the need to release accused persons pending trial, unless their detention is necessary. See *Valente* v. *R.*, [1985] 2 S.C.R. 673 at p. 689 ... .

In my view, the need to maintain confidence in the administration of criminal justice is a value which falls within the ambit of "just cause" in s. 11(e) of the *Charter*. Recognizing this value works to promote the proper functioning of the bail system. It remains to be determined whether that ground for detention is impermissibly vague and overbroad. I now turn to those related issues.

Narrow Set of Circumstances — Vagueness and Overbreadth

The appellant submits that s. 515(10)(c) is defective because it is vague and overbroad. The doctrines of vagueness and overbreadth have been thoroughly reviewed in several decisions of the Supreme Court of Canada. In *R.* v. *Heywood*, [1994] 3 S.C.R. 761 at p. 764, 94 C.C.C. (3d) 481 at p. 516, Cory J. explained the distinction between vagueness and overbreadth:

> Overbreadth and vagueness are related in that both are the result of a lack of sufficient precision by a legislature in the means used to accomplish an objective. In the case of vagueness, the means are not clearly defined. In the case of overbreadth the means are too sweeping in relation to the objective.

He then, for the majority, set out the test for determining when a statute is overbroad:

> Overbreadth analysis looks at the means chosen by the state in relation to its purpose. In considering whether a legislative provision is overbroad, a court must ask the question: Are those means necessary to achieve the state objective? If the state, in pursuing a legitimate objective, uses means which are broader than is necessary to accomplish that objective, the principles of fundamental justice will be violated because the individual's rights will have been limited for no reason. The effect of overbreadth is that in some applications the law is arbitrary or disproportionate.

In *R.* v. *Nova Scotia Pharmaceutical Society*, [1992] 2 S.C.R. 606, Gonthier J. considered the issue of vagueness as a constitutional requirement. He noted that a valid law (that is a law that is not impermissibly vague) must provide a sufficient basis for legal debate. He stated at p. 642 S.C.R.:

> What becomes more problematic is not so much general terms conferring broad discretion, but terms failing to give direction as to how to exercise this discretion, so that this exercise may be controlled. Once more, *an unpermissibly* [sic] *vague law will not provide a sufficient basis for legal debate; it will not give a sufficient indication as to how decisions must be reached, such as factors to be considered or determinative elements.* In giving unfettered discretion, it will deprive the judiciary of means of controlling the exercise of this discretion.

Gonthier J. also made it clear that overbreadth is no more than an analytical tool, that is it has no independent existence. He put it this way, at p. 632 S.C.R.:

> What is referred to as "overbreadth", whether it stems from the vagueness of a law or from another source, remains no more than an analytical tool to establish a violation of a *Charter* right. Overbreadth has no independent existence.

References to a "doctrine of overbreadth" are superfluous.

In addressing the content of the doctrine of vagueness, Gonthier J. explained that vagueness in its constitutional context has two underlying rationales — fair notice of acceptable or prohibited conduct and the limitation of enforcement discretion. In dealing with "fair notice" he said, at p. 635 S.C.R.:

> Fair notice may not have been given when enactments are in somewhat general terms, in a way that does not readily permit citizens to be aware of their substance, when they do not relate to any element of the substratum of values held by society....
>
> Hence, aside from a formal aspect which is in our current system often presumed, fair notice to the citizen comprises a substantive aspect, that is an understanding that certain conduct is the subject of legal restrictions.

Since the *Criminal Code* provision in issue does not prohibit any particular form of conduct, the fair notice rationale for vagueness is of reduced significance. Nonetheless, the statutory criteria for denying bail cannot be vague or imprecise since such deficiencies would, according to *Morales*, result in the provision not meeting the "just cause" constitutional standard set out in s. 11(e) of the *Charter*. The legislation must provide the judiciary with a workable standard, but not a standard of certainty. That is to say the legislation does not have to be so precise that the legal consequences of given conduct can be predicted in advance with absolute certainty: see *Nova Scotia Pharmaceutical, supra*, at p. 639 S.C.R.

In addition, the legislation in question must provide some reasonably structured guidance for legal debate and to the judiciary. In *Nova Scotia Pharmaceutical, supra*, Gonthier J. in summary form said, at p. 643 S.C.R.:

> The doctrine of vagueness can therefore be summed up in this proposition: a law will be found unconstitutionally vague if it so lacks in precision as not to give sufficient guidance for legal debate. This statement of the doctrine best conforms to the dictates of the rule of law in the modern state, and it reflects the prevailing argumentative, adversarial framework for the administration of justice.

Necessary in Order to Maintain Confidence in the Administration of Justice

I accept that the term "confidence in the administration of justice" is open to interpretation. However, this does not render s. 515(10)(c) void for vagueness since the Supreme Court of Canada has held that "[t]he fact that a particular legislative term is open to varying interpretations by the courts is not fatal": see *Reference re Criminal Code ss. 193 and 195.1(1)(c) (Manitoba)*, [1990] 1 S.C.R. 1123 at p. 1157 ("Prostitution Reference").

In my opinion, the term "confidence in the administration of justice" has been given a workable meaning by the courts. The phrase "administration of justice" has been the subject of judicial interpretation in a number of contexts. For example, in *Canadian Broadcasting Corporation* v. *New Brunswick (Attorney General)*, [1996] 3 S.C.R. 480 the Supreme Court of Canada dismissed a constitutional challenge to s. 486(1) of the *Code*. In ruling that the administration of justice provision was not overbroad since it provides the judiciary with a workable standard, La Forest J. considered the meaning to be given to the term "proper administration of justice". He said at p. 511 S.C.R.:

> The phrase "administration of justice" appears throughout legislation in Canada, including the *Charter*. Thus, "proper administration of justice", which of necessity has been the subject of judicial interpretation, provides the judiciary with a workable standard.

In *R.* v. *Farinacci* (1993), 86 C.C.C. (3d) 32 (Ont. C.A.), Arbour J.A. considered the "public interest" standard for denying bail pending appeal in the context of public confidence in the administration of justice. She said, at p. 48:

> Public confidence in the administration of justice requires that judgments be enforced. The public interest may require that a person convicted of a very serious offence, particularly a repeat offender who is advancing grounds of appeal that are arguable but weak, be denied bail.

It is, I think, significant that Parliament did not simply provide in s. 515(10)(c) that an accused could be detained where "necessary in order to maintain confidence in the administration of justice." First, for an accused to be detained under any of s. 515(10)(a), (b) or (c) the accused's detention must be "necessary". Second, Parliament went on to provide guidance by identifying specific factors to be considered by judges when dealing with bail applications. In *MacDougal, supra*, Hall J.A. concluded that the inclusion of the specific factors to be considered in making a decision about pre-trial release or detention militates against finding that the legislation is vague or overbroad. He said, at p. 46:

The question is, is the present provision framed in sufficiently specific language to save it from being found too vague or overbroad?

It is to be noted that Parliament did not simply provide in the new section that a person could be detained *only* for "just cause". Parliament went on to provide that without limiting the generality of this terminology, there were to be considered various other criteria as set forth in the section. These criteria would fall to be considered by judges and lawyers dealing with specific bail applications.

The significance of Parliament having identified a list of factors to be taken into account that may be considered is made clear by contrasting *Morales* and *MacDougal*. In *Morales*, the Supreme Court of Canada held that the third "public interest" ground for detention violated s. 11(e) of the *Charter* because it authorized a "standardless sweep". Lamer C.J.C. put it this way, at p. 732 S.C.R.:

> The term provides no guidance for legal debate [and] authorizes a standardless sweep, as the court can order imprisonment whenever it sees fit ... such unfettered discretion violates the doctrine of vagueness.

By contrast, in *MacDougal*, as I have noted above, Hall J.A. concluded that by providing a list of relevant factors to be considered in the new s. 515(10)(c), Parliament has provided sufficient direction to afford guidance for informed legal debate. Thus, he found that the new section satisfies the *Nova Scotia Pharmaceutical* vagueness test since it gave "... sufficient indication of how a decision must be reached." He said, at p. 48:

> In my judgment, Parliament has not left the legal profession and the judiciary without a road map to use in the interpretation of s. 515(10)(c). The provisions of the section appear to me to require the Crown at a bail hearing to establish a strong *prima facie* case of very bad conduct resulting in serious harm or the potential for serious harm. In such circumstances, there would usually exist a strong likelihood that a significant sentence would be imposed on a person found guilty of such conduct. *I believe that by delineating the list of relevant factors to be considered in the section under review, Parliament has provided sufficient direction to afford guidance for informed legal debate. That, as I noted above, is the standard formulated by the Supreme Court of Canada as being necessary to sustain legislation. I believe lawyers and judges have been afforded sufficient tools to argue and decide specific cases. Hence, I would not conclude that this legislation is either vague or overbroad.* (Emphasis added)

I agree with Hall J.'s conclusion on the issue whether s. 515(10)(c) is vague or overbroad. Section 515(10)(c) provides sufficient direction to afford guidance for informed legal debate and is not void for vagueness.

Necessary to Promote the Proper Functioning of the Bail System

Caputo J. held that s. 515(10)(c) satisfies the second part of the *Morales* test because it provides for the detention of bail for a purpose related to the promotion of the proper functioning of the bail system. In reaching that conclusion, he referred to several Supreme Court of Canada decisions in support of the proposition that public confidence in the administration of justice is necessary to the effective operation of the criminal justice system.

I agree with Caputo J. that "the criminal justice system includes bail". Since the bail system is one of the many components of the criminal justice system, it inevitably follows that decisions on bail have the real capacity to affect confidence in the administration of justice and in the bail system itself. In my opinion, maintaining confidence in the administration of justice, is not a value "extraneous" to the bail system.

I acknowledge that public confidence in the administration of justice (including the bail system) will normally be maintained and enhanced by the pre-trial release of an accused who will attend court when required to do so and who, while on release, will not endanger the public. There are, however, cases such as *R. v. Dakin*, a judgment of the Ontario Court of Appeal, delivered August 14, 1989, [1989] O.J. No. 1348, and there will be cases in the future, where the public confidence in the administration of justice, having regard to the criteria identified in s. 515(10)(c), will be damaged by pre-trial release. When this is the case, the bail system can only function properly if the courts are given the power to deny bail.

Finally, I do not think that the provisions of s. 515(10)(c) in issue represent an re-enactment of the "public interest" ground for detention rejected by the Supreme Court of Canada in *Morales* as being impermissibly vague in the constitutional sense. Contrary to the appellant's submission, in my opinion, the Supreme Court of Canada in *Morales* did not hold that "to maintain a confidence in the administration of justice", on its own was impermissibly vague, in that it authorized a "standardless sweep". The Court referred to that expression as an illustration of one of its formulations that courts used to give meaning to the term "public interest". I think, therefore, that pre-*Morales* decisions such as this court's judgment in *R.* v. *Dakin*, *supra*, remain relevant to the question whether the impugned language is sufficiently precise to give guidance for legal debate.

CONCLUSION

For these reasons, I think Caputo J. was correct in holding that s. 515(10)(c) of the *Criminal Code* complies with the "just cause" requirement for the denial of bail set out in s. 11(e) of the *Charter* and is not constitutionally defective because it is vague or overbroad. Thus, the answer to the constitutional question before us is that s. 515(10)(c), in so far as it permits the denial of bail where detention is necessary to maintain confidence in the administration of justice, does not violate s. 11(e) of the *Charter*. Since there is no violation of s. 11(e) it is not necessary to turn to s. 1 of the *Charter*.

I would dismiss the appeal.

Appeal dismissed.

The following case illustrates the operation of the new tertiary grounds.

R. v. Li[†]

[MACAULAY J.:]

The accused, Li, seeks a review of his detention ordered by a Provincial Court Judge on September 22, 1999, solely on the tertiary ground set out in s. 515(10)(c) of the *Criminal Code*. Li is charged jointly, with another person, with offences of breaking and entering a dwelling, then robbing and confining the occupant in March 1999. The Crown referred to the circumstances at the original hearing as a home invasion. Li was arrested on September 20, 1999.

At the time of Li's arrest, he and his co-accused, were on interim release in relation to charges of extortion and public mischief arising out of events that allegedly occurred about two and one half months after those which give rise to the present charges. In his reasons, the judge expressly declined to consider the later matter as relevant to the issues before him.

Mr. Li was employed locally and resided with his parents who are sureties for him in relation to his earlier release. The Crown raised no concern respecting the primary ground and the judge did not address it. Although the Crown did raise an issue respecting the secondary ground, the judge was not persuaded that there was any merit to it. Instead, the tertiary ground appears to be the sole ground for detention.

The judge concluded that detention was justified on the tertiary ground due to the strength of the Crown's case and [his] concern that public confidence in the administration of justice would be shaken if the accused was released. In regard to the latter, he was obviously concerned about the nature and gravity of home invasions:

> Especially [sic] in a community where there is a considerable amount of wealth, where there are target premises made of particular individuals from a business premise in this town that is a legitimate business premise where people are attacked in the dead of night with weapons involved in their home, where their home is used as a staging ground for a confinement, for the theft of other pieces of property and where people are terrorized, all by young perpetrators who disappear into the woodwork.

In reaching his decision, the judge recognized that the allegations against Li were that he was involved in setting up the offences but that he did not personally enter the victim's home.

. . . .

It is generally accepted that the subsection [ss. 515(10)(c)] was enacted in partial response to the finding by the Supreme Court of Canada in *R.* v.

[†] [1999] B.C.J. No. 2443 (B.C. S.C.), online: QL.

Morales, [1992] 3 SCR 711 that detention in the public interest as then set out in the secondary ground is limited by s. 11(e) of the *Charter*. S. 11(e) expressly guarantees the right not to be denied reasonable bail without just cause. The reference to public interest in the secondary ground was deleted at the same time s. 515(10)(c) was enacted.

Three decisions provide guidance in determining whether detention is justified solely under the tertiary ground: *R. v. Nguyen* (1997), 119 C.C.C. (3d) 269 (B.C.C.A.), *R. v. MacDougal*, [1999] B.C.J. No. 2034, (10 September 1999), Victoria V03432 (B.C.C.A.) and *R. v. Blind*, [1999] S.J. No. 597, (17 September 1999), Regina 7820 (Sask. C.A.). In *Nguyen*, the Chief Justice addressed the public interest issue as it relates to release pending appeal. In doing so, he commented on the "new" definition of public interest found in s. 515(10)(c). He pointed out that the principle that has emerged from the cases is that the law favours release unless there is some factor or factors that would cause ordinary, reasonable, fair-minded members of society, or persons informed about the philosophy of the legislative provisions, *Charter* values and the actual circumstances of the case to believe that detention is necessary to maintain public confidence in the administration of justice.

As an example of a circumstance justifying detention, the Chief Justice offered this:

> Where the offence appears to have been committed with wanton, deliberate or cruel violence, particularly against vulnerable victims such as children or aged persons, or by persons with substantial criminal records or by persons already on bail or parole for similar offences, then the public may well lose respect for the administration of justice if detention is not continued after conviction.

In *MacDougal*, Hall, JA. upheld the constitutionality of ss. 10(c) without reading down the legislation in spite of the problematic opening words. He concluded that the stipulated criteria militated against a finding that the legislation is overly broad.

Hall, JA. also dealt with the circumstances likely to justify detention solely on the tertiary ground. At paragraph 22, he said:

> There are cases, probably fairly infrequent, where in order to maintain public confidence in the administration of justice, detention ought to be ordered to assist in maintaining that public confidence.

The *MacDougal* case also involved an allegation of home invasion and Hall, JA. had no difficulty concluding that detention was justified on the tertiary ground stating:

> In short summary, this accused has an insignificant criminal record, the Crown has a very strong case, the allegations involve entering the home, terrorizing and injuring the occupants who are strangers to the accused, the gravity of the offence and the circumstances surrounding it are horrendous, and are likely to generate a lengthy term of imprisonment. Later, at paragraph 25, he stated that the new provisions require that the Crown establish a strong prima facie case of very bad conduct resulting in serious harm or the potential for serious harm.

The Saskatchewan Court of Appeal released reasons in *Blind* one week after the release of Mr. Justice Hall's reasons and, accordingly, without the benefit of his analysis. After tracking the reasoning in *Nguyen*, the Saskatchewan court proposed a higher test, in my view. The court was concerned that judges would focus unduly on the circumstances and gravity of the offence and said, at paragraph 13:

> It is not sufficient, as was done in this case, to find the Crown has a strong case, that the offence charged is extremely grave, and that a potentially lengthy term of imprisonment is in the offing, or indeed, to list circumstances which could describe any violent crime. More is required. The clause poses the ultimate question, in a case such as this, of whether in all the circumstances, not just the circumstances surrounding the commission of the offence, detention is necessary to maintain confidence in the administration of justice.

And at paragraph 17:

> Parliament must be taken to have contemplated that extraordinary case with respect to which all reasonable individuals armed with the facts would agree that the accused must not be released notwithstanding that attendance at trial and public safety are not concerns. There can be no doubt that the type of case Parliament had in mind is one where the sensibilities of the community are so affected that to have the person free in the community, notwithstanding the presumption of innocence, could lead to real harm to the administration of justice or, indeed, to the accused.

In *Blind*, the accused faced one count of second degree murder and four counts of [attempted] murder arising out of a single firing of a rifle likely while he was drunk. The accused had no record of violent offences.

The difficulty that I have with the test propounded in *Blind* is that it may be interpreted as minimizing the importance of the circumstances and the gravity of the offence or offences charged when considering the tertiary ground. To the extent that *Blind* sets a different test than *MacDougal*, I am bound by the latter. The violent features often present in offences such as home invasions, in my view, become a lightning rod for reducing public confidence in the administration of justice when individuals are released in cases involving very bad conduct resulting in serious harm or risk of harm. Where, in addition, the prosecution appears to have a strong case and there are no mitigating factors to suggest that a conviction may not result in a lengthy term of imprisonment, all these factors provide the underpinnings necessary for maintaining public confidence in the administration of justice through detention orders.

Ms. Gordon argues, on behalf of Li, that the co-accused was released on bail in spite of his more direct involvement but I do not consider that significant. At the conclusion of Li's judicial interim release hearing, the judge referred to the evidence and appeared to conclude that the Crown's case was strong rather than weak. I agree with that assessment. On the other hand, it is apparent, on reviewing the transcript of the co-accused's interim release hearing before another judge, that the evidence against him is somewhat weaker. The judge said that he would have detained on the tertiary ground if the Crown's case was stronger.

Returning to the case at bar, I am not persuaded that the judge erred in principle or that he misapprehended any material facts, or that there has been any change in circumstances justifying a review. Detention was justified on the tertiary ground applying the test set out in *MacDougal*. Furthermore, I agree with that disposition.

I wish to add this. The judge never addressed whether detention was necessary for the safety and protection of the public under the secondary ground having regard to any substantial likelihood that Li would commit a further criminal offence. The allegations of serious criminal conduct on two separate occasions in a relatively brief period of time were factors to be considered, in my respectful view, on the secondary ground. If the judge had done so, he could properly have concluded that detention was justified on that ground as well.

I dismiss the application.

Consider the *Charter* arguments available to challenge detention: ss. 7, 9, 11(e), 12, 15. Will the new tertiary grounds have a disparate impact upon members of certain groups? How would you prepare a challenge to the differential patterns in denial of interim release described in the excerpts from the *Report of the Aboriginal Justice Inquiry of Manitoba* and from the *Report on Systemic Racism*?

14

Powers of Prosecution

Who controls the prosecution of crime? In this section, we examine the powers of prosecution accorded to the actors in the system: police, Crown attorneys, private citizens, and judges. We include some materials that reveal that these discretionary powers are not always used in a "neutral" fashion. It is suggested here that the exercise of prosecutorial discretion is an exercise of *law*. As such, it must be held to public account, and is challengeable under the *Charter*.

Section 2 of the *Criminal Code* defines "prosecutor":

> "Prosecutor" means the Attorney General or, where the Attorney General does not intervene, means the person who institutes proceedings to which this Act applies, and includes counsel acting on behalf of either of them;

The *Rules of Professional Conduct* [(2000) Law Society of Upper Canada, Rule 4(3), Commentary] provide:

> The prosecutor exercises a public function involving much discretion and power, and must act fairly and dispassionately. The prosecutor should not do anything which might prevent the accused from being represented by counsel or communicating with counsel and, to the extent required by law and accepted practice, should make timely disclosure to the accused or defence counsel (or to the court if the accused is not represented) of all relevant and known facts....

Prosecutorial discretion is involved at several stages:

- commencement of action (decision to prosecute) The general sections are:
  - ss. 785–86 and 788 — summary conviction proceedings
  - ss. 574–77 — power to prefer indictment

  There are also a number of sections dealing with specific offences:
  - s. 136(3) witness giving contradictory evidence
  - s. 164(7) warrant of seizure
  - s. 172(4) corrupting children
  - s. 174(3) nudity
  - s. 318(3) advocating genocide
  - s. 319(6) public incitement of hatred
  - s. 320(7) warrant of seizure
  - s. 385(2) fraudulent concealment of title documents
  - s. 422(3) criminal breach of contract
  - s. 478(3) offence committed entirely in one province
- decision to proceed with prosecution
- pre-trial discovery
- plea bargaining
- conduct of trial
- supervisory role over private prosecutions: for example, *Crown Attorneys Act*, R.S.O. 1980, s. 12
- withdrawal of charges (no statutory basis)
- stay of proceedings. The general sections are:
  - s. 795 (on summary conviction)
  - s. 579 (on indictment)

A. POLICE POWERS

As the materials illustrate, certain *offences* are less likely to be the subject of police charges. Given that the police currently constitute the exclusive investigatory body with any authority, what can be done about this phenomenon? In addition, in these materials we have already touched on articles and cases which suggest that certain *groups* within Canada are prosecuted in a way which is not representative of their involvement in crime. That differential enforcement of the law has been challenged using the *Charter*: *Thompson*, *Jane Doe*, *supra*, **Policing**. Finally, the characterization of the victim and her/his membership in certain *groups* affects the characterization of the seriousness of the offence against her/him.

New legislation with respect to sexual assault was introduced in 1983. That legislation replaced the existing offences of rape, attempted rape, and indecent assault with the new offences of sexual assault, sexual assault with a weapon, and aggravated sexual assault. Despite initial reports by the Canadian Centre for Justice Statistics that there had been a consequent significant increase in the reporting of offences ((1991) 11:9 Juristat 6), that increase may have been due to the recategorization of offences: Julian Roberts, "Sexual Assault in Canada: Recent Statistical Trends" (1996) 21 Queen's L.J. 395. It has been well established that the crime of sexual assault is under-reported: see, generally, Lorenne Clark and Debra Lewis, *Rape: The Price of Coercive Sexuality* (Toronto: the Women's Press, 1977); Statistics Canada, "The Violence Against Women Survey," *The Daily* (Ottawa: Minister of Industry, Science and Technology, 1993).

Further, the discrepancy in the treatment of sexual assault by police has been well documented. See, for example, Rita Gunn and Candice Minch, "Unofficial and Official Responses to Sexual Assault" (1985–86) 14:4 Resources for Feminist Research/DRF 47; Rita Gunn and Candice Minch, *Sexual Assault: The Dilemma of Disclosure, the Question of Conviction* (Winnipeg: University of Manitoba Press, 1988). The Gunn and Minch study examined the ways in which sexual assault complaints were filtered by police, prosecutors, and courts. Their study over a two-year period (1976–77) established that at each point in the process, sexual assault complaints were less likely to be proceeded with than other complaints. For a study that tracks the response of the criminal justice system to child abuse cases and identifies similar filtering, see Rita Gunn and Rick Linden, "The Processing of Child Abuse Cases" in Julian Roberts and Renate Mohr, eds., *Confronting Sexual Assault: A Decade of Legal and Social Change* (Toronto: University of Toronto Press, 1994) 84.

Activists had hoped that changes to the legislation might overcome some of the problems. However, as Roberts argues, many of the problems associated with police practices and complaints of sexual assault under the pre-1983 legislation continue: Roberts, "Sexual Assault in Canada," *supra*. He documents filtering by police in terms of the characterization of offences as less serious, the disproportionate determination that complaints are "unfounded," the lower rate of "clearing" offences by proceeding with charging, and concludes that the "attrition" rate from complaint to charge is significantly higher for complaints of sexual assault than for other assaults. The under-reporting of sexual assault complaints compounds this differential treatment. ("The Violence Against Women Survey," *supra*, found that only one in 10 incidents of sexual assault is reported.) Also, critics have argued that the current context of defunding sexual assault centres and victims' services, combined with the challenge to the limited protections to women's security and privacy interests in the courts (Abell and Sheehy, *Proof, Defences, and Beyond*, **Trial Process**) will have a chilling effect on the already limited number of complaints.

Other challenges to prosecutorial discretion have arisen in the context of the various provincial inquiries into racism and Aboriginal justice issues, such as the investigation into the original decision not to charge the men who killed Betty Osborne (see **Policing**, supra), the decision to charge Carney Nerland with manslaughter and to accept a plea bargain (see **Enforcement of the Law**, *supra*), and the abandonment of charges against three white construction bosses in connection with the abduction and sexual assault of three Cree young women during the struggle over the James Bay hydro project: Darcy Henton, "Mystery shrouds assault on Cree girls" *The Toronto Star* (29 March 1992) A1.

B. CROWN ATTORNEYS

Crown attorneys have decision-making powers with respect to accepting or rejecting police choice of charges, and determining which cases they will drop, which they will plea bargain, and which they will pursue. It is important to note that the complainant/victim has no right to challenge a Crown's decision to accept a plea bargain to a lesser offence, nor does the complainant/victim have standing to make submissions at the sentencing hearing: *Re R. and Antler: Re T.(F.)* (1982), 29 C.R. (3d) 283 (B.C.S.C.).

While Crown attorneys have been immune to public challenge to the exercise of prosecutorial discretion, the *Charter* has opened up the possibility of Crown accountability: Donna G. Morgan, "Controlling Prosecutorial Power: Judicial Review, Abuse of Process and Section 7 of the Charter" (1986) 29 Crim. L.Q. 15, and Charles Finkle and Duncan Cameron, "Equal Protection in Enforcement: Towards More Structured Discretion" (1989) 12 Dalhousie L. Rev. 34.

In a number of provinces, the conduct of prosecutions has been criticized as a result of several individual high profile cases. For example, in his article, "Independence and the Director of Public Prosecutions: The Marshall Inquiry and Beyond" (2000) 23 Dal. L.J. 385, Phillip Stenning discusses the impact of the Marshall Inquiry in exposing internal and systemic problems within Nova Scotia's prosecution branch. He reviews the recommendations for reform made by the Inquiry and provides an assessment of implementation. Other Nova Scotia cases, like the failed effort to prosecute Westray for homicide with respect to the deaths of its employees in a mine explosion, the saga of the sexual assault prosecutions against former Premier Gerald Regan, and the effort to prosecute Dr. Nancy Morrison for murder in connection with the death of a patient suffering terminal cancer, have further exposed a department fraught with controversy.

In Saskatchewan, the Justice Minister appointed a review of its prosecutions division to respond to the erosion of public confidence as a result of *Reference Re Milgaard*, *Latimer*, and the Martensville cases, discussed *supra*, **Enforcement of Law**: David Roberts, "Study ordered of criminal prosecutions: Saskatchewan's move hailed as step in right direction but not enough to restore public confidence" *The [Toronto] Globe and Mail* (26 March 1996) A6.

The role of Crown attorneys in the choice and carriage of criminal charges has particular significance in the context of "bias crimes." Several authors have documented the rising incidence of "bias crime" in the United States, and it is reasonable to assume that we are undergoing similar trends in Canada, given the escalation of racial hatred against Jewish people, racialized people, and Aboriginal peoples. Tanya Kateri Hernandez, in "Bias Crimes: Unconscious Racism in the Prosecution of 'Racially Motivated Violence'" (1990) 99 Yale L.J. 845 at 846, documents the known statistics regarding bias-motivated violence, noting that these attackers usually elude prosecution:

> For example, in 1988, in New York City, a city with chronic and highly publicized bias crime, only thirty three bias crimes were prosecuted out of the estimated 800 incidents that were brought to the attention of the New York City Bias Unit.[†]

The author examines state bias crime statutes, and identifies (at 846) the major weakness as *lack of enforcement* on the part of police and prosecutors:

> One factor which accounts for the disparate effect of prosecutorial discretion on bias crimes, is that many of the perpetrators of bias crimes are police officers. Local prosecutors are understandably reluctant [to] prosecute police officers on whom they depend in order to function. This is not a new problem. Within the context of federal and state police brutality cases, "U.S. attorneys ... have consistently opposed ... prosecution...."
>
> ...
>
> The unconscious racism of prosecutors is more of a danger in bias crime prosecution because the premise of bias crime statutes is that racial motivation makes a physical injury more harmful. In order to enforce the statutes, prosecutors must be willing to recognize illegitimate motivation. Unconscious racism,

---

[†] Reproduced by permission of The Yale Law Journal Company and Fred B. Rothman & Company from The Yale Law Journal, Vol. 99, pp. 845–64. Notes omitted.

ingrained in North American culture, makes it difficult for prosecutors to conclude that racially-motivated violence is indeed a crime.

...

Unconscious racism allows many prosecutors not to treat racial violence as a serious crime or consider its victims true victims. One commentator explains: "The social construction of victimhood rests in large measure on the problem that some social theorists would call 'difference' — here, the inability of the dominant culture to understand as victimhood anything not likely to happen to its members." For example, local prosecutors often dismiss bias crimes as "pranks" and in that manner justify sparse investigation. When prosecutors classify bias crimes as mere "pranks," they are unconsciously taking illegitimate factors (like race) into account — as is done in racialist decisionmaking. Racialism can be defined as the belief that "racial categorizations, even oppressive ones, might be acceptable as long as a case can be made for rational fit between ends and means." Because people of color and gay people are marginalized in society, the thinking goes, the victimization of members of such marginalized groups is not accorded the same level of gravity as the victimization of others. The theory of racialist decision making recognizes that this way of thinking can become part of a person's rational decision making process, and is not always a purposefully discriminatory plan.

Hernandez concludes with reform proposals in an effort to increase the effectiveness of bias crimes legislation, including the establishment of a Bias Reporting Agency, reduced prosecutorial discretion, and the development of teams of special prosecutors. *The Report of the Commission on Systemic Racism in the Ontario Criminal Justice System* (Toronto: Queen's Printer, 1995) confirms the transmission of bias into decision-making at a number of points in the criminal justice system (such as Crown elections about how to proceed, at 51-52, discussed *supra*, **Introduction to Criminal Procedure**). In the U.K., the Stephen Lawrence Commission found that the prosecution service was implicated in systemic racism in terms of how that case, discussed *supra*, **Policing**, was handled. Most recently, the chief prosecutor, Sir David Calvert-Smith, is investigating another allegation of racism in the prosecution service that may have been responsible for another failed prosecution, this one regarding the death of a 10-year-old Nigerian boy who bled to death: Pete Harrison, "All Britons racist, chief prosecutor says" *The Ottawa Citizen* (25 June 2002) A12.

At the same time, prosecutors who are attentive to the prevalence of bias crimes, such as violence against women, risk censure for thorough and impassioned representations. In *R. v. Munroe*, [1995] 4 S.C.R. 53, the Court held that Crown counsel's closing address in a murder trial (where the accused had strangled his wife) had been deliberately or recklessly inflammatory and clearly improper. However, the Court concluded that the trial judge had adequately intervened and, therefore, a new trial was not necessary. The address had included references to the rage and hatred that had motivated Marc Lépine and to the risks of violence potentially faced by every family member if provocation as a defence succeeded in the case at bar. The defence counsel had also objected to the wearing of white ribbons in the courtroom by the family of the deceased, at which point the judge asked the Crown attorney to let those individuals know that it was a judge's responsibility to ensure a fair trial. See also the discussion *supra*, **Policing**, with respect to *R. v. R.D.S.*. Are some kinds of "bias" more visible? Does it depend on standpoint?

Cynthia Petersen, in her article "A Queer Response to Bashing: Legislating Against Hate" (1991) 51 Queen's L.J. 237, reviews the statistics that suggest that heterosexist violence against lesbians and gays is of epidemic proportions: in the United States, one national study documented 70,381 such assaults in 1989, and this figure is certainly a drastic under-representation of the incidence of such violence. She describes (at 250) the barriers to the reporting and successful prosecution of heterosexist violence, and cautions against unequivocal support for new hate crimes legislation as a strategy:

> The enactment of hate crimes legislation will not suddenly render the legal system more responsive to heterosexist violence. Hate crimes affect only the small minority of cases which survive the filtering process and actually reach the sentencing stage. Their existence may nevertheless encourage lesbians and gay men to report ... and to enter a system which is fundamentally biased against them. It is irresponsible to encourage victims to pursue avenues which are more likely to result in revictimization than in redress.

C. PRIVATE PROSECUTIONS

Read s. 504 of the *Criminal Code*. Are the private citizen's powers of prosecution an historical anomaly, or are there good reasons to preserve this power? See Barry Wright, Book Review of *Appearing for the Crown* by Phillip Stenning and *Private Prosecutions* by the Law Reform Commission of Canada (1988) 67 Can. Bar Rev. 183.

One of the best-known examples of the invocation of prosecutorial powers by a private citizen is *Dowson* v. *R.*, [1983] 2 S.C.R. 144, where Dowson had laid an information against an officer of the RCMP charging forgery, uttering false documents, and conveying false messages — activities that had been uncovered through the McDonald Commission, described under **Policing**. Dowson undertook this prosecution in response to the failure of the police and the Crown's office to lay and pursue charges against the RCMP even in the light of the Commission's clear findings of criminal conduct on the part of the RCMP. Before the matter was actually heard by the justice of the peace, the AG for Ontario stayed the proceedings under what is now s. 579. The Supreme Court held that with respect to an indictable matter, the AG cannot stay the proceedings until an "indictment has been found" under s. 574.

While this case appears to be a victory for the private citizen, it must be recognized that *Dowson* represents only a technical victory. The end result was that the charges were dismissed. As well, the *Criminal Code* was amended in 1985 and now, under s. 579, the AG can stay proceedings at any time after proceedings have been commenced. The *Kopyto* case, set out under "Judicial Powers to Prosecute," contains more detail about the *Dowson* case.

Generally speaking, if the Crown's office refuses to put its authority behind the prosecution, the judge who hears the case is less likely to make a finding of guilt because of the implicit understanding that, for whatever reason, the Crown did not think the offence warranted prosecution. For instance, in the past, women who were assaulted by their husbands were regularly informed that they could pursue the prosecution privately if they wished. The result was that few such prosecutions were pursued, the conviction rate was low, and the sentences were insignificant. Therefore, in championing the rights of the private prosecutor, one must take account of the fact that the citizen in this role does not have the full authority and legitimacy of the state behind her.

For further examples of private prosecutions as an attempt to force the prosecution of police and prison guards, see: CP, "Charges not resurrected" *The [Toronto] Globe and Mail* (18 May 1996) A3 (Québec Superior Court rejected an application to have dropped charges resurrected against one of the six Montréal officers accused in the Richard Barnabé case, discussed *supra*, **Policing** and **Sentencing**); Henry Hess, "Prison guards to be tried in death of inmate: Lawyers call Kingston case first such prosecution of correctional officers in Canada" *The [Toronto] Globe and Mail* (11 March 1995) A1, A7 (the Robert Gentles case, discussed *supra*, **Prisons and Parole**).

It should be noted that the Attorney General of the province may intervene pursuant to s. 579(1) and either carry the case or, as is more likely in situations such as this, stay the proceedings. For instance, stays of proceedings have been initiated by the AG of Québec and the AG of Ontario, where the government had desisted from prosecuting abortion clinics pending resolution of the constitutionality of the *Criminal Code* provisions on abortion, and members of "Right to Life" groups had initiated private prosecutions. The actions of the Attorney Generals have been unsuccessfully challenged under the *Charter* in the courts in Québec (*Chartrand* v. *Québec (AG)* (1987), 59 C.R. (3d) 388 (Que. C.A.) and in Ontario (*Campbell* v. *Ontario (AG)* (1987), 58 O.R. (2d) 209 (H. Ct.)): AG's decision is only justiciable under the *Charter* if there is evidence of "flagrant impropriety", affirmed by the Ont. C.A. in (1987), 60 O.R. (2d) 617).

In *Kostuch* v. *Alberta (AG)* (1995), 174 A.R. 109 (C.A.), Dr. Kostuch swore a private information to commence an action under the *Fisheries Act* alleging a disruption or destruction of fish habitat at the Old Man River dam site. The Attorney General intervened and stayed the prosecution, and Kostuch applied to set aside the stay, arguing that her rights under s. 7 of the *Charter* had been breached, in that (at 114) "she has not been able to have a court adjudicate on a matter of concern to her," thus causing her emotional stress, and that (at 114) "'security of the person' includes the right to protection from state imposed psychological stress." The court declined to review the exercise of prosecutorial discretion absent proof of "flagrant impropriety," which the court held required (at 116) "proof of misconduct bordering on corruption, violation of the law, bias against or for a particular individual or offence." For some context of the struggle over the Old Man River dam, see the discussion of *R. v. Born With A Tooth* (1993), 81 C.C.C. (3d) 393 (Alta. Q.B.), in Abell and Sheehy, *Proof, Defences, and Beyond*, **The Trial Process**.

Private prosecutions have sometimes been pursued in situations where the state has refused to intervene. For example, the prosecution of Ernst Zundel (*R. v. Zundel*, [1992] 2 S.C.R. 731; (1987), 31 C.C.C. (3d) 97 (Ont. C.A.), appeal from conviction allowed and a new trial ordered) was the first such prosecution of its kind, and it was initiated by a private citizen. The accused's conviction was overturned by the Supreme Court, on the basis that s. 181 (unlike s. 319 in *Keegstra*, *supra*, **Sentencing**) violated s. 2(b) of the *Charter* and was not saved by s. 1. The police declined to lay new charges: Rudy Platiel, "Zundel won't be charged under hate laws, police say" *The [Toronto] Globe and Mail* (9 March 1993) A5; Rudy Platiel, "Jewish Congress annoyed at lack of hate-crime charges" *The [Toronto] Globe and Mail* (6 August 1993) A4, and the discussion *supra*, **Sentencing**.

Most recently, in July 1996, an effort to prosecute a different kind of "hate crime" — "war crimes" involving the mass murder of Jews — was successfully stalled by the defence. The Federal Court of Canada ruled that the prosecutions should be thrown out because of conversations between a Crown prosecutor and the Chief Justice. The private conversations were an attempt to prompt the court to move more quickly (after 17 months of procedural delays), and Justice Bud Cullen held that to allow the case to continue would bring the administration of justice into disrepute: *Canada (Minister of Citizenship and Immigration) v. Tobiass*, [1996] F.C.J. No. 865 (F.C.T.D.), online: QL.

The decision generated considerable controversy as various newspaper editorials attest: Editorial, "How can Mr. Rock stay in office?" *The [Toronto] Globe and Mail* (8 July 1996) A18; Editorial, "Justice not served" *The Toronto Star* (7 July 1996) F2.

David Matas (who is senior counsel to B'Nai B'Rith Canada) and Susan Charendoff argue in *Justice Delayed: Nazi War Criminals in Canada* (Toronto: Summerhill, 1987) that it was easier for a war criminal to get refuge in Canada than it was for a Jew fleeing the Holocaust, and that since 1987, the prosecutions for war crimes have failed "on the most specious of grounds" (citing *R. v. Finta*, [1994] 1 S.C.R. 701). Madeleine Schwarz (who served as counsel with the Department of Justice Crimes Against Humanity and War Crimes Section) agrees that *Finta* set a very high threshold for prosecution of war crimes and crimes against humanity: "Prosecuting Crimes Against Humanity in Canada: What Must Be Proved" (2002) 46 Crim. L.Q. 40. She argues that the new *Crimes Against Humanity Act*, S.C. 2000, c. 24 may overcome some of the hurdles in *Finta*. For example, orders to commit genocide are deemed manifestly unlawful by the new legislation, and thus there is no defence for an accused to argue that he/she was only following what he/she believed to be lawful orders of a government or a superior.

D. CONTEMPT AND JUDICIAL POWERS

Judges too have the power to cite (charge), essentially prosecute, convict, and summarily punish for the common law offence of contempt of court, pursuant to ss. 9 and 10 of the *Criminal Code*, and this does not violate the *Charter*: *R. v. Cohn* (1984), 42 C.R. (3d) 1 (Ont. C.A.). An inferior court is only entitled to cite for contempt committed *in facie* (in the face of the court), whereas superior courts have jurisdiction over *ex facie* contempt: *C.B.C. v. Cordeau* (1979), 48 C.C.C. (2d) 289 (S.C.C.). In "urgent and imperative" circumstances, judges are authorized to initiate summary proceedings and proceed *instanter* to convict and sentence an individual to "preserve the dignity of the court": *R. v. Rarbacki* (1992), 76 C.C.C. (3d) 549 (Que. C.A.); *R. v. B.K.*, [1995] 4 S.C.R. 186. Some of the acts that have been held to amount to criminal contempt include: a witness' refusal to co-operate, swearing, and obscenity (*R. v. Winter* (1986), 53 C.R. (3d) 372 (Alta. C.A.)), drunkenness (*R. v. Perkins* (1980), 51 C.C.C. (2d) 369 (B.C.C.A.)), insulting or criticizing the judge, the publication of materials which might prejudice a trial (*Manitoba (AG)* v. *Groupe Quebecor* (1987), 59 C.R. (3d) 1 (Man. C.A.); *R.* v. *CHEK TV* (1987), 33 C.C.C. (3d) 24 (B.C.C.A.); *R.* v. *Bowes* (1995), 171 A.R. 55 (Q.B.)), and refusal by a journalist to divulge a source (Globe and Mail, "When doing your work can land you in jail" *The [Toronto] Globe and Mail* (26 September 1995) A2; T.R.S. Allan, "Disclosure of Journalists' Sources, Civil Disobedience and the Rule of Law" (1991) 50 C.L.J. 131). For further discussion of the law with respect to the media, see **The Media and the Trial Process**, Abell and Sheehy, *Proof, Defences, and Beyond*.

In December 1993, Chief Katie Rich challenged the authority of the Newfoundland Provincial Court in Davis Inlet. She entered the courtroom accompanied by about 20 women, and presented Judge Hyslop with a letter (reproduced in *Newfoundland (AG)* v. *Rich* (1995), 133 Nfld. & P.E.I.R. 1 (Nfld. C.A.)):

> This letter is to inform you that you are to cease and desist immediately the operation of this court in the Community of Davis Inlet, and withdraw yourselves immediately from this community.
>
> You are further advised that no future holding of the court in our community will be permitted until further notice.
>
> By order of the councillors and community members of Utshimassits.

Chief Rich was charged with contempt: *Nfld.* v. *Rich, supra*. For background to the case, problems in the community, and a discussion of the historical context, including the displacement and relocation of the Innu, see, generally: Michael Valpy, "Courtroom chaos: Justice gets cold feet" *The [Toronto] Globe and Mail* (29 January 1994) D5; Michael Valpy, "One year later: After page 1" *The [Toronto] Globe and Mail* (29 January 1994) D1; CP, "Village of despair: Mass suicide attempt latest crisis for Innu" *The Ottawa Citizen* (28 January 1993) A1; Donald McRae, *Report on the Complaints of the Innu of Labrador to the Canadian Human Rights Commission* (Ottawa: Canadian Human Rights Commission, 1993); Assembly of First Nations, *Violations of Law and Human Rights by the Governments of Canada and Newfoundland in Regard to the Mushuau Innu: A Documentation of Injustice in Utshimassits (Davis Inlet)*, Submission to the Canadian Human Rights Commission (May 1993); and Harold Press, "Davis Inlet in Crisis: Will the Lessons Ever Be Learned?" (1995) 15 Cdn. J. Nat. Stud. 187.

In two other cases, the Supreme Court of Canada held that picketing of a courthouse during a lawful strike by union members (whose workplace it was) constituted criminal contempt because the picketing had the potential to interfere with the proper administration of justice. The Court also held that the resulting violation of union members' s. 2(b) right to freedom of expression was justified under s. 1 of the *Charter*: *B.C. Government Employees Union* v. *B.C. (AG)*, [1988] 2 S.C.R. 1; *Newfoundland Association of Public Employees* v. *Newfoundland (AG)*, [1988] 2 S.C.R. 204.

Compare this treatment of unionized employees' demands to the treatment of judges' demands for better salaries and working conditions: Harry Glasbeek, "Some Strategies for an Unlikely Task: The Progressive Use of Law" (1989) 21 Ottawa L. Rev. 387, footnote 3 and at 411. For some examples, see: *Sask. Prov. Ct. Judges' Assoc.* v. *Sask.* (1995), 133 Sask. R. 115 (Q.B.); *R.* v. *Campbell*, [1995] 2 W.W.R. 469 (Alta. Q.B.); *Mackin* v. *New Brunswick (Minister of Finance)*, [2002] S.C.J. No. 13, online: QL.

Criminal contempt is broadly sketched as any conduct that lessens or demeans the court's authority or interferes with its process or the administration of justice, and it can be either *in facie* (e.g. the refusal of a witness to answer questions) or *ex facie* (e.g publishing comments on a pending case, threatening witnesses). Civil contempt is a breach of the rules of the court, or disobedience of a court order, or other misconduct in a private matter. However, the distinction is somewhat blurred, particularly where the disobedience of the court order is characterized as "public defiance."

Civil contempt converts the ruling of a court in a civil dispute into a potentially criminal matter. What is disturbing about this is the way in which private grievances thus invoke the resources and legitimacy of the state and the sanctions of the criminal process, while bypassing any legislative process. In the discussion that follows, consider how private wrongs (protected by injunctions) escalate into criminal contempt.

The most frequent examples of this occur in relation to trade union disputes, when unions "publicly defy" restrictive labour board orders. See, for example: *United Nurses of Alberta* v. *Alta. (AG)*, [1992] 3 S.C.R. 901. Madam Justice McLachlin defined the elements of the offence (at 933):

> [T]he accused defied or disobeyed a court order in a public way (the *actus reus*), with intent,

knowledge or recklessness as to the fact that the public disobedience will tend to depreciate the authority of the court (the *mens rea*).

For a thoughtful critique of the use of contempt powers against three leaders of the Canadian Union of Postal Workers (C.U.P.W.) in the 1991 national strike, see: Judy Fudge and Harry Glasbeek, "Crossing the Line" *This Magazine* (August 1992) 19. They argue (at 21) that the prosecution of the union leaders for contempt "caused it [the New Democratic Party and the Attorney General] to step into the shoes of a private employer. This allowed the private employer to maintain its stance as a victimized, legitimate actor without any political axe to grind. The union was, as a result, portrayed as a renegade."

Civil contempt has also been invoked in civil disputes involving public protest over environmental destruction. In *MacMillan Bloedel* v. *Simpson*, [1995] 4 S.C.R. 725, the accused contravened an injunction of the B.C. Supreme Court prohibiting protest activities interfering with MacMillan Bloedel's logging operations in the Clayoquot Sound area of Vancouver Island, and was sentenced to 45 days imprisonment and a fine. The Court held that s. 47(2) of the *Young Offenders Act*, which purported to give the youth court exclusive jurisdiction with respect to contempt of court, was unconstitutional and inoperative. Thus, the superior court was not deprived of its jurisdiction to convict the accused of contempt.

The cases emerging from the Clayoquot Sound protests demonstrate the breadth and manipulability of the concept of contempt. One of the only challenges possible is jurisdictional, and *Simpson* demonstrates that such challenges will not readily succeed. For a discussion of the background to the protest (including concerns about the impact on Aboriginal rights and scientific documentation of the environmental impact), the arrest of over 900 people, the trials, and the sentencing, see: Ron MacIsaac and Anne Champagne, eds., *Clayoquot Mass Trials: Defending the Rainforest* (Gabriola: New Society Publishers, 1994). MacIsaac and Champagne describe the widespread protest as one of the largest and broadest in Canadian history. They highlight the way in which Strategic Lawsuits Against Public Participation (SLAPPs) function to attack and inhibit citizens exercising their democratic rights. As they explain (at 28), "SLAPPs are lawsuits in which powerful and wealthy corporations seek civil damages for criticism expressed in a public forum. Targets are private individuals or citizen groups which disagree with the actions of the corporation...." The actions are not dependent (at 28) "upon successful legal arguments, but rather upon exploiting sluggish judicial procedures" and the high costs of litigation. For further critique of the use of injunctions in this case, see also: Hamar Foster and John McLaren, "Clayoquot: the danger of using injunctions" *The [Toronto] Globe and Mail* (5 November 1993) A19.

In *Greenpeace Canada* v. *MacMillan Bloedel*, [1994] 10 W.W.R. 705 (B.C.C.A.), aff'd [1996] 2 S.C.R. 1048, Greenpeace challenged both the breadth of the injunction (covering even the conduct of non-parties) granted to MacMillan Bloedel and the ability of a private party to obtain such an injunction, where the conduct sought to be enjoined may constitute a criminal offence. Greenpeace argued that the relief sought was not connected to any real action, and that the order granted amounted to an *ex parte* warrant of arrest. MacMillan Bloedel argued that the injunction against unnamed and unknown persons was necessary as the only effective mechanism because new people were arriving daily to participate in the blockades. The Court of Appeal held that the injunction was necessary to prevent irreparable harm to a private property interest, without destroying the rights of lawful protest. Wood J.A. dissented on the basis that an injunction could not issue against a non-party or an "ever changing mass of potential defendants" (at paragraph 125) and that the injunction amounted to an *ex parte* order of arrest. He also criticized the slowness of the proceedings and the lack of any genuine action (at paragraph 143–44):

> One cannot view the history of the pleadings in this matter without being struck by the obvious. The formalities of issuing a Writ, amending it from time to time, filing a Statement of Claim and then an amended Statement of Claim, have all been undertaken for the sole purpose of obtaining the interim and interlocutory orders of injunction which, through the facility of their arrest provisions, have then been used to remove protesters interfering with the plaintiff's logging operations.
>
> In response to the appellant's argument that there had been unreasonable delay by the plaintiff in pursuing its action, the judge below said that he saw no evidence that the plaintiff had not moved "at a pace appropriate to the factual situation here." *With respect, there has been no pace whatsoever to the plaintiff's action. It stands today, as it has stood all along, virtually motionless. The factual situa-*

tion here is that the plaintiff brought its action for damages solely because that is the only vehicle by which it could obtain the necessary orders restraining the defendants from interfering ... there is obviously no intention on its part ever to proceed to trial [emphasis added].

Thus, he concluded that the injunction should be set aside.

> It is only because the obligations of the office of Attorney General have not been discharged, in connection with mass public protests ... that the courts have been drawn into a role which they were never intended to perform, and for which they are ill-suited. The inherent jurisdiction of the Supreme Court to punish for contempt of court is essential to the preservation of the due administration of justice. *It is and always has been a jurisdiction to be exercised sparingly and as a last resort. It was never intended to be used to preserve law and order on our streets, or in our forests, any more than equity was ever intended to be used as an instrument of crowd control* [emphasis added].

However, Madam Justice McLachlin, writing for a unanimous Court, upheld the decision of the Court of Appeal to allow the injunction.

It is difficult to challenge a citation for contempt. However, in *Oak Bay Marina* v. *Haida Nation* (1995), 69 B.C.A.C. 132, the court allowed the appeal of the convictions of seven Haida accused, ruling that (at 136) "the injunction order was vague, unenforceable and ambiguous." The injunction sought to prevent the defendants from certain conduct in the vicinity of the plaintiff's fishing camp in the Queen Charlotte Islands, the homeland of the accused.

In another case involving an assertion of Aboriginal sovereignty, *B.C. (AG)* v. *Mount Currie Indian Band*, [1991] 4 W.W.R. 507, aff'd [1991] 4 C.N.L.R. 3 (B.C.C.A.), the British Columbia Supreme Court denied the argument that the court lacked jurisdiction over the 59 accused (the majority of whom were members of the Lil'wat Peoples Movement), characterizing the challenge as a "collateral attack on the injunction." The accused had been involved in a roadblock on "unceded Indian territory." Macdonald J. held (at 524) that:

> The defiance of an order of this court, whether or not the underlying issue is Indian sovereignty, cannot be countenanced. That must be so whether or not the persons involved are acting with the benefit of legal advice and whether or not the order was properly made. To hold otherwise would herald the breakdown of our judicial system.
>
> ...
>
> The persons arrested are not entitled to question, on these contempt proceedings, the authority of the Chief Justice of this court to issue the injunction in question here....
>
> Whether or not this is a court of general jurisdiction in relation to "unceded Indian territory" remains to be determined in this action, although the outcome of that question appears hardly in doubt unless and until *Delgamuukw* [referring to the B.C.C.A. decision] is reversed on appeal.

Finally, contempt proceedings have been used against mothers who were trying to protect their child(ren) and refusing to obey court orders with respect to custody. See, generally, the discussion in Abell and Sheehy, *Proof, Defences, and Beyond*, **Broadening the Defences: Necessity, Self-Defence and Conscience**.

R. v. Kopyto[†]

[CORY, J.A.:]

Harry Kopyto was convicted of contempt of court by scandalizing the court. This appeal is brought from that conviction.

FACTUAL BACKGROUND

For a number of years the appellant acted as the lawyer for his friend, Dr. Dowson. Mr. Dowson was from 1961 to 1972 the executive secretary and subse-

---

[†] (1987), 62 O.R. (2d) 449 (C.A.).

quently chairman of the League for Socialist Action. Allegations have been made that the R.C.M.P. had investigated the activities of the league and Mr. Dowson in an improper manner.

The appellant on behalf of Dowson, brought an action for defamation. The alleged defamation was contained in a summary of the R.C.M.P. investigation of the league that was read by the Attorney-General in the legislature. The claim was struck down by the Federal Court of Appeal [*Dowson* v. *The Queen* (1981), 124 D.L.R. (3d) 260, 37 N.R. 127] and leave to appeal to the Supreme Court of Canada was refused [D.L.R. *loc. cit.*, 39 N.R. 560*n*].

The appellant, again on behalf of Dowson, also sought to have criminal charges brought against members of the R.C.M.P. for purportedly forging letters during their investigation of the league. The legal proceedings involving these charges also had a long and unsuccessful history.

On May 11, 1982, the appellant, still acting for Dowson, instituted civil proceedings in the small claims court against members of the R.C.M.P. The allegation was made that the defendants had conspired to injure Dowson and had made injurious false statements about him. This action too gave rise to a number of well-publicized proceedings. Eventually a truncated version of the case came before Judge Zuker. The decision was reserved. On December 12, 1985, carefully considered reasons were delivered by Judge Zuker [summarized as *Dowson* v. *Chisholm*, 34 A.C.W.S. (2d) 146]. He dismissed the plaintiff's claim, in part on the grounds that the action was not brought within the statutorily prescribed limitation period.

Following the release of the reasons a reporter from the Globe and Mail called the appellant seeking his comments on the judgment. The appellant indicated that he would call the reporter back after he had read the reasons. On the next day, December 17, 1985, the appellant called the reporter. He gave a long statement, portions of which were included in an article published in the Globe and Mail on December 18, 1985, and which form the subject-matter of the charge against him.

The appellant admitted that the Globe and Mail quoted him correctly. The quotations read as follows:

> This decision is a mockery of justice. It stinks to high hell. It says it is okay to break the law and you are immune so long as someone above you said to do it.
>
> Mr. Dowson and I have lost faith in the judicial system to render justice.
>
> We're wondering what is the point of appealing and continuing this charade of the courts in this country which are warped in favour of protecting the police. The courts and the RCMP are sticking so close together you'd think they were put together with Krazy Glue.

THE DECISION AT TRIAL ON THE CHARGE OF CONTEMPT OF COURT

The learned trial judge gave careful, complete and detailed reasons for his conclusion that the appellant was guilty of the offence of contempt of court by scandalizing the court. He observed that there was no doubt about the appellant's sincerity or the *bona fides* of his desire to correct what the appellant perceived to be a social injustice. He rejected the appellant's contention that the remarks had referred to "systemic bias" and that they had not been intended to malign Judge Zuker. He found the appellant's statements to be "a vitriolic unmitigated attack on the trial judge" and, as well, "a blatant attack on all judges of all courts." The appellant's words, he observed, went far beyond criticism and demonstrated an intention to vilify.

The trial judge also concluded that the offence of scandalizing the court did not constitute an infringement of s. 2(*b*) of the *Canadian Charter of Rights and Freedoms* which guarantees freedom of expression. Furthermore, he determined that even if the offence did constitute an infringement of s. 2(*b*), it was a justifiable limitation under s. 1 of the Charter.

It is significant to observe that the Crown did not allege any intended or foreseeable interference with the administration of justice except in so far as it was alleged that the statement brought the over-all administration of justice into disrepute. Further, it was not suggested by the Crown that the appellant's comments were calculated to interfere with the conduct of a specific case presently before the court, or a particular case pending before the courts.

ISSUES TO BE CONSIDERED

A consideration of the following issues is essential to the resolution of this appeal:

1. Do the words of the appellant fall within the purview of s. 8 of the *Criminal Code* so as to constitute contempt of court by scandalizing the court, as that offence has been known at common law?
2. Are the words of the appellant "protected" by the freedom of expression clause set out in s. 2(*b*) of the Charter?

3. If the words of the appellant are protected by s. 2(b) of the Charter, does the offence of contempt of court by scandalizing the court constitute a constitutionally permissible limit on that protection?

. . . .

[Having noted the strong criticisms of the offence itself, Justice Cory continued....]

Despite the harsh criticism, the offence has continued to exist in this province. Equally clearly, the statement of the appellant would constitute the basis of his conviction for that offence prior to the passage of the Charter. The words of the appellant were calculated to bring Judge Zuker into disrepute. Further, the statement that all courts of the country are warped, that is to say, perverted, in favour of the police, was calculated to bring all courts into disrepute.

In his very fair, able and persuasive argument, counsel for the intervenant, Criminal Lawyers' Association, expressed his disapproval of the appellant's statements and conceded that his action was a gross breach of professional responsibility. His assessment was correct. The statement was in the poorest possible taste. It was no more than the whining of an unhappy loser. It was unreasonable, unprofessional and unworthy of even the most marginal and most recent member of the profession. It was, in a word, disgraceful. None the less, the advent of the Charter makes it necessary to review the offence of scandalizing the court in order to ensure that it meets the requisite constitutional standards. The comment, which was no more than the puerile manifestation of petulant pique, nevertheless represented the expression of a sincerely held belief on a matter of public interest. It is not necessary for the purposes of this case to elaborate at length on what constitutes a matter of public interest. The appellant's comment concerned the functioning and operation of a public institution, specifically, the courts. It was thus a comment on a matter of public interest. As a result, it is necessary to consider whether the statement is protected by s. 2(b) of the Charter.

2. Are the words of the appellant "protected" by the freedom of expression clause set out in s. 2(b) of the Charter?

. . . .

How should the ambit of the protection afforded by s. 2(b) of the Charter be determined? First, it is important to note that the rights granted by the Charter were not frozen at the moment of its enactment; the Charter does more than recognize and declare pre-existing rights. The Supreme Court of Canada has on several occasions emphasized that the rights and freedoms contained in the Charter must be ascertained without undue reliance on the pre-Charter view of those rights and freedoms.

. . . .

In my view, statements of a sincerely held belief on a matter of public interest, even if intemperately worded, so long as they are not obscene or criminally libellous, should, as a general rule, come within the protection afforded by s. 2(b) of the Charter. It would, I think, be unfortunate if freedom of expression on matters of public interest so vital to a free and democratic society was to be unduly restricted. The constitutional guarantee should be given a broad and liberal interpretation. The comment of the appellant came within the ambit of that protection. This, I believe, must be the conclusion, whether the two-step procedure described in *R. v. Oakes* is followed or the approach to s. 2(b) set forth in *R. v. Zundel* is adopted.

. . . .

It remains to be determined whether the offence of contempt by scandalizing the court is a constitutionally permissible limit on the protection afforded the appellant's words.

3. If the words are "protected" by s. 2(b) of the Charter does the offence of contempt by scandalizing the court constitute a constitutionally permissible limit on that protection?

It is incumbent upon the Crown to establish, on a balance of probabilities, that the limitation on freedom of expression imposed by the offence of scandalizing the court meets the requirement of s. 1 of the Charter. That section reads:

> 1. The *Canadian Charter of Rights and Freedoms* guarantees the rights and freedoms set out in it subject only to such reasonable limits prescribed by law as can be demonstrably justified in a free and democratic society.

A s. 1 analysis can usefully be divided into three parts: first, is the limit a reasonable limit? Second, is the limit prescribed by law? Third, can the limit be demonstrably justified in a free and democratic society?

. . . .

It may be helpful to summarize what appears to be the approach to the offence of scandalizing the court in other jurisdictions.

The United Kingdom, although recognizing the existence of the offence, has not registered a conviction for over 60 years. Australia and New Zealand which recognize the offence do not have a constitution which guarantees the right of freedom of expression. The European Court of Human Rights has stressed the importance of freedom of expression and limited the scope of the restrictions on that freedom. The United States Supreme Court does not recognize the offence and has found some most intemperate criticisms of the courts and judges to be protected by the constitutional right to free speech. Comments on trials which have been completed have been found almost invariably to come within the protection of the First Amendment.

It would seem that in those free and democratic societies that have either a constitution or a convention which protects freedom of expression that the offence of scandalizing the court, that is to say, to punish as a crime acts done or oral statements made that would tend to bring the courts or the administration of justice into disrepute would not be accepted as a reasonable limit on freedom of expression. It follows that the experience of other free and democratic jurisdictions which possess a constitutional guarantee of freedom of expression, does not support the argument that the offence constitutes a permissible limit on that protection.

It will now be helpful to consider the first aspect of a s. 1 analysis suggested above, that is, whether the offence of contempt of court by scandalizing the court is, as presently defined, a reasonable limit on freedom of expression. In *R.* v. *Oakes, supra*, the Supreme Court of Canada set forth the criteria that were to be considered in determining whether the impugned legislation was a reasonable limit on the particular freedom or right granted by the Charter.

. . . .

It was conceded by counsel for the intervenant and I am satisfied that the first criterion was met in that the objective of protecting the administration of justice was of sufficient importance to warrant overriding a constitutionally protected right or freedom. However, in my view, the second criterion has not been satisfied. Without requiring any proof of the matter, the offence *assumes* that the words which are the subject-matter of the charge will bring the court into contempt or lower its authority. This I take to be an unwarranted and questionable assumption, and leads me to conclude that the offence has not been "carefully designed to achieve the objective in question." By undertaking the proceedings the prosecution must be taken as alleging that the words spoken by the accused which were "calculated to bring the administration of justice into disrepute" will in fact have such an effect. If this is not the basis of the charge then the measure adopted is arbitrary, unfair or based upon irrational considerations. If the essence of the charge is, as it must be, that the words spoken do bring the court into contempt, then it would not be unreasonable to require the prosecution to prove that this is in fact the effect of those words. This requirement is lacking in the offence of scandalizing the court as it is presently known.

It may be helpful in considering this issue to recall that when dealing with contempt cases arising out of statements made pertaining to cases that are pending or under consideration, the courts have *always* required proof that the statements constituted a serious danger to the administration of justice. That is to say that the Crown must show that such statements put the function of the courts in serious question. In *Attorney-General* v. *Times Newspapers Ltd.*, [1973] 1 All E.R. 815, Lord Denning M.R. in the Court of Appeal (reversed in the result by the House of Lords, *supra*) stated at pp. 821–2:

> I regard it as of the first importance that the law which I have just stated should be maintained in its full integrity. We must not allow "trial by newspaper" or "trial by television" or trial by any medium other than the courts of law. But, in so stating the law, I would emphasize that it applies only "when litigation is pending and is actively in suit before the court." To which I would add that there must appear to be *"a real and substantial danger of prejudice"* to the trial of the case or to the settlement of it. (Emphasis added.)

This was essentially the test laid down by the European court later in that same case. That requirement should also be an essential condition of the offence of scandalizing the court, as it would go some distance towards ensuring that the offence: "impairs 'as little as possible' the right or freedom in question." In the absence of such a requirement the limitation imposed by the offence cannot meet the proportionality test as it is both arbitrary and irrational, based as it is on the unproved assumption that the comment will lower the authority of the court. I am confident that the public, if not the media, will take into account the source of the comment before deciding that the court should be regarded with contempt or its authority lowered.

Furthermore, there is some question as to what *mens rea* is required to prove the offence of scandalizing the court. It has been said that the words themselves can constitute the offence. Yet it would seem reasonable to require the Crown to prove that the accused either intended to cause disrepute to the administration of justice or was reckless as to whether that disrepute would follow in spite of the reasonable foreseeability of that result from the words used. Anything less would also seem to be contrary to the proportionality test as it applies too arbitrary a standard.

. . . .

CAN SUCH AN OFFENCE MEET THE REQUIREMENT OF THE CHARTER?

The decision in this case should not be taken as a conclusion that the offence cannot exist. It is in effect a common law offence that, as presently defined, cannot meet the constitutional requirements of the Charter, and not an offence created by statute. The courts created the offence and thus the courts, as well as the legislature, might modify it to meet the requirements of the Charter. For example if the Crown were to prove:

- that an act was done or words were spoken with the intent to cause disrepute to its administration of justice or with reckless disregard as to whether disrepute would follow in spite of the reasonable foreseeability that such a result would follow from the act done or words used;
- and that the evil consequences flowing from the act or words were extremely serious;
- and as well demonstrated the extreme imminence of those evil consequences, so that the apprehended danger to the administration of justice was shown to be real, substantial and immediate;

then the act or words could be punishable as a criminal offence in order to ensure the functioning of the judicial process.

. . . .

[T]here was a submission that the conviction should be set aside on the grounds that the trial judge refused to permit evidence to be given as to the "truth" of the statement made by the appellant. The trial judge held that truth could not be a defence to the charge.

It would seem that historically the defence of truth has not been available to a charge of scandalizing the court. There have been extensive criticisms of this position. Nevertheless there has been and continues to be a vigorous debate on the issue.

I think the criticisms are in some circumstances well founded. For example, let us assume that the statement giving rise to the charge of scandalizing the court was that a judge had taken a bribe. In such a situation it would seem to me to be repugnant to a sense of justice and fairness to refuse to permit the defence of truth to be put forward. However, having said that it would seem that the defence of truth has no real bearing in light of the facts of this case and it is not appropriate to attempt to resolve the issue at this time.

DISPOSITION

In the result, I would allow the appeal and set aside the conviction and direct an acquittal of the appellant.

■

Justices Goodman and Houlden concurred in separate judgments. Justice Goodman stated that the offence of contempt of court was not constitutionally invalid *per se*: the offence might still be prosecuted where justice has been brought into disrepute and that disrepute results in "a clear, significant and imminent or present danger to the fair and effective administration of justice ...." He said, however, that the offence of scandalizing the court could not be similarly salvaged.

Justices Dubin and Brooke, dissenting in part, would have overturned the conviction on the basis that the essential element of the *actus reus* of the offence had not been made out, that is, the reality of the risk to the proper administration of justice:

> The suggestion that there was some over-all conspiracy between all the judiciary in this province and the police to deny a fair trial to the appellant's client, and, indeed, to all those engaged in litigation where the police were involved, is so preposterous that no right-thinking member of society would take it seriously.

Consider whether Mr. Kopyto's assertion was in fact "preposterous" as a substantive matter? Review the materials in **Policing**, in particular, the results of the McDonald Commission Inquiry into the actions of the RCMP What is the *function* of the judicial power to cite for contempt?

All of the Court of Appeal justices stated flatly that Mr. Kopyto's conduct was outrageous and unprofessional. What notion of professionalism underlies such a statement? Consider also which understandings of professionalism are reinforced by, for example, the *Rules of Professional Conduct*, produced by the Law Society of Upper Canada. What sorts of standards ought to be applied to the conduct of judges who wield power to cite for contempt?

Both the Criminal Lawyers' Association and the Canadian Civil Liberties Association were denied leave to intervene in the case: *R. v. Kopyto (Ont. C.A.)*, [1987] O.J. No. 117 (C.A.), online: QL. They had sought to contest the constitutionality of the common law offence of scandalizing the court on the basis of s. 2(b) of the *Charter* and the "chilling effect resulting from the existence of the common law crime of scandalising the Court": Affidavit of the Canadian Civil Liberties Association, Paragraph 8.

William Kunstler was one of the best-known U.S. civil liberties lawyers in the last century. Among others, he represented the Freedom Riders in Mississippi, the Chicago Eight, activists at Wounded Knee, and the Attica prisoners. His vigorous representation of clients and, arguably, his identification with their interests against what he called the "tyranny of judges" led to numerous contempt citations.

Trials and Tribulations[†]

I have been held in contempt by so many courts that it is difficult to remember all of the occasions. In some instances I have spent an hour or so in custody; in others, I have spent as much as a weekend in the cooler. Fortunately, the longest such sentence imposed on me — the four years and thirteen days decreed by Judge Hoffman in the Chicago Conspiracy Trial — was reversed on appeal, thanks to the efforts of my perennial attorney in these matters, Morton Stavis.

Despite the widespread notion that I deliberately court contempt citations, the fact of the matter is that I do not. However, there are some actions by judges which, in my opinion, are so wrong and so hurtful to my clients' interests that I feel compelled to speak out and, indeed, believe it is my duty to do so. Judicial tyranny is no more to be tolerated than that of any other public official, and I will continue to risk imprisonment whenever judges cross the bounds of what I consider to be acceptable conduct.

My philosophy in this regard was perhaps best expressed by me in my remarks to Judge Hoffman just before he sentenced me in Chicago in 1970:

> Your Honor, I have been a lawyer since December of 1948, when I was first admitted to the bar in the state of New York. Since that time I have practised before, among others, the Supreme Court of the United States, the United States Court of Appeals for the First, Second, Third, Fourth, Fifth, Sixth, Seventh, Tenth, and District of Columbia Circuits, Federal District Courts throughout a great deal of the United States, and the United States Court of Military Appeals, as well as a host of state tribunals.
>
> Until today I have never once been disciplined by any judge, federal or state, although a large part of my practice, at least for the last decade, has taken place in hostile southern courts where I was representing black and white clients in highly controversial civil rights cases.
>
> Yesterday, for the first time in my career, I completely lost my composure in a courtroom, as I watched the older daughter of David Dellinger being rushed out of the room because she clapped her hands to acknowledge what amounted to her father's farewell statement to her.
>
> I felt then such a deep sense of utter futility that I could not help crying, something I had not done publicly since childhood.
>
> I am sorry if I disturbed the decorum of the courtroom, but I am not ashamed of my conduct in this court, for which I am about to be punished.
>
> I have tried with all my heart faithfully to represent my clients in the face of what I con-

---

[†] From *Trials and Tribulations* by William Kunstler (New York: Grove Press Inc., 1986) at 93–94. © 1986 by William Kunstler. Used by permission of Grove/Atlantic, Inc.

sider — and still consider — repressive and unjust conduct toward them. If I have to pay with liberty for such representation, then that is the price of my beliefs and my sensibilities.

I can only hope that my fate does not deter other lawyers throughout the country, who, in the difficult days that lie ahead, will be asked to defend clients against a steadily increasing governmental encroachment upon their most fundamental liberties. If they are so deterred, then my punishment will have effects of such terrifying consequences that I dread to contemplate the future domestic and foreign course of this country. However, I have the utmost faith that my beloved comrades at the bar, young and old alike, will not allow themselves to be frightened out of defending the poor, the persecuted, the radicals and the militants, the black people, the pacifists, and the political pariahs of this, our common land.

But to those lawyers who may, in learning what has happened to me, waver, I can only say this: stand firm: remain true to those ideals of the law which, even if openly violated here and in other places, are true and glorious goals, and above all, never desert those principles of equality, justice, and freedom without which life has little if any meaning.

I may not be the greatest lawyer in the world, your Honor, but I think that I am at this moment, along with my colleague, Leonard Weinglass, the most privileged. We are being punished for what we believe in.

■

In *R. v. Bertrand* (1989), 49 C.C.C. (3d) 397, the Québec Superior Court ultimately acquitted a lawyer convicted of contempt for vigorously defending his client's *Charter* rights, including making comments such as, "It is our submission that the person who has infringed the provisions of the Charter is at the same time the person who must pronounce sentence," and, "[W]e believe we cannot have full and complete justice, and in addition there can never be an appearance of justice, regardless of the sentences that you render."

In *R. v. S.B.* (1987), 40 C.C.C. (3d) 242, the Nova Scotia Supreme Court, Appeal Division, overturned the conviction of contempt and sentence of 90 days' imprisonment of an unrepresented 15-year-old for laughing in the courtroom while awaiting sentencing for loitering in a public place. The court did not comment on either the conviction or the sentence, but instead held that the trial judge should have informed the youth of his right to counsel under s. 10(b) of the *Charter* before proceeding to the conviction for contempt.

What different issues are raised by the use of judicial powers of contempt against accused persons, as opposed to lawyers such as Kopyto, Kunstler, and Bertrand?

Now consider the use of contempt as against witnesses and victims in criminal prosecutions in the examples that follow.

When the Victim Goes to Jail: The Law on Contempt of Court†

One January night in 1982 an Ottawa woman named Courtney was allegedly raped repeatedly by two men, who were later apprehended by the police. In November at a preliminary hearing her evidence convinced the judge that the case against them warranted a full trial. A court date was set, postponed, and postponed again until finally the trial began in December 1983 almost two years after the incident. By that time however, Courtney had decided not to give further testimony. She said that threats had been made on her life and the lives of her mother and sister and she feared for their safety. Found in contempt of court for refusing to testify, the witness in a rape trial was sentenced to seven days in jail. The men accused of raping her went free when the charges against them were dropped for lack of evidence.

Then in Orillia last September, neighbours reported that Karen Mitchell, twenty-two years old and a few months pregnant, had been beaten up

---

† By Ellen Adelberg, (1984) 9:3 Status Women News 8 at 8–14. Reproduced by permission of the National Action Committee on Status of Women, Toronto, Ontario.

twice by her fiancé. The Crown Attorney laid two assault charges against Terry Reed. In court in December Karen refused to testify against Reed, claiming that she had never intended to lay charges in the first place but had been told by the police she must in order to receive medical aid and police protection. The judge cited her for contempt of court sentencing her to a three-month term. Karen was freed on bail, pending appeal.

These two incidents have led to varied reactions and serious debate among feminists. Some demonstrated outside courtrooms and the Ontario Parliament Buildings or sent letters to the editor vigorously protesting the judges' actions. Others have been less quick to condemn the use of contempt rulings, arguing that the system must be protected so that it may be used more successfully in the future to prosecute men who commit violent acts against women.

This article will provide more information behind both sides of the debate. It will briefly explore some major related questions such as why rape and wife abuse occur, why women "take it," the laws on contempt and how judges can use them. Are there ways to improve the legal process so that victims are no longer sent to jail? And finally, if the answer does not lie in using and improving the legal process, what needs to be done? In the end, of course, there are not likely to be easy answers. This is just the start of what promises to be a long debate.

First of all, what went wrong? Why did the victims end up in jail and the accused were freed? Chantal Tie, an Ottawa lawyer, notes that these "bizarre and unusual" events in court may be a result of a 1982 directive from the Attorney General of Ontario to judges, to pursue cases of violent assault against women with a new rigor. Wonderful, isn't that what feminists have pressed for during the past ten years? Yes, and no. Feminists have indeed been outraged at the traditional attitude of the judiciary towards women victims of violent male crimes. Judges, lawyers and the police have historically tended to view rape as a result of provocation by women, and wife abuse as a private family matter, not for public scrutiny. Feminists have indeed put pressure on the government to amend sexual assault legislation and to view male violence as criminal, not natural.

However, at the same time, most feminists have argued that men beat and rape women because of their inequality in society, so until women's status is improved, they are likely to continue being abused. According to a study by the Canadian Advisory Council on the Status of Women, one in every five Canadian women is sexually assaulted at some point in her life, and an estimated 500,000 women per year are battered by the men they live with. A 1978 survey of transition houses across Canada revealed that 61% of battered women are below 30 years of age, their average family income is $10,000, their education level Grade 11. Only 22% work outside the home and the majority were beaten when they were pregnant. All these statistics indicate that many, many women who are victims of male violence are in a weak position to take charge of their own lives, or to make a living and provide the necessities of life for their children on their own.

Karen Mitchell has stated publicly that she still intends to marry Terry Reed. At first appearance it seems incredible that she would still want to marry the man who beat her up and after she spent time in jail as an indirect result of his actions. But is it so incredible? She is twenty-two years old and she is pregnant with Reed's child. It is quite possible that Karen sees him as her only ticket to survival in a world where women, especially those who are young and pregnant, have slim chances of finding well-paying jobs, affordable housing and day care — not to mention companionship, love and respect.

And maybe it is not so incredible that Courtney would not testify against the two men charged with repeatedly raping her. One of them is said to be a member of a motorcycle club called "The Outlaws," which has a reputation for violence and involvement in illegal activities, and threats were made against the lives of her and her family. Ottawa is a relatively small city where it is almost impossible to disappear into the woodwork. As she herself explained, she has already suffered through two years waiting for the trial. Should she then jeopardize any future peaceful existence by publicly denouncing the accused?

. . . .

Some feminists make the assumption that the court system can be used as a way of protecting women's rights to live safely among men....

... However, the way the laws are administered [tends] to reflect the unequal status of women in relation to men....

. . . .

Perhaps it is best to explain the contempt of court procedures. Judges have the power to cite a witness for contempt of court if the witness is seen deliberately to obstruct the course of administering justice. In the past witnesses have been cited for refusing to appear in court after they have been subpoenaed, for appearing but refusing to swear to tell the truth, for causing a disturbance in the courtroom, or for refusing to answer questions while under oath. Most witnesses who have been found in contempt of court for refusing to answer questions, have been "parties to the offence," that is, they have been in some way implicated in carrying out the crime. The cases of Courtney and Karen Mitchell are "rather unusual," in the words of a lawyer, because both women were victims of the offences and NOT parties to them. However the sentences they received were not extraordinarily long compared to those imposed on other witnesses for refusing to testify. In fact, Courtney's sentence was considered to be short, given the fact that a preliminary hearing had already occurred.

. . . .

In earlier days, if the woman did not want to go to court, it was standard procedure for the crown attorney to agree to withdraw charges, and the judge would allow the case to be dropped. Now it seems, whether or not the woman agrees, if charges of assault are laid against her husband, lover or acquaintance, she will be subpoenaed into court and expected to give testimony. Codifying the laws governing contempt and appointing female judges will not change that reality, nor make it any easier for a woman to testify.

Proponents of using the legal system to force women to testify after they have been assaulted suggest that improvements can be made within the system to make the process easier. For instance, aside from appointing women judges, victims could be offered immediate police protection — something which did not happen in the case of Courtney; waiting time for trials could be shorter, thereby reducing both the period of agony the victim suffers and the time alleged assailants have to threaten or harass the victim. The accused could be held in custody if he is considered dangerous, thereby allowing the victim to walk outside in relative safety; and finally, court-sponsored support services for the victim could be increased to assist women during the ordeal of waiting for and attending a trial.

Opponents of forcing women to testify at court hearings say that it really doesn't matter if surface changes are made to the legal system because women will still be beaten and raped. Although feminists on this side do not blame the court system for the fact that women are unequal, they look outside of the legal process for ways to redress the inequality and reduce male violence. Providing access to economic security programs, more day care facilities and cheaper housing are crucial steps they say. Educating children and re-educating adults about the immorality of abusing women is another. Providing support services on a wide scale, such as refuges for battered wives, is yet another necessity and so is the control of pornography, if violence against women is to be significantly reduced.

Where are the answers? The arguments on both sides seem to have some relevance. Perhaps what is most important for now is that feminists realize they all share the same goals. Surely every woman recoils in horror when she reads that women victims of male violence are being sent to jail, while alleged attackers go free. Ordeals like those of Courtney and Karen Mitchell may well happen again. What are we going to do about them when they do?

■

In *R. v. D.B.T.* (1996), 147 N.S.R. (2d) 308 (C.A.), the court ordered a new trial on the basis that the trial judge had failed to exercise his jurisdiction (by not considering a citation for contempt) when the complainants/victims (the girlfriend and mother of the accused) refused to testify at a trial for assault and threatening bodily harm (at 310):

> The youth court judge was responsible for the orderly functioning of his court, and for maintaining its dignity and reputation. It is essential to the operation of that court that witnesses must testify; justice cannot be done if persons called as witnesses can refuse with impunity to give evidence, or even to be sworn. A reluctant witness is obviously a problem, but it is a problem the judge must solve; his [sic] discretion for doing so is broad, including contempt proceedings with the possibility of custody or other sanctions as a last resort if cautionary or persuasive efforts fail.
>
> [T]he trial judge erred in fettering his discretion by appearing to adopt a policy of refusing to compel evidence from alleged victims of offences.

Sylvester O'Leary, the accused in the case extracted below, had pleaded guilty on 24 November 1988 to assaulting his wife, before the Provincial Court in Toronto. Mr. O'Leary had himself also laid an assault charge against his wife, but that charge had been dismissed in the 24 November hearing by Judge DiCecco. At the 14 February 1989 sentencing hearing, the same judge decided that he would also dismiss the charges against the husband (with the consent of the Crown, and the wife) in spite of the earlier guilty plea. He then required that both parties enter into a recognizance to keep the peace (s. 810); Ms. O'Leary was under the impression that a counselling clause was to be inserted. Her lawyer had left her to sign the recognizance alone in court. The transcript of what transpired follows.

R. v. O'Leary[†]

The Court: Good. Upon Mr. O'Leary entering into the recognizance as applied, I will dismiss the charge. What does the Crown — dismiss the charge. That would be the best.

Mr. Bains: Yes, Your Honour.

The Court: Thank you.

Mr. Bains: Your Honour, the Crown is not taking a position in opposition to that.

The Court: No it's the fairest position you could have taken.

. . . .

REPORTER'S NOTE: Then other matters resumed.

. . . .

The Court: Mrs. O'Leary, I noticed that you have been trying to approach the bench. Come forward. What is your problem? What disturbs you?

The Witness: Well, Your Honour, I would have assumed that you had still left in place the counselling for my husband and myself —

The Court: But you were making objections to it.

The Witness: No, I wasn't objecting to that. What I was trying to object to was that you were saying something about the breach of the common bail order.

The Court: You should be — it's not the bail order. It's a Common Law Peace Bond Recognizance, and it's obvious if you are ordered to do something if you don't comply, then you have to pay the consequences.

The Witness: Well, since the adjournment, it would be in my best interest and his if it was clearly stated — the requirements.

The Court: Are you agreeable to that?

The Accused: Sir, I don't think we could get anywhere going to a marriage counsellor together. She's getting something else —

The Court: Well, I didn't say together. I never said together.

The Accused: Yes, I know, sir.

The Court: I just said counselling.

The Accused: Yes, I know, sir.

The Witness: Yes, but the problem is within the marriage, and one sees that there's definitely a problem and the other sees that there's no problem except for —

The Court: Well, Madam, do you want me to put on the record who's the problem here? I can see it right away, you are the problem, Madam.

The Witness: Just at this moment. Your Honour —

The Court: You are the problem, Madam. Not at this moment. You were a problem on November the 24th. You were a problem on November the 10th, and I'm quite sure you've been a problem for the last ten years.

The Witness: No, Your Honour. I think you're prejudicing against me here because I do know what has happened to me through the course of ten years of marriage.

The Court: Madam, I have your evidence, given by you —

The Witness: I'm not denying what I stated, sir —

The Court: Madam, I'm advising you —

The Witness: I'm trying to give both of us a chance.

The Court: — Madam, I'm advising you that I did make an order and the order is that you will enter into a recognizance to keep the peace and be of good behaviour for a period of twelve months. Are you refusing to do so?

[†] (14 February 1989), (Ont. Prov. Ct. (Criminal Div.)) [unpublished].

The Witness: I'm requesting, Your Honour, that —

The Court: Are you refusing to do so?

The Witness: I want the marriage counselling put on that. I assumed you left that in place.

The Court: I'm not prepared to put that term. Are you refusing to enter into that recognizance?

The Witness: I don't think it's being fair to me that my husband had assaulted me, not just on the 10th of November, but on numerous other occasions.

The Court: Madam, please answer the question, and I'm not going to go any further because I've given this matter due consideration. I did not rush into making a decision on November 17, I did not rush to make a decision on November 24th. I carefully thought it over. And I'm asking you again, are you refusing to enter into the recognizance as ordered by this Court?

The Witness: I'm questioning it, sir.

The Court: That's not the question. Are you refusing because I ordered you to?

The Witness: Sir, I assumed that you had left that other part of the counselling —

The Court: Step into custody. And you will

The Witness: — that's why I'm back in court.

The Court: — remain in custody for a period of ninety days or until such day as you will sign that recognizance. You're refusing to obey the Court Order.

The Witness: I never said, Your Honour, that I was refusing to.

The Court: Well, then sit down and sign it. Is the recognizance ready?

The Clerk Of The Court: It is.

The Court: You have a choice. You either sign it or you go into the box.

The Witness: Is there counsel I can confer with at the moment?

The Court: You will confer from the box.

The Witness: Can I confer with the counsel?

The Court: You will go into the prisoner's box and you'll have an opportunity to consult counsel. Call Duty Counsel, please, Mr. Clerk, so that this young woman will have an opportunity to be properly informed on what it means to disobey a Court Order.

The Witness: I never said I wouldn't sign it, Your Honour. I am just not understanding all the procedures before me today.

The Court: And Mr. O'Leary you must also understand that I also intend to fully have that order applied to you.

The Accused: Yes, sir. I know.

The Court: You keep the peace and be of good behaviour. If things cannot work out, please leave the residence. And I still urge you greatly to go for counselling.

The Accused: I will, sir.

The Court: Because it will require all your ability to be able to cope with a very difficult situation. I know that you love your wife otherwise you wouldn't be here today. You would have taken off ten years ago. You love your wife, you love your children and you're trying to comply with the responsibility that you promised to fulfill when you got married. And my urgent recommendation is, do go for counselling. Go for it in a controlled type of therapy. Do whatever has to be done, because — for the sake of your own children and yourself. They are entitled to a family where there is tranquility.

The Accused: I know, sir.

The Court: Thank you.

The Court: Do you wish to reconsider, Madam? Do you wish to sign that order?

The Witness: I wanted to ask the Crown if — I apologize I didn't stand before, Your Honour. I wanted to just consult with counsel in terms of what entails this.

The Court: It entails you are to keep the peace and be of good behaviour.

The Witness: Well, Your Honour, it's two times at fault here —

The Court: Oh, well, this one's bound over. Didn't you hear what I said to your husband?

The Witness: Well I feel I'm being persecuted for —

The Court: Nobody's being [persecuted]. I gave both of you direction and the direction is, keep cool both of you.

The Witness: Well, Your Honour, I may argue with the man, but I don't strike the man, unless I've been struck and I hit back in self-defence. It's not my intentions to annoy you, Your Honour.

The Court: She's refusing to sign the order.

The Witness: I don't quite understand —

The Court: Could you explain to her what that order means. Maybe she doesn't believe me.

Mr. Bains: Your Honour, I have no idea what to say.

The Court: The order is to keep the peace and be of good behaviour, enter into a recognizance, and she's refusing to enter into the recognizance.

The Witness: And I was requesting for you to reinstate the counselling which I did not understand you had struck from it.

Mr. Bains: If I may, Your Honour, you do realize that His Honour is merely asking what you are obligated by law to do in this country anyhow, and that's to keep the peace and be of good behaviour.

The Witness: I've no problem with that.

The Court: So why don't you sign it, Madam? Because your husband already signed it and I'm not in a position to get him back and change it. And it's not that I'm asking you to do something that I have not asked your husband to do.

The Witness: Does it protect me?

The Court: It certainly protects you because if he steps out of line, he's going to go in for ninety days.

The Witness: But then Your Honour said that I would go in for ninety days if I argued with my husband.

The Court: Oh, no, no. I didn't say anything about that. I just said keep the peace and be of good behaviour. I didn't say anything about that.

The Witness: The only way I ever breach the peace of tranquility in the home is to argue back with my husband.

The Court: Madam.

The Witness: Is that what you call breaching?

The Court: Madam, on the evidence that you, yourself gave under oath, you did breach the peace and be of good behaviour, you seized your husband's keys. You seized his wallet. You removed several hundred dollars out of his pocket. You, when he tried to retrieve the car keys, stepped on his hands. You —

The Witness: No, Your Honour. That is incorrect.

The Court: Madam, I made those findings of guilty based upon your testimony.

The Witness: I had been knocked over when I landed on my husband.

The Court: Madam, you can only see whatever you want to see.

The Witness: Well, Your Honour, I was —

The Court: Well, I'm not going to argue any more. If you don't sign that order, there will be ninety days.
Good. Take her down —

The Witness: I'll sign the paper.

The Court: Take her down. And when the paper is ready, she'll sign. Take her down.

The Witness: I said I'd sign the paper and you're refusing to let me.

The Court: You will sign the paper.

The Witness: I'm willing to sign it now, but you won't let me, Your Honour.

The Court: When it's ready, you'll sign the paper.

The Witness: Okay.

The Court: Is it ready? Is it ready?

The Clerk Of The Court: Officer.

The Court: Do you see the lady who was just taken out in handcuffs? Mr. Clerk, why don't you go yourself before she faints? Duty Counsel we don't need you any more. The matter got resolved. Thank you.

■

For more information on the action of Judge DiCecco, see Andrew McIntosh, "Judge says woman responsible for her stormy marital situation" *The [Toronto] Globe and Mail* (28 February 1989) A1, A2; "Ontario judge to sue Globe for libel" *The [Toronto] Globe and Mail* (13 March 1989) A14.

There are numerous examples of judicial use of contempt powers that are suggestive of abuse of power:

- Judge Ross of the Ontario Provincial Court ordered a woman spectator into custody for allegedly "disrupting" his court, whereupon she was handcuffed, strip-searched, and held for 90 minutes without charge: Andrew McIntosh, "Toronto courtroom sees Western-style meting out of justice" *The [Toronto] Globe and Mail* (25 February 1989) A1, A6.

- A Nova Scotia justice jailed an assaulted woman for failing to appear to testify against her batterer, without regard for her s. 10(b) *Charter* rights: Monique Conrad, "N.S. justice of the peace lacked jurisdiction to detain witness, woman collects $38,500 award for 6 days' unlawful imprisonment" *The Lawyers Weekly* (15 March 1991) 6.

E. SCRUTINY OF JUDGES

While judges have *almost* free rein when they preside over a courtroom, as some of the foregoing examples illustrate, they are sometimes the subject of complaints to the Canadian Judicial Council (in the case of superior court judges) or provincial judicial councils (in the case of provincial court judges) for their courtroom remarks and actions, and may be disciplined for such behaviour. For example, consider the case of Mr. Justice Jean Bienvenue, who was the subject of an inquiry because of his derogatory remarks about women, lesbians, and the suffering of Jewish people, in presiding over *R. v. Théberge* (December 1995) Trois-Rivières (400-01-002411-940) (Que. S.C.), a prosecution of an African-Canadian woman for killing an abusive husband: Canadian Judicial Council News Release, "Bienvenue Inquiry Committee Report released" (4 July 1996). The Council recommended that he be removed from office, but he retired rather than be impeached, thus preserving his $104,000-a-year pension: Mark Bourrie, "Disgraced judge resigns before impeachment" *Law Times* (30 September–6 October 1996) 1.

The New Brunswick Judicial Council recommended the removal of Judge Jocelyne Moreau-Bérubé, given the impropriety of disparaging remarks, attacking the honesty of Acadian people, that she made during a sentencing hearing: *Decision of the New Brunswick Judicial Council established under the provisions of Section 6.1 of the Provincial Court Act concerning the conduct of Her Honour Judge Jocelyne J. Moreau-Bérubé, a Judge of the New Brunswick Provincial Court* (9 April 1999: Fredericton, New Brunswick). She wondered out loud if she was "surrounded by crooks" on the Acadian peninsula where she lived. While complaints centred on the derogatory nature of the comments with respect to Acadians generally, the comments also could be characterized as reflecting a class bias and welfare-bashing:

> *These are people who live on welfare and we're the ones who support them; they are on drugs and they are drunk day in and day out.* They steal from us left, right and centre and any which way, they find others as crooked as they are to buy the stolen property. It's a pitiful sight. If a survey were taken in the Acadian Peninsula, of the honest people as against the dishonest people, I have the impression that the dishonest people would win.... [L]ook at the honest people in the Acadian Peninsula. They are very few and certainly *very rare."* [As reproduced in the Supreme Court judgment [2002] S.C.J. No. 9, online: QL at paragraph 3, emphasis added].

The Council concluded that the remarks created a reasonable apprehension of bias and would "[shake] public confidence to the point of making the judge unfit to perform her judicial functions" (paragraph 21). They were particularly concerned (at paragraph 21) that:

> ...[A]s the judge often has to *assess the credibility of witnesses* in a trial, or even of an accused, a task which can be particularly difficult, *could such a person think that the judge has linked his or her credibility to pre-conceived opinions or beliefs about the community of which that person may be a member* and for that reason fear that he or she has not benefited from the presumption of innocence. [Emphasis added.]

The Council's decision was overturned by Justice Angers on the basis that the Council recommendation was not sufficiently based on the findings contained in the panel's report, and that the judge had been denied her full right to be heard because she had not been explicitly informed of the possibility of her removal from office as a sanction: *Moreau-Bérubé* v. *New Brunswick* (1999), 218 N.B.R. (2d) 256 (QB); aff'd (2000) 233 N.B.R. (2d) 205 (C.A.); rev'd [2002] S.C.J. No. 9, online: QL. Madam Justice Arbour, writing for a unanimous Court, allowed the appeal and restored the decision of the New Brunswick Judicial Council to recommend removal of the judge. While attentive to the importance of judicial independence and the tension in evaluating integrity, bias and the apprehension of bias in that context, she ruled that the Judicial Council was particularly well situated for such a task (at paragraph 58, 70–71)

> ...When a disciplinary process is launched to look at the conduct of an individual judge, it is alleged that an abuse of judicial independence by a judge has threatened the integrity of the judiciary as a whole. The harm alleged is not curable by the appeal process.
>
> ...
>
> The central issue that the Council had to resolve in deciding to recommend the respondent's dismissal from the bench was whether her comments evidenced bias, or created an apprehension of bias such that she could no longer expect to enjoy the public trust in a fair and independent judiciary....

In my view, it was within the power of the Council to draw its own conclusions, and, in light of the sweeping and generalized nature of Judge Moreau-Bérubé's derogatory comments, it would be difficult to call the conclusion reached by the Council patently unreasonable.... The power to impose the appropriate sanction, which rests solely with the Council presupposes the power to characterize appropriately the nature and seriousness of the misconduct.

In a Nova Scotia case, *R.D.S.*, discussed *supra*, **Policing**, Judge Corinne Sparks (then, the only African-Canadian judge in Nova Scotia) found in favour of a young African-Canadian accused, on the basis that it was possible that police officers "have been known to lie" and to be influenced by racism. Judge Sparks' comments were the subject of a complaint by police and a judicial inquiry. For a thoughtful commentary, see Richard Devlin, "We Can't Go On Together with Suspicious Minds: Judicial Bias and Racialized Perspective in R. v. R.D.S." (1995) 18 Dal. L.J. 408. Devlin compares the treatment of Judge Sparks, and the finding of bias on the basis of her remarks, with the treatment accorded two other cases in which allegations of judicial bias were determined to be "unfounded" (the Donald Marshall, Jr. cases, *supra*, **Aboriginal Peoples and Criminal Law** and the case of Judge Michel Bourassa, discussed *supra*, **Sentencing**). For a thoughtful discussion of *R.D.S.* and the stories presented about race, racial bias, colour blindness and standpoint, see: Sherene Razack, "*R.D.S.* v. *Her Majesty the Queen*: A Case About Home" (1998) Constitutional Forum 59.

In Saskatchewan, complaints against Justice Allyre Sirois led to his resignation shortly before a report by the Canadian Judicial Council was released. The conduct complained of involved victim-blaming comments about women, including a comment that "it takes two to tango" to a woman who had been beaten unconscious by her boyfriend, and a comment that prostitutes were "a different breed" in a case involving a prostitute who was sexually assaulted: CP, "Controversial judge resigns" *The [Toronto] Globe and Mail* (28 February 1998) A10.

Ed Ratushny analyzes the "boundaries of acceptable judicial speech" (at 296) by examining a number of cases (including the wrongful conviction of Donald Marshall, Jr.; *R.* v. *Théberge*, *supra*; *Twinn* v. *Canada* (indexed as *Sawridge Band* v. *R.*, [1997] 3 F.C. 580 (C.A.); *Weatherill* v. *Canada*, [1999] F.C.J. No. 787 (Fed. T.D.), online: QL; *R.* v. *Ewanchuk*, [1998] 1 S.C.R. 493; and *Vriend* v. *Alberta*, [1998] 1 S.C.R. 493): Ed Ratushny, "Speaking as Judges: How Far Can They Go?" (1999–2000) 11 N.J.C.L. 203. In discussing the accountability of judges and remedies for improper conduct, Ratushny highlights the importance of judicial independence, and distinguishes between legal bias and bias reflecting misconduct. He also highlights the way in which understandings of bias, racism and discrimination are shifting:

> As our understanding of systemic discrimination increases, so will the expectations that we have of judges. Public confidence requires that judges be conscious of the pitfalls inherent in systemic discriminatory attitudes and stereotypes. The grave responsibilities of judging conduct, credibility, and relationships between people in a diverse and rapidly changing society require that judges be at the forefront of understanding how to keep an "open mind." It is in the area of judicial speech that discriminatory attitudes on the part of judges are most likely to be revealed ... (at 341–42).

There are numerous examples of misconduct outside the courtroom, for which judges may be disciplined. Also, judges who speak *outside* of the courtroom on issues of public concern are extremely vulnerable to disciplinary action of one form or another. The cases highlight the contingency of bias claims and the limits on judicial independence, and suggest that out-of-court speech may be sanctioned more severely. For a contrary view, see Wayne MacKay, "Judicial Free Speech and Accountability: Should Judges Be Seen and Not Heard?" (1993) 3 N.J.C.L. 159. Consider the following examples.

JUSTICE THOMAS BERGER

As you read the account of Justice Thomas Berger, reconsider earlier examples in the materials, such as the *Inquiry into the Conduct of Judge R.M. Bourassa* under **Sentencing**. What purposes are served by this distinction between courtroom behaviour and public comments? Are the concerns regarding the maintenance of the appearance of judicial neutrality different? What scrutiny and remedies for inappropriate judicial statements and actions should be available?

During the first round of constitutional talks in 1981, Justice Thomas Berger (of the B.C. Supreme Court) made a speech at the University of Guelph denouncing the exclusion of Aboriginal rights from the constitution. Extracts from his speech were reported as follows in "The first Canadians are last" *The [Toronto] Globe and Mail* (12 November 1981) 8:

> The agreement reached in February this year by all parties in the House of Commons, to entrench aboriginal rights and treaty rights in the new Constitution, has been repudiated by the Prime Minister and the premiers.
>
> In fact, they were unanimous on this question. The Prime Minister and all the premiers were in agreement — not only the nine premiers of the English-speaking provinces, but Premier Lévesque, too, for the reasons he gave for his refusal to sign the constitutional agreement did not include any reference to native rights. There was, at the end, not one of our Canadian statesmen willing to make a stand for the rights of the Indians, the Inuit and the Metis.
>
> No one would expect that a Constitution drawn up by the provinces would affirm aboriginal rights and treaty rights ... Now the federal government has, in order to obtain a constitutional agreement, surrendered on the issue of native rights. I confess that I never did believe they would ...
>
> ... It is, in fact, in our relations with the peoples from whom we took this land that we can discover the truth about ourselves and the society we have built....
>
> The constitutional agreement is a defeat for the native peoples, but it is also a defeat for all Canadians. The agreement reveals the true limits of the Canadian conscience and the Canadian imagination.
>
> ... In the end, no matter what ideology they profess, our leaders share one firm conviction: that native rights should not be inviolable; the power of the state must encompass them. Their treatment of native peoples reveals how essential it is to entrench minority rights, without qualification.
>
> ... Under the new Constitution the first Canadians shall be the last....

A judge of the Federal Court complained to the Judicial Council that Berger's speech constituted grave misconduct, and the Council appointed three judges to prepare a report. Their conclusions were reported in John Gray, "Berger can remain on bench, judges say" *The [Toronto] Globe and Mail* (5 June 1982) 1:

> Judges, of necessity, must be divorced from all politics. That does not prevent them from holding strong views on matters of great national importance but they are gagged by the very nature of their independent office, difficult as that may seem.
>
> ... We are prepared to believe that he had the best interests of Canada in mind when he spoke, but a judge's conscience is not an acceptable excuse for contravening a fundamental rule so important to the existence of a parliamentary democracy and judicial independence.
>
> ... It is possible that Justice Berger, and other judges too, have been under a misapprehension as to the nature of the constraints imposed upon judges. That should not be so in the future.
>
> We do not, however, think it would be fair to set standards ex post facto to support a recommendation for removal in this case.

The complaint, the decision of the Judicial Council, the responses of Justice Minister Jean Chrétien and Prime Minister Trudeau, and the comments of Chief Justice Bora Laskin in fact generated considerable controversy and support for Justice Berger. Some suggested that Justice Berger's characterization of the agreement as "mean-spirited and unbelievable" was being attacked for political reasons, including his earlier work as head of the inquiry into the Mackenzie Valley Pipeline: CP, "B.C. lawyers support Berger's comments" *The [Toronto] Globe and Mail* (12 June 1982) 12; Editorial, "Judge Berger's opinion" *The [Toronto] Globe and Mail* (7 June 1982) 6; Marina Strauss, "Laskin lashes out at critics of council's ruling on Berger" *The [Toronto] Globe and Mail* (3 September 1982) 5; Editorial, "Picking at it" *The [Toronto] Globe and Mail* (4 September 1982) 6.

Justice Berger responded in "Fundamental fairness at stake" *The [Toronto] Globe and Mail* (25 May 1982) 8, that a judge had the right, and indeed a duty, to speak out on questions of human rights and fundamental freedoms, particularly minority rights:

> These issues are political in the broadest sense, but they transcend the daily round of partisan politics.... They are questions of fundamental fairness.... It is alleged that this was a breach of judicial convention. If it was, there are precedents for such a breach. Mr. Justice Thorson used to participate in the campaign for nuclear disarmament. Chief Justice Freedman went on television in October, 1970, to declare his support for the invoking of the *War Measures Act*. On the occasion of his visit to Vancouver to open the new Court House in September, 1979, Lord Denning told us that the trade unions in England were a threat to the freedom of that country. No doubt each of these judges felt compelled to speak out. It may be said that it would undermine the independ-

ence of the judiciary if judges were constantly engaged in such activity. But they are not. These interventions by judges are infrequent.

In the end, Justice Berger resigned from the bench, saying he could not accept the ruling of the Judicial Council that there was any impropriety in judges speaking out. His resignation was accepted readily by Ottawa.

Other examples of judicial commentary outside of the courtroom follow:

JUSTICE BERTHA WILSON

Madam Justice Wilson's lecture, "Will Women Judges Really Make a Difference?," delivered in February 1990 as the Fourth Annual Barbara Betcherman Memorial Lecture at Osgoode Hall Law School, and published in (1990) 28 Osgoode Hall L.J. 507, represented a dramatic break with judicial tradition. The talk would have been unimaginable from a Supreme Court judge even 10 years ago, and certainly would have been impossible without the work of the women's movement and the proliferation of feminist legal scholarship. Madam Justice Wilson, drawing heavily on feminist jurisprudence, underlined the masculinist nature of law and, in particular, of criminal law, and challenged assumptions about the possibility of judicial objectivity. The responses to her lecture confirm just how marked a departure from "tradition" this argument was, emanating from a Supreme Court judge, and how provocative to anti-feminists. For example, R.E.A.L. Women of Canada complained to the Canadian Judicial Council that Madam Justice Wilson had violated her oath of impartiality and was biased in favour of feminism. Their remarks were cited in LW, "Judicial council complaint laid over Wilson's address" *The Lawyers Weekly* (23 February 1990) 18:

> It's quite unprecedented that a judge would delve so publicly into public policy, and it certainly does put her position on the court in question ... [Calling into question her impartiality, in particular in criminal, family and tort cases] I don't think any of us would feel comfortable appearing before her now.

The complaint was ultimately rejected. After her retirement, Madam Justice Wilson made another public speech, which again prompted a complaint from R.E.A.L. Women: Lawyers Weekly, "Family violence is manifestation of male power in society: Wilson" *The Lawyers Weekly* (7 June 1991) 15.

JUDGE ANDRÉE RUFFO

Judge Andrée Ruffo, of the youth court of St-Jerome, Québec, has said and done a number of things that have resulted in charges of alleged ethics violations, according to Catherine Buckie, "Here comes the judge" *The Ottawa Citizen* (16 April 1990) F1. Judge Ruffo has published a book critical of the child welfare system in Québec; has made public statements about the inadequacy of state resources available for children in legal difficulties; and has made controversial rulings that defy the prescribed structures and limits of her role: "[S]he sent two boys to the office of Thérèse Lavoie-Roux, then health minister, because there was no room for them in specialized group homes, and order[ed] an abortion for a 14-year-old girl against the advice of youth protection officers." The girl stated that she had herself requested the abortion: "[Judge Ruffo] included in the order that if I changed my mind, the abortion should not be performed." "After ordering the abortion, Ruffo also gave the girl her home telephone number. The judge says she and the girl remain friends today."

As well, "Ruffo once ruled that a child receive psychiatric assessment within 48 hours, that another child undergo a medical examination within 24 hours, and ordered a group home to buy clothes for a child within 48 hours."

Mr. Lapointe, director-general of the Social Services Ministry in the region, filed 58 complaints with the Magistrates Council, 48 of which were dismissed without a hearing. At the hearing for the remaining 10 charges, he argued that her decisions were illegal, and that "he felt that Ruffo was biased against the youth protection department, and he feared she would not judge his cases fairly." The director of youth services has said that "instead of making 'ideal court orders' she should make realistic ones that take the available resources into account."

As a result, the Chief Judge Albert Gobeil complained to the judicial council in 1990. Judge Gobeil was also chairman of the council. Judge Ruffo contested the authority of the Council to hear the disciplinary charges against her, arguing that her rights under ss. 2 and 7 of the *Charter* would be violated. However, her claim was ultimately rejected by the Supreme Court in a lengthy judgment: *Ruffo* v. *Québec (Conseil de la magistrature)*, [1995] 4 S.C.R. 267. She was further reprimanded, again at the instance of Judge Gobeil, in *Cour de Québec (Juge en chef)* v. *Ruffo*, [1997]

No. CM 8-90-30 (Conseil de la magistrature du Québec (Comité d'enquête)).

JUSTICE CHARLES HUBAND

Justice Charles Huband of the Manitoba Court of Appeal gave a speech before a United Church audience that was published in part in the *Winnipeg Free Press* in September 1992. In this speech, he criticized the report of the Manitoba Aboriginal Justice Inquiry as "not simply bad, it is egregiously awful." He stated that the commissioners' conclusion regarding the massive failure of the justice system for Aboriginal peoples is "utterly wrong and completely impractical," blamed the high incarceration rates on a "higher incidence of criminal activity by Aboriginal people," and stated that Judges Sinclair and Hamilton had made "gratuitously insulting statements about their colleagues and their staffs." Thus far, there has been no judicial inquiry into Judge Huband's conduct. For a summary of the remarks and a comparison of Huband's treatment with that of Berger, see Tony Hall, "Judging the Judges" *Can. Forum* (January 1993) 28.

JUSTICE JEAN-CLAUDE ANGERS

Justice Jean-Claude Angers was reprimanded by the Judicial Conduct Committee of the Canadian Judicial Council for his public comments (an open letter to the Prime Minister and members of Parliament, and a radio interview) criticizing proposed gun control legislation: Canadian Judicial Council, "Ruling re Complaints Made to the Canadian Judicial Council Respecting Mr. Justice J.C. Angers" (10 April 1995).

> Your letter and interview criticized the government's proposal for what it called "gun control".... We pause to say, that unlike Mr. Justice Berger, who was commenting on matters of high constitutional importance that would rarely come before him as a judge, yours is a highly partisan attack upon a proposal which, if carried forward into legislation, could well come frequently before you for interpretation or enforcement.

The Committee declined to consider the question of whether a judge may have a defence to formal proceedings against him or her for statements, on the basis of the *Charter*. Although strongly disapproving of the judge's conduct, the Committee did not initiate a formal investigation of Justice Angers, which might have led to a recommendation for removal from office.

JUSTICE JOHN W. McCLUNG

Justice McClung was the subject of numerous complaints to the Canadian Judicial Council for his conduct in relation to *R. v. Ewanchuk* (1998), 132 D.L.R. (4th) 595 (Alta. C.A.), rev'd [1998] 1 S.C.R. 493 and *Vriend v. Alberta* (1996), 57 Alta. L.R. (3d) 235 (C.A.), rev'd [1998] 1 S.C.R. 493, two cases on which he sat at the Court of Appeal.

In *Vriend* (a challenge to the exclusion of "sexual orientation" as a prohibited ground of discrimination under the *Alberta Individual Rights Protection Act*, R.S.A. 1980, c. I-2), the complaint centred on the following excerpts from the judgment of McClung, J.A.:

> I am unable to conclude that it was a forbidden, let alone a reversible, legislative response for the Province of Alberta to step back from the validation of homosexual relations, including sodomy, as a protected and fundamental right, thereby, "rebutting a [millennium] of moral teaching." [at 609]
>
> It is pointless to deny that the Dahmer, Bernardo and Clifford Robert Olsen prosecutions have recently heightened public concern about violently aberrant sexual configurations and how they find expression against their victims. [at 611].

With respect to *Ewanchuk* (a sexual assault case), McClung J.A. took the unprecedented step of penning a venomous attack on Justice L'Heureux-Dubé for her decision overruling him, the day after the Supreme Court decision was released: Justice J.W. McClung, "Right of Reply" *The [Toronto] National Post* (26 February 1999) A19:

> Madam Justice Claire L'Heureux-Dubé's graceless slide into personal invective in Thursday's judgment in the Ewanchuk case allows some response. It issued with "the added bitterness of an old friend." Whether the Ewanchuk case will promote the fundamental right of every accused Canadian to a fair trial will have to be left to the academics. Yet there may be one immediate benefit. The personal convictions of the judge, delivered again from her judicial chair, could provide a plausible explanation for the disparate (and growing number of) male suicides being reported in the Province of Québec.

The following day, a front page story appeared which quoted McClung, J.A. with respect to the victim and Madam Justice L'Heureux-Dubé: S. Ohler, "Judge reiterates belief that teen wasn't assaulted" [Toronto] *National Post* (26 February 1999) A1. He impugned the victim by describing her as someone "not lost on her way home from the nunnery" and took objection to the Supreme Court's ruling that his judgment was based on myths and stereotypes and women and about sexual assault: "I don't like to be accused of living my professional life in a fantasy world of stereotypes and myths. That's going too far." He characterized Madam Justice L'Heureux-Dubé as having "consistent anti-male response[s] on these matters."

The Canadian Judicial Council Panel concluded that the letter was inappropriate, and the remarks in *Ewanchuk*, while problematic, did not "reflect an underlying bias against women" (at 7). They rather generously attributed the impetus for the remarks to the uncertainty of the area of the law: Canadian Judicial Council, Press Release, "Panel expresses strong disapproval of McClung conduct" (21 May 1999). See, also, the *Letter to the Honourable Mr. Justice John W. McClung, Court of Appeal of Alberta from the Chairperson of the Judicial Conduct Committee, Madame Justice C.R. Glube, Chief Justice of Nova Scotia, appointed by the Canadian Judicial Council* (19 May 1999), available online at Canadian Judicial Council website (www.cjc-ccm.gc.ca). His disturbing comments in *Vriend* were characterized as "unnecessary and unfortunate, but not demonstrating an underlying homophobia" (at 7).

Index of Cases

A, B

Abbott v. Canada	**221**
Armstrong v. Warkworth	**217, 224**
B.C. (AG) v. Mount Currie Indian Band	**495**
B.C. Government Employees Union v. B.C. (AG)	**493**
Belczowski v. Canada	**226**
Blueberry River Indian Band v. Canada	**73**
Brandon v. Correctional Service of Canada	**221**
Brown v. Board of Education	**344**
Brown v. Durham Regional Police Force	**338**
Buhlers v. British Columbia	**137**

C

C. (T.L.) v. Vancouver (City)	**278**
C.B.C. v. Cordeau	**492**
Campbell v. Jones	**366**
Campbell v. Ontario (AG)	**491**
Canada (Minister of Citizenship and Immigration) v. Tobiass	**492**
Carr v. Gauthier	**426**
Chartrand v. Québec (AG)	**491**
Cour de Québec (Juge en chef) v. Ruffo	**510**
Coroner's Inquest into the Death of Robert Gentles	**225**

D

Decision of the New Brunswick Judicial Council established under the provisions of Section 6.1 of the Provincial Court Act concerning the conduct of Her Honour Judge Jocelyne J. Moreau-Bérubé, a Judge of the New Brunswick Provincial Court (9 April 1999)	**507**
Delgamuukw v. British Columbia	**50, 73**
Doe v. Metropolitan Toronto Commissioners of Police	**345, 362, 488**
Dowson v. R.	**491**
Dumont v. Canada (AG)	**97**

E

Estate of Maria Teresa Macias v. Ihde	**436**
Estate of Sinthasomphone v. Milwaukee	**364**
Everingham v. Ontario	**224**

F, G

Falkiner v. Ontario (Ministry of Community and Social Services)	**110**
Fieldhouse v. R.	**224, 383**
Garneau v. Québec (Coroner)	**294**

Gazette (The [Montreal]) v. Québec (Coroner)	294
George v. Harris	72, 338
Gonzalez v. Alberta	137
Greenpeace Canada v. MacMillan Bloedel	494

H

Hague v. Deputy Governor of Parkhurst Prison	221
Horsefield v. Ontario	137
Hunter v. Southam	358, 369, 379, 381, 382

I, J

In the Matter of Section 2 of the Individual's Rights Protection Act, R.S.A. 1980, c. I-2	122
In the Matter of The Public Inquiries Act, R.S.A. 1980, c. P-29 between Harvey Kane et al. v. Church of Jesus Christ Christian-Aryan Nations	122
Inquiry into the Conduct of Judge R.M. Bourassa	163, 508
Johnson v. Adamson	314

K, L

Kaplan v. Lasalle	224
Kenora Police Service v. Savino	366
Kostuch v. Alberta (AG)	491
Little Sister's Book and Art Emporium v. Canada	113

M

MacKeigan v. Hickman	93
Mackin v. New Brunswick (Ministry of Finance)	493
MacMillan Bloedel v. Simpson	494
Manitoba (AG) v. Groupe Quebecor Inc.	493
Martineau v. Matsui Disciplinary Board	216
McCleskey v. Kemp	151
McIlkenny v. Chief Constable of the West Midlands	126
Mennes v. Canada	222
Milgaard v. Kujawa	124
Moreau-Bérubé v. New Brunswick	507
Morin v. Canada (AG)	97

N

Nelles v. Ontario (AG)	130
New Brunswick v. G. (J.)	472
Newfoundland Association of Public Employees v. Newfoundland (AG)	493
Newfoundland (AG) v. Rich	493

O, P

Oak Bay Marina v. Haida Nation	495
Ontario (AG) v. Dieleman	35
Popowich v. Saskatchewan	131

R

R. v. A.J.J.	176
R. v. Amauyak	159
R. v. Avadluk	163
R. v. B.K.	492
R. v. Badger	73
R. v. Banks	13, 251
R. v. Bartle	418, 442, 452, 453
R. v. B.(L.C.)	470
R. v. Bata Industries	144
R. v. Belmas	139
R. v. Bertrand	501
R. v. Biron	268, 421, 426
R. v. Black	446, 449
R. v. Blais	74
R. v. Bob	4, 123, 213
R. v. Bonneteau	206
R. v. Borden	368
R. v. Born With A Tooth	492
R. v. Boucher	278
R. v. Bowes	493
R. v. Brennan	278
R. v. Briggs	250
R. v. Brown	338
R. v. Brydges	442, 447, 452
R. v. Burlingham	418
R. v. Burton	413
R. v. C.(M.)	35
R. v. C.A.M.	138
R. v. Campbell	493
R. v. Carker No. 2	225
R. v. Carratt	175
R. v. Carroll	134, 137
R. v. Cayer	427
R. v. CHEK TV	493
R. v. Clarkson	446
R. v. Clay	23, 35, 36, 40
R. v. Cohn	492
R. v. Collins	368, 414, 445
R. v. Coutereille	446
R. v. Curley	163
R. v. Currie	136
R. v. D.B.T.	503
R. v. Daniels (1990) (Sask. Q.B.)	241
R. v. Daniels (1991) (Sask. C.A.)	243
R. v. Deane	318, 325, 338
R. v. Debot	369
R. v. Debraga	138
R. v. Dedman	368, 369
R. v. Deviney	315
R. v. DiPaola	111

Index of Cases

R. v. Downey	225
R. v. Doyle	206
R. v. Drybones	4
R. v. Duguay	427
R. v. Dunn	279
R. v. Durham	315
R. v. Edwards	207
R. v. Evans (1991) (S.C.C.)	446
R. v. Evans (1996) (S.C.C.)	368
R. v. Ewanchuk	508, 511, 512
R. v. Feeney	426
R. v. Ferris	432
R. v. Fiddler	66
R. v. Finta	492
R. v. Ford	466
R. v. Fosseneuve	431
R. v. Généreux	100
R. v. George	324
R. v. Gladstone	74
R. v. Gladue	164, 175
R. v. Glykis	137
R. v. Godoy	368, 426
R. v. Gogol	404, 413
R. v. Golden	392
R. v. Goltz	134
R. v. Gosset	293
R. v. Grafe	429, 431
R. v. Gray	369
R. v. Grant	382
R. v. Groot	279
R. v. Hall	476
R. v. Hamilton	413
R. v. Harper	453
R. v. Hebb	207, 213, 466
R. v. Hemlow	137
R. v. Hill (1990) (Ont. Ct. Just. (Gen. Div.))	214
R. v. Hill (1997) (B.C.C.A.)	221
R. v. Horseman	73
R. v. Hufsky	369, 431
R. v. Ingram	144, 150, 151
R. v. Inwood	188, 204, 206
R. v. J.H.	465
R. v. Jacko	66
R. v. Joe	214
R. v. Johnson (1994) (Y. Terr. C.A.)	176, 177, 181
R. v. Johnson (2000) (B.C.C.A.)	432
R. v. Joseyounen	177, 180
R. v. Keegstra	492
R. v. Kokesch	369
R. v. Kopyto	491, 495, 500
R. v. Kozy	137
R. v. Krachor	222
R. v. Laplante	446
R. v. Latimer	134, 489
R. v. Lavallee	3
R. v. Lavoie	111
R. v. Law	342, 368
R. v. Leclair	442, 443, 446
R. v. Legons	134
R. v. Lelas	144, 150
R. v. Lerke	392, 431
R. v. Levo	207
R. v. Lewis (1992) (Ont. Ct. Just. (Prov. Div.))	316, 413
R. v. Lewis (1996) (S.C.C.)	74
R. v. Li	484
R. v. Lines	316, 365
R. v. Lott	432
R. v. Luxton	134
R. v. M.R.M.	383, 392, 427, 431
R. v. Macooh	426
R. v. Manchester Plastics	140, 143
R. v. Marshall	74
R. v. Matheson	452
R. v. McCallem	453
R. v. McCarthy	413
R. v. McConnell	225
R. v. McDonnell	206
R. v. McGibbon	453
R. v. McKay	225
R. v. McKinney	127
R. v. Mellenthin	369, 418
R. v. Michalowsky	122
R. v. Melaragni	315
R. v. Milne	134
R. v. Miloszewski (1999) (B.C. Prov. Ct.)	145, 150
R. v. Miloszewski (2001) (B.C.C.A.)	150
R. v. Moore	268, 426, 431
R. v. Morales	476
R. v. Moran	430
R. v. Morgentaler (1988) (S.C.C.)	13
R. v. Morgentaler (1993) (S.C.C.)	12
R. v. Morin (1994) (Sask. Q.B.)	178
R. v. Morin (1995) (Sask. C.A.)	176, 177, 178
R. v. Morrisey	134
R. v. Moses	176, 180
R. v. Munson	178, 248
R. v. Munroe	490
R. v. Naappaluk	184
R. v. Naqitarvik	153, 160, 162, 163, 164
R. v. Nepoose	123
R. v. Neve	136
R. v. Nikal	74
R. v. Northwest Territories Power	144
R. v. N.T.C. Smokehouse	74
R. v. O'Connor	3
R. v. O'Leary	504
R. v. Ollenberger	206
R. v. P.(J.A.)	184
R. v. Palmer	128
R. v. Partridge	137
R. v. Paternak	277
R. v. Pati	426
R. v. Patterson	111
R. v. Pearson	476

R. v. Peck	432, 438
R. v. Perkins	492
R. v. Phillips	138
R. v. Ping	136
R. v. Plain	225
R. v. Plant	368, 369
R. v. Pohoretsky	418
R. v. Power	432
R. v. Powley	74
R. v. Pozniak	452, 453
R. v. Prosper	442, 452
R. v. Proulx	135
R. v. R.D.S.	175, 300, 311, 490, 508
R. v. R.H.B.	465
R. v. Rain	454
R. v. Rarbacki	492
R. v. Rehberg	35
R. v. Richards	342
R. v. Rodney	224
R. v. S.B.	501
R. v. Sackanay	175
R. v. Seaboyer	3
R. v. Severight	178
R. v. Shafie	431
R. v. Shaw	447
R. v. Shell Canada Products	144
R. v. Sieben	418
R. v. Shubley	222
R. v. Simard	270
R. v. Simmons	383
R. v. Simpson	418, 431
R. v. Sioui	73
R. v. Smith (1987) (S.C.C.)	134, 242
R. v. Smith (1989) (S.C.C.)	446
R. v. Smith (1996) (Ont. Ct. Just. (Prov. Div.))	426
R. v. Smith (1993) (N.S.C.A.)	299
R. v. Sparrow	73
R. v. Spindell	392
R. v. Sokolowski	317
R. v. Sztuke	143
R. v. Sundown	73
R. v. Taylor	178, 179, 180, 184
R. v. Terrigno	427
R. v. Tesfai	369
R. v. Théberge	507, 508
R. v. Therens	427, 436
R. v. Thompson	296, 300, 466, 488
R. v. Tooze	369
R. v. Tran	465
R. v. Turpin	3, 213
R. v. Vaillancourt	13
R. v. Van-Rob Stampings	143
R. v. Viens	111
R. v. Waugh	426
R. v. Whitfield	420
R. v. White)	111, 466
R. v. Wholesale Travel Group	13, 381
R. v. Wilson	431
R. v. Winter	492
R. v. Wolfe	278
R. v. Wong	369, 419
R. v. Yorke	431
R. v. Young	368, 432
R. v. Zazulak	123
R. v. Zundel	492, 497
R. v. R.E.G.	136
Re Black Action Defence Committee and Huxter, Coroner	315
Re Booth et al. and Huxter	315
Re Ewing and Kearney v. R.	453
Re Kennedy and the Queen et al.	453
Re R. and Antler: Re T.(F.)	489
Re Royal Canadian Mounted Police and Commission of Inquiry	122
Re Urban Alliance on Race Relations for Metropolitan Toronto (Justice) and Huxter	315
Reference Re Milgaard	124
RJR-MacDonald v. Canada (AG)	381
Ruffo v. Québec (Conseil de la magistrature)	510

S

Saint Jacques v. Canada	221
Sask. Prov. Ct. Judges' Assoc. v. Sask.	493
Sauvé v. Canada (Chief Electoral Officer)	226
Sawridge Band v. R.	508
Sweet v. Canada	223

T

Thomson Newspapers v. Canada	382
Thurman v. City of Torrington	432, 436
Trono v. Gallant	221

U, V

United Nurses of Alberta v. Alta. (AG)	493
Veysey v. Correctional Service of Canada	226
Vriend v. Alberta	508, 511

W

Weatherall v. Canada (AG)	213, 224, 508
Weldon v. Home Office	221
Westendorp v. R.	12
Williams v. Canada (Regional Transfer Board, Prairie Region)	221
Wiltshire v. Barrett	422, 424
Winters v. Legal Services Society	465